High-Frequency Financial Econometrics

High-Frequency Financial Econometrics

Yacine Aït-Sahalia and Jean Jacod

Princeton University Press
Princeton and Oxford

Published by Princeton University Press, 41 William Street, Princeton, New Jersey 08540

In the United Kingdom: Princeton University Press, 6 Oxford Street, Woodstock, Oxfordshire OX20 1TW

press.princeton.edu

Library of Congress Cataloging-in-Publication Data

Aït-Sahalia, Yacine.
High-frequency financial econometrics / Yacine Aït-Sahalia, Jean Jacod.
pages cm
Includes bibliographical references and index.
ISBN 978-0-691-16143-3 (hardback)
1. Finance—Econometric models. 2. Econometrics. I. Jacod, Jean. II. Title.
HG106.A3873 2014
332.01'5195—dc23

2013045702

British Library Cataloging-in-Publication Data is available

The publisher would like to acknowledge the authors of this volume for providing the camera-ready copy from which this book was printed.

This book has been composed in LATEX

Printed on acid-free paper ∞

Printed in the United States of America

10 9 8 7 6 5 4 3 2 1

To Sophie and Hadda

and

To Idir, Ines, Olivier, Vincent, Serge and Thomas

Contents

Preface   xvii

Notation   xxiii

I   Preliminary Material   1

1 From Diffusions to Semimartingales   **3**

1.1   Diffusions 5

     1.1.1   The Brownian Motion 5

     1.1.2   Stochastic Integrals 8

     1.1.3   A Central Example: Diffusion Processes 12

1.2   Lévy Processes 16

     1.2.1   The Law of a Lévy Process 17

     1.2.2   Examples 20

     1.2.3   Poisson Random Measures 24

     1.2.4   Integrals with Respect to Poisson Random Measures 27

     1.2.5   Path Properties and Lévy-Itô Decomposition . . 30

1.3   Semimartingales 35

     1.3.1   Definition and Stochastic Integrals 35

     1.3.2   Quadratic Variation 38

     1.3.3   Itô's Formula 40

     1.3.4   Characteristics of a Semimartingale and the Lévy-Itô Decomposition 43

1.4   Itô Semimartingales 44

     1.4.1   The Definition 44

     1.4.2   Extension of the Probability Space 46

     1.4.3   The Grigelionis Form of an Itô Semimartingale . 47

1.4.4   A Fundamental Example: Stochastic Differential
        Equations Driven by a Lévy Process   49
1.5   Processes with Conditionally Independent Increments .   52
      1.5.1   Processes with Independent Increments   53
      1.5.2   A Class of Processes with $\mathcal{F}$-Conditionally Inde-
              pendent Increments   54

2 Data Considerations   57
   2.1   Mechanisms for Price Determination   58
         2.1.1   Limit Order and Other Market Mechanisms . . .   59
         2.1.2   Market Rules and Jumps in Prices   61
         2.1.3   Sample Data: Transactions, Quotes and NBBO .   62
   2.2   High-Frequency Data Distinctive Characteristics   64
         2.2.1   Random Sampling Times   65
         2.2.2   Market Microstructure Noise and Data Errors . .   66
         2.2.3   Non-normality   67
   2.3   Models for Market Microstructure Noise   68
         2.3.1   Additive Noise   68
         2.3.2   Rounding Errors   72
   2.4   Strategies to Mitigate the Impact of Noise   73
         2.4.1   Downsampling   73
         2.4.2   Filtering Transactions Using Quotes   74

II   Asymptotic Concepts   79

3 Introduction to Asymptotic Theory: Volatility Estimation for a Continuous Process   83
   3.1   Estimating Integrated Volatility in Simple Cases   85
         3.1.1   Constant Volatility   85
         3.1.2   Deterministic Time-Varying Volatility   87
         3.1.3   Stochastic Volatility Independent of the Driving
                 Brownian Motion W   88
         3.1.4   From Independence to Dependence for the
                 Stochastic Volatility   90
   3.2   Stable Convergence in Law   91
   3.3   Convergence for Stochastic Processes   96
   3.4   General Stochastic Volatility   99
   3.5   What If the Process Jumps?   106

4 With Jumps: An Introduction to Power Variations   **109**

   4.1   Power Variations 110

      4.1.1   The Purely Discontinuous Case 111

      4.1.2   The Continuous Case 112

      4.1.3   The Mixed Case 113

   4.2   Estimation in a Simple Parametric Example: Merton's

      Model 116

      4.2.1   Some Intuition for the Identification or Lack

             Thereof: The Impact of High Frequency 117

      4.2.2   Asymptotic Efficiency in the Absence of Jumps . 119

      4.2.3   Asymptotic Efficiency in the Presence of Jumps . 120

      4.2.4   GMM Estimation 122

      4.2.5   GMM Estimation of Volatility with Power Varia-

             tions 124

   4.3   References 130

5 High-Frequency Observations: Identifiability and Asymptotic Efficiency   **131**

   5.1   Classical Parametric Models 132

      5.1.1   Identifiability 133

      5.1.2   Efficiency for Fully Identifiable Parametric Models 134

      5.1.3   Efficiency for Partly Identifiable Parametric Mod-

             els 137

   5.2   Identifiability for Lévy Processes and the Blumenthal-

      Getoor Indices 139

      5.2.1   About Mutual Singularity of Laws of Lévy Pro-

             cesses 139

      5.2.2   The Blumenthal-Getoor Indices and Related

             Quantities for Lévy Processes 141

   5.3   Discretely Observed Semimartingales: Identifiable Pa-

      rameters 144

      5.3.1   Identifiable Parameters: A Definition 145

      5.3.2   Identifiable Parameters: Examples 148

   5.4   Tests: Asymptotic Properties 151

   5.5   Back to the Lévy Case: Disentangling the Diffusion Part

      from Jumps 155

  5.5.1   The Parametric Case   155
  5.5.2   The Semi-Parametric Case   156
5.6   Blumenthal-Getoor Indices for Lévy Processes: Efficiency
      via Fisher's Information   160
5.7   References   163

III   Volatility   165

6   **Estimating Integrated Volatility: The Base Case with
    No Noise and Equidistant Observations**   **169**
  6.1   When the Process Is Continuous   171
    6.1.1   Feasible Estimation and Confidence Bounds . . .   173
    6.1.2   The Multivariate Case   176
    6.1.3   About Estimation of the Quarticity   177
  6.2   When the Process Is Discontinuous   179
    6.2.1   Truncated Realized Volatility   180
    6.2.2   Choosing the Truncation Level: The One-
            Dimensional Case   187
    6.2.3   Multipower Variations   191
    6.2.4   Truncated Bipower Variations   194
    6.2.5   Comparing Truncated Realized Volatility and
            Multipower Variations   196
  6.3   Other Methods   197
    6.3.1   Range-Based Volatility Estimators   197
    6.3.2   Range-Based Estimators in a Genuine High-
            Frequency Setting   198
    6.3.3   Nearest Neighbor Truncation   199
    6.3.4   Fourier-Based Estimators   200
  6.4   Finite Sample Refinements for Volatility Estimators . .   202
  6.5   References   207

7   **Volatility and Microstructure Noise**   **209**
  7.1   Models of Microstructure Noise   211
    7.1.1   Additive White Noise   211
    7.1.2   Additive Colored Noise   212
    7.1.3   Pure Rounding Noise   213
    7.1.4   A Mixed Case: Rounded White Noise   215
    7.1.5   Realized Volatility in the Presence of Noise . . .   216

7.2 Assumptions on the Noise 220
7.3 Maximum-Likelihood and Quasi Maximum-Likelihood
    Estimation 224
    7.3.1 A Toy Model: Gaussian Additive White Noise and
          Brownian Motion 224
    7.3.2 Robustness of the MLE to Stochastic Volatility . 228
7.4 Quadratic Estimators 231
7.5 Subsampling and Averaging: Two-Scales Realized
    Volatility 232
7.6 The Pre-averaging Method 238
    7.6.1 Pre-averaging and Optimality 245
    7.6.2 Adaptive Pre-averaging 247
7.7 Flat Top Realized Kernels 250
7.8 Multi-scales Estimators 253
7.9 Estimation of the Quadratic Covariation 254
7.10 References 256

8 Estimating Spot Volatility   259
8.1 Local Estimation of the Spot Volatility 261
    8.1.1 Some Heuristic Considerations 261
    8.1.2 Consistent Estimation 265
    8.1.3 Central Limit Theorem 266
8.2 Global Methods for the Spot Volatility 273
8.3 Volatility of Volatility 274
8.4 Leverage: The Covariation between X and c 279
8.5 Optimal Estimation of a Function of Volatility 284
8.6 State-Dependent Volatility 289
8.7 Spot Volatility and Microstructure Noise 293
8.8 References 296

9 Volatility and Irregularly Spaced Observations   299
9.1 Irregular Observation Times: The One-Dimensional Case 301
    9.1.1 About Irregular Sampling Schemes 302
    9.1.2 Estimation of the Integrated Volatility and Other
          Integrated Volatility Powers 305
    9.1.3 Irregular Observation Schemes: Time Changes . 309
9.2 The Multivariate Case: Non-synchronous Observations . 313
    9.2.1 The Epps Effect 314
    9.2.2 The Hayashi-Yoshida Method 315
    9.2.3 Other Methods and Extensions 320

9.3   References   323

IV   Jumps   325

10 Testing for Jumps   329

10.1 Introduction   331

10.2 Relative Sizes of the Jump and Continuous Parts and
     Testing for Jumps   334

    10.2.1 The Mathematical Tools   334

    10.2.2 A "Linear" Test for Jumps   336

    10.2.3 A "Ratio" Test for Jumps   340

    10.2.4 Relative Sizes of the Jump and Brownian Parts .   342

    10.2.5 Testing the Null $\Omega_T^{(c)}$ instead of $\Omega_T^{(cW)}$ 352

10.3 A Symmetrical Test for Jumps   353

    10.3.1 The Test Statistics Based on Power Variations .   353

    10.3.2 Some Central Limit Theorems   356

    10.3.3 Testing the Null Hypothesis of No Jump   360

    10.3.4 Testing the Null Hypothesis of Presence of Jumps   362

    10.3.5 Comparison of the Tests   366

10.4 Detection of Jumps   368

    10.4.1 Mathematical Background   369

    10.4.2 A Test for Jumps   372

    10.4.3 Finding the Jumps: The Finite Activity Case . .   373

    10.4.4 The General Case   376

10.5 Detection of Volatility Jumps   378

10.6 Microstructure Noise and Jumps   381

    10.6.1 A Noise-Robust Jump Test Statistic   382

    10.6.2 The Central Limit Theorems for the Noise-Robust
     Jump Test   384

    10.6.3 Testing the Null Hypothesis of No Jump in the
     Presence of Noise   386

    10.6.4 Testing the Null Hypothesis of Presence of Jumps
     in the Presence of Noise   388

10.7 References   390

11 Finer Analysis of Jumps: The Degree of Jump Activity   393

11.1 The Model Assumptions   395

11.2 Estimation of the First BG Index and of the Related
     Intensity   399

11.2.1 Construction of the Estimators 399
11.2.2 Asymptotic Properties 404
11.2.3 How Far from Asymptotic Optimality? 407
11.2.4 The Truly Non-symmetric Case 415
11.3 Successive BG Indices 419
11.3.1 Preliminaries 420
11.3.2 First Estimators 422
11.3.3 Improved Estimators 424
11.4 References 427

12 Finite or Infinite Activity for Jumps?   **429**
12.1 When the Null Hypothesis Is Finite Jump Activity . . . 430
12.2 When the Null Hypothesis Is Infinite Jump Activity . . 437
12.3 References 439

13 Is Brownian Motion Really Necessary?   **441**
13.1 Tests for the Null Hypothesis That the Brownian Is
      Present 443
13.2 Tests for the Null Hypothesis That the Brownian Is Absent 446
13.2.1 Adding a Fictitious Brownian 448
13.2.2 Tests Based on Power Variations 449
13.3 References 451

14 Co-jumps   **453**
14.1 Co-jumps for the Underlying Process 453
14.1.1 The Setting 453
14.1.2 Testing for Common Jumps 456
14.1.3 Testing for Disjoint Jumps 459
14.1.4 Some Open Problems 463
14.2 Co-jumps between the Process and Its Volatility 464
14.2.1 Limit Theorems for Functionals of Jumps and
        Volatility 466
14.2.2 Testing the Null Hypothesis of No Co-jump . . . 469
14.2.3 Testing the Null Hypothesis of the Presence of
        Co-jumps 473
14.3 References 474

A Asymptotic Results for Power Variations   **477**
A.1 Setting and Assumptions 477
A.2 Laws of Large Numbers 480

A.2.1 LLNs for Power Variations and Related Functionals 480

A.2.2 LLNs for the Integrated Volatility 484

A.2.3 LLNs for Estimating the Spot Volatility 485

A.3 Central Limit Theorems 488

A.3.1 CLTs for the Processes $B(f, \Delta_n)$ and $\overline{B}(f, \Delta_n)$. 488

A.3.2 A Degenerate Case 490

A.3.3 CLTs for the Processes $B'(f, \Delta_n)$ and $\overline{B}'(f, \Delta_n)$ 492

A.3.4 CLTs for the Quadratic Variation 495

A.4 Noise and Pre-averaging: Limit Theorems 496

A.4.1 Assumptions on Noise and Pre-averaging Schemes 497

A.4.2 LLNs for Noise 498

A.4.3 CLTs for Noise 500

A.5 Localization and Strengthened Assumptions 502

B Miscellaneous Proofs   **507**

B.1 Proofs for Chapter 5 507

B.1.1 Proofs for Sections 5.2 and 5.3 507

B.1.2 Proofs for Section 5.5 513

B.1.3 Proof of Theorem 5.25 520

B.2 Proofs for Chapter 8 531

B.2.1 Preliminaries 531

B.2.2 Estimates for the Increments of X and c 535

B.2.3 Estimates for the Spot Volatility Estimators . . . 538

B.2.4 A Key Decomposition for Theorems 8.11 and 8.14 540

B.2.5 Proof of Theorems 8.11 and 8.14 and Remark 8.15 547

B.2.6 Proof of Theorems 8.12 and 8.17 553

B.2.7 Proof of Theorem 8.20 554

B.3 Proofs for Chapter 10 557

B.3.1 Proof of Theorem 10.12 557

B.3.2 Proofs for Section 10.3 564

B.3.3 Proofs for Section 10.4 568

B.3.4 Proofs for Section 10.5 573

B.4 Limit Theorems for the Jumps of an Itô Semimartingale 578

B.5 A Comparison Between Jumps and Increments 583

B.6 Proofs for Chapter 11 593

B.6.1 Proof of Theorems 11.11, 11.12, 11.18, 11.19, and Remark 11.14 593

B.6.2 Proof of Theorem 11.21 597

B.6.3 Proof of Theorem 11.23 600

B.7   Proofs for Chapter 12   604

B.8   Proofs for Chapter 13   612

B.9   Proofs for Chapter 14   614

    B.9.1   Proofs for Section 14.1   614

    B.9.2   Proofs for Section 14.2   619

Bibliography   **633**

Index   **657**

Preface

Over the past fifteen years or so, the domain of statistical and econometric methods for high-frequency financial data has been experiencing an exponential growth, due to the development of new mathematical methods to analyze these data, the increasing availability of such data, technological developments that made high-frequency trading strategies possible, and the correlative need of practitioners to analyze these data. So, the time seems ripe for a book devoted to this topic.

The purpose of this book is to introduce these recent methods and present some of the main new tools available to analyze high-frequency data, taking into account some of the distinguishing properties of financial data and the constraints they impose on the range of conceivable econometric methods. Indeed, from a statistical perspective, the analysis of high-frequency financial data presents a number of *specific characteristics*. As in many other time series settings, we are observing what is assumed to be an underlying continuous-time stochastic process, but on a grid of *discrete times*. Discrete observation of a path implies in particular that we need to make a distinction between the observed discrete increments and the complete path of the underlying process.

However, although observation times are discrete, the time interval Δ between successive observations is small, or very small: the *high-frequency asymptotics* we consider are all based on limiting results where the time interval Δ tends to zero, or equivalently the sampling frequency tends to infinity. By focusing on asymptotics, we make no real attempt toward an analysis of finite or small samples, although this question is mentioned occasionally. This is not to say that the analysis of small samples is unimportant; this is indeed crucial, since in real life the amount of data available is always finite (even if measured in gigabytes when ultra-high-frequency data is concerned). However, the properties of the various estimators or testing procedures in a small sample situation are always specific to each method, and in most cases can be ascertained only through simulation studies rather than through mathematical analysis. In a few instances, we discuss small sample refinements such as small sample bias corrections or Edgeworth expansions. But a useful treatment of small samples would require hundreds of pages, if at all feasible, hence our quasi exclusive focus on asymptotic theory.

Next, in this book we consider only inference problems on a *finite time horizon*, say $[0, T]$, unlike the usual time series asymptotics where T goes to infinity, or mixed asymptotics where both $\Delta \to 0$ and $T \to \infty$. Our rationale for keeping T fixed is twofold: first, high-frequency asymptotics make it possible to say much, although not everything, about the underlying process when observed within a finite time interval; second, in many cases the underlying models we consider fail to have the type of stationarity or ergodic properties that are crucial for long horizon asymptotics, which then requires different tools. One consequence of observing the price path on a finite horizon is the possibility of being subject to the *peso problem*: when jumps have finite activity, there is a positive probability that the path we observe has no jump on $[0, T]$, although the model itself may allow for jumps.

The class of problems we consider has another specific property: not only is the time horizon finite, but we also observe *a single path* of the process; for example a typical question is the estimation of the so-called integrated volatility, in a model with stochastic volatility: we want the integrated volatility over, say, a specific day, which is of course different from the integrated volatility over the next day, and averaging over many days does not make much sense in that case.

Two final distinguishing characteristics of high-frequency financial data are important, and call for the development of appropriate econometric methods. First, the time interval separating successive observations can be random, or at least time varying. Second, the observations are subject to *market microstructure noise*, especially as the sampling frequency increases. Market microstructure effects can be either information or non-information-related, such as the presence of a bid-ask spread and the corresponding bounces, the differences in trade sizes and the corresponding differences in representativeness of the prices, the different informational content of price changes due to informational asymmetries of traders, the gradual response of prices to a block trade, the strategic component of the order flow, inventory control effects, the discreteness of price changes, data errors, etc. The fact that this form of noise interacts with the sampling frequency raises many new questions, and distinguishes this from the classical measurement error problem in statistics.

Before describing in more detail the contents of this book, let us emphasize at the onset some of its general features:

- Our hope is that the book can be useful to econometricians, statisticians, mathematicians and high-frequency practitioners alike, starting at the graduate level. We have assumed basic knowledge of standard probabilistic and statistical principles, but have otherwise attempted to include the prerequisites that fall outside the standard graduate level econometric curriculum. This motivates the existence of the first two parts, which cover the required relevant elements about stochastic processes, convergence, and statistical experiments, plus a brief description of the specific qualitative features of financial data; a knowledgeable reader can skip these, although they do establish the notation we employ in the remainder of the book. Note that Chapter 5 also contains new material, to which the subsequent chapters occasionally refer.

- Because many methods developed in papers rely on different sets of assumptions, we have made a conscious effort to unify our treatment of the available methods by describing them, and their asymptotic properties, under a *common set of assumptions*. As a result, our proofs will often differ from those in the papers, and the results themselves are sometimes weaker, but more often stronger, than what appeared in the original papers.

- Many different problems are presented and, for most of them, many different methods have been proposed in the literature. However different these statistical methods may appear, they (almost) always hinge upon the same basic techniques and basic limit theorems concerning what we call *power variations*. The mathematical results about these power variations and some related functionals are gathered in Appendix A. They are all taken from Jacod and Protter (2011), and proofs are omitted.

- Apart from Appendix A, we have tried to make this book as self-contained as possible, as far as its mathematical content is concerned. This includes relying as little as possible on specific proofs contained in papers, and providing these proofs instead. On the other hand, writing its proof after each result slows down the exposition and tends to obscure the main ideas, at least for a non-mathematician reader. We have thus chosen to write the main part

of the text without proofs, except when they are very simple and/or
useful for the understanding of what immediately follows. Further,
many results are not stated as formal theorems. Nevertheless, since
this book is also intended to be a mathematical book, the proofs are
given (some of them are new), and they are gathered in Appendix
B.

- Since every rule has its exceptions, for a few results we do not give
  a proof and refer to the appropriate papers. This applies primarily
  to the results on microstructure noise and on non-equally spaced
  observations: these are topics in full development now, and the
  theory is not fully established yet. It also applies in places where
  we only sketch a description of several different methods which have
  been proposed for some specific problems.

- We have included an implementation on real data of some estimators or testing procedures described.

- We have tried to be as comprehensive as possible. This said, even
  under the restrictions imposed by the data (discrete sampling, a
  single path) and by our choice of methods (high-frequency asymptotics, finite horizon), we cannot pretend to cover all or almost all
  recent developments on the topic, let alone an exhaustive comparison between the different methods which have been proposed so
  far, while keeping the length of the book manageable. Inevitably,
  we did not describe *all* the available methods, and the – necessarily
  subjective – choice we made might be viewed as biased by our own
  interests. We apologize in advance to the authors who might feel
  that we have not done full justice to their work.

- We have left out some topics altogether, for instance forecasting (of
  volatility and other related quantities for example) and methods
  for processes driven by fractional Brownian motion or by fractal
  processes.

The book is divided into four parts, plus the two appendices A and
B described above. The first two parts are devoted to preliminary material: the mathematical notions on stochastic processes and especially
semimartingales which are necessary to proceed further, and a chapter
that explains the specificities of financial data are gathered into Part I,
whereas Part II introduces the asymptotic concepts that the analysis in
this book relies upon.

Part III deals with estimation of the volatility part of the model, including methods that are robust to market microstructure noise. Part IV is devoted to estimation and testing questions involving the jump part of the model. The practical importance and relevance of jumps in financial data is universally recognized, but only recently have econometric methods become available to rigorously analyze jump processes. The objective of the methods we will describe here is to decide on the basis of statistical tests applied to high-frequency data which component(s) need to be included in the model (jumps, finite or infinite activity, continuous component, etc.) and determine their relative magnitude. We may then magnify specific components of the model if they are present, so that we can analyze their finer characteristics such as the degree of activity of jumps.

We would like to thank our co-authors of the various papers on which this book is partly based. Without them, most of the book would not exist: many thanks to Jianqing Fan, Arnaud Gloter, Tahaki Hayashi, Jia Li, Yingying Li, Loriano Mancini, Per Mykland, Mark Podolskij, Philip Protter, Markus Reiss, Mathieu Rosenbaum, Viktor Todorov, Matthias Vetter, Dacheng Xiu, Nakahiro Yoshida, Jialin Yu and Lan Zhang. We also thank Yaroslav Yevmenenko-Shul'ts for proofreading parts of the manuscript, and Peter Van Tassel and Michael Sockin for research assistance.

Last but not least, we warmly thank Sophie and Hadda for their love, patience and understanding while we wrote this book.

Yacine Aït-Sahalia, Princeton
Jean Jacod, Paris

Notation

General Notation

for reals $u_n > 0$ and $v_n > 0$:

$u_n \sim v_n$	if u_n/v_n converges to a limit in $(0, \infty)$
$u_n \asymp v_n$	if $\frac{1}{A} \leq u_n/v_n \leq A$ for a constant $A \in (1, \infty)$
$u_n = \mathrm{o}(v_n)$	if $u_n/v_n \to 0$
$u_n = \mathrm{O}(v_n)$	if $\sup_n |u_n|/v_n < \infty$

for random variables U_n and $V_n > 0$:

$U_n = \mathrm{o}_P(V_n)$	if U_n/V_n goes to 0 in probability
$U_n = \mathrm{O}_P(V_n)$	if U_n/V_n is bounded in probability

$\mathcal{M}_d^+$	the set of all $d \times d$ symmetric nonnegative matrices
x^*, A^*	the transpose of a vector or a matrix
$\wedge$	the infimum
$\vee$	the supremum
$[x]$	the integer part of a real x
$\{x\}$	$= x - [x]$, the fractional part of a real x
x^+	$= x \vee 0$, the positive part of a real x
x^-	$= (-x) \vee 0$, the negative part of a real x
$\mathcal{N}(0, 1)$	the standard normal distribution on $\mathbb{R}$
$\mathcal{N}(b, \Sigma)$	the normal distribution on $\mathbb{R}^d$ with mean b and variance-covariance Σ
z_α	the two-sided α-quantile of $\mathcal{N}(0, 1)$
z'_α	the one-sided α-quantile of $\mathcal{N}(0, 1)$

Notation for Convergence

$\xrightarrow{\mathbb{P}}$	convergence in probability (for random variables)
$\xRightarrow{a.s.}$	almost sure convergence (for random variables)
$\xrightarrow{\mathcal{L}}$	convergence in law (for random variables)
$\xrightarrow{\mathcal{L}-s}$	stable convergence in law (for random variables)
$\xRightarrow{\mathbb{P}}$	functional convergence in probability (for processes)
$\xRightarrow{\mathcal{L}}$	functional convergence in probability (for processes)
$\xRightarrow{\mathcal{L}-s}$	functional convergence in probability (for processes)
$\xRightarrow{u.c.p.}$	local uniform convergence in probability (for processes)

Specific Notation

$$\Delta_i^n X = X_{i\Delta_n} - X_{(i-1)\Delta_n} \text{ or } X_{S(n,i)} - X_{S(n,i-1)},$$
the ith return of the process X

$$\Delta X_t = X_t - X_{t-}, \text{ the jump size of the process } X \text{ at } t$$

$$C_t = \int_0^t c_s \, ds, \text{ the integrated volatility}$$

$$C(p)_t = \int_0^t c_s^{p/2} \, ds$$

$$A(p)_t = \sum_{s \le t} |\Delta X_s|^p$$

$$B(f, \Delta_n)_t = \sum_{i=1}^{[t/\Delta_n]-k+1} f(\Delta_i^n X, \cdots, \Delta_{i+k-1}^n X)$$

$$B(f, \Delta_n, u_n)_t = \sum_{i=1}^{[t/\Delta_n]-k+1} f(\Delta_i^n X, \cdots, \Delta_{i+k-1}^n X)$$
$$\times \prod_{j=0}^{k-1} 1_{\{\|\Delta_{i+j}^n X\| \le u_n\}}$$

$$B(p, \Delta_n)_t = \sum_{i=1}^{[t/\Delta_n]} |\Delta_i^n X|^p$$

$$B([p,k], \Delta_n)_t = \sum_{i=1}^{[t/\Delta_n]-k+1} |\Delta_i^n X + \cdots + \Delta_{i+k-1}^n X|^p$$

$$B(p, \Delta_n, u_n)_t = \sum_{i=1}^{[t/\Delta_n]} |\Delta_i^n X|^p 1_{\{|\Delta_i^n X_i^n| \le u_n\}}$$

$$B'(f, \Delta_n)_t = \Delta_n \sum_{i=1}^{[t/\Delta_n]-k+1} f\left(\frac{\Delta_i^n X}{\sqrt{\Delta_n}}, \cdots, \frac{\Delta_{i+k-1}^n X}{\sqrt{\Delta_n}}\right)$$

$$B'(f, \Delta_n, u_n)_t = \Delta_n \sum_{i=1}^{[t/\Delta_n]-k+1} f\left(\frac{\Delta_i^n X}{\sqrt{\Delta_n}}, \cdots, \frac{\Delta_{i+k-1}^n X}{\sqrt{\Delta_n}}\right)$$
$$\times \prod_{j=0}^{k-1} 1_{\{\|\Delta_{i+j}^n X\| \le u_n\}}$$

$$\overline{B}(f, \Delta_n)_t = \sum_{i=1}^{[t/k\Delta_n]} f(\Delta_{ik-k+1}^n X, \cdots, \Delta_{ik}^n X)$$

$$\overline{B}'(f, \Delta_n)_t = \Delta_n \sum_{i=1}^{[t/k\Delta_n]} f\left(\frac{\Delta_{ik-k+1}^n X}{\sqrt{\Delta_n}}, \cdots, \frac{\Delta_{ik}^n X}{\sqrt{\Delta_n}}\right)$$

$$\widehat{C}(\Delta_n)_t^{jl} = \sum_{i=1}^{[t/\Delta_n]} \Delta_i^n X^j \, \Delta_i^n X^l$$

$$\widehat{C}(\Delta_n, u_n)_t^{jl} = \sum_{i=1}^{[t/\Delta_n]} \Delta_i^n X^j \, \Delta_i^n X^l \, 1_{\{\|\Delta_i^n X\| \le u_n\}}$$

Part I

Preliminary Material

Chapter 1

From Diffusions to Semimartingales

This chapter is a quick review of the theory of semimartingales, these processes being those for which statistical methods are considered in this book.

A *process* is a collection $X = (X_t)$ of random variables with values in the Euclidean space $\mathbb{R}^d$ for some integer $d \geq 1$, and indexed on the half line $\mathbb{R}_+ = [0, \infty)$, or a subinterval of $\mathbb{R}_+$, typically $[0, T]$ for some real $T > 0$. The distinctive feature however is that all these variables are defined on *the same probability space* $(\Omega, \mathcal{F}, \mathbb{P})$. Therefore, for any outcome $\omega \in \Omega$ one can consider the *path* (or "trajectory"), which is the function $t \mapsto X_t(\omega)$, and X can also be considered as a single random variable taking its values in a suitable space of $\mathbb{R}^d$-valued functions on $\mathbb{R}_+$ or on $[0, T]$.

In many applications, including the modeling of financial data, the index t can be interpreted as *time*, and an important feature is the way the process evolves through time. Typically an observer knows what happens up to the current time t, that is, (s)he observes the path $s \mapsto X_s(\omega)$ for all $s \in [0, t]$, and wants to infer what will happen later, after time t. In a mathematical framework, this amounts to associating the "history" of the process, usually called the *filtration*. This is the increasing family $(\mathcal{F}_t)_{t \geq 0}$ of σ-fields associated with X in the following way: for each t, $\mathcal{F}_t$ is the σ-field generated by the variables X_s for $s \in [0, t]$ (more precise specifications will be given later). Therefore, of particular interest is the law of the "future" after time t, that is of the family $(X_s : s > t)$, conditional on the σ-field $\mathcal{F}_t$.

3

In a sense, this amounts to specifying the dynamics of the process, which again is a central question in financial modeling. If the process were not random, that would consist in specifying a differential equation governing the time evolution of our quantity of interest, or perhaps a non-autonomous differential equation where $dX_t = f(t, X_s : s \leq t)\, dt$ for a function f depending on time and on the whole "past" of X before t. In a random setting, this is replaced by a "stochastic differential equation."

Historically, it took quite a long time to come up with a class of processes large enough to account for the needs in applications, and still amenable to some simple calculus rules. It started with the Brownian motion, or Wiener process, and then processes with independent and stationary increments, now called Lévy processes after P. Lévy, who introduced and thoroughly described them. Next, martingales were considered, mainly by J. L. Doob, whereas K. Itô introduced (after W. Feller and W. Doeblin) the stochastic differential equations driven by Brownian motions, and also by Poisson random measures. The class of semimartingales was finalized by P.-A. Meyer in the early 1970s only.

In many respects, this class of processes is the right one to consider by someone interested in the dynamics of the process in the sense sketched above. Indeed, this is the largest class with respect to which stochastic integration is possible if one wants to have something like the dominated (Lebesgue) convergence theorem. It allows for relatively simple rules for stochastic calculus. Moreover, in financial mathematics, it also turns out to be the right class to consider, because a process can model the price of an asset in a fair market where no arbitrage is possible only if it is a semimartingale. This certainly is a sufficient motivation for the fact that, in this book, we only consider this type of process for modeling prices, including exchange rates or indices, and interest rates.

Now, of course, quite a few books provide extensive coverage of semimartingales, stochastic integration and stochastic calculus. Our aim in this chapter is not to duplicate any part of those books, and in particular not the proofs therein: the interested reader should consult one of them to get a complete mathematical picture of the subject, for example, Karatzas and Shreve (1991) or Revuz and Yor (1994) for continuous processes, and Dellacherie and Meyer (1982) or Jacod and Shiryaev (2003) for general ones. Our aim is simply to introduce semimartingales and the properties of those which are going to be of constant use in this book, in as simple a way as possible, starting with the most commonly known processes, which are the Brownian motion or Wiener process and the diffusions. We then introduce Lévy processes and Poisson random measures, and finally arrive at semimartingales, presented as a relatively natural extension of Lévy processes.

1.1 Diffusions

1.1.1 The Brownian Motion

The *Brownian motion* (or *Wiener process*), formalized by N. Wiener and P. Lévy, has in fact been used in finance even earlier, by T. N. Thiele and L. Bachelier, and for modeling the physical motion of a particle by A. Einstein. It is the simplest continuous-time analogue of a random walk.

Mathematically speaking, the one-dimensional Brownian motion can be specified as a process $W = (W_t)_{t\geq 0}$, which is Gaussian (meaning that any finite family $(W_{t_1}, \ldots, W_{t_k})$ is a Gaussian random vector), centered (i.e. $\mathbb{E}(W_t) = 0$ for all t), and with the covariance structure

$$\mathbb{E}(W_t\, W_s) = t \wedge s \tag{1.1}$$

where the notation $t \wedge s$ means $\min(t, s)$. These properties completely characterize the law of the process W, by Kolmogorov's Theorem, which allows for the definition of a stochastic process through its finite-dimensional distributions, under conditions known as consistency of the finite-dimensional distributions. And, using for example the Kolmogorov continuity criterion (since $\mathbb{E}(|W_{t+s} - W_s|^4) = 3s^2$ for all nonnegative t and s), one can "realize" the Brownian motion on a suitable probability space $(\Omega, \mathcal{F}, \mathbb{P})$ as a process having *continuous paths*, i.e. $t \mapsto W_t(\omega)$ is continuous and with $W_0(\omega) = 0$ for all outcomes ω. So we will take the view that a Brownian motion always starts at $W_0 = 0$ and has continuous paths.

One of the many fundamental properties of Brownian motion is that it is a *Lévy process*, that is it starts from 0 and has independent and stationary increments: for all $s, t \geq 0$ the variable $W_{t+s} - W_t$ is independent of $(W_r : r \leq t)$, with a law which only depends on s: here, this law is the normal law $\mathcal{N}(0, s)$ (centered with variance s). This immediately follows from the above definition. However, a converse is also true: any Lévy process which is centered and continuous is of the form σW for some constant $\sigma \geq 0$, where W is a Brownian motion.

Now, we need two extensions of the previous notion. The first one is straightforward: a d-dimensional Brownian motion is an $\mathbb{R}^d$-valued process $W = (W_t)_{t\geq 0}$ with components W_t^i for $i = 1, \ldots, d$ (we keep the same notation W as in the one-dimensional case), such that each component process $W^i = (W_t^i)_{t \geq 0}$ is a one-dimensional Brownian motion, and all components are *independent* processes. Equivalently, W is a centered continuous Gaussian process with $W_0 = 0$, and with the following covariance structure:

$$\mathbb{E}(W_t^i \, W_s^j) = \begin{cases} t \wedge s & \text{if } i = j \\ 0 & \text{if } i \neq j. \end{cases} \tag{1.2}$$

A d-dimensional Brownian motion retains the nice property of being a Lévy process.

The second extension is slightly more subtle, and involves the concept of a general *filtered probability space*, denoted by $(\Omega, \mathcal{F}, (\mathcal{F}_t)_{t \geq 0}, \mathbb{P})$. Here $(\Omega, \mathcal{F}, \mathbb{P})$ is a probability space, equipped with a *filtration* $(\mathcal{F}_t)_{t \geq 0}$: this is an increasing family of sub-σ-fields $\mathcal{F}_t$ of $\mathcal{F}$ (that is, $\mathcal{F}_t \subset \mathcal{F}_s \subset \mathcal{F}$ when $t \leq s$), which is right-continuous (that is $\mathcal{F}_t = \cap_{s > t} \mathcal{F}_s$). The right-continuity condition appears for technical reasons, but is in fact an essential requirement. Again, $\mathcal{F}_t$ can be viewed as the amount of information available to an observer up to (and including) time t.

We say that a process X is *adapted* to a filtration $(\mathcal{F}_t)$, or $(\mathcal{F}_t)$-adapted, if each variable X_t is $\mathcal{F}_t$-measurable. The *filtration generated by a process* X is the smallest filtration with respect to which X is adapted. It is denoted as $(\mathcal{F}_t^X)$, and can be expressed as follows:

$$\mathcal{F}_t^X = \cap_{s > t} \, \sigma(X_r : r \in [0, s])$$

(this is right-continuous by construction).

We suppose that the reader is familiar with the notion of a *martingale* (a real process $M = (M_t)_{t \geq 0}$ is a martingale on the filtered space if it is adapted, if each variable M_t is integrable and if $\mathbb{E}(M_{t+s} \mid \mathcal{F}_t) = M_t$ for $s, t \geq 0$), and also with the notion of a *stopping time*: a $[0, \infty]$-valued random variable τ is a stopping time if it is possible to tell, for any $t \geq 0$, whether the event that τ has occurred before or at time t is true or not, on the basis of the information contained in $\mathcal{F}_t$; formally, this amounts to saying that the event $\{\tau \leq t\}$ belongs to $\mathcal{F}_t$, for all $t \geq 0$. Likewise, $\mathcal{F}_\tau$ denotes the σ-field of all sets $A \in \mathcal{F}$ such that $A \cap \{\tau \leq t\} \in \mathcal{F}_t$ for all $t \geq 0$, and it represents the information available up to (and including) time τ.

A process X is called *progressively measurable* if for any t the function $(\omega, s) \mapsto X_s(\omega)$ is $\mathcal{F}_t \otimes \mathcal{B}([0, t])$-measurable on $\Omega \times [0, t]$; here, $\mathcal{B}([0, t])$ denotes the Borel σ-field of the interval $[0, t]$, that is the σ-field generated by the open sets of $[0, t]$. Then, given a stopping time τ and a progressively measurable process X_t, the variable $X_\tau 1_{\{\tau < \infty\}}$ is $\mathcal{F}_\tau$-measurable;

moreover one can define the new process $X_{\tau \wedge t}$, or X stopped at τ, and this process is again adapted. We note the following useful property: if M is a martingale and τ_1 and τ_2 are two stopping times such that $0 \leq \tau_1 \leq \tau_2 \leq T$ a.s. (almost surely), then $\mathbb{E}(M_{\tau_2} \mid \mathcal{F}_{\tau_1}) = M_{\tau_1}$.

Coming back to Brownian motion, we say that a d-dimensional process $W = (W^i)_{1 \leq i \leq d}$ is a *Brownian motion* on the filtered space $(\Omega, \mathcal{F}, (\mathcal{F}_t)_{t \geq 0}, \mathbb{P})$, or an $(\mathcal{F}_t)$ -Brownian motion, if it satisfies the following three conditions:

1. It has continuous paths, with $W_0 = 0$.

2. It is adapted to the filtration $(\mathcal{F}_t)$.

3. For all $s, t \geq 0$ the variable $W_{t+s} - W_t$ is independent of the σ-field $\mathcal{F}_t$, with centered Gaussian law $\mathcal{N}(0, sI_d)$ (I_d is the $d \times d$ identity matrix).

It turns out that a Brownian motion in the previously stated restricted sense is an $(\mathcal{F}_t^W)$-Brownian motion. This property is almost obvious: it would be obvious if $\mathcal{F}_t^W$ were $\sigma(W_r : r \in [0, t])$, and its extension comes from a so-called $0 - 1$ law which asserts that, if an event is in $\mathcal{F}_s^W$ for all $s > t$ and is also independent of $\mathcal{F}_v^W$ for all $v < t$, then its probability can only equal 0 or 1.

Another characterization of the Brownian motion, particularly well suited to stochastic calculus, is the *Lévy Characterization Theorem*. Namely, a continuous $(\mathcal{F}_t)$-adapted process W with $W_0 = 0$ is an $(\mathcal{F}_t)$-Brownian motion if and only if it satisfies

$$\text{the processes } W_t^i \text{ and } W_t^i W_t^j - \delta_{ij} t \text{ are } (\mathcal{F}_t) - \text{martingales} \qquad (1.3)$$

where $\delta_{ij} = 1$ if $i = j$ and 0 otherwise denotes the Kronecker symbol. The necessary part is elementary; the sufficient part is more difficult to prove.

Finally, we mention two well known and important properties of the paths of a one-dimensional Brownian motion:

- *Lévy modulus of continuity*: almost all paths satisfy, for any interval I of positive length,

$$\limsup_{r \to 0} \frac{1}{\sqrt{r \log(1/r)}} \sup_{s,t \in I, |s-t| \leq r} |W_t - W_s| = \sqrt{2}. \qquad (1.4)$$

- *Law of iterated logarithm*: for each finite stopping time T, almost all paths satisfy

$$\limsup_{r\to 0} \frac{1}{\sqrt{r \log\log(1/r)}}\,(W_{T+r} - W_T) = \sqrt{2}. \qquad (1.5)$$

By symmetry, the $\liminf$ in the law of iterated logarithm is equal to $-\sqrt{2}$. Despite the appearances, these two results are not contradictory, because of the different position of the qualifier "almost all." These facts imply that, for any $\rho < 1/2$, almost all paths are locally Hölder with index ρ, but nowhere Hölder with index $1/2$, and *a fortiori* nowhere differentiable.

1.1.2   Stochastic Integrals

A second fundamental concept is stochastic integration. The paths of a one-dimensional Brownian motion W being continuous but nowhere differentiable, *a priori* the "differential" dW_t makes no sense, and neither does the expression $\int_0^t H_s dW_s$. However, suppose that H is a "simple," or piecewise constant, process of the form

$$H_t = \sum_{i\geq 1} H_{t_{i-1}} 1_{[t_{i-1},t_i)}(t), \qquad (1.6)$$

where $0 = t_0 < t_1 < \cdots$ and $t_n \to \infty$ as $n \to \infty$. Then it is natural to set

$$\int_0^t H_s\,dW_s = \sum_{i\geq 1} H_{t_{i-1}}(W_{t\wedge t_i} - W_{t\wedge t_{i-1}}). \qquad (1.7)$$

This would be the usual integral if $t \mapsto W_t$ were the distribution function of a (signed) measure on $[0,t]$, which it is of course not. Nevertheless it turns out that, due to the martingale properties (1.3) of W, this "integral" can be extended to all processes H having the following properties:

$$H \text{ is progressively measurable, and not too big,}$$
$$\text{in the sense that } \int_0^t H_s^2 ds < \infty \text{ for all } t. \qquad (1.8)$$

The extension is still denoted as $\int_0^t H_s dW_s$ or, more compactly, as $H \bullet W_t$. It is called a *stochastic integral*, which emphasizes the fact that it is not a Stieltjes (ω-wise) integral. In particular, it is only defined "up to a null set," meaning that another variable Y is also a version of the stochastic integral if and only if we have $Y = H \bullet W_t$ a.s. So we emphasize that *every* statement about a stochastic integral variable $H \bullet X_t$ or process $(H \bullet X_t)_{t\geq 0}$ is *necessarily* true "up to a null set" only, although for simplicity we usually omit the qualifier "almost surely" (exactly as, for the conditional expectation, one simply writes an equality such as $\mathbb{E}(Y \mid \mathcal{G}) = Z$ without explicitly mentioning "a.s.").

Stochastic integrals enjoy the following properties:

- the process $(H \bullet W_t)_{t \geq 0}$ is a continuous (local) martingale starting at 0
- the process $(H \bullet W_t)^2 - \int_0^t H_s^2 \, ds$ is a (local) martingale
- the map $H \mapsto H \bullet W$ is linear (1.9)
- We have a "dominated convergence theorem": if $H^n \to H$ pointwise and $|H^n| \leq H'$ with H' as in (1.8), then $H^n \bullet W \overset{\text{u.c.p.}}{\Longrightarrow} H \bullet W$.

In this statement, two notions need some explanation. First, $\overset{\text{u.c.p.}}{\Longrightarrow}$ stands for "local uniform convergence in probability," that is we write $X^n \overset{\text{u.c.p.}}{\Longrightarrow} X$ if for all t we have $\sup_{s \leq t} |X_s^n - X_s| \overset{\mathbb{P}}{\longrightarrow} 0$ (convergence in probability). Second, a *local martingale* is a process M for which there exists an increasing sequence of stopping times T_n with infinite limit (called a "localizing sequence"), such that each "stopped" process $t \mapsto M_{t \wedge T_n}$ is a martingale. In other words, M behaves like a martingale up to suitably chosen stopping times; martingales are local martingales but the converse is not true.

Let us also mention that the first statement (1.9) is shorthand for the more correct "one can find versions of the stochastic integrals $H \bullet W_t$ such that almost all paths $t \mapsto H \bullet W_t$ are continuous and start at 0, and further $(H \bullet W_t)_{t \geq 0}$ is a local martingale." And, as mentioned before, the third statement in (1.9) is true "up to null sets."

More generally, let W be a d-dimensional Brownian motion. Then one can integrate "componentwise" a d-dimensional process $H = (H^i)_{1 \leq i \leq d}$ whose components each satisfy (1.8), thus getting the following one-dimensional process:

$$H \bullet W_t = \int_0^t H_s \, dW_s = \sum_{i=1}^d \int_0^t H_s^i \, dW_s^i.$$

We still have the properties (1.9), with the norm of H^n instead of the absolute value in the fourth property. Moreover if H and K are two integrable processes, the process

$$(H \bullet W_t)(K \bullet W_t) - \int_0^t \sum_{i=1}^d H_s^i K_s^i \, ds \text{ is a local martingale.} \quad (1.10)$$

Before stating the "change of variable" formula for stochastic integrals, we give our first (restricted) definition of a semimartingale:

Definition 1.1. *A one-dimensional continuous Itô semimartingale (also called a "generalized diffusion," or a "Brownian semimartingale" sometimes) is an adapted process X which can be written as*

$$X_t = X_0 + \int_0^t b_s \, ds + \int_0^t \sigma_s \, dW_s, \qquad (1.11)$$

where W is a q-dimensional Brownian motion, and σ is a q-dimensional process, integrable in the above sense (i.e., its components satisfy (1.8)), and $b = (b_t)_{t \geq 0}$ is another progressively measurable process such that $\int_0^t |b_s| \, ds < \infty$ for all t.

A d-dimensional continuous Itô semimartingale is a process whose each one of the d components is a continuous Itô semimartingale.

If X is as above, one can integrate a process K with respect to it, by setting

$$K \bullet X_t = \int_0^t K_s \, dX_s = \int_0^t K_s b_s \, ds + \int_0^t K_s \sigma_s \, dW_s$$

(with an obvious interpretation when X and K are q-dimensional). We need $K\sigma$ to be integrable with respect to W, as in (1.8), and also Kb to be integrable with respect to the Lebesgue measure on each finite interval $[0, t]$ (this integral is an "ordinary," or ω-wise, integral). A precise description of all processes K which can thus be integrated is somewhat complicated, but in any case we can integrate all processes K which are progressively measurable and *locally bounded* (meaning we have $|K_s| \leq n$ for any $0 < s \leq T_n$, where T_n is a sequence of stopping times increasing to ∞); note that no condition on K_0 is implied. In this case, the integral process $K \bullet X$ is also a continuous Itô semimartingale.

The last process on the right hand side of (1.11) is called the *continuous martingale part* of X, although it usually is a local martingale only, and it is denoted as X^c (with components $X^{i,c}$ in the multidimensional case). We also associate the family of processes, for $j, l = 1, \ldots, q$ and q the dimension of X:

$$C_t^{jl} = \sum_{i=1}^d \int_0^t \sigma_s^{ji} \sigma_s^{li} \, ds. \qquad (1.12)$$

Another notation for C_t^{jl} is $\langle X^{j,c}, X^{l,c} \rangle_t$ and it is called the *quadratic variation-covariation process*. From this formula, the q^2-dimensional process $C = (C^{jl})_{1 \leq j,l \leq q}$ takes its values in the cone of all positive semi-definite symmetric $q \times q$ matrices, and is continuous in t and increasing (in t again) for the strong order in this cone (that is, $C_t - C_s$ is also positive semi-definite if $t \geq s$). Note also the following obvious but important fact:

If $X = W$ is a Brownian motion, then $X^c = W$ and $C_t^{jl} = \delta_{jl} t$.

This definition of the quadratic variation is based upon the definition (1.11). However, there are two other characterizations. First, one can rewrite (1.10) as

$$X^{j,c} X^{l,c} - C^{jl} \quad \text{is a local martingale.} \tag{1.13}$$

Conversely, C is the *unique* (up to null sets) adapted continuous process, starting at $C_0 = 0$, with path $t \mapsto C_t^{jl}$ having finite variation over compact intervals, and such that (1.13) holds.

Second, the name "quadratic variation" comes from the following property: let $((t(n,i) : i \geq 0) : n \geq 1)$ be a sequence of subdivisions on $\mathbb{R}_+$ with meshes going to 0. This means that for each n we have $t(n,0) = 0 < t(n,1) < \cdots$ and $t(n,i) \to \infty$ as $i \to \infty$, and also $\sup_{i \geq 1} (t(n,i) - t(n,i-1)) \to 0$ as $n \to \infty$. Then we have

$$\sum_{i \geq 1 : t(n,i) \leq t} \left(X_{t(n,i)}^j - X_{t(n,i-1)}^j \right) \left(X_{t(n,i)}^l - X_{t(n,i-1)}^l \right) \xrightarrow{\mathbb{P}} C_t^{jl}. \tag{1.14}$$

Historically this is the way the quadratic variation has been introduced, indeed as a tool for defining stochastic integrals. We will give below a (simple) proof of this property, deduced from Itô's formula, and for general semimartingales. The reason for giving the proof is that from an applied viewpoint (and especially for financial applications) (1.14) is an important property in high-frequency statistics: the left hand side, say when $j = l = 1$, is the so-called *realized quadratic variation*, or realized volatility, of the component X^1, along the observation times $t(n,i)$ for $i \geq 0$, whereas the process C^{11} is what is called "integrated (squared) volatility."

We are now ready to state the change of variable formula, more commonly called *Itô's formula*: for any $\mathcal{C}^2$ real-valued function f on $\mathbb{R}^d$ (twice continuously differentiable) and any d-dimensional continuous Itô semimartingale $X = (X^j)_{1 \leq j \leq d}$, the process $Y = f(X)$ is also a continuous Itô semimartingale; moreover, if f_i' and f_{ij}'' denote the first and second partial derivatives of f, we have

$$f(X_t) \;=\; f(X_0) + \sum_{i=1}^{d} \int_0^t f_i'(X_s)\, dX_s^i \qquad\qquad (1.15)$$

$$+ \frac{1}{2} \sum_{i,j=1}^{d} \int_0^t f_{ij}''(X_s)\, d\langle X^{i,c}, X^{j,c}\rangle_s \;.$$

Note that the processes $f_i'(X_s)$ and $f_{ij}''(X_s)$ are continuous, hence locally bounded, and adapted; so the first integrals in the right hand side above are stochastic integrals with respect to the Itô semimartingales X^i, and the second integrals are ordinary (Stieltjes) integrals with respect to the functions $t \mapsto C_t^{ij} = \langle X^{i,c}, X^{j,c}\rangle_t$, which are absolutely continuous by (1.12).

When $X^c = 0$, that is, when the functions $t \mapsto X_t^i$ are absolutely continuous, the last sum in (1.15) vanishes, and the formula reduces to the usual change of variable formula (then of course f being $\mathcal{C}^1$ would be sufficient). The fact that in general this additional last term is present is one of the key observations made by K. Itô.

1.1.3   A Central Example: Diffusion Processes

As the other name "generalized diffusion processes" for continuous Itô semimartingales suggests, the main examples of such processes are diffusions processes. Historically speaking, they were the first relatively general semimartingales to be considered, and they play a central role in modeling, in the physical sciences and in finance, although in many cases they can be far from sufficient to account for all encountered empirical features of the processes being measured.

Going from general to particular, one can characterize *diffusions* as those continuous Itô semimartingales which are Markov processes. These may be homogeneous or not, and for simplicity we only consider the homogeneous case below, since they are by far the most common ones. More specifically, following for example Çinlar and Jacod (1981), if a continuous d-dimensional Itô semimartingale of the form (1.11) is a homogeneous Markov process, then the two random "infinitesimal coefficients" b_t and σ_t take the form

$$b_t \;=\; b(X_t), \qquad \sigma_t \;=\; \sigma(X_t),$$

where $b = (b^i)_{1 \leq d}$ and $\sigma = (\sigma^{ij})_{1 \leq i \leq d, 1 \leq j \leq q}$ are functions on $\mathbb{R}^d$. That is,

$$X_t = X_0 + \int_0^t b(X_s)\,ds + \int_0^t \sigma(X_s)\,dW_s^j \qquad (1.16)$$

or, componentwise,

$$X_t^i = X_0^i + \int_0^t b^i(X_s)\,ds + \sum_{j=1}^q \int_0^t \sigma^{ij}(X_s)\,dW_s^j, \qquad \forall i = 1,\dots,d.$$

Now, the law of a Markov processes is also characterized by the law of its initial value X_0 and its transition semi-group $(\mathcal{P}_t)_{t\geq 0}$ (defined as the operator which returns $\mathcal{P}_t f(x) = \mathbb{E}(f(X_t)\,|\,X_0 = x)$ when applied to any Borel bounded test function f, and $x \in \mathbb{R}^d$), and in turn the semi-group is characterized by its infinitesimal generator (in general an unbounded operator defined on a suitable domain). Whereas there is no hope in general to have an explicit expression for the semi-group, one can easily compute the infinitesimal generator, at least when the test function is C^2. Namely, with the notation $c(x) = \sigma(x)\sigma(x)^*$ (where σ^* is the transpose of σ), we observe that, by virtue of (1.12), $\langle X^{i,c}, X^{j,c}\rangle_t = C_t^{ij} = \int_0^t c_s^{ij}\,ds$. Then Itô's formula (1.15) implies that

$$
\begin{aligned}
M_t^f &= f(X_t) - f(X_0) - \sum_{i=1}^d \int_0^t b(X_s)^i f_i'(X_s)\,ds \\
&\quad - \frac{1}{2}\sum_{i,j=1}^d \int_0^t c(X_s)^{ij} f_{ij}''(X_s)\,ds
\end{aligned}
$$

is a local martingale. With the notation

$$\mathcal{A}f(x) = \sum_{i=1}^d b(x)^i f_i'(x) + \frac{1}{2}\sum_{i,j=1}^d c(x)^{ij} f_{ij}''(x), \qquad (1.17)$$

we then have $M_t^f = f(X_t) - f(X_0) - \int_0^t \mathcal{A}f(X_s)\,ds$. If further f has compact support, say, and if the coefficients b and σ are locally bounded, then $\mathcal{A}f$ is bounded. Hence M^f is a martingale and not only a local martingale, and by taking the expectation and using Fubini's Theorem we obtain

$$\mathcal{P}_t f(x) = f(x) + \int_0^t \mathcal{P}_s \mathcal{A}f(x)\,ds.$$

In other words, f belongs to the domain of the infinitesimal generator, which is $\mathcal{A}f$ (as defined above) for such a function.

Of course, this does not fully specify the infinitesimal generator: for this we should exhibit its full domain and say how it acts on functions which are in the domain but are not C^2 with compact support (and the domain always contains plenty of such functions). But in the "good" cases, the complete infinitesimal generator is simply the closure of the operator $\mathcal{A}$ acting on C^2 functions with compact support as in (1.17).

Now, diffusions can also be viewed, and historically have been introduced, as solutions of *stochastic differential equation*, or SDE in short. Coming back to (1.16), a convenient way of writing it is in "differential form," as follows, and with the convention $Y = X_0$:

$$dX_t = b(X_t)dt + \sigma(X_t)dW_t, \qquad X_0 = Y \qquad (1.18)$$

despite the fact that the differential dW_t is *a priori* meaningless. Now, we can consider (1.18) as an equation. The "solution" will be a d-dimensional process X, whereas W is a q-dimensional Brownian motion, and the following ingredients are given: the initial condition Y (an $\mathbb{R}^d$-valued random vector, most often a constant $Y = x \in \mathbb{R}^d$) and the coefficients b and σ which are Borel functions on $\mathbb{R}^d$, with the suitable dimensions (they are respectively called the *drift* and *diffusion* coefficients).

The word "solution" for an SDE like (1.18) may have several different meanings. Here we consider the simplest notion, sometimes called solution-process or strong solution. Namely, we are given a q-dimensional $(\mathcal{F}_t)$-Brownian motion W and a d-dimensional $\mathcal{F}_0$-measurable variable Y on some filtered probability space $(\Omega, \mathcal{F}, (\mathcal{F}_t)_{t \geq 0}, \mathbb{P})$, and a *solution* is a continuous adapted process X which satisfies (1.18), which is a shorthand way of writing (1.16) with $X_0 = Y$.

In particular, the integrals on the right side of (1.16) should make sense: so the functions b and σ should be measurable and not "too big"; more important, the process $\sigma(X_t)$ should be progressively measurable, so (unless of course σ is constant) we need X itself to be progressively measurable, and since it is continuous in time this is the same as saying that it is adapted. Finally, it follows in particular that X_0 is $\mathcal{F}_0$-measurable, which is the reason why we impose the $\mathcal{F}_0$-measurability to the initial condition Y.

Of course, as ordinary differential equations, not all SDEs have a solution. Let us simply mention that, if the two functions b and σ are *locally Lipschitz and with at most linear growth* on $\mathbb{R}^d$, then (1.18) has a solution, and furthermore this solution is unique: the uniqueness here means that any two solutions X and X' satisfy $X_t = X'_t$ a.s. for all t, which is the best one can hope since in any case stochastic integrals are defined only up to null sets. An interesting feature is that, under the previous assumptions on b and σ, existence and uniqueness hold for all initial conditions Y.

These Lipschitz and growth conditions are by far not the only available conditions implying existence and/or uniqueness. In fact, existence and/or uniqueness is somehow related to the fact that the operator $\mathcal{A}$ defined by (1.17) for $\mathcal{C}^2$ functions f with compact support can be extended as a *bona fide* infinitesimal generator.

Example 1.2. *The following one-dimensional example ($d = q = 1$):*

$$dX_t = \kappa(\nu - X_t)dt + \eta\sqrt{X_t}dW_t, \qquad X_0 = Y \qquad (1.19)$$

where $\kappa, \eta \in \mathbb{R}$ and $\nu \in \mathbb{R}_+$ are given constants, is known as Feller's equation or in finance the Cox-Ingersoll-Ross (CIR) model, and it shows some of the problems that can occur. It does not fit the previous setting, for two reasons: first, because of the square root, we need $X_t \geq 0$; so the natural state space of our process is not $\mathbb{R}$, but $\mathbb{R}_+$. Second, the diffusion coefficient $\sigma(x) = \eta\sqrt{x}$ is not locally Lipschitz on $[0, \infty)$.

Let us thus provide some comments:

1. In the general setting of (1.18), the fact that the state space is not $\mathbb{R}^d$ but a domain $D \subset \mathbb{R}^d$ is not a problem for the formulation of the equation: the coefficients b and σ are simply functions on D instead of being functions on $\mathbb{R}^d$, and the solution X should be a D-valued process, provided of course that the initial condition Y is also D-valued. Problems arise when one tries to solve the equation. Even with Lipschitz coefficients, there is no guarantee that X will not reach the boundary of D, and here anything can happen, like the drift or the Brownian motion forcing X to leave D. So one should either make sure that X cannot reach the boundary, or specify what happens if it does (such as, how the process behaves along the boundary, or how it is reflected back inside the domain D).

2. Coming back to the CIR model (1.19), and assuming $Y > 0$, one can show that with the state space $D = (0, \infty)$ (on which the coefficients are locally Lipschitz), then the solution X will never reach 0 if and only if $2\kappa\nu > \eta^2$. Otherwise, it reaches 0 and uniqueness fails, unless we specify that the process reflects instantaneously when it reaches 0, and of course we need $\kappa > 0$.

All these problems are often difficult to resolve, and sometimes require *ad hoc* or model-specific arguments. In this book, when we have a diffusion we suppose in fact that it is well defined, and that those difficult

problems have been solved beforehand. Let us simply mention that the
literature on this topic is huge, see for example Revuz and Yor (1994)
and Karatzas and Shreve (1991).

1.2 Lévy Processes

As already said, a *Lévy process* is an $\mathbb{R}^d$-valued process starting at 0 and
having stationary and independent increments. More generally:

Definition 1.3. *A filtered probability space* $(\Omega, \mathcal{F}, (\mathcal{F}_t)_{t\geq 0}, \mathbb{P})$ *being
given, a* Lévy process *relative to the filtration* $(\mathcal{F}_t)$*, or an* $(\mathcal{F}_t)$*-Lévy
process, is an* $\mathbb{R}^d$*-valued process* X *satisfying the following three conditions:*

1. *Its paths are right-continuous with left limit everywhere (we say, a
   càdlàg process, from the French acronym "continu à droite, limité
   à gauche"), with* $X_0 = 0$.

2. *It is adapted to the filtration* $(\mathcal{F}_t)$.

3. *For all* $s, t \geq 0$ *the variable* $X_{t+s} - X_t$ *is independent of the* σ*-field*
   $\mathcal{F}_t$*, and its law only depends on* s.

These are the same as the conditions defining an $(\mathcal{F}_t)$-Brownian motion, except that the paths are càdlàg instead of continuous, and the laws
of the increments are not necessarily Gaussian. In particular, we associate with X its jump process, defined (for any càdlàg process, for that
matter) as

$$\Delta X_t = X_t - X_{t-} \tag{1.20}$$

where X_{t-} is the left limit at time t, and by convention $\Delta X_0 = 0$.

Regarding the nature of the sample paths of a Lévy process, note that
the càdlàg property is important to give meaning to the concept of a
"jump" defined in (1.20) where we need as a prerequisite left and right
limits at each t. When a jump occurs at time t, being right-continuous
means that the value after the jump, X_{t+}, is X_t. In finance, it means
that by the time a jump has occurred, the price has already moved to
$X_t = X_{t+}$ and it is no longer possible to trade at the pre-jump value
X_{t-}.

Although the process can have infinitely many jumps on a finite interval $[0, T]$, the càdlàg property limits the total number of jumps to be at
most countable. It also limits the number of jumps larger than any fixed

value $\varepsilon > 0$ on any interval $[0,t]$ to be at most finite. Further, the paths of a Lévy process are stochastically continuous, meaning that $X_s \xrightarrow{\mathbb{P}} X_t$ (convergence in probability) for all $t > 0$, and as $s \to t$ (here, t is non-random). This condition does not make the paths of X continuous, but it excludes jumps at fixed times. All it says is that at any given *non-random* time t, the probability of seeing a jump at this time is 0.

1.2.1   The Law of a Lévy Process

One can look at Lévy processes *per se* without consideration for the connection with other processes defined on the probability space or with the underlying filtration. We then take the viewpoint of the law, or equivalently the family of all finite-dimensional distributions, that is the laws of any n-tuple $(X_{t_1}, \ldots, X_{t_n})$, where $0 \leq t_1 < \cdots < t_n$.

Because of the three properties defining X above, the law of $(X_{t_1}, \ldots, X_{t_n})$ is the same as the law of $(Y_1, Y_1 + Y_2, \ldots, Y_1 + \cdots + Y_n)$, where the Y_j's are independent variables having the same laws as $X_{t_j - t_{j-1}}$. Therefore the law of the whole process X is completely determined, once the one-dimensional laws $G_t = \mathcal{L}(X_t)$ are known.

Moreover, G_{t+s} is equal to the convolution product $G_t * G_s$ for all $s, t \geq 0$, so the laws G_t have the very special property of being *infinitely divisible*: the name comes from the fact that, for any integer $n \geq 1$, we can write $X_t = \sum_{j=1}^{n} Y_j$ as a sum of n i.i.d. random variables Y_j whose distribution is that of $X_{t/n}$; equivalently, for any $n \geq 1$, the law G_t is the n-fold convolution power of some probability measure, namely $G_{t/n}$ here. This property places a restriction on the possible laws G_t, and is called infinite divisibility. Examples include the Gaussian, gamma, stable and Poisson distributions. For instance, in the Gaussian case, any $X_t \sim \mathcal{N}(m, v)$ can be written as the sum of n i.i.d. random variables $Y_j \sim \mathcal{N}(m/n, v/n)$.

Infinite divisibility implies that the characteristic function $\widehat{G}_t(u) = \mathbb{E}\left(e^{iu^* X_t}\right) = \int e^{iu^* x} G_t(dx)$ (where $u \in \mathbb{R}^d$ and $u^* x$ is the scalar product) does not vanish and there exists a function $\Psi : \mathbb{R}^d \to \mathbb{R}$, called the characteristic exponent of X, such that the characteristic function takes the form

$$\widehat{G}_t(u) = \exp\left(t\Psi(u)\right), \quad u \in \mathbb{R}^d, \ t > 0. \qquad (1.21)$$

Indeed we have $\widehat{G}_{t+s}(u) = \widehat{G}_t(u)\widehat{G}_s(u)$ and $\widehat{G}_t(u)$ is càdlàg in t, which imply that the logarithm of $\widehat{G}_t(u)$ is linear, as a function of t; of course these are complex numbers, so some care must be taken to justify the statement.

In fact it implies much more, namely that $\Psi(u)$ has a specific form given by the *Lévy-Khintchine* formula, which we write here for the variable X_1:

$$\widehat{G}_1(u) = \exp\left(u^*b - \frac{1}{2}u^*cu + \int(e^{iu^*x} - 1 - iu^*x1_{\{\|x\|\leq 1\}})F(dx)\right). \quad (1.22)$$

In this formula, the three ingredients (b, c, F) are as follows:

- $b = (b^i)_{i\leq d} \in \mathbb{R}^d$,

- $c = (c^{ij})_{i,j\leq d}$ is a symmetric nonnegative matrix,   (1.23)
- F is a positive measure on $\mathbb{R}^d$
  with $F(\{0\}) = 0$ and $\int(\|x\|^2 \wedge 1)\, F(dx) < \infty$.

and $u^*cu = \sum_{i,j=1}^d u_i c_{ij} u_j$. The integrability requirement on F in (1.23) is really two different constraints written in one: it requires $\int_{\|x\|\leq 1} \|x\|^2 F(dx) < \infty$, which limits the rate at which F can diverge near 0, and $\int_{\|x\|\geq 1} F(dx) < \infty$. These two requirements are exactly what is needed for the integral in (1.22) to be absolutely convergent, because $e^{iu^*x} - 1 - iu^*x1_{\{\|x\|\leq 1\}} \sim (u^*x)^2$ as $x \to 0$, and $e^{iu^*x} - 1$ is bounded.

We have written (1.2) at time $t = 1$, but because of (1.21), we also have it at any time t. A priori, one might think that the triple (b_t, c_t, F_t) associated with G_t would depend on t in a rather arbitrary way, but this is not so. We have, for any $t \geq 0$, and with the same (b, c, F) as in (1.22),

- $\widehat{G}_t(u) = e^{t\Psi(u)}$,

(1.24)
- $\Psi(u) = u^*b - \frac{1}{2}u^*cu + \int\left(e^{iu^*x} - 1 - iu^*x1_{\{\|x\|\leq 1\}}\right)F(dx)$,

and $\Psi(u)$ is called the *characteristic exponent* of the Lévy process.

In other words, the law of X is completely characterized by the triple (b, c, F), subject to (1.23), thus earning it the name *characteristic triple* of the Lévy process X. And we do have a converse: if (b, c, F) satisfies the conditions (1.23), then it is the characteristic triple of a Lévy process. The measure F is called the *Lévy measure* of the process, c is called the diffusion coefficient (for reasons which will be apparent later), and b is the drift (a slightly misleading terminology, as we will see later again). In Section 1.2.5 below, we will see that the different elements on the right-hand side of (1.22) correspond to specific elements of the canonical decomposition of a Lévy process in terms of drift, volatility, small jumps and big jumps.

We end this subsection by pointing out some moment properties of

Lévy processes. First, for any reals $p > 0$ and $t > 0$ we have

$$\mathbb{E}(\|X_t\|^p) < \infty \quad \Leftrightarrow \quad \int_{\{\|x\|>1\}} \|x\|^p \, F(dx) < \infty. \qquad (1.25)$$

In particular the pth moments are either finite for all t or infinite for all $t > 0$, and they are all finite when F has compact support, a property which is equivalent to saying that the jumps of X are bounded, as we will see later.

Second, cumulants and hence moments of the distribution of X_t of integer order p can be computed explicitly using (1.24) by differentiation of the characteristic exponent and characteristic function. For example, in the one-dimensional case and when $\mathbb{E}(|X_t|^n) < \infty$, the nth cumulant and nth moment of X_t are

$$\kappa_{n,t} = \frac{1}{i^n} \frac{\partial^n}{\partial u^n} (t\Psi(u))_{|u=0} = t\kappa_{n,1},$$

$$\varphi_{n,t} = \frac{1}{i^n} \frac{\partial^n}{\partial u^n} \left(e^{t\Psi(u)}\right)_{|u=0}.$$

The first four cumulants, in terms of the moments and of the centered moments $\mu_{n,t} = \mathbb{E}((X_t - \phi_{1,t})^n)$, are

$$\kappa_{1,t} = \varphi_{1,t} = \mathbb{E}(X_t),$$
$$\kappa_{2,t} = \mu_{2,t} = \varphi_{2,t} - \varphi_{1,t}^2 = \mathrm{Var}(X_t),$$
$$\kappa_{3,t} = \mu_{3,t} = \varphi_{3,t} - 3\varphi_{2,t}\varphi_{1,t} + 2\varphi_{1,t}^3,$$
$$\kappa_{4,t} = \mu_{4,t} - 3\mu_{2,t}^2.$$

In terms of the characteristics (b, c, F) of X, we have

$$\kappa_{1,t} = t\left(b + \int_{|x|\geq 1} x \, F(dx)\right),$$
$$\kappa_{2,t} = t\left(c + \int x^2 \, F(dx)\right),$$
$$\kappa_{p,t} = t \int x^p \, F(dx) \quad \text{for all integers } p \geq 3.$$

All infinitely divisible distributions with a non-vanishing Lévy measure are leptokurtic, that is $\kappa_4 > 0$. The skewness and excess kurtosis of X_t, when the third and fourth moments are finite, are

$$\mathrm{skew}(X_t) = \frac{\kappa_{3,t}}{\kappa_{2,t}^{3/2}} = \frac{\mathrm{skew}(X_1)}{t^{1/2}}$$

$$\mathrm{kurt}(X_t) = \frac{\kappa_{4,t}}{\kappa_{2,t}^2} = \frac{\mathrm{kurt}(X_1)}{t}$$

which both increase as t decreases.

1.2.2   Examples

The Brownian motion W is a Lévy process, with characteristic triple $(0, I_d, 0)$. Another (trivial) example is the pure drift $X_t = bt$ for a vector $b \in \mathbb{R}^d$, with the characteristic triple $(b, 0, 0)$. Then $X_t = bt + \sigma W_t$ is also a Lévy process, with characteristic triple $(b, c, 0)$, where $c = \sigma \sigma^*$. Those are the only *continuous* Lévy processes – all others have jumps – and below we give some examples, starting with the simplest one. Note that the sum of two independent d-dimensional Lévy processes with triples (b, c, F) and (b', c', F') is also a Lévy process with triple $(b'', c+c', F+F')$ for a suitable number b'', so those examples can be combined to derive further ones.

Example 1.4 (Poisson process). *A counting process is an $\mathbb{N}$-valued process whose paths have the form*

$$N_t = \sum_{n \geq 1} 1_{\{T_n \leq t\}}, \tag{1.26}$$

where T_n is a strictly increasing sequence of positive times with limit $+\infty$. The usual interpretation is that the T_n's are the successive arrival times of some kind of "events," and N_t is the number of such events occurring within the interval $[0, t]$. The paths of N are piecewise constant, and increase (or jump) by 1. They are càdlàg by construction.

A Poisson process is a counting process such that the inter-arrival times $S_n = T_n - T_{n-1}$ (with the convention $T_0 = 0$) are an i.i.d. sequence of variables having an exponential distribution with intensity parameter λ. Using the memoryless property of the exponential distribution, it is easy to check that a Poisson process is a Lévy process, and N_t has a Poisson distribution with parameter λt, that is, $\mathbb{P}(N_t = n) = \exp(-\lambda t)\frac{(\lambda t)^n}{n!}$ for $n \in \mathbb{N}$. The converse is also easy: any Lévy process which is also a counting process is a Poisson process.

In particular, $\mathbb{E}(N_t) = \lambda t$ so λ represents the expected events arrival rate per unit of time, and also $\mathrm{Var}(N_t) = \lambda t$. The characteristic function of the Poisson random variable N_t is

$$\widehat{G}_t(u) = \exp\left(t\lambda\left(e^{iu} - 1\right)\right), \tag{1.27}$$

and the characteristic triple of N is $(\lambda, 0, \lambda \varepsilon_1)$, where ε_a stands for the Dirac mass sitting at a; note that (1.27) matches the general formula (1.24). When $\lambda = 1$ it is called the standard Poisson process.

Another property is important. Assume that N is an $(\mathcal{F}_t)$-Poisson process on the filtered space $(\Omega, \mathcal{F}, (\mathcal{F}_t)_{t \geq 0}, \mathbb{P})$; by this, we mean a Poisson process which is also an $(\mathcal{F}_t)$-Lévy process. Because of the independence of $N_{t+s} - N_t$ from $\mathcal{F}_t$, we have $\mathbb{E}(N_{t+s} - N_t \mid \mathcal{F}_t) = \lambda s$. In other words,

$$N_t - \lambda t \ \ is \ an \ (\mathcal{F}_t)\text{-}martingale. \qquad (1.28)$$

This is the analogue of the property (1.3) of the Brownian motion. And, exactly as for the Lévy characterization of the Brownian motion, we have the following: if N is a counting process satisfying (1.28), then it is an $(\mathcal{F}_t)$-Poisson process. This is called the Watanabe characterization of the Poisson process.

$N_t - \lambda t$ is called a compensated Poisson process. Note that the compensated Poisson process is no longer $\mathbb{N}$-valued. The first two moments of $(N_t - \lambda t)/\lambda^{1/2}$ are the same as those of Brownian motion: $\mathbb{E}\left((N_t - \lambda t)/\lambda^{1/2}\right) = 0$ and $\mathrm{Var}\left((N_t - \lambda t)/\lambda^{1/2}\right) = t$. In fact, we have convergence in distribution of $(N_t - \lambda t)/\lambda^{1/2}$ to Brownian motion as $\lambda \to \infty$.

Finally, if N_t and N_t' are two independent Poisson processes of intensities λ and λ', then $N_t + N_t'$ is a Poisson process of intensity $\lambda + \lambda'$.

Example 1.5 (Compound Poisson process). A compound Poisson process is a process of the form

$$X_t = \sum_{n \geq 1} Y_n 1_{\{T_n \leq t\}}, \qquad (1.29)$$

where the T_n's are like in the Poisson case (i.e., the process N associated by (1.26) is Poisson with some parameter $\lambda > 0$) and the two sequences (T_n) and (Y_n) are independent, and the variables (Y_n) are i.i.d. with values in $\mathbb{R}^d \backslash \{0\}$, with a law denoted by G. The T_n's represent the jump times and the Y_n's the jump sizes.

On the set $\{N_t = n\}$, the variable X_t is the sum of n i.i.d. jumps Y_n's with distribution F, so

$$\mathbb{E}\left(e^{iu^* X_t} \mid N_t = n\right) = \mathbb{E}\left[e^{iu^*(Y_1+\dots+Y_n)}\right] = \mathbb{E}\left[e^{iu^* Y_1}\right]^n = \widehat{G}(u)^n$$

where $\widehat{G}(u) = \int_{\mathbb{R}^d} e^{iu^* x} G(dx)$ is the characteristic function of Y_1. Therefore the characteristic function of X_t is

$$\mathbb{E}\left(e^{iu^* X_t}\right) = \sum_{n=0}^{\infty} \mathbb{E}\left(e^{iu^* X_t} \mid N_t = n\right) \mathbb{P}\left(N_t = n\right)$$

$$= e^{-t\lambda} \sum_{n=0}^{\infty} \frac{\left(\lambda \widehat{G}(u) t\right)^n}{n!} = e^{-\lambda t(1 - \widehat{G}(u))}$$

$$= \exp\left(t\lambda \int \left(e^{iu^* x} - 1\right) G(dx)\right).$$

Again, proving that a compound Poisson process is Lévy is a (relatively) easy task, and the above formula shows that its characteristic triple is $(b, 0, \lambda G)$, where $b = \lambda \int_{\{\|x\| \leq 1\}} x G(dx)$. The converse is also true, although more difficult to prove: any Lévy process whose paths are piecewise constant, that is, have the form (1.29), is a compound Poisson process.

Example 1.6 (Symmetrical stable process). *A symmetrical stable process is by definition a one-dimensional Lévy process such that X and $-X$ have the same law, and which has the following scaling (or self-similarity) property, for some index $\beta > 0$:*

$$\text{for all } t > 0, \text{ the variables } X_t \text{ and } t^{1/\beta} X_1 \text{ have the same law.} \quad (1.30)$$

By virtue of the properties of Lévy processes, this implies that for any $a > 0$, the two processes $(X_{at})_{t \geq 0}$ and $(a^{1/\beta} X_t)_{t \geq 0}$ have the same (global) law.

By (1.24), the log-characteristic function of X_t satisfies $\Psi(u) = \Psi(-u)$ because of the symmetry, so (1.30) immediately yields $\Psi(u) = -\phi|u|^\beta$ for some constant ϕ. The fact that ψ is the logarithm of a characteristic function has two consequences, namely that $\phi \geq 0$ and that $\beta \in (0, 2]$, and $\phi = 0$ will be excluded because it corresponds to having $X_t = 0$ identically. Now, we have two possibilities:

1. *$\beta = 2$, in which case $X = \sqrt{2\phi}\, W$, with W a Brownian motion.*

2. *$\beta \in (0, 2)$, and most usually the name "stable" is associated with this situation. The number β is then called the* index, *or stability index, of the stable process. In this case the characteristic triple of X is $(0, 0, F)$, where*

$$F(dx) = \frac{a\beta}{|x|^{1+\beta}} dx \quad (1.31)$$

for some $a > 0$, which is connected with the constant ϕ by

$$\phi = \begin{cases} a\pi & \text{if } \beta = 1 \\ \frac{2a\beta \sin\left(\frac{(1-\beta)\pi}{2}\right)}{(1-\beta)\Gamma(2-\beta)} & \text{if } \beta \neq 1 \end{cases}$$

(Γ is the Euler gamma function). The requirement in (1.23) that F integrates the function $1 \wedge x^2$ is exactly the property $0 < \beta < 2$.

The case $\beta = 1$ corresponds to the Cauchy *process, for which the density of the variable X_t is explicitly known and of the form $x \mapsto 1/\left(ta\pi^2(1 + (x/ta\pi)^2)\right)$.*

*Note that the value of β controls the rate at which F diverges near 0:
the higher the value of β, the faster F diverges, and, as we will see later,
the higher the concentration of small jumps of the process. But the same
parameter also controls the tails of F near ∞. In the case of a stable
process, these two behaviors of F are linked. Of course, this is the price
to pay for the scaling property (1.30).*

*Finally, we note that these processes are stable under addition: if
$X^{(1)}, ..., X^{(n)}$ are n independent copies of X, then there exist numbers
$a_n > 0$ such that $X_t^{(1)} + \cdots + X_t^{(n)} \stackrel{d}{=} a_n X_t$.*

Example 1.7 (General stable process). *As said before, we exclude
the case of the Brownian motion here. The terminology in the non-
symmetrical case is not completely well established. For us, a stable process will be a Lévy process X having the characteristic triple $(b, 0, F)$,
where $b \in \mathbb{R}$ and F is a measure of the same type as (1.31), but not
necessarily symmetrical about 0:*

$$F(dx) = \left(\frac{a^{(+)}\beta}{|x|^{1+\beta}} 1_{\{x>0\}} + \frac{a^{(-)}\beta}{|x|^{1+\beta}} 1_{\{x<0\}} \right) dx, \qquad (1.32)$$

*where $a^{(+)}, a^{(-)} \geq 0$ and $a^{(+)} + a^{(-)} > 0$, and $\beta \in (0,2)$ is again called
the index of the process. This includes the symmetrical stable processes
(take $b = 0$ and $a^{(+)} = a^{(-)} = a$).*

*The scaling property (1.30) is lost here, unless either $\beta = 1$ and $b \in \mathbb{R}$
and $a^{(+)} = a^{(-)}$, or $\beta \neq 1$ and $b = \frac{\beta(a^{(+)}-a^{(-)})}{1-\beta}$. The variables X_t for
$t > 0$ have a density, unfortunately almost never explicitly known, but one
knows exactly the behavior of this density at infinity, and also at 0, as
well as the explicit (but complicated) form of the characteristic function;
see for example the comprehensive monograph of Zolotarev (1986). Note
also that, by a simple application of (1.25), we have for all $t > 0$*

$$p < \beta \quad \Rightarrow \quad \mathbb{E}(|X_t|^p) < \infty, \qquad p \geq \beta \quad \Rightarrow \quad \mathbb{E}(|X_t|^p) = \infty.$$

*Finally, let us mention that the density of the variable X_t is positive
on $\mathbb{R}$ when $\beta \geq 1$, and also when $\beta < 1$ and $a^{(+)}, a^{(-)} > 0$. When
$\beta < 1$ and $a^{(-)} = 0 < a^{(+)}$, (resp. $a^{(+)} = 0 < a^{(-)}$), the density of
X_t is positive on $(b't, \infty)$, resp. $(-\infty, b't)$, and vanishes elsewhere, where
$b' = b - \int_{\{|x|\leq 1\}} x F(dx)$ is the "true drift." If $\beta < 1$ and $b' \geq 0$ and
$a^{(-)} = 0 < a^{(+)}$, almost all paths of X are strictly increasing, and we
say that we have a subordinator.*

Example 1.8 (Tempered stable process). *A tempered stable process of index* $\beta \in (0, 2)$ *is a Lévy process whose characteristic triple is* $(b, 0, F)$, *where* $b \in \mathbb{R}$ *and* F *is*

$$F(dx) = \left(\frac{a^{(+)} \beta e^{-B_+|x|}}{|x|^{1+\beta}} 1_{\{x>0\}} + \frac{a^{(-)} \beta e^{-B_-|x|}}{|x|^{1+\beta}} 1_{\{x<0\}} \right) dx,$$

for some $a^{(+)}, a^{(-)} \geq 0$ *with* $a^{(+)} + a^{(-)} > 0$, *and* $B_-, B_+ > 0$. *The reason for introducing tempered stable processes is that, although they somehow behave like stable processes, as far as "small jumps" are concerned, they also have moments of all orders (a simple application of (1.25) again). Those processes were introduced by Novikov (1994) and extended by Rosiński (2007) to a much more general situation than what is stated here.*

Example 1.9 (Gamma process). *The* gamma process *is in a sense a "tempered stable process with index 0." It is an increasing Lévy process* X *having the characteristics triple* $(0, 0, F)$, *where*

$$F(dx) = \frac{a e^{-Bx}}{x} 1_{\{x>0\}} dx,$$

with $a, B > 0$. *The name comes from the fact that the law of* X_t *is the gamma distribution with density* $x \mapsto \frac{1}{\Gamma(ta)} e^{-Bx} B^{ta} x^{ta-1} 1_{\{x>0\}}$.

1.2.3   Poisson Random Measures

In this subsection we switch to a seemingly different topic, whose (fundamental) connection with Lévy processes will be explained later. The idea is to count the number of jumps of a given size that occur between times 0 and t. We start with a sketchy description of general Poisson random measures, also called Poisson point processes, or "independently scattered point processes." We consider a measurable space $(L, \mathcal{L})$. A *random measure on* L, defined on the probability space $(\Omega, \mathcal{F}, \mathbb{P})$, is a transition measure $\underline{p} = \underline{p}(\omega, dz)$ from $(\Omega, \mathcal{F})$ into $(L, \mathcal{L})$. If for each ω the measure $\underline{p}(\omega, .)$ is an at most countable sum of Dirac masses sitting at pairwise distinct points of L, depending on ω, we say that $\underline{p}$ is associated with a "simple point process" in L, and $\underline{p}(A)$ is simply the number of points falling into $A \subset L$.

Definition 1.10. *A random measure* p *associated with a simple point process is called a* Poisson random measure *if it satisfies the following two properties:*

1. *For any pairwise disjoint measurable subsets $A_1, \ldots, A_n$ of L the variables $\underline{p}(A_1), \ldots, \underline{p}(A_n)$ are independent.*

2. *The intensity measure $\underline{q}(A) = \mathbb{E}(\underline{p}(A))$ is a σ-finite measure on $(L, \mathcal{L})$, without atoms (an atom is a measurable set which has positive measure and contains no subset of smaller but positive measure).*

In this case, if $\underline{q}(A) = \infty$ we have $\underline{p}(A) = \infty$ a.s., and if $\underline{q}(A) < \infty$ the variable $\underline{p}(A)$ is Poisson with parameter $\underline{q}(A)$, that is,

$$\mathbb{P}\left(\underline{p}(A) = n\right) = \exp(-\underline{q}(A)) \frac{(\underline{q}(A))^n}{n!}$$

for $n \in \mathbb{N}$. Hence the "law" of $\underline{p}$ is completely characterized by the intensity measure $\underline{q}$. It is also characterized by the "Laplace functional," which is

$$\Phi(f) := \mathbb{E}\left(e^{-\int f(x)\underline{p}(dx)}\right) = \exp\left(-\int \left(1 - e^{-f(x)}\right) \underline{q}(dx)\right).$$

for any Borel nonnegative (non-random) function f on L, with the convention $e^{-\infty} = 0$.

A last useful (and simple to prove) property is the following one: if $A_1, A_2, \ldots$ are pairwise disjoint measurable subsets of L, we have:

the restrictions of $\underline{p}$ to the A_n's are *independent* Poisson
random measures, whose intensity measures   (1.33)
are the restrictions of $\underline{q}$ to the A_n's.

The situation above is quite general, but in this book we specialize as follows: we let $L = \mathbb{R}_+ \times E$, where $(E, \mathcal{E})$ is a "nice" topological space with its Borel σ-field, typically $E = \mathbb{R}^q$ (it could be a general Polish space as well): for the measure associated with the jumps of a process, see below, $\mathbb{R}_+$ is the set of times and $\mathbb{R}^q$ the set of jump sizes.

Moreover, we only consider Poisson random measures $\underline{p}$ having an intensity measure of the form

$$\underline{q}(dt, dx) = dt \otimes Q(dx), \tag{1.34}$$

where Q is a σ-finite measure on $(E, \mathcal{E})$. In this case it turns out that, outside a null set, the process $a_t = \underline{p}(\{t\} \times E)$ (which *a priori* takes its values in $\overline{\mathbb{N}}$) actually takes only the values 0 and 1, and the (random) set $D = \{t : a_t = 1\}$ is countable: this is the set of times where points occur.

Upon deleting the above null set, it is thus not a restriction to assume that $\underline{p}$ has the representation

$$\underline{p} = \sum_{t \in D} \varepsilon_{(t, Z_t)}, \tag{1.35}$$

where as usual ε_a denotes the Dirac measure sitting at a, and $Z = (Z_t)_{t \geq 0}$ is a measurable process.

When $Q(A) < \infty$, the process $\underline{p}([0, t] \times A)$ is a Poisson process with parameter $Q(A)$. Exactly as in the previous subsection, in which Lévy processes (and in particular Poisson processes) relative to a filtration $(\mathcal{F}_t)$ were defined, we introduce a similar notion for Poisson random measures whose intensity has the form (1.34). Suppose that our random measure $\underline{p}$ is defined on a filtered probability space $(\Omega, \mathcal{F}, (\mathcal{F}_t)_{t \geq 0}, \mathbb{P})$; we then say that $\underline{p}$ is a *Poisson measure relative to* $(\mathcal{F}_t)$, or an $(\mathcal{F}_t)$-*Poisson random measure,* if it is a Poisson measure satisfying also:

1. The variable $\underline{p}([0, t] \times A)$ is $\mathcal{F}_t$-measurable for all $A \in \mathcal{E}$ and $t \geq 0$.

2. The restriction of the measure $\underline{p}$ to $(t, \infty) \times E$ is independent of $\mathcal{F}_t$.

This implies that for all A with $Q(A) < \infty$, the process $\underline{p}([0, t] \times A)$ is an $(\mathcal{F}_t)$-Poisson process, and we have a (not completely trivial) converse: if $\underline{p}$ is a random measure of the form (1.35) such that for any A with $Q(A) < \infty$ the process $\underline{p}([0, t] \times A)$ is an $(\mathcal{F}_t)$-Poisson process with parameter $Q(A)$, then $\underline{p}$ is an $(\mathcal{F}_t)$-Poisson random measure with the intensity measure given by (1.34).

If $E = \{1\}$ the measure $\underline{p}$ is entirely characterized by the process $N_t = \underline{p}([0, t] \times \{1\})$. In this case $\underline{p}$ is an $(\mathcal{F}_t)$-Poisson random measure if and only if N is an $(\mathcal{F}_t)$-Poisson process; this is the simplest example of a Poisson random measure.

Example 1.11. *If X is an $\mathbb{R}^d$-valued càdlàg process, we associate its jump measure, defined as follows (recall the notation (1.20) for the jumps):*

$$\mu^X = \sum_{s > 0: \, \Delta X_s \neq 0} \varepsilon_{(s, \Delta X_s)}, \tag{1.36}$$

which is (1.35) when $E = \mathbb{R}^d$ and $Z_t = \Delta X_t$ and $D = \{t : \Delta X_t \neq 0\}$. Note that $\mu^X([0, t] \times A)$ is the number of jumps of size falling in the measurable set $A \subset E$, between times 0 and t:

$$\mu^X([0, t] \times A) = \sum_{0 < s \leq t} 1_{\{\Delta X_s \in A\}}.$$

Then it turns out that the measure μ^X is a Poisson random measure when X is a Lévy process and an $(\mathcal{F}_t)$-Poisson random measure when X is an $(\mathcal{F}_t)$-Lévy process, and in those cases the measure Q in (1.34) is equal to the Lévy measure of the process; we thus have independence of the number of jumps both serially (over two disjoint time intervals $[t_1, t_2]$ and $[t_3, t_4]$) and cross-sectionally (jump sizes in two disjoint sets A_1 and A_2).

The cross-sectional independence is not simple to prove, but the time independence is quite intuitive: the value $\mu^X((t, t+s] \times A) = \mu^X((0, t+s] \times A) - \mu^X((0, t] \times A)$ is the number of jumps of size in A, in the time interval $(t, t+s]$, so it only depends on the increments $(X_{t+v} - X_t)_{v \geq 0}$. Then, the $(\mathcal{F}_t)$-Lévy property, say, implies that this variable $\mu^X((t, t+s] \times A)$ is independent of $\mathcal{F}_t$, and also that its law only depends on s (by stationarity of the increments of X). Therefore the process $\mu^X((0, t] \times A)$ is an $(\mathcal{F}_t)$-Lévy process, and also a counting process, hence an $(\mathcal{F}_t)$-Poisson process.

1.2.4 Integrals with Respect to Poisson Random Measures

For any random measure μ on $\mathbb{R}_+ \times E$, where $(E, \mathcal{E})$ is a Polish space, and for any measurable function U on $\Omega \times \mathbb{R}_+ \times E$, we set

$$U * \mu_t(\omega) = \int_0^t \int_E U(\omega, s, x) \, \mu(\omega; ds, dx), \qquad (1.37)$$

whenever this makes sense, for example when $U \geq 0$ and μ is positive.

Suppose that $\underline{p}$ is an $(\mathcal{F}_t)$-Poisson random measure, with intensity measure $\underline{q}$ given by (1.34). If $U(\omega, t, x) = 1_A(x)$ with $Q(A) < \infty$, then both $U * \underline{p}_t$ and $U * \underline{q}_t$ are well defined. Keep in mind that $\underline{p}$ is random, but that $\underline{q}$, its compensator, is not. And by (1.28) the compensated difference $U * \underline{p} - U * \underline{q}$ is a martingale on $(\Omega, \mathcal{F}, (\mathcal{F}_t)_{t \geq 0}, \mathbb{P})$. This property extends to any finite linear combination of such U's, and in fact extends much more, as we shall see below.

To this end, we first recall that we can endow the product space $\Omega \times \mathbb{R}_+$ with the predictable σ-field $\mathcal{P}$, that is, the σ-field generated by the sets $B \times \{0\}$ for $B \in \mathcal{F}_0$ and $B \times (s, t]$ for $s < t$ and $B \in \mathcal{F}_s$, or equivalently (although this is not trivial) the σ-field generated by all processes that are adapted and left-continuous, or the σ-field generated by all processes that are adapted and continuous. By extension, the product σ-field $\widetilde{\mathcal{P}} = \mathcal{P} \otimes \mathcal{E}$ is also called the predictable σ-field on $\Omega \times \mathbb{R}_+ \times E$, and a $\widetilde{\mathcal{P}}$-measurable function on this space is called a predictable function.

If U is a predictable function on $\Omega \times \mathbb{R}_+ \times E$ such that $\mathbb{E}(|U| * \underline{q}_t) < \infty$ for all t, the difference $U * \underline{p} - U * \underline{q}$ is again a martingale (this is an easy result, because the linear space spanned by all functions of the form $U(\omega, t, x) = 1_B(\omega)1_{(u,v]}(t)1_A(x)$ is dense in the sets of all predictable functions in $\mathbb{L}^1(\mathbb{P} \otimes \underline{q})$). Slightly more generally, if $|U| * \underline{q}_t < \infty$ for all t, then we have $|U| * \underline{p}_t < \infty$ as well, and the difference $U * \underline{p} - U * \underline{q}$ is a local martingale. Moreover, the càdlàg process $U * \underline{p} - U * \underline{q}$ has jumps obviously satisfying for $t > 0$:

$$\Delta \left(U * \underline{p} - U * \underline{q}\right)_t = \int_E U(t,x)\underline{p}(\{t\} \times dx) = U(t, Z_t)$$

(where we use the representation (1.35) for the last equality, and ΔY is the jump process of any càdlàg process Y).

At this stage, and somewhat similar to stochastic integrals with respect to a Brownian motion, one can define *stochastic integrals* with respect to the Poisson random measure $\underline{p}$, or rather with respect to the compensated measure $\underline{p} - \underline{q}$, as follows: if U is a *predictable* function on $\Omega \times \mathbb{R}_+ \times E$ such that

$$(|U| \wedge U^2) * \underline{q}_t < \infty \quad \forall t \geq 0, \tag{1.38}$$

there exists a local martingale M having the following properties:

- M is orthogonal to all continuous martingales, meaning that the product MM' is a local martingale for any continuous martingale M';

- outside a null set, $M_0 = 0$ and $t > 0$
  $\Rightarrow \Delta M_t = \int_E U(t,x)\underline{p}(\{t\} \times dx) = U(t, Z_t)$.

This local martingale is unique (up to a null set again), and we use either one of the following notations:

$$M_t = U * (\underline{p} - \underline{q})_t = \int_0^t \int_E U(s,x)(\underline{p} - \underline{q})(ds, dx). \tag{1.39}$$

We have the following four properties, quite similar to (1.9):

- the map $U \mapsto U * (\underline{p} - \underline{q})$ is linear;
- we have a "dominated convergence theorem":
  if $U^n \to U$ pointwise and $|U^n| \leq V$ and V satisfies (1.38), then $U^n * (\underline{p} - \underline{q}) \overset{\text{u.c.p.}}{\Longrightarrow} U * (\underline{p} - \underline{q})$;
- if $|U| * \underline{q}_t < \infty$ for all t, then $U * (\underline{p} - \underline{q}) = U * \underline{p} - U * \underline{q}$
  (otherwise, the processes $U * \underline{p}$ and $U * \underline{q}$ may be ill-defined);
- if $U^2 * \underline{q}_t < \infty$ for all t, then $U * (\underline{p} - \underline{q})$ is a locally square-integrable local martingale.

(1.40)

Sometimes, the local martingale $M = U * (\underline{p} - \underline{q})$ is called a "purely discontinuous" local martingale, or a "compensated sum of jumps"; the reason is that in the third property (1.40), $U * \underline{p}_t = \sum_{s \in D} U(s, Z_s) 1_{\{s \leq t\}}$ is a sum of jumps, and $U * \underline{q}$ is the unique predictable process starting at 0 and which "compensates" $U * \underline{p}$, in the sense that the difference becomes a (local) martingale.

The notion of stochastic integral can be extended to random measures of the type (1.35) which are not necessarily Poisson, and below we consider the only case of interest for us, which is the jump measure $\mu = \mu^X$ of an $\mathbb{R}^d$-valued càdlàg adapted process X; see (1.36).

For any Borel subset A of $\mathbb{R}^d$ at a positive distance of 0, the process $\mu([0, t] \times A)$ is an adapted counting process, taking only finite values because for any càdlàg process the number of jumps with size bigger than any $\varepsilon > 0$ and within the time interval $[0, t]$ is finite. Therefore one can "compensate" this increasing process by a *predictable* increasing càdlàg process $Y(A)$ starting at 0, in such a way that the difference $\mu([0, t] \times A) - Y(A)_t$ is a martingale (this is like $U * p - U * q$ in the previous paragraph), and $Y(A)$ is almost surely unique (this is a version of the celebrated Doob-Meyer decomposition of a submartingale). The map $A \mapsto \mu([0, t] \times A)$ is additive, and thus so is the map $A \mapsto Y(A)$, up to null sets. Hence it is not a surprise (although it needs a somewhat involved proof, because of the $\mathbb{P}$-negligible sets) that there exists an almost surely unique random measure ν on $\mathbb{R}_+ \times \mathbb{R}^d$ such that, for all $A \in \mathcal{R}^d$ at a positive distance of 0,

$$\nu([0, t] \times A) \text{ is predictable, and is a version of } Y(A). \qquad (1.41)$$

The measure $\nu = \nu^X$ is called the *compensating measure* of μ. Of course, when μ is further a Poisson random measure, its compensating measure ν is also its intensity, and is thus not random.

We can rephrase the previous statement as follows, with the notation (1.37): If $U(\omega, t, x) = 1_A(x)$, with A Borel and at a positive distance of 0, then $U * \nu$ is predictable and the difference $U * \mu - U * \nu$ is a local martingale. Exactly as in the previous paragraph, this extends to any U which is *predictable* and such that

$$(|U| \wedge U^2) * \nu_t < \infty \quad \forall t \geq 0. \qquad (1.42)$$

Namely, there exists an almost surely unique local martingale M satisfying

- M is orthogonal to all continuous martingales
- outside a null set, we have $M_0 = 0$ and, for all $t > 0$,   (1.43)
  $\Delta M_t = \int_E U(t,x)\mu(\{t\} \times dx) - \int_E U(t,x)\nu(\{t\} \times dx)$.

As in (1.39), we use either one of the following notations:

$$M_t = U * (\mu - \nu)_t = \int_0^t \int_E U(s,x)(\mu - \nu)(ds, dx),$$

and all four properties in (1.40) are valid here, with $\underline{p}$ and $\underline{q}$ substituted with μ and ν.

There is a difference, though, with the Poisson case: the process $\gamma_t = \nu(\{t\} \times \mathbb{R}^d)$ takes its values in $[0,1]$, but it is not necessarily vanishing everywhere. When it is (for example when μ is a Poisson measure), the second property in (1.43) can be rewritten as

$$\Delta M_t = \int_E U(t,x)\mu(\{t\} \times dx) = U(t, \Delta X_t) 1_{\{\Delta X_t \neq 0\}} \qquad (1.44)$$

and the condition (1.42) describes the biggest possible class of predictable integrands U. When γ_t is not identically 0, (1.44) is wrong, and it is possible to define $U * (\mu - \nu)$ for a slightly larger class of integrands (see for example Jacod (1979) for more details).

1.2.5   Path Properties and Lévy-Itô Decomposition

Now we come back to our d-dimensional Lévy processes X, defined on the filtered probability space $(\Omega, \mathcal{F}, (\mathcal{F}_t)_{t \geq 0}, \mathbb{P})$.

A fundamental property, already mentioned in Example 1.11, is that the jump measure $\mu = \mu^X$ of X is a *Poisson random measure* on $L = \mathbb{R}_+ \times \mathbb{R}^d$, with the intensity measure

$$\nu(dt, dx) = dt \otimes F(dx),$$

where F is the Lévy measure of X. Below, we draw some consequences of this fact.

First, since $\mu(A)$ is Poisson with parameter $\nu(A)$ if $\nu(A) < \infty$ and

$\mu(A) = \infty$ a.s. otherwise, we see that

- $F = 0 \Rightarrow X$ is continuous (we knew this already) $\qquad$ (1.45)
- $0 < F(\mathbb{R}^d) < \infty \Rightarrow X$ has a.s. finitely many jumps on any $\qquad$ (1.46)
  interval $[0, t]$ and a.s. infinitely many on $\mathbb{R}_+$
- $F(\mathbb{R}^d) = \infty \Rightarrow X$ has a.s. infinitely many jumps on any $\qquad$ (1.47)
  interval $[t, t + s]$ such that $s > 0$.

Definition 1.12. *In the case of (1.46) we say that we have* finite activity *for the jumps, whereas if (1.47) holds we say that we have* infinite activity.

Next, let g be a nonnegative Borel function on $\mathbb{R}^d$ with $g(0) = 0$. By using the Laplace functional for the functions $f(r, x) = \lambda(g(x) \wedge 1)1_{(t,t+s]}(r)$ and the fact that a nonnegative variable Y is a.s. finite if $\mathbb{E}(e^{-\lambda Y}) \to 1$ as $\lambda \downarrow 0$ and a.s. infinite if and only if $\mathbb{E}(e^{-\lambda Y}) = 0$ for all $\lambda > 0$, we deduce

$$\int (g(x) \wedge 1)F(dx) < \infty \quad \Leftrightarrow \quad \sum_{s \le t} g(\Delta X_s) < \infty,$$
$$\text{a.s. } \forall\, t > 0$$
$$\int (g(x) \wedge 1)F(dx) = \infty \quad \Leftrightarrow \quad \sum_{t < r \le t+s} g(\Delta X_r) = \infty, \qquad (1.48)$$
$$\text{a.s. } \forall\, t \ge 0, s > 0$$

which is particularly useful for the absolute power functions $g(x) = \|x\|^p$ where $p > 0$.

We now set

$$I = \left\{ p \ge 0 : \int_{\{\|x\| \le 1\}} \|x\|^p\, F(dx) < \infty \right\}, \quad \beta = \inf(I). \qquad (1.49)$$

The number β defined above is called the *Blumenthal-Getoor index* of the process X, as introduced by Blumenthal and Getoor (1961), precisely for studying the path properties of Lévy processes. Note that, since the function $p \mapsto \|x\|^p$ is decreasing when $\|x\| \le 1$, the set I is necessarily of the form $[\beta, \infty)$ or (β, ∞), whereas $2 \in I$ always by (1.23), hence $\beta \in [0, 2]$.

There is no conflicting notation here: for a stable or tempered stable process, the stability index and the Blumenthal-Getoor index agree. Those are examples where $I = (\beta, \infty)$. A gamma process has Blumenthal-Getoor index $\beta = 0$ and again $I = (\beta, \infty)$. For a compound Poisson process we have $\beta = 0$ and $I = [\beta, \infty)$. More generally, the jumps have finite activity if and only if $0 \in I$. Later on, we will see that β can be quite naturally generalized, and interpreted as a *jump activity index*: processes

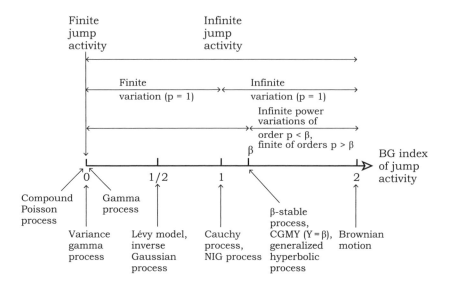

Figure 1.1: Examples of processes and their corresponding BG index of jump activity β.

with higher β tend to jump more frequently. Figure 1.1 provides some examples of processes and the corresponding values of β.

β is a lower bound for the values of p for which the pth power of the jumps are summable. Observing that $\sum_{s\leq t}\|\Delta X_s\|^p 1_{\{\|\Delta X_s\|>1\}} < \infty$ for all t because X has finitely many jumps bigger than 1 on any interval $[0,t]$ (a property of all càdlàg processes), we deduce

$$\begin{aligned} p \in I &\Rightarrow \sum_{s\leq t}\|\Delta X_s\|^p < \infty \ \text{a.s.} \ \forall t \geq 0 \\ p \notin I &\Rightarrow \sum_{s\leq t}\|\Delta X_s\|^p = \infty \ \ \text{a.s.} \ \forall t > 0. \end{aligned} \quad (1.50)$$

With $\mu = \mu^X$ and ν and above, we observe that the predictable function $U(\omega,t,x) = x1_{\{\|x\|\leq 1\}}$ satisfies (1.38), or equivalently (1.38) with $\underline{q} = \nu$. Hence the stochastic integral $U * (\underline{p} - \underline{q})$ is well defined, and will be written below as $(x1_{\{\|x\|\leq 1\}}) * (\mu - \nu)$. With the notation (1.37) we also clearly have

$$(x1_{\{\|x\|>1\}}) * \mu_t = \sum_{s\leq t}\Delta X_s 1_{\{\|\Delta X_s\|>1\}}$$

(a finite sum for each t). On the other hand the symmetric nonnegative matrix c occurring in the Lévy-Khintchine formula can be written as $c = \sigma\sigma^*$ for a $d \times q$ matrix σ, where q is the rank of c.

With all this notation, and with b as in (1.24), one can show that on $(\Omega, \mathcal{F}, (\mathcal{F}_t)_{t\geq0}, \mathbb{P})$ there is a q-dimensional Brownian motion W, *independent* of the Poisson measure μ, and such that the Lévy process X is

$$X_t = bt + \sigma W_t + (x1_{\{\|x\|\leq1\}}) * (\mu - \nu)_t + (x1_{\{\|x\|>1\}}) * \mu_t. \quad (1.51)$$

This is called the *Lévy-Itô decomposition* of X. This decomposition is quite useful for applications, and also provides a lot of insight on the structure of a Lévy process.

A few comments are in order here:

1. When $c = 0$ there is no σ, and of course the Brownian motion W does not show in this formula.

2. The independence of W and μ has been added for clarity, but one may show that if W and μ are an $(\mathcal{F}_t)$-Brownian motion and an $(\mathcal{F}_t)$-Poisson measure on some filtered space $(\Omega, \mathcal{F}, (\mathcal{F}_t)_{t\geq0}, \mathbb{P})$, then they necessarily are independent.

3. The four terms on the right in the formula (1.51) correspond to a canonical decomposition of X_t into a sum of a pure drift term, a continuous martingale, a purely discontinuous martingale consisting of "small" jumps (small meaning smaller than 1) that are compensated, and the sum of the "big" jumps (big meaning bigger than 1). As we will see, this is also the structure of a general semimartingale.

4. The four terms in (1.51) are *independent* of each other; for the last two terms, this comes from (1.33).

5. These four terms correspond to the decomposition of the characteristic function (1.24) into four factors, that is,

$$\mathbb{E}\left(e^{iu^*X_t}\right) = \prod_{j=1}^{4} \phi_j(u),$$

where
$$\phi_1(u) = e^{iu^*bt}, \qquad \phi_2(u) = e^{-\frac{1}{2}tu^*cu},$$
$$\phi_3(u) = e^{t\int_{\{\|x\|\leq1\}}(e^{iu^*x}-1-iu^*x)F(dx)},$$
$$\phi_4(u) = e^{t\int_{\{\|x\|>1\}}(e^{iu^*x}-1)F(dx)}.$$

The terms ϕ_1 and ϕ_2 are the characteristic functions of bt and σW_t, and the last one is the characteristic function of the compound Poisson variable which is the last term in (1.51). For the

third factor, one can observe that on the one hand the variable
$(x1_{(1/n)<\{\|x\|\leq1\}}) * (\mu - \nu)_t$ is a compound Poisson variable minus
$t \int_{\{(1/n)<\|x\|\leq1\}} xF(dx)$, whose characteristic function is

$$\exp t \int_{\{(1/n)<\|x\|\leq1\}} \left(e^{iu^*x} - 1 - iu^*x\right) F(dx),$$

whereas on the other hand it converges to the third term in (1.51)
as $n \to \infty$ by the dominated convergence theorem in (1.40).

6. Instead of truncating jumps at 1 as in (1.51), we can decide to
truncate them at an arbitrary fixed $\varepsilon > 0$, in which case the decomposition formula becomes

$$X_t = b_\varepsilon t + \sigma W_t + (x1_{\{\|x\|\leq\varepsilon\}}) * (\mu - \nu)_t + (x1_{\{\|x\|>\varepsilon\}}) * \mu_t$$

with the drift term changed to

$$b_\varepsilon = b + \int x \left(1_{\{\|x\|\leq\varepsilon\}} - 1_{\{\|x\|\leq1\}}\right) F(dx).$$

We can more generally employ a truncation function $h(x)$ in lieu of
$1_{\{\|x\|\leq\varepsilon\}}$, as long as $h(x) = 1 + o(\|x\|)$ near 0 and $h(x) = O(1/|x|)$
near ∞, so that

$$e^{iu^*x} - 1 - iu \cdot xh(x) = O(\|x\|^2) \quad \text{as } x \to 0$$
$$e^{iu^*x} - 1 - iu \cdot xh(x) = O(1) \quad \text{as } \|x\| \to \infty$$

and $\int(\|x\|^2 \wedge 1)F(dx) < \infty$ ensures that

$$\int \left|e^{iu^*x} - 1 - iu^*xh(x)\right|F(dx) < \infty.$$

The drift needs again to be adjusted to

$$b_h = b + \int x \left(h(x) - 1_{\{\|x\|\leq1\}}\right) F(dx)$$

Different choices of ε or h do not change (c, F) but they are reflected in the drift b_h, which is therefore a somewhat arbitrary
quantity. Since the choice of truncation is essentially arbitrary, so
is the distinction between small vs. big jumps. The only distinguishing characteristic of big jumps is that there are only a finite
number of them, at the most.

7. Recall that the reason we cannot simply take $x * \mu_t$ is that, when the process has infinite jump activity, the series $x * \mu_t = \sum_{s \leq t} \Delta X_s$ may be divergent even though the number of jumps is at most countable. The variable $(x 1_{\{\|x\| > \varepsilon\}}) * \mu_t = \sum_{s \leq t} \Delta X_s 1_{\{\|\Delta X_s\| > \varepsilon\}}$, being a finite sum for all $\varepsilon > 0$, is well defined, but its limit as $\varepsilon \to 0$ may not exist because of the infinitely many jumps. Compensating solves that problem and $(x 1_{\{\varepsilon < \|x\| \leq 1\}}) * (\mu - \nu)_t$ converges as $\varepsilon \to 0$. On the other hand, we cannot simply compensate without truncating and take $x * (\mu - \nu)_t$, because $(x 1_{\{\|x\| > 1\}}) * \nu_t$ may be divergent; hence the solution which consists in breaking the sum (or integrals) into two parts, compensated small jumps, and uncompensated large jumps, both of which are convergent.

8. If the process has finite variation, that is, if $\|x\| * \mu_t < \infty$ almost surely for all t, or equivalently if $\int (\|x\| \wedge 1) F(dx) < \infty$ (note the absence of a square on $\|x\|$), then the integral $x * \mu_t$ is convergent, and the compensation is not needed. The difference between the representation

$$X_t = b't + \sigma W_t + x * \mu_t$$

and (1.51) for a finite variation process consists in a change of drift from b to b'.

1.3   Semimartingales

1.3.1   Definition and Stochastic Integrals

We now reach the main topic of this chapter. Among all processes, the class of semimartingales plays a very special role. For example they are the most general processes with respect to which a (stochastic) integration theory, having the usual "nice" properties like a Lebesgue convergence theorem, can be constructed. This fact may even be used as the definition of semimartingales, according to the Bichteler-Dellacherie-Mokobodski theorem. In mathematical finance they also play a special role, since one of the most basic results (the so-called fundamental asset pricing theorem) says that if no arbitrage is allowed, then the price process should be a semimartingale.

Definition 1.13. *A real-valued process X on the filtered probability space $(\Omega, \mathcal{F}, (\mathcal{F}_t)_{t \geq 0}, \mathbb{P})$ is called a* semimartingale *if it can be written as*

$$X = A + M, \tag{1.52}$$

where M is a local martingale and A is an adapted càdlàg process "with finite variation," which means that the total variation of each path $t \mapsto A_t(\omega)$ is bounded over each finite interval $[0, t]$.

Intuitively, the finite variation process plays the role of a "drift" term (such as $\int_0^t b_s ds$) whereas the local martingale part is "pure randomness" (such as $\int_0^t \sigma_s dW_s$). A deterministic process is a semimartingale if and only if it has finite variation. This decomposition $X = M + A$ is essentially *not* unique, since we can always add to A and subtract from M the same martingale with finite variation. Both A and M may be discontinuous.

A d-dimensional semimartingale $X = (X^i)_{1 \leq i \leq d}$ is a process whose components are real-valued semimartingales. A semimartingale is always adapted and càdlàg. Every adapted process of finite variation (e.g. Poisson or pure drift) is a semimartingale. Every martingale (e.g. Brownian motion) is a semimartingale. By virtue of the Lévy-Itô decomposition (1.51), any Lévy process is a semimartingale, since it is the sum of a square integrable martingale and a finite variation process: one may for example take $A_t = bt + (x1_{\{\|x\|>1\}}) * \mu_t$ to get a decomposition (1.52).

Now we introduce stochastic integrals with respect to a semimartingale X, starting with the one-dimensional case. Exactly as for the Brownian motion, and substituting W with X, one may define the integral $\int_0^t H_s dX_s$ by (1.7) for any simple process H of the form (1.6).

Again as for the Brownian motion, this elementary integral can be extended to a much larger class of integrands. An important difference with the Brownian case is the fact that we need the integrand to be *predictable*, a fundamental requirement without which the whole theory breaks down. More precisely, we consider processes H with the following properties:

H is predictable, and locally bounded in the sense that
we have $|H_t(\omega)| \leq n$ for all $0 < t \leq T_n(\omega)$,   (1.53)
where (T_n) is a sequence of stopping times increasing to ∞.

This is *not* the largest possible class of integrands, but it will be sufficient for our purposes. The extension is of course still denoted by $\int_0^t H_s dX_s$ or $H \bullet X_t$, and is uniquely defined up to a null set again. It has properties analogous to (1.9):

- the process $H \bullet X_t$ is a semimartingale starting at 0
- if X is a local martingale, then so is $H \bullet X$
- the maps $H \mapsto H \bullet X$ and $X \mapsto H \bullet X$ are linear
- we have a "dominated convergence theorem":
  if $H^n \to H$ pointwise and $|H^n| \leq H'$
  where H' satisfies (1.53), then $H^n \bullet X \overset{\text{u.c.p.}}{\Longrightarrow} H \bullet X$.

(1.54)

When X is d-dimensional, one can integrate componentwise a d-dimensional predictable locally bounded process $H = (H^i)_{1 \leq i \leq d}$, thus getting the following one-dimensional process:

$$H \bullet X_t = \int_0^t H_s \, dX_s = \sum_{i=1}^d \int_0^t H_s^i \, dX_s^i.$$

Why the predictability requirement? There are two reasons. A first "mathematical" reason is that, for a general semimartingale, it is impossible to extend integrals of simple integrands to all càdlàg adapted processes while preserving the dominated convergence theorem. Second, in financial applications, trading strategies must be predictable to avoid arbitrage opportunities. Imagine an investor trading an asset with price process X at times T_i, $0 = T_0 < T_1 < \cdots < T_{n+1} = T$, and holding H_{T_i} shares of the asset between T_i and T_{i+1}. The capital gain from that strategy is

$$\sum_{i=0}^n H_{T_i} \left(X_{T_{i+1}} - X_{T_i} \right) = \int_0^T H_t \, dX_t.$$

The transaction times T_i may be fixed, or more generally they may be non-anticipating random times (that is, stopping times). For example the investor may trade the first time X crosses a barrier: this would be a limit order. Also, H_{T_i} is chosen based on information known at T_i: it is $\mathcal{F}_{T_i}$-measurable. The investor's holdings at each time t are given by

$$H_t = H_0 1_0(t) + \sum_{i=0}^n H_{T_i} 1_{(T_i, T_{i+1}]}(t).$$

The investor decides to trade at T_i; immediately afterwards, the portfolio changes from $H_{T_{i-1}}$ to H_{T_i}. Therefore H_t is left-continuous with right-limits (càglàd). This makes it a *predictable* process.

Trading strategies must be predictable when jumps are present, otherwise there may be arbitrage opportunities. Consider for example $X_t = \lambda t - N_t$, where N is a Poisson process with intensity λ. Let T_1 denote the time of the first jump. At that time, X jumps by -1. Consider the strategy that buys 1 unit of the asset at time 0 for price $X_0 = 0$ and sells it right before the crash at T_1. H is not a predictable process, since it is impossible to implement this strategy without knowing ahead the time when T_1 will happen. The holdings H_t are given by 1 between $[0, T_1)$. The fact that the interval is open on the right means that this strategy is not predictable because of the properties of the jump times of a Poisson process. The strategy generates sure profits since

$$\int_0^t H_s dX_s = \begin{cases} \lambda t & \text{for } t < T_1 \\ \lambda T_1 & \text{for } t \geq T_1 \end{cases}$$

and does that with zero initial investment, so it is an arbitrage. This explains why, in the presence of jumps, only predictable strategies are admissible.

1.3.2 Quadratic Variation

For defining the quadratic variation, one needs to recall some properties. The first is that a local martingale M can always be written as $M_t = M_0 + M_t^c + M_t^d$, where $M_0^c = M_0^d = 0$ and M^c is a continuous local martingale, and M^d is a local martingale orthogonal to each continuous (local) martingale. The second is that a local martingale starting from 0, which has bounded variation in the sense explained after (1.52), and which is continuous, is almost surely vanishing everywhere. Therefore, if we consider two decompositions $X = M + A = M' + A'$ as (1.52), then necessarily $M^c = M'^c$ a.s. In other words, we can write the semimartingale X as

$$X_t = X_0 + X_t^c + M_t + A_t,$$

where $A_0 = M_0 = 0$ and where A is of finite variation and M is a local martingale orthogonal to all continuous martingales, and X^c is a continuous local martingale starting at 0. In this decomposition the two processes M and A are still not unique, but the process X^c is unique (up to null sets), and it is called the *continuous martingale part* of X (although it usually is a local martingale only). When X is d-dimensional, so are X^c, M and A, and the components of X^c are denoted $X^{i,c}$.

Now, we saw in Subsection 1.1.2 that, when two continuous local martingales M and M' are stochastic integrals with respect to a (possibly multidimensional) Brownian motion, one can define the quadratic covariation (or variation, if $M' = M$). The same is true of all continuous local martingales: based on the Doob-Meyer decomposition of submartingales again, we have a unique (up to null sets) continuous adapted process $\langle M, M' \rangle$ starting at 0, with finite variation, and such that

$$M M' - \langle M, M' \rangle \text{ is a local martingale,}$$

and further $\langle M, M \rangle$ is increasing.

At this point, we can introduce the *quadratic variation* of a one-dimensional semimartingale X as being

$$[X, X]_t \; = \; \langle X^c, X^c \rangle_t + \sum_{s \leq t} (\Delta X_s)^2. \qquad (1.55)$$

The sum above makes sense, since it is a sum of positive numbers on the countable set $\{s : \Delta X_s \neq 0\} \cap [0, t]$. What is not immediately obvious is that it is a.s. finite, but this fact is one of the main properties of semimartingales. Hence the process $[X, X]$ is increasing and càdlàg, and also adapted (another intuitive but not mathematically obvious property). Another name for $[X, X]$ is the "square bracket." Note that $[X, X] = \langle X, X \rangle$ when X is a continuous local martingale, and in general $[X^c, X^c] = \langle X^c, X^c \rangle$ is the "continuous part" of the increasing process $[X, X]$ (not to be confused with its "continuous martingale part," which is identically 0).

For example, if $X_t = \sigma W_t$, where W is Brownian motion, then $[X, X]_t = \sigma^2 t$. So $[X, X]_t$ is not random, and coincides with the variance of X_t. This is not the case in general: $[X, X]_t$, unlike the variance, is a random variable. It is not defined by taking expectations. For example, for a Poisson process, since N jumps by 1 whenever it does, $[N, N]_t = N_t$ is the number of jumps of the process between 0 and t, and we also have $[X, X]_t = N_t$ for the martingale $X_t = N_t - \lambda t$ if λ is the parameter of the Poisson process N. Moreover, $[X, X]_t$ is well defined for all semimartingales, including those with infinite variance.

If now X and X' are two real-valued semimartingales we set

$$[X, X']_t \; = \; \langle X^c, X'^c \rangle_t + \sum_{s \leq t} \Delta X_s \, \Delta X_s'. \qquad (1.56)$$

Here again the sum above is a.s. absolutely convergent, by the finiteness in (1.55) for X and X' and the Cauchy-Schwarz inequality. The process $[X, X']$ is adapted and of finite variation, but not necessarily increasing any more, and is called the *quadratic covariation process* of X and X'. For example, if $X_t = \int_0^t \sigma_s dW_s$ and $X_t' = \int_0^t \sigma_s' dW_s'$, where W and W' are two Brownian motions with correlation coefficient ρ, then $[X, X']_t = \int_0^t \rho \sigma_s \sigma_s' \, ds$.

For any real a and any other semimartingale X'' we have

$$[X + aX', X''] = [X, X''] + a[X', X''], \qquad [X, X'] = [X', X].$$

Another useful property, which immediately follows from this, is the *polarization identity*:

$$[X, X'] = \frac{1}{4} \left([X + X', X + X'] - [X - X', X - X'] \right) \qquad (1.57)$$

which expresses the quadratic covariation in terms of quadratic variations only. Finally, the following is obvious:

$$[X, X'] = [X - X_0, X' - X_0']. \qquad (1.58)$$

When X is d-dimensional, we thus have a $d \times d$ matrix-valued process $[X, X] = ([X^i, X^j])_{1 \le i,j \le d}$. For all $s, t \ge 0$ the matrix $[X, X]_{t+s} - [X, X]_t$ is symmetric nonnegative.

We end this subsection with a set of inequalities, known under the name of *Burkholder-Gundy inequalities* when $p > 1$ and Davis-Burkholder-Gundy when $p = 1$ (when $p = 2$ it is also a version of Doob's inequality). These inequalities assert that, if X is a *local martingale* and $p \ge 1$ and $S \le T$ are two arbitrary stopping times, then

$$\begin{aligned} \mathbb{E} \left(\sup_{s \in [S,T]} |X_{S+s} - X_s|^p \mid \mathcal{F}_S \right) \\ \le K_p \, \mathbb{E} \left(([X, X]_T - [X, X]_S)^{p/2} \mid \mathcal{F}_S \right), \end{aligned} \qquad (1.59)$$

where K_p is a universal constant depending on p only, and $[X, X]_T$ stands on the set $\{T = \infty\}$ for the increasing (possibly infinite) limit of $[X, X]_t$ as t increases to infinity, and $[X, X]_T - [X, X]_S = 0$ on the set where $S = T = \infty$. As a matter of fact, we also have the inequality (1.59) in the other direction, and with another constant K_p, but this will not be useful for us.

1.3.3 Itô's Formula

We are now ready to state the general form of *Itô's formula*, which extends (1.15). From their very definition, semimartingales form a vector space; linear combinations of a finite number of semimartingales are semimartingales. But the class of semimartingales is closed under much more general transformations, and much of its usefulness comes from this fact. If f is a $\mathcal{C}^2$ function on $\mathbb{R}^d$ and X is a d-dimensional semimartingale, the process $Y = f(X)$ is also a semimartingale and is given by

$$
f(X_t) = f(X_0) + \sum_{i=1}^{d} \int_0^t f_i'(X_{s-}) \, dX_s^i
$$

$$
+ \frac{1}{2} \sum_{i,j=1}^{d} \int_0^t f_{ij}''(X_{s-}) \, d\langle X^{i,c}, X^{j,c} \rangle_s \tag{1.60}
$$

$$
+ \sum_{s \leq t} \left(f(X_s) - f(X_{s-}) - \sum_{i=1}^{d} f_i'(X_{s-}) \Delta X_s^i \right).
$$

The reader will notice that all processes $f_i'(X_{t-})$ and $f_{ij}''(X_{s-})$ are left-continuous with right limits, so they are locally bounded and predictable and the first (stochastic) and second (ordinary) integrals make sense. Moreover, the sth summand in the last sum is smaller than $K_n \|\Delta X_s\|^2$ on the set $\{\sup_{s \leq t} \|X_s\| \leq n\}$, for a constant K_n. Since $\sum_{s \leq t} \|\Delta X_s\|^2 < \infty$ (because the quadratic variation is finite), this last sum is in fact absolutely convergent. In other words, all terms on the right of (1.60) are well defined.

We end this subsection with the promised proof of (1.14), in the general setting of semimartingales. The result is stated in the form of a theorem, which is unusual in this chapter but motivated by its importance in the econometrics literature and more generally for high-frequency statistics.

Theorem 1.14. *Let X and X' be two semimartingales. For each n, let $T(n,0) = 0 < T(n,1) < T(n,2) < \cdots$ be a strictly increasing sequence of stopping time with infinite limit, and suppose that the mesh $\pi_n(t) = \sup_{i \geq 1}(T(n,i) \wedge t - T(n,i-1) \wedge t)$ goes to 0 for all t, as $n \to \infty$. Then we have the following convergence in probability:*

$$
\sum_{i \geq 1} \left(X_{T(n,i) \wedge t} - X_{T(n,i-1) \wedge t} \right) \left(X'_{T(n,i) \wedge t} - X'_{T(n,i-1) \wedge t} \right)
$$
$$
\overset{u.c.p.}{\Longrightarrow} [X, X']_t. \tag{1.61}
$$

Moreover, for any given t we also have

$$
\sum_{i \geq 1, \, T(n,i) \leq t} \left(X_{T(n,i)} - X_{T(n,i-1)} \right) \left(X'_{T(n,i)} - X'_{T(n,i-1)} \right)
$$
$$
\overset{\mathbb{P}}{\longrightarrow} [X, X']_t. \tag{1.62}
$$

in restriction to the set $\{\Delta X_t = 0\} \cup \{\Delta X_t' = 0\}$ on which either X or X' have no jump at time t, and on the whole set Ω when further, for any n, there is an index i such that $T(n,i) = t$.

The convergence (1.62) may actually fail on the set $\{\Delta X_t \neq 0, \Delta X_t' \neq 0\}$. For example, if for all n there is no i such that $T(n, i) = t$, the left side of (1.62) converges in probability (on Ω) to the left limit $[X, X']_{t-}$, which equals $[X, X']_t - \Delta X_t \Delta X_t'$.

The theorem (and its proof below) assumes that $\pi_n(t) \to 0$ pointwise, but the condition $\pi_n(t) \xrightarrow{\mathbb{P}} 0$ is indeed enough for the results to hold.

Proof. In view of (1.58) we can replace X and X' by $X - X_0$ and $X' - X_0'$, or equivalently assume that $X_0 = X_0' = 0$. The proof is based on the elementary equality $(x - y)(x' - y') = xx' + yy' - y(x' - y') - y'(x - y)$ applied with $x = X_{T(n,i)\wedge t}$ and $y = X_{T(n,i-1)\wedge t}$ and $x' = X'_{T(n,i)\wedge t}$ and $y' = X'_{T(n,i-1)\wedge t}$. Summing over all $i \geq 1$, we deduce that the left side of (1.61) is equal to

$$X_t X_t' - \int_0^t H_s^n \, dX_s' + \int_0^t H_s'^n \, dX_s$$

(recall $X_0 = X_0' = 0$), where we have set

$$H_s^n = \sum_{i\geq 1} X_{T(n,i-1)} \, 1_{(T(n,i-1),T(n,i)]}(s)$$

and a similar formula for $H_s'^n$, with X' instead of X. The processes H^n are adapted and left-continuous, hence predictable, and $|H^n| \leq Z$ where Z is the predictable locally bounded process defined by $Z_s = \sup(|X_r| : r \in [0, s))$. Moreover, since the mesh of the subdivision goes to 0, we have $H^n \to X_-$ pointwise. Then the dominated convergence theorem for stochastic integrals, see (1.54), yields $H^n \bullet X' \overset{\text{u.c.p.}}{\Longrightarrow} X_- \bullet X'$, and $H'^n \bullet X \overset{\text{u.c.p.}}{\Longrightarrow} X'_- \bullet X$ holds by the same argument. In other words, the left side of (1.61) converges in the u.c.p. sense to

$$X_t X_t' - \int_0^t X_{s-} \, dX_s + \int_0^t X'_{s-} \, dX_s.$$

It remains to apply Itô's formula to the two-dimensional semimartingale with components X and X' and the function $f(x, x') = xx'$: we deduce from (1.56) that the above expression is equal to $[X, X']_t$, and thus (1.61) is proved. When for each n there is i such that $T(n, i) = t$, the left sides of (1.61) and (1.62) are the same, so (1.62) is proved. Finally, in general, the difference between the left sides of (1.61) and (1.62) is smaller than $\rho(\varepsilon) = \sup(|X_t - X_{t-s}| \, |X_t' - X_{t-s}'| : s \in [0, \varepsilon])$ as soon as $\pi_n(t) \leq \varepsilon$. On the set $\{\Delta X_t = 0\} \cup \{\Delta X_t' = 0\}$ we have $\rho(\varepsilon) \to 0$ as $\varepsilon \to 0$. Then the convergence (1.62) in restriction to this set readily follows from the fact that $\pi_n(t) \to 0$. $\square$

1.3.4   Characteristics of a Semimartingale and the Lévy-Itô Decomposition

Here, X is a d-dimensional semimartingale on $(\Omega, \mathcal{F}, (\mathcal{F}_t)_{t \geq 0}, \mathbb{P})$, and we are now almost ready to define the characteristics of X.

The process $\sum_{s \leq t} \Delta X_s 1_{\{\|\Delta X_s\| > 1\}}$, or equivalently $(x 1_{\{\|x\| > 1\}}) * \mu$ where $\mu = \mu^X$ is the jump measure of X defined by (1.36), is of finite variation. Then we can rewrite (1.52) as

$$X_t = X_0 + A'_t + M_t + \sum_{s \leq t} \Delta X_s 1_{\{\|\Delta X_s\| > 1\}}$$

where $M_0 = A'_0 = 0$ and A' is of finite variation and M is a local martingale. Now, one can show that the semimartingale $A' + M$, which has jumps smaller than 1 by construction, can be written in a *unique* (up to null sets) way as $A' + M = B + N$, where again $N_0 = B_0 = 0$ and N is a local martingale and B is a *predictable* process of finite variation.

Definition 1.15. *The* characteristics *of the semimartingale X are the following triple (B, C, ν):*

(i) $B = (B^i)_{1 \leq i \leq d}$ is the predictable process of finite variation defined above;

(ii) $C = (C^{ij})_{1 \leq i,j \leq d}$ is the quadratic variation of the continuous local martingale part X^c of X, that is, $C^{ij} = \langle X^{i,c}, X^{j,c} \rangle$;

(iii) ν is the (predictable) compensating measure of the jump measure $\mu = \mu^X$ of X, as defined in (1.41).

Sometimes one says "predictable characteristics" or "local characteristics" of the semimartingale X. The name comes from the fact that, when X is a Lévy process with characteristics triple (b, c, F), then its characteristics in the semimartingale sense are

$$B_t(\omega) = bt, \quad C_t(\omega) = ct, \quad \nu(\omega, dt, dx) = dt \otimes F(dx). \qquad (1.63)$$

So (B, C, ν) and (b, c, F) convey the same information. Note that in this case the characteristics (B, C, ν) are *not random*. This turns out to be "necessary and sufficient." More precisely, a semimartingale X has non-random characteristics if and only if it has $(\mathcal{F}_t)$-independent increments; and it has characteristics of the form (1.63) if and only if it is an $(\mathcal{F}_t)$-Lévy process.

The reader should not be misled: unlike for Lévy processes (or more generally for processes with independent increments), the characteristics do *not* characterize the law of the process in general. Whether they do characterize the law in specific cases is an important problem, closely related to the uniqueness of (weak) solutions of some associated SDEs, and we will come back to this point later.

Now, although the characteristics do not always characterize the process X, they provide useful information, especially on the jumps. For example, we have a (partial) analogue of (1.48): for any nonnegative Borel function g on $\mathbb{R}^d$ with $g(0) = 0$ and any $t > 0$,

$$\text{the two sets } \{(g \wedge 1) * \nu_t < \infty\} \text{ and } \{g * \mu_t < \infty\} \tag{1.64}$$
$$\text{are a.s. equal}$$

and in particular, similar to (1.50), for any $p \geq 0$ we have

$$\text{the two sets } \{(\|x\|^p \wedge 1) * \nu_t < \infty\}$$
$$\text{and } \left\{\sum_{s \leq t} \|\Delta X_s\|^p < \infty\right\} \text{ are a.s. equal.} \tag{1.65}$$

The triple (B, C, ν) satisfies a number of structural properties, coming from its definition. The process C is such that $C_{t+s} - C_t$ is a symmetric nonnegative $d \times d$ matrix, as already mentioned. Next, B and ν are predictable, with finite variation for B, but there are other necessary requirements, namely there is a version of (B, ν) satisfying identically

$$(\|x\|^2 \wedge 1) * \nu_t(\omega) < \infty, \qquad \nu(\omega, \{t\} \times \mathbb{R}^d) \leq 1,$$
$$\|\Delta B_t(\omega)\| \leq 1, \qquad \nu(\omega, \{t\} \times \mathbb{R}^d) = 0 \Rightarrow \Delta B_t(\omega) = 0. \tag{1.66}$$

The analogy with Lévy processes goes further; for example we have a formula similar to the Lévy-Itô decomposition, that is,

$$X_t = X_0 + B_t + X_t^c + (x\, 1_{\{\|x\| \leq 1\}}) * (\mu - \nu)_t + (x\, 1_{\{\|x\| > 1\}}) * \mu_t, \tag{1.67}$$

where the stochastic integral above makes sense because of the first property in (1.66). However, this may look like (1.51), but μ is not a Poisson measure and X^c is not a Brownian motion here.

1.4   Itô Semimartingales

1.4.1   The Definition

As seen above, quite a few properties of Lévy processes extend to general semimartingales, but there are also big differences, like the fact that $\nu(\omega, \{t\} \times \mathbb{R}^d)$ may be positive. There is, however, a class of semimartingales which is a more direct extension of Lévy processes:

Definition 1.16. *A d-dimensional semimartingale X is an Itô semi-martingale if its characteristics (B, C, ν) are absolutely continuous with respect to the Lebesgue measure, in the sense that*

$$B_t = \int_0^t b_s ds, \quad C_t = \int_0^t c_s ds, \quad \nu(dt, dx) = dt \, F_t(dx), \qquad (1.68)$$

where $b = (b_t)$ is an $\mathbb{R}^d$-valued process, $c = (c_t)$ is a process with values in the set of all $d \times d$ symmetric nonnegative matrices, and $F_t = F_t(\omega, dx)$ is for each (ω, t) a measure on $\mathbb{R}^d$. The terms (b_t, c_t, F_t) are called the spot characteristics of X.

These b_t, c_t and F_t necessarily have some additional measurability properties, so that (1.68) makes sense: we may choose b_t and c_t predictable (or simply progressively measurable, this makes no difference in the sequel and does not change the class of Itô semimartingales), and F_t is such that $F_t(A)$ is a predictable process for all $A \in \mathcal{R}^d$ (or progressively measurable, again this makes no difference). The last three requirements of (1.66) are automatically fulfilled here, and we can and will choose a version of F_t which satisfies identically

$$\begin{aligned} \int (\|x\|^2 \wedge 1) \, F_t(\omega, dx) &< \infty \\ \text{and } \int_0^t ds \int (\|x\|^2 \wedge 1) \, F_t(\omega, dx) &< \infty. \end{aligned} \qquad (1.69)$$

In view of (1.63), any Lévy process is an Itô semimartingale.

There is an apparent contradiction between Definitions 1.1 and 1.16: a continuous Itô semimartingale in the former sense (or Brownian semimartingale) is also Itô in the latter sense, but the converse is not obvious when X is continuous. However, this contradiction is only apparent.

To be more specific, assume for example that $d = 1$ and that X is continuous, and an Itô semimartingale in the sense of (1.16), and also that $B_t = 0$ identically, so $X = X^c$. The question becomes: can we find a Brownian motion W and a progressively measurable process H such that $X_t = \int_0^t H_s dW_s$? If this is the case, we necessarily have $H_t^2 = c_t$, so since we know that $c_t \geq 0$, natural candidates are

$$H_t = \sqrt{c_t}, \qquad W_t = \int_0^t \frac{1}{H_s} dX_s.$$

Of course the second integral does not make sense if c_t vanishes somewhere, and it should thus be replaced by

$$W_t = \int_0^t \frac{1}{H_s} 1_{\{H_s \neq 0\}} dX_s.$$

This defines a continuous martingale W starting at 0, and with quadratic variation $\int_0^t 1_{\{c_s > 0\}} \, ds$, which may be different from t: hence W is *not* necessarily a Brownian motion; when for example $c_t = 0$ for all $t \leq 1$ it is quite possible that the σ-field $\mathcal{F}_1$ is trivial and thus there simply does *not* exist any $(\mathcal{F}_t)$-Brownian motion on $(\Omega, \mathcal{F}, (\mathcal{F}_t)_{t \geq 0}, \mathbb{P})$.

The solution to this problem needs an extension of the original probability space. The need for an extension also arises in other contexts in this book, so we devote the next subsection to the general question of "extending" the probability space.

1.4.2   Extension of the Probability Space

The space $(\Omega, \mathcal{F}, (\mathcal{F}_t)_{t \geq 0}, \mathbb{P})$ is fixed. Let $(\Omega', \mathcal{F}')$ be another measurable space, and $\mathbb{Q}(\omega, d\omega')$ be a transition probability from $(\Omega, \mathcal{F})$ into $(\Omega', \mathcal{F}')$. We can define the products

$$\widetilde{\Omega} = \Omega \times \Omega', \quad \widetilde{\mathcal{F}} = \mathcal{F} \otimes \mathcal{F}', \quad \widetilde{\mathbb{P}}(d\omega, d\omega') = \mathbb{P}(d\omega)\mathbb{Q}(\omega, d\omega'). \quad (1.70)$$

The probability space $(\widetilde{\Omega}, \widetilde{\mathcal{F}}, \widetilde{\mathbb{P}})$ is called an *extension* of $(\Omega, \mathcal{F}, (\mathcal{F}_t)_{t \geq 0}, \mathbb{P})$. Any variable or process which is defined on either Ω or Ω' is extended in the usual way to $\widetilde{\Omega}$, with the same symbol; for example $X_t(\omega, \omega') = X_t(\omega)$ if X_t is defined on Ω. In the same way, a set $A \subset \Omega$ is identified with the set $A \times \Omega' \subset \widetilde{\Omega}$, and we can thus identify $\mathcal{F}_t$ with $\mathcal{F}_t \otimes \{\emptyset, \Omega'\}$, so $(\widetilde{\Omega}, \widetilde{\mathcal{F}}, (\mathcal{F}_t)_{t \geq 0}, \widetilde{\mathbb{P}})$ is a filtered space.

The filtration $(\mathcal{F}_t)$ on the extended space does not incorporate any information about the second factor Ω'. To bridge this gap we consider a bigger filtration $(\widetilde{\mathcal{F}}_t)_{t \geq 0}$ on $(\widetilde{\Omega}, \widetilde{\mathcal{F}})$, that is with the inclusion property

$$\mathcal{F}_t \subset \widetilde{\mathcal{F}}_t, \qquad \forall t \geq 0.$$

The filtered space $(\widetilde{\Omega}, \widetilde{\mathcal{F}}, (\widetilde{\mathcal{F}}_t)_{t \geq 0}, \widetilde{\mathbb{P}})$ is then called a *filtered extension* of $(\Omega, \mathcal{F}, (\mathcal{F}_t)_{t \geq 0}, \mathbb{P})$.

In many, but not all cases the filtration $(\widetilde{\mathcal{F}}_t)$ has the product form

$$\widetilde{\mathcal{F}}_t = \cap_{s > t} \mathcal{F}_s \otimes \mathcal{F}'_s \quad (1.71)$$

where $(\mathcal{F}'_t)$ is a filtration on $(\Omega', \mathcal{F}')$. Quite often also, the transition probability $\mathbb{Q}$ has the simple form $\mathbb{Q}(\omega, d\omega') = \mathbb{P}'(d\omega')$ for some probability on $(\Omega', \mathcal{F}')$. In the latter case we say that the extension is a *product extension*, and if further (1.71) holds we say that we have a *filtered product extension*, which is simply the product of two filtered spaces.

A filtered extension is called *very good* if it satisfies

$$\omega \mapsto \int 1_A(\omega, \omega') \, \mathbb{Q}(\omega, d\omega') \text{ is } \mathcal{F}_t\text{-measurable}$$
$$\text{for all } A \in \widetilde{\mathcal{F}}_t, \text{ all } t \geq 0. \tag{1.72}$$

Under (1.71), this is equivalent to saying that $\omega \mapsto \mathbb{Q}(\omega, A')$ is $\mathcal{F}_t$-measurable for all $A' \in \mathcal{F}'_t$ and $t \geq 0$. A very good filtered extension is very good because it has the following nice properties:

- any martingale, local martingale, submartingale, supermartingale on $(\Omega, \mathcal{F}, (\mathcal{F}_t)_{t \geq 0}, \mathbb{P})$ is also a martingale, local martingale, submartingale, supermartingale on $(\widetilde{\Omega}, \widetilde{\mathcal{F}}, (\widetilde{\mathcal{F}}_t)_{t \geq 0}, \widetilde{\mathbb{P}})$

$$\tag{1.73}$$

- a semimartingale on $(\Omega, \mathcal{F}, (\mathcal{F}_t)_{t \geq 0}, \mathbb{P})$ is a semimartingale on $(\widetilde{\Omega}, \widetilde{\mathcal{F}}, (\widetilde{\mathcal{F}}_t)_{t \geq 0}, \widetilde{\mathbb{P}})$, with the same characteristics.

Statement (1.72) is equivalent to saying that any bounded martingale on $(\Omega, \mathcal{F}, (\mathcal{F}_t)_{t \geq 0}, \mathbb{P})$ is a martingale on $(\widetilde{\Omega}, \widetilde{\mathcal{F}}, (\widetilde{\mathcal{F}}_t)_{t \geq 0}, \widetilde{\mathbb{P}})$. For example a Brownian motion on $(\Omega, \mathcal{F}, (\mathcal{F}_t)_{t \geq 0}, \mathbb{P})$ is also a Brownian motion on $(\widetilde{\Omega}, \widetilde{\mathcal{F}}, (\widetilde{\mathcal{F}}_t)_{t \geq 0}, \widetilde{\mathbb{P}})$ if the extension is very good, and the same for Poisson random measures.

Many extensions are *not* very good: for example take $\mathbb{Q}(\omega, .)$ to be the Dirac mass $\varepsilon_{U(\omega)}$, on the space $(\Omega', \mathcal{F}') = (\mathbb{R}, \mathcal{R})$ endowed with the filtration $\mathcal{F}'_t = \mathcal{F}'$ for all t, and where U is an $\mathbb{R}$-valued variable on $(\Omega, \mathcal{F})$ which is not measurable with respect to the $\mathbb{P}$-completion of $\mathcal{F}_1$, say. Then $\mathbb{Q}(\omega, A') = 1_{A'}(U(\omega))$ is not $\mathcal{F}_1$-measurable in general, even when $A' \in \mathcal{F}'_1$, and the extension is not very good.

1.4.3 The Grigelionis Form of an Itô Semimartingale

We are now ready to give our representation theorem. The difficult part comes from the jumps of our semimartingale, and it is fundamentally a representation theorem for integer-valued random measure in terms of a Poisson random measure, a result essentially due to Grigelionis (1971). The form given below is Theorem (14.68) of Jacod (1979), and we will call the representation given here the *Grigelionis form* of the semimartingale X.

We have the d-dimensional Itô semimartingale X with characteristics (B, c, ν) given by (1.68). Moreover, d' is an arbitrary integer with $d' \geq d$, and E is an arbitrary Polish space with a σ-finite and infinite measure

λ having no atom, and $\underline{q}(dt, dx) = dt \otimes \lambda(dx)$. Then one can construct a very good filtered extension $(\widetilde{\Omega}, \widetilde{\mathcal{F}}, (\widetilde{\mathcal{F}}_t)_{t\geq 0}, \widetilde{\mathbb{P}})$, on which are defined a d'-dimensional Brownian motion W and a Poisson random measure $\underline{p}$ on $\mathbb{R}_+ \times E$ with intensity measure λ, such that

$$
\begin{aligned}
X_t &= X_0 + \int_0^t b_s ds + \int_0^s \sigma_s dW_s \\
&\quad + (\delta 1_{\{\|\delta\|\leq 1\}}) \star (\underline{p} - \underline{q})_t + (\delta 1_{\{\|\delta\|>1\}}) \star \underline{p}_t,
\end{aligned}
\tag{1.74}
$$

where σ_t is an $\mathbb{R}^d \otimes \mathbb{R}^{d'}$-valued process on $(\Omega, \mathcal{F}, (\mathcal{F}_t)_{t\geq 0}, \mathbb{P})$ which is predictable (or only progressively measurable), and δ is a predictable $\mathbb{R}^d$-valued function on $\Omega \times \mathbb{R}_+ \times E$, both being such that the integrals in (1.74) make sense.

The process b_t is the same here and in (1.68), and we have close connections between $(\sigma_t, \delta(t, z))$ and (c_t, F_t). Namely, a version of the spot characteristics c_t and F_t is given by the following:

- $c_t(\omega) \quad = \quad \sigma_t(\omega)\, \sigma_t^\star(\omega)$
- $F_t(\omega, .) \quad = \quad$ the image of the measure λ
  restricted to the set $\{x : \delta(\omega, t, x) \neq 0\}$
  by the map $x \mapsto \delta(\omega, t, x)$. $\qquad$ (1.75)

Conversely, any process of the form (1.74) (with possibly b, σ and δ defined on the extension instead of $(\Omega, \mathcal{F}, (\mathcal{F}_t)_{t\geq 0}, \mathbb{P})$) is an Itô semimartingale on $(\widetilde{\Omega}, \widetilde{\mathcal{F}}, (\widetilde{\mathcal{F}}_t)_{t\geq 0}, \widetilde{\mathbb{P}})$, and on $(\Omega, \mathcal{F}, (\mathcal{F}_t)_{t\geq 0}, \mathbb{P})$ as well if it is further adapted to $(\mathcal{F}_t)$. Therefore, the formula (1.74) may serve as the definition of Itô semimartingales, if we do not mind extending the space, and for practical applications we do not mind! Therefore, in the sequel we freely use the Grigelionis form above, pretending that it is defined on our original filtered space $(\Omega, \mathcal{F}, (\mathcal{F}_t)_{t\geq 0}, \mathbb{P})$.

There is a lot of freedom in the choice of the extension, of the space E and the function δ, and even of the dimension d' and the process σ: for the latter, for example, the requirement being $\sigma_t \sigma_t^\star = c_t$, we can always take an arbitrary $d' \geq d$, or more generally a d' not smaller than the maximal rank of the matrices $c_t(\omega)$. A natural choice for E is $E = \mathbb{R}^d$, but this is not compulsory and we may take in all cases $E = \mathbb{R}$ with λ being the Lebesgue measure. For example, if we have several Itô semimartingales, and even countably many of them, we can use the same measure $\underline{p}$ for representing all of them at once.

For a Lévy process, the Grigelionis form coincides with its Lévy-Itô representation, upon taking $\underline{p} = \mu$ and $\delta(\omega, t, x) = x$. More generally, in equation (1.74), the term $(\delta 1_{\{\|\delta\|\leq 1\}}) \star (\underline{p} - \underline{q})_t$ corresponds to the small jumps of the process, while the term $(\delta 1_{\{\|\delta\|>1\}}) \star \underline{p}_t$ corresponds to the big jumps of the process.

1.4.4 A Fundamental Example: Stochastic Differential Equations Driven by a Lévy Process

We have already mentioned stochastic differential equations (SDE) of the form (1.18), driven by a Brownian motion. Natural extensions of them are SDEs driven by a Lévy process Z, written as

$$dX_t = a(X_{t-})\, dZ_t, \qquad X_0 = Y. \qquad (1.76)$$

Here Z is a q-dimensional Lévy process, the "solution" X will be d-dimensional, so Y is an $\mathcal{F}_0$-measurable $\mathbb{R}^d$-valued variable, and a is a function from $\mathbb{R}^d$ into $\mathbb{R}^d \times \mathbb{R}^q$. As for (1.18), a (strong) solution is a càdlàg adapted process X which satisfies the following, written componentwise:

$$X_t^i = Y^i + \sum_{j=1}^{q} \int_0^t a(X_{s-})^{ij}\, dZ_s^j. \qquad (1.77)$$

The fact that we take the left limit $a(X_{s-})$ in the integral above, and not $a(X_s)$, is absolutely crucial, because the integrand needs to be predictable, otherwise the stochastic integral *a priori* makes no sense. Of course when Z is continuous, hence the solution X as well, we have $a(X_{s-}) = a(X_s)$.

Note that (1.18) is a special case of (1.76), although it may not be apparent at first glance: in (1.18), if W is q'-dimensional, we take $q = q' + 1$ and $Z^j = W^j$ for $j \leq q'$ and $Z_t^q = t$, and the coefficient a defined by $a^{ij} = \sigma^{ij}$ when $j \leq q'$ and $a^{iq} = b^i$.

Here again, a wide variety of conditions on a imply existence and/or uniqueness of the solution of (1.76). The simplest one is that a is locally Lipschitz with at most linear growth, but many other conditions exist, sometimes related with the specific properties of the driving Lévy process Z.

Now, assuming (1.77), the process X is of course a semimartingale, and even an Itô semimartingale. If (β, γ, F) is the characteristic triple of Z, and using the Lévy-Itô representation of Z with $\underline{p} = \nu^Z$ and $\underline{q} =$

$\nu^X = dt \otimes F(dz)$ and σ such that $\sigma\sigma^* = \gamma$, we can rewrite (1.77) as

$$
\begin{aligned}
X_t^i &= X_0^i + \sum_{j=1}^q \int_0^t a(X_{s-})^{ij} \beta^j \, ds + \sum_{j,k=1}^q \int_0^t a(X_{s-})^{ij} \sigma^{jk} \, dW_s^k \\
&\quad + \sum_{j=1}^q \int_0^t \int_{\mathbb{R}^q} a(X_{s-})^{ij} z^j \, 1_{\{\|z\|\le 1\}} \, (\underline{p} - \underline{q})(ds, dz) \\
&\quad + \sum_{j=1}^q \int_0^t \int_{\mathbb{R}^q} a(X_{s-})^{ij} z^j \, 1_{\{\|z\|>1\}} \, \underline{p}(ds, dz).
\end{aligned}
$$

Therefore, the characteristics (B, C, ν) of X take the form (1.68) with the following (where $a(x)z$ stands for the d-dimensional vector with components $\sum_{j=1}^q a(x)^{ij} z^j$):

$$
\begin{aligned}
b_t^i &= \sum_{j=1}^q a(X_{t-})^{ij} \left(\beta^j + \right. \\
&\qquad \left. + \int_{\mathbb{R}^q} z^j \left(1_{\{\|z\|\le 1\}} - 1_{\{\|a(X_{t-})z\|\le 1\}}\right) F(dz)\right) \\
c_t^{ij} &= \sum_{k,l=1}^q a(X_{t-})^{ik} \gamma^{kl} a(X_{t-})^{jl} \\
F_t(\omega, dx) &= \text{the image of the measure } F \\
&\qquad \text{by the map } z \mapsto a(X_{t-}(\omega))z.
\end{aligned}
\tag{1.78}
$$

These characteristics have a complicated form, although they indeed come naturally as functions of the coefficient a: the problem of finding a process which is an Itô semimartingale with characteristics given a priori in the form (1.78) reduces in fact to solving Equation (1.76).

Now, we also have, in a somewhat more immediate way, the Grigelionis form of X, provided we take for W and $\underline{p}$ the terms coming in the Lévy-Itô decomposition of Z. Namely, in (1.74) the process b_t is the same (complicated) process as above, but σ_t and δ take the simple form

$$
\sigma_t^{ik} = \sum_{j=1}^q a(X_{t-})^{ij} \sigma^{jk}, \qquad \delta(t, z)^i = \sum_{j=1}^q a(X_{t-})^{ij} z^j.
$$

In fact, equations like (1.68) are not really the most natural ones to consider in a discontinuous setting. It is also useful to consider equations which are driven directly by a Brownian motion W and a (general) Poisson random measure $\underline{p}$ on $\mathbb{R}_+ \times E$ for some "abstract" space E and with intensity measure $\underline{q} = dt \otimes \lambda(dz)$. This amounts to considering an equation of the form

$$
\begin{aligned}
X_t \;=\; & Y + \int_0^t b(X_{s-})ds + \int_0^s \sigma(X_{s-})dW_s \\
& + \int_0^t \int_E v(X_{s-}, z)1_{\{\|v(X_{s-},z)\|\le 1\}}\,(\underline{p}-\underline{q})(ds,dz) \quad (1.79) \\
& + \int_0^t \int_E v(X_{s-}, z)1_{\{\|v(X_{s-},z)\|>1\}}\,\underline{p}(ds,dz),
\end{aligned}
$$

where b is an $\mathbb{R}^d$-valued function on $\mathbb{R}^d$ and σ is an $\mathbb{R}^d \otimes \mathbb{R}^q$-valued function on $\mathbb{R}^d$ (where q is the dimension of W) and v is an $\mathbb{R}^d$-valued function on $\mathbb{R}^d \times E$. This type of equation includes (1.77) and immediately gives the Grigelionis form of the solution. When existence and uniqueness hold for all initial conditions Y, the solution is a homogeneous Markov process, and the restriction of its infinitesimal generator to the C^2 functions takes the form

$$
\begin{aligned}
Af(x) \;=\; & \sum_{i=1}^d b(x)^i f_i'(x) + \frac{1}{2}\sum_{i,j=1}^d c(x)^{ij} f_{ij}''(x) \\
& + \int_E \Big(f(x + v(x,z)) - f(x) \quad\quad\quad (1.80) \\
& \quad - \sum_{i=1}^d f_i'(x)v(x,z)^i\, 1_{\{\|v(x,z)\|\le 1\}} \Big)\lambda(dz),
\end{aligned}
$$

where $c = \sigma\sigma^*$. This extends (1.17), and one may show that any homogeneous Markov process which is an Itô semimartingale is of this form.

More generally even, one can interpret the Grigelionis form (1.74) as a generalized SDE similar to (1.79), but with "coefficients" $b_t(\omega)$, $\sigma_t(\omega)$ and $\delta(\omega, t, z)$ which may depend on the whole past of X before time t, and also on ω in an arbitrary (predictable) way. In this setting the infinitesimal generator is replaced by the so-called extended generator

$$
\begin{aligned}
\mathcal{A}_t f(x) \;=\; & \sum_{i=1}^d b_t^i f_i'(x) + \frac{1}{2}\sum_{i,j=1}^d c_t^{ij} f_{ij}''(x) \\
& + \int_E \Big(f(x + \delta(t,z)) - f(x) \\
& \quad - \sum_{i=1}^d f_i'(x)\delta(t,z)^i\, 1_{\{\|\delta(t,z)\|\le 1\}} \Big)\lambda(dz),
\end{aligned}
$$

so $\mathcal{A}_t$ is a second order integro-differential operator mapping the C^2 functions into the set of random variables. This extended generator is no longer the generator of a semi-group, but the characteristic martingale property of the generator is preserved, and it reads as follows: for any $\mathcal{C}^2$ function f, the process

$$M_t^f = f(X_t) - f(X_0) - \int_0^t \mathcal{A}_s f\, ds$$

is a local martingale.

As a consequence of all these considerations, one may state (in a somewhat heuristic way) that the characteristics (B, C, ν), or equivalently (and perhaps more appropriately) (b_t, c_t, F_t), determine the dynamics of the process. They are thus of fundamental importance for modeling purposes. More precisely, the problem of describing the process X is often considered as "solved" when one knows the characteristics (B, C, ν), in connection with X itself and perhaps with other random inputs.

1.5   Processes with Conditionally Independent Increments

In most problems considered in this book we start with an underlying process X which is an Itô semimartingale on some given filtered probability space $(\Omega, \mathcal{F}, (\mathcal{F}_t)_{t\geq 0}, \mathbb{P})$. We then consider various functionals of X, such as the approximate quadratic variation defined as the left side of (1.61) or (1.62). We are interested first in the convergence in probability of these functionals, as in Theorem 1.14, and ultimately in the rate of convergence and, whenever possible, in the "second order" asymptotic behavior, or Central Limit Theorem, associated with the convergence in probability. As it turns out, the limit when such a CLT holds will almost always be defined on an extension of $(\Omega, \mathcal{F}, (\mathcal{F}_t)_{t\geq 0}, \mathbb{P})$, as introduced in (1.70), and what will be available is the law of the limit under the measures $\mathbb{Q}(\omega, d\omega')$, or equivalently the $\mathcal{F}$-conditional law of the limit; the reader can look immediately at Chapter 3 for a (relatively) simple case for which this situation occurs.

Actually, the putative limits will (almost) always be a stochastic process U belonging to a special and relatively restricted class, namely the processes having $\mathcal{F}$-conditionally independent increments. The aim of this section is to describe those processes, which have an interest by themselves and can in fact be defined independently of any limiting procedure. Toward this aim, we first need to consider processes which extend Lévy processes.

1.5.1 Processes with Independent Increments

A q-dimensional process U defined on a space $(\Omega, \mathcal{F}, (\mathcal{F}_t)_{t \geq 0}, \mathbb{P})$ is called a *process with independent increments*, relative to $(\mathcal{F}_t)$, if it is càdlàg, with $U_0 = 0$, adapted, and the increment $U_{t+s} - U_t$ is independent of $\mathcal{F}_t$ for all $s, t \geq 0$. In other words, we have all properties of Definition 1.1 except that the law of $U_{t+s} - U_t$ may depend on both s and t. When $(\mathcal{F}_t) = (\mathcal{F}_t^U)$ is the filtration generated by U we simply say a *process with independent increments*.

When the increments are stationary, U is simply a Lévy process. Otherwise, it still exhibits similar features. In particular, when it is a semimartingale, its characteristics relative to $(\mathcal{F}_t)$ are deterministic (this property characterizes semimartingales with independent increments). We can thus decompose its third (deterministic) characteristic ν as a sum $\nu = \nu^c + \nu^d$, where, using the notation $D = \{t > 0 : \nu(\{t\} \times \mathbb{R}^q) > 0\}$ and its complement D^c in $\mathbb{R}_+$,

$$\nu^c(dt, dx) = \nu(dt, dx) 1_{D^c}(t), \quad \nu^d(dt, dx) = \sum_{s \in D} \varepsilon_s(dt) \otimes \nu(\{s\}, dx)$$

(there is no randomness here). We thus have two types of jumps: those occurring at a time outside the countable set D, which are like the jumps of a Lévy process except that the associated Poisson measure is non-homogeneous (it admits ν^c as its intensity measure), and those occurring at a time in D, which are called *fixed times of discontinuity* because we have

$$\mathbb{P}(\Delta U_t \neq 0) > 0 \quad \Longleftrightarrow \quad t \in D.$$

Although it is possible to describe all processes with independent increments, we restrict our attention to those which are encountered as limits in this book. This class of processes, denoted for short as $\mathcal{L}_0^q$ below (q stands for the dimension), is in fact rather special: it is the class of all processes of the form

$$U_t = \sum_{n: t_n \leq t} v(t_n) Y_n + \int_0^t v'(s) \, dW'_s \tag{1.81}$$

where

- v is a measurable function on $\mathbb{R}_+$, with dimension $q \times Q$
- v' is a measurable locally square-integrable function on $\mathbb{R}_+$, with dimension $q \times Q'$
- W' is a Q'-dimensional Brownian motion
- $t_n \in (0, \infty]$, $t_n \neq t_m$ if $n \neq m$ and $t_n < \infty$
- the $\mathbb{R}^Q$-valued variables Y_n are i.i.d. and independent of W',

and we suppose that at least one of the following two sets of conditions holds:

(i) $0 < \mathbb{E}(\|Y_1\|) < \infty$ and $\sum_{n:\,t_n \leq t} \|v(t_n)\| < \infty$

(ii) $\mathbb{E}(Y_1) = 0,\ 0 < \mathbb{E}(\|Y_1\|^2) < \infty$ and $\sum_{n:\,t_n \leq t} \|v(t_n)\|^2 < \infty$.

Under (i) the first sum in (1.81) is absolutely convergent. Under (ii) this is no longer necessarily true, but it converges in $\mathbb{L}^2$ and the resulting process is a square-integrable martingale. Since $\mathbb{P}(Y_n \neq 0) > 0$, the set of fixed times of discontinuity of U is the set of all finite t_n's such that $v(t_n) \neq 0$.

The following (obvious) fact is important:

> Any U in $\mathcal{L}_0^q$ has independent increments, and its law is
> determined by the functions v and v', the set   (1.82)
> $D = \{t_n : n \geq 1\} \cap (0, \infty)$, and the law η of the variables Y_n,

and we can relabel the sequence t_n at will. Finally, under the previous conditions we have, relative to the filtration $(\mathcal{F}_t^U)$ generated by U:

- U is a centered Gaussian process
  - $\Leftrightarrow$ either η is a centered Gaussian law or $v = 0$ on D
- U is a continuous centered Gaussian martingale   (1.83)
  - $\Leftrightarrow$ $v = 0$ on D.

1.5.2   A Class of Processes with $\mathcal{F}$-Conditionally Independent Increments

Generally speaking, a q-dimensional process U on an extension $(\widetilde{\Omega}, \widetilde{\mathcal{F}}, \widetilde{\mathbb{P}})$ of the original probability space $(\Omega, \mathcal{F}, \mathbb{P})$, see (1.68), is called a *process with $\mathcal{F}$-conditionally independent increments* if, for $\mathbb{P}$-almost all ω, it is a process with independent increments under the measure $\mathbb{Q}(\omega, .)$.

As previously, we restrict our attention to those U which, under $\mathbb{Q}(\omega, .)$, belong to the class $\mathcal{L}_0^q$ described above, and we even suppose that the law η (as in (1.82)) is the same for all ω. Therefore, in order to construct such a process, we start with the following ingredients:

- a progressively measurable process V with dimension $q \times Q$
- a progressively measurable, locally square-integrable process V' with dimension $q \times Q'$
- a probability measure η on $\mathbb{R}^Q$
- a sequence T_n of stopping times, with $T_n \neq T_m$ on the set $\{T_n < \infty\}$ if $n \neq m$.

We also suppose that V and η satisfies at least one of the following two conditions:

$$
\begin{aligned}
&\text{(i)} \quad 0 < \int \|x\|\, \eta(dx) < \infty \text{ and } \sum_{n:T_n \le t} \|V_{T_n}\| < \infty \\
&\text{(ii)} \quad 0 < \int \|x\|^2\, \eta(dx) < \infty, \quad \int x\,\eta(dx) = 0, \\
&\qquad \text{and } \sum_{n:T_n \le t} \|V_{T_n}\|^2 < \infty.
\end{aligned} \tag{1.84}
$$

The construction of a version of the process U is now quite simple. We choose an extra space $(\Omega', \mathcal{F}', \mathbb{P}')$ endowed with the following objects:

- a q'-dimensional Brownian motion W'
- a sequence $(Y_i)_{i\ge 1}$ of i.i.d. variables, (1.85) independent of W', with law η.

Then we define the product extension

$$
\widetilde{\Omega} = \Omega \times \Omega', \quad \widetilde{\mathcal{F}} = \mathcal{F} \otimes \mathcal{F}', \quad \widetilde{\mathbb{P}} = \mathbb{P} \otimes \mathbb{P}'. \tag{1.86}
$$

We also consider the smallest filtration $(\widetilde{\mathcal{F}}_t)_{t\ge 0}$ on $\widetilde{\Omega}$ which contains $(\mathcal{F}_t)_{t\ge 0}$ (recall that any variable on Ω or Ω' can be considered as a variable on the product $\widetilde{\Omega}$, so $\mathcal{F}_t$ is also a σ-field on $\widetilde{\Omega}$), and to which W' is adapted, and such that each Y_n is $\widetilde{\mathcal{F}}_{T_n}$-measurable. Due to the independence built in (1.85) and (1.86), the process W' is an $(\widetilde{\mathcal{F}}_t)$-Brownian motion and the processes V, V' are $(\widetilde{\mathcal{F}}_t)$-progressively measurable. Then it is an easy job to prove that the next formula defines a process U on the extension, with all the required properties:

$$
U_t = \sum_{n:\, T_n \le t} V_{T_n}\, Y_n + \int_0^t V_s'\, dW_s'. \tag{1.87}
$$

It is useful to have explicit formulas for the conditional first and second moments of the process U in this setting. Letting

$$
\begin{aligned}
&M_j = \int x^j \eta(dx), \quad M_{jk} = \int x^j x^k \eta(dx), \\
&C_t'^{jk} = \sum_{l=1}^{q'} \int_0^t V_s'^{jl} V_s'^{kl}\, ds,
\end{aligned} \tag{1.88}
$$

we get

$$
\text{(1.84)-(i)} \quad \Rightarrow \quad \mathbb{E}(U_t^j \mid \mathcal{F}) = \sum_{s\le t} \sum_{k=1}^{q} V_s^{jk} M_k
$$

$$
\text{(1.84)-(ii)} \quad \Rightarrow \quad
\begin{cases}
\mathbb{E}(U_t^j \mid \mathcal{F}) = 0 \\
\mathbb{E}(U_t^j U_t^k \mid \mathcal{F}) = C_t'^{jk} \\
\quad + \sum_{s\le t} \sum_{l,m=1}^{q} V_s^{jl} V_s^{km}\, M_{lm}.
\end{cases}
$$

Finally, if $D(\omega) = \{T_n(\omega) : n \geq 1\} \cap (0, \infty)$, the next two equivalences follow from (1.83):

- U is $\mathcal{F}$-conditionally a centered Gaussian process
  - $\Leftrightarrow$ η is centered Gaussian or $V = 0$ on D
- U is $\mathcal{F}$-conditionally a continuous
  - centered Gaussian martingale $\Leftrightarrow$ $V = 0$ on D.

$$(1.89)$$

We conclude with an important particular case. In many instances, the process U given by (1.87) is continuous, that is, $U_t = \int_0^t V_s' \, dW_s'$. The law of a continuous centered process U with independent increments is completely specified by its covariance matrix $\mathbb{E}(U_t^i U_t^j)$, as a function of time. This is of course still true when U is continuous, with $\mathcal{F}$-conditional mean 0 and with $\mathcal{F}$-conditionally independent increments. That is, the $\mathcal{F}$-conditional law of U in this case is completely specified by the process C' given in (1.88).

In practice, one usually goes the other way around: one starts with a $q \times q$-dimensional process C' of the form

$$C_t' = \int_0^t c_s' \, ds,$$

with c' adapted, with values in the set of nonnegative symmetric $q \times q$ matrices. Then, what precedes gives us a process U which is continuous and $\mathcal{F}$-conditionally centered and with independent increments (equivalently: $\mathcal{F}$-conditionally a centered Gaussian martingale). For this, it suffices to choose a $q \times Q$-dimensional process V which is adapted and is a square root of c', that is, $c_t' = V_t V_t^*$; this is always possible by a measurable selection theorem, up to null sets, and with any choice of Q with $Q \geq q$, or even with $Q \geq \sup_{\omega,t} \operatorname{rank}(c_t'(\omega))$.

Chapter 2

Data Considerations

Semimartingales of the type described in the previous chapter are used as modeling tools in a number of applications including the study of Internet packet flow, turbulence and other meteorological studies, genome analysis, physiology and other biological studies, particle modeling and finance. We will focus in this chapter on the specific characteristics of high-frequency financial data that distinguish them from other, more standard, time series data. The statistical methods we will describe in this book rely on statistics of the process X sampled at times $i\Delta_n$ for $i = 0, \ldots, [T/\Delta_n]$, and sometimes at unevenly spaced times, possibly random. In financial applications, X will typically be the log of an asset price and many statistics will often rely only on the increments of X, or in time series parlance the first differences of X, which are the log-returns from that asset.

The usual rationale for first-differencing a time series is to ensure that when T grows the process does not explode: in many models, the process X may be close to a local martingale and thus the discrete data $X_{i\Delta_n}$ may be close to exhibiting a unit root, whereas the first differences of X will be stationary or at least non-explosive. In this book, the asymptotic perspective we adopt is to have T fixed. As a result, explosive behavior is not a concern. However, as we will see later on, many natural quantities of interest are statistics of the log-returns, but one should be aware that there is no obstacle in principle to using the price process instead of the log-returns. We will see one such example in the discussion of the consequences of rounding, since in most market mechanisms rounding is at the level of the price itself. Let us also add that, when the horizon T is short, such as a day or a week, prices typically change during the whole

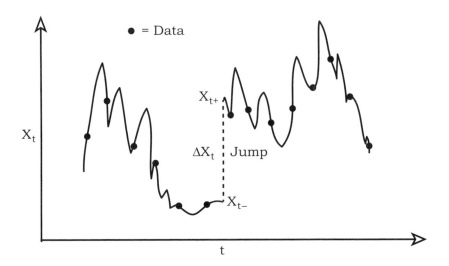

Figure 2.1: A single path observed discretely: discrete increments vs. jumps.

period by a small amount only, whereas the logarithm is a "locally linear" transformation (as is any smooth function): in other words returns and log-returns are roughly proportional.

Finally, we do not assume that we observe the full continuous-time sample path. This distinction is particularly relevant when jumps are present in the underlying price process: observing, say, a relatively large price change as in Figure 2.1 may suggest that a jump was involved, but is not the same as observing the jump of the underlying price process itself.

2.1   Mechanisms for Price Determination

Markets are typically either order-driven or quotes-driven, with hybrid arrangements possible. Order-driven markets typically function through a limit order book, with specific rules determining how and when orders get executed. In a quotes-driven market, orders get routed through a dealer who posts quotes that the customer may or may not accept. These institutional arrangements and the market architecture are constantly evolving, in response to but also under pressure from high-frequency trading firms.

We describe these mechanisms below, very briefly; much more compre-hensive treatments can be found in some of the books that cover market microstructure theory and practice such as O'Hara (1995), Harris (2003) and Hasbrouck (2007). Biais et al. (2005) discuss some of the implications of the price formation and trading process for price discovery and welfare. Let us also mention that microeconomic studies of how prices are formed are drawing increasing attention, due to the availability of ultra-high-frequency data, but we will not touch upon this topic.

2.1.1   Limit Order and Other Market Mechanisms

From the perspective of observing a price, actual recorded transactions are the most straightforward mechanism. In high-frequency data, a transaction is always accompanied by a time stamp that identifies the time at which it was recorded. This time stamp is recorded down to the second, and in some markets now to the millisecond. A transaction is often, but not always, accompanied by a corresponding volume as well as other characteristics that help identify for instance where that transaction took place such as the exchange where it was executed. Rarely, data identifying the parties to the transaction will also be available; this is primarily the case for data collected by market regulators such as the SEC and the CFTC and made available to researchers under stringent conditions.

A limit order specifies a direction for the desired transaction (buy or sell), quantity (number of shares) and price at which the order should be executed (maximal price if this is a buy order, minimal price if this is a sell order). The collection of such orders that are in existence at each time, and have not yet been executed, is the limit order book. When a new order arrives in the market, it is compared to the existing orders in the book. If the new order leads to a possible transaction, for instance because it specifies a buy order and a quantity at a price that are compatible (in this case, higher) with one or more sell orders in the book, a transaction takes place.

Market rules determine in what sequence orders get executed. Typically, the first priority is granted to price, meaning that an order to buy at a higher price will be executed before an order to buy at a lower price. The second priority is often granted to time, so orders at the same price are executed first-in, first-out, although in some markets the second priority is given to order size instead, and in some cases orders are allocated proportionately to each limit order in the book at the best price. Many high-frequency trading strategies are designed to "game" the priority rules by strategically placing multiple orders, many of which the trader has no intention of executing: traders will use their ability to limit orders to hold their place in the queue, and rely on their ability to cancel orders at a lightning fast pace whenever necessary.

Instead of a limit order, a market order may be placed. Such an order specifies only a direction and quantity and is executed at the prevailing price; if the quantity specified exceeds what the book is able to fulfill at the best price, then the order may get executed at progressively worse prices, as it "walks the book."

The price data that get recorded from a limit order market are available in real time using subscription mechanisms for traders, which are an important source of revenue for exchanges, and with a delay of a few minutes for everyone else. While transactions data are readily available, very few data sources contain the limit order book that is in existence at each point in time, that is, the full context in which the transactions actually took place. Reconstructing the limit order book ex post requires a vast amount of computational effort, and access to data (such as messages exchanged between market participants and exchanges to place and cancel orders) that are not readily available.

Although this is rapidly changing, the availability of high-frequency futures data, with the exception of S&P 500 eMini contracts, has so far lagged behind that for equities. One common limitation is that only transactions leading to a price change ("tick data") are being reported, and sometimes no volume data are attached.

In a limit order market, consumers send their orders to the market with minimal role for intermediaries. In a dealer market, by contrast, multiple dealers quote bid and ask prices to potential customers. The bid price is the price at which the dealer is willing to buy from the customer, the ask price the price at which the dealer is willing to sell to the customer. Transactions and quotes data emerge naturally from this market mechanism. Whereas the limit order book is often difficult to reconstruct in a limit order market, the sequence of quotes in effect at each point in time is usually available in a dealer market.

Examples of dealer markets include the markets for foreign exchange, corporate bonds and swaps. The frontier between limit order markets and dealer markets is often fluid. For example, interdealer trade in the foreign exchange market is often conducted via a limit order book. NASDAQ originally operated as a dealer market. It now operates primarily as a limit order market.

Regulatory bodies ask markets to link together to provide the best possible execution irrespectively of where an order is initially placed, while technological developments make it easier to develop a new trading venue and compare in real time price and order information from competing trading venues for the same asset. These forces tend to counteract the effect of market fragmentation. One consequence of market fragmentation for the statistical properties of the price series is to make it more difficult to aggregate price information that emerges from different markets, since the time stamps may not be exactly synchronous and may or may not be reported using the same sets of rules. Some high frequency trading strategies attempt to take advance of any lack of synchronicity.

2.1.2 Market Rules and Jumps in Prices

Both limit order markets and dealers markets are designed to operate continuously. By contrast, a double-sided auction is designed to operate at discrete points in time. Trade then occurs only at periodic auctions, called fixings, once or more often per day. Therefore, by nature, auction markets do not lead to high-frequency transactions data. In other cases, the market operates continuously but with periods of closure such as the night.

One consequence for the price process is that large price increments will often be recorded from the previous close to the new open price. For instance, opening prices will incorporate the cumulative effect of all information revealed overnight. For statistics that are based on price increments, these overnight returns recorded over a long period while the market was closed will often not be included in the sample since they are not comparable to the fixed sampling at Δ_n series. Including them would have the effect of generating an additional, usually large, jump every morning at opening time, in the price series; this would drastically affect the nature of the models for jumps which, when present, are usually thought of as occurring at random and unpredictable times.

Another aspect of market rules that can potentially have an impact on jumps in the price series are rules detailing how the market will operate in case of market disruption, potential or realized. These rules generally specify trading halts and circuit breakers in certain circumstances. For instance, if a firm is about to make a significant announcement, regulators may temporarily halt trading in its stock. The temporary halt in trading is intended to afford agents in the market a chance to assess the information so that once trading resumes the price movement in the stock might be less than it would otherwise have been. Circuit breakers are designed to halt trading in the event of a large market decline.

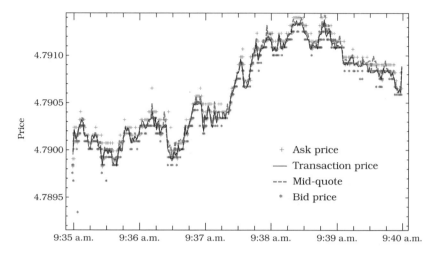

Figure 2.2: Transaction prices and quotes. SPY, December 1, 2010.

2.1.3   Sample Data: Transactions, Quotes and NBBO

Throughout the book, we demonstrate how to implement some of the methods described and report the results using a few high-frequency financial time series obtained from two sources. The first is the NYSE Euronext Trade and Quote (TAQ) database. The TAQ database provides tick-by-tick quote and transaction data for equities listed on the New York Stock Exchange, NYSE American Stock Exchange, NASDAQ National Market System and SmallCap issues. The data are collected between the consolidated tape hours of 4:00 a.m. to 6:30 p.m. EST. We extract from the TAQ data two individual stock price series, Microsoft and Intel, and an exchange traded fund, SPY, that tracks the performance of the S&P500 Index over the four-year period 2005–2010.

Additionally, we employ TickData, Inc., for currency and commodity futures and an equity index.[1] The contracts we consider are EUR/USD futures traded on the CME, NY Light Sweet Crude Oil futures traded on the NYMEX and the Dow Jones Industrial Average cash index. We will use the symbols EC, CL and DJ to denote these contracts respectively. Similar to the equity data, we consider the four-year period from 2007–2010.

---

[1] TickData provides already-filtered high-frequency time series of transaction data including both prices and quantities through its program Tick Write 7. TickData describes its filtering methodology in broad terms in the article "High Frequency Data Filtering," which can be found at http://www.tickdata.com/products/futures/ under "Data Set Generation and Filtering."

As TickData provides filtered high-frequency data we only concern ourselves with filtering the TAQ data. We start by downloading unfiltered data directly from the TAQ database for IBM and SPY into daily files. These data include "good trades" where the TAQ user manual defines good as regular trades which were not corrected, changed or signified as cancel or error, as well as original trades that were later adjusted to correct either the time or data. To construct an unfiltered time series we analyze each day in the sample individually. At each intraday time stamp we check for good transactions. If there are multiple transactions at a time stamp, which is often the case for liquidly traded stocks, we compute an average price weighting each transaction by its volume. If there are no trades at a particular time stamp, we do not change the price from its level at the previous time stamp.

The TAQ database also allows us to download quote data including bids, offers and their respective sizes. When employing quotes data, one possibility consists in constructing a price series by taking the midpoint of the bid and ask quotes, weighted by the quantities for which they are available. One often needs to take care to not include quotes that are far off the mark and may have been posted by a dealer in error or simply to withdraw, perhaps temporarily, from the market (so-called stub quotes). Instead, we use the quotes data to construct a second time series we call NBBO for National Best Bid and Offer. This series is constructed by checking each intraday time stamp for all available bids and offers. The best bid is computed as a volume weighted average of the quotes whose volume and price fall in the highest 90% of all available quotes at that time stamp. The best offer is computed in an analogous manner retaining quotes with the highest volume and lowest price. Then, if the average bid is less than or equal to the average offer, the mid or price is constructed by taking an average of the bid and offer. Hence the NBBO time series consists of a bid, mid and offer for each time stamp. If it happens that the average bid is greater than the average offer, the quotes are removed and we use the quote from the immediately preceding time stamp. Additionally, if no quotes are available at a time stamp, we take the bid, mid and offer from the immediately preceding one.

Finally, we construct a filtered time series using the data from the unfiltered time series and the NBBO time series. At the outset one might argue that any filtering method should err on the side of being conservative, that is, keeping rather than removing transaction data. The unfiltered data are not raw. The TAQ database only reports transactions deemed as good. However, visual inspection of the data may lead one to be concerned about "bouncebacks." These are transactions that visually appear to be outliers, identified as being either higher or lower than both the preceding and following transactions. This is perhaps related to the SEC regulation that exchanges may report trades within 90 seconds of when they actually occur. Reported transaction times may be delayed for a number of reasons. But for our purposes it suffices to realize that at any point t a good transaction may have actually occurred anytime in the window $(t - \tau, : t)$ where τ is a 90 second window. With this in mind we construct our filter by taking at each time t the minimum of the NBBO bid time series and maximum of the NBBO offer time series over the previous 90 seconds, and we remove any transactions that occur outside this window. This filtering method has the advantage that the size of the window will be determined in part by the local volatility of the price process, providing an endogenous method for removing bouncebacks that is hopefully conservative.

We then have three time series, unfiltered, NBBO and filtered, along with the TickData in quarterly files. Each quarterly file pertains to an individual security and it catalogs from 9:30:05 a.m. to 16:00:00 p.m. the day, time, interval between prices in seconds, price and log-return.

2.2   High-Frequency Data Distinctive Characteristics

One of the distinctive characteristics of the data consists of the fact that they are observed at times that are random, or at least not evenly spaced. Complicating matters, the time between observations may be informative about the price process, with trades occurring more or less frequently depending upon the news flow, which itself will generally influence the price process. This form of endogeneity is difficult to deal with, and even to properly formulate mathematically, and will largely be ignored in this book. Related to this question is the fact that when multiple assets are observed, transactions rarely occur at exactly the same time, resulting in asynchronicity.

Observations are also subject to a substantial amount of noise, due to a diverse array of market microstructure effects, either informational or not: bid-ask spread bounces, differences in trade sizes, informational content of price changes, gradual response of prices to a block trade, the strategic component of the order flow, inventory control effects, discreteness of price changes, etc. In some instances, transactions or quotes may be time-stamped to the nearest second, resulting in multiple observations at the same second and a loss of a clear time sequencing, when in fact traders operate on a millisecond time scale.

One additional characteristic that is relevant in practice is the sheer quantity of data available. For example, all transactions on a liquid stock over the course of a year can exceed one gigabyte. Limit order book data can multiply this to a staggering amount of data. While transactions and quotes data are more and more readily available in publicly disseminated databases, reconstructing the limit order book in effect at each point in time remains a time consuming and largely elusive notion, primarily due to the lack of public information about the identity of the accounts behind specific quotes.

Finally, the returns and volatility data may in some cases have distinctive statistical features, such as exhibiting heavy tails, long memory in the case of volatility data, and strong intra-day and intra-week periodicity.

2.2.1   Random Sampling Times

In a limit order market, orders initiated by customers arrive at random times, so it is natural to expect that the transactions will also take place at random times. Creating a series of equally spaced values of X with inter-observations time Δ therefore requires making assumptions. If there is no observed transaction at time $i\Delta$, then we may put in its place the last recorded transaction before that instant. To be effective, this approach requires that Δ be at least slightly longer than the average time separating the actual transactions.

An advantage of quotes data is that they are available continuously, even if slightly stale, so constructing a series of X sampled at equally spaced times $i\Delta$ for $i = 0, 1, \ldots, [T/\Delta]$ is in principle straightforward. Figure 2.3 show histograms of the distribution of inter-transaction and inter-quotes times for the S&P500 and IBM.

An important approach to model irregularly spaced financial data consists of employing point processes, with the times between transactions or quotes labeled as durations, see Hasbrouck (1991), Engle and Russell (1998), Bauwens and Giot (2001), Hautsch (2004, 2012) and Bauwens and Hautsch (2009). Market events tend to be clustered over time, resulting in durations that are typically positively autocorrelated and strongly persistent. These time series properties have given rise to dynamic models

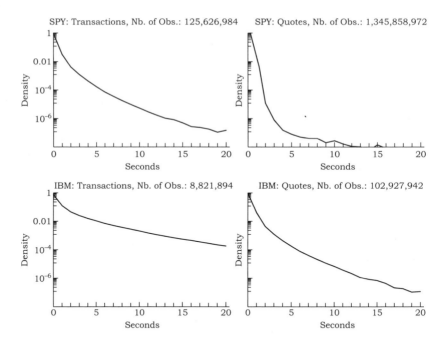

Figure 2.3: Empirical distribution of times between observations, SPY and IBM, 2010.

of intra-trade or intra-quotes durations, often with some features in common with autoregressive volatility models such as Engle's ARCH (1982).

2.2.2   Market Microstructure Noise and Data Errors

A second distinct characteristic of high-frequency financial data is that they are observed with noise, and that the noise interacts with the sampling frequency in complex ways. In an efficient market, X_t is the log of the expectation of the value of the security conditional on all publicly available information at time t. It corresponds to the log-price that would be in effect in a perfect market with no trading imperfections, frictions, or informational effects.

By contrast, market microstructure noise summarizes the discrepancy (often termed as an "observation error") between the efficient log-price and the observed log-price, as generated by the mechanics of the trading process. What we have in mind as the source of noise is a diverse array of market microstructure effects, either information or non-information related, such as the presence of a bid-ask spread and the corresponding

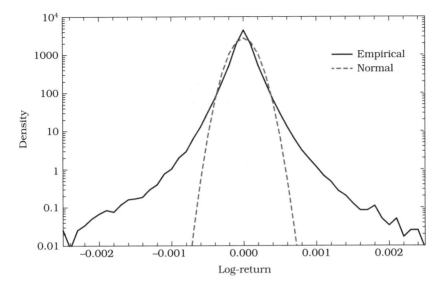

Figure 2.4: Log-plot of the marginal density of log-returns, at a frequency of 5 seconds, empirical compared to Normal with matched variance, filtered SPY transactions, 2010.

bounces, the differences in trade sizes and the corresponding differences in representativeness of the prices, the different informational content of price changes due to informational asymmetries of traders, the gradual response of prices to a block trade, the strategic component of the order flow, inventory control effects, the discreteness of price changes in markets that are subject to a tick size, etc., all summarized into the noise term. That these phenomena are real and important is an accepted fact in the market microstructure literature, both theoretical and empirical. One can in fact argue that these phenomena justify this literature.

2.2.3   Non-normality

A final characteristic of the data, which is of course strongly suggestive of a departure from the Brownian-only paradigm, is non-normality. Log-returns at high frequency can be quite far from being normally distributed, as seen in the Figure 2.4. This non-normality is a well-known feature of empirical returns, dating back to at least the 1960s, and can in fact be seen as having motivated the early introduction of jump processes, such as stable processes, for modeling prices.

This non-normality feature is present at all sufficiently high frequen-

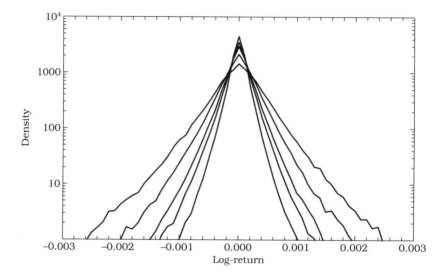

Figure 2.5: Log-plot of the marginal density of log-returns, at frequencies of 5, 10, 15, 30 and 45 seconds, filtered SPY transactions, 2010.

cies, as seen in Figure 2.5. Early evidence on non-normality of returns was produced by Mandelbrot (1963) and Fama (1965).

2.3   Models for Market Microstructure Noise

Although we will consider models with noise in greater detail in Chapter 7, we start now with a brief description of two polar models, which are the most amenable to subsequent analysis.

2.3.1   Additive Noise

The notion that the observed transaction price in high-frequency financial data is the unobservable efficient price plus some noise component due to the imperfections of the trading process is a well established concept in the market microstructure literature (see for instance Black (1986)). A natural assumption is therefore to consider that, instead of observing the process X at dates $\tau_i = i\Delta_n$, we observe X with error:

$$Y_{\tau_i} = X_{\tau_i} + \varepsilon_{\tau_i} \tag{2.1}$$

where in the simplest possible case the $\varepsilon'_{\tau_i}s$ are i.i.d. noise with mean zero and variance a^2 and are independent of the X process. In that context, we view X as the latent efficient log-price, while Y is the observed market log-price. Many market frictions tend to take proportional magnitudes: for instance one may see a transaction cost expressed as some number of basis points. Such a friction would then translate into a multiplicative error for the price, or an additive error for the log-price as specified in (2.1).

We can think of (2.1) as the simplest possible reduced form of structural market microstructure models. The efficient price process X is typically modeled as a semimartingale. This specification coincides with that of Hasbrouck (1993), who discusses the theoretical market microstructure underpinnings of such a model and argues that the parameter a is a summary measure of market quality. Structural market microstructure models do generate (2.1). For instance, Roll (1984) proposes a model where ε is due entirely to the bid-ask spread. Harris (1990b) notes that in practice there are sources of noise other than just the bid-ask spread, and studies their effect on the Roll model and its estimators.

Indeed, a disturbance ε can also be generated by adverse selection effects as in Glosten (1987) and Glosten and Harris (1988), where the spread has two components: one that is due to monopoly power, clearing costs, inventory carrying costs, etc., as previously, and a second one that arises because of adverse selection whereby the specialist is concerned that the investor on the other side of the transaction has superior information. When asymmetric information is involved, the disturbance ε may no longer be uncorrelated with the X process.

Following the analysis of Aït-Sahalia et al. (2005), and assuming that the log-price is a square-integrable martingale, the equality

$$\Delta_i^n Y = \Delta_i^n X + \varepsilon_{\tau_i} - \varepsilon_{\tau_{i-1}}$$

implies the following covariance structure of the observed log-returns $\Delta_i^n Y's$, which are centered variable:

$$\mathbb{E}[\Delta_i^n Y \Delta_{i+j}^n Y] = \begin{cases} \sigma^2 \Delta + 2a^2 & \text{if } j = i \\ -a^2 & \text{if } j = i+1 \\ 0 & \text{if } j > i+1 \end{cases} \qquad (2.2)$$

In other words, the series $\Delta_i^n Y$ is an MA(1) process, as i varies.

Two important properties of the log-returns $\Delta_i^n Y's$ emerge from this equation (2.2). First, microstructure noise leads to spurious variance in observed log-returns, namely $\sigma^2\Delta + 2a^2$ vs. $\sigma^2\Delta$. This is consistent with the predictions of some theoretical microstructure models. For instance Easley and O'Hara (1992) develop a model linking the arrival of information, the timing of trades, and the resulting price process. In their model, the transaction price will be a biased representation of the efficient price process, with a variance that is both overstated and heteroskedastic as a result of the fact that transactions (hence the recording of observations on the process Y) occur at intervals that are time-varying.

Furthermore, the proportion of the total return variance that is market microstructure-induced is

$$\phi = \frac{2a^2}{\sigma^2\Delta + 2a^2} \tag{2.3}$$

at observation interval Δ. As Δ gets smaller, ϕ gets closer to 1, so that a larger proportion of the variance in the observed log-return is driven by market microstructure frictions, and correspondingly a lesser fraction reflects the volatility of the underlying price process X.

Second, (2.2) implies that log-returns are (negatively) autocorrelated with first order autocorrelation $-a^2/(\sigma^2\Delta + 2a^2) = -\phi/2$ and a vanishing higher order autocorrelation. This fact is substantiated in Figure 2.6, which shows that indeed the autocorrelogram of log-returns can be in practice very close to the autocorrelogram of an MA(1) process. It has been noted that market microstructure noise has the potential to explain the empirical autocorrelation of returns. For instance, in the simple Roll model, $\varepsilon_t = (s/2)Q_t$ where s is the bid-ask spread and Q_t, the order flow indicator, is a binomial variable that takes the values $+1$ and -1 with equal probability. Therefore $\text{Var}[\varepsilon_t] = a^2 = s^2/4$. Since $\text{Cov}(\Delta_i^n Y, \Delta_{i-1}^n Y) = -a^2$, the bid-ask spread can be recovered in this model as $s = 2\sqrt{-\rho}$ where $\rho = -a^2$ is the first order autocorrelation of returns. French and Roll (1986) proposed to adjust variance estimates to control for such autocorrelation and Harris (1990b) studied the resulting estimators. Zhou (1996) proposed a bias correcting approach based on the first order autocovariances; see also Hansen and Lunde (2006), who study the Zhou estimator.

In Sias and Starks (1997), ε arises because of the strategic trading of institutional investors, which is then put forward as an explanation for the observed serial correlation of returns. Lo and MacKinlay (1990) show that infrequent trading has implications for the variance and autocorrelations of returns. Other empirical patterns in high-frequency financial

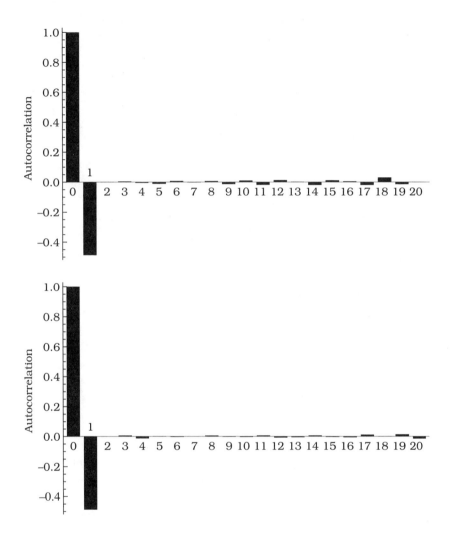

Figure 2.6: Autocorrelogram of log-returns of transaction prices on SPY sampled at a fixed 5 second frequency. For each lag $j = 0, 1, 2, ...$ on the x-axis, the correlation of $\Delta_i^n Y$ and $\Delta_{i-j}^n Y$, estimated from observations $i = j + 1, ..., n$, is reported.

data have been documented: leptokurtosis, deterministic patterns and volatility clustering.

What if the data on log-returns is inconsistent with a simple MA(1) structure? Griffin and Oomen (2008) provide an interesting analysis of the impact of tick vs. transaction sampling. Their results show that the nature of the sampling mechanism can generate fairly distinct autocorrelogram patterns for the resulting log-returns. Now, from a practical perspective, we can view the choice of sampling scheme as one more source of noise, this one attributable to the econometrician who is deciding between different ways to approach the same original transactions or quotes data: should we sample in calendar time? transaction time? tick time? something else altogether? Since the sampling mechanism is not dictated by the data, this argues for working under robust departures from the basic assumptions.

In any case, it is of course possible to generalize the above setup to one where the $\varepsilon'_{\tau_i}s$ are not serially independent, hence modifying the structure given in (2.2). A simple model to capture higher order dependence in the log-returns is

$$\epsilon_{\tau_i} = U_{\tau_i} + V_{\tau_i} \tag{2.4}$$

where U is i.i.d., V is AR(1) with first order coefficient ρ having $|\rho| < 1$, and U and V are independent. Under this model, we obtain an ARMA(1, 1) structure

$$\mathbb{E}[\Delta_i^n Y, \Delta_{i-1}^n Y] = \begin{cases} \sigma^2 \Delta + 2E\left[U^2\right] + 2\left(1 - \rho\right) E\left[V^2\right] & \text{if } j = i \\ -E\left[U^2\right] - \left(1 - \rho\right)^2 E\left[V^2\right] & \text{if } j = i + 1 \\ -\rho^{j-i-1} \left(1 - \rho\right)^2 E\left[V^2\right] & \text{if } j > i + 1 \end{cases}$$

which can generate richer patterns of autocorrelations in the log-returns, all due to serial correlation in the noise, and still assuming that the true log-price is a square-integrable martingale.

2.3.2   Rounding Errors

The second situation we consider is one where the measurement error is primarily due to the fact that transaction prices are multiples of a tick size (e.g., $Y_{\tau_i} = [X_{\tau_i}] = m_i \alpha$ where α is the tick size and m_i is the integer closest to X_{τ_i}/α) and can be modeled as a rounding off problem (see Gottlieb and Kalay (1985), Jacod (1996) and Delattre and Jacod (1997)). Markets often specify a minimum price increment, also known as a tick size, which may be as low as one cent in the case of decimalized stocks in the United States.

The specification of the model in Harris (1990a) combines both the rounding and bid-ask effects as the dual sources of the noise term ε. Finally, structural models, such as that of Madhavan et al. (1997), also give rise to reduced forms where the observed transaction price Y takes the form of an unobserved fundamental value plus error.

Rounding effects are often quite important for many assets and sampling frequencies. On the other hand, this effect can be small for certain data series, such as decimalized stocks at all but the highest frequencies, or liquid currencies which are often rounded to the fourth or fifth decimal point, or indexes which result from computing a weighted average of the rounded prices of a large number of prices. Ceteris paribus, this component of the noise becomes less important as the sampling frequency decreases. Also, it has been noted (see Harris (1991)) that when the tick size is small, priority given to order time can become less effective since a new order can gain priority by offering a slightly better price by one tick; this is the practice known as "pennying."

As noted above, a realistic treatment of rounding effects requires that we operate on price levels instead of log returns.

2.4   Strategies to Mitigate the Impact of Noise

Various strategies are available at the level of data pre-processing, meaning before any of the methods described in the rest of this book, are employed.

2.4.1   Downsampling

High-frequency financial data are often available every second or every few seconds. It has been noted that market microstructure noise is linked to each transaction, and not to the amount of time that separates successive transactions. For instance, the volatility of the underlying efficient price process and the market microstructure noise tend to behave differently at different frequencies. Thinking in terms of signal-to-noise ratio, a log-return observed from transaction prices over a tiny time interval is mostly composed of market microstructure noise and brings little information regarding the volatility of the price process since the latter is (at least in the Brownian case) proportional to the time interval separating successive observations. As the time interval separating the two prices in the log-return increases, the amount of market microstructure noise remains constant, since each price is measured with error, while the informational content of volatility increases. Hence very high-frequency data are mostly composed of market microstructure noise, while the volatility of the price process is more apparent in longer horizon returns.

The simplest method consists then of sampling at a lower frequency, with a time interval typically measured in minutes. In the volatility literature, a value of 5 to 15 minutes has often been employed. One drawback of this approach, however, is that it leads to discarding a substantial amount of the data that were originally available, which in purely statistical terms leads to efficiency losses which can indeed be large. We will discuss this further in Chapter 7.

2.4.2   Filtering Transactions Using Quotes

Different measurements of the stock returns lead to different properties of the constructed price process. One particular issue that deserves careful attention in the data is that of bouncebacks. Bouncebacks are price observations that are either higher or lower than the sequences of prices that both immediately precede and follow them. Such prices generate a log-return from one transaction to the next that is large in magnitude, and is followed immediately by a log-return of the same magnitude but of the opposite sign, so that the price returns to its starting level before that particular transaction. To the extent that we have no reason to believe that those transactions did not actually take place, as we already eliminate transactions known to TAQ to be incorrect, we start with the premise that bouncebacks should not be arbitrarily removed from the sample. However one may think that bouncebacks, although significant in a sense, should not be incorporated in the model for the "true" latent price process, whatever this "true" might mean.

The prevalence of bouncebacks can lead to a large number of relatively small jumps in the raw data and can bias the empirical results toward finding more small jumps than actually happen if the data are correctly measured, or bias the estimated degree of jump activity. By contrast, a true jump can be followed by another jump (due to the prevalence of jump clustering in the data), but these successive jumps will not necessarily be of the same magnitude and of the opposite sign.

One straightforward approach to eliminate bouncebacks would be to eliminate all log-returns that are followed immediately by another log-return of the opposite sign, when both are greater than a predetermined magnitude, such as some number of ticks. There is however typically in

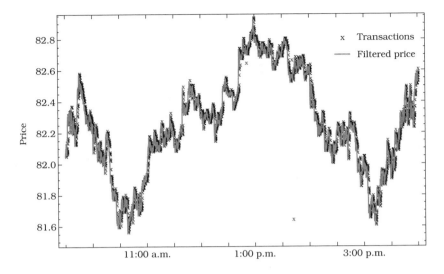

Figure 2.7: Transactions and filtered price, SPY, April 8, 2009.

the data a continuum of bouncebacks in terms of such magnitude, so this approach ends up creating a discontinuity at the arbitrary predetermined magnitude selected: many of them of size less than that level and then none. On the other hand, setting that level within one tick would be extreme and would change the nature of the observed prices.

To deal with bouncebacks endogenously, we can instead make use of the matched quotes data. Transactions that take place outside the currently prevailing quotes are known as "out-trades." A single out-trade will generate a bounceback. We can use the quotes data in order to reduce the incidence rate of bouncebacks in the transactions data, in a manner that is compatible with market rules. Incidentally, bouncebacks can happen in quotes data as well. But they tend to appear when there is only a very small number of quotes at that point in time, with one or more that are off-market for the reasons just described. Quote bouncebacks seem to be unrelated to transaction bouncebacks.

Given the computed NBBO at each point in time, we can take a moving window of, for instance, 90 seconds. This might cover the case of a block trade that might have its reporting delayed. Or opening trades done manually can be delayed, for instance, even at small sizes. The 90-second window we employ is set to reflect the SEC rules that specify that exchanges must report trades within 90 seconds. Trades that are delayed beyond 90 seconds are marked as "late," and already excluded from the starting data by our TAQ filters. We use this 90-second moving

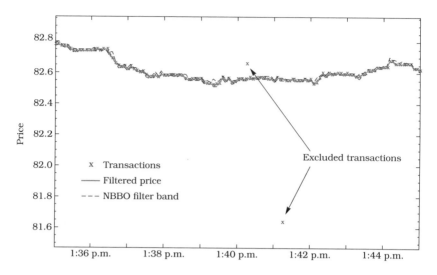

Figure 2.8: Filtering the transaction prices using the NBBO filter constructed from quotes data, SPY, April 8, 2009.

window to construct a running minimum of the national best bid prices and a running maximum of the national best offer prices over the time window. This NBBO bid-offer moving envelope is then used as our filter for transactions: we retain only transactions that take place inside the envelope.

There are many reasons for trades to be delayed, especially when some form of manual execution is involved. For example, in the case of negotiated trades, brokers might work the order over time, leading to a sequence of smaller trades reports. Or the broker might (acting as principal) sell the whole amount to the customer, in which case we would see a single trade report. Another practice involves "stopping" the order: the broker does not execute the order immediately, but does guarantee the buyer a price. The broker can then work the order, deferring any trade reports until the execution is complete, at which time an average price is reported. The average price can appear out of line with the prices around it and lead to a bounceback.

The NBBO filter we employ tends to be conservative – erring on the side of retaining transactions – since there is no guarantee that an out-trade is actually necessarily due to a time delay, or that even if delayed it took place at a time when the bid-ask spread was less than the maximal width of the spread over the 90-second time window. On the other hand, block (negotiated) trades usually carry a price concession and so could be executed outside this envelope and thereby be wrongly excluded. To the extent that, for it to lead to a bounceback, this is by definition a single isolated transaction, it did not have a permanent price impact, but rather was associated with a transient liquidity effect.

We do not make use of the NBBO quotes depth: from the list of prevailing quotes by exchange, we already determine the best (maximum) bid price and the best (minimum) ask price. Using the prevailing quote list, we could sum the bid sizes for quotes at the best bid price, and sum the ask sizes for the quotes at the best ask price. This would produce the NBBO sizes available to trade at each point of time and one could consider filtering out transactions of greater size. However, this might also in some circumstances eliminate legitimate transactions, such as block trades, or for that matter any trade that has a price impact and is executed in one block. In any event, we find empirically that filtering the transactions by the NBBO filter as described above reduces drastically the number of bouncebacks in the data.

We start with the unfiltered transactions data, and this procedure results in a time series of NBBO-filtered transactions. We also produce a series of the midpoint of the just computed NBBO bid and ask prices and use this as our measurement of the quote price at that point in time. We therefore end up with three different measurements of the "price" series, for each stock: the unfiltered transactions; the NBBO-filtered transactions; and the NBBO quotes midpoint. As we will see, statistical procedures applied to these different series tend to yield consistent results, but not always.

Part II

Asymptotic Concepts

This book is about econometric methods for high-frequency data: we want to estimate some parameters of interest, or test some statistical hypotheses, in connection with the model or family of models we use; the "high-frequency" qualifier means that the underlying process X is observed at discrete times, say $0, \Delta_n, 2\Delta_n, \ldots$, with a "small" time interval Δ_n, whereas the observation window $[0, T]$ is not particularly large. Therefore the estimators or tests are based on observations inside a fixed window, T fixed, and we wish them to be at least consistent as Δ_n shrinks to 0; and the faster the convergence of the estimators or tests takes place, the better. Non-regular spacing between observations may also be considered, provided the mesh continues to go to 0.

The aim of this part is to introduce the asymptotic concepts that we employ, and it contains three chapters with very different scopes. The first is devoted to an introduction to the emblematic problem for high-frequency statistics, which is integrated volatility estimation. This chapter concerns a simplified version of the problem and serves as a general introduction to asymptotic theory, whereas the next chapter describes, again in a very simplified setting, the behavior of the so-called power variations, which play a fundamental role later. These two chapters are designed as an introduction to the rest of the book, but the material in them will be re-worked in fuller generality later on; hence they can be skipped without harm (except perhaps for Sections 3.2 and 3.3 in which the stable convergence in law and some basic facts about the convergence of processes are established)

In the third chapter of this part, we introduce in some detail the various quantities or hypotheses which will be estimated or tested later on, starting with the definition of what "estimating" or "testing" a quantity or a hypothesis which is "random" might mean. This includes a number of definitions and examples of "identifiable" parameters or hypotheses. This is done first in the (parametric or semi-parametric) context of Lévy processes, and then for more general Itô semimartingales, which is a fully non-parametric case and for which most "parameters" which one wants to estimate are fundamentally random.

Chapter 3

Introduction to Asymptotic Theory: Volatility Estimation for a Continuous Process

In this chapter, we consider, as an introduction to asymptotic theory, the very simple situation of a one-dimensional continuous martingale of the form

$$X_t = X_0 + \int_0^t \sigma_s \, dW_s. \tag{3.1}$$

Our objective is to "estimate" its integrated volatility, which is

$$C_t = \int_0^t c_s ds, \quad \text{where} \quad c_s = \sigma_s^2,$$

on the basis of discrete observations of X over the time interval $[0, T]$, with the horizon T fixed. The sampling is the simplest possible: equidistant observations, without market microstructure noise. The observation times are $i\Delta_n$ for $i = 0, 1, \ldots, [T/\Delta_n]$, where $[T/\Delta_n]$ is the biggest integer less than or equal to T/Δ_n, and the time interval Δ_n eventually goes to 0: this is what is meant by high-frequency asymptotics, and will be our asymptotic framework throughout.

The parameter C_T to be estimated is in general random, so the word "estimation" is not totally appropriate and should perhaps be replaced by "filtering," but use of "estimation" in the present context is predominant in the econometrics literature. Despite the (possible) randomness of C_T, the notion of estimators is analogous to what one encounters in more standard statistical situations: at stage n, an estimator for C_T is simply a random variable, or statistic, which only depends upon the observations $X_{i\Delta_n}$ for $i = 0, 1, \ldots, [T/\Delta_n]$, and the aim is to find estimators which are (weakly) *consistent*, in the sense that they converge in probability to C_T. We would also like these estimators to converge as fast as possible, and to produce confidence intervals for C_T at any prescribed asymptotic level, hence the need for a Central Limit Theorem.

An important feature of what follows is that *a single path* $t \mapsto X_t(\omega)$ is (partially) observed. Now, should several paths be observed, the quantity of interest C_T would in fact depend on each of those paths and having a good (or even perfect) estimation for one would not entail an improved estimation for the others. So, observing a simple path $X(\omega)$ exactly fits the problem of estimating $C_T(\omega)$ for that particular outcome ω. Then of course having weak consistency does not seem to resolve the question, and strong consistency (that is, almost sure convergence; usually strong consistency does not hold in the context of this book) would not either, but this is in no way different from the same problem in the usual statistical setting.

Here $C_t = [X, X]_t$ is the quadratic variation, so we saw in Theorem 1.14 of Chapter 1 such a consistent sequence of estimators, namely the approximate quadratic variation, often called *"realized volatility"* or "realized variance," although the latter terminology is in fact deeply misleading:

$$\widehat{C}(\Delta_n)_t = \sum_{i=1}^{[t/\Delta_n]} (\Delta_i^n X)^2, \quad \text{where } \Delta_i^n X = X_{i\Delta_n} - X_{(i-1)\Delta_n}. \quad (3.2)$$

Note our notation $\Delta_i^n X$ for the ith return of the process, which is of course different from the notation ΔX_s we would employ to denote the jump at time s, if there were any jump (which is excluded by (3.1) here).

The aim of this chapter is to explain the issues involved when one attempts to derive the rate of convergence and the limiting distribution of the estimation error $\widehat{C}(\Delta_n) - C$, as $\Delta_n \to 0$, at the terminal time T, or at any other time $t \in [0, T]$. We will consider progressively more complex specifications for the process σ_s, starting with the simplest possible case where $\sigma_t = \sigma$ is a constant. As the specifications become more complex, we will see that establishing the limit result requires new tools, including a strengthened mode of convergence known as "stable convergence in law," and we will include the relevant elements about the convergence of processes. All these tools play a crucial role in the rest of the book, and they are explained in details in this chapter.

By contrast with the main part of the book, we try here, for pedagogical reasons, to demonstrate nearly every statement beyond classical probability theory, without appealing to outside results: "demonstrate" is in fact too ambitious a word, since complete proofs are quite intricate in the most general situation, but we always try to give a precise scheme for all proofs, emphasizing methods and ideas. These schematic proofs can serve as a template for the other situations encountered in the book, whose proofs will typically invoke general central limit theorems that are only stated in Appendix A, or elsewhere in the literature.

Let us also mention that the estimation of integrated volatility will be studied again, in a more general context (but with fewer details) in Chapter 6. Therefore, a reader already well acquainted with the convergence of processes and stable convergence in law can skip this chapter without harm.

3.1 Estimating Integrated Volatility in Simple Cases

In this section we consider the model (3.1) and establish the second order asymptotic behavior of the estimators $\widehat{C}(\Delta_n)_t$ in (3.2), or Central Limit Theorem, successively under more and more general assumptions on the volatility process σ_t. In all cases, the process

$$C(4)_t = \int_0^t c_s^2 \, ds = \int_0^t \sigma_s^4 \, ds,$$

called *quarticity* for obvious reasons, plays a key role. For consistency of notation, we could write $C_t = C(2)_t$ but C_t appears so often that it is worth its own designation.

In the model (3.1), the sign of σ_s is irrelevant, so we always assume $\sigma_s = \sqrt{c_s} \geq 0$. We also suppose that c_s is càdlàg, hence σ_s as well; although one could dispense with this additional assumption, it greatly simplifies the arguments below.

3.1.1 Constant Volatility

We begin with the simplest possible situation, where (3.1) holds with $\sigma_t = \sigma$ is a constant. The quantity to be estimated is $C_T = Tc$, where $c = \sigma^2$. It would then look more natural to estimate c itself (estimating c or Tc

are equivalent mathematical problems), but we stick to the estimation of $C_T = Tc$ in order to stay coherent with the more general cases studied below.

We are here in a classical parametric setting. The value X_0 being clearly irrelevant, at stage n we actually observe $[T/\Delta_n]$ i.i.d. returns $\Delta_i^n X$, or equivalently the normalized returns $\Delta_i^n X / \sqrt{\Delta_n}$ which are i.i.d. $\mathcal{N}(0, c)$, with c unknown. This is a particularly simple problem, easily coined in the usual parametric statistical setting where we have a family of probabilities $\mathbb{P}_\theta$ on the space $\mathbb{R}^{\mathbb{N}^*}$, depending on an unknown parameter θ which here is $\theta = Tc$.

At each stage n, the measures $\mathbb{P}_\theta$ restricted to the σ-field generated by the first $[T/\Delta_n]$ variables are all equivalent to the Lebesgue measure on $\mathbb{R}^{[T/\Delta_n]}$. The log-likelihood is

$$l_n(\theta) = -\frac{1}{2} \sum_{i=1}^{[T/\Delta_n]} \left(\frac{(\Delta_i^n X)^2}{c\,\Delta_n} + \log(2\pi\,c\,\Delta_n) \right) \qquad (3.3)$$

and the MLE *(maximum likelihood estimator)* for $\theta = Tc$ is exactly $\widehat{\theta}_n = \frac{T/\Delta_n}{[T/\Delta_n]} \widehat{C}(\Delta_n)_T$. In this simple case the MLE, and thus $\widehat{C}(\Delta_n)_T$ as well (because $1 \leq \frac{T/\Delta_n}{[T/\Delta_n]} \leq 1 + \frac{\Delta_n}{T}$), are well known to be asymptotically efficient (or optimal) in any possible sense of this word in this specific case, with a rate of convergence $1/\sqrt{\Delta_n}$. The term $\frac{T/\Delta_n}{[T/\Delta_n]}$ is simply an adjustment for the end point, or border, of the interval $[0, T]$, since T/Δ_n is not necessarily an integer. In practice, T/Δ_n is most often an integer, but even if it is not the case using the unbiased estimator $\widehat{\theta}_n$ instead of $\widehat{C}(\Delta_n)_T$ does not significantly improve the estimation, except in a situation of very small samples.

Next, the normalized estimation errors are

$$\frac{1}{\sqrt{\Delta_n}} \left(\widehat{C}(\Delta_n)_T - C_T \right) = \frac{1}{\sqrt{\Delta_n}} \sum_{i=1}^{[T/\Delta_n]} \left(\left(\frac{\Delta_i^n X}{\sqrt{\Delta_n}} \right)^2 - c \right) - \frac{T - \Delta_n [T/\Delta_n]}{\sqrt{\Delta_n}}\, c.$$

The last term above is again a border adjustment, obviously going to 0, hence we have (since $C(4)_T = Tc^2$ here) the convergence in law

$$\frac{1}{\sqrt{\Delta_n}} \left(\widehat{C}(\Delta_n)_T - C_T \right) \xrightarrow{\mathcal{L}} \mathcal{N}(0, 2C(4)_T) \qquad (3.4)$$

by an application of the usual CLT (Central Limit Theorem) to the i.i.d. centered variables $(\Delta_i^n X / \sqrt{\Delta_n})^2 - c$, whose variances are $2c^2$.

This fact does not immediately give us a way of constructing confidence intervals for C_T, because the variance $2C(4)_T$ is unknown. However, one can also find consistent estimators V_T^n for $2C(4)_T$, such as

$V_T^n = 2T(\widehat{C}(\Delta_n)_T)^2$ (again the optimal estimators), or

$$V_T^n = \frac{2}{3\Delta_n} \sum_{i=1}^{[T/\Delta_n]} (\Delta_i^n X)^4 \tag{3.5}$$

(these are *not* the optimal estimators, but they are consistent by an application of the Law of Large Numbers, and enjoy a CLT with rate $1/\sqrt{\Delta_n}$ again by the standard CLT). Then a standardization procedure, or Studentization, tells us that

$$\frac{\widehat{C}(\Delta_n)_T - C_T}{\sqrt{\Delta_n V_T^n}} \xrightarrow{\mathcal{L}} \mathcal{N}(0,1). \tag{3.6}$$

At this point, the construction of confidence intervals with asymptotic level $\alpha \in (0,1)$ is straightforward: if z_α denotes the two sided α-quantile of $\mathcal{N}(0,1)$, that is the number such that $\mathbb{P}(|\Phi| > z_\alpha) = \alpha$ where Φ is an $\mathcal{N}(0,1)$ variable, then

$$\left[\widehat{C}(\Delta_n)_T - z_\alpha \sqrt{\Delta_n V_T^n} \, , \, \widehat{C}(\Delta_n)_T + z_\alpha \sqrt{\Delta_n V_T^n} \right] \tag{3.7}$$

is such an interval. So far so good, and this simple case can be treated using only the simplest tools of parametric inference.

3.1.2   Deterministic Time-Varying Volatility

We now extend the model (3.1) by allowing σ_t, hence c_t as well, to be time-dependent, although still non-random. We are now in a semi-parametric model: the function c_t is unknown, but we want to estimate the real parameter $\theta = C_T$, at some fixed time T.

Again, the model fits the usual setting of (semi-parametric) statistical models, although the notion of asymptotic efficiency becomes trickier, and will not be analyzed here. The variables $\widehat{C}(\Delta_n)_T$ of (3.2) are still weakly consistent estimators for C_T. The returns $\Delta_i^n X$ are again independent, centered Gaussian, but no longer identically distributed. Rather, their variances are now

$$v_i^n := \mathbb{E}\left((\Delta_i^n X)^2\right) = \int_{(i-1)\Delta_n}^{i\Delta_n} c_s \, ds.$$

With the notation $\xi_i^n = \frac{1}{\sqrt{\Delta_n}} \left((\Delta_i^n X)^2 - v_i^n\right)$, the normalized estimation error is

$$\frac{1}{\sqrt{\Delta_n}} \left(\widehat{C}(\Delta_n)_T - C_T\right) = \sum_{i=1}^{[T/\Delta_n]} \xi_i^n - \frac{1}{\sqrt{\Delta_n}} \int_{\Delta_n[T/\Delta_n]}^{T} c_s \, ds,$$

and the last term on the right is again a border effect that goes to 0 as $\Delta_n \to 0$.

The variables ξ_i^n form a so-called triangular array of rowwise independent centered variables: this means that within each "row" n the ξ_i^n's are independent and centered when i varies, although in the present case there are complicated dependencies between rows. CLTs for rowwise independent triangular arrays go back to Lindeberg. A set of conditions ensuring the convergence in law of the row sums $\sum_{i=1}^{[T/\Delta_n]} \xi_i^n$ to the normal law $\mathcal{N}(0, V)$ is

$$\sum_{i=1}^{[T/\Delta_n]} \mathbb{E}((\xi_i^n)^2) \to V, \qquad \sum_{i=1}^{[T/\Delta_n]} \mathbb{E}((\xi_i^n)^4) \to 0. \qquad (3.8)$$

Since $\Delta_i^n X$ is $\mathcal{N}(0, v_i^n)$, (3.7) yields $\mathbb{E}((\xi_i^n)^2) = 2\Delta_n^{-1}(v_i^n)^2$ and $\mathbb{E}((\xi_i^n)^4) = 60\,\Delta_n^{-2}(v_i^n)^4$. In view of the càdlàg property of c_t, we readily check (3.8) with $V = 2C(4)_T$, and hence deduce (3.4).

To make this CLT "feasible" (that is, useful for deriving confidence intervals) we need consistent estimators V_T^n for the limiting variance $2C(4)_T$. Taking $V_T^n = 2T(\widehat{C}(\Delta_n)_T)^2$ here does not work, but we can make use of (3.5) for defining V_T^n: applying the criterion (3.8) to the centered variables $\xi_i^n = \frac{1}{\Delta_n^{3/2}}\left((\Delta_i^n X)^4 - 3(v_i^n)^2\right)$, we obtain that $\frac{1}{\sqrt{\Delta_n}}\left(V_t^n - 2C(4)_T\right)$ converges in law to a centered normal variable, and in particular $V_T^n \xrightarrow{\mathbb{P}} 2C(4)_T$.

Therefore, we conclude that (3.6) still holds in the present case, and confidence intervals are derived as in the previous subsection.

3.1.3 Stochastic Volatility Independent of the Driving Brownian Motion W

Our next extension of the class of possible volatility processes in (3.2) allows σ_t to be random but independent of the Brownian motion W that drives the process X in (3.1). In the finance literature, where X_t is the log-price of an asset, this is referred to as the "no-leverage" case.

Heuristically, this case reduces to the previous time varying but deterministic case, by conditioning on the path of c_t: with $\mathcal{G}$ denoting the σ-field generated by all variables c_t, $t \geq 0$, we condition on $\mathcal{G}$. Since without loss of generality one can assume that $\mathcal{F}$ is the σ-field generated by the two processes W and c, this σ-field is nice enough for the existence of a regular version of the $\mathcal{G}$-conditional probability, which we denote as $\mathbb{Q}(\omega, d\omega')$.

Remark 3.1. *We could employ the notation* $\mathbb{P}(d\omega'|\mathcal{G})$, *but this would miss the dependence on the path* ω, *which is essential. Also, the conditional probability of an event* A *given an event* B *requires dividing by the probability of the event* B. *A difficulty arises when the conditioning event* B *is too small to have a non-zero probability, such as when the event represents an* $\mathbb{R}$-*valued random variable taking a given value, as is the case here. The notion of a regular version of the conditional probability is an appropriate definition in such a case:* $\mathbb{Q}(\omega, d\omega')$ *is a transition probability from* $(\Omega, \mathcal{G})$ *into* $(\Omega, \mathcal{F})$ *such that for each* A *in* $\mathcal{F}$, $\omega \longmapsto \mathbb{Q}(\omega, A)$ *is a version of the conditional expectation* $\mathbb{E}(1_A|\mathcal{G})$. *The existence of* $\mathbb{Q}$ *requires nice properties of* $\mathcal{F}$ *which are satisfied here, such as being separable.*

Since W and c are independent, the process W remains a Brownian motion under each $\mathbb{Q}(\omega, .)$: the conditional law of the process W is equal to its unconditional law, and this is the key point of the argument. The conditioning changes the law of X, but X remains the stochastic integral of σ w.r.t. W, with now σ being a non-random function, under $\mathbb{Q}(\omega, .)$.

In other words, we can apply the results of the previous subsection under each $\mathbb{Q}(\omega, .)$, ending up with

$$\text{under each } \mathbb{Q}(\omega, .),$$

$$\begin{cases} \frac{1}{\sqrt{\Delta_n}}(\widehat{C}(\Delta_n)_T - C_T(\omega)) \xrightarrow{\mathcal{L}} \mathcal{N}(0, 2C(4)_T(\omega)) \\ \frac{\widehat{C}(\Delta_n)_T - C_T(\omega)}{\sqrt{\Delta_n} V_T^n} \xrightarrow{\mathcal{L}} \mathcal{N}(0, 1) \end{cases} \tag{3.9}$$

where V_T^n is given by (3.4) again.

In the right side of (3.9) we write $C_T(\omega)$ and $C(4)_T(\omega)$ to emphasize the dependency on the path ω, this dependency being $\mathcal{G}$-measurable. Now, we remove the conditioning and argue under the original measure $\mathbb{P}$ itself. This is not a problem for the second convergence, because the limiting law $\mathcal{N}(0, 1)$ does not depend on ω, and we readily deduce

$$\frac{\widehat{C}(\Delta_n)_T - C_T}{\sqrt{\Delta_n} V_T^n} \xrightarrow{\mathcal{L}} \mathcal{N}(0, 1) \quad \text{under } \mathbb{P}, \tag{3.10}$$

which is (3.6). And, since (3.6) holds, confidence intervals are constructed as before. In other words, our statistical problem is solved in this situation.

However, it is instructive to look at what happens to the first convergence in (3.9). Deconditioning yields

$$Y_n := \frac{1}{\sqrt{\Delta_n}}(\widehat{C}(\Delta_n)_T - C_T) \xrightarrow{\mathcal{L}} Y \tag{3.11}$$

where Y follows the *mixed Gaussian* law $\int \mu(dx)\,\mathcal{N}(0,x)$, with μ being the law of $2C(4)_T$. As usual, one can "realize" the limiting variable Y in many ways, but the most natural one, which takes into account the connection with the variable $C(4)_T$ defined on the original space, is as follows: take the product $(\widetilde{\Omega}, \widetilde{\mathcal{F}}) = (\Omega \times \mathbb{R}, \mathcal{F} \otimes \mathcal{R})$ with the measure $\widetilde{\mathbb{P}}(d\omega, dx) = \mathbb{P}(d\omega) \otimes \mathcal{N}(0,1)$, and set $Y(\omega, x) = x\sqrt{2C(4)_T(\omega)}$. Hence the limit in (3.10) is naturally defined on an extension of the original probability space.

3.1.4   From Independence to Dependence for the Stochastic Volatility

The previous conditioning-on-the-path-of-volatility argument loses its effectiveness when the independence between the volatility and the driving Brownian motion fails, a situation called in finance the leverage effect. To see why the argument fails, let's consider the following, still oversimplified, class of volatility processes, which are random and dependent on W but otherwise piecewise constant in time:

$$\sigma_t = \sqrt{U_0}\, 1_{[0,1)}(t) + \sqrt{U_1}\, 1_{\{t \geq 1\}},$$

where U_0 and U_1 are positive variables, respectively $\mathcal{F}_0$- and $\mathcal{F}_1$-measurable. Then X takes the simple form (without stochastic integrals)

$$X_t = X_0 + \sqrt{U_0}\, W_{1 \wedge t} + \sqrt{U_1}\, (W_t - W_{1 \wedge t}).$$

The law of and the connections between the U_i's and W are left unspecified.

We again want to estimate C_T, which when $T > 1$ is

$$C_T = \int_0^T c_s\, ds = U_0 + (T-1)U_1.$$

The previous method would lead to conditioning on the values U_0 and U_1. Under the simplifying assumption that $1/\Delta_n$ is an integer for all n, the estimator $\widehat{C}(\Delta_n)_T$ splits into two parts,

$$\widehat{C}(\Delta_n)_T = G_0^n + G_1^n,$$

where

$$G_0^n = U_0 \sum_{i=1}^{1/\Delta_n} (\Delta_i^n W)^2, \qquad G_1^n = U_1 \sum_{i=1+1/\Delta_n}^{[T/\Delta_n]} (\Delta_i^n W)^2.$$

If we condition on (U_0, U_1) we have the analogue of the first part of (3.9) for G_1^n, but the analogue for G_0^n breaks down because, under the conditional distribution $\mathbb{Q}(\omega, .)$, the increments $\Delta_i^n W$ for $1 \leq i \leq 1/\Delta_n$ are no longer necessarily independent, due to the fact that the conditioning variable U_1 may depend on those increments. If we simply condition on U_0 we get the first part of (3.9) for both G_0^n and G_1^n, but "separately" in the sense that, although after centering and normalization both converge in law, we have no guarantee that they converge *jointly*, whereas we need the joint convergence to obtain the convergence of the sum.

The conclusion of the analysis of the last two cases is twofold: when the volatility process is dependent of the Brownian motion W driving the process X, the convergence in law of the sequence Y_n of (3.11) does not follow from elementary arguments; moreover, to be able to standardize, we need a stronger form of convergence in law which ensures that, when Y_n converges to Y in this stronger sense and V_n converges in probability to $2C(4)_T$, then the pair (Y_n, V_n) jointly converges in law to $(Y, 2C(4)_T)$.

The requirement stated above leads us to strengthen the notion of convergence in law; we do this in the next section, devoted to introducing the so-called stable convergence in law. As for proving the convergence in law, or stably in law, we need to resort to more sophisticated arguments which rely upon the functional convergence of processes: we actually prove that the sequence of processes $Y_t^n = \frac{1}{\sqrt{\Delta_n}} (\widehat{C}(\Delta_n)_t - C_t)$ converges stably in law, in the "functional sense," that is, considered as random variables taking values in a space of functions on $\mathbb{R}_+$. This gives us a kind of bonus, such as automatically implying that the normalized maximal error $\sup_{s \leq t} |Y_s^n|$ up to time t also converges in law to the supremum over $[0, t]$ of the limiting process, but it is also a necessary step for proving the convergence.

3.2   Stable Convergence in Law

The notion of stable convergence in law was introduced by Rényi (1963), for the very same statistical reason as we need it here. We refer to Aldous and Eagleson (1978) for a very simple exposition and to Jacod and Shiryaev (2003) for more details, and also to Hall and Heyde (1980) for a somewhat different insight on the subject. However, the same notion or very similar ones appear under different guises in control theory for randomized strategies, or for solving stochastic differential equations in the weak sense.

Before getting started, and for the sake of comparison, we recall the notions of convergence in probability and convergence in law, although they have been used previously. Below, E denotes a Polish (that is, metric complete and separable) space, with metric δ and Borel σ-field $\mathcal{E}$. What follows makes sense for more general state spaces, but as soon as we want results we need additional properties, and assuming E to be Polish is not a restriction for this book.

Let Z_n be a sequence of E-valued random variables, all defined on the same probability space $(\Omega, \mathcal{F}, \mathbb{P})$; let Z be an E-valued random variable defined on the same space. We say that Z_n converges in probability to Z if for every fixed $\varepsilon > 0$

$$\mathbb{P}\left(\delta(Z_n, Z) > \varepsilon\right) \rightarrow 0$$

(written $Z_n \xrightarrow{\mathbb{P}} Z$). It is useful to keep in mind that for any continuous function g from E into another metric space E', $Z_n \xrightarrow{\mathbb{P}} Z \Rightarrow g(Z_n) \xrightarrow{\mathbb{P}} g(Z)$. This even holds when g is not continuous, provided it is Borel and $\mathbb{P}(Z \in D_g) = 0$, where D_g is the set of points of discontinuity of g.

As to convergence in law, we let (Z_n) be a sequence of E-valued random variables; we allow each of them to be defined on its own probability space $(\Omega_n, \mathcal{F}_n, \mathbb{P}_n)$. We say that Z_n converges in law if there is a probability measure μ on $(E, \mathcal{E})$ such that

$$\mathbb{E}_n(f(Z_n)) \rightarrow \int f(x)\mu(dx) \tag{3.12}$$

for all functions f on E that are bounded and continuous. Usually one "realizes" the limit as a random variable Z with law μ, on some space $(\Omega, \mathcal{F}, \mathbb{P})$, for example on $(\Omega, \mathcal{F}, \mathbb{P}) = (E, \mathcal{E}, \mu)$ with the canonical variable $Z(x) = x$, and (3.12) reads as

$$\mathbb{E}_n(f(Z_n)) \rightarrow \mathbb{E}(f(Z)) \tag{3.13}$$

for all f as before, and we write $Z_n \xrightarrow{\mathcal{L}} Z$. Unlike convergence in probability, there is no requirement that Z lives on the same space as any of the Z_n's: it is the probability distributions of the random variables that are converging, not the values of the random variables themselves. Note that for $Z_n \xrightarrow{\mathcal{L}} Z$ it is enough to have (3.12) or (3.13) for all functions f which are bounded and Lipschitz, and these convergences also hold when f if bounded Borel with $\mu(D_f) = 0$, see e.g. Parthasarathy (1967). As for convergence in probability, $Z_n \xrightarrow{\mathcal{L}} Z \Rightarrow g(Z_n) \xrightarrow{\mathcal{L}} g(Z)$ when g is continuous, or more generally when g is Borel and $\mu(D_g) = 0$.

For the stable convergence in law, we begin with a formal definition. It applies to a sequence of random variables Z_n, all defined on the *same* probability space $(\Omega, \mathcal{F}, \mathbb{P})$, and taking their values in the state space $(E, \mathcal{E})$, again assumed to be Polish.

Definition 3.2. *We say that Z_n stably converges in law if there is a probability measure η on the product $(\Omega \times E, \mathcal{F} \otimes \mathcal{E})$, such that $\eta(A \times E) = \mathbb{P}(A)$ for all $A \in \mathcal{F}$ and*

$$\mathbb{E}(Y f(Z_n)) \;\rightarrow\; \int Y(\omega) f(x) \, \eta(d\omega, dx) \qquad (3.14)$$

for all bounded continuous functions f on E and all bounded random variables Y on $(\Omega, \mathcal{F})$.

This is an abstract definition, similar to (3.12), and as for the convergence in law it is convenient to "realize" the limit Z in this situation as well. Since, in contrast to convergence in law, all Z_n here are defined on the same space $(\Omega, \mathcal{F}, \mathbb{P})$, it is natural to realize Z on an (arbitrary) extension $(\widetilde{\Omega}, \widetilde{\mathcal{F}}, \widetilde{\mathbb{P}})$ of $(\Omega, \mathcal{F}, \mathbb{P})$, as defined by (1.70). We recall that every variable defined on Ω is automatically extended as a variable on $\widetilde{\Omega}$, with the same symbol, for example $Z_n(\omega, \omega') = Z_n(\omega)$. Letting Z be an E-valued random variable defined on this extension, (3.14) is equivalent to saying (with $\widetilde{\mathbb{E}}$ denoting expectation w.r.t. $\widetilde{\mathbb{P}}$)

$$\mathbb{E}(Y f(Z_n)) \;\rightarrow\; \widetilde{\mathbb{E}}(Y f(Z)) \qquad (3.15)$$

for all f and Y as above, as soon as $\widetilde{\mathbb{P}}(A \cap \{Z \in B\}) = \eta(A \times B)$ for all $A \in \mathcal{F}$ and $B \in \mathcal{E}$. We then say that Z_n converges stably to Z, and this convergence is denoted by $Z_n \overset{\mathcal{L}\text{-s}}{\longrightarrow} Z$. Note that, exactly as for (3.13), the stable convergence in law holds as soon as (3.15) holds for all Y as above and all functions f which are bounded and Lipschitz.

One can always use the following simple way to realize Z: take $\widetilde{\Omega} = \Omega \times E$ and $\widetilde{\mathcal{F}} = \mathcal{F} \otimes \mathcal{E}$ and endow $(\widetilde{\Omega}, \widetilde{\mathcal{F}})$ with the probability η, and put $Z(\omega, x) = x$. However, exactly as in the case of the convergence in law where usually (3.13) is stated with an "arbitrary" Z with law μ, here we prefer to write (3.15) with an arbitrary Z, defined on an arbitrary extension of the original space.

Clearly, when η is given, the property $\widetilde{\mathbb{P}}(A \cap \{Z \in B\}) = \eta(A \times B)$ for all $A \in \mathcal{F}$ and $B \in \mathcal{E}$ simply amounts to specifying the law of Z, conditionally on the σ-field $\mathcal{F}$, that is under the measures $\mathbb{Q}(\omega, .)$ of (1.70). Therefore, saying $Z_n \overset{\mathcal{L}\text{-s}}{\longrightarrow} Z$ amounts to saying that we have stable convergence in law toward a variable Z, defined on any extension $(\widetilde{\Omega}, \widetilde{\mathcal{F}}, \widetilde{\mathbb{P}})$ of $(\Omega, \mathcal{F}, \mathbb{P})$, and with a specified conditional law, knowing $\mathcal{F}$.

Stable convergence in law obviously implies convergence in law. But it implies much more, and in particular the following crucial result: if Y_n and Y are variables defined on $(\Omega, \mathcal{F}, \mathbb{P})$ and with values in the same Polish space E, then

$$Z_n \xrightarrow{\mathcal{L}-\mathrm{s}} Z, \quad Y_n \xrightarrow{\mathbb{P}} Y \quad \Rightarrow \quad (Y_n, Z_n) \xrightarrow{\mathcal{L}-\mathrm{s}} (Y, Z). \qquad (3.16)$$

By contrast, if we use standard convergence in law, $Z_n \xrightarrow{\mathcal{L}} Z$ and $Y_n \xrightarrow{\mathbb{P}} Y$ do *not* imply the joint convergence $(Y_n, Z_n) \xrightarrow{\mathcal{L}} (Y, Z)$ (and to begin with, the law of the pair (Y, Z) is not even well characterized), unless of course one of the two limits Y and Z is a constant. In this sense, stable convergence in law looks like convergence in probability (not a surprise, in view of (3.17) below), for which we have

$$Z_n \xrightarrow{\mathbb{P}} Z, \quad Y_n \xrightarrow{\mathbb{P}} Y \quad \Rightarrow \quad (Y_n, Z_n) \xrightarrow{\mathbb{P}} (Y, Z).$$

Another useful property of the stable convergence in law is the following one. Let F be a bounded function on $\Omega \times E$, measurable with respect to the product σ-field $\mathcal{F} \otimes \mathcal{E}$, and satisfying $\eta(D) = 0$, where D is the set of all (ω, x) such that the function $y \mapsto F(\omega, y)$ is *not* continuous at x. Then

$$Z_n \xrightarrow{\mathcal{L}-\mathrm{s}} Z \quad \Rightarrow \quad \mathbb{E}(F(., Z_n)) \to \widetilde{\mathbb{E}}(F(., Z)).$$

Moreover, when Z is defined *on the same space* Ω as all Z_n, by applying this property for the functions $F(\omega, x) = \delta(Z(\omega), x) \wedge 1$, where δ is a metric on E, we get

$$Z_n \xrightarrow{\mathbb{P}} Z \quad \Longleftrightarrow \quad Z_n \xrightarrow{\mathcal{L}-\mathrm{s}} Z. \qquad (3.17)$$

We also have a simple necessary and sufficient condition for the stable convergence in law:

the sequence Z_n converges stably in law if and only if,
for any $q \geq 1$ and any q-dimensional variable Y on $(\Omega, \mathbb{P})$, $\qquad$ (3.18)
the sequence (Z_n, Y) converges in law.

This criterion gives insight on the notion of stable convergence in law but is rarely useful in practice because it gives no clue on how the limit Z can be constructed.

The property (3.15) should hold for all Y which are $\mathcal{F}$-measurable. Now, it is enlightening (and sometimes useful too!) to see what happens when it holds only for all bounded Y which are measurable with respect to some sub-σ-field $\mathcal{G}$ of $\mathcal{F}$: if this is the case, we say that Z_n converges $\mathcal{G}$-*stably in law* to Z. There are two extreme cases:

- If $\mathcal{G} = \mathcal{F}$, the $\mathcal{G}$-stable convergence in law is the above-defined stable convergence in law.

- If $\mathcal{G} = \{\Omega, \emptyset\}$, the $\mathcal{G}$-stable convergence in law is the usual convergence in law.

Besides these two extremal cases, it might be tempting to consider the $\mathcal{G}$-conditional law of each variable Z_n, say $\mathbb{Q}_n = \mathbb{Q}_n(\omega, dx)$, and also the $\mathcal{G}$-conditional law $\mathbb{Q} = \mathbb{Q}(\omega, dx)$ of Z. Then

$$\begin{aligned} &\mathbb{Q}_n \text{ converges weakly in probability to } \mathbb{Q} \\ &\implies Z_n \text{ converges } \mathcal{G}\text{-stably in law to } Z \end{aligned} \qquad (3.19)$$

is obvious, but the converse is *wrong* in general. It is true (and uninteresting) when $\mathcal{G}$ is the trivial σ-field. When $\mathcal{G} = \mathcal{F}$ then $\mathbb{Q}_n$ is the Dirac mass sitting at Z_n, so the property on the left side of (3.19) amounts to saying that $\mathbb{Q}$ is also a Dirac mass sitting at some Z' and $Z_n \overset{\mathbb{P}}{\longrightarrow} Z'$: so we have $Z = Z'$ a.s. and $Z_n \overset{\mathbb{P}}{\longrightarrow} Z$.

We have also the following (elementary) property:

$$\begin{aligned} &\text{if all } Z_n\text{'s are } \mathcal{G}\text{-measurable, the } \mathcal{G}\text{-stable} \\ &\text{and } \mathcal{F}\text{-stable convergences in law are equivalent.} \end{aligned} \qquad (3.20)$$

We end this section with another extension of stable convergence in law, which will play a fundamental role in what follows. With Z_n defined on $(\Omega, \mathcal{F}, \mathbb{P})$, and if $A \in \mathcal{F}$, we say that Y_n converges *stably in law to Z, in restriction to the set A* if (3.15) holds for all f continuous bounded, and all $\mathcal{F}$-measurable variables Y which are bounded and vanish outside A. The classical notion of convergence in probability in restriction to A is likewise defined by $\mathbb{P}\left(A \cap \{\delta(Z_n, Z) > \varepsilon\}\right) \to 0$. Then, similar with (3.16), we have

$$\begin{aligned} &Z_n \overset{\mathcal{L}-s}{\longrightarrow} Z \text{ in restriction to } A, \quad Y_n \overset{\mathbb{P}}{\longrightarrow} Y \text{ in restriction to } A \\ &\implies \quad (Y_n, Z_n) \overset{\mathcal{L}-s}{\longrightarrow} (Y, Z) \text{ in restriction to } A. \end{aligned} \qquad (3.21)$$

That one can define stable convergence in law in restriction to a set is in deep contrast with convergence in law, for which the sentence "converges in law in restriction to the set A" has no meaning at all.

3.3   Convergence for Stochastic Processes

In this section we briefly review convergence of stochastic processes. We consider a sequence of $\mathbb{R}^q$-valued processes Y^n, for some $q \geq 1$.

The simplest notion of all is "finite-dimensional convergence": this means the convergence of $(Y_{t_1}^n, \dots, Y_{t_k}^n)$ for any choice of the integer k and of the times $t_1, \dots, t_k$, in the appropriate sense (in probability, or in law, or stably in law). When the convergence is in probability, the convergence for any single fixed t implies finite-dimensional convergence, but this is no longer true for convergence in law, or stably in law.

Finite-dimensional convergence is a weak form of convergence, for example if Y^n converges to Y in this sense, the suprema $\sup_{s \leq t} \|Y_s^n\|$ do not converge to the supremum of the limit, in general. To remedy this, we need a stronger form of convergence, called "functional" convergence. This means that we consider each process Y^n as taking its values in a functional space (i.e., a space of functions from $\mathbb{R}_+$ into $\mathbb{R}^q$), and we endow this functional space with a suitable topology: as seen before, we need this functional space to be a Polish space.

Basically, two functional spaces are going to be of interest in this book. One is the space $\mathbb{C}^q = \mathbb{C}(\mathbb{R}_+, \mathbb{R}^q)$ of all continuous functions from $\mathbb{R}_+$ into $\mathbb{R}^q$, endowed with the local uniform topology corresponding for example to the metric $\delta_U(x, y) = \sum_{n \geq 1} 2^{-n} \left(1 \wedge \sup_{s \leq n} \|x(s) - y(s)\| \right)$. The Borel σ-field for this topology is $\sigma(x(s) : s \geq 0)$, and with this topology the space $\mathbb{C}^q$ is a Polish space.

However, although the limiting processes Y we encounter in this book are quite often continuous, this is rarely the case of the pre-limiting processes Y^n, which typically are based upon the discrete observations $X_{i\Delta_n}$: they often come up as partial sums $\sum_{i=1}^{[t/\Delta_n]} f(\Delta_i^n X)$ where $\Delta_i^n X$ are the increments of X defined in (3.2). Such a process has discontinuous, although càdlàg, paths. Therefore, the other functional space of interest for us is the *Skorokhod space*: this is the set $\mathbb{D}^q = \mathbb{D}(\mathbb{R}_+, \mathbb{R}^q)$ of all càdlàg functions from $\mathbb{R}_+$ into $\mathbb{R}^q$.

One possible metric on $\mathbb{D}^q$ is δ_U, which makes $\mathbb{D}^q$ a Banach space, but under which it is unfortunately not separable (hence not Polish). This prompted the development of the *Skorokhod topology*, introduced by Skorokhod (1956) under the name "J1-topology." There is a metric δ_S compatible with this topology, such that $\mathbb{D}^q$ is a Polish space, and again the Borel σ-field is $\sigma(x(s) : s \geq 0)$. We do not need to define this topology here, and the reader is referred to Billingsley (1999) or Ethier and Kurtz (1986) or Jacod and Shiryaev (2003).

We write $x_n \xrightarrow{\text{u.c.p.}} x$ if $\delta_U(x_n, x) \to 0$ (this makes sense for any functions x_n, x), and $x_n \xrightarrow{\text{Sk}} x$ if $\delta_S(x_n, x) \to 0$ (this makes sense for $x_n, x \in \mathbb{D}^q$). The following properties, for $x_n, y_n, x, y \in \mathbb{D}^q$, are worth stating:

$$
\begin{aligned}
x_n \xrightarrow{\text{u.c.p.}} x & \quad\Rightarrow\quad x_n \xrightarrow{\text{Sk}} x \\
x_n \xrightarrow{\text{Sk}} x, \ x \in \mathbb{C}^q & \quad\Rightarrow\quad x_n \xrightarrow{\text{u.c.p.}} x \\
x_n \xrightarrow{\text{Sk}} x, \ y_n \xrightarrow{\text{u.c.p.}} y & \quad\Rightarrow\quad x_n + y_n \xrightarrow{\text{Sk}} x + y.
\end{aligned}
\tag{3.22}
$$

These are nice properties, but the Skorokhod topology also suffers from some drawbacks, of which the reader should be aware:

1. If $x_n \xrightarrow{\text{Sk}} x$ and $y_n \xrightarrow{\text{Sk}} y$ in $\mathbb{D}^q$, it not always true that $x_n + y_n \xrightarrow{\text{Sk}} x + y$: in other words, $\mathbb{D}^q$ is a linear space, but not a topological linear space under this topology.

2. If x_n^i and x^i denote the components of $x_n, x \in \mathbb{D}^q$, the property $x_n \xrightarrow{\text{Sk}} x$ implies $x_n^i \xrightarrow{\text{Sk}} x^i$ for each i (in the space $\mathbb{D}^1$), but the converse is not true.

3. The mapping $x \to x(t)$ is *not* continuous for the Skorokhod topology, although it is continuous at each point x such that $x(t) = x(t-)$ where $x(t-)$ denotes the left limit of x at time t. Given that x is càdlàg, $x(t) = x(t-)$ means that x is continuous at time t.

Therefore, this topology is the one to be used when dealing with càdlàg functions or processes, but a lot of care is needed when using it.

Now we come back to our sequence Y^n of $\mathbb{R}^q$-valued càdlàg processes, and its potential limit Y, another $\mathbb{R}^q$-valued càdlàg process. They can be considered as random variables with values in the space $\mathbb{D}^q$, and we thus have the notions of convergence in law, or stably in law, or in probability, of Y^n toward Y. In the first case, Y is defined on an arbitrary probability space, in the second case it is defined on an extension, and in the third case it is defined on the same space as are all the Y^n's.

The "local uniform convergence" refers to the metric δ_U above on $\mathbb{D}^q$, and we write

$$
Y^n \xRightarrow{\text{u.c.p.}} Y \quad \text{if} \quad \delta_U(Y^n, Y) \xrightarrow{\mathbb{P}} 0,
$$
$$
\text{or equivalently if, for all } T, \ \sup_{t \leq T} \|Y_t^n - Y_t\| \xrightarrow{\mathbb{P}} 0.
\tag{3.23}
$$

This kind of convergence was obtained in the statement of the dominated convergence theorem for stochastic integrals, see (1.9) or (1.54), or for the approximate quadratic variation in (1.61). When we deal with the

Skorokhod topology, and implicitly using the metric δ_S, we write for convergence in probability

$$Y^n \overset{\mathbb{P}}{\implies} Y \quad \text{if} \quad \delta_S(Y^n, Y) \overset{\mathbb{P}}{\longrightarrow} 0.$$

We define similarly $Y^n \overset{\mathcal{L}}{\implies} Y$ and $Y^n \overset{\mathcal{L}\text{-s}}{\implies} Y$ for convergence in law and stable convergence in law, using the Skorokhod topology.

For convenience of notation, we sometimes write $Y^n \overset{\mathbb{P}}{\implies} Y$ as $Y_t^n \overset{\mathbb{P}}{\implies} Y_t$ (and similarly for convergence in law and stable convergence in law). This should not be confused with $Y_t^n \overset{\mathbb{P}}{\to} Y_t$ which means convergence in probability of the variables Y_t^n toward Y_t, for a fixed time t. In other words, a double arrow *always means functional convergence*.

The following property, about one-dimensional processes, is very useful:

$$\begin{array}{c} Y^n \text{ and } Y \text{ non-decreasing, } Y \text{ continuous,} \\ Y_t^n \overset{\mathbb{P}}{\longrightarrow} Y_t \; \forall t \quad \Rightarrow \quad Y^n \overset{\text{u.c.p.}}{\implies} Y. \end{array} \tag{3.24}$$

We now explain some general facts which relate to the convergence of Riemann sums. We have three ingredients here: a d-dimensional semimartingale X (the integrator), a $q \times d$-dimensional adapted and left-continuous process H (the integrand), and for each $n \geq 1$ a strictly increasing sequence of stopping time $T(n,0) = 0 < T(n,1) < T(n,2) < \cdots$, with infinite limit and with meshes $\pi_n(t) = \sup_{i \geq 1}(T(n,i) \wedge t - T(n,i-1) \wedge t)$ going to 0 for all t in probability, as $n \to \infty$. First, we have

$$\sum_{i \geq 1} H_{T(n,i-1)} \left(X_{T(n,i) \wedge t} - X_{T(n,i-1) \wedge t} \right) \overset{\text{u.c.p.}}{\implies} \int_0^t H_s \, dX_s \tag{3.25}$$

(here we use vector notation, so both the left and the right sides are q-dimensional); this result is an obvious consequence of the dominated convergence theorem (1.54), because the processes H^n defined by $H_0^n = H_0$ and $H_t^n = H_{T(n,i-1)}$ for $t \in (T(n,i-1), T(n,i)]$ converge pointwise to H and satisfy $\|H^n\| \leq H'$, where $H_t' = \sup_{s \leq t} \|H_s\|$ is locally bounded.

The left side of (3.25) is not a genuine Riemann sum approximation of the integral since, although the integrand is frozen on each interval $(T(n,i-1), T(n,i)]$, it is not the case of the integrator X which continues to evolve. The behavior of the true Riemann sum is as follows:

$$\sum_{i \geq 1} H_{T(n,i-1)} \left(X_{T(n,i)} - X_{T(n,i-1)} \right) 1_{\{T(n,i) \leq t\}} \overset{\mathbb{P}}{\implies} \int_0^t H_s \, dX_s. \tag{3.26}$$

This is "almost" as good as (3.25): we replace the local uniform topology by the Skorokhod topology. The convergence in (3.26) does *not* hold in

Introduction to Asymptotic Theory

the u.c.p. sense, unless of course X is continuous. In the latter case, the same result also holds when H is right-continuous instead of being left-continuous; those results are proved for example in Jacod and Protter (2011).

Finally, another property will be used from time to time. It is really about càdlàg functions, although it has an immediate extension to càdlàg processes. It asserts that if $x \in \mathbb{D}^q$ and if for each n one has a sequence $0 = t(n,0) < t(n,1) < t(n,2) < \cdots$ of times increasing to infinity, then

$$\sup_{i \geq 1} (t \wedge t(n,i) - t \wedge t(n,i-1)) \to 0 \quad \text{for all } t < \infty$$
$$\implies x^n \xrightarrow{\text{Sk}} x \qquad (3.27)$$
$$\text{where } x^n(t) = x(t(n,i-1)) \quad \text{for } t \in [t(n,i-1), t(n,i)).$$

Remark 3.3. *So far we have considered $\mathbb{R}^q$-valued processes. In the next section we need to consider infinite-dimensional càdlàg processes, and more specifically processes taking their values in the set $E = \mathbb{R}^{\mathbb{N}^*}$ of all infinite sequences $\overline{x} = (x_1, x_2, \ldots)$. Upon using the metric $d(\overline{x}, \overline{y}) = \sum_{n \geq 1} 2^{-n}(1 \wedge |x_n - y_n|)$, for example, the space E is Polish.*

One can define the Skorokhod space $\mathbb{D}(\mathbb{R}_+, E)$ of all càdlàg E-valued functions. All previous considerations extend, word for word, to this situation, and in particular $\mathbb{D}(\mathbb{R}_+, E)$ is again a Polish space.

3.4 General Stochastic Volatility

We now come back to the estimation of the integrated volatility, and consider the general case (3.1), with σ_t being an arbitrary càdlàg (bounded, for simplicity) adapted process on the space $(\Omega, \mathcal{F}(\mathcal{F}_t), \mathbb{P})$ which also supports the Brownian motion W driving the process X.

As before, we want to prove the convergence of the normalized estimation errors

$$Y_t^n = \frac{1}{\sqrt{\Delta_n}} \left(\widehat{C}(\Delta_n)_t - C_t \right)$$

and, again as before, we start by writing $Y^n = Z^n + R^n$, where

$$Z_t^n = \sum_{i=1}^{[t/\Delta_n]} \xi_i^n, \qquad \xi_i^n = \frac{1}{\sqrt{\Delta_n}} ((\Delta_i^n X)^2 - \alpha_i^n),$$
$$\alpha_i^n = \int_{(i-1)\Delta_n}^{i\Delta_n} c_s \, ds, \qquad R_t^n = \frac{1}{\sqrt{\Delta_n}} \int_{\Delta_n [t/\Delta_n]}^{t} c_s \, ds.$$

Since c_t is bounded, we have $\sup_t |R_t^n| \to 0$.

It is thus enough to prove the convergence of the partial sums Z_t^n of the triangular array ξ_i^n above. This array has a priori a nice form, since ξ_i^n is $\mathcal{F}_{i\Delta_n}$-measurable and satisfies $\mathbb{E}(\xi_i^n \mid \mathcal{F}_{(i-1)\Delta_n}) = 0$ by Itô's formula.

However, the discrete-time filtrations $(\mathcal{F}_{i\Delta_n})_{i\geq 0}$ are not comparable as n varies, so the most standard CLTs for martingale differences arrays (see e.g. Hall and Heyde (1980)) do not apply, even those for the so-called nested filtrations and yielding stable convergence in law in that book.

In the case at hand, Theorem IX.7.28 of Jacod and Shiryaev (2003) explicitly gives the desired result, and the reader can refer to that theorem and stop reading this section. However, since more than half the methods and results of this book rely upon limit theorems of the same kind as the stable convergence in law of Z_t^n, we present below a very detailed scheme of the proof. We still do not provide full proofs, which would necessitate many technical arguments, but the general ideas are simple enough to expose.

As for most proofs for the convergence in law, when the laws of the converging variables Z_t^n are not explicitly known, we take two main steps:

1. Prove that the sequence Z_t^n is "tight" (or "uniformly tight," as often expressed), meaning that the family of laws $\mathcal{L}(Z_t^n)$ is relatively compact for the weak convergence of probability measures; equivalently, the sequence is tight if and only if from each subsequence one may extract a further sub-subsequence which converges in law.

2. Prove that all possible limit laws of convergent subsequences of the sequence $\mathcal{L}(Z_t^n)$ are all equal to the same probability measure.

Proving (1) is (relatively) simple. Proving (2) is complicated, and to see why one can refer to Subsection 3.1.3 where, already in that simple case, the limit is difficult to describe, whereas in Subsection 3.1.4 we were unable to describe the putative limit.

The way out of these difficulties is to consider the processes Z^n instead of the values Z_t^n for a specified t. Then one can rely upon the characterization of the limiting distribution as the solution of some "martingale problem," and then prove the uniqueness of the solution.

Step 1. To start with, we observe that, for all $p \geq 2$, we have

$$\mathbb{E}(|\xi_i^n|^p \mid \mathcal{F}_{(i-1)\Delta_n}) \leq K_p \, \Delta_n^{p/2} \tag{3.28}$$

for a constant K_p depending on p (and also on the bound for c_t): this comes from the boundedness of c_t and Burkholder-Gundy inequalities (1.59).

Step 2. As for all CLTs for triangular arrays of martingale differences, the first – necessary – step is to prove the convergence of the "predictable quadratic variation" $A_t^n = \sum_{i=1}^{[t/\Delta_n]} \mathbb{E}((\xi_i^n)^2 \mid \mathcal{F}_{(i-1)\Delta_n})$ of the martingales Z_t^n (they are martingales for the filtration $(\mathcal{F}_t^n)_{t\geq 0}$ defined by $\mathcal{F}_t^n = \mathcal{F}_{i\Delta_n}$ when $i\Delta_n \leq t < (i+1)\Delta_n$). Note that $Z_t^{\prime n} = (Z_t^n)^2 - A_t^n$ is also a martingale, for the same filtration (integrability is ensured by (3.28)).

To evaluate the summands giving A_t^n one uses Itô's formula for the two-dimensional semimartingale (X, C), between the two times $(i-1)\Delta_n$ and $i\Delta_n$, and for the function $f(x, y) = (x^2 - y)^2$. This results in $(\xi_i^n)^2$ being the sum of a martingale increment between these two times, plus

$$\frac{1}{\Delta_n}\left(2(\alpha_i^n)^2 + 8\int_{(i-1)\Delta_n}^{i\Delta_n}(c_s - c_{(i-1)\Delta_n})M_s^{n,i}\,ds\right),$$

where $M_t^{n,i} = \int_{(i-1)\Delta_n}^t (X_s - X_{(i-1)\Delta_n})\sigma_s\,dW_s$. Burkholder-Gundy inequalities (1.59) applied twice yield $\mathbb{E}((M_t^{n,i})^2 \mid \mathcal{F}_{(i-1)\Delta_n}) \leq K\Delta_n^2$ if $(i-1)\Delta_n \leq t \leq i\Delta_n$. Hence, in view of the definition of α_i^n and by Hölder's inequality, and with the notation

$$\eta_i^n = \int_{(i-1)\Delta_n}^{i\Delta_n} \mathbb{E}((c_s - c_{(i-1)\Delta_n})^2 \mid \mathcal{F}_{(i-1)\Delta_n})\,ds,$$

we obtain for some constant K depending on the bound of c_t

$$\left|\mathbb{E}((\xi_i^n)^2 \mid \mathcal{F}_{(i-1)\Delta_n}) - 2\Delta_n\,c_{(i-1)\Delta_n}^2\right| \leq K(\eta_i^n + \sqrt{\Delta_n\,\eta_i^n}).$$

Since c_t is bounded càdlàg we have $\mathbb{E}(\sum_{i=1}^{[t/\Delta_n]}\eta_i^n) \to 0$ (apply Lebesgue's theorem), which in turn implies $\mathbb{E}(\sum_{i=1}^{[t/\Delta_n]}\sqrt{\Delta_n\eta_i^n}) \to 0$ (apply Hölder's inequality). On the other hand, $\Delta_n\sum_{i=1}^{[t/\Delta_n]}c_{(i-1)\Delta_n}^2$ converges for all ω, and locally uniformly in t, to $\int_0^t c_s^2\,ds$ (by Riemann integration). In view of the definition of A^n we thus deduce

$$A_t^n \overset{\text{u.c.p.}}{\Longrightarrow} A_t := 2\int_0^t c_s^2\,ds = 2C(4)_t. \tag{3.29}$$

Remark 3.4. *The main feature is that the limit above is* random. *This is in contrast with the case when the time span T goes to infinity as $\Delta_n \to 0$: under minimal ergodic properties one would then find a non-random limit. The randomness of A_t is the main reason why the forthcoming analysis is somewhat involved.*

Step 3. The proof of the tightness of the sequence of processes Z^n is now simple, thanks to the so-called Aldous' tightness criterion (see Theorem VI.4.13 of Jacod and Shiryaev (2003), the original paper being Aldous (1978) and the specific result used here is by Rebolledo (1979)). Indeed, relative to the filtration $(\mathcal{F}_t^n)$, the process Z^n above is a (locally) square-integrable martingale (use (3.28)) with predictable quadratic variation A^n. Then the above-mentioned criterion tells us that, since A^n converge locally uniformly in time, in probability, to a continuous process (use (3.29)), *the sequence Z^n is tight.*

Step 4. At this stage, it remains to show the uniqueness of the law of the limit of the sequence Z^n. Unfortunately, there seems to be no simple way of doing so, apart from resorting to "martingale problems," and to the following (simple) property of the convergence in law: let V^n be a sequence of martingales, possibly multi-dimensional, each one being defined on some filtered space $(\Omega^n, \mathcal{F}^n, (\mathcal{F}_t^n), \mathbb{P}^n)$, and assume that for each t and each component index i the variables $(V_t^{n,i} : n \geq 1)$ are uniformly integrable. Then, if V^n converges in law to a limit V, this limit is a martingale, relative to the filtration which it generates.

We apply this in the following setting. In view of (3.20), and without loss of generality, we can assume that the filtration $(\mathcal{F}_t)$ is generated by the two processes (W, σ) and that $\mathcal{F} = \bigvee_t \mathcal{F}_t$. Therefore each σ-field $\mathcal{F}_t$ is separable, implying the existence of a sequence $(U(m) : m \geq 3)$ of variables which is dense in $L^1(\Omega, \mathcal{F}, \mathbb{P})$ and such that, for each m and some real number a_m, we have $|U(m)| \leq a_m$ and $U(m)$ is $\mathcal{F}_{a_m}$-measurable. We then consider the càdlàg martingales $U_t^m = \mathbb{E}(U(m) \mid \mathcal{F}_t)$, and the infinite-dimensional process V^n with components

$$V_t^{n,m} = \begin{cases} Z_t^n & \text{if } m = 1 \\ (Z_t^n)^2 - A_t^n & \text{if } m = 2 \\ U_{\Delta_n[t/\Delta_n]}^m & \text{if } m \geq 3. \end{cases}$$

Note that V^n is càdlàg, with values in the Polish space $E = \mathbb{R}^{\mathbb{N}^*}$.

As seen before, the sequence Z^n is tight, and (3.28) with $p = 4$ yields

$$\mathbb{E}\left(\sup_{s \leq t} |\Delta Z_t^n|^4\right) = \mathbb{E}\left(\sup_{1 \leq i \leq [t/\Delta_n]} |\xi_i^n|^4\right) \leq \mathbb{E}\left(\sum_{1 \leq i}^{[t/\Delta_n]} |\xi_i^n|^4\right) \leq K t \Delta_n,$$

hence $\sup_{s \leq t} |\Delta Z_t^n| \xrightarrow{\mathbb{P}} 0$. Therefore, not only is the sequence $V^{n,1} = Z^n$ tight, but all its limits are *continuous* processes. Combining this with (3.29) and also with the general properties (3.22) allows us, by the same argument, to show that the sequence $V^{n,2}$ is also tight and with continuous limiting processes. Moreover, (3.17) and Remark 3.3 imply that $(V^{n,m})_{m \geq 3}$ converges to $(U^m)_{m \geq 3}$ for the Skorokhod topology, for each ω.

At this point, and upon using the last part of (3.22), we deduce that the sequence V^n is tight.

Step 5. Let us choose an arbitrary subsequence V^{n_k} which converges in law. The limiting process V could *a priori* be realized on an arbitrary probability space. However, the first two components $V^{(1)}$ and $V^{(2)}$ of V are necessarily continuous, and $V^{n,m}$ converges to U^m for each ω when $m \geq 3$, and $(V^{n,1})^2 - V^{n,2} = A^n$ converges to A in probability, hence one would like to realize V in such a way that all these properties are preserved. This can be done as follows: Namely, we take an extension $(\widetilde{\Omega}, \widetilde{\mathcal{F}}, \widetilde{\mathbb{P}})$ of the original space, as defined in (1.70), with $\Omega' = \mathbb{C}^1$ and with $Y_t(\omega') = \omega'(t)$ being the canonical process, and with the Borel σ-field $\mathcal{F}'$; the process V is defined, componentwise, as follows:

$$V^{(m)}(\omega, \omega') = \begin{cases} Y(\omega') & \text{if } m = 1 \\ Y(\omega')^2 - A_t(\omega) & \text{if } m = 2 \\ U_t^m(\omega) & \text{if } m \geq 3. \end{cases}$$

With this formulation, what characterizes the law of V is the measure $\widetilde{\mathbb{P}}$ or, equivalently (because $\mathbb{P}$ is fixed), the transition probability $\mathbb{Q}(\omega, d\omega')$ for $\mathbb{P}$-almost all ω.

At this stage, one derives the stable convergence in law of our subsequence Z^{n_k} in a straightforward way. Indeed, if f is a continuous bounded function on $\mathbb{D}^1$ and $m \geq 3$, we have

$$\mathbb{E}(f(Z^n)U(m)) = \mathbb{E}(g_m(V^n)) \to \widetilde{\mathbb{E}}(g_m(V)) = \widetilde{\mathbb{E}}(f(V^{(1)})U(m)), \quad (3.30)$$

where $g_m(x_1, x_2, \ldots) = f(x_1)f_m(x_m(a_m))$ and f_m is an arbitrary bounded continuous function on $\mathbb{R}$ which coincides with the identity on the set $[-a_m, a_m]$: recall that a_m is a bound for the variable $U(m)$, and also that $U_{a_m}^m = U(m)$, hence $g_m(V^n) = f(Z^n)U(m)$ and $g_m(V) = f(V^{(1)})U(m)$. Since the sequence $(U(m) : m \geq 3)$ is dense in L^1, we deduce from (3.30) that $\mathbb{E}(f(Z^n)\,U) \to \widetilde{\mathbb{E}}(f(V^{(1)})\,U)$ for all bounded variables U. In other words, we have proved the following:

$$\text{if } V^{n_k} \text{ converges in law and } \widetilde{\mathbb{P}} \text{ is associated}$$
$$\text{to the limit } V \text{ as above, then } Z^{n_k} \overset{\mathcal{L}\text{-}s}{\Longrightarrow} Y.$$

Step 6. It remains to prove the uniqueness of $\widetilde{\mathbb{P}}$, and this is where martingale problems come into play. We denote by $(\mathcal{F}_t')$ the canonical filtration on Ω' and $(\widetilde{\mathcal{F}}_t)$ is defined by (1.71): this is indeed the filtration generated by the limiting process V.

In this step we explain how the uniqueness follows from the next three properties of the measure $\widetilde{\mathbb{P}}$, to be proved later:

> 1. Y and $Y^2 - A$ are $(\widetilde{\mathcal{F}}_t)$-martingales;
> 2. Each bounded martingale M on $(\Omega, (\mathcal{F}_t), \mathbb{P})$
>   is an $(\widetilde{\mathcal{F}}_t)$-martingale;   (3.31)
> 3. For each M as above, the product YM
>   is an $(\widetilde{\mathcal{F}}_t)$-martingale.

Property (2) implies that $(\widetilde{\Omega}, \widetilde{\mathcal{F}}, (\widetilde{\mathcal{F}}_t), \widetilde{\mathbb{P}})$ is a very good extension of the original filtered space, see after (1.73). It also easily implies (see Jacod and Shiryaev (2003), Section II-7) that all $(\widetilde{\mathcal{F}}_t)$-martingales N on the extended space which are such that MN is also an $(\widetilde{\mathcal{F}}_t)$-martingale for all bounded $(\mathcal{F}_t)$-martingales M enjoy the following property: for almost all ω, the process N is also a martingale under $\mathbb{Q}(\omega, .)$. Henceforth, (1) and (3) imply that under $\mathbb{Q}(\omega, .)$ the two continuous processes Y and $Y^2 - A$ are martingales, whereas $A = A_t(\omega)$ is an increasing continuous non-random function. By a trivial extension (to "non-homogeneous" Brownian motion) of Lévy martingale characterization of Brownian motion (1.3), these properties yield that under $\mathbb{Q}(\omega, .)$ we have

$$\begin{aligned} &Y \text{ is a continuous Gaussian martingale} \\ &\text{with } Y_0 = 0 \text{ and } \langle Y, Y \rangle_t = A_t(\omega). \end{aligned} \qquad (3.32)$$

This completely characterizes the law of Y, hence $\mathbb{Q}(\omega, .)$, which in turn implies the uniqueness of $\widetilde{\mathbb{P}}$ (the existence is ensured as the limit of the laws of the sequence V^{n_k}; it also directly, and more simply, follows from (3.32) because for any continuous increasing function f with $f(0) = 0$ there exists a continuous centered Gaussian process W' with covariance $\mathbb{E}(W'_t W'_{t+s}) = f(t)$ for $s, t \geq 0$).

Step 7. Now we take any subsequence V^{n_k} which converges in law, and let $\widetilde{\mathbb{P}}$ be the associated measure on the extended space. We are left to prove that it satisfies (3.31).

First, each component of V^n is a martingale for the filtration $(\mathcal{F}_t^n)$, whereas (3.28) and the boundedness of each U^m imply that for each t and m the variables $V_t^{n,m}$ are uniformly integrable. Hence, since $(\widetilde{\mathcal{F}}_t)$ is the filtration generated by the process V, we deduce (1) and (2) of (3.31) from the property recalled at the beginning of Step 5 and a density argument.

As for (3), by a density argument again, it is enough to prove it when M belongs to a family $\mathcal{M}$ of square-integrable martingales on the original space, such that the terminal variables M_∞ are total in $L^2(\mathbb{P})$. Let $M \in \mathcal{M}$ and $M_t^n = M_{\Delta_n[t/\Delta_n]}$ be its discretized version, and let also B^n be the predictable compensator of the covariation process $[Z^n, M^n]$ for the filtration $(\mathcal{F}_t^n)$. Suppose for a while that we have proved

$$B_t^n \overset{\text{u.c.p.}}{\Longrightarrow} 0 \tag{3.33}$$

for all t. Since $Z^n M^n - B^n$ is a martingale for the filtration $(\mathcal{F}_t^n)$ with the same uniform integrability property as above, we deduce from (3.33) that YM is a martingale on the extended space, which is (3).

Step 8. The last – and rather technical – step is to prove (3.33). We can choose $\mathcal{M}$ to be the set of all bounded martingales which are orthogonal to W, plus the martingales $W^r = (W_{t \wedge r})_{t \geq 0}$ which are the Brownian motion W itself stopped at any time $r > 0$.

If $M \in \mathcal{M}$ is orthogonal to W, and since ξ_i^n is a stochastic integral with respect to W, we have $\mathbb{E}(\xi_i^n \Delta_i^n M \mid \mathcal{F}_{(i-1)\Delta_n}) = 0$, which in turn implies $B^n \equiv 0$, and thus (3.33) trivially holds. If $M = W^r$, we have $B_t^n = \sum_{i=1}^{[t/\Delta_n]} \zeta_i^n$, where $\zeta_i^n = 0$ when $i > [r/\Delta_n]$ and otherwise is

$$
\begin{aligned}
\zeta_i^n &= \frac{1}{\sqrt{\Delta_n}} \mathbb{E}\big(((\Delta_i^n X)^2 - \alpha_i^n) \Delta_i^n W^r \mid \mathcal{F}_{(i-1)\Delta_n}\big) \\
&= \frac{1}{\sqrt{\Delta_n}} c_{(i-1)\Delta_n} ((\Delta_i^n W)^3 - \Delta_i^n W \mid \mathcal{F}_{(i-1)\Delta_n}) + \zeta_i'^n
\end{aligned}
$$

where $\zeta_i'^n$ is a remainder term which can be shown (more or less as in Step 2) to satisfy $\sum_{i=1}^{[r/\Delta_n]+1} |\zeta_i'^n| \overset{\mathbb{P}}{\longrightarrow} 0$. The first term on the right side above involves the conditional expectation of two odd powers of the increments $\Delta_i^n W$, which is centered Gaussian and independent of $\mathcal{F}_{(i-1)\Delta_n}$, so this term vanishes. This ends the proof of (3.33).

We have thus "proved" (with somewhat heuristic arguments and letting technicalities aside) the following result, which will be restated in a more general context in Chapter 6 as Theorem 6.1:

Fact 3.5. *In the model above, the processes $\frac{1}{\sqrt{\Delta_n}}\big(\widehat{C}(\Delta_n)_t - C_t\big)$ converge stably in law to a limiting process Y which is defined on a very good extension of $(\Omega, \mathcal{F}, (\mathcal{F}_t)_{t \geq 0}, \mathbb{P})$, and which conditionally on $\mathcal{F}$ is a continuous centered Gaussian martingale with (conditional) variance given by*

$$\widetilde{\mathbb{E}}((Y_t)^2 \mid \mathcal{F}) = 2 \int_0^t c_s^2 \, ds.$$

Remark 3.6. *Step 8 is essential in this way: Steps 1–7 go through if one replaces the squared increments $(\Delta_i^n X)^2$ by powers $(\Delta_i^n X)^p$ or absolute powers $|\Delta_i^n X|^p$, upon a suitable renormalization and an appropriate choice of α_i^n. The second part of Step 8 (when $M = W^r$), in contrast, would involve the conditional expectation of $(\Delta_i^n W)^{p+1}$ or $|\Delta_i^n W|^p \Delta_i^n W$, respectively; then the argument still works in the second case but breaks down in the first case unless p is an even integer.*

3.5 What If the Process Jumps?

The continuous model (3.1) is restrictive in many respects, but it is representative of *all continuous* Itô semimartingales. Now, if we have a discontinuous semimartingale, one could also try to understand what happens for an oversimplified, but still representative of the jump case, model. Such a model is

$$X_t = X_0 + \int_0^t \sigma_s \, dW_s + Y_t, \tag{3.34}$$

where Y_t is a compound Poisson process.

In this case, as in all discontinuous cases, the realized volatility $\widehat{C}(\Delta_n)_t$ of (3.2) converges to the quadratic variation $[X, X]_t$, that is,

$$\widehat{C}(\Delta_n)_t \xrightarrow{\mathbb{P}} [X, X]_t = C_t + \sum_{s \leq t} \Delta X_s^2,$$

where $C_t = \int_0^t c_s \, ds = \langle X^c, X^c \rangle_t$ is still the integrated volatility.

We can then consider two different questions. The first one is to assert the quality of $\widehat{C}(\Delta_n)_t$ as estimators of $[X, X]_t$, and this will be considered in the next introductory chapter. The second one is to determine estimators for C_t itself.

For the second question, several methods are available and will be detailed in Chapter 6 in a much more general context. However, one method (the truncation method, described in Section 6.2.1) is very simple to understand and also to explain, in the simplified setting (3.34). It relies upon the two following facts:

1. If an interval $((i-1)\Delta_n, i\Delta_n]$ contains a single jump of size J, the corresponding increment $\Delta_i^n X$ is going to be close to J, which *does not depend* on n and is different from 0.

2. Since X as finitely many jumps on $[0, T]$, say N_T, and when n is large enough, among all intervals $((i-1)\Delta_n, i\Delta_n]$ within $[0, T]$

exactly N_T of them contain a single jump, and all others contain no jump at all.

Eliminating the increments containing jumps is then in principle easy: we choose a sequence u_n decreasing to 0 and throw away all increments with absolute size bigger than u_n; then, we use the other increments as in the no-jump case, and the estimator is

$$\widehat{C}(\Delta_n, u_n)_T = \sum_{i=1}^{[T/\Delta_n]} (\Delta_i^n X)^2 \, 1_{\{|\Delta_i^n X| \leq u_n\}}. \qquad (3.35)$$

In the "finite activity" (for jumps) case (3.34), taking *any* sequence u_n going to 0 eliminates the jumps, by (1) above. However, truncating may also eliminate increments which do not contain jumps. To avoid this, one should take u_n going slowly enough to 0.

Again in the finite activity case, this is quite simple: writing $X' = X - Y$, so X' is indeed given by (3.1), and assuming for simplicity that c_t is bounded (as in the previous section) we have

$$\mathbb{E}(|\Delta_i^n X'|^p) \leq K_p \Delta_n^{p/2}$$

for all $p \geq 0$ (another application of Burkholder-Gundy inequalities (1.59)). Then Markov's inequality yields

$$\sum_{i=1}^{[T/\Delta_n]} \mathbb{P}(|\Delta_i^n X'| > u_n) \leq K_p T \Delta_n^{p/2-1}/u_n^p.$$

This quantity goes to 0, as $n \to \infty$, as soon as $u_n \geq \alpha \Delta_n^\varpi$ for some $\alpha > 0$ and $\varpi \in (0, \frac{1}{2})$, and upon taking $p > \frac{2}{1-2\varpi}$.

If u_n is chosen as above, and by the Borel-Cantelli lemma, for all n large enough we indeed have $|\Delta_i^n X'| \leq u_n$ for all $i \leq [T/\Delta_n]$. Henceforth, $\widehat{C}(\Delta_n, u_n)_T$ is equal for all n large enough to the realized volatility of X', say $\widehat{C}(\Delta_n)'_T$, minus the N_T squared increments of X' corresponding to the intervals containing a jump. Obviously, deleting in (3.2) a finite number of increments, random but *independent of* n, does not affect the asymptotic behavior. Then the following is a consequence of Fact 3.5 above:

Fact 3.7. *In the model above, and with the above-specified choice of the truncation levels u_n, the processes $\frac{1}{\sqrt{\Delta_n}} \left(\widehat{C}(\Delta_n, u_n)_t - C_t \right)$ converge stably in law to the same limiting process as in Fact 3.5.*

Of course, this is not the end of the story: how u_n should be chosen in practice is a crucial issue, and when jumps have infinite activity the result is not as simple as stated above; see Chapter 6 for extensions to more realistic models, weakened assumptions, and practical considerations.

Chapter 4

With Jumps: An Introduction to Power Variations

As seen at the end of Chapter 3, the situation is indeed quite different when the observed process is continuous and when it is not. This is why, in this chapter, we study the simplest possible process having both a non-trivial continuous part and jumps, that is,

$$X_t = X_0 + \sigma W_t + Y_t, \tag{4.1}$$

where Y_t is a compound Poisson process (see Example 1.5), the volatility $\sigma > 0$ is a constant parameter, and W is a standard Brownian motion. The process X is again observed, without microstructure noise, at regularly spaced times $i\Delta_n$ for $i = 0, 1, \ldots, [T/\Delta_n]$ for some fixed time horizon T. As before, the observed returns are denoted as $\Delta_i^n X = X_{i\Delta_n} - X_{(i-1)\Delta_n}$.

The aim of this chapter is mainly to introduce one of the basic building blocks that we employ to analyze processes with jumps: approximate (absolute) *power variations*. These are, for any $p > 0$, the (observable) processes

$$B(p, \Delta_n)_t = \sum_{i=1}^{[t/\Delta_n]} |\Delta_i^n X|^p, \tag{4.2}$$

and they constitute natural extensions of the quadratic variation, corresponding to $p = 2$, that played a central role in Chapter 3. We are interested in the asymptotic behavior of $B(p, \Delta_n)_t$ as $\Delta_n \to 0$.

Why consider powers other than 2? When jumps are present, the quadratic variation involves both the continuous and jump parts of the model. On the other hand, we will see that power variations with $p < 2$ depend on the continuous part of X only (asymptotically, and after a proper normalization), whereas for $p > 2$ they only depend on jumps; this fact allows us to disentangle the two parts of X, continuous and jumps, using appropriate procedures to be explained later in the book. In fact, we will gain quite a bit of mileage from varying the value of p according to the component of the model we seek to identify.

Another set of statistics that play a role in what follows are *truncated versions of the power variations* in (4.2), namely

$$B(p, \Delta_n, u_n)_t = \sum_{i=1}^{[t/\Delta_n]} |\Delta_i^n X|^p 1_{\{|\Delta_i^n X| \le u_n\}}, \qquad (4.3)$$

for very much the same reason that they were useful at the end of Chapter 3.

We start with the asymptotic behavior of these power variations when the model is nonparametric, that is, without specifying the law of the jumps. We do this in the same spirit as in Chapter 3: the ideas for the proofs are explained in details, but technicalities are omitted. Then we consider the use of these variations in a parametric estimation setting based on the generalized method of moments (GMM). There, we study the ability of certain moment functions, corresponding to power variations, to achieve identification of the parameters of the model and the resulting rate of convergence.

We will see that the general nonparametric results have a parametric counterpart in terms of which values of the power p are better able to identify parameters from either the continuous or jump part of the model.

4.1   Power Variations

Below, the model is (4.1), and we write $c = \sigma^2$ and denote by $T_1, T_2, \ldots$, the successive jump times of X (or Y), which form a Poisson process on $\mathbb{R}_+$ with some parameter $\lambda > 0$, independent of W. We also recall that the jump sizes ΔX_{T_q} are an i.i.d. sequence of variables with some law G, and which are independent of W and of the times T_q. Note that X is a Lévy process with characteristics (b, c, F), where $F = \lambda G$ and $b = \int_{\{|x| \le 1\}} x F(dx)$.

As a matter of fact, we begin with the two special cases of purely jump and purely continuous processes, where respectively $\sigma = 0$ and $\lambda =$

0, even though these cases were formally excluded by our assumptions. These two extremal cases are easy to analyze.

4.1.1 The Purely Discontinuous Case

Here we assume that $X = Y$ is a compound Poisson process. It is convenient to introduce the (random) integers $i(n, q)$ defined as

$$i(n, q) = i \quad \text{on the set} \quad \{(i - 1)\Delta_n < T_q \le i\Delta_n\}$$

and also the process $N_t = \sum_{s \le t} 1_{\{T_q \le t\}}$, which is the Poisson process counting the jumps of X.

For any given $t > 0$, when n is sufficiently large (bigger than some random integer $n_t(\omega)$), the N_t jumps before or at time t lie in distinct intervals $((i - 1)\Delta_n, i\Delta_n]$. If this is the case, the returns $\Delta_i^n X$ for $i \le [t/\Delta_n]$ are all equal to 0, except when $i = i(n, q)$ for some q, in which case the return is ΔX_{T_q}. Therefore, we have

$$n \ge n_t, \; s \le t \;\Longrightarrow\; \begin{aligned} B(p, \Delta_n)_s &= \sum_{q \ge 1: \, i(n,q) \le [s/\Delta_n]} |\Delta X_{T_q}|^p \\ &= \sum_{0 < v \le \Delta_n [s/\Delta_n]} |\Delta X_v|^p. \end{aligned} \quad (4.4)$$

We can state this in another way, by introducing the processes

$$A(p)_t = \sum_{0 < s \le t} |\Delta X_s|^p \quad (4.5)$$

(this is of course a finite sum). Then (4.4) is equivalent to saying that, for any $n \ge n_t(\omega)$, we have $B(p, \Delta_n)_s(\omega) = A(p)_s^{(n)}(\omega)$ for all $s \in [0, t]$, where $A(p)_t^{(n)} = A(p)_{\Delta_n [t/\Delta_n]}$ denotes the discretized version of $A(p)$ along the discretization scheme $(i\Delta_n : i \ge 0)$, see (3.27).

The above trivial fact is basically the whole story: indeed, it implies that $B(p, \Delta_n)(\omega) \xrightarrow{\text{Sk}} A(p)(\omega)$ for each ω (convergence in the Skorokhod sense), by (3.27). Moreover, since for any fixed t the probability that X has a jump between $\Delta_n[t/\Delta_n]$ and t goes to 0, it also implies the following:

$$\mathbb{P}\left(B(p, \Delta_n)_t = A(p)_t \right) \;\to\; 1.$$

Henceforth, a Central Limit Theorem for $B(p, \Delta_n)$ is clearly impossible. Instead, one indeed has a perfect fit, on a set of probability going to 1 as $\Delta_n \to 0$.

Remark 4.1. *The "perfect fit" mentioned above is in fact illusory in practice: we have no clue as to whether the number n related to the actual observation scheme is larger than n_t or not. And if it is not, then $B(p, \Delta_n)_t$ and $A(p)_t$ can differ by quite a large amount.*

Remark 4.2. *Models in financial econometrics are not as simple as a compound Poisson process. Realistic models assume either that one has a non-trivial continuous part (see below, the results are then very different), or that the jumps of X have infinite activity, or both, not to speak about a possible drift term.*

When X is a Lévy process without a Gaussian part and with infinite activity for the jumps, things are also very different. First of all, the process $A(p)_t$ is infinite for all $t > 0$ when p is small enough, see (1.50). Otherwise, it is finite-valued, but the equality (4.4) fails for all values of n. In this case we have the convergence in probability $B(p, \Delta_n) \overset{\mathbb{P}}{\Longrightarrow} A(p)$ for the Skorokhod topology, and under additional and rather complicated assumptions we also have a genuine CLT.

4.1.2   The Continuous Case

Now, we assume that $\sigma > 0$ and $\lambda = 0$, the model of Subsection 3.1.1. We then have

$$\Delta_n^{1-p/2} B(p, \Delta_n)_t = \Delta_n \sum_{i=1}^{[t/\Delta_n]} \xi_i^n, \quad \text{where } \xi_i^n = \sigma^p \left(\Delta_i^n W / \sqrt{\Delta_n} \right)^p.$$

The variable $(\xi_i^n)_{i\geq 1}$ are i.i.d., with first and second moments $m_p \sigma^p$ and $m_{2p}\sigma^{2p}$ respectively, where $m_r = \mathbb{E}(|\Phi|^r) = 2^{r/2}\pi^{-1/2}\Gamma\left(\frac{r+1}{2}\right)$ denote the rth absolute moment of an $\mathcal{N}(0,1)$ variable Φ, and Γ denote the gamma function. Then the usual CLT implies, exactly as in Subsection 3.1.1 (which corresponds to the case $p = 2$), that

$$\frac{1}{\sqrt{\Delta_n}} \left(\Delta_n^{1-p/2} B(p, \Delta_n)_t - m_p \sigma^p t \right) \overset{\mathcal{L}}{\longrightarrow} \mathcal{N}\left(0, (m_{2p} - m_p^2)\sigma^{2p} t \right). \quad (4.6)$$

Using Donsker's Theorem, one can obtain a functional convergence, and the same arguments as in the previous chapter allow one to obtain the stable convergence in law (since σ is a constant, the argument can be made much easier). So, we have the following:

Fact 4.3. *In the model above, the processes*

$$\frac{1}{\sqrt{\Delta_n}} \left(\Delta_n^{1-p/2} B(p, \Delta_n)_t - m_p \sigma^p t \right)$$

converge stably in law to a $\sqrt{m_{2p} - m_p^2}\,\sigma^p W'$, where W' is a standard Brownian motion defined on a very good extension of $(\Omega, \mathcal{F}, (\mathcal{F}_t)_{t\geq 0}, \mathbb{P})$ and independent of $\mathcal{F}$.

4.1.3   The Mixed Case

Let us come back to Equation (4.1), with $\sigma > 0$ and $\lambda > 0$. We use the notation $A(p)$ of (4.5), and we write $X^c = \sigma W$ for the continuous part of X, and $B^c(p, \Delta_n)$ denotes the approximate p-power variation of the process X^c at stage n. For simplicity, we restrict our attention to the asymptotic behavior of $B(p, \Delta_n)_t$ at an arbitrarily fixed time t, although a "functional" version of all that follows does exist. We also set the stable convergence in law aside.

With the same notation $n_t(\omega)$ as above, the equality (4.4) fails as such, but is replaced by

$$n \geq n_t \implies B(p, \Delta_n)_t = B^c(p, \Delta_n)_t + B^d(p, \Delta_n)_t, \quad \text{where}$$
$$B^d(p, \Delta_n)_t = \sum_{q \geq 1:\ i(n,q) \leq [t/\Delta_n]} \zeta_q^n,$$
$$\zeta_q^n = |\Delta X_{T_q} + \Delta_{i(n,q)}^n X^c|^p - |\Delta_{i(n,q)}^n X^c|^p.$$

The behavior of $B^c(p, \Delta_n)_t$ is governed by (4.6) and we have, with Φ an $\mathcal{N}(0,1)$ variable,

$$\frac{1}{\sqrt{\Delta_n}} \left(\Delta_n^{1-p/2} B^c(p, \Delta_n)_t - m_p \sigma^p t \right) \xrightarrow{\mathcal{L}} \sqrt{t(m_{2p} - m_p^2)}\, \sigma^p \Phi. \quad (4.7)$$

As for $B^d(p, \Delta_n)_t$, it basically behaves as $B(p, \Delta_n)$ does in the purely discontinuous case $\sigma = 0$, at least at the first order. Namely, for each q, the variable ζ_q^n is never equal to $|\Delta X_{T_q}|^p$, but it converges to it as $n \to \infty$ because $\Delta_{i(n,q)}^n X^c \xrightarrow{\mathbb{P}} 0$. Thus, since there are only $N_t < \infty$ jumps up to time t, one deduces

$$B^d(p, \Delta_n)_t \xrightarrow{\mathbb{P}} A(p)_t.$$

This is not enough for us, and we need the second order behavior, that is, the associated CLT. With the notation $\{x\}^m = |x|^m \operatorname{sign}(x)$, an expansion of the function $x \mapsto |x|^p$ around $\Delta X_{T_q} \neq 0$ gives us

$$\zeta_q^n = |\Delta X_{T_q}|^p + p\,\sigma \{\Delta X_{T_q}\}^{p-1} \Delta_{i(n,q)}^n W + O_P(|\Delta_{i(n,q)}^n W|^2).$$

The random integer $i(n, q)$ only depends on the jumps, hence is independent of W and one has

$$\zeta_q^n = |\Delta X_{T_q}|^p + \sqrt{\Delta_n}\, p\sigma \{\Delta X_{T_q}\}^{p-1} \Phi_q + O_P(\Delta_n) \quad (4.8)$$

where $\Phi_q = \Delta_{i(n,q)}^n W/\sqrt{\Delta_n}$ is independent of the jump process Y and is $\mathcal{N}(0,1)$. We can say more: as soon as $n \geq n_t$, the integers

$i(n,q)$ smaller than $[t/\Delta_n]$ are all distinct, so the corresponding variables Φ_q are independent. Finally, using again the independence of Y and W, we see that the Φ_q's are independent of the process $W_t^{(n)} = W_t - \sum_{q\geq 1,\, i(n,q)\Delta_n \leq t} \Delta_{i(n,q)}^n W$, whereas $W^{(n)} \overset{\text{u.c.p.}}{\longrightarrow} W$ pathwise. Hence "asymptotically" (this is not a precise mathematical statement, but this can be straightened out in a rigorous way) the property (4.8) holds indeed for a sequence Φ_q of i.i.d. $\mathcal{N}(0,1)$ variables, independent of both W and Y, and thus of X as well.

Coming back to the definition of $B^d(p,\Delta_n)$, we then deduce from (4.8), and with Φ_q as above, defined on an extension of the original space and independent of $\mathcal{F}$, that

$$\frac{1}{\sqrt{\Delta_n}} \left(B^d(p,\Delta_n)_t - A(p)_t \right) \overset{\mathcal{L}}{\longrightarrow} \sum_{q=1}^{N_t} p\,\sigma\{\Delta X_{T_q}\}^{p-1}\,\Phi_q. \qquad (4.9)$$

At this point, we use the equality $B(p,\Delta_n)_t = B^c(p,\Delta_n)_t + B'(p,\Delta_n)_t$, valid for n large enough, together with (4.7) and (4.9). As a matter of fact, to get a clear picture of what happens, it is useful to rewrite (4.7) and (4.9) in a somewhat loose form:

$$\begin{pmatrix} B^c(p,\Delta_n)_t \\ B^d(p,\Delta_n)_t \end{pmatrix} \overset{\mathcal{L}}{\simeq} \begin{pmatrix} \Delta_n^{p/2-1} m_p \sigma^p t + \Delta_n^{p/2-1/2}\sqrt{t(m_{2p}-m_p^2)}\sigma^p\Phi \\ A(p)_t + \Delta_n^{1/2}\sum_{q=1}^{N_t} p\,\sigma\{\Delta X_{T_q}\}^{p-1}\,\Phi_q \end{pmatrix} + \begin{pmatrix} o_P(\Delta_n^{p/2-1/2}) \\ o_P(\Delta_n^{1/2}) \end{pmatrix}.$$

For the first order behavior, we simply observe that the leading terms in the expressions giving $B^c(p,\Delta_n)_t$ and $B^d(p,\Delta_n)_t$ are $\Delta_n^{p/2-1} m_p \sigma^p t$ and $A(p)_t$, so the result is simple enough:

$$\begin{aligned} p<2 &\Rightarrow \Delta_n^{1-p/2} B(p,\Delta_n)_t \overset{\mathbb{P}}{\Longrightarrow} m_p \sigma^p t \\ p=2 &\Rightarrow B(2,\Delta_n)_t \overset{\mathbb{P}}{\Longrightarrow} \sigma^2 t + A(2)_t = [X,X]_t \qquad (4.10) \\ p>2 &\Rightarrow B(p,\Delta_n)_t \overset{\mathbb{P}}{\Longrightarrow} A(p)_t \end{aligned}$$

($p=2$ corresponds to the well known convergence of the approximate quadratic variation). For the second order behavior we need to single out seven different cases, and we get

$$p < 1 \quad \Rightarrow \frac{1}{\sqrt{\Delta_n}} \left(\Delta_n^{1-p/2} B(p, \Delta_n)_t - m_p \sigma^p t \right)$$
$$\xrightarrow{\mathcal{L}} \sqrt{t(m_{2p} - m_p^2)} \, \sigma^p \, \Phi$$

$$p = 1 \quad \Rightarrow \frac{1}{\sqrt{\Delta_n}} \left(\Delta_n^{1/2} B(p, \Delta_n)_t - m_1 \sigma t \right)$$
$$\xrightarrow{\mathcal{L}} \sqrt{t(1 - m_1^2)} \, \sigma \, \Phi + A(1)_t$$

$$1 < p < 2 \Rightarrow \frac{1}{\sqrt{\Delta_n}} \left(\Delta_n^{1-p/2} B(p, \Delta_n)_t - m_p \sigma^p t \right.$$
$$\left. - \Delta_n^{1-p/2} A(p)_t \right) \xrightarrow{\mathcal{L}} \sqrt{t(m_{2p} - m_p^2)} \, \sigma^p \, \Phi$$

$$p = 2 \quad \Rightarrow \frac{1}{\sqrt{\Delta_n}} \left(B(2, \Delta_n)_t - A(2)_t - \sigma^2 t \right) \qquad (4.11)$$
$$\xrightarrow{\mathcal{L}} \sqrt{2t} \, \sigma^2 \, \Phi + \sum_{q=1}^{N_t} p \, \sigma \, \Delta X_{T_q} \, \Phi_q$$

$$2 < p < 3 \Rightarrow \frac{1}{\sqrt{\Delta_n}} \left(B(p, \Delta_n)_t - A(p)_t - \Delta_n^{p/2-1} m_p \sigma^p t \right)$$
$$\xrightarrow{\mathcal{L}} \sum_{q=1}^{N_t} p \, \sigma \{ \Delta X_{T_q} \}^{p-1} \, \Phi_q$$

$$p = 3 \quad \Rightarrow \frac{1}{\sqrt{\Delta_n}} \left(B(p, \Delta_n)_t - A(p)_t \right)$$
$$\xrightarrow{\mathcal{L}} m_p \sigma^p t + \sum_{q=1}^{N_t} p \, \sigma \{ \Delta X_{T_q} \}^{p-1} \, \Phi_q$$

$$p > 3 \quad \Rightarrow \frac{1}{\sqrt{\Delta_n}} \left(B(p, \Delta_n)_t - A(p)_t \right)$$
$$\xrightarrow{\mathcal{L}} \sum_{q=1}^{N_t} p \, \sigma \{ \Delta X_{T_q} \}^{p-1} \, \Phi_q$$

All these results are indeed direct consequences of (4.7) and (4.9), except for the case $p = 2$ of the quadratic variation, which needs further a joint convergence for the two left sides of (4.7) and (4.9), and in which the variable Φ is independent of the sequence Φ_q. We will not elaborate further on this question, since much more general results will be stated and used in the rest of the book.

A conclusion of this short analysis is that jumps do really complicate matters, and for power variations we have a *bona fide* Central Limit Theorem only for the powers $p > 3$ or $p = 2$ or $p < 1$ (also $p = 3$ and $p = 1$ if one accepts a biased CLT).

Remark 4.4. *The reader may wonder why we use the* absolute *power variations in (4.3), rather than the (signed) power variations, which can be defined as*

$$B^{signed}(p, \Delta_n)_t = \sum_{i=1}^{[t/\Delta_n]} \{ \Delta_i^n X \}^p$$

(except when p is an integer, the ordinary power $(\Delta_i^n X)^p$ is typically not well defined).

When $p > 2$, the same argument as above yields that $B^{signed}(p, \Delta_n)_t$ converges to $A^{signed}(p)_t = \sum_{s \le t} \{ \Delta X_s \}^p$: in contrast with $A(p)_t$, which is easily interpreted as a cumulative measure of the jump absolute sizes *(with power p), the variable $A^{signed}(p)_t$ does not seem to measure any noteworthy feature of the process: it can be small even when there are many jumps, or big jumps (think of Y being of the form $a(N' - N'')$, where $a > 0$ and N', N'' are two independent Poisson processes).*

Analogously, in the continuous case, the same argument as for (4.6) tells us that

$$\Delta_n^{1/2-p/2} B^{signed}(p, \Delta_n)_t \overset{\mathcal{L}}{\longrightarrow} \mathcal{N}(0, (m_{2p} - m_p^2)\sigma^{2p} t).$$

In contrast with (4.6), which says that $\Delta_n^{1-p/2} B(p, \Delta_n)_t$ is an estimator for σ^p (multiplied by the known quantity $m_p t$) with rate of convergence $1/\sqrt{\Delta_n}$, the above only gives us an estimator of 0, not a very useful statistic indeed.

4.2   Estimation in a Simple Parametric Example: Merton's Model

In this section, we focus on the particular example of the model (4.1), in which the law G of the jumps is the normal law $\mathcal{N}(0, \eta)$. This is a special case of *Merton's model*, without drift. This model is often written in the finance literature in differential form, as

$$dX_t = \sigma dW_t + \alpha J dN_t.$$

Recall that $c = \sigma^2$ and $\eta = \alpha^2$ and that λ is the parameter of the Poisson process N describing the time arrivals of jumps.

Our aim is to explain the intuition which underlies some of the features of estimation in the setting of discrete observations, and some of the methods which are used throughout this book. So, although this section may be skipped without harm, it might also be quite useful for a general comprehension of what follows later on.

This is a parametric model with a three-dimensional parameter $\theta = (c, \lambda, \eta)$. The probability measure is denoted as $\mathbb{P}_\theta$ to emphasize the dependency upon the parameter θ. We could as well replace c and η with σ and α but, at least for the first of those parameters it is more customary and more in line with the rest of this book to consider c. The integrated volatility for this model is ct, and the variance of X_t is $(c + \lambda\eta)t$. Relative to models without jumps, the primary purpose of the model is to generate fat tails for the log-returns, as can be seen in Figure 4.1.

On the basis of discrete observations within the time interval $[0, T]$, the identification problem for the three components of the parameter is

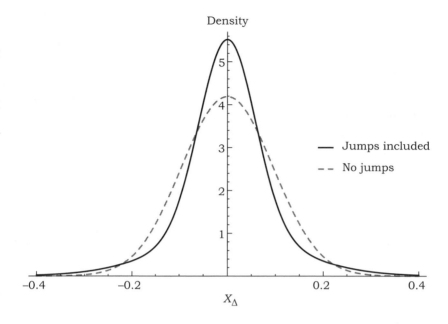

Figure 4.1: Density of increments corresponding to the models $X_t = \sigma W_t + Y_t$ (jumps included) and $X_t = \sigma W_t$ (no jumps). The parameters are such that the two distributions have the same variance.

straightforward (identifiability here means existence of a sequence of estimators which is weakly consistent, as $\Delta_n \to 0$). Namely, c *is identifiable, whereas* λ *and* η *are not*: the identifiability of c follows from Fact 3.7, the non-identifiability of λ and η follows from the fact that on a set of probability $e^{-\lambda T}$ the process X does not jump in $[0, t]$, thus precluding the existence of estimators for λ and η which are consistent on this set.

4.2.1 Some Intuition for the Identification or Lack Thereof: The Impact of High Frequency

As said above, the identifiability problem for λ and η is easy to solve, with a negative answer. However, we might still want to get some information on the jumps, such as their locations or sizes. If for example we knew the exact number N_T of jumps within $[0, T]$, we would take $\frac{1}{T} N_T$ as an estimator for λ: this is not a sequence, and consistency is out of the question, but this is nevertheless the "best" possible estimator for λ (and is in fact the MLE) when X is observed over $[0, T]$, and it is reasonably accurate when T is relatively large.

We may consider inferring jumps from large realized returns, filtered out of the sample path using a (typically endogenously determined) size cutoff; we will discuss formally such a method in Chapter 10. In discretely sampled data, every change in the value of the variable is by nature a discrete jump. Given that we observe in discrete data a change in the asset return of a given magnitude z or larger, what does that tell us about how likely such a change involves a jump, as opposed to just a large realization of the Brownian term? To investigate that question, we see from Bayes' rule that the probability of having had one jump involved in an increment of magnitude greater than a fixed cutoff z in an interval of length Δ is

$$
\mathbb{P}_\theta \left(N_\Delta = 1 \mid X_\Delta \geq z \right) = \mathbb{P}_\theta \left(X_\Delta \geq z \mid N_\Delta = 1 \right) \frac{\mathbb{P}_\theta \left(N_\Delta = 1 \right)}{\mathbb{P}_\theta \left(X_\Delta - X_0 \geq z \right)}
$$

$$
= \frac{e^{-\lambda\Delta} \lambda\Delta \left(1 - \Phi\left(\frac{z - b\Delta}{(\eta + c\Delta)^{1/2}} \right) \right)}{\sum_{n=0}^{+\infty} \frac{e^{-\lambda\Delta} (\lambda\Delta)^n}{n!} \left(1 - \Phi\left(\frac{z - b\Delta}{(n\eta + c\Delta)^{1/2}} \right) \right)}
$$

where Φ denotes the $\mathcal{N}(0,1)$ cumulative distribution function, and an analogous formula holds if we condition upon $X_\Delta < -z$. Similarly, we can compute $\mathbb{P}_\theta(N_\Delta = q \mid X_\Delta \geq z)$ for any other value of q, resulting in Figure 4.2.

The figure shows that as far into the tail as 4 standard deviations, it is still more likely that a large observed log-return was produced by Brownian motion rather than by a jump. So when Δ is not very small this underscores the difficulty of relying on large observed returns as the sole means of identifying jumps. This said, our ability to visually pick out the jumps from the sample path increases rapidly as we increase the sampling frequency by moving from Δ corresponding to one day to one hour to one minute, as seen in Figure 4.3.

The final intuition for the difficulty in telling Brownian motion apart from jumps lies in the effect of time aggregation, which in the present case takes the form of time smoothing. Just like a moving average is smoother than the original series, returns observed over longer time periods are smoother than those observed over shorter horizons, and jumps get averaged out. This effect can be severe enough to make jumps visually disappear from the observed time series of returns. Consider for instance the detection of the October 1987 market crash in data series at different frequencies, in Figure 4.4. As the figure shows, the crash of October 1987 is quite visible at the daily and progressively less so as the frequency decreases, all the way to being invisible at the annual frequency.

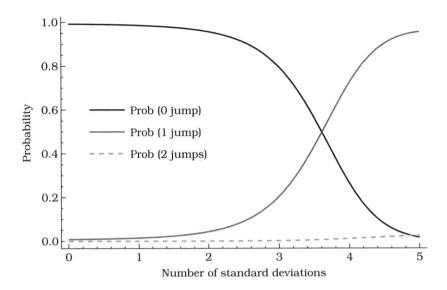

Figure 4.2: Jump probabilities inferred from observing a jump in log-return greater than a given threshold expressed as a number times $\sigma\Delta^{1/2}$. This plot shows that, as the observed log-return grows in absolute value from 0 to a increasingly greater number of standard deviations, the most likely number of jumps is first 0 then 1. The probability of inferring 2 jumps remains marginal in the range of values plotted.

4.2.2 Asymptotic Efficiency in the Absence of Jumps

In order to establish an efficiency benchmark, we start by computing the best possible asymptotic variance (AVAR) that can be achieved for the diffusion parameter $c = \sigma^2$. When $\lambda = 0$, we simply have $X_t = \sigma W_t$. According to the discussion in Subsection 3.1.1 the log-likelihood is given by (3.3) and the MLE is the discrete approximation to the quadratic variation of the process, normalized by T, that is,

$$\widehat{c}_n = \frac{1}{T} \sum_{i=1}^{[T/\Delta_n]} (\Delta_i^n X)^2. \tag{4.12}$$

We have the LAN property, the MLE $\widehat{c}_n$ is efficient, and its asymptotic behavior is given by (3.4) and the asymptotic variance (AVAR) of the estimation error $\widehat{c}_n - c$ is equivalent to the inverse of Fisher's information.

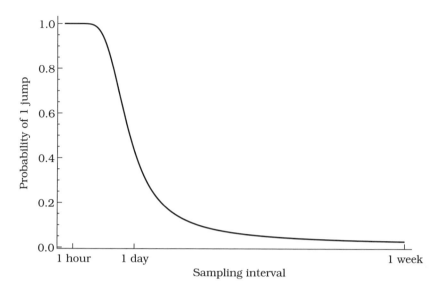

Figure 4.3: Probability that a 5% log-return involves one jump as a function of the sampling interval. This plot shows that the higher the observation frequency, the higher the probability that a jump can be recognized as such from the observation of a large log-return.

We thus have here

$$\frac{1}{\sqrt{\Delta_n}}\,(\widehat{c}_n - c) \xrightarrow{\ \mathcal{L}\ } \mathcal{N}(0, 2c^2/T), \tag{4.13}$$

$$\text{where } \text{AVAR}_{\text{MLE}}^{\text{no jumps}}(c) \;=\; 2c^2\frac{\Delta_n}{T} + \mathrm{o}(\Delta_n).$$

If we are interested in σ rather than c, the MLE is of course $\widehat{\sigma}_n = \sqrt{\widehat{c}_n}$, the rate still $1/\sqrt{\Delta_n}$, and the AVAR becomes equivalent to $c\Delta_n/2T$.

So, in this very simple situation of no jumps, the MLE is asymptotically efficient, the estimation variance decreases as Δ_n decreases and as T increases. It is only natural, since the statistical experiment amounts to observe $[T/\Delta_n]$ i.i.d. $\mathcal{N}(0, c)$-distributed variables (the normalized increments $\Delta_i^n X/\sqrt{\Delta_n}$) with unknown variance c.

4.2.3   Asymptotic Efficiency in the Presence of Jumps

When jumps are present, the first result achieved through a computation of the likelihood function is that, for estimating c when λ and η are arbitrary *but known*, we still have the LAN property, and the MLE, say $\widetilde{c}_n$ (not to be confused with the MLE without jumps, that is, $\widehat{c}_n$ of (4.12)),

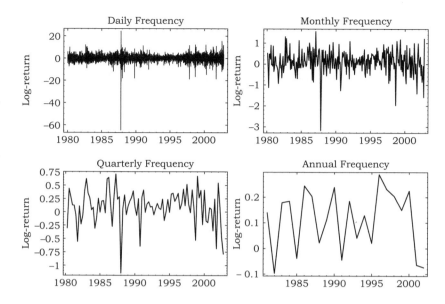

Figure 4.4: Log-returns on the Dow Jones Industrial Average at different observation frequencies, between 1985 and 2002. These plots illustrate the time averaging effect, namely the fact that jumps get averaged out over longer time intervals. For instance, the lower right plot shows that there was no 1987 crash as far as the annual data are concerned.

is asymptotically efficient for estimating c (whatever λ and η are) and satisfies

$$\frac{1}{\sqrt{\Delta_n}}\left(\widehat{c}_n - c\right) \xrightarrow{\mathcal{L}} \mathcal{N}(0, 2c^2/T),$$
$$\text{and } \text{AVAR}_{\text{MLE}}^{\text{with jumps}}(c) = 2c^2\frac{\Delta_n}{T} + \text{o}(\Delta_n). \tag{4.14}$$

In other words, comparing with (4.13), we see that the MLE can in theory perfectly disentangle c from the jumps, when using high-frequency data, where "perfectly" means "as well as if the model contained no jump component." The presence of jumps imposes no cost on our ability to estimate c, in particular the asymptotic variance is still $2c^2/T$ (up to normalization), and not $2(c^2 + \lambda\eta^2)/T$. This can be contrasted with what would happen if, say, we contaminated the Brownian motion with another Brownian motion with known variance c'. In that case, we could also estimate c, but the asymptotic variance of the MLE would be $2(c^2 + c'^2)/T$.

In light of the Cramer-Rao lower bound, the above establishes $2c^2\delta_n/T$ as the asymptotic variance benchmark for alternative estimation methods of c. However, the caveat here is that the MLE for c is efficient, but it is also unfeasible in the usual situation where (λ, η) is unknown. So deriving estimators $\dot{c}_n$ with the proper rate or, better, with the efficient asymptotic behavior described in (4.14) calls for practical methods for disentangling the jumps and the Brownian part.

4.2.4   GMM Estimation

A natural way to address this problem is the generalized method of moments (GMM in short; this is also known by statisticians as the estimating function method). Let us begin with a generic description of GMM (see Hansen (1982)). Below, we will study the estimation of a one-dimensional parameter, c, using a single moment function, but the q-dimensional version version is just as convenient to expose.

In the simplest version we have i.i.d. variables $Y_1, Y_2, \ldots$, having a joint distribution $\mathbb{P}_\theta$ depending on a parameter θ running through an open subset Θ of $\mathbb{R}^q$. At stage n, we observe the first n variables $Y_1, \ldots, Y_n$ which serve as placeholders for the increments $\Delta_i^n X$, and are $\mathbb{R}^d$-valued. We select an m-dimensional function h on $\mathbb{R}^d$, with $m \geq q$, called the moment conditions, such that the expectations

$$\overline{h}(\theta) \;=\; \mathbb{E}_\theta(h(Y_1)) \tag{4.15}$$

are computable under the law $\mathbb{P}_\theta$, preferably in a closed form, and in particular are all well defined. We also assume that $\overline{h}$ is $\mathcal{C}^1$, and a bijection from Θ into the interior of the convex hull generated by all values $h(z)$, where z ranges through the union of the topological supports of the variable Y_1 under all $\mathbb{P}_\theta$.

We then form the centered sample average

$$h_n(\theta) \equiv \frac{1}{n} \sum_{i=1}^{n} \left(h(Y_i) - \overline{h}(\theta) \right) \tag{4.16}$$

and obtain $\widehat{\theta}_n$ by minimizing the quadratic form

$$Q_n(\theta) \equiv h_n(\theta)^* \, \Upsilon_n \, h_n(\theta) \tag{4.17}$$

where Υ_n is an $m \times m$ positive definite, possibly random, weight matrix assumed to converge in probability to a positive definite limit Υ. If the system is exactly identified, that is, $m = q$, the choice of Υ_n is irrelevant and minimizing (4.17) amounts to setting $h_n(\widehat{\theta}_n) = 0$. We let

$$D(\theta) \;=\; \partial_\theta \overline{h}(\theta), \qquad S(\theta) \;=\; \mathbb{E}_\theta\big((h(Y_1) - \overline{h}(\theta))(h(Y_1) - \overline{h}(\theta))^*\big),$$

and we assume that $D(\theta)$ is not degenerate and that the $m \times m$ matrix $S(\theta)$ is positive definite. Then it follows from standard arguments that, under $\mathbb{P}_\theta$,

$$\sqrt{n}(\widehat{\theta}_n - \theta) \xrightarrow{\mathcal{L}} \mathcal{N}\big(0, (D(\theta)^* S(\theta)^{-1} D(\theta))^{-1}\big). \tag{4.18}$$

If $m > q$, this holds if the weight matrix Υ_n is taken to be any consistent estimator of S^{-1}, as this is the efficient choice; choosing Υ_n optimally improves the asymptotic estimation variance, but it does not improve the rate of convergence. A consistent first-step estimator of θ, needed to compute the optimal weight matrix Υ_n, can be obtained by minimizing (4.17) with $\Upsilon_n = Id$.

In practice, the model used to compute the expected value of h may be misspecified. This means that we do not use the correct function $\overline{h}$ in (4.16) but a wrong one, say $\overline{H}$, with still the same smoothness and one-to-one property as $\overline{h}$ has. In other words, the estimator $\widehat{\theta}_n$ is based on the sample averages $H_n(\theta) \equiv \frac{1}{n} \sum_{i=1}^{n} \big(h(\Delta_i^n X) - \overline{H}(\theta)\big)$ and minimizes the quadratic form $H_n(\theta)^* \Upsilon_n H_n(\theta)$.

There is a unique $\overline{\theta}$ such that

$$\overline{H}(\overline{\theta}) = \overline{h}(\theta)$$

and the estimators $\widehat{\theta}_n$ converge to $\overline{\theta}$ instead of the true value θ. Moreover, if $\overline{D}(\theta) = \partial_\theta \overline{H}(\overline{\theta})$ we obtain, instead of (4.18),

$$\sqrt{n}(\widehat{\theta}_n - \overline{\theta}) \xrightarrow{\mathcal{L}} \mathcal{N}\big(0, (\overline{D}(\overline{\theta})^* S(\theta)^{-1} \overline{D}(\overline{\theta}))^{-1}\big). \tag{4.19}$$

Estimating $\overline{\theta}$ instead of θ is not what we want. However, quite often in practice, the misspecification diminishes as n increases. This may seem strange at first glance, but this is typically what happens for the estimation of c in Merton's model when Δ_n goes to 0, as we will see below; this is due to the fact that instead of applying the GMM to an i.i.d. sequence of variables having a fixed law, we apply it to the i.i.d. sequence $(\Delta_i^n X : i \leq n)$, whose law depends on n and is closer and closer to a normal law when Δ_n gets smaller and smaller. In other words, at stage n we use in place of $\overline{H}$ a function $\overline{H}^{(n)}$ which converges as well as its derivative to $\overline{h}$ and its derivative, uniformly on each compact set.

In this case the mean squared error of $\widehat{\theta}_n$ has the following asymptotic behavior, written for simplicity in the univariate case $m = q = 1$:

$$\mathbb{E}_\theta\big((\widehat{\theta}_n - \theta)^2\big) \sim \frac{1}{D(\theta)^2}\Big(\frac{S(\theta)}{n} + |\overline{H}^{(n)}(\theta) - \overline{h}(\theta)|^2\Big). \tag{4.20}$$

We have a bias term, which may be negligible in front of the variance term, or of the same order, or perhaps is the leading term, depending on the case, that is, on the choice of h.

4.2.5 GMM Estimation of Volatility with Power Variations

We now come back to Merton's model, the observation being the increments $\Delta_i^n X$, which for each n are i.i.d., but with a distribution depending on n. Despite this fact, we use the GMM method described above, with moment functions of the following types:

$$
\begin{array}{ll}
\begin{array}{l}\text{absolute} \\ \text{moments}\end{array} & : \quad
\left\{
\begin{array}{l}
h(y) = |y|^p \\
\bar{h}_n(\theta) = \mathbb{E}(|\Delta_i^n X|^p)
\end{array}
\right. , \\[4mm]
\begin{array}{l}\text{truncated} \\ \text{absolute} \\ \text{moments}\end{array} & : \quad
\left\{
\begin{array}{l}
h(y) = |y|^p \, 1_{\{|y| \le u_n\}} \\
\bar{h}_n(\theta) = \mathbb{E}(|\Delta_i^n X|^p 1_{\{|\Delta_i^n X| \le u_n\}})
\end{array}
\right. ,
\end{array}
\tag{4.21}
$$

for various values of the power $p > 0$, not necessarily integers. The truncation levels in (4.21) are of the form

$$
u_n = a \, \Delta_n^\varpi, \qquad \text{for some } \varpi > 0, \ a > 0
$$

(when $a = \infty$, this corresponds to no truncation at all and truncated absolute moments reduce to absolute moments). We could also use the standard moments, $h(y) = y^p$, with $p \in \mathbb{N}$; however, when p is even it is also an absolute moment, and when p is odd the expectation $\mathbb{E}((\Delta_i^n X)^p)$ vanishes for Merton's model (as written here without drift and with centered jump size) for all values of (c, λ, η), so these odd moments give no information in the present example.

In order to implement GMM with correctly centered moments, we need to be able to evaluate the expected values $\bar{h}_n(\theta)$ appearing in (4.21) as explicit functions of the parameters θ of the model. If the correct law $\mathbb{P}_\theta$ of the process is employed to calculate these expected values, then the resulting GMM estimators will be consistent. The question becomes one of comparing their asymptotic variances among themselves, and to that of the MLE.

When λ and η known, the function $\bar{h}_n$ is fully determined. Otherwise, it is unknown and instead we take the expected value of $|\Delta_i^n X|^p$ and $|\Delta_i^n X|^p 1_{\{|\Delta_i^n X| \le u_n\}}$ as if X were actually equal to σW; this is a misspecified, but simpler model, and this gives rise to the function $\overline{H}^{(n)}$ described above.

In any event, we need the form of

$$M(\Delta, p) = \mathbb{E}(|X_\Delta|^p), \quad M_{tr}(\Delta, p, u) = \mathbb{E}\left(|X_\Delta|^p 1_{\{|X_\Delta| \leq u\}}\right). \quad (4.22)$$

One might think that only integer moments are useful, but we will see quite the opposite later on, and considering lower order moments $(0 < p < 2)$ is beneficial for the purpose of identifying the continuous component of a semimartingale. These absolute moments and truncated absolute moments are also available in closed form in this model, using the absolute and truncated absolute moments of $\mathcal{N}(0, 1)$, that is

$$m_p = \mathbb{E}(|U|^p), \quad m_p(x) = \mathbb{E}\left(|U|^p 1_{\{|U| \leq x\}}\right), \quad \text{where } U \text{ is } \mathcal{N}(0, 1).$$

If

$$\Gamma(q) = \Gamma(q, 0), \qquad \Gamma(p, x) = \int_x^\infty e^{-y} y^{q-1} \, dy$$

denote the gamma and incomplete gamma functions of order q, respectively, we have

$$\begin{aligned}
m_p &= \frac{2^{p/2}}{\sqrt{\pi}} \Gamma\left(\frac{1+p}{2}\right), \\
m_p(x) &= \frac{2^{p/2}}{\sqrt{\pi}} \left(\Gamma\left(\frac{1+p}{2}\right) - \Gamma\left(\frac{1+p}{2}, \frac{x^2}{2}\right)\right).
\end{aligned} \quad (4.23)$$

With this notation, the moments of (4.22) are

$$\begin{aligned}
M(\Delta, p) &= m_p \, e^{-\lambda \Delta} \sum_{n=0}^\infty \frac{(\lambda \Delta)^n}{n!} (n\eta + c\Delta)^{p/2} \\
M_{tr}(\Delta, p, u) &= e^{-\lambda \Delta} \sum_{n=0}^\infty \frac{(\lambda \Delta)^n}{n!} (n\eta + c\Delta)^{p/2} m_p\left(\frac{u}{\sqrt{n\eta + c\Delta}}\right).
\end{aligned}$$

The first expression above is of course the limit of the second one, as $u \to \infty$. In particular, we deduce $M(\Delta, 2) = (c + \eta\lambda)\Delta$.

These explicit moment expressions make it possible to compute correctly centered GMM estimators of c, assuming λ and η known. We are not exactly in the setting of the previous subsection, but since the increments $\Delta_i^n X$ are i.i.d. for $i \geq 1$, the fact that their laws depend on n does not impair the results: in this case we still use the correct function $\overline{h}$ of (4.15).

If we do not assume the parameters (λ, η) of the jump part of the model are known, then we instead rely on an approximate centering based on computing expectations assuming that $X = \sigma W$. As discussed above, the effect of the misspecification is to bias the resulting estimator, see

(4.20). Combining this with (4.19), and denoting the estimators as $\widetilde{c}_n$, we have a result of the form

$$\Delta_n^{-v_1}\left(\widetilde{c}_n - \overline{c}_n\right) \xrightarrow{\mathcal{L}} \mathcal{N}(0, v_0), \quad \text{where } \overline{c}_n = c + b_0 \Delta_n^{b_1} + o(\Delta_n^{b_1}), \quad (4.24)$$

with $v_1 \in \left[0, \frac{1}{2}\right]$ (we cannot have $v_1 > \frac{1}{2}$, because of the property (4.18)) and $v_0 > 0$, and also with $b_1 \in \mathbb{R}$ and $b_0 \in \mathbb{R}$ for the bias $\overline{c}_n - c$ incurred by the wrong centering (of course, $\overline{c}_n = c$ when $\lambda = 0$). If $b_1 \leq 0$ and/or $v_1 = 0$ for some choice of (p, a, ϖ), then the parameter c is not identified by a moment function based on that combination.

In what follows, we fully characterize the asymptotic distribution of the semi-parametric estimator of c, that is, the values (b_0, b_1, v_0, v_1) in (4.24) as functions of (p, a, ϖ) and of $\theta = (c, \lambda, \eta)$. We report in the form of AVAR(c) and AVAR$(\overline{c})$ the variances of the difference $\widetilde{c}_n - c$ and $\widetilde{c}_n - \overline{c}_n$, respectively, assuming that the time horizon is $T = 1$. Only the first one is really useful for estimating c, but the second one gives the behavior of the GMM estimators when the two jump parameters (λ, η) are known. We have the following equivalences, as $n \to \infty$:

$$\text{AVAR}_{\text{GMM}}(\overline{c}) \sim v_0 \Delta_n^{2v_1}, \quad \text{AVAR}_{\text{GMM}}(c) \sim v_0 \Delta_n^{2v_1} + b_0^2 \Delta_n^{2b_1}.$$

(In the second expression the leading term is $v_0 \Delta_n^{2v_1}$ when $v_1 < b_1$, and $b_0^2 \Delta_n^{2b_1}$ if $v_1 > b_1$, and the sum of the two terms when $v_1 = b_1$.) Therefore $v_1 = \frac{1}{2}$ and $b_1 \geq \frac{1}{4}$ are the conditions for a convergence rate of $1/\sqrt{\Delta_n}$, otherwise the rate is slower. When $v_1 \leq b_1$ the convergence rate of the semi-parametric estimators is identical to the rate one would obtain in the fully parametric, correctly specified, case where the jump parameters are known, and the same is true of the asymptotic variance itself (at the leading order) when further $v_1 < b_1$. Centering using only the Brownian part is of course the only feasible estimator in the semi-parametric case where the parameters (λ, η) are unknown.

Power Variations without Truncation   In the absence of truncation (equivalently, $a = \infty$), the leading order terms of AVAR$_{\text{GMM}}(\overline{c})$ and AVAR$_{\text{GMM}}(c)$, based on using absolute moments of order p, are given in the following two tables, in which we also report the value obtained when there is no jump, for the sake of comparison:

Moment Function	$M(\Delta_n, 2)$	$M(\Delta_n, p)$ $p \in (1,2]$
$\text{AVAR}_{\text{GMM}}^{\text{with jumps}}(c)$	$3\lambda\eta^2 + \lambda^2\eta^2$	$\frac{4\lambda\eta^p c^{2-p}}{p^2 c^p}\left(m_{2p} + m_p^2\lambda\right)\Delta_n^{2-p}$
$\text{AVAR}_{\text{GMM}}^{\text{with jumps}}(\bar{c})$	$3\lambda\eta^2$	$\frac{4m_{2p}\lambda\eta^p c^{2-p}}{p^2 m_p^2}\Delta_n^{2-p}$
$\text{AVAR}^{\text{no jumps}}(c)$	$2c^2\Delta_n$	$\frac{4c^2(m_{2p}-m_p^2)}{p^2 m_p^2}\Delta_n$

Moment Function	$M(\Delta_n, 1)$	$M(\Delta_n, p)$ $p \in (0,1)$
$\text{AVAR}_{\text{GMM}}^{\text{with jumps}}(c)$	$\frac{4c\left((1-m_1^2)c+\lambda\eta+m_1^2\lambda^2\eta\right)}{m_1^2}\Delta_n$	$\frac{4c^2(m_{2p}-m_p^2)}{p^2 m_p^2}\Delta_n$
$\text{AVAR}_{\text{GMM}}^{\text{with jumps}}(\bar{c})$	$\frac{4c\left((1-m_1^2)c+\lambda\eta\right)}{m_1^2}\Delta_n$	$\frac{4c^2(m_{2p}-m_p^2)}{p^2 m_p^2}\Delta_n$
$\text{AVAR}^{\text{no jumps}}(c)$	$\frac{4c^2(1-m_1^2)}{m_1^2}\Delta_n$	$\frac{4c^2(m_{2p}-m_p^2)}{p^2 m_p^2}\Delta_n$

In all cases with jumps, we have $v_1 = b_1 = 1 - p/2$, so we should never take $p > 2$, explaining why this case is not reported in the table.

Therefore, the estimators based on absolute moments converge at rate $1/\sqrt{\Delta_n}$ only when $p \leq 1$, and are asymptotically unbiased only when $p < 1$. When $1 < p < 2$, the mixture of jumps and volatility slows down the rate of convergence, but identification of c is maintained. We will see later that this a generic behavior of power variations for small powers (less than 2). When $p \geq 2$, the parameter c is no longer identified if we use this method, and when $p > 2$ the absolute difference $|c - \bar{c}_n|$ tends to ∞, as does $|\tilde{c}_n - \bar{c}_n|$ (in probability, and in restriction to the set where there is at least one jump).

When $p < 1$, the asymptotic variance v_0 is identical to the expression obtained without jumps, as is the case when the log-likelihood score is used as a moment function but the GMM estimators are inefficient, not achieving the efficient asymptotic variance $2c^2\Delta_n$ of (4.14), recall that $T = 1$ here, and this is true even in the absence of jumps. When $p = 1$, the rate of convergence remains $n^{1/2}$, but v_0 is larger in the presence of jumps than without jumps, and the bias worsens the picture even more.

To summarize, we find that, although it does not restore full maximum likelihood efficiency, using absolute moments of order less than 2 in GMM helps: When c is estimated using moments of orders greater than 2, then $\text{AVAR}_{\text{GMM}}(c) \to \infty$. If we use $p = 2$ this variance stays bounded but does not vanish asymptotically, which is of course not surprising, since using the second moment exactly amounts to taking the estimator $\widehat{c}_n$ of (4.12), which is the quadratic variation; without jumps, this is the MLE and is efficient, when there are jumps it converges to c *plus* the sum of the squared jumps inside $[0, 1]$. When absolute moments of order $p \in (0, 1)$ are used, we obtain the optimal rate, but not efficiency. When $p \in (1, 2)$, we have an intermediate situation where the rate is $1/\Delta_n^{1-p/2}$.

Note also that these results are consistent with the asymptotic behavior of power variations obtained in (4.11), with distinct behaviors when $p < 1$ or $p = 1$ or $1 < p < 2$ or $p = 2$.

Power Variations With $\Delta_n^{1/2}$ Truncation   Truncating at level $u_n = a\Delta_n^{1/2}$ with $0 < a < \infty$ is natural in the presence of Brownian motion since this is the order of magnitude of its increments. In all cases we find $v_1 = \frac{1}{2}$, whereas $b_1 = \frac{3}{2}$, so the bias is asymptotically negligible for any $p > 0$, in front of the variance term. More precisely, the two variances $\text{AVAR}_{\text{GMM}}(c)$ and $\text{AVAR}_{\text{GMM}}(\bar{c})$ are equivalent, and we have

$$\text{AVAR}_{\text{GMM}}(c) \sim c^2 \frac{m_{2p}(a/\sqrt{c}) - m_p(a/\sqrt{c})^2}{\left(\frac{1}{\sqrt{2\pi}} \left(\frac{a^2}{c} \right)^{(p+1)/2} \exp\left(-\frac{a^2}{2c} \right) - \frac{p}{2} m_p(a/\sqrt{c}) \right)^2} \Delta_n.$$

Truncating at level $\Delta_n^{1/2}$ therefore restores the convergence rate $1/\sqrt{\Delta_n}$ for all values of p, with $\text{AVAR}_{\text{GMM}}(c) = O(\Delta_n)$, and now permits identification of c. We will see the counterpart of this result in the more general nonparametric context later on. When $0 < p < 1$ (where the rate $1/\sqrt{\Delta_n}$ was already achieved without truncation), truncating at level $\Delta_n^{1/2}$ can lead to either a smaller or larger value of v_0 than not truncating, depending upon the values of the ratio $a/\sqrt{c}$ in the truncation level u_n. The value of v_0 is identical to its expression when no jumps are present.

Note also that the value v_0 is *always* bigger than $2c^2$, which would achieve efficiency in (4.14).

Power Variations With Slower Than $\Delta_n^{1/2}$ Truncation   If we now keep too many increments (relative to $\Delta_n^{1/2}$) by truncating according to $0 < \varpi < 1/2$, then we have for $p > 0$

$$v_1 = \frac{1}{2} \bigwedge \frac{2 + (2p+1)\varpi - p}{2}, \qquad b_1 = \frac{2 + (2p+2)\varpi - p}{2}.$$

Again, the bias is asymptotically negligible for any $p > 0$, in front of the variance term, hence again $\mathrm{AVAR}_{\mathrm{GMM}}(c)$ and $\mathrm{AVAR}_{\mathrm{GMM}}(\widetilde{c})$ are equivalent. We have, according to the truncation exponent ϖ adopted:

$$p < \tfrac{1+\varpi}{1-2\varpi} \Rightarrow \mathrm{AVAR}_{\mathrm{GMM}}(c) \sim \frac{4c^2(m_{2p}-m_p^2)}{p^2\, m_p^2}\, \Delta_n$$

$$p = \tfrac{1+\varpi}{1-2\varpi} \Rightarrow \mathrm{AVAR}_{\mathrm{GMM}}(c) \sim \frac{4c^2\left(m_{2p}-m_p^2 + 2\lambda a^{2p+1}/(2p+1)c^{2p}\sqrt{2\eta\pi}\right)}{p^2\, m_p^2}\, \Delta_n$$

$$p > \tfrac{1+\varpi}{1-2\varpi} \Rightarrow \mathrm{AVAR}_{\mathrm{GMM}}(c) \sim \frac{8c^2\lambda a^{2p+1}}{(2p+1)c^{2p}\sqrt{2\eta\pi}p^2\, m_p^2}\, \Delta_n^{2+(2p+1)\varpi - p}.$$

When $0 < p < 1$, we are automatically in the first case above, hence keeping more than $O(\Delta_n^{1/2})$ increments results in the convergence rate $1/\sqrt{\Delta_n}$ and the same asymptotic variance v_0 as when keeping all increments (i.e., not truncating at all). When $p \geq 1$ it is possible to get the convergence rate $1/\sqrt{\Delta_n}$ by keeping more than $O(\Delta_n^{1/2})$ increments, but still "not too many" of them (take ϖ in $\left(\frac{p-1}{2p+1}, \frac{1}{2}\right)$); but even keeping a larger fraction of the increments results in an improvement over keeping all increments since $2 + (2p+1)\varpi - p > (2-p)$ so that the rate of convergence of $\widetilde{c}_n$, although slower than $1/\sqrt{\Delta_n}$, is nonetheless faster (smaller $\mathrm{AVAR}_{\mathrm{GMM}}(\sigma)$) than that obtained without truncation where we had $\mathrm{AVAR}_{\mathrm{GMM}}(\sigma) = O(\Delta_n^{2-p})$.

A *crucial* consequence of these results is what happens when $p = 2$. In this case, and as soon as $\varpi \in \left(\frac{1}{3}, \frac{1}{2}\right)$, we are in the first case above, with $v_0 = 2c^2$. That is, not only do the GMM estimators in this case converge with the efficient rate, but they are efficient. Moreover, since this corresponds to the moment function $h(x) = x^2$, the estimator is particularly simple:

$$\widetilde{c}_n = \sum_{i=1}^{[1/\Delta_n]} (\Delta_i^n X)^2\, 1_{\{|\Delta_i^n X| \leq u_n\}}.$$

This is the same as the truncated estimators (3.35), and it will be encountered often in more general situations later.

Power Variations With Faster Than $\Delta_n^{1/2}$ Truncation   Finally, if we keep too few increments (relative to $\Delta_n^{1/2}$) by truncating according to $\varpi > 1/2$, then $v_1 = \frac{3}{4} - \frac{\varpi}{2}$ and $b_1 = \frac{3}{2}$ for all values of $p > 0$. Once more the bias is negligible and

$$\mathrm{AVAR}_{\mathrm{GMM}}(c) \sim \frac{2(p+1)^2\sqrt{2\pi\, c}}{(2p+1)a}\, \Delta_n^{3/2-\varpi}.$$

Truncating at a rate faster than $\Delta_n^{1/2}$ therefore deteriorates the convergence rate of the estimator from $1/\sqrt{\Delta_n}$ to $1/\Delta_n^{3/4-\varpi/2}$: while we successfully eliminate the impact of jumps on the estimator, we are at the same time reducing the effective sample size utilized to compute the estimator (by truncating "too much"), which increases its asymptotic variance. When $p \in (0,1]$, this is worse than not truncating. When p is larger than 1, then if $p - \varpi > 1/2$ truncating produces a lower asymptotic variance than not truncating.

To conclude, GMM estimators of the continuous part of the model based on absolute moments or power variations of non-integer orders less than 2 or, on absolute moments of any order combined with truncations at the proper rate, do better than traditional integer-based moments such as the variance and kurtosis, a property which we will revisit in the nonparametric context in later chapters.

4.3   References

Lépingle (1976) studied the convergence in probability of the power variations of a discretely sampled general semimartingale, thus providing an analogue of (4.10) (for $p \geq 2$) in a much more general context than here. The first section in this chapter basically follows Jacod (2012), and the second one is taken from Aït-Sahalia (2004).

Chapter 5

High-Frequency Observations: Identifiability and Asymptotic Efficiency

This chapter starts with a brief reminder about a number of concepts and results which pertain to classical statistical models, without specific reference to stochastic processes (although the examples are always stochastic process models). This should help the reader make the connection between classical statistics and the specific statistical situations encountered in this book.

Next, we introduce a general notion of identifiability for a parameter, in a semi-parametric setting. A parameter can be a number (or a vector), as in classical statistics; it can also be a random variable, such as the integrated volatility, as already seen in Chapter 3. The analysis is first conducted for Lévy processes, because in this case parameters are naturally non-random, and then extended to the more general situation of (general or Itô) semimartingales.

We also devote a section to the problem of testing a hypothesis which is "random," such as testing whether a discretely observed path is continuous or discontinuous: the null and alternative are not the usual disjoint subsets of a parameter space, but rather two disjoint subsets of the sample space Ω, which leads us in particular to an *ad hoc* definition of the level, or asymptotic level, of a test in such a context.

Finally, but only in the case of Lévy processes again, we come back to the question of efficient estimation of a parameter, which here is mainly analyzed from the viewpoint of "Fisher efficiency." This is of course far from a general theory of asymptotic efficiency, which at present is not available for semi-parametric Lévy models, let alone general semimartingales.

5.1   Classical Parametric Models

The usual setting of a statistical parametric model is as follows. A sample space $(\Omega, \mathcal{G})$ is endowed with a family of probability measures $\mathbb{P}_\theta$ indexed by a parameter θ in some subspace Θ of $\mathbb{R}^q$. At each stage n, we have an observed σ-field $\mathcal{G}_n$, and we assume that $\bigvee_n \mathcal{G}_n = \mathcal{G}$.

Example 5.1. *Let Ω be the canonical space of all real-valued continuous functions on $\mathbb{R}_+$, with the canonical filtration $(\mathcal{F}_t)_{t\geq 0}$ and $\mathcal{F} = \bigvee_t \mathcal{F}_t$ and the canonical process X. We take $\Theta = \mathbb{R} \times \mathbb{R}_+$ (so $q = 2$), and if $\theta = (b, c)$ and $\sigma = \sqrt{c}$ we denote by $\mathbb{P}_\theta = \mathbb{P}_{(b,c)}$ the unique measure on $(\Omega, \mathcal{F})$ under which*

$$X_t = bt + \sigma W_t,$$

where W is a standard Brownian motion. The time horizon is T, and we set $\mathcal{G} = \mathcal{F}_T$ and $\mathcal{G}_n = \sigma(X_{i\Delta_n} : i = 0, 1, \ldots, [T/\Delta_n])$. So $\mathcal{G}_n$ is generated by the discrete observations of X at times $i\Delta_n$, over the time interval $[0, T]$ (equivalently, by the increments $\Delta_i^n X$). Note that the equality $\bigvee_n \mathcal{G}_n = \mathcal{G}$ holds up to $\mathbb{P}_\theta$-null sets only, but this is of no importance for us.

The quantity θ is usually called the parameter, but we may be interested in estimating one of its components only, or more generally a function of θ. So here a "parameter" is a function g on Θ, say $\mathbb{R}^p$-valued. The function g is known, and an estimator at stage n, say $\widehat{g}_n$, is a priori any $\mathcal{G}_n$-measurable random variable. The sequence $\widehat{g}_n$ is called *consistent* if for all $\theta \in \Theta$ we have

$$\widehat{g}_n \xrightarrow{\mathbb{P}_\theta} g(\theta). \tag{5.1}$$

One should rather term this "weak consistency," but since later we never encounter "strong" consistency, which is the $\mathbb{P}_\theta$-almost sure convergence above instead of convergence in probability, we more simply use the terminology "consistency."

5.1.1   Identifiability

A parameter g, in the above sense, is called *identifiable* if it admits a sequence of consistent estimators. A very simple necessary condition for identifiability is given below:

Theorem 5.2. *If the parameter g is identifiable, then for any two $\theta, \theta' \in \Theta$ such that $g(\theta) \neq g(\theta')$ the measures $\mathbb{P}_\theta$ and $\mathbb{P}_{\theta'}$ are mutually singular.*

Proof. Suppose identifiability and let $\widehat{g}_n$ be a consistent sequence of estimators. Assume $g(\theta) \neq g(\theta')$. Let

$$A_n = \left\{ |\widehat{g}_n - g(\theta)| > \frac{|g(\theta) - g(\theta')|}{2} \right\}.$$

Applying (5.1) for θ and for θ' yields $\mathbb{P}_\theta(A_n) \to 0$ and $\mathbb{P}_{\theta'}(A_n) \to 1$. These two properties imply the mutual singularity of $\mathbb{P}_\theta$ and $\mathbb{P}_{\theta'}$.   □

There are no known sufficient conditions for identifiability, unless one is willing to make the assumption that the measures $\mathbb{P}_\theta$ are all equivalent in restriction to each $\mathcal{G}_n$, plus some regularity and non-degeneracy of the corresponding likelihood functions. However, we do have a weaker form of identifiability: we say that the parameter g is *pairwise identifiable* if for any two θ, θ' with $g(\theta) \neq g(\theta')$, there are estimators $\widehat{g}_n$ satisfying (5.1) for θ and θ'; under $\mathbb{P}_\theta$, $\widehat{g}_n$ consistently estimates $g(\theta)$ and under $\mathbb{P}_{\theta'}$, $\widehat{g}_n$ consistently estimates $g(\theta')$, but this says nothing about the behavior of $\widehat{g}_n$ under the measures $\mathbb{P}_{\theta''}$ when θ'' is neither θ nor θ'.

Theorem 5.3. *The parameter g is pairwise identifiable if and only if, for any two $\theta, \theta' \in \Theta$ with $g(\theta) \neq g(\theta')$, the measures $\mathbb{P}_\theta$ and $\mathbb{P}_{\theta'}$ are mutually singular.*

Proof. If g is pairwise identifiable, it is also pairwise identifiable for any submodel indexed by two points, say $\Theta' = \{\theta, \theta'\}$, in which case identifiability and pairwise identifiability agree. Hence the necessary condition is a consequence of the previous theorem. Conversely, if the measures $\mathbb{P}_\theta$ and $\mathbb{P}_{\theta'}$ are mutually singular, and since $\mathcal{G} = \bigvee_n \mathcal{G}_n$, there exist sets $A_n \in \mathcal{G}_n$ such that $\mathbb{P}_\theta(A_n) \to 0$ and $\mathbb{P}_{\theta'}(A_n) \to 1$. Then

$$\widehat{g}_n = g(\theta) \mathbb{1}_{(A_n)^c} + g(\theta') \mathbb{1}_{A_n}$$

is $\mathcal{G}_n$-measurable and satisfies (5.1) for θ and θ'. This proves the sufficient condition.   □

We will encounter many parameters which are pairwise identifiable. For most of them we come up with consistent estimators, proving *de facto* their identifiability.

Example 5.1 (continued). *In the setting of Example 5.1, it is well known, and also a consequence of Theorem 5.6 below, that the measures* $\mathbb{P}_{(b,c)}$ *and* $\mathbb{P}_{(b',c')}$ *are, in restriction to* $\mathcal{G} = \mathcal{F}_T$, *and excluding the case* $(b',c') = (b,c)$:

- *mutually equivalent if* $c = c' > 0$, *whatever* b, b',

- *mutually singular otherwise.*

Hence c *is pairwise identifiable (and in fact identifiable), whereas* b *is not.*

5.1.2 Efficiency for Fully Identifiable Parametric Models

The most common concepts of optimality or efficiency use the likelihood functions, so we assume that for all n the restrictions $\mathbb{P}_{\theta,n}$ of the measures $\mathbb{P}_\theta$ to the σ-field $\mathcal{G}_n$ are absolutely continuous with respect to a given reference measure μ_n on $(\Omega, \mathcal{G}_n)$. The likelihood at stage n, denoted as $L_n(\theta)$, and relative to μ_n, is the Radon-Nikodym derivative

$$L_n(\theta) = \frac{d\mathbb{P}_{\theta,n}}{d\mu_n}.$$

Apart from the likelihood itself, all notions or results below turn out to be in fact independent of the particular choice of the dominating measure μ_n.

There are two main notions of optimality. The first one, the Cramer-Rao bound, is not asymptotic. It necessitates enough smoothness and integrability on $L_n(\theta)$, so that Fisher's information

$$I_n(\theta) = \int \frac{\partial_\theta L_n(\theta)\, \partial_\theta L_n(\theta)^*}{L_n(\theta)}\, d\mu_n \tag{5.2}$$

is well defined (here $\partial_\theta L_n$ is the gradient of L_n, as a function of θ, and $*$ stands for the transpose). Then $I_n(\theta)$ is a $q \times q$ symmetric nonnegative matrix, which we assume below to be *invertible*. Then if g is a real-valued parameter, differentiable in θ, and as soon as $\widehat{g}_n$ is an unbiased estimator of g (that is, $\mathbb{E}_\theta(\widehat{g}_n) = g(\theta)$ for all θ), we have the Cramer-Rao lower bound on the estimation variance:

$$\mathbb{E}_\theta\left((\widehat{g}_n - g(\theta))^2\right) \geq \partial_\theta g(\theta)^* I_n(\theta)^{-1} \partial_\theta g(\theta). \tag{5.3}$$

There is also a version for biased estimators, which we do not recall here. Then of course if we come up with an estimator $\widehat{g}_n$ which is unbiased and achieves equality in (5.3), it is optimal (or efficient) in the Cramer-Rao sense among all unbiased estimators. Note that this notion of optimality is non-asymptotic: it makes sense for any fixed n.

Now we can look at asymptotic concepts. When θ itself is an identifiable parameter, the Cramer-Rao bound applied to each component $g(\theta) = \theta^j$ yields that all diagonal entries of $I(\theta)_n^{-1}$ go to 0 (provided there exist estimators $\widehat{g}_n$ whose estimation variances go to 0). In most situations, it appears that $I(\theta)_n$ itself explodes at some rate $v_n^2 \to \infty$ (we put a square here, because Fisher's information drives the estimation variance). That is, we have

$$\frac{1}{v_n^2} I(\theta)_n \ \to \ I(\theta) \tag{5.4}$$

for some symmetric nonnegative matrix $I(\theta)$. In this situation, we say that a sequence $\widehat{g}_n$ of unbiased estimators of g is *asymptotically variance-efficient* if for all θ,

$$v_n^2 \, \mathbb{E}_\theta \left((\widehat{g}_n - g(\theta))^2 \right) \ \to \ \partial_\theta g(\theta)^* \, I(\theta)^{-1} \, \partial_\theta g(\theta). \tag{5.5}$$

This concept is not so well defined when $\widehat{g}_n$ is biased, even when the bias is asymptotically negligible. But there is another notion of optimality, developed mainly by Le Cam. This is called *local asymptotic normality*, LAN in short, and goes as follows: letting $l_n = \log L_n$ denote the log-likelihood, under appropriate assumptions, we have both (5.4) and the following convergence in law under $\mathbb{P}_\theta$, for each θ in the interior of Θ (so below $\theta + y/v_n \in \Theta$ for all n large enough):

$$l_n(\theta + y/v_n) - l_n(\theta) \ \xrightarrow{\mathcal{L}} \ y^* \, I(\theta)^{-1/2} \, U - \frac{1}{2} \, y^* \, I(\theta)^{-1} \, y$$

where U is a standard q-dimensional centered Gaussian vector and the convergence holds jointly, with the same U, for any finite family of $y \in \mathbb{R}^q$. In this case, there exist sequences of estimators $\widehat{g}_n$ for g which satisfy (5.5), and also

$$v_n \left(\widehat{g}_n - g(\theta) \right) \ \xrightarrow{\mathcal{L}} \ \Phi \ := \ \partial_\theta g(\theta)^* \, I(\theta)^{-1/2} \, U. \tag{5.6}$$

The sequence v_n going to infinity is called the *rate*, or *speed* of convergence of $\widehat{g}_n$. Moreover, any other "regular" sequence of estimators $\widehat{g}_n'$ is worse than the above, in the sense that either its rate is slower or

$v_n(\widehat{g}'_n - g(\theta))$ converges to a limit which is the sum $\Phi + \Phi'$, where Φ' is independent of Φ (so $\Phi + \Phi'$ is more spread out than Φ, this is the *Hajek convolution theorem*). When this holds, any sequence of estimators satisfying (5.6) is called *asymptotically efficient*. The advantage of this type of optimality is that it is not sensitive to whether the estimators are biased or not, although it somehow implies that the bias is asymptotically negligible. It is also insensitive to the moment properties of $\widehat{g}_n$: these estimators can still be asymptotically efficient even when they have infinite variance (or other infinite moments).

Criteria ensuring the LAN property are too complicated to be fully explained here, and of no real use for us. Let us simply say that they are fulfilled when the observation consists of a sample of n i.i.d. variables with a smooth density, depending smoothly on θ as well, with the rate $v_n = \sqrt{n}$. When we observe a discretized Lévy process, so the increments $\Delta_i^n X$ are also i.i.d., although with a law depending on n, the LAN property also typically holds when θ is fully identifiable.

Finally, suppose that we want to estimate θ itself. When the likelihood function L_n is available one can use the *maximum likelihood estimator*, or MLE, that is, the value (or one of the values) $\widehat{\theta}_n$ achieving the maximum of the function $\theta \mapsto L_n(\theta)$, provided it exists. This method is often considered optimal, for good reasons: if the LAN property holds and the MLE exists, then the latter satisfies (5.6) with $g(\theta) = \theta$. However, the MLE is sometimes difficult to compute, and it has no equivalent for a semi-parametric model. So it usually cannot be used in the situations studied in this book.

Example 5.1 (continued). *In Example 5.1 with $c = \sigma^2 > 0$, and when the observed σ-field is $\mathcal{G}_n = \sigma(X_{i\Delta_n} : i = 0, \ldots, [T_n/\Delta_n])$ with a time horizon T_n which may be fixed, or may go to infinity, the measures $\mathbb{P}_{\theta,n}$ are absolutely continuous with respect to Lebesgue measure on $\mathbb{R}$, and the log-likelihood is*

$$l_n(b,c) = -\frac{1}{2}\sum_{i=1}^{[T_n/\Delta_n]}\left(\frac{(\Delta_i^n X - b\Delta_n)^2}{c\,\Delta_n} + \log(2\pi\,c\,\Delta_n)\right).$$

A simple calculation shows that the Fisher information (5.2) is the matrix with entries

$$I_n(b,c)^{bb} = \frac{\Delta_n[T_n/\Delta_n]}{c}, \quad I_n(b,c)^{cc} = \frac{[T_n/\Delta_n]}{2c^2}, \quad I_n(b,c)^{bc} = 0. \quad (5.7)$$

When b is known, so θ reduces to c, we have (5.4) with $v_n = \sqrt{T_n/\Delta_n}$, and the LAN property is easily checked with the same v_n (it reduces to *the ordinary Central Limit Theorem). The MLE is*

$$\frac{1}{\Delta_n[T_n/\Delta_n]} \sum_{i=1}^{[T_n/\Delta_n]} (\Delta_i^n X - b\Delta_n)^2$$

and satisfies (5.6) with $g(c) = c$. The simpler estimator

$$\frac{1}{\Delta_n[T_n/\Delta_n]} \sum_{i=1}^{[T_n/\Delta_n]} (\Delta_i^n X)^2$$

also satisfies (5.6), as soon as $\Delta_n \to 0$, if for example $T_n = T$ is fixed.

When $c > 0$ is known but $\theta = b$ is unknown, (5.4) and the LAN property hold with $v_n = \sqrt{T_n}$, provided $T_n \to \infty$: this is the condition for identifiability of b, and the MLE $\frac{1}{\Delta_n[T_n/\Delta_n]} X_{\Delta_n[T_n/\Delta_n]}$ then satisfies (5.6).

When both b and c are unknown, so $\theta = (b, c)$ is two-dimensional, (5.4) holds with, necessarily, $v_n = \sqrt{T_n/\Delta_n}$ again, if and only if Δ_n converges to a finite and positive limit Δ. In this case, the two-dimensional MLE satisfies (5.6) with the same v_n.

Remark 5.4. *The previous example is somehow typical of what happens in many practical situations. Supposing for example that $\theta = (\theta_1, \theta_2)$ is two-dimensional, both θ_1 and θ_2 may be identifiable, but the optimal rates for their estimation may be different. That is, (5.4) fails but we have two sequences $v_n^i \to \infty$, such that $I(\theta)_n^{ij} / (v_n^i v_n^j) \to I(\theta)^{ij}$ for $i, j = 1, 2$. Then (5.5) still holds, with $v_n = v_n^j$, when $g(\theta)$ only depends on θ_j.*

In Example 5.1 with $\theta_1 = b$ and $\theta_2 = c$, and when $T_n \to \infty$, we have this with the two rates $v_n^1 = \sqrt{T_n}$ and $v_n^2 = \sqrt{T_n/\Delta_n}$. More generally, this happens for diffusion processes which are discretely observed on $[0, T_n]$, with $T_n \to \infty$, and with a drift coefficient depending on θ_1 and a diffusion coefficient depending on θ_2.

However, in this book we never let $T_n \to \infty$, and such a situation will typically not occur.

5.1.3 Efficiency for Partly Identifiable Parametric Models

Example 5.1 with a fixed time horizon T is a case where the parameter (b, c) is not fully identifiable, although the second component c is. This makes the very definition of optimality for a sequence of estimators difficult to state in a precise mathematical way. This is also the case when, as in Remark 5.4, all components of θ are identifiable but the optimal rates are different for distinct components.

We get around these difficulties in the following manner. Suppose that $\theta = (\theta_1, \theta_2)$, with θ_1 identifiable and one-dimensional, the remaining components being gathered in θ_2 and being identifiable or not. For estimating a function g which depends on θ_1 only, we can proceed as follows:

1. Find estimators $\widehat{g}_n$ which do not depend on θ_1 of course, and neither on θ_2 (as any "estimator" should be!).

2. Prove that the asymptotic estimation variance $V_n(\theta) = \mathbb{E}_\theta \left((\widehat{g}_n - g(\theta))^2 \right)$ satisfies $V_n(\theta)/w_n^2 \to V(\theta)$ for some sequence $w_n \to \infty$.

3. Prove that the first diagonal element of Fisher's information matrix satisfies $I(\theta)_n^{11}/v_n^2 \to I(\theta)^{11} > 0$.

4. Conclude that $\widehat{g}_n$ is asymptotically variance-efficient if $w_n = v_n$ and $V(\theta) = g'(\theta_1)^2/I(\theta)^{11}$.

If instead of (2) and (3) above we have (2'): $w_n((\widehat{g}_n - g(\theta)) \xrightarrow{\mathcal{L}} \Phi$ and (3'): the LAN property when θ_2 is arbitrarily fixed (so we have a statistical experiment with parameter θ_1 only), we conclude that $\widehat{g}_n$ is asymptotically efficient if $w_n = v_n$ and Φ is $\mathcal{N}(0, g'(\theta_1)^2/I(\theta)^{11})$.

The foregoing procedure really amounts to fix θ_2 and consider the submodel $(\mathbb{P}_\theta)$ in which only θ_1 is varying, *except* that we additionally impose that the estimators do *not* depend on the now fixed value θ_2. The above yields asymptotic efficiency for each of these submodels and, loosely speaking, one cannot do better for the global model than for any of its submodels; this is why we conclude asymptotic efficiency for the "global" model.

Remark 5.5. *The reader should be aware that the previous argument, however plausible, is not really mathematically founded. It is correct when $\Theta = \Theta_1 \times \Theta_2$ has a product form. But it may go wrong if the parameter set Θ has a more complicated structure: some information on θ_1 may be gained from a preliminary (or joint) estimation of θ_2. We will see such a (very artificial) example of this later.*

Let us emphasize right now that the above procedure is an idealized one. In many cases we can perform points (1), (2) and (3), but are unable to obtain (4): when $w_n = v_n$ we at least obtain rate-efficient estimators, but even this is not always the case.

5.2 Identifiability for Lévy Processes and the Blumenthal-Getoor Indices

In this section we consider Lévy processes: the basic process X is Lévy, and we study the pairwise identifiability of the three parameters (b, c, F) characterizing the law of X.

5.2.1 About Mutual Singularity of Laws of Lévy Processes

In view of Theorems 5.2 and 5.3, pairwise identifiability is closely connected with the property of two Lévy processes with distinct characteristics to having mutually singular laws. So we give a criterion ensuring that this is the case.

The setting is as follows. We start with the canonical space $(\Omega, (\mathcal{F}_t)_{t\geq 0}, \mathcal{F})$ of all càdlàg $\mathbb{R}^d$-valued functions on $\mathbb{R}_+$, with the canonical process X. For any triple (b, c, F) as in (1.23) we denote by $\mathbb{P}_{(b,c,F)}$ the unique probability measure on $(\Omega, \mathcal{F})$ under which X is a Lévy process with characteristics (b, c, F). Moreover, we let $\mathbb{P}_{(b,c,F)|\mathcal{F}_t}$ be the restriction of $\mathbb{P}_{(b,c,F)}$ to the σ-field $\mathcal{F}_t$.

When F and F' are two Lévy measures, we can write the Lebesgue decomposition

$$F' = f \bullet F + F'^\perp$$

of F' with respect to F: here, f is a nonnegative Borel function on $\mathbb{R}^d$, and $F'^\perp$ is a measure supported by an F-null set. The measure $F'^\perp$ is unique, and the function f is unique up to F-null sets. Then we have

Theorem 5.6. Let (b, c, F) and (b', c', F') be two triples as above.

a) Either the two measures $\mathbb{P}_{(b,c,F)|\mathcal{F}_t}$ *and* $\mathbb{P}_{(b',c',F')|\mathcal{F}_t}$ *are mutually singular for all* $t > 0$, *or they are not mutually singular for all* $t > 0$.

b) Mutual singularity for all $t > 0$ *holds if and only if at least one of the following five properties is violated:*

- $F'^\perp(\mathbb{R}) < \infty$
- $\alpha(F, F') := \int \left(|f(x) - 1|^2 \wedge |f(x) - 1|\right) F(dx) < \infty$
- $\alpha'(F, F') := \int_{\{|x|\leq 1\}} |x|\, |f(x) - 1|\, F(dx) < \infty$ (5.8)
- $b' = b - \int_{\{|x|\leq 1\}} x\,(f(x) - 1)\, F(dx) + c\tilde{b}$ *for some* $\tilde{b} \in \mathbb{R}^d$
- $c' = c.$

This follows from a combination of Theorem IV.4.39 and of the subsequent Remark IV.4.40 of Jacod and Shiryaev (2003). Notice the quite remarkable statement (a), which is usually wrong for semimartingales that are not Lévy processes (and wrong even for "non-homogeneous" Lévy processes), and which is in deep contrast with the following: either $(b, c, F) = (b', c', F')$ or the two measures $\mathbb{P}_{(b,c,F)}$ and $\mathbb{P}_{(b',c',F')}$ are mutually singular on $(\Omega, \mathcal{F})$.

As a – very important – consequence, we deduce the following (well known) property, again for Lévy processes, and when the observations are inside a given finite interval $[0, T]$:

$$\begin{array}{c} \text{The drift } b \text{ is } not \text{ identifiable,} \\ \text{the variance } c \text{ is pairwise identifiable.} \end{array} \tag{5.9}$$

(As a matter of fact, we will come up later, in a much more general situation, with consistent estimators for c, so this parameter is indeed *identifiable*.) In the one-dimensional case for example, the claim about the drift comes from the fact that if (b, c, F) and (b', c, F) are given and if $c > 0$, then the measures $\mathbb{P}_{(b,c,F)|\mathcal{F}_t}$ and $\mathbb{P}_{(b',c,F)|\mathcal{F}_t}$ are *not* mutually singular (they are even equivalent, in this case).

Remark 5.7. *Any statement like (5.9) should be taken with caution. Indeed, the notion of identifiability is relative to a given model, parametric or semi-parametric. In the present situation, identifiability is thus relative to the set $\mathcal{S}$ of all triples (b, c, F) which constitute our statistical model. And the bigger the model is, the harder identifiability becomes.*

For instance (5.9) is correct when $\mathcal{S}$ is the set of all possible triples. More important, it is also correct as soon as $\mathcal{S}$ is such that, for any $b \neq b'$, there are c and F such that (b, c, F) and (b', c, F) are in $\mathcal{S}$, and $c > 0$.

However, it becomes wrong in more restricted models. A trivial (and rather stupid) example is the case where $\mathcal{S}$ is the set of all triple (b, c, F) such that $F = 0$ (say), and $b = c > 0$: then of course b, which equals c, becomes identifiable. A less trivial example is when $\mathcal{S}$ is the set of all $(b, 0, F)$ with F an arbitrary finite measure: then again, b is identifiable for this model.

It remains to examine whether the Lévy measure F is identifiable when X is discretely observed, and as the mesh Δ_n goes to 0. From the study of Merton's model in Chapter 4, it follows that when F is a finite measure it is *not* identifiable. Nonetheless, when F is infinite, some functions of F might be identifiable, and the aim of the next subsection is to study this question, and also to give some variance bounds, using Fisher's information, for some of the identifiable parameters.

5.2.2   The Blumenthal-Getoor Indices and Related Quantities for Lévy Processes

We introduced the *Blumenthal-Getoor index* of a Lévy process, BG index in short, in (1.49). This is sometimes called the BG index of the Lévy measure F, since it only depends on it. There is a characterization of the BG index in terms of the behavior at 0 of the "tail" of F, that is, the function $\overline{F}(x) = F(\{y : \|y\| > x\})$ for $x > 0$. The BG index is the only number β such that, for all $\varepsilon > 0$, we have

$$\lim_{x \to 0} x^{\beta + \varepsilon} \overline{F}(x) = 0, \qquad \limsup_{x \to 0} x^{\beta - \varepsilon} \overline{F}(x) = \infty. \qquad (5.10)$$

Unfortunately we cannot replace the "lim sup" above by a limit, and there exist Lévy measures for which $\liminf_{x \to 0} x^{\beta - \varepsilon} \overline{F}(x) = 0$ for all $\varepsilon \in (0, \beta)$. This makes a general analysis rather difficult and leads us to somewhat restrict the class of Lévy processes under consideration below.

Moreover, β is a "global" index for the d-dimensional process, but each component X^i has its own index β^i, possibly different from the others, and $\beta = \max(\beta^1, \dots, \beta^d)$. Even in the one-dimensional case, β is an index taking care of positive and negative jumps all together, but there is no reason why these two kinds of jumps should behave similarly: we can always write $X = X' + X''$ where X' and X'' are independent Lévy processes having only positive and negative jumps, respectively, and with BG indices β' and β''; then of course $\beta = \max(\beta', \beta'')$. Note that, here, the drift and the continuous Gaussian part of X are, indifferently, put in X' or in X''.

Therefore, we only consider *one-dimensional Lévy processes* in the remainder of this section, and we single out the behavior of positive and negative jumps. Toward this aim, we use the positive and negative tail functions of the Lévy measure, defined as

$$x > 0 \quad \mapsto \quad \overline{F}^{(+)}(x) = F((x, \infty)), \qquad \overline{F}^{(-)}(x) = F((-\infty, -x)).$$

We then have two BG indices $\beta^{(+)}$ and $\beta^{(-)}$, which are the unique numbers satisfying (5.10) with $\overline{F}^{(+)}$ and $\overline{F}^{(-)}$ instead of $\overline{F}$, respectively. Again, we have $\beta = \max(\beta^{(+)}, \beta^{(-)})$. A straightforward extension of (1.25), in which we consider only positive jumps, shows that for any $t > 0$ the variable $\sum_{s \le t} (\Delta X_s)^p \, 1_{\{\Delta X_s > 0\}}$ is almost surely finite if $p > \beta^{(+)}$, and almost surely infinite if $p < \beta^{(+)}$. A quite intuitive consequence of this fact, to be proved below, is that $\beta^{(+)}$, and likewise $\beta^{(-)}$, are identifiable.

Now, (5.10) says that $\overline{F}^{(+)}(x)$, for example, behaves more or less (rather less than more, in fact) as $a^{(+)}/x^{\beta^{(+)}}$ for some $a^{(+)} > 0$, as

$x \to 0$, so identifying the constant $a^{(+)}$ is of interest, as well as identifying the constants appearing in the successive terms of an "expansion" of $\overline{F}^{(+)}(x)$ as a sum of successive (negative) powers of x, if such a thing exists.

Solving this problem in full generality seems to be out of range, so we considerably restrict the class of Lévy measures under consideration. Positive and negative jumps can indeed be studied separately and below we introduce restrictions on, say, the positive jumps only, whereas no restriction is imposed on negative jumps. We consider the class $\mathcal{L}^{(+)}$ of all Lévy processes whose Lévy measure has the form

$$F(dx) = \widetilde{F}(dx) + \sum_{i=1}^{\infty} \frac{\beta_i^{(+)} a_i^{(+)}}{x^{1+\beta_i^{(+)}}} 1_{(0,\eta]}(x)\, dx,$$

where $\eta > 0$ and:

(i) $\quad 0 \le \beta_{i+1}^{(+)} \le \beta_i^{(+)} < 2, \ \beta_i^{(+)} > 0$
$\quad\quad \Rightarrow \beta_i^{(+)} > \beta_{i+1}^{(+)}, \ \lim_{i\to\infty} \beta_i^{(+)} = 0$

(ii) $\quad a_i^{(+)} > 0 \ \Leftrightarrow \ \beta_i^{(+)} > 0$

(iii) $\quad 0 < \sum_{i=1}^{\infty} a_i^{(+)} < \infty$

(iv) $\quad \widetilde{F}$ is a Lévy measure supported by $[0,\eta]^c$.

(5.11)

Here (iv) means that $\widetilde{F}$ is a positive measure with $\int (x^2 \wedge 1)\, \widetilde{F}(dx) < \infty$, and $\widetilde{F}([0,\eta]) = 0$. Conditions (i) and (ii) together ensure the uniqueness of the numbers $(a_i^{(+)}, \beta_i^{(+)})$ in the representation of F, whereas if this representation holds for some $\eta > 0$ it also holds for all $\eta' \in (0,\eta)$, with the same $(a_i^{(+)}, \beta_i^{(+)})$. Condition (iii) ensures that the infinite sum in the representation converges, without being zero (so $a_1^{(+)} > 0$ and $\beta_1^{(+)} > 0$).

Being in $\mathcal{L}^{(+)}$ puts no restriction on negative jumps whatsoever, since the restrictions of F and $\widetilde{F}$ to $\mathbb{R}_-$, which are equal, are unconstrained. If we are interested in negative jumps, we make the "symmetrical" assumption, which amounts to suppose that our process belongs to the class $\mathcal{L}^{(-)}$ of all X such that $-X \in \mathcal{L}^{(+)}$: the relevant indices and intensities are then denoted as $\beta_i^{(-)}$ and $a_i^{(-)}$. And of course the real interest lies in the class $\mathcal{L}^{(+)} \cap \mathcal{L}^{(-)}$.

Clearly, under (5.11) we have $\beta^{(+)} = \beta_1^{(+)}$, and we call $\beta_1^{(+)}, \beta_2^{(+)}, \ldots$ the *successive BG indices* for positive jumps, whereas the $a_i^{(+)}$ are the associated *successive BG intensities*. We also have

$$\overline{F}^{(+)}(x) = \sum_{i=1}^{j} \frac{a_i^{(+)}}{x^{\beta_i^{(+)}}} + o\left(\frac{1}{x^{\beta_j^{(+)}}}\right)$$

(5.12)

as $x \to 0$, for any finite j, and it is this expansion which will be used later to generalize the successive BG indices to semimartingales.

Below, we are interested in the identifiability of $a_i^{(+)}$ and $\beta_i^{(+)}$. The result, whose proof is given on page 507, goes as follows:

Theorem 5.8. *We consider the class of all Lévy processes X with characteristic triple (b, c, F) with F satisfying (5.11). If we observe the path $t \mapsto X_t$ over a finite time interval $[0, T]$, we have the following properties:*

(i) The parameters $\beta_1^{(+)}$ and $a_1^{(+)}$ are pairwise identifiable within the class $\mathcal{L}^{(+)}$.

(ii) If $i \geq 2$ the parameters $\beta_i^{(+)}$ and $a_i^{(+)}$ are pairwise identifiable within the subclass of all $X \in \mathcal{L}^{(+)}$ for which $\beta_i^{(+)} \geq \beta_1^{(+)}/2$, and are not pairwise identifiable on the complement of this subclass.

This theorem only asserts pairwise identifiability, but in Chapter 11 we will exhibit consistent estimators for these parameters in a much more general Itô semimartingales context, thus showing proper identifiability.

Remark 5.9. *As said before, (5.10) is not really the same as having $\overline{F}(x) \sim a/x^\beta$ for some constant $a > 0$, as $x \to 0$. For example it is also compatible with a behavior like $\overline{F}(x) \sim a(\log \frac{1}{x})^\gamma / x^\beta$, where $\gamma \in R$ (and compatible with many other kinds of behavior as well). So we might replace the formula giving F in (5.11) by, for example, the following one:*

$$F(dx) = \widehat{F}(dx) + \sum_{i=1}^{\infty} \frac{\beta_i^{(+)} a_i^{(+)} (\log(1/x))^{\gamma_i^{(+)}}}{x^{1+\beta_i^{(+)}}} 1_{(0,\eta]}(x) \, dx,$$

where $\gamma_i^{(+)} \in R$, and all other ingredients are as in (5.11). Then one may show that all three parameters $(\beta_i^{(+)}, a_i^{(+)}, \gamma_i^{(+)})$ are pairwise identifiable, for $i = 1$ and for all $i \geq 2$ such that $\beta_i^{(+)} \geq \beta_1^{(+)}/2$. The proof is analogous.

Remark 5.10. *One deduces from the theorem that a "part" of the behavior of F near 0 (those $\beta_i^{(+)}$ and $a_i^{(+)}$ for which $\beta_i^{(+)} \geq \beta_1^{(+)}/2$) is identifiable, whereas another part (the $\beta_i^{(+)}$'s smaller than $\beta_1^{(+)}/2$) is not, as illustrated in Figure 5.1. This is a somewhat surprising property.*

On the other hand, if $\eta > 0$, no function of the restriction of F to the complement of the interval $[-\eta, \eta]$ is identifiable: an application of Theorem 5.6 shows that if two Lévy measures F and F' coincide on $[-\eta, \eta]$ and if $c > 0$ and $b \in \mathbb{R}$, the two probabilities $\mathbb{P}_{(b,c,F)|\mathcal{F}_t}$ and $\mathbb{P}_{(b',c,F')|\mathcal{F}_t}$ are not mutually singular (when $c = 0$ this may or may not be the case).

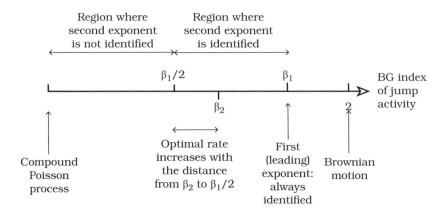

Figure 5.1: Two BG component model: Regions where the components are identified vs. not identified, and optimal rate of convergence.

5.3 Discretely Observed Semimartingales: Identifiable Parameters

Now we suppose that the process of interest is a semimartingale. The most striking difference with the two previous sections, as far as estimation is concerned, lies in the kind of parameters we want to estimate. More precisely, in the Lévy case all parameters of interest are functions of the characteristic triple, since this triple completely characterizes the law of the process. For semimartingales, the situation is similar: although the characteristics do not always characterize the entire law, they are what is closest to this, and the parameters of interest are typically functions of the characteristics. This is where the fundamental difference lies: in the semimartingale case the characteristics are *random*.

In other words, we want to "estimate" parameters which are random, and likewise we want to test hypotheses which are random. The aim of this section is to describe the nature of these "random" parameters and to explain what identifiability might mean in this context and give some examples of parameters that are identifiable, and some that are not.

The setting in this section is as follows. The process X is a d-dimensional semimartingale, on some filtered probability space $(\Omega, \mathcal{F}, (\mathcal{F}_t)_{t \geq 0}, \mathbb{P})$. We denote by $\mu = \mu^X$ its jump measure and by (B, C, ν) its characteristics, as introduced in Chapter 1. We mostly specialize to Itô semimartingales, thus assuming the form (1.63), that is,

$$B_t = \int_0^t b_s ds, \qquad C_t = \int_0^t c_s ds, \qquad \nu(dt, dx) = dt\, F_t(dx),$$

where the spot characteristics are an $\mathbb{R}^d$-valued process $b = (b_t)$, a process $c = (c_t)$ with values in the set of $d \times d$ symmetric nonnegative matrices, and a measure-valued process $F_t = F_t(\omega, dx)$ on $\mathbb{R}^d$.

As for the sampling scheme, at each stage n, observations occur at times $(T(n, i) : 0 \le i \le k_n)$, increasing with i, and within some *fixed* time interval $[0, T]$. Although we occasionally consider observation times $T(n, i)$ which are irregularly spaced, or even random, in most cases we have a *regular sampling scheme*, that is, $T(n, i) = i\Delta_n$ with a (non-random) $\Delta_n > 0$, and $k_n = [T/\Delta_n]$. The term "high-frequency" means that in all cases the mesh of the observation scheme satisfies

$$\pi_n \xrightarrow{\;\mathbb{P}\;} 0, \quad \text{where}$$
$$\pi_n = \max \left(\sup_{1 \le i \le k_n} (T(n, i) - T(n, i - 1)), T - T(n, k_n) \right) \tag{5.13}$$

as $n \to \infty$ (we use convergence in probability to accommodate random schemes, in the regular case this is of course the same as having $\Delta_n \to 0$). Associated with the observation scheme, we introduce the increments of the process X, or returns, as being

$$\Delta_i^n X = X_{T(n,i)} - X_{T(n,i-1)}.$$

5.3.1 Identifiable Parameters: A Definition

The notion of a parameter is strongly connected with the specifications of the model, and a "random" parameter is also connected with the possible outcomes of the experiment. To understand this, we begin with four different and very special situations, in which the basic process X is one-dimensional:

- *Example 1: integrated volatility.* We consider all Itô semimartingales, and the parameter of interest is the integrated volatility, say $Z = C_T = \int_0^T c_s \, ds$.

- *Example 2: jumps or not.* We consider all semimartingales, and the parameter of interest is the indicator function $Z = 1_{\Omega_T^{(c)}}$, where $\Omega_T^{(c)}$ is the set of all ω such that the path $t \mapsto X_t(\omega)$ is continuous on $[0, T]$. Here we still use the terminology "parameter," but it only takes the values 0 and 1 and its estimation really amounts to testing whether it is equal to 0 or to 1.

- *Example 3: Blumenthal-Getoor index.* We consider all semimartingales of the form

$$X_t = \sigma W_t + (Y_t - Y_S) 1_{\{S \leq t\}},$$

where $\sigma \geq 0$ and W is a Brownian motion and Y is a standard symmetric stable process with index β, and S is an arbitrary (unspecified) stopping time. The parameter of interest is $Z = \beta$, which is the BG index of the process X on the interval $[0, T]$, in restriction to the set $\{S < T\}$, whereas there is no jump and the BG index vanishes on the set $\{S \geq T\}$. This is a simple example of a parameter which can (perhaps) be identified if the outcome belongs to some subset (here $\{S < T\}$), but obviously not if the outcome is such that $S(\omega) \geq T$.

- *Example 4: co-jumps for price and volatility.* We consider all Itô semimartingales and the parameter is $Z = 1_{\Omega_T^{\text{co-jumps}}}$, where $\Omega_T^{\text{co-jumps}}$ is the set on which the process X and its spot volatility process c have jumps at the same time.

From a somewhat pedantic viewpoint, one could formalize the notion of a *parameter Z* as follows:

1. We have a class $\mathcal{S}$ of d-dimensional semimartingales. Each process X in this class may be defined on its own probability space $(\Omega, \mathcal{F}, \mathbb{P})$.

2. For each X in this class, the parameter is a given (known) "function" of the path $t \mapsto X_t$, of the path of its characteristics (B, C, ν), and on the law of X.

Statement (2) is still somehow imprecise but could easily be formalized in a rigorous way. However, this is not necessary for us, since in practice, the parameter of interest always has a clear and obvious meaning. For instance in Example 1 the parameter $Z = C_T$ is a function of the characteristics; in Example 2, $Z = 1_{\Omega_T^{(c)}}$ is a function of the path of X; in Example 3, $Z = \beta$ is a function of the law of X; in Example 4, Z is a function of the path of X *and* of the path of its (spot) characteristic $t \mapsto c_t$.

Identifiability (in the asymptotic sense) of a parameter Z is relative to a specific class $\mathcal{S}$, and also to an observation scheme $\mathcal{T} = (T(n, i) : i \geq 0, n \geq 1)$ satisfying (5.13). Moreover, in order to compare processes which may be defined on different spaces it is convenient to suppose that the observation times $T(n, i)$ are *not random* (an extension to random sampling times is possible, at the price of a significantly more complicated setting). Each process X in $\mathcal{S}$ may be considered as a random variable taking its values in the *Skorokhod space*, that is, the space $\mathbb{D}^d = \mathbb{D}(\mathbb{R}_+, \mathbb{R}^d)$ of all càdlàg functions from $\mathbb{R}_+$ into $\mathbb{R}^d$. This space was studied in some detail in Subsection 3.3, and here we simply recall that it is equipped with the σ-field $\mathcal{D}^d$ generated by the maps $x \mapsto x(t)$ for all $t \geq 0$. At stage n one really observes the "discretized" process $X^{(n)}$ defined as

$$X_t^{(n)} = X_{T(n,i)} \quad \text{if} \quad T(n, i) \leq t < T(n, i + 1), \qquad (5.14)$$

which again takes its values in $\mathbb{D}^d$.

Any estimator at stage n is necessarily of the form $G_n(X^{(n)})$ for a function G_n on $\mathbb{D}^d$. With this view on estimators, we can give a definition:

Definition 5.11. *Let A be a measurable subset of $\mathbb{D}^d$. A q-dimensional parameter Z is called $(\mathcal{T}, \mathcal{S})$-identifiable on the set A if there exists a sequence G_n of $\mathbb{R}^q$-valued and $\mathcal{D}_T$-measurable functions on $(\mathbb{D}^d, \mathcal{D}^d)$ such that, for any X in the class $\mathcal{S}$, we have the following convergence in probability, on the space $(\Omega, \mathcal{F}, \mathbb{P})$ on which X is defined:*

$$G_n(X^{(n)}) \xrightarrow{\mathbb{P}} Z \qquad \text{in restriction to the set} \quad X^{-1}(A).$$

It is said pairwise $(\mathcal{T}, \mathcal{S})$-identifiable on the set A *if the above holds in restriction to any subset of $\mathcal{S}$ containing only two processes.*

When $A = \mathbb{D}^d$, we simply say $(\mathcal{T}, \mathcal{S})$-identifiable, or pairwise $(\mathcal{T}, \mathcal{S})$-identifiable. When $Z = 1_{\Omega_0}$ is an indicator function, we rather say *the set Ω_0 is identifiable*, or pairwise identifiable.

When $\mathcal{S}$ is a parametric family indexed by the elements θ of a parameter space Θ, then (pairwise) identifiability for a parameter $Z = g(\theta)$ depending on θ only is the same here and as stated before Theorems 5.2 and 5.3. As for the four previous examples, we will see below identifiability in the first two cases and in the last case, and identifiability in the third case on the set A of all functions in $\mathbb{D}^d$ which are not continuous on $[0, T]$.

Example 5.12. *A very simple case of identifiability is when the parameter Z takes the form $Z = G(X)$ for a function G on $\mathbb{D}^d$, which depends only on the "past" before time T. Then, as soon as G is a continuous function on $\mathbb{D}^d$ (for the Skorokhod topology), the parameter $Z = G(X)$ is* *identifiable; we simply have to take $G_n = G$ and apply the property that $X^{(n)}$ converges to X, see (3.27). The same is true when G is only almost surely continuous relative to the law of any X in the class $\mathcal{S}$.*

This example of identifiability is trivial, mathematically speaking, but not without practical interest. For instance one might be interested in $Z = \sup_{s \leq T} |\Delta X_s|$, the absolute size of the biggest jump up to time T, when the dimension is $d = 1$. This "parameter" is of the above form, with a function G which is almost surely continuous relative to the law of any process X satisfying $\mathbb{P}(\Delta X_T = 0) = 0$ (that is, almost surely X does not jump at our terminal time T). Then if $\mathcal{S}$ is the class of all such processes, we have the following convergence, which even takes place almost surely:

$$G(X^{(n)}) \;=\; \sup_{1 \leq i \leq k_n} |\Delta_i^n X| \;\to\; G(X) \;=\; \sup_{s \leq T} |\Delta X_s|.$$

5.3.2   Identifiable Parameters: Examples

Apart from the class of examples 5.12, deciding whether a given parameter is (pairwise) identifiable or not is usually not a totally trivial matter. One of the problems in the present general situation is that we do not have the analogues of Theorems 5.2 and 5.3, and we also lack criteria for mutual singularity such as Theorem 5.6. However, it is still possible to show identifiability directly, for a number of parameters which are identifiable, and which include the first three examples by which the previous section started.

We start by looking at the *integrated volatility*. More generally, when X is an arbitrary semimartingale, the second characteristic C plays the role of the integrated volatility. This is a crucial "parameter" in finance, so the next result is theoretically very important (we recall that an observation scheme $\mathcal{T}$ is relative to some fixed time horizon T, and that it satisfies (5.13)):

Theorem 5.13. *The second characteristic C_t is $(\mathcal{T}, \mathcal{S})$-pairwise identifiable for any $t \in [0, T]$, when $\mathcal{S}$ is the class of all semimartingales and $\mathcal{T}$ an arbitrary non-random observation scheme.*

This result, proved on page 509, is very close to Theorem 1.14, and in particular to the property (1.62) which exhibits consistent estimators for the quadratic variation-covariation $[X, X]_t$ at any time t at which X does not jump, implying identifiability for the parameter $[X, X]_t$ in the class of all semimartingales X having $\mathbb{P}(\Delta X_t \neq 0) = 0$. So in particular if we restrict $\mathcal{S}$ to be the class of all *continuous* semimartingales, $C_t = [X, X]_t$ is fully identifiable.

For the above theorem, however, we claim pairwise identifiability only, and whether proper identifiability holds in such a general context is unknown. The problem is that, in the proof given on page 509, the consistent estimators explicitly depend on the two processes X and X' which are considered to show pairwise identifiability. However, it will follow from the results in the forthcoming chapters that identifiability (and much more) holds if we restrict ourselves to the class of possibly discontinuous Itô semimartingales.

Next, we go a step further. Since $C_t = \int_0^t c_s\,ds$ when X is an Itô semimartingale, we can ask ourselves whether the spot volatility c_t is also identifiable for a given time $t \le T$.

Posed in such a way, the answer is obviously a *no*, or rather, it is not a well posed problem. Indeed, the process C_t is not unique, but any two versions of this process are almost surely equal, and thus identifiability is not affected by the choice of the version of C_t. For c_t the situation is different, since even when the integral process C_t is fixed, the property $C_t(\omega) = \int_0^t c_s(\omega)\,ds$ characterizes $t \mapsto c_t(\omega)$ only up to Lebesgue-null sets.

Therefore the identifiability problem for c_t is well posed only under some additional regularity assumption on the map $t \mapsto c_t$, and we have the following, proved on page 511:

Theorem 5.14. *The spot volatility c_t is $(\mathcal{T}, \mathcal{S})$-pairwise identifiable for any $t \in [0, T)$, resp. $t \in (0, T]$, for the class $\mathcal{S}$ of all Itô semimartingales for which the process c is right-continuous, resp. left-continuous, and $\mathcal{T}$ is an arbitrary non-random observation scheme.*

In a flagrant contradiction to the title of this subsection, we end it with some facts about the drift, that is, the first characteristic B. In view of the general claim (5.9), the parameter B_t is *not identifiable* for the class of Lévy processes, hence even less for bigger classes of semimartingales. However, according to the subsequent Remark 5.7 it might be identifiable for certain classes $\mathcal{S}$.

For example let $\mathcal{S}$ be the class of all d-dimensional semimartingales X having locally finite variation, that is, of the form

$$X_t = B_t' + \sum_{s \le t} \Delta X_s,$$

where the sum of jumps is absolutely convergent for all t and all ω, and B' is a d-dimensional process with locally finite variation, necessarily continuous and adapted. One can consider B' as the "genuine" drift, sometimes called the *first modified characteristic* of X, whereas the first characteristic B is in this case $B_t = B'_t + \int_0^t \int_{\{\|x\| \le 1\}} x\, \nu(ds, dx)$. Then we have the following theorem, whose proof is analogous to the proof of Theorem 5.13 and is thus omitted:

Theorem 5.15. *The first modified characteristic B'_t is $(\mathcal{T}, \mathcal{S})$-pairwise identifiable for all $t \in [0, T)$, if $\mathcal{S}$ is the class of all d-dimensional semimartingales whose paths have finite variation and $\mathcal{T}$ is an arbitrary nonrandom observation scheme.*

Now we turn to identifiability of parameters related to the jumps of X, and begin with the following processes:

$$A(p)_t = \sum_{s \le t} \|\Delta X_s\|^p \tag{5.15}$$

for $p \ge 0$ (with the convention $0^0 = 0$, so $A(0)_t$ is exactly the number of jumps in $[0, t]$). Each process $A(p)$ is increasing, with $A(p)_0 = 0$, with left and right limits $A(p)_{t-}$ and $A(p)_{t+}$, and is further right-continuous (that is, $A(p)_{t+} = A(p)_t$) at all t, except at $t = S := \inf(t : A(p)_t = \infty)$ if $A(p)_{S-} < \infty$ and $S < \infty$, because in this case $A(p)_S < A(p)_{S+} = \infty$. When $p \ge 2$, however, we always have $S = \infty$ a.s., hence $A(p)$ is almost surely càdlàg.

Theorem 5.16. *Let $p \ge 0$. For each $t < T$ the variable $A(p)_t$ is $(\mathcal{T}, \mathcal{S})$-pairwise identifiable for the class $\mathcal{S}$ of all d-dimensional semimartingales, and any observation scheme $\mathcal{T}$.*

The same is true when $t = T$, on the set $\{\Delta X_T = 0\}$ in general, and also on the set Ω if $T(n, k_n) = T$ for all n large enough.

As a consequence, the set $\Omega_T^{(c)}$ on which X is continuous on the interval $[0, T]$ is pairwise identifiable if we have for example $\mathbb{P}(\Delta X_T = 0) = 1$, as for all Itô semimartingales; this is because $\Omega_T^{(c)} = \{A(p)_T = 0\}$ for any $p \ge 0$. This theorem is proved on page 511.

Next, we associate the following random sets and random variables with the third characteristic of the semimartingale X; the second line below makes sense for any semimartingale, whereas the first line assumes that it is an Itô semimartingale:

$$
\begin{aligned}
I_t &:= \{p \ge 0 : \int \|x\|^p \wedge 1)\, F_t(dx) < \infty\}, & \beta_t &= \inf I_t \\
J_t &:= \{p \ge 0 : (\|x\|^p \wedge 1) * \nu_t < \infty\}, & \gamma_t &= \inf J_t.
\end{aligned}
\tag{5.16}
$$

The set J_t is of the form $[\gamma_t, \infty)$ or (γ_t, ∞); analogously, I_t is of the form $[\beta_t, \infty)$ or (β_t, ∞), and both γ_t and β_t take their values in $[0, 2]$. When t

increases, the set J_t decreases, and it is left-continuous in the sense that $J_t = \cap_{s<t} J_s$, hence γ_t is increasing and left-continuous. The last two properties are of course not true for I_t and β_t, in general.

When X is a Lévy process, $J_t = I_t = I$ and $\gamma_t = \beta_t = \beta$ are non-random and independent of $t > 0$, see (1.49), and β is the Blumenthal-Getoor index. In general, one can interpret γ_t as the "global" Blumenthal-Getoor index on the interval $[0, t]$, and β_t is a "spot" index at time t. Obviously, for each ω we have $\beta_s(\omega) \leq \gamma_t(\omega)$ for Lebesgue-almost all s in $[0, t]$.

The following is proved on page 512.

Theorem 5.17. *For all $t \in [0, T]$ and $p \geq 0$ the variables $1_{J_t}(p)$ and γ_t are $(\mathcal{T}, \mathcal{S})$-pairwise identifiable, when $\mathcal{S}$ is the class of all d-dimensional semimartingales and $\mathcal{T}$ is an arbitrary non-random observation scheme.*

Now we turn to the spot index β_t, when X is an Itô semimartingale. The results are comparable to those for the spot volatility. Namely we need some regularity in time, since the measure F_t, hence the value of β_t at any given fixed time t can be modified in an arbitrary way. For such a restricted class of semimartingale, we have the following result, proved on page 512:

Theorem 5.18. *The spot index β_t and the variables $1_{I_t}(p)$ are $(\mathcal{T}, \mathcal{S})$-pairwise identifiable for all $t \in [0, T)$ and $p \geq 0$, resp. $t \in (0, T]$, for any non-random observation scheme $\mathcal{T}$, and for the class $\mathcal{S}$ of all Itô semimartingales such that, for all $\varepsilon > 0$, the processes $t \mapsto \int (\|x\|^{\beta_t + \varepsilon} \wedge 1) F_t(dx)$ and β_t are all right-continuous, resp. are all left-continuous.*

Theorems 5.17 and 5.18 imply that we can determine, in principle, the "first order" behavior of the measures $\nu(\omega; [0, t] \times dx)$ or $F_t(\omega, dx)$ near 0, in the sense that we know which powers $\|x\|^p$ are integrable near 0. On the other hand, it is fundamental to observe that the restriction of the measure $\nu(\omega; [0, t], dx)$ to the complement of any neighborhood of 0 is *not identifiable*, even when $\mathcal{S}$ is restricted to be a class of Lévy processes, as we saw in the previous section.

5.4   Tests: Asymptotic Properties

As seen above, the estimation problem for a parameter, even a random one, is simple to state. For tests for which the (null and/or alternative) hypotheses are random, it is a different matter; in this section we give an overview of the testing problem when it is "random."

The overall situation is as above: we have a class $\mathcal{S}$ of d-dimensional semimartingales. Each process X in this class may be defined on its own probability space $(\Omega, \mathcal{F}, \mathbb{P})$. However, the random parameter is now replaced by two "random hypotheses," the null and the alternative. That is, for each process X in $\mathcal{S}$ we have two (measurable) disjoint subsets Ω_0 and Ω_1 of the space Ω on which it is defined, and representing respectively the null hypothesis and the alternative hypothesis. As for random parameters, these sets may depend in an implicit way on the law of X or on its characteristics.

Equivalently, we have two "parameters" Z_0 and Z_1 in the previous sense, taking only the values 0 and 1, and such that the product $Z_0 Z_1$ vanishes identically. Then the two hypotheses are the sets $\Omega_0 = \{Z_0 = 1\}$ and $\Omega_1 = \{Z_1 = 1\}$.

Testing the null at stage n amounts to finding a *rejection (critical) region*, that is, a subset $\mathcal{C}_n$ such that if $\omega \in \mathcal{C}_n$ we reject the hypothesis. As before, it should only depend on the observations at stage n, which amounts to saying that $\mathcal{C}_n$ is the set where the discretized process $X^{(n)}$ of (5.14) belongs to a suitably chosen $\mathcal{D}_T$-measurable subset C_n of the Skorokhod space $\mathbb{D}^d$. This notion is of course relative to the discretization scheme $\mathcal{T}$ which is employed (in connection which each X in $\mathcal{S}$). It is then natural to introduce the following definition:

Definition 5.19. *In the previous setting, we say that the sequence $\mathcal{C}_n$ of rejection regions, for testing the null Ω_0 against the alternative Ω_1, is*
- null-consistent *for Ω_0 if $\mathbb{P}(\Omega_0 \cap \mathcal{C}_n) \to 0$ for any X in $\mathcal{S}$,*
- alternative-consistent *for Ω_1 if $\mathbb{P}(\Omega_1 \cap (\mathcal{C}_n)^c) \to 0$ for any X in $\mathcal{S}$.*
When both properties hold, we simply say that the sequence $\mathcal{C}_n$ is consistent.

A consistent sequence of tests "separates" asymptotically the null hypothesis and the alternative hypothesis. As we will see, it is quite often the case that consistent tests can be found. Good as it looks, this does not really solve the problem, however, because it gives absolutely no hint on how close to 0 the probabilities of errors are when n is fixed; this is like consistent estimators, which may in fact converge very slowly and which do not allow at all construction of confidence intervals if there is no associated rate of convergence.

In other words, now comes the problem of determining the size and power of a test $\mathcal{C}_n$ and, to begin with, the mathematical meaning of size and power is *a priori* rather unclear. Consider for example the error of the first kind, at stage n. We mistakenly decide that we are not in Ω_0, that is, the outcome belongs to $\mathcal{C}_n$ and to Ω_0 itself. Measuring the "size" of the error made by this wrong decision, that is the level α_n of the test, can *a priori* be done in several ways.

1. We measure the size on a path basis, that is, for any given ω: the answer is that the size is either 0 or 1, and in any case unknown!

2. We measure it, according to the usual procedure, by the probability that it occurs, that is, $\mathbb{P}(\Omega_0 \cap \mathcal{C}_n)$: this error is always smaller than $\mathbb{P}(\Omega_0)$, even when we take $\mathcal{C}_n = \Omega$ and thus always reject the null hypothesis! So, perhaps a better choice is to "normalize" the error, in such a way that it ranges from 0 in the surely correct decision $\mathcal{C}_n = \emptyset$ (correct from the null viewpoint, of course) to 1 in the surely wrong decision $\mathcal{C}_n = \Omega$. In other words, we may take the size to be $\alpha_n = \mathbb{P}(\mathcal{C}_n \mid \Omega_0) = \frac{\mathbb{P}(\mathcal{C}_n \cap \Omega_0)}{\mathbb{P}(\Omega_0)}$ (assuming $\mathbb{P}(\Omega_0) > 0$, otherwise testing the null Ω_0 makes no real sense).

3. A mid-term choice for the measure of the error, between the two extreme cases above, consists in taking

$$\alpha_n = \sup \left(\mathbb{P}(\mathcal{C}_n \mid A) : \ A \subset \Omega_0, \ \mathbb{P}(A) > 0 \right),$$

where $\mathbb{P}(B \mid A) = \mathbb{P}(A \cap B)/\mathbb{P}(A)$ is the ordinary conditional probability.

Note that the size in the sense 3 cannot be smaller than the size in the sense 2. These two ways of defining the size have one thing in common: for computing the size we have to know $\mathbb{P}$, which seems contradictory with the "model-free" setting we employ here.

Therefore, for us the only feasible possibility is to look at asymptotic properties, when the observed σ-fields $\mathcal{G}_n$ tend as $n \to \infty$ to a σ-field $\mathcal{G}$ (in the sense that $\mathcal{G} = \vee_n \mathcal{G}_n$, up to null sets), with respect to which Ω_0 and Ω_1 are measurable.

So next we take the asymptotic viewpoint, and in view of the previous discussion there are three natural definitions for the asymptotic size:

Definition 5.20. *For a sequence $\mathcal{C}_n$ of tests for the null hypothesis Ω_0, we have the following notions of asymptotic size:*

- *strong asymptotic size:*

$$\alpha = \lim_n \mathbb{P}(\mathcal{C}_n \mid A), \quad \text{for all } A \in \mathcal{F} \text{ with } A \subset \Omega_0 \text{ and } \mathbb{P}(A) > 0$$

- *asymptotic size:*

$$\alpha = \sup \left(\limsup_n \mathbb{P}(\mathcal{C}_n \mid A) : A \in \mathcal{F}, \ A \subset \Omega_0, \ \mathbb{P}(A) > 0 \right)$$

- *weak asymptotic size:*

$$\alpha = \limsup_n \mathbb{P}\left(\mathcal{C}_n \mid \Omega_0\right).$$

The asymptotic and weak asymptotic sizes always exist, the first one being bigger than or equal to the second one. When the strong asymptotic size exists, it is equal to the asymptotic size. Note that, *a priori*, all three kinds of level depend upon the choice of X in $\mathcal{S}$. If we take the supremum of α over all X in $\mathcal{S}$, we obtain a *uniform* asymptotic size. It turns out that in most tests developed in this book, the asymptotic size will actually be a strong asymptotic size, and will also be uniform over the class of semimartingales under consideration.

In practice, we typically go the other way around. We choose some level $\alpha \in (0,1)$ in the usual range, like $\alpha = .05$ or $\alpha = .01$. Then, among all sequences of tests with asymptotic size not bigger than α, we try to find some having the biggest possible power, or asymptotic power. For the notion of asymptotic power, there are two natural counterparts to the definition of the asymptotic size:

$$P_1 = \inf\left(\liminf_n \mathbb{P}(\mathcal{C}_n \mid A) : A \in \mathcal{F}, \ A \subset \Omega_1\right)$$
$$P_2 = \liminf_n \inf\left(\mathbb{P}(\mathcal{C}_n \mid A) : A \in \mathcal{F}, \ A \subset \Omega_1\right).$$

However, the alternative consistency of a sequence of tests is equivalent to saying that $P_1 = 1$, so the version P_1 of the power is kind of weak since when $P_1 < 1$ the tests really behave badly under the alternative. On the other hand, P_2 is typically equal to the asymptotic size of the sequence of tests (as is usual for testing problems with a composite alternative whose closure contains the null, for which the infimum of the power function typically equals the level), and is thus not an adequate measure of the quality of the tests. More sophisticated versions of the power could for example be

$$P_3 = \liminf_n \inf\left(\mathbb{P}(\mathcal{C}_n \mid A) : A \in \mathcal{F}, \ A \subset \Omega_1^n\right),$$

for a suitable sequence Ω_1^n increasing to Ω_1, and at some "distance" from Ω_0 which shrinks to 0. But finding natural sequences Ω_1^n as above seems difficult in the kind of problems considered in this book, and the evaluation of the corresponding power P_3 seems virtually impossible.

In view of this, we will essentially look for sequences of tests such that:

1. The (uniform) asymptotic size is equal to (or not bigger than) some arbitrarily fixed level α, so if n is large enough the actual size of $\mathcal{C}_n$ is approximately equal to (or not bigger than) α.

2. The sequence is alternative-consistent.

5.5 Back to the Lévy Case: Disentangling the Diffusion Part from Jumps

Until the end of this chapter, we consider the problem of asymptotic efficiency, and restrict our attention to Lévy processes, because this problem is still essentially unsolved for discretely observed Itô semimartingales. We suppose that the process is observed at discrete times, but now we ask them to be evenly spread. In other words, we observe the returns

$$\Delta_i^n X \;=\; X_{i\Delta_n} - X_{(i-1)\Delta_n},$$

with Δ_n eventually going to 0, and X will be a Lévy process with characteristic triple (b, c, F). For simplicity, we consider the one-dimensional case only.

As seen in (5.9), the second characteristic c of a Lévy process is always pairwise identifiable, and in fact genuinely identifiable. In the continuous case $F = 0$, and also for Merton's model in Chapter 4, the rate of convergence of optimal estimators has been seen to be $1/\sqrt{\Delta_n}$. In this section, we examine whether the ability to identify c at the same rate, with and without jumps, is specific to Merton's model, or whether it extends to all possible Lévy measures, including those with infinite mass. Intuitively, there must be a limit to how many small jumps can occur in a finite amount of time for this to continue to hold, and in fact this question has two different answers:

1. In a purely parametric situation, with b and F known and c unknown, it is *always* possible (in principle!) to perfectly disentangle the jumps and estimate c with the rate $1/\sqrt{\Delta_n}$, and even the same asymptotic variance, as if there were no jumps.

2. In a semi-parametric situation, with b and F unknown, the problem is more complicated, as we will see in Theorems 5.22 and 5.24 below.

5.5.1 The Parametric Case

We start with the fully parametric case where we know b and F, the only unknown parameter being c. At each stage n, we have a regular statistical experiment where the observed variables are the $[T/\Delta_n]$ i.i.d.

increments distributed as X_{Δ_n}. Hence if $I_\Delta(c;(b,F))$ denotes Fisher's information associated with the observation of the single variable X_Δ, Fisher's information at stage n is simply

$$I(c;(b,F))_n = [\frac{T}{\Delta_n}] I_{\Delta_n}(c;(b,F)). \qquad (5.17)$$

In particular when $b=0$ and $F=0$, so $X=\sqrt{c}\,W$, we have established in (5.7) (with $n=1$ and $\Delta_n=\Delta$) that

$$I_\Delta(c,(0,0)) = \frac{1}{2c^2}. \qquad (5.18)$$

The following gives a complete answer to our questions in the parametric setting (the proof is given on page 513, except for the LAN property whose proof is omitted, since it is not very simple and not really useful for the rest of this book).

Theorem 5.21. *For all $b \in \mathbb{R}$ and all Lévy measures F, and when $c > 0$, we have*

$$\begin{array}{ll} \Delta > 0 & \Rightarrow \quad I_\Delta(c;(b,F)) \leq \frac{1}{2c^2} \\ \Delta \to 0 & \Rightarrow \quad I_\Delta(c;(b,F)) \to \frac{1}{2c^2}. \end{array} \qquad (5.19)$$

Furthermore, for the model in which only c is unknown and we observe X at times $i\Delta_n$ for $i=1,\ldots,[T/\Delta_n]$, if $\Delta_n \to 0$ the LAN property holds at any $c > 0$, with rate $1/\sqrt{\Delta_n}$ and asymptotic Fisher's information $T/(2c^2)$.

Hence in this parametric model there is a sequence of estimators $\tilde{c}_n$ for c such that $\frac{1}{\sqrt{\Delta_n}}(\tilde{c}_n - c)$ converges in law to $\mathcal{N}(0, 2c^2/T)$, and this sequence is efficient. The result is exactly as good as it is when we consider the simple model $X = \sigma W$, and neither the drift nor the jumps impair our ability to efficiently estimate c. Moreover, the MLE is an efficient estimator here. Figure 5.2 illustrates this convergence as the sampling frequency increases.

5.5.2 The Semi-Parametric Case

When b and F are unknown, things are different: in this semi-parametric setting, we need to distinguish jumps from the Brownian part in a somewhat "uniform" way, when F and b vary.

This can be done on the basis of the "uniform" behavior of Fisher's information, where uniformity is relative to reasonable classes of triples (b,c,F), which can be described as follows: we let $A \geq 1$ and ϕ be a

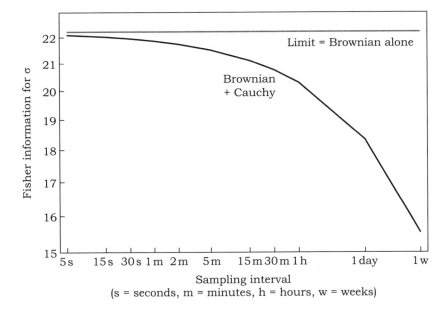

Figure 5.2: Convergence of Fisher's information for $\sigma = \sqrt{c}$ to that of the pure Brownian model as the sampling frequency increases. F corresponds to a Cauchy process.

bounded increasing function on $\mathbb{R}_+$ with $\phi(x) \to 0$ as $x \downarrow 0$, and we set

$$\mathcal{L}_{A,\phi} \;=\; \text{the set of all triples } (b,c,F) \text{ with } 1/A \le c \le A$$
$$\text{and } \textstyle\int_{\{|y| \le x\}} (y^2 \wedge 1)\, F(dy) \le \phi(x) \text{ for all } x > 0.$$

Any Lévy measure satisfies the inequality above for a suitable ϕ, namely $\phi(x) = \int_{\{|y| \le x\}} (y^2 \wedge 1)\, F(dy)$. When $\phi(x) = Ax^{2-\alpha}$ for some $\alpha \in (0,2)$, then $\mathcal{L}_{A,\phi}$ contains all stable processes with index $\beta \le \alpha$, and whose parameters $a^{(+)}$ and $a^{(-)}$ as given in (1.32) satisfy $a^{(+)} + a^{(-)} \le A\left(1 - \frac{2}{\beta}\right)$.

The next theorem contains the second part of (5.19) as a particular case, and is proved on page 513.

Theorem 5.22. *For any $A > 1$ and any function ϕ as above we have, as $\Delta \to 0$,*

$$\sup_{(b,c,F) \in \mathcal{L}_{A,\phi}} \left| I_\Delta(c; (b,F)) - \frac{1}{2c^2} \right| \;\to\; 0. \qquad (5.20)$$

Remark 5.23. *This result is sharp, in the sense that the uniform convergence fails if the function $\phi(x)$ does not go to 0 as $x \to 0$. For example, letting F_β denote the standard symmetric stable Lévy measure with index*

β and parameter $a = 1$ in (1.31), the family $\{F_\beta : \beta \in (0,2)\}$ does not belong to any $\mathcal{G}(\phi)$ as above. And, indeed, if $(2 - \beta_n) \log \Delta_n \to 0$ the numbers $I_{\Delta_n}(c; (0, F_n))$ converge to a limit strictly less than $1/(2c^2)$. In this case the stable processes with index β_n converge in law to a $\sigma'W$, where W is again a standard Brownian motion and $c' = \sigma'^2 > 0$, and the above limit is $1/(2(c + c')^2)$, as if the observed process were $\sqrt{c + c'} \, W$: the information behaves in the limit like that of the superposition of two Gaussian processes, and we cannot identify the variance of one if we only observe the sum of the two.

The lower bound $c \geq 1/A$ is also necessary for (5.20), because of the term $1/2c^2$. In contrast, $\mathcal{L}_{A,\phi}$ puts no restriction on the drift b, which thus does not affect the uniform convergence above. This is because $I_\Delta(c; (b, F)) = I_\Delta(c; (0, F))$.

Theorem 5.22 seems to give us the best possible asymptotic behavior of estimators, at least for the unbiased ones, and in a "uniform" way over large classes of Lévy processes. However, in the present setting the existence of estimators converging with the rate $1/\sqrt{\Delta_n}$, uniformly over the class $\mathcal{L}_{A,\phi}$, is simply *not true*, and the next theorem brings us bad news indeed.

For this we introduce classes of triples, somewhat similar to $\mathcal{L}_{A,\phi}$, where now A is an arbitrary positive constant and r a number in $[0, 2]$:

$$\mathcal{L}(A, r) \;\; = \;\; \text{the set of all triples } (b, c, F) \text{ with } |b| \leq A, \, c \leq A$$
$$\text{and } \int(|x|^r \wedge 1)\,dx \leq A.$$

A sequence of estimators $\widehat{c}_n$ for c, which at stage n only depends on the observations $(X_{i\Delta_n}, i = 0, \ldots, [T/\Delta_n])$, is said to have the *uniform rate* w_n for estimating c, within the class $\mathcal{L}(A, r)$, if the family of variables $w_n(\widehat{c}_n - c)$ is uniformly tight when $n \geq 1$ and when the process X runs through all Lévy processes with characteristic triple in $\mathcal{L}(A, r)$. We then have (see page 515 for the proof):

Theorem 5.24. *Let $A > 0$ and $r \in [0, 2)$. Any uniform rate w_n over the class $\mathcal{L}(A, r)$, for estimating c, satisfies $w_n \leq K\rho_n$ for some constant K, where*

$$\rho_n \;\; = \;\; \begin{cases} 1/\sqrt{\Delta_n} & \text{if } r \leq 1 \\ \left(\frac{1}{\Delta_n} \log\left(\frac{1}{\Delta_n}\right)\right)^{(2-r)/2} & \text{if } r > 1. \end{cases} \qquad (5.21)$$

Moreover, the bound ρ_n is sharp (it is a "minimax rate"), up to a multiplicative constant of course, and in the sense that there exists a sequence of estimators which achieves the rate ρ_n uniformly on the class $\mathcal{L}(A, r)$.

The sets $\mathcal{L}_{A,\phi}$ and $\mathcal{L}(A,r)$ are different, but upon taking $\phi(x) = Ax^{2-r}$ the conditions about the Lévy measure are about the same for the two sets. However, when $r > 1$, the two previous theorems seem in complete contradiction:

1. Theorem 5.22 points toward the existence of estimators converging with the rate $1/\sqrt{\Delta_n}$, uniformly on the class $\mathcal{L}_{A,\phi}$ with ϕ as above.

2. Theorem 5.24 asserts that the uniform rate is at most ρ_n, much slower than $1/\sqrt{\Delta_n}$ if $r > 1$.

So, which is right? Both, of course, but because they indeed solve two very different problems:

1. Theorem 5.22 is basically a *parametric* result, holding uniformly over a non-parametric class of processes; typically, the MLE will achieve this, with the rate $1/\sqrt{\Delta_n}$. But neither the MLE nor any other sequence of estimators which would converge at this rate can be effectively constructed on the sole basis of the observations $X_{i\Delta_n}$ if we have no information on the law of the process other than knowing that its triple belongs to a set such as $\mathcal{L}(A,r)$, or as $\mathcal{L}_{A,\phi}$.

2. Theorem 5.24 is a genuine semi-parametric result. As such, it gives no hint about the "optimal" asymptotic variance, or even about the existence of such a thing. Moreover, as is customary in this kind of setting, it does not prevent the existence of estimators which converge at a faster rate than ρ_n for some, and even for *all*, Lévy processes X in the considered family: as can be seen from the proof, the estimators constructed to show the second part of the theorem are of this sort, converging at a faster rate for each *specified* choice in $\mathcal{L}(A,r)$, but this rate is not uniform, and it has in fact a slower rate than ρ_n when the triple is outside $\mathcal{L}(A,r)$.

Certainly, Fisher's information approach gives overall bounds for the rate and the asymptotic variance, and the former may coincide with the minimax rate, as when $r \leq 1$ above. So if we can come up with estimators achieving the Fisher's information bound we have reached optimality. Otherwise, it seems unreasonable to look for estimators converging faster than the minimax rate. As we will see in Chapter 6, in the case of "general" Itô semimartingales and for estimating the integrated volatility, efficient estimators in Fisher's sense are available for a class of semimartingales satisfying a condition akin to $\mathcal{L}(A, r)$, when $r < 1$. Otherwise, we will construct estimators converging at a rate slower than the minimax rate ρ_n, but "almost" as good, and this is probably the best one can achieve.

5.6 Blumenthal-Getoor Indices for Lévy Processes: Efficiency via Fisher's Information

In the previous section we studied efficient rates for estimating the Gaussian variance c, and here we do the same for the successive BG indices of our Lévy process, and the associated intensity coefficients. For this, we take the viewpoint of Fisher's information, in the same way as in Theorem 5.21 above. As exemplified by comparing Theorems 5.22 and 5.24, the rates obtained in this way are good in a parametric setting, and probably overoptimistic in a genuine semi-parametric situation. Nevertheless, they are useful as overall bounds for the rates in a semi-parametric setting.

In order to be able to compute Fisher's information we need a specific structure of the Lévy process, and the complexity of the computations increases rapidly with the number of BG indices. Since what follows only serves as a benchmark, we thus restrict our attention to a very special, but manageable, situation:

$$X_t = bt + \sqrt{c}\, W_t + Y_t^1 + Y_t^2,$$

where Y^1 and Y^2 are two symmetric stable processes with indices $\beta_1 > \beta_2$, and of course, W, Y^1, Y^2 are independent. Furthermore, each process Y^j depends on a scaling parameter a_j, so that its Lévy measure is

$$F^j(dx) = \frac{a_j \beta_j}{|x|^{1+\beta_j}}\, dx.$$

We have six parameters $(b, c, \beta_1, \beta_2, a_1, a_2)$, among which b is not identifiable, and the behavior of Fisher's information for c is given in Theorem 5.21, so below we are interested in $(\beta_1, \beta_2, a_1, a_2)$ only. A full solution would require the entire Fisher's information matrix, but since our only purpose here is to establish a benchmark we restrict ourselves to considering the diagonal entries only.

Moreover, the relation (5.17) is valid for the full Fisher's information matrix. Therefore, it is enough to establish the asymptotic behavior, as $\Delta \to 0$, of the information for the model in which the single variable X_Δ

is observed. In this setting, the relevant diagonal elements of Fisher's information matrix are denoted as

$$I_\Delta^{\beta_1}, \quad I_\Delta^{\beta_2}, \quad I_\Delta^{a_1}, \quad I_\Delta^{a_2}.$$

Actually, they all depend on $(c, \beta_1, \beta_2, a_1, a_2)$, but not on b.

The essential difficulty in this class of problems is the fact that the density of X_Δ is not known in closed form, since we do not have a closed form for the density of Y_Δ^j (except when $\beta_j = 1$); however, we know its behavior at infinity, which is what matters here, in a very precise way. This allows us to obtain the following theorem, proved on pages 520 et seq.:

Theorem 5.25. *In the previous setting, and as soon as $c > 0$, we have the following equivalences, as $\Delta \to 0$, for the first order BG index and intensity:*

$$I_\Delta^{\beta_1} \sim \frac{a_1}{2(2-\beta_1)^{\beta_1/2}\, c^{\beta_1/2}}\, \Delta^{1-\beta_1/2} \left(\log(1/\Delta)\right)^{2-\beta_1/2}$$

$$I_\Delta^{a_1} \sim \frac{2}{a_1(2-\beta_1)^{\beta_1/2}\, c^{\beta_1/2}\, a_1^2}\, \frac{\Delta^{1-\beta_1/2}}{(\log(1/\Delta))^{\beta_1/2}}.$$

If further $\beta_2 > \beta_1/2$ we also have for the second order BG index and intensity:

$$I_\Delta^{\beta_2} \sim \frac{a_2^2\, \beta_2^2}{2a_1\, \beta_1(2\beta_2-\beta_1)(2-\beta_1)^{\beta_2-\beta_1/2}\, c^{\beta_2-\beta_1/2}}$$
$$\times\, \Delta^{1-\beta_2+\beta_1/2} \left(\log(1/\Delta)\right)^{2-\beta_2+\beta_1/2}$$

$$I_\Delta^{a_2} \sim \frac{2\beta_2^2}{a_1\, \beta_1(2\beta_2-\beta_1)(2-\beta_1)^{\beta_2-\beta_1/2}\, c^{\beta_2-\beta_1/2}}\, \frac{\Delta^{1-\beta_2+\beta_1/2}}{(\log(1/\Delta))^{\beta_2-\beta_1/2}}.$$

Remark 5.26. *The parameter c comes in the denominator of the right sides above, hence the assumption $c > 0$ is essential. When $c = 0$, the leading term of X becomes Y^1, and the behavior of Fisher's information is quite different. One can for example prove that, in this case,*

$$I_\Delta^{\beta_1} \sim \mathcal{I}(\beta_1) \left(\log\frac{1}{\Delta}\right)^2, \qquad I_\Delta^{a_1} \to \frac{1}{a_1^2}\mathcal{I}(\beta_1)$$

for a suitable constant $\mathcal{I}(\beta_1) > 0$.

Remark 5.27. *This theorem provides the (expected) efficient estimation rate for the two pairs of parameters $(\beta_i^{(+)}, a_i^{(+)})$, $i = 1, 2$, in Theorem 5.8, under a very special case of Assumption (5.11): we only have two indices* *(so $\beta_3^{(+)} = 0$) and $\eta = \infty$ and F is symmetrical. If we have more indices (still a finite number), the same analysis is feasible, although significantly more complicated. In contrast, the analysis in the non-symmetrical case, or when η is finite, is probably impossible in full generality.*

As we will see just below, the previous results are compatible with consistent estimators for β_2 and a_2 when $\beta_2 > \beta_1/2$. It says nothing in the case where $\beta_2 = \beta_1/2$, although β_2 and a_2 are still identifiable in this case. Of course, identifiability may occur even when Fisher's information simply does not exist.

Theorem 5.25 is only a partial answer to the global estimation problem of our parameters $(c, \beta_1, \beta_2, a_1, a_2)$. In addition to the asymptotic properties of the off-diagonal entries of Fisher's information, one could wonder whether the LAN property holds separately for each of them (the other being kept fixed), or even globally (but with different rates for each parameter), and whether the MLE is efficient. We do not address these questions here.

However, coming back to the original problem of our discretely observed process and using (5.17), we see that a sequence of estimators is "Fisher-efficient" if we have the following convergences in law:

$$
\left.
\begin{aligned}
\frac{\log(1/\Delta_n)}{\left(\Delta_n \log(1/\Delta_n)\right)^{\beta_1/4}} \left(\widehat{\beta}_1^n - \beta_1\right) &\xrightarrow{\mathcal{L}} \mathcal{N}(0, 1/T\mathcal{I}^{\beta_1}) \\
\frac{1}{\left(\Delta_n^{\beta_1/4} \log(1/\Delta_n)\right)^{\beta_1/4}} \left(\widehat{a}_1^n - a_1\right) &\xrightarrow{\mathcal{L}} \mathcal{N}(0, 1/T\mathcal{I}^{a_1}) \\
\frac{\log(1/\Delta_n)}{\left(\Delta_n \log(1/\Delta_n)\right)^{\beta_2/2-\beta_1/4}} \left(\widehat{\beta}_2^n - \beta_2\right) &\xrightarrow{\mathcal{L}} \mathcal{N}(0, 1/T\mathcal{I}^{\beta_2}) \\
\frac{1}{\left(\Delta_n \log(1/\Delta_n)\right)^{\beta_2/2-\beta_1/4}} \left(\widehat{a}_2^n - a_2\right) &\xrightarrow{\mathcal{L}} \mathcal{N}(0, 1/T\mathcal{I}^{a_2})
\end{aligned}
\right\}
\tag{5.22}
$$

where $\mathcal{I}^{\beta_i}$ and $\mathcal{I}^{a_i}$ are the constants in front of the term involving Δ in the equivalences of the theorem.

We see that the "optimal" rates for estimating β_1 and a_1 are, upon neglecting the logarithmic terms, $1/\Delta_n^{\beta_1/4}$, whereas they are $1/\Delta_n^{\beta_2/2-\beta_1/4}$ for β_2 and a_2: these are much slower than the rate $1/\sqrt{\Delta_n}$ obtained for estimating c.

This is in deep contrast with what happens when $c = 0$, that is, when there is no Brownian part. By virtue of Remark 5.26, in this case the optimal rate for estimating β_1 is $\log(1/\Delta_n)/\sqrt{\Delta_n}$, and it is $1/\sqrt{\Delta_n}$ for a_1. In particular, for β_1 it is (slightly) faster than the usual $1/\sqrt{\Delta_n}$ rate because when we observe the *single* variable Y_Δ^1 and $\Delta \to 0$ we already have consistent estimators for β_1, namely $\widehat{\beta}_{1,\Delta} = -\log(1/\Delta)/\log(|Y_\Delta^1|)$, and the rate of convergence is $\log(1/\Delta)$ in this case. All this follows in a very simple way from the scaling property of Y^1.

5.7 References

The content of Section 5.1 may be found in most textbooks on mathematical statistics, see for example Le Cam and Yang (1990) for a relatively simple account.

There is a large literature devoted to stable processes in finance (starting with the work of Mandelbrot in the 1960s, see for example Rachev and Mittnik (2000) for newer developments). The MLE of stable processes has been studied by DuMouchel (1973a,b, 1975). A variety of other methods have been proposed in the literature for stable processes: using the empirical characteristic function as an estimating equation (see e.g. Press (1972), Fenech (1976), Feuerverger and McDunnough (1981b), Chapter 4 in Zolotarev (1986) and Singleton (2001)), maximum likelihood by Fourier inversion of the characteristic function (see Feuerverger and McDunnough (1981a)), a regression based on the explicit form of the characteristic function (see Koutrouvelis (1980)), and other numerical approximations (see Nolan (1997, 2001)). Some of these methods were compared in Akgiray and Lamoureux (1989).

Section 5.2 follows Aït-Sahalia and Jacod (2012b), while Sections 5.5 and 5.6 follow Aït-Sahalia (2004) and Aït-Sahalia and Jacod (2008), except for Theorem 5.24, which comes from Jacod and Reiß (2013).

For fixed Δ, there exist representations of the density of a stable process in terms of special functions (see Zolotarev (1995) and Hoffmann-Jørgensen (1993)), whereas numerical approximations based on approximations of the densities may be found in DuMouchel (1971, 1973b, 1975), or Nolan (1997, 2001), or Brockwell and Brown (1980).

Part III

Volatility

After all the preliminaries, theoretical considerations and data considerations of the first two parts of the book, we are now ready to start
developing specific statistical methods in the setting of high-frequency
discrete observations. To begin, we consider in the third part of the book
various estimation problems connected with volatility.

That is, we have an Itô semimartingale X, possibly multidimensional,
possibly with jumps, and with second characteristic $C_t = \int_0^t c_s \, ds$. It
is observed at discrete times, over a fixed time interval $[0, T]$, with a
discretization mesh going to 0. Our objects of interest are the integrated
volatility C_T (or C_t, as t varies), and also the "spot" volatility $c = (c_t)$
itself.

Let us mention that, by far, estimation of the integrated volatility
is the topic which has been studied most in high-frequency statistics.
One reason is that, at least when the process X is continuous, it is an
important quantity used for risk management and/or optimal hedging.
Another reason is that in all cases, and as we saw in Chapter 5, the
volatility is always an identifiable parameter, and quite often it is the
only identifiable one.

In Chapter 6 we consider the most basic problem of integrated volatility estimation, when there is no microstructure noise, and when the observations are equidistant. In Chapter 7 the same question is studied when
the observations are contaminated by a noise. Chapter 8 is concerned
with the estimation of the local, or spot, volatility c_t, and in Chapter 9
we study the case when the observation times are no longer necessarily
equidistant, and may be random.

Chapter 6

Estimating Integrated Volatility: The Base Case with No Noise and Equidistant Observations

This chapter covers the various problems arising in the estimation of the integrated volatility, in the idealized situation where the process is observed without error (no microstructure noise) and along a regular observation scheme. In this case the situation is quite well understood, although not totally straightforward when the process has jumps.

The setting is as follows: the underlying process X is a d-dimensional Itô semimartingale (often with $d = 1$), defined on a filtered space $(\Omega, \mathcal{F}, (\mathcal{F}_t)_{t \geq 0}, \mathbb{P})$, and we recall the Grigelionis representation of (1.74):

$$
\begin{aligned}
X_t \;=\; & X_0 + \int_0^t b_s ds + \int_0^t \sigma_s dW_s \\
& + (\delta 1_{\{\|\delta\| \leq 1\}}) \star (\underline{p} - \underline{q})_t + (\delta 1_{\{\|\delta\| > 1\}}) \star \underline{p}_t .
\end{aligned}
\tag{6.1}
$$

Here W is a d'-dimensional Brownian motion and $\underline{p}$ is a Poisson measure on $\mathbb{R}_+ \times E$ with $(E, \mathcal{E})$ an auxiliary Polish space, and with compensator $\underline{q}(dt, dx) = dt \otimes \lambda(dx)$. The "coefficients" are a d-dimensional progressively measurable process b, a $d \times d'$-dimensional progressively measurable process σ, and a d-dimensional predictable function δ on $\Omega \times \mathbb{R}_+ \times E$.

The first two characteristics of X are

$$B_t = \int_0^t b_s ds, \qquad C_t = \int_0^t c_s ds, \qquad \text{where } c_t = \sigma_t \sigma_t^*.$$

Most often, we use the following assumption, in which $r \in [0, 2]$:

Assumption (H-r). *We have (6.1) and*
(i) The process b is locally bounded.
(ii) The process σ is càdlàg.
(iii) There is a sequence (τ_n) of stopping times increasing to ∞ and, for each n, a deterministic *nonnegative function J_n on E satisfying $\int J_n(z)\lambda(dz) < \infty$ and such that $\|\delta(\omega, t, z)\|^r \wedge 1 \leq J_n(z)$ for all (ω, t, z) with $t \leq \tau_n(\omega)$.*

Assumption (H-2) is not much stronger than the property of being an Itô semimartingale, in the sense that, in virtually all models using Itô semimartingales, it is indeed satisfied. (H-r) is basically the same as (H-2), plus the fact that the rth absolute powers of jump sizes are summable over each finite time interval, that is, $\sum_{s \leq t} \|\Delta X_s\|^r < \infty$ almost surely for all $t > 0$. (H-r) for some r implies (H-r') for all $r' > r$, and when X is continuous those assumptions are the same for all r, and reformulated as follows:

Assumption (HC). *We have (6.1) and the process X is continuous, and further the process b is locally bounded and the process σ is càdlàg.*

In this chapter, our aim is to estimate the (random) quantity C_T at a given time T, upon observing the process X without error, at the discrete times $i\Delta_n$ for $i = 0, 1, \ldots, [T/\Delta_n]$, and when the mesh Δ_n of the observation scheme goes to 0. Since the initial value X_0 gives no information at all on C_T, we can equivalently suppose that we observe the returns, or log-returns

$$\Delta_i^n X = X_{i\Delta_n} - X_{(i-1)\Delta_n}. \tag{6.2}$$

Most often, T is a multiple of Δ_n, for example $T = n\Delta_n$, but in some cases one wants to estimate the values C_T and C_S at two (or more) different times, and assuming that both T and S are multiples of Δ_n would be somewhat restrictive.

6.1   When the Process Is Continuous

We start with the simplest case of all: the process X is continuous, that is, of the form

$$X_t = X_0 + \int_0^t b_s ds + \int_0^s \sigma_s dW_s. \qquad (6.3)$$

As a matter of fact, we conduct the estimation of C_t for all $t \geq 0$ simultaneously; this is just as simple as the estimation at a single time, and it provides more insight on the behavior of the integrated volatility C_t as a process. However, an important point is that, when estimating C_t for a particular value t, we do not use observation times $i\Delta_n$ occurring after time t.

We exploit the convergence (1.14) (or (1.61) for the functional convergence) of the *realized volatility*:

$$\widehat{C}(\Delta_n)_t^{jl} = \sum_{i=1}^{[t/\Delta_n]} \Delta_i^n X^j \, \Delta_i^n X^l \overset{\text{u.c.p.}}{\Longrightarrow} C_t^{jl}. \qquad (6.4)$$

Furthermore, Theorem A.15 gives us

Theorem 6.1. *Under Assumption (HC) we have the following functional stable convergence in law*

$$\frac{1}{\sqrt{\Delta_n}} (\widehat{C}(\Delta_n) - C) \overset{\mathcal{L}-s}{\Longrightarrow} \mathcal{W} \qquad (6.5)$$

where $\mathcal{W} = (\mathcal{W}^{jl})_{1 \leq i,j \leq d}$ is a continuous process defined on a very good extension of the space $(\Omega, \mathcal{F}, (\mathcal{F}_t)_{t \geq 0}, \mathbb{P})$ and, conditionally on $\mathcal{F}$, is a continuous centered Gaussian martingale with variance-covariance given by (see page 56):

$$V_t^{ij,kl} := \widetilde{\mathbb{E}}(\mathcal{W}_t^{ij} \, \mathcal{W}_t^{kl} \mid \mathcal{F}) = \int_0^t \left(c_s^{ik} c_s^{jl} + c_s^{il} c_s^{jk} \right) ds. \qquad (6.6)$$

Remark 6.2. *(Optimality)   One does not know whether $\widehat{C}(\Delta_n)_t$ are asymptotically optimal, or "efficient," for estimating C_t, since the very notion of optimality is not even clear in a context as general as (6.3). However, according to the discussion in Subsection 5.1.3, they are efficient for the toy parametric model where $c_t(\omega) = c$ (a constant matrix) and $b_t(\omega) = 0$ (we have the LAN property and $\widehat{C}(\Delta_n)_t$ is the maximum likelihood estimator). For the one-dimensional submodel for which $\sigma_t = f(X_t, Y_t)$ with f a smooth function and Y another continuous Itô*

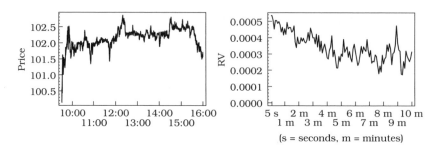

Figure 6.1: The estimator $\widehat{C}(\Delta_n)_t$ at different sampling frequencies (right panel) computed from IBM transactions (left panel) on January 16, 2008.

martingale driven by a Brownian motion independent of X and with non-degenerate diffusion coefficient, Clément et al. (2013) proved a convolution theorem for all possible regular estimators of C_t, with the optimal limiting distribution being conditionally centered Gaussian with exactly the variance given by (6.6); henceforth the estimators $\widehat{C}(\Delta_n)_t$ are also asymptotically efficient within this submodel.

As a consequence, there are good reasons to believe that $\widehat{C}(\Delta_n)_t$ is indeed asymptotically "optimal" for the general non-parametric model (6.3), and it is certainly so in a minimax sense.

Remark 6.3. *(Practical considerations) In financial practice, the estimator $\widehat{C}(\Delta_n)_t$ cannot be employed at a frequency that is too high, due to the presence of market microstructure noise in the data, a topic we will study in detail in Chapter 7. The estimator $\widehat{C}(\Delta_n)_t$ is often constructed from data sampled every few minutes, which presents a number of issues: (i) a large quantity of data is "wasted," resulting in additional sampling error relative to what could be achieved; although the literature often recommends five minutes, the choice of the lower frequency to employ is not clear, and due to smaller sample sizes the difference between the estimators at different sampling frequencies can be large. These effects are illustrated in Figures 6.1 and 6.2. As the frequency decreases, and the sample size correspondingly decreases, the estimator $\widehat{C}(\Delta_n)_t$ tends to be sensitive to the frequency of estimation: implemented at, say, four vs. five vs. six minutes, the estimates turn out to be quite different even though we are only changing by a small amount what is essentially an arbitrary sampling frequency.*

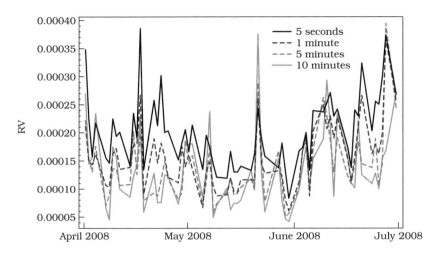

Figure 6.2: The estimator $\widehat{C}(\Delta_n)_t$ at different frequencies, IBM 2008 Q2 filtered data, daily computation of $\widehat{C}(\Delta_n)_t$.

6.1.1   Feasible Estimation and Confidence Bounds

Knowing that $\widehat{C}(\Delta_n)_T$ is an approximation of C_T with an "error" of order of magnitude $\sqrt{\Delta_n}$ is good, but not sufficient for concrete applications. For example, this simple fact does not allow us to construct a confidence interval for C_T at a given level of significance. For this, we also need a precise evaluation of the asymptotic variance which is involved, in order to make the previous CLT "feasible."

Let us first discuss the one-dimensional case, $d = 1$, which by far is the most useful (equivalently, the process X is multidimensional, but we are interested in one of the diagonal parameters C_T^{jj} only). In this case, (6.6) takes the simpler form

$$
\begin{aligned}
\widetilde{\mathbb{E}}\left(\mathcal{W}_T^2 \mid \mathcal{F}\right) &= 2C(4)_T, \quad \text{where} \\
C\left(p\right)_t &= \int_0^t (\sigma_s)^p \, ds = \int_0^t (c_s)^{p/2} \, ds,
\end{aligned}
\tag{6.7}
$$

and in particular, since $C(4)_T > 0$ if and only if $C_T > 0$,

$$
\mathcal{L}\left(\frac{\mathcal{W}_T}{\sqrt{2C(4)_T}} \,\middle|\, \mathcal{F}\right) = \mathcal{N}(0,1)
\tag{6.8}
$$

in restriction to the $\mathcal{F}$-measurable set $\{C_T > 0\}$.

We have very simple consistent estimators for the *quarticity* $C(4)$, and more generally for $C\left(p\right)_t$ for any $p > 0$, under (HC) again. Namely,

Theorem A.2 applied with $k = 1$ and $f(x) = |x|^p$ yields

$$\frac{\Delta_n^{1-p/2}}{m_p} B(p, \Delta_n) \overset{\text{u.c.p.}}{\Longrightarrow} C(p), \quad \text{where } B(p, \Delta_n)_t = \sum_{i=1}^{[t/\Delta_n]} |\Delta_i^n X|^p \quad (6.9)$$

and $m_p = \mathbb{E}(|\Phi|^p)$ denotes the pth absolute moment of the $\mathcal{N}(0, 1)$ variable Φ, and is given by (4.23). Since $m_4 = 3$, if we combine (6.5) and (6.8), we obtain the following result, where for any variable Y and any set $A \in \mathcal{F}$ with $\mathbb{P}(A) > 0$ the notation $\mathcal{L}(Y \mid A)$ stands for the law of the variable Y under the conditional probability $\mathbb{P}(\cdot \mid A)$.

Theorem 6.4. *Under Assumption (HC), if $t > 0$ is fixed, and for all $A \in \mathcal{F}$ such that $\mathbb{P}(A) > 0$ and $A \subset \{C_t > 0\}$, we have*

$$\mathcal{L}(Z_n \mid A) \rightarrow \mathcal{N}(0, 1),$$
$$\text{where } Z_n = \begin{cases} \sqrt{\frac{3}{2}} \dfrac{\widehat{C}(\Delta_n)_T - C_t}{\sqrt{B(4, \Delta_n)_t}} & \text{if } B(4, \Delta_n)_T > 0, \\ 0 & \text{otherwise.} \end{cases} \quad (6.10)$$

This statement is empty when $\mathbb{P}(C_T > 0) = 0$, in which case the estimation of $C_T = 0$ is a trivial and uninteresting problem. It is important to notice that $Z_n = Z_{n,T}$ depends on T. Of course, (6.10) holds for *any* $t > 0$ and not just for the terminal $t = T$, but this convergence cannot hold in any "functional" (in t) sense, even when we have $C_t > 0$ identically for all $t > 0$.

Similar consequences of a Central Limit Theorem such as Theorem 6.1 and of a Law of Large Number such as (6.9) will occur very often in this book, with always the same argument for the proof. This proof illustrates how the stable convergence in (6.5) comes into play, and thus we give a formal proof for this, which will not be repeated later on.

Proof of (6.10). Let $A \in \mathcal{F}$ with $\mathbb{P}(A) > 0$ and $A \subset \{C_T > 0\}$. We set

$$U_n = \frac{1}{\sqrt{\Delta_n}} (\widehat{C}_T(\Delta_n) - C_T),$$
$$V_n = \begin{cases} \sqrt{3\Delta_n / 2B(4, \Delta_n)_T} & \text{if } B(4, \Delta_n)_T > 0 \\ 0 & \text{otherwise.} \end{cases}$$

Since $(2/(3\Delta_n)) B(4, \Delta_n)_T$ converges in probability to $2C(4)_T$ by (6.9) and $C(4)_T > 0$ on A, we deduce that V_n converges in probability to $V = 1/\sqrt{2C(4)_T}$ in restriction to A. We then apply (3.21) and (6.5) to obtain that (V_n, U_n) stably converges in law, in restriction to A, to the

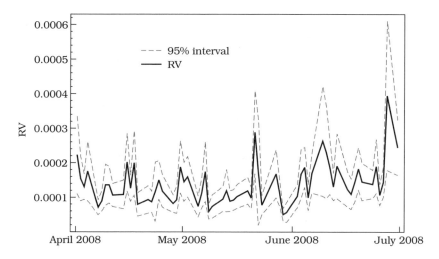

Figure 6.3: The estimator $\widehat{C}(\Delta_n)_t$ and its confidence interval. IBM 2008 Q2 filtered data, daily computation of $\widehat{C}(\Delta_n)_t$, 5 minute frequency.

bidimensional variable $(V, \mathcal{W}_T)$. This implies that, for any continuous bounded function f on $\mathbb{R}$, we have

$$\mathbb{E}(f(Z_n)\, 1_A) = \mathbb{E}(f(U_n V_n)\, 1_A) \to \widetilde{\mathbb{E}}(f(\mathcal{W}_T\, V)\, 1_A).$$

Now, again in restriction to A, the product $\mathcal{W}_T\, V$ is conditionally on $\mathcal{F}$ a centered Gaussian variable with variance $V^2\, \widetilde{\mathbb{E}}(\mathcal{W}_t^2 \mid \mathcal{F})$, which is equal to 1. The right side above is then $\mathbb{E}(f(\Phi))\, \mathbb{P}(A)$ and we deduce that $\mathbb{E}(f(Z_n) \mid A) \to \mathbb{E}(f(\Phi))$, with Φ being an $\mathcal{N}(0, 1)$ variable. This completes the proof.   □

This theorem is the "best" possible, in the following sense: the left side is the conditional law knowing A arbitrary (but fixed, and with a positive probability) in $\mathcal{F}$, whereas the conditional law knowing $\mathcal{F}$ itself is a Dirac mass, because the variables C_T, $\widehat{C}(\Delta_n)_T$ and $B(4, \Delta_n)_T$ are $\mathcal{F}$-measurable. Thus these $\mathcal{F}$-conditional laws *cannot* converge to $\mathcal{N}(0, 1)$.

In practice $B(4, \Delta_n)_T(\omega) > 0$, unless $T < \Delta_n$ or the observed values $X_{i\Delta_n}$ are all equal. Therefore, we slightly (and innocuously) abuse the notation by writing (6.10) as

$$\mathcal{L}\left(\sqrt{\tfrac{3}{2}}\, \frac{\widehat{C}(\Delta_n)_t - C_t}{\sqrt{B(4, \Delta_n)_t}} \;\middle|\; A\right) \to \mathcal{N}(0, 1) \tag{6.11}$$

for all $A \in \mathcal{F}$ with $\mathbb{P}(A) > 0$ and $A \subset \{C_T > 0\}$.

This avoids introducing the auxiliary variables Z_n. In the rest of this book, when a similar situation occurs, we systematically use the formulation (6.11) rather than (6.10).

At this stage we are equipped for constructing a confidence interval for C_T, with a prescribed asymptotic level $\alpha \in (0,1)$. We do it in some detail, because the parameter of interest here is random and thus the situation is not completely customary in statistics. We let z_α be the α-absolute quantile of $\mathcal{N}(0,1)$, that is, the number such that $\mathbb{P}(|\Phi| > z_\alpha) = \alpha$ when Φ is $\mathcal{N}(0,1)$. At stage n the confidence interval will be

$$\mathcal{I}_n = [\widehat{C}(\Delta_n)_T - a_n, \widehat{C}(\Delta_n)_T + a_n],$$
$$\text{with} \quad a_n = z_\alpha \sqrt{\tfrac{2B(4,\Delta_n)_T}{3}}. \tag{6.12}$$

The following property is an obvious consequence of (6.11):

$$\lim_n \mathbb{P}(C_T \notin \mathcal{I}_n \mid A) = \alpha$$
$$\text{for all } A \in \mathcal{F} \text{ with } \mathbb{P}(A) > 0 \text{ and } A \subset \{C_T > 0\}. \tag{6.13}$$

That is, the asymptotic level of this confidence interval is actually α, in the same sense as the strong asymptotic size (or level) of a test, as described in Definition 5.20. Figure 6.3 illustrates the application of Theorem 6.4 to compute pointwise confidence intervals.

6.1.2   The Multivariate Case

We now turn to the multidimensional case $d \geq 2$. Two different questions naturally arise:

1. Find a confidence interval for a given off-diagonal element C_T^{jl} (diagonal entries have been studied above).

2. Find a "confidence region" for the matrix C_T as a whole.

Let us examine the first problem. One needs consistent estimators for the conditional variance $V_T^{jl,jl}$. The simplest way is to make use of Theorem A.8 again. We need to find an integer k and a function f on $(\mathbb{R}^d)^k$ such that $\rho_a^{k\otimes}(f) = a^{jm}a^{lr} + a^{jr}a^{lm}$ for all $a \in \mathcal{M}_d^+$ (the set of all $d \times d$ symmetric nonnegative matrices, recall that ρ_a denotes the normal law $\mathcal{N}(0,a)$ on $\mathbb{R}^d$). Finding such an f with $k = 1$ is not obvious, but using $k = 2$ and $f(x_1, x_2) = x_1^j x_1^m x_2^l x_2^r + x_1^j x_1^r x_2^l x_2^m$ does the job, and we conclude

$$V(\Delta_n)^{jl,mr} \overset{\text{u.c.p.}}{\Longrightarrow} V^{jl,mr}, \quad \text{where}$$
$$V(\Delta_n)_t^{jl,mr} = \tfrac{1}{\Delta_n} \sum_{i=1}^{[t/\Delta_n]-1} \left(\Delta_i^n X^j \, \Delta_i^n X^m \, \Delta_{i+1}^n X^l \, \Delta_{i+1}^n X^r \right. \tag{6.14}$$
$$\left. + \Delta_i^n X^j \, \Delta_i^n X^r \, \Delta_{i+1}^n X^l \, \Delta_{i+1}^n X^m \right).$$

Then, the same argument as for (6.11) gives us:

$$\mathcal{L}\left(\frac{\widehat{C}(\Delta_n)_T^{jl}-C_T^{jl}}{\sqrt{\Delta_n\,|V(\Delta_n)_T^{jl,jl}|}}\,\Big|\,A\right)\to\mathcal{N}(0,1)$$
$$\text{if } A\in\mathcal{F},\ \mathbb{P}(A)>0,\ \ A\subset\{C_T^{jj}>0,C_T^{ll}>0\}. \tag{6.15}$$

(here again the "correct" mathematical statement should be as in (6.10)).

At this stage, the reader should wonder why, in contrast with (6.11), we have written the absolute value $|V(\Delta_n)_T^{jl,jl}|$ above. It is because $V(\Delta_n)_T^{jl,jl}$ may take negative values (in contrast with $V(\Delta_n)_T^{jj,jj}$ when $j=l$), and does so with positive probability if $\mathbb{P}(C_T^{jj}>0,\ C_T^{ll}>0)>0$. This probability goes to 0 as $n\to\infty$, so the result is "mathematically" correct. Nevertheless, for finite samples we might come up with a negative value for $V(\Delta_n)_T^{jl,jl}$; in this case it is thus clearly not a reliable estimator of $V_T^{jl,jl}$ (and for that matter, neither is its absolute value), and we should use another estimator.

We have a similar problem when we try to globally estimate the matrix C_T (question 2 above). Finding confidence regions for a vector or a matrix is typically not a very simple question. But when we have estimators which are consistent, asymptotically mixed normal, and when additionally the consistent estimators for the asymptotic variance are symmetric nonnegative, this is a classical problem and therefore we omit this topic. However, here again we need symmetric nonnegative estimators for the $d^2\times d^2$ matrix with entries $V_T^{jl,km}$, and *this is not the case* of $V(\Delta_n)_T^{jl,km}$.

6.1.3 About Estimation of the Quarticity

In view of what precedes, it becomes necessary to take another view on the estimation of the quarticity. There is even an additional reason for this, which is as follows: apart from the possible lack of positivity, the processes $V(\Delta_n)^{jl,mr}$ have nice asymptotic properties, and in particular enjoy a CLT, with rate $1\sqrt{\Delta_n}$ and a limiting process which is again of the same type as in Theorem 6.1, according to Theorem A.13. However, these processes *never* are asymptotically efficient for estimating $V^{jl,mr}$, as shown by the following example.

Example 6.5. *Consider the simple model* $X=\sigma W$ *where* $d=1$ *and* $\sigma>0$ *is a constant. The quarticity at time 1 is simply* σ^4, *and* $\frac{1}{3\Delta_n}B(4,\Delta_n)_1$ *enjoys a CLT with rate* $1/\sqrt{\Delta_n}$ *and an* $\mathcal{N}(0,32\sigma^4/3)$ *limit. On the other hand, the MLE for* σ^4 *obviously is* $(\widehat{C}(\Delta_n)_1)^2$, *enjoying a CLT with rate* $1/\sqrt{\Delta_n}$ *and an* $\mathcal{N}(0,8\sigma^4)$ *limit: the asymptotic* *variance of the MLE is strictly smaller than the asymptotic variance of the estimators $\frac{1}{3\Delta_n} B(4, \Delta_n)_1$.*

A natural question is thus whether there exist "efficient" ways for estimating $V^{jl,mr}$, where efficiency is taken in the sense of Remark 6.2 (for the toy model of the previous example, and also for the special submodel described in that remark). The answer is yes, and a method consists in using estimators for the "spot volatility" c_t.

These spot estimators will be discussed in detail in Chapter 8, here we simply give the basic definitions. First, we choose a sequence $k_n \geq 1$ of integers satisfying

$$k_n \to \infty, \qquad k_n \Delta_n \to 0, \tag{6.16}$$

and for all $i \geq 0$ we set

$$\widehat{c}(k_n)_i^{jl} = \frac{1}{k_n \Delta_n} \sum_{m=0}^{k_n-1} \Delta_{i+m}^n X^j \, \Delta_{i+m}^n X^l. \tag{6.17}$$

The variable $\widehat{c}(k_n)_i = (\widehat{c}(k_n)_i^{jl})_{1 \leq j,l \leq d}$ takes its values in $\mathcal{M}_d^+$ (the set of nonnegative symmetric $d \times d$ matrices), and the intuition behind this formula will be explained in Chapter 8. Upon applying Theorem A.8 of Appendix A with the functions $g(a) = a^{jl} a^{mr}$ for all possible indices j, l, m, r, we get

$$\overline{V}(\Delta_n)^{jl,mr} \stackrel{\text{u.c.p.}}{\Longrightarrow} V^{jl,mr}, \quad \text{where}$$

$$\overline{V}(\Delta_n)_t^{jl,mr} = \Delta_n \sum_{i=0}^{[t/\Delta_n]-k_n+1} \left(\widehat{c}(k_n)_i^{jm} \widehat{c}(k_n)_i^{lr} \right. \tag{6.18}$$

$$\left. + \widehat{c}(k_n)_i^{jr} \widehat{c}(k_n)_i^{lm} \right).$$

As for (6.15) we now have

$$\mathcal{L}\left(\frac{\widehat{C}(\Delta_n)_T^{jl} - C_T^{jl}}{\sqrt{\Delta_n \overline{V}(\Delta_n)_T^{jl,jl}}} \,\Big|\, A \right) \to \mathcal{N}(0, 1) \tag{6.19}$$

$$\text{if } A \in \mathcal{F}, \ \mathbb{P}(A) > 0, \ A \subset \{C_T^{jj} > 0, C_T^{ll} > 0\}.$$

By construction, all summands for $\overline{V}(\Delta_n)_T^{jl,jl}$ are nonnegative and, even better, for each $s, t \geq 0$ the $d^2 \times d^2$ matrix $\overline{V}(\Delta_n)_{t+s}^{jl,mr} - \overline{V}(\Delta_n)_t^{jl,mr}$ is symmetric nonnegative; hence using these estimators for the (conditional) variance-covariance matrix $V_T^{jl,mr}$ allows us to employ classical methods to derive confidence regions for the matrix-valued integrated volatility C_T.

The rate of convergence of $\overline{V}(\Delta_n)^{jl,mr}$ to $V^{jl,mr}$ depends on the choice of the sequence k_n. However, as seen later in Chapter 8, see in particular

Example 8.23, one has a rate of convergence $1/\sqrt{\Delta_n}$ and also a minimal asymptotic variance, as soon as k_n satisfies $k_n \to \infty$ and $k_n^2 \Delta_n \to 0$, for the modified estimators

$$\overline{V}'(\Delta_n)_t^{jl,mr} = \left(1 - \frac{2}{k_n}\right)\overline{V}(\Delta_n)_t^{jl,mr}, \tag{6.20}$$

and provided that, on top of (HC), the volatility σ_t itself is an Itô semimartingale (possibly with jumps) satisfying (H-2). Note that both $\overline{V}'(\Delta_n)_T^{jl,mr}$ and $\overline{V}(\Delta_n)_T^{jl,mr}$ have the same first order asymptotic behavior.

Another estimator, again based on the spot volatility estimators, is available. Namely, we have

$$\widehat{V}(\Delta_n)^{jl,mr} \overset{\text{u.c.p.}}{\Longrightarrow} V^{jl,mr}, \quad \text{where}$$

$$\widehat{V}(\Delta_n)_t^{jl,mr} = \frac{1}{\Delta_n} \sum_{i=1}^{[t/\Delta_n]-k_n+1} (\Delta_{i+k_n}^n X^j \Delta_{i+k_n}^n X^l - \Delta_n \widehat{c}(k_n)_i^{jl}) \tag{6.21}$$
$$\times (\Delta_{i+k_n}^n X^m \Delta_{i+k_n}^n X^r - \Delta_n \widehat{c}(k_n)_i^{mr}).$$

(To see this, one expands the product in each summand above, and then apply Theorem A.3 for the sum of terms as $\Delta_{i+k_n}^n X^j \Delta_{i+k_n}^n X^l \Delta_{i+k_n}^n X^m \Delta_{i+k_n}^n X^r$ and Theorem A.8 for the sums of the terms which involve $\widehat{c}(k_n)_i$.) Here again, and by construction, the matrix $\widehat{V}(\Delta_n)_t^{jl,mr}$ is symmetric nonnegative, and (6.19) holds with $\widehat{V}(\Delta_n)_T^{jl,jl}$ instead of $\overline{V}(\Delta_n)_T^{jl,jl}$.

So far, the rate of convergence of $\widehat{V}(\Delta_n)^{jl,mr}$ has not been studied, but it is likely to be $1/\sqrt{\Delta_n}$ under the same assumptions as for $\overline{V}(\Delta_n)^{jl,jl}$. These estimators are probably not efficient, but in a sense they are the most intuitive ones among the three families of estimators described so far. Indeed, they look like the empirical covariance of the two time series $\Delta_i^n X^j \, \Delta_i^n X^l$ and $\Delta_i^n X^m \, \Delta_i^n X^r$.

6.2   When the Process Is Discontinuous

Now we turn to the estimation of the same integrated volatility process C_t, when X has the general form (6.1). In this case, the estimators $\widehat{C}(\Delta_n)_t^{jl}$ are not even consistent, since they converge to the total quadratic variation $C_t^{jl} + \sum_{s \le t} \Delta X_s^j \, \Delta X_s^l$. There are basically two methods to overcome this problem, the "truncation" approach and the "multipower" approach.

6.2.1   Truncated Realized Volatility

This method, already mentioned in Section 3.5, amounts to taking the *truncated realized volatility*:

$$\widehat{C}(\Delta_n, u_n)_t^{jl} = \sum_{i=1}^{[t/\Delta_n]} \Delta_i^n X^j \, \Delta_i^n X^l \, 1_{\{\|\Delta_i^n X\| \le u_n\}} \qquad (6.22)$$

where u_n is a suitable sequence going to 0. The idea is that the truncation eliminates the jumps because $u_n \to 0$, whereas if u_n is not "too small," and loosely speaking, it preserves the increments of the continuous part. That is,

$$\text{under (H-2) we have} \quad \widehat{C}(\Delta_n, u_n)^{jl} \overset{\text{u.c.p.}}{\Longrightarrow} C^{jl} \qquad (6.23)$$

as soon as $u_n/\sqrt{\Delta_n \log(1/\Delta_n)} \to \infty$ and $u_n \to 0$. In view of the Lévy modulus of continuity of the Brownian motion (1.4), these conditions on u_n are sharp, but the truncation levels used in this book will always have the following (stronger) property (where $u_n \asymp v_n$ means that both ratios u_n/v_n and v_n/u_n are bounded):

$$u_n \asymp \Delta_n^{\varpi} \quad \text{for some } \varpi \in \left(0, \frac{1}{2}\right), \qquad (6.24)$$

which implies $u_n/\sqrt{\Delta_n \log(1/\Delta_n)} \to \infty$ and $u_n \to 0$, hence (6.23).

Somehow duplicating Section 3.5, we start by explaining, on an intuitive level, why we exactly need $\varpi \in (0, 1/2)$ in (6.24), and the reader can go back to Section 4.2 for additional insight. We consider the case $d = 1$, and the finite jump activity situation when only finitely many jumps occur in $[0, t]$ and $b_t = 0$ and $\sigma_t = \sigma$ is a constant, so $X = \sigma W + J$ where $J_t = \sum_{m \ge 1} Y_m 1_{\{T_m \le t\}}$ is a finite sum. In this situation, the minimum Z_t of all absolute jump sizes between 0 and t is positive and independent of n, as well as the total number N_t of such jumps. Hence for all n large enough any interval $((i-1)\Delta_n, i\Delta_n]$ with $i \le [t/\Delta_n]$ contains a single jump time T_m, or none at all. In the former case, we have $\Delta_i^n X = \sigma \Delta_i^n W + Y_m$, and in the latter $\Delta_i^n X = \sigma \Delta_i^n W$. Moreover, by the Lévy modulus of continuity mentioned above, we have $|\Delta_i^n W| \le 2\sqrt{\Delta_n \log(1/\Delta_n)}$, again for n large enough and all $i \le [t/\Delta_n]$. Then, clearly, if $\varpi > 0$ we have $u_n \to 0$ and thus truncating at u_n eliminates all increments on intervals containing one of the T_m's, whereas all other increments are kept if $\varpi < 1/2$ in (6.24) because then $u_n > 2\sigma\sqrt{\Delta_n \log(1/\Delta_n)}$ for n large.

Moreover, we eventually eliminate only finitely many increments, so $\widehat{C}(\Delta_n, u_n)_t$ is the same as the variable $\widehat{C}(\Delta_n)_t$ of (6.4), computed for σW instead of X, and up to finitely many summands; this does not affect the

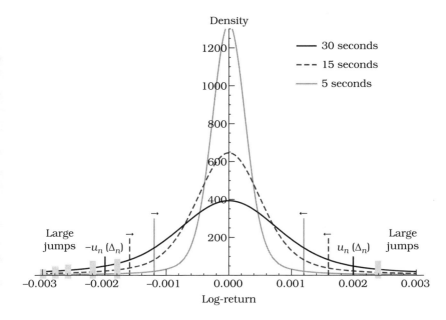

Figure 6.4: Adjusting the truncation rate u_n and the asymptotic elimination of large jumps as $\Delta_n \to 0$.

asymptotic behavior and thus $\widehat{C}(\Delta_n, u_n)_t$ will converge to C_t, which is equal to $\sigma^2 t$ in this case, and even the Central Limit Theorem is not affected.

The behavior of the density of the increments as Δ_n decreases, in the pure Brownian case, is shown in Figure 6.4, illustrating that at some point along the asymptotics all large jumps of the process have been eliminated by the truncation.

If we were taking instead $u_n = \alpha\sqrt{\Delta_n}$ for some $\alpha > 0$, then we would eliminate roughly a proportion of increments due to the Brownian motion equal to the probability $\mathbb{P}(|\Phi| > \alpha/\sigma)$ for a standard normal variable Φ, thus introducing a bias. This is illustrated in Figure 6.5. If we were taking $\varpi > 1/2$, we would eventually eliminate all increments.

Now, the fact that this method also eliminates the jumps in the infinite activity case is less obvious on an intuitive level, but it is true: we will see that the estimators $\widehat{C}(\Delta_n, u_n)_t^{jl}$ are always consistent for estimating C_t^{jl}, but they enjoy an associated CLT with rate $1/\sqrt{\Delta_n}$ only when the degree of activity of the jumps is not too large.

Remark 6.6. *If one does not know whether the process is continuous, one may want to truncate, to be on the safe side. When X is continuous,*

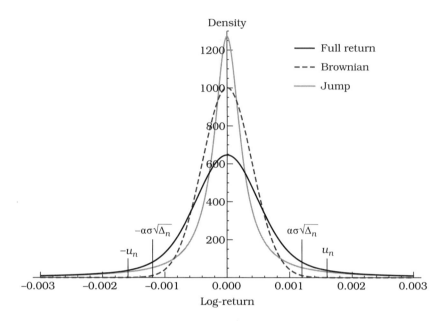

Figure 6.5: Truncating large jumps, at a rate u_n slower than $\sqrt{\Delta_n}$.

for any T we have $\widehat{C}(\Delta_n, u_n)_t = \widehat{C}(\Delta_n)_t$ for all $t \leq T$, as soon as n is large enough. This can be proved rigorously, but also understood by the heuristic considerations above. Thus an unnecessary truncation does no harm.

Remark 6.7. *The truncation in (6.22) is global, in the sense that we truncate the d-dimensional increments $\Delta_i^n X$. One could also truncate the increments of each component separately, the indicator function in (6.22) becoming $1_{\{|\Delta_i^n X^j| \leq u(j)_n, |\Delta_i^n X^l| \leq u(l)_n\}}$, where each sequence $u(j)_n$ is as above. This might be justified if the various components have very different volatilities or different order of magnitudes. Otherwise, there is no special reason to do this. So below we stick to the case where the norm of $\Delta_i^n X$ is truncated.*

Remark 6.8. *(Practical considerations) The condition (6.24) is an asymptotic requirement, necessary for the forthcoming results, but it does not help the statistician to choose the level u_n, especially for finite samples. The stronger condition $u_n = \alpha \Delta_n^\varpi$, for some constant $\alpha > 0$, may look more concrete but still does not really help, because we do not know how to choose α and ϖ, besides $\varpi \in (0, 1/2)$. We will examine how to effectively choose u_n (or, α and ϖ) in Section 6.2.2. In particular we will* *see that it is convenient to express u_n as a given multiple of the "typical" standard deviation of the returns of the Brownian part of the log price, for the asset and the period of time under consideration, and typically this multiple will be between four and eight times the standard deviation.*

Exactly as in the previous section, the convergence (6.23) can be used in a quantitative way only if there is an associated CLT, and this is where things deteriorate. Such a CLT does not hold in general, and for it to be true we need Assumption (H-r) for some $r < 1$: this basically means that the (compensated) sum of "small" jumps of X is *not* too much like a Brownian motion, and it implies that the jumps are summable, that is, $\sum_{s \le t} \|\Delta X_s\| < \infty$ almost surely for all t. The exact formulation is as follows, by virtue of Theorem A.15:

Theorem 6.9. *Under Assumption (H-r) for some $r \in [0, 1)$, and (6.24) with $\frac{1}{2(2-r)} \le \varpi < \frac{1}{2}$, we have the following functional stable convergence in law:*

$$\frac{1}{\sqrt{\Delta_n}} \left(\widehat{C}(\Delta_n, u_n) - C \right) \xLeftrightarrow{\mathcal{L}\text{-}s} \mathcal{W} \tag{6.25}$$

where $\mathcal{W} = (\mathcal{W}^{jl})_{1 \le i, j \le d}$ is the same as in (6.5), and in particular satisfies (6.6).

The optimality of $\widehat{C}(\Delta_n, u_n)_t$ for estimating C_t can be commented on in the same way as in the previous section.

The reader might wonder about the condition $\frac{1}{2(2-r)} \le \varpi < \frac{1}{2}$, implying that the truncation level needs to be small enough. It is always more stringent than (6.24) and impossible to achieve when $r \ge 1$, which explains the restriction $r < 1$. Let us give some insight on the reason of this requirement, in the one-dimensional case. The truncation more or less eliminates all jumps with size bigger than u_n. If (H-r) holds but not (H-q) for some $q < r$, the total contribution to the quadratic variation of the infinitely many jumps of size smaller than u_n has an overall expectation of order of magnitude less than u_n^{2-r}, but bigger than u_n^{2-q}. Thus $\widehat{C}(\Delta_n, u_n)_t$ is approximately equal to C_t plus a term of order $\sqrt{\Delta_n}$ (the "error term" due to the continuous part), plus another term of approximate order bigger than $\Delta_n^{(2-q)\varpi}$, which is due to those small jumps. We want this second error term to be negligible in front of the first one, and this requires $\varpi > \frac{1}{2(2-q)}$. When further we only know that (H-r) holds, this should be true for all $q < r$, hence $\varpi \ge \frac{1}{2(2-r)}$.

To make the CLT in Theorem 6.9 feasible we need consistent estimators for the variance-covariance of $\mathcal{W}_t$, and for this we can modify in an appropriate way all three methods described in the continuous case.

First, in the $d = 1$ case the variables $B(4, \Delta_n)_t$ won't do any more, since by Theorem A.1 they converge to $\sum_{s \leq t} |\Delta X_s|^4$. However, we can again rely upon truncated power functionals, using Theorem A.3 with $k = 1$ and the function $f(x) = |x|^p$ to get, with the notation

$$B(p, \Delta_n, u_n)_t = \sum_{i=1}^{[t/\Delta_n]} |\Delta_i^n X|^p \, 1_{\{|\Delta_i^n X| \leq u_n\}}, \qquad (6.26)$$

and for any $p > 2$,

$$\begin{array}{l} \text{(H-}r) \text{ and } (6.24) \text{ with } r \in [0, 2) \text{ and } \frac{p-2}{2(p-r)} \leq \varpi < \frac{1}{2} \\ \Rightarrow \quad \Delta_n^{1-p/2} \, B(p, \Delta_n, u_n) \overset{\text{u.c.p.}}{\Longrightarrow} m_p \, C(p). \end{array} \qquad (6.27)$$

Then, as for Theorem 6.4, and with the formulation (6.11), we get:

Theorem 6.10. *Under Assumption (H-r) for some $r \in [0, 1)$, and (6.24) with $\frac{1}{2(2-r)} \leq \varpi < \frac{1}{2}$, we have*

$$\mathcal{L}\left(\sqrt{\tfrac{3}{2}} \, \frac{\widehat{C}(\Delta_n, u_n)_T - C_T}{\sqrt{B(4, \Delta_n, u_n)_T}} \, \Big| \, A\right) \to \mathcal{N}(0, 1) \qquad (6.28)$$
$$\text{if } A \in \mathcal{F}, \, \mathbb{P}(A) > 0, \, A \subset \{C_T > 0\},$$

The above choice of u_n is necessary in $\widehat{C}(\Delta_n, u_n)$, but in $B(4, \Delta_n, u_n)$ one could choose a distinct level u_n, which only satisfies the requirement in (6.27). Figure 6.6 illustrates the computation of confidence intervals based on Theorem 6.10.

In the $d \geq 2$ case we can use the following truncated version of (6.18) to get

$$V(\Delta_n, u_n)^{jl, mq} \overset{\text{u.c.p.}}{\Longrightarrow} V^{jl, mq}, \quad \text{where}$$
$$\begin{array}{l} V(\Delta_n, u_n)_t^{jl, mq} = \frac{1}{\Delta_n} \sum_{i=0}^{[t/\Delta_n]-1} \big(\Delta_i^n X^j \, \Delta_i^n X^m \, \Delta_{i+1}^n X^l \, \Delta_{i+1}^n X^q \\ \qquad\qquad + \Delta_i^n X^j \, \Delta_i^n X^q \, \Delta_{i+1}^n X^l \, \Delta_{i+1}^n X^m \big) \\ \qquad\qquad \times 1_{\{\|\Delta_i^n X\| \leq u_n, \, \|\Delta_{i+1}^n X\| \leq u_n\}}. \end{array} \qquad (6.29)$$

Then under the same assumptions as in Theorem 6.10 we have

$$\mathcal{L}\left(\frac{\widehat{C}(\Delta_n, u_n)_T^{jl} - C_T^{jl}}{\sqrt{\Delta_n \, |V(\Delta_n, u_n)_T^{jl, jl}|}} \, \Big| \, A\right) \to \mathcal{N}(0, 1) \qquad (6.30)$$
$$\text{if } A \in \mathcal{F}, \, \mathbb{P}(A) > 0, \, A \subset \{C_T^{jj} > 0, C_T^{ll} > 0\}.$$

Of course, these estimators of the conditional variances suffer from the same drawbacks (lack of positivity) as their non-truncated counterparts for the case where X is continuous.

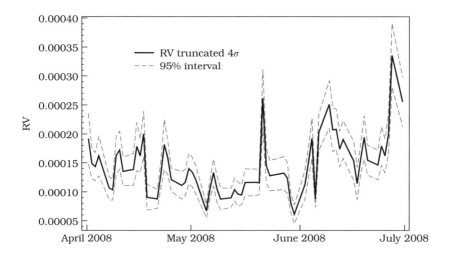

Figure 6.6: The estimator $\widehat{C}(\Delta_n, u_n)_t$ and its confidence interval. IBM 2008 Q2 filtered data, daily computation of $\widehat{C}(\Delta_n, u_n)_t$, 5 minute frequency, with truncation level set at 4σ, see Remark 6.8.

The second possibility consists in using a truncated version of the spot volatility estimators (6.17):

$$\widehat{c}(k_n, u_n)_i^{jl} = \frac{1}{k_n \Delta_n} \sum_{m=0}^{k_n-1} \Delta_{i+m}^n X^j \, \Delta_{i+m}^n X^l 1_{\{\|\Delta_{i+m}^n X\| \leq u_n\}}, \quad (6.31)$$

with u_n as above and k_n as in (6.16). Then Theorem A.8 of Appendix A yields

$$\overline{V}(\Delta_n, u_n)^{jl,mq} \overset{\text{u.c.p.}}{\Longrightarrow} V^{jl,mq}, \quad \text{where}$$

$$\overline{V}(\Delta_n, u_n)_t^{jl,mq} = \Delta_n \sum_{i=0}^{[t/\Delta_n]-k_n+1} \left(\widehat{c}(k_n, u_n)_i^{jm} \widehat{c}(k_n, u_n)_i^{lq} \right.$$
$$\left. + \widehat{c}(k_n, u_n)_i^{jq} \widehat{c}(k_n, u_n)_i^{lm} \right).$$

Here again, it is even better to take

$$\overline{V}'(\Delta_n, u_n)_t^{jl,mq} = \left(1 - \frac{2}{k_n} \right) \overline{V}(\Delta_n, u_n)_t^{jl,mq}$$

(similar to (6.20)) with k_n such that $k_n \to \infty$ and $k_n^2 \Delta_n \to 0$, see Example 8.23 in Chapter 8.

Finally, similar to (6.21), we have

$$\widehat{V}(\Delta_n, u_n)^{jl,mq} \overset{\text{u.c.p.}}{\Longrightarrow} V^{jl,mq}, \quad \text{where}$$

$$\widehat{V}(\Delta_n)_t^{jl,mq} = \frac{1}{\Delta_n} \sum_{i=0}^{[t/\Delta_n]-k_n} \left(\Delta_{i+k_n}^n X^j \, \Delta_{i+k_n}^n X^l - \Delta_n \, \widehat{c}(k_n, u_n)_i^{jl} \right)$$
$$\times \left(\Delta_{i+k_n}^n X^m \, \Delta_{i+k_n}^n X^q - \Delta_n \, \widehat{c}(k_n, u_n)_i^{mq} \right)$$
$$\times 1_{\{\|\Delta_{i+k_n}^n X\| \leq u_n\}}.$$

Then (6.30) holds with $|V(\Delta_n, u_n)_t^{jl,jl}|$ substituted with $\overline{V}(\Delta_n, u_n)_t^{jl,mq}$ or $\overline{V}'(\Delta_n, u_n)_t^{jl,mq}$ or $\widehat{V}(\Delta_n, u_n)_t^{jl,mq}$ (without absolute value). These last estimators are necessarily nonnegative when $(jl) = (mq)$, and considered as $d^2 \times d^2$ matrices they are symmetric nonnegative.

Remark 6.11. *One could show an additional property in Theorem 6.9 (and in Theorem 6.1 as well, in the continuous case). Namely, the convergence in law $\frac{1}{\sqrt{\Delta_n}} (\widehat{C}(\Delta_n, u_n) - C) \overset{\mathcal{L}}{\Longrightarrow} W$ holds uniformly in $X \in \mathcal{S}(r, A)$, for all $A > 0$ and all $r \in [0, 1)$, where $\mathcal{S}(r, A)$ is the class of all semimartingales X satisfying (H-r) with $\|b_t\| + \|c_t\| + \int (\|y\|^r \wedge 1) F_t(dx) \leq A$. This statement is perhaps not very significant from a purely applied viewpoint, but it has great statistical significance: it is indeed similar to the usual semi-parametric statements about "good" estimators, although we are here in a non-classical semi-parametric setting.*

We end this part with a brief look at the situation in which (H-r) holds for some $r \geq 1$, since this is excluded in the previous CLTs. The truncated estimators are still consistent, but the rate of convergence deteriorates, and one no longer has a proper CLT, but only bounds for the rate itself. The result goes as follows:

Proposition 6.12. *Under Assumption (H-r) for some $r \in [1, 2)$, and (6.24) with $0 < \varpi < \frac{1}{2}$, we have the following convergence in probability:*

$$\frac{1}{\Delta_n^{(2-r)\varpi}} (\widehat{C}(\Delta_n, u_n)_T - C_T) \overset{\mathbb{P}}{\Longrightarrow} 0.$$

Exactly as in Remark 6.11, one could even show that the above convergence in probability is uniform in $X \in \mathcal{S}(r, A)$ for any given constant $A > 0$.

By taking ϖ close to $1/2$, we get a rate which approaches $1/\Delta_n^{(2-r)/2}$, as far as the power of Δ_n is concerned. This should be compared with Theorem 5.24, which gives the minimax rate for this question of integrated volatility estimation, in restriction to the class of Lévy processes. This minimax rate is $1/\Delta_n^{1/2}$ when $r = 1$ and

$(\log(1/\Delta_n))^{(2-r)/2}/\Delta_n^{(2-r)/2}$ when $r \in (1, 2)$. Hence the truncated es-timators $\widehat{C}(\Delta_n, u_n)_T$ nearly achieve the minimax rate.

Note that Theorem 5.24 precludes the existence of estimators for C_t which would work with the rate $1/\sqrt{\Delta_n}$, for all $X \in \mathcal{S}(r, A)$ simultane-ously, when $r > 1$. Of course, for any given $X \in \mathcal{S}(r, A)$, a sequence of estimators converging with rate $1/\sqrt{\Delta_n}$ might exist; but such estimators would also depend on the law of X. For example, if X is a Lévy process with known Lévy measure F, the MLE for $C_T = Tc$ has this rate, and other moment estimators as well, but these specific estimators explicitly use F in their construction and usually are not even consistent for a Lévy process with another Lévy measure.

Proposition 6.12 tells us that, even when (H-r) holds for some $r \in [1, 2)$ only, the truncated estimators are reasonably good (and almost as good as possible, in fact). However, since no CLT is available, it seems impossible to derive confidence bounds in that case. Also, note that under the weakest possible assumption (H-2) no rate at all is available.

6.2.2   Choosing the Truncation Level: The One-Dimensional Case

Below we suppose that $d = 1$, since in the multivariate case, the reasoning can be repeated component by component. As we have seen, if $u_n = \alpha \Delta_n^\varpi$ for some $\alpha > 0$, the results hold regardless of the value of α, whereas the value of ϖ is restricted by the assumptions on X. This is obviously due to the asymptotic nature of the result, and for finite (or "small") samples it is a different matter: for any ϖ, by increasing α one increases the empirical value of the estimator $\widehat{C}(\Delta_n, u_n)_T$ from 0 (when α is really small) to the non-truncated value $\widehat{C}(\Delta_n)_T$.

So indeed from a practical viewpoint Δ_n is perhaps small but fixed, and when $u_n = \alpha \Delta_n^\varpi$ the values of α and ϖ are irrelevant *per se*; what matters is the value of u_n itself, in connection with the size Δ_n, the total number of observations n, and the size of the coefficients driving the process X (equivalently, the size of a "typical" increment $\Delta_i^n X$).

As a matter of fact, it is convenient to, and we often do, express the truncation level as a number of standard deviations of the Brownian part of X: the level of truncation u_n is expressed in terms of the number γ of standard deviations of the increments of the continuous martingale part of the process, defined in multiples of the long-term (or average) volatility $\eta^{1/2}$ (that is, η is an "average value" of the squared volatility c_t as t varies). In other words, we write $u_n = \gamma \eta^{1/2} \Delta_n^{1/2}$, so implicitly

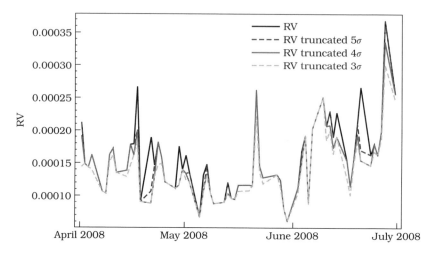

Figure 6.7: The estimators $\widehat{C}(\Delta_n)_t$ and $\widehat{C}(\Delta_n, u_n)_t$ for different truncation levels. IBM 2008 Q2 filtered data, daily computation of the estima-
tors.

γ depends on n and actually should go to ∞ as n increases. Then, we
report the values of the cutoffs u_n in the form of γ (often written as $\gamma\sigma$),
the "number of standard deviations."

We illustrate this in Figure 6.7, which shows the dependence of
$\widehat{C}(\Delta_n, u_n)_t$ on the selection of the truncation level u_n set at 3σ, 4σ and
5σ, with a comparison to the non-truncated $\widehat{C}(\Delta_n)_t$. This has the advantage of providing an easily interpretable size of the cutoff compared
to the size of the increments that would be expected from the Brownian
component of the process; we can then think in terms of truncating at a
level that corresponds to $\gamma = 4, 5, \ldots$, standard deviations of the continuous part of the model. Since the ultimate purpose of the truncation is
either to eliminate or conserve that part, it provides an immediate and
intuitively clear reference point. Of course, this way of expressing the
cutoff level would lose its effectiveness if we were primarily interested in
testing the validity of the asymptotic approximation as the sample size
varies, but for applications, by definition on a finite sample, it seems to
us that the interpretative advantage outweighs this disadvantage.

Now we come back to one possible effective determination of the cutoff
level u_n. Recall the rationale behind truncating increments: eliminate the
jumps, and keep the increments of the continuous part, and this tells us

in which direction to go:

choose u_n as small as possible,
without throwing away too many Brownian increments. $\qquad$ (6.32)

This is still not quite operational, because the aforementioned "Brownian increments" are of course multiplied by the volatility, which is unknown, otherwise there would be no statistical problem. However, the key point in (6.32) is to determine a sort of "lower bound" for u_n such that the last property holds. To get a good insight on this, we can consider the simplified model where X is a continuous Gaussian martingale and the (non-random) volatility c_t is piecewise constant. In this simplified setting we can compare the realized volatility $\widehat{C}(\Delta_n)_T$ (the natural estimator of C_T in this case), with the truncated version $\widehat{C}(\Delta_n, u_n)_T$.

Asymptotically, these two estimators are equally good, since they indeed are *equal* for n large enough, depending on t and ω, as soon as u_n satisfies (6.24). But this gives no hint for finite samples. In this case, provided Δ_n is "reasonably" small (otherwise, no sensible estimation is possible), these two estimators are approximately Gaussian with variance $2\Delta_n \int_0^T c_s^2\,ds$; however, the first one is correctly centered at C_T (up to an error of order Δ_n), the second one is centered (again up to an error of order Δ_n) at $C_T - A_T$, where $A_T = \int_0^T c_s\,g((u_n/\sqrt{c_s\Delta_n}))\,ds$ and $g(u) = \int_{\{|x|>u\}} x^2\,\rho(dx)$ and $\rho = \mathcal{N}(0,1)$. It is thus natural to choose u_n at stage n in such a way that A_T does not exceed a given fraction θ of the standard deviation of the estimation error, that is,

$$\int_0^T c_s\,g(u_n/\sqrt{c_s\Delta_n})\,ds \;\leq\; \theta\left(2\Delta_n \int_0^T c_s^2\,ds\right)^{1/2}.$$

We can choose $\theta = 0.1$ for example (taking θ extremely small does not make much statistical sense here). Moreover, set

$$
\begin{aligned}
c_{\max} &= \sup(c_s : s \in [0,T]),\\
c_{\min} &= \inf(c_s : s \in [0,T]),\\
c_{\text{aver}} &= \frac{1}{T}\int_0^T c_s\,ds.
\end{aligned}
$$

Since g is a decreasing function, the previous inequality is certainly satisfied if the following holds for some number ζ which is bigger than or equal to the ratio $c_{\max}/c_{\min}$:

$$g\left(u_n\sqrt{\zeta/c_{\text{aver}}\,\Delta_n}\right) \;\leq\; \frac{\theta}{\zeta}\sqrt{2\Delta_n/T}. \qquad (6.33)$$

The above model, simplistic as it is, gives us reasonable guidelines for the case of stochastic volatility, provided the volatility does not vary too wildly within the interval of interest $[0, T]$. Suppose that we know (or assume) that the (unknown and random, in the case of a stochastic volatility) ratio $c_{\max}/c_{\min}$ is not more than some known number ζ; such an assumption with $\zeta = 2$ or $\zeta = 3$ seems legitimate when we consider intra-day high-frequency financial data and a horizon T of a day or a week. Then with this kind of heuristics in mind, we can propose the following procedure, in the general case when X has jumps:

1. Find a preliminary estimator c_{aver} of the "average" value of c_s in $[0, T]$. This can be done in several ways. For example one may take

$$c_{\text{aver}} = \frac{1}{T(1 - g(z_\eta))} \, \widehat{C}(\Delta_n, u)_T$$

where u is chosen in such a way that a (relatively large) given proportion η of all increments is thrown away, for example $\eta = 0.25$, and z_η is the absolute η quantile of the standard normal, that is, the number such that $\mathbb{P}(|\Phi| > z_\eta) = \eta$ if Φ is $\mathcal{N}(0, 1)$. Or we may use

$$c_{\text{aver}} = \frac{1}{T} \, C([3], \Delta_n)_T$$

(the estimator based on multipower variations, which will be introduced in the next subsection).

2. Take for u_n the smallest value satisfying (6.33) (this is feasible, since g is a known decreasing function).

We do not claim that this procedure is optimal in any sense, only that it is reasonable. It works well when the assumption that $c_{\max}/c_{\min} \leq \eta$ is likely to hold, together with (H-r) for some $r < 1$.

Remark 6.13. *The above procedure breaks down, of course, in some specific cases. Suppose for example that X is a compound Poisson process with intensity λ and jumps having the law $N(0, a)$. If by luck, or lack of luck, λ and Δ_n are such that $\lambda \Delta_n$ is of order 5 or 10, whereas T/Δ_n is large (say 100 or 1000), then $\widehat{C}(\Delta_n)_T$ and $\widehat{C}(\Delta_n, u_n)_T$ with u_n determined as above will be quite close one to the other, and also quite close to $\lambda a T$, because at our specific observation frequency the process X looks very much like a Brownian motion. When Δ_n becomes much smaller, then $\widehat{C}(\Delta_n, u_n)_T$ will eventually converge to the correct value $C_T = 0$, but when $\Delta_n \sim 10/\lambda$, then $\widehat{C}(\Delta_n, u_n)_T$ is far from 0 and is in fact close to the expected quadratic variation of the whole process.*

Remark 6.14. *Following the discussion above, we can perhaps improve the truncated estimator as follows: Let $\zeta(n,T)$ be the proportion of increments that are thrown away. Since $\widehat{C}(\Delta_n, u_n)_T$ is biased downwards, we could correct it by taking the new estimator*

$$\frac{1}{1 - g(z_{\zeta(n,T)})} \, \widehat{C}(\Delta_n, u_n)_T.$$

When $\zeta(n,T)$ is not small (as in step 1 above), such a correction is advisable. However, when we do the estimation of C_T itself, typically $\zeta(n,T)$ is very small, less or much less than 1%; therefore this correction becomes irrelevant, and it is not even clear that it is going in the right direction — indeed, the increments which are kept are still the sum of a Brownian increment, plus a sum of small jumps, plus of course a (small) drift increment, so its size could very well be systematically bigger in absolute value than the typical Brownian increment.

Remark 6.15. *In any case, using a truncation level u_n which is the same for the whole time period $[0,T]$ is reasonable only when c_s stays in a relatively narrow range over this time interval. Otherwise, one should use an adaptive procedure, which could go as follows:*

1. *Choose $k_n \geq 1$ in such a way that c_s is "not too much varying" on intervals of length $k_n \Delta_n$ (within this restriction, the bigger k_n, the better).*

2. *In the formula (6.22) use a threshold $u_{n,j}$ for the increments $\Delta_i^n X$ such that $(j-1)k_n < i \leq jk_n$, and where $u_{n,j}$ is determined as specified above, with the spot volatility estimator $\widehat{c}(k_n, u_n)_j^n$ of (6.31), constructed on the basis of an a priori arbitrary choice of u_n.*

One could even use an iterative procedure, repeating Step 2 above with the threshold in (6.31) chosen according to the first pass of Step 1.

6.2.3   Multipower Variations

This method is primarily designed for the one-dimensional case $d = 1$. In this case, consider the variables

$$M([p,k], \Delta_n)_t = \sum_{i=1}^{[t/\Delta_n]-k+1} |\Delta_i^n X|^{p/k} |\Delta_{i+1}^n X|^{p/k} \times \ldots |\Delta_{i+k-1}^n X|^{p/k}, \tag{6.34}$$

where $p > 0$ is a real and $k \geq 2$ is an integer (if $k = 1$ we have $M([p,1], \Delta_n) = B(p, \Delta_n)$). We restrict ourselves to the case where all

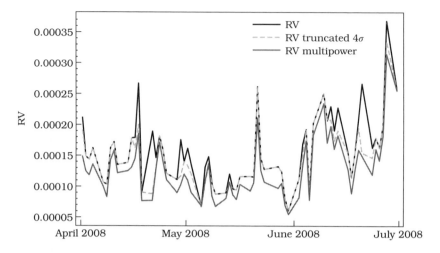

Figure 6.8: The estimators $\widehat{C}(\Delta_n)_t$, $\widehat{C}(\Delta_n, u_n)_t$ truncated at 4σ and $\widehat{C}([k], \Delta_n)_t$ with $p = 2$ and $k = 3$ for different truncation levels. IBM 2008 Q2 filtered data, 5 minute frequency, daily computation of the estimators.

increments in each summand are taken with the same power, although one could also use different powers $p_1, \ldots, p_k$. Such quantities are called *multipower variations*, for an obvious reason.

By virtue of Theorem A.2 we have the following convergence:

$$\text{(H-2) and } p < 2k \;\Rightarrow\; \Delta_n^{1-p/2} \, M([p, k], \Delta_n)_t \overset{\text{u.c.p.}}{\Longrightarrow} (m_{p/k})^k C\,(p)_t. \quad (6.35)$$

Therefore, for any $k \geq 2$ we have the following consistent estimators:

$$\text{(H-2)} \;\Rightarrow\; \widehat{C}([k], \Delta_n) := \frac{1}{(m_{2/k})^k} \, M([2, k], \Delta_n) \overset{\text{u.c.p.}}{\Longrightarrow} C.$$

The reason for this convergence, and more generally for (6.35), is that having two or more "big" jumps within k successive intervals separating observation times is very unlikely, and a single big jump gives a big increment, which is killed by the other (necessarily small) increments in the product, for each summand in (6.34). Figure 6.8 compares the estimator $\widehat{C}([k], \Delta_n)$ with $\widehat{C}(\Delta_n, u_n)$ and $\widehat{C}(\Delta_n)_t$.

The associated CLT requires assumptions significantly stronger than (H-r), although in most models used in practice the non-degeneracy in the first assumption below is satisfied, and if (H-r) holds then (K-r) below also holds with the same real r. For the sake of later use, these assumptions are stated in the d-dimensional case for X; however, we only state (K-r) when $r \in [0, 1]$ (this is simpler than when $r \in (1, 2]$).

Assumption (P). *Both processes c_t and c_{t-} are everywhere invertible.*

Assumption (K-r). *(With $r \in [0,1]$) We have (H-r), the process σ is also an Itô semimartingale satisfying (H-2), and the process $b'_t = b_t - \int_{\{\|\delta(t,z)\| \leq 1\}} \delta(t,z) \, \lambda(dz)$ (which is well defined by (H-r)) is right-continuous with left limits (càdlàg) or left-continuous with right limits (càglàd).*

In (K-r) the requirement on b'_t is rather weak, and the strong requirements are (H-r) and the Itô semimartingale property of the process σ_t.

Remark 6.16. *Assuming (K-r), we have a Grigelionis representation for σ, whose continuous martingale part may be written as $\int_0^t \widetilde{\sigma}_s \, dW_s + \int_0^t \widetilde{\sigma}'_s \, dW'_s$, where W is the same Brownian motion as in (6.1) and W' another Brownian motion independent of W. It follows that we can write*

$$\sigma_t = \sigma_0 + \int_0^t \widetilde{b}_s ds + \int_0^t \widetilde{\sigma}_s dW_s + M_t + \sum_{s \leq t} \Delta \sigma_s \, 1_{\{\|\Delta\sigma_s\| > 1\}}, \quad (6.36)$$

where M is a local martingale with $\|\Delta M_t\| \leq 1$, orthogonal to W, its predictable quadratic covariation process has the form $\langle M, M \rangle_t = \int_0^t a_s ds$ and the predictable compensator of $\sum_{s \leq t} 1_{\{\|\Delta\sigma_s\| > 1\}}$ has the form $\int_0^t \widetilde{a}_s ds$ where $\widetilde{b}$ and M are $d \times d'$-dimensional, and $\widetilde{\sigma}$ is $d \times d' \times d'$-dimensional, and a is d'^4-dimensional and $\widetilde{a}$ is one-dimensional nonnegative. Here, M is the sum of $\int_0^t \widetilde{\sigma}'_s dW'_s$ and the compensated sum of jumps of σ smaller than 1. (K-r) also implies that the processes $\widetilde{b}$, a and $\widetilde{a}$ are locally bounded. The form (6.36) will not be used explicitly, but is given here because it often appears as such in the literature. Moreover, with the previous notation, (K-r) implies that both $\widetilde{\sigma}$ and $\widetilde{\sigma}'$ are càdlàg, although only the càdlàg property of $\widetilde{\sigma}$ is necessary for what follows.

Coming back to our estimation problem, and when $d = 1$, the following result is a particular case of Theorem A.13:

Theorem 6.17. *Assume $k \geq 3$ and Assumptions (P) and (K-2/k). Then we have the following functional stable convergence in law:*

$$\frac{1}{\sqrt{\Delta_n}} \left(\widehat{C}([k], \Delta_n) - C \right) \overset{\mathcal{L}-s}{\Longrightarrow} \mathcal{W}(k), \quad (6.37)$$

where $\mathcal{W}(k)$ is a continuous process defined on an extension of the space $(\Omega, \mathcal{F}, (\mathcal{F}_t)_{t \geq 0}, \mathbb{P})$ and, conditionally on $\mathcal{F}$, is a continuous centered Gaussian martingale with variance

$$\widetilde{\mathbb{E}}((\mathcal{W}(k)_t)^2 \mid \mathcal{F}) = \vartheta(k) \, C(4)_t, \quad (6.38)$$

where $\vartheta(k)$ is the following constant:

$$\vartheta(k) = \frac{1}{(m_{2/k})^{2k}(m_{4/k} - (m_{2/k})^2)}\Big\{(m_{4/k})^{k+1} + (m_{4/k})^k (m_{2/k})^2$$

$$- (2k+1)m_{4/k}(m_{2/k})^{2k} + (2k-1)(m_{2/k})^{2k+2}\Big\}. \quad (6.39)$$

For consistent estimators of $C(4)_T$ we can use (6.26), but it seems more appropriate in this case to also use a multipower-type estimator, that is, to take advantage of the convergence (6.35). There is no special reason to use the same integer k for this as in (6.38) but, if we do, we obtain (same proof as for Theorem 6.4):

Theorem 6.18. *If $k \geq 3$ and under (P) and (K-2/k), we have*

$$\mathcal{L}\Big(\frac{(m_{4/k})^{k/2}}{\sqrt{\vartheta(k)\,M([4,k],\Delta_n)_T}}\,(\widehat{C}([k],\Delta_n)_t - C_T)\,\Big|\,A\Big) \to \mathcal{N}(0,1)$$

if $A \in \mathcal{F}$, $\mathbb{P}(A) > 0$.

Observe that, above, we do not need to specify that A is in the set $\{C_T > 0\}$, since this set is indeed Ω itself because of (P).

We also have a multivariate version, when $d \geq 2$, which is in fact based upon the polarization formula (1.57). We set

$$\widehat{C}([k],\Delta_n)_t^{jl} = \frac{1}{4(m_{2/k})^k}\sum_{i=1}^{[t/\Delta_n]-k+1}\Big(\prod_{m=0}^{k-1}|\Delta_{i+m}^n X^j + \Delta_{i+m}^n X^l|^{2/k}$$

$$- \prod_{m=0}^{k-1}|\Delta_{i+m}^n X^j - \Delta_{i+m}^n X^l|^{2/k}\Big).$$

Then for any $k \geq 2$ we have

$$(\text{H-2}) \quad \Rightarrow \quad \widehat{C}([k],\Delta_n) \overset{\text{u.c.p.}}{\Longrightarrow} C.$$

A CLT holds as well, under the same assumptions as above. However, the conditional variance-covariance of the limiting process is much more difficult to describe, and even more difficult to estimate consistently. We will not elaborate on this, because, as said before, the multipowers are really designed for the one-dimensional case (see the comments in the next subsection).

6.2.4 Truncated Bipower Variations

One can in fact mix the two previous approaches and use "truncated multipower variations." We will do this for bipowers only, for reasons apparent later.

We choose a sequence u_n of truncation levels, satisfying (6.24) as usual. Recalling $m_1 = \sqrt{2/\pi}$, the truncated bipower variation is defined as

$$\widehat{C}([2], \Delta_n, u_n)_t = \frac{\pi}{2} \sum_{i=1}^{[t/\Delta_n]-1} |\Delta_i^n X| \, |\Delta_{i+1}^n X| \, 1_{\{\|\Delta_i^n X\| \leq u_n\}} 1_{\{\|\Delta_{i+1}^n X\| \leq u_n\}}.$$

An application of Theorem A.13 gives us

Theorem 6.19. *Under Assumptions (P) and (K-1), and as soon as u_n satisfies (6.24), we have the following functional stable convergence in law:*

$$\frac{1}{\sqrt{\Delta_n}} \left(\widehat{C}([2], \Delta_n, u_n) - C \right) \overset{\mathcal{L}-s}{\Longrightarrow} \mathcal{W}(2),$$

where $\mathcal{W}(2)$ is as in Theorem 6.17.

At this point, a result analogous to Theorem 6.18 is straightforward, and left to the reader.

Remark 6.20. *If we use the bipower variations without truncation, and again under (P) and (K-1), the previous result fails and Theorem 6.17 does not apply either. However, we still have stable convergence in law of $\widehat{C}([2], \Delta_n)_t$ for each fixed t (or finitely many t's, the functional convergence no longer holds). Moreover, the limit is not $\mathcal{W}(2)_t$, as one could imagine, but it is the sum $\mathcal{W}(2)_t + \mathcal{W}(2)_t'$, where $\mathcal{W}(2)'$ is a (purely discontinuous) process defined on the same extended space as $\mathcal{W}(2)_t$, and taking the form*

$$\mathcal{W}(2)_t' = \sum_{n:\, T_n \leq t} |\Delta X_{T_n}| \, (\sigma_{T_n-} U_n^- + \sigma_{T_n-} U_n^+), \tag{6.40}$$

where $(T_n)_{n \geq 1}$ is a sequence of stopping times weakly exhausting the jumps of X (that is, if $\Delta X_s(\omega) \neq 0$ at time s there is a unique integer $n(\omega)$ such that $T_{n(\omega)}(\omega) = s$), and the variables (U_m^+, U_m^-) are all independent standard normal, defined on the extension, and $\mathcal{F}$-conditionally independent of $\mathcal{W}(2)$. In other words, the limit $\mathcal{W}(2) + \mathcal{W}(2)'$ is of the type described in (1.87), and we will obtain many limiting processes with a form analogous to (6.40) in Chapter 10.

We will not elaborate more on this here; the interested reader can mimic the different methods explained in Subsection 10.2.4 to construct a "feasible" CLT of the form (6.39) (we are here in the case where $\mathcal{W}(2)_t'$ is $\mathcal{F}$-conditionally Gaussian).

6.2.5 Comparing Truncated Realized Volatility and Multipower Variations

So far we have described two (or even three) competing methods for estimating the integrated volatility, in the presence of jumps. There is an immediate difference between truncated realized volatility and multipowers: in the multivariate case, the truncation approach provides estimators $\widehat{C}(\Delta_n, u_n)_T$ which (just as $\widehat{C}(\Delta_n)_T$) are symmetric nonnegative matrices, whereas the multipower estimators $\widehat{C}([k], \Delta_n)_T$ are symmetric but not necessarily nonnegative. This may cause problems when the matrix C_T is replaced by its estimator, especially when this is used as a plug-in inside an optimization problem, such as portfolio choice.

Apart from this difference, which may be considered as a serious drawback for the multipower method in some circumstances, the conditions under which these three methods provide consistent estimators are the same, namely Assumption (H-2). All methods need some tuning parameters, the integer k for multipowers, the truncation levels u_n for the others: in this respect, the multipower method has a strong advantage, since it seems reasonable to take k as small as possible ($k = 2$ in the case of finite activity jumps, and $k = 3$ otherwise). On the other hand, the choice of u_n in the truncated realized volatility or the truncated bipower variation, as discussed in Subsection 6.2.2, is never a totally trivial matter.

When it comes to the associated CLT, we first observe that all methods give us the same convergence rate $1/\sqrt{\Delta_n}$, so they can be compared in terms of the assumptions they need, or in terms of the asymptotic variance they provide:

1. *About the required assumptions*: The multipower method requires (P) and (K-2/3) if we take $k = 3$, and stronger assumptions when $k \geq 4$. The truncated bipower method requires (P) and (K-1). The truncated realized volatility requires (H-r) for some $r < 1$. Now, although formally (K-r) is much stronger than (H-r), for usual models these two assumptions are basically the same. So in practice the multipower method is significantly more restrictive than the other two, which are quite analogous: (P) plus (K-1) is more restrictive than (H-1), but this has little practical importance; conversely (H-r) for some $r < 1$ is more restrictive than (H-1), but since r can be arbitrarily close to 1 the difference is practically insignificant.

2. *About the asymptotic variance*: The asymptotic variances in (6.25)

and (6.37) are $C(4)_T$, multiplied by 2 in the first case and by $\vartheta(k)$ in the second case, and numerical values are

k	2	3	4	5	6	7	8	9
$\vartheta(k)/2$	1.30	1.53	1.69	1.80	1.89	1.96	2.01	2.05

which measure the (quadratic) loss incurred by using the multi-power or truncated bipower (with then $k = 2$ above), *versus* the truncated realized volatility. One may indeed show that the ratio $\vartheta(k)/2$ increases with k, the limit at infinity being $\pi^2/4 \sim 2.465$.

Therefore, from the standpoint of asymptotic estimation variance, the truncated realized volatility is always better than the other two methods.

6.3   Other Methods

Although the approximate quadratic variation is, in the continuous case, the most natural estimator of the integrated variance, a few other estimators have been proposed in the literature, mostly with the aim of eliminating the influence of jumps and/or noise. Below we briefly describe other methods, only in the one-dimensional case $d = 1$ and without proof.

6.3.1   Range-Based Volatility Estimators

Slightly departing from our usual observation schemes framework, we suppose that we can observe the infimum and supremum of the path of the process X within each interval $I(n, i) = ((i - 1)\Delta_n, i\Delta_n]$, that is,

$$\overline{X}_i^n = \sup(X_t : t \in I(n, i)), \qquad \underline{X}_i^n = \inf(X_t : t \in I(n, i)). \qquad (6.41)$$

As we will comment about later, this is somewhat unrealistic in a really high-frequency setting, but in finance it made a lot of sense when only low-frequency observations were available; for example, some forty or thirty years ago, prices were recorded each day, or each hour, *together* with the high and low prices within the day or hour.

The *range* of the path within the interval $I(n, i)$ is the difference

$$R_i^n = \overline{X}_i^n - \underline{X}_i^n.$$

When $X = \sigma W$ is a Brownian motion times a constant $\sigma > 0$, the variables R_i^n are i.i.d. as i varies. They have a density f_n explicitly known as the sum of a series, and moments of the form

$$\mathbb{E}((R_i^n)^p) = \lambda_p \, \sigma^p \, \Delta_n^{p/2},$$

where for all $p \geq 1$ the numbers λ_p are known; for example, $\lambda_2 = 4 \log 2$ and $\lambda_4 = 9\zeta(3)$, where ζ is the Riemann function.

The idea consists in taking the following estimator, at stage n:

$$\widehat{C}^R(\Delta_n)_t = \frac{1}{\lambda_2} \sum_{i=1}^{[t/\Delta_n]} (R_i^n)^2. \tag{6.42}$$

Then as soon as X is a *continuous* Itô semimartingale, we have consistency, that is, $\widehat{C}^R(\Delta_n)_t$ converges in probability to C_t. Moreover, under (HC) plus the continuity of the two processes b_t and σ_t, we have the following stable convergence in law, as $\Delta_n \to 0$.

$$\frac{1}{\sqrt{\Delta_n}} (\widehat{C}^R(\Delta_n) - C) \overset{\mathcal{L}\text{-}s}{\Longrightarrow} \sqrt{\frac{\lambda_4 - (\lambda_2)^2}{2\lambda_2^2}} \, \mathcal{W}, \tag{6.43}$$

where $\mathcal{W}$ has the same description as in Theorem 6.1, in the case $d = 1$.

This is the same as in (6.5), but with a different variance. At this stage, one can standardize and get a convergence similar to (6.11) and construct confidence intervals as in (6.12) and (6.13). In the standardization procedure, for estimating the variable $C(4)_t$ one can use $\frac{1}{3\Delta_n} B(4, \Delta_n)_t$, or (perhaps more appropriately here) the variables

$$\frac{1}{\lambda_4 \Delta_n} \sum_{i=1}^{[t/\Delta_n]} (R_i^n)^4,$$

which also converge in probability to $C(4)_t$.

Remark 6.21. *It is interesting to observe that the rate of convergence is the same $1/\sqrt{\Delta_n}$ for both $\widehat{C}(\Delta_n)_t$ and $\widehat{C}^R(\Delta_n)_t$, but the constant in front of $\mathcal{W}$ is not 1 for the latter, but approximately $1/\sqrt{5}$, implying that the estimation error for $\widehat{C}^R(\Delta_n)_t$ is approximately $1/\sqrt{5}$ the estimation error for $\widehat{C}(\Delta_n)_t$.*

However, the comparison, which rather strongly favors $\widehat{C}^R(\Delta_n)_t$, is not really fair: the observation schemes for the two estimators are indeed quite different.

6.3.2 Range-Based Estimators in a Genuine High-Frequency Setting

In a genuine high-frequency setting we observe the values $X_{i\Delta_n}$, but not the highs and lows (6.41). So instead of the true range R_i^n one has to rely on the following proxies, where $m \geq 2$ is some given integer:

$$\begin{aligned} R(m)_i^n &= \sup(X_{(i+j)\Delta_n} : j = 0, \dots, m) \\ &\quad - \inf(X_{(i+j)\Delta_n} : j = 1, \dots, m). \end{aligned} \tag{6.44}$$

Then, instead of (6.42), we have two possible versions for the estimators:

$$\widehat{C}^{R1}(m, \Delta_n)_t = \frac{1}{\lambda_{m,2}} \sum_{i=1}^{[t/\Delta_n]-m} (R(m)_i^n)^2,$$

$$\widehat{C}^{R2}(m, \Delta_n)_t = \frac{m}{\lambda_{m,2}} \sum_{j=0}^{[t/m\Delta_n]-1} (R(m)_{jm}^n)^2,$$

where $\lambda_{m,2}$ is the expected valued of $(R(m)_1^n)^2$ when $\Delta_n = 1$ and when $X = W$ is a Brownian motion in (6.44). The first estimator uses the $R(m)_i^n$'s on overlapping intervals, the second one does not. Then for any given m we have consistency, and also asymptotic mixed normality, as in (6.43), and under the same assumptions.

However, the asymptotic conditional variance of either one of the two estimators above is bigger than the asymptotic variance of $\widehat{C}(\Delta_n)_t$; this follows from Remark 6.2 for many submodels, including the toy model $X_t = \sigma W_t$ and the "Markov type" model described in that remark; but in fact it *always* holds.

6.3.3 Nearest Neighbor Truncation

Another method, well suited to high-frequency observations when X has jumps, has recently been introduced. It uses ideas in between multipowers and range-based estimators. Namely, one considers the two estimators

$$\widehat{C}^{\mathrm{Min}}(\Delta_n)_t = \frac{\pi}{\pi-2} \sum_{i=1}^{[t/\Delta_n]-1} \min((\Delta_i^n X)^2, (\Delta_{i+1}^n X)^2)$$

$$\widehat{C}^{\mathrm{Med}}(\Delta_n)_t = \frac{\pi}{6-4\sqrt{3}+\pi} \sum_{i=1}^{[t/\Delta_n]-2} \mathrm{med}((\Delta_i^n X)^2, (\Delta_{i+1}^n X)^2, (\Delta_{i+2}^n X)^2),$$

where "$\mathrm{med}(x, y, z)$" stands for the number among the three values x, y, z which is between the other two values. The constants in front of the sums are chosen in such a way that these estimators are consistent: both $\widehat{C}^{\mathrm{Min}}(\Delta_n)_t$ and $\widehat{C}^{\mathrm{Med}}(\Delta_n)_t$ converge in probability to C_t. Moreover, under (K-0) (which implies that the jumps of X have finite activity), we have the following stable convergence in law, as $\Delta_n \to 0$:

$$\frac{1}{\sqrt{\Delta_n}} (\widehat{C}^{\mathrm{Min}}(\Delta_n) - C) \overset{\mathcal{L}-s}{\Longrightarrow} \sqrt{\alpha_{\mathrm{Min}}}\, \mathcal{W}$$

$$\frac{1}{\sqrt{\Delta_n}} (\widehat{C}^{\mathrm{Med}}(\Delta_n) - C) \overset{\mathcal{L}-s}{\Longrightarrow} \sqrt{\alpha_{\mathrm{Med}}}\, \mathcal{W},$$

where $\mathcal{W}$ is as in (6.5) and α_{Min} and α_{Med} are appropriate constants, approximately equal to 1.9 and 1.48, respectively. So the asymptotic estimation variances of these two estimators are bigger than the same for the truncated estimators $\widehat{C}(\Delta_n, u_n)$, by these factors 1.9 and 1.48, and also slightly bigger than the asymptotic variance for the bipower variation, which here can be used because jumps have finite activity. And of course, at this point, one can standardize the statistics and construct confidence intervals as in (6.12) and (6.13).

Therefore, although performing slightly worse than the other methods, the loss in precision is rather small and this method has still reasonable performances. It remains to extend it to infinite activity (for the jumps of X) case, and check whether, if this works out, it does even without the restriction of finite variation of the jumps, which is the main drawback of the truncated and multipowers estimators.

6.3.4 Fourier-Based Estimators

There is still another method, which follows a radically different route. It is based on Fourier transform, or rather, on Fourier series. This method fundamentally supposes that X is continuous, so below we assume (HC).

The method goes as follows. Since it uses Fourier series, the notation would be easier with the terminal time $T = 2\pi$, a convention which is often used in the literature on the subject. However, in order to stay in line with our general setting, we let $T > 0$ be arbitrary here. Below, $i = \sqrt{-1}$ and so we refrain from using i as an index.

There is some arbitrariness in the definition of the Fourier coefficients and for us, for any relative integer $k \in \mathbb{Z}$, the kth Fourier coefficient of the function $t \mapsto c_t^{lm}$ on $[0, T]$ is

$$\mathcal{F}_k(c^{lm}) = \frac{1}{2\pi} \int_0^T e^{-2i\pi kt/T} \, c_t^{lm} \, dt.$$

At stage n, it will be estimated by $\widehat{\mathcal{F}}_k(n, N_n; c^{lm})$ for a suitable sequence N_n of integers going to infinity, and where for any integer N one puts

$$\widehat{\mathcal{F}}_k(n, N; c^{lm}) = \frac{1}{2N+1} \sum_{r=-N}^{N} a_{-r}^{n,l} \, a_{r+k}^{n,m},$$

$$\text{with } a_r^{n,l} = \frac{1}{\sqrt{2\pi}} \sum_{j=1}^{[T/\Delta_n]} e^{-2i\pi rj\Delta_n/T} \, \Delta_j^n X^l. \tag{6.45}$$

The rationale behind this is as follows: suppose that c_t is non-random and continuous, and that X has no drift (recall also that it is continuous). Then, because $\mathbb{E}(\Delta_j^n X^l \Delta_{j'}^n X)$ is approximately $c_{j\Delta_n}^{lm} \Delta_n$ when $j' = j$ and vanishes otherwise, the expectation $\alpha(r, k)_n^{lm} = \mathbb{E}(a_{-r}^{n,l} a_{r+k}^{n,m})$ is easily seen to converge to $\mathcal{F}_k(c^{lm})$, and $\frac{1}{2N+1} \sum_{r=-N}^{N} \alpha(r, k)_n^{lm}$ converges to a quantity $\alpha(k)_n^{lm}$ as $N \to \infty$, which is close to $\mathcal{F}_k(c^{lm})$ when n is big. Of course when r varies the variables $a_{-r}^{n,l} a_{r+k}^{n,m}$ are not independent but they satisfy a kind of Law of Large Numbers: for any given n, $\widehat{\mathcal{F}}_k(n, N; c^{lm})$ itself converges to $\alpha(k)_n^{lm}$ as $N \to \infty$. So, not surprisingly, if we appropriately choose the sequence N_n, we have the consistency

$$\widehat{\mathcal{F}}_k(n, N_n; c^{lm}) \xrightarrow{\mathbb{P}} \mathcal{F}_k(c^{lm}). \tag{6.46}$$

When c_t is random, and in presence of a drift term, the argument is more complicated, but in any case the consistency still holds under (HC) and the continuity of the process c_t, provided $N_n \to \infty$.

We also have a CLT, under the additional assumption that the process σ_t admits a Malliavin derivative with suitable moment bounds (we leave aside the – rather complicated and technical – formulation of the precise assumptions, which can be found in the literature). Then, if N_n is chosen such that $T/N_n\Delta_n$ converges to a limit $a \in (0, \infty)$, the sequence $\frac{1}{\sqrt{\Delta_n}}(\widehat{\mathcal{F}}_k(n, N_n; c^{lm}) - \mathcal{F}_k(c^{lm}))$ converges stably in law to a limit which is, as usual, conditionally on $\mathcal{F}$ a centered Gaussian variable with conditional variance $u(a, k)V_T^{lm,lm}$, with $V_T^{lm,lm}$ given by (6.6) and with $u(a, k)$ depending on k and a only.

At this point, and coming back to integrated volatility, it remains to observe that $C_T^{lm} = 2\pi\mathcal{F}_0(c^{lm})$. This leads us to define

$$\widehat{C}^{\text{Fourier}}(n, N_n)_T^{lm} = 2\pi\,\widehat{\mathcal{F}}_0(n, N_n; c^{lm}) \tag{6.47}$$

as an estimator for C_T^{lm} (note that the complex conjugate of $a_r^{n,l}$ is $a_{-r}^{n,l}$, so the above quantity is necessarily real, and nonnegative when further $l = m$).

Under the same assumptions as above, we then obtain

$$\frac{1}{\sqrt{\Delta_n}}\left(\widehat{C}^{\text{Fourier}}(n, N_n)_T^{lm} - C_T^{lm}\right) \xrightarrow{\mathcal{L}-\text{s}} \alpha(a)\mathcal{W}_T^{lm}, \tag{6.48}$$

where the process $\mathcal{W}^{lm}$ is as in Theorem 6.1, and $\alpha(a)$ is a number, necessarily bigger than or equal to 1, and depending only on the limit a of $T/N_n\Delta_n$ again.

Remark 6.22. *So far, only the CLT for estimating each C_T^{lm} separately is known, although a joint CLT is presumably true as well. Note also that a functional (in time) CLT in this setting is totally out of the question, since the estimators depend in a very special way on the terminal time T, and cannot really be compared one with the others when T varies.*

Remark 6.23. *We always have $\alpha(a) \geq 1$, and $\alpha(a) = 1$ if and only if a is an integer. So if one chooses $N_n = [T/2\Delta_n]$ for example (the so-called*

Nyquist frequency), the Fourier-based estimators achieve asymptotic efficiency for estimating C_T^{lm}, in the same sense as $\widehat{C}(\Delta_n)^{lm}$ does.

We end the subsection with a few concluding comments. Even if we take N_n as in the previous remark, we still have to impose conditions on X, and especially on σ, which are significantly stronger than in Theorem 6.1. Moreover the results break down if X is discontinuous, and there is no obvious way to eliminate the jumps with the Fourier-based method. Since the realized volatility estimator $\widehat{C}(\Delta_n)^{lm}$ is also quite simpler to implement than $2\pi \widehat{\mathcal{F}}_0(n, N_n; c^{lm})$, the latter does not seem to really be competitive for estimating integrated volatility and co-volatility, in the setting of this chapter.

However, we will see later that the Fourier-based estimators still work when there is microstructure noise, and when the observations are irregularly spaced, and even non-synchronous for different components. They also relatively easily provide estimators of the spot volatility, or more precisely of the whole function $t \mapsto c_t$ over $[0, T]$, by Fourier inversion. These questions will be examined in the next three chapters.

6.4 Finite Sample Refinements for Volatility Estimators

As we saw, asymptotic theory predicts that the estimation error for the volatility estimators considered above should be asymptotically mixed normal, whereas the Studentized versions are asymptotically standard normal. However, the simulation evidence suggests that the error distributions of various realized volatility type estimators can be far from normal, for small samples and even for fairly large sample sizes. In particular, they are skewed and heavy-tailed. This non-normality of the estimation error (not to be confused with the non-normality of the estimator itself, which is the rule when stochastic volatility shows up) has an unfortunate and often very significant effect on the confidence interval one may derive for C_t.

Two methods are heavily used in classical statistics for coping with the non-normality for small samples, both being based upon Edgeworth expansion. The general setting is as follows: we have estimators $\widehat{\theta}_n$ for a given one-dimensional parameter θ, such that the estimation error $S_n = w_n(\widehat{\theta}_n - \theta)$, normalized by some sequence $w_n \to \infty$, converges in law to an $\mathcal{N}(0, V)$ variable, for some variance $V > 0$. The aim is to find confidence intervals for θ, with asymptotic level α. Suppose also that we have consistent estimators $\widehat{V}_n$ for V. If Φ is the distribution function of $\mathcal{N}(0,1)$, the confidence intervals

$$\mathcal{I}_n = \left[\widehat{\theta}_n - \frac{z_\alpha}{w_n}\sqrt{\widehat{V}_n}, \widehat{\theta}_n + \frac{z_\alpha}{w_n}\sqrt{\widehat{V}_n}\right], \quad \text{where } 1 - \Phi(z_\alpha) = \frac{\alpha}{2} \qquad (6.49)$$

solve the problem (as we have seen before, see (6.12) and (6.13) for example). The actual level of this confidence interval at stage n is $\alpha_n := \mathbb{P}(\theta \notin \mathcal{I}_n)$, which goes to α as $n \to \infty$. However, for relatively small values of n, α_n may be quite different from α, for two reasons: one is that we replace the (usually) unknown V by $\widehat{V}_n$, the second is that the law of S_n is *not exactly* centered normal.

Now, "under appropriate assumptions" (see below), the ith-cumulant (defined on page 19) of S_n is typically of order of magnitude $\mathrm{Cum}_i(S_n) = O(1/w_n^{i-2})$ for $i \geq 3$, whereas $\mathrm{Var}(S_n) \to V$ and $\mathbb{E}(S_n) \to 0$, and we have an expansion for the distribution function Φ_n of S_n which, given at first and second orders only, is written as

$$\begin{aligned}
\Phi_n(x) &= \widetilde{\Phi}_n\left(\frac{x - \mathbb{E}(S_n)}{\sqrt{\mathrm{Var}(S_n)}}\right)(1 + O(1/w_n^2)) \\
&= \widetilde{\Phi}'_n\left(\frac{x - \mathbb{E}(S_n)}{\sqrt{\mathrm{Var}(S_n)}}\right)(1 + O(1/w_n^3)),
\end{aligned} \qquad (6.50)$$

where

$$\begin{aligned}
\widetilde{\Phi}_n(x) &= \Phi(x)\left(1 - \frac{\mathrm{Cum}_3(S_n)}{6\,\mathrm{Var}(S_n)^{3/2}}(x^2 - 1)\right), \\
\widetilde{\Phi}'_n(x) &= \widetilde{\Phi}_n(x) - \Phi(x)\Big(\frac{\mathrm{Cum}_4(S_n)}{24\,\mathrm{Var}(S_n)^2}(x^3 + 3x) \\
&\quad + \frac{\mathrm{Cum}_3(S_n)^2}{72\,\mathrm{Var}(S_n)^3}(x^5 - 10x^3 + 15x)\Big)
\end{aligned} \qquad (6.51)$$

(those are *Edgeworth expansions*). Taking this into account, one can modify the confidence interval to get an actual level α_n which is closer to the nominal α, in two different ways:

1. Assuming $\mathbb{E}(S_n)$ and $\mathrm{Var}(S_n)$ and $\mathrm{Cum}_3(S_n)$ known, one replaces (6.49) by

$$\mathcal{I}'_n = \left[\widehat{\theta}_n - \frac{z_{n,\alpha}^-\sqrt{\mathrm{Var}(S_n)} + \mathbb{E}(S_n)}{w_n}, \widehat{\theta}_n + \frac{z_{n,\alpha}^+\sqrt{\mathrm{Var}(S_n)} - \mathbb{E}(S_n)}{w_n}\right] \qquad (6.52)$$
$$\text{where } 1 - \widetilde{\Phi}_n(z_{n,\alpha}^-) = \widetilde{\Phi}_n(-z_{n,\alpha}^+) = \alpha/2.$$

The actual level at stage n becomes $\alpha + O(1/w_n)$, much closer to α than previously, and would become $\alpha + O(1/w_n^{3/2})$ if $\widetilde{\Phi}'_n$ were used instead of $\widetilde{\Phi}_n$ (and higher order Edgeworth expansions would lead to actual levels being arbitrarily close to the nominal one).

In practice the moments of S_n are not exactly known, and have to be replaced by estimators, which typically converge at the rate w_n again, so another error of order of magnitude $1/w_n$ should be added, although this additional error is often much smaller than the one occurring if we use $\mathcal{I}_n$ instead of $\mathcal{I}'_n$. So in practice the first order correction is advisable, the second or higher order ones are probably useless.

We should also mention that in some special cases, such as estimation of the mean for an i.i.d. sample, and if one uses the empirical variance to estimate $\mathrm{Var}(S_n)$, then another expansion (with different polynomials in (6.50)) is available and gives us an error which is $O(1/w_n)$.

2. One uses the bootstrap (resampling) method, see for example Hall (1992). We do not explain this method in detail, but it results in the same improvement for confidence intervals as the first order Edgeworth expansion does (and is indeed mathematically based on this expansion). As a rule, it seems that the bootstrap works generally better in practice than the Edgeworth correction, at least in the classical setting of i.i.d. observations.

Of course, we need to say a few words about the "appropriate conditions" under which the expansion (6.50) is valid, and this is where things start deteriorating if we want to apply them to our problem of estimating integrated volatility.

Initially, the validity of the Edgeworth expansion and of the bootstrap were proved for the empirical mean of n i.i.d. variables, and the existence of a fourth moment is enough to imply the result: here θ is the mean, and $w_n = \sqrt{n}$. It also holds under some weak dependence assumption, and versions can be found for non-i.i.d. (but independent or weakly dependent) variables, for both Edgeworth expansion and the bootstrap (one speaks of "wild bootstrap" in this case). So how does this apply to estimation of integrated volatility?

We start with the toy model $X = \sigma W$ and $c = \sigma^2 > 0$ is a constant. In this case, $\widehat{C}(\Delta_n)_T$ is $\Delta_n[t/\Delta_n] = T(1 + O(\Delta_n))$ times the average of the $[T/\Delta_n]$ variables $|\Delta_i^n X|^2/\Delta_n$, which are i.i.d. with the same law as the square of an $\mathcal{N}0, c)$ variable. Therefore what precedes applies to $S_n = (\widehat{C}(\Delta_n)_T - C_T)/\sqrt{\Delta_n}$, and the Edgeworth expansion is still valid for the Studentized version, if we take the empirical variance as the estimator for the variance.

Next, suppose that $X_t = \int_0^t \sigma_s \, dW_s$, with σ_t being time-varying but *non-random*. The variables $|\Delta_i^n X|^2/\Delta_n$ are still independent, but the ith variable has the law of the square of an $\mathcal{N}(0, c_i^n)$ variable, where $c_i^n = \frac{1}{\Delta_n} \int_{(i-1)\Delta_n}^{i\Delta_n} c_s \, ds$, and for any integer $j \geq 2$ we set

$$C(j)_T^n = \Delta_n \sum_{i=1}^{[T/\Delta_n]} (c_i^n)^{j/2},$$

so $C(j)_T^n \to C(j)_T$, with the notation (6.7). Under some regularity conditions on c (unfortunately never given explicitly in the literature, except for the case c is Lipschitz, or piecewise constant), what precedes applies, with $S_n = (\widehat{C}(\Delta_n)_T - C_T)/\sqrt{\Delta_n}$. A simple calculation gives us

$$\mathbb{E}(S_n) = 0, \qquad\qquad \mathrm{Var}(S_n) = 2C(4)_T^n,$$
$$\mathrm{Cum}_3(S_n) = 8\sqrt{\Delta_n}\, C(6)_T^n, \qquad \mathrm{Cum}_4(S_n) = 48\,\Delta_n\, C(8)_T.$$

The first order approximation in (6.50), for instance, takes the form

$$\Phi_n(x) = \widetilde{\Phi}_n\left(\frac{x}{\sqrt{2C(4)_T^n}}\right)(1 + O(\Delta_n)),$$

$$\widetilde{\Phi}_n(x) = \Phi(x)\left(1 - \frac{\sqrt{2\Delta_n}\, C(6)_T^n}{3(C(4)_T^n)^{3/2}}\,(x^2 - 1)\right).$$

Then of course one has to plug in estimators for $C(j)_T^n$, such as $\widehat{C}(j, \Delta_n)_T = m_j \Delta_n^{1-j/2}\, B(j, \Delta_n)_T$. In other words, we use the following approximation for Φ_n:

$$\widehat{\Phi}_n(x) = \Phi\left(\frac{x}{\sqrt{2\widehat{C}(4, \Delta_n)_T}}\right) \tag{6.53}$$
$$\times\left(1 - \frac{\sqrt{2\Delta_n}\, \widehat{C}(6, \Delta_n)_T}{3(\widehat{C}(4, \Delta_n)_T)^{3/2}}\left(\frac{x^2}{2C(4)_T^n} - 1\right)\right).$$

A version of the confidence interval similar with (6.52) (with different notation, though) is as follows:

$$\mathcal{I}_n'' = \left[\widehat{C}(\Delta_n)_T - z_{n,\alpha}'^-\sqrt{\Delta_n},\, \widehat{C}(\Delta_n)_T + z_{n,\alpha}'^+\sqrt{\Delta_n}\right], \tag{6.54}$$
$$\text{where } 1 - \widehat{\Phi}_n(z_{n,\alpha}'^-) = \widehat{\Phi}_n(-z_{n,\alpha}'^+) = \frac{\alpha}{2}.$$

Alternatively, we can use the bootstrap or the wild bootstrap method.

Remark 6.24. *The difference* $\widehat{\Phi}_n(x) - \Phi_n(x)$ *is still of order* $\sqrt{\Delta_n}$, *because* $\widehat{C}(4, \Delta_n)_t - C(4)_t^n = O_P(\sqrt{\Delta_n})$. *However, the difference* $\widehat{\Phi}_n(z_{n,\alpha}'^-) - \Phi_n(z_{n,\alpha}'^-)$ *is of order* $\alpha\sqrt{\Delta_n}$, *much smaller because* α *is typically small.*

So using (6.54) instead of (6.12) significantly improves things, in the sense that the actual level of the new confidence interval is much closer to the nominal α than the level of the previous confidence interval.

For that matter, the bootstrap is a priori much better, since the accuracy becomes of order Δ_n because no estimation of the cumulants is involved.

On the other hand, the triples $(\widehat{C}(j, \Delta_n)_T, j = 2, 4, 6)$ enjoy a joint CLT, as $n \to \infty$, so it is in principle possible to find an Edgeworth expansion for the joint laws of these (centered and normalized) estimators, which translates into an expansion for Φ_n which is different from (6.53) and accurate at order Δ_n, and which involves no unknown parameter.

Now, what happens in the case of a stochastic volatility? We restrict our attention to the one-dimensional case of (6.3), and there are basically two situations:

1. The process σ_t and the driving Brownian motion are *independent* (the "non-leverage" case). According to the discussion of Subsection 3.1.3, we can consider a regular version $\mathbb{Q}(\omega, \cdot)$ of the conditional probability $\mathbb{P}(. \mid \mathcal{G})$, where $\mathcal{G}$ is the σ-field generated by the process σ_T, and we know that the variables S_n defined just above converge in law to $\mathcal{N}(0, 2C(4)_T)$ under $\mathbb{Q}(\omega, \cdot)$ (at least for almost all ω).

   Then of course, as soon as the paths of σ_t are nice enough, one can use the confidence interval (6.54) or the bootstrap, exactly as before. A standing problem is the precise smoothness conditions on the paths of c_t for the validity of Edgeworth expansion or bootstrap: here, typically, the paths of c_t would be Hölder with any index smaller than $\frac{1}{2}$, and the validity of the previous methods has so far not been mathematically established. However, it is likely that these two methods actually improve the determination of the confidence intervals, upon the plain interval given by (6.12), even in that case.

2. The process σ_t and the driving Brownian motion are *dependent*. Going back to the arguments in Subsection 3.1.4 now, we observe that S_n does *not* converge in law to $\mathcal{N}(0, 2C(4)_T)$ under the conditional distributions $\mathbb{Q}(\omega, \cdot)$. In this case the validity of an Edgeworth expansion, hence of a bootstrap procedure as well, is rather questionable, although possibly true. But in any case, this is obviously a topic of further (interesting) inquiries.

6.5   References

Historically speaking, the convergence of the realized volatility toward the integrated volatility is almost as old as stochastic integrals are, and is the cornerstone of the "integration by parts" (or Itô's) formula. The most general statement (Theorem 1.14) goes back to Doléans (1969) for arbitrary martingales and Meyer (1976) for semimartingales, and the CLT for Itô semimartingales is in Jacod and Protter (1998). But for specific submodels, and especially parametric diffusion models, these facts are significantly older with many authors having contributed. On the econometrics side, these facts have been used only relatively recently, mainly since high-frequency data became available. The realized volatility estimator of Section 6.1 has been used in finance (see French et al. (1987)) and popularized in econometrics by Andersen and Bollerslev (1998), Corsi et al. (2001), Andersen et al. (2001, 2003), Barndorff-Nielsen and Shephard (2002), Gençay et al. (2002), Meddahi (2002), see also the survey Andersen and Benzoni (2009). Before that, other estimators based for instance on the range of the process between two successive observation times, for example the high and low daily prices, were widely used and performed much better under the model assumptions than the realized volatility computed on the basis of daily returns; see for example Parkinson (1980), Garman and Klass (1980), Rogers and Satchell (1991), Ball and Torous (1984), Andersen and Bollerslev (1998) or Gallant et al. (1999) or Christensen and Podolskij (2007). Of course, the number of observations in this case is quite small, whereas with high-frequency data one often has from 1,000 to 10,000 times more observations.

When there are jumps, the truncated estimators were introduced by Mancini (2001), see also Mancini (2004, 2009). The corresponding CLT and Proposition 6.12 come from Jacod (2008). The multipower variations were introduced in Barndorff-Nielsen and Shephard (2004), and developed in many subsequent papers, see for example Barndorff-Nielsen and Shephard (2006) and Barndorff-Nielsen et al. (2006). The truncated bipower variations have been studied by Vetter (2010), who also proves the results stated in Remark 6.20. Practical ways for evaluating the truncation level may be found in Shimizu (2010), and an optimal choice is given in Figueroa-López and Nisen (2013) for Lévy processes.

As said above, estimators based on the range have been used before high-frequency methods and data prevailed. The law of the range for the Brownian motion is much older, and due to Feller (1951). The method of Section 6.3.3 is due to Andersen et al. (2012). Fourier-based methods were introduced by Malliavin and Mancino (2002), and the CLTs mentioned above come from Malliavin and Mancino (2009) and Clément and Gloter (2011). See also Cuchiero and Teichmann (2013) for recent developments which allow one to use this method when there are jumps (under (K-r) for some $r < 1$ for the CLT).

Gonçalves and Meddahi (2009) developed an Edgeworth expansion for the RV estimator. Their expansion applies to the Studentized statistic based on the standard RV estimator and it is used for assessing the accuracy of the bootstrap in comparison to the first order asymptotic approach; see also Dovonon et al. (2013). Edgeworth expansions for realized volatility are also developed by Lieberman and Phillips (2008) for inference in the case of long memory.

Corsi (2009) proposed a model where volatility components over different time periods are added together, leading to an autoregressive form for the realized volatility.

Chapter 7

Volatility and Microstructure Noise

In the previous chapter it is assumed that the observations are perfect, in the sense that the value $X_{i\Delta_n}$ of the process of interest at any observation time $i\Delta_n$ is observed *without error*. However, if X_t represents the value at time t of some physical parameter, it is typically observed with a measurement error, which is often assumed to be a "white noise." In finance, as discussed in Chapter 2, things are more complicated, and we can consider at least three types of error, or "noise," in asserting the value of, for example, a log-price X_t at some observation time t.

First, there might be factual errors in recording prices; such errors are reasonably well modeled by using a white noise (not Gaussian, though: most prices are recorded without transcription error, so this type of noise has a high probability of being 0). In any case, these errors are probably relatively easy to eliminate by "cleaning" the data, at the expense of a few missing observations.

Second, there is a rounding error: this type of error occurs in every measurement of any kind, but in physical or biological sciences it is usually small – often negligible – compared to the order of magnitude of the phenomenon which is observed. This is clearly not the case in finance, where prices of an order of magnitude of a few dollars are recorded (and transactions are executed) up to the nearest cent. This results in prices which are often unchanged for a few consecutive observations, a property which is *not* compatible with a semimartingale model with a non-degenerate Brownian part. In other words, the rounding error is a factor

209

which *has to* be taken into consideration, except perhaps in the case of exchange rates (for which many decimal points are given) or indices.

Third, the common paradigm of mathematical finance is that the price is a continuous-time process, and a semimartingale because of the constraint of no arbitrage. However, this is an idealization, since the very existence of a price which would stand *per se*, even in the absence of transactions, is obviously questionable. Since prices are indeed established by the transactions themselves, in between transactions nothing exists, and a continuous-time model really makes sense only as a kind of scaling limit, as transactions become more and more frequent, or as the frequency of observations decreases. The microeconomic mechanism which describes transactions or quotes is called *microstructure*; the scaling limit as time stretches out is the *efficient price*; in between, at high frequency (but not as high as tick-by-tick data), one can consider that the efficient price is polluted by the so-called microstructure *noise*, which is a combination of the difference between the microstructure and its scaling limit, plus the other errors (factual errors, rounding) mentioned before.

As should be clear from the previous discussion, the impact of microstructure noise depends in an essential way upon the frequency of observations. It is considered as negligible, for a typical fairly liquid stock, when the inter-observations time is more than five minutes, or sometimes one minute. It certainly is not so when the inter-observations time is of the order of one, or a few, seconds. This can be seen in a *signature plot*: if one lets Δ_n go to 0, the realized volatility $\widehat{C}(\Delta_n)_T$ of (6.4) at the terminal time T should converge to the integrated volatility when X is continuous, and more generally to the quadratic variation $[X, X,]_T$ when X is an arbitrary semimartingale. However, this is often *not* the case in practice, where $\widehat{C}(\Delta_n)_T$ seems to diverge, increasing when Δ_n decreases, as can be seen in Figure 6.1.

The literature on microstructure noise, and ways to circumvent it, is rather large, but typically focused on specific aspects of the noise, or specific assumptions about it, none of them being overwhelmingly convincing: so far, to our knowledge, there is no comprehensive approach of microstructure noise.

In this chapter, our approach will thus also be quite partial, and fundamentally phenomenological, in contrast with a microeconomical approach. That is, we assume the existence of an underlying (non-observable) efficient price, and what is called *noise* below is by definition the difference between the observed price and the efficient price. Henceforth, it certainly does not apply to tick-by-tick data, even if these were regularly spaced in time (which they are not).

In the whole chapter, with the exception of Section 7.9 in which we briefly indicate how the results extend to the multivariate case, the underlying process X is one-dimensional. We also suppose that it is a continuous Itô semimartingale:

$$X_t = X_0 + \int_0^t b_s \, ds + \int_0^t \sigma_s \, dW_s \qquad (7.1)$$

and make a variety of assumptions, according to the case, but in *all* cases we assume at least (HC).

7.1   Models of Microstructure Noise

As said before, the underlying "efficient" (log-) price process X is one-dimensional, although extending the discussion of this section to the multivariate case would be straightforward.

The assumptions on X are the same as in the previous chapters, depending on the problem at hand, but in all cases it is at least an Itô semimartingale. For simplicity we consider regularly spaced observations, at times $i\Delta_n$ for $i = 0, 1, \ldots$, and again over a finite time interval $[0, T]$. The difference with what precedes is that now we do not observe the variables $X_{i\Delta_n}$, but rather the variables

$$Y_i^n = X_{i\Delta_n} + \epsilon_i^n, \qquad (7.2)$$

where ϵ_i^n is the *noise*. The lower index i for Y_i^n specifies the rank of the observation, the upper index n specifies the frequency, and in principle there is a compatibility relationship expressed by $Y_{i'}^{n'} = Y_i^n$ whenever $i'\Delta_{n'} = i\Delta_n$.

Equation (7.2) is simply a notation, or a definition, of the noise. The problem is now to specify the structure of the noise, and various hypotheses can be considered, which we examine in turn.

7.1.1   Additive White Noise

This is by far the setting which has been studied the most in the literature. In this model, at each stage n, the variables $(\epsilon_i^n)_{i\geq0}$ are *globally independent of the process X* and of the form

$$\epsilon_i^n = \alpha_n \chi_{i\Delta_n} \qquad (7.3)$$

where $(\chi_t)_{t\geq 0}$ is a *white noise*, that is, a family of i.i.d. variables indexed by $\mathbb{R}_+$. Two variants are possible:

1. The law of ϵ_i^n, which by assumption does not depend on i, does not depend on n either (*fixed noise*). In this case, we naturally set

$$\alpha_n = 1 \qquad (7.4)$$

for all n. Of course, the process $(\chi_t)_{t\geq 0}$ is immaterial, only its values at the observation times $i\Delta_n$ are "physically" meaningful. However, the formulation (7.4) is quite convenient, as it automatically ensures the compatibility mentioned above.

2. The law of ϵ_i^n depends on n and shrinks as n increases (*shrinking noise*). In that case, α_n satisfies, as $\Delta_n \to 0$,

$$\alpha_n \to 0. \qquad (7.5)$$

Note that the compatibility relationship between various frequencies no longer holds;

It is customary and not a real restriction in practice to assume that χ_t has finite moments of all orders (although most results only require finite moments up to some order p, typically $p = 4$). Finally, one also assumes that the noise is centered, that is,

$$\mathbb{E}(\chi_t) = 0. \qquad (7.6)$$

This last condition seems restrictive, but one should keep in mind that only the variables Y_i^n in (7.2) are "real," whereas one can always add a constant A to $X_{i\Delta_n}$ and subtract the same A from ϵ_i^n without altering this relationship. Clearly, there is no way of deciding what the value of A might be, hence (7.6) is by no means a restriction in the additive white noise setting.

7.1.2 Additive Colored Noise

In a second kind of setting, one retains the independence between the noise (χ_i^n) and the process X, as well as the zero mean property (7.6), but relax the i.i.d. assumption as i varies. Typically we have (7.4) or (7.5), with a noise process $(\chi_t)_{t\geq 0}$ which is stationary, usually enjoying some mixing properties.

However, even under nice mixing conditions, if the observations are bound to be in a fixed time interval $[0, T]$, essentially *nothing* can be done to "remove" or filter out the noise. For example χ_t could very well be a (centered and mixing) semimartingale by itself, and disentangling the two semimartingales X and χ is a radically impossible task.

In a colored noise setting it is thus more customary to consider the situation where $\epsilon_i^n = \chi_i$ (or $\epsilon_i^n = \alpha_n \chi_i$ in the shrinking noise case), where now the sequence $(\chi_i)_{i \in \mathbb{N}}$ is stationary and (properly) mixing. In this case, disentangling the noise from the underlying is in principle possible, although now the compatibility property between different observation frequencies is violated.

We will not elaborate on this kind of model in this book. The literature is only beginning on this subject, and most statistical questions remain unanswered so far.

7.1.3   Pure Rounding Noise

Another possibility is to consider a "pure rounding noise." This model has the advantage that it matches the way financial data are collected: observed prices are multipleS of a tick size, which can be \$0.01, \$1/32, etc. One implication of rounding is that both observed returns and volatility can be zero over short intervals, an outcome that has zero probability of occurrence in any model that contains a Brownian semimartingale component and with non-noisy observations.

In one version, we take the closest from below rounded-off value of the price. This amounts to having a fixed level of rounding $\beta > 0$, and observing

$$Y_i^n = \beta \left[X_{i\Delta_n} / \beta \right], \tag{7.7}$$

where as usual $[x]$ stands for the *integer part* of $x \in \mathbb{R}$. Then the error ϵ_i^n is defined by (7.2). We could also take the upper rounded-off value $\beta([X_{i\Delta_n}/\beta] + 1)$, or the "middle" value $\beta([X_{i\Delta_n}/\beta] + 1/2)$: this is purely a question of convention, and the formulation (7.7) seems to be the simplest one, from a notational viewpoint. Here again, a variant consists in observing Y_i^n as above, with a rounding level $\beta = \beta_n$ going to 0 as $\Delta_n \to 0$ (a shrinking noise again).

The rounding noise is very different from the additive noise, in many respects. An obvious difference is that, in contrast with the additive noise, it is *not* independent from X: it is even a deterministic and known function of X. A second obvious difference is that the rounding noise is not centered, even if one takes the "middle value" above instead of the lower rounded-off value. A third, less obvious but quite important and rather unfortunate difference is the following one:

> If the observations are given by (7.7), the quadratic
> variation $[X, X]_T$ and the integrated volatility C_T are   (7.8)
> not pairwise-identifiable in the sense of Definition 5.11.

The reason for this is as follows: suppose that we observe the whole path $t \mapsto X_t$ on $[0, T]$, up to rounding. This means that we observe the process $Y_t = \beta [X_t/\beta]$ or, equivalently, the random sets $B(m) = \{t \in [0, T] : m\beta \leq X_t < (m + 1)\beta\}$ for all relative integers m. Knowing all these random sets does not allow us to reconstruct the path $t \mapsto X_t$ itself since we cannot say anything about its behavior when it is between two successive levels $m\beta$ and $(m + 1)\beta$. There is simply *no way* of circumventing this problem: no consistent estimators for the integrated volatility exist, in the case of pure rounding at a fixed level β.

On a more mathematical level, in case X is continuous, observing all sets $B(m)$ amounts to observing the local times $L_t^{m\beta}$ for all $t \in [0, T]$ and $m \in \mathbb{Z}$, so only those local times are identifiable; see (8.53) in the next chapter for a precise definition of local times; in this chapter we only need to know that the local time L^x at level x is an adapted continuous increasing process which is constant on each time interval $[s, t]$ for which $X_u \neq x$ for all $u \in [s, t]$.

Of course, when the rounding level $\beta = \beta_n$ goes to 0 as $\Delta_n \to 0$, (7.8) becomes wrong: all quantities which are identifiable in the perfect observation case are also identifiable under pure rounding, when the rounding level is shrinking. When β_n goes fast enough to 0, we also have that all estimators for the integrated volatility, or for any other identifiable quantity, have exactly the same behavior when we plug in the "true" values $X_{i\Delta_n}$ or the rounded-off variables Y_i^n: it turns out that this holds as soon as $\beta_n/\sqrt{\Delta_n} \to 0$.

When $\beta_n/\sqrt{\Delta_n} \to 0$ fails, but still $\beta_n \to 0$, there are so far very few concrete results, giving for example estimators for the integrated volatility, together with a precise asymptotic behavior. In addition, most of the available results suppose that the process X is a (continuous) diffusion process, and the Markov property usually plays a key role in the proofs.

Remark 7.1. *Rounding affects the price itself, whereas the process X is usually the log-price. Consequently, instead of (7.7) one should rather consider*

$$Y_i'^n = \log\left(\beta' \left[e^{X_{i\Delta_n}}/\beta'\right]\right),   (7.9)$$

where β' is the real rounding level (=1 cent for example). However, as long as the price e^{X_t} stays in some interval $[A - a, A + a]$ with a/A and β/a "small," the right hand sides in (7.7) and (7.9) are very close to one another if $\beta = \beta'/A$. Therefore, in practice it is very often the case that one can use the (simpler) version (7.7) instead of the (more correct) version (7.9).

The same caveat should be made about additive noise as well: it should contaminate the price e^{X_t} itself. If χ'_t is the additive noise contaminating the price (in the non-shrinking case, say), instead of $Y_i^n = X_{i\Delta_n} + \chi_{i\Delta_n}$ one really observes

$$Y_i^n = \log\left(e^{X_{i\Delta_n}} + \chi'_{i\Delta_n}\right).$$

When the noise is small in comparison with the price, this is approximately $Y_i^n = X_{i\Delta_n} + \chi'_{i\Delta_n} e^{-X_{i\Delta_n}}$. The "true" noise is thus $\chi_{i\Delta_n} = \chi'_{i\Delta_n} e^{-X_{i\Delta_n}}$, which is no longer a white noise. However, it is reasonably close to an independent white noise within any time interval in which the price does not vary "too much."

7.1.4 A Mixed Case: Rounded White Noise

Now, rounding is a prevalent feature of financial data, and assuming that the rounding level is small (that is, we are in the asymptotic regime where $\beta_n \to 0$) is probably not adequate, in front of typical price time series observed at ultra-high frequency (say, every few seconds or higher). On the other hand, "pure" rounding, as described just above, implies that all statistical problems studied in this book have *no* solutions.

It is, however, possible to consider an intermediary situation, which combines rounding and the fact that the efficient price is only a kind of limit of the "real price," taken as the transaction frequency goes to infinity. Since we are not exactly in the limiting regime, the difference between efficient and real prices is a first kind of noise, more or less independent of the efficient price itself; and then, on top of this, the "real price" is rounded off. Such considerations lead us to consider a model where the actual observations take the form

$$Y_i^n = \beta\left[(X_{i\Delta_n} + \chi_{i\Delta_n})/\beta\right], \tag{7.10}$$

where as in Subsection 7.1.1 the process $(\chi_t)_{t \geq 0}$ is a white noise independent of X. It is also possible to introduce some dependency between the additive noise above and the process, by taking

$$Y_i^n = \beta\left[(X_{i\Delta_n} + \gamma_{i\Delta_n}\chi_{i\Delta_n})/\beta\right],$$

with χ_t as before and γ a (relatively) arbitrary process, adapted to the filtration with respect to which X itself is a semimartingale.

As it turns out, if the model is (7.10) and the noise χ_t is such that the support of the law of χ_0 contains an interval of length at least β, the "negative" property (7.8) fails, and all quantities which are identifiable in the perfect observation case are also identifiable here.

Indeed, we will often consider such a "mixed" situation, the precise assumptions being stated in Section 7.2 below.

7.1.5 Realized Volatility in the Presence of Noise

We conclude this introductory section with a brief description, without formal proofs, of the behavior of the realized volatility $\widehat{C}(\Delta_n)_t$, when the underlying process X is a continuous semimartingale and when one observes the noisy version Y_i^n, instead of the true values $X_{i\Delta_n}$. This complements the sketchy discussion of Section 2.3. So, instead of (6.4), the (non-corrected) realized volatility becomes

$$\widehat{C}^{\text{noisy}}(\Delta_n)_t = \sum_{i=1}^{[t/\Delta_n]} (\Delta_i^n Y)^2, \quad \text{where } \Delta_i^n Y = Y_i^n - Y_{i-1}^n. \quad (7.11)$$

We consider only the two polar cases of (1) additive noise and (2) pure rounding, with quite restrictive assumptions on X in the latter case. On the other hand, we examine the case where the noise size is constant (that is, (7.4), or (7.7) with α or β constant) and the case of a shrinking noise (with $\alpha = \alpha_n \to 0$ or $\beta = \beta_n \to 0$). Although a fixed size noise (especially in the rounding case) seems more appropriate from a practical viewpoint, it is also intuitively clear that if the noise is very small – whatever this might mean – one can forget about it. It is thus interesting to understand how small the noise should be, so that it does not affect the behavior of $\widehat{C}^{\text{noisy}}(\Delta_n)_t$.

Additive White Noise   Here the noise has the structure (7.5), with α_n either being the constant 1 or going to 0. We have

$$\widehat{C}^{\text{noisy}}(\Delta_n)_t = \sum_{i=1}^{[t/\Delta_n]} (\Delta_i^n X)^2 + 2\alpha_n \sum_{i=1}^{[t/\Delta_n]} \Delta_i^n X \left(\chi_{i\Delta_n} - \chi_{(i-1)\Delta_n}\right)$$
$$- 2\alpha_n^2 \sum_{i=1}^{[t/\Delta_n]} \chi_{(i-1)\Delta_n} \chi_{i\Delta_n} + \alpha_n^2 \sum_{i=1}^{[t/\Delta_n]} \left((\chi_{i\Delta_n})^2 + (\chi_{(i-1)\Delta_n})^2\right).$$

In the right side above, the first term goes to the quadratic variation $[X, X]_t$; by the white noise property of χ_t and (7.6), plus the Law of

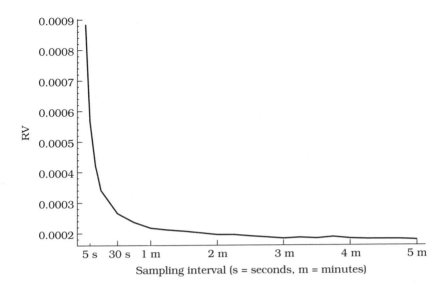

Figure 7.1: Volatility signature plot: Empirical divergence of the RV estimator, $\widehat{C}^{\text{noisy}}(\Delta_n)_t$, as $\Delta_n \to 0$, 30 DJIA stocks, 2007-2010, average pattern. By averaging over time and assets, the plot focuses on the common component, namely the increasing bias of the RV estimator as the sampling frequency increases.

Large Numbers, it is easy to check that, among the last three sums, the last one is the leading term, unless $\Delta_n/\alpha_n^2 \to \infty$; moreover, this leading term converges, after normalization by Δ_n/α_n^2, to $2t\mathbb{E}(\chi_0^2)$ (recall that χ_t has moments of all orders). In other words, we have the following behavior:

$$\Delta_n/\alpha_n^2 \to 0 \quad \Rightarrow \quad \tfrac{\Delta_n}{\alpha_n^2}\widehat{C}^{\text{noisy}}(\Delta_n)_T \xrightarrow{\mathbb{P}} 2\,T\,\mathbb{E}(\chi_0^2)$$

$$\Delta_n/\alpha_n^2 \to \theta \quad \Rightarrow \quad \widehat{C}^{\text{noisy}}(\Delta_n)_T \xrightarrow{\mathbb{P}} [X,X]_T + \tfrac{2\,T}{\theta}\mathbb{E}(\chi_0^2) \qquad (7.12)$$
$$\theta \in (0,\infty)$$

$$\Delta_n/\alpha_n^2 \to \infty \quad \Rightarrow \quad \widehat{C}^{\text{noisy}}(\Delta_n)_T \xrightarrow{\mathbb{P}} [X,X]_T.$$

So the realized volatility tends to $+\infty$, at rate $1/\Delta_n$ when the noise size is constant ($\alpha_n = 1$) and at a slower rate when the noise is shrinking too slowly; it tends to the same limit as without noise when α_n goes to 0 fast enough, and there is a boundary situation for which the limit involves both $[X,X]_T$ and the noise.

The reader will notice that the above argument, which is easy to straighten out in a rigorous way, works regardless of the properties of X: it is enough that it is a semimartingale. For the second order properties

(Central Limit Theorem), though, we need X to be an Itô semimartingale, plus $\Delta_n/\alpha_n^4 \to \infty$, if we want the same limit as without noise.

Figure 7.1 illustrates the corresponding divergence that is observed on empirical data. These theoretical results are in line with the empirical findings, and point very strongly toward the fact that noise *cannot be ignored* at high or especially ultra high frequency.

Sampling Sparsely at a Lower Frequency Faced with the divergence of $\widehat{C}^{\text{noisy}}(\Delta_n)_T$, a popular strategy in empirical work consists of sampling sparsely, that is, constructing lower frequency returns from the available data. For example, from transactions or quotes data observed every second, one might sample every 5 minutes, or every 10 minutes. This involves taking a subsample of n_{sparse} observations. With $T = 1$ day, or 6.5 hours of open trading for stocks, and we start with data sampled every $\Delta_n = 1$ second, then for the full dataset $n = [T/\Delta_n] = 23,400$ observations; but once we sample sparsely every 5 minutes, then we sample every 300th observation, and $n_{\text{sparse}} = 78$.

We assume (7.1) for X, and we want to estimate C_T. The distribution of $\widehat{C}^{\text{noisy,sparse}}(\Delta_n)_T - C_T$, to first approximation, is given by (χ denotes a generic noise variable)

$$
\widehat{C}^{\text{noisy,sparse}}(\Delta_n)_T - C_T \overset{\mathcal{L}}{\approx} \underbrace{2n_{\text{sparse}}\mathbb{E}(\chi^2)}_{\text{bias due to noise}} \tag{7.13}
$$

$$
+ \underbrace{\Big(\underbrace{4n_{\text{sparse}}\mathbb{E}(\chi^4)}_{\text{due to noise}} + \underbrace{\frac{2t}{n_{\text{sparse}}} C(4)_T}_{\text{due to discretization}} \Big)^{1/2} U}_{\text{total variance}}
$$

where U is a standard normal random variable independent of X. The term due to discretization is of course the same term that was already present in the analysis of the basic estimator $\widehat{C}(\Delta_n)_T$ in the absence of noise, in Section 6.1.1, and upon replacing Δ_n by t/n_{sparse}.

So there is potential for using $\widehat{C}^{\text{noisy}}_{\text{sparse}}(\Delta_n)_T$ to estimate C_T. There is a bias $2n_{\text{sparse}}\mathbb{E}(\chi^2)$, but it goes down if one uses fewer observations. But one should avoid sampling too sparsely, since (7.13) shows that decreasing n_{sparse} has the effect of increasing the variance of the estimator via the discretization effect which is proportional to $1/n_{\text{sparse}}$. The tradeoff between sampling too often and sampling too rarely can be formalized, and an optimal frequency at which to sample sparsely can be determined.

It is natural to minimize the mean squared error of $\widehat{C}^{\text{noisy,sparse}}(\Delta_n)_T$,

$$\text{MSE} = (2n_{\text{sparse}}\,\mathbb{E}(\chi^2))^2 + \left(4n_{\text{sparse}}\,\mathbb{E}(\chi^4) + \frac{2T}{n_{\text{sparse}}}\,\mathbb{E}(C(4)_T)\right)$$

over n_{sparse}, leading to

$$8n_{\text{sparse}}\left(\mathbb{E}(\chi^2)\right)^2 + 4\mathbb{E}(\chi^4) - \frac{2T}{n_{\text{sparse}}^2}\,\mathbb{E}(C(4)_T) \approx 0.$$

The optimum n_{sparse}^* is approximately

$$n_{\text{sparse}}^* \simeq \left(\mathbb{E}(\chi^2)\right)^{-2/3}\left(\frac{T}{4}\,\mathbb{E}(C(4)_T)\right)^{1/3}$$

provided that $\mathbb{E}(\chi^4)/(\mathbb{E}(\chi^2))^2$ is not too large. Of course such a choice of n_{sparse}^* is not really feasible in practice because $\mathbb{E}(\chi^2)$ and $\mathbb{E}(C(4)_T)$ are unknown, but they can be roughly pre-estimated. Not surprisingly, one should sample more frequently when the noise is small (smaller $\mathbb{E}(\chi^2)$), and when the signal itself is stronger (larger $C(4)_T$). Of course, some bias remains. The estimator $\widehat{C}^{\text{noisy,sparse}}(\Delta_n)_T$ can be reasonable only if $n_{\text{sparse}}^*\,\mathbb{E}(\chi^2)$ is small.

Pure Rounding Noise   Next, we suppose that the noise has the structure (7.7), with $\beta = \beta_n$ possibly depending on n. In this case the behavior of $\widehat{C}^{\text{noisy}}(\Delta_n)_t$ is not known in general, but it is known when the process X is a (continuous) diffusion, of the form

$$X_t \;=\; X_0 + \int_0^t b_s\,ds + \int_0^t \sigma(X_s)\,dW_s,$$

where b_t is a locally bounded process, and σ is a smooth enough function on $\mathbb{R}$, which never vanishes.

Suppose first that $\beta_n = \beta > 0$ is constant. When n is large enough, for any $i \leq [T/\Delta_n]$ we have $|\Delta_i^n X| \leq \beta$, hence the squared difference $(Y_i^n - Y_{i-1}^n)^2$ is either equal to 0 (when $X_{(i-1)\Delta_n}$ and $X_{i\Delta_n}$ are in the same interval $[m\beta, (m+1)\beta)$), or equal to β^2 (when $X_{(i-1)\Delta_n}$ and $X_{i\Delta_n}$ are in two – necessarily adjacent – such intervals). Thus $\widehat{C}^{\text{noisy}}(\Delta_n)_T$ is simply β^2 times the number of crossings of one of the levels $m\beta$ by the discretized sequence $(X_{i\Delta_n} : 0 \leq i \leq [T/\Delta_n])$. The asymptotic behavior of the number of crossings of a level x by this discretized sequence has to do with the local time L_T^x at this level and time T. More specifically, the number of crossings multiplied by $\sqrt{\Delta_n}$ converges in probability to $\frac{1}{\sigma(x)}\sqrt{2/\pi}\,L_T^x$.

On the other hand, when $\beta_n \to 0$, local times no longer enter the picture, but it is still possible to obtain a limit, after normalization. The general result goes as follows:

$$
\begin{aligned}
&\begin{array}{l} \beta_n = \beta \\ \beta \in (0, \infty) \end{array} \quad \Rightarrow \quad \begin{array}{l} \sqrt{\Delta_n}\,\widehat{C}^{\mathrm{noisy}}(\Delta_n)_T \\ \xrightarrow{\mathbb{P}} \sqrt{\frac{2}{\pi}} \sum_{m \in \mathbb{Z}} \frac{\beta^2}{\sigma(m\beta)} L_T^{m\beta} \end{array} \\[2mm]
&\begin{array}{l} \Delta_n/\beta_n^2 \to 0 \\ \beta_n \to 0 \end{array} \quad \Rightarrow \quad \begin{array}{l} \frac{\sqrt{\Delta_n}}{\beta_n}\,\widehat{C}^{\mathrm{noisy}}(\Delta_n)_T \\ \xrightarrow{\mathbb{P}} \sqrt{\frac{2}{\pi}} \int_0^T \sigma(X_s)\,ds \end{array} \\[2mm]
&\begin{array}{l} \Delta_n/\beta_n^2 \to \theta \\ \theta \in (0, \infty) \end{array} \quad \Rightarrow \quad \begin{array}{l} \widehat{C}^{\mathrm{noisy}}(\Delta_n)_T \\ \xrightarrow{\mathbb{P}} \int_0^T \Gamma(\theta, \sigma(X_s))\,ds \end{array} \\[2mm]
&\begin{array}{l} \Delta_n/\beta_n^2 \to \infty \end{array} \quad \Rightarrow \quad \begin{array}{l} \widehat{C}^{\mathrm{noisy}}(\Delta_n)_T \\ \xrightarrow{\mathbb{P}} [X,X]_t = \int_0^T \sigma(X_s)^2 ds, \end{array}
\end{aligned}
\tag{7.14}
$$

where Γ is a function on $[0, \infty] \times \mathbb{R}$ which is not useful for us here, but which satisfies $\Gamma(\infty, x) = x^2$ and $\theta\Gamma(\theta, x) \to x\sqrt{2/\pi}$ as $\theta \to 0$.

Here again, when $\Delta_n/\beta_n^2 \to 0$ the realized volatility goes to ∞, although with a slower rate than for an additive white noise; when β_n goes to 0 fast enough the noise has no effect, and in a boundary case the noise introduces a bias.

To conclude, we see that, at least in the two special cases described above, ignoring the noise by plugging the noisy observations into the realized volatility results in consistent estimators for $+\infty$ (instead of $[X, X]_T$!) unless the noise size is shrinking at least as fast as $\sqrt{\Delta_n}$. Note also that in the non-shrinking case, no renormalization of $\widehat{C}(\Delta_n)_T$ can result in consistent estimators for $[X, X]_T$: in the additive white noise case $\frac{1}{\Delta_n}\widehat{C}^{\mathrm{noisy}}(\Delta_n)_T$ is a consistent estimator for $2t$ times the variance of the noise, in the pure rounding case, upon dividing by $1/\sqrt{\Delta_n}$ we would "estimate" a sum of local times.

7.2   Assumptions on the Noise

The underlying process X is a one-dimensional Itô semimartingale on a filtered probability space $(\Omega, \mathcal{F}, (\mathcal{F}_t)_{t \geq 0}, \mathbb{P})$, satisfying Assumption (H-2), or (HC) in the continuous case.

As for the noise, we basically consider two different sets of assumptions, corresponding to the additive white noise and to an extension of the "mixed case" described above. In both cases this involves some additional randomness, on top of the randomness describing the evolution of the process X and possible covariates, which is encapsulated in the probability space $(\Omega, \mathcal{F}, \mathbb{P})$. Since in the second case we allow the noise to depend on X, a possible model consists in saying that the noise is defined on an auxiliary space $(\Omega', \mathcal{F}')$ which is endowed with a transition probability $\mathbb{Q}(\omega, d\omega')$, so the pair "process+noise" is defined on the product space $\widetilde{\Omega} = \Omega \times \Omega'$ and evolves according to the probability $\mathbb{P}(d\omega)\,\mathbb{Q}(\omega, d\omega')$; saying that the noise is independent of $\mathcal{F}$ amounts to saying that $\mathbb{Q}(\omega, d\omega') = \mathbb{Q}(d\omega')$ does not depend on ω.

This formulation is somewhat complicated, as far as notation is concerned, because it involves two distinct sample spaces and probabilities. In order to simplify notation as much as we can, we rather suppose that the noise is defined on Ω itself, although it is not measurable with respect to the σ-field $\mathcal{F}$ but with respect to a bigger σ-field $\mathcal{F}'$, and the probability $\mathbb{P}$ is defined on $\mathcal{F}'$. Then, we need to specify the $\mathcal{F}$-conditional distribution of the noise.

We also suppose that the noise is defined at each time t, although of course only the noise at observation times has physical existence. Finally, both sets of assumptions below accommodate constant sized or shrinking noise, the noise size being regulated by a sequence α_n with either $\alpha_n = 1$ for all n (the most interesting case), or $\alpha_n \to 0$.

To summarize, and since we only consider regular observation schemes with mesh size Δ_n below, we have a process $(\chi_t)_{t \geq 0}$ and the observations Y_i^n and noise χ_i^n at stage n are

$$Y_i^n = X_{i\Delta_n} + \epsilon_i^n, \quad \epsilon_i^n = \alpha_n\, \chi_{i\Delta_n}, \text{ either } \alpha_n \equiv 1 \text{ or } \alpha_n \to 0. \quad (7.15)$$

It thus remains to state the assumption on the $\mathcal{F}$-conditional law, of the process $(\chi_t)_{t \geq 0}$. The first one describes the additive white noise, the second one, much weaker, describes an extension of the "mixed case" evoked in the previous section.

Assumption (WN). *The process $(\chi_t)_{t \geq 0}$ is independent of $\mathcal{F}$ and is a white noise satisfying*

$$\mathbb{E}(\chi_t) = 0 \quad \text{and} \quad p \in (0, \infty) \;\Rightarrow\; \mathbb{E}(|\chi_t|^p) < \infty.$$

Assumption (GN). *Conditionally on $\mathcal{F}$, all variables $(\chi_t : t \geq 0)$ are independent, and we have*

- $\mathbb{E}(\chi_t \mid \mathcal{F}) = 0$
- *for all $p > 0$ the process $\mathbb{E}(|\chi_t|^p \mid \mathcal{F})$ is $(\mathcal{F}_t)$-adapted and locally bounded* (7.16)
- *the (conditional) variance process $\gamma_t = \mathbb{E}(|\chi_t|^2 \mid \mathcal{F})$ is càdlàg.*

We do assume moments of all order for the noise. This is mainly for convenience, and a very slight restriction in practice. However, all results would remain true if the pth moment or conditional moment were finite, or locally bounded, for a suitable value of p, typically $p = 4$ or p bigger than but arbitrarily close to 4.

Remark 7.2. *(GN) is much weaker than (WN). It does not imply the independence between the noise and $\mathcal{F}$, or the (unconditional) independence of the variables χ_t when t varies. Note also that the $\mathcal{F}$-conditional and unconditional laws of χ_t may very well depend on t.*

Remark 7.3. *The first part of (7.16) looks innocuous at first glance, but is indeed a very strong assumption. It can trivially be replaced by the assumption $\mathbb{E}(\chi_t \mid \mathcal{F}) = a$ where a is a constant (this really amounts to replacing X_t by $X_t - a$), but the constant a cannot be replaced by a process $a = a_t(\omega)$, and not even by a non-random function $a = a(t)$.*

An example which does not satisfy (GN) is pure rounding noise: all requirements in (GN) are satisfied by the pure rounding noise, except for the first part of (7.16) (even extended as specified above); indeed, we have $\mathbb{E}(\chi_t \mid \mathcal{F}) = X_t - \beta[X_t/\beta]$, which certainly is not a constant.

As we will see below, there are consistent estimators for the integrated volatility under (GN), hence the non-identifiability statement in (7.8) fails. It means that the first part of (7.16) cannot be dispensed with, and weakening this assumption does not seem an easy matter: one can for example read Li and Mykland (2007) to get some deeper insight on this question.

Remark 7.4. *Suppose for example (GN). Not only do we have identifiability of the integrated volatility (by exhibiting consistent estimators), but also identifiability of the integrated conditional moments of the noise, at least when α_n does not go too fast to 0, and up to a fundamental ambiguity: the shrinking parameter α_n is of course unknown, and multiplying it by a constant amounts to dividing the noise χ_t by the same constant.*

So in fact what is identifiable about the noise is the variable $\int_0^t (\alpha_n)^p \gamma(p)_s \, ds$ (in principle, for all t and p).

Example 7.5 (Rounded White Noise). *An example of a situation where (GN) holds is the "mixed case" of the previous section, at least when the noise is not shrinking. That is, we have a white noise independent of $\mathcal{F}$, say $(\chi_t')_{t \geq 0}$ (warning: the notation χ_t in (7.10) is χ_t' here), and the noise in the sense of (7.15) is*

$$\chi_t = \beta[(X_t + \chi_t')/\beta] - X_t. \tag{7.17}$$

If χ'_t has a density which is constant over each interval $[m\beta, (m+1)\beta)$, a simple calculation shows that $\mathbb{E}(\chi_t \mid \mathcal{F})$ is equal to a constant, which further vanishes as soon as $\mathbb{E}(\chi'_t) = 1/2$.

Example 7.6 (Random Allocation on a Tick Grid). *Taking into account the bid-ask spread and the grid $\{m\beta : m \in \mathbb{Z}\}$ of all possible ticks, one could imagine that at any given time t the agents know in which interval $[m\beta, (m+1)\beta)$ the efficient price X_t lies, and set the price at $(m+1)\beta$ with the (conditional) probability $p(X_t) := \frac{1}{\beta}((m+1)\beta - X_t)$ and at $m\beta$ with the probability $1 - p(X_t)$. In other words, the observed value at a sampling time t is $\beta([X_t/\beta] + 1)$ with the probability $p(X_t)$ and $\beta[X_t/\beta]$ with the probability $1 - p(X_t)$.*

In fact, this model coincides with the previous model, upon taking the white noise variables χ'_t to be uniformly distributed over $[0,1]$.

Example 7.7 (Modulated Rounded White Noise). *We still have the form (7.17) for the noise, but now the variables χ'_t are, conditionally on $\mathcal{F}$, independent as t varies, with densities of the form*

$$h_{t,\omega}(x) = \sum_{m\in\mathbb{Z}} \rho(m)(\omega)_t \, 1_{[m\beta,(m+1)\beta)}(x), \qquad (7.18)$$

provided each process $\rho(m)$ is nonnegative $(\mathcal{F}_t)$-adapted, with $\sum_m \rho(m)_t = 1$ and $\sum_m |m|^p \rho(m)_t$ locally bounded for each $p > 0$, and $\sum_m m\rho(m)_t = \frac{1}{2}$.

The following comments are important:

Remark 7.8. *One could argue, quite rightly, that the previous examples are very special; many other examples of noise do satisfy (GN), even among those having the form (7.17). On the contrary, many examples of noise of the form (7.17) with χ'_t a white noise do not satisfy (GN).*

However, when β is small and when the law of each χ'_t has a piecewise Lipschitz-continuous density, the noise (7.17) is well approximated (in the distributional sense) by a noise χ''_t of the same type, with χ''_t having a density like in (7.18) with $\rho(m)$ independent of (ω, t) and equal to the probability that χ_t belongs to $[m\beta, (m+1)\beta)$. Therefore, although the model (7.17) with no special assumption on the law of χ'_t does not satisfy (GN) in general, it approximately does when β is not too large.

Since, as mentioned before, it is probably impossible to forget about the rounding effect, it seems (to us at least) that Example 7.5 is a good substitute to an additive white noise.

Remark 7.9. *Let us also stress the fact that Assumptions (WN) of course, but (GN) as well, require some (conditional or unconditional)* *independence of the variables χ_t as t varies. So they rule out all "colored" noises.*

7.3 Maximum-Likelihood and Quasi Maximum-Likelihood Estimation

7.3.1 A Toy Model: Gaussian Additive White Noise and Brownian Motion

We start our analysis with our usual toy model. The underlying process is a Brownian motion with unknown variance $c = \sigma^2 > 0$, that is,

$$X_t = \sigma W_t.$$

The noise is also the simplest possible, namely an additive white noise (hence (WN) holds), which further is Gaussian: each χ_t follows the normal distribution $\mathcal{N}(0, \gamma)$, where $\gamma \geq 0$ is also unknown. The observations are given by (7.3), with $\alpha_n = \Delta_n^\eta$ for some "shrinking exponent" $\eta \in [0, \infty)$ which is assumed to be known (when $\eta = 0$ the noise is nonshrinking, as in (7.4); when $\eta > 0$ we are in the shrinking noise case of (7.5)).

At stage n, one has in fact the two parameters c and $\gamma_n = \alpha_n^2 \gamma$. Before starting the detailed analysis, let us mention that the computation of the expected value of the estimator based on the observed (noisy) returns, that is, $\widehat{C}^{\mathrm{noisy}}(\Delta_n)$ of (7.11), is simple:

$$\mathbb{E}\left(\widehat{C}^{\mathrm{noisy}}(\Delta_n)_t\right) = (c\Delta_n + 2\gamma_n)\,[t/\Delta_n] \sim ct + \frac{2\gamma_n}{\Delta_n}\,t,$$

which is consistent with the results in (7.12).

If we agree to forget a tiny part of the observations, that is, if we only take into account the observed (noisy) log-returns $\Delta_i^n Y$ defined in (7.11), we are on known grounds: when $\alpha_n = \gamma_n = 0$ these variables are i.i.d. with law $\mathcal{N}(0, c\Delta_n)$, and otherwise the sequence $(\Delta_i^n Y)_{i \geq 1}$ is a moving average of order 1, or MA(1), time series of the form $\Delta_i^n Y = Z_i - v_n Z_{i-1}$, where (Z_i) is a Gaussian white noise with variance v_n', and where

$$\begin{cases} v_n = \frac{2\gamma_n + c\Delta_n - \sqrt{4c\Delta_n\gamma_n + c^2\Delta_n^2}}{2\gamma_n}, \\ v_n' = \frac{\gamma_n}{v_n} = \frac{2\gamma_n + c\Delta_n + \sqrt{4c\Delta_n\gamma_n + c^2\Delta_n^2}}{2} \end{cases} \tag{7.19}$$

(note that $0 < v_n < 1$). Equivalently,

$$\begin{cases} v_n'(1 + v_n^2) = \mathrm{Var}\,(\Delta_i^n Y) = c\Delta_n + 2\gamma_n, \\ -v_n' v_n = \mathrm{Cov}(\Delta_i^n Y, \Delta_{i-1}^n Y) = -\gamma_n. \end{cases} \tag{7.20}$$

Under this model, the log-likelihood function for the $n = [T/\Delta_n]$ observations $(\Delta_i^n Y)_{i=1,...,n}$ is given by

$$l_n(v_n, v_n') = -\frac{1}{2} \log \det(V_n) - \frac{n}{2} \log(2\pi v_n') - \frac{1}{2v_n'} R_n' V_n^{-1} R_n, \quad (7.21)$$

where the covariance matrix for the vector $R_n = (\Delta_1^n Y, ..., \Delta_n^n Y)'$ is $v_n' V_n$, where

$$V_n = \begin{pmatrix} 1+v_n^2 & -v_n & 0 & \cdots & 0 \\ -v_n & 1+v_n^2 & -v_n & \ddots & \vdots \\ 0 & -v_n & 1+v_n^2 & \ddots & 0 \\ \vdots & \ddots & \ddots & \ddots & -v_n \\ 0 & \cdots & 0 & -v_n & 1+v_n^2 \end{pmatrix} \quad (7.22)$$

and $\det(V_n) = (1 - v_n^{2n+2})/(1 - v_n^2)$. The log-likelihood function can be expressed in a computationally efficient form by triangularizing the matrix V_n, yielding an equivalent expression that no longer requires any matrix inversion:

$$l_n(v_n, v_n') = -\frac{1}{2} \sum_{i=1}^{[T/\Delta_n]} \left(\log(2\pi d_i^n) + \frac{(Z_i^n)^2}{d_i^n} \right),$$
$$\text{where } d_i^n = v_n' \frac{1-v_n^{2i+2}}{1-v_n^{2i}}, \quad (7.23)$$
$$Z_1^n = \Delta_1^n Y \text{ and } i \geq 2 \Rightarrow Z_i^n = \Delta_i^n Y + v_n \frac{1-v_n^{2i-2}}{1-v_n^{2i}} Z_{i-1}^n.$$

The corresponding Fisher information matrix for the two parameters v_n and v_n' is

$$I(v_n, v_n')_{n.t} = \begin{pmatrix} \frac{n}{1-v_n^2} - \frac{1+3v_n^2}{(1-v_n^2)^2} + a_n & \frac{v_n}{v_n'}\left(\frac{1}{1-v_n^2} - a_n'\right) \\ \frac{v_n}{v_n'}\left(\frac{1}{1-v_n^2} - a_n'\right) & \frac{n}{2v_n'^2} \end{pmatrix}$$

where (implicitly, all this notation depends on T, through the value of n)

$$\begin{cases} a_n = \frac{v_n^{2wn}}{(1-v_n^{2+2wn})^2}\left(2n^2 + n\frac{3-v_n^2+v_n^{2+2n}-v_n^{4+2n}}{1-v_n^2}\right. \\ \qquad \left. + \frac{1-v_n^4+2v_n^{2+2n}-4v_n^{4+2n}+3v_n^{6+2n}}{(1-v_n^2)^2}\right) \\ a_n' = \frac{(1+n)v_n^{2n}}{1-v_n^{2+2n}}. \end{cases}$$

This holds when $a_n > 0$, whereas in the case $a_n = 0$ the natural reparametrization is $v_n' = c\Delta_n$ and $v_n = 0$, instead of (7.19). The one-dimensional Fisher's information becomes $I(0, v_n')_{n.t} = n/(2v_n'^2)$, as already seen in (5.18) for example.

The parameters of interest are c (or $C_T = cT$) and γ and not v_n and v_n'. By a change of variables, one may express Fisher's information matrix

$$I(c,\gamma)_n = \begin{pmatrix} I(c,\gamma)_n^{cc} & I(c,\gamma)_n^{c\gamma} \\ I(c,\gamma)_n^{c\gamma} & I(c,\gamma)_n^{\gamma\gamma} \end{pmatrix}$$

in terms of (c,γ). The exact expression is somewhat complicated, but results in simple asymptotic as $\Delta_n \to 0$, namely:

$$\eta < \tfrac{1}{2} \quad \Rightarrow \quad \begin{cases} I(c,\gamma)_n^{cc} \sim \dfrac{T}{8\Delta_n^{1/2+\eta}\sqrt{\gamma c^3}}, & I(c,\gamma)_n^{\gamma\gamma} \sim \dfrac{T}{2\gamma^2\Delta_n} \\ I(c,\gamma)_n^{c\gamma} \sim \dfrac{T}{8\Delta_n^{1/2+\eta}\sqrt{\gamma^3 c}} \end{cases}$$

$$\eta = \tfrac{1}{2} \quad \Rightarrow \quad \begin{cases} I(c,\gamma)_n^{cc} \sim \dfrac{TA(c,\gamma)^{cc}}{\Delta_n}, & I(c,\gamma)_n^{\gamma\gamma} \sim \dfrac{TA(c,\gamma)^{\gamma\gamma}}{\Delta_n} \\ I(c,\gamma)_n^{c\gamma} \sim \dfrac{TA(c,\gamma)^{c\gamma}}{\Delta_n} \end{cases} \qquad (7.24)$$

$$\eta > \tfrac{1}{2} \quad \Rightarrow \quad \begin{cases} I(c,\gamma)_n^{cc} \sim \dfrac{T}{2c^2\Delta_n}, & I(c,\gamma)_n^{\gamma\gamma} \sim \dfrac{24\,T}{c^2\Delta_n^{3-4\eta}} \\ I(c,\gamma)_n^{c\gamma} \sim \dfrac{2T}{c^2\Delta_n^{2-2\eta}} \end{cases}$$

for some 2×2 matrix $A(c,\gamma)$ which we do not need to specify here. Moreover, it can be shown that the LAN property holds for the parameter c always, and for the parameter γ when $\eta \le 1/2$. Henceforth, the asymptotic behavior of Fisher's information gives us exactly the characteristics (rate and asymptotic variance) of efficient estimators.

These facts have fundamental consequences about asymptotic estimation:

1. *The case of asymptotically negligible noise*: This corresponds to taking $\eta > 1/2$.

    (a) First, in the limit where there is no noise at all (this corresponds to formally taking $\eta = \infty$), only the entry $I(c,\gamma)_n^{cc}$ of the information matrix makes sense, and it is equal to $T/(2c^2\Delta_n)$ (no approximation is involved in this case).

    (b) Second, if $1/2 < \eta < \infty$, (7.24) tells us that the noise has no influence on the asymptotic rate $1/\sqrt{\Delta_n}$ and the asymptotic (normalized) variance $2c^2/T$ of efficient estimators for c. And it turns out that $(1/T)\sum_{i=1}^{[T/\Delta_n]}(\Delta_i^n Y)^2$ is such an efficient estimator, exactly as if there were no noise.

    (c) Third, concerning the estimation of γ, (7.24) also tells us that one cannot hope for consistent estimators when $\eta \ge 3/4$, whereas if $\eta \in (1/2, 3/4)$ efficient estimators will converge with the rate $1/\Delta_n^{3/2-2\eta}$, with an asymptotic variance $c^2/24$.

2. *The case $\eta = 1/2$*: In this limiting case, both c and γ can efficiently be estimated with the rate $1/\sqrt{\Delta_n}$ and respective asymptotic variances given by the diagonal entries of the inverse of the matrix $A(c, \gamma)$.

3. *The case of large noise*: This correspond to $\eta \in [0, 1/2)$. In this case, efficient estimators for c converge with the rate $1/\Delta_n^{1/4+\eta/2}$ (and thus $1/\Delta_n^{1/4}$ when the noise is not shrinking, $\eta = 0$), and the asymptotic variance is $8\sqrt{\gamma c^3}/T$.

   By contrast, efficient estimators for γ always converge with the rate $1/\sqrt{\Delta_n}$, with asymptotic variance $2\gamma^2/T$, exactly as if only the noise were observed. This is because, in this case, the increments $\Delta_i^n Y$ look more and more like $\chi_{i\Delta_n} - \chi_{(i-1)\Delta_n}$ as n increases.

Of course, the example studied in this section is not realistic for financial data, but it sets up bounds on what can be achieved in a more realistic context. In particular, in the non-shrinking noise case it tells us the optimal rate of convergence $1/\Delta_n^{1/4}$ which we will encounter in a much more general situation. It also tells us that when $\eta > 1/2$ (fast shrinking noise) one can probably forget about the noise.

Equivalently, we can express the results above in the perhaps more intuitive form of asymptotic variances. The asymptotic variance of the MLE is given by the inverse of Fisher's information and we obtain it in the case where the noise is fixed ($\eta = 0$, and so $\gamma_n = \gamma$). In order to keep the same framework as before we estimate $C_T = cT$ instead of the more natural parameter c, and we denote the MLE estimators of the pair (C_T, γ) as $(\widehat{C}^{\mathrm{MLE}}(\Delta_n)_T, \widehat{\gamma}^{\mathrm{MLE}}(\Delta_n)_T)$, and we have the following convergence in law:

$$\left(\frac{1}{\Delta_n^{1/4}} (\widehat{C}^{\mathrm{MLE}}(\Delta_n)_T - C_T), \frac{1}{\Delta_n^{1/2}} (\widehat{\gamma}^{\mathrm{MLE}}(\Delta_n)_T - \gamma) \right)$$

$$\xrightarrow{\mathcal{L}} (U_T, U_T'), \tag{7.25}$$

where the two variables U_T and U_T' are independent, centered normal, with respective variances

$$\mathbb{E}(U_T^2) = 8c^{3/2}\gamma^{1/2}T, \qquad \mathbb{E}(U_T'^2) = 2\gamma^2 t^{-1}. \tag{7.26}$$

So $\widehat{C}^{\mathrm{MLE}}(\Delta_n)_T$ converges to C_T at rate $1/\Delta_n^{1/4}$, and it is optimal to sample as often as possible, unlike for the subsampling method analyzed in Subsection 7.1.5. This should be compared with the rate $1/\Delta_n^{1/2}$ and the asymptotic variance $2c^2T$ of the realized volatility estimators $\widehat{C}(\Delta_n)_T$ which is the MLE when there is no noise.

Remark 7.10. *Remarkably, the assumption that the noise is Gaussian is quite innocuous. Suppose that the noise is erroneously assumed for the MLE computation to be normally distributed when in reality it has a different distribution, but still i.i.d. with mean zero and variance γ_n. Inference is still conducted with the log-likelihood (7.23). This means that the components of the score vector are used as moment functions (or "estimating equations"). Since the first order moments of these moment functions depend only on the second order moment structure of the log-returns $(\Delta_i^n Y)_{i=1,\ldots,n}$, which is unchanged by non-normality of the noise, the moment functions are unbiased under the true distribution of the ϵ_i's.*

Hence the estimator $(\widehat{C}^{MLE}(\Delta_n)_T, \widehat{\gamma}^{MLE}(\Delta_n)_T)$ based on these moment functions is consistent and asymptotically unbiased with the same convergence rates as before (even though the likelihood function is now misspecified). The effect of misspecification solely lies in the variance matrix of the limit (U, U') in (7.25): the two variables U_T and U'_T are still centered normal independent, with variances

$$\mathbb{E}(U_T^2) = 8c^{3/2}\gamma^{1/2}T, \qquad \mathbb{E}(U_T'^2) = 2\gamma^2 T^{-1} + \mathrm{Cum}_4[\epsilon]$$

where the fourth cumulant $\mathrm{Cum}_4[\epsilon] = \mathbb{E}(\epsilon^4) - 3\big(\mathbb{E}(\epsilon^4)\big)^2$ of the noise measures the deviation from normality. In other words, the asymptotic variance of $\widehat{C}^{MLE}(\Delta_n)_T$ is identical to its expression had the noise been Gaussian. And, for the estimation of γ, the asymptotic estimation variance increases when the distribution of the noise departs from normality (recall that $\mathrm{Cum}_4[\epsilon] = 0$ in the normal case).

This estimator, although developed for the toy model where σ is constant, enjoys yet another type of robustness, which we now turn to.

7.3.2   Robustness of the MLE to Stochastic Volatility

This section is concerned with analyzing the MLE described above, but in the context of the more general model (7.1), under Assumption (HC). The observations are given by (7.34) with a non-shrinking white noise satisfying (WN). The variance of the noise is still denoted as $\gamma = \mathbb{E}(\chi_0^2)$. The idea of a quasi-likelihood method applies to semi-parametric models, for which one wants to estimate some parameter. The method consists in pretending that the semi-parametric model is close enough to a parametric model for which the MLE allows for optimal estimation; one can then plug the observed data into the parametric MLE.

The parametric model used here is the toy model of the previous subsection. This toy model is, globally, a very poor approximation of the true model, but "locally in time" it is a reasonable approximation because the drift term plays a negligible role in the estimation of C_t, and the volatility σ_t (or c_t) is càdlàg, hence is in a sense "almost constant" on relatively small time intervals.

Let us revisit the toy model $X_t = \sigma W_t$ with $c = \sigma^2 > 0$ and $C_T = cT$, and the second parameter is the variance γ of the noise, supposed to be Gaussian here. Equation (7.23) gives the log-likelihood at stage n, in terms of the modified parameters (v_n, v'_n), and when the noise is possibly shrinking. However, it is also possible to give an explicit form of the likelihood in terms of the parameters c and $\gamma_n = \gamma$, due to the form of the covariance matrix $\Sigma_n = v'_n V_n$ of the observed (noisy) returns $\Delta_i^n Y = \Delta_i^n X + \Delta_i^n \chi$ for $i = 1, \ldots, n$, which from (7.20) and (7.22) is given for $1 \leq i, j \leq n$ by

$$
\Sigma_n^{ij} = \begin{cases} c\Delta_n + 2\gamma & \text{if } i = j \\ -\gamma & \text{if } i = j \pm 1 \\ 0 & \text{otherwise.} \end{cases} \tag{7.27}
$$

This matrix has an explicit inverse Σ_n^{-1}, and the log-likelihood (7.21) becomes

$$
\begin{aligned}
l(c, \gamma)_n = &-\frac{1}{2}\Big(\log \det(\Sigma_n) + n \log(2\pi) \\
&+ \sum_{i,j=1}^{n} (\Sigma_n^{-1})^{ij} \Delta_i^n Y \Delta_j^n Y \Big).
\end{aligned} \tag{7.28}
$$

After neglecting the end effects, an approximate value of $(\Sigma_n^{-1})^{ij}$ is

$$
(\Sigma_n^{-1})^{ij} = \frac{1}{v'_n} \left(1 - v_n^2\right)^{-1} (v_n)^{|i-j|} \tag{7.29}
$$

(see Durbin (1959)).

Recall that the MLE estimators at stage n for (C_T, γ) are such that $(\frac{1}{t}\widehat{C}^{\mathrm{MLE}}(\Delta_n)_T, \widehat{\gamma}^{\mathrm{MLE}}(\Delta_n)_T)$ maximizes the function $(c, \gamma) \mapsto l(c, \gamma)_n$, and are asymptotically efficient and satisfy (7.25) and (7.26).

Now we come back to the problem at hand. We still define the (random) function $l(c, \gamma)_n$ by the formula (7.28), where the dependency in (c, γ) comes from (7.27), but now the generating data $\Delta_i^n Y$ come from the model with X of the form (7.1). Recall that we want to estimate the integrated volatility C_T, but we will get for free an estimation of the noise variance γ as well.

To this end, at stage n and for the terminal time T, the estimators for C_T and γ will be $\widehat{C}^{\mathrm{QMLE}}(\Delta_n)_T$ and $\widehat{\gamma}^{\mathrm{QMLE}}(\Delta_n)_T$, where

$$\left(\tfrac{1}{t}\widehat{C}^{\mathrm{QMLE}}(\Delta_n)_T, \widehat{\gamma}^{\mathrm{QMLE}}(\Delta_n)_T\right)$$

maximizes the function $(c, \gamma) \mapsto l(c, \gamma)_n$

(in view of the explicit form of l_n, the maximum is always achieved at a single point).

The estimator $\widehat{C}^{\mathrm{QMLE}}(\Delta_n)_T$ is not a quadratic estimator, in the sense of (7.33) below. However, it is obtained, jointly with $\widehat{\gamma}^{\mathrm{QMLE}}(\Delta_n)_T$, and up to the multiplicative factor $1/T$, as the root of the two-dimensional equation $\partial_c l(c, \gamma)_T^n = \partial_\gamma l(c, \gamma)_T^n = 0$. These partial derivatives are complicated functions of c and γ, but they are quadratic in the returns $\Delta_i^n Y$. Therefore, the asymptotic behavior of them, hence the one of their roots as well, relies upon the asymptotic behavior of suitable quadratic functionals. Those functionals are somewhat similar with $B'(f, \Delta_n)$ of (A.8) of Appendix A, with test functions f which are quadratic, but with coefficients depending on n and involving the partial derivatives of the entries of the matrices $\Sigma_n = \Sigma_n(c, \gamma)$ and of their inverses.

The behavior of these coefficients as $n \to \infty$ is known, and relatively easy although tedious to infer. So we will only state the results here, referring to Xiu (2010) for the proofs. As far as assumptions are concerned, (HC) is not enough. We need the process c_t to be locally bounded away from 0 (because in the toy model we accordingly need $c > 0$), that is, Assumption (P) (see page 193). We also need the process σ_t to be an Itô semimartingale satisfying (H-2), hence we assume the following:

Assumption (KC). *We have (HC), the process b is either càdlàg or càglàg, and the process σ is an Itô semimartingale satisfying (H-2).*

Theorem 7.11. *Assume (KC) and (P), and also (WN) with a non-shrinking noise, and set $\Gamma = \mathbb{E}(\chi_0^4) - \gamma^2$. Then we have the following joint stable convergence in law:*

$$\left(\frac{1}{\Delta_n^{1/4}}(\widehat{C}^{QMLE}(\Delta_n)_T - C_T), \frac{1}{\Delta_n^{1/2}}(\widehat{\gamma}^{QMLE}(\Delta_n)_T - \gamma)\right) \xrightarrow{\mathcal{L}-s} (U_T, U_T'),$$

where the two variables U_T and U_T' are defined on an extension of the space $(\Omega, \mathcal{F}, \mathbb{P})$ and, conditionally on $\mathcal{F}$, are independent centered Gaussian variables with respective conditional variances

$$\begin{aligned}
\mathbb{E}(U_T^2 \mid \mathcal{F}) &= \sqrt{\tfrac{\gamma}{T\,C_T}}\left(5T\int_0^T c_s^2\,ds + 3(C_T)^2\right), \\
\mathbb{E}(U_T'^2 \mid \mathcal{F}) &= \tfrac{\Gamma - \gamma^2}{T}.
\end{aligned} \qquad (7.30)$$

Note that if one is interested in γ, there is another, more natural and much simpler, estimator than $\widehat{\gamma}^{\text{QMLE}}(\Delta)_T$, namely

$$\widehat{\gamma}'(\Delta_n)_T = \frac{\Delta_n}{2T} \sum_{i=1}^{[T/\Delta_n]} (\Delta_i^n Y)^2. \tag{7.31}$$

This estimator has the same asymptotic properties as $\widehat{\gamma}^{\text{QMLE}}(\Delta_n)_T$.

When $c_t = c$ is a constant and the noise is Gaussian, we have $\Gamma = 3\gamma^2$ and (7.30) agrees with (7.26). The QMLE estimator is then the MLE, hence is efficient. In the more general situation (7.1), efficiency no longer holds, and later we provide estimators with a strictly smaller asymptotic variance.

This estimator works also when the observations are not regularly spaced, under some conditions, for example when the observation times at each stage n form a renewal process independent of X, and upon modifying the matrix Σ_n of (7.27) and thus l_n in an appropriate way. On the other hand, it does not seem to work if we relax Assumption (WN) according to which the noise is white and homogeneous in time.

7.4   Quadratic Estimators

It is reasonable to expect an estimator of C_t to be homogeneous of degree 2, as a function of the data (that is, if all observed values are multiplied by a constant, the estimator should be multiplied by the squared constant). This does not mean that such estimators are quadratic functions of the data, as seen previously for the quasi-MLE estimator, which is homogeneous of degree 2 but not quadratic. Nevertheless it seems reasonable (and simpler than anything else) to try estimators that are *quadratic functions* of the data, as is $\widehat{C}(\Delta_n)_t$ in the non-noisy case. Such quadratic estimators are the object of our interest in this section, with the (innocuous) restriction that we only consider quadratic functions of the returns.

By construction, quadratic estimators are *local* in nature, unlike the likelihood-based one of Section 7.3, which is *global*. A quadratic estimator at stage n is an estimator of the form

$$\widehat{C}_t^n = \sum_{i,j=1}^{[t/\Delta_n]} a(n,i,j,t)\, \Delta_i^n Y\, \Delta_j^n Y, \tag{7.32}$$

with the notation (7.11) for $\Delta_i^n Y$. Here, the $a(n,i,j,t)$ are suitable weights, which are symmetric in (i,j) and have to be chosen "optimally," and clearly the optimal choice depends on the unknown characteristics of the process and of the noise.

This task being obviously impossible to achieve in full generality, the next simplification consists in taking the sum of "local" quadratic functions, that is, estimators of the form

$$\widehat{C}_t^n = \sum_{i=0}^{[t/\Delta_n]-k_n} \sum_{j,j'=1}^{k_n} h_n\left(\frac{|j-j'|}{k_n}\right) \Delta_{i+j}^n Y \, \Delta_{i+j'}^n Y \qquad (7.33)$$
$$+ \text{ border terms},$$

for appropriately chosen functions h_n on $[0,1]$ which act as a kernel, similar to kernels used in non-parametric density estimation, for example. The unspecified "border terms" are also quadratic and contain increments $\Delta_i^n Y$ for $1 \leq i \leq k_n$ and $[t/\Delta_n] - k_n \leq i \leq [t/\Delta_n]$, and they appear because in the main term above those border increments are not treated on the same footing as the others. Unfortunately, adding border terms is in most cases necessary if we want a nice behavior for $\widehat{C}_t^n$, and they have to be chosen carefully, in connection with the sequence h_n of kernels. Often, but not always, the kernel functions h_n are of the form $h_n = a_n h$ with a kernel h independent of n and a normalizing factor a_n.

Finally, let us mention that the condition that each h_n is supported by $[0,1]$ could be relaxed. It could be a function on $\mathbb{R}$, with (7.33) replaced by

$$\widehat{C}_t^n = \sum_{i,j,j' \in \mathbb{Z}: \, 1 \leq i+j, i+j' \leq [t/\Delta_n]} h_n\left(\frac{|j'-j|}{k_n}\right) \Delta_{i+j}^n Y \, \Delta_{i+j'}^n Y$$
$$+ \text{ border terms}.$$

Basically, what follows holds also in this case, provided h_n goes to 0 fast enough at infinity.

We next turn to various examples of such estimators, including two and multi-scale realized volatility, pre-averaging estimators and realized kernel estimators. Note also that the estimation by a "Fourier transform" type of method is of this kind as well.

7.5   Subsampling and Averaging: Two-Scales Realized Volatility

In this section, we describe a method based on a quadratic estimator, which, historically speaking, was the first consistent estimator of integrated volatility proposed in the literature, in the presence of an additive white noise. This method in its simplest incarnation does not achieve the optimal rate of convergence $\Delta_n^{-1/4}$, but will be extended in the next section to achieve the optimal rate.

We consider the situation of a non-shrinking additive white noise, that is,

$$Y_i^n = X_{i\Delta_n} + \chi_{i\Delta_n}, \qquad (7.34)$$

where $(\chi_t)_{t\geq 0}$ satisfies (WN). The underlying process X is one-dimensional, continuous of the form (7.1), and satisfies (HC).

Since asymptotically the noise cannot be ignored, one might decide to sample at a lower frequency, as described in Subsection 7.1.5: we ignore all data except those occurring at some multiple $\Delta = k_n\Delta_n$ of Δ_n. As analyzed there, if k_n is "large enough" the leading term in the observed return $Y_{i\Delta}^n - Y_{(i-1)\Delta}^n$ is the log-price return $X_{i\Delta} - X_{(i-1)\Delta}$, which is large in comparison with the noise, whereas if k_n is "small enough" the sum $\sum_{i=1}^{[t/\Delta]}(X_{i\Delta} - X_{(i-1)\Delta})^2$ is a reasonable approximation of C_t. These two requirements act in opposite directions, and in any case the method, which could be called *sparse sampling* or *coarse subsampling*, does not enjoy any asymptotic property. Moreover, since c_t and γ are unknown, only a rule of thumb can help us to determine the best Δ, as described in Subsection 7.1.5.

The *two-scales realized volatility* (TSRV), or two scales subsampling method, is an attempt to reconcile the first requirement above (subsampling at a relatively low frequency) and the possibility of having a nice asymptotic behavior. By evaluating the quadratic variation at two different frequencies, averaging the results over the entire sample, and taking a suitable linear combination of the result at the two frequencies, one obtains a consistent estimator of C_T at terminal time T.

TSRV's construction is quite simple: first, partition the original grid of observation times $\mathcal{G} = \{i\Delta_n : i = 0, \ldots, [T/\Delta_n]\}$ into k_n subgrids $\mathcal{G}^{(j)} = \{(j+ik_n)\Delta_n : i = 0, \cdots, [T/k_n\Delta_n - j/k_n]\}$ for $j = 0, \ldots, k_n-1$, for a given sequence k_n of integers, which asymptotically goes to infinity but in such a way that $k_n\Delta_n \to 0$ (in order to ensure the possibility of consistent estimators). The sample size of the subgrids is $\bar{n} = [T/k_n\Delta_n]$ (up to ± 1), which goes to ∞. For example, for $\mathcal{G}^{(0)}$ start at the first observation and take an observation every 5 minutes; for $\mathcal{G}^{(1)}$, start at the second observation and take an observation every 5 minutes, etc. If we start with, say, $23,400$ observations over 6.5 hours at the 1 second frequency, we would then obtain $k_n = 300$ subsamples of $\bar{n} = 78$ observations each. We then average the estimators obtained on these subsamples. To the extent that there is a benefit to sampling at a lower frequency, this benefit can now be retained, while the variation of the estimator will be lessened by the averaging. This reduction in the estimator's variability will open the door to the possibility of doing bias correction.

For each subgrid $j = 0, \ldots, k_n - 1$ we compute the approximate quadratic variation on the basis of the subsample $\mathcal{G}^{(j)}$, and then we average over all j. This leads to a statistic of the form

$$\widehat{C}^{\text{subav}}(\Delta_n, k_n)_t = \frac{1}{k_n} \sum_{j=0}^{k_n-1} \underbrace{\sum_{i=1}^{[t/k_n\Delta_n - j/k_n]} (Y_{j+ik_n}^n - Y_{j+(i-1)k_n}^n)^2}_{\text{RV estimated on the } k\text{th subsample}}. \quad (7.35)$$

Similar to (7.13), the approximate asymptotic properties of this estimator are given by, with U an $\mathcal{N}(0,1)$ variable which is independent of the process X,

$$\widehat{C}^{\text{subav}}(\Delta_n, k_n)_t - C_t \overset{\mathcal{L}}{\approx} \underbrace{\frac{2t}{k_n\Delta_n}\gamma}_{\text{bias due to noise}} \quad (7.36)$$

$$+ \Big(\underbrace{\frac{4t}{k_n^2\Delta_n}\mathbb{E}(\chi^4)}_{\text{due to noise}} + \underbrace{\frac{4k_n\Delta_n}{3}C(4)_t}_{\text{due to discretization}} \Big)^{1/2} U.$$

$$\underbrace{}_{\text{total variance}}$$

While a better estimator than $\widehat{C}^{\text{noisy}}_{\text{sparse}}(\Delta_n)_t$, obtained on a single sparse sample, $\widehat{C}^{\text{subav}}(\Delta_n, k_n)_t$ remains biased, but with much lower bias since $k_n \to \infty$.

However, this bias can be removed by going one step further. As seen before, γ can be consistently estimated for example as in (7.31). The TSRV estimator is then computed as the bias-corrected estimator

$$\underbrace{\widehat{C}^{\text{TSRV}}(\Delta_n, k_n)_t}_{\text{Two Scales RV}} = \underbrace{\widehat{C}^{\text{subav}}(\Delta_n, k_n)_t}_{\text{slow time scale}} - \underbrace{\frac{1}{k_n}\widehat{C}^{\text{noisy}}(\Delta_n)_t}_{\text{fast time scale}}, \quad (7.37)$$

that is,

$$\widehat{C}^{\text{TSRV}}(\Delta_n, k_n)_t = \frac{1}{k_n} \sum_{j=0}^{k_n-1} \sum_{i=1}^{[t/k_n\Delta_n - j/k_n]} \big((Y_{j+ik_n}^n - Y_{j+(i-1)k_n}^n)^2 \quad (7.38)$$
$$- (\Delta_{j+ik_n}^n Y)^2\big).$$

Remark 7.12. *(Practical considerations) Estimators such as TSRV are designed to work for highly liquid assets. Indeed, the bias correction relies on the idea that RV computed with all the high-frequency observations,*

$\widehat{C}^{\text{ noisy}}(\Delta_n)_t$, consists primarily of noise. This is of course true asymptotically as $\Delta_n \to 0$. But if the full data sample frequency is low to begin with (for example, a stock sampled every minute instead of every second), $\widehat{C}^{\text{noisy}}(\Delta_n)_t$ will not be entirely noise, and bias correcting as above may overcorrect, including in extreme cases possibly yielding a negative estimator in (7.38). So care must be taken to apply the estimator to settings which are appropriate. This is designed to work for very high-frequency data, meaning settings where the raw data are sampled every few seconds in the case of typical financial data. If that is not the case, it may be advisable to stop at the estimator $\widehat{C}^{\text{ subav}}(\Delta_n, k_n)_t$ and not attempt the bias correction.

Remark 7.13. *Also, in small samples,*

$$\widehat{C}^{\text{TSRV}}_{\text{adjusted}}(\Delta_n, k_n)_t = (1 - \frac{\bar{n}}{n})^{-1} \widehat{C}^{\text{TSRV}}(\Delta_n, k_n)_t$$

can provide a useful adjustment to the TSRV estimator.

One still has to choose the number k_n of subsamples, and it turns out that the optimal choice is $k_n \sim \kappa\Delta_n^{-2/3}$. We can now use the approximation (7.36) and take into account the bias-correcting term in (7.38) to check the following result (it is stated under (WN), but as far as moments of the noise are concerned, only a finite fourth moment is required):

Theorem 7.14. *Assume (HC) and (WN), with (7.34), and choose the sequence k_n to be*

$$k_n \sim \frac{\kappa}{\Delta_n^{2/3}}, \qquad \text{for some } \kappa \in (0, \infty). \tag{7.39}$$

Then for each $T > 0$ the estimators $\widehat{C}^{\text{TSRV}}(\Delta_n, k_n)_t$ are consistent for estimating C_T, and the variables $\frac{1}{\Delta_n^{1/6}}(\widehat{C}^{\text{TSRV}}(\Delta_n, k_n)_T - C_T)$ converge stably in law to a variable defined on an extension of the space $(\Omega, \mathcal{F}, \mathbb{P})$, which conditionally on $\mathcal{F}$ is centered normal with (conditional) variance

$$\frac{8\gamma^2}{\kappa^2} + \frac{4\kappa T}{3} C(4)_T. \tag{7.40}$$

Unlike the previously considered estimators $\widehat{C}^{\text{noisy}}(\Delta_n)_T$, $\widehat{C}^{\text{noisy}}_{\text{sparse}}(\Delta_n)_T$ and $\widehat{C}^{\text{subav}}(\Delta_n, k_n)_T$, this estimator is now correctly centered at C_T.

Remark 7.15. *If we take k_n such that $k_n\Delta_n^{2/3} \to \infty$, then $\frac{1}{\sqrt{k_n\Delta_n}}(\widehat{C}^{\text{TSRV}}(\Delta_n, k_n)_T - C_T)$ converges stably in law to a variable having the same description as above, but with conditional variance*

$$\frac{4T}{3} C(4)_T$$

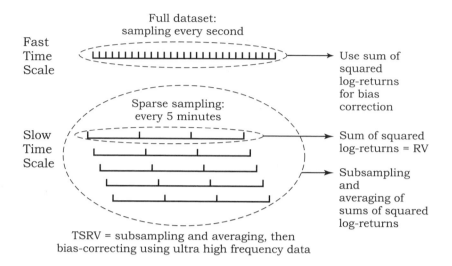

Figure 7.2: Description of TSRV's construction: sample on every grid at the slower 5 minute frequency, average the results, then use the highest frequency available to bias-correct the average.

instead of (7.40). Since $\sqrt{k_n \Delta_n}/\Delta_n^{1/6} \to \infty$ in this case, the rate deteriorates.

In contrast, when $k_n \Delta_n^{2/3} \to 0$ we still have a Central Limit Theorem, but with the centering term involving the noise only, instead of being C_T: we thus cannot do that for estimating C_T.

When $c_s = c$ is a constant, the optimal choice for κ, leading to the smallest asymptotic variance, is $\kappa = (T^2 c^2 / 12\,\gamma^2)^{1/3}$. Of course γ and c are unknown, but it is possible to use preliminary estimators for them (using for example $\frac{\Delta_n}{T}\widehat{C}^{\mathrm{noisy}}(\Delta_n)_T$ for γ and $\frac{1}{T}\widehat{C}^{\mathrm{TSRV}}(\Delta_n, k_n)_T$ for c with a sequence k_n satisfying (7.39) with, say, $\kappa = 1$), and then plug in the "optimal" value of κ thus derived. When c_s is not constant, this does not work, but one may use the same method to derive an "average" value of c_s over $[0, T]$ to plug into the formula for the optimal κ. This of course does *not* result in an optimal value, but probably improves things, in comparison to taking a completely arbitrary κ. This is not the end of the story: in order to have a "feasible" estimator it is necessary to have consistent estimators for the conditional variance (7.40). This is easy for the first term, but more difficult for the second one.

Figure 7.3 illustrates the differences between TSRV and RV, including

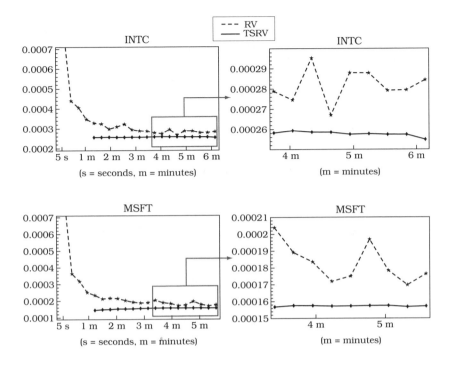

Figure 7.3: Comparison of TSRV and RV.

the divergence of RV when the sampling frequency increases, and the higher variability of RV around the 5mn sampling frequency.

We conclude this section with a few remarks:

Remark 7.16. *Here, we have restricted our attention to one-dimensional and continuous process. The multi-dimensional extension is straightforward, at least when the noises for the different components are independent (and in the regularly spaced observations case, of course). The possibility of an extension to discontinuous processes is not clear.*

Remark 7.17. *One can also wonder whether the method extends to a non-additive white noise. Although this has not been attempted, up to our knowledge, it seems likely that the method works under the general Assumption (GN) as well. It also clearly extends to the case of a shrinking noise, with better rates depending on the sequence α_n.*

Remark 7.18. *(From TSRV to MSRV) TSRV has been extended into what is called as MSRV, for multi-scales realized volatility. The idea is simple: TSRV uses two different scales (the coarsest or slowest one to compute the realized volatility in (7.35), and then the finest or fastest* *one to average these coarse realized volatility estimators). Nothing pre-vents us from computing the estimators $\widehat{C}^{subav}(\Delta_n, k)_T$ for all values k from 1 to some integer M_n, and then using as an estimator a weighted version of these preliminary estimators. Up to appropriately choosing the weights and the integer M_n, and upon adding a de-biasing term again, this "multi-scale" approach allows us to obtain a rate of convergence $1/\Delta_n^{1/4}$, which is the optimal rate for this problem. This method is very close to the pre-averaging method described below. Hence, for the sake of simplicity, we will describe the MSRV method after the pre-averaging method, see Section 7.8.*

7.6   The Pre-averaging Method

In this section, we assume that X satisfies (HC), hence in particular has the form (7.1). The noise satisfies (GN), and we have a possibly shrinking factor which takes the form $\alpha_n = \Delta_n^\eta$ for some known $\eta \in [0, \frac{1}{2})$. The observations are as in (7.15), that is,

$$Y_i^n = X_{i\Delta_n} + \epsilon_i^n, \qquad \epsilon_i^n = \Delta_n^{\mathring{\eta}} \chi_{i\Delta_n}, \tag{7.41}$$

and we use the notation $\Delta_i^n Y = Y_i^n - Y_{i-1}^n$ as before. Although we consider the possibility of a shrinking noise ($\eta > 0$), the reader should keep in mind that the most important case is when $\eta = 0$. Note also that we exclude $\eta \geq 1/2$. This eliminates the case $\eta > 1/2$ where, according to the toy model, the estimation of C_t should not be affected by noise, and it also eliminates the borderline case $\eta = 1/2$.

The heuristic idea is simple. Take a sequence k_n' of integers such that $k_n' \to \infty$ and $k_n' \Delta_n \to 0$, and consider the averages

$$Y_i^{\mathrm{av},n} = \frac{1}{k_n'} \sum_{j=0}^{k_n'-1} Y_{i+j}^n,$$

$$X_i^{\mathrm{av},n} = \frac{1}{k_n'} \sum_{j=0}^{k_n'-1} X_{(i+j)\Delta_n},$$

$$\epsilon_i^{\mathrm{av},n} = \frac{1}{k_n'} \sum_{j=0}^{k_n'-1} \epsilon_{(i+j)\Delta_n}.$$

Because $k_n' \to \infty$ and the ϵ_{i+j}^n's are $\mathcal{F}$-conditionally centered and independent, with essentially bounded moments, $\epsilon_i^{\mathrm{av},n}$ goes to 0 by an extension of the Law of Large Numbers; because $k_n' \Delta_n \to 0$, the variable $X_i^{\mathrm{av},n}$ is close to $X_{i\Delta_n}$, and thus so is $Y_i^{\mathrm{av},n} = X_i^{\mathrm{av},n} + \epsilon_i^{\mathrm{av},n}$. Then, basi-cally one may expect $\sum_{i=1}^{[t/\Delta_n]-2k_n'}(Y_{i+k_n'}^{\mathrm{av},n} - Y_i^{\mathrm{av},n})^2$ to be, after a suitable normalization, a reasonable estimator for C_t.

In reality, things are not quite as simple as in the previous description, but almost. Namely, we will need to add a de-biasing term. Also, the differences $Y^{av,n}_{i+k'_n} - Y^{av,n}_i$ above are averages of $2k'_n$ values of Y^n_j, with weights equal to 1 or -1 and summing up to 0; however, it might be wise to take non-uniform weights, provided they still sum up to 0.

To perform the construction, we basically need two ingredients:

- a sequence of integers k_n satisfying

$$k_n = \frac{1}{\theta \Delta_n^{\eta'}} + o\left(\frac{1}{\Delta_n^{(3\eta'-1)/2}}\right) \text{ as } n \to \infty$$
$$\text{where } \theta > 0, \ \eta' \geq \tfrac{1}{2} - \eta; \tag{7.42}$$

- a real-valued *weight function* g on $\mathbb{R}$, satisfying

$$\begin{aligned} &g \text{ is continuous, null outside } (0,1), \\ &\text{piecewise } C^1 \text{ with a piecewise Lipschitz derivative } g\prime. \end{aligned} \tag{7.43}$$

For any two bounded functions f, h on $\mathbb{R}$ with support in $[0,1]$, and for all integers $n, i \geq 1$ and all $t \in [0,1]$, we set

$$\begin{aligned} \phi(f, h|t) &= \int_t^1 f(s-t)\,h(s)ds, \\ \phi(f) &= \phi(f,f|0) = \int_0^1 f(t)^2 dt, \\ \Phi(f,h) &= \int_0^1 \phi(f,f|t)\,\phi(h,h|t)dt, \end{aligned} \tag{7.44}$$

and

$$\begin{aligned} \phi_{k_n}(h) &= \sum_{i=1}^{k_n} h\left(\tfrac{i}{k_n}\right)^2, \\ \phi'_{k_n}(h) &= \sum_{i=1}^{k_n} \left(h\left(\tfrac{i}{k_n}\right) - h\left(\tfrac{i-1}{k_n}\right)\right)^2. \end{aligned} \tag{7.45}$$

By virtue of (7.43), for any weight function g we have as $n \to \infty$

$$\begin{aligned} \phi_{k_n}(g) &= k_n \phi(g) + O(1), \\ \phi'_{k_n}(g) &= \tfrac{1}{k_n}\phi(g') + O\left(\tfrac{1}{k_n^2}\right). \end{aligned} \tag{7.46}$$

Next, with our observations and with k_n and the weight function g we associate the following variables (recall that $g(0) = g(1) = 0$, hence $\sum_{j=1}^{k_n}\left(g\left(\tfrac{i}{k_n}\right) - g\left(\tfrac{i-1}{k_n}\right)\right) = 0$):

$$\begin{aligned} \overline{Y}^n_i &= \sum_{j=1}^{k_n-1} g\left(\tfrac{j}{k_n}\right)\Delta^n_{i+j-1}Y = -\sum_{j=1}^{k_n}\left(g\left(\tfrac{j}{k_n}\right) - g\left(\tfrac{j-1}{k_n}\right)\right) Y^n_{i+j-2} \\ \widehat{Y}^n_i &= \sum_{j=1}^{k_n}\left(g\left(\tfrac{j}{k_n}\right) - g\left(\tfrac{j-1}{k_n}\right)\right)^2 (\Delta^n_{i+j-1}Y)^2. \end{aligned}$$

Example 7.19 (Triangular kernel). *The simplest weight function is*
$g(s) = 2(s \wedge (1-s))$ *for* $s \in [0,1]$, *for which*

$$\phi(g) = \frac{1}{3}, \quad \phi(g') = 4, \quad \Phi(g,g) = \frac{151}{5040}, \quad \Phi(g,g') = \frac{1}{6}, \quad \Phi(g',g') = \frac{8}{3}.$$

When $k_n = 2k'_n$ is even, we also have

$$\overline{Y}_i^n = \frac{1}{k'_n}(Y_{i+k'_n-1}^n + \cdots + Y_{i+2k'_n-2}^n) - \frac{1}{k'_n}(Y_{i-1}^n + \cdots + Y_{i+k'_n-2}^n)$$

$$\widehat{Y}_i^n = \frac{1}{k'^2_n}\sum_{j=1}^{2k'_n}(\Delta_{i+j-1}^n Y)^2.$$

In this case, $\overline{Y}_i^n$ is simply the difference between two successive (non-overlapping) averages of k'_n values of Y_i^n, that is, $Y_{i+k'_n-1}^{av,n} - Y_{i-1}^{av,n}$ with the notation of the beginning of the section.

We are now ready to exhibit the estimators for C_T. With the previous notation and under the previous assumptions (7.42) and (7.43), they are, as soon as $t > k_n\Delta_n$:

$$\widehat{C}^{\mathrm{Preav}}(\Delta_n, k_n, g)_t = \frac{1}{\phi_{k_n}(g)} \frac{t}{t - k_n\Delta_n} \\ \times \sum_{i=1}^{[t/\Delta_n]-k_n+1}\left((\overline{Y}_i^n)^2 - \frac{1}{2}\widehat{Y}_i^n\right). \tag{7.47}$$

We also set

$$\theta' = \begin{cases} \theta & \text{if } \eta' = 1/2 - \eta \\ 0 & \text{otherwise,} \end{cases} \tag{7.48}$$

and define a nonnegative function $(x,y) \mapsto R(g;x,y)$ on $\mathbf{R}_+^2$ by

$$R(g;u,v) = \frac{4}{\phi(g)^2}\left(\Phi(g,g)x^2 + 2\Phi(g,g')xy + \Phi(g',g')y^2\right). \tag{7.49}$$

We have the following, which combines consistency and the Central Limit Theorem:

Theorem 7.20. *Assume (GN) and (HC) (so in particular X is continuous), and choose k_n and g as in (7.42) and (7.43). Then for each $T > 0$ we have the convergence in probability*

$$\widehat{C}^{\mathrm{Preav}}(\Delta_n, k_n, g)_T \xrightarrow{\mathbb{P}} C_T. \tag{7.50}$$

If further $\eta' > \frac{1}{3}$, we also have the stable convergence in law:

$$\frac{1}{\Delta_n^{(1-\eta')/2}}\left(\widehat{C}^{\mathrm{Preav}}(\Delta_n, k_n, g)_T - C_T\right) \xrightarrow{\mathcal{L}-s} \mathcal{U}_T^{\mathrm{noise}}, \tag{7.51}$$

where $\mathcal{U}^{\text{noise}}$ *is a process defined on an extension of the space* $(\Omega, \mathcal{F}, \mathbb{P})$ *and, conditionally on* $\mathcal{F}$, *is a continuous centered Gaussian martingale with variance given by*

$$V(g)_T = \widetilde{E}\big((\mathcal{U}_T^{\text{noise}})^2 \mid \mathcal{F}\big) = \frac{1}{\theta} \int_0^T R(g; c_s, \theta'^2 \gamma_s) \, ds. \qquad (7.52)$$

Proof. We use the notation (A.58) and (A.59), and observe that $f_{2,0}(x, z) = x^2 - z/2$, so

$$\begin{aligned} \widehat{C}^{\text{Preav}}(\Delta_n, k_n, g)_T &= \frac{k_n \phi(g)}{\phi_{k_n}(g)} \frac{T}{T - k_n \Delta_n} \frac{1}{\phi(g)} \\ &\quad \times B^{\text{noisy}}(2, 0; \Delta_n, k_n, g)_T, \end{aligned} \qquad (7.53)$$

and (7.46) implies that

$$\left| \frac{k_n \phi(g)}{\phi_{k_n}(g)} \frac{T}{T - k_n \Delta_n} - 1 \right| \leq K(\Delta_n^{\eta'} + \Delta_n^{1-\eta'}).$$

Moreover we have here $[X, X] = C$. Hence (7.50) follows from (b) of Theorem A.17 and, since $\Delta_n^{\eta'} + \Delta_n^{1-\eta'} = o(\Delta_n^{(1-\eta')/2})$ when $\eta' > \frac{1}{3}$, (7.51) is a consequence of Theorem A.20 applied with a single component corresponding to the weight function g ($\mathcal{U}^{\text{noise}}$ above is $\frac{1}{\sqrt{\theta}} \mathcal{W}(2)^{\text{noise}}$ there). Moreover, a straightforward (but tedious) computation shows that $R_p(g, h; x, y)$ when $p = 2$ and $g = h$ is exactly $\phi(g)^2 R(g; x, y)$ in (7.49). $\qquad \square$

Remark 7.21. *As seen from the proof,* $\frac{1}{\phi(g)} B^{\text{noisy}}(2, 0; \Delta_n, k_n, g)_T$ *is the key process to study, and was, as such, the first pre-averaged estimator introduced in the literature. However, at least when* $b_t \equiv 0$ *and* $c_t \equiv c$ *is non-random and constant, this variable has expectation*

$$\frac{\phi_{k_n}(g)}{k_n \phi(g)} \frac{[t/\Delta_n]\Delta_n - (k_n - 1)\Delta_n}{T} C_T.$$

This is why we multiply $\frac{1}{\phi(g)} B^{\text{noisy}}(2, 0; \Delta_n, k_n, g)_T$ *in (7.53) by the two correcting factors* $\frac{k_n \phi(g)}{\phi_{k_n}(g)}$ *and* $\frac{T}{T - k_n \Delta_n}$, *the latter being really close to* $\frac{t}{[t/\Delta_n]\Delta_n - (k_n - 1)\Delta_n}$. *The first correction term may be bigger or smaller than* 1, *depending on* k_n *and on* g. *The second correction term is always bigger than* 1, *and without it the estimator is systematically downward biased (of course these correction terms are asymptotically negligible in the CLT above).*

However, although the theorem as stated holds if we replace the terminal time T *by any* $t > 0$, *and in contrast with the processes* $B^{\text{noisy}}(2, 0; \Delta_n, k_n, g)$ *which enjoys a functional limit theorem, this is not the case for* $\widehat{C}^{\text{Preav}}(\Delta_n, k_n, g)_t$, *because of the correcting factor* $\frac{t}{t - k_n}$.

Remark 7.22. *The reader should be aware of the fact that* $\widehat{C}^{\mathrm{Preav}}(\Delta_n, k_n, g)_T$ *may take negative values, and does so with a positive probability in most cases. This property is shared by all estimators proposed in this chapter (TSRV estimator, and the kernel and MSRV estimators to be seen later), and this is in deep contrast with all the estimators introduced in the Chapter 6 when there is no noise. This requires a few comments:*

1. *This can be considered as a serious drawback, but there really is nothing one can do about it, except for saying that if* $\widehat{C}^{\mathrm{Preav}}(\Delta_n, k_n, g)_T < 0$ *the estimator is not reliable (by lack of data, for example).*

2. *It may happen that* $C_T = 0$*, or that* C_T *is positive but very small; in these cases having an estimator with a negative value is not overwhelmingly strange.*

3. *In any case, the estimator by itself is not the only information one can get; we also have confidence bounds, see below. Then, unless the confidence interval at a typical asymptotic level is completely on the negative side, the fact that* $\widehat{C}^{\mathrm{Preav}}(\Delta_n, k_n, g)_T < 0$ *is not redhibitory.*

In order to make this CLT feasible we also need consistent estimators for the conditional variance given in (7.52). Indeed, suppose that we have observable variables V_t^n at stage n, satisfying

$$\frac{1}{\Delta_n^{1-\eta'}} V_T^n \xrightarrow{\mathbb{P}} V(g)_T, \qquad (7.54)$$

with further $V_T^n > 0$ almost surely on the set $\{C_T > 0\}$. Then, analogous with Theorem 6.4 and using a formulation similar to (6.11), we state the following result:

Theorem 7.23. *Under (GN) and (KC) and (7.42) with* $\eta' > \frac{1}{3}$ *and (7.43), and if* V_T^n *satisfies (7.54), we have*

$$\mathcal{L}\left(\frac{\widehat{C}^{\mathrm{Preav}}(\Delta_n, k_n, g)_T - C_T}{\sqrt{V_T^n}} \,\Big|\, A \right) \to \mathcal{N}(0, 1)$$
for all $A \in \mathcal{F}$ *with* $\mathbb{P}(A) > 0$ *and* $A \subset \{C_T > 0\}$.

On the basis of this convergence, it is straightforward to derive confidence intervals for C_t, in exactly the same way as (6.12)–(6.13), and we leave this to the reader.

Our task is now to find processes V^n satisfying (7.54). For this, we rely upon Theorem A.17-(c) of Appendix A, applied with $(p,q) = (4,0), (2,1), (0,2)$. After an elementary calculation, we see that the variables

$$
\begin{aligned}
V^{\mathrm{I}}(\Delta_n, k_n, g)_t = \frac{1}{k_n \, \phi(g)^2} \sum_{i=1}^{[t/\Delta_n]-k_n+1} & \left(\frac{4\Phi(g,g)}{3\phi(g)^2} (\overline{Y}_i^n)^4 \right. \\
& + 4\left(\frac{\Phi(g,g')}{\phi(g)\phi(g')} - \frac{\Phi(g,g)}{\phi(g)^2} \right)(\overline{Y}_i^n)^2 \, \widehat{Y}_i^n \\
& \left. + \left(\frac{\Phi(g,g)}{\phi(g)^2} - \frac{2\Phi(g,g')}{\phi(g)\,\phi(g')} + \frac{\Phi(g',g')}{\phi(g')^2} \right)(\widehat{Y}_i^n)^2 \right)
\end{aligned}
\tag{7.55}
$$

satisfy (7.54) (the convergence is even locally uniform in time).

According to the discussion in Remark 7.21, we can de-bias these estimators in a sense, and use instead

$$
\begin{aligned}
V^{\mathrm{II}}(\Delta_n, k_n, g)_t = \frac{1}{\phi_{k_n}(g)^2} \frac{t}{t - k_n\Delta_n} \sum_{i=1}^{[t/\Delta_n]-k_n+1} & \left(\frac{4\Phi_{k_n}(g)}{3\phi_{k_n}(g)^2} (\overline{Y}_i^n)^4 \right. \\
& + 4\left(\frac{\Phi_{k_n}'(g)}{\phi_{k_n}(g)\phi_n'(g)} - \frac{\Phi_{k_n}(g)}{\phi_{k_n}(g)^2} \right)(\overline{Y}_i^n)^2 \, \widehat{Y}_i^n \\
& \left. + \left(\frac{\Phi_{k_n}(g)}{\phi_{k_n}(g)^2} - \frac{2\Phi_{k_n}'(g)}{\phi_{k_n}(g)\,\phi_{k_n}'(g)} + \frac{\Phi_{k_n}''(g)}{\phi_{k_n}'(g)^2} \right)(\widehat{Y}_i^n)^2 \right),
\end{aligned}
\tag{7.56}
$$

where

$$
\Phi_{k_n}(g) = \sum_{i,j,l=0}^{k_n} g\left(\tfrac{j}{k_n}\right) g\left(\tfrac{j-i}{k_n}\right) g\left(\tfrac{l}{k_n}\right) g\left(\tfrac{l-i}{k_n}\right)
$$

$$
\Phi_{k_n}'(g) = \sum_{i,j,l=0}^{k_n} g\left(\tfrac{j}{k_n}\right) g\left(\tfrac{j-i}{k_n}\right) \left(g\left(\tfrac{l}{k_n}\right) - g\left(\tfrac{l-1}{k_n}\right) \right) \left(g\left(\tfrac{l-i}{k_n}\right) - g\left(\tfrac{l-1-i}{k_n}\right) \right)
$$

$$
\begin{aligned}
\Phi_{k_n}''(g) = \sum_{i,j,l=0}^{k_n} & \left(g\left(\tfrac{j}{k_n}\right) - g\left(\tfrac{j-1}{k_n}\right) \right) \left(g\left(\tfrac{j-i}{k_n}\right) - g\left(\tfrac{j-1-i}{k_n}\right) \right) \\
& \times \left(g\left(\tfrac{l}{k_n}\right) - g\left(\tfrac{l-1}{k_n}\right) \right) \left(g\left(\tfrac{l-i}{k_n}\right) - g\left(\tfrac{l-1-i}{k_n}\right) \right).
\end{aligned}
$$

(To check that $V^{\mathrm{II}}(\Delta_n, k_n, g)$ and $V^{\mathrm{I}}(\Delta_n, k_n, g)$ have the same asymptotic behavior, one may use (7.46) and the analogous properties $\Phi_{k_n}(g) \sim k_n^3 \Phi(g,g)$ and $\Phi_{k_n}'(g) \sim k_n\Phi(g',g)$ and $\Phi_{k_n}''(g) \sim \Phi(g',g')/k_n$.)

Finally, when $\eta' > \frac{1}{2} - \eta$, we can also take the simpler variables

$$
V^{\mathrm{III}}(\Delta_n, k_n, g)_t = \frac{4\Phi(g,g)}{3k_n \, \phi(g)^4} \sum_{i=1}^{[t/\Delta_n]-k_n+1} (\overline{Y}_i^n)^4.
\tag{7.57}
$$

This seems to settle the question, but unless we can use (7.57) we potentially have a problem here, because the variables $V^{\mathrm{I}}(\Delta_n, k_n, g)_T$ and $V^{\mathrm{II}}(\Delta_n, k_n, g)_T$ may take negative values, exactly as in Remark 7.27 for the pre-averaging estimator itself. This problem was already encountered in Subsection 6.1.2. So, again, we have several ways to overcome this problem:

1. Apply Theorem 7.23 with $V_T^n = |V^{II}(\Delta_n, k_n, g)_T|$, which still satisfies (7.54) and also $V_t^n > 0$ almost surely on the set $\{C_T > 0\}$. Although asymptotically correct, this obviously does not work in finite samples when we come up with a negative value for $V^I(\Delta_n, k_n, g)_T$.

2. Choose a sequence $u_n > 0$ going to 0 faster than $\Delta_n^{1-\eta'}$ and take $V_T^n = u_n \vee V^{II}(\Delta_n, k_n, g)_T$. Again, this is mathematically correct, but in practice the choice of u_n is totally unclear, and from a practical viewpoint this method is basically the same as the previous one.

3. Try to find estimators that are nonnegative by construction. This is indeed possible, and an example may be found in Kinnebrock and Podolskij (2008). However, we will not elaborate on this since, should $V^{II}(\Delta_n, k_n, g)_T$ be negative, this would mainly signal that we are far from the asymptotic behavior for estimating the conditional variance and, in this case, there is no reason to suppose that it is not the case for the estimator $\widehat{C}^{\mathrm{Preav}}(\Delta_n, k_n, g)_T$ as well: it might be wiser to give up the estimation, for lack of enough data. There is no difference, in that respect, with the estimation of the integrated cross-volatility, except that here the rate of convergence is much slower $(1/\Delta_n^{1/4}$ in the non-shrinking noise case, instead of $1/\Delta_n^{1/2}$ for the integrated volatility), rendering the problem more acute here.

4. Another, easy to implement method consists of using a non-optimal rate (with $\eta' < \frac{1}{2} - \eta$), and the variance estimators $V^{III}(\Delta_n, k_n, g)_T$ which are positive by construction. We loose accuracy, but in view of the poor rate of convergence mentioned above, it does not make a huge difference from a practical viewpoint.

Remark 7.24. *In the first theorem above, the number θ occurring in (7.42) explicitly appears in the result, through (7.52). In the second theorem it has disappeared from the picture, because in some sense the property (7.54) automatically incorporates θ in V_T^n (note that the versions $V^I(\Delta_n, k_n, g)_T$, $V^{II}(\Delta_n, k_n, g)_T$ and $V^{III}(\Delta_n, k_n, g)_t$ of V_T^n, as well as $\widehat{C}^{\mathrm{Preav}}(\Delta_n, k_n, g)_T$, use g and k_n explicitly, but not θ itself).*

Remark 7.25. *Not only does θ implicitly influence the estimators, but the power η' also does, in a more essential way (although, as before, it does not explicitly shows in the "feasible" theorem 7.23). The smaller the*

η', the more accurate the estimator is, but the constraint $\eta' \geq \frac{1}{2} - \eta$ is essential.

However, assuming that we know the rate of shrinking of the noise, as expressed by η, is in most cases totally unrealistic. So in practice one should probably presume that the noise is not shrinking ($\eta = 0$), and thus take $\eta' = \frac{1}{2}$.

7.6.1 Pre-averaging and Optimality

In this subsection we state a few comments about the quality of the estimator $\widehat{C}^{\mathrm{Preav}}(\Delta_n, k_n, g)$, and in particular about its asymptotic optimality (or lack thereof).

We begin with a first general comment. In (7.47) the numbers $\phi_{k_n}(g)$ appear. From a purely asymptotic viewpoint, it is possible to replace them by $k_n \phi(g)$. However, when k_n is not very large, it is probably more accurate to use $\phi_{k_n}(g)$, which is closer than $k_n \phi(g)$ to the "true" parameter governing the law of the variable $\overline{Y}_i^n$, since the latter is a discrete approximation.

Next, consider the rate of convergence. This rate is $1/\Delta_n^{(1-\eta')/2}$, faster as η' gets smaller, and this number η' is subject to the restrictions $\eta' \geq \frac{1}{2} - \eta$ and $\eta' > \frac{1}{3}$. This leads us to the following comments:

- When $\eta = 0$ (non-shrinking noise) or when $0 < \eta < \frac{1}{6}$ (slowly shrinking noise), one should take $\eta' = \frac{1}{2} - \eta$, leading to the rate $1/\Delta_n^{1/4 + \eta/2}$, and in particular $1/\Delta_n^{1/4}$ in the non-shrinking case. This is in accordance with (7.24), for the toy model seen above. So in these cases one may think that the pre-averaging estimators are *rate-optimal*.

- When $\frac{1}{6} \leq \eta < \frac{1}{2}$ the choice $\eta' = \frac{1}{2} - \eta$ is no longer possible. However, by taking η' very close to, though bigger than, $\frac{1}{3}$, one "approaches" the rate $1/\Delta_n^{1/3}$. In view of (7.24), this is no longer optimal.

Finally, *and only in the non-shrinking noise case* $\eta = 0$, let us discuss optimality, since we already have rate-optimality, upon taking $\eta' = \frac{1}{2}$, so $\theta' = \theta$. We wish to minimize the asymptotic (normalized) variance $V(g)_T$ in (7.52). Since the processes c_t and γ_t are fixed, although unknown, we have two degrees of freedom, namely the choices of the weight function g and of the number θ.

Let us first discuss the (unlikely) situation where both $c_t = c$ and $\gamma_t = \gamma$ are constants. In this situation one knows, see Section 7.3.1 above, that the LAN property for estimating c, or equivalently $C_T = cT$, holds with rate $1/\Delta_n^{1/4}$ and optimal (normalized) asymptotic variance $V_t^{\mathrm{opt}} = 8t\sqrt{c^3\gamma}$, in accordance with (7.24). Coming back to the pre-averaging estimators, for a given kernel g, we may choose θ in an optimal way. Indeed, since

$$V(g)_T = \tfrac{4T}{\phi(g)^2}\left(\Phi(g,g)\,c^2\tfrac{1}{\theta} + 2\Phi(g,g')\,c\,\gamma\,\theta + \Phi(g',g')\,\gamma^2\,\theta^3\right),$$

the optimal choice is $\theta = H_g(c,\gamma)$, where

$$H_g(x,y) = \left(\frac{x}{y}\,\frac{\sqrt{\Phi(g,g')^2 + 3\Phi(g,g)\Phi(g',g')} - \Phi(g,g')}{3\Phi(g',g')}\right)^{1/2}, \qquad (7.58)$$

which leads to $V(g)_t = \alpha(g)V_t^{\mathrm{opt}}$, where

$$\alpha(g) = \frac{6\Phi(g,g)\Phi(g',g') + 2\Phi(g,g')\sqrt{\Phi(g,g')^2 + 3\Phi(g,g)\Phi(g',g')} - 2\Phi(g,g')^2}{3^{3/2}\phi(g)^2\Phi(g',g')^{1/2}\left(\sqrt{\Phi(g,g')^2 + 3\Phi(g,g)\Phi(g',g')} - \Phi(g,g')\right)^{1/2}}. \qquad (7.59)$$

In order to use this, one has to know c and γ, or at least the ratio c/γ: for this, one can follow the method for deriving the optimal θ in (7.39) for the TSRV method.

As for the choice of the weight function g, it amounts to minimizing the number $\alpha(g)$ in (7.59), which cannot be smaller than 1. In the case of the triangular kernel (Example 7.19) one easily sees that $\alpha(g) \sim 1.07$, which is very close indeed to the minimal value 1.

In the more realistic situation where c_t, and perhaps also γ_t, are not constant, one should of course choose the weight function such that $\alpha(g)$ is as close as possible to 1, and then choose a "reasonable" θ, close to the value given by (7.58) with c and γ replaced by average values of c_t and γ_t, as estimated (or roughly guessed) according to a preliminary procedure, as in Section 7.5 above.

There is, however, another method. In fact, minimizing the integrand in (7.52) for each value of time leads one to take $\theta_s = H_g(c_s, \gamma_s)$ for all s, and in this case the conditional variance becomes the following "optimal" value:

$$V^{\mathrm{opt}}(g)_T = 8\,\alpha(g)\int_0^T \sqrt{c_t^3\,\gamma_t}\,dt. \qquad (7.60)$$

This seems unfeasible, for two good reasons: one is that c_t and γ_t are unknown; the other is that θ governs the ratio $1/k_n\Delta_n^{1/2}$ (recall that we take the optimal $\eta' = \tfrac{1}{2}$ since the noise is not shrinking), so if $\theta = \theta_t$ depends on time, then k_n should also depend on time. However, it is possible to straighten out the argument and make it feasible by dividing the time interval $[0, T]$ into blocks on which one can consider c_t and γ_t, hence $H_g(c_t, \gamma_t)$ as well, to be "almost" constant, and then perform the pre-averaging with the optimal value of k_n within each block. This is what we do in the next subsection.

7.6.2   Adaptive Pre-averaging

In this subsection, the noise is not shrinking. We also suppose Assumptions (KC) and (P), as in Theorem 7.11, and a slight reinforcement of (GN), namely

Assumption (GNS). *We have (GN); moreover, the variance process γ_t is an Itô semimartingale satisfying (H-2), and neither γ_t nor γ_{t-} vanishes.*

This assumption ensures that γ is not time-varying too wildly, which is necessary if we want local estimators for it. It could be significantly weakened, but as stated it is not really restrictive when (GN) holds.

We fix the time horizon, say T, and also the weight function g. The estimating procedure is performed through two steps, and we choose two sequences of integers, subject to the conditions

$$l_n \asymp \frac{1}{\Delta_n^w} \ \text{ with } w \in \left(\frac{5}{6}, 1\right), \ k_n \asymp \frac{1}{\Delta_n^{1/2}}, \ 4 \le 2k_n < l_n < T/\Delta_n. \quad (7.61)$$

We split the data into consecutive blocks of data with size l_n each (except for the last one, with size between l_n and $2l_n - 1$). The number of blocks is L_n and the calendar times at which the jth block starts and ends are $T(n, j-1)$ and $T(n, j)$, as given by

$$L_n = \left[\frac{T}{l_n \Delta_n}\right], \qquad T(n, j) = \begin{cases} j l_n \Delta_n & \text{if } j < L_n \\ T & \text{if } j = L_n. \end{cases}$$

Step 1: local estimation of c_t and γ_t. We do the adaptive procedure for the blocks $j = 2, \ldots, L_n$, and for this we use estimators for c_t and γ_t based on the second half of the previous block. More specifically, with $I(n, j) = (T(n, j-2) + l_n \Delta_n/2, T(n, j-1)]$, we estimate the following averages:

$$\overline{c}^n(j) = \frac{2}{l_n \Delta_n} \int_{I(n,j)} c_t \, dt, \qquad \overline{\gamma}^n(j) = \frac{2}{l_n \Delta_n} \int_{I(n,j)} \gamma_t \, dt.$$

The estimators will be

$$
\widehat{c}^n(j) = \frac{2}{l_n \Delta_n \, \phi_{k_n}(g)} \sum_{i=(j-1)l_n-[l_n/2]-k_n}^{(j-1)l_n-k_n} \left((\overline{Z}(k_n)_i^n)^2 - \tfrac{1}{2}\widehat{Z}(k_n)_i^n \right)
$$
$$
\widehat{\gamma}^n(j) = \tfrac{1}{l_n} \sum_{j=(j-1)l_n-[l_n/2]}^{(j-1)l_n} (\Delta_j^n Z)^2
$$

(7.62)

and it turns out that

$$
\begin{aligned}
\widehat{c}^n(j) - \overline{c}^n(j) &= O_{Pu}(\Delta_n^{(2w-1)/4}), \\
\widehat{\gamma}^n(j) - \overline{\gamma}^n(j) &= O_{Pu}(\Delta_n^{w/2}),
\end{aligned}
$$

(7.63)

where $V_i^n = O_{Pu}(v_n)$ means that the variables V_i^n/v_n are bounded in probability, uniformly in i. In turn, with the notation (7.58), this implies

$$
\widehat{\theta}^n(j) - \overline{\theta}^n(j) = O_{Pu}(\Delta_n^{(2w-1)/4}),
$$

where $\widehat{\theta}^n(j) = H_g(\widehat{c}^n(j),\widehat{\gamma}^n(j))$ and $\overline{\theta}^n(j) = H_g(\overline{c}^n(j),\overline{\gamma}^n(j))$.

Step 2: global estimation. We set

$$
k_{n,j} = \begin{cases} k_n & \text{if } j=1 \\ [2\vee(\tfrac{l_n}{2}\wedge\frac{\widehat{\theta}^n(j)}{\sqrt{\Delta_n}})] & \text{if } j\geq 2 \end{cases}
$$

(7.64)

(taking the infimum with $l_n/2$ and the supremum with 2 is irrelevant mathematically speaking, because $\widehat{\theta}^n_{j-1}/\sqrt{\Delta_n}$ goes to infinity at a smaller rate than l_n; however, for small samples, this may be effective, and it would probably be even more appropriate to take the supremum with a value much bigger than 2, such as 10 or 20.

Note that in (7.64) the value $k_{n,1} = k_n$ is as in (7.61) and we do no adaptation within the first block. The other values $k_{n,j}$ are random, but known to the statistician, and our final estimator is

$$
\widehat{C}^{\mathrm{Preav\text{-}Ad}}(\Delta_n,g)_T = \sum_{j=1}^{L_n} \frac{a(n,j)}{\phi_{k_{n,j}}(g)}
$$
$$
\times \sum_{i=J(n,j-1)+1}^{J(n,j)} \left((\overline{Z}(k_{n,j})_i^n)^2 - \tfrac{1}{2}\,\widehat{Z}(k_{n,j})_i^n \right)
$$

(7.65)

where $J(n,0) = 0$ and

$$
\begin{aligned}
1\leq j<L_n \;&\Rightarrow\; \begin{cases} J(n,j) = jl_n \\ a(n,j) = 1 \end{cases} \\
j = L_n \;&\Rightarrow\; \begin{cases} J(n,j) = [T/\Delta_n] - k_{n,L_n} + 1 \\ a(n,j) = \frac{J(n,L_n)-J(n,L_n-1)+k_{n,L_n}}{J(n,L_n)-J(n,L_n-1)}. \end{cases}
\end{aligned}
$$

We also need estimators for the conditional variance encountered below. To this end, we can use

$$
\begin{aligned}
\widehat{V}_T'^n = \sum_{j=1}^{L_n} \frac{a(n,j)}{\phi_{k_{n,j}}(g)^2} \sum_{i=J(n,j-1)+1}^{J(n,j)} & \left(\frac{4\Phi_{k_{n,j}}(g)}{3\phi_{k_{n,j}}(g)^2} (\overline{Z}(k_{n,j})_i^n)^4 \right. \\
+ 4\left(\frac{\Phi'_{k_{n,j}}(g)}{\phi_{k_{n,j}}(g)\phi'_{k_{n,j}}(g)} - \frac{\Phi_{k_{n,j}}(g)}{\phi_{k_{n,j}}(g)^2} \right) & (\overline{Z}(k_{n,j})_i^n)^2 \, \widehat{Z}(k_{n,j})_i^n \\
+ \left(\frac{\Phi_{k_{n,j}}(g)}{\phi_{k_{n,j}}(g)^2} - \frac{2\Phi'_{k_{n,j}}(g)}{\phi_{k_{n,j}}(g)\,\phi'_{k_{n,j}}(g)} + \frac{\Phi''_{k_{n,j}}(g)}{\phi'_{k_{n,j}}(g)^2} \right) & \left. (\widehat{Z}(k_{n,j})_i^n)^2 \right).
\end{aligned}
\tag{7.66}
$$

The behavior of these estimators is given in the following theorem, and we refer to Jacod and Mykland (2012) for a proof:

Theorem 7.26. *Under (KC), (P) and (GNS) the variables* $\widehat{C}^{Preav\text{-}Ad}(\Delta_n, g)_T$ *converge in probability to* C_T, *and we have the following stable convergence in law:*

$$
\frac{1}{\Delta_n^{1/4}} (\widehat{C}^{\text{Preav-Ad}}(\Delta_n, g)_T - C_T) \xrightarrow{\mathcal{L}-s} \mathcal{U}_T'^{\text{noise}},
$$

where $\mathcal{U}_T'^{\text{noise}}$ *is a variable defined on an extension of the space* $(\Omega, \mathcal{F}, \mathbb{P})$ *which, conditionally on* $\mathcal{F}$, *is centered Gaussian with conditional variance*

$$
V^{\text{opt}}(g)_T = \widetilde{E}((\mathcal{U}_T'^{\text{noise}})^2 \mid \mathcal{F}) = 8\,\alpha(g) \int_0^T \sqrt{c_s^3 \gamma_s}\, ds,
$$

where $\alpha(g)$ *is given by (7.59).*

Moreover, we have $\frac{1}{\sqrt{\Delta_n}} \widehat{V}_T'^n \xrightarrow{\mathbb{P}} V^{\text{opt}}(g)_T$, *and thus the variables* $\frac{1}{\sqrt{\widehat{V}_T'^n}} (\widehat{C}^{\text{Preav-Ad}}(\Delta_n, g)_T - C_T)$ *(stably) converge in law to a standard normal variable.*

In particular, the conditional variance achieves the optimal value (relative to the weight function g) given by (7.60). Of course, this leaves open the choice of g, but once more the triangular kernel is nearly optimal.

Remark 7.27. *For simplicity, we have taken the same weight function g for pre-averaging in the two steps, but this is of course not necessary.*

Remark 7.28. *One needs (P) for the estimated value of θ_t to be positive, and the last part of (GNS) for it to be finite. When the process γ is allowed to vanish, and does indeed vanish on some interval, at these places $\widehat{\theta}^n(j)$ tends to be large, and $k_{n,j}$ becomes equal to 2, for n large enough and all j with $jl_n\Delta_n$ in this interval. As easily checked from (7.65), and for the triangular kernel g, it follows that this interval contributes 0 in the sum defining $C^{Preav\text{-}Ad}(\Delta_n, g)_t$, which precludes even the consistency of these* *estimators. For another kernel g, or if we were taking the supremum with a number other than 2 in (7.64), the contribution would be possibly not 0 but still the consistency of the estimators for the integrated volatility would fail.*

7.7 Flat Top Realized Kernels

The pre-averaging estimators are special cases of the general quadratic estimators described in Section 7.4, with a kernel (as in (7.33) for example) having rather specific properties. One can look at more general kernels, still subject to some restrictions of course. This is the aim of this section.

One chooses a sequence k_n of integers satisfying (7.42), and a kernel function f on $[0,1]$ satisfying

$$f \text{ is } C^3, \text{ and } f(0) = 1, \quad f(1) = f'(0) = f'(1) = 0. \tag{7.67}$$

The estimator of C_T at stage n is

$$
\begin{aligned}
\widehat{C}^{\mathrm{FT}}(\Delta_n, k_n, f)_T &= \sum_{i=k_n-1}^{[T/\Delta_n]-k_n+2} \Big((\Delta_i^n Y)^2 \\
&+ \sum_{r=1}^{k_n-2} f\big(\tfrac{r-1}{k_n}\big) \big(\Delta_i^n Y \, \Delta_{i+r}^n Y + \Delta_i^n Y \, \Delta_{i-r}^n Y\big)\Big).
\end{aligned}
\tag{7.68}
$$

The "flat top" qualifier refers to the fact that in each ith summand the weights of $\Delta_i^n Y \, \Delta_{i+j}^n Y$ are equal (to 1) when $j = -1, 0, 1$. We associate with f the numbers

$$
\begin{aligned}
\overline{\Phi}(f) &= \int_0^1 f(s)^2 \, ds, \\
\overline{\Phi}'(f) &= \int_0^1 f'(s)^2 \, ds, \\
\overline{\Phi}''(f) &= \int_0^1 f''(s)^2 \, ds.
\end{aligned}
\tag{7.69}
$$

It is instructive to compare this with the pre-averaging estimator, from the viewpoint of (7.33). Letting aside the border terms (for $i \leq k_n$ or $i \geq [T/\Delta_n] - 2k_n$), and also the asymptotically negligible correcting factor $\frac{t}{t-k_n}$ in the pre-averaging case, both the pre-averaging estimator and the flat top kernel estimator are of that form, with the following function h_n on $[0,1]$:

$$
h_n(x) =
\begin{cases}
\bullet \text{ for the pre-averaging estimator:} \\
\quad \frac{1}{k_n \phi_n(g)} \sum_{j=1}^{[k_n(1-x)]-1} g\big(\tfrac{j}{k_n}\big) g\big(x \vee \tfrac{1}{k_n} + \tfrac{j}{k_n}\big) \\
\bullet \text{ for the flat top kernel estimator:} \\
\quad \frac{1}{k_n} f\big((x - \tfrac{1}{k_n})^+\big)
\end{cases}
$$

(only the values at $x = j/k_n$ really matter here). The functions h_n are different in the two cases. However, as $n \to \infty$ the products $k_n h_n$ converge, with the rate $1/k_n$, to the limit $h^{\text{Preav}}(x) = \phi(g|x)/\phi(g)$ and $h^{\text{FT}} = f$, respectively.

The function $h^{\text{FT}} = f$ is, apart from (7.67), completely general, whereas the function h^{Preav} is restricted, since it is the square of g (up to a normalizing constant) in the convolution sense. When f satisfies (7.67) and has the form $f(x) = \phi(g|x)/\phi(g)$ for a function g satisfying (7.43), we also have $f''(x) = -\phi(g'|x)$ and thus, by an integration by parts, we see that the numbers in (7.69) are indeed

$$\overline{\Phi}(f) = \frac{\Phi(g,g)}{\phi(g)^2}, \quad \overline{\Phi}'(f) = \frac{\Phi(g,g')}{\phi(g)^2}, \quad \overline{\Phi}''(f) = \frac{\Phi(g',g')}{\phi(g)^2}.$$

As it turns out, only the asymptotic behavior of the function h_n defined above really matters for proving a theorem such as Theorem 7.20. So one may expect a result of the following type: under (GN) and (KC) and (7.42), plus (7.67) for f, we have

$$\frac{1}{\Delta_n^{(1-\eta')/2}} \left(\widehat{C}^{\text{FT}}(\Delta_n, k_n, f)_T - C_T \right) \xrightarrow{\mathcal{L}-\text{s}} \mathcal{U}_T^{\prime\text{noise}}, \qquad (7.70)$$

where $\mathcal{U}_T^{\prime\text{noise}}$ is a variable defined on an extension of the space $(\Omega, \mathcal{F}, \mathbb{P})$ which, conditionally on $\mathcal{F}$, is centered Gaussian with variance

$$\begin{aligned} V'(f)_T &= \widetilde{E}\big((\mathcal{U}_T^{\prime\text{noise}})^2 \mid \mathcal{F}\big) \\ &= \tfrac{4}{\theta} \int_0^T \left(\overline{\Phi}(f)\, c_s^2 + 2\overline{\Phi}'(f)\, \theta'^2 c_s \gamma_s + \overline{\Phi}''(f)\, \theta'^4 \gamma_s^2 \right) ds, \end{aligned} \qquad (7.71)$$

with again θ' given by (7.48).

We will not exhibit explicit estimators for the conditional variance occurring in (7.71). But this is of course possible, in the spirit of (7.55).

Remark 7.29. (Warning about border effects) *Only the case of Assumption (WN) with non-shrinking noise ($v_n = 1$) is fully treated in Barndorff-Nielsen et al. (2008) (corresponding to $\eta' = \frac{1}{2}$ and $\theta' = \theta$ in (7.70)), although this paper contains an informal discussion about shrinking noise and about possible extensions of (WN). Moreover, the property (7.70) is not fully correct, as stated above, that is, with the estimators defined exactly by (7.68). This is due to the border effects, which are not negligible at all. As a matter of fact, if one takes $f(x) = \phi(g|x)$ for a C^2 function g satisfying (7.43), so that (7.67) holds, the estimators $\widehat{C}^{\text{FT}}(\Delta_n, k_n, f)_T$ and $\widehat{C}^{\text{Preav}}(\Delta_n, k_n, f)_T$ do not coincide, due to these borders effects. The pre-averaging estimator automatically includes in its*

*definition appropriate borders terms, which allows us to have Theorem
7.20. This is not the case of $\widehat{C}^{\mathrm{FT}}(\Delta_n, k_n, f)_T$: appropriately modifying
the definition in a way that (7.70) holds true is possible, but is a rather
complicated matter, and we refer to the aforementioned paper for a discussion of this issue, resolved by some kind of "jittering" (suitable averaging of the observations near both ends of the observation interval), and
also for a discussion of what happens if one relaxes the flat top assumption, that is, if one takes $f(r/k_n)$ instead of $f((r-1)/k_n)$ in (7.68).*

Remark 7.30. *(Realized kernels and optimality) Observe that
$\widehat{C}^{\mathrm{FT}}(\Delta_n, k_n, f)_T$ (with appropriate additional border terms) and
$\widehat{C}^{\mathrm{Preav}}(\Delta_n, k_n, g)_T$ have exactly the same properties, and in particular enjoy the same Central Limit Theorem, upon replacing the ratios
$\Phi(g,g)/\phi(g)^2$ and $\Phi(g,g')/\phi(g)^2$ and $\Phi(g',g')/\phi(g)^2$ in (7.49) by the
numbers $\overline{\Phi}(f)$ and $\overline{\Phi}'(f)$ and $\overline{\Phi}''(f)$, respectively. Therefore the discussion about optimality in Subsection 7.6.1 can be reproduced here with no
change, except that instead of (7.59) one should use*

$$\alpha'(f) = \frac{6\overline{\Phi}(f)\overline{\Phi}''(f)+2\overline{\Phi}'(f)\sqrt{\overline{\Phi}'(f)^2+3\overline{\Phi}(f)\overline{\Phi}''(f)}-2\overline{\Phi}'(f)^2}{3^{3/2}\,\overline{\Phi}''(f)^{1/2}\left(\sqrt{\overline{\Phi}'(f)^2+3\overline{\Phi}(f\overline{\Phi}''(f)}-\overline{\Phi}'(f)\right)^{1/2}},$$

and f is any function satisfying (7.67).

*Again, the best (smallest) value for $\alpha'(f)$ is 1. A number of possible
kernels f can be studied:*

$$\alpha'(f) = \begin{cases} 1.13 & \text{cubic kernel: } f(x) = 1 - 3x^2 + 2x^3 \\ 1.07 & \text{Parzen kernel: } f(x) = \begin{cases} 1 - 6x^2 + 6x^3 & \text{if } x \le 1/2 \\ 2(1-x)^3 & \text{if } x > 1/2 \end{cases} \\ 1.0025 & \text{Tukey-Hanning kernel of order 16:} \\ & \quad f(x) = \left(\sin(\pi/2(1-x)^{16})\right)^2. \end{cases}$$

*The Parzen kernel is in fact the function $f(x) = \phi(g|x)/\phi(g)$ associ-
ated with the triangular kernel of Example 7.19. The Tukey-Hanning kernel of order 16 is extremely close to optimality (we do not know whether
this kernel is of the form $f(x) = \phi(g|x)$ for a weight function g satisfying
(7.43)).*

*However, in practice, and when c_t and γ_t are varying with time, the
main problem is the choice of the number θ; therefore all choices among
the f's above are essentially equivalent from a practical viewpoint, as is
the choice of the triangular kernel for the pre-averaging method. Note
also that adaptive flat top kernel estimators can probably be constructed,
along the same ideas as in the previous section.*

7.8   Multi-scales Estimators

As mentioned at the end of Section 7.5, the TSRV estimators can be extended to *Multi-Scales Realized Volatility* estimators, or MSRV. This enables one to improve the rate of convergence of the estimator from $\Delta_n^{-1/6}$ to the optimal $\Delta_n^{-1/4}$. The noise is a non-shrinking white noise (Assumption (WN) and $\alpha_n = 1$, or $\eta = 0$ in (7.41)).

These estimators require the choice of a sequence k_n of integers satisfying $k_n \sim 1/\theta\sqrt{\Delta_n}$ for some number $\theta \in (0, \infty)$ (as in (7.42), with $\eta' = \frac{1}{2}$) and of a kernel function f on $[0, 1]$, of class C^3, and subject to

$$\int_0^1 f(s)\,ds = 0, \qquad \int_0^1 s\,f(s)\,ds = 1.$$

The estimator at stage n is then

$$\widehat{C}^{\mathrm{MSRV}}(\Delta_n, k_n, f)_t = \sum_{j=1}^{k_n} \alpha_j^n \sum_{i=j}^{[t/\Delta_n]} \left(Y_i^n - Y_{i-j}^n\right)^2, \tag{7.72}$$

where

$$\begin{aligned} \alpha_j^n &= \frac{1}{k_n^2}\, f\!\left(\tfrac{j}{k_n}\right) - \frac{1}{2k_n^3}\, f'\!\left(\tfrac{j}{k_n}\right) \\ &\quad - \frac{1}{6k_n^3}\,(f'(1) - f'(0)) + \frac{1}{24k_n^4}\,(f''(1) - f''(0)). \end{aligned} \tag{7.73}$$

This is again a quadratic estimator of type (7.33), with

$$\begin{aligned} h_n(x) = \sum_{r=1}^{k_n - j} r\, \Big(&\frac{1}{k_n^2}\, f\!\left(x + \tfrac{r}{k_n}\right) - \frac{1}{2k_n^3}\, f'\!\left(x + \tfrac{r}{k_n}\right) \\ &- \frac{1}{6k_n^3}\,(f'(1) - f'(0)) + \frac{1}{24k_n^4}\,(f''(1) - f''(0)) \Big) \end{aligned}$$

when $x \in [0, 1]$, and provided we set $f(x) = 0$ when $x > 1$. The functions h_n converge to $h(x) = \int_0^{1-x} u\, f(x + u)\, du$. Here, the function h is not necessarily of the form $h(x) = \phi(g|x)$ for some g satisfying (7.43) but, when it is, we have $\phi(g'|x) = h''(x) = f(x)$, and thus with the notation (7.44) we obtain after some calculations

$$\begin{aligned} A(f) &:= \Phi(g, g) = \int_0^1 h(x)^2\, dx \\ &= \tfrac{1}{3} \int_0^1 f(x)\, dx \int_0^x y^2 (3x - y)\, f(y)\, dy \\ A'(f) &:= \Phi(g, g') = \int_0^1 f(x) h(x)\, dx \\ &= \int_0^1 f(x)\, dx \int_0^1 (x \wedge y)\, f(y)\, dy \\ A''(f) &:= \Phi(g', g') = \int_0^1 f(x)^2\, dx. \end{aligned} \tag{7.74}$$

In view of this, the following result gives the asymptotic distribution of the MSRV estimator:

Theorem 7.31. *Assume (HC) and also (WN) with a non-shrinking noise, so in particular $\gamma_t(\omega) = \gamma = \mathbb{E}(\chi_0^2)$ is a constant, and set $\Gamma = \mathbb{E}(\chi_0^4) - \gamma^2$. Then, under (7.68) with a C^3 function f, and if $k_n \sim 1/\theta\sqrt{\Delta_n}$ (that is, (7.42) with $\eta' = \frac{1}{2}$), for each $T > 0$ we have the following stable convergence in law:*

$$\frac{1}{\Delta_n^{1/4}} \big(\widehat{C}^{\mathrm{MSRV}}(\Delta_n, k_n, f)_T - C_t \big) \xrightarrow{\mathcal{L}-s} \mathcal{U}_T^{\mathrm{MSRV}},$$

where $\mathcal{U}_T^{\mathrm{MSRV}}$ is a variable defined on an extension of the space $(\Omega, \mathcal{F}, \mathbb{P})$ and, conditionally on $\mathcal{F}$, is centered Gaussian with variance

$$\widetilde{E}\big((\mathcal{U}_T^{\mathrm{MSRV}})^2 \mid \mathcal{F}\big) = \frac{4}{\theta} \int_0^T \big(A(f)c_s^2 + 2A'(f)c_s\gamma\theta^2 $$
$$+ A''(f)\gamma^2\theta^4 \big)\, ds + 4\Gamma\theta^3 \int_0^1 f(x)^2\, dx. \quad (7.75)$$

In view of (7.74), the first term on the right-hand side of (7.75) is exactly the same as in (7.52), when γ_t is a constant. There is a second term, however. This additional summand is due to the border terms which are implicitly contained in the definition (7.72).

It is likely (but unproved so far) that a similar result holds in the case of shrinking noise $\epsilon_i^n = \Delta_n^\eta \chi_{i\Delta_n}$, provided (7.42) for k_n holds as stated, and with the rate $1/\Delta_n^{(1-\eta')/2}$ instead of $1/\Delta_n^{1/4}$, and θ substituted with θ'. When considering the more general Assumption (GN) for the noise, though, things are more complicated, because the last term in (7.75) has no evident counterpart in this more general case. On the other hand, it is worth noticing that Theorem 7.31 also holds when the observation times are not regularly spaced, but yet not "too far" from this, in an appropriate sense.

7.9 Estimation of the Quadratic Covariation

In this section we briefly review what happens when the underlying process X has dimension $d \geq 2$. Each diagonal element C_T^{jj} of the covariation process is the integrated volatility of the component X^j, so the only thing which needs to be discussed about volatility estimation is the estimation of the off-diagonal elements C_T^{ij}, or more generally of the entire matrix (joint estimation). We make the simplifying hypothesis that all components are observed at the same times $i\Delta_n$, as in the previous chapter (see Chapter 9 for general and possibly non-synchronous observation schemes).

The general discussion of Section 7.1 about microstructure noise can be reproduced word for word, although one should be aware of a specific fact about pure rounding noise: for the off-diagonal elements C_T^{ij}, and assuming that the rounding level β_n is the same for all components, the first two claims in (7.14) become wrong. For example consider the non-shrinking case $\beta_n = \beta$. Then when n is large enough, and at least when the matrix c_t is never degenerate, between two successive observation times a given component may cross one of the level $k\beta$, but it never occurs that two distinct components do this. So indeed the "noisy" realized covariation satisfies

$$C^{jl,\mathrm{noisy}}(\Delta_n)_T = 0 \quad \text{for all } n \text{ large enough, depending on } \omega.$$

Concerning the various assumptions on the noise in Section 7.2, nothing is changed, except of course that the variables χ_t are now d-dimensional, and thus the conditional variance γ_t becomes a $d \times d$ covariance matrix.

Basically, all methods previously explained work as well in the multivariate case, with an appropriately modified version of the estimators, and with CLTs involving multivariate limits.

Let us focus on the pre-averaging estimators, and use all notation of Section 7.6. The definition (7.46) of $\overline{Y}_i^n$ is unchanged, and should be read componentwise (we take the same weight function g for all components, although taking different functions is also possible), so $\overline{Y}_i^n$ is now d-dimensional; in contrast, $\widehat{Y}_i^n$ becomes a $d \times d$ matrix, whose definition is

$$\widehat{Y}_i^{n,lm} = \sum_{j=1}^{k_n} (g_j'^n)^2 \, \Delta_{i+j-1}^n Y^l \, \Delta_{i+j-1}^n Y^m.$$

The estimators for the matrix C_t are now, componentwise:

$$\begin{aligned}
\widehat{C}^{\mathrm{Preav}}(\Delta_n, k_n, g)_t^{lm} &= \frac{1}{\phi_n(g)} \frac{t}{t - k_n \Delta_n} \\
&\times \sum_{i=1}^{[t/\Delta_n] - k_n + 1} \left(\overline{Y}_i^{n,l} \, \overline{Y}_i^{n,m} - \tfrac{1}{2} \widehat{Y}_i^{n,lm} \right).
\end{aligned} \qquad (7.76)$$

This gives matrix-valued estimators, still globally denoted as $\widehat{C}^{\mathrm{Preav}}(\Delta_n, k_n, g)_t$, and which converge in probability, locally uniformly in time, to C_t. A simple extension of Theorem A.20 of Appendix A is as follows:

Theorem 7.32. *Under (GN) and (HC), and under (7.42) and (7.43), for each $t > 0$ we have the same stable convergence in law of*

$\frac{1}{\Delta_n^{(1-\eta')/2}}(\widehat{C}^{\text{ Preav}}(\Delta_n, k_n, g)_T - C_T)$ *toward* $\mathcal{U}_T^{\text{noise}}$ *as in (7.51), except that here* $\mathcal{U}^{\text{noise}}$ *is* d^2*-dimensional, with* $\mathcal{F}$*-conditional variance-covariance given by*

$$
\begin{aligned}
V(g)_T^{lm,l'm'} &= \widetilde{E}(\mathcal{U}_T^{\text{noise},lm}\,\mathcal{U}_T^{\text{noise},l'm'} \mid \mathcal{F}) \\
&= \frac{1}{\theta}\int_0^T R^{lm,l'm'}(g; c_s, \theta'^2\gamma_s)\,ds,
\end{aligned}
\tag{7.77}
$$

where, for all $d \times d$ *matrices* u, v*, we have*

$$
\begin{aligned}
R^{lm,l'm'}(g; u, v) &= \tfrac{2}{\phi(g)^2}\Big(\Phi(g,g)(u^{ll'}u^{mm'} + u^{lm'}u^{ml'}) \\
&\quad + \Phi(g',g')(v^{ll'}v^{mm'} + v^{lm'}v^{ml'}) \\
&\quad + \Phi(g,g')(u^{ll'}v^{mm'} + u^{lm'}v^{l'm} + u^{l'm}v^{lm'} + u^{mm'}v^{ll'})\Big).
\end{aligned}
\tag{7.78}
$$

In the one-dimensional case, (7.78) reduces to (7.49).

7.10   References

Gloter and Jacod (2001a,b) established the optimal rate of convergence of the volatility parameter in the presence of additive noise, proved the LAN property and constructed optimal estimators when the price is a continuous (Markov) diffusion. The analysis of realized volatility and the sparse sampling estimators in Section 7.1.5 follows Zhang et al. (2005) in the case of additive noise. The case of pure rounding was treated in Jacod (1996) and Delattre and Jacod (1997); see also Large (2011) and Corsi and Audrino (2012).

The maximum-likelihood method of Section 7.3 was introduced by Aït-Sahalia et al. (2005); its analysis in the context of stochastic volatility is due to Xiu (2010). The optimal sampling frequency for realized volatility described in Section 7.1.5 follows Aït-Sahalia et al. (2005) and Zhang et al. (2005), with a related result due to Bandi and Russell (2008).

The first consistent volatility estimator in the presence of noise is TSRV of Section 7.5 and was introduced by Zhang et al. (2005); further developments on the two scales approach include Kalnina (2011) and Ikeda (2014). The multi-scales (MSRV) extension of Section 7.8 is due to Zhang (2006).

When the noise is colored (i.e., exhibits time-series dependence), we refer to Kalnina and Linton (2008) and Aït-Sahalia et al. (2011). The properties of TSRV under a different noise structure is analyzed in Taniai et al. (2012). Ubukata and Oya (2009) provide methods to test whether the noise is time-series dependent and/or cross-sectionally depending across assets.

The pre-averaging estimators of Section 7.6 are due to Podolskij and Vetter (2009) and Jacod et al. (2009), with further developments in Hautsch and Podolskij (2010) and Jacod and Mykland (2012). The realized kernel method of Section 7.7 is due to Barndorff-Nielsen et al. (2008) (note that (7.68) is a version of the estimators given in that paper, which does not make use of data outside the time interval $[0, T]$, and with a slight and innocuous change in the summation bounds for r, in order to fit better the notation of this book). The multi-scales method of Section 7.8 is due to Zhang (2006). The estimation of the cross-volatility C_T^{ij} in the presence of noise and for asynchronous observations is studied in Koike (2013), and also in Bibinger et al. (2013) with emphasis on optimality.

Additional models or methods have been proposed. In the constant σ case, French and Roll (1986) proposed adjusting variance estimates to control for the autocorrelation induced by the noise and Harris (1990b) studied the resulting estimators. Zhou (1996) proposed a bias correcting approach based on the first order autocovariances, which is unbiased but inconsistent. The behavior of this estimator has been studied by Zumbach et al. (2002) and Oomen (2005). Hansen and Lunde (2006) proposed extensions of the autocovariance estimator which are also inconsistent. Sun (2006) studied the class of quadratic estimators and derived the best quadratic unbiased estimators of the integrated variance in the presence of independent market microstructure noise. In the same parametric context as Section 7.3.1, Cai et al. (2010) computed estimators for σ^2 and the variance of the noise that achieve the minimax bound. Munk and Schmidt-Hieber (2010) employ a spectral decomposition of the covariance structures to construct series estimators for the variance of the signal and that of the noise when they are time-varying, and they investigate their rates of convergence as a function of their smoothness.

Phillips and Yu (2007) consider a model consisting of a Brownian semimartingale process for the efficient price and a Bernoulli process that determines the extent of "flat price" trading, meaning consecutively sampled prices that remain at the same level, and analyze the properties of the realized volatility estimator in that context. An alternative view of flat prices would attribute the phenomenon to rounding, see Section 7.1.5.

Kinnebrock and Podolskij (2008) and Christensen et al. (2010) developed the multivariate extensions of Section 7.9. Mancino and Sanfelici (2012) extended the Fourier method to the situation of multivariate volatility estimation with noise.

Zhang et al. (2011) developed the Edgeworth expansion, in the spirit of Section 6.4, in the presence of noise, for the realized volatility, TSRV and other estimators. Bandi and Russell (2011) show that the asymptotic properties of the kernel estimators may provide unsatisfactory representations of their finite sample behavior.

Reiß (2011) derives rate-optimal estimators of the volatility function and efficient estimators of the integrated volatility based on a Gaussian shift experiment in terms of the square root of the volatility function.

Forecasting volatility and related quantities has been studied by Andersen et al. (2004, 2005) without noise, and in the presence of market microstructure noise by Aït-Sahalia and Mancini (2008), Bandi et al. (2008), Brownlees and Gallo (2010), Andersen et al. (2011), Ghysels and Sinko (2011), Patton (2011), Maheu and McCurdy (2011) and Sizova (2011). Corradi et al. (2009, 2011) constructed conditional predictive densities and confidence intervals for the integrated variance and estimate these densities using nonparametric kernel estimators. They used different estimators for integrated volatility, including realized volatility and TSRV and derived confidence bands around their kernel estimators.

Koopman and Scharth (2013) use some of these estimators to estimate a stochastic volatility models in a filtering framework. Gatheral and Oomen (2010) compare in a model-free setting the performance of many of the estimators considered in this Chapter.

Chapter 8

Estimating Spot Volatility

The estimation of integrated volatility, studied in Chapter 6, has been the first object of interest in financial econometrics, because of its relevance in finance, and also because it is the simplest object which can be estimated. However, under mild assumptions, such as the volatility being right-continuous or left-continuous, not only is the integrated volatility identifiable, but the volatility process as a whole is identifiable as well, and is potentially quite useful for financial applications. This question of estimating the "spot volatility," that is, the value of the volatility at a given time, deterministic, or possibly random, time, is the object of this chapter.

The setting is as in Chapter 6. The basic process X is observed, at the discrete times $i\Delta_n$, over a finite time interval $[0, T]$, and the returns are $\Delta_i^n X = X_{i\Delta_n} - X_{(i-1)\Delta_n}$. With the exception of Section 8.7, we suppose the observations to be without noise. The process X is a d-dimensional Itô semimartingale on a filtered space $(\Omega, \mathcal{F}, (\mathcal{F}_t)_{t \geq 0}, \mathbb{P})$, which satisfies (H-2) and with the Grigelionis representation

$$
\begin{aligned}
X_t = {} & X_0 + \int_0^t b_s ds + \int_0^t \sigma_s dW_s \\
& + (\delta 1_{\{\|\delta\| \leq 1\}}) \star (\underline{p} - \underline{q})_t + (\delta 1_{\{\|\delta\| > 1\}}) \star \underline{p}_t,
\end{aligned} \tag{8.1}
$$

where W is a d'-dimensional Brownian motion and $\underline{p}$ is a Poisson measure on $\mathbb{R}_+ \times E$ with $(E, \mathcal{E})$ an auxiliary Polish space, and with compensator $\underline{q}(dt, dx) = dt \otimes \lambda(dx)$. Due to (H-2), the d-dimensional process b is progressively measurable and locally bounded, the $d \times d'$-dimensional process σ is càdlàg adapted, and δ is a d-dimensional predictable function

259

$\Omega \times \mathbb{R}_+ \times E$ which satisfies $|\delta(\omega, t, z)| \le J_n(z)$ when $t \le \tau_n(\omega)$, where τ_n is a sequence of stopping times increasing to ∞ and each J_n is a non-random function on E such that $\int (J_n(z) \wedge 1) \lambda(dz) < \infty$.

When the volatility is "state-dependent," that is, of the form $\sigma_t = f(X_t)$, or more generally $\sigma_t = f(Y_t)$ where Y is another process which is also observed at high frequency, with an unknown function f, this is a classical non-parametric estimation of the function f. The literature is vast on this topic, as it is in another specific situation: when σ_t is unknown, but non-random.

These two situations are very special, and in a sense somewhat far from the spirit of this book. So, here, we rather consider a "general" volatility process which, in most of what follows, is also an Itô semimartingale, with unspecified characteristics. Section 8.6, though, is concerned with the state-dependent case $\sigma_t = f(X_t)$, and focuses on the estimation of the function f rather than on the estimation of the path $t \mapsto c_t$, although in this case if f were known exactly one would also know exactly the values $c_{i\Delta_n}$.

We mostly describe how the volatility (or, rather, the matrix $c = \sigma\sigma^*$) can be estimated at a deterministic time t, and also at a random time S, under appropriate assumptions on S. This turns out to be quite simple to do, although the rate of convergence is necessarily slow. After this, we go further in the analysis of the volatility, in several directions. First, when both X and the volatility process are continuous, we estimate the quadratic variation of the volatility process, which is a kind of measure of the variability of the volatility, and the covariation process between the volatility and the (log)-price X itself, which is related to the leverage effect. When the volatility has jumps, it is also possible to detect them, but the techniques are analogous to the detection of jumps of X itself, so this topic is postponed to the part about jumps, in Chapters 10 and 14. Next, we give efficient estimators for variables of the form $\int_0^t g(c_s) \, ds$, in connection with the problems related to quarticity and left unsolved in Chapter 6. Finally, we explain how to modify the various estimators when microstructure noise is present.

All this could be the beginning of a very long story telling us how to estimate the spot volatility of the volatility, and then its volatility, and so on. However, the convergence rates for spot volatility estimators being already very slow, going further seems hopelessly unfeasible in practice, at least for the kind of data and the observation frequencies encountered in finance.

8.1   Local Estimation of the Spot Volatility

Estimating the spot volatility c_t has two aspects. The first is the estimation of the value c_t at a particular time t, or perhaps of c_S for some stopping time S of special interest, or even of the jump size Δc_S when c is càdlàg. The second aspect is the estimation of the path $t \mapsto c_t$ over a given time interval $[0, T]$.

This is very much like non-parametric estimation of a regression function or of a density function: one can emphasize the quality of estimation at one specific point (pointwise estimation); one can instead use global criteria, such as an L^p norm, to assert the quality of the estimation. The first problem is usually solved by kernel methods; the second may be solved by the same kernel methods, and also by global methods such as wavelets or Fourier methods.

In this section we investigate the first question, using kernel methods. As it turns out, we even use a "constant" kernel (the indicator function of an interval), for two reasons. One is simplicity, the other is that in our specific setting this sort of kernel seems to be the most effective one, as we will discuss later.

The literature on this topic was rather scarce until recently, when it exploded. This is mainly because estimating the spot volatility requires a large amount of data, which became available through very high-frequency observations only relatively recently.

8.1.1   Some Heuristic Considerations

The most naïve idea, which turns out to be also quite efficient, is indeed very simple. Suppose that we have estimators $\widehat{C}_t^n$ for C_t, such that $\widehat{C}^n \overset{\text{u.c.p.}}{\Longrightarrow} C$ (convergence in probability, uniform in time on each bounded interval). Then, for any $t \geq 0$ and $s > 0$ we have $\widehat{C}_{t+s}^n - \widehat{C}_t^n \overset{\mathbb{P}}{\longrightarrow} \int_t^{t+s} c_r \, dr$. Now, since c is right-continuous, $\frac{1}{s} \int_t^{t+s} c_r \, dr \to c_t$ as s decreases to 0. Then, one may hope that, for a suitable choice of the sequence s_n going to 0, one has

$$\widehat{c}_t^n := \frac{\widehat{C}_{t+s_n}^n - \widehat{C}_t^n}{s_n} \overset{\mathbb{P}}{\longrightarrow} c_t. \qquad (8.2)$$

Like all estimators for C_t at stage n, $t \mapsto \widehat{C}_t^n$ is constant on each interval $[i\Delta_n, (i+1)\Delta_n)$, hence it is no restriction to take $s_n = k_n \Delta_n$, where $k_n \geq 1$ is an integer. Moreover, $C_{t+s_n} - C_t$ can be reasonably approximated by $\widehat{C}_{t+s_n}^n - \widehat{C}_t^n$ only if the number of returns between times t and $t + s_n$

is large. This leads us to choose the sequence k_n such that

$$k_n \to \infty, \qquad k_n \Delta_n \to 0. \tag{8.3}$$

We will indeed see below that, under appropriate assumptions, (8.3) is enough to yield (8.2).

Getting an idea of the rate of convergence is slightly more complicated, as for all non-parametric estimation problems. We devote the rest of the subsection to heuristic arguments explaining the rates, and for this we use simplifying assumptions: the dimension is $d = 1$, and the process X is continuous and without drift, since the drift should play no role in that matter. Furthermore, we suppose that c_t is non-random, at least for a while.

In this case, it is of course natural to take $\widehat{C}_t^n = \widehat{C}(\Delta_n)_t$ (the realized volatility), as defined by (6.4), so $\widehat{c}_t^n$ in (8.2) becomes

$$\widehat{c}_t^n = \frac{1}{k_n \Delta_n} \sum_{i=[t/\Delta_n]+1}^{[t/\Delta_n]+k_n} (\Delta_i^n X)^2. \tag{8.4}$$

The variables $\Delta_i^n X$ are independent and $\mathcal{N}(0, \alpha_i^n \Delta_n)$-distributed, where $\alpha_i^n = \frac{1}{\Delta_n} \int_{(i-1)\Delta_n}^{i\Delta_n} c_s \, ds$. Arguing for $t = 0$ (but the argument is the same for any t), we see that the estimation error $E_n = \widehat{c}_0^n - c_0$ is the sum $E_n = D_n + S_n$ of a deterministic error and a statistical error:

$$D_n = \frac{1}{k_n} \sum_{i=1}^{k_n} \alpha_i^n - c_0 = \frac{1}{k_n \Delta_n} \int_0^{k_n \Delta_n} (c_s - c_0) \, ds,$$

$$S_n = \frac{1}{k_n} \sum_{i=1}^{k_n} Z_i^n,$$

where the Z_i^n's are independent when i varies, centered, with respective variances $2(\alpha_i^n)^2$ and fourth moments $60\,(\alpha_i^n)^4$. A more appropriate name for D_n would be the "target error," because E_n turns out to be an estimator of $\frac{1}{k_n \Delta_n} \int_0^{k_n \Delta_n} c_s \, ds$, rather than an estimator of c_0.

The statistical error S_n is easy to analyze, as soon as $c_t \to c_0$ as $t \to 0$. Since $k_n \Delta_n \to 0$, this implies that $\alpha_i^n \to c_0$ uniformly in $i = 1, \ldots, k_n$, as $n \to \infty$. Then the usual CLT gives us that $\sqrt{k_n}\, S_n$ converges in law to $\mathcal{N}(0, 2(c_0)^2)$. The deterministic (target) error goes to 0 as well, but the rate of convergence is more difficult to handle and depends on the smoothness of the function c. If for example we assume that c is Hölder with some index $\rho \in (0, 1]$, that is, $|c_t - c_0| \le A t^\rho$ for a constant A, then clearly $|D_n| \le A(k_n \Delta_n)^\rho$.

We thus have two errors with competing rates $\sqrt{k_n}$ for S_n and $1/(k_n\Delta_n)^\rho$ for D_n, and in particular we get for any $A \in (1, \infty)$:

$$k_n^{\rho+1/2}\Delta_n^\rho \to 0 \qquad \Longrightarrow \qquad \begin{cases} S_n \text{ dominates,} \\ \sqrt{k_n}E_n \text{ is tight} \end{cases}$$

$$\frac{1}{A} \leq k_n^{\rho+1/2}\Delta_n^\rho \leq A \quad \Longrightarrow \qquad \begin{cases} S_n \text{ and } D_n \\ \text{are of the same magnitude,} \\ \sqrt{k_n}E_n \text{ is tight} \end{cases} \qquad (8.5)$$

$$k_n^{\rho+1/2}\Delta_n^\rho \to \infty \qquad \Longrightarrow \qquad \begin{cases} D_n \text{ dominates,} \\ \frac{1}{(k_n\Delta_n)^\rho}E_n \text{ is tight.} \end{cases}$$

In the first case $\sqrt{k_n}\,E_n$ converges in law to a centered normal variable; in the second and third cases the existence of a limit theorem depends on the behavior of c_t near 0, besides the mere Hölder property. The biggest possible rate is achieved in the second case above, and it is $1/\Delta_n^{\rho/(1+2\rho)}$.

When $t > 0$ what precedes obviously stays true, but we could also use estimators of the form

$$\widehat{c}_t^n = \frac{1}{k_n\Delta_n} \sum_{i=[t/\Delta_n]+1-l_n}^{[t/\Delta_n]+k_n-l_n} (\Delta_i^n X)^2$$

with an arbitrary sequence l_n of integers between 0 and k_n: we estimate c_t from the right if $l_n = 0$, and from the left if $l_n = k_n$, whereas if $l_n \sim k_n/2$ it is a "symmetrical" estimator around t. Note that when c is piecewise Hölder and càdlàg, everything stays true again, but of course one should either take $l_n = 0$ to estimate c_t, or $l_n = k_n$ to estimate c_{t-}, and any intermediate value for l_n results in an estimation of some average of c_t and c_{t-}.

The same argument applies (up to – not totally trivial – technical details) when c_t is random, and still with ρ-Hölder paths. More generally it applies when, up to some localization, we have

$$\mathbb{E}(|c_{S+s} - c_S| \mid \mathcal{F}_S) \leq K\,s^\rho \qquad (8.6)$$

for some constant K and all finite stopping times S. In particular, this applies when c is an Itô semimartingale satisfying (H-2), upon taking $\rho = \frac{1}{2}$. To stay in the mainstream of this book, as in Chapter 6 for example, later on we will make this assumption on c. It is noteworthy to observe that in this case c_t may jump, but even when it is continuous its paths are ρ'-Hölder for all $\rho' < \frac{1}{2}$, but nowhere $\frac{1}{2}$-Hölder; nonetheless, for the estimation problem at hand the paths behave as if they were $\frac{1}{2}$-Hölder, even when they jump.

Remark 8.1. *(Naïve estimators versus kernel estimators) Instead of taking averaged square returns, as in (8.4), one could take sums weighted by a kernel function ϕ satisfying $\int_{-\infty}^{\infty} \phi(x)\,dx = 1$. Again in the case of X being one-dimensional and continuous, the estimators for c_t could then be*

$$\widehat{c}_t^n = \frac{1}{k_n\Delta_n}\sum_{i\geq 1}\phi\Big(\frac{t - i\Delta_n}{k_n\Delta_n}\Big)(\Delta_i^n X)^2. \tag{8.7}$$

Although ϕ could be arbitrary, usually it is chosen with compact support, say $[-1,1]$ or $[0,1]$, in which case the above sum is finite. The naïve estimator $\frac{1}{k_n\Delta_n}\sum_{i=[t/\Delta_n]+1}^{[t/\Delta_n]+k_n}(\Delta_i^n X)^2$ is the kernel estimator with $K(x) = 1_{(0,1]}(x)$.

Basically, the previous discussion applies for all kernel estimators, at least with kernels having a bounded support. Now, in non-parametric estimation it is usually the case that taking a well-behaved kernel, in connection with the smoothness of the function to estimate, improves things, such as the rate of convergence of the estimators. However, two additional remarks are in order here:

Remark 8.2. *If the function to estimate is $C^{m+\rho}$, meaning m times differentiable, with ρ-Hölder mth derivative, taking a kernel satisfying $\int x^j \phi(x)\,dx = 0$ for $j = 1,\dots,m-1$ improves the rate. But, here, the function (or path) $t \mapsto c_t$ is typically behaving (in "expectation," as explained before) as if it were Hölder with exponent $\frac{1}{2}$; so all (piecewise continuous) kernels give the same convergence rate.*

Remark 8.3. *The rate is thus in fact given by (8.5), in all cases of interest. Without much loss of generality we can take $k_n \asymp 1/\Delta_n^\tau$ for some $\tau \in (0,1)$, hence the fastest rate is $1/\Delta_n^{\rho/(1+2\rho)}$, corresponding to taking $\tau = \frac{2\rho}{1+2\rho}$. With this optimal choice for τ, an appropriate choice of the kernel results in a smaller asymptotic estimation variance, provided of course that the variables $(\widehat{c}_t^n - c_t)/\Delta_n^{\rho/(1+2\rho)}$ actually converge in law. However, such a convergence is not guaranteed and, even if it holds (as it will under the stronger assumptions made below), the asymptotic variance cannot be practically estimated and deriving confidence bounds is thus impossible.*

With a suboptimal value $\tau < \frac{2\rho}{1+2\rho}$, in contrast, we will see that we always obtain a Central Limit Theorem, with an asymptotic variance which can be estimated, hence allowing us to construct confidence bounds. But, in this case, it turns out that the minimal asymptotic variance is indeed achieved by kernels which are indicator functions of intervals, whereas all other kernels give bigger asymptotic variances, see Remark 8.10 below.

Consequently, and although a large amount of the literature about spot volatility estimation is about kernel estimators with more or less general kernels, we consider the use below of the "naïve" kernel $\phi(x) = 1_{(0,1]}(x)$ better.

8.1.2   Consistent Estimation

At this stage, we define the spot volatility estimators which will be used later on, and we use the naïve approach (8.2). There are several possible versions, according to the choice of $\widehat{C}_t^n$, which in turn depends on whether X is continuous. Moreover, again following the previous discussion, we may want to estimate c_t, or c_{t-}, resulting in two possible estimators.

We choose a sequence of integers k_n satisfying (at least) (8.3). We also choose a sequence $u_n \asymp \Delta_n^\varpi$ of truncation levels, with $0 < \varpi < \frac{1}{2}$, see (6.23), and define componentwise the following $\mathcal{M}_d^+$-valued variables, as in (6.17) and (6.31):

$$\begin{aligned}
\widehat{c}(k_n)_i^{jl} &= \frac{1}{k_n\Delta_n} \sum_{m=0}^{k_n-1} \Delta_{i+m}^n X^j \, \Delta_{i+m}^n X^l \\
\widehat{c}(k_n,u_n)_i^{jl} &= \frac{1}{k_n\Delta_n} \sum_{m=0}^{k_n-1} \Delta_{i+m}^n X^j \, \Delta_{i+m}^n X^l \, 1_{\{\|\Delta_{i+m}^n X\|\le u_n\}}
\end{aligned} \tag{8.8}$$

There is also a version based on multipowers, which we give in the one-dimensional case only (since multipowers are designed for this case). For any integer $k \geq 2$ this is

$$\widehat{c}(k_n,[k])_i = \frac{1}{(m_{2/k})^k k_n\Delta_n} \sum_{m=0}^{k_n-1} |\Delta_{i+m}^n X|^{2/k} \cdots |\Delta_{i+m+k-1}^n X|^{2/k}.$$

All these variables are *a priori* defined for all $i \geq 1$, but it will prove handy to extend the definition to all relative integers $i \in \mathbb{Z}$ by the same formulas, with the convention

$$\Delta_i^n X = 0 \quad \text{if } i \le 0. \tag{8.9}$$

Since the first estimators $\widehat{c}(k_n)_i$ are not suitable when X has jumps (see, however, Remark 8.5 below), and since the multipower estimators are (theoretically) not as good as the truncated ones, we will pursue the discussion with $\widehat{c}(k_n,u_n)_i$ only. But it should be understood that similar statements are valid for the other two estimators as well, plus X continuous for the first one.

The variable $\widehat{c}(k_n,u_n)_i$ is an estimator for c_t at time $t = i\Delta_n$; this statement does not make much sense if i is fixed, because then $i\Delta_n$ goes to 0 and $\widehat{c}(k_n, u_n)_i$ is really an estimator for c_0. To straighten things up, we set

$$\left.\begin{aligned}
\widehat{c}(t; k_n, u_n) &= \widehat{c}(k_n, u_n)_{i+1} \\
\widehat{c}(t-; k_n, u_n) &= \widehat{c}(k_n, u_n)_{i-k_n}.
\end{aligned}\right\} \quad \text{if } (i-1)\Delta_n < t \leq i\Delta_n. \quad (8.10)$$

According to the convention (8.9), this is defined for all $t \in \mathbb{R}$, and totally uninteresting when $t < 0$. When $t = 0$ only $\widehat{c}(t; k_n, u_n)$ is meaningful. When $t > 0$, we have $i - k_n \geq 1$ for all n large enough in (8.10). These estimators are usually called *local spot volatility estimators*, by opposition to global estimators, to be introduced later.

The notation (8.10) also applies when $t = S(\omega)$ is a random time. Then, according to Theorem A.6 of Appendix A, for any *stopping time* S we have

$$\left\{\begin{aligned}
\widehat{c}(S; k_n, u_n) &\xrightarrow{\mathbb{P}} c_S && \text{on the set } \{S < \infty\} \\
\widehat{c}(S-; k_n, u_n) &\xrightarrow{\mathbb{P}} c_{S-} && \text{on the set } \{0 < S < \infty\}.
\end{aligned}\right. \quad (8.11)$$

Remark 8.4. *This applies in particular for $S = t$, a deterministic positive time. In this case, as soon as the process c has no fixed time of discontinuity, we have $c_{t-} = c_t$ almost surely. We can therefore use either $\widehat{c}(t; k_n, u_n)$ or $\widehat{c}(t-; k_n, u_n)$ to estimate c_t, and for that matter we could even use $\widehat{c}(k_n, u_n)_{i(n,t)}$ for any sequence $i(n,t)$ of integers such that $t/\Delta_n - pk_n \leq i(n,t) \leq t/\Delta_n + pk_n$, for any fixed $p \geq 1$.*

Remark 8.5. *As said before, (8.11) holds for the estimators based on the multipowers $\widehat{c}(k_n, [k])_i$, and for those based on $\widehat{c}(k_n)_i$ when X is continuous. More surprisingly it holds as well for $\widehat{c}(k_n)_i$ when X jumps, provided $S = t$ is deterministic, or is an arbitrary stopping time for the first convergence, or is a jump time of X for the second convergence; this is due to the fact that, for example in the case S is a jump time (last case above), the contribution of the jumps occurring in the time interval $(S, S + (k_n + 1)\Delta_n]$ is asymptotically negligible in front of the contribution of the Brownian part. The CLT stated below, though, does not hold with $\widehat{c}(k_n)_i$ when X is discontinuous.*

8.1.3   Central Limit Theorem

According to the discussion in Subsection 8.1.1 and in particular to the comments after (8.6), we assume that c (or σ) is itself an Itô semimartingale. It is useful to have a "joint" Grigelionis representation for X, together with c and/or σ. That is, we are given a d'-dimensional Brownian motion W and a Poisson measure $\underline{p}$ on $\mathbb{R}_+ \times E$, with intensity measure $\underline{q}(dt, dx) = dt \otimes \lambda(dx)$, and we have

$$
\begin{aligned}
X_t &= X_0 + \int_0^t b_s \, ds + \int_0^t \sigma_s \, dW_s \\
&\quad + (\delta 1_{\{\|\delta\| \leq 1\}}) \star (\underline{p} - \underline{q})_t + (\delta 1_{\{\|\delta\| > 1\}}) \star \underline{p}_t \\
\sigma_t &= \sigma_0 + \int_0^t b_s^{(\sigma)} \, ds + \int_0^t \sigma_s^{(\sigma)} \, dW_s \\
&\quad + (\delta^{(\sigma)} 1_{\{\|\delta^{(\sigma)}\| \leq 1\}}) \star (\underline{p} - \underline{q})_t + (\delta^{(\sigma)} 1_{\{\|\delta^{(\sigma)}\| > 1\}}) \star \underline{p}_t \\
c_t &= c_0 + \int_0^t b_s^{(c)} \, ds + \int_0^t \sigma_s^{(c)} \, dW_s \\
&\quad + (\delta^{(c)} 1_{\{\|\delta^{(c)}\| \leq 1\}}) \star (\underline{p} - \underline{q})_t + (\delta^{(c)} 1_{\{\|\delta^{(c)}\| > 1\}}) \star \underline{p}_t .
\end{aligned}
\tag{8.12}
$$

We use here a matrix-type notation, and perhaps it is useful to recall the dimension of the various coefficients (below the indices run through $\{1, \ldots, d\}$ for i, j, k and through $\{1, \ldots, d'\}$ for l, m)

- $X = (X^i)$, $b = (b^i)$, $\delta = (\delta^i)$ are d-dimensional
- $\sigma = (\sigma^{il})$, $b^{(\sigma)} = (b^{\sigma, il})$, $\delta^{(\sigma)} = (\delta^{(\sigma), il})$ are $d \times d'$-dimensional
- $c = (c^{ij})$, $b^{(c)} = (b^{(c), ij})$, $\delta^{(c)} = (\delta^{(c), ij})$ are $d \times d$-dimensional
- $\sigma^{(\sigma)} = (\sigma^{(\sigma), il, m})$ is $d \times d' \times d'$-dimensional
- $\sigma^{(c)} = (\sigma^{(c), ij, l})$ is $d \times d \times d'$-dimensional.

In (8.12) the third equation is a consequence of the second one, by $c = \sigma\sigma^*$ and Itô's formula. Therefore any assumption made on the coefficients of the second equation automatically translate into an assumption on the coefficients of the third one, whereas the other way around is not necessarily true, in case the matrix c_t is degenerate at some points. One could express $b^{(c)}, \sigma^{(c)}, \delta^{(c)}$ as (deterministic) functions of $\sigma, b^{(\sigma)}, \sigma^{(\sigma)}, \delta^{(\sigma)}$, but we do not need this now.

The formulation (8.12) allows us to easily express not only the integrated volatility of X (the second characteristic $C_t = \int_0^t c_s \, ds$), but also the (integrated and spot) volatility of the volatility c, and co-volatility between X and c:

$$
\begin{aligned}
C_t^{(c)} &= \int_0^t c_s^{(c)} ds, &\text{where } c_s^{(c), ij, i'j'} &= \textstyle\sum_{l=1}^{d'} \sigma_s^{(c), ij, l} \sigma_s^{(c), i'j', l}, \\
C_t^{(X, c)} &= \int_0^t c_s^{(X, c)} ds, &\text{where } c_s^{(X, c), i, i'j'} &= \textstyle\sum_{l=1}^{d'} \sigma_s^{il} \sigma_s^{(c), i'j', l}.
\end{aligned}
\tag{8.13}
$$

Concerning the various coefficients above, we need Assumption (K-r), which was stated on page 193 when $r \leq 1$. We state it again below to take care of the case when $r > 1$, and for more clarity we formulate it in terms of all three equations (8.12), but it is equivalent to the apparently shorter formulations given in Appendix A, and in Chapter 6 when $r \leq 1$. Namely, for any $r \in [0, 2]$ we set

Assumption (K-r). *We have (8.12) and*

(i) The processes $b, b^{(\sigma)}, b^{(c)}$ are locally bounded.

(ii) The processes $\sigma^{(\sigma)}, \sigma^{(c)}$ are càdlàg.

(iii) There is a sequence (τ_n) of stopping times increasing to ∞ and, for each n, a deterministic nonnegative function J_n on E satisfying $\int J_n(z)\,\lambda(dz) < \infty$, such that if $t \leq \tau_n(\omega)$ then

$$\|\delta(\omega,t,z)\|^r \wedge 1 \leq J_n(z),$$
$$\|\delta^{(\sigma)}(\omega,t,z)\|^2 \wedge 1 \leq J_n(z),$$
$$\|\delta^{(c)}(\omega,t,z)\|^2 \wedge 1 \leq J_n(z).$$

(iv) Moreover, with the notation

$$\widehat{b}_s = \int_{\{\|\delta(s,z)\|\leq 1\}} \|\delta(s,z)\|\lambda(dz),$$
$$S = \inf\left(t : \int_0^t \widehat{b}_s\,ds = \infty\right)$$
$$b'_t = b_t - \int_{\{\|\delta(t,z)\|\leq 1\}} \delta(t,z)\,\lambda(dz) \quad if \ t \leq S$$

$(\widehat{b}_t$ is well defined and $[0,\infty]$-valued), *then*

$$\sup_{(\omega,t):\,t\leq\tau_n(\omega)\wedge S(\omega)} \widehat{b}_t(\omega) < \infty,$$

and the paths $t \mapsto b'_t$ on $[0,S]$, and $t \mapsto b_t$ on $\mathbb{R}_+$ as well when further $r > 1$, are either càdlàg or càglàd.

We also single out the case where X is continuous:

Assumption (KC). *We have (K-2) and the process X is continuous (which is equivalent to having $\delta \equiv 0$, so (iv) above reduces to b being either càdlàg or càglàg.*

Now we come to the Central Limit Theorem associated with (8.11). As said before, the estimation error $\widehat{c}(t;k_n,u_n) - c_t$ is the sum of a statistical error $\widehat{c}(t;k_n,u_n) - \Phi_n$, where $\Phi_n = \frac{1}{k_n\Delta_n}\left(C_{t+k_n\Delta_n} - C_t\right)$ plus a target error $\Phi_n - c_t$ which, under the present assumption, is not only of order of magnitude $\sqrt{k_n\Delta_n}$, but also enjoys a CLT involving the volatility of the volatility $c_t^{(c)}$. We are thus in the situation of (8.5), with $\rho = \frac{1}{2}$ and a CLT holds in all three cases.

In order to state this CLT, we need to describe the limit. It is made up of two processes Z and Z', defined on an extension $(\widetilde{\Omega}, \widetilde{\mathcal{F}}, \widetilde{\mathbb{P}})$ of the probability space $(\Omega, \mathcal{F}, \mathbb{P})$, and which conditionally on $\mathcal{F}$ are two independent $\mathbb{R}^{d^2}$-valued *Gaussian white noises* (that is, the values at distinct times are independent and centered Gaussian), with the following conditional covariances:

$$\widetilde{\mathbb{E}}\big(Z_t^{ij}\,Z_t^{kl}\mid\mathcal{F}\big)=c_t^{ik}\,c_t^{jl}+c_t^{il}\,c_t^{jk},\qquad\widetilde{\mathbb{E}}\big(Z_t'^{ij}\,Z_t'^{kl}\mid\mathcal{F}\big)=c_t^{(c),ij,kl}.\qquad(8.14)$$

These limits being a (conditional) white noise, they are "very bad" processes, with for example almost all paths $t\mapsto Z_t$ being *not* even measurable functions, and the supremum of Z over any time interval of positive length being almost surely infinite. Therefore a functional convergence in law in the previous theorem is meaningless, and we rather use the *finite-dimensional stable convergence in law* already mentioned in Section 3.2 and denoted as $\overset{\mathcal{L}_{f-s}}{\longrightarrow}$: we say that $Y^n\overset{\mathcal{L}_{f-s}}{\longrightarrow}Y$, where Y^n and Y are q-dimensional processes, if for any finite family $t_1<\cdots<t_l$ of times we have the following stable convergence in law on $(\mathbb{R}^q)^l$:

$$\big(Y_{t_1}^n,\cdots,Y_{t_l}^n\big)\overset{\mathcal{L}-s}{\longrightarrow}\big(Y_{t_1},\ldots,Y_{t_l}\big).$$

We start with the continuous case for X, hence use the non-truncated versions of the estimators, see (8.8):

Theorem 8.6. *Under (KC) and if $k_n\sqrt{\Delta_n}\to\beta\in[0,\infty]$, we have the following finite-dimensional stable convergence in law, with Z and Z' as above:*

$$\begin{aligned}\beta=0\quad&\Rightarrow\quad\big(\sqrt{k_n}\,(\widehat{c}(t;k_n)-c_t)\big)_{t\geq0}\overset{\mathcal{L}_{f-s}}{\longrightarrow}(Z_t)_{t\geq0}\\[4pt]\beta\in(0,\infty)\quad&\Rightarrow\quad\big(\sqrt{k_n}\,(\widehat{c}(t;k_n)-c_t)\big)_{t\geq0}\overset{\mathcal{L}_{f-s}}{\longrightarrow}(Z_t+\beta Z_t')_{t\geq0}\qquad(8.15)\\[4pt]\beta=\infty\quad&\Rightarrow\quad\Big(\tfrac{1}{\sqrt{k_n\Delta_n}}\,(\widehat{c}(t;k_n)-c_t)\Big)_{t\geq0}\overset{\mathcal{L}_{f-s}}{\longrightarrow}(Z_t')_{t\geq0}.\end{aligned}$$

This result is a part of Theorem 13.3.7 of Jacod and Protter (2011). The two limiting variables have a clear interpretation: if we come back to the discussion around (8.5), Z_t is the limit of the (normalized) statistical error $\sqrt{k_n}\,S_n$, and Z_t' the limit of $\sqrt{k_n}\,D_n=\frac{\sqrt{k_n}}{k_n\Delta_n}\int_{t0}^{t+k_n\Delta_n}(c_s-c_t)\,ds$. Although not immediately obvious, it turns out that in the second case, when the two errors have the same order of magnitude, they are asymptotically independent.

The previous theorem stays valid if we replace $\widehat{c}(t;k_n)$ by the truncated versions $\widehat{c}(t;k_n,u_n)$, as soon as $u_n/\Delta_n^\varpi\to\infty$ for some $\varpi\in(0,\frac{1}{2})$. In contrast, when X is discontinuous, we need the truncated estimators, plus some additional conditions stated below (both forthcoming theorems are consequences of (c) of Theorem 13.3.3 of Jacod and Protter (2011)), with an innocuous weakening of the assumption on k_n when $\tau\neq\frac{1}{2}$ below.

Theorem 8.7. *Assume (K-r) for some $r \in [0, 2)$. Choose $u_n \asymp \Delta_n^\varpi$ and $k_n \asymp 1/\Delta_n^\tau$ for some ϖ and τ satisfying*

$$0 < \tau \wedge (1 - \tau) < \frac{2-r}{r}, \qquad \frac{\tau \wedge (1-\tau)}{2(2-r)} < \varpi < \frac{1}{2},$$
$$\text{if } \tau = \tfrac{1}{2} \text{ then } k_n \sqrt{\Delta_n} \to \beta \in (0, \infty) \tag{8.16}$$

(so $0 < \tau < 1$). Then we have the following finite-dimensional stable convergence in law, with Z and Z' as above:

$$\tau < \tfrac{1}{2} \;\Rightarrow\; \left(\sqrt{k_n}\,(\widehat{c}(t; k_n, u_n) - c_t)\right)_{t \geq 0} \xrightarrow{\mathcal{L}_f - s} (Z_t)_{t \geq 0}$$
$$\tau = \tfrac{1}{2} \;\Rightarrow\; \left(\sqrt{k_n}\,(\widehat{c}(t; k_n, u_n) - c_t)\right)_{t \geq 0} \xrightarrow{\mathcal{L}_f - s} (Z_t + \beta Z'_t)_{t \geq 0} \tag{8.17}$$
$$\tau > \tfrac{1}{2} \;\Rightarrow\; \left(\tfrac{1}{\sqrt{k_n \Delta_n}}\,(\widehat{c}(t; k_n, u_n) - c_t)\right)_{t \geq 0} \xrightarrow{\mathcal{L}_f - s} (Z'_t)_{t \geq 0}.$$

We have the same convergences (8.15) and (8.17) for $\widehat{c}(t-; k_n) - c_t$ and $\widehat{c}(t-; k_n, u_n) - c_t$, upon replacing $c_t^{(c)}$ by $c_{t-}^{(c)}$ in (8.14) (recall from Remark 8.4 that $c_{t-} = c_t$ almost surely, for any given t). We even have the joint convergence of $(\widehat{c}(t-; k_n, u_n) - c_t, \widehat{c}(t; k_n, u_n) - c_t)$, suitably normalized, toward two (conditionally) independent white noises, although this joint convergence is not useful in the previous context.

In contrast, the joint convergence is useful if we replace the fixed times t above by stopping times, which may be jump times of the process c. So below we consider a finite or countable family of finite stopping times S_q, with pairwise disjoint graphs in the sense that $S_{q'} \neq S_q$ for all $q' \neq q$. Somewhat surprisingly, one cannot replace the t's in (8.17) by the S_q's without very specific assumptions on these stopping times. Namely, we have to assume that each one has the form $S_s = s_q \wedge S'_q$ where $s_q \in (0, \infty]$ is non-random and S'_q is a "jump time" of a Poisson random measure p (for example the one driving X and σ as in (8.12)), that is, $\underline{p}(\{S'_q\} \times E) = 1$. Note that necessarily $S_q > 0$ in this framework.

For instance, this structural assumption is satisfied if we have finite stopping times S_q such that $\|\Delta X_{S_q}\| + \|\Delta c_{S_q}\| > 0$.

We then have the following (when X is continuous we can also use the non-truncated estimators):

Theorem 8.8. *Under the assumptions of the previous theorem, and if S_q is a sequence of finite stopping times satisfying the hypotheses stated* *above, we have the following stable convergence in law:*

$$\tau < \tfrac{1}{2} \Rightarrow \begin{array}{c}\left(\sqrt{k_n}\left(\widehat{c}(S_q-;k_n,u_n)-c_{S_q-}\right),\sqrt{k_n}\left(\widehat{c}(S_q;k_n,u_n)-c_{S_q}\right)\right)_{q\geq1}\\ \overset{\mathcal{L}-s}{\longrightarrow}(U_{q-},U_{q+})_{q\geq1}\end{array}$$

$$\tau = \tfrac{1}{2} \Rightarrow \begin{array}{c}\left(\sqrt{k_n}\left(\widehat{c}(S_q-;k_n,u_n)-c_{S_q-}\right),\sqrt{k_n}\left(\widehat{c}(S_q;k_n,u_n)-c_{S_q}\right)\right)_{q\geq1}\\ \overset{\mathcal{L}-s}{\longrightarrow}\left(U_{q-}+\beta U'_{q-},U_{q+}+\beta U'_{q+}\right)_{q\geq1}\end{array}$$

$$\tau > \tfrac{1}{2} \Rightarrow \begin{array}{c}\left(\frac{1}{\sqrt{k_n\Delta_n}}\left(\widehat{c}(S_q-;k_n,u_n)-c_{S_q-}\right),\right.\\ \left.\frac{1}{\sqrt{k_n\Delta_n}}\left(\widehat{c}(S_q;k_n,u_n)-c_{S_q}\right)\right)_{q\geq1}\overset{\mathcal{L}-s}{\longrightarrow}(U'_{q-},U'_{q+})_{q\geq1}\end{array}$$

where the variables $U_{q-},U'_{q-},U_{q+},U'_{q+}$ are defined on an extension $(\widetilde{\Omega},\widetilde{\mathcal{F}},\widetilde{\mathbb{P}})$ of $(\Omega,\mathcal{F},\mathbb{P})$ and, conditionally on $\mathcal{F}$, are all independent centered Gaussian with covariances

$$\widetilde{\mathbb{E}}\left(U_{q-}^{ij}U_{q-}^{kl}\mid\mathcal{F}\right)=c_{S_q-}^{ik}c_{S_q-}^{jl}+c_{S_q-}^{il}c_{S_q-}^{jk},$$
$$\widetilde{\mathbb{E}}\left(U_{q+}^{ij}U_{q+}^{kl}\mid\mathcal{F}\right)=c_{S_q}^{ik}c_{S_q}^{jl}+c_{S_q}^{il}c_{S_q}^{jk},$$
$$\widetilde{\mathbb{E}}\left(U_{q-}'^{ij}U_{q-}'^{kl}\mid\mathcal{F}\right)=c_{S_q-}^{(c),ij,kl},$$
$$\widetilde{\mathbb{E}}\left(U_{q+}'^{ij}U_{q+}'^{kl}\mid\mathcal{F}\right)=c_{S_q}^{(c),ij,kl}.$$

When we restrict our attention to the single variable $\widehat{c}(S;k_n,u_n)$ (so there is no longer any joint convergence), the result holds for any finite stopping time (no need for $\underline{p}(\{S\}\times E)=1$, see Remark 13.3.2 in Jacod and Protter (2011)). However, this is not true for the variable $\widehat{c}(S-;k_n,u_n)$.

The rate of convergence is always $1/\Delta_n^{(\tau\wedge(1-\tau))/2}$, the best rate being thus $1/\Delta_n^{1/4}$, achieved with $\tau=\tfrac{1}{2}$. The reader should notice the restrictions in (8.16). When $r\leq\tfrac{4}{3}$, the first condition is automatically satisfied, we can take $\tau=\tfrac{1}{2}$, and a conservative choice of ϖ is any value strictly between $\tfrac{3}{8}$ and $\tfrac{1}{2}$. When $r>\tfrac{4}{3}$ things are different, since $\tau\wedge(1-\tau)$ should be chosen smaller than $\frac{2-r}{r}$. Thus, in order to put these estimators into use, we need to assume that the activity index of the jumps of X is bounded from above by a *known* constant $r<2$.

In case $\tau\geq\tfrac{1}{2}$ the limiting variables involve $c_t^{(c)}$, which is nearly impossible to estimate (see Section 8.3 below, however). When $\tau<\tfrac{1}{2}$, though, or when $k_n\sqrt{\Delta_n}\to0$ when X is continuous, these theorems allow us to construct confidence intervals for c_t, or c_S when S is a stopping time, or c_{S-} when S is a jump time of the $(d+d^2)$-dimensional process (X,c), at least in restriction to the set where c does not vanish. For example in dimension one, for any finite stopping time S, and in restriction to the set $\{c_S>0,S<\infty\}$, the standardized variables $\sqrt{k_n}\left(\widehat{c}(S;k_n,u_n)-c_S\right)/\sqrt{2}\,\widehat{c}(S;k_n,u_n)$ converge stably in law to $\mathcal{N}(0,1)$;

hence, under the assumption that c does not vanish and upon taking $\tau < \frac{1}{2}$, a confidence interval for c_S at asymptotic level α is

$$\left[\widehat{c}(S; k_n, u_n) - \sqrt{2}\,\widehat{c}(S; k_n, u_n)\, z_\alpha\,,\, \widehat{c}(S; k_n, u_n) + \sqrt{2}\,\widehat{c}(S; k_n, u_n)\, z_\alpha\right],$$

where z_α is the symmetric α-quantile of $\mathcal{N}(0, 1)$.

Let us emphasize once more that this can be done for any given t or S, or any finite family of such, but the "confidence bounds" one might be tempted to deduce for the path $t \mapsto c_t$ are genuine confidence intervals for each fixed t, but not for the path itself.

Remark 8.9. *As mentioned in Subsection 8.1.1, one can replace Assumption (H-2) for σ or c which is implicit in (K-r) by (8.6) (for all components c^{ij}). Then the results of Theorems 8.7 and 8.8 hold when $\tau < \frac{2\rho}{1+2\rho}$. When $\tau \geq \frac{2\rho}{1+2\rho}$, though, the convergence in law is generally not true, but we do have the convergence rate $1/\Delta_n^{\rho(1-\tau)}$.*

Remark 8.10. *All the previous results hold if we use a kernel ϕ on $[0, 1]$ which is piecewise continuous and $\int_0^1 \phi(x)\, dx = 1$ and modify (8.8) as follows:*

$$\begin{aligned}
\widehat{c}(\phi; k_n, u_n)_i^{jl} &= \frac{1}{k_n \Delta_n} \\
&\times \sum_{m=0}^{k_n - 1} \phi\left(\tfrac{m}{k_n}\right) \Delta_{i+m}^n X^j\, \Delta_{i+m}^n X^l\, 1_{\{\|\Delta_{i+m}^n X\| \leq u_n\}}
\end{aligned} \tag{8.18}$$

as in (8.7). More precisely, the results hold, upon replacing Z and Z' by $a(\phi)Z$ and $a'(\phi)Z'$, where

$$a(\phi)^2 = \int_0^1 \phi(x)^2\, dx, \quad a'(\phi) = \int_0^1 \left(\int_x^1 \phi(y)\, dy\right)^2 dx.$$

In the situation of Theorem 8.6 for example, and unless $\phi(x) \equiv 1$, we have $a(\phi)^2 > 1$ and thus the asymptotic (conditional) variance obtained in the case $k_n \sqrt{\Delta_n} \to 0$ is always bigger than for the naïve version (8.8). In contrast, when $k_n \sqrt{\Delta_n} \to \infty$, upon choosing ϕ appropriately, one can make this variance as small as one wishes to. When $k_n \sqrt{\Delta_n} \to \beta \in (0, \infty)$, this variance for (8.18) may be bigger or smaller than the one for (8.8), but in any case it can be made as close to the variance in the case $k_n \sqrt{\Delta_n} \to 0$ as one wishes to by choosing β small. However, since when $k_n \sqrt{\Delta_n}$ does not go to 0 we obtain in fact an "unfeasible" CLT anyway, it seems that for spot volatility estimation the naïve estimators (8.8) actually perform better than "general" kernel estimators.

8.2   Global Methods for the Spot Volatility

Now we turn to the "global" estimation of the spot volatility, and the shortness of this section reflects the fact that near to nothing is known on this topic.

The kernel estimators give us a global estimation, in the sense that the function $t \mapsto \widehat{c}(t; k_n, u_n)$ can be considered as an estimator of the function $t \mapsto c_t$. However, there seems to be no result on the behavior of the error function $\widetilde{c}(t; k_n) - c_t$, except for one very interesting but relatively restricted result.

For this result to hold, we need (KC) (so X is continuous), and the drift b_t must satisfy a condition similar to (8.6). We also need the (rather strong, and preventing leverage) requirement that the Brownian motion driving X is independent of the process c: in the setting of (8.12), this amounts to saying that σ_s^{ij} vanishes identically for all $j > j_0$ for some index $j_0 < d'$, and that the process c_t is independent of $(W^j)_{1 \leq j \leq j_0}$. Then, for all $T > 0$, we have

$$
\text{the sequence} \quad \frac{\sqrt{k_n}}{\sqrt{\log(1/\Delta_n)}} \, \sup_{t \in [0,T]} \| \widetilde{c}(t; k_n) - c_t \| \tag{8.19}
$$
is bounded in probability.

Another powerful global method is the Fourier-based method, as described in Subsection 6.3.4. Like all global methods, it is not performing so well for "point estimation" (here, the estimation of c_t at a specific time t), but it works well for "functional estimation," that is, the estimation of the path $t \mapsto c_t$ on the interval of interest $[0, T]$.

Below, we assume that both X and c are *continuous*, so in particular (KC) holds. The horizon T is kept fixed, and it plays a fundamental role, as in all global methods. Let us recall the estimators (6.45) of the (random) kth Fourier coefficient $\mathcal{F}_k(c^{lm})$ of the function $t \mapsto c_t^{lm}$ on the interval $[0, T]$:

$$
\widehat{\mathcal{F}}_k(n, N_n; c^{lm}) = \frac{1}{2N_n + 1} \sum_{r=-N_n}^{N_n} a_{-r}^{n,l} \, a_{r+k}^{n,m},
$$
$$
\text{with} \quad a_r^{n,l} = \frac{1}{\sqrt{2\pi}} \sum_{j=1}^{[T/\Delta_n]} e^{-2i\pi r j \Delta_n / T} \, \Delta_j^n X^l, \tag{8.20}
$$

where N_n is a sequence of integers increasing to ∞.

The idea for estimating c_t is then quite simple: we pretend that $\widehat{\mathcal{F}}_k(n, N_n; c^{lm})$ is really the kth Fourier coefficient, and construct the estimator of $t \mapsto c_t^{lm}$ by Fourier inversion. Using Fejer's formula, this leads us to take

$$\widehat{c}^{\text{Fourier}}(T, n, N_n)_t^{lm} = \frac{1}{2N_n+1}$$
$$\times \sum_{r=-N_n}^{N_n} \left(1 - \frac{|r|}{N_n}\right) e^{2i\pi rt/T} \, \widehat{\mathcal{F}}_r(n, N_n; c^{lm}) \tag{8.21}$$

which, as in (6.47), is necessarily a real, and is nonnegative when $l = m$. We plug T as an argument in this estimator, to emphasize the fact that it *fundamentally* depends on this terminal time, and is of course relevant for $t \leq T$ only.

Then, as soon as $N_n \Delta_n \to 0$ we have the following uniform convergence in probability (which is deduced from the convergence (6.46) for each k, plus some estimates):

$$\sup_{t \in [0,T]} \|\widehat{c}^{\text{Fourier}}(T, n, N_n)_t - c_t\| \xrightarrow{\mathbb{P}} 0. \tag{8.22}$$

So far, no rate of convergence in (8.22) is available. Another, still open, interesting (and related) question is whether we have a rate of convergence in L^p, in the sense that

$$w_n^p \int_0^T |\widehat{c}^{\text{Fourier}}(T, n, N_n)_t^{lm} - c_t^{lm}|^p \, dt \quad \text{is bounded in probability,}$$

for some sequence $w_n \to \infty$. Here p could be 2, or perhaps any real in $[1, \infty)$.

8.3   Volatility of Volatility

Now that we have seen that spot volatility can be estimated, many natural questions arise: What is the quadratic variation of c, or its continuous part (volatility of volatility)? What is the quadratic covariation between X and c (sometimes referred to as a measure of the leverage effect)? Does c jump? Where?

For the time being we set aside all questions about the jumps of c, which will be examined in Part IV. In this section and the next we concentrate on the quadratic variation-covariation. Although results could be derived when X and/or c have jumps, upon appropriate modifications such as truncations and appropriate assumptions on the jumps, such as (H-r) for X and/or c with $r < 1$, below we restrict our attention to the case where both X and c are *continuous*.

Everything can be done for an arbitrary dimension d, at the expense of extremely cumbersome notation. For simplicity, and also because practical interest mainly lies in the volatility of a single asset and its connections with the asset log-price itself, we restrict our attention to the $d = 1$ dimensional case. Note, however, that in (8.12) we still may have $d' \geq 2$, and we *should have* $d' \geq 2$ in the case of a genuine stochastic volatility, since there should be at least two independent linear Brownian motions to drive the pair (X, σ).

In addition to the continuity of X and c, we need some weak smoothness assumptions on the drift. We gather all these in the following, where the double "C" in the name (KCC) refers to the fact that both the log-price process X and the volatility process σ are continuous:

Assumption (KCC). *We have (8.12), the processes $b, b^{(\sigma)}, \sigma^{(\sigma)}$ are càdlàg, and the two coefficients $\delta, \delta^{(\sigma)}$ vanish identically.*

Then of course $\delta^{(c)}$ also vanishes identically, and we may rewrite (8.12) as

$$
\begin{aligned}
X_t &= X_0 + \int_0^t b_s \, ds + \int_0^t \sigma_s \, dW_s \\
\sigma_t &= \sigma_0 + \int_0^t b_s^{(\sigma)} \, ds + \int_0^t \sigma_s^{(\sigma)} \, dW_s \\
c_t &= c_0 + \int_0^t b_s^{(c)} \, ds + \int_0^t \sigma_s^{(c)} \, dW_s.
\end{aligned}
\tag{8.23}
$$

The processes $b^{(c)}$ and $\sigma^{(c)}$ are also càdlàg, since the following holds because $c_t = \sum_{l=1}^{d'} (\sigma_t^l)^2$:

$$
b_t^{(c)} = 2 \sum_{l=1}^{d'} \sigma_t^l b_t^{(\sigma),l} + \sum_{l,m=1}^{d'} (\sigma^{(\sigma),l,m})^2, \qquad \sigma_t^{(c),m} = \sum_{l=1}^{d'} \sigma_t^l \sigma_t^{(\sigma),l,m}.
$$

The quadratic variation of c_t is then the same as (8.13), namely $[c, c]_t = C_t^{(c)} = \int_0^t c_s^{(c)} \, ds$ with $c_s^{(c)} = \sum_{l=1}^{d'} (\sigma_s^{(c),l})^2$.

The idea for estimating $C_T^{(c)}$ is indeed very simple. We know that

$$
\begin{aligned}
\sum_{i=1}^{[T/l_n\Delta_n]} \left(c_{il_n\Delta_n} - c_{(i-1)l_n\Delta_n} \right)^2 &\xrightarrow{\mathbb{P}} [c, c]_T \\
\frac{1}{l_n} \sum_{i=1}^{[T/\Delta_n]-l_n+1} \left(c_{(i-1+l_n)\Delta_n} - c_{(i-1)\Delta_n} \right)^2 &\xrightarrow{\mathbb{P}} [c, c]_T
\end{aligned}
\tag{8.24}
$$

for any sequence $l_n \geq 1$ of integers such that $l_n\Delta_n \to 0$. These convergences hold with the rate of convergence $1/\sqrt{l_n\Delta_n}$ and an asymptotic variance for the second estimator (slightly) less than for the first one. Of course, if the variables $c_{i\Delta_n}$ were observed we would use this with $l_n = 1$, which would guarantee the minimal estimation variance. This is not the case, but it seems natural to substitute $c_{i\Delta_n}$ with the estimators $\hat{c}(k_n)_i$ given in (8.8), without truncation because X is continuous. This leads us to take

$$\widehat{[c,c]}(\Delta_n, k_n, l_n)_T = \frac{1}{l_n} \sum_{i=1}^{[T/\Delta_n]-l_n-k_n+1} \left(\widehat{c}(k_n)_{i+l_n} - \widehat{c}(k_n)_i\right)^2, \quad (8.25)$$

which only depends on the observations within $[0, T]$, and in view of Theorem 8.6 the optimal choice for k_n is

$$k_n \sim \frac{\beta}{\sqrt{\Delta_n}} \quad \text{for some } \beta \in (0, \infty). \quad (8.26)$$

In contrast, the choice of l_n is more subtle. From the insight given by the convergence (8.24) it might appear that taking $l_n = 1$ is the best choice. However, when $l_n < k_n$, basically $k_n - l_n$ terms in the difference $\widehat{c}(k_n)_{i+l_n} - \widehat{c}(k_n)_i$ cancel out; for example, if $l_n = 1$ the estimator becomes

$$\widehat{[c,c]}(\Delta_n, k_n, 1)_T = \frac{2}{(k_n \Delta_n)^2} \left(B(4, \Delta_n)_T - \sum_{i=1}^{[T/\Delta_n]-k_n} (\Delta_i^n X)^2 (\Delta_{i+k_n}^n X)^2\right)$$
$$+ \text{ negligible border terms.}$$

Hence, by virtue of (6.9) and of a relatively simple extension of Theorem A.2 of Appendix A, one can show that $\widehat{[c,c]}(\Delta_n, k_n, 1)_T$ consistently estimates $\frac{4}{\beta^2} C(4)_T$, and not $C_T^{(c)}$ at all! More generally, it consistently estimates a suitable multiple of $C(4)_T$ when $l_n = l$, and still the same (after normalization) when $l_n \to \infty$ with $l_n/k_n \to 0$.

On the contrary, $\widehat{[c,c]}(\Delta_n, k_n, l_n)_T$ consistently estimates $\alpha C_T^{(c)}$ when $l_n/k_n \to w \in (0, \infty]$, for a suitable constant $\alpha > 0$. To understand what α is, one should be aware that $\widehat{c}(k_n)_{i+1}$ is a good estimator of $\frac{1}{k_n \Delta_n} \int_{(i-1)\Delta_n}^{(i+k_n-1)\Delta_n} c_s \, ds$, rather than of $c_{i\Delta_n}$ itself. Therefore, $\widehat{[c,c]}(\Delta_n, k_n, l_n)_T$ is a proxy for

$$\frac{1}{l_n(k_n\Delta_n)^2} \sum_{i=0}^{[T/\Delta_n]-l_n-k_n} \left(\int_{(i+l_n-1)\Delta_n}^{(i+l_n+k_n-1)\Delta_n} c_s ds - \int_{(i-1)\Delta_n}^{(i+k_n-1)\Delta_n} c_s ds\right)^2.$$

We can obtain α by computing the limit of the expected value of the above, in the case of c a martingale with constant volatility $c^{(c)}$ (not a very realistic model indeed, since in this case c can become negative, but it is enough to understand what happens). Recalling $l_n/k_n \to w \geq 1$, one gets $\alpha = 1 - 1/3w$, whereas the asymptotic minimal variance increases when w increases, and the rate becomes $1/\sqrt{l_n\Delta_n}$, slower than $1/\Delta_n^{1/4}$ when $w = \infty$ and equivalent to $1/\Delta_n^{1/4}$ otherwise.

Therefore if we want an estimator that approaches $C_T^{(c)}$ as fast as possible, we should choose $l_n = k_n$, hence $w = 1$, and multiply

$\widehat{[c,c]}(\Delta_n, k_n, l_n)_T$ by $1/\alpha = 3/2$. In other words, a proper estimator is indeed

$$\widehat{C^{(c)}}^n_T = \frac{3}{2k_n} \sum_{i=1}^{[T/\Delta_n]-2k_n+1} \left((\widehat{c}(k_n)^n_{i+k_n} - \widehat{c}(k_n)^n_i)^2 - \frac{4}{k_n}(\widehat{c}(k_n)^n_i)^2\right) \quad (8.27)$$

(this is (8.25) with $l_n = k_n$, up to the multiplicative factor $3/2$, plus a de-biasing term).

We then have the following – consistency and CLT together – result (this is proved in Appendix B, see Section B.2, as all the results in this section):

Theorem 8.11. *Assume (KCC) and take k_n as in (8.26). Then for each $T > 0$ we have the consistency $\widehat{C^{(c)}}^n_T \overset{\mathbb{P}}{\longrightarrow} C^{(c)}_T$. We also have the following stable convergence in law:*

$$\frac{1}{\Delta_n^{1/4}} \left(\widehat{C^{(c)}}^n_T - C^{(c)}_T\right) \overset{\mathcal{L}-s}{\Longrightarrow} \mathcal{U}_T^{(C^{(c)})}, \qquad (8.28)$$

where $\mathcal{U}_T^{(C^{(c)})}$ is a random variable defined on an extension of the space $(\Omega, \mathcal{F}, \mathbb{P})$, which conditionally on $\mathcal{F}$ is centered Gaussian with variance

$$\mathbb{E}((\mathcal{U}_T^{(C^{(c)})})^2 \mid \mathcal{F}) = \int_0^T \left(\frac{48}{\beta^3}(c_s)^4 + \frac{12}{\beta}(c_s)^2 c_s^{(c)} + \frac{151\,\beta}{70}(c_s^{(c)})^2\right) ds. \qquad (8.29)$$

The rate $1/\Delta_n^{1/4}$ is optimal, in the same minimax sense as $1/\Delta_n^{1/2}$ is the optimal rate for estimating the integrated volatility C_T itself. To see this, one can consider the parametric submodel for which, in (8.23), one has $b_t = \tilde{b}_t = \tilde{\sigma}_t = 0$ identically, and $\tilde{\sigma}'_t = f(\theta, \sigma_t)$ for a smooth and non-vanishing function f depending on a real parameter θ. Then it is proved in Hoffmann (2002) that $1/\Delta_n^{1/4}$ is the optimal rate for estimating θ, hence also for estimating $\int_0^T f(\theta, \sigma_s)^2 ds$.

Finally, a feasible (standardized) CLT associated with (8.28), in the same way as Theorem 6.4, is available. For this, we need consistent estimators for the right side of (8.29), which amounts to finding consistent estimators for the quarticity $C(4)_t = \int_0^t (c_s)^2 ds$, and for the two variables $F_t = \int_0^t (c_s)^2 c_s^{(c)} ds$ and $G_t = \int_0^t (c_s^{(c)})^2 ds$. As seen in (6.9), we know how to estimate $C(4)_t$. The estimation of F_t is also simple; the estimation of G_t is more difficult. However, we are concerned here with consistent estimators only and, although accurate estimators are of course preferable to poor ones, the actual rate of convergence is not our primary concern.

Henceforth, we propose simple – and not really accurate – estimators, globally for the right side of (8.29). We first choose a sequence $l_n \geq 1$ of integers satisfying

$$l_n \asymp \frac{1}{\Delta_n^{1/4}}. \tag{8.30}$$

Note that $k_n l_n \Delta_n \to 0$. With k_n and l_n as above, we use the simplifying notation

$$\Delta_i'^n X = X_{ik_n l_n \Delta_n} - X_{(i-1)k_n l_n \Delta_n}, \tag{8.31}$$
$$\Delta_i'^n \widehat{c} = \widehat{c}(k_n)_{1+ik_n l_n} - \widehat{c}(k_n)_{1+(i-1)k_n l_n},$$

and define the estimators by

$$V_t^{C^{(c)},n} = \frac{1}{\Delta_n^{3/2}} \sum_{i=1}^{[t/k_n l_n \Delta_n]-2} \left(\frac{16}{3k_n^6 l_n^3} (\Delta_i'^n X)^4 (\Delta_{i+1}'^n X)^4 \right. \tag{8.32}$$
$$\left. + \frac{4}{k_n^3 l_n^2} (\Delta_i'^n X)^4 (\Delta_{i+1}'^n \widehat{c})^2 + \frac{151}{70\, l_n} (\Delta_i'^n \widehat{c})^2 (\Delta_{i+1}'^n \widehat{c})^2 \right).$$

Then we have the following, which allows us to construct confidence intervals in the usual way:

Theorem 8.12. *Under the assumptions of Theorem 8.11, we have*

$$V_T^{C^{(c)},n} \xrightarrow{\mathbb{P}} \mathbb{E}((\mathcal{U}_T^{(C^{(c)})})^2 \mid \mathcal{F}) \tag{8.33}$$

and thus

$$\mathcal{L}\left(\frac{\widehat{C^{(c)}}_T^n - C_T^{(c)}}{\sqrt{V_T^{C^{(c)},n}}} \,\Big|\, A \right) \to \mathcal{N}(0,1)$$
for all $A \in \mathcal{F}$ with $\mathbb{P}(A) > 0$ and $A \subset \{C_T + C_T^{(c)} > 0\}$.

Remark 8.13. *One can show that the rate of convergence of $V_T^{C^{(c)},n}$ is $1/\Delta_n^{1/8}$, quite slow indeed, and the choice (8.30) gives the best possible rate for estimators of the form (8.31). However, these estimators still satisfy the consistency (8.33), as long as $l_n \to \infty$ and $k_n l_n \Delta_n \to 0$. Better estimators (with rate $1/\Delta_n^{1/4}$) could be constructed, according to the scheme proposed in Section 8.5 below or to Vetter (2011), but the proof of the consistency would be significantly more involved, and it is not necessary for us here.*

At this juncture, the reader may wonder about the difference between the estimator (8.27) and the sum of the second summands in the estimator (8.32). As is easily proved, we have the convergence

$$\sum_{i=1}^{[T/k_n l_n \Delta_n]-1} (\Delta_i'^n \widehat{c})^2 \xrightarrow{\mathbb{P}} C_T^{(c)} = \int_0^T c_s^{(c)} \, ds.$$

The left side above and the right side of (8.27) differ in many ways, although they estimate the same quantity. Apart from the different normalization, due to the fact that the sums in the two cases extend over different sets of integers, the expression in (8.27) is similar to the above with $l_n = 1$, *plus a de-biasing term*. De-biasing is not necessary in the present case, because $l_n \to \infty$, but of course the rate of convergence becomes (much) slower.

8.4 Leverage: The Covariation between X and c

The setting is the same as in the previous section, including dimension $d = 1$ and Assumption (KCC), and we now are concerned with the estimation of the quadratic covariation $[X, c]$ between the process X and its volatility c, that is, $C^{(X,c)}$ of (8.13).

This covariation is called, or related to, the "leverage effect." The terminology originates in the fact that an asset's volatility tends to be negatively correlated with the asset's returns. Typically, rising asset prices are accompanied by declining volatility, and vice versa. The term "leverage" refers to one possible economic interpretation of this phenomenon, developed in Black (1976) and Christie (1982): as asset prices decline, companies become mechanically more leveraged since the relative value of their debt rises relative to that of their equity. As a result, it is natural to expect that their stock becomes riskier, hence more volatile. While this is only a hypothesis, this explanation is sufficiently prevalent in the literature that the term "leverage effect" has been adopted to describe the statistical regularity in question. It has also been documented that the effect is generally asymmetric: other things equal, declines in stock prices are accompanied by larger increases in volatility than the decline in volatility that accompanies rising stock markets (see, e.g., Nelson (1991) and Engle and Ng (1993)). Various discrete-time models with a leverage effect have been estimated by Yu (2005).

The magnitude of the effect, however, seems too large to be attributable solely to an increase in financial leverage: Figlewski and Wang (2000) noted among other findings that there is no apparent effect on volatility when leverage changes because of a change in debt or number of shares, only when stock prices change, which questions whether the effect is linked to financial leverage at all. As always, correlation does not imply causality. Alternative economic interpretations have been suggested: an anticipated increase in volatility requires a higher rate of return from the asset, which can only be produced by a fall in the asset price (see, e.g., French et al. (1987) and Campbell and Hentschel (1992)).

The terminology somehow drifted away, and by now "leverage effect" qualifies the connection between the behavior of the volatility $c = \sigma^2$ and the log-price X, beyond the necessary connection $dX_s = b_t dt + \sigma_t dW_t$. The phenomenon described above would then be reflected by the fact that, loosely speaking, the increments of X and of c are negatively correlated; in a more mathematical way, this amounts to saying that the covariation $[X, c]$ is a decreasing process: again, this property is not well established from an empirical viewpoint, and so there is a clear necessity of being able to estimate the variables $[X, c]_T$ and check whether they are negative or not.

The method for estimating $C_T^{(X,c)}$ is basically the same as in Section 8.3, and it can be introduced in the same way. For any sequence $l_n \geq 1$ such that $l_n \Delta_n \to 0$, we have

$$\frac{1}{l_n} \sum_{i=1}^{[T/\Delta_n]-l_n+1} \left(X_{(i+l_n-1)\Delta_n} - X_{(i-1)\Delta_n}\right)\left(c_{(i+l_n-1)\Delta_n} - c_{(i-1)\Delta_n}\right)$$
$$\xrightarrow{\mathbb{P}} [X,c]_T,$$

with the rate of convergence $1/\sqrt{l_n \Delta_n}$, the best choice (giving rise to the fastest convergence rate and smallest asymptotic variance) being $l_n = 1$. Exactly as before, we substitute $c_{i\Delta_n}$ with the estimators $\widehat{c}(k_n)_{i+1}$, which leads us to take k_n satisfying (8.26) and define

$$\widehat{[X,c]}(\Delta_n, k_n, l_n)_T =$$
$$\frac{1}{l_n} \sum_{i=1}^{[T/\Delta_n]-l_n-k_n+1} \left(X_{(i+l_n-1)\Delta_n} - X_{(i-1)\Delta_n}\right)\left(\widehat{c}(k_n)_{i+l_n} - \widehat{c}(k_n)_i\right). \tag{8.34}$$

Again as in the previous section, if we take $l_n = 1$ above we obtain

$$\widehat{[X,c]}(\Delta_n, k_n, 1)_T = \frac{1}{k_n \Delta_n} \sum_{i=1}^{[T/\Delta_n]-k_n} \Delta_i^n X \left((\Delta_{i+k_n}^n X)^2 - (\Delta_i^n X)^2\right).$$

A simple extension of Theorem A.2 of Appendix A shows that, once multiplied by $1/\sqrt{\Delta_n}$, this converges in law to a non-trivial variable which only depends on the volatility c and not at all on the process of interest $[X, c] = C^{(X,c)}$. The same holds for any constant sequence $l_n = l$. Hence, in order to estimate $C^{(X,c)}$ we need $l_n \geq k_n$. Then, as in the previous section again, (8.34) behaves like

$$\frac{1}{l_n k_n \Delta_n} \sum_{i=1}^{[T/\Delta_n]-l_n-k_n+1} \left(X_{(il_n+\kappa k_n-1)\Delta_n} - X_{(i-1)\Delta_n} \right)$$
$$\times \left(\int_{(i+l_n-1)\Delta_n}^{(i+l_n+k_n-1)\Delta_n} c_s \, ds - \int_{(i-1)\Delta_n}^{(i+k_n-1)\Delta_n} c_s \, ds \right) \tag{8.35}$$

where $\kappa = 0$, but we allow ourselves to use this with $\kappa = 1$ as well, since with $\kappa = 1$ the above expression is somewhat more symmetric. Exactly as in the previous section again, if $l_n/k_n \to w \in (0, \infty]$, (8.35) converges to $\alpha C_T^{(X,c)}$, and for calculating α one can consider the case where both X and c are martingales, with $[X, c]_t = t$, in which case α is simply the expectation of (8.35) when $T = 1$. This gives us $\alpha = 1 - \frac{1-\kappa}{2w}$. Moreover, the rate is $1/\sqrt{l_n \Delta_n}$, slower than $1/\Delta_n^{1/4}$ when $w = \infty$ and equivalent to $1/\Delta_n^{1/4}$ otherwise, and the normalized asymptotic variance increases with w.

Consequently, the best one can do, from an asymptotic viewpoint and for estimators similar with (8.34), is to take $l_n = k_n$, and thus to consider the following estimator:

$$\widehat{C^{(X,c)}}_T^n = \frac{1}{k_n} \sum_{i=1}^{[T/\Delta_n]-2k_n+1} \left(X_{(i+2k_n-1)\Delta_n} - X_{(i-1)\Delta_n} \right)$$
$$\times \left(\widehat{c}(k_n)_{i+k_n} - \widehat{c}(k_n)_i \right), \tag{8.36}$$

which corresponds to taking $\kappa = 1$ above. One could also take the version associated with $\kappa = 0$, but it turns out that because of its lack of "symmetry" it exhibits a bigger asymptotic variance, see Remark 8.16 below.

The main result is as follows (see Section B.2 of Appendix B for the proof of all results in the present section):

Theorem 8.14. *Assume (KCC) and take k_n as in (8.26). Then for each $T > 0$ we have $C_T^{(X,c)} \xrightarrow{\mathbb{P}} C_T^{(X,c)}$ and also the following stable convergence in law:*

$$\frac{1}{\Delta_n^{1/4}} \left(\widehat{C^{(X,c)}}_T^n - C_T^{(X,c)} \right) \xrightarrow{\mathcal{L}-s} \mathcal{U}_T^{(C^{(X,c)})}, \tag{8.37}$$

where $\mathcal{U}_T^{(C^{(X,c)})}$ is a random variable defined on an extension of the space $(\Omega, \mathcal{F}, \mathbb{P})$, which conditionally on $\mathcal{F}$ is centered Gaussian with variance

$$\mathbb{E}((\mathcal{U}_T^{(C^{(X,c)})})^2 \mid \mathcal{F}) = \int_0^T \left(\frac{8}{3\beta} (c_s)^3 + \frac{23\beta}{15} c_s^{(c)} c_s \right.$$
$$\left. + \frac{23\beta}{30} (c_s^{(X,c)})^2 \right) ds. \tag{8.38}$$

The rate is again $1/\Delta_n^{1/4}$ and, although there is no proof for this so far, it is probably optimal, exactly as it is optimal for Theorem 8.11.

Remark 8.15. *It is possible to obtain a joint Central Limit Theorem asserting that*

$$\left(\frac{1}{\Delta_n^{1/4}}\left(\widehat{C^{(c)}}_T^n - C_T^{(c)}\right), \frac{1}{\Delta_n^{1/4}}\left(\widehat{C^{(X,c)}}_T^n - C_T^{(X,c)}\right)\right) \xrightarrow{\mathcal{L}-s} \left(\mathcal{U}_T^{(C^{(c)})}, \mathcal{U}_T^{(C^{(X,c)})}\right),$$

with a limit which, conditionally on $\mathcal{F}$, is jointly Gaussian, centered, with (conditional) variances given by (8.29) and (8.38) and covariance

$$\mathbb{E}(\mathcal{U}_T^{(C^{(.c)})} \mathcal{U}_T^{(C^{(X,c)})} \mid \mathcal{F}) = \int_0^T \left(\frac{5}{\beta}(c_s)^2 c_s^{(X,c)} + \frac{151\,\beta}{120} c_s^{(c)} c_s^{(X,c)}\right) ds. \qquad (8.39)$$

This will be proven together with the previous theorem.

Remark 8.16. *As written before, one could use another version of the estimator, corresponding to choosing $\kappa = 0$ in (8.35), and explicitly given by*

$$\frac{2}{k_n} \sum_{i=1}^{[T\Delta_n]-2k_n+1} \left(X_{(i+k_n-1)\Delta_n} - X_{(i-1)\Delta_n}\right)\left(\widehat{c}(k_n)_{i+k_n} - \widehat{c}(k_n)_i\right).$$

This is the estimator proposed by Wang and Mykland (2012). It enjoys the same properties as $\widehat{C^{(X,c)}}_T^n$ in the previous theorem, except that its conditional variance is

$$\int_0^T \left(\frac{72}{3\beta}(c_s)^3 + \frac{64\,\beta}{15} c_s^{(c)} c_s + \frac{4\,\beta}{5}(c_s^{(X,c)})^2\right) ds,$$

which is always bigger than the variance given in (8.38).

Notice also that these authors propose to replace $\widehat{c}(k_n)_i$ in (8.36) by

$$\widehat{c}(k_n)_i' = \frac{1}{k_n \Delta_n} \sum_{m=0}^{k_n-1} \left(\Delta_{i+m}^n X - \overline{\Delta}_i^n X\right)^2,$$

where

$$\overline{\Delta}_i^n X = \frac{1}{k_n \Delta_n}\left(X_{(i+k_n)\Delta_n} - X_{i\Delta_n}\right).$$

The reason for this correction is that $\overline{\Delta}_i^n X$ is a kind of estimator of the drift, or of the averaged drift, over the interval $[(i-1)\Delta_n, (i+k_n-1)\Delta_n]$. It turns out that, asymptotically speaking, $\widehat{c}(k_n)_i'$ has exactly the same properties as $\widehat{c}(k_n)_i$ in (8.10) and in Theorem 8.7 or 8.8, as is fairly easy *to check. However, although we are in a situation where no consistent estimation of the drift is possible, "on average" the correcting variables $\overline{\Delta}_i^n X$ are proper de-biasing terms, and making this correction is probably advisable.*

Note that the same correction could also be applied to the estimators $\widehat{C^{(c)}}_T^n$ of (8.27).

A feasible (standardized) CLT is associated with (8.37). Namely, with (8.30) and the notation (8.31), we set

$$V_T^{C^{(X,c)},n} = \frac{1}{\Delta_n^{3/2}} \sum_{i=1}^{[T/k_n l_n \Delta_n]-2} \left(\frac{8}{9 k_n^3 l_n^2} (\Delta_i'^n X)^2 (\Delta_{i+1}'^n X)^4 \right.$$
$$+ \frac{23}{15\, l_n} (\Delta_i'^n X)^2 (\Delta_{i+1}'^n \widehat{c})^2$$
$$\left. + \frac{23}{30\, l_n} \Delta_i'^n X\, \Delta_i'^n \widehat{c}\, \Delta_{i+1}'^n X\, \Delta_{i+1}'^n \widehat{c} \right). \qquad (8.40)$$

Then we have the following, which allows us to construct confidence intervals in the usual way:

Theorem 8.17. *Under the assumptions of Theorem 8.14, we have*

$$V_T^{C^{(X,c)},n} \xrightarrow{\;\mathbb{P}\;} \mathbb{E}\big((\mathcal{U}_T^{(C^{(X,c)})})^2 \mid \mathcal{F}\big) \qquad (8.41)$$

and thus

$$\mathcal{L}\left(\frac{\widehat{C^{(X,c)}}_T^n - C_T^{(X,c)}}{\sqrt{V_T^{C^{(X,c)},n}}} \,\Big|\, A \right) \to \mathcal{N}(0,1)$$
for all $A \in \mathcal{F}$ with $\mathbb{P}(A) > 0$ and $A \subset \{C_T + C_T^{(c)} > 0\}$.

Back to leverage. As mentioned before, what is usually called "leverage effect" is not the covariation $[X, c]$, but rather the "correlation" between X and c. Of course, the correlation is in principle a non-random quantity, which has very little to do with any particular outcome of the pair (X, c), and the correlation *stricto sensu* has to be replaced by either one of the two following quantities:

$$R_T = \frac{C_T^{(X,c)}}{\sqrt{C_T\, C_T^{(c)}}}, \qquad r_t = \frac{c_t^{(X,c)}}{\sqrt{c_t\, c_t^{(c)}}}. \qquad (8.42)$$

Here, r_t is a kind of "spot" correlation at time t, and R_T is a "global" correlation (up to time T): both are random, although in an ergodic situation for σ_t and for the increments of X_t, then both R_T and $\frac{1}{T} \int_0^T r_s\, ds$ converge to the stationary correlation between c and the returns, as $T \to \infty$.

Example 8.18. *(Leverage in the Heston Model) In some examples, such as the Heston model, it turns out that in* (8.42) *we have* $R_T = r_t = \rho$ *non-random, for all* t, T. *The stochastic volatility model of Heston (1993) specifies:*

$$
\begin{aligned}
dX_t &= (\mu - c_t/2)dt + c_t^{1/2}dW_t \\
dc_t &= \kappa(\alpha - c_t)dt + \gamma c_t^{1/2}dW_t',
\end{aligned}
\tag{8.43}
$$

where W and W' are two Brownian motions with correlation ρ, that is, $\mathbb{E}(W_t W_t') = \rho t$, and the parameters μ, α, κ and γ are constants. Note that in this model

$$
[X, X]_t = C_t, \qquad [X, c]_t = \gamma\rho C_t, \qquad [c, c]_t = \gamma^2 C_t, \tag{8.44}
$$

so that in (8.42) *we have* $R_T = r_t = \rho$ *and this number ρ summarizes the leverage effect. Therefore, if we use the estimators $\widehat{C^{(c)}}_T^{\,n}$ and $\widehat{C^{(X,c)}}_T^{\,n}$ for $C_T^{(c)}$ and $C_T^{(X,c)}$, as well as the realized volatility estimator $\widehat{C}(\Delta_n)_T$ of* (6.4) *for C_T, the statistic*

$$
\widehat{\rho}_T^{\,n} = \frac{\widehat{C^{(X,c)}}_T^{\,n}}{\sqrt{\widehat{C^{(c)}}_T^{\,n}}\sqrt{\widehat{C}(\Delta_n)_T}} \tag{8.45}
$$

is a consistent estimator for ρ, and by the delta method it enjoys a CLT with convergence rate $1/\Delta_n^{1/4}$ and with stable convergence in law to a limit which conditionally on $\mathcal{F}$ is centered Gaussian. We leave to the reader the task of computing the asymptotic variance of the limit, and also to derive consistent estimators for this (conditional) variance, so that it becomes possible to construct confidence intervals.

This type of result is of course not restricted to the Heston model, but holds for any model enjoying (8.44) *for some constant γ.*

8.5 Optimal Estimation of a Function of Volatility

Let us recall that the problem of estimating the quarticity was only partly solved in Chapter 6, in the sense that the proposed estimators were in no way efficient in the sense of Remark 6.2. In this section we come back to this question and, more generally, we consider the estimation of a functional of the form

$$
U(g)_t = \int_0^t g(c_s)\,ds
$$

for an arbitrary (smooth enough) test function g on the set $\mathcal{M}_d^+$. By virtue of Theorem A.8 of Appendix A (applied with $f \equiv 1$, hence $p' = 0$), natural estimators are

$$U(\Delta_n, g)_t = \Delta_n \sum_{i=1}^{[t/\Delta_n]-k_n+1} g(\widehat{c}(k_n, u_n)_i)$$

(in (A.26) the indicator function $1_{\{\|\Delta_{i+k_n}^n X\| \leq u_n\}}$ shows up, but it is useful only when the function f appearing there is not constant). More specifically we have $U(\Delta_n, g) \overset{\text{u.c.p.}}{\Longrightarrow} U(g)$ (consistency), under (H-r) and for any continuous function g on $\mathcal{M}_d^+$ satisfying $|g(x)| \leq K(1 + \|x\|^p)$, under any one of the following sets of conditions:

- X continuous and $p \geq 0$
  and either $u_n \equiv \infty$ or $u_n \asymp \Delta_n^\varpi$ with $0 < \varpi < \frac{1}{2}$
- $p < 1$ and $u_n \equiv \infty$ (8.46)
- $p \leq 1$ and $u_n \asymp \Delta_n^\varpi$ with $0 < \varpi < \frac{1}{2}$
- $p > 1$ and $u_n \asymp \Delta_n^\varpi$ with $\frac{p-1}{2p-r} < \varpi < \frac{1}{2}$.

Moreover, this is true for any sequence $k_n \to \infty$ such that $k_n \Delta_n \to 0$.

Remark 8.19. *Let us emphasize that Theorems A.2 or A.3 (for the consistency) and A.13 or A.14 (for the CLT) give us another method to estimate $U(g)_t$. It consists in finding a function f on $\mathbb{R}^d$, or more generally on $(\mathbb{R}^d)^k$, such that $g(x) = \mathbb{E}(f(\Phi_1, \dots, \Phi_k))$ where the Φ_j's are i.i.d. $\mathcal{N}(0, x)$. In this case,*

$$\overline{B}'(f, \Delta_n)_t = \Delta_n \sum_{i=1}^{[t/k\Delta_n]} f\left(\frac{\Delta_{ik-k+1}^n X}{\sqrt{\Delta_n}}, \dots, \frac{\Delta_{ik}^n X}{\sqrt{\Delta_n}}\right)$$

converges locally uniformly in time, in probability, to $U(g)$, and under appropriate assumptions a CLT holds, with rate $1/\sqrt{\Delta_n}$. This method is the most widely used in practice, so far. For example, this is what the estimator $\frac{1}{3\Delta_n} B(4, \Delta_n)$ of the quarticity does when $d = 1$.

However, the asymptotic variance of these estimators is always bigger than the one obtained in the CLT for the appropriate de-biased version of $U(\Delta_n, g)$ given below. More important, perhaps, is that there does not always exist a function f associated with g as above; for instance, if it exists, then necessarily g is C^∞. Moreover, even when it exists it is often difficult to find, except for functions g that are of the product form $g(x) = \prod_{i,j=1}^d (x^{ij})^{l(i,j)}$ (with $l(i,j)$ nonnegative integers) or $g(x) = \prod_{i,j=1}^d |x^{ij}|^{l(i,j)}$ (with $l(i,j)$ nonnegative reals), or linear combinations of such products.

In view of this remark, it is natural to try to find "optimal" estimators for the variables $U(g)_t$, in the sense that they achieve not only the optimal rate $1/\sqrt{\Delta_n}$, but also the minimal asymptotic (conditional) variance. When $g(x) = x$ this amounts to estimating the integrated volatility, and a simple calculation shows that in this case $U(\Delta_n, g)_t$ is equal to the truncated realized volatility $\widehat{C}(\Delta_n, u_n)_t$, plus some (negligible) border terms. Since it is out of the question to do any better for a general function g (even a smooth one) than for $g(x) = x$, we thus need at least Assumption (H-r) for some $r \in [0, 1)$, and in fact we even need the stronger assumption (K-r).

Now, we have to choose the window size k_n in the definition of the spot volatility estimators. A natural choice seems to be $k_n \sim \beta/\sqrt{\Delta_n}$, because it ensures rate optimality for the spot volatility estimators, by virtue of Theorem 8.7. With this choice, we do obtain a CLT, in the sense that $\frac{1}{\sqrt{\Delta_n}} (U(\Delta_n, g)_t - U(g)_t)$ converges stably in law for each fixed t. Moreover, the limit is $\mathcal{F}$-conditionally Gaussian, with the optimal (minimal) variance which will be described below, but *not centered*, and the $\mathcal{F}$-conditional mean of the limit consists of four bias terms, of the following form (in the one-dimensional case, for simplicity):

1. A first term of the form $-\frac{\beta}{2}(g(c_0) + g(c_t))$, due to a border effect;

2. A second term of the form $\frac{1}{\beta} \int_0^t g''(c_s)(c_s)^2\, ds$ (with g'' the second derivative of g);

3. A third term of the form $-\frac{\beta}{12} \int_0^t g''(c_s)\, c_s^{(c)}\, ds$, where $c_t^{(c)}$ is the volatility of the volatility;

4. A fourth term of the form $\beta \sum_{s \leq t} G(c_{s-}, c_s)$ for a suitable function G depending on g and which vanishes on the diagonal.

It is possible to consistently estimate these four terms, and thus bias-correct $U(\Delta_n, g)$ and obtain a CLT with a conditionally centered Gaussian limit. Consistent estimators for the first and second terms are easy to derive (note that the second term is of the form $U(f)_t$ for the function $f(x) = g''(x) x^2$). Consistent estimators for the last two terms, involving the volatility and the jumps of c_t, are more complicated to describe, especially the last one, and also likely to have poor performances in terms of rate, as we saw in the previous section.

Now, if we let β go to 0, we kill the first, third and fourth bias terms and inflate the second one. Letting $\beta \to 0$ indeed amounts to choosing k_n going to infinity slower than $1/\sqrt{\Delta_n}$, and it turns out that doing so greatly simplifies the analysis, without affecting the efficient rate and asymptotic variance. We need, though, for k_n not to go to ∞ "too slowly," and the necessary assumptions are as such

$$k_n^2 \Delta_n \to 0, \qquad k_n^3 \Delta_n \to \infty. \tag{8.47}$$

The test function g is a C^3 function on $\mathcal{M}_d^+$, and the two first partial derivatives are denoted as $\partial_{jk} g$ and $\partial^2_{jk,lm} g$, since any $x \in \mathcal{M}_d^+$ has d^2 components x^{jk}. The family of all partial derivatives of order j is simply denoted as $\partial^j g$. The modified, de-biased, estimators will be

$$
\begin{aligned}
U'(\Delta_n, g)_t^n = \Delta_n & \sum_{i=1}^{[t/\Delta_n]-k_n+1} \Big(g(\widehat{c}(k_n, u_n)_i) \\
& - \frac{1}{2k_n} \sum_{j,k,l,m=1}^{d} \partial^2_{jk,lm}\, g(\widehat{c}(k_n, u_n)_i) \\
& \times \big(\widehat{c}(k_n, u_n)_i^{jl}\, \widehat{c}(k_n, u_n)_i^{km} + \widehat{c}(k_n, u_n)_i^{jm}\, \widehat{c}(k_n, u_n)_i^{kl} \big) \Big).
\end{aligned}
\tag{8.48}
$$

The main result of this section, proved in Section B.2 of Appendix B (as are all results of this section), is as follows:

Theorem 8.20. *Assume (K-r) for some $r < 1$. Let g be a C^3 function on $\mathcal{M}_d^+$ such that*

$$\| \partial^j g(x) \| \le K(1 + \|x\|^{(p-j)^+}), \qquad j = 0, 1, 2, 3 \tag{8.49}$$

for some constants $K > 0$, $p > 1$. Either suppose that X is continuous and $u_n/\Delta_n^\epsilon \to \infty$ for some $\epsilon \in [0, 1/2)$ (for example $u_n \equiv \infty$, so there is no truncation at all), or suppose that

$$u_n \asymp \Delta_n^\varpi, \qquad \frac{2p-1}{2(2p-r)} \le \varpi < \frac{1}{2}. \tag{8.50}$$

Finally, assume (8.47) for k_n. Then we have the functional stable convergence in law

$$\frac{1}{\sqrt{\Delta_n}} \left(U'(\Delta_n, g) - U(g) \right) \overset{\mathcal{L}-s}{\Longrightarrow} Z,$$

where Z is a process defined on an extension $(\widetilde{\Omega}, \widetilde{\mathcal{F}}, (\widetilde{\mathcal{F}}_t), \widetilde{\mathbb{P}})$ of $(\Omega, \mathcal{F}, (\mathcal{F}_t), \mathbb{P})$ and which, conditionally on $\mathcal{F}$, is a continuous centered Gaussian martingale with variance

$$
\widetilde{\mathbb{E}}((Z_t)^2 \mid \mathcal{F}) = \sum_{j,k,l,m=1}^{d} \int_0^t \partial_{jk} g(c_s)\, \partial_{lm} g(c_s) \\
\times \big(c_s^{jl} c_s^{km} + c_s^{jm} c_s^{kl} \big)\, ds.
\tag{8.51}
$$

   The restriction $r < 1$, necessary for (8.50) to be non-empty, is exactly
the same as in Theorem 6.9 for estimating the integrated volatility of
X in the presence of jumps. Observe also that $g(x) = x$ satisfies (8.49)
with $p = 1$, so (8.50) is exactly the condition on u_n needed in Theorem
6.9; and of course when $g(x) = x$ the de-biasing term vanishes and, as
mentioned before, $U'(\Delta_n, g) = U(\Delta_n, g)$ is $\widehat{C}(\Delta_n, u_n)_t$ plus negligible
border terms. The two results here and in Theorem 6.9 agree, except
that the assumptions here are stronger.

Remark 8.21. *The C^3 property of g is somewhat restrictive; for example, in the one-dimensional case it rules out the power functions
$g(x) = x^r$ on $[0, \infty)$ with $r \in (0,3) \backslash \{1, 2\}$. It could be proved that, in
the one-dimensional case again, and under (P) (that is, the processes c_t
and c_{t-} do not vanish), the result still holds when g is C^3 on $(0, \infty)$ and
satisfies (8.49) with an arbitrary $p > 0$. Here again, Assumption (P) is
also necessary for having a CLT for the functionals of Remark 8.19 (say,
with $k = 1$) when the test function f is C^1 outside 0 only.*

   It is simple to make this CLT "feasible." Indeed, we associate with g
the following function on $\mathcal{M}_d^+$:

$$h(x) = \sum_{j,k,l,m=1}^{d} \partial_{jk}\, g(x)\, \partial_{lm}\, g(x) \left(x^{jl} x^{km} + x^{jm} x^{kl} \right),$$

which is continuous with $h(x) \leq K(1 + \|x\|^{2p-2})$, and nonnegative (and
positive at each x such that $\partial g(x) \neq 0$). Equation (8.50) implies the last
conditions in (8.46) and we have $U(\Delta_n, h) \stackrel{\text{u.c.p.}}{\Longrightarrow} U(h)$, with $U(h)_t$ being
the right hand side of (8.51). Then we readily deduce for any $T > 0$

$$\mathcal{L}\left(\frac{U'(\Delta_n, g)_t - U(g)_t}{\sqrt{\Delta_n\, U(\Delta_n, h)_t}} \,\Big|\, A \right) \to \mathcal{N}(0, 1)$$
for all $A \in \mathcal{F}$ with $\mathbb{P}(A) > 0$ and $A \subset \{U(h)_T > 0\}$.

Therefore the estimators $U'(\Delta_n, g)_T$ are feasible, and deducing confidence bounds is then straightforward, and done as for the previous analogous situations.

Example 8.22 (Quarticity). *Suppose $d = 1$ and take $g(x) = x^2$, so we
want to estimate the quarticity $C(4)_t = \int_0^t c_s^2\, ds$. In this case "optimal"
estimators for the quarticity are*

$$\Delta_n \left(1 - \frac{2}{k_n}\right) \sum_{i=1}^{[t/\Delta_n] - 2k_n + 1} \left(\widehat{c}(k_n, u_n)_i\right)^2.$$

The asymptotic variance is $8 \int_0^t c_s^4 \, ds$, to be compared with the asymptotic variance of the more usual estimators $\frac{1}{3\Delta_n} \sum_{i=1}^{[t/\Delta_n]} (\Delta_i^n X)^4$, which is $\frac{32}{3} \int_0^t c_s^4 \, ds$.

It turns out that, in this case, the condition (8.47) is not necessary for the CLT to hold. It is indeed enough that $k_n^2 \Delta_n \to 0$ and $k_n \to \infty$. However, this is because the second derivative of g is a constant, and in all other cases one needs (8.47).

Example 8.23 (Quarticity in the Multidimensional Case). *Now we suppose $d \geq 1$ and wish to estimate the variables of (6.6), that is,*

$$V_t^{jk,lm} = \int_0^t \left(c_s^{jl} \, c_s^{km} + c_s^{jm} \, c_s^{kl} \right) ds.$$

We take $g(x) = x^{jl} x^{km} + x^{jm} x^{kl}$, and a simple calculation yields that the "optimal" estimators are

$$\Delta_n \left(1 - \frac{2}{k_n} \right) \sum_{i=1}^{[t/\Delta_n]-2k_n+1} \left(\widehat{c}(k_n, u_n)_i^{jl} \, \widehat{c}(k_n, u_n)_i^{km} + \widehat{c}(k_n, u_n)_i^{jm} \, \widehat{c}(k_n, u_n)_i^{kl} \right).$$

Here again, the condition (8.47) is not necessary, and $k_n^2 \Delta_n \to 0$ and $k_n \to \infty$ are enough.

Finally, let us come back to *optimality*. In the case of the toy model $X_t = \sigma W_t$ with $\sigma > 0$ a constant and $d = 1$, the MLE for estimating $U(g)_T = Tg(c)$ is of course $Tg(\widehat{C}_T^n/T)$, which converges to $U(g)_t$ with rate $1/\sqrt{\Delta_n}$ and a limiting variable which is centered Gaussian with variance $2Tc^2g'(c)^2$ (here g' is the derivative of g). This is exactly the conditional variance of Z_T in this special case, so the estimators $\overline{U}(\Delta_n, g)_T$ are asymptotically efficient for the toy model. They are also efficient for the submodel described in Remark 6.2, again because they achieve the bound provided by the convolution theorem of Clément et al. (2013). Moreover, in view of Theorem 5.24, the restriction $r < 1$ is (almost) necessary for having convergence with rate $1/\sqrt{\Delta_n}$, uniformly in reasonable non-parametric families (the case $r = 1$ also, perhaps, allows for the same rate, but this is not mathematically established for the time being).

8.6   State-Dependent Volatility

The setting of this section is in a sense quite special, with respect to the rest of this book. Besides assuming X to be continuous one-dimensional, we suppose that it is of "Markov type." at least as far as volatility is concerned. That is, instead of (8.1), we suppose that

$$X_t = X_0 + \int_0^t b_s \, ds + \int_0^t \sqrt{f(X_s)} \, dW_s, \qquad (8.52)$$

where f is an unknown function on $\mathbb{R}$ and b_t is a locally bounded optional process. We assume throughout that f is positive and C^r for some $r \geq 1$ (when r is not an integer, this means that f is $[r]$ times differentiable, and its $[r]$th derivative is locally Hölder with index $r - [r]$). Since b_t is locally bounded, we thus have (HC).

The aim is to estimate the function f. This is a classical non-parametric problem, for which there exist basically two methods, exactly as described in Section 8.1: one is global, based for example on wavelets' decompositions, and is well-suited for the so-called adaptive estimation, when the function f has an unknown degree of smoothness. The other one is kernel estimation, which supposes a known minimal degree of smoothness (although adaptive estimation is also feasible); this is much easier to explain and we will concentrate on it. In any case, our aim is a simple and quick review of this question, which in a sense is somehow marginal with respect to the mainstream of this book, and we make no attempt toward completeness.

Whatever method is used, estimating f at some point x on the basis of observations within the time interval $[0, T]$ is of course possible only if X visits this point before time T; the quality of the estimation is related with the "number of visits" of x. Actually, as for any diffusion-type process, if $X_t = x$ at some time t then we also have $X_s = x$ for infinitely (uncountably) many times s in any interval $[t - \varepsilon, t + \varepsilon]$ with $\varepsilon > 0$. So the proper version of the "number of visits" of x during the time interval $[0, t]$ is the *local time* L_t^x at level x and time t. We recall (see for example Protter (2004)) that a version of the local time is the process

$$L_t^x = |X_t - x| - |X_0 - x| - \int_0^t \operatorname{sign}(X_s - x) \, dX_s. \qquad (8.53)$$

With this definition of local time, the density of the occupation measure at time t is $x \mapsto L_t^x / f(x)$, that is, $\int_0^t 1_A(X_s) \, ds = \int_A \frac{L_t^x}{f(x)} \, dx$ for any Borel set A. Thus, we consider estimating $f(x)$ at some point x only if we are inside the following subset of Ω, implicitly depending on the time horizon T:

$$\Omega(x, w) = \{\omega : L_T^x(\omega) \geq w \, T \, f(x)\} \qquad (8.54)$$

where $w > 0$ is arbitrarily chosen: the estimation is done only if the time spent by X around x, in the time interval $[0, T]$, is more than a minimal value "measured" by w. On the other hand, if we want a "functional" estimation of f over a subset A of $\mathbb{R}$, we restrict our attention to the set

$$\Omega(w)_A = \cap_{x \in A} \Omega(x, w). \tag{8.55}$$

If A is included into an open interval (y, z), the set on which the path $t \mapsto X_t$ for $t \in [0, T]$ hits both points y and z is included into the union $\cup_{w>0}\Omega(w)_A$; so, despite the fact that the intersection (8.55) defining $\Omega(w)_A$ is uncountable, this set is typically not empty when $w > 0$ is small enough.

To perform the estimation, we choose a function g on $\mathbb{R}$, the *kernel*, satisfying

- g is continuously differentiable with support in $[-1, 1]$
- $\int_{\mathbb{R}} g(x)\, dx = 1$.

For any $x \in \mathbb{R}$ we consider the processes

$$V(x, \Delta_n)_t = \sqrt{\Delta_n} \sum_{i=1}^{[t/\Delta_n]} g\left(\frac{X_{(i-1)\Delta_n} - x}{\sqrt{\Delta_n}}\right)$$
$$V'(x, \Delta_n)_t = \frac{1}{\sqrt{\Delta_n}} \sum_{i=1}^{[t/\Delta_n]} g\left(\frac{X_{(i-1)\Delta_n} - x}{\sqrt{\Delta_n}}\right) (\Delta_i^n X)^2.$$

For any $w > 0$ we also define the stopping times

$$S_n(x, w) = T \wedge \inf(s : V(x, \Delta_n)_T \geq wT).$$

The estimator of $f(y)$ involves the preceding processes for all x on a grid of mesh $\sqrt{\Delta_n}$, and at a distance of y smaller than $\Delta_n^{1/(1+2r)}$. To this effect, we set $z_j^n = 2j\sqrt{\Delta_n}$ for $j \in \mathbb{Z}$. If $x \in \mathbb{R}$; we set $j_n(x) = \sup(j \in \mathbb{Z} : z_j^n \leq x)$ and $v_n = [\Delta_n^{(2r-1)/(2+4r)}]$. Then we choose numbers (ξ_j^n) such that

$$\sum_{j=-v_n}^{v_n} \xi_j^n = 1 + 2v_n, \qquad \sup_{j,n} |\xi_j^n| < \infty$$
$$i = 1, \cdots, [r] \ \Rightarrow\ \sum_{j=-v_n}^{v_n} \xi_j^n j^i = 0. \tag{8.56}$$

(Such a choice is clearly possible.) The point estimator at x is then

$$\widehat{f(x)}_T^n = \frac{1}{v_n} \sum_{j=-v_n}^{v_n} \xi_j^n \frac{V'(z_{j_n(x)+j}^n, w, \Delta_n)_{T \wedge S_n(x,w)}}{V(z_{j_n(x)+j}^n, w, \Delta_n)_{T \wedge S_n(x,w)}}. \tag{8.57}$$

The key point here is that the processes $V(x, \Delta_n)$ converge in the u.c.p. sense to $\frac{1}{f(x)} L^x$, so for $w > 0$ the following sets are related to the sets in (8.54) and (8.55):

$$\Omega(x, w)_n = \cap_{j=-v_n}^{v_n} \{V(z_{j_n(x)+j}^n, \Delta_n)_T \geq w\},$$
$$\Omega(w)_{A,n}^n = \cap_{x \in A} \Omega(x, w)_n,$$

and those subsets only depend on the observations at stage n. The results, proved in Jacod (2000), are as follows, where $F \bigtriangleup G$ denotes the symmetrical difference between two sets F and G:

Theorem 8.24. *Suppose that f is C^r for some $r \geq 1$ and is positive, and that b_t is locally bounded, in the model (8.52). Let $w > 0$ and A be a compact subset of $\mathbb{R}$ and $t > 0$.*

a) We have $\sup_{x \in A} \mathbb{P}(\Omega(x, w)_n \bigtriangleup \Omega(x, w)) \to 0$ and $\mathbb{P}(\Omega(w)_{A,n} \bigtriangleup \Omega(w)_A) \to 0$.

b) The variables $\frac{1}{\Delta_n^{r/(1+2r)}} (\widehat{f(x)}_T^n - f(x))$, in restriction to the set $\Omega(x, w)$, or equivalently to the sets $\Omega(x, w)_n$, are bounded in probability, uniformly in $n \in \mathbb{N}$ and in $x \in A$.

c) For any $p \geq 1$ the variables $\int_A | \frac{1}{\Delta_n^{r/(1+2r)}} (\widehat{f(x)}_T^n - f(x))|^p dx$, in restriction to the set $\Omega(w)_A$, or equivalently to the sets $\Omega(w)_{A,n}$, are bounded in probability, uniformly in $n \in \mathbb{N}$ and in $x \in A$.

The claims (b) and (c) with the sets $\Omega(x, w)$ and $\Omega(w)_A$ remain true when g is only bounded with support in $[-1, 1]$. Then if we take $g(x) = \frac{1}{2} 1_{[-1,1]}(x)$, the stopping procedure involved in (8.57) simply amounts to stopping the two processes $V(x, \Delta_n)$ and $V'(x, \Delta_n)$ at the time where $2w/\sqrt{\Delta_n}$ observations of X have been found inside the interval $[x - \sqrt{\Delta_n}, x + \sqrt{\Delta_n}]$.

Note that, on the set $\Omega(x, w)_n$, the variable $V(x, w, \Delta_n)_{T \wedge S_n(x,w)}$ is approximately equal to wT, allowing us control of the denominator in (8.57); this is why one stops the processes. Although necessary for the proof, this trick is damageable because it leads us to discard some observations, which has no effect on the convergence rate, but using all available data should give better estimators.

The choice of w is rather arbitrary: the bigger w, the smaller the error, but on the other hand if w increases, the "useful" set $\Omega(x, w)$ on which estimation is possible shrinks. The choice of the ξ_j^n in (8.56) is also relatively arbitrary. Here is an example of possible choice: if $1 \leq r < 2$, take $\xi_j^n = 1$ for all j. If $r \geq 2$, let $q = [r/2]$ and $\delta_n = [(v_n - 1)/2(q + 1)]$; then take $\xi_0^n = 1$ and $\xi_j^n = \alpha_m^n$ if $m = 0, \ldots, q$ and $m\delta_n < |j| \leq (m+1)\delta_n$ and $\xi_j^n = 0$ if $|j| > (q + 1)\delta_n$, where the α_m^n for $m = 0, \ldots, q$ are the unique solutions of the system of $q + 1$ linear equations:

$$\sum_{m=0}^{q} \alpha_m^n = \frac{v_n - 1}{2\delta_n}, \qquad \sum_{m=0}^{q} \alpha_m^n \sum_{j=m\delta_n+1}^{(m+1)\delta_n} j^{2i} = 0, \quad i = 1, \ldots, q.$$

Remark 8.25. *The rate, for the point estimation and the functional estimation (respectively (b) and (c) of the theorem), is the usual nonparametric rate obtained in density estimation, for example. And it can be shown that it is the optimal (minimax) rate.*

On the other hand, the major drawback of what precedes is the lack of a Central Limit Theorem for the point estimators.

Remark 8.26. *There exist estimators for f which enjoy a Central Limit Theorem, at any point x (again, conditional on the fact that X visits the state x before time t), see Florens-Zmirou (1993). However, for this one needs $r \geq 2$ (a very slight restriction), and more importantly the rate is $1/\Delta_n^{1/3}$, not depending on r and always slower than $1/\Delta_n^{r/(2+r)}$.*

8.7 Spot Volatility and Microstructure Noise

All methods described so far in this chapter suppose that the underlying process is observed without noise. However, for spot volatility one needs data recorded at much higher frequency than for integrated volatility, in order to obtain reasonably accurate estimators. In practice, this means that we have to cope with the fact that data are noisy even more than for estimating integrated volatility.

We thus devote this last section to this problem. Quite a few authors have examined the question, but the given answers are often with a "qualitative" flavor, without clear-cut conditions, or only stating the consistency of the estimators, without attempts to reach a convergence rate.

As a consequence, we will be rather brief and, after a few comments on the Fourier-based method, will mainly focus on the method explained in Section 8.1. We totally skip the extension of Sections 8.3–8.6 to the noisy case. We suppose that X is d-dimensional and continuous, and more precisely satisfies (KC).

In principle, the Fourier-based method is quite appropriate for automatically eliminating the microstructure noise, at least when the noise is additive, that is, (WN) holds. The reason is as follows: the Fourier coefficients (8.20) of the observed noisy process are the sum of the Fourier coefficients of the (unobserved) process X, plus those of the (again unobserved) noise itself, plus a "cross term" (because the coefficients are quadratic functions of the observations) which turns out to be negligible in front of the others. Since the noise is assumed to be white, its Fourier coefficients are "small" at low frequency (that is, for small values of the coefficient index k). Since in (8.21) one restricts the sum to the coefficients with index smaller than N_n, one thus "automatically" eliminates the noise, as long as N_n is not too large.

Of course, N_n should go to infinity, so there is an optimal choice of N_n balancing the approximation error (the discrepancy between the finite sum and its limit for the non-noisy case), and the error due to the presence of noise.

In any case, upon appropriately choosing N_n, it can be shown that the estimators (8.21) are robust against noise: if in (8.20) one plugs the observed noisy returns instead of $\Delta_i^n X$, then $\widehat{c}^{\text{Fourier}}(T, n, N_n)_t^{lm}$ still converges to c_t, and even satisfies (8.22). Unfortunately, so far one does not know exactly the rate of convergence (at each t, or uniform over $t \in [0, T]$), in connection with the choice of N_n.

Let us now turn to the local estimators of c_t. In principle, one can de-noise the data by using any of the methods described in the previous chapter. We focus on the pre-averaging method, but probably the quasi-likelihood method works well in this case also, because "locally" the processes c_t and γ_t (conditional variance of the noise) are approximately constant, at least in many instances. This allows us to use the relatively weak Assumption (GN), for which we refer to page 221. For simplicity we only consider the (most useful) case of non-shrinking noise, that is, $\eta = 0$. At stage n the observations are

$$Y_i^n = X_{i\Delta_n} + \chi_{i\Delta_n},$$

and we use the notation $\Delta_i^n Y^l = Y_i^n - Y_{i-1}^{n,l}$ as before, with $Y_i^{n,l}$ the lth component of Y_i^n.

For pre-averaging we choose a function g satisfying (7.43), so it is continuous, null outside $(0, 1)$, piecewise C^1 with a piecewise Lipschitz derivative g'. We also use a sequence k_n of integers satisfying (7.42) with $\eta = 0$ and $\eta' = \frac{1}{2}$ (which gives the best rate), that is, $k_n = 1/\theta\sqrt{\Delta_n}+o(1/\Delta_n^{1/4})$, where $\theta > 0$ is fixed. Then we set

$$\overline{Y}_i^{n,l} = \sum_{j=1}^{k_n-1} g\left(\tfrac{j}{k_n}\right) \Delta_{i+j-1}^n Y^l,$$
$$\widehat{Y}_i^{n,lm} = \sum_{j=1}^{k_n} \left(g\left(\tfrac{j}{k_n}\right) - g\left(\tfrac{j-1}{k_n}\right)\right)^2 \Delta_{i+j-1}^n Y^l \Delta_{i+j-1}^n Y^m.$$

With $\phi_{k_n}(g) = \sum_{i=1}^{k_n} |g(i/k_n)|^2$, we recall the pre-averaged estimator (7.76) of integrated volatility:

$$\widehat{C}^{\text{Preav}}(\Delta_n, k_n, g)_t^{lm} = \frac{1}{\phi_{k_n}(g)} \frac{t}{t-k_n}$$
$$\times \sum_{i=1}^{[t/\Delta_n]-k_n+1} \left(\overline{Y}_i^{n,l} \overline{Y}_i^{n,m} - \tfrac{1}{2}\widehat{Y}_i^{n,lm}\right). \tag{8.58}$$

Since X is continuous, those consistently estimate C_t^{lm} and enjoy a CLT with rate $1/\Delta_n^{1/4}$.

For estimating c_t we utilize the heuristic approach of Subsection 8.1.2, based on (8.2) with $\widehat{C}_t^n = \widehat{C}^{\mathrm{Preav}}(\Delta_n, k_n, g)_t$, thus using $\frac{1}{s_n}(\widehat{C}_{t+s_n}^n - \widehat{C}_t^n)$. As before, one must choose $s_n \to 0$ appropriately. For this, we observe that the normalized difference above is actually an estimator of $\frac{1}{s_n}(C_{t+s_n} - C_t)$, and we thus have a target error (the difference between this and c_t) of order $\sqrt{s_n}$. On the other hand Theorem 7.32 with $\eta' = \frac{1}{2}$ implies that the statistical error $\frac{1}{s_n}((\widehat{C}_{t+s_n}^n - \widehat{C}_t^n) - (C_{t+s_n} - C_t))$ has approximately the same law as $\frac{\Delta_n^{1/4}}{s_n}(\mathcal{U}_{t+s_n}^{\mathrm{noise}} - \mathcal{U}_t^{\mathrm{noise}})$, whose order of magnitude is $\Delta_n^{1/4}/\sqrt{s_n}$. Equalling the rates of the two kinds of errors leads us to take $s_n \asymp \Delta_n^{1/4}$, or equivalently $s_n = h_n\Delta_n$ with a sequence h_n of integers behaving as $1/\Delta_n^{3/4}$ and providing us with the overall rate $1/\Delta_n^{1/8}$. We can also take a different behavior for h_n or s_n, leading to sub-optimal rates, although in any case we must impose $h_n/k_n \to \infty$ and $h_n\Delta_n \to 0$.

Before giving the estimators we state two further remarks.

Remark 8.27. *In (8.58) the factor $\frac{t}{t-k_n}$ accounts for the "wrong" number of summands, but for the spot volatility, and exactly as (7.62), this problem does not occur, hence this factor is omitted.*

Remark 8.28. *Second, the term $\frac{1}{2}\widehat{Y}_i^n$ is a de-biasing term which, when $[t/\Delta_n] < i \le [(t + s_n)/\Delta_n]$ and s_n is small, is approximately equal to $\frac{a}{k_n}\gamma_t$ for some constant a depending on g (recall that γ_t is the conditional variance of the noise at time t and is càdlàg). Since $\phi_{k_n}(g) \asymp k_n$, the contribution of these de-biasing terms to the ratio $\frac{1}{s_n}(\widehat{C}_{t+s_n}^n - \widehat{C}_t^n)$ is of order $s_n/k_n^2\Delta_n \asymp s_n$, in all cases negligible in front of the expected rate of convergence. Therefore, one can propose the following estimators, where by a convention analogous to (8.9) we set $\overline{Y}_i^n = 0$ when $i \le 0$:*

$$\widehat{c}^{\mathrm{Preav}}(k_n, h_n)_i^{lm} = \frac{1}{h_n\Delta_n\,\phi_{k_n}(g)} \sum_{j=i}^{i+h_n-1} \overline{Y}_{i+j+k_n}^{n,l}\, \overline{Y}_{i+j+k_n}^{n,m} \tag{8.59}$$

and, if $(i-1)\Delta_n < t \le i\Delta_n$,

$$\widehat{c}^{\mathrm{Preav}}(t; k_n, h_n) = \widehat{c}^{\mathrm{Preav}}(k_n, h_n)_{i+1}$$
$$\widehat{c}^{\mathrm{Preav}}(t-; k_n, h_n) = \widehat{c}^{\mathrm{Preav}}(k_n, h_n)_{i-(h_n+1)k_n}.$$

Formula (8.59) is the same as in (7.62), up to the de-biasing term, and with different upper and lower limits in the sum (hence a different normalization as well); however, it would not hurt to keep the de-biasing term.

At this point, one can fairly easily straighten out the previous heuristic argument and obtain a CLT analogous to Theorem 8.6, hence *de facto* the consistency. We need to modify the characterization of the variables Z_t to incorporate the variance given by (7.77), whereas Z_t' is unchanged. Namely, with the notation (7.78), we simply replace the first property (8.14) by

$$\widetilde{\mathbb{E}}(Z_t^{ij} Z_t^{kl} \mid \mathcal{F}) = \frac{1}{\theta} R^{ij,kl}(g; c_t, \theta^2 \gamma_t).$$

Then, under (KC) and (GN) one can show that, similar to (8.15) but unfortunately with much slower rates, as necessarily $h_n \Delta_n \to 0$ and $h_n \sqrt{\Delta_n} \to \infty$, and assuming $h_n \Delta_n^{3/4} \to \beta \in [0, \infty]$:

$$\beta = 0 \qquad \Rightarrow \quad \left(h_n^{1/2} \Delta_n^{1/4}(\widehat{c}^{\,\mathrm{Preav}}(t; k_n, h_n) - c_t)\right)_{t \geq 0} \xrightarrow{\mathcal{L}_f - s} (Z_t)_{t \geq 0}$$

$$\beta \in (0, \infty) \Rightarrow \left(h_n^{1/2} \Delta_n^{1/4}(\widehat{c}^{\,\mathrm{Preav}}(t; k_n, h_n) - c_t)\right)_{t \geq 0} \xrightarrow{\mathcal{L}_f - s} (Z_t + \beta Z_t')_{t \geq 0}$$

$$\beta = \infty \qquad \Rightarrow \quad \left(\frac{1}{\sqrt{h_n \Delta_n}}(\widehat{c}^{\,\mathrm{Preav}}(t; k_n, h_n) - c_t)\right)_{t \geq 0} \xrightarrow{\mathcal{L}_f - s} (Z_t')_{t \geq 0}.$$

Once more, the fastest rate corresponds to the (basically unfeasible) second case above, and is $1/\Delta_n^{1/8}$, not very fast indeed. Similar properties hold for the left-hand estimators $\widehat{c}^{\,\mathrm{Preav}}(t-; k_n, h_n)$, and also for spot estimators evaluated at a stopping time.

A noticeable characteristic of this result is that the choices of the two sequences k_n and h_n are independent: we take $k_n \sim 1/\theta \sqrt{\Delta_n}$ and θ appears in the characterization of Z. We take h_n independently, such as $h_n \sim \beta/\Delta_n^{3/4}$, or close to this, depending on whether one requires a feasible estimator or not.

8.8 References

Estimation of the spot volatility started in a Markov setting (continuous diffusion processes), in which case it amounts to estimating the diffusion coefficient, and corresponds to state-dependent volatility. In this setting, parametric estimation is a classic topic, non-parametric estimation is more recent and started (in the case of discrete observations on a finite time interval) with Genon-Catalot et al. (1992), Hoffmann (1999a,b) for wavelets methods, and Florens-Zmirou (1993), who uses kernel estimators. In Section 8.6 here, we follow Jacod (2000), which provides rate improvements on the previously quoted paper, whereas Jiang and Knight (1997) contains comparable results, based on the same method. In this setting, Renò (2008) uses a Fourier-based method.

For general continuous Itô semimartingales without noise, the first paper about estimating spot volatility seems to be Foster and Nelson (1996), which basically uses the method explained in Section 8.1, under the name of rolling volatility estimators; see also Andreou and Ghysels (2002) and Kristensen (2010). The treatment here follows Section 13.3 of Jacod and Protter (2011), other papers being for example Fan and Wang (2008), which contains the global statement (8.19), Ogawa and Hoang-Long (2010), Alvarez et al. (2012), and Bandi and Renò (2011). For a thorough study with general kernel-type estimators, combining local and global estimation, one can consult Mancini et al. (2012). The main aim of these papers is estimating spot volatility, but in many other places such an estimation (without an associated rate of convergence) is performed as a tool for solving other problems: see for example Mykland and Zhang (2008), Lee and Mykland (2008), Aït-Sahalia and Jacod (2009b) and Bos et al. (2012).

The Fourier-based method for spot volatility, without or with noise, is discussed in Malliavin and Mancino (2009) and Mancino and Sanfelici (2008, 2011). Local estimators in the presence of noise are studied for example in Kalnina and Linton (2008), Ogawa and Sanfelici (2011) and Zu and Boswijk (2014). Wavelets methods have been used in Hoffmann et al. (2012).

Apart from the early paper by Gloter (2000), where in a semi-parametric setting the parameter in the volatility of volatility is estimated, estimation of the quadratic variation and covariation $[c, c]$ and $[X, c]$ and related questions are rather recent, and one can quote Vetter (2011), Wang and Mykland (2012) (who also consider the case of noisy data), Aït-Sahalia et al. (2013), Vetter (2012) for a slightly different but related problem, and Bandi and Renò (2012). Dufour et al. (2012) separate the leverage and the volatility feedback effects.

A functional method for estimating trajectories of volatility is proposed by Müller et al. (2011). Dahlhaus and Neddermeyer (2013) employ a particle filter.

For the efficient estimation of integrals of functions of the volatility we follow Jacod and Rosenbaum (2013), and the convolution theorem which serves to establish efficiency is in Clément et al. (2013). Let us also mention that Mykland and Zhang (2009) have proposed using the same method, with $k_n = k$ a constant; for the quarticity or more generally for estimating $C(p)_t$, they obtain a CLT with rate $1/\sqrt{\Delta_n}$ and an asymptotic variance which approaches the optimal when k is large.

Chapter 9

Volatility and Irregularly Spaced Observations

Up to now, we only considered regularly spaced observation times. This is pertinent in many cases, like in physical or biological sciences where measurement devices are set to record data every minute, or second, or millisecond. In finance, this is also pertinent for indices, which are computed often, but typically at regular times.

For asset prices, things are different. For example transaction prices are recorded at actual transaction times, these times being also recorded (in principle, although there might be some delays or approximations, see Chapter 2). So, at least theoretically, we observe the values of X at successive times S_i, as well as the times S_i themselves. Here, $S_i < S_{i+1}$, and $S_i \to \infty$ as $i \to \infty$ because there are only finitely many transactions occurring before any finite time.

There are mainly two ways of dealing with this question. The first is to pretend that the observations occur at regular times $i\Delta_n$, with $X_{i\Delta_n}$ being set equal to X_{S_j} for the largest S_j smaller than or equal to $i\Delta_n$. An error is involved here, but if the asset is very liquid and Δ_n moderately small, the difference $i\Delta_n - S_j$ is typically small in front of Δ_n, hence the error is small, hopefully negligible. This method is quite common in practice: it is easy to implement and has the additional advantage of weakening the impact of microstructure noise by downsampling.

However, this method has a fundamental drawback: it uses only a small part of the data (for instance, if an average of 10 transactions occur in intervals of length Δ_n, we only use one tenth of the data), and thus incurs a large loss of information. It is thus fundamental to develop statistical tools allowing the use of irregularly spaced observations.

Besides the purely mathematical difficulties, such an approach raises a few practical or methodological problems. First, it requires users to know exactly the times S_i, which in practice is not always possible. Second, it requires assumptions on the structure of the sequence S_i; for example, are the times irregularly spaced but non-random, or are they themselves random? In the latter case, how are they related to the underlying X? Moreover, in the multivariate setting, the observation times of the various components are usually different, and one needs to model the global behavior of the observation times for all components at once.

As a matter of fact, many authors evoked these questions, often suggesting empirical solutions, but so far relatively few actually made significant mathematical contributions to the subject. It is nevertheless a very active and growing (and important) field, quite far from being in a mature stage. Therefore, our ambition in this chapter is rather modest, and we quickly review some basic results only. These results concern first the estimation of the integrated volatility for a one-dimensional process, and second the estimation of the covariation process for two prices observed at non-synchronous times. The only situation which we consider is the case where the underlying process is continuous. Moreover, we assume that there is no observation noise. A fully realistic approach would necessitate a mix between the content of the previous chapter and of this one.

In the whole chapter, except for Subsection 9.1.3, the – possibly d-dimensional – underlying process X satisfies Assumption (HC): it is a continuous Itô semimartingale of the form

$$X_t = X_0 + \int_0^t b_s ds + \int_0^t \sigma_s dW_s, \qquad (9.1)$$

defined on a filtered space $(\Omega, \mathcal{F}, (\mathcal{F}_t)_{t\geq 0}, \mathbb{P})$ which supports the q-dimensional Brownian motion W, and b_t is a locally bounded progressively measurable process, and σ_t an adapted càdlàg process. As usual, $c_t = \sigma_t\sigma_t^*$, and we are (mostly) interested in the process $C_t = \int_0^t c_s\, ds$.

Finally, let us mention that the results of this chapter are stated without formal proofs, and we refer to the relevant papers for these proofs.

9.1 Irregular Observation Times: The One-Dimensional Case

In the real world, observation times are given once and for all. However, exactly as in the previous chapters, we are after asymptotic results, and thus envision the (theoretical) possibility that the frequency of observations does increase to infinity. Hence at each stage n we have strictly increasing observation times $(S(n, i) : i \geq 0)$, and without restriction we may assume $S(n, 0) = 0$. We associate the notation

$$
\begin{aligned}
\Delta(n, i) &= S(n, i) - S(n, i - 1), \\
N_t^n &= \sup(i : S(n, i) \leq t), \\
\pi_t^n &= \sup_{i=1, \cdots, N_t^n + 1} \Delta(n, i).
\end{aligned}
\tag{9.2}
$$

That is, π_t^n is the "mesh" up to time t, by convention $\sup(\emptyset) = 0$, and N_t^n is the number of observation times within $(0, t]$. We will assume throughout that, with T the time horizon,

$$
\lim_{i \to \infty} S(n, i) = \infty \text{ for all } n, \qquad \pi_T^n \xrightarrow{\mathbb{P}} 0 \text{ as } n \to \infty. \tag{9.3}
$$

These properties ensure that at each stage n there are finitely many observations, and that the mesh goes to 0 as $n \to \infty$, thus permitting us to obtain asymptotic results.

The underlying process X satisfies (HC), without further mention. By analogy with our general notation $\Delta_i^n Y$ of (6.2), for any process Y the returns are still written as

$$
\Delta_i^n Y = Y_{S(n,i)} - Y_{S(n,i-1)}.
$$

Estimating the integrated volatility C_t, in the one-dimensional case, say, is still apparently very simple for this observation scheme. Indeed, by Theorem 1.14 we know that, under (9.3) and as soon as all $S(n, i)$ are stopping times, the realized volatility $\sum_{i=1}^{N_t^n} (\Delta_i^n X)^2$ converges in the u.c.p. sense to C_t. The stopping time property of $S(n, i)$ is totally innocuous to assume, from a practical viewpoint, since an observation or trade cannot (in principle) take place at some time which anticipates the future.

Where things deteriorate and additional assumptions are needed is when we want to provide a rate of convergence and exhibit a Central Limit Theorem. We devote the next subsection to describing and commenting about these additional assumptions.

9.1.1   About Irregular Sampling Schemes

To begin with, we need to decide whether we consider the sampling times $S(n,i)$ as being random or not, although in all cases they should be observable. This very first question has no obvious answer, but most authors consider random sampling schemes, which indeed makes a lot of sense: for example one may suppose that the transaction times are distributed according to a Poisson process, with some intensity increasing to ∞ as $n \to \infty$; or one may suppose that an observation occurs as soon as the price crosses some barriers. So below we generally assume that the $S(n,i)$'s are random, which of course includes as a particular case deterministic sampling.

Next, we have to decide whether we only allow "endogenous" sampling (that is, $S(n,i)$ only depends on the process X and possible covariates, such as the volatility itself) or we allow for extra randomness in the sampling scheme; sampling at Poisson points independent of X is an example of the second situation, whereas sampling at hitting times is an example of the first situation. And of course there are "mixed" cases where sampling occurs at times $S(n,i)$ depending on X and involving also extra randomness, if for example one samples according to a Poisson process modulated by the underlying X.

There are various ways of mathematically modeling these endogenous and exogenous components, exactly as for microstructure noise. Below, for simplicity and as we did in Chapter 7, we suppose that the $S(n,i)$'s are defined on the original space Ω, but measurable with respect to a σ-field which may be bigger than $\mathcal{F}$. The structural assumptions are then conveniently expressed as follows:

Assumption (A). *The probability measure $\mathbb{P}$ is defined on a σ-field $\mathcal{F}'$ bigger than or equal to $\mathcal{F}$ and we have a filtration $(\mathcal{F}'_t)$ which contains $(\mathcal{F}_t)$ and with respect to which W is still a Brownian motion, and each $S(n,i)$ is an $(\mathcal{F}'_t)$-stopping time which, conditionally on $\mathcal{F}'_{S(n,i-1)}$, is independent of the σ-field $\mathcal{F}$, and finally (9.3) holds.*

This is satisfied, under (9.3), when the $S(n,i)$'s are non-random (*deterministic schemes*), or when the $S(n,i)$'s are independent of the $\mathcal{F}$ (*independent schemes*). It is satisfied in many other cases as well. However it rules out some *a priori* interesting situations: when (A) holds and the stopping time $S(n,i)$ is measurable with respect to $\mathcal{F}$, then it is "strongly predictable" in the sense that it is $\mathcal{F}'_{S(n,i-1)}$-measurable. This is quite restrictive, excluding for example the case where the $S(n,i)$'s are the successive hitting times of a spatial grid by X, but in a financial context it might be a reasonable assumption: an agent decides to buy or sell at time $S(n, i)$ on the basis of the information available before, that is, up to the previous transaction time $S(n, i - 1)$.

(A) is a purely structural assumption, which needs to be complemented by additional requirements. One of them is that not only does the "overall" mesh π_T^n go to 0, but it does so at a rate which is non-random, and that the partial meshes π_t^n converge to 0 at the same rate, for all $t \in (0, T]$. Another one is that, at each stage n, the times $S(n, i)$ are sufficiently evenly distributed in time. To express these requirements, we need a preliminary notation, where $q \geq 0$ is arbitrary:

$$D(q)_t^n = \sum_{i=1}^{N_t^n} \Delta(n, i)^q.$$

Note that $D(0)_t^n = N_t^n$, and $D(1)_t^n = S(n, N_t^n)$, and $D(2)_t^n$ is a kind of "quadratic variation" of the sampling intervals. We will need the following assumption for one or several values of q, depending on the problem at hand:

Assumption (D-q). *We have (A), and there is a (necessarily nonnegative) process $a(q)$ which is progressively measurable with respect to the filtration $(\mathcal{F}_t)_{t \geq 0}$, and a sequence δ_n of positive numbers, going to 0, such that for all t we have*

$$\delta_n^{1-q} D(q)_t^n \overset{\mathbb{P}}{\longrightarrow} \int_0^t a(q)_s \, ds. \qquad (9.4)$$

The normalization δ_n^{1-q} is motivated by the regular schemes $S(n, i) = i\Delta_n$, for which $D(q)_t^n = \Delta_n^q [t/\Delta_n]$, and which thus satisfies (D-q) for all $q \geq 0$ with $\delta_n = \Delta_n$ and $a(q)_t = 1$. Note also that, since $t - \pi_t^n \leq D(1)_t^n \leq t$, (9.3) implies (D-1) with $a(1)_t = t$, and irrespective of the sequence δ_n.

Note that (D-q) for some sequence δ_n implies (D-q) for any other sequence δ_n' satisfying $\delta_n'/\delta_n \to \alpha \in [0, \infty)$, and the new limit in (9.4) and when $q > 1$ is then $\alpha^{q-1} a(q)$, and in particular vanishes when $\delta_n'/\delta_n \to 0$; the forthcoming theorems which explicitly involve δ_n are true but "empty" when the limit in (9.4) vanishes identically.

The processes $D(q)^n$ are of course connected which each other. For instance, if $0 \leq q < p < q'$, Hölder's inequality implies that, for any $s \leq t$,

$$D(p)_t^n - D(p)_s^n \leq \left(D(q)_t^n - D(q)_s^n\right)^{\frac{q'-p}{q'-q}} \left(D(q')_t^n - D(q')_s^n\right)^{\frac{p-q}{q'-q}}. \qquad (9.5)$$

Thus, if (D-q) holds for some $q \neq 1$ and a sequence δ_n, then if $1 < p < q$ or $q < p < 1$, and from any subsequence, one may extract a further subsequence which satisfies (D-p) with the same δ_n, and we have versions of $a(q)$ and $a(p)$ satisfying $a(p)_t \leq a(q)_t^{(p-1)/(q-1)}$.

For a deterministic scheme, (D-q) may or may not be satisfied, but there is no simple criterion ensuring that it holds when $q \neq 1$. No general criterion for random schemes exists either, but it is possible to describe a reasonably large class of random schemes for which this assumption holds. These schemes are called *mixed renewal schemes* and are constructed as follows: we consider a double sequence $(\varepsilon(n,i) : i, n \geq 1)$ of i.i.d. positive variables on $(\Omega, \mathcal{F}', \mathbb{P})$, independent of $\mathcal{F}$, with moments

$$m'_q = \mathbb{E}(\varepsilon(n,i)^q).$$

We may have $m'_q = \infty$ for $q > 1$, but we assume $m'_1 < \infty$. We also have a sequence v^n of positive $(\mathcal{F}_t)$-progressively measurable processes such that both v^n and $1/v^n$ are locally bounded, and a sequence δ_n of positive numbers, going to 0. The sampling times $S(n,i)$ are defined by induction on i as follows:

$$S(n,0) = 0, \qquad S(n, i+1) = S(n,i) + \delta_n \, v^n_{S(n,i)} \, \varepsilon(n, i+1). \qquad (9.6)$$

The following lemma, showing some connections between the various hypotheses above, is simple to prove:

Lemma 9.1. *Any mixed renewal scheme satisfies (A). If further the processes v^n in (9.6) converge in the u.c.p. sense to a càdlàg process v such that both v and v_- do not vanish, and if $m'_q < \infty$ for some $q \geq 1$ (this is always true for $q = 1$), then (D-p) holds for all $p \in (0, q]$ with $a(p)_t = \frac{m'_p}{m'^p_1} (v_t)^{p-1}$ and the same sequence δ_n as in (9.6).*

Example 9.2. *When the $\varepsilon(n,i)$ above are exponential with parameter 1 and $v^n \equiv 1$, the times $(S(n,i) : i \geq 1)$ form a Poisson process with parameter $1/\delta_n$, independent of $\mathcal{F}$, and we have independent Poisson sampling. When v^n is not constant, it becomes a kind of "modulated Poisson scheme." However, conditionally on $\mathcal{F}$, the $(S(n,i) : i \geq 1)$ are no longer (non-homogeneous) Poisson.*

A genuine modulated Poisson scheme is rather a double sequence $S(n,i)$ such that, for each n and conditionally on $\mathcal{F}$, the points times $(S(n,i) : i \geq 1)$ form a non-homogeneous Poisson process with intensity function $t \mapsto \delta_n v^n_t$. Lemma 9.1 holds for such schemes, for all $q \geq 0$ under the same assumptions on v^n.

Both notions of a modulated Poisson scheme make sense, from a practical viewpoint. And of course if the v^n's in some sense smooth in time, both notions are very close one to the other.

Finally, let us mention that, among all irregular schemes, there is the special class of all schemes obtained by time-changing a regular scheme. However, we postpone this topic until we have studied some estimation problems for the general schemes introduced above.

9.1.2 Estimation of the Integrated Volatility and Other Integrated Volatility Powers

In the remainder of this section, we assume that X is one-dimensional and satisfies (HC), without further mention. We extend the family of realized power variations $B(p, \Delta_n)_t$ by setting, for arbitrary nonnegative reals p, q,

$$B^n(p,q)_t = \sum_{i=1}^{N_t^n} \Delta(n,i)^{q+1-p/2} |\Delta_i^n X|^p. \tag{9.7}$$

In the regular sampling case we have $B^n(p,q) = \Delta_n^{q+1-p/2} B(p, \Delta_n)$, so when q varies these processes all convey the same information, but this is no longer the case in the irregular sampling case.

These modified power variations enjoy a law of large numbers which extends (6.9): namely, if $p > 0$ and $q \geq 0$ and if Assumptions (A) and (D-$(q+1)$) hold, we have

$$\frac{1}{\delta_n^q} B^n(p,q) \overset{\text{u.c.p.}}{\Longrightarrow} m_p\, C(p,q), \tag{9.8}$$

where

$$C(p,q)_t = \int_0^t c_s^{p/2}\, a(q+1)_s\, ds.$$

In particular, since (D-1) with $a(1)_t = 1$ is always true (recall that (9.3) is assumed) and $C(p,0) = C(p)$, where as previously

$$C(p)_t = \int_0^t c_s^{p/2}\, ds,$$

we have under (A)

$$B^n(p,0) \overset{\text{u.c.p.}}{\Longrightarrow} m_p\, C(p). \tag{9.9}$$

(When $p = 2$, and because $B^n(2,0)$ is the approximate quadratic variation built upon the discretization scheme $S(n,i) : i \geq 0$), the full force of

(A) is not necessary for this; we need only (9.3) and the stopping times property of all $S(n,i)$.)

A Central Limit Theorem associated with the convergence (9.9) goes as follows (recall that the σ-field $\mathcal{F}'$ on which $\mathbb{P}$ is defined may be strictly bigger than $\mathcal{F}$; however, the $\mathcal{F}$-stable convergence was introduced on page 95). The most interesting case is the estimation of the integrated volatility $C = C(2)$, but the results are just as easy to state for any $C(p)$ with $p \geq 2$:

Theorem 9.3. *Let $p \geq 2$, and assume (HC) when $p = 2$ and (KC) when $p > 2$. Assume (D-2) for the sampling scheme. Then the processes $\frac{1}{\sqrt{\delta_n}}\left(B^n(p,0)-m_p\,C(p)\right)$ converge $\mathcal{F}$-stably in law to a process $\mathcal{V}(p)$ which is defined on a very good extension of $(\Omega, \mathcal{F}', (\mathcal{F}'_t), \mathbb{P})$ and, conditionally on $\mathcal{F}$, is a continuous centered Gaussian martingale with variance*

$$\mathbb{E}(\mathcal{V}(p)_t^2 \mid \mathcal{F}) = (m_{2p} - m_p)\,C(2p,1)_t.$$

Moreover, for any $T > 0$ we have

$$\mathcal{L}\left(\frac{\sqrt{m_{2p}}\,(B^n(p,0)_T - m_p\,C(p)_T)}{\sqrt{(m_{2p}-m_p)\,B^n(2p,1)_T}}\bigg|A\right) \to \mathcal{N}(0,1) \tag{9.10}$$
for all $A \in F$ with $P(A) > 0$ and $A \subset \{C_T > 0\}$.

Finally, when the $S(n,i)$'s are strongly predictable in the sense that each $S(n,i)$ is $\mathcal{F}'_{S(n,i-1)}$-measurable, the stable convergence above holds relative to the whole σ-field $\mathcal{F}'$.

Remark 9.4. *For estimating the integrated volatility C_T we use $B^n(2,0)_T$, and of course this is the same as the realized volatility:*

$$B^n(2,0)_T = \sum_{i=1}^{N^n_T}(\Delta^n_i X)^2.$$

When we want to estimate the quarticity, or other power functionals $C(p)_T$, then $B^n(p,0)$ is no longer the same as the normalized approximate p-power variation $\delta_n^{1-p/2}\sum_{i=1}^{N^n_T}|\Delta^n_i X|^p$.

Our reason for introducing the processes $B^n(p,q)$ for $q \geq 0$, instead of $B^n(p,0)$ only, is the standardization in (9.10). This property, to be interpreted as (6.11), allows us to derive confidence bounds in the usual way. Note that A in (9.10) should belong to $\mathcal{F}^{X,W,b,\sigma}$ and not only to $\mathcal{F}$, and due to (D-2) the variable $C(2p,1)_T$ is $\mathcal{F}$-measurable.

If one wants the rate $1/\sqrt{\delta_n}$ for the convergence of $B^n(p,1)$ toward $m_p\,C(p,1)$, one needs stronger assumptions than (D-2): for example (D-3), plus a rate faster than $1/\sqrt{\delta_n}$ in the convergence (9.4), or the convergence $v^n \to v$ when the sampling is a mixed renewal scheme. More generally, it is possible to obtain a CLT for $B^n(p,q)$, for all reals $p \geq 2$ and $q \geq 0$; we do not further elaborate on this here.

Remark 9.5. *This theorem has a multidimensional extension, in the sense that we can consider a finite family $(p_j)_{1 \leq j \leq q}$ of reals with $p_j \geq 2$. We then have the $\mathcal{F}$-stable convergence in law of the q-dimensional processes with components $\frac{1}{\sqrt{\delta_n}} (B^n(p_j, 0) - m_{p_j} C(p_j))$. Another easy extension consists of taking a smooth enough test function f on $\mathbb{R}$ and then considering the "normalized" functionals*

$$\sum_{i=1}^{N_t^n} \Delta(n,i) \, f(\Delta_i^n X / \sqrt{\Delta(n,i)}). \tag{9.11}$$

Remark 9.6. *The Law of Large Numbers and the associated CLT for functionals of the form (9.11) also hold when the underlying process X is d-dimensional (under appropriate assumptions on f and on the sampling scheme). This extension is nearly obvious, but it should be emphasized that dealing with functionals like (9.11) requires that all components of X are observed at the same times $S(n,i)$.*

An interesting – and crucial – feature of the standardized version (9.10) is that the properties of the observation scheme are not showing explicitly in the result itself: the process $a(2)$ and even the rates δ_n are absent from the ratio

$$\frac{B^n(p,0)_T - m_p C(p)_T}{\sqrt{(m_{2p} - m_p)\, B^n(2p,1)_T}},$$

which only features variables which are observed by the statistician, plus of course the quantity $C(p)_T$ to be estimated. This is fortunate, since for example the rate δ_n is an abstract quantity, *a priori* unknown. This is also dangerous because one might be tempted to use the result without checking that the assumptions on the sampling scheme are satisfied (which means, in this context, "reasonable" on the basis of the known observation times). In any case, and although the rate δ_n does not explicitly show up, it still governs the "true" speed of convergence.

Once more, δ_n is unknown, but N_t^n is known (that is, observed). Then as soon as (D-0) also holds, we have $\delta_n N_t^n \xrightarrow{\mathbb{P}} \int_0^t a(0)_s ds$, and so the actual rate of convergence for the estimators is $1/\sqrt{N_t^n}$, as it should be.

We end the subsection with a few comments:

About the proofs: The proof of Theorem 9.3 is rather complicated, at least when the sampling is random, and omitted (as are indeed all formal proofs for this chapter). In contrast, proving (9.8) is rather simple and somewhat enlightening, as to the role of Assumption (D-$(q+1)$): there are (tedious, and usual for this sort of problem) estimates which reduce the problem to proving the convergence of

$$\frac{1}{\delta_n^q} \sum_{i=1}^{N_t^n} \Delta(n,i)^{q+1-p/2} \, c_{S(n,i-1)}^{p/2} |\Delta_i^n W|^p,$$

which is equivalent to the convergence of

$$\frac{1}{\delta_n^q} \sum_{i=1}^{N_t^n} \Delta(n,i)^{q+1} \, c_{S(n,i-1)}^{p/2} m_p$$

(because of (ii) in Assumption (A): this equivalence is wrong in general, if the structural assumption (A) fails). At this stage, one observes that (D-$(q+1)$) is in fact equivalent to the convergence

$$\frac{1}{\delta_n^q} \sum_{i=1}^{N_t^n} \Delta(n,i)^{q+1} \, H_{S(n,i-1)} \;\xrightarrow{\mathbb{P}}\; \int_0^t H_s \, a(q+1)_s \, ds$$

for *all* càdlàg processes H.

About optimality, or asymptotic efficiency: We focus here on estimation of $C = C(2)$. For regular sampling the question of optimality has been (more or less) answered in Remark 6.2, and for irregular sampling schemes we again consider the toy model $X = \sigma W$ with $c = \sigma^2$ a constant, and $C_T = cT$.

For regular sampling we have $\widehat{C}(\Delta_n)_T = B^n(2,0)_T$ and the MLE for C_T is $\frac{T/\Delta_n}{[T/\Delta_n]} B^n(2,0)_T$, which behaves as $B^n(2,0)_T$ (up to a term of order of magnitude Δ_n). When the sampling is non-random but not regular, we still have a Gaussian experiment for our toy model and the MLE becomes

$$A_T^n \;=\; \frac{T}{N_T^n} \sum_{i=1}^{N_T^n} \frac{1}{\Delta(n,i)} |\Delta_i^n X|^2 \;=\; \frac{T}{N_T^n} B^n(2,0)_T.$$

This is again asymptotically efficient, and for each n the variance of $A_T^n - C_T$ is $2c^2 T^2 / N_T^n$. Now, if further (D-2) holds, the asymptotic variance of $\frac{1}{\sqrt{\delta_n}}(B^n(2,0)_T - C_T)$ is $2c^2 \int_0^T a(2)_s ds$, and if (D-0) also holds we have $\delta_n N_T^n \to \int_0^T a(0)_s ds$. Therefore, under both (D-0) and (D-2), the two asymptotic variances Σ and Σ' of $\frac{1}{\sqrt{\delta_n}}(B^n(2,0)_T - C_T)$ and $\frac{1}{\sqrt{\delta_n}}(A_T^n - C_T)$ satisfy

$$\Sigma \;=\; \alpha \Sigma', \quad \text{where} \quad \alpha \;=\; \frac{1}{T^2} \Big(\int_0^T a(2)_s ds \Big) \Big(\int_0^T a(0)_s ds \Big).$$

If we use (9.5) with $q = 0$ and $p = 1$ and $q' = 2$ and go the limit, we see that $\alpha \geq 1$, as it should be because A_T^n is asymptotically efficient. It may happen that $\alpha = 1$, of course, but this property is equivalent to saying that $D(0)_T^n D(2)_T^n - (D(1)_T^n)^2 \to 0$, and the equality $D(0)_T^n D(2)_T^n = (D(1)_T^n)^2$ implies that the $\Delta(n,i)$'s for $i \leq N_T^n$ are all equal (by Cauchy-Schwarz inequality); therefore *the realized volatility $B^n(2,0)_T$ is asymptotically efficient only when the sampling scheme is "asymptotically" a regular sampling.*

At this stage, one might wonder why we do not use A_T^n instead of $B^n(2,0)_T$ in general. This is because, and coming back to the general stochastic volatility situation, under (D-0) we have

$$A_T^n \xrightarrow{\mathbb{P}} T \, \frac{\int_0^T c_s \, a(0)_s \, ds}{\int_0^T a(0)_s \, ds},$$

which is different from $C_T = \int_0^T c_s \, ds$ unless either c_s or $a(0)_s$ do not depend on time. In other words, A_T^n is not even consistent for estimating C_T in general. The reason is of course that if A_T^n is the MLE for the toy model with $c_s = c$ constant (and for deterministic sampling), it is no longer the MLE when c_s is time-varying and non-random, not to speak about the stochastic volatility case.

9.1.3 Irregular Observation Schemes: Time Changes

Below, we give a quick overview of the special class of observation schemes which are obtained by time-changing a regular scheme. There are two ingredients: a sequence of numbers $\delta_n > 0$ which goes to 0 and represents the meshes of the regular scheme to be time-changed; and the time change itself, which comes in several distinct versions, in increasing order of generality:

1. The simplest one consists of taking a function $\Lambda = (\Lambda_t)_{t \geq 0}$ from $\mathbb{R}_+$ into itself, with the following properties for some constant $A > 1$:

   $$\Lambda_0 = 0, \quad \Lambda \text{ is } C^1 \text{ with a derivative } \lambda \text{ satisfying} \tag{9.12}$$
   $$\tfrac{1}{A} \leq \lambda_t \leq A \text{ and } |\lambda_t - \lambda_s| \leq A|t - s|.$$

   Then of course Λ is a bijection, and the reciprocal function is denoted as $\overline{\Lambda}$ and is also C^1.

2. Another version consists of assuming that Λ is random, with all paths satisfying (9.12) (with A possibly random as well), and inde-

pendent of all the processes of interest (the log-price X, its volatility, its drift, its Lévy measures when it jumps, and so on). Up to enlarging the filtered space, one can suppose that Λ is defined on $(\Omega, \mathcal{F}, (\mathcal{F}_t), \mathbb{P})$ and $\mathcal{F}_0$-measurable.

3. A third – slightly more general – version is basically as above, except that Λ is simply assumed to be $\mathcal{F}_0$-measurable: it is then independent of the terms W and $\underline{p}$ which drive X and possibly its volatility process, but it is no longer necessarily independent of X itself. Then the "constant" A may be random, and taken to be $\mathcal{F}_0$-measurable.

4. The fourth and most general version consists of assuming that Λ is random, defined on $(\Omega, \mathcal{F}, (\mathcal{F}_t), \mathbb{P})$, with paths satisfying (9.12) with A being $\mathcal{F}_0$-measurable, and such that for each t the variable Λ_t is *a stopping time*. This last requirement, jointly with (9.12), is in fact *rather restrictive*, although automatically satisfied by the first three versions above.

Now, with such a Λ, plus the sequence δ_n, we associate the observation scheme with observation times given by

$$S(n, i) = \Lambda_{i\delta_n}. \tag{9.13}$$

Such a scheme is naturally called a *time-changed regular scheme*.

What is important here is that the function or process Λ is *fixed*. Because of this, it is deeply different from the renewal or mixed renewal schemes, unless of course $\Lambda_t = at$ for some constant $a > 0$ (but then (9.13) is a regular scheme). Would Λ be allowed to depend on n, all schemes satisfying (A) (and many more) would be of this type, but the whole idea here is precisely that it does *not* depend on n. The Lipschitz condition on λ could be weakened and the boundedness of λ and $1/\lambda$ could be replaced by local boundedness but here, for simplicity, we stick to the above requirements.

Like all schemes in this section, when X is multi-dimensional time-changed regular schemes rule out asynchronous observations of the various components. When X is one-dimensional, though, and in the absence of a specific mechanism which would describe how observation times occur, time-changed regular schemes are reasonably general and probably account for many schemes encountered in practice. Note, however, that such a scheme implies that the inter-observation time $\Delta_n(n, i)$ is between δ_n/A and $\delta_n A$, which can be viewed as a serious restriction.

Now, a time-changed regular scheme obviously satisfies (9.3). The first three versions described above satisfy Assumption (A), with $\mathcal{F}' = \mathcal{F}$, although the fourth might violate it. However, arguing pathwise, it is easy to check the following:

$$\begin{aligned} &\text{it satisfies (D-}q\text{) for all } q \geq 0, \\ &\text{with } a(q)_t = (\lambda_{\overline{\Lambda}_t})^{q-1} \text{ and with the sequence } \delta_n. \end{aligned} \tag{9.14}$$

The feature which makes these schemes mathematically appealing is as follows. Suppose that X is an Itô semimartingale with spot characteristics (b_t, c_t, F_t), and consider the time-changed process

$$\overline{X}_t = X_{\Lambda_t}. \tag{9.15}$$

This process is adapted to the time-changed filtration $\overline{\mathcal{F}}_t = \mathcal{F}_{\Lambda_t}$ (this is why we need each Λ_t to be a stopping time). Classical properties of time changes, see Jacod (1979) for example, give us the following fundamental property:

$$\begin{aligned} &\overline{X} \text{ is an Itô semimartingale relative to the time-changed} \\ &\text{filtration } (\overline{\mathcal{F}}_t)_{t \geq 0}, \text{with characteristics } (\overline{B}, \overline{C}, \overline{\nu}) \\ &\text{and spot characteristics } (\overline{b}, \overline{c}, \overline{F}) \text{ given by} \\ &\overline{B}_t = B_{\Lambda_t}, \quad \overline{C}_t = C_{\Lambda_t}, \quad \overline{\nu}((0, t \times A) = \nu((0, \Lambda_t] \times A) \\ &\overline{b}_t = \lambda_t \, b_{\Lambda_t}, \quad \overline{c}_t = \lambda_t \, c_{\Lambda_t}, \quad \overline{F}_t = \lambda_t \, F_{\Lambda_t}. \end{aligned} \tag{9.16}$$

Now we come to the estimation of C_T, say in the one-dimensional case, when X is of the form (9.1) with (HC). More generally, we estimate the variables $C(p, q)_T$ of (9.8) (recall $C_T = C(2, 0)_T$); in view of (9.14), the processes $C(p, q)$ are now

$$C(p, q)_T = \int_0^T c_s^{p/2} (\lambda_{\overline{\Lambda}_s})^q \, ds. \tag{9.17}$$

In practice, only $C(p, 0)$ seem to be of interest, but as before the estimation of $C(p, q)$ for $q \neq 0$ proves useful technically.

Set, for $a \in \mathbb{R}$,

$$\begin{aligned} &\delta_i^n \overline{X} = \overline{X}_{i\delta_n} - \overline{X}_{(i-1)\delta_n}, \qquad \lambda_i^n = \tfrac{1}{\delta_n} \int_{(i-1)\delta_n}^{i\delta_n} \lambda_s \, ds \\ &B^{\overline{X}}(p, a; \delta_n)_t = \sum_{i=1}^{[t/\delta_n]} |\delta_i^n \overline{X}|^p \, (\lambda_i^n)^{ap}, \end{aligned} \tag{9.18}$$

so $B^{\overline{X}}(p, 0; \delta_n)$ is simply the process $B(p, \delta_n)$ associated with $\overline{X}$ by (6.9), with δ_n instead of Δ_n. In view of the Lipschitz property of λ, and by virtue of the extensions of Theorems A.2 and A.13 to the case of "random weights," as in Chapter 7 of Jacod and Protter (2011), the processes $B^{\overline{X}}(p, a; \delta_n)$ enjoy exactly the same limit theorem (LNN and CLT) as $B(p, \Delta_n)$ does (for X), provided in all statements we replace Δ_n by δ_n and make the substitution

$$C^{\overline{X}}(r, a)_t = \int_0^t (\lambda_s)^{ar} (\overline{c}_s)^{r/2} ds \quad \text{instead of} \quad C(r)_t = \int_0^t c_s^{r/2} ds$$

(this occurs with $r = p/2$ for the LNN and with $r = p/2$ and $r = p$ for the CLT).

Observing that $N_t^n = [\overline{\Lambda}_t / \delta_n]$ and $\delta_i^n \overline{X} = \Delta_i^n X$, and recalling (9.7), we readily get

$$B^n(p, q)_t = \delta_n^{q+1-p/2} B^{\overline{X}}\left(p, \frac{q+1}{p} - \frac{1}{2}; \delta_n\right)_{\overline{\Lambda}_t}. \tag{9.19}$$

Theorem 9.7. *Assume (HC) and let $(S(n, i))$ be a time-changed regular scheme with meshes δ_n and time change process Λ. Then all claims of Theorem 9.3 hold here, with the definition (9.17) for $C(2p, 1)$.*

Proof. The CLT, extended as before, tells us that $\frac{1}{\sqrt{\delta_n}}(\delta_n^{1-p/2} B^{\overline{X}}(p, a; \delta_n) - C^{\overline{X}}(p, a))$ stably converges in law to some process $\overline{\mathcal{W}}$ which conditionally on $\mathcal{F}$ is a continuous centered Gaussian martingale (for the time-changed extended filtration) with conditional variance $\overline{V}_t = (m_{2p} - m_p^2)C^{\overline{X}}(2p, a)_t$. We will use this with $a = \frac{1}{p} - \frac{1}{2}$, so (9.19) yields $B^n(p, 0)_t = \delta_n^{1-p/2} B^{\overline{X}}(p, a; \delta_n)_{\overline{\Lambda}_t}$, whereas (9.16) and a change of variable imply $C^{\overline{X}}(p, a)_t = C(p, 0)_{\overline{\Lambda}_t} = C(p)_{\overline{\Lambda}_t}$ and $C^{\overline{X}}(2p, a)_t = C(2p, 1)_{\overline{\Lambda}_t}$. Since stable convergence in law is preserved by any continuous strictly increasing time change, we deduce from what precedes that $\frac{1}{\sqrt{\delta_n}}(B^n(p, 0) - C(p))$ stably converges in law to $\mathcal{W}_t = \overline{\mathcal{W}}_{\overline{\Lambda}_t}$. It is elementary to check that $\mathcal{W}$ is a continuous centered Gaussian martingale with conditional variance $V_t = (m_{2p} - m_p^2)C(2p, 1)_t$. This ends the proof of the first part of the theorem. A similar argument, using the LLN for $\delta_n^{1-p} B^{\overline{X}}(2p, a; \delta_n)$, with the same a as above, allows us to deduce that $\frac{1}{\delta_n} B^n(2p, 1) \overset{\text{u.c.p.}}{\Longrightarrow} m_{2p}C(2p, 1)$. Then a standard argument yields the last result. $\square$

What precedes shows that this result may hold in some cases where (A) fails. But what is really important is that the argument of the previous proof carries over in many other situations. Namely, if X satisfies one of the assumptions stated before, such as (H-r), (K-r), (P) and (KC), then by (9.16) $\overline{X}$ satisfies the same assumption, relative to the time-changed filtration $(\overline{\mathcal{F}}_t)$, of course. All results stated in the previous chapters apply to $\overline{X}$ observed along the regular grids $(i\delta_n : i \geq 1)$. Then, for all such results which hinge upon a functional LLN or CLT, the previous time-change argument and the fact that a relation similar with (9.19) holds most functionals of X and of $\overline{X}$ yield that the same results hold for X observed along a time-changed regular grid.

In other words, we have:

Meta Theorem: *A result which holds for regular observation schemes holds as well, under the same assumptions on the underlying process, for time-changed regular schemes.*

This applies to *all* results in Subsections 6.1 and 6.2, and to most results in Chapters 7 and 8. There is an important caveat, though: the various standardized CLTs and the associated confidence intervals hold for time-changed regular schemes, exactly as they are stated in the regular case, but the non-standardized limits typically exhibit a variance which involves the function or process λ_t, or rather $\lambda_{\overline{\Lambda}_t}$. So each result has to be specifically reworked (but in all cases this is very simple to do). An – unfortunate – consequence is that all considerations made previously about optimality become wrong in this case, as we saw at the end of the previous subsection for example (but of course rate-optimality is preserved).

Finally, the "meta theorem" above also applies to the analysis of jumps which is done in the last part of this book.

9.2 The Multivariate Case: Non-synchronous Observations

As said in Remark 9.6, the previous section extends without problem to the multivariate case for the underlying process X, *provided all components are observed at the same times*. However, in high frequency financial data, when observation times are unevenly distributed, they are also typically different for different components of the (log) price process. In this case, things are *very* different, as we briefly sketch below.

We again restrict our attention to integrated volatility estimation, and focus on the estimation of the off-diagonal elements C_T^{ij} of the integrated (co)volatility. We then can, and will, suppose that X is two-dimensional, and try to estimate C_T^{12}. At stage n, the sampling times of the component X^j are the $(S_j(n, i) : i \geq 0)$, as described in the previous section. Other assumptions on the observation times will be specified later.

9.2.1 The Epps Effect

Recall once more that, by Theorem 1.14,

$$\sum_{i\geq 1:\, R(n,i)\leq T} (X^1_{R(n,i)} - X^1_{R(n,i-1)})(X^1_{R(n,i)} - X^1_{R(n,i-1)}) \xrightarrow{\mathbb{P}} C^{12}_T \quad (9.20)$$

as $n \to \infty$, for *any* scheme $R(n,i)$ of stopping times which satisfies (9.3). Here the $R(n,i)$'s are *the same* for both components, and historically speaking, the first attempts for estimating C^{12}_T used (9.20): one pretends that one actually observes both X^1 and X^2 at common times $R(n,i)$, often called *refresh times*. There are several ways of performing this task; the most popular one consists of taking $R(n,i) = i\delta_n$ for some $\delta_n > 0$ (a regular grid) and replacing the "true" (unobserved) $X^j_{R(n,i)}$ by $X^j_{S_j(n,k)}$ where $S_j(n,k)$ is the largest actual observation time of X^j not bigger than $R(n,i)$. One could also rearrange the two sequences $S_1(n,i)$ and $S_2(n,i)$ into a single strictly increasing sequence $S(n,i)$ (for any given n), and take for $R(n,i)$ the value $S(n,ki)$ for some $k \geq 1$. Other variants are possible.

This class of methods induces obvious errors, which are small only when, for *all* i and for $j = 1,2$, the differences $R(n,i) - \sup_{k:S_j(n,k)\leq R(n,i)} S_j(n,k)$ are small in front of δ_n. Unless the actual sampling times are very close to being regular, this requirement implies that one should choose δ_n quite large, say 5 or 10 to 20 times bigger than the maximum of the meshes $\pi^n_{1,T}$ and $\pi^n_{2,T}$ of the two schemes $S_1(n,i)$ and $S_2(n,i)$. Analogously, for the rearrangement method described above, the integer k should be large enough. In all cases, this results in a *huge* loss of data.

Worse: when we let δ_n decrease (while staying bigger than $\pi^n_{1,T} \vee \pi^n_{2,T}$, of course), we observe the so-called *Epps effect*, which features estimators for C^{12}_T that become smaller and smaller in absolute value. This effect is easy to understand, as seen in the following (simple and intuitive, albeit totally unrealistic from a practical viewpoint) example.

Example 9.8. *The sampling scheme is*

$$S_1(n,i) = \frac{i}{n}, \qquad S_2(n,i) = \begin{cases} 0 & \text{if } i = 0 \\ \frac{i}{n} - \frac{1}{2} & \text{if } i \geq 1, \end{cases}$$

and $X^1 = X^2 = W$ and $T = 1$, so $C^{12}_T = 1$. Let $\Phi(n,k)$ be the left side of (9.20) when $T = 1$ and $R(n,i) = ik/n$ (corresponding to taking $\delta_n = k/n$) and when we replace the "true" $X^j_{R(n,i)}$ by $X^j_{S_j(n,i)}$ for the biggest $S_j(n,i)$ smaller than $R(n,i)$.

The expectation of $\Phi(n,k)$ is easily seen to be $\frac{2k-1}{2n}\left[\frac{n}{k}\right]$. For n large, this is about $\frac{2k-1}{k}$, close to 1 if k is (relatively) large, but equal to $\frac{1}{2}$ if $k = 1$. And actually, in this simple case, one easily checks that not only the expectations, but the random variables $\Phi(n,k)$ themselves, behave in this way, and more specifically converge in probability to $\frac{2k-1}{2k}$.

Other choices of the regular grid $R(n,i)$ with mesh δ_n generate similar results: when δ_n is not much larger than $1/n$ the estimators (9.20) are far from the true value 1, and if we take $\delta_n = 1/n$ (the smallest possible value, which apparently makes use of all available data), the left side of (9.20) is a consistent estimator for $1/2$ instead of 1.

This example is representative of the general situation: when C_t^{12} is increasing in t (hence nonnegative, because $C_0^{12} = 0$) the estimators (9.20) used with the refresh times, as described above, are downward biased for estimating C_T^{12}, and the bias becomes drastically more severe when the mesh between refresh times becomes closer to the mesh $\pi_T^n \vee \pi_T'^n$. When C_t^{12} is decreasing, hence nonpositive, we analogously get an upward bias.

9.2.2   The Hayashi-Yoshida Method

The reason why (9.20) with "refresh times" is not consistent for estimating C_T^{12} is apparent in Example 9.8, because in this case the two components X^1, X^2 are martingales: the expectation of the product of two increments $(X_{t+s}^1 - X_t^1)(X_{t'+s'}^2 - X_{t'}^2)$ is the expected value of $\int_{[t,t+s]\cap[t',t'+s']} c_u^{12}\,du$, which in the Brownian case is simply a constant times the Lebesgue measure of $[t,t+s]\cap[t',t'+s']$. Therefore, (9.20) is an estimator for $\int_{A_{\delta_n}} c_s^{12}\,ds$, where A_{δ_n} is a subset of $[0,T]$ whose Lebesgue measure is a fraction of T (actually $T/2$ in the previous example) when δ_n is "small."

The idea of Hayashi-Yoshida estimator is to replace A_{δ_n} above by a set which is indeed $[0,T]$ itself, up to (negligible) border terms near T. This is achieved by taking the following:

$$\widehat{C}^{\mathrm{HY}}(n)_T^{12} = \sum_{(i,i')\in J(n,T)} \Delta_i^n X^1\,\Delta_{i'}^n X^2, \qquad (9.21)$$

where

$$\Delta_i^n X^j = X_{S_j(n,i)}^j - X_{S_j(n,i-1)}^j$$
$$I_j(n,i) = (S_j(n,i-1), S_j(n,i)]$$
$$J(n,T) = \{(i,i') : 0 < S_1(n,i) \le T, 0 < S_2(n,i') \le T,$$
$$I_1(n,i) \cap I_2(n,i') \ne \emptyset\}.$$

We then have

Theorem 9.9. *Assume that the two-dimensional process X satisfies (HC) and that the observation times $(S_j(n,i))$ for $j = 1,2$ are stopping times and satisfy (9.3). Then the estimators $\widehat{C}^{\mathrm{HY}}(n)_T^{12}$ are consistent for estimating C_T^{12}, that is,*

$$\widehat{C}^{\mathrm{HY}}(n)_T^{12} \xrightarrow{\mathbb{P}} C_T^{12}.$$

Note that when $S_2(n,i) = S_1(n,i)$ identically, the estimator $\widehat{C}^{\mathrm{HY}}(n)_T^{12}$ is simply the realized co-volatility

$$\sum_{i=1}^{N_T^n} \Delta_i^n X^1 \, \Delta_i^n X^2,$$

as in Remark 9.4 for the realized volatility in case of a single asset price.

If we want a rate of convergence, and an associated CLT, we need additional assumptions on the sampling scheme and on X. There are several versions for the assumptions on the sampling schemes, and we only describe the simplest one below:

Assumption (DD-2). *For a sequence δ_n of positive numbers converging to 0, and two numbers $0 \le v < v' < 1$ with further $v' > \frac{4}{5}$, we have:*

(i) Both schemes $(S_1(n,i))$ and $(S_2(n,i))$ satisfy (9.3) and are constituted of stopping times relative to the filtration $(\mathcal{F}_{(t-\delta_n^v)^+})_{t\ge0}$.

(ii) With $|I|$ denoting the length of any interval I, there are four (necessarily nonnegative) $(\mathcal{F}_t \cap \mathcal{F}^{X,W,b,\sigma})_{t\ge0}$-progressively measurable processes $a^1, a^2, \overline{a}, \overline{a}'$ (with $\mathcal{F}$ as specified in Assumption (A)) such that for all t and $j = 1,2$ we have

$$\frac{1}{\delta_n} \sum_{i\ge1} |I_j(n,i)|^2 \, 1_{\{S_j(n,i)\le t\}} \xrightarrow{\mathbb{P}} \int_0^t a_s^j \, ds$$

$$\frac{1}{\delta_n} \sum_{i,i'\ge1} |I_1(n,i) \cap I_2(n,i')|^2 \, 1_{\{S_1(n,i)\vee S_2(n,i')\le t\}} \xrightarrow{\mathbb{P}} \int_0^t \overline{a}_s \, ds \qquad (9.22)$$

$$\frac{1}{\delta_n} \sum_{i,i'\ge1} |I_1(n,i)| \, |I_2(n,i')| \, 1_{\{I_1(n,i)\cap I_2(n,i')\neq\emptyset, \, S_1(n,i)\vee S_2(n,i')\le t\}}$$
$$\xrightarrow{\mathbb{P}} \int_0^t \overline{a}'_s \, ds.$$

(iii) The meshes $\pi_{1,t}^n$ and $\pi_{2,t}^n$ of the two schemes satisfy $\frac{1}{\delta_n^{v'}} \pi_{j,t}^n \xrightarrow{\mathbb{P}} 0$.

The first convergence above is exactly (9.2) in (D-2) for the scheme $S_j(n,i)$, with a^j playing the role of $a(2)$, and with the *same* sequence δ_n for $j = 1,2$; this can be interpreted as a nice asymptotic behavior of the "quadratic variation" of the sampling times, and the last two properties in (9.22) are statements about the "quadratic covariation" between the two schemes.

Note also that, by (iii), the number δ_n^v is (much) bigger than the two meshes π_t^n and $\pi_t'^n$ on a set $\Omega_{n,t}$ whose probability goes to 1, so (i) implies, loosely speaking, that "in restriction to this set" the times $S(n,i)$ and $S'(n,i)$ are strongly predictable in an even stronger sense than as stated after Assumption (A). So although the two schemes do not necessarily satisfy (A) as stated, they do satisfy an essentially stronger assumption.

Note that this assumption allows for sampling X^1, say, more frequently than X^2, by allowing for example a_s' to be significantly larger than a_s, but the ratio of the sampling frequencies of the two components should stay approximately constant. The next example illustrates this fact.

Example 9.10. *If $S_1(n,i) = S_2(n,i) = i\Delta_n$ are two regular schemes with the same mesh, (DD-2) obviously holds, with $\delta_n = \Delta_n$ and $a_s^1 = a_s^2 = \overline{a}_s = \overline{a}_s' = 1$.*

If $S_1(n,i) = i\Delta_n$ and $S_2(n,i) = ik\Delta_n$, so both schemes are regular with respective meshes Δ_n and $k\Delta_n$ for some integer $k \geq 2$, we still have (DD-2) with $\delta_n = \Delta_n$, but now $a_s^1 = \overline{a}_s = 1$ and $a_s^2 = \overline{a}_s' = k$.

When $S_1(n,i) = i\Delta_n$ and $S_2(n,i) = i\alpha\Delta_n$ when $\alpha > 1$ is not an integer, we still have (DD-2) with $a_s = 1$ and $a_s^2 = \alpha$, and $\overline{a}_s$, and $\overline{a}_s'$ are independent of s but rather complicated functions of α.

Example 9.11. *This example shows that, although (DD-2) implies a form of strong predictability, it nevertheless accommodates sampling schemes with exogenous randomness. For each n one takes two independent sequences $S_1(n,i)$ and $S_2(n,i)$ which are the arrival times of Poisson processes with intensities $n\alpha_1$ and $n\alpha_2$, for two constants $\alpha_j > 0$, those processes being also independent of (X, W, b, σ). Then upon enlarging the filtration, without impairing the Brownian property of W and Equation (9.1), one may assume that all $S_j(n,i)$'s are $\mathcal{F}_0$-measurable. Then (DD-2) is satisfied with $\delta_n = 1/n$ and $v = 0$ and $v' \in (4/5, 1)$, and with*

$$a_s^j = \frac{2}{\alpha_j}, \qquad \overline{a}_s = \frac{2}{\alpha_1 + \alpha_2}, \qquad \overline{a}_s' = \frac{2}{\alpha_1} + \frac{2}{\alpha_2}.$$

We can now state the CLT for estimating C_T^{12}:

Theorem 9.12. *Assume that the two-dimensional process X satisfies (9.1) with two processes b_t and σ_t having paths which are uniformly Hölder of index $\frac{1}{2} - \varepsilon$ on $[0, T]$ for all $\varepsilon > 0$. Assume also that the observation times $S_j(n,i)$ satisfy (DD-2). Then for any $T > 0$ the variables*

$\frac{1}{\sqrt{\delta_n}} \left(\widehat{C}^{\mathrm{HY}}(n)_T^{12} - C_T^{12} \right)$ *converge stably in law to a variable defined on an extension of the original probability space and which conditionally on $\mathcal{F}$ is centered Gaussian with variance*

$$V_T = \int_0^T \left(c_s^{11} \, c_s^{22} \, \overline{a}_s' + (c_s^{12})^2 \, (a_s^1 + a_s^2 - \overline{a}_s) \right) ds. \qquad (9.23)$$

In view of the comments made before, and since when $X^1 = X^2$ Assumption (DD-2) is essentially stronger than (D-2), with $a^1 = a^2 = \overline{a} = \overline{a}' = a(2)$, in this case the previous result is basically Theorem 9.3 for $p = 2$.

Remark 9.13. *The above result is exactly Theorem 8.1 of Hayashi and Yoshida (2011), to which we refer for the proof, and upon observing that a process Y has path which are almost surely uniformly Hölder of index $\frac{1}{2} - \varepsilon$ on $[0, T]$ for all $\varepsilon > 0$ if and only if, for all $\varepsilon > 0$, the variables $\frac{1}{v^{1/2-\varepsilon}} \sup(\|Y_{t+s} - Y_t\| : 0 \le t \le t + s \le (t + v) \wedge T)$ are bounded in probability as v varies in $(0, 1)$.*

In particular, the above assumptions on X are met when both processes b and σ are themselves (continuous Itô) semimartingales satisfying (HC).

However, a look at the proof in the above-mentioned paper shows that the result also holds when b and σ are possibly discontinuous Itô semi-martingales, provided they satisfy (H-2). Let us also mention that this paper contains analogous results under weaker (but probably difficult to check practically) sets of assumptions.

For practical purposes, one needs consistent estimators for the conditional variance given in (9.23). Here again, the problem is not completely obvious for the same reason as before: the non-synchronicity of observation. However, consistency only is required, and not a CLT.

Following again Hayashi and Yoshida (2011), one can proceed as follows. As mentioned before, the estimators $\widehat{C}^{\mathrm{HY}}(n)_T^{11}$ and $\widehat{C}^{\mathrm{HY}}(n)_T^{22}$ are defined in a way similar to (9.21) and coincide with $B^n(2, 0)_T$ written for the one-dimensional processes X^1 and X^2 respectively. Then for a suitable sequence $h_n > 0$ eventually going to 0, we consider the following "spot volatility estimators" at (or, around) time t:

$$\widehat{c}^{\mathrm{HY}}(t; h_n)^{ij} = \frac{1}{h_n} \left(\widehat{C}^{\mathrm{HY}}(n)_{t+h_n}^{ij} - \widehat{C}^{\mathrm{HY}}(n)_t^{ij} \right). \qquad (9.24)$$

These estimators are well suited to the non-regular sampling situation, but in the regular sampling case $S_1(n, i) = S_2(n, i) = i\Delta_n$ they indeed coincide with the spot estimators given in (8.10), with no truncation because X is continuous, and with h_n here playing the role of $k_n \Delta_n$ in that formula.

The idea is then to approximate (9.23) by Riemann sums, and replace c_t there by $\widehat{c}^{\text{HY}}(t; h_n)$. We also have to approximate the unknown processes $a^j, \overline{a}, \overline{a}'$, and for this we use the convergences (9.22), in which the left side are indeed known at stage n, up to the (unknown) normalization $1/\delta_n$. Since the estimators (9.24) are observable only when $t + h_n$ is smaller than the horizon T, this leads us to take

$$
\begin{aligned}
\widehat{V}(h_n)_T = {} & \sum_{i,i' \geq 1} \widehat{c}^{\text{HY}}(S_1(n,i) \vee S_2(n,i'); h_n)^{11} \\
& \times \widehat{c}^{\text{HY}}(S_1(n,i) \vee S_2(n,i'); h_n)^{22} \\
& \times |I_2(n,i')| \, 1_{\{I_1(n,i) \cap I_2(n,i') \neq \emptyset\}} \, 1_{\{S_1(n,i) \vee S_2(n,i') \leq T - h_n\}} \\
& + \sum_{i \geq 1} \left(\widehat{c}^{\text{HY}}(S_1(n,i); h_n)^{12}\right)^2 |I_1(n,i)|^2 \, 1_{\{S_1(n,i) \leq T - h_n\}} \\
& + \sum_{i \geq 1} \left(\widehat{c}^{\text{HY}}(S_2(n,i); h_n)^{12}\right)^2 |I_2(n,i)|^2 \, 1_{\{S_2(n,i) \leq T - h_n\}} \\
& - \sum_{i,i' \geq 1} \left(\widehat{c}^{\text{HY}}(S_1(n,i) \vee S_2(n,i'); h_n)^{12}\right)^2 |I_1(n,i) \cap I_2(n,i')|^2 \\
& \times 1_{\{S_1(n,i) \vee S_2(n,i') \leq T - h_n\}}.
\end{aligned}
$$

We then have the following result:

Theorem 9.14. *Under the assumptions of Theorem 9.12, and as soon as $\delta_n / h_n^2 \to 0$, we have*

$$
\frac{1}{\delta_n} \widehat{V}(h_n)_T \xrightarrow{\ \mathbb{P}\ } V_T,
$$

and thus

$$
\mathcal{L}\left(\frac{\widehat{C}^{\text{HY}}(n)_T^{12} - C_T^{12}}{\sqrt{\widehat{V}(h_n)_T}} \,\Big|\, A\right) \to \mathcal{N}(0,1)
$$

for all $A \in \mathcal{F}$ with $\mathbb{P}(A) > 0$ and $A \subset \{C_T^{11} + C_T^{22} > 0\}$.

Since $\widehat{C}^{\text{HY}}(n)_T^{12}$ and $\widehat{V}(h_n)_T$ are observable at stage n, this result allows us to derive confidence bounds in the usual way. Let us note, however, that we have the tuning parameter h_n to choose, subject to δ_n/h_n^2 and h_n going to 0, which in practice means that those numbers should be small. There seems to be a problem here, since δ_n is *a priori* unknown, but as seen in the previous section δ_n is of the order of magnitude $1/N_T^n$, where N_T^n is the number of observations (of the first, or of the second, or of both, components) up to time T. So one should choose h_n is such a way that $h_n^2 N_T^n$ is large and h_n is small, for example $h_n \simeq 1/(N_T^n)^{1/3}$ should work because N_T^n itself is supposed to be reasonably large (otherwise no accurate estimation is possible anyway).

Remark 9.15. *Good as they are, the Hayashi-Yoshida estimators suffer from an unfortunate drawback. Namely, the matrix-valued estimators $\widehat{C}^{HY}(n)_T^{i,j})_{i,j=1,2}$ are symmetrical by construction but not necessarily nonnegative. So far, only methods based on refresh time lead to nonnegative symmetric matrix-valued estimators in the case of non-synchronous observations.*

9.2.3   Other Methods and Extensions

Integrated Volatility Estimation   For estimating the integrated volatility, another method allows us to deal with observations that are irregularly spaced and/or asynchronous in the multidimensional case. This is the Fourier-based method, for which the only difference with the evenly spaced case is in the formula giving the Fourier coefficients.

The setting is the same as in the previous section, with a two-dimensional process X whose component X^j is sampled at the times $0 < S_j(n,1) < \cdots < S_j(n,i) < \cdots$, at stage n. Of course, this accommodates the one-dimensional case as well, by taking $X^2 = X^1$ and $S_2(n,i) = S_1(n,i)$.

We then modify the definition (6.45) of the estimator of the kth Fourier coefficient of the spot (cross) volatility c^{lm}, at stage n and truncation N, by taking instead:

$$\widehat{\mathcal{F}}_k(n,N;c^{lm}) = \frac{1}{2N+1}\sum_{r=-N}^{N} a_{-r}^{n,l}\, a_{r+k}^{n,m},$$
$$\text{where} \quad a_r^{n,l} = \frac{1}{\sqrt{2\pi}}\sum_{j\geq 1:\, S_l(n,j)\leq T} e^{-2i\pi r S_l(n,j)/T}\,\Delta_j^n X^l.$$

Here, $\Delta_j^n X^l$ is still the jth observed return of the component X^l, as defined by (9.21). The integrated volatility estimators are still

$$\widehat{C}^{\text{Fourier}}(n,N_n)_T^{lm} = 2\pi\,\widehat{\mathcal{F}}_0(n,N_n;c^{lm}).$$

With this notation, the results stated in Subsection 6.3.4 are still valid, under appropriate assumptions.

The problem here is in fact how to specify those assumptions. For X this is simple: as far as consistency results are concerned, it is enough to have (HC) and c continuous; for the Central Limit Theorem (6.48) one additionally needs that σ_t admits a Malliavin derivative with suitable moment bounds. Things are more difficult for the hypotheses on the sampling schemes:

1. They should satisfy (9.3), of course;

2. They should be *non-random*, or (perhaps) random but independent of X;

3. In the synchronous $(S_1(n,i) = S_2(n,i))$ but irregular case, one should have (D-2), with some sequence δ_n.

When all three conditions hold, in the synchronous case, and upon choosing N_n such that $T/N_n\delta_n \to a \in (0,\infty)$, we have the same CLT as in (6.48), except that the limit takes the form $\int_0^T \alpha(a, a(2)_s)\, dW_s$, where $a(2)_s$ is the function (or process) showing in (9.4) and α is here a (easily computable) function on $\mathbb{R}^2$.

In the non-synchronous case, conditions resembling (DD-2) ensure a CLT of the same type, but they are somewhat difficult to state, and even more difficult to check; details can be found in Clément and Gloter (2011), under the name of Hypothesis A4.

Spot Volatility Estimation The above Fourier-based method also gives, in principle, reasonable estimators for the spot volatility, given by (8.21) again, that is,

$$\widehat{c}^{\,\mathrm{Fourier}}(T, n, N_n)_t^{lm} = \frac{1}{2N_n + 1} \sum_{r=-N_n}^{N_n} \left(1 - \frac{|r|}{N_n}\right) e^{2i\pi rt/T} \widehat{\mathcal{F}}_r(n, N_n; c^{lm}).$$

On the other hand, one can adapt the method of Section 9.1 or the Hayashi-Yoshida method to spot volatility estimation, under Assumption (HC). Since X is continuous, truncated estimators are irrelevant. We have an estimator $\widehat{C}_t^n$ for C_t, which is either the realized volatility (that is, $B^n(2,0)_t$ in the one-dimensional case) when we have a single component, or two components observed synchronously, or the Hayashi-Yoshida estimator $\widehat{C}^{\mathrm{HY}}(n)_t^{lm}$ in the asynchronous case. Then, for any sequence $s_n > 0$ we set

$$\widetilde{c}^{\,\mathrm{irr}}(t; s_n) = \frac{1}{s_n}\,(\widehat{C}_{t+s_n}^n - \widehat{C}_t^n),$$

which is the same as (9.22) in the case of the Hayashi-Yoshida estimator.

Under (HC), plus (A) and (D-2) or for time-changed regular schemes in the synchronous case, or (DD-2) and the additional conditions on X imposed in Theorem 9.12 in the asynchronous case, Theorem 8.7 holds for $\widetilde{c}^{\,\mathrm{irr}}(t; s_n)$, with the following changes: First, assuming $s_n/\sqrt{\delta_n} \to \beta$

for some $\beta \in [0, \infty]$, (8.17) is replaced by

$$
\begin{aligned}
\beta = 0 \quad &\Rightarrow \left(\sqrt{\tfrac{s_n}{\delta_n}} \left(\widetilde{c}^{\,\mathrm{irr}}(t; s_n) - c_t \right) \right)_{t \geq 0} \xrightarrow{\mathcal{L}_f - s} (Z_t)_{t \geq 0} \\
0 < \beta < \infty \quad &\Rightarrow \left(\sqrt{\tfrac{s_n}{\delta_n}} \left(\widetilde{c}^{\,\mathrm{irr}}(t; s_n) - c_t \right) \right)_{t \geq 0} \xrightarrow{\mathcal{L}_f - s} (Z_t + \beta Z_t')_{t \geq 0} \quad (9.25) \\
\beta = \infty \quad &\Rightarrow \left(\tfrac{1}{\sqrt{s_n}} \left(\widetilde{c}^{\,\mathrm{irr}}(t; s_n) - c_t \right) \right)_{t \geq 0} \xrightarrow{\mathcal{L}_f - s} g(Z_t')_{t \geq 0}.
\end{aligned}
$$

Second, Z and Z' are as in (8.17), except that the conditional variance (8.14) of Z_t is modified and becomes (with the notation $a^j, \overline{a}, \overline{a}'$ of (9.23) when (DD-2) holds, and $a^1 = a^2 = \overline{a} = \overline{a}' = a(2)$ in the synchronous case with (D-2))

$$
\mathbb{E}(Z_t^{ij} Z_t^{kl} \mid \mathcal{F}) = \left(c_t^{ii} c_t^{jj} \, \overline{a}_t' + (c_t^{ij})^2 \left(a_t^i + a_t^j - \overline{a}_t \right) \right).
$$

Noisy Observations   When microstructure noise is present and observations are irregularly spaced, many papers propose consistent estimators for integrated, or even spot, volatility. A few recent papers analyze associated Central Limit Theorems, under various assumptions on the sampling times and/or the noise.

We will not report any specific method here, referring to the relevant papers for details, and will simply make a few comments. Basically, most "mixtures" of one of the methods proposed above for irregular schemes, and one of the de-noising methods explained in Chapter 7, result in consistent estimators.

Now, a nice fact about kernel methods for eliminating the noise, such as pre-averaging, is that not only do they wipe out the noise but they also smooth out the sampling irregularities; this is a simple effect of taking weighted averages of successive observations. So the assumptions on the sampling schemes need to be much less stringent in the presence of noise than when observations are totally accurate, in order to obtain "similar" CLTs. For instance the use of refresh times combined with a simple average of the observations between successive refresh times leads to reasonable estimators, because in any case the presence of noise implies that estimators converge with a much slower rate than without noise. In the case of non-shrinking noise, with δ_n being again a kind of average time between successive observations, the best achievable rates are now $1/\delta_n^{1/4}$ for the integrated volatility and $1/\delta_n^{1/8}$ for the spot volatility.

What is still not clear at this stage is how far one can relax assumptions like the structural Assumption (A), when noise is present. In the literature, several variants are proposed, but one lacks a thorough analysis of the "minimal" assumptions that are required.

9.3   References

The topic of irregularly spaced observation times is relatively recent in the literature. In a parametric setting, early works in that direction are Dacunha-Castelle and Florens-Zmirou (1986) and, more in line with what we do here, Genon-Catalot and Jacod (1994). Aït-Sahalia and Mykland (2003, 2004), and Duffie and Glynn (2004) consider the case of parametric estimators with irregular observation times.

Papers dealing explicitly with the estimation of integrated volatility in a non-parametric setting and with irregular observations are Barndorff-Nielsen and Shephard (2005), in which time-changed regular schemes were introduced, Mykland and Zhang (2006) in the one-dimensional (or multidimensional with synchronous observations) case, and Hayashi and Kusuoka (2008) and Hayashi and Yoshida (2005) for the consistency of co-volatility estimators under asynchronous observations. The corresponding Central Limit Theorems are in Hayashi and Yoshida (2008, 2011), and also in Hayashi et al. (2011) for the case studied in Section 9.1. One can find additional discussions in Griffin and Oomen (2011) and also in Oomen (2006), which considers the behavior of the approximate quadratic variation in the presence of additive microstructure noise, but with a purely discontinuous price process.

The Fourier-based method for irregular sampling is studied in Malliavin and Mancino (2002), and then in the subsequent papers referred to in Chapters 6 and 8.

The statement in (9.25) appears to be new.

The noisy case has been considered in some of the previously quoted papers, including those on the Fourier method, and also, often for time-changed regular schemes, in Barndorff-Nielsen et al. (2008, 2011), Christensen et al. (2010, 2011), Bibinger (2012) and Koike (2013) the last three papers also providing an associated Central Limit Theorem. Bibinger and Reiß (2014) propose localized spectral estimators for the quadratic covariation and the spot co-volatility of a diffusion, in the presence of additive noise. In Bibinger et al. (2013) the authors use a kind of moments method, and put emphasis on optimality.

Finally, we should mention that what precedes applies to specific (basically strongly predictable observation times, or observation times that are independent of X). This excludes sampling at hitting times, which can also be viewed as a reasonable alternative for modeling irregular sampling. This topic has been totally skipped in this book, but quite significant work on this has been done recently, and the reader can con-

sult Fukasawa (2010a,b) or Fukasawa and Rosenbaum (2011). One can
in fact construct a model which combines microstructure noise, including
rounding noise, and sampling at transaction times on the basis of suitably defined hitting times, and then estimate the integrated volatility,
see Robert and Rosenbaum (2011, 2012). A different approach with tests
for endogenous sampling times can be found in Li et al. (2009).

Part IV

Jumps

So far, we have been interested in volatility, integrated or spot, hence in the second characteristic C_t of the log-price process X, which describes its continuous martingale part. Jumps of X were not excluded, but were viewed as a nuisance for the purpose of estimating the volatility component of the model and we tried to eliminate them in one way or another.

In this part, jumps become our main interest. We first try to answer the fundamental question of whether there are jumps at all. When the answer is positive, our aim is to estimate as many features of these jumps as we can. Of course, since the overall setting is still the same, discrete observations at high frequency of a single path of the process, up to a finite fixed time horizon T, by necessity we have to stay modest: as seen in Chapter 5, it is out of the question to consistently estimate the law of the jumps, or (more to the point) the Lévy measures themselves. We can, however, say something about the concentration of these Lévy measures near 0, and in particular estimate the Blumenthal-Getoor index, or successive indices, of the process, under appropriate (and unfortunately somehow restrictive) assumptions.

Still assuming that there are jumps, we can next try to find out where they are and which size they have. It is also possible, in the multivariate case, to decide whether two different components jump at the same time or not, or whether one component jumps at the same time as its volatility process.

All these questions are analyzed below. In Chapter 10 we develop various tests for deciding whether there are jumps or not, and procedures which allow us to pin down the jump times and sizes. Chapter 11 is devoted to the estimation of the Blumenthal-Getoor indices, and Chapter 12 to the related question of deciding whether jumps have finite activity. When we find that jumps have infinite activity it becomes legitimate to ask ourselves whether the Brownian motion itself is present or if the jumps by themselves are enough to account for the variability of the process, and this is done in Chapter 13. Finally, Chapter 14 is concerned with the question of the existence of co-jumps of two different prices, or of a price process and its volatility process.

Many of the seemingly disparate problems studied in this part of the book can be understood as part of a common framework, relying on an analogy with spectrography (see Aït-Sahalia and Jacod (2012a)). We observe a time series of high-frequency returns, that is, a single path, over a finite length of time $[0, T]$. Using that time series as input, we design a set of statistical tools that can tell us something about specific components of the process that produced the observations. These tools play the role of the measurement devices used in astrophysics to analyze the light emanating from a star, for instance. Our observations are the high-frequency returns; in astrophysics it would be the light, visible or not. Here, the data generating mechanism is assumed to be a semimartingale; in astrophysics it would be whatever nuclear reactions inside the star are producing the light that is collected. Astrophysicists can look at a specific range of the light spectrum to learn about specific chemical elements present in the star. Here, we design statistics that focus on specific parts of the distribution of high-frequency returns in order to learn about the different components of the semimartingale that produced those returns. From the time series of returns, we can get the distribution of returns at time interval Δ_n. Based on the information contained in that distribution, we would like to figure out which components should be included in the model (continuous? jumps? which types of jumps?) and in what proportions. That is, we would like to deconstruct the observed series of returns back into its original components, continuous and jumps. We need to run the raw data through some devices that will emphasize certain components to the exclusion of others, magnify certain aspects of the model, etc. In spectrography, one needs to be able to recognize the visual signature of certain chemical elements. Here, we need to know what to expect to see if a certain component of the model is present or not in the observed data. This means that we will need to have a law of large numbers, obtained by imagining that we had collected a large number of sample paths instead of a single one. This allows us to determine the visual signature of specific components of the model.

Chapter 10

Testing for Jumps

This chapter is devoted to the most basic question about jumps: are they present at all? As seen in Chapter 5, this question can be answered unambiguously when the full path of the underlying process X is observed over the time interval of interest $[0, T]$. However, we suppose that X is discretely observed along a regular scheme with lag Δ_n, so no jump can actually be exactly observed, since observing a large discrete increment $\Delta_i^n X$ may be suggestive that a jump took place, but provides no certitude. We wish to derive testing procedures which are at least consistent (that is, give the right answer as $\Delta_n \to 0$). This can only be done under some structural hypotheses on X, and the property of being an Itô semimartingale is a suitable one.

A priori X could be multidimensional. However, if it jumps, then at least one of its components jumps. Hence we can test for jumps separately for each component, and the question really is about one-dimensional processes. So in the whole chapter, and without loss of generality, we suppose that X is *one-dimensional*. It is defined on a filtered space $(\Omega, \mathcal{F}, (\mathcal{F}_t)_{t \geq 0}, \mathbb{P})$, with the usual Grigelionis representation described in Section 1.4:

$$X_t = X_0 + \int_0^t b_s ds + \int_0^t \sigma_s dW_s \qquad (10.1)$$
$$+ (\delta 1_{\{|\delta| \leq 1\}}) \star (\underline{p} - \underline{q})_t + (\delta 1_{\{|\delta| > 1\}}) \star \underline{p}_t.$$

Here W is a one-dimensional Brownian motion and $\underline{p}$ is a Poisson measure on $\mathbb{R}_+ \times E$ with $(E, \mathcal{E})$ an auxiliary Polish space, and with compensator $\underline{q}(dt, dx) = dt \otimes \lambda(dx)$. The processes b and σ are progressively measurable, and δ is a predictable function $\Omega \times \mathbb{R}_+ \times E$. It is no restriction to assume $\sigma_t \geq 0$ identically, and as usual $c_t = \sigma_t^2$. We briefly recall (with any $r \in [0, 2]$) the Assumptions (H-r), (K-r) and (P) (in the one-dimensional case, and (K-r) below is indeed the same as in Chapter 8, despite the different formulation), and also introduce a new Assumption (H$'$). In the whole chapter we assume at least (H-2).

Assumption (H-r). *We have (10.1) with b locally bounded and σ càdlàg, and $|\delta(\omega, t, z)|^r \wedge 1 \le J_n(z)$ whenever $t \le \tau_n(\omega)$, where (τ_n) is a sequence of stopping times increasing to ∞, and (J_n) is a sequence of deterministic nonnegative functions satisfying $\int J_n(z) \lambda(dz) < \infty$.*

Next, we introduce the notation

$$
\begin{aligned}
\widehat{b}_s &= \int_{\{\|\delta(s,z)\| \le 1\}} \|\delta(s, z)\| \lambda(dz), \\
S &= \inf \left(t : \int_0^t \widehat{b}_s \, ds = \infty \right) \\
b'_t &= b_t - \int_{\{\|\delta(t,z)\| \le 1\}} \delta(t, z) \, \lambda(dz) \quad \text{if } t \le S,
\end{aligned}
\tag{10.2}
$$

so $\widehat{b}_t$ is well defined and $[0, \infty]$-valued, and b'_t is well defined as a process when $S = \infty$. The following is implied by (H-1), but not by (H-r) when $r > 1$:

Assumption (H$'$). *We have (H-2) and there is a sequence (τ_n) of stopping times increasing to ∞, such that $\sup_{(\omega,t):\, t \le \tau_n(\omega) \wedge S(\omega)} \widehat{b}_t(\omega) < \infty$.*

Assumption (K-r). *We have (H-r) and (H$'$) and the process σ is an Itô semimartingale satisfying (H-2) (hence the process c as well). Moreover, all paths $t \mapsto b'_t$ on $[0, S]$, and when $r > 1$ all paths $t \mapsto b_t$ on $\mathbb{R}_+$ as well, are either right-continuous with left limits (càdlàg) or left-continuous with right limits (càglàd).*

Assumption (P). *The processes c_t and c_{t-} never vanish.*

Let us also recall the notation (where p is a positive real)

$$
C(p)_t = \int_0^t \sigma_s^p \, ds \qquad (\text{so } C = C(2)),
\tag{10.3}
$$

and, for the jumps, as in (5.15) when $d = 1$,

$$
A(p)_t = \sum_{s \le t} |\Delta X_s|^p,
\tag{10.4}
$$

which may be infinite when $0 < p < 2$, but is finite when $p \ge 2$.

10.1   Introduction

It is important to stress from the onset that the question is not whether
jumps are possible, but whether jumps actually took place. A process
with finite jump activity (more on that in Chapter 11) will have at most
a finite number of jumps in $[0, T]$, but may very well have none in that
particular time interval. This does not mean that jumps are impossible
for this process. In economics, this situation corresponds to the classical
peso problem whereby a currency may be subject to a big devaluation
risk, but, as long as its peg to another currency remains effective, no
jump in the exchange rate would be observed. So any answer we give to
that question may be specific to the interval $[0, T]$.

This said, the question of whether the path of X has jumps over $[0, T]$
can be understood in two ways:

1. In a strict sense: we decompose the sample space Ω into two disjoint
   subsets:

$$
\begin{aligned}
\Omega_T^{(c)} &= \{\omega : \ t \mapsto X_t(\omega) \text{ is continuous on } [0, T]\} \\
\Omega_T^{(j)} &= \{\omega : \ t \mapsto X_t(\omega) \text{ is discontinuous on } [0, T]\},
\end{aligned}
\tag{10.5}
$$

   and we want to know whether the observed outcome ω belongs to
   $\Omega_T^{(c)}$ or to $\Omega_T^{(j)}$.

2. In an approximate sense: is the contribution of jumps significant,
   compared to the contribution of the "continuous part"? Here, the
   contribution of jumps is the sum of the last two terms in (10.1),
   whereas the continuous part is the sum of the first two terms.

Put this way, the first question seems more appealing than the second
one. However, since the path is not fully observed, any effective procedure
is likely to recognize whether there are "big" jumps, and to miss the small
or very small ones. And the notion of "big" is of course relative to the
variability of the continuous part. This means that any procedure has to
somehow compare, explicitly or implicitly, the relative sizes of the jumps
(if any) and the continuous part, and the two ways of understanding the
problem are perhaps not as different as they might first appear.

Observe also that one can refine the first question above, by asking
the following third question:

3. At which times in $[0, T]$ do the jumps occur, and what are their
   sizes ?

If we can solve the third question then we clearly can deduce an answer to the first question. However, it is immediately clear that, at a given stage n, the third question can be answered only if there is at most one jump within each interval $((i-1)\Delta_n, i\Delta_n]$; worse: if all or nearly all of these intervals contain a jump, in practice it becomes impossible to answer the question, so the third question can only be answered (asymptotically) if there are at most finitely many jumps on $[0, T]$. However, as we will see, it is still possible in practice to use a method based on a solution to the third question to solve, or partially solve, the basic first question.

Comparing the relative sizes of the jump part and of the continuous part is not an immediately obvious matter. The most natural way, which can be put in use for all Itô semimartingales, seems to be using the quadratic variation, to which both the continuous martingale part and the jump part contribute, with the same weight, unlike what happens with other power variations where one or the other part dominates (see Chapter 4). That is, $[X, X]_t = C_t + A(2)_t$ and one may think of C_t and $A(2)_t$ as being the "total (squared) sizes" of the continuous and discontinuous parts. Such a statement is somewhat imprecise, but it can be substantiated when X is a Lévy process with all X_t's being square-integrable, as follows: if $X = X^c + X^d$ with X^d being a purely discontinuous martingale (so there is no drift and $X^c = \sigma W$), then $C_t = ct$ is the second moment of X_t^c, and $A(2)_t$, although random, is approximately the second moment of X_t^d (assumed to be finite) when t is large, in the sense that $t^{-1} A(2)_t$ converges a.s. to the second moment of X_1^d.

In any event, in all the literature we are aware of, the sizes of "the continuous part" and "the jump part" are always quantified by C_t and $A(2)_t$, or by relatively simple transformations of these. For example we can "weight" the quadratic variation, as is sometimes done in measuring the quadratic risk in portfolio management. More precisely, with some (random, nonnegative) predictable weight process H, usually related to delta-hedging, one considers

$$C(H)_t = \int_0^t H_s \, dC_s,$$

$$A(2, H)_t = \int_0^t H_s \, dA(2)_s,$$

and $C(H)_t$ and $A(2, H)_t$ are interpreted as the quadratic hedging error due to the continuous and discontinuous parts, respectively. Apart from this question of hedging risk, one can also take H to be a function of the form $H_t = f(t, X_{t-})$. In this case the measures $C(H)_t$ and $A(2, H)_t$ put more or less weight, depending on the time t and on the value of the price.

In this chapter, we first consider in Section 10.2 tests that address the second question, that is, we estimate C_t and $A(2)_t$ and construct a test based on these estimators. These procedures suffer from an intrinsic drawback: they allow us to construct tests (with a given asymptotic level) only when the null hypothesis is $\Omega_T^{(c)}$, that is, "no jump." It is impossible with this approach to test the null hypothesis that "jumps are present" since that would require specifying as part of the null hypothesis that a certain percentage of quadratic variation is due to jumps. On the other hand, these tests have the advantage that, if the test results in rejecting $\Omega_T^{(c)}$, they also give estimators for the relative sizes of the jump and continuous parts, that is, of the ratio $A(2)_T / C_T$ (or, equivalently, of $A(2)_T / [X, X]_T$, for the contribution of jumps to the overall variability of the process).

Next, we introduce in Section 10.3 procedures which allow us to treat the two possible hypotheses $\Omega_T^{(c)}$ and $\Omega_T^{(j)}$ in an almost symmetrical way. This approach also has the advantage of having model-free limits: they depend neither on the law of the process nor on the coefficients of the equation (10.1), and it does not require any preliminary estimation of these coefficients. In Section 10.4 we explain how to estimate the location and size of the jumps, at least for those whose size is bigger than a positive prescribed value, that is, we (partially) solve the third question; we also use this method to construct tests for jumps. Section 10.5 is concerned with the jumps of the volatility process, and in Section 10.6 we examine what happens when the price process is contaminated by microstructure noise.

Before proceeding, we must state a theoretically important caveat. Although the interest lies in the two complementary subsets $\Omega_T^{(c)}$ and $\Omega_T^{(j)}$, it is in fact impossible with the methods developed below to provide results when the outcome ω is such that $C_T(\omega) = 0$, that is, when the Brownian part has been completely inactive on $[0, T]$ because the volatility vanishes. In other words, if

$$
\begin{aligned}
\Omega_T^{(W)} &= \{\omega : C_T(\omega) > 0\}, \\
\Omega_T^{(cW)} &= \Omega_T^{(c)} \cap \Omega_T^{(W)}, \\
\Omega_T^{(jW)} &= \Omega_T^{(j)} \cap \Omega_T^{(W)},
\end{aligned}
\tag{10.6}
$$

our sets of interest will usually be $\Omega_T^{(cW)}$ and/or $\Omega_T^{(jW)}$ instead of $\Omega_T^{(c)}$ and/or $\Omega_T^{(j)}$. Here, the superscripts W stand for "the continuous martingale (or Wiener) part is not vanishing identically." The notion of a set $\Omega_T^{(cW)}$ may seem curious at first, but it is possible for a process to have continuous paths without a Brownian component if the process consists only of a pure drift. Let us finally mention that, in many models used in finance, we have $\Omega_T^{(W)} = \Omega$, but such models exclude all pure jump models. Of course, in a pure jump model, the question of whether jumps are present or not is meaningless.

10.2 Relative Sizes of the Jump and Continuous Parts and Testing for Jumps

This section is mainly concerned with the construction of a test based on the measure of the relative sizes of the "jump part" and the "continuous (or, Brownian) part" of the observed process X. The key point is obviously to find estimators for C_t and $A(2)_t$, or equivalently for C_t and $[X, X]_t = C_t + A(2)_t$. This question has essentially been solved in Chapter 6, although we need some complements, given in the first subsection below.

10.2.1 The Mathematical Tools

We start by recalling some notation. With $k \geq 2$ an integer, and a sequence of truncation levels u_n satisfying $u_n \asymp \Delta_n^\varpi$ 'for some $\varpi \in \left(0, \frac{1}{2}\right)$, that is, (6.24), we set

$$\widehat{C}(\Delta_n)_t = \sum_{i=1}^{[t/\Delta_n]} (\Delta_i^n X)^2$$
$$\widehat{C}(\Delta_n, u_n)_t = \sum_{i=1}^{[t/\Delta_n]} (\Delta_i^n X)^2 \, 1_{\{|\Delta_i^n X| \leq u_n\}}$$
$$\widehat{C}([k], \Delta_n)_t = \frac{1}{(m_{2/k})^k} \sum_{i=1}^{[t/\Delta_n]-k+1} \prod_{j=1}^{k} |\Delta_{i+j-1}^n X|^{2/k}.$$

Under Assumption (H-2), and as already mentioned, we have

$$\widehat{C}(\Delta_n) \overset{\mathbb{P}}{\Longrightarrow} [X, X],$$
$$\widehat{C}(\Delta_n, u_n) \overset{\text{u.c.p.}}{\Longrightarrow} C, \qquad\qquad (10.7)$$
$$\widehat{C}([k], \Delta_n) \overset{\text{u.c.p.}}{\Longrightarrow} C.$$

We also have associated Central Limit Theorems. The CLTs for $\widehat{C}(\Delta_n, u_n)$ and $\widehat{C}([k], \Delta_n)$ have been mentioned in Chapter 6, but here we need a joint CLT for these processes, together with $\widehat{C}(\Delta_n)$, which is stated as Theorem A.16. Namely, we have (recall that (KC) is (K-2) plus the continuity of X)

$$\text{under (H-}r\text{)}, \quad r < 1, \quad \tfrac{1}{2(2-r)} \leq \varpi < \tfrac{1}{2} :$$
$$(\tfrac{1}{\sqrt{\Delta_n}}(\widehat{C}(\Delta_n) - [X,X]), \tfrac{1}{\sqrt{\Delta_n}}(\widehat{C}(\Delta_n, u_n) - C))$$
$$\overset{\mathcal{L}\text{-}s}{\Longrightarrow} (\mathcal{U} + \mathcal{W}, \mathcal{W})$$

$$\text{under (P), (K-}r\text{)}, \quad k \geq 3, \quad r \leq \tfrac{2}{k}, \quad \tfrac{1}{2(2-r)} \leq \varpi < \tfrac{1}{2} :$$
$$(\tfrac{1}{\sqrt{\Delta_n}}(\widehat{C}(\Delta_n) - [X,X]), \tfrac{1}{\sqrt{\Delta_n}}(\widehat{C}(\Delta_n, u_n) - C), \qquad (10.8)$$
$$\tfrac{1}{\sqrt{\Delta_n}}(\widehat{C}([k], \Delta_n) - C)) \overset{\mathcal{L}\text{-}s}{\Longrightarrow} (\mathcal{U} + \mathcal{W}, \mathcal{W}, \mathcal{W}(k))$$

$$\text{under (P), (KC)}, \quad k \geq 2 :$$
$$(\tfrac{1}{\sqrt{\Delta_n}}(\widehat{C}(\Delta_n) - C), \tfrac{1}{\sqrt{\Delta_n}}(\widehat{C}([k], \Delta_n) - C)) \overset{\mathcal{L}\text{-}s}{\Longrightarrow} (\mathcal{W}, \mathcal{W}(k)).$$

Here, $\mathcal{U}$, $\mathcal{W}$, $\mathcal{W}(k)$ are defined on an extension $(\widetilde{\Omega}, \widetilde{\mathcal{F}}, (\widetilde{\mathcal{F}}_t)_{t \geq 0}, \widetilde{\mathbb{P}})$ of $(\Omega, \mathcal{F}, (\mathcal{F}_t)_{t \geq 0}, \mathbb{P})$ and, conditionally on $\mathcal{F}$, the process $\mathcal{U}$ is independent of the pair $(\mathcal{W}, \mathcal{W}(k))$, which is a continuous centered Gaussian martingale with variances-covariances given by

$$\widetilde{\mathbb{E}}((\mathcal{W}_t)^2 \mid \mathcal{F}) = 2C(4)_t$$
$$\widetilde{\mathbb{E}}((\mathcal{W}(k)_t)^2 \mid \mathcal{F}) = \vartheta(k)C(4)_t$$
$$\widetilde{\mathbb{E}}(\mathcal{W}_t \, \mathcal{W}(k)_t \mid \mathcal{F}) = \vartheta'(k)C(4)_t,$$

with $\vartheta(k)$ given by (6.39) and

$$\vartheta'(k) = \frac{k\,(m_{2+2/k} - m_{2/k})}{m_{2/k}}.$$

(Note that $\mathcal{W}$ and $\mathcal{W}(k)$ are as in Chapter 6, but here we provide the joint $\mathcal{F}$-conditional distribution.) Moreover, $\mathcal{U}$ is given by

$$\mathcal{U}_t = 2 \sum_{q \geq 1: T_q \leq t} \Delta X_{T_q} \big(\sqrt{\kappa_q}\, \sigma_{T_q -} \Psi_{q-} + \sqrt{1 - \kappa_q}\, \sigma_{T_q} \Psi_{q+} \big), \qquad (10.9)$$

with $(T_q)_{q \geq 1}$ a sequence of stopping times exhausting the jumps of X and κ_q, Ψ_{q-}, Ψ_{q+} being defined on the extension and mutually independent, independent of $\mathcal{F}$ and $(\mathcal{W}, \mathcal{W}(k))$, and κ_q is uniform over $[0, 1]$ and Ψ_{q+}, Ψ_{q-} are standard normal. So conditionally on $\mathcal{F}$ it is a centered process and, as soon as the processes X and σ never jump at the same times, it is Gaussian (but of course discontinuous).

The sum $\mathcal{U} + \mathcal{W}$ is of the form (1.87), with $V'_t = \sqrt{2}\,c_t$ and V_t being two-dimensional with the two components $2\Delta X_t \sigma_{t-}$ and $2\Delta X_t \sigma_t$, and the variables Y_q having the two components $\sqrt{\kappa_q}\,\Psi_{q-}$ and $\sqrt{1-\kappa_q}\,\Psi_{q+}$, and $V_{T_q}Y_q$ standing for the scalar product. In particular, we have the conditions (ii) of (1.84), and $\mathcal{U}$ is indeed well defined.

We do not give the joint CLT for $(\widehat{C}(\Delta_n),\widehat{C}(\Delta_n,u_n))$ when X is continuous, because in this case for any t we have $\widehat{C}(\Delta_n)_s = \widehat{C}(\Delta_n,u_n)_s$ for all $s \leq t$, as soon as n is large enough (depending on ω). The last statement in (10.8) with $k=1$ also holds, but reduces to the convergence of $\frac{1}{\sqrt{\Delta_n}}(\widehat{C}(\Delta_n)-C)$, because $\widehat{C}([1],\Delta_n) = \widehat{C}(\Delta_n)$ and $\mathcal{W}(1)=\mathcal{W}$.

10.2.2   A "Linear" Test for Jumps

A test for jumps can be constructed using the statistics $\widehat{C}(\Delta_n)$ (realized quadratic variation), which estimates $[X,X]$, and $\widehat{C}([k],\Delta_n)$ (multipower variations), which estimates C. We do not present all the different versions of those tests here since, although they have different practical characteristics, their mechanism boils down to either one of two procedures: the first one consists of using a "linear" test statistic; the second one consists of using "ratio" test statistics. We will show in particular that these two kinds of tests work under our current assumptions, which are significantly weaker than those in the existing literature.

The aim is to test the null hypothesis "no jump," that is, the outcome belongs to the set $\Omega_T^{(c)}$ of (10.5), where T is the (fixed) time horizon. The simplest idea consists of taking an integer $k \geq 2$ and using the following fact, under (H-2):

$$S^{(\mathrm{J-MP1})}(k,\Delta_n) := \widehat{C}(\Delta_n)_T - \widehat{C}([k],\Delta_n)_T$$

$$\xrightarrow{\ \mathbb{P}\ } \begin{cases} 0 & \text{on } \Omega_T^{(c)} \\ A(2)_T = \sum_{s\leq T}(\Delta X_s)^2 > 0 & \text{on } \Omega_T^{(j)}. \end{cases}$$

In view of (10.8), under (P) and (KC) (hence when X is continuous) the normalized statistics $\frac{1}{\sqrt{\Delta_n}}S^{(\mathrm{J-MP1})}(k,\Delta_n)$ converge stably in law to $\mathcal{W}_T - \mathcal{W}(k)_T$. When X has jumps but nevertheless the set $\Omega_T^{(c)}$ has a positive probability, we expect the same result, but only "in restriction to this set." Let us recall that, in contrast with the concept of convergence in law in restriction to a subset A of Ω, which is meaningless, stable convergence in law in restriction to A was discussed on page 95: we say that $Z_n \xrightarrow{\mathcal{L}-s} Z$ in restriction to A if

$$\mathbb{E}(f(Z_n)\,1_{A'}) \rightarrow \widetilde{\mathbb{E}}(f(Z)\,1_{A'})$$

for all bounded continuous functions f and all measurable subsets $A' \subset A$.

However, it turns out that the stable convergence in law of $\frac{1}{\sqrt{\Delta_n}} S^{(\text{J-MP1})}(k, \Delta_n)$ in restriction to $\Omega_T^{(c)}$ is *not* a straightforward consequence of (10.8), unless $\Omega_T^{(c)} = \Omega$ of course, and in view of the problem at hand we do not want to assume this equality here. We then explicitly show how to deduce this stable convergence in law in restriction to $\Omega_T^{(c)}$ from the same convergence when we have $\Omega_T^{(c)} = \Omega$ in the proof of the following theorem, at the end of the subsection. The same type of arguments will be used quite often later, and no proofs will be provided since they all are of the same sort.

Theorem 10.1. *Assuming (P) and (K-2), we have the following stable convergence in law:*

$$\frac{1}{\sqrt{\Delta_n}} S^{(\text{J-MP1})}(k, \Delta_n) \xrightarrow{\mathcal{L}-s} \widetilde{\mathcal{W}}(k) := \mathcal{W}_T - \mathcal{W}(k)_T \tag{10.10}$$
in restriction to the set $\Omega_T^{(c)}$,

and in particular the variable $\widetilde{\mathcal{W}}(k)_T$ is $\mathcal{F}$-conditionally centered normal with variance

$$\mathbb{E}(\widetilde{\mathcal{W}}(k)_T^2 \mid \mathcal{F}) = \vartheta''(k) C(4)_T, \quad \text{where } \vartheta''(k) = \vartheta(k) + 2(1 - \vartheta'(k)).$$

Let us come back to the construction of a test based on the statistic $S^{(\text{J-MP1})}(k, \Delta_n)$. Exactly as for (6.11), we need to standardize. To estimate the variable $C(4)_T$ we can use the variables $B^n(4, \Delta_n, u_n)_T / 3\Delta_n$ with a suitable cutoff sequence u_n, or $M([4, k'], \Delta_n)_T / (m_{4/k'})^{k'} \Delta_n$ (as defined by (6.34)) for some integer $k' \geq 2$, or $U'(\Delta_n, g)_T$ with $g(x) = x^2$, according to (8.48). Using for example the multipower estimator, which is natural here, we then obtain

$$\mathcal{L}\left(\frac{(m_{4/k'})^{k'/2}}{\sqrt{\vartheta''(k) M([4,k'],\Delta_n)_T}} S^{(\text{J-MP1})}(k, \Delta_n) \Big| A\right) \to \mathcal{N}(0,1), \tag{10.11}$$
if $A \in \mathcal{F}$, $A \subset \Omega_T^{(cW)}$, $\mathbb{P}(A) > 0$

(as usual, see e.g. (6.10), the ratio on the left side above is taken to be 0, or 1, or any other dummy value, when the denominator vanishes).

With a prescribed asymptotic level $\alpha \in (0, 1)$, we take at stage n the following critical (rejection) region:

$$C_n = \left\{ S^{(\text{J-MP1})}(k, \Delta_n) > z'_\alpha \sqrt{\frac{\vartheta''(k)}{(m_{4/k'})^{k'}}} \sqrt{M([4, k'], \Delta_n)_T} \right\}, \tag{10.12}$$

where z'_α is the α-quantile of $\mathcal{N}(0,1)$, that is, the number such that $\mathbb{P}(\Psi > z'_\alpha) = \alpha$ when Ψ is $\mathcal{N}(0,1)$. This test has the following property (we refer to Section 5.4 for the meaning of "strong asymptotic size" and "consistent" in the present setting, where the null and alternative hypotheses are subsets of the sample space Ω):

Theorem 10.2. *Assuming (P) and (K-2), the tests $\mathcal{C}_n$ defined above have the strong asymptotic size α for the null hypothesis $\Omega_T^{(cW)}$, and are consistent for the alternative $\Omega_T^{(j)}$.*

Proof. The claim about asymptotic size is a straightforward consequence of (10.11). The second claim amounts to $\mathbb{P}(\Omega_T^{(j)} \cap (\mathcal{C}_n)^c) \to 0$, and since $S^{(\text{J-MP1})}(k, \Delta_n)$ converges in probability to a positive limit in restriction to $\Omega_T^{(j)}$, it is clearly enough to prove that $M([4, k'], \Delta_n)_T \xrightarrow{\mathbb{P}} 0$. When $k' \geq 3$, this comes from Theorem A.2 of Appendix A with the test function $f(x_1, \ldots, x_{k'}) = \prod_{j=1}^{k'} |x_j|^{4/k'}$. For the case $k' = 2$ we observe that $M([4, 2], \Delta_n)_T \leq 2A_n^2 \widehat{C}(\Delta_n)_T$, where $A_n = \sup(\min(|\Delta_i^n X|, |\Delta_{i+1}^n X|) : i = 1, \ldots, [T/\Delta_n])$. The paths of X being càdlàg, we have $A_n \to 0$, and the property for $k' = 2$ follows. $\qquad\square$

Remark 10.3. *As mentioned before, we may use other estimators for $C(4)_T$. For example, with $u_n \asymp \Delta_n^\varpi$ for some $\varpi \in (0, \frac{1}{2})$, we can take $\frac{1}{3\Delta_n} B(4, \Delta_n, u_n)_T$, leading to the critical region*

$$\left\{ |S^{(\text{J-MP1})}(k, \Delta_n)| > z'_\alpha \sqrt{\vartheta''(k)/3} \sqrt{B(4, \Delta_n, u_n)_T} \right\}$$

(we have $B(4, \Delta_n, u_n)_T \leq u_n^2 \widehat{C}(\Delta_n)_T$, hence $B(4, \Delta_n, u_n)_T \xrightarrow{\mathbb{P}} 0$, hence the alternative-consistency).

Remark 10.4. *One might also think of taking the untruncated $\frac{1}{3\Delta_n} B(4, \Delta_n)_T$ as an estimator for $C(4)_T$, since the convergence is taken in restriction to the set $\Omega_T^{(c)}$. This leads to taking*

$$\left\{ |S^{(\text{J-MP1})}(k, \Delta_n)| > z'_\alpha \sqrt{\vartheta''(k)/3} \sqrt{B(4, \Delta_n)_T} \right\}.$$

These tests again have asymptotic size α. However, they are not consistent for the alternative $\Omega_T^{(j)}$, because $B(4, \Delta_n)_T$ does not go to 0 on the set $\Omega_T^{(j)}$. Hence such tests should be avoided.

Remark 10.5. *In the same line of thought, one could imagine taking advantage of the following convergence:*

$$S_n = \widehat{C}(\Delta_n)_T - \widehat{C}(\Delta_n, u_n)_T \xrightarrow{\mathbb{P}} \begin{cases} 0 & \text{on } \Omega_T^{(c)} \\ A(2)_T > 0 & \text{on } \Omega_T^{(j)} \end{cases}$$

when $u_n \asymp \Delta_n^\varpi$ for some $\varpi \in \left(0, \frac{1}{2}\right)$. However, not only do we have the first convergence above, but actually $S_n = 0$ for all n large enough (depending on ω) on the set $\Omega_T^{(c)}$ and, of course, there is no associated Central Limit Theorem.

In a sense this property looks like a wonderful thing, since asymptotically one can decide without error whether ω lies in $\Omega_T^{(c)}$ or in $\Omega_T^{(j)}$. But of course this is "too nice to be true" The problem lies here with the choice of the truncation level u_n: if it is large enough, all increments are kept and $S_n = 0$, whereas if it is too small, most increments are thrown away in $\widehat{C}(\Delta_n, u_n)_T$ and S_n is (artificially) large.

One could think of using the empirical rules established in Subsection 6.2.2 for choosing u_n. This typically leads to finding a positive value for S_n above, but there seems to be no way of mathematically asserting the size of S_n under the null $\Omega_T^{(c)}$ if we apply this rule. In other words, it seems impossible to base a test on S_n which achieves a prescribed asymptotic level.

Remark 10.6. *The previous tests work for testing the null $\Omega_T^{(cW)}$. Although we could derive from (10.8) a Central Limit Theorem for $S^{(J-MP1)}(k, \Delta_n)$ in restriction to the set $\Omega_T^{(jW)}$ as well, the centering term in this CLT is the unknown variable $A(2)_T$. Therefore it is not possible to base a test for the null $\Omega_T^{(jW)}$ on these statistics, if we want a given asymptotic level.*

Proof of Theorem 10.1. Suppose that there is a process X' such that

$$X' \text{ satisfies (KC) and (P) and } \mathbb{P}(\Omega_T^{(c)} \cap D_T^c) = 0, \qquad (10.13)$$
$$\text{where } D_T = \{\omega : X_s(\omega) = X'_s(\omega) \ \forall s \in [0,T]\}.$$

Letting $S'^{(J-MP1)}(k, \Delta_n)$ be the statistic associated with X' as $S^{(J-MP1)}(k, \Delta_n)$ is associated with X, we observe the following facts: on the one hand, $S'^{(J-MP1)}(k, \Delta_n) = S^{(J-MP1)}(k, \Delta_n)$ a.s. on $\Omega_T^{(c)}$ because $\mathbb{P}(\Omega_T^{(c)} \cap D_T^c) = 0$; on the other hand, we can apply (10.8) to X', yielding the stable convergence in law to a limit $\widetilde{\mathcal{W}}'(k)$ which, conditionally on $\mathcal{F}$, is centered Gaussian with variance $(m_{4/k})^k \vartheta''(k) C'(4)_T$, where $C'(4)$ is associated with X' as $C(4)$ is with X. The property $X'_s = X_s$ for all $s \leq T$ on the set $\Omega_T^{(c)}$ implies that the volatility σ' of X' satisfies $\sigma'_s = \sigma_s$ for $s \leq T$ on $\Omega_T^{(c)}$, up to a null set. Thus $C'(4)_T = C(4)_T$ a.s. on $\Omega_T^{(c)}$ and, conditional on $\mathcal{F}$ and on $\Omega_T^{(c)}$, the variables $\widetilde{\mathcal{W}}(k)$ and $\widetilde{\mathcal{W}}'(k)$ have the same law. It follows that $\mathbb{E}(f(S^{(J-MP1)}(k, \Delta_n)/\sqrt{\Delta_n}) 1_A) \to \widetilde{\mathbb{E}}(f(\widetilde{U}) 1_A)$ for all measurable subsets $A \subset \Omega_T^{(c)}$, which is (10.10). It remains to show

(10.13). We use the notation S and b_t' of (10.2), and the process X' will be

$$X_t' = X_0 + \int_0^t b_{s \wedge S}' \, ds + \int_0^t \sigma_s \, dW_s,$$

which satisfies (P) and (KC), because X satisfies (P) and (K-2). Then we set $R = \inf(t : \Delta X_t \neq 0)$, and let μ be the jump measure of X and ν be its compensator. Recall (1.67), that is,

$$X_t = X_0 + \int_0^t b_s \, ds + \int_0^t \sigma_s \, dW_s \tag{10.14}$$
$$+ (x \, 1_{\{|x| \le 1\}}) * (\mu - \nu)_t + (x \, 1_{\{|x| > 1\}}) * \mu_t.$$

By definition of R we have $1 * \mu_R \le 1$, hence $\mathbb{E}(1 * \nu_R) \le 1$ and $1 * \nu_R < \infty$ a.s. It follows first that $R \le S$ a.s., and second that we can rewrite (10.14) for $t \le R$ as

$$X_t = X_0 + B_t' + \int_0^t \sigma_s \, dW_s + x * \mu_t,$$

where

$$B_t' = \int_0^t b_s \, ds - (x \, 1_{\{|x| \le 1\}}) * \nu_t.$$

Moreover, $x * \mu_t = 0$ when $t < R$, whereas the connection between the representation (10.14) and the Grigelionis representation of X shows that indeed $B_t' = \int_0^t b_s' \, ds$ when $t \le S$. In other words, we have $X_t = X_t'$ a.s. for all $t < R$. Since obviously $R > T$ on the set $\Omega_T^{(c)}$, we have proved the last part of (10.13), and the proof is complete. $\qquad \square$

10.2.3 A "Ratio" Test for Jumps

The test (10.12) is "scale-free" in the sense that if we multiply the process X by a constant γ, the critical region $\mathcal{C}_n$ is unchanged. The statistic $S^{(\text{J-MP1})}(k, \Delta_n)$, though, is multiplied by γ^2. One might expect, perhaps, more stability if one chooses right away a scale-free statistic. This is achieved, for example, by the following ratio statistic:

$$S^{(\text{J-MP2})}(k, \Delta_n) = \frac{\widehat{C}([k], \Delta_n)_T}{\widehat{C}(\Delta_n)_T}. \tag{10.15}$$

The behavior of these statistics is easily deduced from (10.7), although we must be careful because of the presence of the denominator. Once more, we arbitrarily take $S^{(\text{J-MP2})}(k, \Delta_n) = 1$, for example, when $\widehat{C}(\Delta_n)_T = 0$ (that is, when $X_{i\Delta_n} = X_0$ for all i, a situation which *never* occurs in practice). In the limit, the denominator $[X, X]_T$ vanishes if and only if

$X_t = X_0 + \int_0^t b_s ds$ for all $t \leq T$. Again, this situation never occurs for any model used in finance. Then we have under (H-2)

$$S^{(\text{J-MP2})}(k, \Delta_n) \overset{\mathbb{P}}{\longrightarrow} \begin{cases} 1 & \text{on } \Omega_T^{(cW)} \\ C_T/[X, X]_T < 1 & \text{on } \Omega_T^{(j)}. \end{cases} \qquad (10.16)$$

The behavior on $\Omega_T^{(c)} \backslash \Omega_T^{(cW)}$ is not interesting for us, and not known in general, although when the process b is càdlàg the limit is known to be again 1 on this set.

Next, since $S^{(\text{J-MP2}))}(k, \Delta_n) = 1 - S^{(\text{J-MP1})}(k, \Delta_n)/\widehat{C}(\Delta_n)_T$, we deduce from $\widehat{C}(\Delta_n)_T \overset{\mathbb{P}}{\longrightarrow} C_T$ on $\Omega_T^{(c)}$ and from (10.10) that, as soon as X satisfies (P) and (K-2),

$$\frac{1}{\sqrt{\Delta_n}} \left(S^{(\text{J-MP2})}(k, \Delta_n) - 1 \right) \overset{\mathcal{L}-s}{\longrightarrow} - \frac{\widetilde{\mathcal{W}}(k)}{C_T} = - \frac{\widetilde{\mathcal{W}}(k)}{[X, X]_T}$$
in restriction to the set $\Omega_T^{(cW)}$.

The standardized version, analogous to (10.11), goes as follows:

$$\mathcal{L}\left(\frac{(m_{4/k})^{k/2} \sqrt{\widehat{C}(\Delta_n)_T}}{\sqrt{\vartheta''(k) \, M([4, k], \Delta_n)_T}} \left(S^{(\text{J-MP2})}(k, \Delta_n) - 1 \right) \Big| A \right) \to \mathcal{N}(0, 1)$$
if $A \in \mathcal{F}$, $A \subset \Omega_T^{(cW)}$, $\mathbb{P}(A) > 0$,

and a natural critical region at stage n is then

$$\mathcal{C}_n = \left\{ S^{(\text{J-MP2})}(k, \Delta_n) < 1 - z'_\alpha \frac{\sqrt{\vartheta''(k) \, M([4, k], \Delta_n)_T}}{\sqrt{(m_{4/k})^k \, \widehat{C}(\Delta_n)_T}} \right\}. \qquad (10.17)$$

Note that we could substitute $\widehat{C}(\Delta_n)_T$ in these two formulas with $\widehat{C}(\Delta_n, u_n)_T$ or $\widehat{C}([k], \Delta_n)_T$.

Exactly as for Theorem 10.2, we then have

Theorem 10.7. *Assuming (P) and (K-2), the tests $\mathcal{C}_n$ defined in (10.17) have the strong asymptotic level α for the null hypothesis $\Omega_T^{(cW)}$, and are consistent for the alternative $\Omega_T^{(j)}$.*

Mutatis mutandis, Remarks 10.3, 10.5 and 10.6 are valid here. We can also observe that it is possible to use other ratios. Indeed, $S^{(\text{J-MP2})}(k, \Delta_n)$ measures the ratio between the (squared) contribution of the continuous martingale part, versus the global contribution. One could prefer the ratios $(\widehat{C}(\Delta_n)_T - \widehat{C}([k], \Delta_n)/C(\Delta_n)_T$ or $(\widehat{C}(\Delta_n)_T - \widehat{C}([k], \Delta_n)_T)/\widehat{C}([k], \Delta_n)_T$, the latter being the ratio between the jump part and the continuous part, for example. The first ratio above is of course $1 - S^{(\text{J-MP2})}(k, \Delta_n)$. The second has an interesting practical meaning, and its behavior is

$$\frac{\widehat{C}(\Delta_n)_T - \widehat{C}([k], \Delta_n)_T}{\widehat{C}([k], \Delta_n)_T} \xrightarrow{\mathbb{P}} \begin{cases} 0 & \text{on } \Omega_T^{(cW)} \\ A(2)_T/C_T & \text{on } \Omega_T^{(j)} \end{cases}$$

with the last expression equal to $+\infty$ on the set $\Omega_T^{(j)} \cap \{C_T = 0\}$. The construction of tests based on these other ratios is completely similar to what precedes, and those tests have the same asymptotic properties.

10.2.4 Relative Sizes of the Jump and Brownian Parts

In this part, we compare the (cumulative) sizes of jumps to the size of the Brownian part, and, as noted before, this is usually done by comparing the respective contributions to the quadratic variation, which are $A(2)_T$ and C_T.

This can be achieved by using the ratios $A(2)_T/[X,X]_T$ or $C_T/[X,X]_T$ (which compare the jump part, or the continuous part, to the overall quadratic variation), or the ratios $A(2)_T/C_T$ or $C_T/A(2)_T$ (which compare the jump part to the continuous part, and vice versa). There are obvious relationships between these various ratios, so for concreteness we focus on the percentage of quadratic variation (QV) due to the continuous part:

$$S = \frac{C_T}{[X,X]_T},$$

which is well defined on the set $\Omega_T^{(cW)} \cup \Omega_T^{(j)} = \{[X,X]_T > 0\}$.

This ratio can be estimated by the statistics $S^{(\text{J-MP2})}(k, \Delta_n)$ of (10.16), and also by

$$S^{(\text{J-TR})}(\Delta_n, u_n) = \frac{\widehat{C}(\Delta_n, u_n)_T}{\widehat{C}(\Delta_n)_T}. \tag{10.18}$$

While $S^{(\text{J-TR})}(\Delta_n, u_n)$ splits C_T into a continuous and a jump component, it is possible to further split the jump part of $[X,X]_T$ into a small and a big jump component, as illustrated in Figure 10.1, based on any arbitrary finite cutoff ε for the jump size. The split between the continuous and jump parts is properly defined; that between small and big jumps depends on the definition of "small" and "big", namely on ε.

Both $S_n^{(\text{J-MP2})}$ and $S_n^{(\text{J-TR})}$ go in probability to S, in restriction to the set $\{[X,X]_T > 0\}$.

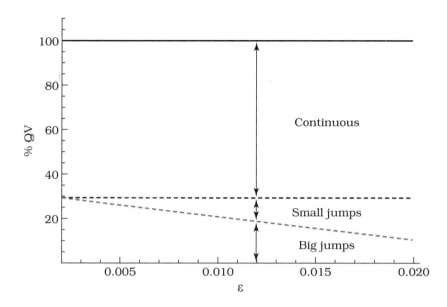

Figure 10.1: Splitting up the QV into continuous and jump components, and into small and big jumps as a function of the jump size cutoff ε.

Figure 10.2 shows the empirical results for the statistics (10.18) obtained from computing the fraction of quadratic variation from the Brownian component using the four quarters of the years, values of u_n ranging from 2 to 5 standard deviations, in increments of 1, and Δ_n from 5 seconds to 2 minutes in the same increments as earlier. Unfiltered transactions are marked U, filtered transactions are marked F and the NBBO midpoint quotes are marked M. We find values around 75% for F and U, and somewhat lower for M, around 60% with some stock/quarter samples leading to values that are in fact indicative of an almost pure jump process in the quotes data.

In the middle right panel (similar but as a function of Δ_n), we see that the estimated fraction is fairly stable as we vary the sampling frequency. It is also quite stable for the two different measurements of the transactions data, F and U, and the quotes data M, going up slightly as the sampling frequency decreases. The lower panels show a more pronounced increase in the Brownian-driven part of QV as a function of the asset's liquidity: using both measures, we find that more liquid assets are associated with a higher proportion of Brownian-driven QV.

In the case of the DJIA index, we find values that range from 85% to 95%, suggesting in line with the previous evidence that jumps are less

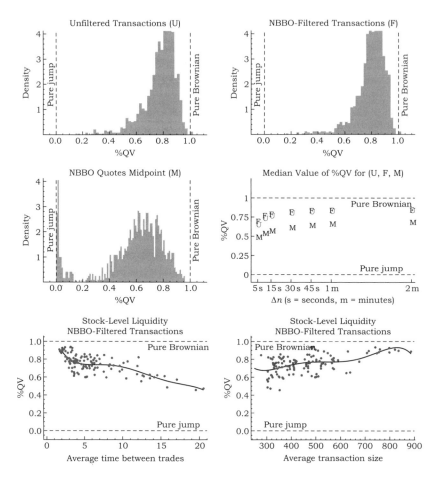

Figure 10.2: Estimating the proportion of QV attributable to the continuous component: Empirical distribution of the proportion of QV attributable to the continuous component for the 30 DJIA stocks, 2006, measured using transactions (unfiltered, U, and NBBO-filtered, F) and NBBO quotes midpoint (M), median value of $\%QV$ as a function of the sampling interval Δ_n, and nonlinear regression of $\%QV$ against stock-level liquidity measures.

of a factor for the index. Incidentally, one could imagine measuring the proportion of jumps that are systematic vs. those that are idiosyncratic on the basis of the comparison between %QV estimated for the index and for its components.

As seen before, on $\Omega_T^{(cW)}$ we have a Central Limit Theorem for $S_n^{(\text{J-MP2})}$, whereas $S_n^{(\text{J-TR})} = 1$ for all n large enough (see Remark 10.5 for comments about this – too good – result). However, when X is continuous it does not make much sense to evaluate the proportion of jumps. In other words, one really would like to estimate S only when this number is strictly between 0 and 1, that is, in restriction to the set $\Omega_T^{(jW)}$ defined in (10.6). In a sense, this supposes that, prior to estimating S, one has performed a test about the presence of jumps and concluded that there were jumps on $[0, T]$ (for example the null hypothesis in one of the tests described in the previous subsections has been rejected).

Now, (10.8) and the "delta method" allow us to get the following CLTs for the two statistics $S^{(\text{J-MP2})}(k, \Delta_n)$ and $S^{(\text{J-TR})}(\Delta_n, u_n)$, and *in restriction to the set* $\Omega_T^{(jW)}$:

$$
\begin{aligned}
\text{(P), (K-2/}k), \ k \geq 3 \quad &\Rightarrow \quad \frac{1}{\sqrt{\Delta_n}}\left(S^{(\text{J-MP2})}(k, \Delta_n) - S\right) \\
&\qquad\qquad \xrightarrow{\mathcal{L}\text{-}s} \mathcal{S}^{(\text{J-MP2})}(k) \\[2ex]
\text{(H-}r), r < 1, \quad &\Rightarrow \quad \frac{1}{\sqrt{\Delta_n}}\left(S^{(\text{J-TR})}(\Delta_n, u_n) - S\right) \\
\tfrac{1}{2(2-r)} \leq \varpi < \tfrac{1}{2}, \quad &\qquad\qquad \xrightarrow{\mathcal{L}\text{-}s} \mathcal{S}^{(\text{J-TR})}
\end{aligned}
\tag{10.19}
$$

(recall $u_n \asymp \Delta_n^{\varpi}$), where the variables $\mathcal{S}^{(\text{J-MP2})}(k)$ and $\mathcal{S}^{(\text{J-TR})}$ are defined on the extended space, with the help of the processes $\mathcal{U}$, $\mathcal{W}$ and $\mathcal{W}(k)$ described in Subsection 10.2.1, by the following formulas:

$$
\begin{aligned}
\mathcal{S}^{(\text{J-MP2})}(k) &= -\frac{C_T}{[X,X]_T^2}\,\mathcal{U}_T + \frac{1}{[X,X]_T}\,\mathcal{W}(k)_T - \frac{C_T}{[X,X]_T^2}\,\mathcal{W}_T \\
\mathcal{S}^{(\text{J-TR})} &= -\frac{C_T}{[X,X]_T^2}\,\mathcal{U}_T + \frac{A(2)_T}{[X,X]_T^2}\,\mathcal{W}_T.
\end{aligned}
\tag{10.20}
$$

It is interesting to observe that the CLT for $S^{(\text{J-TR})}(\Delta_n, u_n)$ needs far fewer assumptions than the CLT for $S^{(\text{J-MP2})}(k, \Delta_n)$, and in particular it needs no assumption on the stochastic volatility σ_t other than being càdlàg (and even this could be relaxed, and replaced by the fact that $C(4)_t < \infty$ for all t: see Theorem 5.4.2 of Jacod and Protter (2011)). Moreover, the next proposition shows that when both CLTs hold, the estimators $S^{(\text{J-TR})}(\Delta_n, u_n)$ are *always asymptotically better* than the estimators $S^{(\text{J-MP2})}(k, \Delta_n)$, in the sense that the asymptotic $\mathcal{F}$-conditional variance of the former is less than that of the latter. We even have a *convolution theorem*, as in asymptotic statistics in a situation where the so-called LAMN property holds, see Jeganathan (1982) or Le Cam and Yang (1990). This is of course not surprising since, were we in a usual parametric setting (as when $\sigma_t = \sigma$ is simply a constant to be estimated, or in the state-dependent case $\sigma_t = f(t, X_t, \theta)$ with an unknown parameter θ and a known function f), the (parametric) LAMN property typically would hold; see Dohnal (1987) or Genon-Catalot and Jacod (1994).

Proposition 10.8. *When $k \geq 3$ and (P) and (K-2/k) hold, and in restriction to the set $\Omega_T^{(jW)}$, the $\mathcal{F}$-conditional distribution of the limiting variables $\mathcal{S}^{(\text{J-MP2})}(k)$ is the convolution of the $\mathcal{F}$-conditional distribution of $\mathcal{S}^{(\text{J-TR})}$ and of the law $\mathcal{N}(0, \Sigma_k^2)$, where Σ_k^2 is an $\mathcal{F}$-measurable positive variable.*

Proof. Not only do we have the two convergences in (10.19), but the joint convergence also holds by (10.8). With the simplifying notation $\alpha = -C_T/[X, X]_T^2$ and $\beta = 1/[X, X]_T$ (two positive random variables on $\Omega_T^{(jW)}$), and observing that $A(2)_T/[X, X]_T^2 = \alpha + \beta$, the limit of the pair of normalized centered statistics is $(\mathcal{S}^{(\text{J-MP2})}(k), \mathcal{S}^{(J-TR)})$, where

$$
\begin{aligned}
\mathcal{S}^{(\text{J-MP2})}(k) &= \alpha \mathcal{U}_T + \beta \mathcal{W}(k)_T + \alpha \mathcal{W}_T, \\
\mathcal{S}^{J-TR} &= \alpha \mathcal{U}_T + (\alpha + \beta) \mathcal{W}_T.
\end{aligned}
$$

These two variables are the sums of a "common summand" $\alpha \mathcal{U}_T$, plus two $\mathcal{F}$-conditionally centered Gaussian variables, independent of $\mathcal{U}_t$, and with respective variances

$$
\begin{aligned}
a &= \left(\beta^2 \vartheta(k) + 2\alpha\beta\vartheta'(k) + 2\alpha^2 \right) C(4)_T, \\
a' &= 2(\alpha + \beta)^2 C(4)_T .
\end{aligned}
$$

Then the result will follow with $\Sigma^2 = a - a'$, provided we can show that $a > a'$ on $\Omega_T^{(jW)}$. This amounts to having $f(\alpha/\beta) > 0$, where $f(x) = \vartheta(k) + 2x(\vartheta'(k) - 2) - 2$. Since $\alpha/\beta \in (-1, 0)$ on the set $\Omega_T^{(jW)}$, it is enough to prove that $f(0) \geq 0$ and $f(-1) \geq 0$. The first one of these two properties is $\vartheta(k) \geq 2$, which was seen in Chapter 6; the second one follows from the fact that $f(-1)$ is the $\mathcal{F}$-conditional variance of $\mathcal{W}(k)_T - \mathcal{W}_T$, divided by $C(4)_T$. $\quad\square$

Taking this result into account, we use $S^{(\text{J-TR})}(\Delta_n, u_n)$ for estimating S below, but the following arguments would apply exactly as well for $S^{(\text{J-MP2})}(k, \Delta_n)$, would one prefer to use it (on the basis, for example, that it does not require the tuning parameter u_n).

Since (weakly) consistent estimators are available, the next step is to give a *confidence interval*, which is very similar to deriving tests. However, we need to single out two cases, and before doing this we introduce the following notation, for any $p \geq 2$:

$$D(p)_t = \sum_{s \leq t} |\Delta X_s|^p (c_{s-} + c_s). \tag{10.21}$$

Case 1: The Processes X and σ Do Not Jump Together

The reason for singling out this case is that it allows us to rewrite $\mathcal{U}$ as

$$\mathcal{U}_t = 2 \sum_{q \geq 1} \Delta X_{T_q} \sigma_{T_q} \Psi_q 1_{\{T_q \leq t\}}, \tag{10.22}$$

where $\Psi_q = \sqrt{\kappa_q} \Psi_{q-} + \sqrt{1 - \kappa_q} \Psi_{q+}$ is again standard normal. An important consequence of this specific form is that the process $\mathcal{U}$ is $\mathcal{F}$-conditionally a centered Gaussian martingale, with (conditional) variance given by (since $c_{s-} = c_s$ when $\Delta X_s \neq 0$)

$$\mathbb{E}(\mathcal{U}_t^2 \mid \mathcal{F}) = 2D(2)_t = 4 \sum_{s \leq t} (\Delta X_s)^2 c_s$$

(the main difference between $\mathcal{U}$ and $\mathcal{W}$ here is that $\mathcal{W}$ is continuous, whereas $\mathcal{U}$ is purely discontinuous). Therefore, the limiting variable $\mathcal{S}^{(\text{J-TR})}$ is $\mathcal{F}$-conditionally a centered Gaussian variable with (conditional) variance

$$\mathbb{E}((\mathcal{S}^{(\text{J-TR})})^2 \mid \mathcal{F}) = 2 \frac{C_T^2 D(2)_T + A(2)_T^2 C(4)_T}{[X, X]_T^4}. \tag{10.23}$$

Exactly as for the tests described before, we need weakly consistent estimators for this expression. To this end, we use the following convergences (see (6.26) for the latter one):

$$\widehat{C}(\Delta_n)_T \xrightarrow{\mathbb{P}} [X, X]_T,$$
$$\widehat{C}(\Delta_n, u_n)_T \xrightarrow{\mathbb{P}} C_T, \tag{10.24}$$
$$\frac{1}{\Delta_n} B(4, \Delta_n, u_n)_T \xrightarrow{\mathbb{P}} 3 C(4)_T,$$

which have already been used before, and we need also estimators for $D(2)_T$, which is more difficult.

To solve this problem, we use the spot volatility estimators of Chapter 8, see (8.8). More specifically, we choose a sequence k_n of integers with the following property:

$$k_n \to \infty, \qquad k_n \Delta_n \to 0. \tag{10.25}$$

Then we set

$$
\begin{aligned}
\widehat{c}(k_n, [k])_i &= \frac{1}{(m_{2/k})^k k_n \Delta_n} \\
&\quad \times \sum_{m=0}^{k_n-1} |\Delta_{i+m}^n X|^{2/k} \cdots |\Delta_{i+m+k-1}^n X|^{2/k} \\
\widehat{c}(k_n, u_n)_i &= \frac{1}{k_n \Delta_n} \sum_{m=0}^{k_n-1} (\Delta_{i+m}^n X)^2 \, 1_{\{|\Delta_{i+m}^n X| \le u_n\}}.
\end{aligned}
\tag{10.26}
$$

Next, we take a sequence $w_n \asymp \Delta_n^{\varpi'}$ for some $\varpi' \in (0, 1/2)$. We choose $\widehat{c}_i^n$ to be either $\widehat{c}(k_n, [k])_i$ or $\widehat{c}(k_n, u_n)_i$, as defined above, and set $k = 1$ in the second case. Finally, we set for any $p > 0$

$$
\begin{aligned}
D(\Delta_n, p)_t &= \sum_{i=k_n+k}^{[t/\Delta_n]-k_n-k+1} |\Delta_i^n X|^p \, 1_{\{|\Delta_i^n X| > w_n\}} \\
&\quad \times \big(\widehat{c}_{i-k_n-k+1}^n + \widehat{c}_{i+1}^n\big).
\end{aligned}
\tag{10.27}
$$

(The bounds are designed in such a way that these variables, for any given t, use all increments of X within $[0, t]$, and no increment extending after time t.) Then, by Theorem A.7 of Appendix A, applied with the function $g(y, y') = y + y'$, we have the following convergences (for the Skorokhod topology), as soon as $p \ge 2$:

$$
D(\Delta_n, p) \overset{\mathbb{P}}{\Longrightarrow} D(p).
\tag{10.28}
$$

Remark 10.9. *The upward truncation at level w_n serves the same purpose of "separating" the increments due to relatively big jumps from the others, as the truncation u_n in $\widehat{c}(k_n, u_n)_i$. Therefore it is natural (although not necessary) to take here the version $\widehat{c}_i^n = \widehat{c}(k_n, u_n)_i$, and also $w_n = u_n$, and again the same u_n in the definition of $B(4, \Delta_n, u_n)$.*

Let us now come back to the problem at hand. In view of (10.19) and (10.23), we obtain under (H-r) for some $r < 1$ and u_n such that $\frac{1}{2(2-r)} \le \varpi < \frac{1}{2}$

$$
\begin{aligned}
&\mathcal{L}\Big(\tfrac{1}{\sqrt{V_n}} \big(S^{(\text{J-TR})}(\Delta_n, u_n) - S\big) \,\big|\, A\Big) \to \mathcal{N}(0, 1), \\
&\text{for all } A \in \mathcal{F} \text{ with } A \subset \Omega_T^{(jW)} \text{ and } \mathbb{P}(A) > 0,
\end{aligned}
$$

where

$$
\begin{aligned}
V_n &= \frac{1}{3(\widehat{C}(\Delta_n)_T)^4} \Big\{ 6\Delta_n (\widehat{C}(\Delta_n, u_n)_T)^2 \, D(\Delta_n, 2)_T \\
&\quad + 2(\widehat{C}(\Delta_n)_T - \widehat{C}(\Delta_n, u_n)_T)^2 \, B(4, \Delta_n, u_n)_T \Big\}.
\end{aligned}
\tag{10.29}
$$

At this point, it is straightforward to construct a confidence interval with asymptotic level $\alpha \in (0,1)$ for S. Denoting again by z_α the α-absolute quantile of $\mathcal{N}(0,1)$, at stage n we take the following confidence interval for the ratio $S = C_T/[X,X]_T$:

$$
\mathcal{I}_n = [S^{(\text{J-TR})}(\Delta_n, u_n) - a_n, S^{(\text{J-TR})}(\Delta_n, u_n) + a_n], \\
\text{where } a_n = z_\alpha \sqrt{V_n}.
\tag{10.30}
$$

Then, exactly as in (6.13), we have

Theorem 10.10. *Under (H-r) for some $r < 1$ and $\frac{1}{2(2-r)} \leq \varpi < \frac{1}{2}$ in (10.8), the confidence interval (10.30) has asymptotic level α in restriction to $\Omega_T^{(jW)}$, in the sense that*

$$
\lim_n \mathbb{P}(S \notin \mathcal{I}_n \mid A) = \alpha \\
\text{for all } A \in \mathcal{F} \text{ with } \mathbb{P}(A) > 0 \text{ and } A \subset \Omega_T^{(jW)}.
\tag{10.31}
$$

Case 2: The Processes X and σ May Jump Together

In this case (10.22) fails, and the process $\mathcal{U}$ is no longer $\mathcal{F}$-conditionally Gaussian. The previous argument for constructing a confidence interval breaks down, and there are two ways to solve the problem.

A conservative confidence interval Although the limiting variable $\mathcal{S}^{(\text{J-TR})}$ is no longer $\mathcal{F}$-conditionally Gaussian in this case, it is still $\mathcal{F}$-conditionally centered and satisfies (10.23). Hence its $\mathcal{F}$-conditional variance is again estimated by the variables V_n of (10.29), and we deduce from (10.24) and (10.28) that

$$
\mathcal{L}\Big(\frac{1}{\sqrt{V_n}}\big(S^{(\text{J-TR})}(\Delta_n, u_n) - S\big) \,\big|\, A\Big) \to \mathcal{L}_A, \\
\text{for all } A \in \mathcal{F} \text{ with } A \subset \Omega_T^{(jW)} \text{ and } \mathbb{P}(A) > 0
$$

where $\mathcal{L}_A$ is a distribution which *a priori* depends on the set A and is in general unknown, but whose mean and variance are known and equal respectively to 0 and 1. Therefore, if we define a confidence interval for S by

$$
\mathcal{I}_n = [S^{(\text{J-TR})}(\Delta_n, u_n) - a_n, S^{(\text{J-TR})}(\Delta_n, u_n) + a_n], \\
\text{where } a_n = \sqrt{V_n/\alpha},
\tag{10.32}
$$

and by virtue of the Bienaymé-Tchebycheff inequality, we obtain the following:

Theorem 10.11. *Under (H-r) for some $r < 1$ and $\frac{1}{2(2-r)} \le \varpi < \frac{1}{2}$ in (10.8), the confidence interval (10.32) satisfies*

$$\limsup_n \ \mathbb{P}(S \notin \mathcal{I}_n \mid A) \ \le \ \alpha$$
$$\textit{for all } A \in \mathcal{F} \textit{ with } \mathbb{P}(A) > 0 \textit{ and } A \subset \Omega_T^{(jW)}. \tag{10.33}$$

This has to be compared with (10.31), and here the inequality is strict in general.

A sharp confidence interval In order to avoid a strict inequality in (10.33), which leads to an unnecessarily large confidence interval, we can also use a Monte Carlo approach.

Indeed, what we really need is the α-absolute quantile of the limiting variable $\mathcal{S}^{(\text{J-TR})}$, that is, the (random, $\mathcal{F}$-measurable) number Z_α such that

$$\widetilde{\mathbb{P}}(|\mathcal{S}^{(\text{J-TR})}| > Z_\alpha \mid \mathcal{F}) \ = \ \alpha.$$

This variable cannot be exactly calculated, but it can be estimated by means of a Monte Carlo technique which we now explain. Recall from (10.20) that

$$\mathcal{S}^{(\text{J-TR})} = \frac{2C_T}{[X,X]_T^2} \sum_{q \ge 1} \Delta X_{T_q} \left(\sqrt{\kappa_q} \sigma_{T_q-} \Psi_{q-} + \sqrt{1-\kappa_q} \sigma_{T_q} \Psi_{q+} \right) 1_{\{T_q \le t\}}$$
$$+ \frac{\sqrt{2C(4)_T \, A(2)_T}}{[X,X]_T^2} \, \Psi',$$

where $(\Psi_{q-}, \Psi_{q+}, \kappa_q)$ are as in (10.9) and Ψ' is another $\mathcal{N}(0,1)$ variable, independent of everything else (the sign in front of the first term of the right side above has been changed, but this is immaterial because Ψ_{q-} and Ψ_{q+} are symmetrical). We also use once more the notation (10.26) and choose $\widehat{c}_i^n$ to be either $\widehat{c}(k_n, [k])_i$ or $\widehat{c}(k_n, u_n)_i$, in which case we set $k = 1$. Then, the procedure is as follows:

1. We replace C_T, $[X, X]_T$, $C(4)_T$ and $A(2)_T$ by their estimators, namely $\widehat{C}(\Delta_n, u_n)_T$, $\widehat{C}(\Delta_n)_T$, $B(4, \Delta_n, u_n)/3\Delta_n$ and $\widehat{C}(\Delta_n)_T - \widehat{C}(\Delta_n, u_n)_T$. Then we set $\Omega_n = \{\widehat{C}(\Delta_n)_T > \widehat{C}(\Delta_n, u_n)_T > 0\}$, and we observe that 1_{Ω_n} converges in probability to $1_{\Omega_T^{(jW)}}$ (equivalently, one could use $\widehat{C}([k], \Delta_n)_T$ and/or $M([4, k], \Delta_n)_T/(m_{4/k})^k \Delta_n$ instead of $\widehat{C}(\Delta_n, u_n)_T$ and $B(4, \Delta_n, u_n)/3\Delta_n$, but for simplicity we use the truncated versions below).

2. If the observed outcome ω is not in Ω_n, we should stop here: perhaps we are not in $\Omega_T^{(jW)}$, or we do not have enough data to go on. Otherwise, we proceed.

3. We pretend that the jump times T_q which are "significant" are in intervals $((i-1)\Delta_n, i\Delta_n]$ for which $|\Delta_i^n X| > u_n$ and $k + k_n \leq i \leq [T/\Delta_n] - k_n - k + 1$. These i's are labeled $i_1, i_2, \ldots, i_{r(n)}$ ($r(n)$ is the (random) total number of such i's, and $r(n) \geq 1$ because $\widehat{C}(\Delta_n)_T > \widehat{C}(\Delta_n, u_n)_T)$. Then we "replace" $(\Delta X_{T_q}, \sigma_{T_q-}, \sigma_{T_q})$ by $(\Delta_{i_q}^n X, \sqrt{\widetilde{c}_{i_q - k_n - k}^n}, \sqrt{\widetilde{c}_{i_q}^n})$.

4. We draw N_n copies of $(\Psi_{q-}, \Psi_{q+}, \kappa_q, \Psi')$, for q running from 1 to $r(n)$, say $(\Psi_{q-}^j, \Psi_{q+}^j, \kappa_q^j, \Psi'^j)$ for $j = 1, \ldots, N_n$, all independent.

5. We compute the N_n variables (well defined on Ω_n), for $j = 1, \ldots, N_n$:

$$S_n^j = \frac{2\widehat{C}(\Delta_n, u_n)_T}{\widehat{C}(\Delta_n)_T^2} \sum_{q=1}^{r(n)} \Delta_{i_q}^n X \left(\sqrt{\kappa_q^j \widehat{c}_{i_q - k_n}^n} \, \Psi_{q-}^j \right.$$
$$\left. + \sqrt{(1 - \kappa_q^j) \widehat{c}_{i_q + 1}^n} \, \Psi_{q+}^j \right) \tag{10.34}$$
$$+ \frac{\sqrt{2B^n(4, \Delta_n, u_n)_T / 3\Delta_n}}{\widehat{C}(\Delta_n)_T^2} \left(\widehat{C}(\Delta_n)_T - \widehat{C}(\Delta_n, u_n)_T \right) \Psi'^j.$$

6. We denote by Z_n^α the α-absolute quantile of the empirical distribution of the family $(S_n^j : 1 \leq j \leq N_n)$, that is, we reorder these N_n variables so that $|S_n^1| \geq |S_n^2| \geq \cdots \geq |S_n^{N_n}|$, and we set $Z_n^\alpha = |S_n^{[\alpha N_n]}|$.

7. We terminate the procedure by taking the following confidence interval:
$$\mathcal{I}_n = [S^{(\text{J-TR})}(\Delta_n, u_n) - a_n, S^{(\text{J-TR})}(\Delta_n, u_n) + a_n], \tag{10.35}$$
where $a_n = Z_n^\alpha \sqrt{\Delta_n}$.

As stated in the following theorem, this confidence interval has the asymptotic level α. In this theorem one has to be careful about the notation, since we have introduced some extra randomness through the Monte Carlo. It is of course not a restriction to suppose that the additional variables $(\Psi_{q-}^j, \Psi_{q+}^j, \kappa_q^j, \Psi'^j)$ are defined on the same extension $(\widetilde{\Omega}, \widetilde{\mathcal{F}}, \widetilde{\mathbb{P}})$ of the original probability space, and they all are independent of the σ-field $\mathcal{F}$. But now the confidence interval $\mathcal{I}_n$ is defined on the extension, although it is a "feasible" interval (the proof of the next theorem is rather involved, and provided in Appendix B, Subsection B.3.1).

Theorem 10.12. *Assume (H-r) for some $r \in [0, 1)$, and take $u_n \asymp \Delta_n^\varpi$ with $\frac{1}{2(2-r)} \leq \varpi < \frac{1}{2}$. Then, as soon as the number of Monte Carlo experiments N_n goes to infinity as $n \to \infty$, the interval (10.35) satisfies*
$$\widetilde{\mathbb{P}}(S \notin \mathcal{I}_n \mid A) \to \alpha \quad \text{if } A \in \mathcal{F}, \, P(A) > 0, \, A \subset \Omega_T^{(jW)}. \tag{10.36}$$

Remark 10.13. *The reader will have noticed that we always assume* $(H\text{-}r)$ *for some* $r < 1$ *and* $\frac{1}{2(2-r)} \leq \varpi < \frac{1}{2}$, *when we construct a confidence interval. If* $(H\text{-}r)$ *fails for all* $r < 1$, *no Central Limit Theorem is available, and no confidence interval as well: this fact is of course of the same nature as the restriction* $r < 1$ *in Theorem 6.9, for example.*

10.2.5   Testing the Null $\Omega_T^{(c)}$ instead of $\Omega_T^{(cW)}$

As the reader already noticed, in the previous tests the null hypothesis is $\Omega_T^{(cW)}$ and not $\Omega_T^{(c)}$. This will also be the case for the forthcoming tests below, for which the null may be $\Omega_T^{(cW)}$ or $\Omega_T^{(jW)}$, but never $\Omega_T^{(c)}$ or $\Omega_T^{(j)}$. This is due to the fact that all the Central Limit Theorems which we use are "trivial" (= with a vanishing limit) when the Brownian motion is absent and the volatility identically 0.

One can overcome this problem by using the following procedure, which we explain in the setting of the previous tests, but which works equally well for the tests to come later. The idea is to add a *fictitious* Brownian motion to the observed data. More precisely, one simulates a Brownian motion W' independent of everything else, taking some $\sigma' > 0$ (a constant) and setting $c' = \sigma'^2$. The observed increments $\Delta_i^n X$ are replaced by

$$\Delta_i^n X' \;=\; \Delta_i^n X + \sigma' \Delta_i^n W'.$$

(Actually, one does not simulate the whole path of W', only the increments $\Delta_i^n W'$ are relevant, so getting the $\Delta_i^n X'$ is very simple.) Note that, mathematically speaking, it is clearly not a restriction to suppose that W' is defined on $(\Omega, \mathcal{F}, (\mathcal{F}_t)_{t \geq 0}, \mathbb{P})$ and, up to enlarging the filtration, that it is adapted to the filtration $(\mathcal{F}_t)$. This correspond to the observation of the process

$$X' \;=\; X + \sigma' W',$$

which is of course an Itô semimartingale, with the same first and third characteristics as X, whereas its second characteristic is $C_t' = C_t + tc'$.

We denote by $\Omega_T'^{(c)}$, $\Omega_T'^{(j)}$, $\Omega_T'^{(cW)}$ and $\Omega_T'^{(jW)}$ the sets associated with the new process X' by (10.5) and (10.6). Since we add a continuous non-vanishing Brownian component to X, we obviously have

$$\Omega_T^{(c)} = \Omega_T'^{(cW)}, \qquad \Omega_T^{(j)} = \Omega_T'^{(jW)}.$$

Therefore, one can construct the tests described previously on the basis of the new increments $\Delta_i^n X'$, and this gives tests for the null hypothesis $\Omega_T^{(c)}$ in an obvious way.

We lose something, though, in the following sense: if we let c' increase, then the strong asymptotic size of the tests is still the prescribed value α; but if there are jumps, we reject the null less and less often. To see this, consider for example the first test, based on $\mathcal{S}^{(\text{J-MP1})}(k, \Delta_n)$, which we denote as $\mathcal{S}'^{(\text{J-MP1})}(k, \Delta_n)$ if we use the observations $X'_{i\Delta_n}$ instead of $X_{i\Delta_n}$. This statistic is approximately equal to $A(2)_T > 0$ when there are jumps, so we basically reject when the multipower $M'[4, k], \Delta_n)_T$ associated with X' is smaller than $A(2)_T^2 (m_{4/k})^k / z_\alpha'^2 \vartheta''(k)$. Now, $M'[4, k], \Delta_n)_T$ is approximately $\Delta_n (m_{4/k})^k (C(4)_T + c'^2 T)$ and rejection occurs less often when c' increases. So the "genuine" asymptotic power decreases.

This effect is weak when c' is small, relative to the average size of the volatility c_t on $[0, T]$. But since the procedure is designed to cover the case when $c_t \equiv 0$, it is obviously a difficult task to choose the tuning parameter c'. In a sense, if one suspects that c_t might vanish, it is probably wiser to first test for the presence of the Brownian motion, according to the procedures explained in Chapter 13 below.

10.3   A Symmetrical Test for Jumps

The tests developed in the previous section are by necessity non-symmetrical, in the sense that we can test the null hypothesis "no jumps" (that is, $\Omega_T^{(c)}$ or $\Omega_T^{(cW)}$) against $\Omega_T^{(j)}$, but not the other way around. In this section, we introduce a "symmetrical" test statistics which allow us to test both null hypotheses $\Omega_T^{(cW)}$ and $\Omega_T^{(jW)}$.

10.3.1   The Test Statistics Based on Power Variations

The tests presented here rely on power variations, which were introduced in (6.9) as

$$B(p, \Delta_n)_t = \sum_{i=1}^{[t/\Delta_n]} |\Delta_i^n X|^p,$$

where p is a positive real, and here we will choose $p > 2$, and even $p > 3$ later.

Let us begin with some intuition, based on the asymptotic behavior of $B(p, \Delta_n)_T$. As we will see more precisely below, these variables basically behave as follows when Δ_n is small:

$$X \text{ has jumps on } [0, T] \quad \Rightarrow \quad B(p, \Delta_n)_T \approx A(p)_T > 0$$

$$X \text{ is continuous on } [0, T] \quad \Rightarrow \quad \begin{array}{l} B(p, \Delta_n)_T \approx \Delta_n^{p/2-1} m_p \, C(p)_T, \\ \text{and } C(p)_T > 0 \text{ on } \Omega_T^{(W)}. \end{array}$$

The idea is then simple: we sample at two different frequencies, the highest one with time lag Δ_n, and a lower one with time lag $k\Delta_n$ for some integer $k \geq 2$, which amounts to using a subsample. We thus have the power variations $B(p, \Delta_n)_T$ and $B(p, k\Delta_n)_T$ at these two frequencies, and their ratio $B(p, k\Delta_n)_T / B(p, \Delta_n)_T$ has the following asymptotic behavior:

1. If X has jumps, both power variations go to the same positive limits, so the ratio goes to 1.

2. If X is continuous and $C(p)_T > 0$, hence on $\Omega_T^{(cW)}$, both variations go to zero, but at rates that depend upon the sampling frequency and the ratio goes to $k^{p/2-1} > 1$.

Thus, sampling at two different frequencies let us distinguish between the two situations of jumps and no jumps. The key advantage of using a ratio is that we do not need to know or estimate $A(p)_T$ or $C(p)_T$. All we need is for the null hypothesis to specify whether $A(p)_T > 0$ or $A(p)_T = 0$. That is, in the context of Figure 10.3, on $\Omega_T^{(j)}$, both variations converge to the *same* finite limit $A(p)_T > 0$ and so the ratio tends to 1 (the middle situation depicted in the figure), whereas on $\Omega_T^{(cW)}$ the variation converges to 0 and the ratio tends to a limit greater than 1, with value specifically depending upon the rate at which the variation tends to 0 (the lower situation depicted in the figure).

There are in fact two possible versions for the power variation with the time lag $k\Delta_n$, according to whether we only use the observations $X_{ik\Delta_n}$ for $i \geq 0$, or compute the variation with time lag $k\Delta_n$ and all starting points $0, \Delta_n, \ldots, (k-1)\Delta_n$ and then sum up over all starting points, hence using again all data:

$$
\begin{aligned}
B([p, k], \Delta_n)_t &= \sum_{i=1}^{[t/\Delta_n]-k+1} |X_{(i+k-1)\Delta_n} - X_{(i-1)\Delta_n}|^p \\
B(p, k\Delta_n)_t &= \sum_{i=1}^{[t/k\Delta_n]} |X_{ik\Delta_n} - X_{(i-1)k\Delta_n}|^p.
\end{aligned}
\tag{10.37}
$$

Clearly, $B([p, 1], \Delta_n) = B(p, \Delta_n)$. The behavior of these power variations is known and stated in Appendix A; indeed, $B([p, k], \Delta_n) = B(g, \Delta_n)$ and

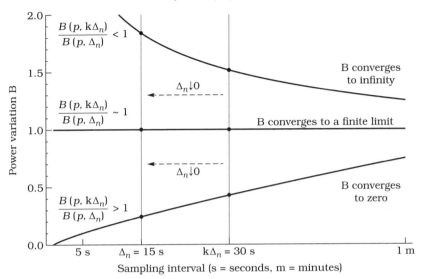

Figure 10.3: The three possible asymptotic behaviors of the power variation $B(p, \Delta_n)$ (diverge to infinity, converge to a finite limit, converge to zero) are identified by the asymptotic behavior of the ratio $B(p, k\Delta_n)/B(p, \Delta_n)$, without the need to estimate the actual limit.

$B(p, k\Delta_n) = \overline{B}(g, \Delta_n)$, the function g on $\mathbb{R}^k$ being

$$g(x_1, \cdots, x_k) = |x_1 + \cdots + x_k|^p.$$

Then, since $g(x) = \mathrm{O}(\|x\|^p)$ as $x \to 0$ in $\mathbb{R}^k$, Theorem A.1 tells us that, for any time T and as soon as $p > 2$, we have

$$B([p, k], \Delta_n)_T \xrightarrow{\ \mathbb{P}\ } kA(p)_T, \qquad B(p, k\Delta_n)_T \xrightarrow{\ \mathbb{P}\ } A(p)_T. \qquad (10.38)$$

This holds for any semimartingale, at any point T such that $\mathbb{P}(\Delta X_T \neq 0) = 0$, hence for all T if X is an Itô semimartingale.

On the other hand, the test function g is homogeneous with degree p, so with the notation of Appendix A we have $B([p, k], \Delta_n) = \Delta_n^{p/2-1} B'(g, \Delta_n)$ and $B(p, k\Delta_n) = \Delta_n^{p/2-1} \overline{B}'(g, \Delta_n)$. Hence Theorem A.2 and the property $\rho_a^{k\otimes}(g) = (ka)^{p/2} m_p$ (with the notation of this theorem) yield that, under (H'),

$$\Delta_n^{1-p/2} B([p, k], \Delta_n)_T \xrightarrow{\ \mathbb{P}\ } k^{p/2} m_p C(p)_T$$
$$\Delta_n^{1-p/2} B(p, k\Delta_n)_T \xrightarrow{\ \mathbb{P}\ } k^{p/2-1} m_p C(p)_T \qquad (10.39)$$
both in restriction to the set $\Omega_T^{(c)}$.

Here, $C(p)_t = \int_0^t |\sigma_s|^p \, ds$ is as usual, and $p > 0$. In fact, the aforementioned theorem states this result when X is continuous, and when it is not we apply the same argument as for Theorem 10.1, hence the necessity of (H′) instead of (H-2).

This leads us to introduce the following two test statistics, for any integer $k \geq 2$ and real $p > 2$:

$$S^{(\text{J-PV1})}(p, k, \Delta_n) = \frac{B([p, k], \Delta_n)_T}{kB(p, \Delta_n)_T}, \tag{10.40}$$

$$S^{(\text{J-PV2})}(p, k, \Delta_n) = \frac{B(p, k\Delta_n)_T}{B(p, \Delta_n)_T}.$$

By virtue of (10.38) and (10.39), and since $\Omega_T^{(j)} = \{A(p)_T > 0\}$ and $\Omega_T^{(cW)} = \{C(p)_T > 0 = A(p)_T\}$ (for any p), we deduce that

$$S^{(\text{J-PV1})}(p, k, \Delta_n) \xrightarrow{\mathbb{P}} \begin{cases} 1 & \text{on } \Omega_T^{(j)} \text{ under (H-2)} \\ k^{p/2-1} & \text{on } \Omega_T^{(cW)} \text{ under (H′)} \end{cases}$$

$$\tag{10.41}$$

$$S^{(\text{J-PV2})}(p, k, \Delta_n) \xrightarrow{\mathbb{P}} \begin{cases} 1 & \text{on } \Omega_T^{(j)} \text{ under (H-2)} \\ k^{p/2-1} & \text{on } \Omega_T^{(cW)} \text{ under (H′)} \end{cases}$$

Since $k^{p/2-1} > 1$ (because $p > 2$), this immediately leads to tests of the following form, for the two possible null hypotheses: we reject the null $\Omega_T^{(cW)}$, resp. the null $\Omega_T^{(j)}$, if $S^{(\text{J-PV1})}(p, k, \Delta_n)$ or $S^{(\text{J-PV1})}(p, k, \Delta_n)$ is smaller, resp. bigger, than a value between 1 and $k^{p/2-1}$. However, exactly as for the previous tests, if we want to achieve a prescribed asymptotic level $\alpha \in (0, 1)$, we need a Central Limit Theorem for these statistics, and this begins with a *joint* CLT for the pairs $(B(p, \Delta_n), B([p, k], \Delta_n))$ or $(B(p, \Delta_n), B(p, k\Delta_n))$.

10.3.2   Some Central Limit Theorems

We start with the CLT when X has jumps. This needs $p > 3$ and Assumption (H-2), and we have the following stable convergence in law, for any fixed time T (see page 564 for the proof):

$$\left(\tfrac{1}{\sqrt{\Delta_n}}(B([p, k], \Delta_n)_T - kA(p)_T), \tfrac{1}{\sqrt{\Delta_n}}(B(p, \Delta_n)_T - A(p)_T)\right)$$
$$\xrightarrow{\mathcal{L}\text{-}s} (\mathcal{U}(p, k)_T, \mathcal{U}(p)_T)$$
$$\left(\tfrac{1}{\sqrt{\Delta_n}}(B(p, k\Delta_n)_T - A(p)_T), \tfrac{1}{\sqrt{\Delta_n}}(B(p, \Delta_n)_T - A(p)_T)\right) \tag{10.42}$$
$$\xrightarrow{\mathcal{L}\text{-}s} (\overline{\mathcal{U}}(p, k)_T, \mathcal{U}(p)_T).$$

Here, the limiting processes have a description similar to (10.9), with a few more ingredients:

$$
\begin{aligned}
\mathcal{U}(p)_T &= p \sum_{q\geq 1: T_q \leq T} |\Delta X_{T_q}|^{p-1} \operatorname{sign}(\Delta X_{T_q}) \\
&\quad \times \left(\sqrt{\kappa_q}\, \sigma_{T_q-}\, \Psi_{q-} + \sqrt{1-\kappa_q}\, \sigma_{T_q}\, \Psi_{q+} \right), \\
\mathcal{U}(p,k)_T &= p \sum_{q\geq 1: T_q \leq T} |\Delta X_{T_q}|^{p-1} \operatorname{sign}(\Delta X_{T_q}) \\
&\quad \times \left(\sigma_{T_q-} \left(\sqrt{\tfrac{k(k-1)}{2}}\, \Psi'_{q-} + k\,\sqrt{\kappa_q}\, \Psi_{q-} \right) \right. \\
&\qquad \left. + \sigma_{T_q} \left(\sqrt{\tfrac{k(k-1)}{2}}\, \Psi'_{q+} + k\,\sqrt{1-\kappa_q}\, \Psi_{q+} \right) \right) \\
\overline{\mathcal{U}}(p,k)_T &= p \sum_{q: T_q \leq T} |\Delta X_{T_q}|^{p-1} \operatorname{sign}(\Delta X_{T_q}) \\
&\quad \times \left(\sigma_{T_q-} \left(\sqrt{\kappa_q}\, \Psi_{q-} + \sqrt{L_q}\, \Psi'_{q-} \right) \right. \\
&\qquad \left. + \sigma_{T_q} \left(\sqrt{1-\kappa_q}\, \Psi_{q+} + \sqrt{k-1-L_q}\, \Psi'_{q+} \right) \right),
\end{aligned}
$$

where $(T_q)_{q\geq 1}$ is a sequence of stopping times exhausting the jumps of X, and

$$
\begin{aligned}
&\kappa_q, \Psi_{q-}, \Psi_{q+}, \Psi'_{q-}, \Psi'_{q+}, L_q \text{ are defined on an extension of} \\
&\text{the space, mutually independent, independent of } \mathcal{F}, \\
&\text{with } \kappa_q \text{ uniform over } [0,1], \ L_q \text{ uniform on } \{0,1,\ldots,k-1\} \\
&\text{and } \Psi_{q\pm} \text{ and } \Psi'_{q\pm} \text{ standard normal.}
\end{aligned} \tag{10.43}
$$

We deduce a CLT for our statistics $S^{(\text{J-PV1})}(p,k,\Delta_n)$ and $S^{(\text{J-PV2})}(p,k,\Delta_n)$, in restriction to the set $\Omega_T^{(j)}$. Namely, by the same argument as in Theorem 10.1, we get

$$
\begin{aligned}
\tfrac{1}{\sqrt{\Delta_n}} \left(S^{(\text{J-PV1})}(p,k,\Delta_n) - 1 \right) &\xrightarrow{\mathcal{L}\text{-s}} S_{(j)}^{(\text{J-PV1})}(p,k) \\
\tfrac{1}{\sqrt{\Delta_n}} \left(S^{(\text{J-PV2})}(p,k,\Delta_n) - 1 \right) &\xrightarrow{\mathcal{L}\text{-s}} S_{(j)}^{(\text{J-PV2})}(p,k),
\end{aligned} \tag{10.44}
$$

both in restriction to $\Omega_T^{(j)}$, with

$$
\begin{aligned}
S_{(j)}^{(\text{J-PV1})}(p,k) &= \tfrac{p}{A(p)_T} \sum_{q\geq 1: T_q \leq T} |\Delta X_{T_q}|^{p-1} \operatorname{sign}(\Delta X_{T_q}) \\
&\quad \times \left(\sigma_{T_q-} \sqrt{\tfrac{k-1}{2k}}\, \Psi'_{q-} + \sigma_{T_q} \sqrt{\tfrac{k-1}{2k}}\, \Psi'_{q+} \right) \\
S_{(j)}^{(\text{J-PV2})}(p,k) &= \tfrac{p}{A(p)_T} \sum_{q\geq 1: T_q \leq T} |\Delta X_{T_q}|^{p-1} \operatorname{sign}(\Delta X_{T_q}) \\
&\quad \times \left(\sigma_{T_q-} \sqrt{L_q}\, \Psi'_{q-} + \sigma_{T_q} \sqrt{k-1-L_q}\, \Psi'_{q+} \right).
\end{aligned}
$$

Now we turn to the case where X is continuous. Letting Ψ, Ψ' and Ψ'' be three independent $\mathcal{N}(0,1)$-variables on the space $(\Omega', \mathcal{F}', \mathbb{P}')$, we set for $k \geq 1$ and $j = 0, \ldots, k$,

$$\overline{m}_{2p}(k,j) = \mathbb{E}'\big(|\sqrt{j}\Psi + \sqrt{k-j}\Psi'|^p \, |\sqrt{j}\Psi + \sqrt{k-j}\Psi''|^p\big)$$

$$\widetilde{m}_{2p}(k) = \mathbb{E}'\big(|\Psi|^p \, |\Psi + \sqrt{k-1}\Psi'|^p\big) - k^{p/2}(m_p)^2 \qquad (10.45)$$

$$\widehat{m}_{2p}(k) = \overline{m}_{2p}(k,k) + 2\sum_{j=1}^{k-1} \overline{m}_{2p}(k,j) - (2k-1)\overline{m}_{2p}(k,0).$$

(Note that $\widetilde{m}_{2p}(1) = \widehat{m}_{2p}(1) = m_{2p} - (m_p)^2$ and $\overline{m}_{2p}(k,0) = k^p(m_p)^2$ and $\overline{m}_{2p}(k,k) = k^p \, m_{2p}$.) Then, under (KC), and with $p > 1$, we have the following (functional) stable convergence in law (see page 566 for the proof):

$$\Big(\tfrac{1}{\sqrt{\Delta_n}}\,(\Delta_n^{1-p/2} B([p,k],\Delta_n) - k^{p/2} m_p\, C\,(p)),$$
$$\tfrac{1}{\sqrt{\Delta_n}}\,(\Delta_n^{1-p/2} B(p,\Delta_n) - m_p\, C\,(p))\Big)$$
$$\overset{\mathcal{L}-\mathrm{s}}{\Longrightarrow} (\mathcal{W}(p,k),\mathcal{W}(p))$$

$$(10.46)$$

$$\Big(\tfrac{1}{\sqrt{\Delta_n}}\,(\Delta_n^{1-p/2} B(p,k\Delta_n) - k^{p/2-1} m_p\, C\,(p)),$$
$$\tfrac{1}{\sqrt{\Delta_n}}\,(\Delta_n^{1-p/2} B(p,\Delta_n) - m_p\, C\,(p))\Big)$$
$$\overset{\mathcal{L}-\mathrm{s}}{\Longrightarrow} (\overline{\mathcal{W}}(p,k),\mathcal{W}(p)),$$

where the limiting processes $(\mathcal{W}(p,k), k\mathcal{W}(p))$ and $(\overline{\mathcal{W}}(p,k), \mathcal{W}(p))$ are defined on an extension $(\widetilde{\Omega}, \widetilde{\mathcal{F}}, (\widetilde{\mathcal{F}}_t)_{t \geq 0}, \widetilde{\mathbb{P}})$ of the space $(\Omega, \mathcal{F}, (\mathcal{F}_t)_{t \geq 0}, \mathbb{P})$ and, conditionally on the σ-field $\mathcal{F}$, are centered Gaussian martingales, with the following $\mathcal{F}$-conditional variance-covariance:

$$\begin{aligned}
\widetilde{\mathbb{E}}\big((\mathcal{W}(p,k)_T)^2 \mid \mathcal{F}\big) &= \widehat{m}_{2p}(k)\, C\,(2p)_T \\
\widetilde{\mathbb{E}}\big((\mathcal{W}(p)_T)^2 \mid \mathcal{F}\big) &= (m_{2p} - (m_p)^2)\, C\,(2p)_T \\
\widetilde{\mathbb{E}}\big(\mathcal{W}(p,k)_T\, \mathcal{W}(p)_T \mid \mathcal{F}\big) &= k\, \widetilde{m}_{2p}(k)\, C\,(2p)_T \qquad (10.47)\\
\widetilde{\mathbb{E}}\big((\overline{\mathcal{W}}(p,k)_T)^2 \mid \mathcal{F}\big) &= k^{p-1}(m_{2p} - (m_p)^2)\, C\,(2p)_T \\
\widetilde{\mathbb{E}}\big(\overline{\mathcal{W}}(p,k)_T\, \mathcal{W}(p)_T \mid \mathcal{F}\big) &= \widetilde{m}_{2p}(k)\, C\,(2p)_T\,.
\end{aligned}$$

We deduce a CLT for our ratio statistics, using once more the same argument as in Theorem 10.1 to extend the convergence from the case when X is continuous to the general case, but in restriction to the set $\Omega_T^{(cW)}$. We then have under (K-2)

$$\tfrac{1}{\sqrt{\Delta_n}}\big(S^{(\text{J-PV1})}(p,k,\Delta_n) - k^{p/2-1}\big) \overset{\mathcal{L}-\mathrm{s}}{\longrightarrow} \mathcal{S}_{(c)}^{(\text{J-PV1})}(p,k)$$
$$\tfrac{1}{\sqrt{\Delta_n}}\big(S^{(\text{J-PV2})}(p,k,\Delta_n) - k^{p/2-1}\big) \overset{\mathcal{L}-\mathrm{s}}{\longrightarrow} \mathcal{S}_{(c)}^{(\text{J-PV2})}(p,k),$$

$$(10.48)$$

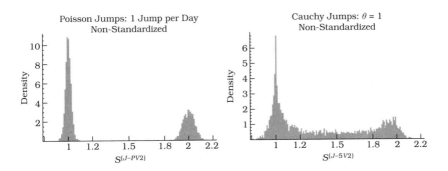

Figure 10.4: Tiny jumps or no jumps: Monte Carlo distribution of the non-standardized test statistic $S^{(\text{J--PV2})}(p,k,\Delta_n)$ for $p = 4$ and $k = 2$ and $\Delta_n = 1$ second, computed using a data generating process with either one Poisson jump per day on average including paths that contain no jumps (left panel) or tiny Cauchy jumps (right panel).

both in restriction to $\Omega^{(cW)}$, where the variables $\mathcal{S}^{(\text{J-PV1})}_{(c)}(p,k)$ and $\mathcal{S}^{(\text{J-PV1})}_{(c)}(p,k)$ are defined on an extension of the space, and are $\mathcal{F}$-conditionally centered Gaussian with the following conditional variances:

$$
\begin{aligned}
\widetilde{\mathbb{E}}((\mathcal{S}^{(\text{J-PV1})}_{(c)}(p,k))^2 \mid \mathcal{F}) &= \alpha(p,k)_1 \frac{C(2p)_T}{(C(p)_T)^2}, \\
\text{with } \alpha(p,k)_1 &= \frac{\widehat{m}_{2p}(k)+k^p(m_{2p}-(m_p)^2)-2k^{p/2+1}\,\widetilde{m}_{2p}(k)}{k^2(m_p)^2} \\
\widetilde{\mathbb{E}}((\mathcal{S}^{(\text{J-PV2})}_{(c)}(p,k))^2 \mid \mathcal{F}) &= \alpha(p,k)_2 \frac{C(2p)_T}{(C(p)_T)^2}, \\
\text{with } \alpha(p,k)_2 &= \frac{k^{p-2}(k+1)(m_{2p}-(m_p)^2)-2k^{p/2-1}\,\widetilde{m}_{2p}(k)}{(m_p)^2}.
\end{aligned}
\tag{10.49}
$$

In Figure 10.4 we give the histogram of the statistic $S^{(\text{J-PV2})}(p,k,\Delta_n)$ for $p = 4$ and $k = 2$, for 1000 Monte Carlo trials: the left panel exhibits the case of a Brownian motion plus a Poisson process, the peak at 1 corresponding to the paths having at least one jump on the time interval, the peak at 2 corresponding to the simulated paths with no jump, and the two kinds of paths are clearly well separated by the statistic. The right panel shows the same when X is a Brownian motion plus a Cauchy process: the peak at 1 corresponds to paths with at least one "large" jump, the (small) peak at 2 corresponds to those paths with only very small jumps; we see that the statistic is able to distinguish between relatively big jumps or not, but fails to distinguish when all jumps are small (recall that in the right panel, *all paths* have infinitely many jumps, most of them tiny ones.

10.3.3   Testing the Null Hypothesis of No Jump

In this subsection, we construct a test for the null hypothesis $\Omega_T^{(c)}$, or rather $\Omega_T^{(cW)}$, which in most practical cases is equal to $\Omega_T^{(c)}$.

Consider for example $S^{(\text{J-PV1})}(p, k, \Delta_n)$. Under the null, this statistic is asymptotically centered around $k^{p/2-1}$ and $\mathcal{F}$-conditionally Gaussian, and we need to estimate the conditional variance $\alpha(p, k) \, C(2p)_T / (C(p)_T)^2$. This amounts to estimating $C(p)_T$ and $C(2p)_T$, and for this we know several methods, such as truncated power variations or multipower variations. Both choices lead to the same theoretical results, and for concreteness we choose the truncated variations:

$$B(q, \Delta_n, u_n)_T = \sum_{i=1}^{[T/\Delta_n]} |\Delta_i^n X|^q \, 1_{\{|\Delta_i^n X| \leq u_n\}},$$

with $u_n \asymp \Delta_n^\varpi$ and some $\varpi \in \left(0, \frac{1}{2}\right)$.

As a matter of fact, we really need the consistency on $\Omega_T^{(cW)}$ only, so in that respect even non-truncated power variations work. So we have at least four natural candidates

$$
\begin{aligned}
V_n^{(1)} &= \alpha(p, k)_1 \frac{(m_p)^2 \, B(2p, \Delta_n)_T}{\Delta_n \, m_{2p} \, (B(p, \Delta_n)_T)^2}, \\
V_n^{(2)} &= \alpha(p, k)_1 \frac{(m_p)^2 \, B(2p, \Delta_n, u_n)_T}{\Delta_n \, m_{2p} \, (B(p, \Delta_n)_T)^2}, \\
V_n^{(3)} &= \alpha(p, k)_1 \frac{(m_p)^2 \, B(2p, \Delta_n)_T}{\Delta_n \, m_{2p} \, (B(p, \Delta_n, u_n)_T)^2}, \\
V_n^{(4)} &= \alpha(p, k)_1 \frac{(m_p)^2 \, B(2p, \Delta_n, u_n)_T}{\Delta_n \, m_{2p} \, (B(p, \Delta_n, u_n)_T)^2},
\end{aligned}
\tag{10.50}
$$

which all converge in probability to the conditional variance on the set $\Omega_T^{(cW)}$. Actually, other variants are possible, such as taking in the denominators above the product $B(p, \Delta_n)_T \, B(p, \Delta_n, u_n)_T$.

On the other hand, under the alternative hypothesis $\Omega_T^{(j)}$, $S^{(\text{J-PV1})}(p, k, \Delta_n)$ converges to 1, smaller than $k^{p/2-1}$. This leads us to use one of the following critical regions at stage n:

$$\mathcal{C}_n^{(l)} = \left\{ S^{(\text{J-PV1})}(p, k, \Delta_n) < k^{p/2-1} - z_\alpha' \sqrt{\Delta_n \, V_n^{(l)}} \right\} \tag{10.51}$$

for $l = 1, 2, 3, 4$ and where, as usual, z_α' is the α-quantile of the standard normal distribution $\mathcal{N}(0, 1)$.

Theorem 10.14. *Assuming (K-2) and $p > 3$ and $k \geq 2$, the tests $\mathcal{C}_n^{(l)}$ defined above have the strong asymptotic size α for the null hypothesis $\Omega_T^{(cW)}$, for $l = 1, 2, 3, 4$. Moreover,*

- *The tests $\mathcal{C}_n^{(2)}$ are consistent for the alternative $\Omega_T^{(j)}$ if $u_n \asymp \Delta_n^\varpi$ with $\varpi \in \left(0, \frac{1}{2}\right)$.*

- *The tests $\mathcal{C}_n^{(4)}$ are consistent for the alternative $\Omega_T^{(jW)}$ if $u_n \asymp \Delta_n^\varpi$ with $\varpi \in \left(\frac{1}{2} - \frac{1}{p}, \frac{1}{2} \right)$.*

- *The tests $\mathcal{C}_n^{(1)}$ and $\mathcal{C}_n^{(3)}$ are not consistent for the alternative $\Omega_T^{(jW)}$ in general.*

One should thus *absolutely avoid* using the tests with $l = 1$ or $l = 3$, and probably the test with $l = 2$ is more powerful than the one with $l = 4$ in the presence of infinitely many small jumps. On the other hand, under the null, all $V_n^{(l)}$'s behave in the same way, and are indeed all equal when n is large enough.

Proof of Theorem 10.14. The first claim readily follows from (10.48) and from the convergence in probability, in restriction to the set $\Omega_T^{(cW)}$, toward the conditional variance (10.49), in all cases $l = 1, 2, 3, 4$. For the second claim, since $S^{(\text{J-PV1})}(p, k, \Delta_n) \overset{\mathbb{P}}{\longrightarrow} 1$ on $\Omega_T^{(jW)}$, the consistency under the alternative is obviously implied by $\Delta_n V_n^{(l)} \overset{\mathbb{P}}{\longrightarrow} 1$ on $\Omega_T^{(jW)}$ or $\Omega_T^{(j)}$, according to the case, whereas if this fails the consistency also fails, at least when z_α' is large (which is true when α is small). By (10.38) we see that $\Delta_n V_n^{(l)}$ converge to a positive limit when $l = 1$, whereas $V_n^{(3)} \geq V_n^{(1)}$ by construction. So alternative consistency fails in these two cases. We now prove the consistency in the case $l = 2$, and leave out the case $l = 4$, which is not very simple to prove (a proof can be found in Aït-Sahalia and Jacod (2009b)). The inequality $B(2p, \Delta_n, u_n)_T \leq u_n^p B(p, \Delta_n)_T$ is obvious, and $B(p, \Delta_n)_T$ converge in probability to a positive limit on $\Omega_T^{(j)}$. Then $\Delta_n V_n^{(2)} \overset{\mathbb{P}}{\longrightarrow} 1$ on $\Omega_T^{(j)}$ follows from the fact that $u_n \to 0$. □

In a similar way, one can use the statistics $S^{(\text{J-PV2})}(p, k, \Delta_n)$. This gives us the following (we only state the case corresponding to $l = 2$ in the previous theorem):

Theorem 10.15. *Assuming (K-2) and $p > 3$ and $k \geq 2$, the tests with critical regions*

$$\mathcal{C}_n = \left\{ S^{(\text{J-PV2})}(p, k, \Delta_n) < k^{p/2-1} \right. \tag{10.52}$$

$$\left. -z_\alpha' \sqrt{\alpha(p,k)_2 \frac{(m_p)^2 \, B(2p, \Delta_n, u_n)_T}{m_{2p} \, (B(p, \Delta_n)_T)^2}} \right\}$$

have the strong asymptotic size α for the null hypothesis $\Omega_T^{(cW)}$ and are consistent for the alternative $\Omega_T^{(j)}$ if $u_n \asymp \Delta_n^\varpi$ with $\varpi \in \left(0, \frac{1}{2}\right)$.

10.3.4 Testing the Null Hypothesis of Presence of Jumps

Now, we turn to the other the null hypothesis $\Omega_T^{(j)}$, or rather $\Omega_T^{(jW)}$, which again in most practical cases is equal to $\Omega_T^{(j)}$. We start with a test based on the statistic $S^{(\text{J-PV1})}(p, k, \Delta_n)$, which is easier to handle.

Using $S^{(\text{J-PV1})}(p, k, \Delta_n)$ for the Test

A significant advantage of $S^{(\text{J-PV1})}(p, k, \Delta_n)$ is the following: after centering and normalization, its limiting variable $\mathcal{S}_{(j)}^{(\text{J-PV1})}(p, k)$ is $\mathcal{F}$-conditionally centered Gaussian, with conditional variance

$$\widetilde{\mathbb{E}}((\mathcal{S}_{(j)}^{(\text{J-PV1})}(p, k))^2 \mid \mathcal{F}) = p^2 \frac{k-1}{2k} \frac{D(2p-2)_T}{(A(p)_T)^2}, \qquad (10.53)$$

where

$$D(2p-2)_T = \sum_{s \leq T} |\Delta X_s|^{2p-2} (c_{s-} + c_s),$$

is as in (10.21). Note that (10.27) provides us the estimators $D(\Delta_n, 2p-2)_T$ for $D(2p-2)_T$:

$$D(\Delta_n, 2p-2)_T \xrightarrow{\mathbb{P}} D(2p-2)_T.$$

Here, in (10.27), we take $\widehat{c}_i^n = \widehat{c}(k_n, u_n)_i$, as given by (10.26) with a truncating sequence $u_n \asymp \Delta_n^{\varpi}$ for some $\varpi \in (0, \frac{1}{2})$. As for $A(p)_T$, a natural sequence of estimators is $B(p, \Delta_n)_T$, by virtue of (10.38) (which also tells us that we could choose $B(p, k\Delta_n)_T$ or $B([p, k], \Delta_n)_T / k$, instead of $B(p, \Delta_n)_T$).

Now, in view of (10.41) and of the CLT described above, together with the suggested estimators for $D(2p-2)_T$ and $A(p)_T$, we are led to use the following critical region at stage n:

$$\mathcal{C}_n = \Big\{ S^{(\text{J-PV1})}(p, k, \Delta_n) > 1 \qquad (10.54)$$

$$+ z_\alpha' \, p \sqrt{\Delta_n \frac{(k-1) \, D(\Delta_n, 2p-2)_T}{2k \, (B(p, \Delta_n)_T)^2}} \Big\}$$

where z_α' is the α-quantile of the standard normal distribution $\mathcal{N}(0, 1)$.

Theorem 10.16. *Assuming (H-2) and $p > 3$ and $k \geq 2$, the tests $\mathcal{C}_n$ defined by (10.54) have the strong asymptotic size α for the null hypothesis $\Omega_T^{(jW)}$, and are consistent for the alternative $\Omega_T^{(cW)}$ if further (H') holds.*

Proof. The first claim follows from (10.44) and the fact that $(k - 1)p^2 D(\Delta_n, 2p - 2)_T / 2k(B(p, \Delta_n)_T)^2$ estimates the variance in (10.53). Note that the argument works for testing $\Omega_T^{(jW)}$, but not for testing $\Omega_T^{(j)}$: although the CLT in (10.44) holds on the latter set, on the set-difference $\Omega_T^{(j)} \backslash \Omega_T^{(jW)}$ the limiting variable $\mathcal{S}_{(j)}^{(\text{J-PV1})}(p, k)$ vanishes and there is no standardized version of the CLT. For the second claim we use that, in restriction to $\Omega_T^{(c)}$ and for all n large enough, we have $|\Delta_i^n X| \le u_n$ for all $i \le [T/\Delta_n]$, implying $D(\Delta_n, 2p - 2)_T = 0$, whereas $B(p, \Delta_n)_T > 0$ for all n large enough on $\Omega_T^{(cW)}$; in this case, rejecting is the same as having $\mathcal{S}^{(\text{J-PV1})}(p, k, \Delta_n) > 1$, so $\mathbb{P}(\Omega_T^{(cW)} \cap (\mathcal{C}_n)^c) \to 0$ follows from the property $\mathcal{S}^{(\text{J-PV1})}(p, k, \Delta_n) \xrightarrow{\mathbb{P}} k^{p/2} > 1$ on $\Omega_T^{(cW)}$. $\qquad \square$

Using $\mathcal{S}^{(\text{J-PV2})}(p, k, \Delta_n)$ for the Test

When the processes X and σ do not jump together, the limiting variables $\mathcal{S}_{(j)}^{(\text{J-PV2})}(p, k)$ is $\mathcal{F}$-conditionally centered Gaussian, with conditional variance

$$\widetilde{\mathbb{E}}((\mathcal{S}_{(j)}^{(\text{J-PV2})}(p, k))^2 \mid \mathcal{F}) = (k - 1)p^2 \frac{D(2p - 2)_T}{2(A(p)_T)^2}. \tag{10.55}$$

Exactly as above, this leads us to consider the following critical region at stage n:

$$\mathcal{C}_n = \Big\{ S^{(\text{J-PV2})}(p, k, \Delta_n) > 1 \tag{10.56}$$
$$+ z'_\alpha \, p \sqrt{\Delta_n \frac{(k - 1) D(\Delta_n, 2p - 2)_T}{2(B(p, \Delta_n)_T)^2}} \Big\},$$

and we have the analogue of Theorem 10.16, with the same proof:

Theorem 10.17. *Assume (H-2) and that the processes X and σ do not jump together. If $p > 3$ and $k \ge 2$, the tests $\mathcal{C}_n$ defined by (10.56) have the strong asymptotic size α for the null hypothesis $\Omega_T^{(jW)}$, and are consistent for the alternative $\Omega_T^{(cW)}$ if further (H') holds.*

When the processes X and σ have some jumps at the same times, the variable $\mathcal{S}_{(j)}^{(\text{J-PV2})}(p, k)$ is no longer $\mathcal{F}$-conditionally Gaussian, but still is conditionally centered with a variance given by (10.55). Then, using Markov's inequality, we can take the following critical regions:

$$\mathcal{C}_n = \Big\{ S^{(\text{J-PV2})}(p, k, \Delta_n) > 1 \tag{10.57}$$
$$+ \frac{p}{\sqrt{\alpha}} \sqrt{\Delta_n \frac{(k - 1) D(\Delta_n, 2p - 2)_T}{2(B(p, \Delta_n)_T)^2}} \Big\}.$$

Then the following result is again proved as were the previous ones:

Theorem 10.18. *Assuming (H-2) and $p > 3$ and $k \geq 2$, the tests C_n defined by (10.57) have an asymptotic size not bigger than α for the null hypothesis $\Omega_T^{(jW)}$, and they are consistent for the alternative $\Omega_T^{(cW)}$ if further (H') holds.*

The actual asymptotic level is in general much less than α, so this test has a "conservative" level and much less power than if the actual level were exactly α. To remedy this situation, we could do as for the "sharp confidence interval" in Theorem 10.12. We will not do this here, because as we will see just below the tests based upon $S^{(\text{J-PV1})}(p, k, \Delta_n)$ are always more accurate than those based on $S^{(\text{J-PV2})}(p, k, \Delta_n)$.

Finally, we report the empirical values of $S^{(\text{J-PV2})}(p, k, \Delta_n)$, abbreviated as S_J in the next discussion, in the form of a histogram in Figure 10.5 for each of the three possible measurements of the data. The data for the histogram are produced by computing S_J for the four quarters of the year, the 30 stocks, and for a range of values of p from 3 to 6 (in increments of 0.25), Δ_n from 5 seconds to 2 minutes (with values 5, 15, 30, 60, 90 and 120 seconds), and $k = 2, 3$. The top left histogram corresponds to the unfiltered transactions, the top right to the NBBO-filtered transactions and the lower left to the NBBO midpoint quotes. In this and the plots that follow, the values of the parameters k and p are varied across the experiments; the "noise dominates" region consists of the range of possible values of the limits of the statistic being implemented, when k and p vary, for the two cases where the noise dominates.

As indicated in (10.82), values below 1 are indicative of noise of one form or another dominating. We find that this is the case only for the unfiltered transactions data, and only at the highest sampling frequencies, the histogram then displaying a left tail. For the other data measurements, the histograms display very little mass in the regions where the noise dominates. The conclusion from S_J is that the noise is not the major concern, except for the unfiltered transactions at the ultra high frequencies, but once past this domain, the evidence points toward the presence of jumps with the histograms centered around 1.

One potential caveat needs to be raised. The evidence for values around 1 is compelling at the highest frequencies, but this is where it is possible for the noise to exert downward pressure on the point estimates, since the noise results in lower limits. It is possible that in small samples we obtain estimates around one as a result of a procedure that is biased downward from higher values by residual amounts of noise. This

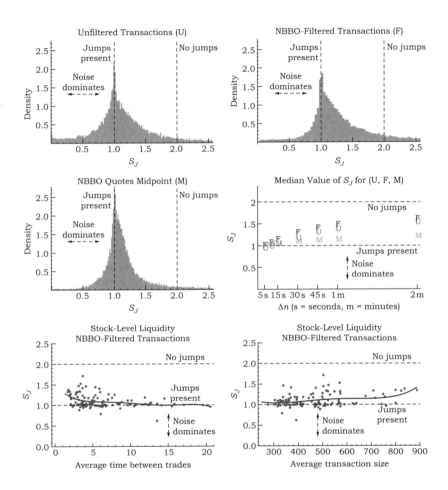

Figure 10.5: Testing for Jumps: Empirical distribution of $S^{(J-PV2)}(p, k, \Delta_n)$ for all 30 DJIA stocks, 2006, measured using transactions (unfiltered, U, and NBBO-filtered, F) and NBBO quotes midpoint (M), median value of $S^{(J-PV2)}(p, k, \Delta_n)$ as a function of the sampling interval Δ_n, and nonlinear regression of S_J against stock-level liquidity measures.

conclusion is not surprising *per se*, even for the index and a fortiori for the individual assets. A power law fits the data quite well and a continuous component alone (with typically exponentially decaying tails) would be rather unlikely to generate such returns.

The middle right panel in Figure 10.5 displays the median value of S_J (across values of p and k, and the four quarters) as a function of the sampling interval Δ_n. Unfiltered transactions are marked U, filtered transactions are marked F and the NBBO midpoint quotes are marked M. In all cases, the median value of S_J starts around 1 at the highest frequencies and then rises. Comparing different data measurements, we find that S_J is generally highest for F (meaning less evidence of jumps there), then for U and then for M. Similar results obtain if the mean is employed instead of the median. But as the sampling frequency decreases, the evidence in favor of the presence of jumps becomes more mixed, when the 30 components of the DJIA are taken in the aggregate. When implemented on the DJIA index itself, we find values of S_J that range between 1.5 and 2.5, providing between less evidence in favor of jumps and evidence against them for the index at the lower frequencies and for the time period considered.

However, a point should be emphasized here. The histogram is more spread out when frequency decreases because less data are used and the statistical error increases, so that the procedure becomes less conclusive.

Finally, we check if any cross-sectional differences in S_J can be explained by cross-sectional differences in liquidity among the 30 stocks. To this aim, the lower two panels on Figure 10.5 show the results of a nonlinear regression of the statistic S_J on two stock-level measures of liquidity, the average time between successive trades, and the average size of the transactions. Both regressions show a slight decrease in S_J values as the asset becomes less liquid, meaning higher time between trades and lower transaction size, but neither result is strong enough to be noticeable.

10.3.5   Comparison of the Tests

The families of tests above are equally good under the null hypothesis (at least asymptotically), except for those defined by (10.57). They behave differently, though, under the alternative.

Consider for example the tests (10.51) and (10.52) for the null $\Omega_T^{(cW)}$. We have these two tests for any given pair (p, k) with $p > 3$ real and $k \geq 2$ integer, and those two numbers also have to be chosen. However, we start with p and k fixed. The key point for a comparison of the tests based on $S^{(\text{J-PV1})}(p, k, \Delta_n)$ and $S^{(\text{J-PV2})}(p, k, \Delta_n)$ is the following proposition:

Proposition 10.19. *Assuming (H-2), and with $p > 3$ and $k \geq 2$ fixed, the $\mathcal{F}$-conditional variances of the limits satisfy*

$$\widetilde{\mathbb{E}}((\mathcal{S}_{(c)}^{(\text{J-PV1})}(p, k))^2 \mid \mathcal{F}) = \frac{\alpha(p,k)_1}{\alpha(p,k)_2} \widetilde{\mathbb{E}}((\mathcal{S}_{(c)}^{(\text{J-PV2})}(p, k))^2 \mid \mathcal{F}) \quad on \quad \Omega_T^{(cW)}$$

$$\widetilde{\mathbb{E}}((\mathcal{S}_{(j)}^{(\text{J-PV1})}(p, k))^2 \mid \mathcal{F}) = \frac{1}{k} \widetilde{\mathbb{E}}((\mathcal{S}_{(j)}^{(\text{J-PV2})}(p, k))^2 \mid \mathcal{F}) \quad on \quad \Omega_T^{(jW)},$$

and $\alpha(p, k)_1 < \alpha(p, k)_2$.

The first equality follows from (10.49), the second follows from comparing (10.53) and (10.55); the last claim $\alpha(p, k)_1 < \alpha(p, k)_2$ is not obvious, and is proved on page 567.

It follows that the statistic $S^{(\text{J-PV1})}(p, k, \Delta_n)$ is (asymptotically) less spread out around its limiting value (1 or $k^{p/2-1}$ on $\Omega_T^{(jW)}$ and $\Omega_T^{(cW)}$, respectively,) than $S^{(\text{J-PV2})}(p, k, \Delta_n)$. In other words, under either null hypothesis, the two tests based on $S^{(\text{J-PV1})}(p, k, \Delta_n)$ and $S^{(\text{J-PV2})}(p, k, \Delta_n)$ have the same asymptotic size, but those based on $S^{(\text{J-PV1})}(p, k, \Delta_n)$ have systematically a bigger power than the others, for both possible null hypotheses. So, it is advisable to always use the tests (10.51) and (10.54) based on $S^{(\text{J-PV1})}(p, k, \Delta_n)$ (not to mention the fact that under the null $\Omega_T^{(jW)}$ the statistic $S^{(\text{J-PV2})}(p, k, \Delta_n)$ is usually *not* asymptotically normal).

The choice of p and k is more difficult. When p and/or k increase, the two limits 1 and $k^{p/2-1}$ become further apart, thus appearing to be easier to distinguish. However, this is counterbalanced by the fact that the limiting variances may also be increasing.

When p is fixed and k varies: Let us consider first the case where $p > 3$ is fixed, but k varies. Under the null $\Omega_T^{(jW)}$ the variance (10.53) increases with k, and the limit as $k \to \infty$ is three times the value for $k = 2$; this has to be compared with the squared distance $(k^{p/2-1} - 1)^2$, which increases much faster and goes to ∞ as $k \to \infty$. So if we wish to test the null $\Omega_T^{(jW)}$ it is probably advisable to take k "as large as possible," in order to improve on the power.

Under the null $\Omega_T^{(cW)}$ the variance (10.49) is proportional to $\alpha(p, k)_1$, whose behavior as k increases is not transparent. However, $\alpha(p, k)_1$ is equivalent to $\alpha(p)_1 k^{p-1}$ for some constant $\alpha(p)_1$ (as $k \to \infty$), whereas the square $(k^{p/2-1} - 1)^2$ behaves as k^{p-2}, so in this case we should choose a value of k which is not too large.

In conclusion, the "optimal" choice of k depends on the hypothesis to be tested. And of course it also depends on the data, since in order to have some chance to be in the asymptotic regime, k should be much smaller than the number $[T/\Delta_n]$ of observed increments.

When k is fixed and p varies: The situation here is much more difficult to analyze, because the asymptotic variance depends on p through $\alpha(p,k)_1$ for the first tests, but also on the (random) numbers $C\,(2p)_T\,/(C\,(p)_T)^2$ or $p^2 D(2p-2)_T/(A(p)_T)^2$. Therefore there seems to be no "theoretical" rule for the choice of p.

Let us, however, mention that in the simple case where the volatility process $\sigma_t = \sigma$ is a constant, then $C\,(2p)_T\,/(C\,(p)_T)^2 = 1/T$, so the choice of p for the test with the null $\Omega_T^{(cW)}$ amounts to optimizing $\alpha(p,k)_1$, in connection with $(k^{p/2-1} - 1)^2$. For the other null, we then have $p^2 D(2p-2)_T/(A(p)_T)^2 = p^2\,\sigma^2\,A(2p-2)_T/(A(p)_T)^2$, whose precise behavior is again unpredictable, but which behaves as $p^2/\sup_{s\leq T}|\Delta X_s|^2$ as $p \to \infty$.

So the choice of p is, overall, rather unclear. The bigger p is, the more emphasis is put on "big" jumps (when there are jumps, of course), and in all cases on "big" increments (or big outliers, when there is microstructure noise). We thus advocate choosing a moderate value for p, like $p = 4$. It is also possible (and perhaps advisable) to construct a series of tests with different values of p.

10.4 Detection of Jumps

The main aim of this section is not testing for jumps, but estimating the size and location of "relatively big" jumps. As a by-product, however, we can derive a test for the null hypothesis "the process X is continuous." Unfortunately, this test is not exactly of the same type as the previous ones, as will be explained later. We mainly follow Lee and Mykland (2008) and Lee and Hannig (2010) with suitable modifications to fit our setting. In particular, and in contrast with these papers, we do not want the volatility process σ to be necessarily continuous, since when X jumps it is often the case that σ jumps at the same time.

The idea is straightforward. If X jumps at some time S in the interval $((i_n - 1)\Delta_n, i_n\Delta_n]$ for some (random) integer i_n, then $\Delta_{i_n}^n X$ is equal to ΔX_S (a non-vanishing variable, independent of n), plus a variable which tends to 0 as $n \to \infty$; in contrast, if X does not jump on $((i-1)\Delta_n, i\Delta_n]$, then $\Delta_i^n X$ is of order $\sqrt{\Delta_n}$, multiplied by the volatility, or a kind of average of the volatility on the corresponding interval, plus a negligible drift term. Hence, for deciding whether $\Delta_i^n X$ is small or not, we have to compare it with the volatility, and thus with an estimator of it if we want feasibility.

To this end, we use one of the estimators given in (10.26) and, as before, we write $\widehat{c}_i^n$ for either $\widehat{c}(k_n, [k])_i$ (with an integer $k \geq 2$) or $\widehat{c}(k_n, u_n)_i$ (and then we set $k = 1$, and u_n satisfies (6.24)), and in all cases we assume a rather innocuous reinforcement of (10.25):

$$k_n \Delta_n^\eta \to \infty, \quad k_n \Delta_n^{\eta'} \to 0 \quad \text{for some} \ \ 0 < \eta < \eta' < 1. \qquad (10.58)$$

Then we set

$$Z_i^n = \frac{\Delta_i^n X}{\sqrt{\Delta_n \, \widehat{c}_{i+1}^n}}, \quad S^{(\text{J-DET})}(\Delta_n) = \sup_{1 \leq i \leq [T/\Delta_n] - k_n - k + 1} |Z_i^n|. \qquad (10.59)$$

Remark 10.20. *Lee and Mykland (2008) use $\widehat{c}_{(i-k_n-k+1)^+}^n$ in the definition of Z_i^n, instead of $\widehat{c}_{i+1}^n$, and for that matter one could take $\widehat{c}_j^n$ for any integer j between $(i - k_n - k + 1)^+$ and i, at least when both X and σ are continuous, which is the case under the null hypothesis to be tested below. Our choice of $\widehat{c}_{i+1}^n$ slightly simplifies the analysis.*

At this stage, we notice the following:

1. In all cases, we will see that the statistics $S^{(\text{J-DET})}(\Delta_n)$ explode ($=$ go to ∞) as $n \to \infty$. However, this occurs with the rate $1/\sqrt{\Delta_n}$ when there are jumps, by virtue of what precedes. In contrast, in the absence of jumps the rate of convergence is $\log(1/\Delta_n)$. Thus we decide that there is no jump if $S^{(\text{J-DET})}(\Delta_n)$ is "not too large".

2. If, on the basis of what precedes, we conclude that there are jumps, then we decide that a jump occurs inside $((i - 1)\Delta_n, i\Delta_n]$ if $|Z_i^n|$ is large enough: this gives us the approximate location of the jump (inside the above interval; clearly, specifying a more precise location is simply out of reach with discrete observations), and the corresponding increment $\Delta_i^n X$ is an estimator of the size of the jumps.

Before giving concrete specifications for the procedures heuristically described above, we need some mathematical background.

10.4.1 Mathematical Background

To start, let us mention that in this section we assume at least (H-2), and also (P) (that is, σ_t and σ_{t-} do not vanish); this is to ensure that the denominators in (10.59) do not go to 0 faster than $\sqrt{\Delta_n}$. Assuming (P) is in contrast with the assumptions prevailing in most of the previous sections, and it implies $\Omega_T^{(W)} = \Omega$.

For describing the results, we need the same ingredients $(\kappa_q, \Psi_{q+}, \Psi_{q-})$ as in (10.9), defined on an extension $(\widetilde{\Omega}, \widetilde{\mathcal{F}}, \widetilde{\mathbb{P}})$ of the space, and also another sequence $(\Psi_q : q \geq 1)$ of independent standard normal variables, independent of the previous ones and of $\mathcal{F}$. Also, $(T_q)_{q \geq 1}$ denotes a sequence of stopping times exhausting the jumps of X and, without loss of generality, we can assume that $T_q < \infty$ a.s. (indeed, since we are interested in what happens on $[0, T]$ only, it is always possible to add fictitious jumps after time T). Then, as before, we set

$$i(n, q) \text{ is the random integer such that}$$
$$(i(n, q) - 1)\Delta_n < T_q \leq i(n, q)\Delta_n. \tag{10.60}$$

Next, studying Z_i^n as $n \to \infty$ for any fixed i has no real interest, because it is related to the behavior of X near 0 only. What is really meaningful is the following variable, defined for each $t > 0$:

$$Z^n(t) = Z_i^n \quad \text{when } (i - 1)\Delta_n < t \leq i\Delta_n. \tag{10.61}$$

Then, not surprisingly, the asymptotic behavior is as follows (the proofs for this section are often of a technical nature, and all gathered in Subsection B.3.3 of Appendix B, see page 568 for the forthcoming one):

Theorem 10.21. *Assume (H-2) and (P).*

(a) For any finite family of (non-random) times $0 < t_1 < \cdots < t_q$ such that $\mathbb{P}(\Delta\sigma_{t_j} = 0) = 1$, we have the following convergence in law:

$$\left(Z^n(t_j)\right)_{1 \leq j \leq q} \xrightarrow{\mathcal{L}} \left(\Psi_j\right)_{1 \leq j \leq q}. \tag{10.62}$$

(b) We have the following stable convergence in law:

$$\left(\frac{1}{\sqrt{\Delta_n}} \left(\Delta_{i(n,q)}^n X - \Delta X_{T_q}\right)\right)_{q \geq 1}$$
$$\xrightarrow{\mathcal{L}\text{-}s} \left(\sqrt{\kappa_q}\, \sigma_{T_q-}\Psi_{q-} + \sqrt{1 - \kappa_q}\, \sigma_{T_q}\Psi_{q+}\right)_{q \geq 1}, \tag{10.63}$$

and, for all $\varepsilon > 0$:

$$\lim_{\varepsilon \to 0} \sup_n \mathbb{P}\left(\{S^{(J-DET)}(\Delta_n) \leq \varepsilon/\sqrt{\Delta_n}\} \cap \Omega_T^{(j)}\right) = 0. \tag{10.64}$$

The convergence (10.62) holds true for all choices of t_j when the process σ has no fixed times of discontinuity, for example if it is itself

an Itô semimartingale. In contrast, (10.62) for a single $t_j = t$ *fails* if
$\mathbb{P}(\Delta\sigma_t \neq 0) > 0$: in this case, the sequence $Z^n(t)$ converges in law if the
"fractional part" $t/\Delta_n - [t/\Delta_n]$ converges to a limit, and otherwise the
sequence $Z^n(t)$ does not converge in law at all.

The claims (a) and (b) look incompatible with one another, since
the first implies that the sequences $Z^n(t)$ are bounded in probability
and the second implies $|Z^n_{i(n,q)}| \xrightarrow{\mathbb{P}} \infty$ on the set $\{\Delta X_{T_q} \neq 0\}$. This
apparent contradiction is resolved by noticing that for any fixed t we
have $\mathbb{P}(T_q = t) = 0$. Note that a "joint" convergence for (10.62) and
(10.63) also holds, but we will not need this below.

Assuming that σ has no fixed time of discontinuity, we have finite-
dimensional convergence in law of the processes $Z^n(t)$, to a limit $Z(t)$
which is a standard "white noise," of the same type as the one encountered in Theorem 8.7, with no possibility of a "functional" convergence.

The previous theorem gives us a lower bound for $S^{(\text{J-DET})}(\Delta_n)$ on the
set $\Omega_T^{(j)}$, but no real insight about its behavior on $\Omega_T^{(c)}$. For this, we need
a supplementary result related to the theory of extreme values. We recall
that a random variable ξ is called a *Gumbel* variable (see e.g. Embrechts
et al. (1997)) if its distribution function is

$$\mathbb{P}(\xi \leq x) = \exp{-e^{-x}}.$$

The following result is proven on page 571.

Theorem 10.22. *Assume (KCC) (that is, both X and σ satisfy
(H-2) and are continuous) and (P). Then, with the notation $l_n = \sqrt{2\log(1/\Delta_n)}$, and if k_n satisfies (10.58), we have*

$$l_n\left(S^{(\text{J-DET})}(\Delta_n) - l_n + \frac{\log(2\pi l_n)}{2l_n} - \frac{\log 2T}{l_n}\right) \xrightarrow{\mathcal{L}} \xi, \qquad (10.65)$$

and in particular $\frac{1}{l_n}S^{(\text{J-DET})}(\Delta_n) \xrightarrow{\mathbb{P}} 1$.

Remark 10.23. *The reader will notice the – necessary – hypothesis
that the volatility σ is continuous, the result being wrong otherwise. One
could, on the other hand, relax the Itô semimartingale assumption for σ,
provided the path of σ remains Hölder with index $(1/2) - \varepsilon$ for all $\varepsilon > 0$
(as is the case when it is a continuous Itô semimartingale).*

*An important drawback of this result is that (10.65) asserts conver-
gence in law, but not stable convergence in law (or, at least, this is not
known to us). This will have unfortunate consequences on the testing
procedure below.*

10.4.2   A Test for Jumps

Based on the previous considerations, it becomes quite simple to build a test for the null hypothesis "no jump." With a prescribed asymptotic level α, we consider the α-upper quantile of the Gumbel distribution, that is, the number

$$g_\alpha \;=\; \log\Big(1/\log\frac{1}{1-\alpha}\Big),$$

which is such that $\mathbb{P}(U > g_\alpha) = \alpha$ when U is a Gumbel variable. We introduce the critical (rejection) region (with $l_n = \sqrt{2\log(1/\Delta_n)}$ again):

$$\mathcal{C}_n = \Big\{ S^{(\text{J-DET})}(\Delta_n) > l_n - \frac{\log(2\pi l_n)}{2l_n} + \frac{\log(2T) + g_\alpha}{l_n}\Big\}. \qquad (10.66)$$

The following immediately results from Theorem 10.22 for (a), and from (10.64) for (b):

Theorem 10.24. *(a) Under (KCC) and (P), the critical regions (10.66) satisfy* $\mathbb{P}(\mathcal{C}_n) \to \alpha$.

(b) Under (H-2) and (P), the critical regions (10.66) are consistent for the alternative $\Omega_T^{(j)}$.

The consistency for the alternative has the usual meaning of Definition 5.19, namely $\mathbb{P}(\Omega_T^{(j)} \cap (\mathcal{C}_n)^c) \to 0$, and from that perspective the result above is in line with the results for the other tests developed so far.

This is, unfortunately, *not the case at all* for the asymptotic size. Here, we only have a *weaker form* of the asymptotic size, different from Definition 5.20, and only when $\mathbb{P}(\Omega_T^{(c)}) = 1$. In other words, we are performing a test in the usual statistical sense: the null hypothesis is the family of all models (or processes) satisfying (KC) and (P), with σ being continuous. And, even in this case, the sequence $\mathbb{P}(\mathcal{C}_n \mid A)$ may very well converge to a limit bigger than α, for some A with $\mathbb{P}(A) > 0$ (so we have no control on the "asymptotic size" in the sense of Definition 5.20). These problems are due to the lack of stable convergence in law in Theorem 10.22.

Example 10.25. *Suppose that we have a model with finite activity for the jumps, that is, (10.1), with the assumptions (K-0) and (P) and with further σ continuous. We can rewrite (10.1) as*

$$X_t \;=\; X_0 + \int_0^t b_s' ds + \int_0^s \sigma_s dW_s + \delta \star \underline{p}_t, \qquad (10.67)$$

where

$$b_t' = b_t - \int \delta(t,z) 1_{\{|\delta(t,x)|\le 1\}} \lambda(dx),$$

and consider the continuous process

$$X'_t = X_t - \sum_{s \leq t} \Delta X_s = X_0 + \int_0^t b'_s \, ds + \int_0^t \sigma_s \, dW_s. \qquad (10.68)$$

Typically, here, both sets $\Omega_T^{(j)}$ and $\Omega_T^{(c)}$ have positive probability.

Our theorem says that, should we consider the continuous process X' with the corresponding statistic $S'^{(\mathrm{J-DET})}(\Delta_n)$ and critical region $\mathcal{C}'_n$, then $\mathbb{P}(\mathcal{C}'_n) \to \alpha$. Moreover, $S'^{(\mathrm{J-DET})}(\Delta_n) = S^{(\mathrm{J-DET})}(\Delta_n)$ on $\Omega_T^{(c)}$, hence also $\Omega_T^{(c)} \cap \mathcal{C}_n = \Omega_T^{(c)} \cap \mathcal{C}'_n$. Then, the most we can say about the size of the test is that $\limsup_n \mathbb{P}(\mathcal{C}_n \mid \Omega_T^{(c)}) \leq \alpha/\mathbb{P}(\Omega_T^{(c)})$, which may be large when $\mathbb{P}(\Omega_T^{(c)})$ is small.

On the other hand, the theorem also says that $\mathbb{P}(\Omega_T^{(j)} \cap (\mathcal{C}_n)^c) \to 0$. And, as a matter of fact, this test is typically more powerful than the tests developed in the previous sections.

Another possibility for testing the null of "no jump" stems from Theorem 10.21: this theorem asserts that the variables $Z^n(t)$ of (10.61) are asymptotically normal, and also asymptotically independent for distinct values of t, under the minimal assumptions (H-2) and (P), plus the fact that σ has no fixed time of discontinuity. This remains a "finite-dimensional" result in the sense that it does not hold for all times at once. However, it turns out that, *when X is continuous*, the variables $(Z_i^n)_{i \geq 1}$ are also asymptotically normal and independent. Therefore, one can follow Lee and Hannig (2010) and use a normality test, such as a QQ-plot technique.

We will not elaborate on this, though, because the asymptotic theory is in fact quite difficult to establish in a rigorous way, in view of the non-functional convergence obtained in (a) of Theorem 10.21, and not solved yet.

10.4.3   Finding the Jumps: The Finite Activity Case

Now we come to the problem of finding jumps, a task obviously much easier when there are only finitely many of them. So, to start with, we suppose finite activity for jumps in this subsection: the setting is as in Example 10.25, except that the continuity of σ is not assumed, we have (K-0) and (P) and the equations (10.67) and (10.68).

For each n, we let

$$A_n = \{i \in \{1, \ldots, [T/\Delta_n]\} : i \neq i(n, q) \; \forall q \geq 1\}$$

be the set of indices i such that the interval $((i-1)\Delta_n, i\Delta_n]$ contains no jump. By an application of Theorem 10.22 to the continuous process X', and when the Itô semimartingale σ is *continuous*, we have (recall $l_n = \sqrt{2\log(1/\Delta_n)}$, and (10.58) is assumed, see page 571 for a proof)

$$\mathbb{P}\Big(\sup_{i \in A_n} |Z_i^n| > l_n \Big) \;\to\; 0. \tag{10.69}$$

When σ has jumps, whether this still holds is unknown (probably not, unless the jump times of σ are also jump times of X). However, to deal with this case we take a sequence $v_n > 0$ such that

$$v_n \;\asymp\; \Delta_n^{-\varpi} \qquad \text{for some } \varpi \in \Big(0, \frac{1}{2}\Big), \tag{10.70}$$

so $1/v_n$ satisfies (6.24), and we set

$$\overline{Z}_i^n \;=\; \Delta_i^n X / \sqrt{\Delta_n}.$$

Since X' is continuous with paths being Hölder with index ρ for any $\rho \in (0, \frac{1}{2})$, whereas $\Delta_i^n X = \Delta_i^n X'$ when $i \in A_n$, we readily deduce from (10.70) that

$$\mathbb{P}\Big(\sup_{i \in A_n} |\overline{Z}_i^n| > v_n \Big) \;\to\; 0. \tag{10.71}$$

By assuming (10.69) or (10.71), the problem of finding the location and size of all jumps is quite easily solved (in principle!), according to the following procedure:

- Denote by $I_n(1) < \cdots < I_n(\widehat{R}_n)$ the indices i
  in $\{1, \ldots, [T/\Delta_n]\}$ such that either $|Z_i^n| > l_n$ if we
  know that σ is continuous, or $|\overline{Z}_i^n| > v_n$ otherwise; $\qquad$ (10.72)
- Set $\widehat{T}(n,q) = I_n(q)\Delta_n$ and $\widehat{J}(n,q) = \Delta_{I_n(q)}^n X$
  for $q = 1, \ldots, \widehat{R}_n$.

We then conclude that the number of jumps is $\widehat{R}_n$, located in the discretization intervals preceding the times $\widehat{T}(n,q)$, and with (estimated) sizes $\widehat{J}(n,q)$. This is substantiated by the following result, in which the S_q's denote the successive jump times of X (see page 572 for a proof).

Theorem 10.26. *Assume (K-0) and (P) and, when one does not want to assume σ to be continuous, choose any sequence v_n satisfying (10.70). Let $R = \sup(q : T_q \leq T)$ be the number of jumps of X within $[0,T]$ (recall that $\mathbb{P}(T_R = T) = 0$ because X is an Itô semimartingale). Then we have*

$$\mathbb{P}\big(\widehat{R}_n = R, \, T_q \in (\widehat{T}(n,q)-\Delta_n, \widehat{T}(n,q)] \;\forall q \in \{1,\ldots,R\}\big) \;\to\; 1 \tag{10.73}$$

and also the following stable convergence in law:

$$\left(\frac{1}{\sqrt{\Delta_n}}\left(\widehat{J}(n,q) - \Delta X_{T_q}\right)\right)_{q \leq R} \tag{10.74}$$
$$\xrightarrow{\mathcal{L}-s} \left(\sqrt{\kappa_q}\,\sigma_{T_q -}\Psi_{q-} + \sqrt{1 - \kappa_q}\,\sigma_{T_q}\,\Psi_{q+}\right)_{q \leq R}$$

where $(\kappa_q, \Psi_{q-}, \Psi_{q+})$ are as in Theorem 10.21.

The convergence (10.74) might look meaningless at first glance, because the number R is random; however, due to the properties of stable convergence in law, it should be interpreted as follows: for each integer k the stable convergence holds in restriction to the set $\{R = k\}$. Hence (10.74) makes perfect sense, in contrast to the similar statement in which stable convergence in law is substituted with convergence in law.

As far as the number and location of jumps are concerned, (10.73) is obviously the best one can achieve. In particular, due to the observation scheme, it is clearly impossible to specify a location any better than asserting that it lies in some of the inter-observation intervals.

Concerning the estimation of the jump size, (10.74) is also the best one can do, asymptotically speaking. This result can be converted into feasible confidence intervals: first we estimate c_{T_q} and $c_{T_q -}$ by the approximate spot volatilities $\widehat{c}^{n}_{I_n(q)+1}$ and $\widehat{c}^{n}_{I_n(q)-k_n-k}$, see (8.11) for example. Next, if we believe that σ is continuous, or at least continuous at time T_q (a property which can be assumed if $\widehat{c}^{n}_{I_n(q)+1}$ and $\widehat{c}^{n}_{I_n(q)-k_n-k}$ are close to one another) we construct a confidence interval based on the fact that the limit of each term in (10.74) is approximately Gaussian centered with variance $\widehat{c}^{n}_{I_n(q)+1}$. Otherwise, we can build a "conservative" confidence interval, in the same way as in (10.32), using the fact that the asymptotic (conditional) variance is $\frac{1}{2}\left(\widehat{c}^{n}_{I_n(q)} + \widehat{c}^{n}_{I_n(q)-k_n-k}\right)$. Or we may use a more sophisticated method, based on Monte Carlo, as in Theorem 10.12. We somehow doubt, however, the usefulness of a sophisticated method here, since in any case the approximations of c_{T_q} and $c_{T_q -}$ by $\widehat{c}^{n}_{I_n(q)}$ and $\widehat{c}^{n}_{I_n(q)-k_n-k}$ are not really accurate.

Remark 10.27. *This theorem is typically an asymptotic result. In practice, some jumps of X may be small. In the finite sample case, it may thus happen that the size of the jump at time T_q, say, is quite smaller than $l_n \sqrt{\Delta_n}\, c_{T_q}$ or $v_n \sqrt{\Delta_n}\, c_{T_q}$ (according to the case), and the previous procedure does not allow us to detect this jump. On the contrary, an increment $\Delta^n_i X$ may be very large, even though it does not contain any jump, so that $|Z^n_i| > l_n$ or $|\overline{Z}^n_i| > v_n$, and we then wrongly conclude the presence of a jump (spurious jump, or false alarm).*

To detect all jumps the cutoff level for Z_i^n or $\overline{Z}_i^n$ should be as small as possible: in that respect, if we know that σ is continuous, using $|Z_i^n| > l_n$ rather than $|\overline{Z}_i^n| > v_n$ is clearly preferable, and otherwise one should use a v_n with ϖ as small as possible (bigger than 0). In any case, there is nothing one can do about very small jumps, obviously. In the case of finite activity, this is perhaps not a very serious issue, since in most such models used in practice the jumps do have a significantly large size, in comparison with the volatility. In the infinite activity case, most jumps are small or very small, and thus are beyond any possibility of detection, as we will see in the next subsection.

On the other hand, to avoid detecting spurious jumps, one should use a "large" cutoff, that is, in all cases $|\overline{Z}_i^n| > v_n$, with $\varpi > 0$ as large as possible (smaller than $1/2$). This does not totally rule out the possibility of detection of spurious jumps, but it drastically reduces the probability of doing so.

Remark 10.28. The choice between the two versions with Z_i^n or $\overline{Z}_i^n$, and of v_n in the second case, is very much like the choice of the cutoff level u_n in the estimation of the volatility, see page 187. This is of course not a surprise.

In a sense, using Z_i^n and l_n, when possible, is optimal, because the (necessary, but unknown and random and time-varying) "scaling parameter" σ is automatically included in the statistic itself, which is not the case for $\overline{Z}_i^n$ and v_n. When σ jumps, the problem comes from the fact that there is no good control of the supremum of the differences $|\hat{c}_i^n - c_{(i-1)\Delta_n}|$. Hence it could be that some $\hat{c}_i^n$, although always positive, is very small, leading to a large value for Z_i^n and to a spurious jump if one uses Z_i^n in this case instead of $\overline{Z}_i^n$.

10.4.4   The General Case

Below, we drop the finite activity assumption and simply assume (K-2) and (P). We will not consider the case where σ is continuous, since very few models with infinite activity jumps for the price exhibit a continuous volatility.

As noted before, it is of course impossible to reach all jumps of X. The only sensible thing seems to be to look for jumps with absolute size bigger than some prescribed (fixed) level, say $a > 0$.

For this type of problem, the situation is very similar to the finite activity case. Let $T_1, T_1, \ldots$ be the successive jump times of X with $|\Delta X_s| > a$

and $R = \sup(q : T_q \leq T)$. Somewhat analogous with (10.72), we

- Let $I_n(1) < \cdots < I_n(\widehat{R}_n)$ be the indices i
  in $\{1, \cdots, [T/\Delta_n]\}$ such that $|\Delta_i^n X| > a$.
- Set $\widehat{T}(n,q) = I_n(q)\Delta_n$ and $\widehat{J}(n,q) = \Delta_{I_n(q)}^n X$
  for $q = 1, \ldots, \widehat{R}_n$. \hfill (10.75)

Then, by virtue of the following theorem, we conclude that $R = \widehat{R}_n$ and that each T_q for $q \leq T$ is in the interval $(\widehat{T}(n,q) - \Delta_n, \widehat{T}(n,q)]$, with the (estimated) size $\widehat{J}(n,q)$ (see page 573 for a proof).

Theorem 10.29. *Assuming (K-2) and (P), and with the previous notation, both (10.73) and (10.74) hold as soon as*

$$\mathbb{P}(|\Delta X_{T_q}| = a) = 0, \quad \forall q \geq 1. \tag{10.76}$$

The condition (10.76) may look restrictive, but it is satisfied for all $a > 0$ except countably many values (unfortunately, unknown). Moreover, as soon as the Lévy measures $F_t(dx)$ of X have a density, a situation which prevails in all models with infinite jump activity used in finance, then (10.76) holds for all $a > 0$.

The procedure (10.75) is much simpler than the procedure (10.72), because we are only looking for jumps with size bigger than a: there is no cutoff level (going to 0 at an appropriate rate) to choose here, and we do not use estimators of the spot volatility. For the estimation of the size ΔX_{T_q}, the discussion given after Theorem 10.26 can be reproduced here without any change.

However, this is again an "asymptotic" result. In the finite sample case, one may detect spurious big jumps: we may have $|\Delta_i^n X| > a$ because there was a jump in the interval $((i-1)\Delta_n, i\Delta_n]$ with size slightly smaller than a, and likewise we can miss a jump with size slightly bigger than a. We can also detect a spurious jump because in the interval there are two jumps of size approximately $a/2$, and with the same sign. A good idea is probably to do the detection at level a, and also at some other levels $a' < a$. Denote by $\widehat{R}_n(a')$ the number of "detected" jumps at level a'. Then:

1. Consider the biggest $a' < a$ such that $\widehat{R}_n(a') > \widehat{R}_n(a)$. If $\widehat{T}$ is one of the jumps detected at level a', but not at level a, one can use the confidence intervals for the size of this jump to evaluate the probability that its real size is bigger than a, thus asserting the probability of a missed jump.

2. For any $\widehat{T}(n,q)$ detected at level a, the corresponding confidence intervals give us the probability that it is a jump of size smaller than a.

10.5   Detection of Volatility Jumps

In this section, we turn to the question of estimating the jumps (location and size) of the squared volatility process c_t.

In contrast with the low-performing results about the estimation of the quadratic variation $[c, c]$ obtained in Section 8.3, finding the jumps of the process c is easier. Of course, one cannot expect the same rates as for the jumps of the underlying process X itself, as described in Theorems 10.26 and 10.29. But we still can do something. As before, we consider the one-dimensional case only, and assume (K-r) for some $r \in [0, 2)$.

Exactly as in the previous section, we fix a level $a > 0$ and try to detect all jumps of c with size bigger than a. We set

$$T_0 = 0, \quad T_{q+1} = \inf(t > T_q : |\Delta c_t| > a),$$
$$R = \sup(q : T_q \le T).$$

We use below the estimators $\widehat{c}(k_n, u_n)_i$ of (10.26), associated with the sequence $k_n \sim \beta / \Delta_n^{\tau}$ for some $\beta > 0$, and $u_n \asymp \Delta_n^{\varpi}$, subject to the conditions (8.16) (and with $u_n = \infty$, that is no truncation at all, if X is known to be continuous). Recall that $\widehat{c}(k_n, u_n)_{i+1}$ is really an estimator of the averaged volatility

$$\overline{c}_i^n = \frac{1}{k_n \Delta_n} \int_{i\Delta_n}^{(i+k_n)\Delta_n} c_s \, ds.$$

Let us first argue in the simple case where c is equal to the constant u on $[0, S)$, and to the constant $v > u$ on $[S, \infty)$, so $T_1 = S$ with the above notation. When i increases the average volatility $\overline{c}_i^n$ stays equal to u for $i \le [S/\Delta_n] - k_n$, then increases "linearly" in i, and finally stays constant again, equal to v, for $i \ge [S/\Delta_n] + 1$. Consequently, the jump of c results in $k_n + 1$ successive small increments of $\overline{c}_i^n$, hardly discernible when k_n is large. In contrast, the differences $\Delta \overline{c}_i^n = \overline{c}_{(i+2)k_n}^n - \overline{c}_{ik_n}^n$ behave as such: letting j be such that $S \in (jk_n\Delta_n, (j+1)k_n\Delta_n]$, we see that $\Delta \overline{c}_i^n$ vanishes when $i \le j-3$ or $i \ge j+1$, and equals $v - u$ when $i = j-1$, whereas $\Delta \overline{c}_{j-2}^n + \Delta \overline{c}_j^n = v - u$ again.

The previous argumentation, simplistic as it looks, leads us to consider the following differences, which estimate the increments $\Delta \overline{c}_i^n$:

$$L_i^n = \widehat{c}(k_n, u_n)_{(i+2)k_n+1} - \widehat{c}(k_n, u_n)_{ik_n+1}. \tag{10.77}$$

Up to time T, those increments are observable for $i =$ $0, 1, \ldots, [T/k_n \Delta_n] - 3$. In case of a jump Δc_S with $S \in$ $(jk_n\Delta_n, (j+1)k_n\Delta_n]$ we may hope that L^n_{j-1} and $L^n_{j-2} + L^n_j$ are close to Δc_S and, when i is sufficiently close to j but different from $j-2, j-1, j$, then $|L^n_i|$ is much smaller. This theoretical behavior is blurred out by the estimation error incurred by using $\widehat{c}(k_n, u_n)_i$, and also by the intrinsic variation of the process c itself, which is of course not constant right before or right after time S. Nevertheless, and among many slightly different possibilities, one way to detect the jumps of c with size bigger than a is as follows:

We start with $I_n(0) = 0$ and define by induction on q (as usual, $\inf(\emptyset) = \infty$; we recall that below τ is such that $k_n \sim \beta/\Delta_n^\tau$):

$$I_n(q) = \inf\big(i \in \{I_n(q-1) + 3, \ldots, [T/k_n\Delta_n] - k - 3\} :$$
$$|L^n_{i-1}| > a, \ |L^n_{i-1} - L^n_{i-2} - L^n_i| \leq \Delta_n^{\frac{\tau \wedge (1-\tau)}{4}}\big)$$
$$\widehat{R}_n = \sup(q : I_n(q) < \infty),$$

and

$$\widehat{T}(n, q) = I_n(q)k_n\Delta_n,$$
$$\widehat{J}(n, q) = \tfrac{1}{2}\big(L^n_{I_n(q)-2} + L^n_{I_n(q)-1} + L^n_{I_n(q)}\big)$$

for $q = 1, \ldots, \widehat{R}_n$. Although not explicitly mentioned, these quantities also depend on the number $a > 0$, and on Δ_n, k_n, u_n.

The following theorem gives us the behavior of these estimators. It is related to both Theorem 10.29 and Theorem 8.7, and in particular the volatility $c^{(c)}$ of the volatility process c_t appears: since (K-r) holds, the quadratic variation of c is $[c, c]_t = \int_0^t c_s^{(c)}\, ds + \sum_{s \leq t}(\Delta c_s)^2$, see for example (8.13). The proof is given in Subsection B.3.4 of Appendix B.

Theorem 10.30. *Assume (K-r) with some $r \in [0, 2)$, and let $a > 0$ be such that*

$$\mathbb{P}(\exists t > 0 : |\Delta c_t| = a) = 0, \quad \forall q \geq 1. \tag{10.78}$$

We also choose $k_n \sim \beta/\Delta_n^\tau$ with $\beta > 0$ and $u_n \asymp \Delta_n^\varpi$ with the following conditions, which imply (8.16):

$$\tfrac{2(r-1)^+}{r} < \tau < 1, \quad \tau \wedge (1-\tau) < \tfrac{2-r}{r}, \quad \tfrac{1-\tau}{2(2-r)} < \varpi < \tfrac{1}{2}. \tag{10.79}$$

Then we have

$$\mathbb{P}\big(\widehat{R}_n = R, \ T_q \in [\widehat{T}(n, q), \widehat{T}(n, q) + k_n\Delta_n]$$
$$\text{for all } q = 1, \ldots, R\big) \ \to \ 1 \tag{10.80}$$

and also the following stable convergence in law:

$$\tau < \tfrac{1}{2} \;\Rightarrow\; \begin{array}{c} \left(\sqrt{k_n}\,\big(\widehat{J}(n,q) - \Delta c_{T_q}\big)\right)_{q \leq R} \\ \xrightarrow{\;\mathcal{L}-s\;} \left(\sqrt{c_{T_q-}^2 + c_{T_q}^2}\,\Psi_q\right)_{q \leq R} \end{array}$$

$$\tau = \tfrac{1}{2} \;\Rightarrow\; \begin{array}{c} \left(\sqrt{k_n}\,\big(\widehat{J}(n,q) - \Delta c_{T_q}\big)\right)_{q \leq R} \\ \xrightarrow{\;\mathcal{L}-s\;} \left(\sqrt{c_{T_q-}^2 + c_{T_q}^2 + \tfrac{\beta^2}{2}c_{T_q-}^{(c)} + \tfrac{\beta^2}{2}c_{T_q}^{(c)}}\,\Psi_q\right)_{q \leq R} \end{array} \qquad (10.81)$$

$$\tau > \tfrac{1}{2} \;\Rightarrow\; \begin{array}{c} \left(\frac{1}{\sqrt{k_n \Delta_n}}\big(\widehat{J}(n,q) - \Delta c_{T_q}\big)\right)_{q \leq R} \\ \xrightarrow{\;\mathcal{L}-s\;} \left(\sqrt{\tfrac{1}{2}c_{T_q-}^{(c)} + \tfrac{1}{2}c_{T_q}^{(c)}}\,\Psi_q\right)_{q \leq R} \end{array}$$

where the variables Ψ_q are defined on an extension of the space $(\Omega, \mathcal{F}, \mathbb{P})$, and are independent of $\mathcal{F}$ and i.i.d. standard normal.

Moreover, when the process X is continuous one can dispense with the condition (10.79): the results hold as soon as $\tau \in (0,1)$ and $\varpi \in (0, \tfrac{1}{2})$, and also if in (10.77) we use the non-truncated estimators $\widehat{c}(k_n)_i$.

Exactly as for Theorem 10.29 the condition (10.78) may look restrictive, but it is satisfied for all $a > 0$ except countably many values. It is also satisfied for all $a > 0$ as soon as the Lévy measures $F_t^{(c)}(dx)$ of c have a density.

The reader will notice that the detection of jumps, that is, the localization of all the times T_q, is always possible. However, we need to choose τ and ϖ (the latter when X is discontinuous only), subject to (10.79). This is possible only if we know that r does not exceed a specified value $r_0 < 2$ because (10.79) cannot hold when $r = 2$. The precision of the jump localization is $k_n \Delta_n$, so for this purpose we should use a value of τ as small as possible, for example τ very close to $\tfrac{1}{3}$ if we know that $r \leq \tfrac{4}{3}$ (when r is bigger, then τ is also bigger and the precision deteriorates). In the limit (not really feasible), the asymptotic precision of the localization for the jumps is $\Delta_n^{2/3}$, when $r \leq \tfrac{4}{3}$.

For the estimation of the jump sizes, things are different: the best rate is achieved by taking $\tau = \tfrac{1}{2}$, the estimation rate being $1/\Delta_n^{1/4}$ in this case. Achieving this rate necessitates $r < \tfrac{4}{3}$.

However, the estimation of Δc_{T_q} can be considered as accomplished only if it goes together with confidence intervals. For this, we again need consistent estimators for the $\mathcal{F}$-conditional variance and, when $\tau < \tfrac{1}{2}$, such estimators are for example $\widehat{c}(k_n, u_n)_{(I_n(q)-1)k_n}$ and $\widehat{c}(k_n, u_n)_{(I_n(q)+1)k_n}$ for c_{T_q-} and c_{T_q}, respectively. When $\tau \geq \tfrac{1}{2}$ we need estimators for $c_{T_q-}^{(c)}$ and $c_{T_q}^{(c)}$ as well. But, as suggested in Section 8.3, such an estimation cannot be performed with any kind of reasonable accuracy. This supports a choice $\tau < \tfrac{1}{2}$, whenever this is possible.

Remark 10.31. *When X is continuous, the situation is significantly better, because there is no restriction on τ, apart from being in $(0,1)$. In this case the localization of (big) jumps is asymptotically correct within an interval of size $\Delta_n^{1-\tau}$, with τ arbitrarily close to 0. We can almost exactly determine in which interval $((i-1)\Delta_n, i\Delta_n]$ each jump of size bigger than a occurs.*

Remark 10.32. *The best (theoretical) rate $\Delta_n^{1/4}$ for the estimation of jump sizes is probably optimal. To see that, one might consider the example where*

$$\sigma_t = W'_t + \alpha\, N_t, \qquad X_t = \int_0^t \sigma_s\, dW_s$$

where W and W' are two independent Brownian motions and N is a standard Poisson process, and α is an unknown parameter. We are in a classical parametric setting, and it is relatively simple to check that, in restriction to the set $\{N_T = 1\}$ on which a single jump of σ occurs on the time interval $[0, T]$, for example, the optimal rate at which α can be estimated is $1/\Delta_n^{1/4}$.

On the other hand, even when X is discontinuous it should be possible to obtain localization intervals for each jump with a precision arbitrarily close to Δ_n. For instance, instead of considering the increments L_i^n one might consider $L_j'^n = \widehat{c}(k_n, u_n)_{j+2k_n} - \widehat{c}(k_n, u_n)_j$ and base estimators on the whole family of these increments, indexed by $j = 0, \ldots, [T/\Delta_n] - 3k_n$, instead of only considering $L_i^n = L_{ik_n}'^n$ for $i = 0, \ldots, [T/k_n\Delta_n] - 3$. Unfortunately, this would require significantly more sophisticated methods, which have not been developed so far.

10.6   Microstructure Noise and Jumps

In contrast to the estimation of integrated volatility, tests or estimation methods for jumps in the presence of noise have been the object of very few investigations so far. In this section we record a single problem, the most basic one, which concerns tests for the existence of jumps. We also expound a single type of test, the "symmetrical tests" of Section 10.3, and use a single de-noising method, which is pre-averaging. However, the other "kernel type" de-noising methods expounded in Chapter 7 can probably be used in this context equally well.

The setting is the same as in previous discussions, plus the noise. For simplicity, we only consider the case of non-shrinking noise, satisfying Assumption (GN), see page 221. The observations and their returns thus have the form

$$Y_i^n = X_{i\Delta_n} + \chi_{i\Delta_n}, \qquad \Delta_i^n Y = Y_i^n - Y_{i-1}^n.$$

Our aim is still to decide whether the outcome ω lies in $\Omega_T^{(c)}$ or in $\Omega_T^{(j)}$. As before, we need to restrict our attention to the subsets $\Omega_T^{(cW)}$ and/or $\Omega_T^{(jW)}$ on which the Brownian motion is active.

Before starting, let us briefly mention the behavior of the two statistics $S^{(\text{J-PV1})}(p, k, \Delta_n)$ and $S^{(\text{J-PV2})}(p, k, \Delta_n)$ when we plug in the noisy returns $\Delta_i^n Y$ instead of the true ones $\Delta_i^n X$. This of course depends on the structure of the noise, and so far only the additive white noise case is fully understood: we then denote the statistics as $S^{\text{noisy}-(\text{J-PV1})}(p, k, \Delta_n)$ and $S^{\text{noisy}-(\text{J-PV2})}(p, k, \Delta_n)$, and the power variations which are used for defining these statistics as $B^{\text{noisy}}([p, k], \Delta_n)$ and $B^{\text{noisy}}(p, k\Delta_n)$.

In the case of an additive white noise with finite pth moment, and with χ, χ' denoting two independent variables with the same law as all χ_i^n, it can be (easily) proved that, under (H-2),

$$\Delta_n B^{\text{noisy}}([p, k], \Delta_n)_T \xrightarrow{\mathbb{P}} T \mathbb{E}(|\chi - \chi'|^p)$$
$$\Delta_n B^{\text{noisy}}(p, k\Delta_n)_T \xrightarrow{\mathbb{P}} \tfrac{T}{k} \mathbb{E}(|\chi - \chi'|^p)$$

for all $p > 0$. This readily implies, under (H-2),

$$\begin{aligned}
S^{\text{noisy}-(\text{J-PV1})}(p, k, \Delta_n) &\xrightarrow{\mathbb{P}} \tfrac{1}{k}, \\
S^{\text{noisy}-(\text{J-PV2})}(p, k, \Delta_n) &\xrightarrow{\mathbb{P}} \tfrac{1}{k}.
\end{aligned} \qquad (10.82)$$

In particular, and similar to the fact that the "noisy" realized volatility is not an estimator of integrated volatility, the previous statistics cannot be used for telling whether there are jumps or not, because they have the same asymptotic behavior in both cases (at least at first order).

10.6.1   A Noise-Robust Jump Test Statistic

We will use below the pre-averaging method. For this, we take a sequence of integers $k_n \geq 1$ satisfying

$$k_n \sim \frac{1}{\theta \sqrt{\Delta_n}} + o\left(\frac{1}{\Delta_n^{1/4}}\right) \qquad (10.83)$$

for some $\theta > 0$. We also choose a function g on $\mathbb{R}$ which is continuous, null outside $(0, 1)$, piecewise C^1 with a piecewise Lipschitz derivative g', that is, (7.43), and we set

$$\overline{Y}(g)^n_i = \sum_{j=1}^{k_n-1} g\left(\tfrac{j}{k_n}\right) \Delta^n_{i+j-1} Y,$$

$$\widehat{Y}^n(g)_i = \sum_{j=1}^{k_n} \left(g\left(\tfrac{j}{k_n}\right) - g\left(\tfrac{j-1}{k_n}\right)\right)^2 (\Delta^n_{i+j-1} Y)^2.$$

Next, we choose an *even integer* $p \geq 4$ and we define $(\zeta_{p,j})_{j=0,\ldots,p/2}$ as the unique numbers solving the following triangular system of linear equations:

$$\zeta_{p,0} = 1,$$

$$\sum_{l=0}^{j} 2^l\, m_{2j-2l}\, C^{p-2j}_{p-2l}\, \zeta_{p,l} = 0, \qquad j = 1, 2, \ldots, p/2,$$

where as usual m_r is the rth absolute moment of the law $\mathcal{N}(0,1)$. These could be explicitly computed, and for example when $p = 4$ (the case used in practice),

$$\zeta_{4,0} = 1, \quad \zeta_{4,1} = -3, \quad \zeta_{4,2} = \frac{3}{4}.$$

Finally, we define the following processes, which depend on p, q, k_n, g where $q \geq 0$ is an additional integer parameter, and which when $q = 0$ are a kind of de-noised and de-biased power variations of order p:

$$B^{\text{noisy}}(p, q, \Delta_n, k_n, g)_t = \frac{1}{k_n} \sum_{l=0}^{p/2} \zeta_{p,l} \qquad (10.84)$$
$$\times \sum_{i=1}^{[t/\Delta_n]-k_n+1} |\overline{Y}(g)^n_i|^{p-2l}\, |\widehat{Y}(g)^n_i|^{q+l}.$$

We can now introduce the ratio statistics which will be used for testing jumps and which are analogous with $S^{(\text{J-PV1})}(p, k, \Delta_n)$ or $S^{(\text{J-PV2})}(p, k, \Delta_n)$. The difference is that we do not take two distinct time lags Δ_n and $k\Delta_n$, but work instead with the same time lag and *two distinct weight functions* g and h. Then we set, with T being the time horizon,

$$S^{\text{J-noisy}}(p, g, h; \Delta_n) = \frac{B^{\text{noisy}}(p, 0, \Delta_n, k_n, g)_T}{B^{\text{noisy}}(p, 0, \Delta_n, k_n, h)_T}.$$

Theorem A.17 of Appendix A (with $\eta = 0$ because the noise is not shrinking, and $\eta' = \frac{1}{2}$ because of (10.83)) yields that, for any T fixed, the variables $B^{\text{noisy}}(p, 0, \Delta_n, k_n, g)_T$ converge in probability to $\phi(g^{p/2})A(p)_T$ (recall the notation $\phi(g) = \int_0^1 g(x)^2\, dx$), whereas if further X is continuous the variables $(k_n\Delta_n)^{1-p/2} B^{\text{noisy}}(p, 0, \Delta_n, k_n, g)_T$

converge to $m_p \phi(g)^{p/2} C(p)_T$. Using the same argument as in Theorem 10.1, one deduces the following property, analogous with (10.41):

$$S^{\text{J-noisy}}(p, g, h; \Delta_n)$$
$$\xrightarrow{\;\mathbb{P}\;} \begin{cases} \eta_j := \frac{\phi(g^{p/2})}{\phi(h^{p/2})} & \text{on the set } \Omega_T^{(j)} \text{ under (H-2)} \\ \eta_c := \frac{\phi(g)^{p/2}}{\phi(h)^{p/2}} & \text{on the set } \Omega_T^{(cW)} \text{ under (H')} \end{cases} \qquad (10.85)$$

Unless g and h are proportional, the two numbers η_j and η_c are different. They are *known*, and for concreteness we can always suppose that $\eta_c > \eta_j$. Henceforth, we are in the same situation as in Section 10.3 and decide that the path X is continuous if $S^{\text{J-noisy}}(p, g, h; \Delta_n)$ is bigger than some well chosen number in (η_j, η_c), and discontinuous otherwise. And, in order to make this procedure feasible, one needs the second order behavior of the test statistic, which is given in the next subsection.

Example 10.33. *The simplest choice for the pair g, h is as follows. First, choose g, for example the triangular kernel discussed in Example 7.19. Next, take $h(x) = g(\lambda x)$ for some $\lambda > 1$, so the support of h is $[0, 1/\lambda] \subset [0, 1]$). A straightforward computation shows $\eta_c = \lambda^{p/2} > \eta_j = \lambda$.*

10.6.2 The Central Limit Theorems for the Noise-Robust Jump Test

Unfortunately, it is necessary to begin with a long series of notation. For any four bounded functions $g, h, \overline{g}, \overline{h}$ on $\mathbb{R}$ with support in $[0, 1]$ we set for all $t \in \mathbb{R}$ and integers p, l with $0 \le l \le p$ and p even

$$\phi(g, h|t) = \int g(s - t) h(s) \, ds$$

hence $\phi(g, g|0) = \phi(g) = \int_0^1 g(s)^2 \, ds$, and

$$\Phi(g, \overline{g}; h, \overline{h})_{p-} = \int_0^1 \phi(g^{p-1}, \overline{g}|t - 1) \, \phi(h^{p-1}, \overline{h}|t - 1) \, dt$$
$$\Phi(g, \overline{g}; h, \overline{h})_{p+} = \int_0^1 \phi(g^{p-1}, \overline{g}|t) \, \phi(h^{p-1}, \overline{h}|t) \, dt$$
$$\overline{\Phi}(g, h; p, l|t) = \sum_{j=0}^{[(p-l)/2]} C_{p-l}^{2l} \, m_{2j} \, m_{p-2j} \, \phi(g)^{l-p/2} \, \phi(g, h|t)^{p-l-2j}$$
$$\times \left(\phi(g)\phi(h) - \phi(g, h|t)^2 \right)^j.$$

Next, with g, h being two weight functions and with p and r as above and $x, y \ge 0$ we set

$$a(g, h : p, l|t) = \sum_{i,j=0}^{p/2} 2^{i+j} \, \zeta_{p,i} \zeta_{p,j} \, \phi(g')^i \, \phi(h')^j$$
$$\times \sum_{w=(2l+2j-p)+}^{(2l)\wedge(p-2i)} C_{p-2i}^{w} \, C_{p-2j}^{2l-w}$$
$$\times \overline{\Phi}(g, h; 2l, w|t) \, \overline{\Phi}(g', h'; 2p - 2j - 2i - 2l, p - 2i - w|t)$$

$$A(g, h; p, l) = \int_{-1}^{1} a(g, h : p, l | t)\, dt - 2(m_p)^2\, \phi(g)^{p/2}\, \phi(h)^{p/2}\, x^p\, 1_{\{l=0\}},$$
$$R_p(g, h; x, y) = \sum_{l=0}^{p} A(g, h; p, l)\, x^l\, y^{p-l},$$

and finally

$$\begin{aligned}
\Xi(p; g, h)_t &= p^2 \sum_{s \le t} |\Delta X_s|^{2p-2} \\
&\quad \times \big(c_{s-}\,\Phi(g, g; h, h)_{p-} + c_s\,\Phi(g, g; h, h)_{p+}\big), \\
\Xi(p; g, h)_t' &= p^2 \sum_{s \le t} |\Delta X_s|^{2p-2} \\
&\quad \times \big(\gamma_{s-}\Phi(g, g'; h, h')_{p-} + \gamma_s\,\Phi(g, g'; h, h')_{p+}\big).
\end{aligned} \qquad (10.86)$$

These notations may look, and are, extremely cumbersome. However, the numbers $\Phi(g, \overline{g}; h, \overline{h})_{p\pm}$ and $A(g, h; p, r)$ are quite simple to compute numerically for explicit test functions, such as g being the triangular kernel or its derivative. The interested reader will find an interpretation of $R_p(g, h; x, y)$ on pages 500 et seq. of Appendix A.

We then have two basic CLTs, coming from Theorem A.19. We use the simplifying notation $B^{(n)}(p; g) = B^{\mathrm{noisy}}(p, 0, , \Delta_n, k_n, g)$. Besides Assumption (GN) on the noise, the first one requires (H-2) only. Since $p \ge 4$ and $\eta' = \frac{1}{2}$, so $\theta' = \theta$ in the pre-averaging notation, it asserts the joint stable convergence in law (recall (10.38) for $A(p)_T$)

$$\frac{1}{\Delta_n^{1/4}}\big(B^{(n)}(p; g)_T - \phi(g^{p/2})A(p)_T, B^{(n)}(p; h)_T - \phi(h^{p/2})A(p)_T\big) \xrightarrow{\mathcal{L}\text{-s}}$$
$$\big(\tfrac{1}{\sqrt{\theta}}\mathcal{U}(p; g)_T^{\mathrm{noisy}} + \sqrt{\theta}\,\mathcal{U}'(p; g)_T^{\mathrm{noisy}}, \tfrac{1}{\sqrt{\theta}}\mathcal{U}(p; h)_T^{\mathrm{noisy}} + \sqrt{\theta}\,\mathcal{U}'(p; h)_T^{\mathrm{noisy}}\big)$$

for any fixed time T, and where $(\mathcal{U}(p; g)_T^{\mathrm{noisy}}, \mathcal{U}(p; h)_T^{\mathrm{noisy}})$ and $(\mathcal{U}'(p; g)_T^{\mathrm{noisy}}, \mathcal{U}'(p; h)_T^{\mathrm{noisy}})$ are two two-dimensional variables defined on an extension of the space which, conditionally on $\mathcal{F}$, are independent centered Gaussian, with the covariance structure

$$\widetilde{E}(\mathcal{U}(p; g)_T^{\mathrm{noisy}}\,\mathcal{U}(p; h)_T^{\mathrm{noisy}} \mid \mathcal{F}) = \Xi(p; g, h)_T$$
$$\widetilde{E}(\mathcal{U}'(p; g)_T^{\mathrm{noisy}}\,\mathcal{U}'(p; h)_T^{\mathrm{noisy}} \mid \mathcal{F}) = \Xi'(p; g, h)_T.$$

The second CLT is under (KC), so X is continuous. It asserts the joint stable convergence in law

$$\frac{1}{\Delta_n^{1/4}}\big((k_n\Delta_n)^{1-p/2}\, B^{(n)}(p; g)_T - m_p\phi(g)^{p/2}C(p)_T,$$
$$(k_n\Delta_n)^{1-p/2}\, B^{(n)}(p; h)_T - m_p\phi(h)^{p/2}C(p)_T\big)$$
$$\xrightarrow{\mathcal{L}\text{-s}} \big(\tfrac{1}{\sqrt{\theta}}\,\mathcal{W}(p; g)_T^{\mathrm{noisy}}, \tfrac{1}{\sqrt{\theta}}\,\mathcal{W}(p; h)_T^{\mathrm{noisy}}\big)$$

for any fixed time T, and where $(\mathcal{W}(p; g)_T^{\mathrm{noisy}}, \mathcal{W}(p; h)_T^{\mathrm{noisy}})$ is again a two-dimensional variable defined on an extension of the space which, conditionally on $\mathcal{F}$, is centered Gaussian, with the covariance structure

$$\widetilde{E}(\mathcal{W}(p; g)_T^{\mathrm{noisy}}\,\mathcal{W}(p; h)_T^{\mathrm{noisy}} \mid \mathcal{F}) = \int_0^T R_p(g, h; c_s, \theta^2\gamma_s)\, ds.$$

At this point, the same argument (the delta method) as for (10.44) allows us to deduce the following partial stable convergence in law, under (H-2):

$$\frac{1}{\Delta_n^{1/4}}\left(S^{\text{J-noisy}}(p,g,h;\Delta_n) - \eta_j\right) \xrightarrow{\mathcal{L}-\mathrm{s}} \mathcal{S}^{\text{J-noisy}}_{(j)}(p,g,h) \qquad (10.87)$$
in restriction to $\Omega_T^{(j)}$

in restriction to $\Omega_T^{(j)}$, where the variable $\mathcal{S}^{\text{J-noisy}}_{(j)}(p,g,h)$ is defined on an extension of the space, and is $\mathcal{F}$-conditionally centered Gaussian with conditional variance:

$$
\begin{aligned}
V^{\text{J-noisy}}_{(j)}(p,g,h) &:= \widetilde{\mathbb{E}}\big((\mathcal{S}^{\text{J-noisy}}_{(j)}(p,g,h))^2 \mid \mathcal{F}\big) \\
&= \frac{1}{\phi(h^{p/2})^4\, A(p)_T^2}\Big(\tfrac{1}{\theta}\,(\phi(h^{p/2})^2\, \Xi(p;g,g)_T \\
&\quad -2\phi(g^{p/2})\phi(h^{p/2})\Xi(p;g,h)_T + \phi(g^{p/2})^2\, \Xi(p;h,h)_T \\
&\quad +\theta\,(\phi(h^{p/2})^2\, \Xi'(p;g,g)_T - 2\phi(g^{p/2})\phi(h^{p/2})\Xi'(p;g,h)_T \\
&\quad +\phi(g^{p/2})^2\, \Xi'(p;h,h)_T)\Big).
\end{aligned}
\qquad (10.88)
$$

In the same way, one gets under (K-2), and with the same argument as for Theorem 10.1:

$$\frac{1}{\Delta_n^{1/4}}\left(S^{\text{J-noisy}}(p,g,h;\Delta_n) - \eta_c\right) \xrightarrow{\mathcal{L}-\mathrm{s}} \mathcal{S}^{\text{J-noisy}}_{(c)}(p,g,h) \qquad (10.89)$$
in restriction to $\Omega_T^{(cW)}$

where $\mathcal{S}^{\text{J-noisy}}_{(c)}(p,g,h)$ is defined on an extension and is $\mathcal{F}$-conditionally centered Gaussian with conditional variance:

$$
\begin{aligned}
V^{\text{J-noisy}}_{(c)}(p,g,h) &:= \widetilde{\mathbb{E}}\big((\mathcal{S}^{\text{J-noisy}}_{(c)}(p,g,h))^2 \mid \mathcal{F}\big) \\
&= \frac{1}{\theta\,\phi(h)^{2p}\,(m_p)^2\, C(p)_T^2}\int_0^T\big(\phi(h)^p\, R_p(g,g;c_s,\theta^2\gamma_s) \\
&\quad -2\phi(g)^{p/2}\phi(h)^{p/2}\, R_p(g,h;c_s,\theta^2\gamma_s) \\
&\quad +\phi(g)^p\, R_p(h,h;c_s,\theta^2\gamma_s)\big)\,ds.
\end{aligned}
\qquad (10.90)
$$

10.6.3 Testing the Null Hypothesis of No Jump in the Presence of Noise

Here we construct tests for the null hypothesis $\Omega_T^{(cW)}$. The idea is of course the same as in Subsection 10.3.3, based on (10.89), and we need consistent estimators for $V^{\text{J-noisy}}_{(c)}(p,g,h)$, at least in restriction to $\Omega_T^{(cW)}$. The problem is similar to the variance estimation in Subsection 10.3.3 and we will use below the version corresponding to $V_n^{(2)}$ in (10.50). That is, we estimate $C(p)_T$ in the denominator of (10.48) by using a non-truncated estimator and taking advantage of the property

$$(k_n\Delta_n)^{1-p/2}\, B^{\text{noisy}}(p,0;\Delta_n,k_n,g)_T \xrightarrow{\mathbb{P}} m_p\,\phi(g^{p/2})\, C(p)_T$$
in restriction to $\Omega_T^{(cW)}$,

which follows from Theorem A.17 in the usual way.

For estimating the integral in (10.90) we observe that $R_p(g, h; x, y)$ is a polynomial in (x, y), and we make use of the truncated versions of (10.84), which are

$$B^{\text{noisy}}(p, q; \Delta_n, k_n, g; u_n)_t = \frac{1}{k_n} \sum_{l=0}^{p/2} \zeta_{p,l}$$
$$\times \sum_{i=1}^{[t/\Delta_n]-k_n+1} |\overline{Y}(g)_i^n|^{p-2l} \, |\widehat{Y}(g)_i^n|^{q+l} \, 1_{\{|\overline{Y}(g)_i^n| \leq u_n\}}$$

where $u_n \asymp \Delta_n^{\varpi}$ for some $\varpi \in (0, \frac{1}{4})$ (note that here ϖ is more restricted than in the usual truncation procedure, due to the fact that the typical size of $|\overline{Y}(g)_i^n|$ is $\Delta_n^{1/4}$, instead of $\Delta_n^{1/2}$ for $|\Delta_i^n X|$). Let us also pick another weight function f (which can be g or h, for example) and set

$$\widehat{R}(g, h)_n = \frac{1}{(k_n \Delta_n)^{p-1}} \sum_{l=0}^{p} \frac{A(g, h; p, l)}{m_{2l} \, 2^{p-l} \phi(f)^l \, \phi(f')^{p-l}}$$
$$\times B^{\text{noisy}}(2l, p - l; \Delta_n, k_n, f; u_n)_T.$$

In view of the last equation in (10.42), Theorem A.18-(a) of Appendix A gives us

$$\widehat{R}(g, h)_n \xrightarrow{\mathbb{P}} \int_0^T R_p(g, h; c_s, \theta^2 \gamma_s) \, ds,$$
in restriction to $\Omega_T^{(cW)}$.

All these properties imply that the variables

$$\widehat{V}_{(c)}^n = \frac{k_n \sqrt{\Delta_n} \, \phi(g^{p/2})^2}{\phi(h)^{2p} \, (m_p)^2 \, (B^{\text{noisy}}(p, 0; \Delta_n, k_n, g)_T)^2} \left(\phi(h)^p \widehat{R}(g, g)_n \right.$$
$$\left. - 2\phi(g)^{p/2} \phi(h)^{p/2} \widehat{R}(g, h)_n + \phi(g)^p \, \widehat{R}(h, h)_n \right) \tag{10.91}$$

converge in probability to $V_{(c)}^{\text{J-noisy}}(p, g, h)$, in restriction to the set $\Omega_T^{(cW)}$. Recalling that $\eta_c > \eta_j$, this leads us to use the following critical region at stage n:

$$\mathcal{C}_n = \left\{ S^{\text{J-noisy}}(p, g, h; \Delta_n) < \eta_c - z'_\alpha \, \Delta_n^{1/4} \sqrt{\widehat{V}_{(c)}^n} \right\} \tag{10.92}$$

where z'_α is the α-quantile of the standard normal distribution $\mathcal{N}(0, 1)$.

Theorem 10.34. *Assume (K-2) and (GN). Let $p \geq 4$ be an even integer and choose g, h, f as above, and k_n satisfying (10.83), and $u_n \asymp (\Delta_n)^{\varpi}$ for some $\varpi \in (0, \frac{1}{4})$. Then the tests (10.92) have the strong asymptotic size α for the null hypothesis $\Omega_T^{(cW)}$. They are also consistent for the alternative $\Omega_T^{(j)}$, as soon as $\varpi > \frac{p-2}{4(p-1)}$.*

Proof. The first claim follows from (10.89) and $\widehat{V}_{(c)}^n \xrightarrow{\mathbb{P}} V_{(c)}^{\text{J-noisy}}(p, g, h)$ on $\Omega_T^{(cW)}$. For the second claim, by the first part of (10.85) and $\eta_j < \eta_c$, it suffices to show that $\sqrt{\Delta_n}\,\widehat{V}^n_{(c)} \xrightarrow{\mathbb{P}} 0$ on $\Omega^{(jW)}_T$. Toward this aim, we first observe that the denominator of (10.91) converges in probability to a limit which is positive on $\Omega^{(jW)}_T$, by an application of (A.61). Hence it is indeed enough to prove that $\sqrt{\Delta_n}\,\widehat{R}(g,h)_n \xrightarrow{\mathbb{P}} 0$ for any two functions g, h. Now, we set

$$H(l)_n = \sum_{i=1}^{[T/\Delta_n]-k_n+1} |\overline{Y}(f)^n_i|^{2p-2l}\,|\widehat{Y}(f)^n_i|^l\,1_{\{|\overline{Y}(f)^n_i|\leq u_n\}}.$$

We clearly have $\sqrt{\Delta_n}\,|\widehat{R}(g,h)_n| \leq K\Delta_n^{3/2-p/2}\sum_{l=0}^p H(l)_n$, whereas Hölder's inequality implies $H(l)_n \leq (H(0)_n)^{(p-l)/p}\,(H(p)_n)^{l/p}$. Henceforth we are left to prove that $\Delta_n^{3/2-p/2}H(l)_n \xrightarrow{\mathbb{P}} 0$ for $l = 0$ and for $l = p$. For this, we can rely upon the localization procedure mentioned in Section A.5 of Appendix A, which allows us to assume the strengthened assumptions (SH-2) and (SGN) instead of (H-2) and (GN). In this case, the estimates (A.79) give us $\mathbb{E}(|\overline{Y}(f)^n_i|^2) \leq K\Delta_n^{1/2}$ and $\mathbb{E}(|\widehat{Y}(f)^n_i|^p) \leq K\Delta_n^{p/2}$, from which we deduce

$$\mathbb{E}(H(0)_n) \leq u_n^{2p-2}\sum_{i=1}^{[T/\Delta_n]-k_n+1}\mathbb{E}(|\overline{Y}(f)^n_i|^2) \leq KT\Delta_n^{(2p-2)\varpi-1/2},$$
$$\mathbb{E}(H(p)_n) \leq KT\Delta_n^{p/2-1}.$$

Since $\varpi > \frac{p-2}{4(p-1)}$, we obtain the result. $\qquad\square$

10.6.4 Testing the Null Hypothesis of Presence of Jumps in the Presence of Noise

Based on the behavior (10.85) of the statistic $S^{\text{J-noisy}}(p,g,h;\Delta_n)$ and on its associated CLT (10.87), we now test the null hypothesis $\Omega^{(jW)}_T$. We need consistent estimators for the conditional variance (10.88), which amounts to consistent estimators for the variables $\Xi(p;g,h)_T$ and $\phi(h)^{p/2}A(p)_T$. For the latter, and as seen before, we can use $B^{\text{noisy}}(p,0,\Delta_n,k_n,h)_T$. For the former, we use Theorem A.18-(b) of Appendix A: if $u_n > 0$ and $k'_n \in \mathbb{N}$ satisfy

$$\frac{k'_n}{k_n} \to \infty, \quad k'_n\Delta_n \to 0, \quad u_n \asymp \Delta_n^{\varpi/2} \text{ for some } \varpi \in \left(0,\frac{1}{2}\right), \quad (10.93)$$

and if

$$F_{n+} = \frac{1}{k_n^2 k_n' \Delta_n} \sum_{i=1}^{[t/\Delta_n]-k_n'-k_n+1} |\overline{Y}(f)_i^n|^{2p-2}$$
$$\times \sum_{j=1}^{k_n'} \left((\overline{Y}(f)_{i+j}^n)^2 - \frac{1}{2}\widehat{Y}(f)_{i+j}^n \right) 1_{\{|\overline{Y}(g)_{i+j}^n| \le u_n\}}$$

$$F_{n-} = \frac{1}{k_n^2 k_n' \Delta_n} \sum_{i=k_n+k_n'}^{[t/\Delta_n]-k_n+1} |\overline{Y}(f)_i^n|^{2p-2}$$
$$\times \sum_{j=1}^{k_n'} \left((\overline{Y}(f)_{i-j}^n)^2 - \frac{1}{2}\widehat{Y}^n(f)_{i-j} \right) 1_{\{|\overline{Y}(f)_{i-j}^n| \le u_n\}}$$

$$F_{n+}' = \frac{1}{k_n^2 k_n' \Delta_n} \sum_{i=1}^{[t/\Delta_n]-k_n'-k_n+1} |\overline{Y}(f)_i^n|^{2p-2}$$
$$\times \sum_{j=1}^{k_n'} \widehat{Y}^n(f)_{i+j} 1_{\{|\overline{Y}(f)_{i+j}^n| \le u_n\}}$$

$$F_{n-}' = \frac{1}{k_n^2 k_n' \Delta_n} \sum_{i=k_n+k_n'}^{[t/\Delta_n]-k_n+1} |\overline{Y}(f)_i^n|^{2p-2} \sum_{j=1}^{k_n'} \widehat{Y}(f)_{i-j}^n 1_{\{|\overline{Y}(f)_{i-j}^n| \le u_n\}},$$

for an arbitrary weight function f (for example $f = g$ or $f = h$), we have

$$F_{n+} \xrightarrow{\mathbb{P}} \phi(f)\,\phi(f^{p-1}) \sum_{s \le t} c_s |\Delta X_s|^{2p-2}$$
$$F_{n-} \xrightarrow{\mathbb{P}} \phi(f)\,\phi(f^{p-1}) \sum_{s \le t} c_{s-} |\Delta X_s|^p$$
$$F_{n+}' \xrightarrow{\mathbb{P}} 2\theta^2 \phi(f')\,\phi(f^{p-1}) \sum_{s \le t} \gamma_s |\Delta X_s|^{2p-2}$$
$$F_{n-}' \xrightarrow{\mathbb{P}} 2\theta^2 \phi(f')\,\phi(f^{p-1}) \sum_{s \le t} \gamma_{s-} |\Delta X_s|^{2p-2}.$$

Then, in view of (10.86) and (10.88), the next variables converge in probability to $V_{(j)}^{\text{J-noisy}}(p, g, h)$:

$$\widehat{V}_{(j)}^n = \frac{p^2 k_n \sqrt{\Delta_n}}{\phi(h^{p/2})^2 \phi(f^{p-1}) (B^{\text{noisy}}(p,0,\Delta_n,k_n,h)_T)^2}$$
$$\times \Big(\frac{1}{\phi(f)} \big((\phi(h^{p/2})^2 \Phi(g,g;g,g)_{p-} - 2\phi(g^{p/2})\phi(h^{p/2})\,\Phi(g,g;h,h)_{p-}$$
$$+ \phi(g^{p/2})^2\,\Phi(h,h;h,h)_{p-} \big)\, F_{n-}$$
$$+ \frac{1}{\phi(f)} \big((\phi(h^{p/2})^2\,\Phi(g,g;g,g)_{p+} - 2\phi(g^{p/2})\phi(h^{p/2})\,\Phi(g,g;h,h)_{p+}$$
$$+ \phi(g^{p/2})^2\,\Phi(h,h;h,h)_{p+} \big)\, F_{n+}$$
$$+ \frac{1}{2\phi(f')} \big((\phi(h^{p/2})^2\,\Phi(g,g';g,g')_{p-} - 2\phi(g^{p/2})\phi(h^{p/2})\,\Phi(g,g';h,h')_{p-}$$
$$+ \phi(g^{p/2})^2\,\Phi(h,h';h,h')_{p-} \big)\, F_{n-}'$$
$$+ \frac{1}{2\phi(f')} \big((\phi(h^{p/2})^2\,\Phi(g,g';g,g')_{p+} - 2\phi(g^{p/2})\phi(h^{p/2})\,\Phi(g,g';h,h')_{p+}$$
$$+ \phi(g^{p/2})^2\,\Phi(h,h';h,h')_{p+} \big)\, F_{n+}' \Big).$$

Note that although these formulas are rather lengthy, the quantities involved are easy to compute numerically. The main result is then as follows:

Theorem 10.35. *Assume (H-2) and (GN). Let $p \ge 4$ and choose g, h, f as above, and k_n, k_n', u_n satisfying (10.83) and (10.93). Then the tests* *with critical regions*

$$\mathcal{C}_n \;=\; \Big\{ S^{\text{J-noisy}}(p, g, h; \Delta_n) > \eta_j + z'_\alpha \Delta_n^{1/4} \sqrt{\widehat{V}^n_{(j)}} \;\Big\},$$

have the strong asymptotic size α for the null hypothesis $\Omega_T^{(jW)}$, and are consistent for the alternative $\Omega_T^{(cW)}$ if further (H$'$) holds.

Proof. Since $\widehat{V}^n_{(j)} \xrightarrow{\;\mathbb{P}\;} V^{\text{J-noisy}}_{(j)}(p, g, h) > 0$ on $\Omega_T^{(W)}$, the first claim follows from (10.87), and the second one from the second part of (10.85) and from $\eta_c > \eta_j$.   □

10.7   References

The literature about tests for jumps is not as abundant as for the estimation of integrated volatility, but still quite vast, and the above account is not exhaustive. Among the procedures which have not been analyzed here, one may mention the following ones: the first test for jumps of a discretely sampled process was proposed by Aït-Sahalia (2002); that test is designed for diffusion (Markov) processes and is based on properties of the transition density of the process over discrete time intervals and as such is not specific to high-frequency data, and it involves techniques that are different from those that are the main subject of this book. Using high-frequency data, Carr and Wu (2003b) exploit the differential behavior of short dated options to test for the presence of jumps. Of course, the structure of the data in such tests is different from here, as it is in Jiang and Oomen (2008), who use variance swaps. Podolskij and Ziggel (2011) provide a test based on a form of bootstrap is given while Christensen et al. (2011) features an overview of empirical results on jumps from Press (1967) up to the most recent work.

The "linear" test and some forms of the "ratio" test of Section 10.2 are due to Barndorff-Nielsen and Shephard (2006) and Huang and Tauchen (2005); for multipowers, the first authors use $k = 2$ while the second ones propose several versions, using $k = 2$ and $k = 3$. Corsi et al. (2010) use a ratio test based on truncated multipowers.

The estimators of the ratio based on truncations in Section 10.2 was proposed in Aït-Sahalia and Jacod (2012a), while the method underlying the "sharp confidence intervals" and based on Monte Carlo in Subsection 10.2.4 was developed by Jacod and Todorov (2009) for a different purpose. The idea of adding an extra Brownian motion in Subsection 10.2.5 is due to Corsi et al. (2010), again for a different purpose.

The symmetrical tests of Section 10.3 for jumps vs. continuous and continuous vs. jumps are due to Aït-Sahalia and Jacod (2009b) for the statistic $S^{(\text{J-PV2})}(p, k, \Delta_n)$, and the improvement consisting in using $S^{(\text{J-PV1})}(p, k, \Delta_n)$ is due to Fan and Fan (2011).

Section 10.4 mainly follows Lee and Mykland (2008) and Lee and Hannig (2010) with suitable modifications to fit our setting. In particular, and in contrast with these papers, we do not want the volatility process σ to be necessarily continuous, since when X jumps it is often the case that σ jumps at the same time. Andersen et al. (2007) modify Lee and Mykland (2008) by taking in the denominator the estimated average volatility over the time interval, instead of the estimated spot volatility.

Subsections 10.4.3 and 10.4.4 contain essentially new material, although a connected study in the finite activity case may be found in Clément et al. (2014). Section 10.5 about detection of volatility jumps is also new, whereas Section 10.6 about jump tests in the presence of microstructure noise is taken, without proofs, from Aït-Sahalia et al. (2012), while Li (2013) contains some additional material.

Finally, two papers, by Dumitru and Urga (2012) and Theodosiou and Zikes (2011), propose a comparison of some of the tests, including those descried in this chapter and some of those which have only been mentioned here.

Chapter 11

Finer Analysis of Jumps: The Degree of Jump Activity

After having developed tests for deciding whether the underlying process X has jumps, we go further in the statistical analysis of the jumps. This of course makes sense only if we believe that jumps exist, for example because one of the tests of the previous chapter rejects the "continuous" hypothesis.

The previous analysis can be extended in two different directions. One direction amounts to studying the same kind of testing problems in more complex situations, such as finding whether two components of a multi-dimensional process have jumps at the same times (always, sometimes, never?), or whether a process and its volatility have jumps at the same times, or, when this is the case, whether the sizes of the jumps of the price and of the volatility are correlated or not. These sorts of questions will be (partially) answered in Chapter 14.

In this chapter, we pursue another direction. The underlying process is one-dimensional again, but our aim is to estimate the parameters governing the jumps (that is, which are constitutive of the Lévy measure of the process) and which are identifiable in the sense of Chapter 5.

Theorem 5.8, which solves the identifiability question for Lévy processes, serves as a guideline for the forthcoming investigations: basically, for a Lévy process X which is (discretely or continuously) observed on a fixed time interval $[0, T]$, the Lévy measure F, which describes the law of the jumps, *can never* be identified on the basis of the observation of a single path. However, one may still say something about the behavior of F near 0. More specifically, the behavior near 0 of the Lévy measure is related with small and very small jumps, and in particular it somehow describes the concentration of these small jumps. For example, the "explosion" rate at 0 of the measure F is characterized by the following objects:

$$ I = \left\{ p \geq 0 : \int (|x|^p \wedge 1)\, F(dx) < \infty \right\}, \qquad \beta = \inf I $$

(this is (1.49)), and according to (1.50), we have $p \in I$ if and only if $A(p)_t = \sum_{s \leq t} |\Delta X_s|^p < \infty$ almost surely for all t, and otherwise $A(p)_t = \infty$ almost surely for all $t > 0$. In particular, jumps have finite activity if and only if $0 \in I$, in which case $\beta = 0$ (we may have $\beta = 0$ and jumps with infinite activity, in the case of a gamma process for example). The number β is called the Blumenthal-Getoor (BG) index and belongs to $[0, 2]$. Furthermore I is either (β, ∞) or $[\beta, \infty)$, and $2 \in I$ always. So the bigger β, the faster the measure F diverges near 0, hence, in a sense, the more small or tiny jumps we have. These properties are what motivate our calling β a jump activity index, and our interest in estimating it.

Coming back to identifiability of F, the restriction of F to the complement of any neighborhood of 0 is *never* identifiable. On the other hand, β and the set I are identifiable, because the variables $A(p)_T$ are observed (in the case of continuous observations) or approximated (when observations are discrete), for all p. Even more, if F enjoys a kind of "expansion" near 0 we have not only β, but also further BG indices $\beta_2 > \beta_3 > \cdots$, all smaller than $\beta = \beta_1$, and those (together with their associated intensities) are identifiable as long as they are bigger than $\beta/2$. Clearly β, its associated intensity, and even the successive BG indices and associated intensities, are only a tiny part of the whole measure F. But one should understand that they are essentially the only parts of F which can be identified, or consistently estimated: this is for Lévy processes, but it is of course even more true for more general semimartingales.

The notions of BG indices can be extended to Itô (or even, general) semimartingales, see (5.16) for example, and successive BG indices also make sense for semimartingales. Our primary concern in this chapter is the estimation of those quantities, together with the related intensities. For general Itô semimartingales the problem seems utterly intractable, so we need some assumptions on the process, which may be considered as restrictive from a theoretical point of view. However, in practice *all* models used by practitioners fulfill these assumptions. Our objective in doing so is to provide specification tools for financial models, where the presence or at least the possibility of large jumps is generally accepted. There is much less consensus in the literature regarding the nature or even the need for small jumps, and this is where knowing the BG index might prove very useful for modeling.

11.1   The Model Assumptions

The underlying process X is our usual one-dimensional Itô semimartingale, defined on some filtered space $(\Omega, \mathcal{F}, (\mathcal{F}_t)_{t\geq 0}, \mathbb{P})$. It has the Grigelionis representation (1.74), that is,

$$X_t = X_0 + \int_0^t b_s ds + \int_0^t \sigma_s dW_s \tag{11.1}$$
$$+ (\delta 1_{\{|\delta|\leq 1\}}) \star (\underline{p} - \underline{q})_t + (\delta 1_{\{|\delta|>1\}}) \star \underline{p}_t,$$

with the usual notation: W is a one-dimensional Brownian motion, $\underline{p}$ is a Poisson measure on $\mathbb{R}_+ \times E$ with $(E, \mathcal{E})$ a Polish space, and with compensator $\underline{q}(dt, dx) = dt \otimes \lambda(dx)$.

The Blumenthal-Getoor index is most easily expressed in terms of the characteristics of the process. These characteristics are of the form (1.68), that is,

$$B_t = \int_0^t b_s ds, \qquad C_t = \int_0^t c_s ds, \qquad \nu(dt, dx) = dt\, F_t(dx),$$

where b is the same as in (11.1), and $c = \sigma^2$, and $F_t(\omega, dx)$ is the restriction to $\mathbb{R}\backslash\{0\}$ of the image of λ by the map $z \mapsto \delta(\omega, t, z)$.

The main assumption in this chapter is the same as in (H-2) for the processes b and σ, but is quite stronger for δ (or for the Lévy measures F_t, as it is expressed), and as stated below it only makes sense when X is one-dimensional. We first need to introduce the "tail" functions of the Lévy measure F_t: they are the functions on $(0, \infty)$ (also depending implicitly on ω) given by

$$\overline{F}_t^{(+)}(x) = F_t((x, \infty)),$$
$$\overline{F}_t^{(-)}(x) = F_t((-\infty, -x)),$$
$$\overline{F}_t(x) = \overline{F}_t^{(+)}(x) + \overline{F}_t^{(+)}(x).$$

There is *a priori* no reason for which positive and negative jumps should behave in the same way, so we have two indices, one for positive jumps and the other for negative jumps, as explained for Lévy processes in Subsection 5.2.2. However, for a clearer exposition, we start with the (partly) symmetrical case where positive and negative jumps have the same index, the non-symmetrical case being examined in Subsection 11.2.4 below. So we introduce the following assumption:

Assumption (L). *The process X is of the form (11.1), with b_t locally bounded and σ_t càdlàg, and there are two constants $0 \leq \beta' < \beta < 2$ such that*

$$x \in (0,1] \quad \Rightarrow \quad \left| x^\beta \, \overline{F}_t^{(\pm)}(x) - a_t^{(\pm)} \right| \leq L_t \, x^{\beta - \beta'}, \tag{11.2}$$

where $a_t^{(+)}$ and $a_t^{(-)}$ and L_t are nonnegative predictable (or optional) and locally bounded processes.

Under (L) we introduce the following increasing processes:

$$\begin{aligned}
A_t^{(+)} &= \int_0^t a_s^{(+)} \, ds, \\
A_t^{(-)} &= \int_0^t a_s^{(-)} \, ds, \\
A_t &= A_t^{(+)} + A_t^{(-)}.
\end{aligned} \tag{11.3}$$

Note that for any Lévy process satisfying (L), $a_t^{(\pm)}(\omega) = a^{(\pm)}$ are constants.

Recalling the "global" Blumenthal-Getoor index γ_t (on the time interval $[0,t]$) and the "spot" index β_t (at time t) defined in (5.16), we see that under Assumption (L) we have $\gamma_t = \beta$ on the set $\{A_t > 0\}$, whereas $\gamma_t \leq \beta'$ on the complement $\{A_t = 0\}$. Analogously, we have $\beta_t = \beta$ on the set $\{a_t^{(+)} + a_t^{(-)} > 0\}$ and $\beta_t \leq \beta'$ on its complement.

Example 11.1. *We first give examples of Lévy processes which satisfy (L). This is clearly true of a stable process with index β (the assumption is designed for that!), and also of a tempered stable process whose Lévy measure has the form*

$$F(dx) = \frac{\beta}{|x|^{1+\beta}} \left(f_+(x) 1_{\{x>0\}} + f_-(x) 1_{\{x<0\}} \right) dx \tag{11.4}$$

with $f_\pm(x) = a^{(\pm)} e^{-B_\pm |x|}$ for some constants $a^{(+)}, a^{(-)}, B_{(+)}, B_{(-)} > 0$. It turns out that the measure F given by (11.4) satisfies (L) for much more general functions $f_\pm$ than the negative exponentials. Namely, as soon as $\int_1^\infty f_+(x) x^{-1-\beta} \, dx < \infty$ and $|f_+(x) - 1| \leq K x^{\beta - \beta'}$ and all $x \in (0,1]$, plus the same conditions on f_-, on the negative side, then (L) is satisfied.

Example 11.2. *Still about Lévy processes: if X and Y are two independent Lévy processes, with X satisfying (L), and Y having a Blumenthal-Getoor less than β', then $X + Y$ also satisfies (L), with the same $\beta, \beta', a^{(+)}, a^{(-)}$ as X.*

Example 11.3. *Many examples of Lévy models proposed in finance for asset returns satisfy (L), with either fixed values of β, or β being a free parameter. (We will discuss estimating β below.) Examples are included in Figure 1.1. They include compound Poisson-based models starting with Merton (1976), the normal inverse Gaussian model of Barndorff-Nielsen (1998) ($\beta = 1$), the variance gamma model of Madan and Seneta (1990) and Madan et al. (1998) ($\beta = 0$), the hyperbolic model of Eberlein and Keller (1995), the generalized hyperbolic model of Barndorff-Nielsen (1977) and the CGMY model of Carr et al. (2002) (in which β is a free parameter).*

Example 11.4. *Very often semimartingales are obtained by stochastic integration against a Lévy process. In this case, Assumption (L) is preserved. That is, if Z is a Lévy process satisfying (L) and without Brownian part, and if H is a locally bounded predictable process, the semimartingale*

$$X_t = X_0 + \int_0^t b_s \, ds + \int_0^t \sigma_s \, dW_s + \int_0^t H_s \, dZ_s \qquad (11.5)$$

satisfies (L) as well, with the same indices β and β', as soon as b is locally bounded and σ is càdlàg.

Example 11.5. *A similar type of assumption on F_t consists of assuming that we have*

$$F_t(dx) = \frac{\beta}{|x|^{1+\beta}} \left(a_t^{(+)} 1_{\{x>0\}} + a_t^{(-)} 1_{\{x<0\}} \right) dx + F_t'(dx),$$

where $a_t^{(+)}$ and $a_t^{(-)}$ are as in (L) and F_t' is a signed measure with the following property: if $|F_t'|$ denotes the absolute value of F_t', that is, the smallest positive measure such that both $|F_t'| - F_t'$ and $|F_t'| + F_t'$ are positive measures, then

$$\text{the process} \quad \int (|x|^{\beta'} \wedge 1) |F_t'|(dx) \quad \text{is locally bounded.}$$

(Of course, although F_t' may be a signed measure, the measure F_t should be a positive measure.) This assumption implies (L), with the same $\beta, \beta', a_t^{(\pm)}$, and is in fact "almost" the same as (L).

Remark 11.6. *The previous examples suggest that (L) is a reasonably weak assumption, and in any case it is satisfied by all models used in finance, when they have jumps.*

The latter fact does not really mean, though, that it is a reasonable assumption to model real data. Indeed, (L) contains two (intertwined) hypotheses:

(L1). The measure F_t is close to a stable Lévy measure, by an amount measured by $\beta - \beta'$ (see the previous comments), as far as small jumps are concerned (it says nothing about the finiteness of moments of the jumps, in contrast with the Lévy stable case).

(L2). The index β, which a priori could be $\beta_t(\omega)$, is indeed not random and not time-dependent.

Hypothesis (L1) seems reasonable (although from a mathematical viewpoint one could replace $|x|^\beta$ in (11.2) by $L(x)|x|^\beta$, with L a slowly varying function, and accordingly modify the forthcoming results; note that if, for example, $L(x) = (\log |x|)^\gamma$ for some $\gamma \in \mathbb{R}$, then not only β but γ as well are identifiable on the basis of the observation of a single path on a finite time interval).

On the other hand, hypothesis (L2) is less likely to hold. One would rather expect $\beta = \beta_t$ to be varying (slowly?) with time. The dependence upon ω would also be a natural hypothesis, but in contrast with the dependency upon t, it is irrelevant in the context of the observation of a single path.

A last mention: although we need β to be non-random and constant over time, we do not require $a_t^{(\pm)}$ to be strictly positive at all times. We may have "intermittencies": when $a_t^{(+)} = a_t^{(-)} = 0$ the spot Blumenthal-Getoor index is not bigger than β' at those times.

Remark 11.7. *It is also worth mentioning that having (L) plus $a_t^{(+)} = a_t^{(-)} = 0$ identically amounts to saying that the BG index of all spot Lévy measures F_t does not exceed the fixed number β'. In this case, the index β itself has no relevant meaning for the process X.*

Under (L), Theorem 5.17 tells us that the parameter β, which here is non-random and equal to γ_T in (5.16) on the set

$$\Omega_T^{(\beta)} = \{A_T > 0\}, \tag{11.6}$$

is identifiable, or at least pairwise identifiable, on the basis of the observation over $[0, T]$.

Moreover, although stated only for Lévy processes, Theorem 5.8 suggests that the variables $A_t^{(\pm)}$ are also identifiable for all $t \leq T$ (and the two processes $a_t^{(\pm)}$ as well, when they are càdlàg or càglàd). Therefore, there should exist estimators for β and $A_T^{(\pm)}$, at each stage n, when the process is discretely observed with observation lag Δ_n, which are consistent as $\Delta_n \to 0$, and hopefully enjoy good distributional properties, so that we can for example construct confidence intervals: this is the object of the next section. We could also construct estimators for $a_t^{(\pm)}$ (somehow looking like the spot volatility estimators), but we will not touch upon this topic below.

There is a strong connection between (H-r) and (L), or rather between (H-r) and the following assumption, which is obviously weaker than (L) for any given index β:

Assumption (L'). *The process X is of the form (11.1), with b_t locally bounded and σ_t càdlàg and, for some constant $\beta \in [0,2]$, the process $\sup_{x \in (0,1]} x^\beta \, \overline{F}_t(x)$ is locally bounded.*

We then have the following lemma (proved on page 583), which yields that under (L) we have (H-r) for all $r > \beta$; it also yields that (L') with $\beta = 0$ is the same as (H-0).

Lemma 11.8. *If (H-r) holds for some $r \in [0,2]$, we have (L') for all $\beta \in [r,2]$, and conversely if (L') holds for some $\beta \in [0,2)$, there exists a Grigelionis decomposition (11.1) which satisfies (H-r) for all $r \in (\beta,2]$, and also for $r = 0$ when $\beta = 0$.*

11.2 Estimation of the First BG Index and of the Related Intensity

Below we suppose that X satisfies (L) and that it is observed at regularly spaced times $i\Delta_n$ within the time interval $[0,T]$. As always, the returns are denoted as $\Delta_i^n X = X_{i\Delta_n} - X_{(i-1)\Delta_n}$.

11.2.1 Construction of the Estimators

One of the main challenges raised by the estimation of β and $A_T^{(\pm)}$ is that these quantities are related to the small (or, rather, very small) jumps, because they describe the behavior of the Lévy measures "at 0" in the sense that the "tail" functions at 0 of the Lévy measure F_t satisfy $\overline{F}_t^{(\pm)}(x) \sim a_t^{(\pm)}/x^\beta$ as $x \downarrow 0$. Hence it is natural to expect that the small increments of the process are going to be the ones that are most informative about β. On the other hand (see Subsection 10.4.4), recovering small jumps is an impossible task, because there are infinitely many of them, and also they are blurred out by the "Brownian increments" due to the continuous martingale part in (11.1). Being able to "see through" the continuous part of the semimartingale in order to say something about the number and concentration of small jumps is therefore going to be the challenge we face as we attempt to estimate β.

The key ideas for deriving estimators are as follows:

- Throw away small increments, because those are mainly due to the Brownian part, plus the sum of infinitely many infinitesimal jumps; those small increments provide no useful information on "individual" small jumps. This step is performed by choosing a cutoff level u_n going to 0 and deleting all increments with size smaller than u_n. Note that the truncation is now to the right, unlike that of Section 6.2.1.

- Pretend that increments bigger than u_n are jumps: that is, if $|\Delta_i^n X| > u_n$, then the interval $((i-1)\Delta_n, i\Delta_n]$ contains a jump with size bigger than u_n, and only one, and further $\Delta_i^n X$ itself is a good approximation for this jump size. This property is of course not literally true, and is even quite wrong in a sense, but one of our main tasks is to show that it is "right enough."

- Estimate β and $A_t^{(\pm)}$, as if we had observed exactly all jumps with size bigger than u_n, and also as if the sizes of these jumps were independent.

The choice of the cutoff levels u_n raises the same problems as those for estimating the integrated volatility when there are jumps, except that we are now interested in the jumps instead of trying to eliminate them; it is natural for the same reasons to take a sequence satisfying (6.24), that is,

$$ u_n \asymp \Delta_n^\varpi \qquad \text{for some } \varpi \in \left(0, \frac{1}{2}\right). \tag{11.7} $$

The rationale behind this choice of ϖ is that increments of order of magnitude less than or equal to $\sqrt{\Delta_n}$ are mainly "Brownian increments," thus giving no or very little information on the jumps themselves. Since $\Delta_n^{1/2} \ll \Delta_n^\varpi$, the upward truncation at level u_n eliminates these uninformative (for jumps) returns, while still keeping some information about small jumps because $u_n \to 0$ so the number of kept increments goes to infinity as soon as there are infinite activity jumps.

***First estimators based on counting increments greater than the
truncation cutoff*** For these first estimators, the main role is played
by the following integer-valued functionals:

$$
\begin{aligned}
J(\Delta_n, u_n)_t^{(+)} &= \sum_{i=1}^{[t/\Delta_n]} 1_{\{\Delta_i^n X > u_n\}} \\
J(\Delta_n, u_n)_t^{(-)} &= \sum_{i=1}^{[t/\Delta_n]} 1_{\{\Delta_i^n X < -u_n\}} \\
J(\Delta_n, u_n)_t &= J(\Delta_n, u_n)_t^{(+)} + J(\Delta_n, u_n)_t^{(-)}.
\end{aligned}
\tag{11.8}
$$

These are very simple-minded functionals: they simply count how many
increments are bigger than u_n, or smaller than $-u_n$, or bigger than u_n
in absolute value. They lead to empirical quantiles of the distribution of
log-returns. By using the statistic $J(\Delta_n, u_n)_t$, which simply counts the
number of large increments – those greater than u_n – we are retaining
only those increments of X that are not predominantly made of contributions from its continuous martingale part, which are $O_p(\Delta_n^{1/2})$, and
instead are predominantly made of contributions due to a jump.

The key property of the functionals $J(\Delta_n, u_n)_t$ is their convergence in
probability

$$
u_n^\beta J(\Delta_n, u_n)_t \xrightarrow{\mathbb{P}} A_t,
\tag{11.9}
$$

which we will show holds under Assumption (L). This property leads to
an estimator of β at each stage n. Fix $\gamma > 1$ and, recalling the time
horizon T, define

$$
\widehat{\beta}_n(\gamma; u_n) = \frac{\log(J(\Delta_n, u_n)_T / J(\Delta_n, \gamma u_n)_T)}{\log(\gamma)}
\tag{11.10}
$$

if $J(\Delta_n, \gamma u_n)_T > 0$, and 0 otherwise. $\widehat{\beta}_n(\gamma; u_n)$ is at least consistent
for estimating β on the set $\{A_T > 0\}$. Note that 0 in the definition
of $\widehat{\beta}_n(\gamma; u_n)$ when $J(\Delta_n, \gamma u_n)_T = 0$ is a dummy value, which could be
replaced by anything else.

This $\widehat{\beta}_n$ is constructed from a suitably scaled ratio of two J's evaluated
on the same time scale Δ_n but at two different truncation levels. In a
way, this construction is in the same spirit as the classical estimator of
Hill (1975), who conducts inference about the tails of a distribution based
on ratios of various extremes.

A number of variants are possible. Taking $k \geq 1$ an integer and two
sequences u_n and v_n of truncation levels, and with a fixed time horizon
T, we can set

$$
\widehat{\beta}_n'(u_n; v_n; k) = \frac{\log(J(\Delta_n, u_n)_T / J(k\Delta_n, v_n)_T)}{\log(v_n/u_n)}
\tag{11.11}
$$

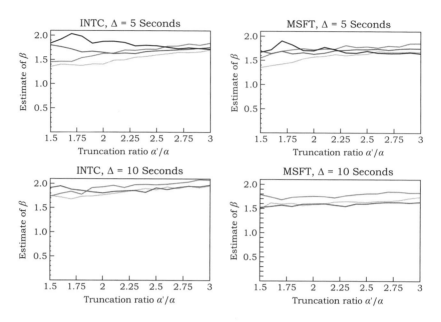

Figure 11.1: Estimates of the jump activity index β obtained from $\hat{\beta}_n$ at 5 and 10 seconds for Intel and Microsoft, all 2006 transactions.

if $J(\Delta_n, u_n)_T > 0$ and $J(k\Delta_n, v_n)_T) > 0$, and 0 otherwise. These more general estimators have the same asymptotic properties as the former ones have. In this formulation, k seems to play no role, but it indeed does in the associated Central Limit Theorem. A natural choice could be $k \geq 2$ and either $v_n = u_n\sqrt{k}$ or $v_n = u_n k^\varpi$ (recall (11.7)). However, it seems that $\hat{\beta}_n(\gamma; u_n) = \hat{\beta}'_n(u_n; \gamma u_n; 1)$ already offers enough flexibility, with γ ranging from 1 to ∞.

Note that for any given n it may happen that $\hat{\beta}_n(\gamma; u_n)$ is not informative. This is of course the case when $J(\Delta_n, \gamma u_n)_T = 0$, but also when this variable is relatively small: indeed, $J(\Delta_n, \gamma u_n)_T$ is the number of returns which are really used in the statistical analysis, and thus it should be reasonably large. If this is not the case, one may take a smaller value for the truncation level u_n.

For example, Figure 11.1 shows the results of implementing the estimator $\hat{\beta}_n$.

Improved estimators based on a smooth truncation In the heuristic justification of the pertinence of the previous estimators based on counting "large" returns, it is of course not exactly true that the jumps bigger than u_n are in one-to-one correspondence with the returns $\Delta_i^n X$ bigger than u_n: by using $J(\Delta_n, u_n)_t$ we quite likely miss some jumps slightly bigger than u_n, and mistakenly count some jumps slightly smaller than u_n. To partly alleviate this, we can use a smooth test function g to construct a smooth approximation to the indicator functions $1_{(u_n, \infty)}$ or $1_{(-\infty, -u_n)}$ in (11.8). We then set

$$J(g; \Delta_n, u_n)_t = \sum_{i=1}^{[t/\Delta_n]} g(\Delta_i^n X / u_n). \qquad (11.12)$$

We will assume that, for some real $p \geq 1$, the test function g satisfies

- g is bounded, even, nonnegative, continuous,
  piecewise C^1, with $g(0) = 0$;
- $|g'(x)| \leq K(|x|^{p-1} \wedge 1)$, $\int |g'(y)| \, dy < \infty$;   (11.13)
- $x, x + y \in [-1, 1]$
  $\Rightarrow |g'(x+y) - g'(x)| \leq K|x|^{(p-2)^+} |y|^{(p-1) \wedge 1}$.

In particular, we have $|g(x)| \leq K(|x|^p \wedge 1)$. The evenness assumption is rather innocuous: it means that we treat the positive and the negative jumps in exactly the same way, and it simplifies notation. Note that if (11.13) holds with p, it also holds with all $p' > p$. For example, we may take

$$g(x) = |x|^p \wedge 1, \quad \text{or} \quad g(x) = (|x| - 1)^+ \wedge 1. \qquad (11.14)$$

The first one satisfies (11.13) with p equal to the exponent of $|x|$; the second one, like any bounded continuous and piecewise C^1 even function vanishing on $[-1, 1]$, satisfies (11.13) for *all* $p > 0$.

Before exhibiting the estimators, we also associate with any g satisfying (11.13) the following functions, where $x \in \mathbb{R}$ and $y \in (0, p)$ and $z > 1$:

$$\begin{aligned}
g_+(x) &= g(x) 1_{\{x > 0\}}, \\
g_-(x) &= g(x) 1_{\{x < 0\}} = g_+(-x), \\
v_g(y) &= y \int_0^\infty \frac{g(x)}{x^{1+y}} \, dx, \\
\overline{v}_g(y, z) &= \frac{y}{(\log z)^2 \, v_g(y)^2} \int_0^\infty \frac{(g(x) - z^y \, g(x/z))^2}{x^{1+y}} \, dx.
\end{aligned} \qquad (11.15)$$

The estimation is performed through two successive steps, by estimating β first and then $A_T^{(\pm)}$. We fix a sequence u_n satisfying (11.7), a number $\gamma > 1$, and a function g satisfying (11.13) and not identically equal to 0. As usual, the time horizon T is fixed, and not explicitly mentioned in the estimators which we presently introduce:

$$\widehat{\beta}(\gamma, g; u_n) = \frac{\log \left(J(g; \Delta_n, u_n)_T / J(g; \Delta_n, \gamma u_n)_T \right)}{\log \gamma} \qquad (11.16)$$

if $J(g; \Delta_n, u_n)_T > 0$ and $J(g; \Delta_n, \gamma u_n)_T > 0$, and 0 otherwise, where 0 is a dummy value, as in (11.10), which could indeed be replaced by any arbitrary number. Next, with the convention $v_g(0) = 1$ (again a dummy value!), we set

$$\widehat{A}^{(\pm)}(\gamma, g; u_n) = \frac{(u_n)^{\widehat{\beta}(\gamma, g; u_n)}}{v_g(\widehat{\beta}(\gamma, g; u_n))} \, J(g_\pm; \Delta_n, u_n)_T. \qquad (11.17)$$

Remark 11.9. *As we will see below, it is best to choose a test function g which satisfies $g(x) > 0$ for all $x \neq 0$, in which case $\widehat{\beta}(\gamma, g; u_n)$ takes the dummy value 0 on the set where $\Delta_i^n X = 0$ for all $i \leq [T/\Delta_n]$, a set with vanishing probability in all practical situations. Otherwise, one may have $\widehat{\beta}(\gamma, g; u_n) = 0$ on a set with positive probability. However, the limit theorems obtained below are in restriction to the set $\Omega_T^{(\beta)} = \{A_T > 0\}$, and on this set both $J(g; \Delta_n, u_n)_T$ and $J(g; \Delta_n, \gamma u_n)_T$ (properly normalized) go to a positive limit. Thus, asymptotically at least, this dummy value 0 is immaterial.*

In practice, $\widehat{\beta}(\gamma, g; u_n) = 0$ means that the estimation of β is impossible at stage n with the chosen test function g and truncation level u_n, and we stop here: this could be because u_n is not small enough, but more likely it is because we are outside the set $\Omega_T^{(\beta)}$, and probably even because the observed path has finitely many jumps, or even none at all.

Remark 11.10. *The above estimators estimate β, $A_T^{(+)}$ and $A_T^{(-)}$, under (L). Now, in this assumption we allow for $a_t^{(+)}$ and $a_t^{(-)}$ to be different, whereas the BG index β is the same for positive and negative jumps, although when $a_t^{(+)} > 0 = a_t^{(-)}$ for example, β is the BG index for positive jumps, and the BG index for negative jumps is at most β'. The situation where the indices for positive and negative jumps are distinct, with the necessary specific assumptions, is considered in some detail in Subsection 11.2.4.*

11.2.2 Asymptotic Properties

The key point is the asymptotic behavior of the functionals $J(g_\pm; \Delta_n, u_n)$: here $u_n \asymp \Delta_n^\varpi$ with ϖ allowed to be an arbitrary positive number (instead of $\varpi \in (0, \frac{1}{2})$, we will need this wider generality later), and g is a function satisfying (11.13), with the exponent p.

First, by Theorem B.20-(a) with $\beta_+ = \beta_- = \beta$, we have the following convergence in probability, locally uniform in time:

$$u_n^\beta \, J(g; \Delta_n, u_n) \overset{\text{u.c.p.}}{\Longrightarrow} v_g(\beta) \, A \qquad (11.18)$$

(recall that $v_g(\beta)$ is finite when $p > \beta$, as is the case below; this extends (11.9) upon noticing that $v_g(\beta) = 1$ when $g(x) = 1_{\{|x| \geq 1\}}$, although this particular function does not satisfy (11.13)), under (L) and either one of the following two conditions on the triple (β, p, ϖ):

(i) $p > 2$, $\varpi < \frac{p-2}{2(p-\beta)}$

(ii) $\sigma_t \equiv 0$ and $\begin{cases} p > 1, \; \varpi < \frac{p-1}{p-\beta} & \text{if } \beta < 1 \\ p > \beta, \; \varpi < \frac{1}{\beta} & \text{if } \beta \geq 1. \end{cases}$ $\qquad$ (11.19)

Moreover, we have a CLT associated with (11.18), with the rate $u_n^{\beta/2}$, as soon as $\beta' < \beta/2$ and either one of the following two conditions is satisfied:

(i) $p > 2$, $\varpi < \frac{1}{2+\beta} \wedge \frac{p-2}{2p-\beta}$

(ii) $\sigma_t \equiv 0$ and $\begin{cases} p > 1, \; \varpi < \frac{2}{2+\beta} \wedge \frac{2p-2}{2p-\beta} & \text{if } \beta < 1 \\ p > \beta, \; \varpi < \frac{2}{\beta(2+\beta)} \wedge \frac{2p-2\beta}{\beta(2p-\beta)} & \text{if } \beta \geq 1. \end{cases}$ $\qquad$ (11.20)

In view of the form of our estimators, the following result is now (almost) evident, and formally proved, together with the next CLT, on pages 593 et seq.

Theorem 11.11. *Assume (L) and let $u_n \asymp \Delta_n^\varpi$ for some $\varpi \in (0, \frac{1}{2})$. Then for all $\gamma > 1$ and g satisfying (11.13) with $p > \frac{2-\beta\varpi}{1-2\varpi}$ (always satisfied when $p \geq 4$ if $\varpi \leq \frac{1}{4}$) we have*

$$\left. \begin{array}{l} \widehat{\beta}(\gamma, g; u_n) \xrightarrow{\;\mathbb{P}\;} \beta \\ \widehat{A}^{(\pm)}(\gamma, g; u_n) \xrightarrow{\;\mathbb{P}\;} A_T^{(\pm)} \end{array} \right\} \text{ in restriction to the set } \Omega_T^{(\beta)}.$$

The associated Central Limit Theorem is less obvious, and it takes the following form:

Theorem 11.12. *Assume (L) with $\beta' < \beta/2$, and let $u_n \asymp \Delta_n^\varpi$ for some $\varpi \in (0, \frac{1}{2+\beta})$ and $\gamma > 1$ and g satisfying (11.13) with $p > \frac{2-\beta\varpi}{1-2\varpi}$ (these conditions on (p, ϖ) are satisfied for all $\beta \in (0, 2)$ if $p \geq 4$ and $\varpi \leq \frac{1}{4}$). Then the following joint stable convergence in law holds, in restriction to the set $\Omega_T^{(\beta)}$, and where Φ is a standard normal variable, defined on an extension of the space $(\Omega, \mathcal{F}, \mathbb{P})$ and independent of $\mathcal{F}$:*

$$\left(\frac{\widehat{\beta}(\gamma, g; u_n) - \beta}{u_n^{\beta/2}}, \; \frac{\widehat{A}^{(+)}(\gamma, g; u_n) - A_T^{(+)}}{u_n^{\beta/2} \log(1/u_n)}, \; \frac{\widehat{A}^{(-)}(\gamma, g; u_n) - A_T^{(-)}}{u_n^{\beta/2} \log(1/u_n)} \right)$$
$$\xrightarrow{\mathcal{L}-s} \left(\sqrt{\frac{\overline{v}_g(\beta, \gamma)}{A_T}} \Phi, \; -\sqrt{\frac{\overline{v}_g(\beta, \gamma)}{A_T}} A_T^{(+)} \Phi, \; -\sqrt{\frac{\overline{v}_g(\beta, \gamma)}{A_T}} A_T^{(-)} \Phi \right).$$
$\qquad$ (11.21)

A striking feature of this result is the degeneracy of the three-dimensional limit. The estimation errors for all three quantities β, $A_T^{(+)}$ and $A_T^{(-)}$ are the same, up to multiplicative $\mathcal{F}$-measurable variables. The error in the estimation of β actually drives the other two errors, because in (11.17) the term involving the biggest error is $u_n^{\widehat{\beta}(\gamma,g;u_n)}$.

The rate of convergence is $1/u_n^{\beta/2} \asymp 1/\Delta_n^{\beta\varpi/2}$, so we should use ϖ as large as possible, that is, $\varpi = \frac{1}{4}$. In this case the rate becomes $1/\Delta_n^{\beta/8}$. This is a conservative result, assuming that *a priori* β ranges through the whole interval $(0,2)$. However, if for some reason we "know" that β is strictly smaller than a given value β_0, we can choose ϖ bigger than $\frac{1}{4}$, hence improving the estimation. More specifically, in this case the CLT holds for all $\beta \in (0,\beta_0)$ under the following conditions:

$$\varpi = \frac{1}{2+\beta_0}, \qquad p \geq \frac{4-2\beta_0}{\beta_0} \qquad (11.22)$$

and the rate becomes $1/\Delta_n^{\beta/(4+2\beta_0)}$.

Remark 11.13. *If we take $g(x) = 1_{\{|x|>1\}}$ we have $\widehat{\beta}(\gamma,g;u_n) = \widehat{\beta}(\gamma;u_n)$, as given by (11.9). This function g satisfies (11.13) for all $p > 0$, except that it is discontinuous at the two points -1 and 1. Nevertheless, one has exactly the same results (consistency and CLT), although we need stronger requirements on ϖ, due to the lack of smoothness of g: for example the CLT holds for all $\beta \in (0,2)$ when $\varpi \leq \frac{1}{5}$ only. So the best rate of convergence with these estimators is significantly lower, and it is not advisable to use (11.9) in practice.*

Remark 11.14. *As mentioned above, the rate improves when one knows that $\beta < \beta_0$ for some value $\beta_0 < 2$. When further β is known (a rather unlikely event in practice, but perhaps true in other contexts than finance), we can do better for the estimation of $A_T^{(\pm)}$. In this case, we substitute $\widehat{\beta}(\gamma,g;u_n)$ with β in (11.17). Then, with $\widehat{A}_n^{(\pm)}$ denoting the new estimators, the rate of convergence becomes the slightly faster $u_n^{-\beta/2}$ (the log term disappears), and we have*

$$\left(\frac{\widehat{A}_n^{(+)}-A_T^{(+)}}{u_n^{\beta/2}}, \frac{\widehat{A}_n^{(-)}-A_T^{(-)}}{u_n^{\beta/2}}\right) \xrightarrow{\mathcal{L}-s} \left(\frac{\sqrt{v_{g^2}(\beta)A_T^{(+)}}}{v_g(\beta)}\Phi_+, \frac{\sqrt{v_{g^2}(\beta)A_T^{(-)}}}{v_g(\beta)}\Phi_-\right)$$

in restriction to the set $\Omega_T^{(\beta)}$, and where Φ_+ and Φ_- are two standard normal variables, independent, and independent of $\mathcal{F}$ (see page 597 for the proof).

In order to make the estimations above feasible, one needs consistent estimators for the (conditional) asymptotic variances in (11.21).

For example, the variance of $\widehat{\beta}(\gamma, g; u_n) - \beta$ is asymptotically equivalent to $u_n^\beta \overline{v}_g(\gamma, \beta)/A_T$, which involves A_T and also the unknown value β in two ways: in $\overline{v}_g(\beta, \gamma)$ and in the rate $u_n^{\beta/2}$. Since $\beta \mapsto \overline{v}_g(\beta, \gamma)$ and $\beta \mapsto v_g(\beta)$ are continuous functions we can plug in the estimator of β; for $u_n^\beta/v_g(\beta)A_T$ we can use the consistency result (11.18) and approximate this quantity by $1/J(g; \Delta_n, u_n)_T$.

Putting these ideas to use, we can then give confidence bounds for β and $A_T^{(\pm)}$. Namely, if z_α is the α-absolute quantile of $\mathcal{N}(0, 1)$, the interval

$$\mathcal{I}_n = \left[\widehat{\beta}(\gamma, g; u_n) - a_n z_\alpha, \widehat{\beta}(\gamma, g; u_n) + a_n z_\alpha\right],$$

$$\text{with } a_n = \sqrt{\frac{\overline{v}_g(\gamma, \widehat{\beta}(\gamma, g; u_n)) \, v_g(\gamma, \widehat{\beta}(\gamma, g; u_n))}{J(g; \Delta_n, u_n)_T}} \tag{11.23}$$

is a confidence interval for β, at stage n, with asymptotic significance level α in the sense that

$$\lim_n \mathbb{P}(\beta \notin I_n \mid B) = \alpha$$
$$\text{for all } B \in \mathcal{F} \text{ with } \mathbb{P}(B) > 0 \text{ and } B \subset \Omega_T^{(\beta)} = \{A_T > 0\}.$$

In the same way, confidence intervals for $A_T^{(+)}$ and $A_T^{(-)}$ with asymptotic significance level α are given, at stage n, by

$$\mathcal{I}_n^{(\pm)} = \left[\widehat{A}^{(\pm)}(\gamma, g; u_n)\left(1 - a_n z_\alpha \log(1/u_n)\right), \right.$$
$$\left. \widehat{A}^{(\pm)}(\gamma, g; u_n)\left(1 + a_n z_\alpha \log(1/u_n)\right)\right]$$

with a_n as in (11.23).

Remark 11.15. *The reader will have noticed that the asymptotic properties of the three estimators above hold on the set $\Omega_T^{(\beta)}$ (under (L)), and thus they work as well if there is no Brownian motion at all, that is, when σ_t is identically 0.*

If we know that there is no Brownian motion (tests for this eventuality are given in Chapter 13), and if we also know that β does not exceed some known value β_0 (as before Remark 11.13) we can even improve the rate. Indeed, instead of (11.22) we can take ϖ to be smaller than $\frac{p-1}{p} \wedge \frac{2}{(\beta_0 \vee 1)(2+\beta_0)}$, but as close to this value as we wish to, and $p \geq 3$ (this follows from Theorem B.20 and the same proof as for the previous theorem).

11.2.3   How Far from Asymptotic Optimality?

This subsection is devoted to various comments about the optimality, or lack thereof, of the estimators constructed above. This concerns in particular the choice of the tuning "parameters" $\gamma > 1$ and u_n and of the function g itself.

About the Rate of Convergence   The most important parameter
is the one governing the rate of convergence, that is the sequence u_n:
the rate for estimating β being $u_n^{\beta/2}$, one should take u_n "as small" as
possible, in comparison with Δ_n of course. That is, since $u_n \asymp \Delta_n^\varpi$,
one should take ϖ as large as possible, that is, $\varpi = \frac{1}{4}$ (or bigger when
possible, as in the situation described in (11.22)). More precisely, the
squared estimation errors have the following order of magnitude: if $u_n =
\alpha \Delta_n^\varpi$, then

$$
\begin{aligned}
(\widehat{\beta}(\gamma, g; u_n) - \beta)^2 &\approx \tfrac{\overline{v}_g(\beta,\gamma)\,\alpha^\beta}{A_T}\,\Delta_n^{\beta\varpi} \\
(\widehat{A}^{(\pm)}(\gamma, g; u_n) - A_T^{(\pm)})^2 &\approx \tfrac{\overline{v}_g(\beta,\gamma)\,\alpha^\beta\varpi^2(A_T^{(\pm)})^2}{A_T}\,\Delta_n^{\beta\varpi}\left(\log\tfrac{1}{\Delta_n}\right)^2
\end{aligned}
\tag{11.24}
$$

(the right sides above are the asymptotic conditional variances). These
convergence rates are quite slow. To understand why they are so slow,
and how close to (or far from) optimality they are, one can consider the
model studied in Section 5.2, with only one stable process. That is, our
underlying process has the form

$$ X = \sigma W + Y, \tag{11.25} $$

where $\sigma > 0$ and Y is a symmetric stable process with Lévy measure
$F(dx) = (a\beta/2|x|^{1+\beta})\,dx$ (this differs from the model in Section 5.2 by
a factor $1/2$, in order to fit the notation of the present chapter). There
are three parameters in this model: $c = \sigma^2 > 0$, $\beta \in (0,2)$, and $a > 0$.
Further, (L) holds, with the same β and $a_t^{(\pm)} = a/2$, hence $A_T = Ta$.

   In such a parametric model, an overall lower bound for the estimation variance of a parameter at stage n is given by the inverse of the
corresponding Fisher information at this stage. Theorem 5.25 and (5.22)
provide us with the rate at which Fisher-efficient estimators $\widehat{\theta}_n$ converge
to θ, that is, such that the normalized sequence $r_n(\widehat{\theta}_n - \theta)$ converge to
a proper limit, for the two parameters $\theta = \beta$ and $\theta = a$ (or equivalently
$\theta = aT$):

- for β: $r_n(\text{opt}) \sim 1/\Delta_n^{\beta/4}(\log(1/\Delta_n))^{\beta/4-1}$
- for a: $r_n(\text{opt}) \sim 1/\Delta_n^{\beta/4}(\log(1/\Delta_n))^{\beta/4}.$

$$\tag{11.26}$$

   A comparison between (11.24) and (11.26) shows how far from rate
optimality our estimators are, in the setting of (11.25): if we neglect the
logarithmic terms, the rates $r_n = 1/\Delta_n^{\beta\varpi/2}$ in (11.24) and $r_n(\text{opt}) =
1/\Delta_n^{\beta/4}$ in (11.26) satisfy

$$ r_n \approx r_n(\text{opt})^{2\varpi}. $$

When β ranges through $(0, 2)$, we need $\varpi = \frac{1}{4}$ and the rate r_n is roughly (up to logarithmic terms again) the square root of the optimal rate. If we know that $\beta \in (0, \beta_0)$ for some $\beta_0 < 2$, then we can take $\varpi = \frac{1}{2+\beta_0}$, see (11.22), hence the rate r_n approaches the optimal rate when β_0 is small. One should, however, be aware that the rates deteriorate as β decreases, but this is an intrinsic property already of the optimal rates above.

This comparison is perhaps not totally fair, since (11.26) holds when σ is known, and for a very special parametric submodel. However, the situation here is in deep contrast with the estimation of the integrated volatility, which can be done with the same rate, and even the same asymptotic variance as the optimal estimation of σ^2 in the model (11.25).

Remark 11.16. *One should be aware that any estimator for β which uses only the increments bigger than u_n, as the estimators $\widehat{\beta}(\gamma, g; u_n)$ basically do (because $g(x)$ is small, when $|x|$ is small) is likely to have a rate not faster than $1/u_n^{\beta/2}$ (as again our estimators do): indeed, the number of increments bigger than u_n is of order of magnitude A_T/u_n^{β} as soon as u_n is large enough to eliminate the "Brownian increments" (this is what taking $\varpi < \frac{1}{2}$ does), hence the rate can hardly be faster than the square root $1/u_n^{\beta/2}$.*

The Asymptotic Variance   Once the rate is fixed, that is, once ϖ with $u_n \asymp \Delta_n^{\varpi}$ is chosen (typically $\varpi = \frac{1}{4}$), we still have to choose the tuning parameters α if $u_n = \alpha\Delta_n^{\varpi}$, and $\gamma > 1$, and the test function g.

First, one should choose α as small as possible. Since the truncation is mainly aimed at eliminating the "Brownian increments," and as for the truncations occurring in the previous chapters, in practice u_n is chosen to be something like three to five times the standard deviation of a typical Brownian increment, that is, $\sqrt{\overline{\sigma}^2 \Delta_n}$, where $\overline{\sigma}^2$ is the average squared volatility.

Next we should choose g and γ which minimize the variance $\overline{v}_g$ (note that this quantity, as well as the estimators, are invariant if we multiply g by a constant, so if we restrict our attention to bounded test functions we can always standardize in such a way that $\sup|g| = 1$). A complete study seems to be out of reach, but we can consider the first example of (11.14), that is, $g(x) = g_p(x) = |x|^p \wedge 1$ with $p > \beta$. A calculation shows that

$$v_g(\beta) = \frac{p}{p-\beta}, \qquad \overline{v}_g(\beta, \gamma) = \frac{2(p-\beta)}{(\log \gamma)^2} \times \frac{p(\gamma^{\beta} - 1) - \beta\gamma^{\beta}(1 - \gamma^{-p})}{p(2p - \beta)}.$$

When p is fixed, $\overline{v}_g(\beta, \gamma)$ decreases from $+\infty$ to some positive value when

γ increases from 0 to some value $\gamma(p, \beta)$, and then it increases back to ∞. When γ is fixed, $\overline{v}_g(\beta, \gamma)$ increases with p in (β, ∞), from 0 up to $(\gamma^\beta - 1)/2$: consequently, it is best to use the test function $g(x) = |x|^p \wedge 1$ with s as small as possible, that is, $p = 4$ when no prior knowledge on β is assumed, and $p = \frac{4 - 2\beta_0}{\beta_0}$ if we know that β is smaller than a given value β_0.

Practical Considerations and Results   In practice, and apart from the choice of u_n which has been discussed above, one should be aware that the rate is low, hence confidence bounds are wide apart. We suggest using the previous procedure for g as described above (with $p = 4$) and with several values of γ, ranging from 1.5 to 5 for example. Then one can perform a regression on the different values of γ.

Estimating β requires large sample size due to the reliance on truncating from the right to eliminate the contributions from the continuous part of the model. That is, the estimators of β discard by construction a large fraction of the original sample, and to retain a sufficient number of observations to the right of a cutoff u_n, we need to have a large sample to begin with. So we will generally estimate β using only the highest sampling frequencies. Of course, these sampling frequencies are the most likely to be subject to market microstructure noise. Because we are only retaining the increments larger than the cutoff u_n instead of those smaller than the cutoff, this could be less of a concern despite the ultra high sampling frequencies.

We find in practice estimated β's in the range from 1.5 to 1.8, indicating a very high degree of jump activity, in effect much closer to Brownian motion than to compound Poisson. The filtered transactions produce the highest estimates of β, leading on average to a process that effectively looks like Brownian motion. Figure 11.2 reports the values of the estimator $\hat{\beta}$ computed for the four quarters of the year, a range of values of α from 5 to 10 standard deviations, and Δ_n from 5 to 10 seconds. The middle right plot reports the corresponding data against the limited range of Δ_n employed. The lower panels, relating the estimated values of β to stock-level liquidity, do not display strong patterns. Looking at the DJIA index itself, to the extent that an infinite activity component is present, we find that it is less active, with estimated values of β ranging from 0.9 to 1.4. But in light of the results of the test of finite vs. infinite jump activity (see the next chapter) it is even likely that the jumps of the index have finite activity.

This discrepancy between the behavior of the DJIA index and its

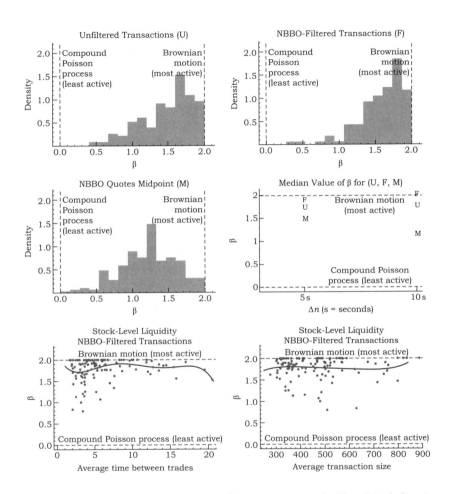

Figure 11.2: Estimating the index of jump activity β : Empirical distribution of β for all 30 DJIA stocks, 2006, measured using transactions (unfiltered, U, and NBBO-filtered, F) and NBBO quotes midpoint (M), and median value of the estimated β as a function of the sampling interval Δ_n, and nonlinear regression of the estimated β against stock-level liquidity measures.

individual stock components can be interpreted in light of *a factor model with systematic and idiosyncratic components*. If we further decompose the jump part of individual stocks into a common component and an idiosyncratic component, then when an idiosyncratic jump occurs the other stock prices do not jump, so the influence of this particular jump on the index, which is an average, is essentially wiped out: the index will not exhibit a jump of significant size. In contrast, a systematic jump will typically occur at the same time (and often with the same sign) for most or all stocks, resulting in a jump of the index. Therefore, the absence of empirical evidence in favor of infinite activity jumps in the index, combined with their presence in the individual components, point toward purely idiosyncratic small jump components in the individual assets.

This makes sense if we think of most systematic, that is, market-wide, price moves as driven by important macroeconomic news and therefore likely to be large. On the other hand, small infinite activity jumps are more likely to reflect individual stock-level considerations, such as stock-specific information and its immediate trading environment, and therefore are more likely to be idiosyncratic.

Consistent with this, we also found that the proportion of quadratic variation attributable to jumps is lower for the index than for its individual components. One could conceivably measure the proportion of jumps that are systematic vs. those that are idiosyncratic on the basis of the comparison between the proportions of quadratic variation estimated for the index and for its components. Doing this using the empirical results above would suggest a proportion of systematic jumps representing about 10% of the total quadratic variation, and a proportion of idiosyncratic jumps representing about 15% of total quadratic variation, with the remaining 75% representing the continuous part of the total quadratic variation. This breakdown ultimately determines the empirical importance of (different types of) jumps as a source of asset returns variance.

A Bias Correction   By construction, we are forced by the presence of a continuous martingale part to rely on a small fraction of the sample – those increments larger than $u_n = \alpha \Delta_n^{\varpi}$ or using smoother cutoff function – for the purpose of estimating β. As a result, the effective sample size utilized by the estimator of β is small, even if we sample at a relatively high frequency. This situation calls for an analysis of the small sample behavior of the estimator.

Such a small sample analysis is out of reach in general but it can be carried out explicitly for the model $X_t = \sigma W_t + Y_t$, where W is a Wiener process and Y is a symmetric β-stable process, hence with the process A_t of (11.3) of the form $A_t = at$ and the Lévy measure $F(dx) = a\beta/2|x|^{1+\beta}$ for some $a > 0$. We denote as h and h_β the respective densities of the variables W_1 and Y_1. Following Zolotarev (1986), Theorem 2.4.2 and Corollary 2 of Theorem 2.5.1, we have the expansion

$$h_\beta(x) = \frac{a\beta}{2|x|^{1+\beta}}\left(1 - \frac{a'}{|x|^\beta} + O\left(\frac{1}{|x|^{2\beta}}\right)\right), \qquad \text{as } |x| \to \infty \quad (11.27)$$

for a suitable constant $a' > 0$ depending on a and β. By the scaling properties of W and Z, the expected value of $g(\Delta_i^n X/u_n)$, for a test function g satisfying (11.14) with some $p \geq 4$, is

$$\alpha_n = \int\int h(y)\, h_\beta(z)\, g\left(\frac{y\sigma\Delta_n^{1/2} + z\Delta_n^{1/\beta}}{u_n}\right) dy\, dz$$

$$= \frac{u_n}{\Delta_n^{1/\beta}} \int\int h(y)\, g(x)\, h_\beta\left(\Delta_n^{-1/\beta}(xu_n - y\sigma\Delta_n^{1/2})\right) dx\, dy,$$

where the last formula results from a change of variables. Since $u_n \asymp \Delta_n^\varpi$ with $\varpi \in (0, 1/2)$ and $\beta \in (0, 2)$, for all $x, y \neq 0$ we have $\Delta_n^{-1/\beta}\frac{u_n}{\Delta_n^{1/\beta}}(xu_n - y\sigma\Delta_n^{1/2}) \to \infty$ and also $y\sigma\Delta_n^{1/2}/xu_n \to 0$. Thus (11.27) and an expansion of $(1 - y\sigma\Delta_n^{1/2}/xu_n)^{-(1+j\beta)}$ for $j = 1, 2$, yield

$$\frac{u_n}{\Delta_n^{1/\beta}} h_\beta\left(\frac{xu_n - y\sigma\Delta_n^{1/2}}{\Delta_n^{1/\beta}}\right) = \frac{a\beta\Delta_n}{2u_n^\beta|x|^{1+\beta}}\left(1 + \sigma y\frac{\Delta_n^{1/2}}{u_n x} + \sigma^2 y^2\frac{\Delta_n}{u_n^2 x^2}\right.$$

$$\left. -a'\frac{\Delta_n}{u_n^\beta|x|^\beta} + o\left(\frac{\Delta_n^{3/2}}{u^3}\right)\right)$$

for suitable positive constants $\alpha, \alpha', \alpha''$ (the remainder term above depends on x, y, of course).

Arguing somewhat heuristically (the argument can be made rigorous), and taking advantage of $\int yh(y)\, dy = 0$ and $\int y^2 h(y)\, dy = 1$, recalling v_g as defined in (11.15), and using the fact that the expectation of $J(g; \Delta_n, u_n)_t$ is $[t/\Delta_n]\,\alpha_n$, we deduce that, for two positive constants d_1, d_2 (depending on a, β, σ, g),

$$u_n^\beta\, \mathbb{E}(J(g; \Delta_n, u_n)_t) = a\,t\,v_g(\beta)\left(1 + d_1\frac{\Delta_n}{u_n^2} - d_2\frac{\Delta_n}{u_n^\beta}\right) + \text{smaller terms}.$$

The two correction terms partly compensate each other, although the first one is bigger asymptotically than the second one (but not necessarily for finite samples). The first correction term is due to the interaction between the Wiener and the stable processes, while the second one is due to the more accurate approximation of the tail of the stable process in (11.27) compared to the leading order term.

For more insight on the first correction term, one can consider the function $g(x) = 1_{\{|x|>1\}}$, corresponding to using the first estimators $\widehat{\beta}_n(\gamma; u_n)$ of (11.10): we are just counting the increments $\Delta_i^n X$ bigger than u_n, and pretending that it is the same as counting the increments $\Delta_i^n Y$ bigger than u_n. But in fact we may have $\Delta_i^n X > u_n$ and $\Delta_i^n Y \leq u_n$, when the latter increment is close but smaller than u_n, or have $\Delta_i^n X \leq u_n$ and $\Delta_i^n Y > u_n$. These two sources of error somehow compensate each other, but not completely, so the need for a correction for g as above, and for a smooth function g as well.

Turning now to the general case of a semimartingale satisfying (L), the same argument shows that, for $u_n^\beta \, J(g; \Delta_n, u_n)_t$, a more accurate centering than $v_g(\beta)A_t$ is as follows, where D_1 and D_2 are two nonnegative random variables:

$$v_g(\beta)A_t \left(1 + D_1 \frac{\Delta_n}{u_n^2} - D_2 \frac{\Delta_n}{u_n^\beta}\right). \tag{11.28}$$

The effect on the estimator $\widehat{\beta}(\gamma, g; u_n)$ itself is that, instead of β, a corrected centering term is

$$\beta + \frac{1}{\log\gamma}\left(D_1\left(1 - \frac{1}{\gamma^2}\right)\frac{\Delta_n}{u_n^2} + D_2\left(\frac{1}{\gamma^\beta} - 1\right)\frac{\Delta_n}{u_n^\beta}\right). \tag{11.29}$$

Asymptotically, the first of the two correcting terms above is the larger one.

This suggests a small sample bias correction for the estimator $\widehat{\beta}(\gamma, g; u_n)$ obtained by subtracting from it an estimator of the two correction terms on the right hand side of (11.29). As seen in simulation studies, this correction is quite effective in practice. We also note that the two correcting terms are asymptotically negligible at the rate $1/u_n^{\beta/2}$ at which the central limit occurs. Consequently, the bias-corrected estimator has the same asymptotic distribution as the original estimator.

To implement the bias correction in practice, we need to estimate the two variables D_1 and D_2. One can rewrite (11.28) as

$$u_n^\beta \, J(g; \Delta_n, \gamma u_n)_t \sim w_0 \frac{1}{\gamma^\beta} + w_1 \frac{1}{\gamma^{2+\beta}} + w_2 \frac{1}{\gamma^{2\beta}}$$
$$+ \text{ a conditionally centered Gaussian term}, \tag{11.30}$$
$$\text{where } w_0 = v_g(\beta)A_t, \; w_1 = w_0 D_1 \frac{\Delta_n}{u_n^2}, \; w_2 = -w_0 D_2 \frac{\Delta_n}{u_n^\beta}$$

(of course, the w_j's are random variables, depending on n). A concrete procedure is then as follows:

1. Compute the preliminary estimator $\widehat{\beta}_n = \widehat{\beta}(\gamma, g; u_n)$, for some given $\gamma > 1$.

2. For a bunch of distinct $\gamma_1, \ldots, \gamma_k$ compute $u_n^\beta J(g; \Delta_n, \gamma_j u_n)_t$ and estimate the unknown coefficients w_0, w_1, w_2 in (11.30) by a straightforward linear regression of $u_n^\beta J(g; \Delta_n, \gamma_j u_n)_t$ on $1/\gamma^{\widehat{\beta}_n}$, $1/\gamma^{2+\widehat{\beta}_n}$ and $1/\gamma^{2\widehat{\beta}_n}$.

3. Given the estimators $\widehat{w}_j$ of the regression coefficients, a bias-corrected estimator is given by

$$\widehat{\beta}(\gamma, g; u_n)^{\text{bias-corrected}} = \widehat{\beta}(\gamma, g; u_n) - \frac{1}{\log \gamma} \left(\frac{\widehat{w}_1}{\widehat{w}_0} \left(1 - \frac{1}{\gamma^2} \right) \right.$$
$$\left. + \frac{\widehat{w}_2}{\widehat{w}_0} \left(1 - \frac{1}{\gamma^\beta} \right) \right).$$

11.2.4 The Truly Non-symmetric Case

In this subsection we consider a situation where positive and negative jumps possibly have different degrees of activity. In this case, the two types of jumps are treated completely independently, and below we put more emphasis on positive jumps, with of course no loss of generality.

Note that if, even without compelling evidence, we suspect that positive and negative jumps might behave differently, we should do the analysis as described below. This is in particular true if, after a "symmetrical" analysis, we come out with an estimate for $A_T^{(-)}$ which is "much smaller" or "much bigger" than the one for $A_T^{(+)}$.

We have two different assumptions, according to whether we are interested in positive jumps or in negative jumps. In the first case, the assumption for the restrictions of the Lévy measures F_t to $\mathbb{R}_+$ is the same as in (L), whereas the assumption on their restrictions to $\mathbb{R}_-$ is minimal, and the other way around in the second case.

Assumption (L_+). *The process X is of the form (11.1), with b_t locally bounded and σ_t càdlàg, and there are three constants $0 \le \beta'_+ < \beta_+ \le \beta < 2$ such that*

$$x \in (0, 1] \Rightarrow \begin{cases} \left| x^{\beta_+} \overline{F}_t^{(+)}(x) - a_t^{(+)} \right| \le L_t\, x^{\beta_+ - \beta'_+} \\ x^\beta \overline{F}_t^{(-)}(x) \le L_t, \end{cases} \qquad (11.31)$$

where $a_t^{(+)}$ and L_t are nonnegative predictable (or optional) and locally bounded processes.

Assumption (L_−). *The process X is of the form (11.1), with b_t locally bounded and σ_t càdlàg, and there are three constants $0 \leq \beta'_- < \beta_- \leq \beta < 2$ such that*

$$x \in (0,1] \Rightarrow \begin{cases} |x^{\beta_-}\, \overline{F}_t^{(-)}(x) - a_t^{(-)}| \leq L_t\, x^{\beta_- - \beta'_-} \\ x^{\beta}\, \overline{F}_t^{(+)}(x) \leq L_t, \end{cases} \tag{11.32}$$

where $a_t^{(-)}$ and L_t are nonnegative predictable (or optional) and locally bounded processes.

Remark 11.17. *If (L) holds with $\beta, \beta', a_t^{(\pm)}$ we have both (L_+) and (L_−), with the same β as in (L) and $\beta_+ = \beta_- = \beta$ and $\beta'_+ = \beta'_- = \beta'$ and also the same processes $a_t^{(\pm)}$.*

Conversely, if (L_+) and (L_−) hold with respectively $\beta_+, \beta'_+, a_t^{(+)}$ and $\beta_-, \beta'_-, a_t^{(-)}$, the second inequalities in (11.31) and (11.32) hold with $\beta = \beta_+ \vee \beta_-$, and we have (L) with this β. The specification of β' in (L), and of the two processes in (11.2), which we denote as $a_t^{(\pm,L)}$ in this remark for clarity, is as follows:

1. *If $\beta_+ = \beta_-(= \beta)$, then $a_t^{(\pm,L)} = a_t^{(\pm)}$ and $\beta' = \beta'_+ \vee \beta'_-$.*

2. *If $\beta_+ \neq \beta_-$, we may assume for example that $\beta_- < \beta_+(= \beta)$, the other case being similar. Then $a_t^{(+,L)} = a_t^{(+)}$ and $a_t^{(-,L)} = 0$ and $\beta' = \beta'_+ \vee \beta_-$.*

Under (L_+), resp. (L_−), we define $A_t^{(+)}$, resp. $A_t^{(-)}$, as in (11.3), whereas we replace (11.6) by the sets

$$\Omega_T^{(\beta_+,+)} = \{A_T^{(+)} > 0\}, \qquad \Omega_T^{(\beta_-,-)} = \{A_T^{(-)} > 0\},$$

according to the case. Assuming for example (L_+), our aim is to estimate β_+ and $A_T^{(+)}$, in restriction to the set $\Omega_T^{(\beta_+,+)}$. The procedure is of course the same as previously, except that we only consider (truncated) positive increments. With a sequence $u_n \asymp \Delta_n^\varpi$ of truncation levels, and with a test function g satisfying (11.13) (except that g need not be even, since below we only consider its restriction $g_+(x) = g(x)\,1_{\{x>0\}}$ to $\mathbb{R}_+$), and with any $\gamma > 1$, we construct the estimators

$$\widehat{\beta}_+(\gamma, g; u_n) = \frac{\log\left(J(g_+; \Delta_n, u_n)_T / J(g_+; \Delta_n, \gamma u_n)_T\right)}{\log \gamma} \tag{11.33}$$

if $J(g_+; \Delta_n, u_n)_T > 0$ and $J(g_+; \Delta_n, \gamma u_n)_T > 0$, and 0 otherwise, and

$$\widehat{A}^{(+)}(\gamma, g; u_n) = \frac{(u_n)^{\widehat{\beta}_+(\gamma,g;u_n)}}{v_g(\widehat{\beta}_+(\gamma, g; u_n))}\, J(g_+; \Delta_n, u_n)_T. \tag{11.34}$$

The last formula is the same as (11.17), except that we use $\widehat{\beta}_+(\gamma, g; u_n)$ instead of $\widehat{\beta}(\gamma, g; u_n)$.

When (L_-) holds, we define $\widehat{\beta}_-(\gamma, g; u_n)$ and $\widehat{A}^{(-)}(\gamma, g; u_n)$ in the same way, except that we are using $g_-(x) = g(x) 1_{\{x<0\}}$ instead of g_+.

Exactly as in the "symmetrical" case, Theorem B.20 yields $u_n^{\beta_+} J(g_+; \Delta_n, u_n) \overset{\text{u.c.p.}}{\Longrightarrow} v_g(\beta_+) A^{(+)}$ as soon as $\varpi < \frac{1}{2(1+\beta-\beta_+)}$ and $p > \frac{2-2\beta_+\varpi}{1-2\varpi}$, whereas the associated CLT requires $\varpi < \frac{1}{2+2\beta-\beta_+}$ and $p > \frac{2-\beta_+\varpi}{1-2\varpi}$. Then we have the analogues of Theorems 11.11 (consistency) and 11.12 (the CLT for the estimators), and these results are proved simultaneously with the preceding theorems, on pages 593 et seq. (we only give the results under (L_+), but the analogous result under (L_-) is straightforward).

Theorem 11.18. *Let $u_n \asymp \Delta_n^\varpi$ for some $\varpi \in \left(0, \frac{1}{2(1+\beta-\beta_+)}\right]$, and $\gamma > 1$ and g be a function satisfying (11.13) with some $p > \frac{2-2\beta_+\varpi}{1-2\varpi}$ (those conditions hold for all $0 \le \beta_+ < \beta < 2$ if $\varpi \le \frac{1}{6}$ and $p \ge 3$). Then under (L_+) we have*

$$\left.\begin{array}{c} \widehat{\beta}_+(\gamma, g; u_n) \overset{\mathbb{P}}{\longrightarrow} \beta_+ \\[2mm] \widehat{A}^{(+)}(\gamma, g; u_n) \overset{\mathbb{P}}{\longrightarrow} A_T^{(+)} \end{array}\right\} \text{ in restriction to the set } \Omega_T^{(\beta_+, +)}.$$

Theorem 11.19. *Let $u_n \asymp \Delta_n^\varpi$ for some $\varpi > 0$ and $\gamma > 1$ and g be a function satisfying (11.13) with some p.*

a) Under (L_+) with $\beta'_+ < \beta_+/2$ and if further $\varpi < \frac{1}{2+2\beta-\beta_+}$ and $p > \frac{2-\beta_+\varpi}{1-2\varpi}$ (those conditions hold for all $0 \le 2\beta_+ < \beta < 2$ if $\varpi \le \frac{1}{6}$ and $p \ge 3$), we have the following joint stable convergence in law, in restriction to the set $\Omega_T^{(\beta_+, +)}$, and where Φ_+ is a standard normal variable, defined on an extension of the space $(\Omega, \mathcal{F}, \mathbb{P})$ and independent of $\mathcal{F}$:

$$\left(\frac{\widehat{\beta}_+(\gamma, g; u_n) - \beta_+}{u_n^{\beta_+/2}}, \frac{\widehat{A}^{(+)}(\gamma, g; u_n) - A_T^{(+)}}{u_n^{\beta_+/2} \log(1/u_n)}\right)$$
$$\overset{\mathcal{L}-s}{\longrightarrow} \left(\sqrt{\frac{\overline{v}_g(\beta_+, \gamma)}{A_T^{(+)}}}\, \Phi_+, \; -\sqrt{\overline{v}_g(\beta_+, \gamma)}\, A_T^{(+)}\, \Phi_+\right).$$

b) If both (L_+) and (L_-) hold, with $\beta'_\pm < \beta_\pm/2$ and $\varpi < \frac{1}{2+2\beta_+\vee\beta_- - \beta_+\wedge\beta_-}$ and $p > \frac{2-\beta_+\wedge\beta_-\varpi}{1-2\varpi}$ (again automatically satisfied if $\varpi \le \frac{1}{6}$ and $p \ge 3$), we also have the following joint stable convergence in law, in restriction to the set $\Omega_T^{(\beta_+, +)} \cap \Omega_T^{(\beta_-, -)}$, with Φ_- another standard *normal variable independent of Φ_+ above and of $\mathcal{F}$:*

$$
\left(\frac{\widehat{\beta}_+(\gamma,g;u_n)-\beta_+}{u_n^{\beta_+/2}}, \; \frac{\widehat{\beta}_-(\gamma,g;u_n)-\beta_-}{u_n^{\beta_-/2}}, \right.
$$
$$
\left. \frac{\widehat{A}^{(+)}(\gamma,g;u_n)-A_T^{(+)}}{u_n^{\beta_+/2}\,\log(1/u_n)}, \; \frac{\widehat{A}^{(-)}(\gamma,g;u_n)-A_T^{(-)}}{u_n^{\beta_-/2}\,\log(1/u_n)} \right)
$$
$$
\xrightarrow{\mathcal{L}-s} \left(\sqrt{\frac{\overline{v}_g(\beta_+,\gamma)}{A_T^{(+)}}}\,\Phi_+, \; \sqrt{\frac{\overline{v}_g(\beta_-,\gamma)}{A_T^{(-)}}}\,\Phi_-, \right.
$$
$$
\left. -\sqrt{\overline{v}_g(\beta_+,\gamma)A_T^{(+)}}\,\Phi_+, \; -\sqrt{\overline{v}_g(\beta_-,\gamma)A_T^{(-)}}\,\Phi_- \right).
$$

$$(11.35)$$

Even more in this non-symmetric case, there is no reason to take the same constant γ, or the same test function g, for positive and negative jumps. The statement as well as the proof are modified in an obvious way if we take different γ and/or g.

The various comments or remarks stated after Theorem 11.12 are obviously valid in the present situation, *including* the construction of confidence intervals: the precise formulation is left to the reader.

Remark 11.20. *It is interesting to compare Theorem 11.12 with (b) of Theorem 11.19, when $\beta_+ = \beta_-$. In this case, (L) is the same as (L_+) and (L_-), and the restrictions on ϖ and p are also the same in the two theorems. However, the results differ in two respects:*

1. *In (b) above we have two asymptotically ($\mathcal{F}$-conditionally) independent estimators for the same parameter $\beta = \beta_+ = \beta_-$, both with a bigger asymptotic variance than $\widehat{\beta}(\gamma,g;u_n)$. And any convex linear combination $a\widehat{\beta}_+(\gamma,g;u_n) + (1-a)\widehat{\beta}_-(\gamma,g;u_n)$ also has a bigger asymptotic variance than $\widehat{\beta}(\gamma,g;u_n)$, so it is better to use $\widehat{\beta}(\gamma,g;u_n)$ if for some reason we know that $\beta_+ = \beta_-$.*

2. *In (b) above the estimators for $A_T^{(+)}$ and $A_T^{(-)}$ are asymptotically ($\mathcal{F}$-conditionally) independent, unlike in Theorem 11.12. This is due to the asymptotic independence of the estimators for β_+ and β_-.*

This theorem allows us to construct a test for the null hypothesis that $\beta_+ = \beta_-$, under (L_+) and (L_-), and in restriction to the set $\Omega_T^{(\beta_+,+)} \cap \Omega_T^{(\beta_-,-)}$. Toward this aim, by (11.35) and under the null (so $\beta_+ = \beta_- = \beta$), the variables $u_n^{-\beta/2}\big(\widehat{\beta}_+(\gamma,g;u_n) - \widehat{\beta}_-(\gamma,g;u_n)\big)$ converge stably in law to $\sqrt{\overline{v}_g(\beta_+,\gamma)}\,(\Phi_+/\sqrt{A_T^{(+)}} - \Phi_-/\sqrt{A_T^{(-)}})$, which is $\mathcal{F}$-conditionally centered Gaussian with variance $\overline{v}_g(\beta_+,\gamma)(1/A_T^{(+)} + 1/A_T^{(-)})$. This variance is consistently estimated by $u_n^{-\beta} V_n$, where

$$
V_n = \overline{v}_g(\beta_+,\gamma)\, v_g(\beta) \left(\frac{1}{J(g_+;\Delta_n,u_n)T} + \frac{1}{J(g_-;\Delta_n,u_n)T} \right)
$$

(recall (11.18), note that V_n is observable, whereas the unobservable $u_n^{-\beta}$ cancels out below).

Hence, with z_α denoting as usual the α-absolute quantile of $\mathcal{N}(0,1)$, the critical regions

$$\mathcal{C}_n = \left\{ |\widehat{\beta}_+(\gamma, g; u_n) - \widehat{\beta}_-(\gamma, g; u_n)| > z_\alpha \sqrt{V_n} \right\}$$

have the strong asymptotic size α for testing the null hypothesis $\beta_+ = \beta_-$, and they are consistent for the alternative hypothesis $\beta_+ \neq \beta_-$ (because $u_n^{-\varepsilon} |\widehat{\beta}_+(\gamma, g; u_n) - \widehat{\beta}_-(\gamma, g; u_n)|$ converge in probability to $+\infty$ for any $\varepsilon > 0$ when $\beta_+ \neq \beta_-$.

Likewise, one may construct tests for the unilateral hypotheses $\beta_+ \leq \beta_-$ or $\beta_+ \geq \beta_-$, and also tests for $A_T^{(+)} = A_T^{(-)}$ (the latter when $\beta_+ = \beta_-$, otherwise this makes no practical sense).

11.3   Successive BG Indices

The notion of successive Blumenthal-Getoor indices was been introduced in Subsection 5.2.2 of Chapter 5, for Lévy processes. The usual BG index β for a semimartingale satisfying Assumption (L), for example, describes how Lévy measures F_t diverge near 0, in the sense that it basically imposes the following behavior for the tail functions $\overline{F}_t$:

$$\overline{F}_t(x) \sim \frac{a_t}{x^\beta}, \qquad \text{as } x \downarrow 0, \tag{11.36}$$

where $a_t \geq 0$ is a process.

We can think of (11.36) as providing the leading term, near 0, of the jump measure of X. Given that this term is identifiable, but that the full Lévy measures are not, our aim is to examine where the boundary between what can vs. cannot be identified lies. Toward this aim, one direction to go is to view (11.36) as giving the first term of the expansion of the "tail" $\overline{F}_t(\omega, u)$ near 0, and go further by assuming a series expansion such as

$$\overline{F}_t(x) \sim \sum_{i \geq 1} \frac{a_t^i}{x^{\beta_i}}, \qquad \text{as } x \downarrow 0, \tag{11.37}$$

with successive powers $\beta_1 = \beta > \beta_2 > \beta_3 > \cdots$ (this extends (5.12)). Those β_i's are the "successive BG indices." This series expansion can for example result from the superposition of processes with different BG indices, in a model consisting of a sum of such processes.

The question then becomes one of identifying the successive terms in that expansion. As seen in Theorem 5.8, for Lévy processes we have the somewhat surprising result that the first index β_1 is always identifiable and that the subsequent indices β_i are identifiable if they are bigger than $\beta_1/2$, whereas those smaller are not. An intuition for this particular value of the identifiability boundary can be gained from Theorem 11.12 or, rather, from its proof: the estimation of β is based on a preliminary estimation of the processes $u_n^\beta \int_0^t \overline{F}_s(u_n)\, ds$ for a sequence $u_n \downarrow 0$, at least when one uses the version (11.10) with the test function $g(x) = 1_{\{|x|>1\}}$. Moreover, in this estimation the rate of convergence is $u_n^{-\beta/2}$. This means that any term contributing to $\overline{F}_t(u_n)$ by an amount less than $u_n^{-\beta/2}$, as $u_n \to 0$, is fundamentally unreachable. This shows that there are limits to our ability to identify these successive terms.

Our aim below is to show that, in accordance with Theorem 5.8 but in a more general Itô semimartingale setting, one can indeed construct estimators which are consistent for estimating the successive indices β_i, as long as they are bigger than $\beta/2$. We also determine their rate of convergence, which we will see are slow.

11.3.1   Preliminaries

Our first task is to extend Assumption (L) to the case of successive indices, as in (11.37). To avoid complicated notation, we restrict our attention to the case where the jumps are "asymptotically" symmetric near 0, that is, when both $\overline{F}_t^{(+)}$ and $\overline{F}_t^{(-)}$ have an expansion near 0 with the same negative powers of x; however, it would also be possible to treat positive and negative jumps separately, in the spirit of Subsection 11.2.4 above. With j is an integer, we set

Assumption (L-j). *The process X is of the form (11.1), with b_t locally bounded and σ_t càdlàg, and there are constants $0 \le \beta_{j+1} < \beta_j < \dots < \beta_1 < 2$ with $\beta_j > \beta_1/2$ and such that*

$$x \in (0,1] \;\Rightarrow\; \left| \overline{F}_t^{(\pm)}(x) - \sum_{i=1}^{j} \frac{a_t^{i\pm}}{x^{\beta_i}} \right| \le \frac{L_t}{x^{\beta_{j+1}}}, \qquad (11.38)$$

where a_t^{i+} and a_t^{i-} and L_t are nonnegative predictable (or optional) and locally bounded processes.

As with (L), we associate with this assumption the following increasing processes:

$$A_t^{i+} \;=\; \int_0^t a_s^{i+}\, ds, \quad A_t^{i-} \;=\; \int_0^t a_s^{i-}\, ds, \quad A_t^i \;=\; A_t^{i+} + A_t^{i-}.$$

Under this assumption, the β_i's for $i = 1,\ldots,j$ are naturally called the successive *Blumenthal-Getoor indices*. They should rather be referred to as "potential" BG indices, since if for example $A_T^i(\omega) = 0$ the index β_i is immaterial for the process X, up to time T and for the specific outcome ω. Note that β_{j+1} is usually *not* by itself a BG index.

When X is a Lévy process, we know by Theorem 5.8 that β_i and A_T^i are pairwise identifiable for $i = 1,\ldots,j$ because $\beta_j > \beta_1/2$, whereas if $\beta_j < \beta_1/2$ were allowed the parameter β_j would *not* be identifiable. We will in fact exhibit consistent estimators for β_i, and for the variables A_T^{i+} and A_T^{i-}, when X is an Itô semimartingale satisfying (L-j). In particular, this will ensure that those quantities are identifiable.

(L-j) implies (L), with $\beta = \beta_1$ and $\beta' = \beta_2$ and $a_t^{(\pm)} = a_t^{1\pm}$, and (L-1)=(L): below we restrict our attention to the case $j \geq 2$, since the case $j = 1$ is established in the previous sections.

For example, if X is the sum of a (continuous) Itô semimartingale satisfying (HC), plus j independent symmetrical stable (or tempered stable) processes with indices β_i, then (L-j) is satisfied. It is also satisfied by the process

$$X_t = X_0 + \int_0^t b_s\, ds + \int_0^t \sigma_s\, dW_s + Z_t + \sum_{i=1}^j \int_0^t H_s^i\, dY_s^i,$$

if the sum of the four first terms on the right above define a semimartingale satisfying (H-β_{j+1}), and the Y^i's are stable or tempered stable processes with indices β_i, mutually independent and independent of W, and the H^i's are predictable locally bounded processes.

Clearly, the estimation of all the β_i's, for example, cannot be more accurate than the estimation of $\beta = \beta_1$ in the previous section. Worse, even: as soon as $j \geq 2$ we have (L) with $\beta' > \frac{\beta}{2}$, hence Theorem 11.12 does *not* apply as is, and the available rates are much slower than previously.

The "natural" assumption (L-j) is in fact not quite enough for us, and we will need the following, where $\varepsilon > 0$:

Assumption (L-j-ε). *We have (L-j), and furthermore:*
- *There is a* known *number $\varepsilon > 0$ such that $\beta_i - \beta_{i+1} > \varepsilon$ for all $i = 1,\ldots,j-1$;*
- *We have $A_T^i > 0$ almost surely for $i = 1,\ldots,j$.*

This assumption contains two requirements. One is that the various BG indices are sufficiently far apart; that the minimal distance is bigger than some $\varepsilon > 0$ is of course always true, but the point here is that this ε

is *known*: this number is explicitly used for constructing the estimators, The other requirement implies that the "component parts" of the process X corresponding to each index β_i are all "active" at some point in the interval $[0, T]$. In other words, the β_i's are the genuine successive BG indices on the time interval $[0, T]$. This is of course a little bit restrictive, but it greatly simplifies the analysis. It also implies that in the forthcoming limit results one does *not* have the usual qualifier "in restriction to a suitable subset" of Ω.

The estimation is based on a two-step procedure, the first step being devoted to preliminary estimators $\widetilde{\beta}_n^i$ and $\widetilde{A}_n^{i\pm}$ for β_i and $A_T^{i\pm}$, the final estimators being denoted $\widehat{\beta}_n^i$ and $\widehat{A}_n^{i\pm}$.

11.3.2   First Estimators

As before, we choose a sequence $u_n \asymp \Delta_n^{\varpi}$ of truncation levels, with some $\varpi \in (0, 1/4)$. We also take a test function g satisfying (11.13) for some $p \geq 4$. These bounds on ϖ and p are those needed in Theorem 11.12 and are thus *a fortiori* needed here.

The preliminary estimators for β_1 and $A_T^{1\pm}$ are the same as in (11.16) and (11.17), namely

$$\widetilde{\beta}_n^1 = \frac{\log\left(J(g; \Delta_n, u_n)_T / J(g; \Delta_n, \gamma u_n)_T\right)}{\log \gamma}$$

$$\widetilde{A}_n^{1\pm} = \frac{(u_n)^{\widetilde{\beta}_n^1}}{v_g(\widetilde{\beta}_n^1)} J(g_\pm; \Delta_n, u_n)_T,$$

where $\gamma > 1$ is chosen arbitrarily. As usual, the above definition of $\widetilde{\beta}_n^1$ holds if $J(g; \Delta_n, u_n)_T > 0$ and $J(g; \Delta_n, \gamma u_n)_T > 0$; $\widetilde{\beta}_n^1$ is defined to be 0 otherwise.

Next, the estimators for $j \geq 2$ are constructed by induction on j in the following way. We use the number ε for which Assumption (L-j-ε) holds and set for all $i \geq 1$:

$$u_{n,i} = u_n^{(\varepsilon/2)^{i-1}} \tag{11.39}$$

(so $u_{n,1} = u_n$). We denote by $I(k, l)$ the set of all subsets of $\{1, \ldots, j\}$ having l elements. Then, assuming that $\widetilde{\beta}_i^n$ and $\widetilde{A}_{i\pm}^n$ are already known for $i = 1, \ldots, k-1$, we set (with $x \geq 1$ below)

$$U^n(k, x) = \sum_{l=0}^{k-1} (-1)^l J(g; \Delta_n, x\gamma^l u_{n,k})_T \sum_{R \in I(k-1,l)} \gamma^{\sum_{i \in R} \tilde{\beta}_n^i}$$

$$\tilde{\beta}_n^k = \begin{cases} \frac{\log\left(U^n(k,1)/U^n(k,\gamma)\right)}{\log \gamma} & \text{if } U^n(k, 1) > 0, \ U^n(k, \gamma) > 0 \\ 0 & \text{otherwise} \end{cases} \quad (11.40)$$

$$\tilde{A}_n^{k\pm} = \frac{u_{n,k}^{\tilde{\beta}_n^k}}{v_g(\tilde{\beta}_n^k)} \left(J(g_\pm; \Delta_n, u_{n,k})_T - \sum_{i=1}^{k-1} v_g(\tilde{\beta}_n^i) \tilde{A}_n^{i\pm} u_{n,k}^{-\tilde{\beta}_n^i} \right).$$

Finally, in order to state the result, we need a further notation for $i = 1, \ldots, j-1$:

$$H_i = \frac{A_T^{i+1} v_g(\beta_{i+1})}{A_T^i v_g(\beta_i) \log \gamma} \frac{\prod_{l=1}^i \left(\gamma^{\beta_l - \beta_{i+1}} - 1\right)}{\prod_{l=1}^{i-1} \left(\gamma^{\beta_l - \beta_i} - 1\right)} \quad (11.41)$$

(recall that we assume $A_T^i > 0$ here). The asymptotic behavior of our preliminary estimators is described in the following theorem:

Theorem 11.21. *Assume (L-j-ε) for some $j \geq 2$ and $\varepsilon > 0$, choose $u_n \asymp \Delta_n^\varpi$ for some $\varpi \in (0, \frac{1}{4})$ and a function g satisfying (11.8) with some $p \geq 3$, and finally let $\gamma > 1$. Then the estimators defined above satisfy, for $i = 1, \ldots, j-1$,*

$$\frac{\tilde{\beta}_n^i - \beta_i}{u_{n,i}^{\beta_i - \beta_{i+1}}} \xrightarrow{\mathbb{P}} -H_i, \qquad \frac{\tilde{A}_n^{i\pm} - A_T^i}{u_{n,i}^{\beta_i - \beta_{i+1}} \log(1/u_{n,i})} \xrightarrow{\mathbb{P}} H_i A_T^{i\pm}, \quad (11.42)$$

and furthermore the following variables are bounded in probability as n varies:

$$\frac{\tilde{\beta}_n^j - \beta_j}{u_{n,j}^{\beta_j - (\beta_1/2) \vee \beta_{j+1}}}, \qquad \frac{\tilde{A}_n^{j\pm} - A_T^{j\pm}}{u_{n,j}^{\beta_j - (\beta_1/2) \vee \beta_{j+1}} \log(1/u_{n,j})}. \quad (11.43)$$

(See page 597 for the proof.) Note the differences between this result and Theorem 11.11 for example: in the latter we have a stable convergence in law, allowing us to construct confidence intervals. Here the convergence takes place in probability, with a limit which is a function of the quantities to be estimated. Hence this result gives us a rate of convergence, but no feasible way to construct a confidence interval. In other words, this type of result is potentially much less useful than the previous ones.

Remark 11.22. *It is possible for the estimators $\tilde{A}_n^{i\pm}$ to be negative, in which case we may replace them by 0, or by any other positive number.*

It may also happen that the sequence $\widetilde{\beta}_n^i$ is not decreasing, and we can then reorder the whole family to obtain a decreasing family (we relabel the estimators of $A_T^{i\pm}$ accordingly, of course). All these modifications are asymptotically immaterial.

11.3.3 Improved Estimators

The preliminary estimators not only do not provide us with confidence intervals, but their rates are exceedingly slow, especially for higher order indices. If we start with the "optimal" choice $\varpi = \frac{1}{4}$ for the truncation levels $u_n \asymp \Delta_n^\varpi$, the convergence rate for $\widetilde{\beta}_n^i$ for example is $1/\Delta_n^{(\beta_i - \beta_{i-1})\varepsilon^{i-1}/2^{i+1}}$, with ε as in Assumption (L-j-ε). Even when $j = 2$, that is, when we have two BG indices, the rate for β_2 is $1/\Delta_n^{(\beta_1 - \beta_2)\varepsilon/8}$ and ε is smaller than $\beta_1 - \beta_2$ and should in fact be chosen much smaller than this, because the β_i's are unknown.

This is why we propose improved estimators, constructed on the basis of the previous preliminary estimators. Those new estimators are still not amenable to constructing confidence intervals, and their rates are still slow, but not so far from the optimal rates, as we will see below: it will appear that the slow rates of convergence are partly a defect of the estimators we construct, but also are an inherent limitation imposed by the problem at hand.

The method consists of minimizing, at each stage n, a suitably chosen contrast function Φ_n. We still assume (L-j-ε) for some $j \geq 2$ and some $\varepsilon > 0$. First we take an integer $L \geq 2j$ and numbers $1 = \delta_1 < \delta_2 < \cdots < \delta_L$. We also choose positive weights w_k (typically $w_k = 1$, but any choice is indeed possible), and we take truncation levels $u_n \asymp \Delta_n^\varpi$ with $\varpi \in \left(0, \frac{1}{4}\right)$ (unfortunately, the "optimal" $\varpi = \frac{1}{4}$ is excluded). We also let D be the set of all $(x_i, y_i^+, y_i^-)_{1 \leq i \leq j}$ with $0 \leq x_j \leq x_{j-1} \leq \cdots \leq x_1 \leq 2$ and $y_i^\pm \geq 0$. Finally, g is a function satisfying (11.13) with some $p \geq 3$, and the contrast function is defined on D by

$$\Phi_n(x_1, y_1^+, y_1^-, \ldots, x_j, y_j^+, y_j^-) = \sum_{l=1}^{L} w_l \Bigg(\Big(J(g_+; \Delta_n, \delta_l u_n)_T$$
$$- \sum_{i=1}^{j} \frac{y_i^+ v_g(x_i)}{(\delta_l u_n)^{x_i}} \Big)^2 + \Big(J(g_-; \Delta_n, \delta_l u_n)_T - \sum_{i=1}^{j} \frac{y_i^- v_g(x_i)}{(\delta_l u_n)^{x_i}} \Big)^2 \Bigg).$$

Then the estimation consists of the following two steps:

1. We construct preliminary estimators $\widetilde{\beta}_n^i$ (decreasing in i) and $\widetilde{A}_n^{i\pm}$ (nonnegative) for β_i and $A_T^{i\pm}$ for $i = 1, \ldots, j$, such that $(\widetilde{\beta}_n^i - \beta_i)/u_n^\eta$ and $(\widetilde{A}_n^{i\pm} - A_T^{i\pm})/u_n^\eta$ go to 0 in probability for some $\eta > 0$. For

example, we may choose those described in the previous section, see Remark 11.22; the consistency requirement is then fulfilled for any $\eta < (\varepsilon/2)^j$.

2. We denote by D_n the (compact and non-empty) random subset of D defined by

$$D_n = \{(x_i, y_i^+, y_i^-) \in D : |x_i - \widetilde{\beta}_n^i| \le \zeta u_n^\eta,$$
$$|y_i^+ - \widetilde{A}_n^{i+}| \le \zeta u_n^\eta, \ |y_i^- - \widetilde{A}_n^{i-}| \le \zeta u_n^\eta, \ \forall i = 1, \dots, j\}$$

for some arbitrary (fixed) $\zeta > 0$. Then the final estimators $\widehat{\beta}_n^i$ and $\widehat{A}_n^{i\pm}$ will be

$$(\widehat{\beta}_n^i, \widehat{A}_n^{i+}, \widehat{A}_n^{i-})_{1 \le i \le j} = \underset{D_n}{\operatorname{argmin}} \ \Phi_n(x_1, y_1^+, y_1^-, \dots, x_j, y_j^+, y_j^-),$$

which always exists, because D_n is compact and Φ_n is a continuous (random) function on D.

Theorem 11.23. *Assume (L-j-ε) for some $j \ge 2$ and $\varepsilon > 0$. Choose $u_n \asymp \Delta_n^\varpi$ for some $\varpi \in \left(0, \frac{1}{4}\right)$, and a function g satisfying (11.8) with some $p \ge 3$, and the number $\gamma > 1$. Then, for all choices of $\delta_2, \dots, \delta_L$ outside a Lebesgue-null subset of the set $\{(z_i)_{2 \le i \le L} : 1 < z_2 < \cdots < z_L\}$ (depending on the β_i's), the sequences of variables*

$$\frac{\widehat{\beta}_n^i - \beta_i}{u_n^{\beta_i - (\beta_1/2) \vee \beta_{j+1} - \mu}}, \quad \frac{\widehat{A}_n^{i+} - A_T^{i+}}{u_n^{\beta_i - (\beta_1/2) \vee \beta_{j+1} - \mu}}, \quad \frac{\widehat{A}_n^{i-} - A_T^{i-}}{u_n^{\beta_i - (\beta_1/2) \vee \beta_{j+1} - \mu}} \qquad (11.44)$$

are bounded in probability for all $i = 1, \dots, j$ and all $\mu > 0$.

The rates obtained here are much better than in Theorem 11.21. For example, for β_1 the rate is faster than $1/u_n^{\beta_1/2 - \mu}$ for any $\mu > 0$ instead of being $1/u_n^{\beta_1 - \beta_2}$. And for β_j it is faster than $1/u_n^{\beta_j - \beta_1/2 - \mu}$ instead of $1/u_n^{(\varepsilon/2)^{j-1}(\beta_j - \beta_1/2)}$.

For example, consider $j = 2$ and extend (11.25) as

$$X = \sigma W + Y^1 + Y^2$$

with $\sigma > 0$ and Y^1, Y^2 two stable symmetric processes with indices $\beta_1 > \beta_2$ and intensities a_i. We have (L-2-ε) and $A_t^i = t a_i$. In this case, (5.22) shows that the optimal rates are given by (11.26) for β_1 and a_1, whereas for β_2 and a_2 they are

- for β_2: $\quad r_n(\text{opt}) = 1/\Delta_n^{\beta_2/2 - \beta_1/4} (\log(1/\Delta_n))^{\beta_2/2 - \beta_1/4 - 1}$
- for a_2: $\quad r_n(\text{opt}) = 1/\Delta_n^{\beta_2/2 - \beta_1/4} (\log(1/\Delta_n))^{\beta_2/2 - \beta_1/4}$.

Hence, exactly as in the previous section, and upon taking $u_n \asymp \Delta_n^{\varpi}$ with ϖ very close to $\frac{1}{4}$, we see that the rates in Theorem 11.23 are roughly the square roots of the optimal rates, in this very special case.

Remark 11.24. *As stated, we only need $L = 2j$, and choosing $L > 2j$ does not improve the asymptotic properties. However, from a practical viewpoint it is probably wise to take L bigger than $2j$ in order to smooth out the contrast function somehow, especially for (relatively) small samples. A choice of the weights $w_l > 0$ other than $w_l = 1$, such as w_l decreasing in l, may serve to put less emphasis on the large truncation values $u_n \delta_l$ for which less data are effectively used.*

Remark 11.25. *The result does not hold for all choices of the δ_l's, but only when $(\delta_2, \ldots, \delta_L)$ (recall $\delta_1 = 1$) does not belong to some Lebesgue-null set $G(\beta_1, \ldots, \beta_j)$. This seems a priori a serious restriction, because $(\beta_1, \ldots, \beta_j)$ and this set $G(\beta_1, \ldots, \beta_j)$ are unknown. In practice, we choose a priori $(\delta_2, \ldots, \delta_L)$, so we may have bad luck, just as we may have bad luck for the particular outcome ω which is drawn ...; we can also perform the estimation several times, for different values of the δ_i's, and compare the results.*

Remark 11.26. *In the last theorem we impose the assumption (L-j-ε), although ε does not show in the result itself and can thus be taken arbitrarily small (recall that (L-j-ε) with ε arbitrarily small amounts to (L-j) plus the fact that all variables A_T^i are strictly positive); this is in principle enough to ensure that Theorem 11.23 holds.*

However, we need (L-j-ε) to construct the preliminary estimators, hence it is also stated as an assumption in the theorem. Were we able to come up with other preliminary estimators satisfying the required hypotheses in Step 1 of our algorithm, then (L-j-ε) could be replaced by (L-j) and $A_T^i > 0$ for all $i \leq j$. On the other hand, relaxing $A_T^i > 0$ does not seem to be obvious.

Remark 11.27. *We have a rate of convergence for our estimators, but no associated Central Limit Theorem. Such a CLT is radically impossible to obtain since, as seen in the subsection devoted to preliminary estimators, the first order terms for the normalized estimation errors are bias terms.*

As a consequence, we can estimate the successive indices β_i, but we cannot provide confidence bounds for them.

11.4   References

As already mentioned, the Blumenthal-Getoor index was introduced in Blumenthal and Getoor (1961) in the context of Lévy processes. There is a large literature about estimation of the stability index for a sample of stable variables and about the Hill or similar estimators, in various contexts; however, the methods always rely upon analyzing large T, and are thus not relevant in the context of this book. Recently a number of authors have studied the estimation of the Lévy measure of a Lévy process which is sampled at high frequency, but when simultaneously the time horizon goes to infinity, see for example Basawa and Brockwell (1982), Figueroa-López and Houdré (2006), Nishiyama (2008), Neumann and Reiß (2009), Figueroa-López (2009), Comte and Genon-Catalot (2009, 2011).

By contrast, the literature about estimation of the identifiable part of the Lévy measure from high-frequency data on a fixed time interval is more limited. The extension of the BG index to semimartingales and the corresponding estimation method in Section 11.2 originates in Aït-Sahalia and Jacod (2009a), and was subsequently improved in Jing et al. (2011).

Successive BG indices, studied in Section 11.3, were introduced and estimated in Aït-Sahalia and Jacod (2012b).

Belomestny (2010) considered the BG index of a Lévy process. Reiß (2013) proposes tests on the volatility, the jump measure and the BG index of a Lévy process, using the empirical characteristic function. Other papers are concerned with the "overall' activity index of a semimartingale discretely observed on a finite time interval, which equals 2 when there is a Brownian motion and otherwise is the BG index; see for example Woerner (2011) and Todorov and Tauchen (2010).

Chapter 12

Finite or Infinite Activity for Jumps?

The previous chapter was concerned with the estimation of the degree of activity of the jumps of a process X, that is, of its Blumenthal-Getoor index. If the resulting confidence interval does not contain the value 0, one may conclude that the genuine activity index is positive, and thus the jumps have *infinite activity* (infinitely many jumps inside the observation interval $[0, T]$). Otherwise the true BG index may be equal to 0, and then a natural question to ask oneself is whether or not the observed path has infinitely many jumps on $[0, T]$. As we know, if this is the case the BG index vanishes, whereas the converse is not quite true: a gamma process has jumps with infinite activity and yet a vanishing BG index. Of course, it is possible to reverse the order of the questions, and ask first whether X has jumps with finite or infinite activity, and only in the latter case attempt to estimate the BG index.

The question posed above is quite important in practice. Indeed, a process with jumps of finite activity looks pretty much like Merton's model (including a drift, of course, and with jumps which are not necessarily Gaussian), and in any case is much simpler to specify and also to understand than a process with jumps of infinite activity.

In other words, our aim in this chapter is to construct tests which allow us to decide in which of the following two subsets of the sample space the observed path lies:

$$\Omega_T^{(fa)} = \{\omega : t \mapsto X_t(\omega) \text{ has finitely many jumps in } [0, T]\}$$
$$\Omega_T^{(ia)} = \{\omega : t \mapsto X_t(\omega) \text{ has infinitely many jumps in } [0, T]\}. \tag{12.1}$$

Note that, by virtue of Theorem 5.16, these sets are identifiable (at least pairwise), because for example $\Omega_T^{(ia)} = \{A(0)_T = \infty\}$, with the notation (5.15). These two subsets are the "null hypotheses" for which we construct tests, successively, in the two sections of this chapter.

As for the process X, as previously it is a one-dimensional Itô semimartingale on some filtered space $(\Omega, \mathcal{F}, (\mathcal{F}_t)_{t \geq 0}, \mathbb{P})$, with Grigelionis representation

$$X_t = X_0 + \int_0^t b_s ds + \int_0^t \sigma_s dW_s \qquad (12.2)$$
$$+ (\delta 1_{\{|\delta| \leq 1\}}) \star (\underline{p} - \underline{q})_t + (\delta 1_{\{|\delta| > 1\}}) \star \underline{p}_t$$

and characteristics of the form

$$B_t = \int_0^t b_s ds, \qquad C_t = \int_0^t c_s ds, \qquad \nu(dt, dx) = dt \, F_t(dx)$$

(same notation as in the previous chapters). Additional assumptions will be made as required.

12.1   When the Null Hypothesis Is Finite Jump Activity

We start with the null hypothesis of "finite activity" of jumps. Exactly as for testing for the existence of jumps, here we cannot test the null hypothesis $\Omega_T^{(fa)}$ as stated in (12.1) and we will take the null to be $\Omega_T^{(fa)} \cap \Omega_T^{(W)}$, where $\Omega_T^{(W)} = \{C_T > 0\}$ is the set (already encountered in (10.6)) on which the Brownian motion is active.

Next, exactly as in Theorems 10.14 and 10.15 for testing for jumps, if we want alternative consistency we must restrict the alternative to $\Omega_T^{(ia)} \cap \Omega_T^{(W)}$ as well. But this is not enough: we need additional assumptions on the structure of the jumps of X, in the spirit of Assumption (L) of the previous chapter, and accordingly reduce further, if necessary, the alternative hypothesis. We basically have two ways to do this:

1. Assume (L), see page 396, in which case the alternative hypothesis will not be $\Omega_T^{(ia)} \cap \Omega_T^{(W)}$ but rather the set $\Omega_T^{(\beta)} \cap \Omega_T^{(W)}$; see (11.5). This method has the advantage of being coherent with the tests when the null is "infinite activity," as constructed later and for which (L) is really needed. However, (L) supposes that the putative BG index β is positive; hence it rules out some interesting cases, such as when the jumps of X are those of a gamma process, which has infinite activity and at the same time a vanishing BG index.

2. Consider the "global" BG index γ_t up to time t, defined in (5.16) as

$$\gamma_t = \inf(p \geq 0 : \int_0^t ds \int (|x|^p \wedge 1) F_s(dx) < \infty),$$

and which is non-decreasing in t. Then the additional assumption is expressed in terms of this global index, as follows:

Assumption (J). *The process X is of the form (12.2) with b_t locally bounded and σ_t càdlàg. Moreover, the global BG index γ_t takes its values in $[0, 2)$ (the value 2 is excluded), and for all $\varepsilon > 0$ the process $\sup_{x \in (0,1]} x^{\gamma_t + \varepsilon} \overline{F}_t(x)$ is locally bounded, where $\overline{F}_t$ is the two-sided tail function $\overline{F}_t(x) = F_t((-\infty, -x) \cup (x, \infty))$ for $x > 0$.*

This assumption is a mild local boundedness assumption, which is made even weaker by the fact that we use the global BG index γ_t instead of the (perhaps more natural) instantaneous index β_t.

Even under (J), the alternative still cannot be $\Omega_T^{(ia)} \cap \Omega_T^{(W)}$, but a subset of it. It has a somewhat complicated description, and we first need a notation (for $u \in (0, 1]$ and $q \geq 0$):

$$G(q, u)_t = \inf_{x \in (0, u/2]} x^q \left(\overline{F}_t(x) - \overline{F}_t(u) \right). \tag{12.3}$$

Then we set

$$\Omega_T^{(iia)} = \Omega_T^{(i, \gamma > 0)} \cup \Omega_T^{(i, \gamma = 0)}, \tag{12.4}$$

where, with l_T denoting the Lebesgue measure on $[0, T]$,

$$\Omega_T^{(i, \gamma > 0)} = \Big\{ \omega : \gamma_T(\omega) > 0,$$
$$l_T \big(\{ t : \liminf_{u \to 0} G(q, u)_t(\omega) = \infty \} \big) > 0 \text{ for all } q < \gamma_T(\omega) \Big\},$$
$$\Omega_T^{(i, \gamma = 0)} = \Big\{ \omega : \gamma_T(\omega) = 0,$$
$$l_T \big(\{ t : \lim_{x \to 0} (\overline{F}_t(x^{1+\rho}) - \overline{F}_t(x))(\omega) = \infty \} \big) > 0 \text{ for all } \rho > 0 \Big\}.$$

Remark 12.1. *The sets $\Omega_T^{(i, \gamma > 0)}$ and $\Omega_T^{(i, \gamma = 0)}$ are often easy to describe in particular examples, as shown below, but it is not so easy to grasp their meaning in general. The former set is basically the set on which there are "enough" times t in $[0, T]$ at which the local BG index β_t is arbitrarily close to γ_T, plus some (implicit) condition implying that $\overline{F}_t(x)$ converges to $+\infty$ "regularly enough," for enough times t, as $x \to 0$.*

In contrast, the latter set says that, again for "enough" times t, $\overline{F}_t(x)$ is large enough.

The connections between (L) and (J) and between $\Omega_T^{(ia)}$ and either $\Omega_T^{(\beta)}$ or $\Omega_T^{(iia)}$ are explicated in the next lemma, which, like all results of this subsection, is proved on pages 604 et seq.

Lemma 12.2. *We have the following implications:*

a) If (J) holds, then $\Omega_T^{(iia)} \subset \Omega_T^{(ia)}$ almost surely.

b) If (L) holds with either $\beta' = 0$ or $A_t > 0$ for all $t > 0$, then (J) holds.

c) If (L) holds, then $\Omega_T^{(\beta)} \subset \Omega_T^{(ia)}$ almost surely.

d) If (L) holds with $\beta' = 0$, then $\Omega_T^{(\beta)} = \Omega_T^{(ia)} = \Omega_T^{(iia)}$ almost surely.

The reader should not be misled by this statement: Assumption (J) is fundamentally *much weaker* than (L), although formally we may have (L) and not (J). By part (b) of this lemma, we see that all examples of Section 11.1, except Example 11.5, satisfy (J).

Example 12.3. *When X is a Lévy process, so $\gamma_t(\omega) = \beta$ is the BG index of the Lévy measure F, and both $\Omega_T^{(i,\gamma>0)}$ and $\Omega_T^{(i,\gamma=0)}$ are either empty or equal to Ω itself, according to the following:*

1. $\Omega_T^{(i,\gamma>0)} = \Omega$ *if and only if $\beta > 0$ and $x^{\beta-\varepsilon}\overline{F}(x) \to \infty$ for all $\varepsilon > 0$, as $x \to 0$.*

2. $\Omega_T^{(i,\gamma=0)} = \Omega$ *if and only if $\beta = 0$ and $\overline{F}(x^{1+\rho}) - \overline{F}(x) \to \infty$ for all $\rho > 0$, as $x \to 0$.*

The latter condition is satisfied if $\overline{F}(x) \sim a\big(\log(1/x)\big)^v$ for any $v > 0$ and $a > 0$ (the case $v = 1$ includes gamma processes), but not when $v = 0$ (that is, X is a compound Poisson process, with $\beta = 0$ and $\Omega_T^{(i,\gamma=0)} = \emptyset$). It is also not satisfied when $\overline{F}(x) \sim a\log(\log(1/x))$, in which case $\beta = 0$ again and $\Omega_T^{(i,\gamma=0)} = \emptyset$, although $\Omega_T^{(ia)} = \Omega$.

Example 12.4. *This is similar to Example 11.4, with X of the form (11.5) and the Lévy measure F of the Lévy process Z satisfying*

$$\overline{F}(x) \sim \frac{(\log(1/x))^v}{x^w} \qquad as \ x \downarrow 0$$

for some $w \in [0,2)$ and $v \in \mathbb{R}$, with $v \geq 0$ when $w = 0$. Then we have (L) with $\beta = w$, if and only if $w > 0$ and $v = 0$, whereas (J) holds in all cases. Note that $\gamma_t = w$ if $\overline{H}_t = \int_0^t |H_s|\,ds$ is positive, and $\gamma_t = 0$ otherwise.

In this example we have the following equalities, up to null sets of course:

$$w > 0 \quad \Rightarrow \quad \Omega_T^{(ia)} = \Omega_T^{(iia)} = \Omega_T^{(i,\gamma>0)} = \{\overline{H}_T > 0\}$$
$$w = 0, \ v > 0 \quad \Rightarrow \quad \Omega_T^{(ia)} = \Omega_T^{(iia)} = \Omega_T^{(i,\gamma=0)} = \{\overline{H}_T > 0\},$$

whereas when $w = v = 0$ the measure F is finite, hence $\Omega_T^{(ia)} = \emptyset$. Note also that $\Omega_T^{(ia)} = \Omega_T^{(\beta)}$ as well when $w = \beta > 0$ and $v = 0$ (so (L) holds).

After these preliminaries, we turn to the description of the tests. The idea is very close to what was done in Section 10.3, except that here we truncate the increments at some cutoff levels u_n which, as usual, satisfy (11.7). The rationale is that, on the set $\Omega_T^{(fa)}$, for n large enough, all increments $\Delta_i^n X$ on intervals without jumps and inside $[0, T]$ are smaller than u_n, whereas all the (finitely many) others are bigger than u_n, and are thus eliminated by the truncation. Thus the statistics used in Section 10.3, once increments are substituted with truncated increments, behave on the set $\Omega_T^{(fa)}$ as they behaved without truncation on the set $\Omega_T^{(c)}$.

As a matter of fact, using statistics like $B(p, \Delta_n, u_n)$ (see (6.26)), is possible but, exactly as for the estimation of the BG index, it looks preferable to take "smooth" test functions, provided they behave as $|x|^p$ near 0 and vanish far from 0. This is why we suggest taking the function

$$g_p(x) = |x|^p \bigwedge (2 - |x|)^+, \tag{12.5}$$

but any function satisfying (11.13) and equal to $|x|^p$ on a neighborhood of 0 and with compact support could be used here. The building blocks for constructing the estimators are thus the following modifications of the functionals $J(g; \Delta_n, u_n)$ given by (11.12):

$$J([g_p, k], \Delta_n, u_n)_t = \sum_{i=1}^{[t/\Delta_n]-k+1} g_p\left(\frac{X_{(i+k-1)\Delta_n} - X_{(i-1)\Delta_n}}{u_n}\right)$$

$$J(g_p, k\Delta_n, u_n)_t = \sum_{i=1}^{[t/k\Delta_n]} g_p\left(\frac{X_{ik\Delta_n} - X_{(i-1)k\Delta_n}}{u_n}\right),$$

where $p > 0$ and k is a positive integer. Of course when $k = 1$ we have $J([g_p, k], \Delta_n, u_n) = J(g_p, k\Delta_n, u_n) = J(g_p, \Delta_n, u_n)$, so below we take $k \geq 2$. The statistics are then defined in a similar way to (10.40):

$$S^{(FA-PV1)}(p, k, \Delta_n, u_n) = \frac{J([g_p, k], \Delta_n, u_n)_T}{kJ(g_p, \Delta_n, u_n)_T}$$
$$S^{(FA-PV2)}(p, k, \Delta_n, u_n) = \frac{J(g_p, k\Delta_n, u_n)_T}{J(g_p, \Delta_n, u_n)_T}. \tag{12.6}$$

The asymptotic behavior of these statistics is given by the following theorem (compare with (10.41) and (10.48); the proof is on page 613):

Theorem 12.5. *Assume (K-2) and let $p > 2$ and $k \geq 2$ and let $u_n \asymp \Delta_n^\varpi$ with $\varpi \in \left(0, \frac{1}{2}\right)$.*

a) In restriction to the set $\Omega_T^{(fa,W)} = \Omega_T^{(fa)} \cap \Omega_T^{(W)}$ we have

$$S^{(FA-PV1)}(p, k, \Delta_n, u_n) \xrightarrow{\mathbb{P}} k^{p/2-1},$$
$$S^{(FA-PV2)}(p, k, \Delta_n, u_n) \xrightarrow{\mathbb{P}} k^{p/2-1} \tag{12.7}$$

and also the following stable convergences in law, again on $\Omega_T^{(fa,W)}$:

$$\frac{1}{\sqrt{\Delta_n}}\left(S^{(\text{FA}-\text{PV1})}(p,k,\Delta_n,u_n) - k^{p/2-1}\right) \xrightarrow{\mathcal{L}_s} S_{(c)}^{(\text{FA}-\text{PV1})}(p,k)$$
$$\frac{1}{\sqrt{\Delta_n}}\left(S^{(\text{FA}-\text{PV2})}(p,k,\Delta_n,u_n) - k^{p/2-1}\right) \xrightarrow{\mathcal{L}_s} S_{(c)}^{(\text{FA}-\text{PV2})}(p,k), \tag{12.8}$$

where $S^{(\text{J}-\text{PV1})}(p,k)$ *and* $S^{(\text{J}-\text{PV2})}(p,k)$ *are the variables of (10.48).*

b) *Assume further that* $\varpi < \frac{p-2}{2p}$. *Then, in restriction to the set* $\Omega_T^{(iia)}$ *if (J) holds, and in restriction to the set* $\Omega_T^{(\beta)}$ *if (L) holds, we have*

$$S^{(\text{FA}-\text{PV1})}(p,k,\Delta_n,u_n) \xrightarrow{\mathbb{P}} 1,$$
$$S^{(\text{FA}-\text{PV2})}(p,k,\Delta_n,u_n) \xrightarrow{\mathbb{P}} 1. \tag{12.9}$$

As usual, in order to construct the tests we need consistent estimators for the conditional variances of the limits in (12.8). To this aim, and if for example we use the first test statistics $S^{(\text{FA}-\text{PV1})}(p,k,\Delta_n,u_n)$, we can take one of the estimators provided by formula (10.50). In view of Theorem 10.14 and of the subsequent comments, it is presumably best to take the second among those estimators, that is, $V_n^{(2)}$.

At this point, we can reproduce word for word the proof of Theorems 10.14 and 10.15 and we obtain the following result, where z_α' is the α-quantile of the standard normal distribution $\mathcal{N}(0,1)$ (the critical regions below are identical to those in the two previously mentioned theorems):

Theorem 12.6. *Assume (K-2), and let* $p > 2$ *and* $k \geq 2$ *and* $u_n \asymp \Delta_n^\varpi$. *Let also* $\alpha(p,k)_1$ *and* $\alpha(p,k)_2$ *be given by (10.49).*

a) *The tests with critical regions*

$$\mathcal{C}_n = \Big\{ S^{(\text{FA}-\text{PV1})}(p,k,\Delta_n,u_n) < k^{p/2-1}$$
$$- z_\alpha' \sqrt{\alpha(p,k)_1 \frac{(m_p)^2 \, B(2p,\Delta_n,u_n)_T}{m_{2p} \, (B(p,\Delta_n,u_n)_T)^2}} \Big\} \tag{12.10}$$

have the strong asymptotic level α *for the null hypothesis* $\Omega_T^{(fa)} \cap \Omega_T^{(W)}$. *If further* $\varpi < \frac{p-2}{2p}$, *then under (J) they are consistent for the alternative* $\Omega_T^{(iia)} \cap \Omega_T^{(W)}$, *and under (L) they are consistent for the alternative* $\Omega_T^{(\beta)} \cap \Omega_T^{(W)}$.

b) *The same properties hold for the following critical regions:*

$$\mathcal{C}_n = \Big\{ S^{(\text{FA}-\text{PV2})}(p,k,\Delta_n,u_n) < k^{p/2-1}$$
$$- z_\alpha' \sqrt{\alpha(p,k)_2 \frac{(m_p)^2 \, B(2p,\Delta_n,u_n)_T}{m_{2p} \, (B(p,\Delta_n,u_n)_T)^2}} \Big\}. \tag{12.11}$$

Proposition 10.19 and all the subsequent comments (concerning the null $\Omega_T^{(cW)}$) apply here without change. In particular, the tests (12.10) are better than the tests (12.11), from the viewpoint of the power of the test, and we should choose a small value for k, such as $k = 2$. Although the asymptotic size is not affected by the choice of ϖ, in order to achieve alternative consistency one should choose $\varpi < \frac{p-2}{2p}$.

Remark 12.7. *Since our statistics $S^{(\mathrm{FA-PV1})}(p, k, \Delta_n, u_n)$ and $S^{(\mathrm{FA-PV2})}(p, k, \Delta_n, u_n)$ are based on the variables $J(g_p; \Delta_n, u_n)_T$, it is perhaps more coherent to use the same in the estimators of the asymptotic variances. In other words, we could replace $B(p, \Delta_n, u_n)_T$ and $B(2p, \Delta_n, u_n)_T$ by $J(g_p; \Delta_n, u_n)_T$ and $J(g_{2p}; \Delta_n, u_n)_T$, respectively, in the above definitions of the critical regions. Such a substitution does not alter the results.*

Now we turn to empirical considerations. Each one of the statistics below is computed separately for each quarter of 2006 and for each asset. The data for the histogram in Figure 12.1 are produced by computing for the four quarters of the year and each stock the value of $S^{(\mathrm{FA-PV2})}(p, k, \Delta_n, u_n)$, abbreviated as S_{FA} in the forthcoming discussion, for a range of values of p from 3 to 6, α from 5 to 10 standard deviations, Δ_n from 5 seconds to 2 minutes, and $k = 2, 3$. We find that the empirical values of S_{FA} are distributed around 1, which is indicative of infinite activity jumps. That is, even as we truncate, the statistic continues to behave as if jumps are present. If only a finite number of jumps had been present, then the statistic should have behaved as if the process were continuous. But the histograms do display a fat right tail, indicative of finite activity jumps for at least some of the DJIA components. The histograms are quite similar for all three data measurements, suggesting that they tend to differ only because of the larger increments: those are indeed the ones that are filtered in F compared to U, but since they are truncated away by S_{FA} anyway, then for the purpose of computing S_{FA} the two data measurements produce close results.

The middle right panel in Figure 12.1 displays the mean value of S_{FA} (across the four quarters, two stocks, and values of p, α and k) as a function of Δ_n. A pattern similar to the corresponding plot in Figure 10.5 emerges. Even for very small values of Δ_n, the noise does not dominate (limits below 1); instead the limit is around 1 as Δ_n increases away from the frequencies where the noise would have been expected to dominate. Unless we start downsampling more (reaching 5 to 10 minutes), the limit does not get close to $k^{p/2-1}$. The lower panels examine any patterns linking S_{FA} to stock-level measures of liquidity; no strong cross-sectional pattern emerges.

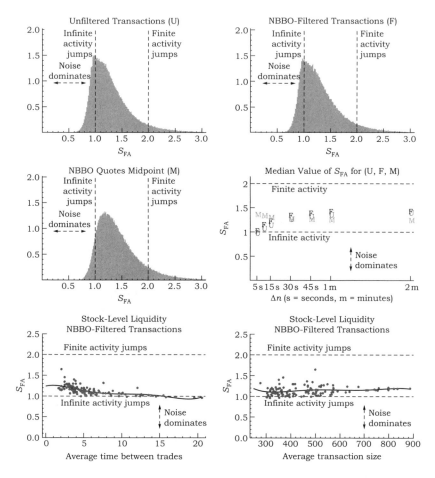

Figure 12.1: Testing whether jumps have finite or infinite activity: Empirical distribution of $S^{(FA-PV2)}(p, k, \Delta_n, u_n)$ for all 30 DJIA stocks, 2006, measured using transactions (unfiltered, U, and NBBO-filtered, F) and NBBO quotes midpoint (M), median value of $S^{(FA-PV2)}(p, k, \Delta_n, u_n)$ as a function of the sampling interval Δ_n, and nonlinear regression of S_{FA} against stock-level liquidity measures.

Overall, the evidence suggests the presence of infinite activity jumps in the DJIA 30 components. To the extent that jumps are present in the DJIA index itself, the evidence is in favor of finite activity jumps: we find values of S_{FA} ranging from 1.7 to 2.2 for the index.

12.2 When the Null Hypothesis Is Infinite Jump Activity

Now we turn to the other possible null hypothesis, that of "infinite activity" of jumps. For this problem, we must be able to evaluate the asymptotic level of our tests, and to do so we need some rather strong assumptions on X, namely (L): the situation is in fact quite similar to the estimation of the BG index. However, and as before, even though we assume (L) we do not want to suppose that the index β is known.

Under this assumption, the null hypothesis will be $\Omega_T^{(\beta)}$, which is included in $\Omega_T^{(ia)}$, and the alternative will be $\Omega_T^{(fa,W)} = \Omega_T^{(fa)} \cap \Omega_T^{(W)}$.

The construction of the test statistics is slightly complicated, because we want an asymptotic behavior which is model-free within the class of models satisfying (L), and in particular does not depend on the unknown value of β under the null. To achieve this, we take two powers $p > p' > 2$ and a real $\gamma > 1$; we use the variables $J(g; \Delta_n, u_n)_T$ of (11.12), with a sequence $u_n \asymp \Delta_n^\varpi$ for some $\varpi \in (0, \frac{1}{2})$, and with the test functions g_p and $g_{p'}$ defined by (12.5). With all these ingredients we construct the statistics as follows:

$$S^{(\text{IA-PV})}(p, p', \gamma, \Delta_n, u_n) = \frac{J(g_p; \Delta_n, \gamma u_n)_T \, J(g_{p'}; \Delta_n, u_n)_T}{J(g_p; \Delta_n, u_n)_T \, J(g_{p'}; \Delta_n, \gamma u_n)_T}.$$

In other words, unlike for the previous statistic $S^{(\text{FA-PV1})}(p, k, \Delta_n, u_n)$, we now play with different powers p and p', and different levels of truncation u_n and γu_n, but otherwise sample at the same frequency Δ_n.

The next theorem, proved on page 610, gives us the asymptotic behavior of our statistics, and we need some preliminary notation. Each of the following four functions satisfies (11.13), as well as any product of them:

$$\begin{aligned} h_1(x) &= g_p(x/\gamma), \quad h_2(x) = g_p(x), \\ h_3(x) &= g_{p'}(x), \quad h_4(x) = g_{p'}(x/\gamma). \end{aligned} \quad (12.12)$$

Observe that, with the notation (11.15), we have $v_{h_j}(\beta) = v_{h_{j+1}}(\beta)/\gamma^\beta$ when $j = 1, 3$. The functions h_i are "known," in the sense that they depend only on the parameters p, p', γ chosen by the statistician. In contrast, we introduce the following functions, which also depend on the unknown β and thus cannot be used directly, but are convenient for stating the result:

$$l_j = \frac{h_j}{v_{h_j}(\beta)} \quad \text{for} \quad j = 1, 2, 3, 4,$$

$$g = (l_1 - l_2 + l_3 - l_4)^2 = \sum_{i,j=1}^{4}(-1)^{i+j}l_i l_j. \tag{12.13}$$

Note that the function g also satisfies (11.13), with the exponent $2p'$, so $v_{l_j}(\beta)$ is well defined. We have $v_{l_j}(\beta) = 1$ by construction.

Theorem 12.8. *Assume (K-2) and (L), and let $p > p' \geq 4$ and $\gamma > 1$ and $u_n \asymp \Delta_n^\varpi$ with $\varpi \in (0, \frac{1}{4}]$.*

a) We have

$$S^{(\text{IA-PV})}(p, p', \gamma, \Delta_n, u_n) \xrightarrow{\mathbb{P}} \begin{cases} 1 & \text{on the set } \Omega_T^{(\beta)} \\ \gamma^{p'-p} & \text{on the set } \Omega_T^{(fa,W)} \end{cases}. \tag{12.14}$$

b) When $\beta' < \frac{\beta}{2}$ in (L), the variables

$$u_n^{-\beta/2}\big(S^{(\text{IA-PV})}(p, p', \gamma, \Delta_n, u_n) - 1\big)$$

converge stably in law, in restriction to the set $\Omega_T^{(\beta)}$, to a variable defined on an extension of the space, which, conditionally on the σ-field $\mathcal{F}$, is centered Gaussian with the following (conditional) variance, where g is given by (12.13) and depending on β:

$$V = v_g(\beta)/A_T.$$

c) The variables

$$V_n = \sum_{i,j=1}^{4}(-1)^{i+j}\frac{J(h_i h_j; \Delta_n, u_n)_T}{J(h_i; \Delta_n, u_n)_T\, J(h_j; \Delta_n, u_n)_T} \tag{12.15}$$

satisfy

$$u_n^{-\beta} V_n \xrightarrow{\mathbb{P}} \begin{cases} V & \text{on the set } \Omega_T^{(\beta)} \\ 0 & \text{on the set } \Omega_T^{(fa,W)} \end{cases}. \tag{12.16}$$

The functions h_j are known, so the statistic V_n can be explicitly computed using the data only. According to the established scheme, we deduce that the normalized statistics

$$\frac{S^{(\text{IA-PV})}(p, p', \gamma, \Delta_n, u_n) - 1}{\sqrt{V_n}}$$

converge stably in law, in restriction to the set $\Omega_T^{(\beta)}$, to a standard normal law. Since the second limit in (12.14) is smaller than 1, we are thus led to use the following rejection region, at stage n:

$$\mathcal{C}_n = \{S^{(\text{IA-PV})}(p, p', \gamma, \Delta_n, u_n) < 1 - z'_\alpha / \sqrt{V_n}\}, \tag{12.17}$$

where z'_α is again the α-quantile of $\mathcal{N}(0,1)$, and of course V_n is given by (12.15). The same proof as for the previous analogous results readily yields the result (for the consistency for the alternative, one may use the fact that, on $\Omega_T^{(fa,W)}$, the standardized variable $(S^{(\mathrm{IA\text{-}PV})}(p,p',\gamma,\Delta_n,u_n)-1)/\sqrt{V_n}$ converges in probability to $-\infty$, as a consequence of (12.14) and (12.16)).

Theorem 12.9. *Assume (K-2) and (L) with $\beta' < \frac{\beta}{2}$, and let $p' > p \geq 4$ and $\gamma > 1$ and $u_n \asymp \Delta_n^\varpi$ with $\varpi \in \left(0, \frac{1}{4}\right]$. The tests with critical regions given by (12.17) have the strong asymptotic level α for the null hypothesis $\Omega_T^{(\beta)}$, and they are consistent for the alternative $\Omega_T^{(fa,W)}$.*

Some comments are in order here. First, the structure of the sum (12.15), indeed a quadratic form, implies that $V_n \geq 0$ always. So the critical region is well defined.

Second, the rate under the null is not apparent in the definition of the critical region, since it is automatically "absorbed" by the estimator V_n; however, the true rate is $u_n^{\beta/2}$, so it is best to take u_n as small as possible, hence $\varpi = \frac{1}{4}$. Note that all these results are still valid when p' is smaller than 4, although bigger than 2; in this case we need $\varpi \leq \frac{p'-2}{2p'} < \frac{1}{4}$, so it is *not* advisable to choose $p' \in (2,4)$ and one should take $p' \geq 4$.

Finally, the assumptions are rather strong because we need (L), exactly as for estimating the BG index. This is of course not a surprise, and the proofs show that indeed the two types of result (this test and the estimation of β) are very closely related. On the other hand, we need not incorporate $\Omega_T^{(W)}$ into the null hypothesis here.

12.3 References

The tests presented here are borrowed from Aït-Sahalia and Jacod (2011), and are improved here using the same approach as Jing et al. (2011) for the BG estimation. A related problem, namely testing whether jumps have finite variation or not, has been studied by Cont and Mancini (2011).

Chapter 13

Is Brownian Motion Really Necessary?

So far we have explained how to test the presence of jumps and, when the answer to this question is positive, how to test whether the jumps have finite activity or not, and how to estimate the activity index (or BG index) of the jumps.

Now suppose that these procedures end up with the answer that jumps have infinite activity, and perhaps, even, that the BG index is "high" (on its scale: between 0 and 2). In the latter case, high-activity (compensated) jumps look pretty much like a Brownian motion plus occasional large jumps. It is thus legitimate to ask oneself the question of whether, in addition to those very active jumps, there is also a driving Brownian motion, or whether the process is "pure jump," that is, without a continuous martingale part.

When there are no jumps, or finitely many jumps, and no Brownian motion, X reduces to a pure drift plus occasional jumps, and such a model is fairly unrealistic in the context of most financial data series, although it may be realistic in some other situations. But for financial applications one can certainly consider models that consist only of a jump component, plus perhaps a drift, if that jump component is allowed to be infinitely active.

Many models in mathematical finance do not include jumps. But among those that do, the framework most often adopted consists of a jump-diffusion: these models include a drift term, a Brownian-driven continuous part, and a finite activity jump part; see for example Merton (1976), Ball and Torous (1983) and Bates (1991). When infinitely many jumps are included, however, a number of models in the literature dispense with the Brownian motion altogether. The log-price process is then a purely discontinuous Lévy process with infinite activity jumps, or more generally is driven by such a process; see for example Madan and Seneta (1990), Eberlein and Keller (1995) and Carr and Wu (2003a).

The mathematical treatment of models relying on pure jump processes is quite different from the treatment of models where a Brownian motion is present. For instance, risk management procedures, derivative pricing and portfolio optimization are all significantly altered, so there is interest from the mathematical finance side in finding out which model is more likely to have generated the data.

The aim of this short chapter is thus to provide explicit testing procedures to decide whether the Brownian motion is necessary to model the observed path, or whether the process is entirely driven by its jumps.

The structural assumption is the same as in the previous two chapters, with the underlying process X being a one-dimensional Itô semimartingale, since in the multi-dimensional case we can again perform the test on each component separately. The process is defined on a filtered space $(\Omega, \mathcal{F}, (\mathcal{F}_t)_{t \geq 0}, \mathbb{P})$ and has the Grigelionis representation (1.74), that is,

$$X_t = X_0 + \int_0^t b_s ds + \int_0^t \sigma_s dW_s \tag{13.1}$$
$$+ (\delta 1_{\{|\delta| \leq 1\}}) \star (\underline{p} - \underline{q})_t + (\delta 1_{\{|\delta| > 1\}}) \star \underline{p}_t,$$

with the usual notation (W is a one-dimensional Brownian motion, $\underline{p}$ is a Poisson measure on $\mathbb{R}_+ \times E$ with $(E, \mathcal{E})$ a Polish space, and with compensator $\underline{q}(dt, dx) = dt \otimes \lambda(dx)$). The characteristics of X are thus

$$B_t = \int_0^t b_s ds, \qquad C_t = \int_0^t c_s ds, \qquad \nu(dt, dx) = dt\, F_t(dx),$$

where b is the same as in (13.1), and $c = \sigma^2$, and $F_t(\omega, dx)$ is the restriction to $\mathbb{R} \backslash \{0\}$ of the image of λ by the map $z \mapsto \delta(\omega, t, z)$. We often use Assumptions (H-r) and (K-r) and (H$'$), defined at the beginning of Chapter 10 (page 330), and (L) defined page 396.

Our aim is to construct a test allowing us to separate the following two disjoint hypotheses:

$$\Omega_T^{(W)} = \{C_T > 0\}, \qquad \Omega_T^{(noW)} = \{C_T = 0\},$$

with the idea that if we decide that the observed outcome is in $\Omega_T^{(W)}$, the Brownian motion in (13.1) is really necessary, whereas otherwise one can omit it. The observations are, as before, regularly spaced at times $i\Delta_n$, over the fixed time interval $[0, T]$, and Δ_n goes to 0.

13.1 Tests for the Null Hypothesis That the Brownian Is Present

We start with testing the null hypothesis $\Omega_T^{(W)}$, under which the Brownian is necessary.

Probably, the most natural idea to do this is as follows. In Chapter 10 we introduced two statistics, $S^{(\text{J-MP2})}(k, \Delta_n)$ in (10.15) and $S^{(\text{J-TR})}(\Delta_n, u_n)$ in (10.18), to test the null hypothesis that there is no jump, in which case they are close to 1. When there are jumps, but no Brownian motion, both of them are close to 0, whereas if there are jumps *and* Brownian motion, both converge to the positive (random) ratio $S = C_T / [X, X]_T$. One can thus try to use these statistics for testing whether the outcome ω is in $\Omega_T^{(W)}$ as well.

Using statistics which converge to S above induces serious problems, though: when the null is $\Omega_T^{(noW)}$, that is, $S = 0$, we have nothing like a Central Limit Theorem which would give us some help finding the asymptotic size. All CLTs at our disposal, so far, give degenerate results when the Brownian part vanishes. When, as in this section, the null is $\Omega_T^{(W)} = \{S > 0\}$, we still have a problem: we do have a CLT, under suitable assumptions on the process, but since S is unknown under the null (apart from the fact that it is positive) we cannot properly center the statistics $S^{(\text{J-MP2})}(k, \Delta_n)$ or $S^{(\text{J-TR})}(\Delta_n, u_n)$ in order to construct a test, even.

To overcome this difficulty, we may look for statistics which converge to a known (non-random) limit on the set $\Omega_T^{(W)}$, and for this we resort again to some ratio of power, or rather truncated power, variations. More precisely, we consider the same test functions g_p as in the previous chapter:

$$g_p(x) = |x|^p \bigwedge (2 - |x|)^+, \tag{13.2}$$

but any function satisfying (11.13) and equal to $|x|^p$ on a neighborhood of 0 could be used here (we do not need this function to have compact support below, in contrast to the requirements in the previous chapter). We associate the same processes as in (11.12), that is,

$$
\begin{aligned}
J([g_p, k], \Delta_n, u_n)_t &= \sum_{i=1}^{[t/\Delta_n]-k+1} g_p\left(\frac{X_{(i+k-1)\Delta_n} - X_{(i-1)\Delta_n}}{u_n}\right) \\
J(g_p, k\Delta_n, u_n)_t &= \sum_{i=1}^{[t/k\Delta_n]} g_p\left(\frac{X_{ik\Delta_n} - X_{(i-1)k\Delta_n}}{u_n}\right),
\end{aligned}
\tag{13.3}
$$

Here, $k \geq 1$ is an integer, and u_n is a sequence of truncation levels satisfying $u_n \asymp \Delta_n^\varpi$ for some $\varpi \in (0, \frac{1}{2})$.

The statistics we will use are those of (12.6), which we recall:

$$S^{(\text{FA-PV1})}(p, k, \Delta_n, u_n) = \frac{J([g_p, k], \Delta_n, u_n)_T}{k J(g_p, \Delta_n, u_n)_T}$$
$$S^{(\text{FA-PV2})}(p, k, \Delta_n, u_n) = \frac{J(g_p, k\Delta_n, u_n)_T}{J(g_p, \Delta_n, u_n)_T}.$$

There is a big difference, however: for testing for finite activity of jumps we were using a power $p > 2$, whereas here we will use $p < 2$, and the reason is as follows: if we take $p > 2$ and assume (L) for example, then these ratios converge to 1 on the set $\Omega_T^{(\beta)}$, as seen in (12.9), irrespective of whether we are in $\Omega_T^{(\beta)} \cap \Omega_T^{(W)}$ or in $\Omega_T^{(\beta)} \cap \Omega_T^{(noW)}$. In other words, with $p > 2$ these statistics cannot distinguish between the null and the alternative.

When $p < 2$, things are totally different. On $\Omega_T^{(W)}$ the Brownian part plays the main role and the convergence (12.7) holds (that is, the above statistics converge in probability to $k^{p/2-1}$), irrespective of the properties of the jumps. On the other hand, on the set $\Omega_T^{(\beta)} \cap \Omega_T^{(noW)}$, when (L) holds and $p > \beta$, these statistics still converge to 1, as in (12.9) again.

We state all these consistency results, together with the associated Central Limit Theorem under the null, in the next theorem (all results of this chapter are proved on pages 612 et seq.).

Theorem 13.1. *Let $p \in (1, 2)$ and $k \geq 2$ and $u_n \asymp \Delta_n^\varpi$ with $\varpi \in (0, \frac{1}{2})$.*

a) Under (K-2), and in restriction to the set $\Omega_T^{(W)}$, we have

$$S^{(\text{FA-PV1})}(p, k, \Delta_n, u_n) \xrightarrow{\mathbb{P}} k^{p/2-1},$$
$$S^{(\text{FA-PV2})}(p, k, \Delta_n, u_n) \xrightarrow{\mathbb{P}} k^{p/2-1}. \tag{13.4}$$

b) Assuming (K-r) for some $r \in [0, 1)$ and $\varpi \geq \frac{p-1}{2(p-r)}$, we have the following stable convergences in law, in restriction to the set $\Omega_T^{(W)}$:

$$\frac{1}{\sqrt{\Delta_n}} \left(S^{(\text{FA-PV1})}(p, k, \Delta_n, u_n) - k^{p/2-1} \right) \xrightarrow{\mathcal{L}-s} S_{(c)}^{(\text{J-PV1})}(p, k)$$
$$\frac{1}{\sqrt{\Delta_n}} \left(S^{(\text{FA-PV2})}(p, k, \Delta_n, u_n) - k^{p/2-1} \right) \xrightarrow{\mathcal{L}-s} S_{(c)}^{(\text{J-PV1})}(p, k),$$

where $S^{(\text{J-PV1})}(p, k)$ and $S^{(\text{J-PV1})}(p, k)$ are the variables of (10.48).

c) Assuming (K-r) for some $r \in [0, 1)$ and (L) with some β (necessarily $\beta \in (0, 1)$), and $\varpi \leq \frac{p-1}{p}$, then in restriction to the set $\Omega_T^{(\beta)} \cap \Omega_T^{(noW)}$, we have

$$S^{(\text{FA-PV1})}(p, k, \Delta_n, u_n) \xrightarrow{\mathbb{P}} 1,$$
$$S^{(\text{FA-PV2})}(p, k, \Delta_n, u_n) \xrightarrow{\mathbb{P}} 1. \tag{13.5}$$

Once more, to apply this result for a concrete test, we need to standardize our statistics. This is done exactly as in Theorem 12.6, and with

z'_α denoting the α-quantile of the standard normal distribution $\mathcal{N}(0,1)$ we construct our tests and obtain their properties in the next theorem (it looks exactly the same as Theorem 12.6, but beware of the conditions, which are significantly different; notice also the sign change in the critical regions, which occurs because $k^{p/2-1}$ is smaller than 1 here instead of being bigger as in Theorem 12.6).

Theorem 13.2. *Assume (K-r) for some $r \in [0,1)$ and let $p \in [2r,2)$ and $k \geq 2$ and $u_n \asymp \Delta_n^\varpi$ with $\frac{p-1}{2(p-r)} \leq \varpi \leq \frac{p-1}{p}$. Let also $\alpha(p,k)_1$ and $\alpha(p,k)_2$ be given by (10.49).*
    a) The tests with critical regions

$$\mathcal{C}_n = \Big\{ S^{(\mathrm{FA-PV1})}(p,k,\Delta_n,u_n) > k^{p/2-1}$$
$$+ z'_\alpha \sqrt{\alpha(p,k)_1 \frac{(m_p)^2 \, B(2p,\Delta_n,u_n)_T}{m_{2p} \, (B(p,\Delta_n,u_n)_T)^2}} \Big\}$$

have strong asymptotic size α for the null hypothesis $\Omega_T^{(W)}$. If further (L) holds they are consistent for the alternative $\Omega_T^{(\beta)} \cap \Omega_T^{(noW)}$.
    b) The same properties hold for the following critical regions:

$$\mathcal{C}_n = \Big\{ S^{(\mathrm{FA-PV2})}(p,k,\Delta_n,u_n) > k^{p/2-1}$$
$$+ z'_\alpha \sqrt{\alpha(p,k)_2 \frac{(m_p)^2 \, B(2p,\Delta_n,u_n)_T}{m_{2p} \, (B(p,\Delta_n,u_n)_T)^2}} \Big\}.$$

Exactly as in Remark 12.7, one could replace $B(p,\Delta_n,u_n)_T$ and $B(2p,\Delta_n,u_n)_T$ in the above definitions of the critical regions by $J(g_p;\Delta_n,u_n)_T$ and $J(g_{2p};\Delta_n,u_n)_T$, respectively.

An *important drawback* of these tests should be emphasized. Apart from the somewhat restrictive assumption (L) needed for the alternative consistency, the previous tests can be used only when one knows that (K-r) holds for some $r < 1$. This is quite unfortunate, because one is more likely to test whether a Brownian motion is necessary in the case where the jump activity is relatively close to 2; here, it *should be* smaller than 1. Note that, as already mentioned in (c) of Theorem 13.1, this implies that when (L) holds for the alternative consistency, necessarily $\beta < 1$ (this comes from Lemma 11.8).

The conditions on ϖ above exactly combine the conditions for (b) and (c) in Theorem 13.1, and if they are satisfied we must have $p \geq 2r$. So, not only do we have to assume (K-r) for some $r < 1$, but we need an *a priori* bound $r_0 < 1$ such that the unknown r does not exceed r_0, in order to choose p.

As we will see below, testing the null $\Omega_T^{(noW)}$ does *not* suffer from the same drawback: we will need (L), but without the restriction that $\beta < 1$.

Figure 13.1 displays histograms of the distribution of $S^{(\text{FA-PV1})}$ obtained by computing its value for the four quarters of the year for a range of values of p from 1 to 1.75, α in $u_n = \alpha\Delta_n^\varpi$ from 5 to 10 standard deviations, Δ_n from 5 seconds to 2 minutes, and $k = 2,3$. The empirical estimates are always on the side of the limit arising in the presence of a continuous component. Even as the sampling frequency increases, the noise does not seem to be a dominant factor, although as usual, lower values of $S^{(\text{FA-PV1})}$ below 1 are now obtained, and for very high sampling frequencies the results are consistent with some mixture of the noise driving the asymptotics.

This is confirmed by the middle right panel in Figure 13.1 which displays the median value of $S^{(\text{FA-PV1})}$ (across the four quarters, two stocks, and values of p, α and k) as a function of Δ_n. As we downsample away from the noise-dominated frequencies, the average value of the statistic settles down toward the one indicating the presence of a Brownian motion.

Because values of p less than 2 are employed by the statistic $S^{(\text{W}-\text{PV1})}$, we find relatively small differences between the results for filtered and unfiltered transactions: since they differ mainly by a few of their large increments, but values of $p < 2$ tend to underemphasize large increments, we obtain similar results for F and U. The lower panels look at the relationship between $S^{(\text{FA}-\text{PV1})}$ and the underlying asset's liquidity. Like $S^{(\text{J}-\text{PV1})}$, we find that there is a very slight increase in the value of the statistic as the asset becomes more liquid. In the case of the DJIA index, we find that a Brownian motion is likely present, except at the highest frequencies. Indeed, increments of the index tend to be very smooth owing to the nature of the index as an average. It is possible that the averaging involved in the construction of the index may enable us to detect a spurious Brownian component in the index.

13.2 Tests for the Null Hypothesis That the Brownian Is Absent

There are two ways to our knowledge to test for the null hypothesis "there is no Brownian motion." The first is quite simple and, exactly as for the previous tests, it needs (H-r) for some $r < 1$, but it does *not* need (L) at all, and neither does it need (K-r). The second one needs (L), but without restriction on the value of β.

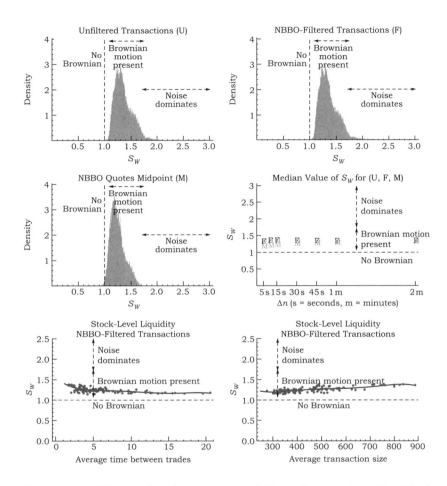

Figure 13.1: Testing for the presence of Brownian motion: Empirical distribution of $S^{(W-PV1)}(p, k, \Delta_n, u_n)$ for all 30 DJIA stocks, 2006, measured using transactions (unfiltered, U, and NBBO-filtered, F) and NBBO quotes midpoint (M), median value of $S^{(W-PV1)}(p, k, \Delta_n, u_n)$ as a function of the sampling interval Δ_n, and nonlinear regression of S_W against stock-level liquidity measures.

13.2.1   Adding a Fictitious Brownian

Here the null hypothesis is $\Omega_T^{(noW)}$. The idea is to add a *fictitious* Brownian motion to the observed data, exactly as in Subsection 10.2.5. More precisely, one simulates a Wiener process W', independent of everything else, and takes some $\sigma' > 0$ (a constant, and we set $c' = \sigma'^2$). Then the observed increments $\Delta_i^n X$ are replaced by the following increments:

$$\Delta_i^n Y = \Delta_i^n X + \sigma' \Delta_i^n W' \tag{13.6}$$

which are those of the process $Y = X + \sigma' W'$ (without restriction we can assume that W' is defined on $(\Omega, \mathcal{F}, \mathbb{P})$ and adapted to the filtration $(\mathcal{F}_t)$. This simply amounts to replacing the second characteristic C_t of X by the second characteristic $C_t' = C_t + tc'$ of Y.

Our null hypothesis can now be expressed as

$$\Omega_T^{(noW)} = \{C_T' = c'T\}. \tag{13.7}$$

It follows that since c' is a *known* number, we can test whether C_T' is bigger than $c'T$. For this, we can use the estimators for the integrated volatility, developed in Chapter 6 with their associated distributional theories, but put to use with the increments $\Delta_i^n Y$ of (13.6) instead of $\Delta_i^n X$.

In other words, we can use the estimator $\widehat{C}(\Delta_n, u_n)$ of (6.22), based on truncated increments (we are in the one-dimensional case here); or we may use the estimator $\widehat{C}([k], \Delta_n)$ of (6.35), based on multipower variations. The analysis is of course the same in the two cases, and in view of the discussion in Subsection 6.2.5 we conduct the test on the basis of truncated realized volatility only.

As usual, we take a sequence $u_n \asymp \Delta_n^\varpi$ for some $\varpi \in (0, \frac{1}{2})$. The associated truncated realized volatility of the process Y is

$$\widehat{C}^Y(\Delta_n, u_n)_T = \sum_{i=1}^{[T/\Delta_n]} (\Delta_i^n Y)^2 1_{\{|\Delta_i^n Y| \le u_n\}}.$$

We also need the following estimators for the quarticity:

$$B^Y(4, \Delta_n, u_n)_T = \sum_{i=1}^{[T/\Delta_n]} (\Delta_i^n Y)^4 1_{\{|\Delta_i^n Y| \le u_n\}},$$

which converges in probability to $3\int_0^T (c_s + c')^2 \, ds$ (we could replace this by the other, more efficient, estimators for the quarticity discussed in Section 8.5).

With these notations, we can reformulate (6.28) as follows: Assuming (H-r) for some $r \in (0,1)$, and provided $\varpi \geq \frac{1}{2(2-r)}$, we have that

$$\sqrt{\frac{3}{2}} \frac{\widehat{C}^Y(\Delta_n, u_n)_T - C'_T}{\sqrt{B^Y(4, \Delta_n, u_n)_T}}$$

converges stably to an $\mathcal{N}(0,1)$ variable, independent of $\mathcal{F}$.

Recalling (13.7), plus the fact that $C'_T \geq c'T$, we straightforwardly deduce the following result (as always, z'_α is the one-sided α-quantile of $\mathcal{N}(0,1)$):

Theorem 13.3. *Assume (H-r) for some $r \in [0,1)$ and let $u_n \asymp \Delta_n^\varpi$ with $\frac{1}{2(2-r)} \leq \varpi < \frac{1}{2}$. The tests with critical regions*

$$\mathcal{C}_n = \left\{ \widehat{C}^Y(\Delta_n, u_n)_T > c'T + \frac{z'_\alpha}{\sqrt{3}} \sqrt{2B^Y(4, \Delta_n, u_n)_T} \right\}$$

have the strong asymptotic size α for the null hypothesis $\Omega_T^{(noW)}$, and they are consistent for the alternative $\Omega_T^{(W)}$ under (H').

Once again, a nice thing about this procedure is that it tests exactly the null and the alternative which we want, without extra restriction like being in $\Omega_T^{(\beta)}$. But it suffers the same kind of drawback as the tests of the previous section, namely the jump activity index has to be smaller than 1; this is especially bad if we take the null to be "no Brownian motion," as here.

This test needs specifying the truncation levels u_n, as do most tests in this book, and for this one can take advantage of the procedure outlined in Subsection 6.2.2, of course replacing the true volatility c_t by $c_t + c'$. There is another tuning parameter, which is the number c'. Clearly, the actual power of the test increases as c' decreases, so one should take $c'T$ "small," relative to the total quadratic variation $[X,X]_T$ (estimated by $\widehat{C}(\Delta_n)_T$, for the process X of course).

13.2.2 Tests Based on Power Variations

The null hypothesis is still $\Omega_T^{(noW)}$ here, and we want tests which do not require any restriction on the activity index of jumps, or as little as possible. The price we have to pay is that we need Assumption (L).

We use the same ratio test statistics as for testing for infinite activity, except that instead of taking two powers $p > p' > 2$ we now take $p > p' = 2$. In other words, we use the following test statistics:

$$S^{(IA-PV)}(p, 2, \gamma, \Delta_n, u_n) = \frac{J(g_p; \Delta_n, \gamma u_n)_T \, J(g_2; \Delta_n, u_n)_T}{J(g_p; \Delta_n, u_n)_T \, J(g_2; \Delta_n, \gamma u_n)_T}.$$

The truncation levels are $u_n \asymp \Delta_n^\varpi$ as before, and the functions g_p of (13.2), and $\gamma > 1$.

Here again, the key point is the behavior of $J(g_p; \Delta_n, u_n)_T$, as described by (11.18), when (L) holds: under appropriate conditions on ϖ, we have that $u_n^\beta J(g_p; \Delta_n, u_n)_T$ converges in probability to $v_{g_p}(\beta)$, if $p > 2$ always, and if $p = 2$ when there is no Brownian motion, in which case our statistics go to 1. On the other hand, in the presence of the Brownian motion, $u_n^2 J(g_2; \Delta_n, u_n)_T$ is also basically the same as the truncated realized volatility $B(2, \Delta_n, u_n)_T$, which converges to $C_T > 0$; this results in a limit equal to γ^β for our statistics.

We state the conditions for this, and also the associated Central Limit Theorem, in the next result, proved on page 613. First, we recall the notation (12.12):

$$h_1(x) = g_p(x/\gamma), \quad h_2(x) = g_p(x),$$
$$h_3(x) = g_2(x/\gamma), \quad h_4(x) = g_2(x).$$

Theorem 13.4. *Assume (L) with some β strictly smaller than a given number $\beta_0 \in (0, 2)$, and let $p \geq 4$ and $\gamma > 1$ and $u_n \asymp \Delta_n^\varpi$ with $\varpi \in (0, \frac{1}{4} \wedge \frac{4-2\beta_0}{\beta_0(4-\beta_0)}]$.*

a) We have

$$S^{(\mathrm{IA-PV})}(p, 2, \gamma, \Delta_n, u_n) \overset{\mathbb{P}}{\longrightarrow} \begin{cases} 1 & \text{on the set } \Omega_T^{(noW)} \cap \Omega_T^{(\beta)} \\ \gamma^{2-\beta} & \text{on the set } \Omega_T^{(W)} \cap \Omega_T^{(\beta)}. \end{cases} \tag{13.8}$$

b) Assuming $\beta' < \frac{\beta}{2}$ in (L), the variables

$$u_n^{-\beta/2}\big(S^{(\mathrm{IA-PV})}(p, 2, \gamma, \Delta_n, u_n) - 1\big)$$

converge stably in law, in restriction to the set $\Omega_T^{(noW)} \cap \Omega_T^{(\beta)}$, to a variable defined on an extension of the space, which, conditionally on the σ-field $\mathcal{F}$, is centered Gaussian with (conditional) variance

$$V = \sum_{i,j=1}^{4} (-1)^{i+j} \frac{v_{h_i h_j}(\beta)}{v_{h_i}(\beta) \, v_{h_j}(\beta) \, A_T}.$$

c) The variables

$$V_n = \sum_{i,j=1}^{4} (-1)^{i+j} \frac{J(h_i h_j; \Delta_n, u_n)_T}{J(h_i; \Delta_n, u_n)_T \, J(h_j; \Delta_n, u_n)_T} \tag{13.9}$$

satisfy, for some strictly positive variable V',

$$u_n^{-\beta} V_n \overset{\mathbb{P}}{\longrightarrow} \begin{cases} V & \text{on the set } \Omega_T^{(noW)} \cap \Omega_T^{(\beta)} \\ V' & \text{on the set } \Omega_T^{(W)} \cap \Omega_T^{(\beta)}. \end{cases} \tag{13.10}$$

Observe that the second limit in (13.8) is unknown, because it involves β, but it is always bigger than 1. Therefore, for testing the null hypothesis "no Brownian motion" we can take the following critical (rejection) region, with again z'_α the one-sided α-quantile of $\mathcal{N}(0,1)$ and V_n given by (13.9):

$$\mathcal{C}_n \ = \ \left\{ S^{(\text{IA-PV})}(p, 2, \gamma, \Delta_n, u_n) > 1 + z'_\alpha / \sqrt{V_n} \right\}. \tag{13.11}$$

The following result is thus obtained in the same way as all our results about tests:

Theorem 13.5. *Assume (L) with $\beta' < \beta/2$, and assume also that $\beta < \beta_0$ for some given $\beta_0 \in (0,2)$. Let $p > 2$ and $\gamma > 1$ and $u_n \asymp \Delta_n^\varpi$ with $\varpi \in \left(0, \frac{1}{4} \wedge \frac{4-2\beta_0}{\beta_0(4-\beta_0)}\right]$.*
 The tests with critical regions given by (13.11) have the strong asymptotic size α for the null hypothesis $\Omega_T^{(\beta)} \cap \Omega_T^{(noW)}$, and they are consistent for the alternative $\Omega_T^{(\beta)} \cap \Omega_T^{(W)}$.

As seen above, we need to assume the unknown β is smaller than some known (or chosen by the statistician) number β_0. This is needed to effectively construct the test, in the sense that it comes in the choice of ϖ (in practice, ϖ, or rather u_n, is often chosen as described in Subsection 6.2.2, so this question may seem slightly immaterial).

The fact that β should be smaller than this number β_0 is, again, a theoretical restriction, somewhat of the same nature as the restriction $\beta < 1$ in the previous tests of this chapter. It is, however, much less serious, in the sense that β_0 can be chosen arbitrarily close to 2. In other words, whatever β is, there is always a choice of ϖ for which the tests described here work.

Finally, as often for those tests, the actual rate of convergence of the tests under the null is not apparent in Theorem 12.9. It is indeed $1/u_n^{\beta/2} \asymp 1/\Delta_n^{\beta\varpi/2}$. Thus, as usual, it is best to take ϖ as large as possible.

13.3   References

The test for the null "the Brownian is present" in Section 13.1, and the test for the other possible null in Section 13.2.1, are taken from Aït-Sahalia and Jacod (2010), with the smooth truncation modification analogous to Jing et al. (2011). The test for the null "the Brownian is absent" of Section 13.2.2 is taken from Cont and Mancini (2011). Implicitly, Woerner (2011) and Todorov and Tauchen (2010), which deal with the overall activity of the process, could also be concerned with the presence or absence of the Brownian motion, although they do not ask that question and do not provide tests for these occurrences. In the context of a specific parametric model, allowing for jump components of finite or infinite activity on top of a Brownian component, Carr et al. (2002) find that the time series of index returns are likely to be devoid of a continuous component. For the null hypothesis Ω_T^W, Jing et al. (2012) propose another ratio test based on counting returns smaller than u_n, with $u_n \asymp \Delta_n^\varpi$ but now $\varpi > 1/2$, under an assumption stronger than (L) but which works also when $\beta \geq 1$.

Let us also mention that another question, not treated here at all, is connected with the problem studied in this chapter. This is, in the multi-dimensional case, the determination of the rank of the volatility matrix c_t, or rather the maximal rank of this matrix over the interval $[0, T]$: if this rank is $r < d$, then an r-dimensional Brownian motion is enough to drive X (model with r factors) and, if $r = 0$, there is no Brownian motion at all. In this direction, one may look at Jacod et al. (2008) and Jacod and Podolskij (2013).

Chapter 14

Co-jumps

So far, and except for Chapter 6 about volatility estimation, we have mainly considered one-dimensional processes, or at least addressed one-dimensional questions. The real (financial) world, however, is multidimensional. This is why, in this chapter, we study some questions which only make sense in a multivariate setting.

We will be concerned with two problems: one is about a multidimensional underlying process X, and we want to decide whether two particular components of X jump at the same time: this can happen always, or never, or for some but not all jump times. The second problem is again about a one-dimensional underlying process X, but we study the pair (X, σ), with the second component being the volatility of the first component X; again, we want to decide whether X and σ jump at the same times, always or never, or sometimes.

As usual, the process X is observed at the regularly spaced observation times $i\Delta_n$, within a finite time interval $[0, T]$.

14.1   Co-jumps for the Underlying Process

14.1.1   The Setting

The question of finding whether the components of a multidimensional process jump at the same times or not is a rather intricate problem. A complete answer to this question involves all possible subsets of components and tells us whether all those particular components jump together or not, always, or sometimes. Our aim here is much more modest, as we only consider pairs of components: the problem is basically two-dimensional, and we can suppose that the underlying process $X = (X^1, X^2)$ is two-dimensional (or, discard the other components).

This underlying Itô semimartingale X is defined on a filtered space $(\Omega, \mathcal{F}, (\mathcal{F}_t)_{t \geq 0}, \mathbb{P})$, with the Grigelionis representation

$$X_t \;=\; X_0 + \int_0^t b_s ds + \int_0^t \sigma_s dW_s \qquad\qquad (14.1)$$
$$+ \; (\delta 1_{\{\|\delta\| \leq 1\}}) \star (\underline{p} - \underline{q})_t + (\delta 1_{\{\|\delta\| > 1\}}) \star \underline{p}_t.$$

Here W is a d'-dimensional Brownian motion and $\underline{p}$ is a Poisson measure on $\mathbb{R}_+ \times E$ with $(E, \mathcal{E})$ an auxiliary Polish space, and with compensator $\underline{q}(dt, dx) = dt \otimes \lambda(dx)$. The two-dimensional and $2 \times d'$-dimensional processes $b = (b^i)_{i=1,2}$ and $\sigma = (\sigma^{ij})_{i=1,2; 1 \leq j \leq d'}$ are progressively measurable, and $\delta = (\delta^i)_{i=1,2}$ is a predictable $\mathbb{R}^2$-valued function $\Omega \times \mathbb{R}_+ \times E$. As usual, we set $c_t = \sigma_t \sigma_t^*$, which here takes its values in the set of all 2×2 symmetric nonnegative matrices. In the whole chapter we make Assumption (H-r), which we briefly recall:

Assumption (H-r). *We have (10.1) with b locally bounded and σ càdlàg, and $\|\delta(\omega, t, z)\|^r \wedge 1 \leq J_n(z)$ whenever $t \leq \tau_n(\omega)$, where (τ_n) is a sequence of stopping times increasing to ∞, and (J_n) is a sequence of deterministic nonnegative functions satisfying $\int J_n(z) \lambda(dz) < \infty$.*

We also sometimes need the following additional hypothesis:

Assumption (CoJ). *If $\tau = \inf(: \Delta X_t^1 \Delta X_t^2 \neq 0)$ is the infimum of the common jump times of the two components, the process*

$$1_{\{t \leq \tau\}} \int_{\{\|\delta(t,z)\| \leq 1, \; \delta^1(t,z)\delta^2(t,z) \neq 0\}} \|\delta(t,z)\| \, \lambda(dz)$$

is locally bounded.

This is implied by (H-1), but not by (H-r) when $r > 1$. In any case, it is a mild additional assumption, since it turns out that we always have

$$\int_0^\tau dt \int_{\{\|\delta(t,z)\| \leq 1, \; \delta^1(t,z)\delta^2(t,z) \neq 0\}} \|\delta(t,z)\| \, \lambda(dz) \; < \; \infty \quad \text{a.s.}$$

Finally, for simplicity we make the following assumption (one could dispense with it, at the expense of much more complicated statements, and it is most often satisfied in practice):

Assumption (P). *The processes c_t and c_{t-} are everywhere invertible.*

Now we introduce the subsets of Ω which we want to test. Below, a "common jump," say at time t, means that both components jump at this time, but *not* that their jump sizes are the same. In principle, X^1 or X^2 or both could be continuous on $[0,T]$, in which case there is no possibility of common jumps. However, we suppose that in a first stage we have tested each component (according to one of the tests described in Chapter 10 for example) for jumps, and that we have decided that both have jumps. In other words, we are *a priori* interested in the following four sets:

$$\Omega_T^{(Coj)} = \{\omega : \sup_{t\in[0,T]} |\Delta X_t^1(\omega)\Delta X_t^2(\omega)| > 0\}$$
$$\Omega_T^{(noCoj)} = \{\omega : t \mapsto X_t^i(\omega) \text{ for } i = 1,2$$
$$\quad \text{are discontinuous and never jump together on } [0,T]\}$$
$$\Omega_T^{(1\Rightarrow2)} = \{\omega : X^1 \text{ is discontinuous} \tag{14.2}$$
$$\quad \text{and if } t \leq T \text{ and } \Delta X_t^1(\omega) \neq 0, \text{ then } \Delta X_t^2(\omega) \neq 0\}$$
$$\Omega_T^{(2\Rightarrow1)} = \{\omega : X^2 \text{ is discontinuous}$$
$$\quad \text{and if } t \leq T \text{ and } \Delta X_t^2(\omega) \neq 0, \text{ then } \Delta X_t^1(\omega) \neq 0\}.$$

The two sets $\Omega_T^{(Coj)}$ on which we have "co-jumps," and $\Omega_T^{(noCoj)}$ on which we have no co-jumps, are disjoint; their union is not Ω but the set on which both components have at least a jump on $[0,T]$. Unlike in Chapter 10, we do not need to consider the set $\Omega_T^{(W)}$ (or its two-dimensional counterpart) on which the Brownian motion is active, because we assume (P), which implies $\Omega_T^{(W)} = \Omega$.

Although knowing whether we are in the set $\Omega_T^{(1\Rightarrow2)}$ for example is interesting for modeling purposes, tests for this set considered as the null hypothesis are so far unavailable. So below we will test the two null hypotheses $\Omega_T^{(noCoj)}$ and $\Omega_T^{(Coj)}$ against the corresponding alternative hypotheses $\Omega_T^{(Coj)}$ and $\Omega_T^{(noCoj)}$, respectively (note that $\Omega_T^{(i\Rightarrow j)} \subset \Omega_T^{(Coj)}$).

For these tests we use power functionals again, but with specific powers of the two components of our process. Given an arbitrary Borel function g on $\mathbb{R}^2$ and an integer $k \geq 1$, we set

$$B(f, \Delta_n)_t = \sum_{i=1}^{[t/\Delta_n]} f(\Delta_i^n X)$$
$$B(f, [k], \Delta_n)_t = \sum_{i=1}^{[t/\Delta_n]-k+1} f(X_{(i+k-1)\Delta_n} - X_{(i-1)\Delta_n}).$$

We have $B(f, [1], \Delta_n) = B(f, \Delta_n)$, and this notation is similar to (10.37). According to Theorem A.1 of Appendix A one applies (A.15) to the symmetrical function $g(x_1, \ldots, x_k) = f(x_1 + \cdots + x_k)$, and as soon as g

is continuous and $f(x) = \mathrm{o}(\|x\|^2)$ as $x \to 0$, we get

$$B(f, [k], \Delta_n)_T \xrightarrow{\mathbb{P}} k\, f * \mu_T = k \sum_{s \leq T} f(\Delta X_s). \qquad (14.3)$$

Below, we mainly use these functionals with the following power test function:

$$x = (x^1, x^2) \in \mathbb{R}^2 \quad \mapsto \quad h(x) = (x^1 x^2)^2. \qquad (14.4)$$

14.1.2   Testing for Common Jumps

Unlike in Section 10.3, we cannot find a single test statistic allowing us to test both possible null hypotheses, and here we introduce the statistic used for testing the null $\Omega_T^{(Coj)}$, that is, there are common jumps. This statistic needs to choose an integer $k \geq 2$, and it is

$$S^{(\mathrm{CoJ})}(k, \Delta_n) = \frac{B(h, [k], \Delta_n)_T}{k\, B(h, \Delta_n)_T}.$$

In view of (14.3), and since $\Omega_T^{(Coj)}$ is exactly the set $\{h * \mu_T > 0\}$, we readily obtain

$$S^{(\mathrm{CoJ})}(k, \Delta_n) \xrightarrow{\mathbb{P}} 1 \quad \text{on } \Omega_T^{(Coj)}. \qquad (14.5)$$

This is true without any assumption on X besides being a semimartingale; but from now on we suppose at least (H-2) and (P).

The behavior of the statistic outside $\Omega_T^{(Coj)}$ is more complicated to establish, because both numerator and denominator go to 0 as $n \to \infty$. We can use the "second order CLT" stated in Appendix A as Theorem A.10 to get the following convergence (*warning:* in contrast with (14.5), the convergence below does not take place in probability, but is the weaker stable convergence in law):

$$S^{(\mathrm{CoJ})}(k, \Delta_n) \xrightarrow{\mathcal{L}\text{-}\mathrm{s}} \widetilde{\mathcal{S}}^{(\mathrm{CoJ})} \quad \text{in restriction to } \Omega_T^{(noCoj)}, \qquad (14.6)$$

where $\widetilde{\mathcal{S}}^{(\mathrm{CoJ})}$ is a variable defined on an extension of the space, satisfying

$$\mathbb{P}(\widetilde{\mathcal{S}}^{(\mathrm{CoJ})} = 1) = 0.$$

See page 614 and seq. for a proof of this result, as well as of the other results of this subsection.

Combining (14.5) and (14.6) allows us to use $S^{(\mathrm{CoJ})}(k, \Delta_n)$ to construct tests which asymptotically separate the two hypotheses. Going further and constructing tests with a prescribed asymptotic level needs a feasible Central Limit Theorem under the null, which is available. First, as a consequence of Theorem A.9 of Appendix A, under (H-2) we have the following stable convergence in law:

$$\frac{1}{\sqrt{\Delta_n}} \left(S^{(\text{CoJ})}(k, \Delta_n) - 1 \right) \xrightarrow{\mathcal{L}-\text{s}} \mathcal{S}^{(\text{CoJ})} \quad \text{in restriction to } \Omega_T^{(\text{Coj})}, \quad (14.7)$$

where $\mathcal{S}^{(\text{CoJ})}$ is a variable defined on an extension of the space and is, conditionally on the σ-field $\mathcal{F}$, a centered Gaussian variable with (conditional) variance

$$\begin{aligned}
\mathbb{E}\big((\mathcal{S}^{(\text{CoJ})})^2 \mid \mathcal{F}\big) = \frac{4k^2 - 6k + 2}{3k \left(\sum_{s \leq T} (\Delta X_s^1 \Delta X_s^2)^2 \right)^2} \sum_{s \leq T} (\Delta X_s^1 \Delta X_s^2)^2 \\
\times \big((\Delta X_s^1)^2 (c_{s-}^{22} + c_s^{22}) + (\Delta X_s^2)^2 (c_{s-}^{11} + c_s^{11}) \\
+ 2 \Delta X_s^1 \Delta X_s^2 (c_{s-}^{12} + c_s^{12}) \big).
\end{aligned} \quad (14.8)$$

Now, we need consistent estimators for the above conditional asymptotic variance. Such estimators are available, on the basis of the convergences (14.3) and (A.25). We first set

$$\begin{aligned}
\widehat{c}(k_n, u_n)_i^{jl} &= \frac{1}{k_n \Delta_n} \sum_{m=1}^{k_n} \Delta_{i+m}^n X^j \, \Delta_{i+m}^n X^l \, 1_{\{\|\Delta_{i+m}^n X\| \leq u_n\}} \\
\widehat{G}_n &= \sum_{i=k_n+1}^{[T/\Delta_n] - k_n} \left(\Delta_i^n X^1 \, \Delta_i^n X^2 \right)^2 1_{\{\|\Delta_i^n X\| > u_n\}} \\
&\quad \times \sum_{j,l=1}^{2} \Delta_i^n X^j \, \Delta_i^n X^l \big(\widehat{c}(k_n, u_n)_{i-k_n-1}^{jl} + \widehat{c}(k_n, u_n)_i^{jl} \big),
\end{aligned} \quad (14.9)$$

where as usual $u_n \asymp \Delta_n^\varpi$ for some $\varpi \in (0, \frac{1}{2})$ and $k_n \geq 1$ is a sequence of integers increasing to infinity and such that $k_n \Delta_n \to 0$. Here, $\widehat{c}(k_n, u_n)_i^{jl}$ is the spot volatility estimator introduced in (6.31) and thoroughly studied in Chapter 8. Then the following observable variables converge in probability to the right side of (14.8), in restriction to the set $\Omega_T^{(\text{Coj})} = \{h * \mu_T > 0\}$:

$$V_n = \frac{4k^2 - 6k + 2}{3k} \frac{\widehat{G}_n}{(B(h, \Delta_n)_T)^2}.$$

Again, we have a problem here: on the alternative set $\Omega_T^{(\text{noCoj})}$, both G_n and $B(h, \Delta_n)_T$ go to 0 in probability. As explained in Remark 14.3 below, it turns out that the product $\Delta_n V_n$ converges stably in law to a non-trivial limit on this set, and this might affect the alternative consistency of the tests defined below. This is why we consider a modified estimator, involving a sequence w_n of numbers and defined as

$$V_n' = V_n \bigwedge w_n, \quad \text{with } w_n \to \infty, \quad w_n \Delta_n \to 0.$$

Note that since $w_n \to \infty$, we still have the convergence in probability of V_n' to the right side of (14.8), in restriction to the set $\Omega_T^{(Coj)}$.

At this stage, the critical regions for the tests can be constructed as follows, where z_α is the α-absolute quantile of the law $\mathcal{N}(0, 1)$. We indeed have two critical regions, corresponding to V_n and V_n' above:

$$\begin{aligned}
\mathcal{C}_n &= \left\{ \left| S^{(\mathrm{CoJ})}(k, \Delta_n) - 1 \right| > z_\alpha \sqrt{\Delta_n V_n} \right\} \\
\mathcal{C}_n' &= \left\{ \left| S^{(\mathrm{CoJ})}(k, \Delta_n) - 1 \right| > z_\alpha \sqrt{\Delta_n V_n'} \right\}.
\end{aligned} \tag{14.10}$$

Note that here we reject when the test statistic is too small or too large, because on the alternative it converges stably in law to a limit which is almost surely different from 1, but may be bigger or smaller than 1.

The following result is proved beginning on page 614:

Theorem 14.1. *Assume (H-2) and (P). Both tests $\mathcal{C}_n$ and $\mathcal{C}_n'$ defined above have the strong asymptotic size α for the null hypothesis $\Omega_T^{(Coj)}$. Moreover, under the additional assumption (CJ), the second tests $\mathcal{C}_n'$ are consistent for the alternative $\Omega_T^{(noCoj)}$.*

Remark 14.2. *The second test $\mathcal{C}_n'$ is difficult to apply, because one has to choose the sequence w_n. Although any choice is possible, subject to the very weak conditions $w_n \to \infty$ and $w_n \Delta_n \to 0$, in practice Δ_n is given and we need to choose the single number w_n. One has really no clue for this choice: the important thing is whether it is smaller or bigger than the observed value V_n, but again there seems to be no specific reason to choose either possibility.*

One way out of this problem is probably to compute V_n for the highest frequency observations, corresponding to Δ_n, and also for various sub-sampling grids, corresponding to $j\Delta_n$ for a few (small) values of the integer j: we thus have estimators $V_n(j)$ for $j = 1, 2, \ldots, J$, where J is reasonable, say $J = 5$. If these computations lead to approximately the same values $V_n(j)$, then one takes $V_n' = V_n$. If, in contrast, the values $V_n(j)$ clearly increase when j decreases, this might mean either that the number of observations is too small to estimate the conditional variance accurately, or that V_n is actually going to infinity as $n \to \infty$ and thus one should reject the null hypothesis.

Remark 14.3. *The previous remark leads us to examine the asymptotic power of the first tests $\mathcal{C}_n$ more closely. Similar to the convergence (14.6) and as mentioned before, one can prove that in restriction to the alternative $\Omega_T^{(noCoj)}$ the normalized variables $\Delta_n V_n$ converge stably in law to* *some limiting variable $\mathcal{V}$. We even have, in restriction to $\Omega_T^{(noCoj)}$ again, the joint convergence of $(S^{(CoJ)}(k, \Delta_n), \Delta_n V_n)$ to $(\mathcal{S}^{(CoJ)}, \mathcal{V})$. Moreover, it turns out that the $\mathcal{F}$-conditional joint law of the limit admits a density on $\mathbb{R}^2$ in restriction to $\Omega_T^{(noCoj)}$. We call this density $\varphi = \varphi(\omega; x, y)$.*

Therefore, if $A \subset \Omega_T^{(noCoj)}$ with $\mathbb{P}(A) > 0$, we have for the (ordinary) conditional probabilities

$$\mathbb{P}(\mathcal{C}_n \mid A) \rightarrow \frac{1}{\mathbb{P}(A)} \mathbb{E}\Big(1_A \int_{\{(x,y): |x-1| > z_\alpha \sqrt{y}\}} \varphi(.; x, y) \, dx \, dy\Big).$$

This is unavailable in practice because, of course, the density φ is not computable, but in all cases it is strictly smaller than 1, preventing those tests $\mathcal{C}_n$ to be alternative-consistent.

Remark 14.4. *The statistic $S^{(CoJ)}(k, \Delta_n)$ here looks like $S^{(J-PV1)}(p, k, \Delta_n)$ in (10.40), with $p = 4$ (the degree of the polynomial h here). One could also use a statistic similar to $S^{(J-PV2)}(p, k, \Delta_n)$, namely the ratio $B(h, k\Delta_n)_T / B(h, \Delta_n)_T$, as in Jacod and Todorov (2009); but, in view of the discussion in Subsection 10.3.5, it is better to use $S^{(CoJ)}(k, \Delta_n)$.*

14.1.3 Testing for Disjoint Jumps

Now we turn to the null hypothesis "disjoint jumps," that is the null set $\Omega_T^{(noCoj)}$. The method is based on the following very simple statistic, where h is the same function as in (14.4):

$$S^{(NoCoJ)}(\Delta_n) = B(h, \Delta_n)_T.$$

We can specialize (14.3) as follows:

$$S^{(NoCoJ)}(\Delta_n) \xrightarrow{\mathbb{P}} \begin{cases} 0 & \text{on } \Omega_T^{(noCoj)} \\ h * \underline{p}_T & \text{on } \Omega_T^{(Coj)}. \end{cases} \tag{14.11}$$

Again, this is true without any assumption on X besides being a semi-martingale, but below we assume (H-2), (P) and (CoJ).

In this setting, we have a Central Limit Theorem associated with both convergences above. The one of interest for us here is associated with the first part of (14.11) and is given by the second order CLT stated as Theorem A.9 of Appendix A. To state the result, we need some notation. First, we set

$$H_t = \int_0^t \big(c_s^{11} c_s^{22} + 2(c_s^{12})^2\big) \, ds,$$

an increasing process. Our second notation is very close to (10.9), but in a two-dimensional setting and adapted to the result at hand (below, R_q is two-dimensional, with components R_q^1 and R_q^2):

$$\widetilde{\mathcal{U}}_t = \sum_{q \geq 1 : T_q \leq t} \left(\left(\Delta X_{T_q}^2 R_q^1 \right)^2 + \left(\Delta X_{T_q}^1 R_q^2 \right)^2 \right),$$
$$R_q = \sqrt{\kappa_q} \, \sigma_{T_q -} \Psi_{q-} + \sqrt{1 - \kappa_q} \, \sigma_{T_q} \Psi_{q+},$$

where $(T_q)_{q \geq 1}$ is a sequence of stopping times exhausting the jumps of X and $\kappa_q, \Psi_{q-}, \Psi_{q+}$ are defined on an extension of the space and are mutually independent, independent of $\mathcal{F}$, with κ_q uniform over $[0, 1]$ and $\Psi_{q\pm}$ standard normal d'-dimensional.

The process $\widetilde{\mathcal{U}}$ is nondecreasing and nonnegative. Its $\mathcal{F}$-conditional mean is

$$\widetilde{\mathbb{E}}(\widetilde{\mathcal{U}}_t \mid \mathcal{F}) = H_t' := \frac{1}{2} \sum_{s \leq t} \left((\Delta X_s^2)^2 (c_{s-}^{11} + c_s^{11}) + (\Delta X_s^1)^2 (c_{s-}^{22} + c_s^{22}) \right).$$

With all this notation, the following stable convergence in law holds:

$$\frac{1}{\Delta_n} S^{(\mathrm{NoCoJ})}(\Delta_n) \xrightarrow{\mathcal{L} - \mathrm{s}} S^{(\mathrm{NoCoJ})} := \widetilde{\mathcal{U}}_T + H_T$$
$$\text{in restriction to } \Omega_T^{(noCoj)}. \tag{14.12}$$

Unfortunately, conditionally on $\mathcal{F}$ the limiting variable $S^{(\mathrm{NoCoJ})}$, being nonnegative, is not Gaussian. When the two processes X and σ do not jump at the same time, it is basically a weighted sum of squared Gaussian variables, with weights related to the (non-observable) jumps of X. In the general case it is even more difficult to describe. Therefore, for designing a test based on the above statistic, with a prescribed asymptotic level, we face the same difficulties as for the test for jumps in the one-dimensional case, using $S^{(\mathrm{J\text{-}PV1})}(p, k_n, \Delta_n)$. And, exactly as in that case, we have two ways to solve the problem.

A Conservative Test   The first method, not a very efficient one, uses Markov's inequality to bound the actual level of the test. This can be done because one has consistent estimators for the $\mathcal{F}$-conditional mean $H_T + H_T'$ of the limit $S^{(\mathrm{NoCoJ})}$. First, as in (14.9), consistent estimators for H_T' are

$$\widehat{H}_n' = \frac{1}{2} \sum_{i=k_n+1}^{[T/\Delta_n]-k_n} \left(\left(\Delta_i^n X^2 \right)^2 \left(\widehat{c}(k_n, u_n)_{i-k_n-1}^{11} + \widehat{c}(k_n, u_n)_i^{11} \right) \right.$$
$$\left. + \left(\Delta_i^n X^1 \right)^2 \left(\widehat{c}(k_n, u_n)_{i-k_n-1}^{22} + \widehat{c}(k_n, u_n)_i^{22} \right) \right) 1_{\{\|\Delta_i^n X\| > u_n\}}$$

where the sequence u_n satisfies $u_n \asymp \Delta_n^\varpi$ for some $\varpi \in (0, \frac{1}{2})$ and $k_n \geq 1$ is a sequence of integers increasing to infinity and such that $k_n \Delta_n \to 0$. As for the estimation of H_T, on the basis of Section 8.5 one can use (among many other possible choices) the following estimators:

$$\widehat{H}_n = \Delta_n \sum_{i=1}^{[T/\Delta_n]-k_n+1} \left(\widehat{c}(k_n, u_n)_i^{11} \widehat{c}(k_n, u_n)_i^{22} \right. \tag{14.13}$$
$$\left. +2 \left(\widehat{c}(k_n, u_n)_i^{12} \right)^2 \right).$$

The standardized statistics $S^{(\mathrm{NoCoJ})}(\Delta_n)/(\widehat{H}_n + \widehat{H}'_n)$ converge stably in law, in restriction to the set $\Omega_T^{(noCoj)}$, to a variable, again defined on an extension of the space, and with $\mathcal{F}$-conditional mean equal to 1. Therefore, in view of (14.11), a natural family of critical regions for testing the null hypothesis $\Omega_T^{(noCoj)}$ is as follows, where $\alpha \in (0, 1)$ is the intended asymptotic level:

$$\mathcal{C}_n = \left\{ S^{(\mathrm{NoCoJ})}(\Delta_n) > \Delta_n \frac{\widehat{H}_n + \widehat{H}'_n}{\alpha} \right\}.$$

We reject when the test statistic is too large, because it is positive on the alternative and vanishes on the null. The following result is proved on page 617:

Theorem 14.5. *Assume (H-2), (P) and (CoJ). The tests $\mathcal{C}_n$ defined above have an asymptotic size not bigger than α for the null hypothesis $\Omega_T^{(noCoj)}$, and are consistent for the alternative $\Omega_T^{(Coj)}$.*

Typically, these tests have no strong asymptotic sizes. More important, the actual asymptotic size is usually significantly smaller than the prescribed level α. So we advise the procedure described next.

A Sharp Test This family of tests uses a Monte Carlo approach, already described before and in Theorem 10.12. Let us rewrite the limit $S^{(\mathrm{NoCoJ})}$ more explicitly as

$$S^{(\mathrm{NoCoJ})} = H_T + \sum_{q \geq 1: T_q \leq T} \left(\Delta X_{T_q}^2 \left(\sqrt{\kappa_q} \left(\sigma_{T_q-} \Psi_{q-} \right)^1 \right. \right.$$
$$+ \sqrt{1 - \kappa_q} \left(\sigma_{T_q} \Psi_{q+} \right)^1 \right) + \Delta X_{T_q}^1 \left(\sqrt{\kappa_q} \left(\sigma_{T_q-} \Psi_{q-} \right)^2 \right.$$
$$\left. \left. + \sqrt{1 - \kappa_q} \left(\sigma_{T_q} \Psi_{q+} \right)^2 \right) \right)$$

where $(\Psi_{q-}, \Psi_{q+}, \kappa_q)$ are mutually independent, and independent of $\mathcal{F}$, with $\Psi_{q\pm}$ being $\mathcal{N}(0, I_{d'})$ and κ_q being uniform on $(0, 1)$. Note that here d' and σ_t are somewhat arbitrary, subject to $\sigma_t \sigma_t^* = c_t$. It is always possible to choose $d' = 2$, and we will do this below.

The procedure is as follows:

1. We replace H_T by its estimator $\widehat{H}_n$, given in (14.13).

2. We pretend that the jump times T_q which are "significant" correspond to the intervals $((i-1)\Delta_n, i\Delta_n]$ for which $\|\Delta_i^n X\| > u_n$ and $k + k_n \le i \le [T/\Delta_n] - k_n - k + 1$. Those i's are labeled $i_1, i_2, \ldots, i_{r(n)}$, where $r(n)$ is the (random) total number of such i's. Observing that by construction the estimating matrices $\widehat{c}(k_n, u_n)_i$ are symmetric nonnegative, for each one we choose a 2×2 square root, denoted as $\widetilde{\sigma}_i^n$.

3. We draw N_n copies of $(\Psi_{q-}, \Psi_{q+}, \kappa_q)$, for q running from 1 to $r(n)$, say $(\Psi(j)_{q-}, \Psi(j)_{q+}, \kappa(j)_q)$ for $j = 1, \ldots, N_n$, all independent (recall that the $\Psi_{q\pm}^j$ are two-dimensional standard Gaussian).

4. We compute the following variables, for $j = 1, \ldots, N_n$:

$$
\begin{aligned}
S_n^j = \widehat{H}_n + \sum_{q=1}^{r(n)} \Big(\Delta_{i_q}^n X^2 \big(\sqrt{\kappa(j)_q}\, (\widetilde{\sigma}_{i_q - k_n}^n\, \Psi(j)_{q-})^1 \\
+ \sqrt{1 - \kappa(j)_q}\, (\widetilde{\sigma}_{i_q+1}^n\, \Psi(j)_{q+})^1 \big) + \Delta_{i_q}^n X^1 \big(\sqrt{\kappa(j)_q}\, (\widetilde{\sigma}_{i_q - k_n}^n\, \Psi(j)_{q-})^2 \\
+ \sqrt{1 - \kappa(j)_q}\, (\widetilde{\sigma}_{i_q+1}^n\, \Psi(j)_{q+})^2 \big) \Big).
\end{aligned}
$$

5. We denote by Z_n^α the α-quantile of the empirical distribution of the family $(S_n^j : 1 \le j \le N_n)$, that is, we re-order these N_n variables so that $S_n^1 \ge S_n^2 \ge \cdots \ge S_n^{N_n}$, and we set $Z_n^\alpha = S_n^{[\alpha N_n]}$.

6. We terminate the procedure by taking the following rejection region:

$$
\mathcal{C}_n = \{ S^{(\mathrm{NoCoJ})}(\Delta_n) > Z_n^\alpha \Delta_n \}. \tag{14.14}
$$

It is not a restriction to suppose that the additional variables $(\Psi(j)_{q-}, \Psi(j)_{q+}, \kappa(j)_q)$ are defined on the same extension of the original probability space, and they all are independent of the σ-field $\mathcal{F}$. Hence, although the critical region $\mathcal{C}_n$ is also defined on this extension, it is nevertheless a "feasible" critical region.

We then have the following result, proved on page 618:

Theorem 14.6. *Assume (H-2), (P) and (CoJ), and choose any sequence N_n which goes to infinity. The tests $\mathcal{C}_n$ defined by (14.14) have a strong asymptotic size α for the null hypothesis $\Omega_T^{(noCoj)}$, and are consistent for the alternative $\Omega_T^{(Coj)}$.*

14.1.4 Some Open Problems

We end this section with the description of a few open problems which could be solved in a similar fashion, but are not detailed in this book, and so far have not been explicitly worked out with all mathematical details.

1. The first open problem is to construct a test for the null hypothesis $\Omega_T^{(1\Rightarrow2)}$, introduced in (14.2). Often for this kind of problem, the question amounts to finding test statistics which behave differently under the null, and under the alternative, which here might be $\Omega_T^{(Coj)}\backslash\Omega_T^{(1\Rightarrow2)}$ because one would not address this question unless one was sure that there are common jumps.

One might think for instance to use

$$S^{(1\Rightarrow2,V1)}(\Delta_n, u_n) = \sum_{i=1}^{[t/\Delta_n]} |\Delta_i^n X^1|^p 1_{\{|\Delta_i^n X^2|\leq u_n\}}$$

for a suitable power $p > 2$ and a sequence $u_n \asymp \Delta_n^\varpi$ for some $\varpi \in \left(0, \frac{1}{2}\right)$. Indeed, we have

$$S^{(1\Rightarrow2,V1)}(\Delta_n, u_n)$$
$$\xrightarrow{\;\mathbb{P}\;} \sum_{s\leq T} |\Delta X_s^1|^p 1_{\{\Delta X_s^2=0\}} \begin{cases} = 0 & \text{on } \Omega_T^{(1\Rightarrow2)} \\ > 0 & \text{on } \Omega_T^{(Coj)}\backslash\Omega_T^{(1\Rightarrow2)}. \end{cases}$$

Another possibility consists of using a ratio test statistic, for example of the form

$$S^{(1\Rightarrow2,V2)}(\Delta_n, u_n) = \frac{S^{(1\Rightarrow2,V1)}(\Delta_n, u_n)}{\sum_{i=1}^{[t/\Delta_n]} |\Delta_i^n X^1|^p},$$

which basically has the same asymptotic behavior as $S^{(1\Rightarrow2,V1)}(\Delta_n, u_n)$, but is probably more stable.

However, so far, no Central Limit Theorem is available for this type of variable, although we may expect one if we take $p > 3$.

2. Another type of – interesting – problem is to determine whether, under the hypothesis of common jumps, the two components of the jump are related to one another. This may take various forms:

(i) One question is whether, conditionally on the fact that there is a common jump time, and also conditionally on the past before this time, the two jump sizes are independent or not. This is related to the behavior of the Lévy measures F_t of the two-dimensional process X, and more precisely to the fact that these Lévy measures on $\mathbb{R}^2$ are products of two measures on $\mathbb{R}$, or not.

However, this question cannot be answered if the observation interval $[0, T]$ is kept fixed, by virtue of the identifiability (or, rather, non-identifiability) of the Lévy measure when the time horizon is fixed. When $T = T_n \to \infty$ as $\Delta_n \to 0$, though, and under some appropriate stationarity or ergodicity assumptions, this question could probably be answered.

(ii) On the opposite side of the spectrum of all related questions, one may ask whether there is a "functional relationship" between the jumps of X^1 and those of X^2. For example, for a given function ϕ from $\mathbb{R}$ into itself, do we necessarily have $\Delta X_t^2 = \phi(\Delta X_t^1)$ for all t, or perhaps $\Delta X_t^2 = a\phi(\Delta X_t^1)$ for an unknown constant a? When the function ϕ is totally unknown, there seems to be no way for testing this property. In contrast, if ϕ is known, or belongs to some known parametric family, it is possible to develop such tests.

14.2 Co-jumps between the Process and Its Volatility

Now we come back to the one-dimensional case for the underlying process X. We still have (14.1), with now W a one-dimensional Brownian motion. The processes b and σ and the function δ are one-dimensional as well, and $c_t = \sigma_t^2$. In all this section, we suppose that X satisfies (K-r) for some $r \in [0, 2)$, an assumption already encountered several times before.

Our aim is to test whether X and the volatility σ, or equivalently c, have jumps in common.

We can do this for "all" jumps of X and c, over the fixed time interval $[0, T]$. However, although this looks at first glance as the best thing to do, one may argue the following: the spot volatility is estimated with quite a slow convergence rate, so when one tries to determine the volatility jumps it is rather likely that many spurious jumps are detected and many genuine jumps are missed. When the jumps of X have finite activity, they are rather accurately detected, see Section 10.4, and, asymptotically, spurious jumps of c will typically not occur at the same time as a jump of X. In the infinite activity case, things are different, and it might be more appropriate to test whether there are jump times t of c that are also jump times of X with $|\Delta X_t|$ bigger than some *a priori* given size $a > 0$.

However, as we will see, it is still possible to asymptotically discriminate whether X and c have common jumps or not, even in the infinite activity case. Therefore, to accommodate the two situations above, we consider a subset A of $\mathbb{R}$ of the following type:

$$A = (-\infty, -a) \cup (a, \infty) \quad \text{for some} \quad a \geq 0, \tag{14.15}$$

and restrict our attention to those jumps of X which lie in A, that is, all jumps when $a = 0$, and only those with size bigger than a when $a > 0$. In the latter case, and exactly as in Theorem 10.29, one needs the additional assumption (10.76) on X, which we state again:

$$\mathbb{P}(\exists t > 0 \text{ with } |\Delta X_t| = a) = 0. \tag{14.16}$$

Recall that this is satisfied for any $a > 0$ under very weak assumptions, such as the Lévy measures F_t of X having a density.

Now, in connection with A above, the subsets of Ω which we want to test are the following ones:

$$
\begin{aligned}
\Omega_T^{(A,cj)} &= \{\omega : \exists s \in (0, T] \text{ with } \Delta X_s(\omega) \in A \backslash \{0\} \\
&\quad \text{and } \Delta c_s(\omega) \neq 0\} \\
\Omega_T^{(A,dj)} &= \{\omega : \forall s \in (0, T], \ \Delta X_s(\omega) \in A \backslash \{0\} \Rightarrow \Delta c_s(\omega) = 0 \\
&\quad \text{and } \exists s \in (0, T] \text{ with } \Delta X_s(\omega) \in A \backslash \{0\}\}.
\end{aligned}
\tag{14.17}
$$

So $\Omega_T^{(A,cj)}$ is the set on which X and c have common jumps, with additionally the jump size of X being in A, and $\Omega_T^{(A,dj)}$ is the set on which this does not occur, although there are jumps of X with size in A. When $a = 0$, testing one of the above as the null hypothesis against the other one makes sense only if we already know that X jumps. When $a > 0$, it additionally requires that X has jumps with size bigger than a: hence, prior to doing these tests, one should check whether there are such jumps for X, by using for example the techniques developed in Section 10.4.

Remark 14.7. *The set A in (14.15) is just an example. It is possible to conduct the tests with A being any subset of $\mathbb{R}$ such that, almost surely, X has no jump with size in the topological boundary of A. However, in this case the assumptions are (slightly) more complicated to state, whereas this example with an arbitrary $a \geq 0$ undoubtedly covers the most useful practical situations.*

Remark 14.8. *It is also possible to take into consideration the jumps of c whose size lies inside another set A' as in (14.15), with some $a' \geq 0$, or even a more general set A'. The first set in (14.17) would then be*

$$\Omega_T^{(A,A',cj)} = \{\omega : \exists s \in (0,T] \text{ with } \Delta X_s(\omega) \in A\backslash\{0\}$$
$$\text{and } \Delta c_s(\omega) \in A'\backslash\{0\}\},$$

with a similar modification for the second one.

For example it would be interesting to test whether jumps of X result in positive jumps of c, as is often postulated in financial statistics. This would happen if we accept $\Omega_T^{(\mathbb{R}^\star,(0,\infty),cj)}$ and reject $\Omega_T^{(\mathbb{R}^\star,(-\infty,0),cj)}$, where $\mathbb{R}^\star = \mathbb{R}\backslash\{0\}$.

14.2.1 Limit Theorems for Functionals of Jumps and Volatility

The tests presented below are constructed on the basis of functionals of the following type. We consider two test functions f on $\mathbb{R}$ and g on $\mathbb{R}^2$, and the associated process

$$A(f,g)_t \;=\; \sum_{s \leq t} f(\Delta X_s)\, g(c_{s-}, c_s),$$

provided of course that the potentially infinite series above is absolutely convergent, for example when g is of linear growth and $f(x) = O(x^2)$ as $x \to 0$. The – unfortunately unobservable – variable $A(f,g)_T$ tells us whether we are in $\Omega_T^{(A,dj)}$ or $\Omega_T^{(A,cj)}$ if we choose f and g appropriately. For example, if f, g are nonnegative, and $g(y,y') > 0$ if and only if $y \neq y'$, and $f(x) > 0$ if and only if $x \in A\backslash\{0\}$, then $A(f,g)_T > 0$ on $\Omega_T^{(A,cj)}$ and $A(f,g)_T = 0$ on $\Omega_T^{(A,dj)}$.

We can approximate $A(f,g)_T$ by functionals of the observed returns $\Delta_i^n X$ and the spot volatility estimators constructed in (8.8) and recalled in (14.9). Namely, with $k_n \to \infty$ and $k_n \Delta_n \to 0$, and truncation levels $u_n \asymp \Delta_n^\varpi$ for some $\varpi \in (0, \frac{1}{2})$, and any two functions f on $\mathbb{R}$ and g on $\mathbb{R}^2$, we set

$$D(f,g;k_n,u_n,\Delta_n)_t = \sum_{i=k_n+1}^{[t/\Delta_n]-k_n} f(\Delta_i^n X) \tag{14.18}$$
$$\times g(\widehat{c}(k_n,u_n)_{i-k_n}, \widehat{c}(k_n,u_n)_{i+1})\, 1_{\{|\Delta_i^n X| > u_n\}}.$$

Next, we state the assumptions needed on f and g. With the notation ∂f for the first derivative of f and $\partial_i g$ and $\partial_{ij}^2 g$ (for $i,j = 1,2$) for the first and second partial derivatives of g, those assumptions (in connection with the set A in (14.15), and also with the index r for which Assumption (K-r) needed below holds) are:

- f is C^1 and positive on A, null on the complement $[-a, a]$, locally bounded,
  and if $a = 0$ we have $|\partial f(x)| \leq K|x|$ for $|x| \leq 1$
- g is C^2, null on the diagonal of $\mathbb{R}^2$ and positive outside,   (14.19)
  with $\partial_i g(y, y) = 0$, $\partial_{11}^2 g(y, y) + \partial_{22}^2 g(y, y) > 0$,
  and if $a = 0$ and $r > 0$ in (K-r),
  the first and second derivatives of g are bounded.

According to Theorem A.7 of Appendix A, if we assume (H-2) and (14.19), or if we assume (H-r) for some $r \in [0, 2)$ and replace the conditions on g by the property that it is continuous and satisfies $|g(y, z)| \leq K(1 + |y|^p + |y|^p))$ for some $p \geq 1$, plus $\varpi \geq \frac{p-1}{2p-r}$, we have

$$D(f, g; k_n, u_n, \Delta_n)_t \xrightarrow{\mathbb{P}} A(f, g)_t. \qquad (14.20)$$

Next, we turn to the associated Central Limit Theorem or, rather, theorems: there is a "first order" CLT and also, when the limit in it vanishes, a "second order" CLT. Since we will use the functionals (14.18) associated with k_n and, at the same time, those associated with wk_n for some integer $w \geq 2$, we need a joint CLT. To state the first CLT, we introduce the following processes:

$$
\begin{aligned}
\widetilde{\mathcal{U}}_t &= \sqrt{2} \sum_{q \geq 1 : T_q \leq t} f(\Delta X_{T_q}) \\
&\quad \times \left(\partial_1 g(c_{T_q-}, c_{T_q}) c_{T_q-} \Psi_{q-} + \partial_2 g(c_{T_q-}, c_{T_q}) c_{T_q} \Psi_{q+} \right) \\
\widetilde{\mathcal{U}}'_t &= \sqrt{2} \sum_{q \geq 1 : T_q \leq t} f(\Delta X_{T_q}) \\
&\quad \times \left(\partial_1 g(c_{T_q-}, c_{T_q}) c_{T_q-} \Psi'_{q-} + \partial_2 g(c_{T_q-}, c_{T_q}) c_{T_q} \Psi'_{q+} \right)
\end{aligned}
\qquad (14.21)
$$

where $(T_q)_{q \geq 1}$ is a sequence of stopping times exhausting the jumps of X and $\Psi_{q-}, \Psi_{q+}, \Psi'_{q-}, \Psi'_{q+}$ are defined on an extension of the space and are mutually independent, independent of $\mathcal{F}$, and $\mathcal{N}(0, 1)$-distributed. These two processes are, conditionally on $\mathcal{F}$, centered (discontinuous) Gaussian martingales and independent with the same law, characterized by the conditional variances

$$
\begin{aligned}
\widetilde{\mathbb{E}}((\widetilde{\mathcal{U}}_t)^2 \mid \mathcal{F}) &= A(f^2, G)_t, \\
\text{where } G(y, z) &= 2(\partial_1 g(y, z)^2 y^2 + \partial_2 g(y, z)^2 z^2).
\end{aligned}
\qquad (14.22)
$$

The next two theorems are basically the same as Theorems 13.4.1 and 13.4.2 of Jacod and Protter (2011), in a special situation. However, the conditions on the test functions are weaker here (and we need this below), so we provide a proof for them, on pages 621 and 629, respectively.

Theorem 14.9. *Assume (K-r) for some $r \in [0,2)$ and choose f and g satisfying (14.19) with A as in (14.15), with further (14.16) when $a > 0$. Let u_n and k_n satisfy*

$$u_n \asymp \Delta_n^\varpi, \quad k_n \asymp \Delta_n^{-\tau},$$

with

- *if $a > 0$ or $r = 0$:*
- *otherwise :*

$$
\begin{cases}
0 < \varpi < \frac{1}{2} \\
0 < \tau < ((\varpi(4 - 2r)) \wedge \frac{2-r}{r} \wedge \frac{1}{2} \\
\frac{1}{4-r} < \varpi < \frac{1}{2} \wedge \frac{1}{2r} \\
0 < \tau < ((\varpi(4 - r) - 1) \wedge \frac{1}{2}.
\end{cases}
\tag{14.23}
$$

Then, for any given time $T > 0$ and any integer $w \geq 2$, the two-dimensional variables

$$
\begin{aligned}
\Big(\sqrt{k_n} \left(D(f, g; k_n, u_n \Delta_n)_T - A(f, g)_T \right), \\
\sqrt{k_n} \left(D(f, g; w k_n, u_n \Delta_n)_T - A(f, g)_T \right) \Big)
\end{aligned}
$$

converge stably in law to the variables $(\widetilde{\mathcal{U}}_T, \frac{1}{w} (\widetilde{\mathcal{U}}_T + \sqrt{w-1} \widetilde{\mathcal{U}}_T'))$.

Remark 14.10. *The condition on ϖ and τ is weaker when $a > 0$ or $r = 0$ than in the other cases, as expected.*

The conditions (14.19) on f, g are designed in view of the tests to come. However, for the previous result, one can relax the properties $f > 0$ on A and $g(y,y) = \partial_j g(y,y) = 0$ and $g(y,z) > 0$ when $y \neq z$. These assumptions, however, are needed for what follows.

On the set $\Omega_T^{(A,dj)}$, not only does the limit $A(f,g)_T$ vanish, but the variables $\widetilde{\mathcal{U}}(1)_T$ and $\widetilde{\mathcal{U}}'(1)_T$ vanish as well. However, we have another CLT with normalization k_n instead of $\sqrt{k_n}$. For stating the result we again need to describe the limiting processes. With $(T_q, \Psi_{q-}, \Psi_{q+}, \Psi_{q-}', \Psi_{q+}')$ as in (14.21), for any integer $w \geq 1$ we set

$$
\begin{aligned}
\widetilde{\mathcal{U}}(w)_t = \frac{1}{w^2} \sum_{q \geq 1: T_q \leq t\}} c_{T_q}^2 \, f(\Delta X_{T_q}) \\
\times \Big(\partial_{11}^2 \, g(c_{T_q}, c_{T_q})(\Psi_{q-} + \sqrt{w-1}\, \Psi_{q-}')^2 \\
+ 2\partial_{12}^2 \, g(c_{T_q}, c_{T_q})(\Psi_{q-} + \sqrt{w-1}\, \Psi_{q-}')(\Psi_{q+} + \sqrt{w-1}\, \Psi_{q+}') \\
+ \partial_{22}^2 \, g(c_{T_q}, c_{T_q})(\Psi_{q+} + \sqrt{w-1}\, \Psi_{q+}')^2 \Big).
\end{aligned}
\tag{14.24}
$$

This process is of finite variation and with $\mathcal{F}$-conditional mean given by

$$
\begin{aligned}
&\widetilde{\mathbb{E}}(\widetilde{\mathcal{U}}(w)_t \mid \mathcal{F}) = \tfrac{1}{w}\, A(f, G')_T, \\
&\text{where} \quad G'(y, z) = z^2 \left(\partial_{11}^2\, g(z, z) + \partial_{22}^2\, g(z, z) \right).
\end{aligned}
\tag{14.25}
$$

Theorem 14.11. *Assume (K-r) for some $r \in [0, 2)$ and choose f and g satisfying (14.19), with further (14.16) when $a > 0$. Let u_n and k_n satisfy (14.23). Then, for any given time $T > 0$ and any integer $w \geq 2$, the variables*

$$
\left(k_n\, D(f, g; k_n, u_n\Delta_n)_T,\, k_n\, D(f, g; wk_n, u_n\Delta_n)_T \right)
$$

converge stably in law, in restriction to the set $\Omega_T^{(A,dj)}$ to the variables $(\widetilde{\mathcal{U}}(1)_T, \widetilde{\mathcal{U}}(w)_T)$.

Remark 14.12. *The reader will observe that in these two theorems we do not claim the "functional" stable convergence, which is an open question in general, although of no importance for us below. When $a > 0$ or $r = 0$, though, this functional convergence does hold.*

14.2.2   Testing the Null Hypothesis of No Co-jump

Here we take the null hypothesis to be "X and σ have no common jump" with jump size of X in A, that is, $\Omega_T^{(A,dj)}$, for A either being at a positive distance of 0, or containing a neighborhood of 0. We construct two families of tests.

Some General Tests   Below, we assume (K-r) for some $r \in [0, 2)$. We choose two functions f and g satisfying (14.19), and use the fact that $\Omega_T^{(A,dj)} = \{D(f, g)_T = 0\}$. We choose k_n and u_n satisfying (14.23). We will also need another sequence u_n' of truncation levels subject to

$$
u_n' \asymp \Delta_n^{\varpi'}, \qquad \frac{1}{4 - r} < \varpi' < \frac{1}{2}.
\tag{14.26}
$$

On the basis of the convergence (14.20), we use the statistics $D(f, g; k_n, u_n\Delta_n)_T$, which satisfy

$$
D(f, g; k_n, u_n\Delta_n)_T \xrightarrow{\;\mathbb{P}\;}
\begin{cases}
0 & \text{on } \Omega_T^{(A,dj)} \\
A(f, g)_T > 0 & \text{on } \Omega_T^{(A,cj)}.
\end{cases}
$$

In order to assert the size of a test based on $D(f, g; k_n, u_n\Delta_n)_T$ we need a CLT in restriction to $\Omega_T^{(A,dj)}$, and it is provided by Theorem 14.11 since in Theorem 14.9 the limit vanishes. On the set $\Omega_T^{(A,dj)}$ the limit $\widetilde{\mathcal{U}}(1)_T$ of

$k_n D(f,g;k_n,u_n\Delta_n)_T$ has an unknown $\mathcal{F}$-conditional distribution, but its conditional expectation is $A(f,G')_T$ by (14.25). Observe also that, because of (14.19), we have $A(f,G')_T \geq 0$, and even $A(f,G')_T > 0$ on $\Omega_T^{(A,dj)} \cup \Omega_T^{(A,cj)}$.

We need now to construct an estimator for $A(f,G')_T$. The function G has a quadratic growth, so (14.20) yields that the statistics $D(f,G';k_n,u'_n,\Delta_n)_T$ are consistent estimators of $A(f,G')_T$, but only because we assume (14.26), which is the reason for introducing these new truncation levels. Note that we can take $u'_n = u_n$, or $\varpi' = \varpi$ only when $r < \frac{4}{3}$. So, by our usual argument using stable convergence in law, plus the fact that $A(f,G')_T > 0$ on the set $\Omega_T^{(A,dj)} \cup \Omega_T^{(A,cj)}$ (use the last property in (14.19)), we deduce that

$$\frac{k_n\, D(f,g;k_n,u_n\Delta_n)_T}{D(f,G';k_n,u'_n,\Delta_n)_T} \xrightarrow{\mathcal{L}-\mathfrak{s}} \frac{\widetilde{\mathcal{U}}(1)_T}{A(f,G')_T} \quad \text{in restriction to } \Omega_T^{(A,dj)},$$

and the limiting variable above is nonnegative, with $\mathcal{F}$-conditional expectation equal to 1. On the other hand, the left side above goes to $+\infty$ on $\Omega_T^{(A,cj)}$ in probability, because its numerator does so by Theorem 14.9. Thus, using Markov's inequality, we obtain the following result:

Theorem 14.13. *Assume (K-r) for some $r \in [0,2)$, choose f and g satisfying (14.19), with further (14.16) when $a > 0$, and let k_n and u_n satisfy (14.23) and u'_n satisfy (14.26). For all $\alpha \in (0,1)$ the tests*

$$C_n = \left\{ D(f,g;k_n,u_n\Delta_n)_T > \frac{D(f,G';k_n,u'_n,\Delta_n)_T}{\alpha\, k_n} \right\}.$$

have an asymptotic size not bigger than α for the null hypothesis $\Omega_T^{(A,dj)}$, and are consistent for the alternative $\Omega_T^{(A,cj)}$.

Remark 14.14. *As in many of the previous tests, in order to choose τ, ϖ and ϖ' in such a way that (14.23) and (14.26) hold, one must have a prior knowledge of the value of r for which (K-r) holds, or at least of a number $r_0 < 2$ which r cannot exceed.*

Observing that the actual rate of convergence is k_n, it is advisable to choose τ as large as possible. We should then choose ϖ as large as possible, close to $\frac{1}{2} \wedge \frac{1}{2r_0}$, and then τ close to $((\varpi(4-r_0)-1) \wedge \frac{1}{2}$. As for ϖ', we take any value satisfying (14.26) with $r = r_0$. We end up with a rate which is close to $1/\Delta_n^{1/2}$ when $r_0 < 1$ and to $1/\Delta_n^{(2-r_0)/2}$ otherwise.

The actual asymptotic size of this test is usually much lower than α, because Markov's inequality is a crude approximation, and it is not a strong asymptotic size. However, one can use a Monte Carlo approach similar to the "sharp test" of Theorem 14.6. It goes as follows:

1. The indices i of the intervals $((i-1)\Delta_n, i\Delta_n]$ for which $|\Delta_i^n X| > u_n$ and $k + k_n \leq i \leq [T/\Delta_n] - k_n - k + 1$. are labeled $i_1, i_2, \ldots, i_{r(n)}$.

2. We draw N_n independent copies of (Ψ_{q-}, Ψ_{q+}), for q running from 1 to $r(n)$, denoted as $(\Psi(j)_{q-}, \Psi(j)_{q+})$, for $j = 1, \ldots, N_n$ (those are $\mathcal{N}(0,1)$).

3. We compute the following variables, for $j = 1, \ldots, N_n$, and with the shorthand notation $\widehat{c}_i^n = \widehat{c}(k_n, u_n)_i$:

$$Y_n^j = \sum_{q=1}^{r(n)} (\widehat{c}_{i_q+1}^n)^2 \, f(\Delta_{i_q}^n X) \left(\partial_{11}^2 \, g(\widehat{c}_{i_q+1}^n, \widehat{c}_{i_q+1}^n) \Psi(j)_{q-}^2 \right.$$
$$\left. + 2\partial_{12}^2 \, g(\widehat{c}_{i_q+1}^n, \widehat{c}_{i_q+1}^n) \Psi(j)_{q-} \Psi(j)_{q+} + \partial_{22}^2 \, g(\widehat{c}_{i_q+1}^n, \widehat{c}_{i_q+1}^n) \Psi(j)_{q+}^2 \right).$$

4. We denote by Z_n^α the α-quantile of the empirical distribution of the family $(Y_n^j : 1 \leq j \leq N_n)$.

5. We terminate the procedure by taking the following rejection region:
$$\mathcal{C}_n = \{D(f, g; k_n, u_n\Delta_n)_T > Z_n^\alpha / k_n\}. \tag{14.27}$$

We then have the following result, whose proof is exactly as the proof of Theorem 14.6 and thus omitted:

Theorem 14.15. *Assume (K-r) for some $r \in [0,2)$, choose f and g satisfying (14.19), with further (14.16) when $a > 0$, and let k_n and u_n satisfy (14.26). Choose any sequence N_n going to infinity. The tests defined by (14.27) have strong asymptotic size α for the null hypothesis $\Omega_T^{(A,dj)}$, and are consistent for the alternative $\Omega_T^{(A,cj)}$.*

A Specific Test Among all possible tests of the type above (that is, among all possible choices of the test functions f and g), and although they seem to perform asymptotically in exactly the same way, some are better than others in terms of the actual power. Deriving optimality in this context is a difficult, even impossible, task.

Nevertheless, there are specific choices which are easier to handle, and in this part we describe such a choice, for which we do not need the Monte Carlo procedure in order to achieve a strong asymptotic size.

This choice applies when $a > 0$ (then we assume (14.16)), and also when $a = 0$ in the case (K-0) holds, meaning, basically, that the jumps of X are *known* to be of finite activity. We choose the functions

$$f(x) = 1_A(x), \qquad g(y,z) = 2\log\frac{y+z}{2} - \log y - \log z, \qquad (14.28)$$

which clearly satisfy the conditions in (14.19) when $a > 0$, or when $r = 0$ in Assumption (K-r).

This g corresponds to the log-likelihood ratio test for testing that two independent samples of i.i.d. zero-mean normal variables have the same variance. The link with our testing comes from the fact that around a jump time the high-frequency increments of X are "approximately" i.i.d. normal.

With the choice (14.28), the first expression (14.24) is written as

$$\widetilde{\mathcal{U}}(1)_t = \frac{1}{2}\sum_{q\geq 1:\, T_q\leq t}(\Psi_{q-} - \Psi_{q+})^2\, 1_{\{|\Delta X_{T_q}|>a\}}.$$

So the limiting distribution of the test statistics depends only on the number of jumps, and is thus straightforward to implement. Conditionally on $\mathcal{F}$, this variable has the same law as a chi-square variable with N_T degrees of freedom, where $N_T = \sum_{p\geq 1}1_{\{|\Delta X_{T_p}|>a\}}$ is the number of jumps of X taken into consideration. The variable N_T is not observable. However, we have

$$N_T^n = \sum_{i=1}^{[T/\Delta_n]}1_{\{|\Delta_i^n X|>a\vee u_n\}} \;\xrightarrow{\mathbb{P}}\; N_T,$$

due to (14.16), and since these are integer-valued variables we even have $\mathbb{P}(N_T^n = N_T) \to 1$.

Thus, denoting by $z(\alpha, n)$ the α-quantile of a chi-square variable χ_n^2 with n degrees of freedom, that is, the number such that $\mathbb{P}(\chi_n^2 > z(\alpha, n)) = \alpha$, we may take the following critical region at stage n:

$$\mathcal{C}_n = \{D(f,g;k_n,u_n\Delta_n)_T > z(\alpha, N_t^n)/k_n\}. \qquad (14.29)$$

These critical regions enjoy the following properties (the alternative consistency holds because $z(\alpha, N_t^n)$ is eventually equal to $z(\alpha, N_t) > 0$, so $z(\alpha, N_t^n)/k_n \xrightarrow{\mathbb{P}} 0$, whereas $D(f,g;k_n,u_n\Delta_n)_T \xrightarrow{\mathbb{P}} A(f,g)_T > 0$ on $\Omega_T^{(A,cj)}$).

Theorem 14.16. *Assume that (K-r) holds with $r \in (0,2)$ and $a > 0$, or with $r = 0$, and also (14.16) when $a > 0$. Choose f and g as in (14.28)* *and let k_n and u_n satisfy (14.23) (first condition). Then the tests (14.29) have strong asymptotic size α for the null hypothesis $\Omega_T^{(A,dj)}$, and are consistent for the alternative $\Omega_T^{(A,cj)}$.*

14.2.3 Testing the Null Hypothesis of the Presence of Co-jumps

Now we consider the null hypothesis to be "X and σ have common jumps" with jump sizes in A for X, that is, $\Omega_T^{(A,cj)}$. We still assume (K-r) for some $r \in [0,2)$. We take an integer $w \geq 2$ and a pair (f,g) satisfying (14.19), together with k_n and u_n satisfying (14.23), and with u'_n satisfying (14.26).

The test statistics will be

$$S_n(k_n, w)^{(\text{CJ-Vol})} = \frac{D(f,g; wk_n, u_n, \Delta_n)_T}{D(f,g; k_n, u_n, \Delta_n)_T},$$

which implicitly depends upon f, g, u_n, Δ_n.

If we combine (14.20) and Theorem 14.11, we first obtain

$$S_n(k_n, w)^{(\text{CJ-Vol})} \xrightarrow{\mathbb{P}} 1 \quad \text{on the set } \Omega_T^{(A,cj)}$$

$$S_n(k_n, w)^{(\text{CJ-Vol})} \xrightarrow{\mathcal{L}-s} \mathcal{S}^{(\text{CJ-Vol})} = \frac{\widetilde{\mathcal{U}}(w)_T}{\widetilde{\mathcal{U}}(1)_T} \neq 1 \text{ a.s. on the set } \Omega_T^{(A,dj)}$$

(that $\mathcal{S}^{(\text{CJ-Vol})} \neq 1$ almost surely on $\Omega_T^{(A,dj)}$ comes from the fact that the pair $(\widetilde{\mathcal{U}}(w)_T, \widetilde{\mathcal{U}}(1)_T)$ has a density, conditionally on $\mathcal{F}$). Next, Theorem 14.9 yields

$$\sqrt{k_n}\left(S_n(k_n, w)^{(\text{CJ-Vol})} - 1\right) \xrightarrow{\mathcal{L}-s} \mathcal{S}^{(\text{CJ-Vol})} = \frac{\sqrt{w-1}\,\widetilde{\mathcal{U}}'_T - (1-w)\widetilde{\mathcal{U}}_T}{w\,A(f,g)_T},$$

in restriction to the set $\Omega_T^{(A,cj)}$. By virtue of (14.22), the limit is, conditionally on $\mathcal{F}$, centered Gaussian with variance

$$\mathbb{E}\left((\mathcal{S}^{(\text{CJ-Vol})})^2 \mid \mathcal{F}\right) = \frac{(w-1)A(f,G)_T}{w\,A(f,g)_T^2}$$

and, as in the previous subsection, this conditional variance may be consistently estimated on $\Omega_T^{(A,cj)}$ by $k_n V_n$, where

$$V_n = \frac{(w-1)\,D(f,G; k_n, u'_n, \Delta_n)_T}{k_n\,w\,(D(f,g; k_n, u_n, \Delta_n)_T)^2}.$$

Hence $(S_n(k_n, w)^{(\text{CJ-Vol})} - 1)/\sqrt{V_n}$ converges stably in law to an $\mathcal{N}(0,1)$ variable on $\Omega_T^{(A,cj)}$. We are thus led to choose the following critical regions, with z_α the α-absolute quantile of $\mathcal{N}(0,1)$:

$$\mathcal{C}_n = \left\{|S_n(k_n, w)^{(\text{CJ-Vol})} - 1| > z_\alpha \sqrt{V_n}\right\}. \qquad (14.30)$$

Similar to Theorem 14.9, we have a problem with this choice under the alternative $\Omega_T^{(A,dj)}$ on which, by Theorem 14.11, V_n/k_n converges stably in law and thus $(S_n(k_n, w)^{\text{(CJ-Vol)}} - 1)/\sqrt{V_n}$ converges to 0 on this set. Thus the tests above are not alternative-consistent and the "asymptotic power" is even 0. However, we can "truncate" V_n and define new critical regions as follows:

$$\mathcal{C}'_n = \left\{ |S_n(k_n, w)^{\text{(CJ-Vol)}} - 1| > z_\alpha \sqrt{V_n \wedge \sqrt{k_n}} \right\}. \qquad (14.31)$$

Then, with exactly the same proof as for 14.1, we have:

Theorem 14.17. *Assume (K-r) for some $r \in [0, 2)$, choose f and g satisfying (14.19), and let k_n and u_n satisfy (14.23) and u'_n satisfy (14.26). Both tests $\mathcal{C}_n$ and $\mathcal{C}'_n$ defined above have the strong asymptotic size α for the null hypothesis $\Omega_T^{(A,cj)}$.*

Moreover, the second tests $\mathcal{C}'_n$ are consistent for the alternative $\Omega_T^{(A,dj)}$.

All comments of Remark 14.14 are valid here, except that the "rate" under the null is $\sqrt{k_n}$ instead of k_n.

Remark 14.18. *Exactly as in the previous subsection, if $a > 0$ or if (K-0) holds we can take the test function f, g given by (14.28). But for this test there does not seem to be a real advantage in doing so: the simplest test functions in this case are probably $f = 1_A$ and $g(y, z) = (y - z)^2$.*

Remark 14.19. *For implementing this test, and in addition to the choice of k_n, u_n and u'_n discussed in Remark 14.14, we also have to choose the integer w.*

Under the null $\Omega_T^{(A,cj)}$ the asymptotic $\mathcal{F}$-conditional variance of $\sqrt{k_n}(S_n(k_n, w)^{\text{(CJ-Vol)}} - 1)$ takes the form $\frac{w-1}{w} \Phi$, where $\Phi = A(f, G)_T/(Q(f, g)_T)^2$ does not depend on w. The minimum of $\frac{w-1}{w}$ for $w \geq 2$ is achieved at $w = 2$, so it is probably advisable to always choose $w = 2$.

14.3   References

The content of this chapter is mainly borrowed from two papers by Jacod and Todorov (2009, 2010), with a few simplifications. Co-jumps between two prices have also been considered in Gobbi and Mancini (2012) where the correlation between co-jumps is studied, and in Bibinger and Winkelmann (2013) in the case of noisy observations. Price and volatility co-jumps are also considered in Bandi and Renò (2012, 2013).

The existence of a functional relationship between co-jumps of the price and volatility is studied in Jacod et al. (2013a), and Jacod et al. (2013b) provides tests for non-zero correlation between these co-jumps.

Appendix A

Asymptotic Results for Power Variations

In this appendix, we gather most Laws of Large Numbers and Central Limit Theorems needed in the book and relative to the power variations, truncated or not, for Itô semimartingales, as well as some useful limiting results for a few other processes. We do not aim toward completeness, and unless otherwise specified the proofs can be found in Jacod and Protter (2011), abbreviated below as [JP].

A.1 Setting and Assumptions

We have a d-dimensional semimartingale $X = (X^i)_{1 \leq i \leq d}$, defined on a given filtered probability space $(\Omega, \mathcal{F}, (\mathcal{F}_t)_{t \geq 0}, \mathbb{P})$. Although a few of the subsequent results may be true without further assumptions on X, we nevertheless assume throughout that X is an Itô semimartingale, with jump measure μ and characteristics (B, C, ν), with

$$B_t = \int_0^t b_s ds, \qquad C_t = \int_0^t c_s ds, \qquad \nu(dt, dx) = dt\, F_t(dx), \qquad \text{(A.1)}$$

where $b = (b_t)$ is an $\mathbb{R}^d$-valued process, $c = (c_t)$ is a process with values in the set of $d \times d$ symmetric nonnegative matrices, and $F_t = F_t(\omega, dx)$ is for each (ω, t) a measure on $\mathbb{R}^d$, all those being progressively measurable in (ω, t).

We also use the Grigelionis form of X:

$$X_t = X_0 + \int_0^t b_s ds + \int_0^t \sigma_s dW_s$$
$$+ (\delta 1_{\{\|\delta\| \leq 1\}}) \star (\underline{p} - \underline{q})_t + (\delta 1_{\{\|\delta\| > 1\}}) \star \underline{p}_t. \qquad (A.2)$$

Recall that W is a d'-dimensional Brownian motion and $\underline{p}$ is a Poisson measure on $\mathbb{R}_+ \times E$ with $(E, \mathcal{E})$ an auxiliary Polish space, and b is as in (A.1) and σ is a $d \times d'$-dimensional progressively measurable process, and δ is a predictable function on $\Omega \times \mathbb{R}_+ \times E$, with

- $c_t(\omega) = \sigma_t(\omega) \sigma_t^\star(\omega)$
- $F_t(\omega, .) = $ the image of the measure λ restricted to the set $\{x : \delta(\omega, t, x) \neq 0\}$ by the map $x \mapsto \delta(\omega, t, x)$.

Quite often we need the process σ_t to be an Itô semimartingale as well. In this case, and upon modifying $\underline{p}$ and W, and especially upon increasing the dimension of the latter, we can write the Grigelionis form of σ as follows, with the same $W, \underline{p}, \underline{q}$ as above:

$$\sigma_t = \sigma_0 + \int_0^t b_s^{(\sigma)} ds + \int_0^t \sigma_s^{(\sigma)} dW_s$$
$$+ (\delta^{(\sigma)} 1_{\{|\delta^{(\sigma)}\| \leq 1\}}) \star (\underline{p} - \underline{q})_t + (\delta^{(\sigma)} 1_{\{\|\delta^{(\sigma)}\| > 1\}}) \star \underline{p}_t. \qquad (A.3)$$

This automatically implies

$$c_t = c_0 + \int_0^t b_s^{(c)} ds + \int_0^t \sigma_s^{(c)} dW_s$$
$$+ (\delta^{(c)} 1_{\{|\delta^{(c)}\| \leq 1\}}) \star (\underline{p} - \underline{q})_t + (\delta^{(c)} 1_{\{\|\delta^{(c)}\| > 1\}}) \star \underline{p}_t$$

where the coefficients can be explicitly computed in terms of those in (A.3) and σ_t itself.

Now we state a variety of assumptions on X, which will be used in the various limit theorems. Some of them involve a real r, always in the interval $[0, 2]$.

Assumption (H-r). *We have (A.2) and*

(i) The process b is locally bounded.

(ii) The process σ is càdlàg.

(iii) There is a sequence (τ_n) of stopping times increasing to ∞ and, for each n, a deterministic nonnegative function J_n on E satisfying $\int J_n(z) \lambda(dz) < \infty$ and such that $\|\delta(\omega, t, z)\|^r \wedge 1 \leq J_n(z)$ for all (ω, t, z) with $t \leq \tau_n(\omega)$.

Assumption (H'). *We have (H-2) and there is a sequence* (τ_n) *of stopping times increasing to* ∞, *such that if*

$$
\begin{aligned}
S &= \inf \left(t : \int_0^t \widehat{b}_s \, ds = \infty \right), \\
\text{where } \widehat{b}_s &= \int_{\{\|\delta(s,z)\| \leq 1\}} \|\delta(s,z)\| \lambda(dz)
\end{aligned}
\tag{A.4}
$$

(the process $\widehat{b}_t$ is well defined but it may be infinite for some, or even all, values of (ω, t)), then $\sup_{(\omega,t):\, t \leq \tau_n(\omega) \wedge S(\omega)} \widehat{b}_t(\omega) < \infty$.

Assumption (H-2) is little more than assuming simply that X is an Itô semimartingale. (H-r) becomes stronger as r decreases, and (H-1) implies (H') with $S = \infty$ because under (H-1) we have $|\widehat{b}_s| \leq \int J_n(z)\lambda(dz)$ if $s \leq \tau_n$.

Under (H-2) the variables

$$
b_t' = b_t - \int_{\{\|\delta(t,z)\| \leq 1\}} \delta(t,z) \, \lambda(dz)
\tag{A.5}
$$

are well defined on the set $\{S \geq t\}$. Under (H-1), and since then $S = \infty$, the process b_t' is well defined at all times, and we can rewrite X as

$$
X_t = X_0 + \int_0^t b_s' \, ds + \int_0^t \sigma_s \, dW_s + \delta * \underline{p}_t,
\tag{A.6}
$$

and so the process b' can be viewed as the *genuine drift*.

Assumption (K-r). *We have (H-r) and (H') and the process* σ *is an Itô semimartingale satisfying (H-2) (hence the process c as well). Moreover, with the notation (A.5), all paths $t \mapsto b_t'$ on $[0, S]$ as well as all paths $t \mapsto b_t$ on $\mathbb{R}_+$ when further $r > 1$ are either right-continuous with left limits (càdlàg) or left-continuous with right limits (càglàd).*

When X is continuous, if it satisfies (H-2), resp. (K-2), then it also satisfies (H-r), resp. (K-r), for all $r \in [0, 2]$. For convenience, we reformulate the assumptions in this case:

Assumption (HC). *We have (A.1) and X is continuous, the process b is locally bounded and the process σ is càdlàg (equivalently, we have (H-2) and X is continuous).*

Assumption (KC). *We have (HC), the process b is either càdlàg or càglàd, and the process σ is an Itô semimartingale satisfying (H-2) (equivalently, we have (K-2) and X is continuous).*

Assumption (KCC). *We have (KC), the process σ is also continuous, and the process $b^{(\sigma)}$ in (A.3) is càdlàg.*

Another type of assumption is sometimes needed:

Assumption (P). *Both processes c_t and c_{t-} are everywhere invertible.*

Next, we turn to another kind of assumption, which says more or less that the small jumps are somewhat similar to those of a stable process. The two assumptions below make sense as stated only when $d = 1$, which is implicitly assumed. We introduce the "tail" functions of the Lévy measure F_t as being the following functions on $(0, \infty)$:

$$\begin{aligned}
\overline{F}_t^{(+)}(x) &= F_t((x, \infty)), \\
\overline{F}_t^{(-)}(x) &= F_t((-\infty, -x)), \\
\overline{F}_t(x) &= \overline{F}_t^{(+)}(x) + \overline{F}_t^{(+)}(x).
\end{aligned}$$

Assumption (L). *We have (A.2) with b_t locally bounded and σ_t càdlàg, and there are two constants $0 \le \beta' < \beta < 2$ such that*

$$x \in (0, 1] \quad \Rightarrow \quad \left| x^\beta \, \overline{F}_t^{(\pm)}(x) - a_t^{(\pm)} \right| \le L_t \, x^{\beta - \beta'}, \qquad (A.7)$$

where $a_t^{(+)}$ and $a_t^{(-)}$ and L_t are nonnegative predictable (or optional) locally bounded processes.

This assumption is rather strong, in the sense that, for example, it implies that the local BG index β_t defined in (5.16) equals β (a constant, depending neither on t nor on ω) as soon as $a_t^{(+)} + a_t^{(-)} > 0$, and the global index γ_t also equals β if $\int_0^t (a_s^{(+)} + a_s^{(-)}) \, ds > 0$. As proved in Lemma 11.8, it also implies (H-r) for all $r > \beta$. The next assumption, although not formally weaker than (L), is indeed much weaker in spirit:

Assumption (J). *We have (A.2) with b_t locally bounded and σ_t càdlàg. Moreover, the global BG index $\gamma_t = \inf(p \ge 0 : \int_0^t ds \int (|x|^p \wedge 1) \, F_s(dx) < \infty)$ takes its values in $[0, 2)$ (the value 2 is excluded), and for all $\varepsilon > 0$ the process $\sup_{x \in (0, 1]} x^{\gamma_t + \varepsilon} \overline{F}_t(x)$ is locally bounded.*

A.2   Laws of Large Numbers

A.2.1   LLNs for Power Variations and Related Functionals

We recall the following notation, associated with the sequence Δ_n going to 0 as $n \to \infty$:

$$\Delta_i^n X = X_{i\Delta_n} - X_{(i-1)\Delta_n}.$$

With any function f on $(\mathbb{R}^d)^k$, where $k \geq 1$, we associate the processes

$$
\begin{aligned}
B(f, \Delta_n)_t &= \sum_{i=1}^{[t/\Delta_n]-k+1} f(\Delta_i^n X, \ldots, \Delta_{i+k-1}^n X) \\
B'(f, \Delta_n)_t &= \Delta_n \sum_{i=1}^{[t/\Delta_n]-k+1} f\left(\frac{\Delta_i^n X}{\sqrt{\Delta_n}}, \ldots, \frac{\Delta_{i+k-1}^n X}{\sqrt{\Delta_n}}\right).
\end{aligned}
\tag{A.8}
$$

When $k \geq 2$, each increment $\Delta_i^n X$ appears in several summands, so one could also consider the processes

$$
\begin{aligned}
\overline{B}(f, \Delta_n)_t &= \sum_{i=1}^{[t/k\Delta_n]} f(\Delta_{ik-k+1}^n X, \ldots, \Delta_{ik}^n X) \\
\overline{B}'(f, \Delta_n)_t &= \Delta_n \sum_{i=1}^{[t/k\Delta_n]} f\left(\frac{\Delta_{ik-k+1}^n X}{\sqrt{\Delta_n}}, \ldots, \frac{\Delta_{ik}^n X}{\sqrt{\Delta_n}}\right).
\end{aligned}
\tag{A.9}
$$

When $k = 1$ there is no difference between (A.8) and (A.9).

We also consider the truncated versions, with a sequence of truncation levels $u_n > 0$ satisfying

$$
u_n \asymp \Delta_n^{\varpi}, \quad \text{where } 0 < \varpi < \frac{1}{2},
\tag{A.10}
$$

and which are

$$
\begin{aligned}
B(f, \Delta_n, u_n)_t &= \sum_{i=1}^{[t/\Delta_n]-k+1} f(\Delta_i^n X, \ldots, \Delta_{i+k-1}^n X) \\
&\quad \times \prod_{j=0}^{k-1} 1_{\{\|\Delta_{i+j}^n X\| \leq u_n\}} \\
B'(f, \Delta_n, u_n)_t &= \Delta_n \sum_{i=1}^{[t/\Delta_n]-k+1} f\left(\frac{\Delta_i^n X}{\sqrt{\Delta_n}}, \ldots, \frac{\Delta_{i+k-1}^n X}{\sqrt{\Delta_n}}\right) \\
&\quad \times \prod_{j=0}^{k-1} 1_{\{\|\Delta_{i+j}^n X\| \leq u_n\}}.
\end{aligned}
\tag{A.11}
$$

When the test function f, depending on k successive increments, has the form $f(x_1, \ldots, x_k) = g(x_1 + \cdots + x_k)$, then, instead of $B'(f, \Delta_n, u_n)$ above it is more natural to consider the following truncated version:

$$
\begin{aligned}
B'([g, k], \Delta_n, u_n)_t &= \Delta_n \sum_{i=1}^{[t/\Delta_n]-k+1} g\left(\frac{\Delta_i^n X + \cdots + \Delta_{i+k-1}^n X}{\sqrt{\Delta_n}}\right) \\
&\quad \times 1_{\{\|\Delta_i^n X + \cdots + \Delta_{i+k-1}^n X\| \leq u_n\}}.
\end{aligned}
\tag{A.12}
$$

For all these functionals, the test function f may be q-dimensional: the associated functionals are also q-dimensional, and the previous definitions should be read componentwise. Recall that $\overset{\mathbb{P}}{\Longrightarrow}$ stands for the convergence in probability for processes, relative to the Skorokhod topology.

Theorem A.1. *[JP, Theorems 3.3.1 and 7.3.3] Assume that X is a semimartingale and that the q-dimensional function f on $(\mathbb{R}^d)^k$ is continuous and satisfies $\|f(z)\| = o(\|z\|^2)$ as $z \to 0$ in $(\mathbb{R}^d)^k$.*

(a) If $k = 1$ we have

$$B(f, \Delta_n) \overset{\mathbb{P}}{\Longrightarrow} f * \mu. \tag{A.13}$$

(b) If $k \geq 1$ and with the functions f_j on $\mathbb{R}^d$ defined by $f_j(x) = f(0, \ldots, 0, x, 0, \ldots, 0)$ with $x \in \mathbb{R}^d$ occurring as the jth argument, we have for each t

$$B(f, \Delta_n)_t \overset{\mathbb{P}}{\longrightarrow} \sum_{j=1}^{k} f_j * \mu_t \quad \text{on the set } \{\Delta X_t = 0\}. \tag{A.14}$$

(c) If $k \geq 2$ and if f is invariant by permutation of its k arguments (we also say "symmetrical"), so $f_j = f_1$ for all $j = 2, \ldots, k$, we have

$$\overline{B}(f, \Delta_n) \overset{\mathbb{P}}{\Longrightarrow} f_1 * \mu. \tag{A.15}$$

In contrast with (A.13), the convergence of $B(f, \Delta_n)$ when $k \geq 2$ does *not* take place for the Skorokhod topology in general. Moreover, even when $k = 1$, the convergence in (A.14) usually fails on the set $\{\Delta X_t \neq 0\}$. However, if X is an Itô semimartingale, this set is negligible, so the convergence in (A.14) holds on the whole space Ω. Note also that when $k \geq 2$ the sequence $\overline{B}(f, \Delta_n)$ does *not* converge (functionally, or even for fixed times t) when the functions f_j are not all the same.

For the next theorem we need some notation. If a is any matrix in the set $\mathcal{M}_d^+$ of all $d \times d$ symmetric nonnegative matrices, we denote by ρ_a the law $\mathcal{N}(0, a)$ on $\mathbb{R}^d$. We write $\rho_a(f) = \int f(x) \rho_a(dx)$ when f is a function on $\mathbb{R}^d$ and, more generally, $\rho_a^{k\otimes}(f) = \int f(x_1, \ldots, x_k) \, \rho_a(dx_1) \cdots \rho_a(dx_k)$ when f is a function on $(\mathbb{R}^d)^k$. In (A.16) below the convergence is, as stated in (3.23), in probability and locally uniform in time, despite the fact that on the right side we write the time t in order to define the limiting process.

Theorem A.2. *[JP, Theorems 3.4.1 and 7.2.2] Assume (H-2) and that the q-dimensional function f on $(\mathbb{R}^d)^k$ is continuous and of polynomial growth. Then we have*

$$B'(f, \Delta_n) \overset{u.c.p.}{\Longrightarrow} \int_0^t \rho_{c_s}^{k\otimes}(f) \, ds \tag{A.16}$$

$$\overline{B}'(f, \Delta_n) \overset{u.c.p.}{\Longrightarrow} \frac{1}{k} \int_0^t \rho_{c_s}^{k\otimes}(f) \, ds \tag{A.17}$$

in the following two cases:

(a) When X is continuous (that is, (HC) holds).

(b) When $\|f(x_1,\dots,x_k)\| \le \prod_{j=1}^{k} \Psi(\|x_j\|)(1 + \|x_j\|^2)$ for some continuous function Ψ on $\mathbb{R}_+$ tending to 0 at infinity.

Now we turn to the truncated functionals:

Theorem A.3. *[JP, Theorems 9.2.1] Assume (H-r) for some $r \in [0,2]$ and that the q-dimensional function f on $(\mathbb{R}^d)^k$ is continuous and of polynomial growth. Then we have*

$$B'(f, \Delta_n, u_n) \overset{u.c.p.}{\Longrightarrow} U'(f)_t = \int_0^t \rho_{c_s}^{k\otimes}(f) \, ds$$

and also, when $f(x_1, \cdots, x_k) = g(x_1 + \dots + x_k)$,

$$B'([g,k], \Delta_n, u_n) \overset{u.c.p.}{\Longrightarrow} U'([g,k])_t = \int_0^t \rho_{kc_s}(g) \, ds,$$

in the following two cases:

(a) When X is continuous (that is, (HC) holds).

(b) When $\|f(x_1,\dots,x_k)\| \le K \prod_{j=1}^{k}(1 + \|x_j\|^p)$ for some constant K and the pair (p, ϖ) satisfies

$$either \quad p \le 2 \quad or \quad r < 2 < p, \quad \varpi \ge \frac{p-2}{2(p-r)}.$$

The conditions on f above are much weaker than in Theorem A.2. For the functionals truncated from below, that is $B(f, \Delta_n) - B(f, \Delta_n, u_n)$, the conditions are also much weaker than in Theorem A.1 (but X should satisfy (H-r) instead of being an arbitrary semimartingale), and we have:

Theorem A.4. *[JP, Theorem 9.1.1] Assume (H-r) for some $r \in [0,2]$ and that the q-dimensional function f on $\mathbb{R}^d$ is continuous with $\|f(x)\| = O(\|x\|^r)$ as $x \to 0$. Then we have*

$$B(f, \Delta_n) - B(f, \Delta_n, u_n) \overset{\mathbb{P}}{\Longrightarrow} U(f) = f * \mu.$$

We could also truncate the functionals $\overline{B}'(f, \Delta_n)$ when $k \ge 2$, and obtain similar results, but those are of no interest for us in this book.

Remark A.5. *All the LLNs above still hold when we relax the continuity assumption on the test function, in the following way (we keep, however, the various growth conditions or behavior near 0). Namely, we can replace the continuity by the property that it is "almost surely continuous," in* *the following sense, and where D_f denotes the set of all points where the function f is not continuous:*

(a) For Theorems A.1 and A.4 the function f (or f_j, according to the case) is such that $\mathbb{P}(\exists t > 0$ with $\Delta X_t \in D_f) = 0$.

(b) For Theorems A.2 and A.3 we have $\int_0^\infty \rho_{c_s}^{k\otimes}(D_f)\, ds = 0$; this condition is implied, when (P) holds, by the fact that the Lebesgue measure of D_f equals 0; without (P) and in the one-dimensional case $d = k = 1$ it is also implied by the same property, plus the additional property that $0 \notin D_f$.

The same remark holds as well for all *convergences in probability encountered in the sequel.*

A.2.2   LLNs for the Integrated Volatility

When the test function is quadratic, that is, f is the d^2-dimensional function on $\mathbb{R}^d$ (so $k = 1$) with components $f(x)^{jl} = x^j x^l$, we have

$$B(f^{jl}, \Delta_n)_t = B'(f^{jl}, \Delta_n)_t = \widehat{C}(\Delta_n)_t^{jl} := \sum_{i=1}^{[t/\Delta_n]} \Delta_i^n X^j \, \Delta_i^n X^l. \quad \text{(A.18)}$$

The d^2-dimensional process $\widehat{C}(\Delta_n)$ with components $\widehat{C}(\Delta_n)^{jl}$ is the *realized quadratic variation*, which would perhaps be more appropriately denoted as $[X, X]^n$. Neither Theorem A.1 nor Theorem A.2 applies in this case, unless X is continuous. Nevertheless (1.61) and the fact that for any given càdlàg process its discretized versions converge to the process for the Skorokhod topology give

$$\widehat{C}(\Delta_n) \overset{\mathbb{P}}{\Longrightarrow} [X, X]$$

(where $[X, X]$ has components $[X^j, X^l]$). This is true without any assumption on X, other than being a semimartingale. The convergence $\widehat{C}(\Delta_n)_t \overset{\mathbb{P}}{\longrightarrow} [X, X]_t$ does not necessarily hold for each t. It does, however, when X is an Itô semimartingale, because $\Delta X_t = 0$ a.s. for any given t.

Next, if we apply Theorem A.3 with the quadratic f as above, we get under (A.10)

$$\begin{aligned} \widehat{C}(\Delta_n, u_n)_t^{jl} &= B'(f^{jl}, \Delta_n, u_n)_t \\ &= \sum_{i=1}^{[t/\Delta_n]} \Delta_i^n X^j \, \Delta_i^n X^l \, 1_{\{\|\Delta_i^n X\| \le u_n\}} \overset{\text{u.c.p.}}{\Longrightarrow} C_t^{jl}. \end{aligned} \quad \text{(A.19)}$$

Finally, we can consider the multipower variations, defined for any integer

$k \geq 2$, as

$$
\begin{aligned}
\widehat{C}([k], \Delta_n)_t^{jl} = \frac{1}{4(m_{2/k})^k} \sum_{i=1}^{[t/\Delta_n]-k+1} & \left(|\Delta_i^n X^j + \Delta_i^n X^l|^{2/k} \right. \\
& \cdots |\Delta_{i+k-1}^n X^j + \Delta_{i+k-1}^n X^l|^{2/k} \\
& - |\Delta_i^n X^j - \Delta_i^n X^l|^{2/k} \\
& \left. \cdots |\Delta_{i+k-1}^n X^j - \Delta_{i+k-1}^n X^l|^{2/k} \right),
\end{aligned}
\tag{A.20}
$$

where m_p denotes the pth absolute moment of $\mathcal{N}(0, 1)$. Then, Theorem A.2 applied with the function

$$
f(x_1, \ldots, x_k) = \prod_{m=1}^k |x_m^j + x_m^l|^{2/k} - \prod_{m=1}^k |x_m^j - x_m^l|^{2/k}
$$

gives us

$$
\widehat{C}([k], \Delta_n) \overset{\text{u.c.p.}}{\Longrightarrow} C.
\tag{A.21}
$$

A.2.3   LLNs for Estimating the Spot Volatility

We assume (H-2) throughout the whole subsection. For estimating the spot volatility c_t there are mainly three possible estimators, all based on the choice of a sequence k_n of integers with the following properties:

$$
k_n \to \infty, \qquad k_n \Delta_n \to 0,
\tag{A.22}
$$

and those estimators are (with $k \geq 2$ an integer, for the second one)

$$
\begin{aligned}
\widehat{c}(k_n)_i^{jl} &= \frac{1}{k_n \Delta_n} \sum_{m=0}^{k_n-1} \Delta_{i+m}^n X^j \, \Delta_{i+m}^n X^l \\
\widehat{c}(k_n, [k])_i^{jl} &= \frac{1}{4(m_{2/k})^k k_n \Delta_n} \sum_{m=0}^{k_n-1} \left(|\Delta_{i+m}^n X^j + \Delta_{i+m}^n X^l|^{2/k} \right. \\
& \qquad \cdots |\Delta_{i+m+k-1}^n X^j + \Delta_{i+m+k-1}^n X^l|^{2/k} \\
& \qquad - |\Delta_{i+m}^n X^j - \Delta_{i+m}^n X^l|^{2/k} \\
& \qquad \left. \cdots |\Delta_{i+m+k-1}^n X^j - \Delta_{i+m+k-1}^n X^l|^{2/k} \right) \\
\widehat{c}(k_n, u_n)_i^{jl} &= \frac{1}{k_n \Delta_n} \sum_{m=0}^{k_n-1} \Delta_{i+m}^n X^j \, \Delta_{i+m}^n X^l \, 1_{\{\|\Delta_{i+m}^n X\| \leq u_n\}}.
\end{aligned}
\tag{A.23}
$$

These are *a priori* defined when $i \geq 1$, but for convenience we extend the definition to all relative integers i, by the same formulas, and with the convention that $\Delta_i^n X \equiv 0$ when $i \leq 0$. This convention is in force all the way below. Note that the matrix-valued variables $\widehat{c}(k_n)_i$ and $\widehat{c}(k_n, u_n)_i$ take their values in the set $\mathcal{M}_d^+$, but this is not the case of $\widehat{c}(k_n, [k])_i$.

Next, for any time $t \geq 0$ (possibly random), we set if $(i-1)\Delta_n < t \leq i\Delta_n$

$$
\begin{array}{ll}
\widehat{c}(t-;k_n) = \widehat{c}(k_n)_{i-k_n}, & \widehat{c}(t;k_n) = \widehat{c}(k_n)_{i+1} \\
\widehat{c}(t-;k_n,[k]) = \widehat{c}(k_n,[k])_{i-k_n-k+1}, & \widehat{c}(t;k_n,[k]) = \widehat{c}(k_n,[k])_{i+1} \\
\widehat{c}(t-;k_n,u_n) = \widehat{c}(k_n,u_n)_{i-k_n}, & \widehat{c}(t;k_n,u_n) = \widehat{c}(k_n,u_n)_{i+1}.
\end{array}
$$

where i runs through $\mathbb{N}$. So when t is non-random for example, $\widehat{c}(t-;k_n)$ is really meaningful only when $t > (k_n+1)\Delta_n$, which holds for n large enough when $t > 0$.

Theorem A.6. [*JP, Theorem 9.3.2*] *Assume (H-2), and let k_n satisfy (A.22) and u_n satisfy (A.10). Then, for any finite stopping time T, we have*

$$
\begin{array}{l}
\widehat{c}(T;k_n) \xrightarrow{\mathbb{P}} c_T \\
\widehat{c}(T;k_n,[k]) \xrightarrow{\mathbb{P}} c_T \\
\widehat{c}(T;k_n,u_n) \xrightarrow{\mathbb{P}} c_T.
\end{array}
$$

If further T is positive, and if either $T > S$ identically for some other stopping time S and T is $\mathcal{F}_S$-measurable, or the process c_t is an Itô semimartingale and $\underline{p}(\{T\} \times E) = 1$ a.s. ($\underline{p}$ is any Poisson random measure driving both X and σ, so this means that T is a "jump time" of $\underline{p}$), then

$$
\begin{array}{ll}
\widehat{c}(T-;k_n) \xrightarrow{\mathbb{P}} c_{T-} & \\
\widehat{c}(T-;k_n,[k]) \xrightarrow{\mathbb{P}} c_{T-} & \text{(A.24)} \\
\widehat{c}(T-;k_n,u_n) \xrightarrow{\mathbb{P}} c_{T-}.
\end{array}
$$

This result is remarkable because we do not need to truncate or take multipowers to obtain consistent estimators, *even when there are jumps.*

In some places, we need to approximate quantities such as

$$
\sum_{s \leq t} f(\Delta X_s) g(c_{s-}, c_s)
$$

for suitable functions f and g. This is of course related to the estimation of the spot volatility, and natural estimators take the form

$$
\begin{aligned}
D(f,g;k_n,u_n,w_n,\Delta_n)_t &= \sum_{i=k_n+1}^{[t/\Delta_n]-k_n} f(\Delta_i^n X) \\
&\quad \times g(\widehat{c}(k_n,u_n)_{i-k_n}, \widehat{c}(k_n,u_n)_{i+1}) \, \mathbf{1}_{\{\|\Delta_i^n X\| > w_n\}} \\
D(f,g;k_n,[k],w_n\Delta_n)_t &= \sum_{i=k_n+1}^{[t/\Delta_n]-k_n-k} f(\Delta_i^n X) \\
&\quad \times g(\widehat{c}(k_n,[k])_{i-k_n}, \widehat{c}(k_n,[k])_{i+1}) \, \mathbf{1}_{\{\|\Delta_i^n X\| > w_n\}}.
\end{aligned}
$$

Theorem A.7. [*JP, Theorem 9.5.1 and Remark 9.5.2-(c)*] *Assume that* X *satisfies* (H-r) *for some* $r \in [0,2]$. *Let* f *and* g *be as follows:*

- f *is a continuous function on* $\mathbb{R}^d$ *such that* $f(x) = o(\|x\|^r)$ *as* $x \to 0$;
- g *is a continuous function on* $(\mathbb{R}^d \otimes \mathbb{R}^d)^2$ *such that* $|g(z,z')| \le K(1 + \|z\|^p)(1 + \|z'\|^p)$.

Let w_n *satisfy either* $w_n \asymp \Delta_n^{\varpi'}$ *with* $0 < \varpi' < \frac{1}{2}$, *or* $w_n = 0$ *for all* n *in the case when* $f(x) = o(\|x\|^2)$ *as* $x \to 0$. *Then:*

(i) For any sequence $u_n \asymp \Delta_n^{\varpi}$ *with* $\frac{p-1}{2p-r} \le \varpi < \frac{1}{2}$ *when* $p > 1$, *we have the following Skorokhod convergence in probability:*

$$D(f,g; k_n, u_n, w_n, \Delta_n)_t \overset{\mathbb{P}}{\Longrightarrow} \sum_{s \le t} f(\Delta X_s) g(c_{s-}, c_s). \qquad (A.25)$$

(ii) For any integer $k > p$, *we have the following Skorokhod convergence in probability:*

$$D(f,g; k_n, [k], w_n\Delta_n) \overset{\mathbb{P}}{\Longrightarrow} \sum_{s \le t} f(\Delta X_s) g(c_{s-}, c_s).$$

Finally, one may be interested in approximating $\int_0^t g(c_s)\,ds$ for some function g on the set $\mathcal{M}_d^+$. When g takes the form $g(a) = \rho_a^{k\otimes}(f)$ for a continuous function f on $(\mathbb{R}^d)^k$ with polynomial growth, for some integer k, one can use $B'(f, \Delta_n)_t$ and take advantage of (A.16). However, this puts some restriction on g, for instance that it is C^∞. Moreover, if $g \ge 0$ for example, one may wish for an approximation which is always nonnegative, and this is not necessarily the case of $B'(f, \Delta_n)_t$. So the following, which is Theorem 9.4.1 of [JP] when $f \equiv 1$ and a simple extension of it otherwise, will be useful for us:

Theorem A.8. *Assume that* X *satisfies* (H-r) *for some* $r \in [0,2]$. *Let* g *be a continuous function on* $\mathcal{M}_d^+$, *such that* $|g(a)| \le K(1 + \|a\|^p)$ *for some* $p \ge 0$. *Let also* f *be a continuous function on* $\mathbb{R}^d$ *such that* $|f(x)| \le K(1 + \|x\|^{p'})$ *for some* $p' \ge 0$.

(i) If either X *is continuous, or* $p < 1$ *and* $p' < 2$, *we have*

$$\Delta_n \sum_{i=0}^{[t/\Delta_n]-k_n+1} g(\widehat{c}(k_n)_i)\, f\!\left(\frac{\Delta_{i+k_n}^n X}{\sqrt{\Delta_n}}\right) \overset{u.c.p.}{\Longrightarrow} \int_0^t g(c_s)\, \rho_{c_s}(f)\, ds.$$

(ii) If either $p \le 1$ *and* $p' \le 2$, *or* $p > 1$ *and* $p' > 2$ *and* (H-r) *holds for some* $r \in [0,2)$ *and the sequence* u_n *satisfies* (A.10) *with* $\varpi \ge \frac{p-1}{2p-r} \wedge \frac{p'-2}{2(p'-r)}$, *we have*

$$\Delta_n \sum_{i=0}^{[t/\Delta_n]-k_n+1} g(\widehat{c}(k_n, u_n)_i)\, f\!\left(\frac{\Delta_{i+k_n}^n X}{\sqrt{\Delta_n}}\right) 1_{\{\|\Delta_{i+k_n}^n X\| \le u_n\}}$$
$$\overset{u.c.p.}{\Longrightarrow} \int_0^t g(c_s)\, \rho_{c_s}(f)\, ds. \qquad (A.26)$$

A.3   Central Limit Theorems

A.3.1   CLTs for the Processes $B(f, \Delta_n)$ and $\overline{B}(f, \Delta_n)$

We now consider the Central Limit Theorems (CLTs) associated with
each LLN of the previous section. In all cases, the limiting process is de-
fined on an extension $(\widetilde{\Omega}, \widetilde{\mathcal{F}}, \widetilde{\mathbb{P}})$ of the original probability space $(\Omega, \mathcal{F}, \mathbb{P})$
of type (1.86), with a variety of processes V' and V'' and of probability
measures η, but always with the same sequence T_n of stopping times
which we now specify.

The sequence of stopping times $(T_n)_{n \geq 1}$ *weakly exhausts* the jumps
of X, in the following sense:

- $n \neq m \ \Rightarrow \ \{T_n = T_m < \infty\} \ = \ \emptyset$
- $\Delta X_t(\omega) \neq 0 \ \Rightarrow \ \exists n = n(\omega, t)$ such that $t = T_n(\omega)$.   (A.27)

Such a sequence always exists, due to the fact that X is càdlàg adapted,
and many different ones exist. The qualifier "weakly" stands for the fact
that we do *not* require that X actually jumps at each finite T_n, that
is, ΔX_{T_n} may vanish on a subset of $\{T_n < \infty\}$. It would be possible to
impose this additional condition (then (T_n) would be called an *exhausting
sequence* for the jumps). Again, many different such sequences exist in
general, unless X is continuous (in this case the only exhausting sequence
is of course $T_n \equiv \infty$).

The reason for using a weakly exhausting sequence is the greater flexibility; for example, we can choose a sequence that weakly exhausts the
jumps of X, and perhaps also those of another process of interest. In any
case, we *fix below the weakly exhausting sequence T_n*, and the results do
not depend on this particular choice.

For the CLT associated with Theorem A.1 we need some notation, in
connection with the number k of arguments of the test function f which
is used. We set $\mathcal{K}_- = \{-k+1, -k+2, \ldots, -1\}$ and $\mathcal{K}_+ = \{1, 2, \ldots, k-1\}$
and $\mathcal{K} = \mathcal{K}_- \cup \mathcal{K}_+$. We consider variables $\Psi_{n,j}$, Ψ_{n-}, Ψ_{n+}, κ_n, L_n on an
auxiliary space $(\Omega', \mathcal{F}', \mathbb{P}')$, all independent and with the following laws:

$\Psi_{n,j}, \Psi_{n-}, \Psi_{n+}$ are d'-dimensional, $\mathcal{N}(0, I_{d'})$
κ_n is uniform on $[0, 1]$ (A.28)
L_n is integer-valued, uniform on $\{0, 1, \ldots, k - 1\}$.

On the product extension (1.86) we define the following d-dimensional random variables

$$
R_{n,j} = \begin{cases} \sigma_{T_{n-}} \Psi_{n,j} & \text{if } j \in \mathcal{K}_{-} \\ \sqrt{\kappa_n}\sigma_{T_{n-}} \Psi_{n-} + \sqrt{1-\kappa_n}\sigma_{T_n} \Psi_{n+} & \text{if } j = 0 \\ \sigma_{T_n} \Psi_{n,j} & \text{if } j \in \mathcal{K}_{+}. \end{cases} \qquad (A.29)
$$

The test function f is an $\mathbb{R}^q$-valued function on $(\mathbb{R}^d)^k$, where $k \geq 2$. When it is C^1 the first derivatives are globally denoted by ∇f, but we also need some more specific notation: the d-dimensional arguments of f are $x_1, \ldots, x_k$, and x_j has the components x_j^i for $i = 1, \ldots, d$. Then we write (with $x \in \mathbb{R}^d$)

$$
\begin{aligned}
f_j(x) &= f(0, \ldots, 0, x, 0, \ldots, 0) \\
\partial_i f_{(l);j}(x) &= \tfrac{\partial f}{\partial x_l^i}(0, \ldots, 0, x, 0, \ldots, 0) \qquad (A.30) \\
\partial_{ii'}^2 f_{(ll');j}(x) &= \tfrac{\partial^2 f}{\partial x_l^i \partial x_{l'}^{i'}}(0, \ldots, 0, x, 0, \ldots, 0)
\end{aligned}
$$

where x is at the jth place.

With all this notation, the limiting processes will be the q-dimensional processes defined on the product extension $(\widetilde{\Omega}, \widetilde{\mathcal{F}}, \widetilde{\mathbb{P}})$ as

$$
\begin{aligned}
\mathcal{U}(f)_t &= \sum_{n:\, T_n \leq t} \sum_{j,l=1}^{k} \sum_{i=1}^{d} \partial_i f_{(l);j}(\Delta X_{T_n}) R_{n,l-j}^i \\
\overline{\mathcal{U}}(f)_t &= \sum_{n:\, T_n \leq t} \sum_{j,l=1}^{k} \sum_{i=1}^{d} \partial_i f_{(l);j}(\Delta X_{T_n}) R_{n,l-j}^i \mathbf{1}_{\{L_n = j-1\}}.
\end{aligned} \qquad (A.31)
$$

These are of the form (1.87) with $V' = 0$, and for $\mathcal{U}(f)$, say, with $q'' = 2kd' + 1$ and the variables Y_n having the components $\Psi_{n,j}^i$ and $\sqrt{\kappa_n}\, \Psi_{n-}^i$ and $\sqrt{1-\kappa_n}\, \Psi_{n+}^i$, and the components of the process V'' being linear combinations of $\sigma_{T_n-}^{ij}$ and $\sigma_{T_n}^{ij}$ times $\partial_i f_{(l);j}(\Delta X_{T_n})$. Therefore, as soon as f is such that $\|\partial_i f_{(l);j}\| = O(\|x\|)$ as $x \to 0$, the processes $\mathcal{U}(f)$ (and $\overline{\mathcal{U}}(f)$ as well) are well defined and are martingales on the extended space. Furthermore the $\mathcal{F}$-conditional variance-covariances are

$$
\begin{aligned}
&\widetilde{\mathbb{E}}(\mathcal{U}(f^i)_t\, \mathcal{U}(f^{i'})_t \mid \mathcal{F}) = \\
&\sum_{s \leq t} \sum_{r,r'=1}^{d} \Big(\tfrac{1}{2} \sum_{j,j'=1}^{k} (\partial_r f_{(j);j}^i\, \partial_{r'} f_{(j');j'}^{i'})(\Delta X_s)\, (c_{s-}^{rr'} + c_s^{rr'}) \\
&\quad + \sum_{j=2}^{k} \sum_{l=1}^{j-1} \sum_{l'=1}^{k+l-j} (\partial_r f_{(l);j}^i\, \partial_{r'} f_{(l');j+l'-l}^{i'})(\Delta X_s)\, c_{s-}^{rr'} \\
&\quad + \sum_{j=1}^{k-1} \sum_{l=j+1}^{k} \sum_{l'=1+l-j}^{k} (\partial_r f_{(l);j}^i\, \partial_{r'} f_{(l');j+l'-l}^{i'})(\Delta X_s)\, c_s^{rr'} \Big)
\end{aligned}
$$

$$
\begin{aligned}
&\widetilde{\mathbb{E}}(\overline{\mathcal{U}}(f^i)_t\, \overline{\mathcal{U}}(f^{i'})_t \mid \mathcal{F}) = \\
&\sum_{s \leq t} \sum_{r,r'=1}^{d} \tfrac{1}{2} \big(\partial_r f^i\, \partial_{r'} f^{i'} + (k-1)\partial_r^* f^i\, \partial_{r'}^* f^{i'}\big)(\Delta X_s)(c_{s-}^{rr'} + c_s^{rr'}).
\end{aligned}
$$

Theorem A.9. *[JP, Theorem 11.1.1] Assume (H-2), and let f be a C^2 function from $(\mathbb{R}^d)^k$ into $\mathbb{R}^q$, satisfying*

$$f(0) = 0, \quad \nabla f(0) = 0, \quad \|\nabla^2 f(z)\| = \text{o}(\|z\|) \text{ as } z \to 0 \text{ in } (\mathbb{R}^d)^k. \quad (A.32)$$

(a) For each fixed t we have

$$\frac{1}{\sqrt{\Delta_n}} \left(B(f, \Delta_n)_t - \sum_{j=1}^k f_j \star \mu_t \right) \overset{\mathcal{L}-s}{\longrightarrow} \mathcal{U}(f)_t. \quad (A.33)$$

(b) If f is invariant by permutation of its k arguments, we have the following functional convergence

$$\frac{1}{\sqrt{\Delta_n}} \left(\overline{B}(f, \Delta_n)_t - f_1 \star \mu_{k\Delta_n [t/k\Delta_n]} \right) \overset{\mathcal{L}-s}{\Longrightarrow} \overline{\mathcal{U}}(f), \quad (A.34)$$

and for each fixed t we also have

$$\frac{1}{\sqrt{\Delta_n}} \left(\overline{B}(f, \Delta_n)_t - f_1 \star \mu_t \right) \overset{\mathcal{L}-s}{\longrightarrow} \overline{\mathcal{U}}(f)_t. \quad (A.35)$$

Moreover, the processes $\mathcal{U}(f)$ and $\overline{\mathcal{U}}(f)$ are $\mathcal{F}$-conditionally Gaussian as soon as the two processes X and σ have no common jumps.

A functional convergence like (A.34) for $B(f, \Delta_n)$ does *not* hold, unless of course $k = 1$.

A.3.2   A Degenerate Case

The functional $B(f, \Delta_n)$ may be "degenerate," in the sense that the limit $\overline{\mathcal{U}}(f)$ in the previous CLT vanishes identically. We will encounter this situation in a special case, which we explain below.

The test function f is a two-dimensional function on $(\mathbb{R}^d)^k$ with components

$$f^j(x_1, \cdots, x_k) = \begin{cases} h(x_1) & \text{if } j = 1 \\ h(x_1 + \cdots + x_k) & \text{if } j = 2. \end{cases} \quad (A.36)$$

where $h(x) = (x^1 x^2)^2$. This function is C^2 with $f(z) = \text{O}(\|z\|^4)$ as $z \to 0$, is globally homogeneous with degree 4, and satisfies

$$\partial_1 h(x) = 2x^1 (x^2)^2, \quad \partial_2 h(x) = 2(x^1)^2 x^2$$
$$\partial_{11}^2 h(x) = 2(x^2)^2, \quad \partial_{22}^2 h(x) = 2(x^1)^2, \quad \partial_{12}^2 h(x) = 4x^1 x^2. \quad (A.37)$$

The functions associated with f in (A.30) become

$$f_1^1 = f_j^2 = h, \quad \partial_i f_{(1);1}^1 = \partial_i f_{(l);j}^2 = \partial_i h,$$
$$\partial_{i,i'}^2 f_{(1,1);1}^1 = \partial_{i,i'}^2 f_{(l,l');1}^2 = \partial_{ii'}^2 h, \quad (A.38)$$

with all other functions f_j^1, $\partial_i f_{(l);j}^1$ and $\partial_{i,i'}^2 f_{(l,l');j}^1$ being 0.

We also assume the following property for the process X, which is at least two-dimensional:

$$\Delta X_t^1 \, \Delta X_t^2 \; = \; 0 \quad \text{identically}, \tag{A.39}$$

that is, the two components X^1 and X^2 *never jump at the same times*. In this case, the special form of f implies that $f_j * \mu = 0$ and $\overline{U}(f) = 0$ identically, so the result (A.33) is degenerate.

The next result may be considered in view of the convergence rate $1/\Delta_n$ instead of $1/\sqrt{\Delta_n}$ as a "second order" Central Limit Theorem.

Theorem A.10. *[JP, Theorem 15.2.4] Assume (H-2) and the condition (A.39). Let f be the function defined by (A.36). Then for each t, we have the following stable convergence in law:*

$$\frac{1}{\Delta_n} B^n(f, \Delta_n)_t \; \overset{\mathcal{L}-s}{\longrightarrow} \; \widetilde{\mathcal{U}}(f)_t + \overline{C}(f)_t,$$

where $\overline{C}(f)$ is the following two-dimensional process:

$$\overline{C}(f)_t^j = \begin{cases} H_t & \text{if } j = 1 \\ k^2 H_t & \text{if } j = 2, \end{cases} \quad \text{where } H_t = \int_0^t \left(c_s^{11} c_s^{22} + 2(c_s^{12})^2 \right) ds$$

and where $\mathcal{U}(f)$ is defined on an extension of the probability space by the following formula, where the R_n's are as in (A.31):

$$\widetilde{\mathcal{U}}(f)_t = \frac{1}{2} \sum_{n=1}^{\infty} \left(\sum_{j,l,l'=1}^{k} \sum_{i,i'=1}^{2} \partial_{i,i'}^2 f_{(l,l'),j}(\Delta X_{T_n}) R_{n,l-j}^i \, R_{n,l'-j}^{i'} \right) 1_{\{T_n \le t\}}.$$

Moreover, conditionally on $\mathcal{F}$, the process $\mathcal{U}(f)$ has independent increments, with mean function

$$\widetilde{\mathbb{E}}(\widetilde{\mathcal{U}}(f^j, X)_t \mid \mathcal{F}) \; = \; \begin{cases} H_t' & \text{if } j = 1 \\ k^2 H_t' & \text{if } j = 2, \end{cases} \tag{A.40}$$

where $H_t' = \frac{1}{2} \sum_{s \le t} \left((\Delta X_s^1)^2 (c_{s-}^{11} + c_s^{11}) + (\Delta X_s^2)^2 (c_{s-}^{22} + c_s^{22}) \right)$.

Here, $\overline{C}(f)$ plays the role of a drift, since it is $\mathcal{F}$-measurable. The process $\widetilde{\mathcal{U}}(f)$ is of the form (1.87) with $V' = 0$, and with the sequence V_n satisfying (i) of (1.84).

A.3.3   CLTs for the Processes $B'(f, \Delta_n)$ and $\overline{B}'(f, \Delta_n)$

For the CLT associated with Theorem A.8 we again need some preliminary notation for describing the limit. Before this, we describe the class **TF** of test functions f which will be considered. This class looks complicated, because we want to accommodate a number of different situations.

Definition A.11. *A test function in* **TF** *is a possibly multidimensional function on* $(\mathbb{R}^d)^k$, *for an arbitrary integer* $k \geq 1$. *Each of its components is a linear combination of functions of the type*

$$
\begin{aligned}
either \quad &(x_1, \ldots, x_k) \mapsto \textstyle\prod_{j \in I} g_j(x_j) \\
or \quad &(x_1, \ldots, x_k) \mapsto g_1(x_1 + \cdots + x_k),
\end{aligned}
\tag{A.41}
$$

where I *is a non-empty subset of* $\{1, \ldots, k\}$ *and where each* g_j *is a function of the following form:*

$$
g_j(x) = g_j(x^1, \ldots, x^d) = h_j(x) \prod_{i=1}^d |x^i|^{w_{j,i}}, \quad w_{i,j} \geq 0, \quad \sum_{i=1}^d w_{j,i} > 0
$$

(with the convention $0^0 = 1$*), where* h_j *is a* C^2 *function, bounded as well as its first and second partial derivatives, and which is a globally even function on* $\mathbb{R}^d$.

Here, *globally even* means that $h_j(-x) = h_j(x)$ for any $x \in \mathbb{R}^d$. If f is a test function in the above sense, each component is a linear combination of functions of type (A.41), each one of these involving a number of exponents of the form $w_{j,i}$: denoting by $\mathbb{W}$ the family of *all* exponents appearing in at least one of those functions, we then set

$$
\overline{w} = \max(\mathbb{W}), \qquad \underline{w} = \min(w : w \in \mathbb{W}, w > 0).
\tag{A.42}
$$

Note that the functionals $\widehat{C}^n$ and $\widehat{C}^n(k)$ defined before are equal to $B'(f, \Delta_n)$ for functions f in **TF**, as well as the multipowers $\widehat{C}^n([k], \Delta_n)$ of (A.20).

Next, we describe the limiting process. It will be a continuous process of the form (1.87), with $V'' = 0$ (so there is no law η), and we need to describe the process V'. To this end, for any $d \times d$ symmetric nonnegative matrix a we consider a sequence Φ_n of independent $\mathcal{N}(0, a)$ variable on some space $(\Omega'', \mathcal{F}'', \mathbb{P}'')$, and the σ-fields $\mathcal{G}$ and $\mathcal{G}'$, respectively generated by $\Phi_1, \ldots, \Phi_{k-1}$ and $\Phi_1, \ldots, \Phi_k$. Then, with $f^1, \ldots, f^q$ being the components of f, we set

$$R_a(f)^{il} = \sum_{j,j'=0}^{k-1} \mathbb{E}''\Big(\mathbb{E}''\big(f^i(\Phi_{k-j},\dots,\Phi_{2k-j-1}) \mid \mathcal{G}'\big)$$
$$\times \mathbb{E}''\big(f^l(\Phi_{k-j'},\dots,\Phi_{2k-j'-1}) \mid \mathcal{G}'\big)$$
$$-\mathbb{E}''\big(f^i(\Phi_{k-j},\dots,\Phi_{2k-j-1}) \mid \mathcal{G}\big)$$
$$\times \mathbb{E}''\big(f^l(\Phi_{k-j'},\dots,\Phi_{2k-j'-1}) \mid \mathcal{G}\big)\Big)$$

$$\overline{R}_a(f)^{jl} = \tfrac{1}{k}\Big(\mathbb{E}''\big((f^j f^l)(\Phi_1,\dots,\Phi_k)\big)$$
$$-\mathbb{E}''\big(f^j(\Phi_1,\dots,\Phi_k)\big)\,\mathbb{E}''\big(f^l(\Phi_1,\dots,\Phi_k)\big)\Big).$$

(A.43)

With the notation ρ_a used in the previous section, we also have

$$\overline{R}_a(f)^{jl} = \tfrac{1}{k}\big(\rho_a^{\otimes k}(f^j f^l) - \rho_a^{\otimes k}(f^j)\rho_a^{\otimes k}(f^l)\big)$$
$$k=1 \;\Rightarrow\; \overline{R}_a(f)^{jl} = R_a(f)^{jl} = \rho_a(f^j f^l) - \rho_a(f^j)\rho_a(f^l).$$

Both $R_a(f)$ and $\overline{R}_a(f)$ are $q\times q$ symmetric nonnegative matrices, continuous as a function of a (recall that any test function f is continuous with polynomial growth). We can thus find progressively measurable $q\times q$-measurable processes H_t and $\overline{H}_t$ which are square roots of $R_{c_t}(f)$ and $\overline{R}_{c_t}(f)$ respectively. Then we set

$$\mathcal{W}(f)_t = \int_0^t H_s\, dW_s', \qquad \overline{\mathcal{W}}(f)_t = \int_0^t \overline{H}_s\, dW_s', \qquad (A.44)$$

on the product extension $(\widetilde{\Omega}, \widetilde{\mathcal{F}}, \widetilde{\mathbb{P}})$ of $(\Omega,\mathcal{F},\mathbb{P})$ defined by (1.86), and where W' is a q-dimensional Brownian motion on $(\Omega',\mathcal{F}',\mathbb{P}')$. Note that $\mathcal{W}(f)$ and $\overline{\mathcal{W}}(f)$ are continuous locally square-integrable martingales on the extension, with

$$\widetilde{\mathbb{E}}(\mathcal{W}'(f^i)_t\,\mathcal{W}(f^j)_t \mid \mathcal{F}) = \int_0^t R_{c_s}(f)^{ij}\,ds$$
$$\widetilde{\mathbb{E}}(\overline{\mathcal{W}}'(f^i)_t\,\overline{\mathcal{W}}'(f^j)_t \mid \mathcal{F}) = \int_0^t \overline{R}_{c_s}(f)^{ij}\,ds.$$

(A.45)

Remark A.12. *The multipowers $\widehat{C}^n([k],\Delta_n)$ of (A.20) are of particular interest in dimension $d=1$. More generally one can consider the same expression, with $2/k$ substituted with p/k for an arbitrary $p>0$. This corresponds to considering $B'^n(f_{p,k})$ with the test function $f_{k,p}(x_1,\dots,x_k) = \prod_{j=1}^k |x_j|^{p/k}$. It is then worth noticing that the quantities $R_a(f)$ and $\overline{R}_a(f)$ take a simple form (here, a is simply a nonnegative real number):*

$$R_a(f_{p,k}) = \vartheta(k,p)\,a^{p/2},$$
$$\overline{R}_a(f_{k,p}) = \big((m_{2p/k})^k - (m_{p/k})^{2k}\big)a^{p/2},$$

(A.46)

where

$$\vartheta(p,k) = \tfrac{1}{m_{2p/k} - (m_{p/k})^2} \left\{ (m_{2p/k})^{k+1} + (m_{2p/k})^k (m_{p/k})^2 \right.$$
$$\left. - (2k+1)m_{2p/k} (m_{p/k})^{2k} + (2k-1)(m_{p/k})^{2k+2} \right\}.$$

Note that $\vartheta(2,k)$ is the number $\vartheta(k)$ defined in (6.39).

Theorem A.13. *[JP, Theorem 11.2.2] Let f be a q-dimensional test function on $(\mathbb{R}^d)^k$, belonging to the class **TF**, and we associate the notation (A.42). Suppose that X satisfies (K-r) for some $r \in [0,1)$ and also (P) when $\underline{w} \leq 1$.*

(i) If X is continuous (that is, (KC) holds), we have

$$\frac{1}{\sqrt{\Delta_n}} \left(B'(f,\Delta_n)_t - \int_0^t \rho_{c_s}^{\otimes k}(f)\, ds \right) \overset{\mathcal{L}-s}{\Longrightarrow} \mathcal{W}(f) \qquad (A.47)$$

$$\frac{1}{\sqrt{\Delta_n}} \left(\overline{B}'(f,\Delta_n)_t - \frac{1}{k}\int_0^t \rho_{c_s}^{\otimes k}(f)\, ds \right) \overset{\mathcal{L}-s}{\Longrightarrow} \overline{\mathcal{W}}(f), \qquad (A.48)$$

where $\mathcal{W}(f)$ and $\overline{\mathcal{W}}(f)$ are defined in (A.44), and in particular are $\mathcal{F}$-conditionally continuous Gaussian centered martingales with conditional variance-covariances given by (A.45).

(ii) The same is true when X is discontinuous, if $r \leq \underline{w}$ and $\overline{w} < 1$.

The conditions on f are reasonably weak when X is continuous. Otherwise, (K-r) with $r < 1$ is a strong restriction on the degree of activity of the jumps, and the condition $\overline{w} < 1$ is also a very strong restriction on f. The latter can be substantially weakened if we consider the truncated functionals, and the limit is still the same as in the previous theorem:

Theorem A.14. *[JP, Theorem 13.2.1] Let f be a q-dimensional test function on $(\mathbb{R}^d)^k$, belonging to the class **TF**, and with the associated notation (A.42). Let $u_n \asymp \Delta_n^\varpi$ and suppose that X satisfies (P) when $\underline{w} \leq 1$, and that any one of the following three conditions is satisfied:*

- *(KC) holds (so X is continuous) and $0 < \varpi < \frac{1}{2}$.*
- *(K-1) holds and $\underline{w} = \overline{w} = 1$ and $0 < \varpi < \frac{1}{2}$.*
- *(K-r) holds for some $r \in [0,1) \cap [0,\underline{w}]$ and $\frac{1 \vee \overline{w} - 1}{2(1 \vee \overline{w} - r)} < \varpi < \frac{1}{2}$.*

Then we have

$$\frac{1}{\sqrt{\Delta_n}} \left(B'(f,\Delta_n,u_n)_t - \int_0^t \rho_{c_s}^{\otimes k}(f)\, ds \right) \overset{\mathcal{L}-s}{\Longrightarrow} \mathcal{W}(f)$$

with $\mathcal{W}(f)$ as in the previous theorem. Moreover, for any real $\gamma > 0$ we have

$$\frac{1}{\sqrt{\Delta_n}} \left(B'(f,\Delta_n,u_n)_t - B'(f,\Delta_n,\gamma u_n)_t \right) \overset{u.c.p.}{\Longrightarrow} 0, \qquad (A.49)$$

and also, when $f(x_1, \ldots, x_k) = g(x_1 + \cdots + x_k)$,

$$\frac{1}{\sqrt{\Delta_n}} \left(B'(f, \Delta_n, u_n)_t - B'([g, k], \Delta_n, \gamma u_n)_t \right) \overset{u.c.p.}{\Longrightarrow} 0. \qquad (A.50)$$

A.3.4   CLTs for the Quadratic Variation

The CLT associated with the convergence (A.18) does not follow from the previous theorems, but it exists, and it mixes the limits $\mathcal{U} = \mathcal{U}(f)$ and $\mathcal{W} = \mathcal{W}(f)$ in Theorems A.9 and A.13, as given by (A.31) and (A.44) (with $k = 1$ and f the quadratic function with components $f(x)^{jl} = x^j x^l$). These limits use as ingredients the variables of (A.28) and a d^2-dimensional Brownian motion W', all defined on the auxiliary space $(\Omega', \mathcal{F}', \mathbb{P}')$, and with W' being independent of all the other variables. In other words, using our specific form of f, we have with the notation (A.28)

$$\mathcal{U}_t^{ij} = \sum_{q \geq 1} \sum_{l=1}^{d'} \left(\Delta X_{T_q}^i \left(\sqrt{\kappa_q} \, \sigma_{T_q-}^{jl} \Psi_{q-}^l + \sqrt{1-\kappa_q} \, \sigma_{T_q}^{jl} \Psi_{q+}^l \right) \right.$$
$$\left. + \Delta X_{T_q}^j \left(\sqrt{\kappa_q} \, \sigma_{T_q-}^{il} \Psi_{q-}^l + \sqrt{1-\kappa_q} \, \sigma_{T_q}^{il} \Psi_{q+}^l \right) \right) 1_{\{T_q \leq t\}}$$

$$\mathcal{W}_t^{ij} = \sum_{k,l=1}^{d} \int_0^t H_s^{ij,kl} \, dW_s'^{kl},$$

where $\sum_{u,v=1}^d H_s^{ij,uv} H_s^{kl;uv} = c_s^{ik} c_s^{jl} + c_s^{il} c_s^{jk}$. Moreover, conditionally of $\mathcal{F}$ the two processes $\mathcal{U}$ and $\mathcal{W}$ are *independent*, with independent increments and centered, and $\mathcal{W}$ is a Gaussian martingale, as is $\mathcal{U}$ when the two processes X and σ *have no jumps at the same times*. Hence the $\mathcal{F}$-conditional law of $\mathcal{W}$, and that of $\mathcal{U}$ as well when X and σ have no common jumps, is characterized by the (conditional) variances-covariances given by

$$\mathbb{E}(\mathcal{U}_t^{ij} \mathcal{U}_t^{kl} \mid \mathcal{F}) = \tfrac{1}{2} \sum_{s \leq t} \left(\Delta X_s^i \Delta X_s^k (c_{s-}^{jl} + c_s^{jl}) \right.$$
$$+ \Delta X_s^i \Delta X_s^l (c_{s-}^{jk} + c_s^{jk}) + \Delta X_s^j \Delta X_s^k (c_{s-}^{il} + c_s^{il})$$
$$\left. + \Delta X_s^j \Delta X_s^l (c_{s-}^{ik} + c_s^{ik}) \right) \qquad (A.51)$$
$$\mathbb{E}(\mathcal{W}_t^{ij} \mathcal{W}_t^{kl} \mid \mathcal{F}) = \int_0^t \left(c_s^{ik} c_s^{jl} + c_s^{il} c_s^{jk} \right) ds.$$

Theorem A.15. *[JP, Theorem 5.4.2] Under (H-2), and with $\mathcal{U}$ and $\mathcal{W}$ as defined above, we have*

$$\frac{1}{\sqrt{\Delta_n}} \left(\widehat{C}(\Delta_n)_t - [X, X]_{\Delta_n [t/\Delta_n]} \right) \overset{\mathcal{L}-s}{\Longrightarrow} \mathcal{U} + \mathcal{W}.$$

If we want to estimate the continuous part C_t of the quadratic variation $[X, X]_t$, we can use either $\widehat{C}(\Delta_n, u_n)$ or $\widehat{C}([k], \Delta_n)$ as defined by (A.19) and (A.20). We then have a joint CLT for the triple $(\widehat{C}(\Delta_n), \widehat{C}([k], \Delta_n), \widehat{C}(\Delta_n, u_n))$. Since we do not have an "explicit" form for the conditional covariance of the limit in the CLT for $\widehat{C}^n([k], \Delta_n)$, except when $d = 1$, the joint CLT below is given without restriction on d when only $\widehat{C}^n$ and $\widehat{C}^n(u_n-)$ are considered, and for $d = 1$ otherwise.

Theorem A.16. [JP, Theorem 13.2.6] Assume (H-r) for some $r \in [0, 1)$, and let u_n be given by (A.10) with $\frac{1}{2(2-r)} \leq \varpi < \frac{1}{2}$. Then

$$
\begin{pmatrix} \frac{1}{\sqrt{\Delta_n}} (\widehat{C}(\Delta_n)_t - [X, X]_{\Delta_n[t/\Delta_n]}) \\ \frac{1}{\sqrt{\Delta_n}} (\widehat{C}(\Delta_n, u_n)_t - C_t) \end{pmatrix} \xRightarrow{\mathcal{L}-s} \begin{pmatrix} \mathcal{U} + \mathcal{W} \\ \mathcal{W} \end{pmatrix},
$$

where $\mathcal{U}$ and $\mathcal{W}$ are as in Theorem A.15.

When further $d = 1$ and (P) holds, as well as either $k \geq 3$ and (K-2/k), or $k \geq 2$ and (KC) (so X is continuous), we also have

$$
\begin{pmatrix} \frac{1}{\sqrt{\Delta_n}} (\widehat{C}(\Delta_n)_t - [X, X]_{\Delta_n[t/\Delta_n]}) \\ \frac{1}{\sqrt{\Delta_n}} (\widehat{C}(\Delta_n, u_n)_t - C_t) \\ \frac{1}{\sqrt{\Delta_n}} (\widehat{C}([k], \Delta_n)_t - C_t) \end{pmatrix} \xRightarrow{\mathcal{L}-s} \begin{pmatrix} \mathcal{U} + \mathcal{W} \\ \mathcal{W} \\ \mathcal{W}(k) \end{pmatrix},
$$

with $\mathcal{U}$ as above and where the pair $(\mathcal{W}, \mathcal{W}(k))$ is, conditionally on $\mathcal{F}$, independent of $\mathcal{U}$, and a centered continuous Gaussian martingale whose variance-covariance is given by

$$
\begin{aligned}
\widetilde{\mathbb{E}}((\mathcal{W}_t)^2 \mid \mathcal{F}) &= 2 \int_0^t c_s^2 \, ds \\
\widetilde{\mathbb{E}}((\mathcal{W}(k)_t)^2 \mid \mathcal{F}) &= \frac{\vartheta(2,k)}{(m_{2/k})^{2k}} \int_0^t c_s^2 \, ds \\
\widetilde{\mathbb{E}}(\mathcal{W}_t \, \mathcal{W}(k)_t \mid \mathcal{F}) &= \frac{k \, (m_{2+2/k} - m_{2/k})}{m_{2/k}} \int_0^t c_s^2 \, ds.
\end{aligned}
\tag{A.52}
$$

The first line in (A.52) is the same as the last line in (A.51) when $d = 1$, and $\vartheta(2, k) = \vartheta(k)$ is as in (6.39) or (A.46).

A.4   Noise and Pre-averaging: Limit Theorems

In this section we restrict our attention to the one-dimensional case, $d = 1$. We only record the results which are strictly needed in the main part of this book.

A.4.1 Assumptions on Noise and Pre-averaging Schemes

The noise $(\chi_t)_{t \geq 0}$ is a process defined on Ω, and each χ_t is measurable with respect to a σ-field $\mathcal{F}'$ bigger than $\mathcal{F}$, and $\mathbb{P}$ is a probability on $(\Omega, \mathcal{F}')$. The observed variables are

$$Y_i^n = X_{i\Delta_n} + \Delta_n^\eta \chi_{i\Delta_n}, \qquad \text{where } \eta \in \left[0, \frac{1}{2}\right). \qquad (A.53)$$

The assumptions on $(\chi_t)_{t \geq 0}$ are as follows:

Assumption (GN). *Conditionally on $\mathcal{F}$, all variables $(\chi_t : t \geq 0)$ are independent and satisfy*

- $\mathbb{E}(\chi_t \mid \mathcal{F}) = 0.$
- *For all $p > 0$ the process $\mathbb{E}(|\chi_t|^p \mid \mathcal{F})$ is $(\mathcal{F}_t)$-adapted and locally bounded.*
- *The (conditional) variance process $\gamma_t = \mathbb{R}((\chi_t)^2 \mid \mathcal{F})$ is càdlàg.*

We choose integers $k_n \geq 1$ satisfying

$$\begin{array}{c} k_n = \frac{1}{\theta\,\Delta_n^{\eta'}} + o\left(\frac{1}{\Delta_n^{(3\eta'-1)/2}}\right) \quad \text{as } n \to \infty \\ \text{where } \theta > 0, \ \eta' > 0, \ \eta + \eta' \geq \frac{1}{2}, \\ \text{and we set } \theta' = \begin{cases} \theta & \text{if } \eta + \eta' = 1/2 \\ 0 & \text{if } \eta + \eta' > 1/2. \end{cases} \end{array} \qquad (A.54)$$

A *weight function* is a real-valued, not identically vanishing, function g on $\mathbb{R}$, satisfying

$$\begin{array}{l} g \text{ is continuous, null outside } (0,1), \text{ piecewise } C^1 \\ \text{with a piecewise Lipschitz derivative } g\prime. \end{array} \qquad (A.55)$$

For any continuous function h on $\mathbb{R}$, we set

$$\phi_n(h) = \sum_{i=1}^{k_n} h\left(\frac{i}{k_n}\right)^2, \quad \phi_n'(h) = \sum_{i=1}^{k_n} \left(h\left(\frac{i}{k_n}\right) - h\left(\frac{i-1}{k_n}\right)\right)^2,$$
$$\phi(h) = \int_0^1 h(s)^2\, ds,$$

and for any weight function g we have as $n \to \infty$

$$\phi_n(g) = k_n \phi(g) + O(1), \qquad \phi_n'(g) = \frac{1}{k_n} \phi(g') + O\left(\frac{1}{k_n^2}\right). \qquad (A.56)$$

Finally, with our observations and with k_n and the weight function g we associate the following variables (recall that $g(0) = g(1) = 0$, hence

$\sum_{j=1}^{k_n} \left(g\left(\frac{i}{k_n}\right) - g\left(\frac{i-1}{k_n}\right) \right) = 0)$:

$$\overline{Y}_i^n = \sum_{j=1}^{k_n-1} g\left(\tfrac{i}{k_n}\right) \Delta_{i+j-1}^n Y = -\sum_{j=1}^{k_n} \left(g\left(\tfrac{i}{k_n}\right) - g\left(\tfrac{i-1}{k_n}\right) \right) Y_{i+j-2}^n$$

$$\widehat{Y}_i^n = \sum_{j=1}^{k_n} \left(g\left(\tfrac{i}{k_n}\right) - g\left(\tfrac{i-1}{k_n}\right) \right)^2 (\Delta_{i+j-1}^n Y)^2. \tag{A.57}$$

A.4.2   LLNs for Noise

We restrict our attention to a very special kind of test function: polynomials in $\overline{Y}_i^n$ and $\widehat{Y}_i^n$. For each *even* nonnegative integer p (including $p = 0$) we let the sequence $\zeta_{p,l}$ for $l = 0, \ldots, p/2$ be the solution of the following triangular system of linear equations ($C_p^q = \frac{p!}{q!(p-q)!}$ is the binomial coefficient, and m_q is the qth absolute moment of $\mathcal{N}(0,1)$):

$$\zeta_{p,0} = 1$$
$$\sum_{l=0}^j 2^l \, m_{2j-2l} \, C_{p-2l}^{p-2j} \, \zeta_{p,l} = 0, \qquad j = 1, 2, \ldots, \tfrac{p}{2},$$

hence $\zeta_{p,1} = -\frac{1}{2} C_p^2$, and $\zeta_{p,2} = \frac{3}{4} C_p^4$ if $p \geq 4$. We define the function $f_{p,q}$ on $\mathbb{R} \times \mathbb{R}$ by

$$f_{p,q}(x, z) = \sum_{l=0}^{p/2} \zeta_{p,l} \, x^{p-2l} \, z^{l+q}, \tag{A.58}$$

and in particular $f_{0,q}(x, z) = z^q$. The (non-truncated and truncated) processes of interest are

$$B^{\mathrm{noisy}}(p, q; \Delta_n, k_n, g)_t = \tfrac{1}{k_n} \sum_{i=1}^{[t/\Delta_n]-k_n+1} f_{p,q}(\overline{Y}_i^n, \widehat{Y}_i^n), \tag{A.59}$$

$$B^{\mathrm{noisy}}(p, q; \Delta_n, k_n, g; u_n)_t = \tfrac{1}{k_n} \sum_{i=1}^{[t/\Delta_n]-k_n+1} f_{p,q}(\overline{Y}_i^n, \widehat{Y}_i^n) 1_{\{|\overline{Y}_i^n| \leq u_n\}}. \tag{A.60}$$

Since $B^{\mathrm{noisy}}(p, q; \Delta_n, k_n, g)$ equals $(k_n \Delta_n)^{q+p/2-1} V'^n(f_{p/2,q}, g, k_n, Z^n)$ with the notation of [JP], by combining Theorems 16.5.3, 16.6.1 and 16.5.1 of that reference, respectively (recall that $\phi(g^{p/2}) = \int_0^1 g(x)^p \, dx$), plus (A.54) and (A.56), we get

Theorem A.17. *Let X be a semimartingale and assume (GN) for the noise. Let p be an even integer, and assume (A.54).*
(a) If $p \geq 4$ and $\eta' \geq 2 \frac{1-p\eta}{2+p}$, for each $t \geq 0$ we have

$$B^{\mathrm{noisy}}(p, 0; \Delta_n, k_n, g)_t \xrightarrow{\mathbb{P}} \phi(g^{p/2}) \sum_{s < t} |\Delta X_s|^p. \tag{A.61}$$

(b) *Under (H-2), for each $t \geq 0$ we have*

$$B^{\text{noisy}}(2, 0; \Delta_n, k_n, g)_t \xrightarrow{\mathbb{P}} \phi(g) [X, X]_t.$$

(c) *Under (HC), so X is continuous, and with $q \in \mathbb{N}$, we have*

$$(k_n \Delta_n)^{1-p/2-q} B^{\text{noisy}}(p, q; \Delta_n, k_n, g) \tag{A.62}$$
$$\xRightarrow{u.c.p.} m_p \, 2^q \, \phi(g)^{p/2} \, \phi(g')^q \, \theta'^{2q} \int_0^t c_s^{p/2} \, \gamma_s^q \, ds.$$

Finally, we need the behavior of the truncated functionals (A.60) and an analogue of Theorem A.7. For this, and besides k_n satisfying (A.54), one considers another sequence $k_n' \geq 1$ of integers and a sequence $u_n > 0$ of truncation levels, such that

$$k_n'/k_n \to \infty, \quad k_n' \Delta_n \to 0, \quad u_n \asymp \Delta_n^{\varpi} \tag{A.63}$$
$$\text{for some } \varpi \in (0, \tfrac{1-\eta'}{2}).$$

Theorems 16.4.2 and 16.5.4 and Remark 16.5.5 of [JP], plus the fact that in both theorems one may take $\varpi' > 1 - \eta'$, which amounts to no truncation for $\widehat{Y}_i^n$ below, give us the following (note also that ϖ here is $(1 - \eta')\varpi$ in those theorems):

Theorem A.18. *Assume (H-2) and (GN), and also (A.54) and (A.63), and let p be an even integer and q an integer, with $p + 2q \geq 2$.*

(a) If X is continuous (and in other cases, not useful for us, as well), we have

$$(k_n \Delta_n)^{1-p/2-q} B^{\text{noisy}}(p, q; \Delta_n, k_n, g; u_n)$$
$$\xRightarrow{u.c.p.} m_p \, 2^q \, \phi(g)^{p/2} \, \phi(g')^q \, \theta'^{2q} \int_0^t c_s^{p/2} \, \gamma_s^q \, ds.$$

(b) For each $t \geq 0$ we have

$$\frac{1}{k_n^2 \, k_n' \, \Delta_n} \sum_{i=1}^{[t/\Delta_n]-k_n'-k_n+1} |\overline{Y}_i^n|^p \sum_{j=1}^{k_n'} \left((\overline{Y}_{i+j}^n)^2 - \tfrac{1}{2} \widehat{Y}_{i+j}^n \right) \mathbf{1}_{\{|\overline{Y}_{i+j}^n| \leq u_n\}}$$
$$\xrightarrow{\mathbb{P}} \phi(g) \, \phi(g^{p/2}) \sum_{s \leq t} c_s |\Delta X_s|^p,$$

$$\frac{1}{k_n^2 \, k_n' \, \Delta_n} \sum_{i=k_n+k_n'}^{[t/\Delta_n]-k_n+1} |\overline{Y}_i^n|^p \sum_{j=1}^{k_n'} \left((\overline{Y}_{i-j}^n)^2 - \tfrac{1}{2} \widehat{Y}_{i-j}^n \right) \mathbf{1}_{\{|\overline{Y}_{i-j}^n| \leq u_n\}}$$
$$\xrightarrow{\mathbb{P}} \phi(g) \, \phi(g^{p/2}) \sum_{s \leq t} c_{s-} |\Delta X_s|^p,$$

$$\frac{1}{k_n^2 \, k_n' \, \Delta_n} \sum_{i=1}^{[t/\Delta_n]-k_n'-k_n+1} |\overline{Y}_i^n|^p \sum_{j=1}^{k_n'} \widehat{Y}_{i+j}^n \, \mathbf{1}_{\{|\overline{Y}_{i+j}^n| \leq u_n\}}$$
$$\xrightarrow{\mathbb{P}} 2\theta'^2 \phi(g') \, \phi(g^{p/2}) \sum_{s \leq t} \gamma_s |\Delta X_s|^p,$$

$$\frac{1}{k_n^2 \, k_n' \, \Delta_n} \sum_{i=k_n+k_n'}^{[t/\Delta_n]-k_n+1} |\overline{Y}_i^n|^p \sum_{j=1}^{k_n'} \widehat{Y}_{i-j}^n \, \mathbf{1}_{\{|\overline{Y}_{i-j}^n| \leq u_n\}}$$
$$\xrightarrow{\mathbb{P}} 2\theta'^2 \phi(g') \, \phi(g^{p/2}) \sum_{s \leq t} \gamma_{s-} |\Delta X_s|^p.$$

A.4.3   CLTs for Noise

For the CLTs associated with the LLNs in Theorem A.17 one needs quite a lot of notation. For any four bounded functions $g, h, \overline{g}, \overline{h}$ on $\mathbb{R}$ with support in $[0,1]$ we set for all $t \in \mathbb{R}$ and integers p, r with $0 \leq r \leq p$ and p even

$$
\begin{aligned}
&\phi(g, h|t) = \int g(s-t)\, h(s)\, ds \qquad (\text{hence } \phi(g, g|0) = \phi(g)) \\
&\Phi(g, \overline{g}; h, \overline{h})_{p-} = \int_0^1 \phi(g^{p-1}, \overline{g}|t-1)\, \phi(h^{p-1}, \overline{h}|t-1)\, dt \\
&\Phi(g, \overline{g}; h, \overline{h})_{p+} = \int_0^1 \phi(g^{p-1}, \overline{g}|t)\, \phi(h^{p-1}, \overline{h}|t)\, dt \qquad\qquad (A.64) \\
&\overline{\Phi}(g, h; p, r|t) = \sum_{l=0}^{[(p-r)/2]} C_{p-r}^{2l}\, m_{2l}\, m_{p-2l} \\
&\qquad\qquad \times \phi(g)^{r-p/2}\, \phi(g, h|t)^{p-r-2l} \left(\phi(g)\phi(h) - \phi(g, h|t)^2\right)^l.
\end{aligned}
$$

To understand the last formula, consider on some filtered space a Brownian motion W and the two Gaussian processes $L_t^g = \int_0^\infty g(u-t)\, dW_u$ and similarly for L_t^h. They are jointly stationary, centered, and with covariance $\mathbb{E}(L_s^g\, L_{s-t}^h) = \phi(g, h|t)$ (here $t \in \mathbb{R}$, but $s \geq 0$ and $s - t \geq 0$). Then $\overline{\Phi}(g, h; p, r|t) = \mathbb{E}((L_s^g)^r\, (L_{s-t}^h)^{p-r})$, which does not depend on s.

Next, with g, h being two weight functions and with p and r as above and $x, y \geq 0$ we set

$$
\begin{aligned}
a(g, h : p, r|t) &= \sum_{l,j=0}^{p/2} 2^{l+j}\, \zeta_{p,l} \zeta_{p,j}\, \phi(g')^l\, \phi(h')^j \\
&\quad \times \sum_{w=(2r+2j-p)^+}^{(2r)\wedge(p-2l)} C_{p-2l}^{w}\, C_{p-2j}^{2r-w} \\
&\quad \times \overline{\Phi}(g, h; 2r, w|t)\, \overline{\Phi}(g', h'; 2p-2j-2l-2r, p-2l-w|t) \\
A(g, h; p, r) &= \int_{-1}^1 a(g, h : p, r|t)\, dt \\
R_p(g, h; x, y) &= \sum_{r=0}^{p} A(g, h; p, r)\, x^r\, y^{p-r} - 2(m_p)^2\, \phi(g)^{p/2}\, \phi(h)^{p/2}\, x^p.
\end{aligned}
$$

The interpretation of $R(g, h; x, y)$ is as follows: we consider the previous Gaussian processes L^g, L^h, and construct two other processes (globally independent of the others) $L'^{g'}, L'^{h'}$, associated in the same way with the derivatives g' and h' and another independent Brownian motion W'. Then $R_p(g, h; x, y) = \int_{-1}^1 a_t\, dt$, where a_t is the covariance of the two variables $f_p(\sqrt{x}\, L_1^g + \sqrt{y}\, L_1'^{g'}, 2y\phi(g'))$ and $f_p(\sqrt{x}\, L_{1-t}^h + \sqrt{y}\, L_{1-t}'^{h'}, 2y\phi(h'))$, with f_p given by (A.58). In particular, if $g^1, \ldots, g^q$ is a family of weight functions, for all $x, y \geq 0$ the matrix $(R_p(g^i, g^j; x, y))_{i,j}$ is symmetric nonnegative.

Now, we are ready to explain the limits which are found in the CLT. We fix a family $g^1, \ldots, g^q$ of weight functions satisfying (A.55). First, the matrices $\Phi_{p\pm} = (\Phi(g^i, g^i; g^j, g^j)_{p\pm})$ and $\Phi'_{p\pm} = (\Phi(g^i, (g^i)'; g^j, (g^j)')_{p\pm})$ are symmetric nonnegative. We can then associate four processes which also take their values in the set of $q \times q$ symmetric nonnegative matrices (the series defining $\Xi(p)_t$ and $\widetilde{\Xi}(p)_t$ are absolutely convergent because the maps $s \mapsto c_s$ and $s \mapsto \gamma_s$ are locally bounded and $\sum_{s \le t} |\Delta X_s|^{2p-2} < \infty$ because $p \ge 2$):

$$\xi(p)_s = p^2 |\Delta X_s|^{2p-2} (c_{s-} \Phi_{p-} + c_s \Phi_{p+}), \qquad \Xi(p)_t = \sum_{s \le t} \xi(p)_s$$
$$\xi'(p)_s = p^2 |\Delta X_s|^{2p-2} (\gamma_{s-} \Phi'_{p-} + \gamma_s \Phi'_{p+}), \qquad \Xi'(p)_t = \sum_{s \le t} \xi'(p)_s.$$

We consider an auxiliary space $(\Omega', \mathcal{F}', \mathbb{P}')$ supporting two sequences (Ψ_n) and (Ψ'_n) of i.i.d. $\mathcal{N}(0, I_q)$-distributed q-dimensional variables, and a q-dimensional Brownian motion W', all these being independent. We choose a weakly exhausting sequence (T_n) for the jumps of X, as in (A.27). We also choose two processes $\alpha(p)_s$ and $\alpha'(p)_s$ which are $q \times q$-dimensional (measurable) square roots of the processes $\xi(p)_s$ and $\xi'(p)_s$ above, and a (measurable) square root $R_p^{1/2}(x, y)$ of the symmetric non-negative matrix $(R_p(g^i, g^j; x, y))$. Then, on the product extension (1.86), one may define (componentwise) three q-dimensional processes as follows:

$$\mathcal{U}(p)_t^{\text{noisy},j} = \sum_{m \ge 1:\, T_m \le t} \sum_{l=1}^{q} \alpha(p)_{T_m}^{jl} \Psi_m^l$$
$$\mathcal{U}'(p)_t^{\text{noisy},j} = \sum_{m \ge 1:\, T_m \le t} \sum_{l=1}^{q} \widetilde{\alpha}(p)_{T_m}^{'jl} \Psi_m^{'l}$$
$$\mathcal{W}(p)_t^{\text{noisy},j} = \sum_{l=1}^{q} \int_0^t R_p^{1/2}(c_s, \theta'^2 \gamma_s)^{jl} \, dW_s^{''l}.$$

These depend on p, but also implicitly on the weight functions g^j. They have the form (1.87), the first two being purely discontinuous, and the last being continuous. Conditionally on $\mathcal{F}$, they are independent, centered Gaussian martingales, with the following (conditional) covariances:

$$\widetilde{E}(\mathcal{U}(p)_t^{\text{noisy},j} \mathcal{U}(p)_t^{\text{noisy},l} \mid \mathcal{F}) = \Xi(p)_t^{jl}$$
$$\widetilde{E}(\mathcal{U}'(p)_t^{\text{noisy},j} \mathcal{U}'(p)_t^{\text{noisy},l} \mid \mathcal{F}) = \Xi'(p)_t^{jl}$$
$$\widetilde{E}(\mathcal{W}(p)_t^{\text{noisy},j} \mathcal{W}(p)_t^{\text{noisy},l} \mid \mathcal{F}) = \int_0^t R_p(g^j, g^l; c_s, \theta'^2 \gamma_s) \, ds.$$

The following result is a combination of Theorems 16.5.6 and 16.5.7 of [JP] (warning: the notation is slightly different, for example p here is $2p$ there; we also have a single p here instead of a family $p_1, \ldots, p_q$), plus (A.54). Below, all previous notation is in force.

Theorem A.19. *Assume (GN) and (A.54). Let $p \ge 2$ be an even integer, and let $g^1, \ldots, g^q$ be q weight functions satisfying (A.55).*

(a) Under (H-2) and if $p \ge 4$ and If $\eta' > \frac{3 - 2p\eta}{3 + p} \vee \frac{1}{3}$, for each $t > 0$ we have the following stable convergence in law:

$$\frac{1}{\Delta_n^{(1-\eta')/2}} \left(B^{\text{noisy}}(p, 0, \Delta_n, k_n, g^j)_t - \phi((g^j)^{p/2} \sum_{s \le t} |\Delta X_s|^p) \right)_{1 \le j \le q}$$
$$\xrightarrow{\mathcal{L}-s} \frac{1}{\sqrt{\theta}} \left(\mathcal{U}(p)_t^{\text{noisy}} + \theta' \mathcal{U}'(p)_t^{\text{noisy}} \right).$$

b) Under (KC) (so X is continuous) and $\eta' > \frac{1}{3}$, we have the (following) functional stable convergence in law:

$$\frac{1}{\Delta_n^{(1-\eta')/2}} \Big((k_n \Delta_n)^{1-p/2} B^{\text{noisy}}(p, 0, \Delta_n, k_n, g^j)_t$$
$$- m_p \phi(g^j)^{p/2} \int_0^t c_s^{p/2} ds \Big)_{1 \leq j \leq q}$$
$$\overset{\mathcal{L}-s}{\Longrightarrow} \frac{1}{\sqrt{\theta}} \mathcal{W}(p)^{\text{noisy}}.$$

This theorem clearly distinguishes between the continuous and the discontinuous cases, the latter holding when $p \geq 4$ only. But, as in Theorem A.16, when $p = 2$ we still have a CLT which mixes the two kinds of limits above:

Theorem A.20. *[JP, Theorem 16.6.2] Assume (H-2), (GN), (A.54) and $\eta' > \frac{1}{3}$. Let g be a weight function satisfying (A.55). Then for each $t > 0$ we have the following stable convergence in law:*

$$\frac{1}{\Delta_n^{(1-\eta')/2}} \Big(B^{\text{noisy}}(p, 0; \Delta_n, k_n, g)_t - \phi(g) [X, X]_t \Big)$$
$$\overset{\mathcal{L}-s}{\Longrightarrow} \frac{1}{\sqrt{\theta}} (\mathcal{U}(2)_t^{\text{noisy}} + \theta' \mathcal{U}'(2)_t^{\text{noisy}} + \mathcal{W}(2)_t^{\text{noisy}}). \tag{A.65}$$

A.5 Localization and Strengthened Assumptions

The results recalled above, both LLNs and CLTs, are proved under strengthened assumptions first, and extended to the *ad hoc* assumptions by a procedure called *localization*. This localization procedure has been used many times in the literature and it is fully described in Subsection 4.4.1 of [JP] (the following, inconsequential, correction is needed on page 117: in Assumption 4.4.7 one should require $\|\Delta X_t(\omega)\| \leq A$ instead of $\|X_t(\omega)\| \leq A$). The same procedure will also be used, when necessary, in the proofs given in the Appendix B, and will shortly be refereed to, without further explanation, as follows: "by the localization procedure, we can use the strengthened assumptions..."

Now, we describe below these strengthened assumptions, which bear the same names as the original ones, preceded by the letter S. They are in fact the original assumptions, *plus* a boundedness property for some of the ingredients. The list is as follows:

Assumption (SH-r). *We have (H-r), and the processes b and σ are bounded, and $\|\delta(\omega, t, z)\|^r \leq J(z)$ for all (ω, t, z), where J is a bounded function satisfying $\int J(z) \lambda(dz) < \infty$.*

Assumption (SK-r). *We have (K-r) and (SH-r) and the process σ satisfies (SH-2), and further $\sup(\|\widehat{b}'_t(\omega)\| : \omega \in \Omega, t \leq S(\omega)) < \infty$ (with the notation (A.4), the latter condition being implied by the others when $r \leq 1$).*

Assumption (SKC). *We have (SK-0) and the process X is continuous.*

Assumption (SKCC). *We have (SKC), the process σ is continuous, and $b^{(\sigma)}$ is càdlàg or càglàd.*

Assumption (SP). *There is $\varepsilon > 0$ such that for all $\omega \in \Omega$ and $x \in \mathbb{R}^d$ we have $x^* c_t(\omega) x \geq \varepsilon\|x\|^2$ if $t \geq 0$ and $x^* c_{t-}(\omega) x \geq \varepsilon\|x\|^2$ if $t > 0$.*

Assumption (SGN). *We have (GN) and the conditional moments $\mathbb{E}(|\chi_t|^p \mid \mathcal{F})$ are bounded for all p.*

An important property is that, under (SH-2), we may rewrite (A.2) as

$$X_t = X_0 + \int_0^t \overline{b}_s \, ds + \int_0^t \sigma_s \, dW_s + \delta * (\underline{p} - \underline{q})_t, \qquad (A.66)$$

where $\overline{b}_t = b_t + \int_{\{\|\delta(t,z)\|>1\}} \delta(t,z) \lambda(dz)$ is again bounded. Under (SH-1) we have (A.6) and b'_t is bounded.

Remark A.21. *In this book, a process H is called locally bounded if $|H_s| \leq n$ for all $0 < s \leq S_n$, where S_n is a sequence of stopping times increasing to infinity, and this tells us nothing about the initial variable H_0; it is more common in the literature to call H locally bounded if it satisfies $|H_s| \leq a_n$ for all $0 \leq s \leq S_n$ with S_n as above and with constants a_n (so then $|H_0| \leq a_1$). However, when the specific value H_0 is irrelevant, the two notions coincide, because we can replace the original H_0 by $H_0 = 0$. This explains why we can for example replace (H-r) by (SH-r) (by localization), since the value of b at any specific time is irrelevant and can be arbitrarily set to 0.*

Finally, we end this appendix with a few estimates for the increments of the processes X and the volatility σ, under these strengthened assumptions. We let T be a finite stopping time and $t > 0$. We also have an arbitrary exponent $p > 0$, and the constant K below (varying from line to line) depends on the various bounds appearing in the relevant strengthened assumptions, and on p as well.

First, we assume (SH-2). We then have by (2.1.44) of [JP]:

$$\mathbb{E}\big(\sup_{s\leq t}\|X_{T+s}-X_T\|^p \mid \mathcal{F}_T\big) \leq \begin{cases} K\,t^{p/2} & \text{if } X \text{ is continuous} \\ K\,t^{1\wedge(p/2)} & \text{otherwise.} \end{cases} \tag{A.67}$$

In the same way, under (SK-2),

$$\mathbb{E}\big(\sup_{s\leq t}\|\sigma_{T+s}-\sigma_T\|^p \mid \mathcal{F}_T\big) \leq \begin{cases} K\,t^{p/2} & \text{if } \sigma \text{ is continuous} \\ K\,t^{1\wedge(p/2)} & \text{otherwise.} \end{cases} \tag{A.68}$$

Next, Lemmas 2.1.4–2.1.7 of [JP] give us the following. Let $\alpha(q)$, $\alpha(q,y)$, $\alpha'(q)$ and $\alpha''(q)$ be (non-random, possibly infinite) numbers such that

$$\begin{aligned} &\int_{\{\|\delta(\omega,t,z)\|\leq y\}}\|\delta(\omega,t,z)\|^q\lambda(dz) \leq \alpha(q,y), \\ &\alpha(q)=\alpha(q,\infty) \\ &\int\big(\|\delta(\omega,t,z)\|^q \wedge \|\delta(\omega,t,z)\|\big)\,\lambda(dz) \leq \alpha'(q) \\ &\int\big(\|\delta(\omega,t,z)\|^q \wedge 1\big)\lambda(dz) \leq \alpha''(q) \end{aligned} \tag{A.69}$$

identically. Let also H be a predictable process. Then, if $\alpha(2)<\infty$ and $\int_0^t H_s^2\,ds<\infty$ for all t, the process $Y=(H\delta)*(\underline{p}-\underline{q})$ is well defined (it is a square-integrable martingale) and satisfies

$$\begin{aligned} &\mathbb{E}\big(\sup_{s\leq t}\|Y_{T+s}-Y_T\|^p \mid \mathcal{F}_T\big) \\ &\leq \begin{cases} K\alpha(p)\mathbb{E}\big(\int_T^{T+t}|H_s|^p ds \mid \mathcal{F}_T\big) & \text{if } 1\leq p\leq 2 \\ K\big(\alpha(p)+t^{p/2-1}\alpha(2)^{p/2}\big)\mathbb{E}\big(\int_T^{T+t}|H_s|^p ds \mid \mathcal{F}_T\big) & \text{if } p\geq 2, \end{cases} \end{aligned} \tag{A.70}$$

and the process $Z=\delta*(\underline{p}-\underline{q})$, when $r\in[1,2]$ and $\chi\in(0,1/r]$, satisfies

$$p\geq r \quad\Rightarrow\quad \begin{cases} \mathbb{E}\big(\sup_{s\leq t}\big(\frac{\|Z_{T+s}-Z_T\|}{t^\chi}\wedge 1\big)^p \mid \mathcal{F}_T\big) \\ \leq K\,t^{1-\chi r}\big(\alpha(r,t^{\frac{\chi}{2}})+t^{\frac{\chi(r-1)}{2}}\alpha'(r)\big). \end{cases} \tag{A.71}$$

When $\alpha(1)<\infty$ and $\int_0^t|H_s|\,ds<\infty$ for all t, the process $Y=(H\delta)*\underline{p}$ is well defined and satisfies

$$\begin{aligned} &\mathbb{E}\big(\sup_{s\leq t}\|Y_{T+s}-Y_T\|^p \mid \mathcal{F}_T\big) \\ &\leq \begin{cases} K\alpha(p)\mathbb{E}\big(\int_T^{T+t}|H_s|^p ds \mid \mathcal{F}_T\big) & \text{if } 0<p\leq 1 \\ K\big(\alpha(p)+t^{p-1}\alpha(1)^p\big)\mathbb{E}\big(\int_T^{T+t}|H_s|^p ds \mid \mathcal{F}_T\big) & \text{if } p\geq 1, \end{cases} \end{aligned} \tag{A.72}$$

and the process $Z=\delta*\underline{p}$, when $r\in[0,1]$ and $\chi\in(0,1/r]$, satisfies

$$p\geq r \quad\Rightarrow\quad \begin{cases} \mathbb{E}\big(\sup_{s\leq t}\big(\frac{\|Z_{T+s}-Z_T\|}{t^\chi}\wedge 1\big)^p \mid \mathcal{F}_T\big) \\ \leq K\,t^{1-\chi r}\big(\alpha(r,t^{\frac{\chi}{2}})+t^{\frac{\chi r}{2}}\alpha''(r)\big). \end{cases} \tag{A.73}$$

The previous estimates yield, if $|\delta(\omega, t, z)|^r \leq J(z)$ with $[0, 2]$, and if $w > 0$, that the process Z equal to $(\delta 1_{\{J \leq w\}}) * (p - q)$ when $r > 1$ and to $(\delta 1_{\{J \leq w\}}) * p$ when $r \leq 1$ satisfies

$$p \geq r, \ t \leq w^r \quad \Rightarrow \quad \begin{cases} \mathbb{E}\big(\sup_{s \leq t} \|Z_{T+s} - Z_T\|^p \mid \mathcal{F}_T\big) \\ \qquad \leq \ K \, t \, w^{p-r} \, (\alpha \vee \alpha^p). \end{cases} \tag{A.74}$$

In the same setting, but with $w = \infty$ above in the definition of Z, Corollary 2.1.9 of [JP] gives us, with ϕ a function depending on J, r, p but not on δ and satisfying $\phi(t) \to 0$ as $t \to 0$,

$$\left.\begin{array}{c} p \geq r, \ t \leq 1, \\ 0 < \chi < \frac{1}{r} \end{array}\right\} \quad \Rightarrow \quad \begin{cases} \mathbb{E}\big(\sup_{s \leq t} \big(\frac{\|Z_{T+s} - Z_T\|}{t^\chi} \wedge 1\big)^p \mid \mathcal{F}_T\big) \\ \qquad \leq \ K \, t^{1 - \chi r} \, \phi(t). \end{cases} \tag{A.75}$$

It is sometimes useful to extend these inequalities to stopping times T with respect to a bigger filtration. Below, we consider a measurable subset A of E, and p^A denotes the restriction of p to the set $\mathbb{R}_+ \times A$. Then we introduce two σ-fields and two filtrations on Ω, as follows:

- $\mathcal{H}^W = \sigma(W_t : t \geq 0), \quad \mathcal{H}^A = \sigma(p^A(D) : D \in \mathcal{R}_+ \otimes \mathcal{E})$
- $(\mathcal{G}_t^A)$ is the smallest filtration containing $(\mathcal{F}_t)$
  and with $\mathcal{H}^A \subset \mathcal{G}_0^A$ $\hspace{3cm}$ (A.76)
- $(\mathcal{G}_t^{A,W})$ is the smallest filtration containing $(\mathcal{G}_t^A)$
  and with $\mathcal{H}^W \subset \mathcal{G}_0^{A,W}$.

Then Proposition 2.19 of [JP] yields, with T any stopping time relative to the relevant extended filtration,

$$\delta(\omega, s, x) = 0 \ \text{ if } T < s \leq T + t, \ z \in A \quad \Rightarrow \\ \begin{cases} \bullet \ (\text{A.67}) \text{ holds with } (\mathcal{G}_t^A) \text{ instead of } (\mathcal{F}_t) \\ \bullet \ (\text{A.70}), (\text{A.71}), (\text{A.72}), (\text{A.73}), (\text{A.74}) \\ \quad \text{and (A.75) hold with } (\mathcal{G}_t^{A,W}) \text{ instead of } (\mathcal{F}_t). \end{cases} \tag{A.77}$$

Analogously, when (SK-2) holds, and with the notation δ^σ of (A.3), we have

$$\delta^\sigma(\omega, s, x) = 0 \ \text{ if } T < s \leq T + t, \ z \in A \\ \Rightarrow (\text{A.68}) \text{ holds with } (\mathcal{G}_t^A) \text{ instead of } (\mathcal{F}_t). \tag{A.78}$$

Our last estimates are in the presence of noise, under Assumptions (SH-2) and (SGN) and (A.53). Then, with the notation (A.57) we have, by Lemma 16.4.3 of [JP] (those are quite elementary estimates, close to (A.67))

$$\mathbb{E}(|\overline{Y}_i^n|^2) \leq K \, k_n \Delta_n, \qquad \mathbb{E}(|\widehat{Y}_i^n|^p) \leq K (k_n \Delta_n)^p. \tag{A.79}$$

Appendix B

Miscellaneous Proofs

We now provide the proof of many results left unproven in the main text. Some are more or less reproduced from published papers, most with improvements and quite a few are new. This is not to say that *all* results stated in this book are given a full proof (either in the main text or below). The choice of giving a proof or not is of course arbitrary, and our choice certainly reflects our preferences but is also motivated by our concern about writing a self-contained book. In a field such as this, and with the wish of describing or at least mentioning many different methods, a totally self-contained book is virtually impossible to write, but we tried to be as self-contained as possible. Here again, we abbreviate the reference Jacod and Protter (2011) as [JP].

B.1 Proofs for Chapter 5

B.1.1 Proofs for Sections 5.2 and 5.3

Proof of Theorem 5.8. Here we consider one-dimensional Lévy processes with characteristic (b, c, F), with F satisfying (5.11), and for simplicity we omit the index $^{(+)}$ stressing that this condition, which we recall for the reader's convenience, concerns positive jumps only:

$$F(dx) = \widetilde{F}(dx) + \sum_{i=1}^{\infty} \frac{\beta_i \, a_i}{x^{1+\beta_i}} \, 1_{(0,\eta]}(x) \, dx, \quad \text{where } \eta > 0 \text{ and}$$

(i) $0 \leq \beta_{i+1} \leq \beta_i < 2, \quad \beta_i > 0 \Rightarrow \beta_i > \beta_{i+1}, \quad \lim_{i \to \infty} \beta_i = 0$

(ii) $a_i > 0 \iff \beta_i > 0$ (B.1)

(iii) $0 < \sum_{i=1}^{\infty} a_i < \infty$

(iv) $\widetilde{F}$ is a Lévy measure supported by $(0, \eta]^c$.

We fix the time horizon $T > 0$ and observe the paths $t \mapsto X_t$ over the interval $[0, T]$.

(i) For the first claim, and in view of Theorem 5.2, we need to show the following property: let (b, c, F) and (b', c', F') be two characteristic triples such that F and F' satisfy (B.1) with $(a_i, \beta_i, \eta, \widetilde{F})$ and $(a'_i, \beta'_i, \eta', \widetilde{F}')$, respectively. We also set

$$j = \inf \left(i \geq 1 : (\beta_i, a_i) \neq (\beta'_i, a'_i) \right) \tag{B.2}$$

and let $\mathbb{P}_{(b,c,F)|\mathcal{F}_t}$ be the restriction to $\mathcal{F}_t$ of the unique measure on the canonical space $(\Omega, \mathcal{F}, (\mathcal{F}_t)_{t \geq 0})$ under which the canonical process is Lévy with characteristic triple (b, c, F). Then we need to prove that, where $\mathbb{P} \perp \mathbb{Q}$ denotes mutual singularity,

$$\beta_j \geq \frac{\beta_1}{2} \quad \Rightarrow \quad \mathbb{P}_{(b,c,F)|\mathcal{F}_T} \perp \mathbb{P}_{(b',c',F')|\mathcal{F}_T}. \tag{B.3}$$

Upon exchanging (b, c, F) and (b', c', F') if necessary, we can assume that

$$\beta_1 > 0 \quad \text{(hence } a_1 > 0\text{)},$$
$$\text{and either } \beta_j > \beta'_j, \quad \text{or} \quad \beta_j = \beta'_j \text{ and } a_j > a'_j. \tag{B.4}$$

Upon incorporating the restriction of F to $(\eta', \eta]$ into $\widetilde{F}$ if $\eta' < \eta$, or the restriction of F' to $(\eta, \eta']$ into $\widetilde{F}'$ if $\eta' > \eta$, it is no restriction to suppose $\eta = \eta'$. Set

$$\widehat{F}(dx) = \sum_{i=1}^{\infty} \frac{\beta_i a_i}{x^{1+\beta_i}} 1_{(0,\eta]}(x) \, dx, \quad \widehat{F}'(dx) = \sum_{i=1}^{\infty} \frac{\beta'_i a'_i}{x^{1+\beta'_i}} 1_{(0,\eta]}(x) \, dx$$

$$H(x) = \sum_{i=1}^{j-1} \frac{\beta_i a_i}{x^{1+\beta_i}} 1_{(0,\eta]}(x), \quad G(x) = \sum_{i=j}^{\infty} \frac{\beta_i a_i}{x^{1+\beta_i}} 1_{(0,\eta]}(x),$$
$$G'(x) = \sum_{i=j}^{\infty} \frac{\beta'_i a'_i}{x^{1+\beta'_i}} 1_{(0,\eta]}(x).$$

If $g = H + G$ and $g' = H + G'$ and $f = g'/g$ (with the convention $\frac{0}{0} = 1$), we have $\widehat{F}' = f \bullet \widehat{F}$. Then $f - 1 = \frac{G'-G}{g}$ on $(0, \eta)$, and

$$G(x) - G'(x) = \frac{\beta_j a_j}{x^{1+\beta_j}} \left(1 - \frac{\beta'_j a'_j}{\beta_j a_j} x^{\beta_j - \beta'_j} + \sum_{i=j+1}^{\infty} \frac{\beta_i a_i}{\beta_j a_j} x^{\beta_j - \beta_i} \right.$$
$$\left. - \sum_{i=j+1}^{\infty} \frac{\beta'_i a'_i}{\beta_j a_j} x^{\beta_j - \beta'_i} \right) 1_{(0,\eta]}(x).$$

Conditions (ii), (iii) and (iv) of (B.1) and (B.4) imply, for some constants $A_+ > A_- > 0$ and $\varepsilon \in (0, \eta]$,

$$\frac{A_-}{x^{1+\beta_1}} 1_{(0,\eta]}(x) \leq g(x) \leq \frac{A_+}{x^{1+\beta_1}} 1_{(0,\eta]}(x)$$
$$A_- x^{\beta_1 - \beta_j} 1_{(0,\varepsilon]}(x) \leq |f(x) - 1| \leq A_+ x^{\beta_1 - \beta_j} 1_{(0,\eta]}(x). \tag{B.5}$$

We now use the singularity criterion given in Theorem 5.6, and the notation therein, in particular the numbers $\alpha(F, F')$. We have

$$\alpha(F, F') \geq \alpha(\widehat{F}, \widehat{F}') = \int_0^\eta g(x)\big(|f(x) - 1| \wedge |f(x) - 1|^2\big)\, dx$$
$$\geq \int_0^\varepsilon \frac{A^2}{x^{1+\beta_2}} \wedge \frac{A^3}{x^{1+2\beta_j-\beta_1}}\, dx,$$

and the last integral is infinite when $\beta_j \geq \beta_1/2$, hence (B.3) follows.

(ii) For the second claim, and again because of Theorem 5.2, it is enough to show the following property: letting (b, c, F) be as above, and assuming the existence of a j such that $0 < \beta_j < \beta_1/2$, one can find $b' \in \mathbb{R}$ and a Lévy measure F' satisfying (B.1) with some $(a'_i, \beta'_i, \eta', \widetilde{F}')$, such that $(a'_i, \beta'_i) = (a_i, \beta_i)$ for all $i < j$ and $(a'_j, \beta'_j) \neq (a_j, \beta_j)$, and such that

$$\mathbb{P}_{(b,c,F)|\mathcal{F}_T} \not\perp \mathbb{P}_{(b',c,F')|\mathcal{F}_T}. \tag{B.6}$$

To this aim, we take for F' the measure given by (B.1) with the same η, $\widetilde{F}$, and with $(a'_i, \beta'_i) = (a_i, \beta_i)$ for all $i \neq j$, whereas either $\beta'(j)$ is arbitrary in (β_{j+1}, β_j) and $a'_j > 0$ is arbitrary, or $\beta'(j) = \beta_j$ and a'_j is arbitrary in $(0, a_j)$. Then, with the notation of the first part of the proof, we have (B.2), (B.4) and (B.5), and also $F' = f \bullet F$, so

$$\alpha'(F, F') = \int_0^\eta x\, |f(x) - 1|\, g(x)\, dx \leq A_+^2 \int_0^\eta x^{-\beta_j}\, dx,$$

which is finite because $\beta_j < \beta_1/2 < 1$. Therefore the number $b' = b - \int_0^{\eta \wedge 1} x(f(x) - 1)g(x)\, dx$ is well defined. The two triples (b, c, F) and (b', c, F') satisfy the first and the last three properties in (5.8), whereas (B.5) yields

$$\alpha(F, F') = \int_0^\eta (|f(x) - 1|^2 \wedge |f(x) - 1|)g(x)dx \leq \int_0^\eta \frac{A_+^3}{x^{1+2\beta_j-\beta_1}}dx,$$

which is finite because $\beta_j < \beta_1/2$. Then all conditions in (5.8) are satisfied, and we have (B.6). $\qquad\square$

Proof of Theorem 5.13. We let X and X' be two d-dimensional semimartingales on $(\Omega, \mathcal{F}, \mathbb{P})$ and $(\Omega', \mathcal{F}', \mathbb{P}')$, respectively, with second characteristics C and C'. Consider the d^2-dimensional processes $V(n)$ with components

$$V(n)_t^{jl} = \sum_{i \geq 1} \left(X_{T(n,i)\wedge t}^j - X_{T(n,i-1)\wedge t}^j\right)\left(X_{T(n,i)\wedge t}^l - X_{T(n,i-1)\wedge t}^l\right).$$

By Theorem 1.14 we have $V(n) \overset{\text{u.c.p.}}{\Longrightarrow} V$, where the components of V are $V^{jl} = [X^j, X^l]$, and thus $(X, V(n)) \overset{\text{u.c.p.}}{\Longrightarrow} (X, V)$ also. Then Proposition VI.6.37 of Jacod and Shiryaev (2003) yields that the discretized versions satisfy $(X^{(n)}, V(n)^{(n)}) \overset{\mathbb{P}}{\Longrightarrow} (X, V)$ (convergence in probability for the Skorokhod topology), and where $V(n)^{(n)}$ is the discretized process associated with $V(n)$ by (5.14). Set

$$
\begin{aligned}
y \in \mathbb{R}_+ &\mapsto \phi(y) = (y-1)^+ \wedge 1, \\
x \in \mathbb{R}^d, \ u > 0 &\mapsto \phi_u(x) = \phi(\|x\|/u)
\end{aligned}
\tag{B.7}
$$

and, for any integer $m \geq 1$,

$$
\begin{aligned}
Z(m)^n_t &= V(n)^{(n)}_t - \sum_{s \leq t} \phi_{1/m}(\Delta X^{(n)}_s) \Delta V(n)^{(n)}_s, \\
Z(m)_t &= V_t - \sum_{s \leq t} \phi_{1/m}(\Delta X_s) \Delta V_s.
\end{aligned}
$$

Since $\phi_{1/m}$ vanishes on a neighborhood of 0, another property of the Skorokhod topology, see for example Corollary VI.2.28 in Jacod and Shiryaev (2003), allows us to deduce from $(X^{(n)}, V(n)^{(n)}) \overset{\mathbb{P}}{\Longrightarrow} (X, V)$ that $Z(m)^n \overset{\mathbb{P}}{\Longrightarrow} Z(m)$ for each fixed m. On the other hand, $\phi_{1/m}$ converges to the indicator function of the singleton $\{0\}$, hence by (1.56) we have

$$
Z(m)^{jl}_t = C^{jl}_t + \sum_{s \leq t} \Delta X^j_s \Delta X^l_s \left(1 - \phi_{1/m}(\Delta X_s)\right) \ \rightarrow \ C^{jl}_t \quad \text{as } m \to \infty
$$

where the convergence holds locally uniformly in t, hence a fortiori for the Skorokhod topology. The same properties hold for X', with C' and the similar processes $Z'(m)^n, Z'(m)$. Now, we recall a well known fact: if $U_n(m), U(m), U$ and $U'_n(m), U'(m), U'$ are random variables on $(\Omega, \mathcal{F}, \mathbb{P})$ and $(\Omega', \mathcal{F}', \ \mathbb{P}')$ respectively, with values in a metric space E, then

$$
\left\{
\begin{aligned}
&\bullet \ U(m) \overset{\mathbb{P}}{\longrightarrow} U \text{ and } U'(m) \overset{\mathbb{P}'}{\longrightarrow} U' \text{ as } m \to \infty, \\
&\bullet \ U_n(m) \overset{\mathbb{P}}{\longrightarrow} U(m) \text{ and } U'_n(m) \overset{\mathbb{P}'}{\longrightarrow} U'(m) \\
&\quad \text{as } n \to \infty \text{ for each } m, \\
&\Longrightarrow \ \text{there is a sequence } m_n \text{ such that} \\
&\qquad U_n(m_n) \overset{\mathbb{P}}{\longrightarrow} U \text{ and } U'(m_n) \overset{\mathbb{P}'}{\longrightarrow} U'.
\end{aligned}
\right.
\tag{B.8}
$$

Applying this with $U_n(m) = Z(m)^n$, $U(m) = Z(m)$ and $U = C$, which take their values in $\mathbb{D}^{d^2}$, and with the analogous processes related with X', we deduce the existence of a sequence m_n such that $Z(m_n)^n \overset{\mathbb{P}}{\Longrightarrow} C$ and $Z'(m_n)^n \overset{\mathbb{P}'}{\Longrightarrow} C'$. If $t_n = \sup(T(n,i) : i \geq 0, T(n,i) \leq t)$, and because C and C' are continuous in time, we deduce $Z(m_n)^n_{t_n} \overset{\mathbb{P}}{\longrightarrow} C_t$ and $Z'(m_n)^n_{t_n} \overset{\mathbb{P}'}{\longrightarrow} C'_t$. Observing that $Z(m_n)^n_{t_n} = G_n(X^{(n)})$ and $Z'(m_n)^n_{t_n} = G_n(X'^{(n)})$ for a suitable $\mathcal{D}^d_T$-measurable function G_n on $\mathbb{D}^d$ when $t \leq T$, we deduce the claim. $\qquad\qquad\square$

Proof of Theorem 5.14. We use the notation and assumptions of the previous proof, and assume for example that the spot volatilities c_t and c_t' are right-continuous, and we take $t \in [0, T]$. What precedes implies that $\frac{1}{s} (Z(m_n)^n_{(t+s)_n} - Z(m_n)^n_{t_n}) \xrightarrow{\mathbb{P}} \frac{1}{s} (C_{t+s} - C_t)$ as $n \to \infty$, for any $s > 0$, whereas $\frac{1}{s} (C_{t+s} - C_t) \to c_t$ as $s \to 0$. The same holds for the process X' and c_t', with the same sequence m_n. So again, one can find a sequence s_n such that $\frac{1}{s_n} (Z(m_n)^n_{(t+s_n)_n} - Z(m_n)^n_{t_n}) \xrightarrow{\mathbb{P}} c_t$ and $\frac{1}{s_n} (Z'(m_n)^n_{(t+s_n)_n} - Z'(m_n)^n_{t_n}) \xrightarrow{\mathbb{P}} c_t'$, which yields the result. □

Proof of Theorem 5.16. When $p > 2$, and when the sampling scheme is a regular scheme, the result is an obvious consequence of Theorem A.1 in Appendix A, which in addition gives proper identifiability (and proper identifiability could also be proved when $p \leq 2$). However, below we give the proof for an arbitrary (non-random) scheme $\mathcal{T}$, and for any $p > 0$.

We introduce some notation, unnecessarily complicated for the present proof but which will be useful for the proof of the next results. Let X and X' be two semimartingales, defined on the spaces $(\Omega, \mathcal{F}, \mathbb{P})$ and $(\Omega', \mathcal{F}', \mathbb{P}')$. Let g be an increasing continuous function on $\mathbb{R}_+$, with $g(x) = x$ for all $x \in [0, \eta]$ and some $\eta > 0$. This function does not show in the notation, and will be specified later. With the notation ϕ_u of (B.7), for all integers $m \geq 1$ and reals $t \geq s \geq 0$ we define the following functions on the Skorokhod space $\mathbb{D}^d$:

$$\overline{A}(p)_{s,t}(x) = \sum_{r \in (s,t]} g(\|\Delta x(r)\|)^p,$$
$$\overline{A}(p, m)_{s,t}(x) = \sum_{r \in (s,t]} g(\|\Delta x(r)\|)^p \, \phi_{1/m}(\Delta x(r)).$$

In particular, when $g(x) = x$ we see that $A(p)_t = \overline{A}(p)_t(X)$ (composition of mappings, if we consider X as a mapping from Ω into $\mathbb{D}^d$). The reason for introducing $\overline{A}(p)_{s,t}$ for all $t \geq s \geq 0$ and not simply $\overline{A}(p)_{0,t}$ for $t \geq 0$ is that the equality $\overline{A}(p)_{s,t} = \overline{A}(p)_{0,t} - \overline{A}(p)_{0,s}$ obviously holds if $\overline{A}(p)_{0,s} < \infty$, but is meaningless otherwise. We also associate with t the sequence $t_n = \inf(T(n, i) : i \geq 0, T(n, i) \geq t)$, and analogously the sequence s_n with s (note that t_n here differs from t_n in the proof of Theorem 5.13). On the one hand, observing that $\overline{A}(p, m)_{s,t}$ is a finite sum, we see that for each $m \geq 1$ and $p \geq 0$ we have $\overline{A}(p, m)_{s_n, t_n}(X^{(n)}) \to \overline{A}(p, m)_{s,t}(X)$ pointwise, as $n \to \infty$, and also $\overline{A}(p, m)_{s_n, t_n}(X) \to \overline{A}(p, m)_{s,t}(X)$ on the set $\{\Delta X_t = \Delta X_s = 0\}$. On the other hand, $\overline{A}(p, m)_{s,t}$ increases to $\overline{A}(p)_{s,t}$ (either finite or infinite) as $m \to \infty$. Then, for any subset D of $\mathbb{R}_+$ which is at most countable we can apply (B.8) with $E = [0, \infty]^D$ to obtain a sequence m_n such that

$$p \in D \Rightarrow \begin{cases} \bullet \ \overline{A}(p, m_n)_{s_n, t_n}(X^{(n)}) \to \overline{A}(p)_{s,t}(X) \\ \bullet \ \overline{A}(p, m_n)_{s,t}(X^{(n)}) \to \overline{A}(p)_t(X) \\ \text{on } \{\Delta X_t = \Delta X_s = 0\} \end{cases} \tag{B.9}$$

(these convergences hold for each ω), and the same for X', with the same sequence m_n. Then, since $A(p)_t = \overline{A}(p)_t(X)$ if $g(x) = x$, and upon taking $s = s_n = 0$ and $D = \{p\}$, we deduce the first claim of the theorem. The last claim is an easy consequence of the first one and of the previous proof. □

Proof of Theorem 5.17. Due to the left continuity of J_t and γ_t, it is enough to prove the identifiability when $t \le T$ is such that $\mathbb{P}(\Delta X_t = 0) = \mathbb{P}'(\Delta X'_t = 0) = 1$. We use the notation of the previous proof. First, take $g(x) = x$ and $s = s_n = 0$ and $D = \{p\}$. Then (B.9) and $\mathbb{P}(\Delta X_t = 0) = \mathbb{P}'(\Delta X'_t = 0) = 1$ yield the existence of a sequence $u_n \to \infty$ such that $1_{\{\overline{A}(p,m_n)_{0,t}(X^{(n)}) \le u_n\}}$ and $1_{\{\overline{A}(p,m_n)_{0,t}(X'^{(n)}) \le u_n\}}$ converge in probability under $\mathbb{P}$ and $\mathbb{P}'$, to $1_{\{A(p)_t < \infty\}}$ and $1_{\{A'(p)_t < \infty\}}$ respectively, where $A'(p)_t = \sum_{s \le t} \|\Delta X'_s\|^p$: this proves pairwise identifiability of the "parameter" $1_{\{A(p)_t < \infty\}}$. Since by (1.65) we have $J_t = \{p \ge 0 : A(p)_t < \infty\}$ outside a null set, we deduce pairwise identifiability of $1_{J_t}(p)$. Second, we take for g a function which is strictly increasing and bounded by 1. Then $p \mapsto \overline{A}(p)_{0,t}$ is decreasing, and even strictly decreasing unless $\overline{A}(p)_{0,t} = 0$ for all p (note that $\overline{A}(p)_{0,t}(x) = 0$ for some $x \in \mathbb{D}^d$ and all $p \ge 0$ if and only if x is continuous on $[0, t]$). Then we pick a countable subset D which is dense in $\mathbb{R}_+$. Applying (B.9) with this function g, and still with $s = s_n = 0$, and using the fact that $p \mapsto \overline{A}(p, m)_{0,t}$ is strictly decreasing for all m large enough, we see that the measurable functions $H_{n,k,t}(x) = \sup(p \in D : \overline{A}(p, m_n)_{0,t}(x) > k)$ on $\mathbb{D}^d$ satisfy $H_{n,k,t}(X^{(n)}) \xrightarrow{\mathbb{P}} G(k)_t := \sup(p \in D : \overline{A}(p)_t(X) > k)$ as $n \to \infty$ for all $k > 0$, and a similar statement holds for X' with the same sequence m_n. Now, $G(k)_t \to \gamma_t$ as $k \to \infty$. Then we can find a sequence $k_n \to \infty$ such that $H_{n,k_n,t}(X^{(n)}) \xrightarrow{\mathbb{P}} \gamma_t$, and the same for X': this shows pairwise identifiability for the parameter γ_t. □

Proof of Theorem 5.18. We consider below the right-continuous case only, so we fix $t \in [0, T]$. Again, we use the notation of the proof of Theorem 5.16. We set $\gamma_{t,s} = \inf (p \ge 0 : \int_t^s dr \int f(\|x\|^p \wedge 1) F_r(dx) < \infty)$ when $s > t$, and $\Phi_\varepsilon = \int f(\|x\|^{\beta_t + \varepsilon} \wedge 1) F_t(dx)$. By the assumed regularity properties, for any $\eta > 0$ we have $\int f(\|x\|^{\beta_t - \eta} \wedge 1) F_r(dx) = \infty$ and

$\int(\|x\|^{\beta_t+\eta} \wedge 1) F_r(dx) < \Phi_\eta + 1$, for all r in a (random) interval of positive length starting at t. Therefore, for each ω we have for some $s = s(\omega) > t$

$$\int_t^s dr \int (\|x\|^{\beta_t+\eta} \wedge 1) F_r(dx) \le \Phi_\varepsilon + 1,$$
$$\int_t^s dr \int (\|x\|^{\beta_t-\eta} \wedge 1) F_r(dx) = \infty.$$

In view of (5.16), we deduce $\gamma_{t,s} \ge \beta_t - \eta$ and $\gamma_{t,s} \le \beta_t + \eta$. This being true for all $\eta > 0$, it follows that $\gamma_{t,s} \ge \beta_t$ for all $s > t$, and also $\gamma_{t,s} \to \beta_t$, as s decreases to t. Now, we reproduce the proof of the previous theorem, using (B.9) with (t,s) instead of $(0,t)$, to obtain that, for any $s \in (t,T)$ the variable $\gamma_{t,s}$ is pairwise identifiable, so we have measurable functions $G_{t,s,n}$ on $\mathbb{D}^d$ such that $G_{t,s,n}(X^{(n)}) \xrightarrow{\;\mathbb{P}\;} \gamma_{t,s}$, and also $G_{t,s,n}(X^{(n)}) \xrightarrow{\;\mathbb{P}'\;} \gamma'_{t,s}$, where $\gamma'_{t,s}$ is associated with X'. Since $\gamma_{t,s} \to \beta_t$ as $s \downarrow t$, we deduce the existence of a sequence t_n decreasing to t and such that $G_{t,t_n,n}(X^{(n)}) \xrightarrow{\;\mathbb{P}\;} \beta_t$, and the same for X' (with the same sequence t_n), thus implying pairwise identifiability for β_t.   □

B.1.2 Proofs for Section 5.5

We recall that $I_\Delta(c;(b,F))$ denotes Fisher's information of the statistical model where the single variable X_Δ is observed, and where X is a one-dimensional Lévy process whose characteristic triple is (b,c,F), with b and F fixed, whereas the parameter is c and varies through $(0,\infty)$.

Proof of Theorems 5.21 and 5.22. Step 1. As already mentioned, we omit the proof of the LAN property. We need to prove the following two properties:

(a) We have

$$
\begin{aligned}
\Delta > 0 &\quad\Rightarrow\quad I_\Delta(c;(b,F)) \le \tfrac{1}{2c^2} \\
\Delta \to 0 &\quad\Rightarrow\quad I_\Delta(c;(b,F)) \to \tfrac{1}{2c^2}.
\end{aligned}
\tag{B.10}
$$

(b) For any $A > 1$ and any bounded increasing function ϕ on $[0,\infty)$ such that $\phi(x) \to 0$ as $x \to 0$, we have, as $\Delta \to 0$,

$$\sup_{(b,c,F)\in\mathcal{L}_{A,\phi}} \left| I_\Delta(c;(b,F)) - \frac{1}{2c^2} \right| \to 0. \tag{B.11}$$

where $\mathcal{L}_{A,\phi}$ is the set of all triples (b,c,F) with $\frac{1}{A} \le c \le A$ and $\int_{\{|y|\le x\}}(y^2 \wedge 1)\,F(dy) \le \phi(x)$ for all $x > 0$.

The second part of (B.10) is a special case of (B.11). Observing that $I_\Delta(c;(b,F)) = I_\Delta(c;(0,F))$, by translation invariance, we may assume without loss of generality that $b = 0$.

Step 2. We begin with an auxiliary result. We may write $X = \sigma W + Y$, where $\sigma = \sqrt{c}$ and Y is a Lévy process independent of W and with characteristic triple $(0, 0, F)$, and also $Y = M + N$, where $N_t = \sum_{s \leq t} \Delta Y_s 1_{\{|\Delta Y_s| > 1\}}$ and M is a martingale with $|\Delta M| \leq 1$. We will apply to these processes M and N the estimates (A.71) and (A.73) of Appendix A, respectively. The jump measure μ of Y is a Poisson random measure with compensator $\nu(dt, dx) = dt \otimes F(dx)$, so M is as Z in (A.71) with $\delta(\omega, t, x) = x 1_{\{|x| \leq 1\}}$; moreover, if $(b, c, F) \in \mathcal{L}_{A,\phi}$, one can take the bounds in (A.69) to be $\alpha(2, y) = \phi(y)$ and $\alpha'(2) = \phi(1)$. Similarly, N is as Z in (A.73) with $\delta(\omega, t, x) = x 1_{\{|x| > 1\}}$, and the bounds in (A.69) can be taken to be $\alpha(1, y) = 0$ for $y < 1$ and $\alpha''(1) = \phi(\infty)$ (recall that ϕ is increasing and bounded). Therefore (A.71) applied to M with $p = r = 2$ and (A.73) applied to N with $p = 2$, $r = 1$, and $\chi = 1/2$ in both cases, give us

$$\mathbb{E}\left(\frac{Y_\Delta^2}{\Delta} \bigwedge 1\right) \leq K\left(\phi(\Delta^{1/4}) + \phi(\infty)\Delta^{1/4}\right). \tag{B.12}$$

Step 3. Next, we compute Fisher's information. Below, h is the standard normal density, and G_Δ is the law of the variable Y_Δ, so the law of X_Δ admits the following convolution product as a density $x \mapsto p_\Delta(c, x)$:

$$p_\Delta(c, x) = \frac{1}{\sqrt{c\Delta}} \int h\left(\frac{x - y}{\sqrt{c\Delta}}\right) G_\Delta(dy). \tag{B.13}$$

Clearly, p_Δ is C^∞ in (c, x) on $(0, \infty) \times \mathbb{R}$ and, with the notation $\check{h}(x) = h(x) + h'(x) = (1 - x)h(x)$, the first partial derivative with respect to c is

$$\partial_c p_\Delta(c, x) = -\frac{1}{2c\sqrt{c\Delta}} \int \check{h}\left(\frac{x - y}{\sqrt{c\Delta}}\right) G_\Delta(dy). \tag{B.14}$$

Recall that Fisher's information $I_\Delta(b, (c, F)) = I_\Delta$ is

$$I_\Delta = \int \frac{(\partial_c p_\Delta(c, x))^2}{p_\Delta(c, x)} dx. \tag{B.15}$$

Next, we denote by G_Δ' the distribution of the variable $Y_\Delta/\sqrt{\Delta}$. By the change of variable $x \leftrightarrow x/\sqrt{c\Delta}$ in (B.15), and taking advantage of (B.13) and (B.14), we deduce

$$\begin{aligned} I_\Delta &= \frac{1}{4c^2} \int \psi(G_\Delta', x) \, dx \\ \text{where } \psi(G_\Delta', x) &= \frac{\left(\int \check{h}(x - u/\sqrt{c}) G_\Delta'(du)\right)^2}{\int h(x - u/\sqrt{c}) G_\Delta'(du)}. \end{aligned} \tag{B.16}$$

Step 4. We now turn to the first part of (B.10). We have

$$\psi(G'_\Delta, x) \leq \int \widetilde{h}(x - u/\sqrt{c})\, G'_\Delta(du), \text{ where } \widetilde{h}(x) = \frac{\check{h}(x)^2}{h(x)} = (1-x)^2 h(x)$$

by the Cauchy-Schwarz inequality applied to $\check{h}/\sqrt{h}$ and $\sqrt{h}$. Hence (B.16) yields

$$\begin{aligned}
I_\Delta &\leq \tfrac{1}{4c^2} \int dx \int \widetilde{h}(x - u/\sqrt{c})\, G'_\Delta(du) \\
&= \tfrac{1}{c^2} \int \widetilde{h}(x)\, dx = \tfrac{1}{c^2} \int (1-x)^2 h(x)\, dx = \tfrac{1}{2c^2}.
\end{aligned}$$

Step 5. Finally, in order to obtain (B.11), it is enough to show that if a sequence $(0, c_n, F_n)$ in $\mathcal{L}_{A,\phi}$ is such that $c_n \to c > 0$, then

$$I_{\Delta_n}(c_n; (0, F_n)) \to \frac{1}{2c^2}. \tag{B.17}$$

Toward this aim, we observe that the Lévy process with characteristic triple $(0, c_n, F_n)$ can be written as $\sqrt{c_n}\, W + Y^n$. We deduce from (B.12) and the property $\phi(x) \to 0$ as $x \to 0$ that the laws $G''^n_{\Delta_n}$ of the variables $Y^n_{\Delta_n}$ weakly converge to the Dirac measure ε_0. Since h and $\check{h}$ are bounded continuous, $\psi(G''^n_{\Delta_n}, x) \to \widetilde{h}(x)$ for all x follows. Then (B.16) and Fatou's lemma yield $\liminf_n I_{\Delta_n}(c_n; (0, F_n)) \geq 1/2c^2$. Combining this with Step 3 above, we get (B.17). □

Proof of Theorem 5.24. With $A > 0$ and $r \in [0, 2]$ we associate the set $\mathcal{L}(A, r)$ of all triples (b, c, F) with $|b| \leq A$, $c \leq A$ and $\int (|x|^r \wedge 1)\, dx \leq A$. We need to prove that if we have a sequence of estimators $\widehat{c}_n$ for c and a sequence of numbers $w_n > 0$ such that the family of variables $w_n(\widehat{c}_n - c)$ is uniformly tight when $n \geq 1$ and when the process X runs through all Lévy processes with $(b, c, F) \in \mathcal{L}(A, r)$, then necessarily $w_n \leq K\rho_n$ for some constant K, where

$$\rho_n = \begin{cases} 1/\sqrt{\Delta_n} & \text{if } r \leq 1 \\ \left(\tfrac{1}{\Delta_n} \log(\tfrac{1}{\Delta_n})\right)^{(2-r)/2} & \text{if } r > 1. \end{cases} \tag{B.18}$$

We also need to exhibit estimators which achieve the rate ρ_n uniformly for all X as above.

Step 1. We start with the proof of the bound (B.18). By the results of Subsection 3.1.1 the optimal rate is $1/\sqrt{\Delta_n}$ for the subclass of continuous Lévy processes, so we necessarily have $w_n \leq K/\sqrt{\Delta_n}$. It thus suffices to prove that $w_n \leq \left(\log(1/\Delta_n)/\Delta_n\right)^{(2-r)/2}$, up to a multiplicative constant, of course, and when $r > 1$.

By scaling, if the result holds for one $A > 0$, it holds for all $A > 0$. So below we will construct two sequences X^n and Y^n of Lévy processes, with respective characteristics $(0, 1 + a_n, F_n)$ and $(0, 1, G_n)$, with $a_n = (\Delta_n / \log(1/\Delta_n))^{(2-r)/2}$ and with the two Lévy measures F_n and G_n satisfying

$$\int (|x|^r \wedge 1) \, F_n(dx) \leq K, \qquad \int (|x|^r \wedge 1) \, G_n(dx) \leq K \qquad \text{(B.19)}$$

for some constant K (possibly changing from line to line, but not depending on n). Hence all X^n, Y^n belong to $\mathcal{L}(A, r)$, if A is the supremum of K in (B.19) and of all $1 + a_n$ (note that $a_n \to 0$). For any process X we write $\mathbb{P}_X^n$ for the joint law of the increments $\overline{X}_n = (\Delta_i^n X : i = 1, \ldots, [T/\Delta_n])$. We claim that, if further

$$\begin{array}{c} \text{the total variation distance} \\ \text{between the laws } \mathbb{P}_{X^n}^n \text{ and } \mathbb{P}_{Y^n}^n \text{ tends to } 0, \end{array} \qquad \text{(B.20)}$$

then the result holds.

To see this, we recall that an estimator at stage n, evaluated for a process X, is simply a function $\widehat{c}_n(\overline{X}_n)$. If a sequence of such estimators has uniform rate $w_n \to \infty$ on $\mathcal{L}(A, r)$ for estimating the second characteristic, then the two sequences $w_n(\widehat{c}_n(\overline{X}^n)^n - (1 + a_n))$ and $w_n(\widehat{c}_n(\overline{Y}^n)^n - 1)$ are tight under $\mathbb{P}_{X^n}^n$ and $\mathbb{P}_{Y^n}^n$, respectively, and thus (B.20) implies that the sequence $w_n(\widehat{c}_n(\overline{Y}^n)^n - (1 + a_n))$ is also tight under $\mathbb{P}_{Y^n}^n$. This is possible only if $\sup_n w_n a_n < \infty$, which is the desired result.

Step 2. We take $u_n = 2/a_n^{1/(2-r)}$ and the even and C^2 functions h_n on $\mathbb{R}$ defined by

$$h_n(u) = a_n \left(1_{\{|u| \leq u_n\}} + e^{-(|u| - u_n)^3} 1_{\{|u| > u_n\}} \right).$$

For the Fourier transform we use the convention $\mathcal{F}g(u) = \int e^{iux} g(x) \, dx$, so the inverse is $\mathcal{F}^{-1}h(x) = \frac{1}{2\pi} \int e^{-iux} h(u) \, du$, and $g^{(p)}$ denotes the pth derivative of g, when it exists.

Since $h_n^{(q)} \in \mathbb{L}^p$ for all $p \geq 1$ and $q = 0, 1, 2$, we can define $H_n = \mathcal{F}^{-1}h_n$, and we have $h_n^{(q)} = i^q \mathcal{F}H_{n,q}$, where $H_{n,q}(x) = x^q H_n(x)$. Plancherel identity yields (since also $u_n \to \infty$)

$$\begin{array}{c} \|H_n\|_{\mathbb{L}^2} \leq K a_n u_n^{1/2} \leq K a_n^{(3-2r)/(4-2r)}, \\ q = 1, 2 \implies \|H_{n,q}\|_{\mathbb{L}^2} \leq \|h_n^{(q)}\|_{\mathbb{L}^2} \leq K a_n. \end{array} \qquad \text{(B.21)}$$

Then the Cauchy-Schwarz inequality applied to the functions $\frac{1}{\sqrt{1+x^2}}$ and $H_n(x)\sqrt{1 + x^2}$ yields

$$\int |H_n(x)| \, dx \leq K(1 + a_n^{(3-2r)/(4-2r)}) \leq K. \qquad \text{(B.22)}$$

(Note, however, that $H_n(0) > a_n u_n \to \infty$.) Therefore the two measures

$$F_n(dx) = \frac{|H_n(x)|}{x^2}\,dx, \qquad G_n(dx) = F_n(dx) + \frac{H_n(x)}{x^2}\,dx$$

are nonnegative and integrate x^2, hence are Lévy measures. Moreover, splitting the integration domain in the integral $\int e^{-iux}\,h_n(u)\,du$ into the sets $\{|u| \le u_n\}$ and $\{|u| > u_n\}$, we get

$$|H_n(x)| \;\le\; Ka_n\left(\frac{|\sin(u_n x)|}{|x|} + 1\right)$$

$$\le\; Ka_n\left(u_n\,1_{\{|x|\le 1/u_n\}} + \frac{1}{|x|}\,1_{\{1/u_n<|x|\le1\}} + 1_{\{|x|>1\}}\right).$$

In turn, the integration domain in $\int \frac{|x|^r\wedge 1}{x^2}\,|H_n(x)|\,dx$ can be split into $\{|x| \le 1/u_n\}$, $\{1/u_n < |x| \le 1\}$ and $\{|x| > 1\}$, and recalling $1 < r < 2$ we deduce from the above that

$$\int \frac{|x|^r \wedge 1}{x^2}\,|H_n(x)|\,dx \;\le\; Ka_n(u_n^{2-r} + 1) \;\le\; K.$$

It follows that the measures F_n and G_n satisfy (B.19), and it remains to prove (B.20).

Step 3. We denote by ϕ_n and ψ_n the characteristic functions of $X_{\Delta_n}^n$ and $Y_{\Delta_n}^n$, and $\eta_n = \phi_n - \psi_n$. These functions are real (because H_n is an even function) and given by

$$\phi_n(u) = \exp\left(-\tfrac{\Delta_n}{2}\left(u^2 + a_n u^2 + 2\widetilde{\phi}_n(u)\right)\right),$$
$$\psi_n(u) = \exp\left(-\tfrac{\Delta_n}{2}\left(u^2 + 2\widetilde{\phi}_n(u) + 2\widetilde{\eta}_n(u)\right)\right)$$

where

$$\widetilde{\phi}_n(u) = \int(1-\cos(ux))\,\frac{|H_n(x)|}{x^2}\,dx,$$
$$\widetilde{\eta}_n(u) = \int(1-\cos(ux))\,\frac{H_n(x)}{x^2}\,dx.$$

Equation (B.21) implies that $\widetilde{\phi}_n$ and $\widetilde{\eta}_n$ are twice differentiable. Since $\widetilde{\phi}_n'(u) = \int \sin(ux)\,\frac{|H_n(x)|}{x}\,dx$ and $|\sin(ux)| \le |ux|$, (B.22) yields

$$0 \le \widetilde{\phi}_n(u) \le K(1 + a_n^{(3-2r)/(4-2r)})\,u^2,$$
$$|\widetilde{\phi}_n'(u)| \le K(1 + a_n^{(3-2r)/(4-2r)})\,|u| \tag{B.23}$$

(since $1 < r < 2$ the exponent of a_n in the right sides above may be positive or negative). Moreover, $\widetilde{\eta}_n''(u) = \int \cos(ux)\,H_n(x)\,dx = h_n(u)$ and $\widetilde{\eta}(0) = \widetilde{\eta}'(0) = 0$, hence by the definition of h_n one deduces

$$\begin{aligned}
|u| \le u_n \;&\Rightarrow\; \widetilde{\eta}_n(u) = \tfrac{a_n u^2}{2}, \qquad \widetilde{\eta}_n'(u) = a_n u \\
|u| \ge u_n \;&\Rightarrow\; |\widetilde{\eta}_n(u)| \le \tfrac{a_n u^2}{2}, \qquad |\widetilde{\eta}_n'(u)| \le a_n|u|.
\end{aligned} \tag{B.24}$$

Step 4. Since X^n and Y^n have a non-vanishing Gaussian part, the variables $X_{\Delta_n}^n$ and $Y_{\Delta_n}^n$ have densities, denoted by f_n and g_n, and we set $k_n = f_n - g_n$. Since X^n and Y^n are Lévy processes, the variation distance between $\mathbb{P}_{X^n}^n$ and $\mathbb{P}_{Y^n}^n$ is not more than $[T/\Delta_n]$ times $\int |k_n(x)|\, dx$, and we are thus left to show that $\frac{1}{\Delta_n} \int |k_n(x)|\, dx \to 0$.

To check this, we use the same argument as for (B.22): if $k_{n,1}(x) = x k_n(x)$, by the Cauchy-Schwarz inequality we have $\int |k_n(x)|\, dx \leq K(\|k_n\|_{\mathbb{L}^2} + \|k_{n,1}\|_{\mathbb{L}^2})$, whereas $\eta_n = \mathcal{F}k_n$ and also, since η_n is twice differentiable, $\eta_n' = i\mathcal{F}k_{n,1}$. By Plancherel identity, it is thus enough to prove that

$$\frac{1}{\Delta_n^2} \int |\eta_n(u)|^2\, du \to 0, \qquad \frac{1}{\Delta_n^2} \int |\eta_n'(u)|^2\, du \to 0. \tag{B.25}$$

We have $\widetilde{\phi}_n + \widetilde{\eta}_n \geq 0$, which implies $\psi_n(u) \leq e^{-u^2\Delta_n/2}$, hence (B.24) yields

$$\begin{aligned}
|\eta_n(u)| &= \psi_n(u)\left|1 - \frac{\phi_n(u)}{\psi_n(u)}\right| \\
&= \psi_n(u)\left|1 - e^{-\Delta_n(a_n u^2 - 2\widetilde{\eta}_n(u))/2}\right| \\
&\leq \frac{\Delta_n a_n u^2}{2} e^{-\Delta_n u^2/2}\, 1_{\{|u| > u_n\}},
\end{aligned}$$

and

$$\begin{aligned}
|\eta_n'(u)| &= \Delta_n \big| (u + u a_n + \widetilde{\phi}_n'(u))\phi_n(u) \\
&\quad - (u + \widetilde{\phi}_n'(u) + \widetilde{\eta}_n'(u))\psi_n(u)\big|\, 1_{\{|u| > u_n\}}.
\end{aligned}$$

Then, upon using (B.24) again and (B.23) and $\phi_n(u) \leq e^{-u^2\Delta_n(1+a_n)/2}$ (because $\widetilde{\phi}_n \geq 0$), we get

$$\begin{aligned}
|\eta_n'(u)| &\leq \Delta_n\Big(a_n |u| e^{-\Delta_n u^2/2} + |\widetilde{\eta}_n'(u)| e^{-\Delta_n u^2/2} \\
&\quad + |u + \widetilde{\phi}_n'(u)|\, |\eta_n(u)|\Big) 1_{\{|u| > u_n\}} \\
&\leq K\Delta_n a_n |u| e^{-\Delta_n u^2/2}\Big(1 + (1 + a_n^{\frac{3-2r}{4-2r}})\Delta_n u^2\Big) 1_{\{|u| > u_n\}}.
\end{aligned}$$

Now, since $u_n = 2\big(\frac{\log(1/\Delta_n)}{\Delta_n}\big)^{1/2}$, a change of variables gives us for $q \geq 1$

$$\begin{aligned}
\int_{\{|u| > u_n\}} (\Delta_n u^2)^q e^{-\Delta_n u^2}\, du &= \frac{1}{\sqrt{\Delta_n}} \int_{4\log(1/\Delta_n)}^{\infty} x^{q-1/2} e^{-x}\, dx \\
&\leq K\Delta_n^{7/2} (\log(1/\Delta_n))^{q-1/2}.
\end{aligned}$$

Hence, using the definition of a_n and $r < 2$, we obtain (with K below depending on r):

$$\int |\eta_n(u)|^2\, du \leq K a_n^2 \Delta_n^{7/2} \big(\log(1/\Delta_n)\big)^{3/2} \leq K\Delta_n^{7/2}$$

$$\int |\eta_n'(u)|^2\, du \leq K\big(a_n^2 + a_n^{\frac{7-2e}{2-r}}\big)\Delta_n^{9/2} \big(\log(1/\Delta_n)\big)^{7/2} \leq K\Delta_n^{9/2}.$$

Then (B.25) follows, and this completes the proof of (5.21).

Step 5. It remains to show that the bound (5.21) is sharp, and for this we need to exhibit estimators achieving this bound. These are based on the empirical characteristic function of the observed returns, that is,

$$\widehat{\phi}_n(u) = \frac{1}{[T/\Delta_n]} \sum_{j=1}^{[T/\Delta_n]} e^{iu\Delta_j^n X}$$

for $u \in \mathbb{R}$. We are concerned with the set of Lévy processes whose characteristic triples belong to $\mathcal{L}(A, r)$ for some $A > 0$ and $r \in [0, 2)$, and the estimators for c will be

$$\widehat{c}_n = -\frac{2}{\Delta_n v_n^2} \left(\log |\widehat{\phi}_n(v_n)| \right) 1_{\{\widehat{\phi}_n(v_n) \neq 0\}},$$

where

$$v_n = \begin{cases} \frac{1}{\sqrt{\Delta_n}} & \text{if } r \leq 1 \\ \frac{\sqrt{(r-1)\log(1/\Delta_n)}}{\sqrt{2A\Delta_n}} & \text{if } r > 1. \end{cases}$$

Let ϕ_n denote the characteristic function of X_{Δ_n}, with X a Lévy process with characteristics (b, c, F) in $\mathcal{L}(A, r)$. Its modulus at $u = v_n$ is $e^{-\frac{\Delta_n}{2}\left(cv_n^2 + \gamma_n\right)}$, where $\gamma_n = 2 \int (1 - \cos(v_n x)) F(dx)$. The estimation error $\widehat{c}_n - c$ is the sum $G_n + H_n$ of the deterministic and stochastic errors:

$$G_n = -\frac{2}{\Delta_n v_n^2} \log |\phi_n(v_n)| - c = \frac{\gamma_n}{v_n^2},$$
$$H_n = \frac{2}{\Delta_n v_n^2} \left(\log |\phi_n(v_n)| - \left(\log |\widehat{\phi}_n(v_n)| \right) 1_{\{\widehat{\phi}_n(v_n)\neq 0\}} \right).$$

We study these two errors separately, and below the constants K and n_0 may depend on r and A, but on nothing else, and in particular not on (b, c, F). We have $1 - \cos y \leq 1 \wedge y^2 \leq |y|^r \wedge 1$, and by hypothesis $\int (|x|^r \wedge 1) F(dx) \leq A$, hence $0 \leq \gamma_n \leq 2 \int (|v_n x|^r \wedge 1) F(dx) \leq 2Av_n^r$. With the notation (5.21), this implies, for all n large enough to have $v_n^r \leq v_n^2/2$,

$$|G_n| \leq \frac{2A}{v_n^{2-r}} \leq \frac{K}{\rho_n},$$
$$\frac{1}{|\phi_n(v_n)|} = e^{\Delta_n(cv_n^2 + \gamma_n)/2} \leq e^{A\Delta_n v_n^2} \leq \frac{K}{\Delta_n^{(r-1)^+/2}}. \tag{B.26}$$

Next, the variables $\exp(v_n \Delta_j^n X)$ are i.i.d. as j varies, with modulus 1 and expectation $\phi_n(v_n)$, hence $V_n = \widehat{\phi}_n(v_n) - \phi_n(v_n)$ satisfies $\mathbb{E}(|V_n|^2) \leq T\Delta_n$. Thus, on the set $\{|V_n| \leq \Delta_n^{r/4}\}$, we have $|V_n/\phi_n(v_n)| \leq 1/2$ and $\widehat{\phi}_n(v_n) = V_n + \phi_n(v_n) \neq 0$ for all $n \geq n_0$, by (B.26), yielding

$$|H_n| = \frac{2}{\Delta_n v_n^2} \left| \log \left| 1 + \frac{V_n}{\phi_n(v_n)} \right| \right| \leq K \frac{|V_n|}{\Delta_n v_n^2 |\phi_n(v_n)|},$$

$$\mathbb{E}\big(|H_n|\,1_{\{|V_n|\le\Delta_n^{1/4}\}}\big) \le \begin{cases} K\sqrt{T}\,\sqrt{\Delta_n} & \text{if } r \le 1 \\ K\sqrt{T}\,\dfrac{\Delta_n^{(2-r)/2}}{\log(1/\Delta_n)} & \text{if } r > 1. \end{cases}$$

The latter estimate and the first part of (B.26), plus the fact that $\mathbb{P}(|V_n| > \Delta_n^{r/4}) \le T\Delta_n^{(2-r)/4}$ (by Bienaymé-Tchebycheff inequality), and the equality $\widehat{c}_n - c = G_n + H_n$, yield that the variables $\rho_n(\widehat{c}_n - c)$ are tight, uniformly in n and also in the choice of the triple (b, c, F) in $\mathcal{L}(A, r)$. $\quad\square$

B.1.3   Proof of Theorem 5.25

For this theorem the underlying process is $X_t = bt + \sqrt{c}\,W_t + Y_t^1 + Y_t^2$, where Y^1 and Y^2 are two symmetric stable processes with indices $\beta_1 > \beta_2$, the three processes W, Y^1, Y^2 being independent, and the Lévy measure of Y^j is

$$F^j(dx) = \frac{a_j\,\beta_j}{|x|^{1+\beta_j}}\,dx.$$

Our aim is to prove the following equivalences, as $\Delta \to 0$, for the diagonal element of Fisher's information matrix, for the statistical model where X_Δ is observed and $(\beta_1, \beta_2, a_1, a_2)$ vary:

$$I_\Delta^{\beta_1} \sim \frac{a_1}{2(2-\beta_1)^{\beta_1/2}\,c^{\beta_1/2}}\,\Delta^{1-\beta_1/2}\,(\log(1/\Delta))^{2-\beta_1/2} \qquad (B.27)$$

$$I_\Delta^{a_1} \sim \frac{2}{a_1(2-\beta_1)^{\beta_1/2}\,c^{\beta_1/2}\,a_1^2}\,\frac{\Delta^{1-\beta_1/2}}{(\log(1/\Delta))^{\beta_1/2}}. \qquad (B.28)$$

$$I_\Delta^{\beta_2} \sim \frac{a_2^2\,\beta_2^2}{2a_1\,\beta_1(2\beta_2-\beta_1)(2-\beta_1)^{\beta_2-\beta_1/2}\,c^{\beta_2-\beta_1/2}} \qquad (B.29)$$
$$\times\,\Delta^{1-\beta_2+\beta_1/2}\,(\log(1/\Delta))^{2-\beta_2+\beta_1/2}$$

$$I_\Delta^{a_2} \sim \frac{2\beta_2^2}{a_1\,\beta_1(2\beta_2-\beta_1)(2-\beta_1)^{\beta_2-\beta_1/2}\,c^{\beta_2-\beta_1/2}} \qquad (B.30)$$
$$\times\,\frac{\Delta^{1-\beta_2+\beta_1/2}}{(\log(1/\Delta))^{\beta_2-\beta_1/2}},$$

and when further $\beta_2 > \beta_1/2$ for the last two equivalences.

The proof is analogous to the proof of Theorem 5.21, although with many more steps. As in that theorem, we may and will assume that $b = 0$.

Fisher's Information   In our first step we compute the Fisher informations $I_\Delta^{\beta_i}$ and $I_\Delta^{a_i}$. We start with some notation. Recall that h is the density of $\mathcal{N}(0,1)$, and denote by h_β the density of the symmetric stable variable with index β, standardized in such a way that the Lévy measure of its distribution has the density $\beta/|x|^{1+\beta}$; if the Lévy density were $\beta a/|x|^{1+\beta}$, the density of the variable itself would then be $a^{1/\beta} h_\beta(a^{1/\beta}x)$. The function $(\beta, x) \mapsto h_\beta(x)$ is C^∞ on $(0, 2) \times \mathbb{R}$, and if $\check{h}_\beta(x) = h_\beta(x) + x\, \partial_x h_\beta(x)$ the following behavior as $|x| \to \infty$ is know, see for example Zolotarev (1995):

$$
\begin{aligned}
h_\beta(x) &= \tfrac{\beta}{|x|^{1+\beta}} + O\left(\tfrac{1}{|x|^{1+2\beta}}\right) \\
\check{h}_\beta(x) &= -\tfrac{\beta^2}{|x|^{1+\beta}} + O\left(\tfrac{1}{|x|^{1+2\beta}}\right) \\
\partial_\beta h_\beta(x) &= -\tfrac{\beta \log|x| - 1}{|x|^{1+\beta}} + O\left(\tfrac{\log|x|}{|x|^{1+2\beta}}\right).
\end{aligned}
\tag{B.31}
$$

Let $\overline{Y}^j$ be the stable process with index β_j and scaling parameter 1 instead of a_j, so that Y_Δ^j has the same law as $(\Delta a_j)^{1/\beta_j}\, Y_1^j$. Hence, similar to (B.13), and omitting the dependency upon the five parameters $(c, \beta_1, \beta_2, a_1, a_2)$, the density $x \mapsto p_\Delta(x)$ of X_Δ is written as

$$
p_\Delta(x) = \tfrac{1}{\sqrt{c\Delta}} \int h\left(\tfrac{x - (\Delta a_1)^{1/\beta_1} y_1 - (\Delta a_2)^{1/\beta_2} y_2}{\sqrt{c\Delta}}\right) h_{\beta_1}(y_1) h_{\beta_2}(y_2)\, dy_1 dy_2.
$$

Set

$$
u_i = \tfrac{\Delta^{\frac{1}{\beta_i} - \frac{1}{2}} a_i^{\frac{1}{\beta_i}}}{\sqrt{c}}, \qquad v_i = \tfrac{1}{\beta_i(2 - \beta_i)}\left(2 + \tfrac{\log(a_i/c)}{\log(1/u_i)}\right),
$$
$$
a = \left(\tfrac{c^{\beta_1 - \beta_2} a_2^{2 - \beta_1}}{a_1^{2 - \beta_2}}\right)^{\frac{1}{2 - \beta_1}},
\tag{B.32}
$$

so $u_i \to 0$ and $\tfrac{u_2}{u_1} \to 0$ and $v_i \to \tfrac{2}{\beta_i(2 - \beta_i)}$ as $\Delta \to 0$. Differentiating the expression giving p_Δ, integrating by part, and using $\partial_x(x h_\beta(x)) = \check{h}_\beta(x)$, we get with h' the derivative of h:

$$
\begin{aligned}
\partial_{a_i} p_\Delta(x) &= -\tfrac{1}{a_i \beta_i \sqrt{c\Delta}} \int h'\left(\tfrac{x}{\sqrt{c\Delta}} - u_i y - u_{3-i} z\right) u_i y h_{\beta_i}(y) h_{\beta_{3-i}}(z)\, dy dz \\
&= -\tfrac{1}{a_i \beta_i \sqrt{c\Delta}} \int h\left(\tfrac{x}{\sqrt{c\Delta}} - u_i y - u_{3-i} z\right) \check{h}_{\beta_i}(y) h_{\beta_{3-i}}(z)\, dy dz,
\end{aligned}
$$

and in the same way, upon using $\tfrac{\log(\Delta a_i)}{\beta_i^2} = -v_i \log\tfrac{1}{u_i}$,

$$
\begin{aligned}
\partial_{\beta_i} p_\Delta(x) = \tfrac{1}{\sqrt{c\Delta}} \int h\left(\tfrac{x}{\sqrt{c\Delta}} - u_i y - u_{3-i} z\right) \\
\times \left(\partial_\beta h_{\beta_i}(y) - v_i \log\tfrac{1}{u_i} \check{h}_{\beta_i}(y)\right) h_{\beta_{3-i}}(z)\, dy dz.
\end{aligned}
$$

We introduce now a family of functions on $\mathbb{R}$, for $i = 1, 2$:

$$
\begin{aligned}
S_\Delta(x) &= \int h(x - u_1 y_1 - u_2 y_2) h_{\beta_1}(y_1) h_{\beta_2}(y_2)\, dy_1 dy_2 \\
R_\Delta^{i,0}(x) &= \tfrac{1}{u_i^{\beta_i}} \int h(x - u_i y - u_{3-i} z) \check{h}_{\beta_i}(y_i) h_{\beta_{3-i}}(y_j)\, dy dz \\
R_\Delta^{i,1}(x) &= \tfrac{1}{u_i^{\beta_i} \log(1/u_i)} \int h(x - u_i y - u_{3-i} z) \partial_\beta h_{\beta_i}(y) h_{\beta_{3-i}}(z)\, dy dz,
\end{aligned}
$$

and the following numbers, where $l, m \in \{0, 1\}$:

$$
J_\Delta^{i,lm} = \int \tfrac{R_\Delta^{i,l}(x)\, R_\Delta^{i,m}(x)}{S_\Delta(x)}\, dx.
$$

At this point, the formulas giving the various entries of the Fisher information matrix, and the previous formulas for p_Δ and its derivatives, plus a change of variables, readily yield

$$I_\Delta^{\beta_i} = u_i^{2\beta_i} \left(\log(1/u_i)\right)^2 \left(J_\Delta^{i,11} - 2v_i J_\Delta^{i,01} + v_i^2 J_\Delta^{i,00}\right),$$
$$I_\Delta^{a_i} = \frac{u_i^{2\beta_i}}{a_i^2 \beta_i^2} J_\Delta^{i,00}.$$

$$(B.33)$$

Some Auxiliary Functions   We now proceed to studying a few auxiliary functions. In the whole discussion, ϕ denotes a continuous increasing bounded function on $\mathbb{R}_+$ with $\phi(0) = 0$, which may vary from line to line, or even within a line, as does the constant K. Also here $\beta > 0$, p is either 0 or 1, and θ is either 1 or 2.

Step 1. Set

$$g_\theta(x) = \frac{1}{\theta} h\left(\frac{x}{\theta}\right), \qquad f_\beta^p(x) = \begin{cases} 1 & \text{if } |x| \le 1 \\ \frac{1 \vee (\log|x|)^p}{|x|^{1+\beta}} & \text{if } |x| > 1. \end{cases}$$

$$D^{\theta,\beta,p}(x) = \int_{\{|z|>1\}} g_\theta(x-z) f_\beta^p(z)\, dz.$$

$$(B.34)$$

The function $D^{\theta,\beta,p}$ takes its values in $(0,1)$ and can be decomposed as $D^{\theta,\beta,p} = D' + D''$, where, with the notation $A'_x = \{z : |z| > 1, |x - z| \ge \sqrt{|x|}\}$ and $A''_x = \{z : |z| > 1, |x - z| < \sqrt{|x|}\}$,

$$D'(x) = \int_{A'_x} g_\theta(x-z) f_\beta^p(z)\, dz, \qquad D''(x) = \int_{A''_x} g_\theta(x-z) f_\beta^p(z)\, dz.$$

On the one hand, $g_\theta(x - z) \le K e^{-|x|/2\theta^2}$ on A'_x, hence $D'(x) \le K e^{-|x|/2\theta^2}$, and $D'(x)/f_\beta^p(x) \to 0$ as $|x| \to \infty$. On the other hand,

$$\frac{D''(x)}{f_\beta^p(x)} = \int g_\theta(x-z) k_x(z)\, dz, \quad \text{where } k_x(z) = \frac{f_\beta^p(z)}{f_\beta^p(x)} 1_{A''_x}(z).$$

If $|x| \ge 3$ we have $|z| > 1$ if $|x - z| < \sqrt{|x|}$, hence the function k_x converges pointwise to 1 as $|x| \to \infty$, and $|k_x(z)| \le K$ for all $|x| \ge 3$. Then the dominated convergence theorem yields

$$D^{\theta,\beta,p}(x) \sim f_\beta^p(x) \quad \text{as } |x| \to \infty.$$

$$(B.35)$$

Since $0 < D^{\theta,\beta,p} < 1$, (B.34) and (B.35) imply the existence of a constant $C > 1$ such that

$$\frac{1}{C} f_\beta^p \le D^{\theta,\beta,p} \le C f_\beta^p.$$

$$(B.36)$$

Step 2. In this step we fix p (either 0 or 1) and consider two numbers $b \in \mathbb{R}$ and $\bar{b} \geq 0$, and a bounded continuous even function l on $\mathbb{R}$, satisfying

$$\int l(x)\,dx = \bar{b}, \qquad l(x) = b f_\beta^p(x)\Big(1 + \mathrm{O}\Big(\frac{1}{|x|^\beta}\Big)\Big) \quad \text{as } |x| \to \infty. \tag{B.37}$$

For all $w \in \big(0, 1 \wedge \tfrac{1}{3}\big]$ we set

$$T_w^{\theta,l}(x) = \int g_\theta(x - wy)\,l(y)\,dy. \tag{B.38}$$

In the following estimates we use the facts that a primitive of $x^q (\log x)^p$ (for $x \geq 1$) is $x^{q+1}/(q+1)$ when $p = 0$ and $(-1+(q+1)\log x)x^{q+1}/(q+1)^2$ when $p = 1$, and that when $|z| > 3$ then $f_\beta^p(z) = (\log|z|)^p/|z|^{1+\beta}$, and otherwise $f_\beta^p(z) \leq K/|z|^{1+\beta}$. An easy calculation shows that $|\partial_x^2 g_\theta(x - y)| \leq K g_{2\theta}(x)$ for all $x \in \mathbb{R}$, $|y| \leq 1$. Then, since $g_\theta'(x) = -\frac{x}{\theta^2}\,g_\theta(x)$, we have

$$|y| \leq 1 \quad \Rightarrow \quad \Big|g_\theta(x - y) - g_\theta(x) + \frac{y}{\theta^2}\,g_\theta(x)\Big| \leq K y^2\, g_{2\theta}(x).$$

Since l is an even function, and in view of (B.37), we deduce

$$\begin{aligned}
\Big|\int_{\{|z| \leq \frac{1}{w}\}} \big(g_\theta(x - wz) - g_\theta(x)\big)\,l(z)\,dz\Big| & \\
\leq K g_{2\theta}(x) \int_{\{|z| \leq \frac{1}{w}\}} (wz)^2\,|l(z)|\,dz & \\
\leq K g_{2\theta}(x) w^\beta \Big(1 + p \log \tfrac{1}{w}\Big). &
\end{aligned} \tag{B.39}$$

We also have (recall $p \in \{0, 1\}$ and $w \leq \tfrac{1}{3}$, so $f_\beta^p(x/w) = w^{1+\beta}(f_\beta^p(x) + p f_\beta^0(x) \log \tfrac{1}{w})$ if $|x| > 1$),

$$\begin{aligned}
\int_{\{|z| > \frac{1}{w}\}} |l(z)|\,dz &\leq K w^\beta \Big(1 + p \log \tfrac{1}{w}\Big) \\
\int_{\{|z| > \frac{1}{w}\}} g_\theta(x - wz) \frac{f_\beta^p(z)}{|z|^\beta}\,dz &\leq w^{\beta-1} \int_{\{|x| > 1\}} g_\theta(x - x) f_\beta^p\big(\tfrac{x}{w}\big)\,dz \\
&\leq K w^{2\beta}\big(D^{\theta,\beta,p}(x) + p D^{\theta,\beta,0}(x) \log \tfrac{1}{w}\big)
\end{aligned}$$

and since (B.37) implies $|l(x) - b f_\beta^p(x)| \leq K f_\beta^p(x)/|x|^\beta$ we deduce

$$\begin{aligned}
\Big|\int_{\{|z| > \frac{1}{w}\}} g_\theta(x - wz)\,l(z)\,dz - b\,w^\beta\big(D^{\theta,\beta,p}(x) + p\,D^{\theta,\beta,0}(x) \log \tfrac{1}{w}\big)\Big| & \\
\leq K w^{2\beta}\big(D^{\theta,\beta,p}(x) + p\,D^{\theta,\beta,0}(x) \log \tfrac{1}{w}\big). &
\end{aligned}$$

Putting all these estimates together, and using also (B.36) and $g_\theta \leq K g_{2\theta} \leq K f_\beta^0$, we obtain

$$\begin{aligned}
\Big|T_w^{\theta,l} - \bar{b}\,g_\theta - b\,w^\beta\big(D^{\theta,\beta,p} + p\,D^{\theta,\beta,0} \log \tfrac{1}{w}\big)\Big| & \\
\leq K w^\beta\Big(\big(1 + p \log \tfrac{1}{w}\big)(g_{2\theta} + w^\beta f_\beta^0) + p w^\beta f_\beta^1\Big). &
\end{aligned} \tag{B.40}$$

In particular, this implies

$$
\begin{aligned}
|T_w^{\theta,l}| &\leq K\bar{b}\,g_\theta + Kw^\beta\left((1+p\log\tfrac{1}{w})f_\beta^0 + pf_\beta^1\right) \\
|T_w^{\theta,l} - \bar{b}_p\,g_\theta| &\leq Kw^\beta\left((1+p\log\tfrac{1}{w})f_\beta^0 + pf_\beta^1\right),
\end{aligned}
\tag{B.41}
$$

and also (using (B.36) again) the existence of two constants $C_0, w_0 > 0$ (depending on $b, \bar{b}, \beta, \theta$) such that

$$
\bar{b} > 0, \ p = 0, \ w \in (0, w_0] \quad \Rightarrow \quad T_w^{\theta,l} \geq C_0(g_\theta + w^\beta f_\beta^0).
\tag{B.42}
$$

Step 3. Here we consider two continuous even functions l and l' satisfying

$$
l(x) \sim b f_\beta^p(x), \quad l'(x) \sim b' f_{\beta'}^{p'}(x), \qquad \text{as } |x| \to \infty,
\tag{B.43}
$$

where again p and p' are either 0 or 1. For $w \in (0, 1/3]$ we set

$$
H_w(l, l')(x) = \int l(x - wy)l'(y)\,dy.
\tag{B.44}
$$

We will give various estimates and study the behavior at infinity of $H_w(l, l')$ and, since this function is bounded (uniformly in w), continuous and even, it suffices to consider what happens when $x > 3$.

We begin with a lower bound. If $x > 3$ and $|wy| \leq \frac{1}{3}$ (B.34) readily implies $f_\beta^0(x - wy) \geq f_\beta^0(x)/8$, hence

$$
H_w(f_\beta^0, h_{\beta'})(x) \geq \frac{1}{8} f_\beta^0(x) \int_{-1/3w}^{1/3w} h_{\beta'}(y)\,dy = C f_\beta^0(x)
$$

for some constant $C > 0$ (independent of w). Since $H_w(f_\beta^0, h_{\beta'}) > 0$ everywhere, we deduce

$$
f_\beta^0 \leq K\,H_w(f_\beta^0, h_{\beta'}).
\tag{B.45}
$$

Next, coming back to general functions l, l', we consider the function $k_x(y) = l(x - wy)l'(y)$ and the four sets, for $x > 3$:

$$
\begin{aligned}
A_x^1 &= (-\infty, -x/2w] \cup [3x/2w, \infty), \\
A_x^2 &= ((x-1)/w, (x+1)/w) \\
A_x^3 &= [x/2w, (x-1)/w] \cup [(x+1)/w, 3x/2w) \\
A_x^4 &= (-x/2w, x/2w).
\end{aligned}
$$

We have $|k_x(y)| \leq K\dfrac{(\log|y|)^{p'}}{x^{1+\beta/2}|y|^{1+\beta'}}$ if $y \in A_x^1$, hence $\int_{A_x^1} |k_x(y)|dy \leq Kw^{\beta'} f_{\beta'}^0(x)\left(\log\tfrac{1}{w}\right)^{p'}$ is obvious. If $y \in A_x^2$ we have $|k_x(y)| \leq K f_{\beta'}^{p'}(y)$,

and

$$\int_{A_x^2} f_{\beta'}^{p'}(y)dy =$$

$$\frac{w^{\beta'}}{\beta'^2}\left(\frac{\beta' + p'(\beta'\log\frac{x-1}{w} + 1 - \beta')}{(x-1)^{\beta'}} - \frac{\beta' + p'(\beta'\log\frac{x+1}{w} + 1 - \beta')}{(x+1)^{\beta'}}\right),$$

which is smaller than $Kw^{\beta'}(f_{\beta'}^{p'}(x) + p'f_{\beta'}^0(x)\log\frac{1}{w})$. If $y \in A_x^3$ we have $|k_x(y)| \leq Kw^{1+\beta'}(f_{\beta'}^{p'}(x) + p'f_{\beta'}^0(x)\log\frac{1}{w})m_x(y)$, where $m_x(y) = f_\beta^p(x - wy)$, and by a change of variables we get

$$\int_{A_x^3} m_x(y)dy = \frac{2}{w}\int_0^{x/2-1}\frac{(1 \vee \log(u+1))^p}{(u+1)^{1+\beta}}\,du \leq \frac{K}{w}.$$

In other words, we have proved so far that

$$\int_{A_x^1 \cup A_x^2 \cup A_x^3}|k_x(y)|\,dy \leq Kw^{\beta'}\left(f_{\beta'}^{p'}(x) + p'f_{\beta'}^0(x)\log\frac{1}{w}\right). \qquad (B.46)$$

It remains to consider the integral on A_x^4. On this set, $|k_x(y)| \leq Kf_\beta^p(x)|l'(y)|$, and l' is integrable, so the integral is smaller than $Kf_\beta^p(x)$. Therefore (recalling that the above holds when $x > 3$, and also when $x < -3$, and $H_w(l, l')$ is bounded, and $\inf_{|x|\leq 3}f_\beta^p(x) > 0$),

$$|H_w(l, l')| \leq Kf_\beta^p + Kw^{\beta'}\left(f_{\beta'}^{p'} + p'f_{\beta'}^0\log\frac{1}{w}\right). \qquad (B.47)$$

Now we study the behavior at infinity, when $l' = h_{\beta'}$. For this we write $A_x^5 = (-\sqrt{x}/w, \sqrt{x}/w)$, which is included into A_x^4, and we set $A_x^6 = A_x^4\backslash A_x^5$. On the one hand,

$$\int_{A_x^6}|k_x(y)|\,dy \leq Kf_\beta^p(x)\int_{\{y:|y|>\sqrt{x}/w\}}h_{\beta'}(y)dy \leq Kf_\beta^p(x)\frac{w^{\beta'/2}}{x^{\beta'/2}},$$

where the last inequality follows from (B.31). On the other hand, recalling (B.43), if $y \in A_x^5$ we have $k_x(y) = m_x(y)h_{\beta'}(y)$, where $m_x(y) = bf_\beta^p(x)(1 + \varepsilon_x(y, w))$ and $\sup_{y\in A_x^5, w\in(0,1/3]}|\varepsilon_x(y, w)| \to 0$ as $x \to \infty$. Hence

$$\frac{1}{f_\beta^p(x)}\int_{A_x^5}k_x(y)dy = b\int_{A_x^5}(1 + \varepsilon_x(y, w))h_{\beta'}(y)dy \to b \quad \text{uniformly in } w$$

because A_x^5 increases to $\mathbb{R}$ as $x \to \infty$. These two properties, plus (B.46), imply the following:

$$|H_w(l, h_{\beta'})(x) - bf_\beta^p(x)| \leq f_\beta^p(x)\phi(1/x) + Kw^{\beta'}f_{\beta'}^0(x) \qquad (B.48)$$

(recall that ϕ denotes a generic continuous bounded function with $\lim_{x\downarrow 0}\phi(x) = 0$).

Estimates for S_Δ With the notation (B.38), we can write S_Δ in two ways:

$$\begin{aligned}
S_\Delta(x) &= \int T_{u_2}^{1,h_{\beta_2}}(x - u_1 y)\, h_{\beta_1}(y)\, dy \\
&= \int T_{u_1}^{1,h_{\beta_1}}(x - u_2 y)\, h_{\beta_2}(y)\, dy.
\end{aligned} \tag{B.49}$$

First, if $i = 1,2$ the function $l = h_{\beta_i}$ satisfies (B.37) with $p = 0$, hence (B.42) yields $T_{u_i}^{1,h_{\beta_i}} \geq C_0 h$, implying in turn $S_\Delta \geq C_0\, T_{u_{3-i}}^{1,h_{\beta_{3-i}}}$. Then, another application of (B.42) shows that $g \leq K S_\Delta$, where $g = h + u_1^{\beta_1} f_{\beta_1}^0 + u_2^{\beta_2} f_{\beta_2}^0$. On the other hand, (B.41) yields $T_{u_2}^{1,h_{\beta_2}} \leq K(h + u_2^{\beta_2} f_{\beta_2}^0)$, hence (B.47) and (B.41) again give us $S_\Delta \leq K g$. In other words, there is a constant $C > 1$ such that, if $\Delta \leq 1$,

$$\frac{1}{C}\left(h + u_1^{\beta_1} f_{\beta_1}^0 + u_2^{\beta_2} f_{\beta_2}^0\right) \leq S_\Delta \leq C\left(h + u_1^{\beta_1} f_{\beta_1}^0 + u_2^{\beta_2} f_{\beta_2}^0\right). \tag{B.50}$$

Second, (B.40) and (B.49) yield, by integration, and by using the first part of (B.31),

$$\begin{aligned}
&\left|S_\Delta - T_{u_2}^{1,h_{\beta_2}} - \beta_1\, u_1^{\beta_1}\, H_{u_2}(D^{1,\beta_1,0}, h_{\beta_2})\right| \\
&\qquad \leq K u_1^{\beta_1}\left(T_{u_2}^{2,h_{\beta_2}} + u_1^{\beta_1} H_{u_2}(f_{\beta_1}^0, h_{\beta_2})\right).
\end{aligned}$$

Another application of (B.40), plus (B.47) and $u_2^{\beta_2} \leq K u_2^{\beta_1}$ (because $\beta_2 < \beta_1$), gives

$$\begin{aligned}
&\left|S_\Delta - h - \beta_2 u_2^{\beta_2} D^{1,\beta_2,0} - \beta_1 u_1^{\beta_1} H_{u_2}(D^{1,\beta_1,0}, h_{\beta_2})\right| \\
&\qquad \leq K(u_2^{\beta_2} g_2 + u_1^{\beta_1} h + u_1^{2\beta_1} f_{\beta_1}^0 + u_1^{\beta_1} u_2^{\beta_2} f_{\beta_2}^0).
\end{aligned} \tag{B.51}$$

The last estimate will be used as follows: taking (B.35), (B.36), (B.48) and (B.50) into consideration, together with the properties $u_2^{\beta_2}/u_1^{\beta_1} \leq K\Delta^{(\beta_1-\beta_2)/2}$ and $g_\theta(x)/f_{\beta_i}^0(x) \to 0$ as $|x| \to \infty$, we deduce that for all $\Gamma \geq 1$ (recalling that ϕ is a generic increasing bounded continuous function on $\mathbb{R}_+$, vanishing at 0):

$$\begin{aligned}
&|x| \leq \Gamma \;\Rightarrow\; S_\Delta(x) \geq h(x)/2 \text{ if } \Delta < C_\Gamma \text{ , for some } C_\Gamma > 0 \\
&|x| \geq \Gamma \;\Rightarrow\; |S_\Delta(x) - S_\Delta'(x)| \leq S_\Delta(x)(\phi(1/\Gamma) + \phi(\Delta)) \\
&\qquad \text{where } S_\Delta' = h + \beta_1 u_1^{\beta_1} f_{\beta_1}^0 + \beta_2 u_2^{\beta_2} f_{\beta_2}^0.
\end{aligned} \tag{B.52}$$

Estimates for $R_\Delta^{i,0}$ Below, we fix $\Gamma \geq 1$. If $i = 1$ we set $\psi = h_{\beta_2}$ and $\Psi = \check{h}_{\beta_1}$, whereas if $i = 2$ we set $\psi = \check{h}_{\beta_2}$ and $\Psi = h_{\beta_1}$. We then have

$$R_\Delta^{i,0}(x) = \frac{1}{u_i^{\beta_i}} \int T_{u_2}^{1,\psi}(x - u_1 y)\, \Psi(y)\, dy.$$

Suppose first $i = 1$. Since $u_2^{\beta_2}/u_1^{\beta_1} \leq K\Delta^{(\beta_1-\beta_2)/2}$, (B.41) applied to $T_{u_2}^{1,\hbar_{\beta_2}}$ (so with $p = 0$ and $\bar{b} = 1$) and an integration give

$$\left|R_\Delta^{1,0} - \frac{1}{u_1^{\beta_1}}T_{u_1}^{1,\check{h}_{\beta_1}}\right| \leq K\Delta^{(\beta_1-\beta_2)/2}H_{u_1}(f_{\beta_2}^0, \check{h}_{\beta_1}).$$

Then (B.31) and (B.40) and (B.47), plus $\int \check{h}_\beta(x)dx = 0$, yield

$$|R_\Delta^{1,0} + \beta_1^2 D^{1,\beta_1,0}| \leq K(g_2 + u_1^{\beta_1}f_{\beta_1}^0 + \Delta^{(\beta_1-\beta_2)/2}f_{\beta_2}^0).$$

Finally, since $g_2(x)/f_{\beta_1}^0(x) \to 0$ as $|x| \to \infty$, we deduce from (B.35) that

$$\begin{aligned}|R_\Delta^{1,0}| &\leq K(g_2 + f_{\beta_1}^0 + f_{\beta_2}^0)\\ |x| \geq \Gamma \Rightarrow &\begin{cases} |R_\Delta^{1,0}(x) + \beta_1^2 f_{\beta_1}^0(x)|\\ \leq K(f_{\beta_1}^0(x)\phi(1/\Gamma) + \Delta^{(\beta_1-\beta_2)/2}f_{\beta_2}^0(x)).\end{cases}\end{aligned} \quad \text{(B.53)}$$

Now, we turn to $R_\Delta^{2,0}$. By the same arguments as above, we have

$$\begin{aligned}|R_\Delta^{2,0} + \beta_2^2 H_{u_1}(D^{1,\beta_2,0}, h_{\beta_1})| &\leq K(T_{u_1}^{2,h_{\beta_1}} + u_2^{\beta_2}H_{u_1}(f_{\beta_2}^0, h_{\beta_1}))\\ &\leq K(g_2 + u_1^{\beta_1}f_{\beta_1}^0 + u_2^{\beta_2}f_{\beta_2}^0).\end{aligned}$$

Then (B.35) and (B.48) and the above estimates yield

$$\begin{aligned}|R_\Delta^{2,0}(x)| &\leq K(g_2 + f_{\beta_1}^0 + f_{\beta_2}^0)\\ |x| \geq \Gamma \Rightarrow |R_\Delta^{2,0}(x) + \beta_2^2 f_{\beta_2}^0(x)| &\leq f_{\beta_2}^0(x)\phi(1/\Gamma).\end{aligned} \quad \text{(B.54)}$$

Estimates for $R_\Delta^{i,1}$ We argue as in the previous part. For notational purposes we write here $\dot{h}_\beta = \partial_\beta h_\beta$. We take below $\psi = h_{\beta_2}$ and $\Psi = \dot{h}_{\beta_1}$ when $i = 1$, and $\psi = \dot{h}_{\beta_2}$ and $\Psi = h_{\beta_1}$ when $i = 2$, to get

$$R_\Delta^{i,1}(x) = \frac{1}{u_i^{\beta_i}\log(1/u_i)}\int T_{u_2}^{1,\psi}(x - u_1 y)\Psi(y)\,dy.$$

The estimates in (B.41) yields

$$\left|R_\Delta^{1,1} - \frac{1}{u_1^{\beta_1}\log(1/u_1)}T_{u_1}^{1,\dot{h}_{\beta_1}}\right| \leq K\frac{\Delta^{(\beta_1-\beta_2)/2}}{\log(1/u_1)}H_{u_1}(f_{\beta_2}^0, \dot{h}_{\beta_1}).$$

Note that (B.31) implies $\dot{h}_{\beta_1} = l_0 + l_1$ for two functions l_i satisfying (B.37) with $p = i$ and with the constants b_i and $\bar{b}_i$ such that $\bar{b}_0 + \bar{b}_1 = \int \dot{h}_{\beta_1}(x)dx = 0$ and $b_0 = 1$ and $b_1 = -\beta_1$. Then (B.40) and (B.47) again yield

$$\begin{aligned}&\left|R_\Delta^{1,1} + \beta_1\left(D^{1,\beta_1,0} + \frac{D^{1,\beta_1,1}}{\log(1/u_1)}\right)\right|\\ &\leq K\left(g_2 + u_1^{\beta_1}f_{\beta_1}^0 + \frac{u_1^{\beta_1}f_{\beta_1}^1 + f_{\beta_1}^0 + \Delta^{(\beta_1-\beta_2)/2}f_{\beta_2}^0}{\log(1/u_1)}\right).\end{aligned}$$

Hence, since $f^0_{\beta_1}(x)/f^1_{\beta_1}(x) \to 0$ as $|x| \to \infty$,

$$|R^{1,1}_\Delta| \leq K(g_2 + f^1_{\beta_1} + f^1_{\beta_2})$$

$$|x| \geq \Gamma \Rightarrow \begin{cases} |R^{1,1}_\Delta(x) + \beta_1 f^0_{\beta_1}(x)| \\ \leq f^0_{\beta_1}(x)\phi(1/\Gamma) \\ + \frac{f^1_{\beta_1}(x)}{\log(1/u_1)} + K\frac{\Delta^{(\beta_1-\beta_2)/2}}{\log(1/u_1)}f^0_{\beta_2}(x). \end{cases} \tag{B.55}$$

In the same way, we have

$$|R^{2,1}_\Delta + \beta_2 H_{u_1}(D^{1,\beta_2,0}, h_{\beta_1})|$$
$$\leq K\left(T^{2,h_{\beta_1}}_{u_1} + \frac{H_{u_1}(f^1_{\beta_1}, h_{\beta_1})}{\log(1/u_2)} + u^{\beta_2}_2 H_{u_1}(f^1_{\beta_2}, h_{\beta_1})\right)$$
$$\leq K\left(g_2 + \frac{f^1_{\beta_1}}{\log(1/u_2)} + u^{\beta_2}_2 f^1_{\beta_2}\right),$$

implying

$$|R^{2,1}_\Delta| \leq K(g_2 + f^1_{\beta_1} + f^1_{\beta_2})$$

$$|x| \geq \Gamma \Rightarrow \begin{cases} |R^{2,1}_\Delta(x) + \beta_2 f^0_{\beta_2}(x)| \\ \leq f^0_{\beta_2}(x)\phi(1/\Gamma) + \frac{f^1_{\beta_2}(x)}{\log(1/u_2)}. \end{cases} \tag{B.56}$$

Some Useful Integrals Before proceeding to the proof of Theorem 5.25 we still need to study the behavior, as $\Delta \to 0$, of integrals of the following type (recall (B.52) for S'_Δ):

$$\Theta^{\beta,p}_{\Delta,\Gamma} = \int_{\{|x|>\Gamma\}} \frac{f^p_\beta(x)^2}{S'_\Delta(x)}\,dx, \tag{B.57}$$

where as above $p \in \{0,1\}$ and $\beta \in (\beta_1/2, \beta_1]$ and $\Gamma > 3$.

We will use the following (easy) property: for $y \geq 1$ and $y' \in (y, \infty]$,

$$\psi^p_\beta(y,y') = \int_{\{y<|x|<y'\}} \frac{f^p_\beta(x)^2}{f^0_{\beta_1}(x)}\,dx \sim \Psi^p_\beta(y) = \frac{2(\log y)^{2p}}{(2\beta-\beta_1)y^{2\beta-\beta_1}} \tag{B.58}$$
as $y \to \infty$, $\frac{y'}{y} \to \infty$.

Since both functions $h/f^0_{\beta_1}$ and $f^0_{\beta_1}/f^0_{\beta_2}$ are ultimately strictly decreasing, for all $u > 0$ small enough there are unique numbers L_u and M_u such that, with a given by (B.32),

$$|x| > L_u \Leftrightarrow f^0_{\beta_1}(x) < au^{\beta_1 \frac{\beta_1-\beta_2}{2-\beta_1}} f^0_{\beta_2}(x),$$
$$|x| > M_u \Leftrightarrow h(x) < u^{\beta_1} f^0_{\beta_1}(x) \tag{B.59}$$

and of course the inequalities above become equalities when $x = L_u$ and $x = M_u$, respectively. The following properties are easy to check:

$$L_u = \frac{1}{a^{\frac{1}{\beta_1-\beta_2}}u^{\frac{\beta_1}{2-\beta_1}}}, \qquad u \to 0 \Rightarrow M_u \sim \sqrt{2\beta_1 \log(1/u)}. \tag{B.60}$$

Let $\mu \in (0,1)$. If $M_{u_1\mu} < |x| < L_{u_1/\mu}$, (B.59) yields $h(x) < (u_1\mu)^{\beta_1} f^0_{\beta_1}(x)$ and $u_2^{\beta_2} f^0_{\beta_2}(x) < \mu^{\beta_1(\beta_1-\beta_2)/(2-\beta_1)} u_1^{\beta_1} f^0_{\beta_1}(x)$, the latter inequality using also (B.32) and a simple calculation. Thus if $\delta(\mu) = 1 + \left(\mu^{\beta_1}/\beta_1 + \beta_2 \mu^{\beta_1(\beta_1-\beta_2)/(2-\beta_1)}\right)/\beta_1$, and in view of the definition of S'_Δ, we get $S'_\Delta(x) \le \beta_1 u_1^{\beta_1} \delta(\mu) f^0_{\beta_1}(x)$. It follows that, for u_1 (hence Δ) small enough so that $M_{u_1\mu} > \Gamma$,

$$\Theta^{\beta,p}_{\Delta,\Gamma} \ge \int_{\{M_{u_1\mu}<|x|<L_{u_1/\mu}\}} \frac{f^p_\beta(x)^2}{S'_\Delta(x)}\,dx \ge \frac{1}{\delta(\mu)}\frac{1}{\beta_1 u_1^{\beta_1}}\psi^p_\beta(M_{u_1\mu}, L_{u_1/\mu}).$$

By (B.60) we have $L_{u_1/\mu}/M_{u_1\mu} \to \infty$ for each μ, whereas $\Psi^p_\beta(M_{u_1\mu})/\Psi^p_\beta(M_{u_1}) \to 1$. Thus (B.58) and the fact that $\delta(\mu) \to 1$ as $\mu \to 0$ give

$$\liminf_{\Delta\to 0} \frac{\beta_1 u_1^{\beta_1}}{\Psi^p_\alpha(M_{u_1})}\,\Theta^{\beta,p}_{\Delta,\Gamma} \ge 1. \qquad (B.61)$$

On the other hand, let $\gamma \in (0,1)$. We have $h(x) \ge h(M_{u_1})^{\gamma^2}$ if $|x| \le \gamma M_{u_1}$, whereas S'_Δ is bigger than both h and $\beta_1 u_1^{\beta_1} f^0_{\beta_1}$. Then we deduce from (B.59) and $\alpha := \int f^p_\beta(x)^2\,dx < \infty$ that

$$\Theta^{\beta,p}_{\Delta,\Gamma} \le \int_{\{|x|\le\gamma M_{u_1}\}} \frac{f^p_\beta(x)^2}{h(x)}\,dx + \frac{1}{\beta_1 u_1^{\beta_1}} \int_{\{|x|>\gamma M_{u_1}\}} \frac{f^p_\beta(x)^2}{f^0_{\beta_1}(x)}\,dx$$
$$\le \frac{\psi^p_\beta(\gamma M_{u_1}, \infty)}{\beta_1 u_1^{\beta_1}}(1 + \psi'^p_\beta(\gamma, u_1)),$$

where

$$\psi'^p_\beta(\gamma, u_1) = \frac{\alpha\,\beta_1 u_1^{\beta_1}}{\psi^p_\beta(\gamma M_{u_1},\infty)\,h(M_{u_1})^{\gamma^2}} = \frac{\alpha\,\beta_1 u_1^{(1-\gamma^2)\beta_1}\,M_{u_1}^{\gamma^2(1+\beta_1)}}{\psi^p_\beta(\gamma M_{u_1},\infty)}$$

(recall $h(M_{u_1}) = u_1^{\beta_1}/M_{u_1}^{1+\beta_1}$ for u_1 small enough, which gives the last equality above). We deduce from (B.58) that $\psi^p_\beta(\gamma M_{u_1}, \infty)/\Psi^p_\beta(\gamma M_{u_1}) \to 1$, and we draw two consequences: first, $\psi'^p_\beta(\gamma, u_1) \asymp u_1^{\beta_1} M_{u_1}^{\gamma^2(1+\beta_1)+2\beta-\beta_1}/(\log M_{u_1})^{2p}$, hence $\psi'^p_\beta(\gamma, u_1) \to 0$ by (B.60); second, we have

$$\limsup_{\Delta\to 0} \frac{\beta_1 u_1^{\beta_1}}{\Psi^p_\beta(M_{\gamma u_1})}\,\Theta^{\beta,p}_{\Delta,\Gamma} \le 1.$$

This holds for any $\gamma \in (0,1)$, whereas (B.58) again implies $\Psi^p_\beta(\gamma M_{u_1})/\Psi^p_\beta(M_{u_1}) \to 1/\gamma^{2\beta-\beta_1}$. Hence, letting $\gamma \to 1$ above, and combining with (B.61), we obtain $\Theta^{\beta,p}_{\Delta,\Gamma} \sim \Psi^p_\beta(M_{u_1})/\beta_1 u_1^{\beta_1}$, as $\Delta \to 0$. In view of (B.58), and after some calculations, this leads us to

$$\Theta^{\beta,p}_{\Delta,\Gamma} \sim \overline{\psi}^p_\beta(\Delta) := \frac{2^{1-2p} c^{\beta_1/2}}{a_1 \beta_1 (2\beta-\beta_1)(2-\beta_1)^{\beta-\beta_1/2}} \times \frac{(\log\log(1/\Delta))^{2p}}{\Delta^{1-\beta_1/2}(\log(1/\Delta))^{\beta-\beta_1/2}}. \qquad (B.62)$$

Proof of Theorem 5.25 We are finally in a position to prove the result. We let $\Gamma > 3$ and $i \in \{1,2\}$ and $l, m \in \{0,1\}$, and we write $\gamma_{i,0} = \beta_i^2$ and $\gamma_{i,1} = \beta_i$. Then, we set

$$\overline{J}_{\Delta,\Gamma}^{i,lm} = \int_{\{|x| \leq \Gamma\}} \frac{R_\Delta^{i,l}(x)\, R_\Delta^{i,m}(x)}{S_\Delta(x)}\, dx,$$

$$L_{\Delta,\Gamma}^{i,lm} = \int_{\{|x| > \Gamma\}} \frac{(R_\Delta^{i,l}(x) + \gamma_{i,l} f_{\beta_i}^0(x))(R_\Delta^{i,m}(x) + \gamma_{i,m} f_{\beta_i}^0(x))}{S_\Delta(x)}\, dx,$$

$$\overline{L}_{\Delta,\Gamma}^{i,m} = \int_{\{|x| > \Gamma\}} \frac{f_{\beta_i}^0(x)(R_\Delta^{i,m}(x) + \gamma_{i,m} f_{\beta_i}^0(x))}{S_\Delta(x)}\, dx,$$

and

$$M_{\Delta,\Gamma}^{i,m} = \int_{\{|x| > \Gamma\}} \frac{f_{\beta_i}^m(x)^2}{S_\Delta(x)}\, dx.$$

With this notation, we have by a simple calculation

$$J_\Delta^{i,lm} = \overline{J}_{\Delta,\Gamma}^{i,lm} + \gamma_{i,l}\gamma_{i,m} M_{\Delta,\Gamma}^{i,0} + L_{\Delta,\Gamma}^{i,lm} - \gamma_{i,l}\overline{L}_{\Delta,\Gamma}^{i,m} - \gamma_{i,m}\overline{L}_{\Delta,\Gamma}^{i,l}. \quad (B.63)$$

Now, we proceed with some estimates. First, if we apply the estimates (B.52)–(B.56), we see that for any Γ, and with C_Γ as in (B.52), we have $\sup\left(\frac{R_\Delta^{i,l}(x)\, R_\Delta^{i,m}(x)}{S_\Delta(x)} : \Delta < C_\Gamma, |x| \leq \Gamma\right) < \infty$. Hence there is a constant K_Γ depending on Γ, such that

$$|\overline{J}_{\Delta,\Gamma}^{i,lm}| \leq K_\Gamma \quad \text{for all } \Delta \text{ small enough.} \quad (B.64)$$

Next, the Cauchy-Schwarz inequality yields

$$|\overline{L}_{\Delta,\Gamma}^{i,m}| \leq \sqrt{L_{\Delta,\Gamma}^{i,mm} M_{\Delta,\Gamma}^{i,0}}, \qquad |L_{\Delta,\Gamma}^{i,lm}| \leq \sqrt{L_{\Delta,\Gamma}^{i,ll} L_{\Delta,\Gamma}^{i,mm}}. \quad (B.65)$$

Equation (B.52) yields $|M_{\Delta,\Gamma}^{i,m} - \Theta_{\Delta,\Gamma}^{\beta_i,m}| \leq \Theta_{\Delta,\Gamma}^{\beta_i,m}(\phi(1/\Gamma) + \phi(\Delta))$. Thus, applying (B.62), we first deduce $\Theta_{\Delta,\Gamma}^{\beta_i,m} \to \infty$, and therefore

$$\lim_{\Gamma \to \infty} \limsup_{\Delta \to 0} \left|\frac{M_{\Delta,\Gamma}^{i,m}}{\overline{\psi}_{\beta_i}^m(\Delta)} - 1\right| = 0. \quad (B.66)$$

Moreover, (B.53)–(B.56) yield

$$L_{\Delta,\Gamma}^{i,mm} \leq M_{\Delta,\Gamma}^{i,0}(\phi(1/\Gamma) + \Delta^{(\beta_1-\beta_2)/2}) + \frac{M_{\Delta,\Gamma}^{i,m}}{\log(1/u_i)}.$$

By (B.62), we have $\overline{\psi}_{\beta_i}^1(\Delta)/\overline{\psi}_{\beta_i}^0(\Delta) \log(1/u_i) \to 0$. Hence by (B.66),

$$\lim_{\Gamma \to \infty} \limsup_{\Delta \to 0} \frac{L_{\Delta,\Gamma}^{i,mm}}{\overline{\psi}_{\beta_i}^0(\Delta)} = 0.$$

This and (B.64)–(B.66), plus $\lim_{\Delta \to 0} \overline{\psi}^p_\beta(\Delta) = \infty$, yield for all i, m, l

$$\lim_{\Gamma \to \infty} \limsup_{\Delta \to 0} \frac{1}{\overline{\psi}^0_{\beta_i}(\Delta)} (|\overline{J}^{i,lm}_{\Delta,\Gamma}| + |\overline{L}^{i,m}_{\Delta,\Gamma}| + |L^{i,lm}_{\Delta,\Gamma}|) = 0.$$

At this stage, we use (B.63) to deduce $J^{i,lm}_\Delta \sim \gamma_{i,l}\,\gamma_{i,m}\,\overline{\psi}^0_{\beta_i}(\Delta)$ when $\Delta \to 0$. This, combined with (B.33) and the definition (B.62), plus the fact that $v_i \to \frac{2}{\beta_i(2-\beta_i)}$ as $\Delta \to 0$, yield all results in Theorem 5.25. $\square$

B.2   Proofs for Chapter 8

After an introductory part, we first prove a number of useful estimates and then study some properties of the spot volatility estimators. Then we proceed to the proofs for Subsections 8.3–8.5, in a somewhat different order than in the main text.

B.2.1   Preliminaries

Below we assume at least (K-r) for some $r \in [0, 2]$. For the sake of clarity, we recall the setting. We have the following structure, in matrix notation:

$$
\begin{aligned}
X_t &= X_0 + \int_0^t b_s\, ds + \int_0^t \sigma_s\, dW_s \\
&\quad + (\delta 1_{\{\|\delta\|\le 1\}}) \star (\underline{p} - \underline{q})_t + (\delta 1_{\{\|\delta\|>1\}}) \star \underline{p}_t \\
\sigma_t &= \sigma_0 + \int_0^t b^{(\sigma)}_s\, ds + \int_0^t \sigma^{(\sigma)}_s\, dW_s \\
&\quad + (\delta^{(\sigma)} 1_{\{\|\delta^{(\sigma)}\|\le 1\}}) \star (\underline{p} - \underline{q})_t + (\delta^{(\sigma)} 1_{\{\|\delta^{(\sigma)}\|>1\}}) \star \underline{p}_t \\
c_t &= c_0 + \int_0^t b^{(c)}_s\, ds + \int_0^t \sigma^{(c)}_s\, dW_s \\
&\quad + (\delta^{(c)} 1_{\{\|\delta^{(c)}\|\le 1\}}) \star (\underline{p} - \underline{q})_t + (\delta^{(c)} 1_{\{\|\delta^{(c)}\|>1\}}) \star \underline{p}_t.
\end{aligned}
\tag{B.67}
$$

We emphasize that the third equation above follows by Itô's formula from the second one, and $b^{(c)}, \sigma^{(c)}, \delta^{(c)}$ are deterministic functions of $\sigma, b^{(\sigma)}, \sigma^{(\sigma)}, \delta^{(\sigma)}$. We also recall the (integrated and spot) volatility of the volatility c, and co-volatility between X and c:

$$
\begin{aligned}
C^{(c)}_t &= \int_0^t c^{(c)}_s\, ds, & c^{(c),ij,i'j'}_s &= \sum_{l=1}^{d'} \sigma^{(c),ij,l}_s \sigma^{(c),i'j',l}_s \\
C^{(X,c)}_t &= \int_0^t c^{(X,c)}_s\, ds, & c^{(X,c),i,i'j'}_s &= \sum_{l=1}^{d'} \sigma^{il}_s \sigma^{(c),i'j',l}_s.
\end{aligned}
\tag{B.68}
$$

We assume (K-r), or (KC), or (KCC), according to the case. However, by a "localization procedure" we can replace these assumptions by strengthened ones, as explained on page 502. Upon using the notation

$$
\begin{aligned}
S &= \inf\left(t : \int_0^t \widehat{b}_s\, ds = \infty\right), \quad \text{where} \\
\widehat{b}_s &= \int_{\{\|\delta(s,z)\|\le 1\}} \|\delta(s, z)\| \lambda(dz) \\
t \in [0, \infty) \cap [0, S] &\Rightarrow b'_t = b_t - \int_{\{\|\delta(t,z)\|\le 1\}} \delta(t, z)\, \lambda(dz),
\end{aligned}
\tag{B.69}
$$

these assumptions, denoted as (SK-r), (SKC) and (SKCC), can be described in terms of the coefficients of the first two equations of (B.67), as follows:

Assumption (SK-r). *We have (B.67), the processes $b, b^{(\sigma)}, \sigma, \sigma^{(\sigma)}$ are bounded, as well as $\widehat{b}_t$ on $\{t \leq S\}$; the processes $\sigma^{(\sigma)}$, and b when $r > 1$, and b' in restriction to $[0, S]$ are càdlàg or càglàd; we have $\|\delta(t, z)\|^r \leq J(z)$ and $\|\delta^{(\sigma)}(t, z)\|^2 \leq J(z)$ identically, where J is a bounded nonnegative function on E with $\int J(z) \lambda(dz) < \infty$.*

Assumption (SKC). *We have (SK-0) with δ identically vanishing, so X is continuous.*

Assumption (SKCC). *We have (B.67), and $\delta, \delta^{(\sigma)}$ are identically vanishing, and $b, b^{(\sigma)}$ are bounded càdlàg or càglàd, and $\sigma^{(\sigma)}$ is bounded càdlàg, and σ is bounded (of course continuous).*

In the sequel, the constant K may change from line to line and may depend on the bounds in the previous assumptions, but never on n or on the various indices $i, j, \ldots$; when it depends on an extra parameter p it is denoted as K_p. We also use the shorthand notation $\mathcal{F}_i^n$ for $\mathcal{F}_{i\Delta_n}$.

Under (SK-r), and by (A.66), one may rewrite (B.67) as

$$\begin{aligned}
X_t &= X_0 + \int_0^t \overline{b}_s \, ds + \int_0^t \sigma_s \, dW_s + \delta \star (\underline{p} - \underline{q})_t \\
\sigma_t &= \sigma_0 + \int_0^t \overline{b}_s^{(\sigma)} \, ds + \int_0^t \sigma_s^{(\sigma)} \, dW_s + \delta^{(\sigma)} \star (\underline{p} - \underline{q})_t \qquad \text{(B.70)} \\
c_t &= c_0 + \int_0^t \overline{b}_s^{(c)} \, ds + \int_0^t \sigma_s^{(c)} \, dW_s + \delta^{(c)} \star (\underline{p} - \underline{q})_t.
\end{aligned}$$

Here, $\overline{b}_t = b_t + \int \delta(t, z) 1_{\{\|\delta(t,z)\| > 1\}} \lambda(dz)$, and likewise for $\overline{b}_t^{(\sigma)}$ and $\overline{b}_t^{(c)}$. Observe that we have (upon multiplying the function J by a constant)

$$\begin{aligned}
\|\overline{b}_t\| + \|\sigma_t\| + \|\overline{b}_t^{(\sigma)}\| + \|\sigma_t^{(\sigma)}\| & \\
+ \, \|c_t\| + \|\overline{b}_t^{(c)}\| + \|\sigma_t^{(c)}\| + \|c_t^{(X,c)}\| &\leq K, \qquad \text{(B.71)} \\
\|\delta(t, z)\|^r + \|\delta^{(\sigma)}(t, z)\|^2 + \|\delta^{(c)}(t, z)\|^2 &\leq J(z).
\end{aligned}$$

When (SK-r) with $r \leq 1$ holds, the process b_t' of (B.69) is defined for all times and bounded, and according to (A.6), we also have

$$X_t = X_0 + \int_0^t b_s' \, ds + \int_0^t \sigma_s \, dW_s + \delta \star \underline{p}_t. \qquad \text{(B.72)}$$

We end this introduction with three general results. In the first two we have a sequence $k_n \geq 1$ of integers satisfying $k_n \Delta_n \to 0$.

First, with any q-dimensional càdlàg bounded process Y we associate the variables

$$\eta_{i,j}^n = \sqrt{\mathbb{E}(\sup_{s\in(0,j\Delta_n]} \|Y_{(i-1)\Delta_n+s} - Y_{(i-1)\Delta_n}\|^2 \mid \mathcal{F}_{i-1}^n)},$$
$$\eta_i^n = \eta_{i,1}^n, \qquad \eta_i'^n = \eta_{i,2k_n}^n.$$
(B.73)

Lemma B.1. *For all $i \le i' < i+j \le i'+2k_n$ we have $\mathbb{E}(\eta_{i',j}^n \mid \mathcal{F}_{i-1}^n) \le 2\eta_i'^n$, and for all t we have $\Delta_n\mathbb{E}(\sum_{i=1}^{[t/\Delta_n]} \eta_i'^n) \to 0$ and $\Delta_n\mathbb{E}(\sum_{i=1}^{[t/\Delta_n]} \eta_i^n) \to 0$.*

Proof. The first claim follows from Cauchy-Schwarz inequality. For the second one, setting $\gamma_t^n = \sup_{s\in(0,(2k_n+1)\Delta_n]} \|Y_{t+s} - Y_s\|^2$, we observe that $\mathbb{E}((\eta_i'^n)^2)$ is smaller than a constant always, and smaller than $\frac{1}{\Delta_n}\int_{(i-2)\Delta_n}^{(i-1)\Delta_n} \mathbb{E}(\gamma_s^n)\,ds$ when $i \ge 2$. Hence

$$\Delta_n\mathbb{E}\left(\sum_{i=1}^{[t/\Delta_n]} \eta_i'^n\right) \le \sqrt{t}\left(\mathbb{E}\left(\Delta_n\sum_{i=1}^{[t/\Delta_n]}(\eta_i'^n)^2\right)\right)^{1/2}$$
$$\le \sqrt{t}\left(K\Delta_n + \mathbb{E}\left(\int_0^t \gamma_s^n\,ds\right)\right)^{1/2}.$$

We have $\gamma_s^n \le K$ and the càdlàg property of Y yields that $\gamma_s^n(\omega) \to 0$ for all ω, and all s except for countably many strictly positive values (depending on ω). Then, the second claim follows by the dominated convergence theorem, and it clearly implies the third. $\square$

Lemma B.2. *For any reals a_i^n with $|a_i^n| \le L$ for all n, i, and any array ξ_i^n of q-dimensional variables such that each ξ_i^n is $\mathcal{F}_i^n$-measurable and satisfies*

$$\|\mathbb{E}(\xi_i^n \mid \mathcal{F}_{i-1}^n)\| \le L', \qquad \mathbb{E}(\|\xi_i^n\|^q \mid \mathcal{F}_{i-1}^n) \le L_q,$$

where $q \ge 2$ and L, L', L_q are constants, we have

$$\left\|\mathbb{E}\left(\sum_{j=1}^{2k_n-1} a_j^n \xi_{i+j}^n \mid \mathcal{F}_{i-1}^n\right)\right\| \le LL'k_n,$$
$$\mathbb{E}\left(\left\|\sum_{j=1}^{2k_n-1} a_j^n \xi_{i+j}^n\right\|^q \mid \mathcal{F}_{i-1}^n\right) \le K_q L^q(L_q k_n^{q/2} + L'^q k_n^q).$$

Proof. Set $\xi_i'^n = \mathbb{E}(\xi_i^n \mid \mathcal{F}_{i-1}^n)$ and $\xi_i''^n = \xi_i^n - \xi_i'^n$, and also $A_n' = \sum_{j=1}^{2k_n-1} a_j^n \xi_{i+j}'^n$ and $A_n'' = \sum_{j=1}^{2k_n-1} a_j^n \xi_{i+j}''^n$. We obviously have $\|A_n'\| \le LL'k_n$, implying the first claim.

The variables $\xi_{i+j}''^n$ are martingale increments for the discrete-time filtration $(\mathcal{F}_{i+j}^n)_{j\ge 0}$. Then Burkholder-Gundy and Hölder inequalities give us

$$\mathbb{E}(\|A_n^l{}''\|^q \mid \mathcal{F}_{i-1}^n) \leq K_q \mathbb{E}\Big(\big(\sum_{j=0}^{2k_n-1} \|a_j^n \xi_{i+j}''^n\|^2\big)^{q/2} \mid \mathcal{F}_{i-1}^n\Big)$$
$$\leq L^q K_q k_n^{q/2-1} \mathbb{E}\Big(\sum_{j=0}^{2k_n-1} \|\xi_{i+j}''^n\|^q \mid \mathcal{F}_{i-1}^n\Big),$$

which, since $\mathbb{E}(\|\xi_{i+j}'^n\|^q \mid \mathcal{F}_{i-1}^n) \leq \mathbb{E}(\|\xi_{i+j}^n\|^q \mid \mathcal{F}_{i-1}^n)$, is smaller than $K_q L^q L_q k_n^{q/2}$. The second claim readily follows. □

Finally, we prove some estimates which are slightly finer than those in Appendix A, for a q-dimensional continuous semimartingale of the form

$$Y_t = \int_0^t b_s^Y \, ds + \int_0^t \sigma_s^Y \, dW_s.$$

Note that $Y_0 = 0$ here. Here, W is a q'-dimensional Brownian motion, with q' arbitrary, and $c^Y = \sigma^Y \sigma^{Y\star}$. We assume that for some constant A we have

$$\|b^Y\| \leq A, \qquad \|\sigma^Y\| \leq A. \tag{B.74}$$

In connection with (B.73), we associate with any process Z the variables

$$\eta(Z)_t = \sqrt{\mathbb{E}\big(\sup_{s \leq t} \|Z_s - Z_0\|^2 \mid \mathcal{F}_0\big)}.$$

Lemma B.3. *In the previous setting, and with the constant K below only depending on A in (B.74), we have for $t \in [0,1]$*

$$\|\mathbb{E}(Y_t \mid \mathcal{F}_0) - t\,b_0^Y\| \leq t\,\eta(b^Y)_t \leq Kt$$
$$|\mathbb{E}(Y_t^j Y_t^m \mid \mathcal{F}_0) - t\,c_0^{Y,jm}| \tag{B.75}$$
$$\leq Kt(t + \sqrt{t}\,\eta(b^Y)_t + \eta(c^Y)_t) \leq Kt.$$

If further

$$\|\mathbb{E}(c_t^Y - c_0^Y \mid \mathcal{F}_0)\| + \mathbb{E}(\|c_t^Y - c_0^Y\|^2 \mid \mathcal{F}_0) \leq At \tag{B.76}$$

for all t, we also have

$$|\mathbb{E}(Y_t^j Y_t^m \mid \mathcal{F}_0) - t\,c_0^{Y,jm}| \leq K\,t^{3/2}(\sqrt{t} + \eta(b^Y)_t) \leq K\,t^{3/2}. \tag{B.77}$$

$$\big|\mathbb{E}\big(Y_t^j Y_t^k Y_t^l Y_t^m \mid \mathcal{F}_0\big)$$
$$-t^2(c_0^{Y,jk} c_0^{Y,lm} + c_0^{Y,jl} c_0^{Y,km} + c_0^{Y,jm} c_0^{Y,kl})\big| \leq K\,t^{5/2}. \tag{B.78}$$

Proof. The first part of (B.75) follows by taking the $\mathcal{F}_0$-conditional expectation in the decomposition $Y_t = M_t + tb_0^Y + \int_0^t (b_s^Y - b_0^Y) \, ds$, where M

is a q-dimensional martingale with $M_0 = 0$. For the second part, we deduce from Itô's formula that $Y^j Y^m$ is the sum of a martingale vanishing at 0, plus the process

$$b_0^{Y,j} \int_0^t Y_s^m \, ds + b_0^{Y,m} \int_0^t Y_s^j \, ds + \int_0^t Y_s^m (b_s^{Y,j} - b_0^{Y,j}) \, ds$$
$$+ \int_0^t Y_s^j (b_s^{Y,m} - b_0^{Y,m}) \, ds + c_0^{Y,jm} t + \int_0^t (c_s^{Y,jm} - c_0^{Y,jm}) \, ds.$$

Since $\mathbb{E}(\|Y_t\| \mid \mathcal{F}_0) \leq K \sqrt{t}$ by (A.67) of Appendix A, we deduce both the second part of (B.75) and (B.77) by taking again the conditional expectation and by using the Cauchy-Schwarz inequality and the first part.

For any indices $j_1, \ldots, j_4$ Itô's formula yields that, with M a martingale vanishing at 0,

$$\prod_{l=1}^4 Y_t^{j_l} = M_t + \sum_{l=1}^p \int_0^t b_s^{Y,j_l} \prod_{1 \leq m \leq p, m \neq l} Y_s^{j_m} \, ds$$
$$+ \tfrac{1}{2} \sum_{1 \leq l, l' \leq d, l \neq l'} c_0^{Y,j_l j_{l'}} \int_0^t \prod_{1 \leq m \leq 4, m \neq l, l'} Y_s^{j_m} \, ds$$
$$+ \tfrac{1}{2} \sum_{1 \leq l, l' \leq d, l \neq l'} \int_0^t (c_s^{Y,j_l j_{l'}} - c_0^{Y,j_l j_{l'}})$$
$$\times \prod_{1 \leq m \leq 4, m \neq l, l'} Y_s^{j_m} \, ds.$$

Again, we take the $\mathcal{F}_0$-conditional expectation; using $\mathbb{E}(\|Y_t\|^q \mid \mathcal{F}_0) \leq K_q t^{q/2}$ for all $q \geq 0$ (see (A.67)) and (B.76), plus Fubini's theorem and the Cauchy-Schwarz inequality, one checks that the contribution of the second and fourth terms on the right side above is smaller than $K t^{5/2}$. For the third term we additionally use (B.77), and a simple calculation yields (B.78).   □

B.2.2   Estimates for the Increments of X and c

In all this subsection we suppose X to be *continuous*, thus assuming at least (SKC). The estimates of Appendix A give us for all $q \geq 0$

$$\begin{aligned}
\mathbb{E}\big(\sup_{w \in [0,s]} \|X_{t+w} - X_t\|^q \mid \mathcal{F}_t\big) &\leq K_q s^{q/2}, \\
\|\mathbb{E}(X_{t+s} - X_t \mid \mathcal{F}_s)\| &\leq K s, \\
\mathbb{E}\big(\sup_{w \in [0,s]} \|c_{t+w} - c_t\|^q \mid \mathcal{F}_t\big) &\leq K_q s^{1 \wedge (q/2)}, \\
\|\mathbb{E}(c_{t+s} - c_t \mid \mathcal{F}_s)\| &\leq K s.
\end{aligned} \tag{B.79}$$

This is unfortunately not enough for us, and we proceed to giving a series of other estimates. For simpler notation later on, we define the following multidimensional variables

$$\zeta(1)_i^n = \tfrac{1}{\Delta_n} \Delta_i^n X \, \Delta_i^n X^* - c_{(i-1)\Delta_n}, \quad \zeta(2)_i^n = \Delta_i^n c, \quad \zeta(3)_i^{n,j} = \Delta_i^n X$$
$$\zeta'(r)_i^n = \mathbb{E}(\zeta(r)_i^n \mid \mathcal{F}_{i-1}^n), \quad \zeta''(r)_i^n = \zeta(r)_i^n - \zeta'(r)_i^n$$

and

$$\begin{aligned}
\alpha_i^n &= \tfrac{1}{k_n} \sum_{j=0}^{k_n-1} \zeta(1)_{i+j}^n, \\
\beta_i^n &= \tfrac{1}{k_n} \sum_{j=0}^{k_n-1} c_{(i+j-1)\Delta_n} \\
\overline{\beta}_i^n = \beta_i^n - c_{(i-1)\Delta_n} &= \tfrac{1}{k_n} \sum_{j=0}^{k_n-1} (c_{(i+j-1)\Delta_n} - c_{(i-1)\Delta_n}) \\
&= \tfrac{1}{k_n} \sum_{j=0}^{k_n-1} (k_n - j - 1)\,\zeta(2)_{i+j}^n.
\end{aligned} \tag{B.80}$$

Here, k_n is the sequence of integers used to construct the spot volatility estimators, and it either satisfies $k_n \sim \beta/\sqrt{\Delta_n}$ for some $\beta > 0$, or $k_n\sqrt{\Delta_n} \to 0$.

Estimates Under (SKCC)   We first assume (SKCC), and set

$$\begin{aligned}
&\eta_i^n,\ \eta_i'^n\ \text{ associated by (B.73)} \\
&\text{with the process } Y = (b, b^{(c)}, \sigma^{(c)}, c^{(c)}, c^{(X,c)}).
\end{aligned} \tag{B.81}$$

We apply (B.79) and also Lemma B.3 to the processes $Y_t = X_{(i-1)\Delta_n+t} - X_{(i-1)\Delta_n}$ or $Y_t = c_{(i-1)\Delta_n+t} - c_{(i-1)\Delta_n}$, to obtain

$$\begin{aligned}
\|\zeta'(1)_i^n\| &\le K\sqrt{\Delta_n}\left(\sqrt{\Delta_n} + \eta_i^n\right) \le K\sqrt{\Delta_n}, \\
\mathbb{E}(\|\zeta(1)_i^n\|^q \mid \mathcal{F}_{i-1}^n) &\le K_q \\
\|\zeta'(2)_i^n - b_{(i-1)\Delta_n}^{(c)}\Delta_n\| &+ \|\zeta'(3)_i^n - b_{(i-1)\Delta_n}\Delta_n\| \\
&\le K\Delta_n(\sqrt{\Delta_n} + \eta_i^n) \le K\Delta_n \\
\mathbb{E}(\|\zeta(2)_i^n\|^q \mid \mathcal{F}_{i-1}^n) &+ \mathbb{E}(\|\zeta(3)_i^n\|^q \mid \mathcal{F}_{i-1}^n) \le K_q\Delta_n^{q/2}
\end{aligned} \tag{B.82}$$

and also, with $\overline{\zeta}(r)_i^n$ denoting either $\zeta(r)_i^n$ or $\zeta''(r)_i^n$:

$$\begin{aligned}
\Big|\mathbb{E}(\overline{\zeta}(1)_i^{n,jk}\,\overline{\zeta}(1)_i^{n,lm} \mid \mathcal{F}_{i-1}^n) & \\
-(c_{(i-1)\Delta_n}^{jl} c_{(i-1)\Delta_n}^{km} + c_{(i-1)\Delta_n}^{jm} c_{(i-1)\Delta_n}^{kl})\Big| &\le K\sqrt{\Delta_n} \\
\Big|\mathbb{E}(\overline{\zeta}(2)^{n,jl}\,\overline{\zeta}(2)^{n,km} \mid \mathcal{F}_{i-1}^n) - c_{(i-1)\Delta_n}^{(c),jl,km}\Delta_n\Big| &\le K(\Delta_n^2 + \Delta_n^{3/2}\eta_i^n) \\
\Big|\mathbb{E}(\overline{\zeta}(3)_i^{n,j}\,\overline{\zeta}(3)_i^{n,k} \mid \mathcal{F}_{i}^{(n)}) - c_{(i-1)\Delta_n}^{jk}\Delta_n\Big| &\le K(\Delta_n^2 + \Delta_n^{3/2}\eta_i^n) \\
\Big|\mathbb{E}(\overline{\zeta}(2)_i^{n,jk}\,\overline{\zeta}(3)_i^{n,l} \mid \mathcal{F}_{i-1}^n) - c_{(i-1)\Delta_n}^{(X,c),jk,l}\Delta_n\Big| &\le K(\Delta_n^2 + \Delta_n^{3/2}\eta_i^n) \\
\Big|\mathbb{E}(\overline{\zeta}(1)_i^{n,jk})\,\overline{\zeta}(2)_i^{n,lm}) \mid \mathcal{F}_{i-1}^n)\Big| &\le K\Delta_n \\
\Big|\mathbb{E}(\overline{\zeta}(1)_i^{n,jk})\,\overline{\zeta}(3)_i^{n,l} \mid \mathcal{F}_{i-1}^n)\Big| &\le K\Delta_n.
\end{aligned} \tag{B.83}$$

Finally, for any bounded martingale N which is orthogonal to W, and with the notation $N_t^{*n} = \big(\mathbb{E}(\sup_{t\in((i-1)\Delta_n,i\Delta_n]}|N_t - N_{(i-1)\Delta_n}|^2 \mid \mathcal{F}_{i-1}^n)\big)^{1/2}$, and upon using Itô's formula, one gets

$$\begin{aligned}
\big|\mathbb{E}(\zeta''(1)_i^{n,jk}\,\Delta_i^n N \mid \mathcal{F}_{i-1}^n)\big| &\le K\sqrt{\Delta_n}\,N_i^{*n} \\
\big|\mathbb{E}(\zeta''(2)_i^{n,jk}\,\Delta_i^n N \mid \mathcal{F}_{i-1}^n)\big| &\le K\Delta_n\,N_i^{*n} \\
\big|\mathbb{E}(\zeta''(3)_i^{n,j}\,\Delta_i^n N \mid \mathcal{F}_{i-1}^n)\big| &\le K\Delta_n\,N_i^{*n},
\end{aligned} \tag{B.84}$$

whereas when $N = W^l$ is one of the components of W, we have instead

$$
\begin{aligned}
&\left|\mathbb{E}(\zeta''(1)_i^{n,jk} \Delta_i^n W^l \mid \mathcal{F}_{i-1}^n)\right| \leq K\Delta_n \\
&\left|\mathbb{E}(\zeta''(2)_i^{n,jk} \Delta_i^n W^l \mid \mathcal{F}_{i-1}^n) - \sigma_{(i-1)\Delta_n}^{(c),jk,l} \Delta_n\right| \leq K\Delta_n \eta_i^n \\
&\left|\mathbb{E}(\zeta''(3)_i^{n,j} \Delta_i^n W^l \mid \mathcal{F}_{i-1}^n) - \sigma_{(i-1)\Delta_n}^{jl} \Delta_n\right| \leq K\Delta_n^{3/2},
\end{aligned}
\tag{B.85}
$$

Estimates Under (SKC)   Here we no longer assume (SKCC), but only (SKC). We set

$$
\overline{\eta}_i^n, \; \overline{\eta}_i'^n \quad \text{associated by (B.73) with the process } Y = b.
\tag{B.86}
$$

Some of the estimates in (B.82) or (B.83) fail, but we now have the following ones, for $q \geq 2$:

$$
\begin{aligned}
&\|\zeta'(1)_i^n\| \leq K\sqrt{\Delta_n}\left(\sqrt{\Delta_n} + \overline{\eta}_i^n\right), \\
&\mathbb{E}(\|\zeta(1)_i^n\|^q \mid \mathcal{F}_{i-1}^n) \leq K_q \\
&\|\zeta'(2)_i^n\| \leq K\Delta_n \mathbb{E}(\|\zeta(2)_i^n\|^q \mid \mathcal{F}_{i-1}^n) \leq K_q\Delta_n \\
&\left|\mathbb{E}(\zeta(1)_i^{n,jk} \zeta(1)_i^{n,lm} \mid \mathcal{F}_{i-1}^n)\right. \\
&\quad \left. - (c_{(i-1)\Delta_n}^{jl} c_{(i-1)\Delta_n}^{km} + c_{(i-1)\Delta_n}^{jm} c_{(i-1)\Delta_n}^{kl})\right| \leq K\sqrt{\Delta_n} \\
&\left|\mathbb{E}(\zeta(1)_i^{n,jk}) \zeta(2)_i^{n,lm}) \mid \mathcal{F}_{i-1}^n)\right| \leq K\Delta_n.
\end{aligned}
\tag{B.87}
$$

Recalling the definition of α_i^n and $\overline{\beta}_i^n$ in (B.80), we then have:

Lemma B.4. *Under (SKC) we have for all* $q \geq 2$

$$
\begin{aligned}
&\left\|\mathbb{E}(\alpha_i^n \mid \mathcal{F}_{i-1}^n)\right\| \leq K\sqrt{\Delta_n}\left(\sqrt{\Delta_n} + \overline{\eta}_i'^n\right) \\
&\left|\mathbb{E}(\alpha_i^{n,jk} \alpha_i^{n,lm} \mid \mathcal{F}_{i-1}^n) - \frac{1}{k_n}(c_{(i-1)\Delta_n}^{jl} c_{(i-1)\Delta_n}^{km} + c_{(i-1)\Delta_n}^{jm} c_{(i-1)\Delta_n}^{kl})\right| \\
&\quad \leq K\sqrt{\Delta_n}\left(\frac{1}{k_n} + \overline{\eta}_i'^n\right) \\
&\mathbb{E}(\|\alpha_i^n\|^q \mid \mathcal{F}_{i-1}^n) \leq K_q(\Delta_n^{q/2} + k_n^{-q/2}) \\
&\left|\mathbb{E}(\alpha_i^{n,jk} \overline{\beta}_i^{n,lm} \mid \mathcal{F}_{i-1}^n)\right| \leq K k_n \Delta_n \\
&\left\|\mathbb{E}(\overline{\beta}_i^n \mid \mathcal{F}_{i-1}^n)\right\| \leq K k_n \Delta_n, \\
&\mathbb{E}(\|\overline{\beta}_i^n\|^q \mid \mathcal{F}_{i-1}^n) \leq \begin{cases} K_q(k_n\Delta_n)^{q/2} & \text{if } c \text{ is continuous} \\ K_q k_n \Delta_n & \text{otherwise.} \end{cases}
\end{aligned}
$$

Proof. The first claim above directly follows from (B.87). For the second claim, we set $\xi_i^n = c_{(i-1)\Delta_n}^{jl} c_{(i-1)\Delta_n}^{km} + c_{(i-1)\Delta_n}^{jm} c_{(i-1)\Delta_n}^{kl}$ and write $\alpha_i^{n,jk} \alpha_i^{n,lm}$ as

$$
\begin{aligned}
&\frac{1}{k_n^2} \sum_{u=0}^{k_n-1} \zeta(1)_{i+u}^{n,jk} \zeta(1)_{i+u}^{n,lm} \\
&+ \frac{1}{k_n^2} \sum_{u=0}^{k_n-2} \sum_{v=u+1}^{k_n-1} (\zeta(1)_{i+u}^{n,jk} \zeta(1)_{i+v}^{n,lm} + \zeta(1)_{i+u}^{n,lm} \zeta(1)_{i+v}^{n,jk}).
\end{aligned}
$$

By (B.87) and successive conditioning and the first part of Lemma B.1, the $\mathcal{F}_{i-1}^n$-conditional expectation of the last term above is smaller than $K\sqrt{\Delta_n}\,(\sqrt{\Delta_n}+\overline{\eta}_i'^n)$. The conditional expectation of the first term, up to $K\sqrt{\Delta_n}/k_n$, is $\frac{1}{k_n^2}\sum_{u=0}^{k_n-1}\mathbb{E}(\xi_{i+u}^n\mid\mathcal{F}_{i-1}^n)$. Using the boundedness of c_t and (B.79), we easily check that $\bigl|\mathbb{E}(\xi_{i+u}^n\mid\mathcal{F}_{i-1}^n)-\xi_i^n\bigr|\le Kk_n\Delta_n$ when $u\le k_n$, and the second claim follows.

For the third claim, we use (B.87) and Hölder's inequality, plus Burkholder-Gundy inequality applied to the martingale increments $\zeta(1)_{i+j}''^n$. For the fourth claim, we use (B.87) and Hölder's inequality again, plus successive conditioning. The last two claims are obvious consequences of (B.79). $\qquad\square$

B.2.3 Estimates for the Spot Volatility Estimators

Let us recall the spot volatility estimators, associated with the sequence of integers k_n and possibly a truncation sequence $u_n>0$:

$$\begin{aligned}
\widehat{c}(k_n)_i^{jl} &= \frac{1}{k_n\Delta_n}\sum_{m=0}^{k_n-1}\Delta_{i+m}^n X^j\,\Delta_{i+m}^n X^l\\
\widehat{c}(k_n,u_n)_i^{jl} &= \frac{1}{k_n\Delta_n}\sum_{m=0}^{k_n-1}\Delta_{i+m}^n X^j\,\Delta_{i+m}^n X^l\,1_{\{\|\Delta_{i+m}^n X\|\le u_n\}}.
\end{aligned}\tag{B.88}$$

Since $\widehat{c}(k_n)_i-c_{(i-1)\Delta_n}=\overline{\beta}_i^n+\alpha_i^n$, Lemma B.4 yields for $q\ge2$ and under (SKC)

$$\begin{aligned}
&\bigl\|\mathbb{E}(\widehat{c}(k_n)_i-c_{(i-1)\Delta_n}\mid\mathcal{F}_{i-1}^n)\bigr\|\le K(\sqrt{\Delta_n}+k_n\Delta_n)\\
&\mathbb{E}(\|\widehat{c}(k_n)_i^n-c_{(i-1)\Delta_n}\|^q\mid\mathcal{F}_{i-1}^n)\\
&\quad\le\begin{cases}K_q((k_n\Delta_n)^{q/2}+k_n^{-q/2}) & \text{if }c_t\text{ is continuous}\\ K_q(\Delta_n^{q/2}+k_n^{-q/2}+k_n\Delta_n) & \text{otherwise.}\end{cases}
\end{aligned}\tag{B.89}$$

Lemma B.5. *Assume (SH-r) for some $r\in[0,2)$, and let X' be the continuous Itô semimartingale equal to $X-\delta\star(\underline{p}-\underline{q})$ when $r>1$ and to $X-\delta\star\underline{p}$ if $r\le1$. Let also $\widehat{c}'(k_n)_i$ be the non-truncated spot volatility estimators associated with the process X'. Then if $u_n\asymp\Delta_n^{\varpi}$ with $0<\varpi<\frac12$, for all $q>0$ we have*

$$\mathbb{E}\bigl(\|\widehat{c}(k_n,u_n)_i-\widehat{c}'(k_n)_i\|^q\mid\mathcal{F}_{i-1}^n\bigr)\le\begin{cases}\Delta_n^{(2q-r)\varpi-q+1}\psi_n & \text{if }q>\frac{2r(1-r\varpi)}{2+r-4r\varpi}\\ K_{q,\varepsilon}\Delta_n^{\frac{2-r}{2r}-\varepsilon} & \text{if }q\le\frac{2r(1-r\varpi)}{2+r-4r\varpi}\end{cases}\tag{B.90}$$

(when $q\ge r$ we are in the first case above) for all $\varepsilon>0$ and where ψ_n is a sequence (depending on q) going to 0 as $n\to\infty$.

Of course, for this result to have any interest at all, the exponents of Δ_n in the right side should be positive, implying $q < \frac{1-r\varpi}{1-2\varpi}$.

Proof. By (B.79) applied to X' and (A.75) to $X - X'$ we have for all $q > 0$ and $p \geq r$

$$\mathbb{E}\big(\|\Delta_i^n X'\|^q \mid \mathcal{F}_{i-1}^n\big) \leq K_q \Delta_n^{q/2},$$
$$\mathbb{E}\Big(\frac{\|\Delta_i^n (X-X')\|^p}{u_n^p} \wedge 1 \mid \mathcal{F}_{i-1}^n\Big) \leq K_p \Delta_n^{1-r\varpi}\,\psi_n$$

with ψ_n as in the statement of the lemma (this sequence will change from line to line, with always $\psi_n \to 0$). On the other hand, for any $x, y \in \mathbb{R}^d$ and $u, v, q > 0$ we have

$$\big\| (x+y)(x+y)^\star 1_{\{\|x+y\|>u\}} - xx^\star \big\|^q$$
$$\leq K_{q,v}\Big(u^{2q} \big(\tfrac{\|y\|}{u} \wedge 1\big)^{2q} + \|x\|^q u^q \big(\tfrac{\|y\|}{u} \wedge 1\big)^q + \tfrac{\|x\|^{q(2+v)}}{u^{qv}}\Big).$$

Applying this with $x = \Delta_i^n X'$ and $y = \Delta_i^n (X - X')$, we deduce from the previous estimates and Hölder's inequality that, for some $\varepsilon > 0$ arbitrarily small,

$$\mathbb{E}\big(\big\| (\Delta_i^n X \Delta_i^n X^\star) 1_{\{\|\Delta_i^n X\| \leq u_n\}} - (\Delta_i^n X' \Delta_i^n X'^\star)\big\|^q \mid \mathcal{F}_{i-1}^n\big|$$
$$\leq K_{q,\varepsilon,v}\big(\Delta_n^{(2q-r)\varpi+1}\,\psi_n + \Delta_n^{\frac{q}{2}+q\varpi+(1-r\varpi)(1\wedge\frac{q}{r})-\varepsilon} + \Delta_n^{q(1+\frac{v}{2}(1-2\varpi))}\big),$$

and the same is of course true if we condition with respect to $\mathcal{F}_{i-j}^n$ for $j > 1$. Then it follows from (B.88) and Hölder's inequality that the left side of (B.90) is smaller than

$$K_{q,\varepsilon,v}\big(\Delta_n^{(2q-r)\varpi+1-q}\,\psi_n + \Delta_n^{-\frac{q}{2}+q\varpi+(1-r\varpi)(1\wedge\frac{q}{r})-\varepsilon} + \Delta_n^{q\frac{v}{2}(1-2\varpi)}\big).$$

The last summand above is negligible in front of the other two summands if v is chosen large enough, and the second summand is negligible in front of the first one when $\varepsilon > 0$ is small enough if and only if $q > \frac{2r(1-r\varpi)}{2+r-4r\varpi}$, and in particular when $q \geq r$. This yields (B.90). $\qquad\square$

This lemma has the following important consequence:

Lemma B.6. *If Theorem 8.20 holds under (SKC) and for the nontruncated estimators $\widehat{c}(k_n)_i^n$, it also holds under (K-r) with $r < 1$ and for the truncated estimators $\widehat{c}(k_n, u_n)_i^n$, as soon as u_n satisfies (8.50).*

Proof. By localization we may and will assume (SK-r). We use the notation X' and $\widehat{c}'(k_n)_i$ of the previous lemma, and observe that X' satisfies (SKC).

By (8.49), we have

$$|g(\widehat{c}(k_n, u_n)_i) - g(\widehat{c}'(k_n)_i)|$$
$$\leq K(1 + \|\widehat{c}(k_n, u_n)_i\| + \|\widehat{c}'(k_n)_i\|)^{p-1} \|\widehat{c}(k_n, u_n)_i - \widehat{c}'(k_n)_i\| \leq K\xi_i^n$$

where

$$\xi_i^n = (1 + \|\widehat{c}'(k_n)_i\|)^{p-1} \|\widehat{c}(k_n, u_n)_i - \widehat{c}'(k_n)_i^n\| + \|\widehat{c}(k_n, u_n)_i - \widehat{c}'(k_n)_i^n\|^p.$$

Note that (B.89) implies $\mathbb{E}(\|\widehat{c}'(k_n)_i\|^q) \leq K_q$, since c is bounded. Hence, since $r < 1 < p$ we deduce from (B.90) and Hölder's inequality that, for all $q > 1$ and some sequence $\psi_n \to 0$ depending on p and q,

$$\mathbb{E}(\xi_i^n) \leq \left(\Delta_n^{\frac{(2q-r)\varpi - q + 1}{q}} + \Delta_n^{(2p-r)\varpi - p + 1}\right)\psi_n.$$

By taking q close enough to 1, the right side above is smaller than $\Delta_n^{(2p-r)\varpi - p + 1}\psi_n$. Therefore, if $\overline{U}'(\Delta_n, g)_t^n$ is given by (8.48) with $\widehat{c}'(k_n)_i$ instead of $\widehat{c}(k_n, u_n)_i$, we have

$$\mathbb{E}(|\overline{U}'(\Delta_n, g)_t^n - U'(\Delta_n, g)_t^n|) \leq t\, \psi_n \Delta_n^{(2p-r)\varpi + 1 - p} = \mathrm{o}\left(\frac{1}{\sqrt{\Delta_n}}\right),$$

where the last part comes from (8.50). This shows the result for Theorem 8.20. $\square$

B.2.4 A Key Decomposition for Theorems 8.11 and 8.14

In this subsection we make the specific choice (8.26) for the sequence k_n of integers, that is,

$$k_n \sim \frac{\beta}{\sqrt{\Delta_n}} \qquad \text{for some } \beta \in (0, \infty). \tag{B.91}$$

Some Auxiliary Sequences We will prove both Theorems 8.11 and 8.14 together, and toward this aim we first introduce some useful specific sequences of numbers. With $m \in \{0, \ldots, 2k_n - 1\}$ and $j, l \in \mathbb{Z}$ and $u, v, u', v' \in \{1, 2, 3\}$ we set

$$\varepsilon(1)_m^n = \begin{cases} -1 & \text{if } 0 \leq m < k_n \\ 1 & \text{if } k_n \leq m < 2k_n, \end{cases}$$

$$\varepsilon(2)_m^n = \sum_{q=m+1}^{2k_n - 1} \varepsilon(1)_q^n = (m+1) \wedge (2k_n - m - 1), \quad \varepsilon(3)_m^n = 1$$

$$y_{u,v}^n = \begin{cases} 3/2k_n^3 & \text{if } u, v \in \{1, 2\} \\ 1/k_n^2 & \text{otherwise} \end{cases}, \quad z_{u,v}^n = \begin{cases} 1/\Delta_n & \text{if } u = v = 1 \\ 1 & \text{otherwise} \end{cases}$$

and

$$\gamma(u,v;m)_{j,l}^n = y_{u,v}^n \sum_{q=0\vee(j-m)}^{(l-m-1)\wedge(2k_n-m-1)} \varepsilon(u)_q^n \, \varepsilon(v)_{q+m}^n,$$

$$\Gamma(u,v)_m^n = \gamma(u,v;m)_{0,2k_n}^n$$

$$H(u,v;u'v')_n = z_{u,u'}^n \, z_{v,v'}^n \sum_{m=1}^{2k_n-1} \Gamma(u,v)_m^n \, \Gamma(u',v')_m^n$$

which clearly satisfy (we never need the – trivial – case $u=v=3$)

$$j \le m, \; l \ge 2k_n \;\Rightarrow\; \gamma(u,v;m)_{j,l}^n = \Gamma(u,v)_m^n$$

$$\widetilde{\gamma}_{u,v}^n = \sup_{j,l,m} |\gamma(u,v;m)_{j,l}^n|$$

$$\le \begin{cases} K & \text{if } (u,v) = (2,2),(2,3),(3,2) \\ K/k_n & \text{if } (u,v) = (1,2),(2,1),(1,3),(3,1) \\ K/k_n^2 & \text{if } (u,v) = (1,1). \end{cases} \tag{B.92}$$

We also need, for $m \in \{0,\dots,k_n-1\}$ and $j,l \in \mathbb{Z}$ and $u,v \in \{1,2\}$, the numbers

$$\overline{\varepsilon}(1)_m^n = 1, \quad \overline{\varepsilon}(2)_m^n = k_n - m - 1,$$

$$\overline{\gamma}(u,v;m)_{j,l}^n = \frac{6}{k_n^4} \sum_{q=0\vee(j-m)}^{(l-m-1)\wedge(k_n-m-1)} \overline{\varepsilon}(u)_q^n \, \overline{\varepsilon}(v)_{q+m}^n,$$

which satisfy

$$|\overline{\gamma}(u,v;m)_{j,l}^n| \le \begin{cases} K/k_n & \text{if } (u,v) = (2,2) \\ K/k_n^2 & \text{if } (u,v) = (1,2),(2,1) \\ K/k_n^3 & \text{if } (u,v) = (1,1). \end{cases} \tag{B.93}$$

We need to compute the numbers $\Gamma(u,v)_m^n$: a tedious but elementary calculation shows that they are as follows, when $m \le k_n - 1$ and when $m \ge k_n$ (these two values being separated by $\|$ below):

$$
\begin{array}{llll}
\Gamma(1,1)_m^n = & \dfrac{6k_n-9m}{2k_n^3} & \| & -\dfrac{6k_n-3m}{2k_n^3} \\[2mm]
\Gamma(1,3)_m^n = & -\dfrac{m}{k_n^2} & \| & -\dfrac{2k_n-m}{k_n^2} \\[2mm]
\Gamma(3,1)_m^n = & \dfrac{m}{k_n^2} & \| & \dfrac{2k_n-m}{k_n^2} \\[2mm]
\Gamma(1,2)_m^n = & -\dfrac{12k_nm-9m^2+6k_n-9m}{4k_n^3} & \| & -\dfrac{3(2k_n-m)(2k_n-m-1)}{4k_n^3} \\[2mm]
\Gamma(2,1)_m^n = & \dfrac{12k_nm-9m^2-6k_n+9m}{4k_n^3} & \| & \dfrac{3(2k_n-m)(2k_n-m+1)}{4k_n^3} \\[2mm]
\Gamma(2,2)_m^n = & \dfrac{4k_n^3-6k_nm^2+3m^3+2k_n-3m}{4k_n^3} & \| & \dfrac{(2k_n-m)^3-2k_n+m}{4k_n^3} \\[2mm]
\Gamma(2,3)_m^n = & \dfrac{2k_n^2-m^2+m}{2k_n^2} & \| & \dfrac{(2k_n-m)(2k_n-m+1)}{2k_n^2} \\[2mm]
\Gamma(3,2)_m^n = & \dfrac{2k_n^2-m^2-m}{2k_n^2} & \| & \dfrac{(2k_n-m)(2k_n-m-1)}{2k_n^2}.
\end{array}
$$

This yields the following behavior of $H(u,v;u';v')_n$, as $n \to \infty$, stated for $(u,v) \le (u',v')$ only because of the obvious symmetry $H(u,v;u',v')_n =$

$H(u', v'; u, v)_n$ (recall also (B.91)):

$$\sqrt{\Delta_n}\, H(u, v; u', v')_n \qquad\qquad\qquad\qquad\qquad\qquad\qquad (B.94)$$

$$\rightarrow \begin{cases} 3/\beta^3 & \text{if } (u, v, u', v') = (1, 1, 1, 1) \\ 3/4\beta & \text{if } (u, v, u', v') = (1, 2, 1, 2), (2, 1, 2, 1) \\ 5/8\beta & \text{if } (u, v, u', v') = (1, 2, 1, 3), (2, 1, 3, 1) \\ 2/3\beta & \text{if } (u, v, u', v') = (1, 3, 1, 3), (3, 1, 3, 1) \\ 151\,\beta/280 & \text{if } (u, v, u', v') = (2, 2, 2, 2) \\ 151\,\beta/240 & \text{if } (u, v, u', v') = (2, 2, 2, 3), (2, 2, 3, 2) \\ 23\,\beta/30 & \text{if } (u, v, u', v') = (2, 3, 2, 3), (2, 3, 3, 2), (3, 2, 3, 2) \\ 0 & \text{otherwise.} \end{cases}$$

The Decomposition Recall (SKCC) and $d = 1$. We have

$$\widehat{c}(k_n)_i = c_{(i-1)\Delta_n} + \frac{1}{k_n} \sum_{j=0}^{k_n-1} \sum_{u=1}^{2} \overline{\varepsilon}(u)_j^n \zeta(u)_{i+j}^n$$

$$\widehat{c}(k_n)_{i+k_n} - \widehat{c}(k_n)_i = \frac{1}{k_n} \sum_{j=0}^{2k_n-1} \sum_{u=1}^{2} \varepsilon(u)_j^n \zeta(u)_{i+j}^n$$

$$X_{(i+2k_n-1)\Delta_n} - X_{(i-1)\Delta_n} = \sum_{j=0}^{2k_n-1} \varepsilon(3)_j^n \zeta(3)_{i+j}^n.$$

Thus

$$(\widehat{c}(k_n)_i)^2 = (c_{(i-1)\Delta_n})^2 + \frac{2c_{(i-1)\Delta_n}}{k_n} \sum_{u=1}^{2} \sum_{j=0}^{k_n-1} \overline{\varepsilon}(u)_j^n \zeta(u)_{i+j}^n$$

$$+ \frac{1}{k_n^2} \sum_{u,v=1}^{2} \Big(\sum_{j=0}^{k_n-1} \overline{\varepsilon}(u)_j^n\, \overline{\varepsilon}(v)_j^n\, \zeta(u)_{i+j}^n\, \zeta(v)_{i+j}^n$$

$$+ 2 \sum_{j=0}^{k_n-2} \sum_{l=j+1}^{k_n-1} \overline{\varepsilon}(u)_j^n\, \zeta(u)_{i+j}^n\, \overline{\varepsilon}(v)_l^n\, \zeta(v)_{i+l}^n \Big)$$

$$(\widehat{c}(k_n)_{i+k_n} - \widehat{c}(k_n)_i)^2 = \frac{1}{k_n^2} \sum_{u,v=1}^{2} \Big(\sum_{j=0}^{2k_n-1} \varepsilon(u)_j^n\, \varepsilon(v)_j^n\, \zeta(u)_{i+j}^n\, \zeta(v)_{i+j}^n$$

$$+ 2 \sum_{j=0}^{2k_n-2} \sum_{l=j+1}^{2k_n-1} \varepsilon(u)_j^n\, \zeta(u)_{i+j}^n\, \varepsilon(v)_l^n\, \zeta(v)_{i+l}^n \Big)$$

$$(\widehat{c}(k_n)_{i+k_n} - \widehat{c}(k_n)_i)(X_{(i+2k_n-1)\Delta_n} - X_{(i-1)\Delta_n}^n)$$

$$= \frac{1}{k_n} \sum_{u=1}^{2} \Big(\sum_{j=0}^{2k_n-1} \varepsilon(u)_j^n\, \varepsilon(3)_j^n\, \zeta(u)_{i+j}^n\, \zeta(3)_{i+j}^n$$

$$+ \sum_{j=0}^{2k_n-2} \sum_{l=j+1}^{2k_n-1} \big(\varepsilon(u)_j^n\, \zeta(u)_{i+j}^n\, \varepsilon(3)_l^n\, \zeta(3)_{i+l}^n$$

$$+ \varepsilon(3)_j^n\, \zeta(3)_{i+j}^n\, \varepsilon(u)_l^n\, \zeta(u)_{i+l}^n \big) \Big).$$

Then we set, with the convention $\sum_{i=a}^{a'} = 0$ when $a > a'$,

$$\overline{A}(0)_t^n = \frac{6}{k_n^2} \sum_{i=1}^{[t/\Delta_n]-2k_n+1} (c_{(i-1)\Delta_n})^2,$$

$$\overline{A}(1;u)_t^n = \frac{12}{k_n^3} \sum_{i=1}^{[t/\Delta_n]-2k_n+1} c_{(i-1)\Delta_n} \sum_{j=0}^{k_n-1} \overline{\varepsilon}(u)_j^n \zeta(u)_{i+j}^n$$

$$\overline{A}(2;u,v)_t^n = \sum_{i=1}^{[t/\Delta_n]-k_n} \overline{\gamma}(u,v;0)_{i-1-[t/\Delta_n],i}\, \zeta(u)_i^n\, \zeta(v)_i^n$$

$$\overline{A}(3;u,v)_t^n = \sum_{i=2}^{[t/\Delta_n]-k_n} \left(\sum_{m=1}^{(i-1)\wedge(k_n-1)} \overline{\gamma}(u,v;m)_{i-1-[t/\Delta_n],i}^n \zeta(u)_{i-m}^n \right) \zeta(v)_i^n$$

and

$$\rho(u,v)_i^n = \sum_{m=1}^{2k_n-1} \Gamma(u,v)_m^n\, \zeta(u)_{i-m}^n, \qquad Z(u,v)_t^n = \sum_{i=2k_n}^{[t/\Delta_n]} \rho(u,v)_i^n\, \zeta''(v)_i^n$$

$$A(1;u,v)_t^n = \Gamma(u,v)_0^n \sum_{i=1}^{[t/\Delta_n]} \zeta(u)_i^n\, \zeta(v)_i^n$$

$$A(2;u,v)_t^n = \sum_{i=1}^{[t/\Delta_n]} \left(\gamma(u,v;0)_{i+2k_n-1-[t/\Delta_n],i} - \Gamma(u,v)_0^n \right)\zeta(u)_i^n\, \zeta(v)_i^n$$

$$A(3;u,v)_t^n = \sum_{i=2}^{[t/\Delta_n]} \left(\sum_{m=1}^{(i-1)\wedge(2k_n-1)} \gamma(u,v;m)_{i-1+2k_n-[t/\Delta_n],i}^n \zeta(u)_{i-m}^n \right.$$
$$\left. -\rho(u,v)_i^n\, 1_{\{i\geq 2k_n\}} \right)\zeta(v)_i^n$$

$$A(4;u,v)_t^n = \sum_{i=2k_n}^{[t/\Delta_n]} \rho(u,v)_i^n\, \zeta'(v)_i^n.$$

If we do the appropriate changes of order of summations, and after some tedious computations, we arrive at the following decompositions for the estimators $\widehat{C^{(c)}}_T^n$ and $\widehat{C^{(X,c)}}_T^n$ given by (8.27) and (8.36):

$$\widehat{C^{(c)}}_T^n = A_T^n + U_T^n - \overline{A}_T^n, \qquad \widehat{C^{(X,c)}}_T^n = A_T'^n + U_T'^n, \qquad \text{(B.95)}$$

where

$$A^n = \sum_{u,v=1}^{2} \left(A(1;u,v)^n + A(2;u,v)^n + 2A(3;u,v)^n + 2A(4;u,v)^n \right)$$

$$\overline{A}^n = \overline{A}(0)^n + \sum_{u=1}^{2} \overline{A}(1;u)^n + \sum_{u,v=1}^{2} \left(\overline{A}(2;u,v)^n + 2\overline{A}(3;u,v)^n \right)$$

$$A'^n = \sum_{u=1}^{2} \left(A(1;u,3)^n + A(2;u,3)^n + A(3;u,3)^n \right.$$
$$\left. + A(3;3,u)^n + A(4;u,3)^n + A(4;3,u)^n \right)$$

$$U^n = 2 \sum_{u,v=1}^{2} Z(u,v)^n, \qquad U'^n = \sum_{u=1}^{2} \left(Z(u,3)^n + Z(3,u)^n \right).$$

The Negligible Terms The aim of this part is to show the following negligibility result.

Proposition B.7. *Under (SKCC), and for all t, both $\frac{1}{\Delta_n^{1/4}} (A_t^n - \overline{A}_t^n - C_t^{(c)})$ and $\frac{1}{\Delta_n^{1/4}} (A_t'^n - C_t^{(X,c)})$ go to 0 in probability.*

We first recall a simple criterion for asymptotic negligibility of a triangular array:

Lemma B.8. *If $m_n, l_n \geq 1$ are arbitrary integers, and if for all $n \geq 1$ and $1 \leq i \leq m_n$ the variable ξ_i^n is $\mathcal{F}_{i+l_n}^n$-measurable, we have*

$$\left.\begin{array}{r} \sum_{i=1}^{m_n} |\mathbb{E}(\xi_i^n \mid \mathcal{F}_{i-1}^n)| \xrightarrow{\mathbb{P}} 0 \\ l_n \sum_{i=1}^{m_n} \mathbb{E}(|\xi_i^n|^2) \longrightarrow 0 \end{array}\right\} \;\Rightarrow\; \sup_{j \leq m_n} \left| \sum_{i=1}^{j} \xi_i^n \right| \xrightarrow{\mathbb{P}} 0. \qquad (B.96)$$

Proof. With the convention $\xi_i^n = 0$ when $i > m_n$, we set

$$\xi_i'^n = \mathbb{E}(\xi_i^n \mid \mathcal{F}_{i-1}^n), \qquad \xi_i''^n = \xi_i^n - \xi_i'^n,$$
$$A_n = \sum_{i=1}^{m_n} |\xi_i'^n|,$$
$$M(k)_i^n = \sum_{j=0}^{i} \xi_{k+l_n j}''^n, \qquad \overline{M}(k)_n = \sup_{i \leq [(m_n - k)/l_n]} |M(k)_i^n|,$$

so

$$\sup_{j \leq m_n} \left| \sum_{i=1}^{j} \xi_i^n \right| \leq A_n + \sum_{k=1}^{l_n} \overline{M}(k)_n.$$

The first condition in (B.96) implies $A_n \xrightarrow{\mathbb{P}} 0$. On the other hand, each sequence $M(k)^n$ is a martingale, relative to the discrete-time filtration $(\mathcal{F}_{k+il_n}^n)_{i \geq 0}$, hence Doob's inequality gives us $\mathbb{E}(|\overline{M}(k)_n|^2) \leq 4 \sum_{j=0}^{[(m_n - k)/l_n]} \mathbb{E}(|\xi_{k+l_n j}''^n|^2)$, which in turn is smaller than $4 \sum_{j=0}^{[(m_n - k)/l_n]} \mathbb{E}(|\xi_{k+l_n j}^n|^2)$. Since $\mathbb{E}(|\sum_{k=1}^{l_n} \overline{M}(k)_n|^2) \leq l_n \sum_{k=1}^{l_n} \mathbb{E}(|\overline{M}(k)_n|^2)$, the second condition in (B.96) yields that this expectation goes to 0, and this completes the proof. $\qquad\square$

We also state the following consequence of Lemma B.2 and (B.82). If the a_i^n's are reals, all bounded by some constant L, then for all $q \geq 2$ we have (recall $k_n \sqrt{\Delta_n} \leq K$)

$$\mathbb{E}\left(\left| \sum_{j=0}^{2k_n - 1} a_j^n \zeta(u)_{i+j}^n \right|^q\right) \leq \begin{cases} K_q L^q k_n^{q/2} & \text{if } u = 1 \\ K_q L^q / k_n^{q/2} & \text{if } u = 2, 3. \end{cases} \qquad (B.97)$$

Proof of Proposition B.7. Step 1. We first study the "non-trivial" terms $A(1;1,1)^n$, $A(1;2,2)^n$, $A(1;2,3)^n$ and $\overline{A}(0)^n$. First, $\Gamma(2,2)_0^n = 1 + O(1/k_n^2)$ and $\Gamma(2,3)_0^n = 1$, hence the CLT for the approximate quadratic variation of the process (X,c), see Theorem A.15, yields

$$\frac{1}{\Delta_n^{1/4}} \left(A(1;2,2)^n - C^{(c)} \right) \overset{\text{u.c.p.}}{\Longrightarrow} 0, \qquad \frac{1}{\Delta_n^{1/4}} \left(A(1;2,3)^n - C^{(X,c)} \right) \overset{\text{u.c.p.}}{\Longrightarrow} 0.$$

Next, Theorem 10.3.2 of [JP] for the function $\overline{F}((x,y),(x',y')) = (x'^2 - y)^2$ and the process (X,c), plus $\Gamma(1,1)_0^n = 3/k_n^2$, yield (with $C(4)_t = \int_0^t (c_s)^2\,ds$ being the quarticity)

$$\frac{1}{\Delta_n^{1/4}} \left(k_n^2 \Delta_n\, A(1;1,1)_t^n - 6C(4)_t \right) \overset{\text{u.c.p.}}{\Longrightarrow} 0.$$

Finally, since c satisfies (HC), Theorem 6.1.2 of [JP] yields

$$\frac{1}{\Delta_n^{1/4}} \left(k_n^2 \Delta_n\, \overline{A}(0)_t^n - 6C(4)_t \right) \overset{\text{u.c.p.}}{\Longrightarrow} 0.$$

In view of these and of the definition of A^n, $\overline{A}^n$ and A'^n, it remains to prove

$$\frac{1}{\Delta_n^{1/4}} B_t^n \overset{\mathbb{P}}{\longrightarrow} 0 \qquad\qquad (\text{B.98})$$

in the cases

(a) $B^n = \overline{A}(1;u)^n$, $u = 1,2$
(b) $B^n = \overline{A}(j;u,v)^n$, $j = 2,3$, $u = 1,2$, $v = 1,2$
(c) $B^n = A(1;u,v)^n$, $(u,v) = (1,2),(2,1),(1,3)$
(d) $B^n = A(j;u,v)^n$, $j = 2,3,4$, all (u,v) except $(u,v) = (3,3)$.

Step 2. Here we consider case (a) in (B.98). The variable $\chi_i^n = \sum_{j=0}^{k_n-1} \overline{\varepsilon}(u)_j^n \zeta(u)_{i+j}^n$ is $\mathcal{F}_{i+k_n}^n$-measurable, and by (B.82) and (B.97) it satisfies for both $u = 1,2$

$$|\mathbb{E}(\chi_i^n \mid \mathcal{F}_{i-1}^n)| \le K, \qquad \mathbb{E}(|\chi_i^n|^2 \mid \mathcal{F}_{i-1}^n) \le K k_n.$$

The result readily follows from (B.96) applied to the array $\xi_i^n = \frac{12}{k_n^3 \Delta_n^{1/4}} c_{(i-1)\Delta_n} \chi_i^n$.

Step 3. Here we prove (B.98) in case (b), first when $j = 2$. Upon using (B.82) and (B.93), we see that the variable $\xi_i^n = \overline{\gamma}(u,v;0)_{i+k_n-1-[t/\Delta_n],i}\, \zeta(u)_i^n\, \zeta(v)_i^n$ has $\mathbb{E}(|\xi_i^n|) \le K/k_n^3$ for all $u,v = 1,2$, and $\mathbb{E}(|B_t^n|) \le K t \sqrt{\Delta_n}$ follows, implying (B.98).

Next suppose $j = 3$, and denote by χ_i^n the ith summand in the sum defining $\overline{A}(3; u, v)_t^n$, which is $\mathcal{F}_i^n$-measurable. By (B.82), (B.93) and successive conditioning one gets for all $u, v = 1, 2$:

$$\mathbb{E}\left(\left|\mathbb{E}(\chi_i^n \mid \mathcal{F}_{i-1}^n)\right|\right) \leq K\Delta_n^{3/2}, \qquad \mathbb{E}(|\chi_i^n|^2) \leq K\Delta_n^{5/2},$$

and (B.98) follows from (B.96) applied to the array $\xi_i^n = \chi_i^n/\Delta_n^{1/4}$.

Step 4. Here we consider case (c), say for $(u, v) = (1, 2)$. As in step 1, Theorem 10.3.2 of [JP] applied to the process (X, c) and the function $\overline{F}((x, y), (x', y')) = (x'^2 - y)y'$ implies that $\sqrt{\Delta_n} \sum_{i=1}^{[t/\Delta_n]} \zeta(1)_i^n \zeta(2)_i^n$ converges in law to some limiting process. Since $\Gamma(1, 2)_0^n = -3/2k_n^2$, we deduce that B^n satisfies (B.98). A similar argument shows the result for $(u, v) = (2, 1), (1, 3)$.

Step 5. Here we prove (B.98) in case (d), when $j = 2$. By the first part of (B.92) all summands in B_t^n vanish, except for $4k_n - 2$ of them, namely those for i between 1 and $2k_n - 1$, and between $[t/\Delta_n] - 2k_n + 2$ and $[t/\Delta_n]$, and for the summands which are non-vanishing the coefficient in front of $\zeta(u)_i^n \zeta(v)_i^n$ is smaller than $\widetilde{\gamma}_{u,v}^n$. In view of (B.92) and (B.82), it follows (using the Cauchy-Schwarz inequality when $u \neq v$) that in all cases $\mathbb{E}(|B_t^n|) \leq K\sqrt{\Delta_n}$, and (B.98) follows.

Step 6. Next, we prove (B.98) in case (d), when $j = 3$. As above, all summands in B_t^n vanish, except for $4k_n - 2$ values of i. Below we treat only the first $2k_n - 1$ summand (for simplicity of notation), but the last $2k_n - 2$ are treated analogously. We can rewrite the sum of these first summands as

$$B_t^{n,(1)} = \sum_{i=1}^{(2k_n-1)\wedge([t/\Delta_n])} \chi_i^n, \quad \chi_i^n = \delta_i^n \, \zeta(v)_i^n, \quad \delta_i^n = \sum_{m=1}^{i-1} a_{i,m}^n \, \zeta(u)_{i-m}^n,$$

where the $a_{i,m}^n$ are reals such that $|a_{i,m}^n| \leq 2\widetilde{\gamma}_{u,v}^n$, and of course depend on (u, v). We can then apply (B.97) with $L = 2\widetilde{\gamma}_{u,v}^n$ and (B.92) to get

$$\mathbb{E}(|\delta_i^n|^p) \leq \begin{cases} K_p/k_n^{3p/2} & \text{if } v = 1 \\ K_p/k_n^{p/2} & \text{if } v = 2, 3. \end{cases} \tag{B.99}$$

Moreover δ_i^n is $\mathcal{F}_{i-1}^n$-measurable, so (B.82) yields

$$\mathbb{E}\left(\left|\mathbb{E}(\chi_i^n \mid \mathcal{F}_{i-1}^n)\right|\right) \leq K\Delta_n^{5/4}, \qquad \mathbb{E}(|\chi_i^n|^2) \leq K\Delta_n^{3/2},$$

and $B_t^{n,(1)} \xrightarrow{\mathbb{P}} 0$ follows from (B.96) applied with $m_n = 2k_n - 1$ and $l_n = 1$ and $\xi_i^n = \chi_i^n/\Delta_n^{1/4}$.

Step 7. Finally, we show (B.98) in Case (d), when $j = 4$. Exactly as for (B.99), we have

$$\mathbb{E}(|\rho(u,v)_i^n|^p \mid \mathcal{F}_{i-2k_n}^n) \leq \begin{cases} K_p/k_n^{3p/2} & \text{if } v = 1 \\ K_p/k_n^{p/2} & \text{if } v = 2,3. \end{cases} \quad (B.100)$$

In view of (B.82), we have for $u = 1,2,3$:

$$\mathbb{E}(|A(4;u,1)_t^n|) \leq K\Delta_n^{5/4} \mathbb{E}\Big(\sum_{i=1}^{[t/\Delta_n]} (\sqrt{\Delta_n} + \eta_i^n)\Big).$$

By Lemma B.1, this implies $A(4;u,1)_t^n/\Delta_n^{1/4} \xrightarrow{\mathbb{P}} 0$.

Now, let $v = 2,3$. If $V(2) = b^{(c)}$ and $V(3) = b$, and using (B.82) and the first part of Lemma B.1, we see that $\mathbb{E}(|\zeta'(v)_i^n - V(v)_{(i-2k_n)\Delta_n}\Delta_n|^2 \mid \mathcal{F}_{i-2k_n}^n) \leq K(\Delta_n \eta_{i-2k_n+1}^{\prime n})^2$. Then the Cauchy-Schwarz inequality and (B.100) for $p = 2$, plus Lemma B.1, yield

$$\mathbb{E}\Big(\Big|\frac{1}{\Delta_n^{1/4}} \sum_{i=2k_n}^{[t/\Delta_n]} \rho(u,v)_i^n \big(\zeta'(v)_i^n - V(v)_{(i-2k_n)\Delta_n}^{(n)}\Delta_n\big)\Big|\Big)$$
$$\leq K\Delta_n \mathbb{E}\Big(\sum_{i=2k_n}^{[t/\Delta_n]} (\sqrt{\Delta_n} + \eta_i^{\prime n})\Big) \to 0.$$

Observe that $\Delta_n^{3/4} \sum_{i=2k_n}^{[t/\Delta_n]} \rho(u,v)_i^n V(v)_{(i-2k_n)\Delta_n} = G^n + M^n$, where

$$\xi_{i,t}^n = \sum_{m=(2k_n-i)\vee 1}^{[t/\Delta_n]-i)\wedge(2k_n-1)} \Gamma(u,v)_m^n V(s)_{(i+m-2k_n)\Delta_n}$$
$$G_t^n = \Delta_n^{3/4} \sum_{i=1}^{[t/\Delta_n]-1} \xi_{i,t}^n \zeta'(u)_i^n, \qquad M_t^n = \Delta_n^{3/4} \sum_{i=1}^{[t/\Delta_n]-1} \xi_{i,t}^n \zeta''(u)_i^n.$$

We have $|\xi_{i,t}^n| \leq Kk_n\widetilde{\gamma}_{u,v}^n$, so (B.82) and (B.92) yield $\mathbb{E}(|\xi_{i,t}^n \zeta'(u)_i^n|) \leq K\sqrt{\Delta_n}$ in all cases, and $G_t^n \xrightarrow{\mathbb{P}} 0$ follows. On the other hand, $\xi_{i,t}^n$ is $\mathcal{F}_{i-1}^n$-measurable, hence Doob's inequality and (B.82) and (B.92) again yield $\mathbb{E}\big(\sup_{s\leq t}|M_s^n|^2\big) \leq Kt\sqrt{\Delta_n} \to 0$ in all cases. The proof is complete. □

B.2.5 Proof of Theorems 8.11 and 8.14 and Remark 8.15

Scheme of the Proof In view of (B.95) and Proposition B.7, we are left to prove a CLT for the processes U^n and U'^n. To this end, suppose that we have proved the following (joint) stable convergence in law, where (u,v) runs through the set $P = \{1,2,3\}^2\setminus\{(3,3)\}$:

$$\Big(\frac{1}{\Delta_n^{1/4}} Z(u,v)^n\Big)_{(u,v)\in P} \xrightarrow{\mathcal{L}-s} Z = (Z(u,v))_{(u,v)\in P}, \quad (B.101)$$

where Z is defined on a very good extension $(\widetilde{\Omega}, \widetilde{\mathcal{F}}, (\widetilde{\mathcal{F}}_t), \widetilde{\mathbb{P}})$ of $(\Omega, \mathcal{F}, (\mathcal{F}_t), \mathbb{P})$ and is, conditionally on $\mathcal{F}$, a continuous centered Gaussian martingale with covariance structure

$$
\begin{aligned}
\widetilde{\mathbb{E}}(Z(u,v)_t\, Z(u',v')_t \mid \mathcal{F}) &= G(u,v;u',v')_t \\
&= \int_0^t g(u,v;u',v')_s\, ds, \quad \text{(B.102)}
\end{aligned}
$$

where the process $g(u,v;u',v')$ is given in the following display:

$$
g(u,v;u',v')_t =
\begin{cases}
\frac{12}{\beta^3}(c_t)^4 & \text{if } (u,v;u',v') = (1,1;1,1) \\[4pt]
\frac{3}{2\beta}(c_t)^2 c_t^{(c)} & \text{if } (u,v;u',v') = (1,2;1,2),\,(2,1;2,1) \\[4pt]
\frac{151\beta}{280}(c_t^{(c)})^2 & \text{if } (u,v;u',v') = (2,2;2,2) \\[4pt]
\frac{5}{4\beta}(c_t)^2 c_t^{(X,c)} & \text{if } \begin{cases} (u,v;u',v') = (1,2;1,3), \\ (2,1;3,1),(1,3;1,2),(3,1;2,1) \end{cases} \\[10pt]
\frac{4}{3\beta}(c_t)^3 & \text{if } (u,v;u',v') = (1,3;1,3),\,(3,1;3,1) \\[4pt]
\frac{151\beta}{240} c_t^{(c)} c_t^{(X,c)} & \text{if } \begin{cases} (u,v;u',v') = (2,2;2,3), \\ (2,2;3,2),(2,3;2,2),(3,2;2,2) \end{cases} \\[10pt]
\frac{23\beta}{30} c_t^{(c)} c_t & \text{if } (u,v;u',v') = (2,3;2,3),\,(3,2;3,2) \\[4pt]
\frac{23\beta}{30}(c_t^{(X,c)})^2 & \text{if } (u,v;u',v') = (2,3;3,2) \\[4pt]
0 & \text{otherwise.}
\end{cases}
\quad \text{(B.103)}
$$

Indeed, suppose that (B.101) holds. We thus have (8.28) and (8.37) with

$$
\mathcal{U}_T^{(C^{(c)})} = 2\sum_{u,v=1}^{2} Z(u,v)_T, \qquad \mathcal{U}_T^{(C^{(X,c)})} = \sum_{u=1}^{2}(Z(u,3)_T + Z(3,u)_T).
$$

Then both $\mathcal{U}_T^{(C^{(c)})}$ and $\mathcal{U}_T^{(C^{(X,c)})}$ are, conditionally on $\mathcal{F}$, centered Gaussian variables with variances given by (8.29) and (8.38), respectively, as a simple calculation shows: thus both Theorems 8.11 and 8.14 are proved, and Remark 8.15 as well.

We are thus left to prove (B.101). We have

$$
\frac{1}{\Delta_n^{1/4}} Z(u,v)_t^n = \sum_{i=2k_n}^{[t/\Delta_n]} \xi(u,v)_i^n, \qquad \xi(u,v)_i^n = \frac{1}{\Delta_n^{1/4}}\, \rho(u,v)_i^n\, \zeta''(v)_i^n,
$$

and the $\xi(u,v)_i^n$ are martingale increments, relative to the discrete time filtration $(\mathcal{F}_i^n)$. Then, using a standard criterion for the stable convergence of triangular arrays of martingale increments (see e.g. Theorem

2.2.15 of [JP]), in order to obtain the convergence (B.101), it suffices to prove the following three properties: for all $t > 0$, all $(u, v), (u', v') \in \mathcal{R}$, and all martingales N which are either bounded and orthogonal to W, or equal to one component W^j:

$$G(u, v; u', v')^n_t \quad := \quad \sum_{i=2k_n}^{[t/\Delta_n]} \mathbb{E}\big(\xi(u, v)^n_i \, \xi(u', v')^n_i \mid \mathcal{F}^n_{i-1}\big)$$

$$\xrightarrow{\ \mathbb{P}\ } \ G(u, v; u', v')_t \qquad\qquad (B.104)$$

$$\sum_{i=2k_n}^{[t/\Delta_n]} \mathbb{E}\big(|\xi(u, v)^n_i|^4 \mid \mathcal{F}^n_{i-1}\big) \xrightarrow{\ \mathbb{P}\ } 0 \qquad\qquad (B.105)$$

$$B(N; u, v)^n_t := \sum_{i=2k_n}^{[t/\Delta_n]} \mathbb{E}\big(\xi(u, v)^n_i \, \Delta^n_i N \mid \mathcal{F}^n_{i-1}\big) \xrightarrow{\ \mathbb{P}\ } 0. \qquad (B.106)$$

The property (B.105) is simple. If we combine (B.82) and (B.100), by successive conditioning, we see that $\mathbb{E}\big(|\xi(u, v)^n_i|^4\big) \leq K\Delta^2_n$ in all cases, obviously implying (B.105).

Proof of (B.106) When N is a bounded martingale orthogonal to W, we apply the estimates (B.84), successive conditioning, and (B.100), to get

$$\mathbb{E}\big(|B(N; u, v)^n_t|\big) \leq K\Delta_n \sum_{i=1}^{[t/\Delta_n]} \mathbb{E}(N^{*n}_i).$$

Doob's inequality yields $(N^{*n}_i)^2 \leq 4\mathbb{E}((\Delta^n_i N)^2 \mid \mathcal{F}^n_{i-1})$, hence by the Cauchy-Schwarz inequality

$$\mathbb{E}\big(|B(N; u, v)^n_t|\big) \quad \leq \quad K\sqrt{t\Delta_n} \left(\mathbb{E}\Big(\sum_{i=1}^{[t/\Delta_n]} (\Delta^n_i N)^2\Big)\right)^{1/2}$$

$$= \quad K\sqrt{t\Delta_n} \left(\mathbb{E}([N, N]_{\Delta_n[t/\Delta_n]})\right)^{1/2}.$$

Since N is a bounded martingale, $\mathbb{E}([N, N]_t) \leq K$ for all t, and (B.106) follows.

We now turn to the case $N = W^j$ for some $j = 1, \ldots, d'$, and we will essentially reproduce step 7 of the proof of Proposition B.7, with a different meaning for the notation $V(v)$. Namely, we set $V(1) = 0$ and $V(2) = \sigma^{(c), j}$ and $V(3) = \sigma^j$ and also

$$B'(N; u, v)^n_t = \Delta^{3/4}_n \sum_{i=2k_n}^{[t/\Delta_n]} \rho(u, v)^n_i \, V(v)_{(i-2k_n-1)\Delta_n}.$$

Then (B.85) and the property

$$\mathbb{E}((V(v)_{i\Delta_n} - V(v)_{(i-2k_n-1)\Delta_n})^2 \mid \mathcal{F}^n_{i-2k_n-1}) \leq K(\Delta_n + (\eta'^n_{i-2k_n-1})^2),$$

plus again (B.100), the Cauchy-Schwarz inequality and Lemma B.1, yield

$$\mathbb{E}\big(|B(N;u,v)^n_t - B'(N;u,v)^n_t|\big) \leq K\Delta_n \mathbb{E}\Big(\sum_{i=1}^{[t/\Delta_n]} \eta'^n_i \Big) \to 0.$$

Moreover, $B'(N;u,1)^n \equiv 0$, so it remains to show that $B'(N;u,v)^n_t \xrightarrow{\mathbb{P}} 0$ when $v = 2,3$. This is proved as in Step 7 of the proof of Proposition B.7, since here $B'(N;u,v)^{n,\delta}$ is exactly $G^n + M^n$ there (the processes $V(s)$ are different but still bounded). □

Proof of (B.104) We fix the two pairs (u,v) and (u',v') and begin with a reduction of the problem, in the same spirit as in the previous proof. Set

$$V_t = \begin{cases} 2(c_t)^2 & \text{if } (v,v') = (1,1) \\ c_t^{(c)} & \text{if } (v,v') = (2,2) \\ c_t^{(X,c)} & \text{if } (v,v') = (2,3),(3,2) \\ c_t & \text{if } (v,v') = (3,3) \\ 0 & \text{otherwise} \end{cases}$$

and

$$\overline{V}_t = \begin{cases} 2(c_t)^2 & \text{if } (u,u') = (1,1) \\ c_t^{(c)} & \text{if } (u,u') = (2,2) \\ c_t^{(X,c)} & \text{if } (u,u') = (2,3),(3,2) \\ c_t & \text{if } (u,u') = (3,3) \\ 0 & \text{otherwise.} \end{cases}$$

Recall that $z^n_{v,v'}$ is $1/\Delta_n$ if $v = v' = 1$ and is 1 otherwise. Then, with the notation

$$\overline{G}^n_t = z^n_{v,v'} \sqrt{\Delta_n} \sum_{i=2k_n}^{[t/\Delta_n]} \rho(u,v)^n_i \, \rho(u',v')^n_i \, V_{(i-1)\Delta_n},$$

we deduce from (B.83) and (B.100) that

$$\mathbb{E}(|G(u,v;u',v')^n_t - \overline{G}^n_t|) \leq Kt\sqrt{\Delta_n}.$$

So it remains to prove that $\overline{G}^n_t \xrightarrow{\mathbb{P}} G(u,v;u',v')_t$, and the only non-trivial cases are when $(v,v') = (1,1),(2,2),(2,3),(3,2),(3,3)$, since otherwise these processes are identically vanishing.

A further reduction is amenable. Namely, set

$$\overline{G}_t^{\prime n} = z_{v,v'}^n \sqrt{\Delta_n} \sum_{i=2k_n}^{[t/\Delta_n]} \rho(u,v)_i^n \, \rho(u',v')_i^n \, V_{(i-2k_n)\Delta_n}. \qquad (\text{B.107})$$

We have $\mathbb{E}(|V_{(i-1)\Delta_n} - V_{(i-2k_n)\Delta_n}|^2) \le K\mathbb{E}(\Delta_n + (\eta_{i-2k_n}^{\prime n})^2)$. Then, Lemma B.1 and (B.100) and the Cauchy-Schwarz inequality yield

$$\mathbb{E}(|\overline{G}_t^n - \overline{G}_t^{\prime n}|) \le K\sqrt{t}\left(\Delta_n \sum_{i=1}^{[t/\Delta_n]} \mathbb{E}((\eta_i^{\prime n})^2)\right)^{1/2} \to 0.$$

So we are left to show that for $(v,v') = (1,1),(2,2),(2,3),(3,2),(3,3)$, we have

$$\overline{G}_t^{\prime n} \xrightarrow{\mathbb{P}} G(u,v;u',v')_t. \qquad (\text{B.108})$$

In view of (B.107) we need to express the product $\rho(u,v)_i^n \, \rho(u',v')_i^n$ in a more tractable way. We have

$$\overline{G}_t^{\prime n} = \sum_{j=1}^3 \widehat{G}(j)_t^n, \qquad \widehat{G}(j)_t^n = z_{v,v'}^n \sqrt{\Delta_n} \sum_{i=2k_n}^{[t/\Delta_n]} \widehat{\rho}(j)_i^n \, V_{(i-2k_n)\Delta_n}$$

$$\widehat{\rho}(1)_i^n = \sum_{m=1}^{2k_n-1} \Gamma(u,v)_m^n \, \Gamma(u',v')_m^n \, \zeta(u)_{i-m}^n \, \zeta(u')_{i-m}^n$$

$$\widehat{\rho}(2)_i^n = \sum_{m=1}^{2k_n-2} \Gamma(u,v)_m^n \, \zeta(u)_{i-m}^n \sum_{m'=m+1}^{2k_n-1} \Gamma(u',v')_{m'}^n \, \zeta(u')_{i-m'}^n$$

$$\widehat{\rho}(3)_i^n = \sum_{m'=1}^{2k_n-2} \Gamma(u',v')_{m'}^n \, \zeta(u')_{i-m'}^n \sum_{m=m'+1}^{2k_n-1} \Gamma(u,v)_m^n \, \zeta(u)_{i-m}^n.$$

Observe that $\widehat{G}(2)_t^n = \sum_{i=2}^{[t/\Delta_n]-1} \xi_i^n \, \zeta(u)_i^n$, where

$$\xi_i^n = z_{v,v'}^n \sqrt{\Delta_n} \sum_{m=1\vee(2k_n-i)}^{([t/\Delta_n]-i)\wedge(2k_n-2)} \Gamma(u,v)_m^n \, V_{(i+m-2k_n)\Delta_n}$$
$$\times \sum_{m'=m+1}^{2k_n-1} \Gamma(u',v')_{m'}^n \, \zeta(u')_{i-m'}^n$$

is $\mathcal{F}_{i-1}^n$-measurable. Then $\sum_{m'=m+1}^{2k_n-1} \Gamma(u',v')_w^n \, \zeta(u')_{i-m'}^n$ satisfies (B.97) with $L = \widetilde{\gamma}_{u',v'}^n$ and u' instead of u, whereas V_t is bounded, hence we obtain for $p = 1,2$, and with $a = 1/2$ if $u' = 1$ and $a = -1/2$ when $u' \ge 2$, that $\mathbb{E}(|\xi_i^n|^p) \le K_p(z_{s,s'}^n \widetilde{\gamma}_{u,v}^n \widetilde{\gamma}_{u',v'}^n k_n^a)^p$. An examination of all possible cases (recall that $(v,v') = (1,1),(2,2),(2,3),(3,2)$) leads us to

$$\mathbb{E}(|\xi_i^n|^p) \le \begin{cases} K\Delta_n^{3p/4} & \text{if } u = 1 \\ K\Delta_n^{p/4} & \text{if } u = 2,3. \end{cases}$$

If we combine this with (B.82), plus the martingale increment property of $\zeta''(u)_i^n$, we obtain by our usual argument

$$\mathbb{E}\left(\left|\sum_{i=2}^{[t/\Delta_n]-1} \xi_i^n \zeta'(u)_i^n\right|\right) \to 0,$$

$$\mathbb{E}\left(\left|\sum_{i=2}^{[t/\Delta_n]-1} \xi_i^n \zeta''(u)_i^n\right|^2\right) \to 0.$$

Therefore $\widehat{G}(2)_t^n \xrightarrow{\mathbb{P}} 0$, and the property $\widehat{G}(3)_t^n \xrightarrow{\mathbb{P}} 0$ is obtained in exactly the same way.

At this stage it remains to prove that $\widehat{G}(1)_t^n \xrightarrow{\mathbb{P}} G(u,v;u',v')_t$. Letting now $\xi_i^n = \zeta(u)_i^n \zeta(u')_i^n$ and $\xi_i'^n = \mathbb{E}(\xi_i^n \mid \mathcal{F}_{i-1}^n)$ and $\xi_i''^n = \xi_i^n - \xi_i'^n$, we have

$$\widehat{G}(1)^n = \widehat{G}'^n + \widehat{G}''^n, \quad \widehat{G}_t'^n = \sum_{i=1}^{|t/\Delta_n|-1} \mu_{i,t}^n \xi_i'^n, \quad \widehat{G}_t''^n = \sum_{i=1}^{|t/\Delta_n|-1} \mu_{i,t}^n \xi_i''^n$$

with

$$\mu_{i,t}^n = z_{v,v'}^n \sqrt{\Delta_n} \sum_{w=1\vee(2k_n-i)}^{[t/\Delta_n]-i)\wedge(2k_n-1)} \Gamma(u,v)_m^n \Gamma(u',v')_w^n V_{(i+m-2k_n)\Delta_n}.$$

It thus suffices to show that

$$\widehat{G}_t'^n \xrightarrow{\mathbb{P}} G(u,v;u',v')_t, \qquad \widehat{G}_t''^n \xrightarrow{\mathbb{P}} 0. \tag{B.109}$$

We observe that $\mu_{i,t}^n$ is $\mathcal{F}_{i-1}^n$-measurable and

$$|\mu_{i,t}^n| \le K z_{v,v'}^n \widetilde{\gamma}_{u,v}^n \widetilde{\gamma}_{u',v'}^n \le \begin{cases} K\Delta_n & \text{if } u = u' = 1 \\ K\sqrt{\Delta_n} & \text{if } u \wedge u' = 1 < u \vee u' \\ K & \text{if } u, u' \ge 2. \end{cases} \tag{B.110}$$

In view of (B.82) and the martingale increment property of $\xi_i''^n$, we deduce $\mathbb{E}((\widehat{G}_t''^n)^2) \le Kt\Delta_n$ in all cases, implying the second part of (B.109).

For the first part of (B.109) we use (B.83) and (B.110) and our usual argument (as above for $\widehat{G}(2)_t^n$) to obtain $\mathbb{E}(|\widehat{G}_t'^n - \widehat{G}_t^n|) \to 0$ in all cases, where

$$\widehat{G}_t^n = \Delta_n \sum_{i=1}^{|t/\Delta_n|-1} \overline{\mu}_{i,t}^n V_{(i-1)\Delta_n} \overline{V}_{(i-1)\Delta_n},$$

$$\overline{\mu}_{i,t}^n = z_{v,v'}^n z_{u,u'}^n \sqrt{\Delta_n} \sum_{m=1\vee(2k_n-i)}^{([t/\Delta_n]-i)\wedge(2k_n-1)} \Gamma(u,v)_m^n \Gamma(u',v')_m^n.$$

We have $|\overline{\mu}_{i,t}^n| \le K z_{v,v'}^n z_{u,u'}^n \widetilde{\gamma}_{u,v}^n \widetilde{\gamma}_{u',v'}^n$, which is bounded by (B.84). We also have the equality $\overline{\mu}_{i,t}^n = \sqrt{\Delta_n} H(u,v;u',v')_n$ except when $i \le 2k_n - 2$ or $i \ge [t/\Delta_n] - 2k_n + 2$. Therefore, in view of (B.94), in which the limit is denoted by $H(u,v;u',v')$, and by Riemann integration, we obtain (B.109) with $G(u,v,u',v')_t = H(u,v;u',v') \int_0^t V_s \overline{V}_s \, ds$, and the proof of (B.104) is complete. $\qquad \square$

B.2.6   Proof of Theorems 8.12 and 8.17

As for all standardized CLTs, and on the basis of Theorems 8.11 and 8.14, it is enough to prove the two convergences (8.33) and (

Below, we use the notation (8.31), and also $\Delta_i''^n c = c_{ik_n l_n \Delta_n} - c_{(i-1)k_n l_n \Delta_n}$ and $\Delta_n' = k_n l_n \Delta_n$, and we set

$$H(j)_n = \tag{B.111}$$

$$\begin{cases} \frac{1}{(\Delta_n')^3} \sum_{i=1}^{[T/k_n l_n \Delta_n]-2} (\Delta_i'^n X)^4 (\Delta_{i+1}'^n X)^4 & \text{if } j = 1 \\ \frac{1}{(\Delta_n')^2} \sum_{i=1}^{[T/k_n l_n \Delta_n]-2} (\Delta_i'^n X)^4 (\Delta_{i+1}'^n \widehat{c})^2 & \text{if } j = 2 \\ \frac{1}{\Delta_n'} \sum_{i=1}^{[T/k_n l_n \Delta_n]-2} (\Delta_i'^n \widehat{c})^2 (\Delta_{i+1}'^n \widehat{c})^2 & \text{if } j = 3 \\ \frac{1}{(\Delta_n')^2} \sum_{i=1}^{[T/k_n l_n \Delta_n]-2} (\Delta_i'^n X)^2 (\Delta_{i+1}'^n X)^4 & \text{if } j = 4 \\ \frac{1}{\Delta_n'} \sum_{i=1}^{[T/k_n l_n \Delta_n]-2} (\Delta_i'^n X)^2 (\Delta_{i+1}'^n \widehat{c})^2 & \text{if } j = 5 \\ \frac{1}{\Delta_n'} \sum_{i=1}^{[T/k_n l_n \Delta_n]-2} \Delta_i'^n X \Delta_{i+1}'^n \widehat{c} \Delta_{i+1}'^n X \Delta_{i+1}'^n \widehat{c} & \text{if } j = 6. \end{cases}$$

In view of (8.29) and (8.38), plus $k_n \sim \gamma/\sqrt{\Delta_n}$ and the definitions (8.32) and (8.40) of the estimators, it is clearly enough to show that $H(j)_n \overset{\mathbb{P}}{\longrightarrow} H(j)$, where

$$\begin{aligned} H(1) &= 9 \int_0^T (c_s)^4 \, ds, & H(2) &= 3 \int_0^T (c_s)^2 c_s^{(c)} \, ds, \\ H(3) &= \int_0^T (c_s^{(c)})^2 \, ds, & H(4) &= 3 \int_0^T (c_s)^3 \, ds, \\ H(5) &= \int_0^T c_s c_s^{(c)} \, ds, & H(6) &= \int_0^T (c_s^{(X,c)})^2 \, ds. \end{aligned}$$

Let us denote as $H'(j)_n$ the same variables as in (B.111), upon substituting $\Delta_i'^n \widehat{c}$ and $\Delta_{i+1}'^n \widehat{c}$ with $\Delta_i'^n c$ and $\Delta_{i+1}'^n c$ everywhere. It is obviously sufficient to prove that

$$H(j)_n - H'(j)_n \overset{\mathbb{P}}{\longrightarrow} 0, \qquad H'(j)_n \overset{\mathbb{P}}{\longrightarrow} A(j) \tag{B.112}$$

as $n \to \infty$, and for $j = 1, 2, 3, 4, 5, 6$.

Let us examine the definition of each $H'(j)_n$: comparing with (A.8) of Appendix A, we observe that $H'(j)_n = B'(f_j, \Delta_n')_{T-2\Delta_n'}$, with time lag Δ_n' instead of Δ_n, with $k = 2$, with the two-dimensional continuous semimartingale process (X, c) instead of X, and with the test functions $f_j((x, y), (z, v))$ given as follows, successively for $j = 1, 2, 3, 4, 5, 6$:

$$x^4 z^4, \quad x^4 v^2, \quad y^2 v^2, \quad x^2 z^4, \quad x^2 v^2, \quad xyzv.$$

Then the second part of (B.112) is an immediate consequence of Theorem A.2.

As to the first part of (B.112), it is trivial when $j = 1, 4$, since then $H(j)_n = H'(j)_n$. Otherwise, we use the estimates $\mathbb{E}(|\Delta_i'^n X|^q) \leq$

$K_q(\Delta_n')^{q/2}$ and $\mathbb{E}(|\Delta_i'^n c|^q) \leq K_q(\Delta_n')^{q/2}$ for all $q > 0$ (since both X and c are continuous semimartingales with bounded coefficients), together with the second part of (B.89). An applications of Hölder's inequality gives us $\mathbb{E}'|H(j)_n - H'(j)_n|) \leq KT/\sqrt{l_n}$, in all cases $j = 2, 3, 5, 6$: hence the first part of (B.112) holds true, and the proof is complete. $\square$

B.2.7   Proof of Theorem 8.20

We recall that we want to estimate the variable $U(g)_t = \int_0^t g(c_s)\, ds$ for a test function g on $\mathcal{M}_d^+$ which is C^3 and satisfies

$$\|\partial^j g(x)\| \leq K(1 + \|x\|^{(p-j)^+}), \qquad j = 0, 1, 2, 3. \tag{B.113}$$

In the context of Theorem 8.20, the window size k_n for spot volatility estimators satisfies

$$k_n^2 \Delta_n \to 0, \qquad k_n^3 \Delta_n \to \infty. \tag{B.114}$$

By localization and Lemma B.6, it is enough to consider the case when (SKC) holds and when we use the non-truncated estimators for the spot volatility. So we aim toward a CLT for the variables

$$
\begin{aligned}
U'(\Delta_n, g)_t^n = \Delta_n \sum_{i=1}^{[t/\Delta_n]-k_n+1} \Bigg(& g(\widehat{c}(k_n)_i) \\
& - \frac{1}{2k_n} \sum_{j,k,l,m=1}^{d} \partial^2_{jk,lm}\, g(\widehat{c}(k_n)_i) \\
& \times \big(\widehat{c}(k_n)_i^{jl}\, \widehat{c}(k_n)_i^{km} + \widehat{c}(k_n)_i^{jm}\, \widehat{c}(k_n)_i^{kl}\big) \Bigg).
\end{aligned}
\tag{B.115}
$$

We now derive a decomposition for $U'(\Delta_n, g) - U(g)$, in the spirit of Subsection B.2.4, with a few negligible terms, plus a leading term which enjoys a CLT. We still use the notation (B.80), so $\widehat{c}(k_n)_i - c_{(i-1)\Delta_n} = \alpha_i^n + \overline{\beta}_i^n$, as soon as $t > k_n \Delta_n$, and thus

$$\frac{1}{\sqrt{\Delta_n}}\left(U'(\Delta_n, g)_t^n - U(g)_t\right) = \sum_{r=1}^{4} U(r)_t^n,$$

where, with all sums over j, k, l, m below extending from 1 to d,

$$U(1)_t^n = \frac{1}{\sqrt{\Delta_n}} \sum_{i=1}^{[t/\Delta_n]-k_n+1} \int_{(i-1)\Delta_n}^{i\Delta_n} (g(c_{(i-1)\Delta_n}) - g(c_s)) \, ds$$
$$- \frac{1}{\sqrt{\Delta_n}} \int_{\Delta_n([t/\Delta_n]-k_n+1)}^{t} g(c_s) \, ds$$

$$U(2)_t^n = \sqrt{\Delta_n} \sum_{i=1}^{[t/\Delta_n]-k_n+1} \sum_{l,m} \partial_{lm} g(c_{(i-1)\Delta_n}) \overline{\beta}_i^{n,lm}$$

$$U(3)_t^n = \sqrt{\Delta_n} \sum_{i=1}^{[t/\Delta_n]-k_n+1} \left(g(\widehat{c}(k_n)_i) - g(c_{(i-1)\Delta_n}) \right.$$
$$- \sum_{l,m} \partial_{lm} g(c_{(i-1)\Delta_n}) (\alpha_i^{n,lm} + \overline{\beta}_i^{n,lm})$$
$$\left. - \frac{1}{2k_n} \sum_{j,k,l,m} \partial_{jk,lm}^2 g(\widehat{c}(k_n)_i) \left(\widehat{c}(k_n)_i^{jl} \widehat{c}(k_n)_i^{km} + \widehat{c}(k_n)_i^{jm} \widehat{c}(k_n)_i^{kl} \right) \right)$$

$$U(4)_t^n = \sqrt{\Delta_n} \sum_{i=1}^{[t/\Delta_n]-k_n+1} \sum_{l,m} \partial_{lm} g(c_{(i-1)\Delta_n}) \alpha_i^{n,lm}.$$

Therefore, Theorem 8.20 readily follows from the next two lemmas:

Lemma B.9. *Under (SKC) and (B.114) we have* $U(j)^n \overset{u.c.p.}{\Longrightarrow} 0$ *for* $j = 1, 2, 3$.

Lemma B.10. *Under (SKC) we have the functional stable convergence in law* $U(4)^n \overset{\mathcal{L}-s}{\Longrightarrow} Z$, *where* Z *is as described in Theorem 8.20.*

Proof of Lemma B.9. The case $j = 1$: Since $g(c_s)$ is bounded, the absolute value of the last term in $U(1)_t^n$ is smaller than $K k_n \sqrt{\Delta_n}$, which goes to 0 by (8.47). The first term of $U(1)_t^n$ is $\sum_{i=1}^{[t/\Delta_n]-k_n+1} \xi_i^n$, where $\xi_i^n = \frac{1}{\sqrt{\Delta_n}} \int_{(i-1)\Delta_n}^{i\Delta_n} (g(c_{(i-1)\Delta_n}) - g(c_s)) \, ds$ is $\mathcal{F}_i^n$-measurable, and the process $g(c_t)$ is itself an Itô semimartingale satisfying (SH-2). We deduce from (B.79) applied to $g(c_t)$ instead of c_t that $|\mathbb{E}(\xi_i^n \mid \mathcal{F}_{i-1}^n)| \leq K\Delta_n^{3/2}$ and $\mathbb{E}(|\xi_i^n|^2 \mid \mathcal{F}_{i-1}^n)| \leq K\Delta_n^2$. Then $U(1)^n \overset{u.c.p.}{\Longrightarrow} 0$ follows from (B.96) applied with $l_n = 1$ and $m_n = [t/\Delta_n]$.

The case $j = 2$: Here we set $\xi_i^n = \sqrt{\Delta_n} \sum_{l,m} \partial_{lm} g(c_{(i-1)\Delta_n}) \overline{\beta}_i^n$, which is $\mathcal{F}_{i+k_n-1}^n$-measurable, and satisfies $|\mathbb{E}(\xi_i^n \mid \mathcal{F}_{i-1}^n)| \leq K\Delta_n^{3/2}$ and $\mathbb{E}(|\xi_i^n|^2 \mid \mathcal{F}_{i-1}^n)| \leq K\Delta_n^2$ by Lemma B.4. Then $U(2)^n \overset{u.c.p.}{\Longrightarrow} 0$ follows from (B.96) applied with $l_n = k_n$ and $m_n = [t/\Delta_n]$.

The case $j = 3$: Using (B.113) and a Taylor expansion of g, plus the property $\widehat{c}(k_n)_i - c_{(i-1)\Delta_n} = \alpha_i^n + \overline{\beta}_i^n$ again, we easily check that the ith summand in the definition of $U(3)_t^n$ is $v_i^n + w_i^n$, where

$$v_i^n = \frac{\sqrt{\Delta_n}}{2} \sum_{j,k,l,m} \partial^2_{jk,lm} g(c_i^n) \left(\alpha_i^{n,jk} \alpha_i^{n,lm} + \alpha_i^{n,jk} \overline{\beta}_i^{n,lm} + \overline{\beta}_i^{n,jk} \alpha_i^{n,lm} \right.$$
$$\left. - \frac{1}{k_n} \left(c_{(i-1)\Delta_n}^{jl} c_{(i-1)\Delta_n}^{km} + c_{(i-1)\Delta_n}^{jm} c_{(i-1)\Delta_n}^{kl} \right) \right)$$
$$|w_i^n| \le K\sqrt{\Delta_n} \left(\|\alpha_i^n\|^p + \|\alpha_i^n\|^3 + \|\overline{\beta}_i^n\| \frac{1 + \|\alpha_i^n\|^{p-1}}{k_n} \right.$$
$$\left. + \|\overline{\beta}_i^n\|^2 (1 + \|\alpha_i^n\|^{(p-3)^+}) \right)$$

and we thus have $U(3)_t^n = G_t^n + H_t^n$, with

$$G_t^n = \sum_{i=1}^{[t/\Delta_n]-k_n+1} (w_i^n + \mathbb{E}(v_i^n \mid \mathcal{F}_{i-1}^n)),$$
$$H_t^n = \sum_{i=1}^{[t/\Delta_n]-k_n+1} (v_i^n - \mathbb{E}(v_i^n \mid \mathcal{F}_{i-1}^n)).$$

In view of Lemma B.4 and Hölder's inequality, we have

$$|w_i^n + \mathbb{E}(v_i^n \mid \mathcal{F}_{i-1}^n)| \le K\Delta_n \left(\frac{1}{\sqrt{k_n}} + \frac{1}{\sqrt{k_n^3 \Delta_n}} + k_n\sqrt{\Delta_n} + \overline{\eta}_i'^n \right),$$
$$\mathbb{E}(|v_i^n|^2) \le \frac{K\Delta_n}{k_n} \left(\frac{1}{k_n} + \sqrt{k_n\Delta_n} \right),$$

and we readily deduce from Lemma B.1, from (B.96) and the $\mathcal{F}_{i+k_n-1}^n$-measurability of v_i^n, and from the properties $k_n^2\Delta_n \to 0$ and $k_n^3\Delta_n \to \infty$, that both G^n and H^n converge to 0 in the u.c.p. sense, thus implying the result. $\qquad \square$

Proof of Lemma B.10. Using the definition of α_i^n, and upon a change of the order of summation, we have

$$U(4)_t^n = \sqrt{\Delta_n} \sum_{i=1}^{[t/\Delta_n]} \sum_{l,m} w_i^{n,lm} \zeta(1)_i^{n,lm},$$

where

$$w_i^{n,lm} = \frac{1}{k_n} \sum_{j=(i-[t/\Delta_n]+k_n-1)^+}^{(i-1)\wedge(k_n-1)} \partial_{lm}g(c_{(i-j-1)\Delta_n}).$$

We set

$$U'(1)_t^n = \sqrt{\Delta_n} \sum_{i=1}^{[t/\Delta_n]} \sum_{l,m} \partial_{lm}g(c_{(i-1)\Delta_n}) \zeta(1)_i^{n,lm}$$
$$v_i^{n,lm} = \frac{1}{k_n} \sum_{j=(i-[t/\Delta_n]+k_n-1)^+}^{(i-1)\wedge(k_n-1)} \partial_{lm}g(c_{(i-j-1)\Delta_n}) - \partial_{lm}g(c_{(i-1)\Delta_n}).$$

Equation (B.113) and the boundedness of c yield $|v_i^{n,lm}| \le K \sup_{s \in [(i-1)\Delta_n, (i+k_n-1)\Delta_n]} \|c_s - c_{(i-1)\Delta_n}\|$, hence (B.79) implies $\mathbb{E}(|v_i^{n,lm}|^2) \le K\sqrt{\Delta_n}$ when $k_n \le i \le [t/\Delta_n] - k_n$ and

$|v_i^{n,lm}| \leq K$ always, whereas $v_i^{n,lm}$ is $\mathcal{F}_{i-1}^n$-measurable. Therefore $\xi_i^n = \sqrt{\Delta_n} \sum_{l,m} v_i^{n,l,m} \zeta(1)_i^{n,lm}$ satisfies $|\mathbb{E}(\xi_i^n \mid \mathcal{F}_{i-1}^n)| \leq K\Delta_n^{5/4}$ and $\mathbb{E}(|\xi_i^n|^2 \mid \mathcal{F}_{i-1}^n) \leq K\Delta_n^{3/2}$ when $k_n \leq i \leq [t/\Delta_n] - k_n$, and $|\mathbb{E}(\xi_i^n \mid \mathcal{F}_{i-1}^n)| \leq K\Delta_n^{3/4}$ and $\mathbb{E}(|\xi_i^n|^2 \mid \mathcal{F}_{i-1}^n) \leq K\Delta_n$ otherwise. It then follows that (B.96) holds with $l_n = 1$ and $m_n = [t/\Delta_n]$ and thus $U(1)_t^n - U'(1)_t^n \overset{\mathbb{P}}{\longrightarrow} 0$.

It remains to show that $U'(1)^n \overset{\mathcal{L}-s}{\longrightarrow} Z$: this is exactly what Theorem 10.3.2 of [JP] tells us, when applied to the pair (X,c) and the function $\overline{F}$ on $\mathbb{R}^d \times \mathcal{M}_d^+$ with components $\overline{F}^{lm}((x,y),(x',y')) = \partial_{lm}g(y)(x''x'^m - y^{lm})$, up to one point: the component X of (X,c) satisfies (K-r) for some $r < 1$ (and even (K-0), but not the component c. However, in the function $\overline{F}^{lm}((x,y),(x',y'))$ the argument y' does not show up, so a close look at the proof reveals that one does not need (K-r) for the component c of (X,c), and (H-2) for c is enough. Hence the aforementioned theorem applies here, and the proof is complete. $\qquad\square$

B.3   Proofs for Chapter 10

B.3.1   Proof of Theorem 10.12

This theorem is rather intuitive, but its formal proof is somewhat involved. We use the notation of Section 10.2 without special mention, and in particular the processes $\mathcal{U}$ or $\mathcal{W}$ introduced in (10.8).

We begin with an auxiliary result showing how to approximate the $\mathcal{F}$-conditional law of a variable such as $\mathcal{U}_T$ or $\mathcal{W}_T$ by quantities involving only the observed increments $\Delta_i^n X$. Since we need this type of result in various circumstances, we consider below a rather general (and complicated) setting which answers all our needs. We fix some integer $k \geq 1$ and set $\overline{\mathcal{K}} = \{-k+1, \ldots, k-1\}$ (this is $\mathcal{K} \cup \{0\}$ with the notation introduced before (A.28)). We also take another finite set $\overline{\mathcal{K}}'$ of indices, and real functions $g_{j,l}$ on $\mathbb{R}^d$ and $g'_{j,l}$ on $\mathbb{N}$, indexed by $(j,l) \in \mathcal{L} = \overline{\mathcal{K}} \times \overline{\mathcal{K}}'$ and three $\mathcal{F}$-measurable real-valued variables $\gamma, \gamma', \gamma''$. With the notation (A.27), (A.28) and (A.29) for $T_n, \Psi_{n,j}, \Psi_{n\pm}, \kappa_n, L_n, R_{n,j}$ and with Ψ denoting another $\mathcal{N}(0,1)$ variable, independent of everything else, we consider the real-valued variable

$$Y = \gamma \sum_{m: T_m \leq T} \sum_{(j,l) \in \mathcal{L}} g_{j,l}(\Delta X_{T_m}, R_{m,j}) g'_{j,l}(L_m) + \gamma' \Psi + \gamma'' \quad \text{(B.116)}$$

on the extended space, provided the $g_{j,l}$'s are such that this makes sense. Note that $T > 0$ is fixed throughout the whole subsection.

Next, we have to describe the variables which will approximate Y. Since $R_{m,j}$ involves the volatility, we need to incorporate one of the estimators (A.23) for the (squared) spot volatility and then take a square root. The non-truncated $\widehat{c}_i^n$ will not work (as it does not in Theorem A.7). The multipower version $\widehat{c}_i^n(k_n, [k])$ is not so easy to deal with, because it is typically not symmetric nonnegative when $d > 1$, hence we use the truncated version below. However, when $d = 1$ the same arguments work exactly in the same way with the multipower version $\widehat{c}_i^n(k_n, [k])$. We set

$$\widetilde{\sigma}_i^n \text{ is a (measurable) } d \times d' \text{ matrix, with } \widetilde{\sigma}_i^n \, \widetilde{\sigma}_i^{n*} = \widehat{c}_i^n(k_n, u_n). \quad \text{(B.117)}$$

Next, with the variables $(\kappa_m, \Psi_{m\pm}, \Psi_{m,j})$ of (A.28) again, we set

$$\widetilde{R}_{m,j}^n = \begin{cases} \widetilde{\sigma}_{m-k_n}^n \Psi_{m,j} & \text{if } j \in \mathcal{K}_- \\ \sqrt{\kappa_m}\widetilde{\sigma}_{m-k_n}^n \Psi_{m-} + \sqrt{1-\kappa_m}\widetilde{\sigma}_{m+1}^n \Psi_{m+} & \text{if } j = 0 \\ \widetilde{\sigma}_{m+1}^n \Psi_{m,j} & \text{if } j \in \mathcal{K}_+. \end{cases} \quad \text{(B.118)}$$

The variables γ, γ' and γ'', to be used later, are not necessarily observable at stage n, but we assume that they enjoy consistent estimators: we have $\mathcal{F}$-measurable variables γ_n, γ_n', γ_n'' with

$$\gamma_n \xrightarrow{\mathbb{P}} \gamma, \qquad \gamma_n' \xrightarrow{\mathbb{P}} \gamma', \qquad \gamma_n'' \xrightarrow{\mathbb{P}} \gamma''. \quad \text{(B.119)}$$

Finally we choose a sequence $w_n \geq 0$, and the approximation to Y is

$$Y_n = \gamma_n \sum_{i=k_n+1}^{[T/\Delta_n]-k_n} \sum_{(j,l)\in\mathcal{L}} g_{j,l}(\Delta_i^n X, \widetilde{R}_{i,j}^n) \, g_{j,l}'(L_i) \, 1_{\{|\Delta_i^n X|>w_n\}} \quad \text{(B.120)}$$
$$+ \gamma_n'\Psi + \gamma_n''.$$

We then have an auxiliary result, which is of some interest on its own:

Theorem B.11. *Assume (H-r) for some* $r \in [0,2]$ *and (B.117), and that each* $g_{j,l}$ *is continuous and satisfies* $|g_{j,l}(x,y)| \leq h(x)h'(y)$, *for two nonnegative continuous functions* h *and h' such that*
- $h(x) = \mathrm{o}(\|x\|^r)$ *as* $x \to 0$;
- $h'(x) = \mathrm{O}(\|x\|^p)$ *as* $\|x\| \to \infty$, *for some* $p \geq 0$.

Choose u_n *and* w_n *such that* $u_n \asymp \Delta_n^\varpi$ *with* $0 < \varpi < \frac{1}{2}$ *and also* $\varpi \geq \frac{p-1}{2p-2r}$ *when* $p > 2$, *and* $w_n \asymp \Delta_n^{\varpi'}$ *with* $0 < \varpi' < \frac{1}{2}$, *or* $w_n = 0$ *when* $h(x) = \mathrm{o}(\|x\|^2)$ *as* $x \to 0$. *Then, the* $\mathcal{F}$-conditional distributions Γ *and* Γ_n *of* Y *and* Y_n *satisfy*

$$\Gamma_n \xrightarrow{\mathbb{P}} \Gamma \text{ (convergence in probability, for the weak topology).} \quad \text{(B.121)}$$

Proof. Step 1. First we perform several simplifications. First, by a localization procedure, we may assume the strengthened assumption (SH-r). Next, we set $Y' = \gamma'\Psi + \gamma''$ and $Y'_n = \gamma'_n\Psi + \gamma''_n$, and also $Y'' = Y - Y'$ and $Y''_n = Y_n - Y'_n$. We also denote by $\Gamma', \Gamma'', \Gamma'_n, \Gamma''_n$ the $\mathcal{F}$-conditional distributions of the variables Y', Y'', Y'_n, Y''_n.

In view of (B.119), the convergence $\Gamma'_n \xrightarrow{\mathbb{P}} \Gamma'$ is clear, and since $\Gamma = \Gamma' * \Gamma''$ and $\Gamma_n = \Gamma'_n * \Gamma''_n$ (convolution products) we are left to prove $\Gamma''_n \xrightarrow{\mathbb{P}} \Gamma''$. By (B.119) again, it is also clear that we may assume $\gamma_n = \gamma = 1$ identically. In other words, we can come back to Y and Y_n, under the following additional assumptions:

$$\gamma_n = \gamma = 1, \qquad \gamma'_n = \gamma' = 0, \qquad \gamma''_n = \gamma'' = 0. \qquad (B.122)$$

Step 2. In a second step we prove the result when, for some $\varepsilon > 0$, all functions $g_{j,l}$ satisfy $g_{j,l}(x,y) = 0$ when $\|x\| \leq \varepsilon$. In this case, as soon as $w_n < \varepsilon$, we have $\|\Delta_i^n X\| > w_n$ when $g_{j,l}(\Delta_i^n X, \widetilde{R}_{i,j}^n) \neq 0$, so we can dispense with the truncation in (B.120).

Let $S_1, S_2, \ldots$ be the successive jump times of X with jump sizes bigger than $\varepsilon/2$. We also write $i(n,p)$ for the unique integer such that $(i(n,p)-1)\Delta_n < S_p \leq i(n,p)\Delta_n$, and $M = \sup(p : S_p \leq T)$. Let Ω_n be the set (depending on T) of all ω satisfying the following properties:

(a) $\|\Delta_i^n X\| \leq \varepsilon$ for all integers i between 1 and $[T/\Delta_n] + 1$ which are not one of the $i(n,p)$'s;

(b) $i(n,M) \leq [T/\Delta_n]$ and $i(n,p) < i(n,p+1)$ for all $p \leq M$.

On the one hand, $\mathbb{P}(\Omega_n) \to 1$ as $n \to \infty$. On the other hand, in restriction to Ω_n, we have (up to relabeling the variables $(R_{m,j})_{j\in\overline{\mathcal{K}}}$, which does not change their joint $\mathcal{F}$-conditional distribution):

$$
\begin{aligned}
Y &= \sum_{(j,l)\in\mathcal{L}} \sum_{m=1}^{M} g_{j,l}(\Delta X_{S_m}, R_{m,j})\, g'_{j,l}(L_m) \\
Y_n &= \sum_{(j,l)\subset\mathcal{L}} \sum_{m=1}^{M} g_{j,l}(\Delta_{i(n,m)}^n X, \widetilde{R}_{i(n,m),j}^n)\, g'_{j,l}(L_{i(n,m)}).
\end{aligned}
\qquad (B.123)
$$

As an obvious consequence of the definition (A.29), the variables $((R_{m,j} : j \in \overline{\mathcal{K}}), L_m)$, conditionally on $\mathcal{F}$, are independent when m varies and each one has a law which only depends on the pair (c_{T_m-}, c_{T_m}), in a continuous way. That is, this (conditional) law has the form $F(c_{T_m-}, c_{T_m}; dx)$, where $(z, z') \mapsto F((z, z'), dx)$ is (weakly) continuous. Analogously, conditionally on $\mathcal{F}$, the variables $((\widetilde{R}_{i(n,m),j}^n : j \in$

$\overline{\mathcal{K}}), L_{i(n,m)})$ are independent when m varies, with the law

$$F\big(\widehat{c}^n_{i(n,m)-k_n}(k_n, u_n), \widehat{c}^n_{i(n,m)+1}(k_n, u_n); dx\big).$$

Here, F is the same as for $R_{m,j}$, and this property does *not* depend on the particular choice of $\widetilde{\sigma}^n_i$ which is made in (B.117). Therefore, the two conditional laws Γ and Γ_n are indeed of the form

$$\begin{aligned}
\Gamma(dx) &= \overline{F}\big(M, (\Delta X_{S_m}, c_{T_m-}, c_{T_m})_{1\leq m\leq M}, dx\big)\\
\Gamma_n(dx) &= \overline{F}\big(M, (\Delta^n_{i(n,m)} X, \widehat{c}^n_{i(n,m)-k_n}(k_n, u_n),\\
&\qquad \widehat{c}^n_{i(n,m)+1}(k_n, u_n))_{1\leq m\leq M}, dx\big)
\end{aligned}$$

with *the same* $\overline{F}$, which further depends (weakly) continuously on the various arguments, because the $g_{j,l}$'s are continuous functions. Therefore, (B.121) is a straightforward consequence of the following convergences:

$$\begin{aligned}
\Delta^n_{i(n,m)} X &\xrightarrow{\ \mathbb{P}\ } \Delta X_{S_m},\\
\widehat{c}^n_{i(n,m)-k_n}(k_n, u_n) &\xrightarrow{\ \mathbb{P}\ } c_{T_m-},\\
\widehat{c}^n_{i(n,m)+1}(k_n, u_n) &\xrightarrow{\ \mathbb{P}\ } c_{T_m}.
\end{aligned} \tag{B.124}$$

The first convergence above comes from the definition of $i(n,m)$ (it holds in fact for each ω). The two others come from Theorem A.6, once observed that $\widehat{c}^n_{i(n,m)-k_n}(k_n, u_n) = \widehat{c}^n(k_n, u_n)_{(S_m-)}$ and $\widehat{c}^n_{i(n,m)+1}(k_n, u_n) = \widehat{c}^n(k_n, u_n)_{(S_m)}$.

Step 3. We now remove the assumption that each $g_{j,l}$ vanishes on a neighborhood of 0. To this effect, we truncate the functions $g_{j,l}$ in the following way. We take a continuous function ψ on $\mathbb{R}_+$, with $1_{[0,1/2]} \leq \psi \leq 1_{[0,1]}$ and, for any $\varepsilon > 0$, we set

$$g^\varepsilon_{j,l}(x,y) = g_{j,l}(x,y)\psi(\|x\|/\varepsilon), \quad g'^\varepsilon_{j,l}(x,y) = g_{j,l}(x,y)(1 - \psi(\|x\|/\varepsilon)),$$

so $g_{j,l} = g^\varepsilon_{j,l} + g'^\varepsilon_{j,l}$. We also write Y and Y_n as Y^ε and Y^ε_n if we substitute all $g_{j,l}$ with $g^\varepsilon_{j,l}$, and as Y'^ε and Y'^ε_n if it is with $g'^{\varepsilon}_{j,l}$, and accordingly the $\mathcal{F}$-conditional distributions are written as $\Gamma^\varepsilon, \Gamma^\varepsilon_n, \Gamma'^\varepsilon, \Gamma'^\varepsilon_n$.

The previous step gives us that, for any $\varepsilon > 0$ fixed, $\Gamma'^\varepsilon_n \xrightarrow{\ \mathbb{P}\ } \Gamma'^\varepsilon$ as $n \to \infty$. So, (B.121) will hold if we prove the following two properties, for any bounded Lipschitz function f on $\mathbb{R}$ and any $\eta > 0$:

$$\begin{aligned}
&\lim_{\varepsilon\to 0} \mathbb{P}\big(\Gamma^\varepsilon(f) - \Gamma(f)| > \eta\big) = 0,\\
&\lim_{\varepsilon\to 0} \limsup_{n\to\infty} \mathbb{P}\big(|\Gamma'^\varepsilon_n(f) - \Gamma^\varepsilon(f)| > \eta\big) = 0.
\end{aligned}$$

Since $Y = Y^\varepsilon + Y'^\varepsilon$ and $Y_n = Y^\varepsilon_n + Y'^\varepsilon_n$, these two properties are obviously satisfied if

$$\begin{aligned}
&\widetilde{\mathbb{E}}\big(|Y'^\varepsilon| \,|\, \mathcal{F}\big) \xrightarrow{\ \mathbb{P}\ } 0 \quad \text{as } \varepsilon \to 0,\\
&\lim_{\varepsilon\to 0} \limsup_{n\to\infty} \mathbb{P}\big(\widetilde{\mathbb{E}}(|Y'^\varepsilon_n| \,|\, \mathcal{F}) > \eta\big) = 0.
\end{aligned} \tag{B.125}$$

In view of the properties of the functions $g_{j,l}$, plus the boundedness of the process c (because of (SH-r)) and the definition of $R_{m,j}$ and $\widetilde{R}_{m,j}^n$, a simple calculation shows that, with $h_\varepsilon(x) = h(x)\psi(\|x\|/\varepsilon)$, we have

$$\widetilde{\mathbb{E}}(|Y'^\varepsilon| \mid \mathcal{F}) \leq K \sum_{s \leq t} h_\varepsilon(\Delta X_s), \qquad \widetilde{\mathbb{E}}(|Y_n'^\varepsilon| \mid \mathcal{F}) \leq K Z_n^\varepsilon,$$

where

$$Z_n^\varepsilon = \sum_{i=k_n+1}^{[t/\Delta_n]-k_n} h_\varepsilon(\Delta_i^n X) \, 1_{\{\|\Delta_i^n X\| > w_n\}}$$
$$\times (1 + \|\widehat{c}_{i-k_n}^n(u_n-)\|^{p/2} + \|\widehat{c}_{i+1}^n(u_n-)\|^{p/2}).$$

(H-r) implies that $\sum_{s \leq t} h(\Delta X_s) < \infty$, so the first part of (B.125) follows from the dominated convergence theorem because $h_\varepsilon \leq h$ and $h_\varepsilon \to 0$ pointwise. For the second part, we use Theorem A.7 with ϕ_ε and $g(z) = 1 + \|z\|^{p/2}$ (so p is substituted with $p/2$), to obtain

$$Z_n^\varepsilon \overset{\mathbb{P}}{\longrightarrow} \sum_{s \leq t} h_\varepsilon(\Delta X_s) \left(\|c_{s-}\|^{p/2} + \|c_s)\|^{p/2} \right)$$

as $n \to \infty$, and the right side above goes to 0 as $\varepsilon \to 0$. This gives the second part of (B.125), and the proof is complete. $\qquad\square$

Proof of Theorem 10.12. In this proof we use all notation preceding the statement of Theorem 10.12, without special mention.

Step 1. The algorithm for constructing the confidence interval $\mathcal{I}_n$ in (10.35) stops at Step 2 when $\omega \notin \Omega_n$, and the result only concerns what happens on $\Omega_T^{(jW)}$, which is also the limit (in probability) of Ω_n. However, for the proof it is convenient to complete the algorithm "outside Ω_n," that is, we skip Step 2 and proceed even if $\omega \notin \Omega_n$. Analogously, the limiting variable $\mathcal{S}^{(\text{J-TR})}$ is in principle irrelevant outside $\Omega_T^{(jW)}$, so we can change it at will outside this set. Therefore, recalling Ψ'^j in Step 4 of the algorithm, we set

$$S_n^j = \Psi'^j \text{ outside } \Omega_n, \text{ and } \mathcal{S}^{(\text{J-TR})} = \Psi'^1 \text{ outside } \Omega_T^{(jW)}. \qquad (\text{B.126})$$

Then Steps 5 and 6 of the algorithm are performed with this definition.

We denote below Γ and Γ_n the $\mathcal{F}$-conditional distributions of $\mathcal{S}^{(\text{J-TR})}$ and S_n^1, respectively. In (10.20) and in the second formula in (10.34), the last summand is $\mathcal{F}$-conditionally independent of the first one and is an $\mathcal{N}(0,1)$ variable independent of $\mathcal{F}$, multiplied by a positive $\mathcal{F}$-measurable variable, whereas in (B.126) the variables are $\mathcal{N}(0,1)$. This allows us to deduce that

$$\Gamma \text{ and } \Gamma_n \text{ have positive densities on } \mathbb{R}. \qquad (\text{B.127})$$

Therefore the functions $\overline{\Gamma}(x) = \Gamma([-x,x)^c)$ and $\overline{\Gamma}_n(x) = \Gamma'_n[-x,x]^c)$ on $\mathbb{R}_+$ are continuous and strictly decreasing from 1 to 0. We denote their inverses by G^x and G_n^x, which are continuous strictly decreasing functions on $(0,1)$, and are of course $\mathcal{F}$-measurable as functions of ω.

Step 2. We observe that $\mathcal{S}^{(\text{J-TR})}$ is exactly the variable Y of (B.116), with $k=1$ and $\mathcal{L} = \{(0,0)\}$, and provided we take $g(x,y) = xy$ and $g'(l) = 1$, and

$$\gamma = -\frac{2C_T}{[X,X]_T^2}\,1_{\Omega_T^{(jW)}},$$
$$\gamma' = \frac{A(2)_T\,\sqrt{2C(4)_T}}{[X,X]_T^2}\,1_{\Omega_T^{(jW)}} + 1_{(\Omega_T^{(jW)})^c},$$
$$\gamma'' = 0.$$

Similarly, the variable S_n^1 is Y_n of (B.120), with the same g, h, h' and $\gamma''_n = 0$ and

$$\gamma_n = -\frac{2\widehat{C}(\Delta_n,u_n)_T}{\widehat{C}(\Delta_n)_T^2}\,1_{\Omega_n},$$
$$\gamma'_n = \frac{(\widehat{C}(\Delta_n)_T - \widehat{C}(\Delta_n,u_n)_T)\,\sqrt{2B^n(4,\Delta_n,u_n)_T/3\Delta_n}}{\widehat{C}(\Delta_n)_T^2}\,1_{\Omega_n} + 1_{(\Omega_n)^c}.$$

The condition (B.119) is implied by (10.24) and the property $1_{\Omega_n} \xrightarrow{\mathbb{P}} 1_{\Omega_T^{(jw)}}$. Since (H-$r$) holds for some $r < 1$, all assumptions of Theorem B.11 are fulfilled, and we conclude that $\Gamma_n \xrightarrow{\mathbb{P}} \Gamma$ weakly.

This property yields $\overline{\Gamma}_n(x) \xrightarrow{\mathbb{P}} \overline{\Gamma}(x)$ for each x, and even uniformly in x. This and the fact that $x \mapsto G^x$ is continuous strictly decreasing readily give us for each $\varepsilon > 0$

$$\sup_{x \in [\varepsilon, 1-\varepsilon]} |G_n^x - G^x| \xrightarrow{\mathbb{P}} 0. \tag{B.128}$$

Step 3. Now we prove an auxiliary result, which goes as follows: let $(Z_j)_{1 \leq j \leq N}$ be an i.i.d. sequence of positive variables with a purely non-atomic law, and denote by ϕ the unique right-continuous (decreasing) function such that $\mathbb{P}(Z_i > \phi(x)) = x$ for all $x \in (0,1)$. Fix $\alpha \in (0,1)$ and an integer N such that $N > 4/\alpha(1-\alpha)$. Set $U(x) = \frac{1}{N}\sum_{i=1}^N 1_{\{Z_i > x\}}$ and call $Z'(\alpha)$ the $[\alpha N]^{\text{th}}$ variable in the family $(Z_j : j = 1, \ldots, N)$, after they have been rearranged in decreasing order. Then, if $\varepsilon \in (4/N, \alpha(1-\alpha))$ and $Z'(\alpha) > \phi(\alpha - \varepsilon)$, we have

$$U(\phi(\alpha - \varepsilon)) \geq U(Z'(\alpha)) = \frac{[\alpha N] - 1}{N} \geq \alpha - \frac{2}{N} \geq \alpha - \frac{\varepsilon}{2},$$

that is, $U(\phi(\alpha - \varepsilon)) - (\alpha - \varepsilon) \geq \varepsilon/2$. In a similar way, if $Z'(\alpha) < \phi(\alpha + \varepsilon)$ we have $U(\phi(\alpha + \varepsilon)) - (\alpha + \varepsilon) \leq -\varepsilon$. Since the variables $U(\phi(x))$ have mean x and variance smaller than $1/4N$, it follows from the Bienaymé-Tchebycheff inequality that

$$
\begin{aligned}
\mathbb{P}(Z'(\alpha) &\notin [\phi(\alpha + \varepsilon), \phi(\alpha - \varepsilon)]) \\
&\leq \mathbb{P}(U(\phi(\alpha - \varepsilon)) - (\alpha - \varepsilon) \geq \varepsilon/2) \\
&\quad + \mathbb{P}(U(\phi(\alpha + \varepsilon)) - (\alpha + \varepsilon) \leq \varepsilon) \\
&\leq \tfrac{5}{4N\varepsilon^2}.
\end{aligned}
\tag{B.129}
$$

Step 4. We come back to the problem at hand. With any $\alpha \in (0,1)$ we apply the previous auxiliary result with N_n large enough to have $\frac{4}{N_n} < \frac{1}{N_n^{1/4}} < \alpha(1-\alpha)$ and with $\varepsilon = v_n = 1/N_n^{1/4}$ and the variables $|S_n^j|$ under their $\mathcal{F}$-conditional laws Γ_n. Observe that $\phi(x)$ is now G_n^x, and $Z'(\alpha)$ is the empirical quantile Z_n^α defined in Step 6 of our algorithm. Then (B.129) is read as

$$
\widetilde{\mathbb{P}}\big(Z_n^\alpha \notin [G_n^{\alpha+v_n}, G_n^{\alpha-v_n}] \mid \mathcal{F}\big) \;\leq\; \frac{5}{4N_n^{1/2}}.
\tag{B.130}
$$

Letting $T_n = (S^{(\text{J-TR})}(\Delta_n, u_n) - S)/\sqrt{\Delta_n}$, the claim amounts to the convergence

$$
\begin{aligned}
\widetilde{\mathbb{P}}(\{|T_n| > Z_\alpha^n\} \cap A) &\to \alpha\,\mathbb{P}(A) \\
&\text{if } A \in \mathcal{F},\ P(A) > 0,\ A \subset \Omega_T^{(jW)}.
\end{aligned}
\tag{B.131}
$$

If $B_n = \{Z_n^\alpha \notin [G_n^{\alpha+v_n}, G_n^{\alpha-v_n}]\}$, we have

$$
\begin{aligned}
\mathbb{P}(\{|T_n| > G_n^{\alpha-v_n}\} \cap A) - \widetilde{\mathbb{P}}(B_n) &\leq \widetilde{\mathbb{P}}(\{|T_n| > Z_\alpha^n\} \cap A) \\
&\leq \mathbb{P}(\{|T_n| > G_n^{\alpha+v_n}\} \cap A) + \widetilde{\mathbb{P}}(B_n).
\end{aligned}
$$

Then, since (B.130) implies $\widetilde{\mathbb{P}}(B_n) \to 0$, in order to get (B.131) it is enough to prove that

$$
\begin{aligned}
\mathbb{P}(\{|T_n| > G_n^{\alpha-v_n}\} \cap A) &\to \alpha\,\mathbb{P}(A), \\
\mathbb{P}(\{|T_n| > G_n^{\alpha+v_n}\} \cap A) &\to \alpha\,\mathbb{P}(A).
\end{aligned}
\tag{B.132}
$$

If $y \in (0,1)$ and $D = \{(\omega, x) : \omega \in A, |x| > G^y(\omega)\}$, the function $F(\omega, x) = 1_D$ is bounded, $\mathcal{F} \otimes \mathcal{R}$-measurable, and $x \mapsto F(\omega, x)$ is continuous for $\Gamma(\omega, dx)$-almost all x because of (B.127). Since $T_n \xrightarrow{\mathcal{L}-\mathfrak{s}} S$ (J-TR) by (10.19) on the set $\Omega_T^{(jW)}$ and $A \subset \Omega_T^{(jW)}$, it follows from (3.16) that

$$
\mathbb{P}(\{|T_n| > G^y\} \cap A) \;\to\; \widetilde{\mathbb{P}}(\{|S^{(\text{J-TR})} > G^y\} \cap A) \;=\; y\,\mathbb{P}(A), \tag{B.133}
$$

where the last equality comes from the definition of G^y and by conditioning on $\mathcal{F}$. If $a > 0$ we have

$$
\begin{aligned}
\widetilde{\mathbb{P}}\left(\{|T_n| > G^{\alpha-a}\} \cap A\right) &- \mathbb{P}\left(G^{\alpha-a} < G_n^{\alpha-v_n}\right) \\
&\leq \mathbb{P}\left(\{|T_n| > G^{\alpha-v_n}\} \cap A\right) \\
&\leq \mathbb{P}\left(\{|T_n| > G^{\alpha+v_n}\} \cap A\right) \\
&\leq \widetilde{\mathbb{P}}\left(\{|T_n| > G^{\alpha+a}\} \cap A\right) + \mathbb{P}\left(G^{\alpha+a} > G_n^{\alpha+v_n}\right).
\end{aligned}
$$

Now, (B.128) and the fact that $x \mapsto G^x$ is strictly decreasing implies $\mathbb{P}(G^{\alpha-a} < G_n^{\alpha-v_n}) \to 0$ and $\mathbb{P}(G^{\alpha+a} > G_n^{\alpha+v_n}) \to 0$. Therefore, we deduce (B.132) from (B.133) and from the fact that $a > 0$ is arbitrarily small. This completes the proof. $\qquad\square$

B.3.2   Proofs for Section 10.3

Below we provide the proofs for the properties left unproven in Section 10.3, namely (10.42), (10.46) and Proposition 10.19.

Proof of (10.42). We assume $p > 3$. With the two-dimensional test function with components

$$
\begin{aligned}
f^1(x_1, \ldots, x_k) &= |x_1 + \cdots + x_k|^p, \\
f^2(x_1, \ldots, x_k) &= |x_1|^p + \cdots + |x_k|^p,
\end{aligned}
\tag{B.134}
$$

we have

$$
\begin{aligned}
B([p,k], \Delta_n)_t &= B(f^1, \Delta_n)_t, \\
kB(p, \Delta_n)_t &= B(f^2, \Delta_n)_t + H_t^n, \\
B(p, k\Delta_n)_t &= \overline{B}(f^1, \Delta_n)_t, \\
B(p, \Delta_n)_t &= \overline{B}(f^2, \Delta_n)_t + \overline{H}_t^n,
\end{aligned}
\tag{B.135}
$$

where $\overline{H}_t^n = \sum_{i=k[t/k\Delta_n]+1}^{[t/\Delta_n]} |\Delta_i^n X|^p$ and H_t^n is a similar border term (slightly more complicated to express). Observe that

$$
\begin{aligned}
H_t^n + \overline{H}_t^n &\leq k^{2+p/2} \Delta_n^{p/2} \left(X(0; k\Delta_n) + X(t; k\Delta_n)\right), \\
\text{where } X(t; v) &= \sup_{s \in [0,v]} \frac{|X_{t+s} - X_t|}{\sqrt{v}},
\end{aligned}
\tag{B.136}
$$

and under (SH-2), which we can assume by a localization argument (see page 502), the family of variables $(X(t; v) : v \in [0,1])$ is bounded in probability for any fixed $t \geq 0$ (see for example (2.1.33), (2.1.34) and Lemma 2.1.5 of [JP]. Since $p > 3$, it follows that

$$
\begin{aligned}
kB(p, \Delta_n)_t - B(f^2, \Delta_n)_t &= o_{\mathbb{P}}(\sqrt{\Delta_n}), \\
B(p, \Delta_n)_t - \overline{B}(f^2, \Delta_n)_t &= o_{\mathbb{P}}(\sqrt{\Delta_n}).
\end{aligned}
\tag{B.137}
$$

The conditions (A.32) needed in Theorem A.9 hold because $p > 3$. With the notation (A.30) we have

$$f_j^1(x) = f_j^2(x) = |x|^p,$$
$$\partial f^1_{(l);j}(x) = p|x|^{p-1}\,\text{sign}(x),$$
$$\partial f^2_{(l);j}(x) = p|x|^{p-1}\,\text{sign}(x)\,\delta_{lj}$$

(δ_{lj} is the Kronecker symbol). Since f is invariant by a permutation of its arguments, (A.33) and (A.35) yield that, for any fixed t, and with the notation (A.27) and (A.28),

$$\left(\tfrac{1}{\sqrt{\Delta_n}}(B(f^1,\Delta_n)_t - kA(p)_t),\ \tfrac{1}{\sqrt{\Delta_n}}(B(f^2,\Delta_n)_t - kA(p)_t)\right)$$
$$\xrightarrow{\mathcal{L}-s} (\mathcal{U}(f^1)_t, \mathcal{U}(f^2)_t)$$
$$\left(\tfrac{1}{\sqrt{\Delta_n}}(\overline{B}(f^1,\Delta_n)_t - A(p)_t),\ \tfrac{1}{\sqrt{\Delta_n}}(\overline{B}(f^2,\Delta_n)_t - A(p)_t)\right)$$
$$\xrightarrow{\mathcal{L}-s} (\overline{\mathcal{U}}(f^1)_t, \overline{\mathcal{U}}(f^2)_t)$$

where

$$\mathcal{U}(f^1)_t = p\sum_{q:\,T_q\le t} |\Delta X_{T_q}|^{p-1}\,\text{sign}(\Delta X_{T_q})$$
$$\times\left(\sigma_{T_q-}\left(k\sqrt{\kappa_q}\,\Psi_{q-} + \sum_{j=1-k}^{-1}(j+k)\Psi_{q,j}\right)\right.$$
$$\left.+\sigma_{T_q}\left(k\sqrt{1-\kappa_q}\,\Psi_{q+} + \sum_{j=1}^{k-1}(k-j)\Psi_{q,j}\right)\right)$$
$$\mathcal{U}(f^2)_t = kp\sum_{q:\,T_q\le t} |\Delta X_{T_q}|^{p-1}\,\text{sign}(\Delta X_{T_q})$$
$$\times\left(\sigma_{T_q-}\sqrt{\kappa_q}\,\Psi_{q-} + \sigma_{T_q}\sqrt{1-\kappa_q}\,\Psi_{q+}\right)$$

and

$$\overline{\mathcal{U}}(f^1)_t = p\sum_{q:\,T_q\le t} |\Delta X_{T_q}|^{p-1}\,\text{sign}(\Delta X_{T_q})$$
$$\times\left(\sigma_{T_q-}\left(\sqrt{\kappa_q}\,\Psi_{q-} + \sum_{j=-L_n}^{-1}\Psi_{q,j}\right)\right.$$
$$\left.+\sigma_{T_q}\left(\sqrt{1-\kappa_q}\,\Psi_{q+} + \sum_{j=1}^{k-1-L_n}\Psi_{q,j}\right)\right)$$
$$\overline{\mathcal{U}}(f^2)_t = \sum_{q:\,T_q\le t} |\Delta X_{T_q}|^{p-1}\,\text{sign}(\Delta X_{T_q})$$
$$\times\left(\sigma_{T_q-}\sqrt{\kappa_q}\,\Psi_{q-} + \sigma_{T_q}\sqrt{1-\kappa_q}\,\Psi_{q+}\right).$$

The pairs

$$\left(\sum_{j=1-k}^{-1}(j+k)\Psi_{q,j},\ \sum_{j=1}^{k-1}\Psi_{q,j}\right)\text{ and }\left(\sqrt{k(k-1)/2}\,\Psi'_{q-},\ \sqrt{k(k-1)/2}\,\Psi'_{q+}\right)$$

(notation (10.43)), resp. the pairs

$$\left(\sum_{j=-L_n}^{-1}\Psi_{q,j},\ \sum_{j=1}^{k-1-L_n}\Psi_{q,j}\right)\text{ and }\left(\sqrt{L_n}\,\Psi'_{q-},\ \sqrt{k-1-L_n}\,\Psi'_{q+}\right),$$

have the same law. Thus in view of (B.135) and (B.137) we deduce (10.42). □

Proof of (10.46). Here we assume (KC), so X is continuous. The two-dimensional test function f given by (B.134) is globally even and homogeneous of degree p, and as for (B.135) we have

$$
\begin{aligned}
\Delta_n^{1-p/2} B([p,k], \Delta_n)_t &= B'(f^1, \Delta_n)_t, \\
\Delta_n^{1-p/2} k B'(p, \Delta_n)_t &= B'(f^2, \Delta_n)_t + \Delta_n^{1-p/2} H_t^n, \\
\Delta_n^{1-p/2} \overline{B}'(p, k\Delta_n)_t &= \overline{B}'(f^1, \Delta_n)_t, \\
\Delta_n^{1-p/2} \overline{B}'(p, \Delta_n)_t &= \overline{B}'(f^2, \Delta_n)_t + \Delta_n^{1-p/2} \overline{H}_t^n,
\end{aligned}
$$

with appropriate border terms H_t^n and $\overline{H}_t^n$. Exactly as for (B.137), one deduces from (B.136) that

$$
\begin{aligned}
\Delta_n^{1-p/2} k B'(p, \Delta_n)_t - B'(f^2, \Delta_n)_t &= \mathrm{o_P}(\sqrt{\Delta_n}) \\
\Delta_n^{1-p/2} \overline{B}'(p, \Delta_n)_t - \overline{B}'(f^2, \Delta_n)_t &= \mathrm{o_P}(\sqrt{\Delta_n}).
\end{aligned}
\tag{B.138}
$$

Next, we need to compute $R_a(f)$ and $\overline{R}_a(f)$, as given by (A.43). This is elementary but rather tedious, and we only give the result here. With the notation (10.45), it turns out that

$$
\begin{aligned}
R_a(f)^{11} &= a^p\, \widehat{m}_{2p}(k) \\
\overline{R}_a(f)^{11} &= a^p\, k^{p-1}(m_{2p} - (m_p)^2) \\
R_a(f)^{12} &= a^p\, k^2\, \widetilde{m}_{2p}(k) \\
\overline{R}_a(f)^{12} &= a^p\, \widetilde{m}_{2p}(k) \\
R_a(f)^{22} &= a^p\, k^2(m_{2p} - (m_p)^2) \\
\overline{R}_a(f)^{22} &= a^p\, (m_{2p} - (m_p)^2).
\end{aligned}
\tag{B.139}
$$

An application of (A.47) yields the following functional stable convergences in law:

$$
\left(\tfrac{1}{\sqrt{\Delta_n}} \left(B'(f^1, \Delta_n) - k^{p/2} m_p\, C\,(p) \right), \tfrac{1}{\sqrt{\Delta_n}} \left(B'(f^2, \Delta_n)_t - k m_p\, C\,(p) \right) \right)
$$
$$
\overset{\mathcal{L}-s}{\Longrightarrow} (\mathcal{W}(f^1), \mathcal{W}(f^2))
$$
$$
\left(\tfrac{1}{\sqrt{\Delta_n}} \left(\overline{B}'(f^1, \Delta_n) - k^{p/2-1} m_p\, C\,(p) \right), \tfrac{1}{\sqrt{\Delta_n}} \left(\overline{B}'(f^2, \Delta_n)_t - m_p\, C\,(p) \right) \right)
$$
$$
\overset{\mathcal{L}-s}{\Longrightarrow} (\overline{\mathcal{W}}(f^1), \overline{\mathcal{W}}(f^2))
$$

where the limiting processes are defined on an extension of the space and, conditionally on $\mathcal{F}$, are centered Gaussian martingales with variance-covariance given by (A.45). Then (10.46) follows, upon using (B.138) and observing that a version of $\mathcal{W}(f^2)$ is $k\overline{\mathcal{W}}(f^2)$ and renaming the limiting processes as $\mathcal{W}(f^1) = \mathcal{W}(p,k)$ and $\overline{\mathcal{W}}(f^1) = \overline{\mathcal{W}}(p,k)$ and $\mathcal{W}(f^2) = \mathcal{W}(p)$. The covariance formula (10.47) follows from (B.139). $\qquad\square$

Proof of Proposition 10.19. The only claim to prove is $\alpha(p,k)_1 < \alpha(p,k)_2$. Let $U_0, U_1, U_2, \ldots$ be i.i.d. standard normal variables. With p and k fixed, and for $j, l \geq 0$ with $j + l \leq k$, $x \in \mathbb{R}$, we introduce functions F_j on $\mathbb{R}^j$, numbers γ_j and variables $Y_{j,l}(x)$ by

$$
\begin{aligned}
F_j(x_1, \ldots, x_j) &= \mathbb{E}\big(|x_1 + \cdots + x_j + \sqrt{k-j}\,U_0|^p\big), \\
\gamma_j &= \mathbb{E}\big(|F_j(U_1 + \cdots + U_j) - F_0|^2\big) \\
Y_{j,l}(x) &= F_k(U_1, \ldots, U_k) + x F_j(U_1, \ldots, U_j) \\
&\quad + x F_l(U_{j+1}, \ldots, U_{j+l}) - (1 + 2x)F_0.
\end{aligned}
$$

Note that $F_0 = k^{p/2} m_p$ is a constant, and $\mathbb{E}(F_j(U_1, \ldots, U_j)) = \mathbb{E}(F_l(U_{j+1}, \ldots, U_{j+l})) = F_0$. By successive conditioning, we also have

$$
\begin{aligned}
\mathbb{E}\big(F_j(U_1, \ldots, U_j)\, F_k(U_1, \ldots, U_k)\big) &= \mathbb{E}\big(F_j(U_1, \ldots, U_j)^2\big) \\
\mathbb{E}\big(F_l(U_{j+1}, \ldots, U_{j+l})\, F_k(U_1, \ldots, U_k)\big) &= \mathbb{E}\big(F_l(U_{j+1}, \ldots, U_{j+l})^2\big).
\end{aligned}
$$

Then a simple computation shows that

$$
\mathbb{E}(Y_{j,l}(x)^2) = \gamma_k + 2x(\gamma_j + \gamma_l) + x^2(\gamma_j + \gamma_l).
$$

The variables $Y_{j,l}(x)$ are non-degenerate, implying $\mathbb{E}(Y_{l,j}(x)^2) > 0$. Thus the polynomial $x \mapsto \mathbb{E}(Y_{l,j}(x)^2)$ of degree 2 has no real root, hence its discriminant is strictly negative, that is,

$$
\gamma_j + \gamma_l \ < \ \gamma_k.
$$

Adding up these inequalities for all pairs $(j, k-j)$ for $j = 1, \ldots, \frac{k-1}{2}$ when k is odd, and for $j = 1, \ldots, \frac{k}{2}$ when k is even, we obtain in all cases

$$
2\sum_{j=1}^{k-1} \gamma_j \ < \ (k-1)\gamma_k.
$$

Coming back to the notation (10.45), we see that $\overline{m}_{2p}(k, j) = \gamma_j + (F_0)^2$, whereas $\gamma_0 = 0$. Thus

$$
\widehat{m}_{2p}(k) \ = \ \gamma_k + 2\sum_{j=1}^{k-1} \gamma_j \ < \ k\gamma_k.
$$

Since

$$
\alpha(p,k)_2 - \alpha(p,k)_1 \ = \ \frac{k^{p+1}(m_{2p} - (m_p)^2) - \widehat{m}_{2p}(k)}{k^2\,(m_p)^2},
$$

and $k^{p+1}(m_{2p} - (m_p)^2) = k\gamma_k$, we deduce $\alpha(p,k)_1 < \alpha(p,k)_2$, and the proof is complete. $\square$

B.3.3   Proofs for Section 10.4

Below, we give a (sketchy) proof of the results of Section 10.4. By localization one can replace any assumption, such as (H-2) or (P), by its
strengthened version (SH-2) or (SP).

Proof of Theorem 10.21. Let $i[n,t]$ be the integer such that $(i[n,t] -
1)\Delta_n < t \le i[n,t]\Delta_n$, and $\widehat{c}^n_{(t)} = \widehat{c}^n_{i[n,t]}$, so

$$Z^n(t) \;=\; \Delta^n_{i[n,t]} X / \sqrt{\Delta_n \, \widehat{c}^n_{(t)}}. \tag{B.140}$$

On the one hand, $(\Delta^n_{i[n,t_j]} W / \sqrt{\Delta_n})_{1 \le j \le q}$ stably converges in law to
$(\Psi_j)_{1 \le j \le q}$, by an elementary result on stable convergence. On the other
hand, $\widehat{c}^n_{(t)} \overset{\mathbb{P}}{\longrightarrow} c_t$ by Theorem A.6, and if $\mathbb{P}(\Delta\sigma_t = 0) = 1$ we have
$\sigma_{(i[n,t]-1)\Delta_n} \overset{\mathbb{P}}{\longrightarrow} \sigma_t$ as well. Thus, in view of (SP), (a) follows from the
property

$$\begin{aligned}
\mathbb{P}(\Delta\sigma_t = 0) &= 1 \\
\Rightarrow \;\; \Delta^n_{i[n,t]} X &- \sigma_{(i[n,t]-1)\Delta_n} \Delta^n_{i[n,t]} W \;=\; \mathrm{o}_\mathbb{P}(\sqrt{\Delta_n}).
\end{aligned} \tag{B.141}$$

To check this, we observe that by (A.66),

$$\Delta^n_i X - \sigma_{(i-1)\Delta_n} \Delta^n_i W \;=\; \xi^n_i + \xi'^n_i + \xi''^n_i,$$

where

$$\begin{aligned}
\xi^n_i &= \int_{(i-1)\Delta_n}^{i\Delta_n} \bar{b}_s \, ds, \\
\xi'^n_i &= \int_{(i-1)\Delta_n}^{i\Delta_n} \left(\sigma_s - \sigma_{(i-1)\Delta_n}\right) dW_s, \\
\xi''^n_i &= \Delta^n_i(\delta * (\underline{p} - \underline{q})).
\end{aligned}$$

We have $\xi^n_{i[n,t]}/\sqrt{\Delta_n} \to 0$ because $\bar{b}$ is bounded. By Doob's inequality,

$$\mathbb{E}\!\left(\left(\xi'^n_{i[n,t]}/\sqrt{\Delta_n}\right)^2\right) \le \tfrac{1}{\Delta_n} \mathbb{E}\!\left(\int_{(i[n,t]-1)\Delta_n}^{i[n,t]\Delta_n} \left(\sigma_s - \sigma_{(i[n,t]-1)\Delta_n}\right)^2\right),$$

which goes to 0 by the dominated convergence theorem when $\mathbb{P}(\Delta\sigma_t =
0) = 1$. Finally, an application of (A.75) with $p = r = 2$ shows that
$\mathbb{E}\!\left(\left(1 \wedge (\xi''^n_{i[n,t]}/\sqrt{\Delta_n})\right)^2\right) \le K\phi(\Delta_n)$, which goes to 0 as $n \to \infty$. Therefore
we conclude (B.141).

Now we turn to (b). Equation (10.63) is a known result, which is the
main building block of the proof of Theorem A.9; see Proposition 4.4.5
in [JP]. Next, (10.63) implies that

$$\begin{aligned}
S^{(\text{J-DET})}(\Delta_n) &\ge \frac{1}{\sqrt{\widehat{c}^n_{i(n,q)+1}}} \left(\frac{|\Delta X_{T_q}|}{\sqrt{\Delta_n}} + \mathrm{O}_\mathbb{P}(1)\right) \\
&\text{on } \Omega_{n,q} = \{T_q < T - (k_n + k - 1)\Delta_n\},
\end{aligned}$$

whereas $\hat{c}^n_{i(n,q)+1} \xrightarrow{\mathbb{P}} c_{T_q}$, and $c_{T_q} > 0$ by (P). Therefore, for all q we have

$$\lim_{\varepsilon \to 0} \sup_n \, \mathbb{P}\big(\{S^{\,(\mathrm{J-DET})}(\Delta_n) \le \varepsilon/\sqrt{\Delta_n}\} \cap \Omega_{n,q} \cap \{\Delta X_{T_q} \ne 0\}\big) \;=\; 0.$$

Since the sets $\cup_{q \ge 1}(\Omega_{n,q} \cap \{\Delta X_{T_q} \ne 0\})$ converge almost surely to $\Omega_T^{(j)}$ as $n \to \infty$, (10.64) follows.   □

Before proving Theorem 10.22 we need a few auxiliary results, for which k_n and k are as in the theorem and X and σ are continuous. We use the following notation:

$$\begin{aligned}
M_n &= \sup_{i \le [T/\Delta_n]} |\Delta_i^n W|/\sqrt{\Delta_n} \\
M_n(1) &= \sup_{i \le [T/\Delta_n]} |\Delta_i^n X - \sigma_{(i-1)\Delta_n} \Delta_i^n W|/\sqrt{\Delta_n} \\
M_n(2) &= \sup_{i \le [T/\Delta_n]} \sup_{t \in (0,(k_n+k-1)\Delta_n]} |\sigma_{(i-1)\Delta_n+t} - \sigma_{(i-1)\Delta_n}| \\
M_n(3) &= \sup_{i \le [T/\Delta_n]-k_n-k+1} |\hat{c}^n_{i+1} - c_{(i-1)\Delta_n}|.
\end{aligned}$$

Lemma B.12. *Recalling* $l_n = \sqrt{2\log(1/\Delta_n)}$, *we have the following convergence in law:*

$$l_n\left(M_n - l_n + \frac{\log(2\pi l_n)}{2l_n} - \frac{\log 2T}{l_n}\right) \xrightarrow{\mathcal{L}} \xi, \tag{B.142}$$

where ξ is a Gumbel variable, and in particular $M_n/l_n \xrightarrow{\mathbb{P}} 1$.

Proof. We set $v_n = [T/\Delta_n]$ for the number of increments taken into consideration in M_n, and $w_n = \sqrt{2\log v_n}$. One easily checks that $w_n = l_n + (\log T)/l_n + O(1/l_n^3)$, so (B.142) amounts to

$$\overline{M}_n := w_n\left(M_n - w_n - \frac{\log 2}{w_n} + \frac{\log(2\pi w_n)}{2w_n}\right) \xrightarrow{\mathcal{L}} \xi,$$

Classical results on extremes, see e.g. page 147 of Embrechts et al. (1997), plus the fact that the variables $\Delta_i^n W/\sqrt{\Delta_n}$ for $i \ge 1$ are i.i.d. standard normal, and that we use the maximum of the absolute values of the increments instead of the maximum of the increments, which explains the additional term with $\log 2$ above, yield that the variables $\overline{M}_n$ above converge in law to ξ. The last claim readily follows from (B.142).   □

Lemma B.13. *Under (KC) and if σ is continuous, we have* $l_n^\rho M_n(j) \xrightarrow{\mathbb{P}} 0$ *for all $\rho \ge 0$ and $j = 1, 2, 3$.*

Proof. Without restriction we may assume (SKC). We have

$$\Delta_i^n X - \sigma_{(i-1)\Delta_n} \Delta_i^n W = \zeta_i^n + \zeta_i'^n,$$

where

$$\zeta_i^n = \int_{(i-1)\Delta_n}^{i\Delta_n} b_s \, ds,$$
$$\zeta_i'^n = \int_{(i-1)\Delta_n}^{i\Delta_n} (\sigma_s - \sigma_{(i-1)\Delta_n}) \, dW_s.$$

We have $|\zeta_i^n| \leq K\Delta_n$ because b_t is bounded. When $p \geq 2$, by virtue of (A.68) and the Burkholder-Gundy inequality, $\mathbb{E}(|\zeta_i'^n|^p) \leq K\Delta_n^p$. Thus

$$\mathbb{E}((M_n(1))^p) \leq K\Delta_n^{p/2} + \frac{K}{\Delta_n^{p/2}} \sum_{i=1}^{[T/\Delta_n]} \mathbb{E}(|\zeta_i'^n|^p) \leq K(\Delta_n^{p/2} + T\Delta_n^{p/2-1})$$

and, since $l_n^\rho \Delta_n^\varepsilon \to 0$ for all $\rho, \varepsilon > 0$, the claim about $M_n(1)$ follows upon taking $p > 2$.

In the same way, another application of (A.68) yields, when σ is continuous,

$$\mathbb{E}((M_n(2))^p) \leq \sum_{i=1}^{[T/\Delta_n]} \mathbb{E}\left(\sup_{t \in ((i-1)\Delta_n, (i+k_n-1)\Delta_n)} |\sigma_t - \sigma_{(i-1)\Delta_n}|^p \right)$$
$$\leq KT \frac{(k_n\Delta_n)^{p/2}}{\Delta_n}.$$

Hence, in view of (10.58) and $l_n^\rho \Delta_n^\varepsilon \to 0$ for all $\rho, \varepsilon > 0$ again, the claim about $M_n(2)$ follows upon taking $p > 2/\eta'$.

Now we turn to $M_n(3)$. We prove the result in the case $\widehat{c}_i^n = \widehat{c}_i^n(k_n, u_n)$ only (so $k = 1$), the other case being similar. First, $|\Delta_i^n X| \leq (M_n(1) + M_n)\sqrt{\Delta_n}$ for all $i \leq [T/\Delta_n]$. Hence Lemma B.12 and $l_n M_n(1) \overset{\mathbb{P}}{\longrightarrow} 0$ yield $\sup_{i \leq [T/\Delta_n]} |\Delta_i^n X| \leq 2l_n\sqrt{\Delta_n}$ on a set Ω_n whose probability goes to 1. Since $u_n \asymp \Delta_n^\varpi$ for some $\varpi \in (0, \frac{1}{2})$ we deduce that, with the notation (A.23), we have $\widehat{c}_i^n = \widehat{c}(k_n)_i^n$ (the estimator without truncation) for all $i \leq [T/\Delta_n]$ on Ω_n. It is thus enough to prove the result when, in the definition of $M_n(3)$, we substitute $\widehat{c}(k_n)_i^n$ with $\widehat{c}_i^n$. Moreover,

$$\Delta_{i+m}^n X = \sigma_{(i-1)\Delta_n}\Delta_{i+m}^n W + (\sigma_{(i+m-1)\Delta_n} - \sigma_{(i-1)\Delta_n})\Delta_{i+m}^n W$$
$$+ \Delta_{i+m}^n X - \sigma_{(i+m-1)\Delta_n}\Delta_{i+m}^n W.$$

Hence, since σ is bounded, we have for $m = 1, \ldots, k_n$:

$$\left| (\Delta_{i+m}^n X)^2 - c_{(i-1)\Delta_n}(\Delta_{i+m}^n W)^2 \right|$$
$$\leq K\Delta_n(M_n(1)^2 + M_nM_n(1) + M_n^2M_n(2)).$$

Then we deduce from Lemma B.12 and from $l_n^{\rho+2} M_n(j) \overset{\mathbb{P}}{\longrightarrow} 0$ for $j = 1, 2$ that

$$l_n^\rho \sup_{i \leq [T/\Delta_n]-k_n-k+1} \left| \widehat{c}(k_n)_{i+1}^n - \frac{c_{(i-1)\Delta_n}}{k_n\Delta_n} \sum_{m=1}^{k_n} (\Delta_{i+m}^n W)^2 \right| \overset{\mathbb{P}}{\longrightarrow} 0$$

Thus, letting $C_i^n = \frac{1}{k_n \Delta_n} \sum_{m=1}^{k_n} (\Delta_{i+m}^n W)^2 - 1$ and $N_n = \sup_{i \le [T/\Delta_n] - k_n} |C_i^n|$, it remains to prove that $l_n^\rho N_n \xrightarrow{\mathbb{P}} 0$. Observe that C_i^n has the same law as $\frac{1}{k_n} \sum_{j=1}^{k_n} (U_j^2 - 1)$, where the U_j are i.i.d. $\mathcal{N}(0,1)$, so the Burkholder-Gundy inequality yields $\mathbb{E}((C_i^n)^p) \le K/k_n^{p/2}$ for all $p > 1$. Hence $\mathbb{E}(N_n^p) \le KT/\Delta_n k_n^{p/2}$ and, since $k_n \Delta_n^\eta \to \infty$ by (10.58), the result follows by choosing $p > 2/\eta$. $\qquad\square$

Proof of Theorem 10.22. We assume (SKC) and (SP). The latter implies that $A = \inf_{t,\omega} c_t(\omega) > 0$, and also that one can choose σ to be always positive. By Lemma B.12, we only have to prove that

$$l_n \left(S^{(\text{J-DET})}(\Delta_n) - M_n \right) \xrightarrow{\mathbb{P}} 0. \tag{B.143}$$

For all $i \le [T/\Delta_n] - k_n + k + 1$ we have $|\widehat{c}_{i+1}^n - c_{(i-1)\Delta_n}| \le M_n(3)$, hence $\widehat{c}_i^n \ge A/2$ on the set $\Omega_n = \{M_n(3) \le A/2\}$, which satisfies $\mathbb{P}(\Omega_n) \to 1$ by Lemma B.13.

Now,

$$\left| Z_i^n - \frac{\Delta_i^n W}{\sqrt{\Delta_n}} \right| \le \frac{|\Delta_i^n X - \sigma_{(i-1)\Delta_n} \Delta_i^n W|}{\sqrt{\Delta_n \widehat{c}_{i+1}^n}} + \frac{|\Delta_i^n W|}{\sqrt{\Delta_n}} \left| \frac{\sigma_{(i-1)\Delta_n}}{\sqrt{\widehat{c}_{i+1}^n}} - 1 \right|.$$

We have $|1 - \sqrt{x/y}| \le K|x - y|$ when $x, y \ge A/2$, and $|\sup x_i - \sup y_i| \le \sup |x_i - y_i|$ when $x_i, y_i \ge 0$, hence

$$l_n \left| S^{(\text{J-DET})}(\Delta_n) - M_n \right| \le K l_n \left(M_n(1) + M_n M_n(3) \right) \quad \text{on the set } \Omega_n.$$

At this stage, (B.143) follows from $\mathbb{P}(\Omega_n) \to 1$ and from the previous two lemmas. $\qquad\square$

Proof of (10.69). We prove the result only in the case when we take for $\widehat{c}_i^n$ in (10.59) the version $\widehat{c}_i^n = \widehat{c}_i^n(k_n, u_n)$. We may assume (SP) and (SK-0). Recall that σ is continuous. We consider the process X' of (10.68), the associated variables $Z_i'^n$ and statistics $S'^{(\text{J-DET})}(\Delta_n)$, and

$$\xi_n = l_n \left(S'^{(\text{J-DET})})(\Delta_n) - l_n + \frac{\log(2\pi l_n)}{2l_n} - \frac{\log 2T}{l_n} \right),$$

which converges in law to the Gumbel variable ξ by (10.65) because X' satisfies (KC) and (P). Since $S'^{(\text{J-DET})}(\Delta_n) > \frac{l_n^2}{1+l_n}$ implies $\xi_n > \frac{\log(2\pi l_n)}{2} - \log 2T - \frac{1}{2}$ as soon as $l_n \ge 1$, we deduce

$$\mathbb{P} \left(S'^{(\text{J-DET})}(\Delta_n) > \frac{l_n^2}{1+l_n} \right) \to 0. \tag{B.144}$$

Of course, the $Z_i'^n$ are computed with the estimators $\widehat{c}_i'^n = \widehat{c}_i'^n(k_n, u_n)$ associated with the process X'. We thus have to compare $\widehat{c}_i^n$ and $\widehat{c}_i'^n$. To this end, we recall that (SK-0) implies $1_{\{\delta(t,z)\neq 0\}} \leq J(z)$ for some λ-integrable function J on E. We can thus replace the Poisson measure $\underline{p}$ by its restriction to $\mathbb{R}_+ \times \{J \geq 1\}$, hence λ by its restriction to $\{J \geq 1\}$, without modifying X. In other words, we may assume that λ is a finite measure. The sequence $S_q = \inf(t : 1 * \underline{p}_t = q)$ is then strictly increasing to ∞, and the number $Q = \max(q : S_q \leq T)$ of S_q's in $[0, T]$ is a Poisson random variable, and we associate $i'(n, q)$ with S_q as $i(n, q)$ is associated with T_q in (10.60). For simplicity we write below $I_n = \{1, \ldots, [T/\Delta_n]\}$, and I_n' for the set of all i such that $i = i'(n, q) - m$ for some $q \leq Q$ and some $m \in \{0, \ldots, k_n\}$, and $I_n'' = I_n \backslash I_n'$.

As in the proof of Theorem 10.22 there is a constant $A > 0$ such that $\Omega_n = \{\inf_{i \leq [T/\Delta_n]} \widehat{c}_i'^n \geq A/2\}$ satisfies $\mathbb{P}(\Omega_n) \to 1$. The set $\Omega_{n,\varepsilon}$ on which, for any $q = 1, \ldots, Q$, we have either $|\Delta X_{S_q}| > \varepsilon$ or $\Delta X_{S_q} = 0$, and also $|\Delta_i^n X'| \leq u_n/2$ for all $i \leq [T/\Delta_n]$, satisfies $\lim_{\varepsilon \to 0} \liminf_n \mathbb{P}(\Omega_{n,\varepsilon}) = 1$. On $\Omega_{n,\varepsilon}$, and as soon as $u_n < \varepsilon/2$, for all $i \in I_n$ we have either $\Delta_i^n X = \Delta_i^n X'$ or $|\Delta_i^n X| > u_n$, the latter occurring only if $i = i'(n, q)$ for some $q \leq Q$. Then on $\Omega_{n,\varepsilon}$ we have

$$i \in I_n'' \;\Rightarrow\; \widehat{c}_i'^n = \widehat{c}_i^n,$$
$$i \in I_n' \;\Rightarrow\; 0 \leq \widehat{c}_i'^n - \widehat{c}_i^n \leq V_n = \frac{1}{k_n \Delta_n} \sum_{m=1}^{Q} (\Delta_{i'(n,m)}^n X')^2.$$

If we use the first part of (A.77) (with $(\mathcal{G}_t^A)$ and $A = E$), plus the fact that Q is $\mathcal{G}_t^A$-measurable and has finite expectation, we obtain $\mathbb{E}(V_n) \leq K/k_n$, hence $l_n^\rho V_n \overset{\mathbb{P}}{\longrightarrow} 0$ for all $\rho > 0$ because of (10.58). Thus $\Omega_{n,\varepsilon}' = \Omega_n \cap \Omega_{n,\varepsilon} \cap \{V_n < A/4l_n\}$ satisfies $\lim_{\varepsilon \to 0} \liminf_n \mathbb{P}(\Omega_{n,\varepsilon}') = 1$.

Now, on $\Omega_{n,\varepsilon}'$ and if $u_n \leq \varepsilon/2$, we have $\widehat{c}_i'^n > A/2$ and $\widehat{c}_i^n > A/4$ if $i \in I_n$, whereas $\Delta_i^n X = \Delta_i^n X'$ when $i \in A_n$, hence $|Z_i'^n - Z_i^n| \leq 4Z_i'^n V_n/A \leq Z_i'^n/l_n$ for all $i \in A_n$, implying $\sup_{i \in A_n} |Z_i^n| \leq \frac{1+l_n}{l_n} S'^{(\text{J-DET})}(\Delta_n)$. Therefore, as soon as $u_n \leq \varepsilon/2$,

$$\mathbb{P}\left(\sup_{i \in A_n} |Z_i^n| > l_n\right) \leq \mathbb{P}(\Omega_{n,\varepsilon}') + \mathbb{P}\left(S'^{(\text{J-DET})}(\Delta_n) > \frac{l_n^2}{1+l_n}\right)$$

and (10.69) follows from (B.144) and $\lim_{\varepsilon \to 0} \liminf_n \mathbb{P}(\Omega_{n,\varepsilon}') = 1$. $\square$

Proof of Theorem 10.26. We use the notation $i(n, q)$ of (10.60), with T_q being the successive jump times of X, and first assume that σ is continuous. In view of (10.63) and $\widehat{c}_{i(n,q)+1}^n \overset{\mathbb{P}}{\longrightarrow} c_{T_q} > 0$ (recall (A.24)) and $l_n \sqrt{\Delta_n} \to 0$ and $|\Delta X_{T_q}| > 0$, we obtain $\mathbb{P}(|Z_{i(n,q)}^n| > l_n) \to 1$ for all q.

Hence the set

$$\Omega_n = \Big\{ T_R \le \Delta_n[T/\Delta_n], \ \sup_{i \in A_n} |Z_i^n| \le l_n,$$
$$q \le R \Rightarrow i(n,q) < i(n,q+1) \text{ and } |Z_{i(n,q)}^n| > l_n \Big\}$$

satisfies $\mathbb{P}(\Omega_n) \to 1$ by (10.69).

On Ω_n we have $\widehat{R}_n = R$ and $I_n(q) = i(n,q)$ (hence $T_q \in (\widehat{T}(n,q) - \Delta_n, \widehat{T}(n,q)])$ for all $q \le R$ by the definition (10.72). Hence (10.73) follows from $\mathbb{P}(\Omega_n) \to 1$. On Ω_n we also have $\widehat{J}(n,q) = \Delta_{i(n,q)}^n X$ for $q \le R$, so (10.74) follows from (10.64) and the fact that $\sigma_{T_q-} = \sigma_{T_q}$ under our assumptions.

In the case where σ may jump, we simply replace $\sup_{i \in A_n} |Z_i^n| \le l_n$ by $\sup_{i \in A_n} |\overline{Z}_i^n| \le v_n$ in the definition of Ω_n, and observe that $\mathbb{P}(|\overline{Z}_{i(n,q)}^n| > v_n) \to 1$ for all q because of (10.70). $\qquad\square$

Proof of Theorem 10.29. We use again the notation $i(n,q)$ of (10.60), with T_q now being as in Theorem 10.26. Let also

$$X_t'' = X_t - \sum_{s \le t} \Delta X_s \mathbf{1}_{\{|\Delta X_s| > a\}}.$$

Since X is càdlàg, we have for all sample paths in the set $\Omega_a = \{\omega : |\Delta X_s(\omega)| \ne a \ \forall s > 0\}$ and all $q \ge 1$

$$\limsup_{n \to \infty} \ \sup_{i \le [T/\Delta_n]} |\Delta_i^n X''| < a, \qquad \lim_{n \to \infty} |\Delta_{i(n,q)}^n X''| = 0.$$

This implies that on this set Ω_a we have $\widehat{R}_n = R$ and $I_n(q) = i(n,q)$ for all $q \le R$, as soon as n is large enough. Since (10.76) amounts to $\mathbb{P}(\Omega_a) = 1$, we deduce (10.73). Finally, (10.74) is proved as in the previous theorem. $\qquad\square$

B.3.4 Proofs for Section 10.5

In this subsection we prove Theorem 10.30, and as before it is no restriction to assume the strengthened Assumption (SK-r). In particular, we have (B.70) and (B.71) with J bounded.

We are given the number $a > 0$, and we suppose that $k_n \sim \beta/\Delta_n^\tau$ with $\beta > 0$ and $u_n \asymp \Delta_n^\varpi$ with

$$\frac{2(r-1)^+}{r} < \tau < 1, \quad \tau \wedge (1-\tau) < \frac{2-r}{r}, \quad \frac{1-\tau}{2(2-r)} < \varpi < \frac{1}{2}. \quad \text{(B.145)}$$

We start with an auxiliary lemma. Set $A = \{z \in E : J(z) > a^2/16\}$ and let $S_1, S_2, \ldots$ be the successive jump times of the process $\mathbf{1}_A * \underline{p}$.

Any jump of c with size bigger than $a/4$ occurs at some time S_p, because $|\delta^{(c)}(t,z)|^2 \le J(z)$. Note that all S_p's are almost surely finite when $\lambda(A) > 0$, and almost surely infinite otherwise, in which case the next result is void. For convenience we set $S_0 = 0$. We denote by $m(n,p)$ the unique (random) integer such that $m(n,p)k_n\Delta_n < S_p \le (m(n,p)+1)k_n\Delta_n$. Recall also that $R \le R' = \max(p : S_p < T)$.

The next lemma is closely related to Theorem 8.8, which exhibits a different behavior as τ is smaller than, equal to, or greater than $\frac{1}{2}$; recall that $k_n \sim \beta/\Delta_n^\tau$ here. In order to unify the statement, we make the following convention:

$$
\begin{aligned}
\tau < \tfrac{1}{2} &\Rightarrow w_n = 1/\sqrt{k_n}, \quad \bar{c}_t = c_t \\
\tau = \tfrac{1}{2} &\Rightarrow w_n = 1/\sqrt{k_n}, \quad \bar{c}_t = \sqrt{c_t^2 + \beta^2 c_t^{(c)}/2} \\
\tau > \tfrac{1}{2} &\Rightarrow w_n = \sqrt{k_n\Delta_n}, \quad \bar{c}_t = \sqrt{c_t^{(c)}/2}.
\end{aligned}
\tag{B.146}
$$

With the shorthand notation $\widehat{c}_i^n = \widehat{c}(k_n, u_n)_i$, we also recall that $L_i^n = \widehat{c}_{(i+2)k_n+1}^n - \widehat{c}_{ik_n+1}^n$, see (10.77).

Lemma B.14. *Under the previous assumption we have the following stable convergences in law:*

$$
\begin{aligned}
&\left(\frac{1}{w_n} \left(\frac{L_{m(n,p)-2}^n + L_{m(n,p)-1}^n + L_{m(n,p)}^n}{2} - \Delta c_{S_p} \right) \right)_{p \ge 1} \\
&\qquad \overset{\mathcal{L}\text{-}s}{\longrightarrow} \left(\bar{c}_{S_p-} U_p^- + \bar{c}_{S_p} U_p^+ \right)_{p \ge 1} \\
&\left(L_{m(n,p)-2}^n, L_{m(n,p)-1}^n, L_{m(n,p)}^n \right)_{p \ge 1} \\
&\qquad \overset{\mathcal{L}\text{-}s}{\longrightarrow} \left((1-\kappa_p)\Delta c_{S_p}, \Delta c_{S_p}, \kappa_p \Delta c_{S_p} \right)_{p \ge 1}
\end{aligned}
\tag{B.147}
$$

where the variables $(U_p^-, U_p^+, \kappa_p)_{p \ge 1}$ are defined on an extension of the space $(\Omega, \mathcal{F}, \mathbb{P})$ and are all mutually independent and independent of $\mathcal{F}$, with $U_p^\pm$ standard normal and κ_p uniform on $(0,1)$. Moreover, for all $p \ge 1$,

$$
\begin{aligned}
L_{m(n,p)-1}^n - \Delta c_{S_p} &= O_\mathbb{P}(w_n) \\
L_{m(n,p)-1}^n - L_{m(n,p)-2}^n - L_{m(n,p)}^n &= O_\mathbb{P}(w_n) \\
j \in \mathbb{Z}\backslash\{0,1,2\} \Rightarrow L_{m(n,p)-j}^n &= O_\mathbb{P}(w_n).
\end{aligned}
\tag{B.148}
$$

Proof. The proof is based on the following extension of Theorem 8.8, which is proved exactly as Theorem 13.3.3 of [JP]. Namely, recalling that (B.145) implies (8.16), for any finite subset $J \subset \{1,2,\dots\}$ we have the following stable convergence in law:

$$\left(\frac{1}{w_n}\left(\widehat{c}^{\,n}_{1+(m(n,p)-j)k_n} - c_{S_p-}\right), \frac{1}{w_n}\left(\widehat{c}^{\,n}_{1+(m(n,p)+j)k_n} - c_{S_p}\right)\right)_{p\geq 1, j\in J}$$
$$\xrightarrow{\mathcal{L}-s} \left(\sqrt{2}\,\overline{c}_{S_p-}\, U_p^{j-},\ \sqrt{2}\,\overline{c}_{S_p}\, U_p^{j+}\right)_{p\geq 1, j\in J}$$
$$\left(\widehat{c}^{\,n}_{1+m(n,p)k_n}\right)_{p\geq 1} \xrightarrow{\mathcal{L}-s} \left(\kappa_p\, c_{S_p-} + (1-\kappa_p)c_{S_p}\right)_{p\geq 1}$$

where the variables $(U_p^{j-}, U_p^{j+}, \kappa_p)_{p\geq 1, j\in J}$ are defined on an extension of the space, are mutually independent and also independent of $\mathcal{F}$, and $U_p^{j\pm}$ are standard normal and κ_p are uniform on $(0,1)$.

Recall that for any $k \in \mathbb{Z}$,

$$L^n_{m(n,p)+k} = \widehat{c}^{\,n}_{1+(m(n,p)+2+k)k_n} - \widehat{c}^{\,n}_{1+(m(n,p)+k)k_n}$$
$$L^n_{m(n,p)-2} + L^n_{m(n,p)-1} + L^n_{m(n,p)} = -\widehat{c}^{\,n}_{1+(m(n,p)-2)k_n}$$
$$- \widehat{c}^{\,n}_{1+(m(n,p)-1)k_n} + \widehat{c}^{\,n}_{1+(m(n,p)+1)k_n} + \widehat{c}^{\,n}_{1+(m(n,p)+2)k_n}$$
$$L^n_{m(n,p)-1} - L^n_{m(n,p)-2} - L^n_{m(n,p)} = \widehat{c}^{\,n}_{1+(m(n,p)-2)k_n}$$
$$- \widehat{c}^{\,n}_{1+(m(n,p)-1)k_n} + \widehat{c}^{\,n}_{1+(m(n,p)+1)k_n} - \widehat{c}^{\,n}_{1+(m(n,p)+2)k_n}.$$

Then (B.148) readily follows, as well as (B.147). For the later we take $U_p^- = -(U_p^{2-} + U_p^{1-})/\sqrt{2}$ and $U_p^+ = (U_p^{2+} + U_p^{1+})/\sqrt{2}$ for the first convergence, whereas we also use $\widehat{c}^{\,n}_{(m(n,p)+2)k_n} \xrightarrow{\mathbb{P}} c_{S_p}$ for the second convergence. $\qquad\square$

Proof of Theorem 10.30. We need a number of steps.

Step 1. Suppose that (10.80) holds, and we prove (10.81). The key point is of course the convergence (B.147), but one has to be careful; indeed, the S_p's are the jump times of $1_A * \underline{p}$, whereas the T_q's in (10.81) are the jump times of c with jump size bigger than a. As already mentioned, any T_q is also a jump time of $1_A * \underline{p}$, but usually not the other way around, so we need some care. We also use the simplifying notation (B.146).

For any $q \geq 1$ we let p_q be the unique (random) integer such that $T_q = S_{p_q}$. Then, for $l \geq 1$ and $1 \leq j_1 < \cdots < j_l$ we denote by $D(l; j_1, \ldots, j_l)$ the $\mathcal{F}$-measurable set on which $R = l$ and $p_q = j_q$ for $q = 1, \ldots, l$. These sets are pairwise disjoint and constitute a partition of Ω, so by virtue of the properties of the stable convergence in law it is enough to prove the convergence (10.81) in restriction to each of those sets $D(l; j_1, \ldots, j_l)$.

On the set $D(l; j_1, \ldots, j_l)$ we have $L^n(I_n(q) - j) = L^n_{m(n,j_q)}$ and $T_q = S_{j_q}$ for $q = 1, \ldots, l$. Thus (B.147) yields that, in restriction to $D(l; j_1, \ldots, j_l)$,

$$\left(\sqrt{k_n}\left(\frac{L^n_{I_n(q)-2} + L^n_{I_n(q)-1} + L^n_{I_n(q)}}{2} - \Delta c_{S_p}\right)\right)_{1\leq q\leq l}$$
$$\xrightarrow{\mathcal{L}-s} \left(\overline{c}_{T_q-} U_{j_q}^- + \overline{c}_{T_q} U_{j_q}^+\right)_{1\leq q\leq l}.$$

Since the sequence $\left(\bar{c}_{T_q-}U^-_{j_q} + \bar{c}_{T_q}U^+_{j_q}\right)_{q\geq1}$ has the same $\mathcal{F}$-conditional distribution as the sequence $\left(\sqrt{\bar{c}^2_{T_q-} + \bar{c}^2_{T_q}}\,\Psi_q\right)_{q\geq1}$, where the variables Ψ_q are again i.i.d., $\mathcal{N}(0,1)$, and independent of $\mathcal{F}$, we deduce the convergence (10.81) on the set $D(l; j_1, \ldots, j_l)$, and this proves the result.

Therefore, it remains to prove (10.80), which is the difficult part of the proof. For simplicity, we rewrite this property as $\mathbb{P}(\Omega_n) \to 1$, where

$$\Omega_n = \left\{\widehat{R}_n = R,\ T_q \in [\widehat{T}(n,q), \widehat{T}(n,q) + k_n\Delta_n]\ \forall q \in \{1, \cdots, R\}\right\}.$$

Step 2. We set $\rho_n = \Delta_n^{(\tau\wedge(1-\tau))/4}$, and we recall that by (10.78), and up to throwing away a null set, we have $|\Delta c_t| \neq a$ identically. We denote by $\mathcal{I}_n = \{0, \ldots, [T/k_n\Delta_n] - 3\}$ the family of all possible indices i for the variables L^n_i which are taken into consideration. We also introduce some other (random, possibly empty) families of indices (recall that $R' = \max(p : S_p < T)$):

$$I_+ = \{p \in \{1, \ldots, R'\} : |\Delta c_{S_p}| > a\},$$
$$I_- = \{p \in \{1, \ldots, R'\} : |\Delta c_{S_p}| < a\},$$

$$I_0 = \{p \in \{1, \ldots, R'\} : \Delta c_{S_p} = 0\},$$
$$I'_0 = \{p \in \{1, \ldots, R'\} : \Delta c_{S_p} \neq 0\},$$

and

$$J_n = \left\{i \in \mathcal{I}_n : \forall p \in \{1, \ldots, R'\}\ \text{we have}\ |j - m(n,p)| \geq 3\right\}$$

With the usual conventions $\inf_{p\in\emptyset} x_p = \infty$ and $\sup_{p\in\emptyset} x_p = 0$ when $x_p \geq 0$, we define the following subsets of Ω:

$$
\begin{aligned}
A(n,1) &= \left\{\inf_{p\in I_+} |L^n_{m(n,p)-1}| \leq a\right\}\\
A(n,2) &= \left\{\sup_{p\in I_-} |L^n_{m(n,p)-1}| > a\right\}\\
A(n,3) &= \left\{\sup_{1\leq p\leq R'} |L^n_{m(n,p)-1} - L^n_{m(n,p)-2} - L^n_{m(n,p)}| > \rho_n\right\}\\
A(n,4) &= \cup_{j=-1,1} \left\{\sup_{p\in I_0} |L^n_{m(n,p)+j-1}| > a\right\}\\
A(n,5) &= \cup_{j=-1,1} \left\{\inf_{p\in I'_0} |L^n_{m(n,p)+j-1} - L^n_{m(n,p)+j-2}\right.\\
&\qquad\qquad\qquad \left. - L^n_{m(n,p)+j}| \leq \rho_n\right\}\\
A(n,6) &= \cup_{j=-2,2} \left\{\sup_{1\leq p\leq R'} |L^n_{m(n,p)+j-1}| > a\right\}\\
A(n,7) &= \left\{\exists i \in J_n\ \text{with}\ |L^n_{i-1}| > a\ \text{and}\ |L^n_{i-1} - L^n_{i-2} - L^n_i| \leq \rho_n\right\}.
\end{aligned}
$$

Then, a thorough – and rather tedious – examination of the definition of Ω_n (using in particular the fact that any jump of c of size bigger than a occurs at some S_p) reveals that its complement is contained in

$\cup_{j=1}^{7} A(n,j)$. Therefore, it remains to prove that, for $k \in \{1, \ldots, 7\}$, we have

$$\mathbb{P}(A(n,k)) \rightarrow 0. \tag{B.149}$$

Step 3. This step is devoted to proving (B.149) for $k \in \{1, \ldots, 6\}$. Since R' is finite, we have

$$\sup_{p \leq R'} \left(|L_{m(n,p)-1}^n - \Delta c_{S_p}| + |L_{m(n,p)-1}^n - L_{m(n,p)-2}^n - L_{m(n,p)}^n| \right)$$
$$= O_{\mathrm{P}}(w_n) = O_{\mathrm{P}}(\rho_n^2)$$

from (B.148). We also have $\inf_{p \in I_+} |\Delta c_{S_p}| > a$ and $\sup_{p \in I_-} |\Delta c_{S_p}| < a$, when the sets I_+ and I_-, respectively, are not empty. Therefore (B.149) follows when $k = 1, 2, 3$. Next, the second part of (B.147) implies that $L_{m(n,p)+j}^n \xrightarrow{\mathbb{P}} 0$ for $j = -1, 1$ when $\Delta c_{S_p} = 0$, hence the same argument as above yields (B.149) for $k = 4$. In the same way we get the result for $k = 6$ by applying the last part of (B.148).

Finally, if we combine the last parts of (B.147) and (B.148), we see that

$$Y_j^n := \inf_{p \in I_0'} |L_{m(n,p)+j-1}^n - L_{m(n,p)+j-2}^n - L_{m(n,p)+j}^n|$$
$$\xrightarrow{\mathcal{L}-s} Y_j = \begin{cases} \inf_{p \in I_0'} (1 - \kappa_p) |\Delta c_{S_p}| & \text{if } j = -1 \\ \inf_{p \in I_0'} \kappa_p |\Delta c_{S_p}| & \text{if } j = 1, \end{cases}$$

and $Y_j > 0$ almost surely (note that $Y_j = \infty$ is $I_0' = \emptyset$). It follows that $\mathbb{P}(Y_j^n \leq \rho_n) \rightarrow 0$. This clearly yields (B.149) for $k = 5$.

Step 4. For the proof of (B.149) for $k = 7$ we need another auxiliary result. We fix $\theta > 0$, to be specified later. Set $\zeta_i^n = \widehat{c}_{ik_n}^n - c_{(ik_n-1)\Delta_n}$. Two successive applications of (B.89) and (B.90) with $q = 1$, for the index $j_2 k_n$ first, and then for the index $j_1 k_n$ (note that the variable $\zeta_{j_1}^n$ is $\mathcal{F}_{j_2 k_n \Delta_n}$-measurable), plus the Markov's inequality, yield

$$\mathbb{P}(|\zeta_{j_1}^n| > \theta, \ |\zeta_{j_2}^n| > \theta) \leq \frac{K_\varepsilon}{\theta^2} \eta(n, \varepsilon)^2$$

for all $\varepsilon > 0$ and all $0 \leq j_1 < j_2$, and where $\eta(n, \varepsilon) = \Delta_n^{(2-r)(\varpi \wedge (1/2r)) - \varepsilon}$.

The number of pairs (j_1, j_2) in $\{0, \ldots, [T/k_n \Delta_n]\}$ with $j_1 < j_2 \leq j_1 + 4$ being smaller than $4[T/k_n \Delta_n]$, and since $\eta(n, \varepsilon)^2 / k_n \Delta_n \rightarrow 0$ for $\varepsilon > 0$ small enough, by virtue of (B.145), we deduce from the Borel-Cantelli lemma that $\mathbb{P}(\Omega_T^n(\theta)) \rightarrow 1$, where

$$\Omega_T^n(\theta) = \begin{array}{l} \text{the set on which, for any } i \in \{0, \cdots, [T/k_n \Delta_n]\} \\ \text{we have } |\zeta_j^n| > \theta \text{ for at most one value of } j \\ \text{in } \{i, i+1, i+2, i+3, i+4\}. \end{array}$$

Therefore, it remains to prove that

$$\mathbb{P}\big(\Omega_T^n(\theta) \cap A(n,7)\big) \;\to\; 0. \tag{B.150}$$

Step 5. In this last step, we recall that the process c has no jump bigger than $a/4$ outside the set $\mathcal{S} = \{S_1, S_2, \ldots\}$. We introduce the "modulus of continuity" of the function $s \mapsto c_s$ on $[0,T]$ and outside the set $\mathcal{S}$, for the time lag $4k_n\Delta_n$:

$$\zeta_n = \sup\big(|c_{r+s} - c_r| : 0 \le r \le r+s \le T, \; s \le 4k_n\Delta_n, \; (r, r+s) \cap \mathcal{S} = \emptyset\big).$$

The key property used here is that, for all ω, $\limsup_n \zeta_n \le \frac{a}{4}$. Hence $\mathbb{P}(\zeta_n \le \frac{a}{4} + \theta) \to 0$ for any $\theta > 0$, and instead of (B.150) it is thus enough to prove that, for some $\theta > 0$, we have

$$\begin{aligned} \mathbb{P}(\Omega_T^{\prime n}(\theta) \cap A(n,7)) \;&\to\; 0, \\ \text{where } \Omega_T^{\prime n}(\theta) = \Omega_T^n(\theta) &\cap \{\zeta_n \le \tfrac{a}{4} + \theta\}. \end{aligned} \tag{B.151}$$

Now we choose $\theta \in \big(0, \frac{a}{36}\big)$. We also suppose that n is large enough to have $\rho_n < \theta$, and we write

$$\overline{L}_i^n \;=\; c_{(i+2)k_n\Delta_n} - c_{ik_n\Delta_n}.$$

By the definition of $A(n,7)$ we see that on the set $\Omega_T^n(\theta) \cap A(n,7)$ there exists a (random) $i \in \mathcal{I}_n$ such that $((i-2)k_n\Delta_n, (i+3)k_n\Delta_n) \cap \mathcal{S} = \emptyset$ and satisfying the following properties for at least one j in $\{-1, 1\}$:

$$\begin{aligned} |L_{i-1}^n| > a, \; |L_{i-1+j}^n| > \tfrac{a-\rho_n}{2} \;&\Rightarrow\; \min(|L_{i-1}^n|, |L_{i-1+j}^n|) > \tfrac{a}{3} \\ &\Rightarrow\; \max(|\overline{L}_{i-1}^n|, |\overline{L}_{i-1+j}^n|) > \tfrac{a}{3} - 2\theta \end{aligned}$$

(here we have used the fact that among all $|\zeta_j^n|$ for $j = i-2, i-1, i, i+1, i+2$, at most one is bigger than θ). But if further $\zeta_n \le \frac{a}{4} + \theta$, for all i as above we have $|\overline{L}_{i-1+j}^n| \le \frac{a}{4} + \theta$ for $j = -1, 0, 1$, whereas $\frac{a}{3} - 2\theta > \frac{a}{4} + \theta$ if $\theta < \frac{a}{36}$. It follows that indeed $\Omega_T^{\prime n}(\theta) \cap A(n,7) = \emptyset$, implying (B.151) and thus (B.149) for $k = 7$, and the proof is complete □

B.4   Limit Theorems for the Jumps of an Itô Semimartingale

In this section we prove a few results which are scattered in the literature, and are about some functionals of the jumps of the process X, supposed to be a one-dimensional Itô semimartingale X. No discretization is involved here, but the results will be used later in the framework of discretely observed processes.

Our functionals of interest are the following, for $u > 0$ and g a function on $\mathbb{R}$:

$$J(g; u)_t = \sum_{s \leq t} g(\Delta X_s / u). \tag{B.152}$$

Our aim is to describe their behavior as $u = u_n$ goes to 0, under suitable assumptions on g and X. We assume the condition (11.13) on g, which we recall here for the reader's convenience:

$$\begin{aligned}
&g \text{ is bounded, even, nonnegative, continuous,} \\
&\text{piecewise } C^1, \text{ with } g(0) = 0, \\
&|g'(x)| \leq K(|x|^{p-1} \wedge 1), \qquad \int |g'(y)|\, dy < \infty, \\
&\text{and } x, x + y \in [-1, 1] \\
&\Rightarrow \ |g'(x+y) - g'(x)| \leq K|x|^{(p-2)^+} |y|^{(p-1)\wedge 1},
\end{aligned} \tag{B.153}$$

which in particular implies $g(x) \leq K(|x|^p \wedge 1)$: here, $p \geq 1$ is a real, subject to various conditions later. The results of this section do not require the last property in (B.153), but for simplicity we stick to this condition, since it will be needed later. We associate with such a function g and with any $\beta \in [0, 2]$ and $z > 1$ the following quantities, as in (11.15):

$$\begin{aligned}
g_+(x) &= g(x) 1_{\{x>0\}}, \\
g_-(x) &= g(x) 1_{\{x<0\}} = g_+(-x) \\
v_g(\beta) &= \beta \int_0^\infty \frac{g(x)}{x^{1+\beta}}\, dx, \\
\overline{v}_g(\beta, z) &= \frac{\beta}{((\log z)\, v_g(\beta))^2} \int_0^\infty \frac{(g(x) - z^\beta\, g(x/z))^2}{x^{1+\beta}}\, dx.
\end{aligned} \tag{B.154}$$

Note that, in general, $p > \beta$ is required for $v_g(\beta) < \infty$ and for $\overline{v}_g(\beta, z)$ to be well defined.

As for the process X, we suppose that it is an Itô semimartingale, although here we only need conditions on the jumps, expressed in terms of the Lévy measures. Namely, if F_t denotes the spot Lévy measure of X, we introduce the following assumptions, where for $x > 0$ the tail functions are

$$\begin{aligned}
\overline{F}_t^+(x) &= F_t((x, \infty)), \\
\overline{F}_t^-(x) &= F_t((-\infty, -x)), \\
\overline{F}_t(x) &= \overline{F}_t^+(x) + \overline{F}_t^-(x).
\end{aligned}$$

Assumption (L''$_+$). *We have nonnegative predictable (or optional) processes $a_t^{(+)}$ and L_t and numbers $0 \leq \beta'_+ < \beta_+ \leq 2$ such that*

$$x \in (0, 1] \quad \Rightarrow \quad \left| x^{\beta_+} \overline{F}_t^{(+)}(x) - a_t^{(+)} \right| \leq L_t\, x^{\beta_+ - \beta'_+}.$$

Assumption (L''_). *We have nonnegative predictable (or optional) processes $a_t^{(-)}$ and L_t and numbers $0 \le \beta'_- < \beta_- \le 2$ such that*

$$x \in (0,1] \quad \Rightarrow \quad \left| x^{\beta_-} \, \overline{F}_t^{(-)}(x) - a_t^{(+)} \right| \le L_t \, x^{\beta_- - \beta'_-}.$$

Below, we treat positive and negative jumps separately, by using for example $J(g_+; u)_t$ with g_+ as given by (B.154) for positive jumps. As is natural for this kind of problem, the key role will be played by the compensators of the processes $J(g_+; u)$, which are

$$
\begin{aligned}
\widetilde{J}(g_+; u)_t &= \int_0^t F_s(g_+; u) \, ds, \\
\text{where } \; F_t(f; u) &= \int f(x/u) \, F_t(dx),
\end{aligned}
\tag{B.155}
$$

as soon as the process $F_s(g_+; u)$ is locally bounded, which is for example the case under (L''_+) if g satisfies (B.153) with $p > \beta_+$. As a rule, we put emphasis on positive jumps, negative jumps being treated in a completely symmetric way.

Our first result is a bound on the difference $J(g_+; u) - \widetilde{J}(g_+; u)$:

Lemma B.15. *If the process $\sup_{x \in (0,1]} x^{\beta_+} \, \overline{F}_t^+(x)$ is locally bounded for some $\beta_+ \in [0,2]$, and g satisfies (B.153) with some $p > \beta$, then for all t we have*

$$\sup_{s \le t} |J(g_+; u)_s - \widetilde{J}(g_+; u)_s| \;=\; O_P(u^{-\beta_+/2}), \qquad \text{as } u \to 0. \tag{B.156}$$

Proof. Our usual localization argument allows us to assume that $x^{\beta_+} \overline{F}_t^+(x) \le K$ for all $x \in (0,1]$. Fubini's theorem yields

$$
\begin{aligned}
F_t(g_+; u) &= \int_0^\infty F_t(dx) \int_0^{\frac{x \wedge 1}{u}} g'(y) dy \\
&\quad + \int_1^\infty \left(g(x/u) - g(1/u) \right) F_t(dx) \\
&= \int_0^{1/u} g'(y) \, \overline{F}_t^{(+)}(uy) \, dy \\
&\quad + \int_1^\infty \left(g(x/u) - g(1/u) \right) F_t(dx).
\end{aligned}
\tag{B.157}
$$

Then $g'(x) \le K(|x|^{p-1} \wedge 1$ and $g(x) \le K$ and $\int |g'(x)| dx < \infty$ yield, if $p > \beta_+$ and $u \in (0,1]$,

$$F_t(g_+; u) \;\le\; K u^{-\beta_+}. \tag{B.158}$$

The process $M(u) = J(g_+; u) - \widetilde{J}(g_+; u)$ is a locally square-integrable martingale with predictable quadratic variation $\langle M(u), M(u) \rangle = \widetilde{J}(g_+^2; u)$ (because $(\Delta J(g_+; u)_s)^2 = \Delta J(g_+^2; u)_s$). Hence (B.158) and the fact that the function g^2 also satisfy (B.153), with $2p$ instead of p, yield by Doob's inequality

$$\mathbb{E}\left(\sup_{s \le t} |M(u)_s|^2 \right) \;\le\; 4\mathbb{E}\left(\widetilde{J}(g_+^2; u)_t \right) \;\le\; K t u^{-\beta_+}. \tag{B.159}$$

This gives us (B.156).   □

Theorem B.16. *Assume (L''_+) and set $A_t^{(+)} = \int_0^t a_s^{(+)} ds$. Let g satisfy (B.153) with $p > \beta_+$. Then we have the following convergence in probability, locally uniform in time, as $u \to 0$:*

$$u^{\beta_+} J(g_+; u) \overset{u.c.p.}{\Longrightarrow} \overline{A}^{(+)}(g) := v_g(\beta_+) A^{(+)}. \tag{B.160}$$

The same result holds under (L''_-), upon replacing β_+, $A^{(+)}$ and $\overline{A}^{(+)}(g)$ by β_-, $A_t^{(-)} = \int_0^t a_s^{(-)} ds$ and $\overline{A}^{(-)}(g) = v_g(\beta_-) A^{(-)}$.

Proof. We prove only the first claim. By localization, we may assume that $|x^{\beta_+} \overline{F}_t^+(x) - a_t^{(+)}| \leq K x^{\beta_+ - \beta'_+}$ for some $\beta'_+ < \beta_+$ and some constant K. We have (B.157), and also by the same argument

$$v_g(\beta_+) = \int_0^{1/u} \frac{g'(y)}{y^{\beta_+}} dy + \int_{1/u}^\infty \big(g(x) - g(1/u)\big) \frac{\beta_+}{x^{1+\beta_+}} dx.$$

Then in view of (B.153) and (A.7) with L_t being a constant (due to our strengthened assumption),

$$\begin{aligned}
&\big|u^{\beta_+} F_t(g_+; u) - v_g(\beta_+) a_t^{(+)}\big| \\
&\leq \int_0^{1/u} |g'(y)| \big|u^{\beta_+} \overline{F}_t^{(+)}(uy) - \tfrac{a_t^{(+)}}{y^{\beta_+}}\big| dy \\
&\quad + K u^{\beta_+} \overline{F}_t(1) + K \int_{1/u}^\infty \frac{\beta_+}{x^{1+\beta_+}} dx \\
&\leq K u^{\beta_+ - \beta'_+} \int_0^\infty \frac{|g'(y)|}{y^{\beta'_+}} dy + K u_+^\beta \\
&\leq K u^{\beta_+ - \beta'_+},
\end{aligned} \tag{B.161}$$

where we also applied $p > \beta_+ > \beta'_+$ and $\int |g'(x)| dx < \infty$ and $|g'(x)| \leq K(|x|^{p-1} \wedge 1)$. Recalling (B.155), we deduce

$$\sup_{s \leq t} \big|u^{\beta_+} \widetilde{J}(g_+; u)_x - \overline{A}^{(+)}(g)_s\big| \leq K t u^{\beta_+ - \beta'_+}. \tag{B.162}$$

Combining this and (B.156) gives us the result.   □

We also have an associated Central Limit Theorem, in the form of a joint convergence for several processes of the type (B.152). Below, we consider a sequence $u_n \downarrow 0$ and a family $(g^j)_{1 \leq j \leq q}$ of functions satisfying (B.153). Assume (L''_+), and associate the q-dimensional process $Z^{n,+}$ with components

$$Z^{n,+i} = u_n^{-\beta_+/2} \big(u_n^{\beta_+} J(g_+^j; u_n) - \overline{A}^{(+)}(g^j)\big). \tag{B.163}$$

If further we have (L''_-), we also have another q-dimensional process $Z^{n,-}$ with components

$$Z^{n,-i} = u_n^{-\beta_-/2} \big(u_n^{\beta_-} J(g_-^j; u_n) - \overline{A}^{(-)}(g^j)\big). \tag{B.164}$$

Theorem B.17. *Assume (L''_+) with $\beta'_+ < \beta_+/2$, and suppose that all functions g_j satisfy (B.153) with $p > \beta_+$. Then the q-dimensional processes $Z^{n,+}$ converge stably in law to a limiting process $\mathcal{Z}^+$, defined on an extension $(\widetilde{\Omega}, \widetilde{\mathcal{F}}, (\widetilde{\mathcal{F}}_t)_{t\geq 0}, \widetilde{\mathbb{P}})$ of $(\Omega, \mathcal{F}, (\mathcal{F}_t)_{t\geq 0}, \mathbb{P})$, and which is continuous and, conditionally on $\mathcal{F}$, is a centered Gaussian martingale with variance-covariances given by*

$$\widetilde{\mathbb{E}}(\mathcal{Z}_t^{+i}\,\mathcal{Z}_t^{+j} \mid \mathcal{F}) \ = \ \overline{A}^{(+)}(g^i g^j)_t. \tag{B.165}$$

If further (L''_-) holds with $\beta'_- < \beta_-/2$ and $p > \beta_-$, then the 2q-dimensional processes $(Z^{n,+}, Z^{n,-})$ converge stably in law to a limiting process $(\mathcal{Z}^+, \mathcal{Z}^-)$ having the same description as above, with additionally

$$\widetilde{\mathbb{E}}(\mathcal{Z}_t^{-i}\,\mathcal{Z}_t^{-j} \mid \mathcal{F}) \ = \ \overline{A}^{(-)}(g^i g^j)_t, \qquad \widetilde{\mathbb{E}}(\mathcal{Z}_t^{+i}\,\mathcal{Z}_t^{-j} \mid \mathcal{F}) \ = \ 0. \tag{B.166}$$

Proof. We will prove the second claim only, and by localization we may assume $|x^{\beta_+}\overline{F}_t^+(x) - a_t^{(+)}| \leq Kx^{\beta_+ - \beta'_+}$ and $|x^{\beta_-}\overline{F}_t^-(x) - a_t^{(-)}| \leq Kx^{\beta_- - \beta'_-}$ for all $x \in (0, 1]$. We consider the 2q-dimensional processes M^n with components

$$M^{n,+i} = u_n^{-\beta_+/2}\big(u_n^{\beta_+} J(g_+^i; u_n) - \widetilde{J}(g_+^j; u_n)\big),$$
$$M^{n,-i} = u_n^{-\beta_-/2}\big(u_n^{\beta_-} J(g_-^i; u_n) - \widetilde{J}(g_-^i; u_n)\big).$$

Since $\beta'_\pm < \beta_\pm/2$, one deduces from (B.162) that $Z^{n,\pm i} - M^{n,\pm i} \overset{\text{u.c.p.}}{\Longrightarrow} 0$, so it is enough to prove the stable convergence in law of the processes M^n.

Each component $M^{n,\pm i}$ is a locally square-integrable martingale, and in fact a compensated sum of jumps with jumps smaller than $Ku_n^{\beta_\pm/2}$ by construction, and $u_n^{\beta_\pm/2} \to 0$. Therefore, by Theorem IX.7.3 of Jacod and Shiryaev (2003) applied with $Z = Z(n) = 0$ and with the truncation function $h(x) = x$, we see that it is enough to show the following properties, where ε and η are either $+$ or $-$ and $\delta^{\varepsilon,\eta}$ is 1 if $\varepsilon = \eta$ and 0 otherwise:

$$\langle M^{n,\varepsilon i}, M^{n,\eta j}\rangle_t \ \overset{\mathbb{P}}{\longrightarrow} \ \delta^{\varepsilon,\eta}\,\overline{A}^{(\varepsilon)}(g_\varepsilon^i g_\varepsilon^j)_t \tag{B.167}$$

$$\langle M^{n,\varepsilon i}, N\rangle_t \ \overset{\mathbb{P}}{\longrightarrow} \ 0, \tag{B.168}$$

for any $t > 0$ and any N is a class $\mathcal{N}$ of bounded martingales which is total in the $\mathbb{L}^2$ sense in the set of all bounded martingales.

Since $\Delta M_s^{n,\varepsilon i}\Delta M_s^{n,\eta j}$ vanishes when $\varepsilon \neq \eta$ and otherwise is equal to $u_n^{\beta_\varepsilon}\Delta J(g_\varepsilon^i g_\varepsilon^j; u_n)_s$, we have

$$\langle M^{n,\varepsilon i}, M^{n,\eta j}\rangle \ = \ \delta^{\varepsilon,\eta}\,u_n^{\beta_\varepsilon}\,\widetilde{J}(g_\varepsilon^i g_\varepsilon^j; u_n).$$

Then (B.167) follows from (B.162), because the product $g_\varepsilon^i g_\varepsilon^j$ satisfies (B.153) with some $p > \beta_\varepsilon$.

Next we turn to (B.168). The jump measure μ of X has the compensator $\nu(dt, dx) = dt \, F_t(dx)$, so $\nu(\{t\} \times \mathbb{R}) = 0$ for all t and a decomposition theorem for martingales (Theorem III.4.20 of Jacod and Shiryaev (2003)) tells us that we can take for $\mathcal{N}$ the union $\mathcal{N} = \mathcal{N}_1 \cup \mathcal{N}_2$, where $\mathcal{N}_1$ is the class of all bounded martingales which are orthogonal (in the martingale sense) to all stochastic integrals of the form $\psi * (\mu - \nu)$ and $\mathcal{N}_2$ is the class of all bounded martingales of the form $N = (\psi \, 1_{\{|x|>a\}}) * (\mu - \nu)$, with $a > 0$ arbitrary (and ψ bounded, since N is).

When $N \in \mathcal{N}_1$ we have $\langle M^{n,\varepsilon i}, N \rangle_t = 0$, hence (B.168) holds. When $N = (\psi \, 1_{\{|x|>a\}}) * (\mu - \nu)$ is in $\mathcal{N}_2$, and since $M^{n,\varepsilon i} = \phi_n * (\mu - \nu)$, where $\phi_n(\omega, t, x) = u_n^{\beta_\varepsilon/2} \, g_\varepsilon^i(x/u_n)$, We have

$$\langle M^{n,\varepsilon i}, N \rangle_t = u_n^{\beta_\varepsilon/2} \int_0^t ds \int_{\{|x|>a\}} \psi(s, x) \, g_\varepsilon^i(x/u_n) \, F_s(dx).$$

Since g_ε^i and ψ are bounded, the absolute value of the above variable is smaller than $K u_n^{\beta_\varepsilon/2} \nu([0, t] \times \{x : |x| > a\})$, and (B.168) follows again. □

B.5   A Comparison Between Jumps and Increments

The main object of this section is to compare the functionals

$$J(g; \Delta_n, u_n)_t = \sum_{i=1}^{[t/\Delta_n]} g(\Delta_i^n X/u_n) \qquad (B.169)$$

with the functionals $J(g; u_n)$ of the previous section, for suitable test functions g. We assume throughout that X is a one-dimensional Itô semimartingale of the (usual) form (A.2), satisfying (H-r) for some $r \in [0, 2]$, although the càdlàg property of σ is not needed (only the boundedness is).

However, we begin with the proof of Lemma 11.8.

Proof of Lemma 11.8. We first assume (H-r) for some $r \in [0, 2]$. By localization we can assume (SH-r), so that $|\delta(\omega, t, z)|^r \leq J(z)$ for some bounded and λ-integrable function $J \geq 0$. Using (1.75) and Markov's inequality, for $x \in (0, 1]$ we come up with

$$\overline{F}_t(x) = \lambda(\{z : |\delta(t, z)| > x\})$$
$$\leq \lambda(\{z : J(z) > x^r\}) \leq \tfrac{1}{x^r} \int J(z) \, \lambda(dz)$$

for any $x \in (0, 1]$. Then (L') for $\beta = r$, hence for all $\beta \in [r, 2]$, follows.

Conversely, we assume (L') for some $\beta \in [0, 2]$, and again by localization we may assume that

$$x \in (0, 1] \quad \Rightarrow \quad x^\beta \overline{F}_t(x) \leq L \tag{B.170}$$

for a constant L. As mentioned in Chapter 1, there are many Grigelionis representations for X, and to begin with there is a large choice for the driving Poisson measure $\underline{p}$. However, in the one-dimensional case, it is always possible to choose the following one: we take $E = \mathbb{R}$ and

$$\delta(\omega, t, z) = \begin{cases} \inf(x : \overline{F}^{(+)}_{\omega,t}(x) > z) & \text{if } z > 0 \\ 0 & \text{if } z = 0 \\ -\inf(x : \overline{F}^{(-)}_{\omega,t}(x) > -z) & \text{if } z < 0, \end{cases}$$

with the convention $\inf(\emptyset) = 0$. It follows that the measure $F_{\omega,t}$ is the restriction to $\mathbb{R}\backslash\{0\}$ of the image of the Lebesgue measure $\lambda(dz) = dz$ by the mapping $z \mapsto \delta(\omega, t, z)$. Therefore, by Theorem (14.56) of Jacod (1979), X admits the representation (A.2) with this δ and $\underline{p}$ a Poisson random measure on $\mathbb{R}_+ \times \mathbb{R}$ with intensity measure $\underline{q}(dt, dx) = dt \otimes dx$.

Now, (B.170) and the definition of δ yield that $|\delta(\omega, t, z)|^r \wedge 1 \leq J(z)$, where $J(z) = \frac{L^{r/\beta}}{|z|^{r/\beta}} \wedge 1$. Then (H-$r$) holds for all $r > \beta$ because in this case $\int J(z) \, dz < \infty$. Finally, when $\beta = 0$, (B.170) again implies $|\delta(\omega, t, z)|^0 \wedge 1 = 1_{\{\delta(\omega,t,z)\neq 0\}} \leq 1_{[-L,L]}(z)$, which in turn implies implies (H-0). $\qquad\square$

Next, we look for the numbers η for which the difference $J(g; \Delta_n, u_n) - J(g; u_n)$ multiplied by Δ_n^η goes to 0. In view of the convergence results in Theorems B.16 and B.17, and when $u_n \asymp \Delta_n^\varpi$ for some $\varpi > 0$ and (L$_+$) for example holds, this has interest only if we find that $\eta < \beta_+\varpi$ and $\eta < \beta_+\varpi/2$, respectively. In view of Lemma 11.8, we are thus led to compare the possible exponents η with $r\varpi$ or $r\varpi/2$, when (H-r) holds.

Proposition B.18. *Assume (H-r) for some $r \in [0, 2]$, and let $p > r \vee 1$ and g be a function satisfying (B.153). Let $u_n \asymp \Delta_n^\varpi$ for some $\varpi \in \left(0, \frac{1}{r}\right]$. Then*

$$\Delta_n^\eta \left(J(g_\pm; \Delta_n, u_n) - J(g_\pm; u_n) \right) \overset{u.c.p.}{\Longrightarrow} 0, \tag{B.171}$$

under any one of the following conditions:

(a) $X^c \equiv 0$ and either $r \leq 1$ and $B - (\delta 1_{\{|\delta| \leq 1\}}) * \underline{q} \equiv 0$ (that is, $X_t = X_0 + \sum_{s \leq t} \Delta X_s$, recall that B is the first characteristic of X) or

$r > 1$, and in all cases (with the convention $\frac{(p-1)\wedge r}{r} = 1$ when $r = 0$) $\eta > \eta_a = \eta_a(p, r, \varpi)$ where

$$\eta_a(p, r, \varpi) := \tag{B.172}$$
$$\begin{cases} \varpi + (r\varpi - 1)\frac{(p-1)\wedge r}{r} & \text{if } r \leq 1 \\ \left(r\varpi + (r\varpi - 1)\frac{(p-r)\wedge 1}{r}\right) \vee \left(\frac{r\varpi}{2} + (r\varpi - 1)\frac{(2p-2)\wedge r}{2r}\right) & \text{if } r > 1. \end{cases}$$

(b) $r \leq 1$ and $X^c \equiv 0$ and $\eta > \eta_b = \eta_b(p, r, \varpi)$ where

$$\eta_b(p, r, \varpi) := (\varpi + r\varpi - 1) \bigvee (p\varpi + 1 - p). \tag{B.173}$$

(c) $\varpi < \frac{1}{2}$ and $\eta > \eta_c = \eta_c(p, r, \varpi)$ where

$$\eta_c(p, r, \varpi) := \left(\varpi + r\varpi - \frac{1}{2}\right) \bigvee \left(p\varpi + 1 - \frac{p}{2}\right). \tag{B.174}$$

Note that $\eta_c \geq \eta_b$ when $r \leq 1$, and $\eta_c \geq \eta_a$ always, as it should be (these inequalities are obvious when $r \leq 1$, and the latter is tedious but straightforward to check when $r > 1$). All three bounds η_a, η_b, η_c are increasing, as functions of r: when we have (H-r') for some $r' > r$ but not (H-r), the process X is "closer" in a sense to the Brownian part, so it is "more difficult" for $J(g_\pm; \Delta_n, u_n)$ to be close to $J(g_\pm; u_n)$, and in order to have (B.171) the exponent η should be bigger.

Proof. The proof of this result is given only for g_+, the case of g_- being similar. It is divided into a number of technical steps, which are conducted under the strengthened assumption (SH-r): by localization, this is not a restriction.

Step 1. By (SH-r) we have $|\delta(t, z)|^r \leq J(z)$, where J is bounded and λ-integrable. As soon as n is large enough to have $u_n < 1$ we have the following decompositions of X:

$$X = X_0 + Z + X^n + Y^n, \quad \text{where } X^n = (\delta 1_{\{J > u_n^r/2\}}) * \underline{p}$$

and

$$r > 1 \Rightarrow \begin{cases} Z = X^c \\ Y^n = B - (\delta 1_{\{J > u_n^r/2, |\delta| \leq 1\}}) * \underline{q} + (\delta 1_{\{J \leq u_n^r/2\}}) * (\underline{p} - \underline{q}) \end{cases}$$
$$r \leq 1 \Rightarrow \begin{cases} Z = X^c + B - (\delta 1_{\{|\delta| \leq 1\}}) * \underline{q} \\ Y^n = (\delta 1_{\{J \leq u_n^r/2\}}) * \underline{p}. \end{cases}$$

We write $g_n(x) = g_+(x/u_n)$, so $J(g_+; \Delta_n, u_n) = J(g_n; \Delta_n, 1)$ and $J(g_+; u_n) = J(g_n; 1)$. We introduce the intervals $I(n, i) = ((i -$

$1)\Delta_n, i\Delta_n]$, and $\tau(n,i)$ denotes the number of jumps of the Poisson process $1_{\{J>u_n^r/2\}} * \underline{p}$ in the time interval $I(n,i)$. Note that

$$\tau(n,i) \text{ is independent of } \mathcal{F}_{(i-1)\Delta_n}, \text{ and Poisson} \atop \text{with parameter smaller than } K\Delta_n^{1-r\varpi}. \tag{B.175}$$

Step 2. We derive some consequences of (SH-r). Since $0 \le g(x) \le K(|x| \wedge 1)^p$, we have for $w \in (0, \infty]$

$$
\begin{aligned}
pq \ge r \;\Rightarrow\; & \int g_n(\delta(t,z))^q \, \lambda(dz) \\
& \le K \int \left(\frac{J(z)^{pq/r}}{u_n^{pq}} \wedge 1 \right) \lambda(dz) \\
& \le K \int \frac{J(z)^r}{u_n^r} \, \lambda(dx) \le \frac{K}{u_n^r} \\
q \ge 0 \;\Rightarrow\; & \int |\delta(t,z)|^q \, 1_{\{J(z)>u_n^r/2\}} \, \lambda(dz) \le \frac{K_q}{u_n^{(r-q)^+}}, \\
q \ge r \;\Rightarrow\; & \int |\delta(t,z)|^q \, 1_{\{J(z)\le u_n^r/2\}} \, \lambda(dz) \le K_q u_n^{q-r}.
\end{aligned}
\tag{B.176}
$$

Let $(\mathcal{G}_t^n)$ be the smallest filtration containing ($\mathcal{F}_t$) and such that the variables $\tau(n,i)$ for $i \ge 1$ are all $\mathcal{G}_0^n$-measurable.

We first deduce from (B.176) that both functions $g_n(\delta)$ and $g_n(\delta) 1_{\{J>u_n^r/2\}}$ on $\Omega \times \mathbb{R}_+ \times E$ satisfy (A.69) with $\alpha(q) = K_q/u_n^r$ when $q \ge 1$ (recall $p > r$), hence by from (A.72) and its improvement (A.77) we get, for $q \ge 1$,

$$
\begin{aligned}
& T \text{ a finite } (\mathcal{F}_t)\text{-stopping time} \\
& \Rightarrow \mathbb{E}\left(\left(\sum_{s\in(T,T+\Delta_n]} g_n(\Delta X_s) \right)^q \;\Big|\; \mathcal{F}_T \right) \le K_q \Delta_n^{1-r\varpi} \\
& T \text{ a finite } (\mathcal{G}_t^n)\text{-stopping time} \\
& \Rightarrow \mathbb{E}\left(\left(\sum_{s\in(T,T+\Delta_n]} g_n(\Delta Y_s^n) \right)^q \;\Big|\; \mathcal{G}_T^n \right) \le K_q \Delta_n^{1-r\varpi}.
\end{aligned}
\tag{B.177}
$$

Analogously, the function $\delta 1_{\{J>u_n^r/2\}}$ satisfies (A.69) with $\alpha(q) = \alpha'(q) = \alpha''(q) = K_q$ when $q \ge r$, and with $\alpha(1) = K u_n^{1-r}$ when $r > 1$. We also have $X^n = (\delta 1_{\{J(x)>u_n^r/2\}}) * (\underline{p} - \underline{q}) + U^n$ with $U^n = (\delta 1_{\{J(x)>u_n^r/2\}}) * \underline{q}$ and $\sup_{s\le\Delta_n} |U_{t+s}^n - U_t^n| \le K\Delta_n u_n^{1-r}$ when $r > 1$ (use again (B.176)). Hence (A.72) for the first estimate below, and (A.71) when $r > 1$ and (A.73) when $r \le 1$ for the second one yield for $q \ge r$, and since $r\varpi < 1$,

$$
\begin{aligned}
& \mathbb{E}\left(\sup_{s\le\Delta_n} |X_{T+s}^n - X_T^n|^q \;\Big|\; \mathcal{F}_T \right) \le K_q \Delta_n \\
& \mathbb{E}\left(\sup_{s\le\Delta_n} \left(\frac{|X_{T+s}^n - X_T^n|}{u_n} \wedge 1 \right)^q \;\Big|\; \mathcal{F}_T \right) \le K_q \Delta_n^{1-r\varpi}.
\end{aligned}
\tag{B.178}
$$

In the same way, the function $\delta 1_{\{J\le u_n/2\}}$ satisfies (A.69) with $\alpha(q) = \alpha'(q) = \alpha''(q) = K_q u_n^{q-r}$ when $q \ge r$. Upon using the improvement

(A.77), we then obtain after some calculation using again (B.176) and the boundedness of the first spot characteristic b_t that, for any finite $(\mathcal{G}_t^n)$-stopping time T and any bounded predictable process H and for $q \geq r$,

$$
\mathbb{E}\left(\sup_{s \leq \Delta_n} | \int_T^{T+s} H_u \, dY_u^n |^q \mid \mathcal{G}_T^n \right)
$$
$$
\leq K_q \Delta_n^{(q-r)\varpi} \, \mathbb{E}\left(\int_T^{T+\Delta_n} |H_u|^q \, du \mid \mathcal{G}_T^n \right) \tag{B.179}
$$
$$
\mathbb{E}\left(\sup_{s \leq \Delta_n} \left(\frac{|Y_{T+s}^n - Y_T^n|}{u_n} \wedge 1 \right)^q \mid \mathcal{G}_T^n \right) \leq K_q \Delta_n^{1-r\varpi}.
$$

Step 3. Coming back to the processes of interest, we have the decomposition

$$
J(g_+; \Delta_n, u_n) - J(g_+; u_n) = \sum_{j=1}^5 V^n(j)
$$

where $V^n(j)_t = \sum_{i=1}^{[t/\Delta_n]} \zeta_i^n(j)$ and

$$
\zeta_i^n(1) = g_n(\Delta_i^n X) - g_n(\Delta_i^n X^n + \Delta_i^n Y^n)
$$
$$
\zeta_i^n(2) = \left(g_n(\Delta_i^n Y^n) - \sum_{s \in I(n,i)} g_n(\Delta Y_s^n) \right) 1_{\{\tau(n,i)=0\}}
$$
$$
\zeta_i^n(3) = \left(g_n(\Delta_i^n X^n + \Delta_i^n Y^n) - \sum_{s \in I(n,i)} g_n(\Delta X_s) \right) 1_{\{\tau(n,i) \geq 2\}}
$$
$$
\zeta_i^n(4) = \left(g_n(\Delta_i^n X^n + \Delta_i^n Y^n) - g_n(\Delta_i^n X^n) \right) 1_{\{\tau(n,i)=1\}}
$$
$$
\zeta_i^n(5) = - \sum_{s \in I(n,i)} g_n(\Delta Y_s^n) 1_{\{\tau(n,i)=1\}}
$$

(use $\Delta X_s = \Delta X_s^n + \Delta Y_s^n$, plus the fact that Y^n and X^n do not jump together, and the fact that if $\tau(n,i) = 1$ the increment $\Delta_i^n X^n$ is equal to the unique jump of X^n on the interval $I(n,i)$, whereas $\Delta_i^n X^n = 0$ when $\tau(n,i) = 0$). Then, the proof consists in showing that

$$
\forall \varepsilon > 0, \ t > 0 : \quad \mathbb{E}\left(\sup_{s \leq t} |V^n(j)_s| \right) \leq K_{t,\varepsilon} \Delta_n^{\theta_j - \varepsilon} \tag{B.180}
$$

for $j = 1, 2, 3, 4, 5$, for some θ_j, with the following properties: $\theta_j \geq -\eta_a$ for $j = 2, 3, 4, 5$, and $\theta_1 \geq -\eta_b$ in Case (b), and $\theta_1 \geq -\eta_c$ in case (c) (note that in Case (a) we have $Z = 0$, hence $V^n(1) \equiv 0$).

Step 4. Here we prove (B.180) for $j = 3$. Since $0 \leq g_n \leq K$, we deduce from (B.175) that

$$
\mathbb{E}\left(g_n(\Delta_i^n X^n + \Delta_i^n Y^n) 1_{\{\tau(n,i) \geq 2\}} \right)
$$
$$
\leq K \mathbb{P}(\tau(n,i) \geq 2) \leq K \Delta_n^{2-2r\varpi}. \tag{B.181}
$$

Since $r < p$, Hölder's inequality and the last inequality above and (B.177) give for conjugate exponents u, w

$$
\mathbb{E}\left(1_{\{\tau(n,i) \geq 2\}} \sum_{s \in I(n,i)} g_n(\Delta X_s) \right) \leq K_v \Delta_n^{(1-r\varpi)/u + 2(1-r\varpi)/w}.
$$

Taking w close to 1, and using again (B.181), we deduce that $\mathbb{E}(|\zeta_i^n(3)|) \leq K_\varepsilon \Delta_n^{2(1-r\varpi)-\varepsilon}$ for any $\varepsilon > 0$, hence (B.180) holds with $\theta_3 = 1 - 2r\varpi$, which clearly satisfies $\theta_3 \geq -\eta_a$.

Step 5. Here we prove (B.180) for $j = 5$. We use the second part of (B.177) and (B.175) and successive conditioning to obtain $\mathbb{E}(|\zeta_i^n(5)|) \leq K\Delta_n^{2(1-r\varpi)}$. So (B.180) holds with $\theta_5 = \theta_3$.

Step 6. Next we prove (B.180) for $j = 4$. Equation (B.153) yields $|g(x + y) - g(x)| \leq K(|y| \wedge 1)$, hence

$$|\zeta_i^n(4)| \leq K\Big(\frac{|\Delta_i^n Y^n|}{u_n} \bigwedge 1\Big) 1_{\{\tau(n,i)=1\}}.$$

By (B.179), plus Hölder's inequality when $r > 1$, and (B.175) and successive conditioning, we obtain $\mathbb{E}(|\zeta_i^n(4)|) \leq K\Delta_n^{(1-r\varpi)(1+1/(r\vee 1))}$. Thus (B.180) holds with $\theta_4 = (1 - r\varpi)\frac{1}{r\vee 1} - r\varpi$, which is easily checked to satisfy $\theta_4 \geq -\eta_a$.

Step 7. The proof of (B.180) for $j = 2$ is the most delicate part, accomplished through several steps.

Sub-step (i). We need additional notation. For $t \geq (i - 1)\Delta_n$ we set

$$Y_t^{n,i} = Y_t^n - Y_{(i-1)\Delta_n}^n,$$
$$U_t^{n,i} = g_n(Y_t^{n,i}) - \sum_{s\in((i-1)\Delta_n,t]} g_n(\Delta Y_s^{n,i}).$$

If $S(n,i) = (i\Delta_n) \wedge \inf(t > 0 : |Y^{n,i}| > u_n/2)$, we then have

$$\zeta_i^n(2) = (v_i^n + w_i^n)1_{\{\tau(n,i)=0\}},$$

with $v_i^n = U_{S(n,i)}^{n,i}$ and $w_i^n = U_{i\Delta_n}^{n,i} - U_{S(n,i)}^{n,i}$.

We can further decompose v_i^n as follows. We set $B^n = B - (\delta 1_{\{J>u_n^r/2, |\delta|\leq 1\}}) * \underline{q}$ and $M^n = (\delta 1_{\{J\leq u_n^r/2\}}) * (\underline{p} - \underline{q})$ when $r > 1$ (so $Y^n = B^n + M^n$), and $B^n = 0$ when $r \leq 1$, and also

$$k_n(x,y) = \begin{cases} g_n(x + y) - g_n(x) - g_n(y) & \text{if } r \leq 1 \\ g_n(x + y) - g_n(x) - g_n(y) - g_n'(x)y & \text{if } r > 1. \end{cases}$$
$$\chi_i^n = \begin{cases} 0 & \text{if } r \leq 1 \\ \int_{(i-1)\Delta_n}^{S(n,i)} g_n'(Y_s^{n,i})dM_s^n & \text{if } r > 1. \end{cases}$$

Since $p > 1 \vee r$, (B.154) implies that the restriction of g to $[-1, 1]$, hence of g_n to $[-u_n, u_n]$ as well, is C^r: this means C^1 in the usual sense when $r = 1$, and Hölder with index r when $r \in [0, 1)$, and C^1 with its derivative Hölder with index $r - 1$ when $r \in (1, 2]$. On the other hand, $|\Delta Y^n| \leq u_n/2$, so the semimartingale $Y_{t\wedge S(n,i)}^{n,i}$, which is without a continuous martingale part, takes its values in $[-u_n, u_n]$, and $Y_{s-}^{n,i} \in [-u_n/2, u_n/2]$ if $s \le S(n,i)$. In other words, the function g_n and the process $Y^{n,i}$ satisfy the properties required to apply the extension of Itô's formula given in Theorem 3.3.2 of [JP], and this formula gives us the decomposition

$$v_i^n = \xi_i^n + \chi_i^n$$

where

$$\xi_i^n = \int_{(i-1)\Delta_n}^{S(n,i)} g_n'(Y_s^{n,i}) dB_s^n + \sum_{s \in ((i-1)\Delta_n, S(n,i)]} k_n(Y_{s-}^{n,i}, \Delta Y_s^n).$$

We thus end up with $\zeta_i^n(2) = (\xi_i^n + \chi_i^n + w_i^n) 1_{\{\tau(n,i)=0\}}$.

Suppose for a while that, for some $\theta \in \mathbb{R}$,

$$\begin{aligned}
\mathbb{E}(|w_i^n|) &\le K\Delta_n^{\theta+1}, \\
\mathbb{E}(|\xi_i^n|) &\le K\Delta_n^{\theta+1}, \\
\mathbb{E}(|\chi_i^n|^2) &\le K\Delta_n^{2\theta+1}.
\end{aligned} \tag{B.182}$$

This implies $\mathbb{E}\left(\sum_{i=1}^{[t/\Delta_n]}(|w_i^n| + |\xi_i^n|)\right) \le Kt\Delta_n^\theta$. Moreover, $\chi_i^n = 0$ when $r \le 1$, and otherwise M^n is a martingale, hence $\mathbb{E}(\chi_i^n \mid \mathcal{F}_{i-1}) = 0$. Then when $r > 1$ Doob's inequality yields

$$\mathbb{E}\left(\sup_{s \le t} \left|\sum_{i=1}^{[t/\Delta_n]} \chi_i^n\right|^2\right) \le 4 \sum_{i=1}^{[t/\Delta_n]} \mathbb{E}(|\chi_i^n|^2) \le Kt\Delta_n^{2\theta}.$$

Thus (B.180) holds with $K_t = K(t + \sqrt{t})$ and $\theta_2 = \theta$. Hence it remains to prove (B.182) with $\theta \ge -\eta_a$.

Sub-step (ii). For the first claim of (B.182) we use $g_n(x) \le K(1 \wedge (|x|/u_n)^p)$ and combine (B.177) and (B.179) with $T = S(n,i)$, to get $\mathbb{E}(|w_i^n| \mid \mathcal{G}_{S(n,i)}^n) \le K\Delta_n^{1-r\varpi} 1_{\{S(n,i)<i\Delta_n\}}$, whereas $\mathbb{P}(S(n,i) < i\Delta_n) \le K\Delta_n^{1-r\varpi}$ by (B.179) again. Hence $\mathbb{E}(|w_i^n|) \le K\Delta_n^{2-2r\varpi}$, and the first part of (B.182) holds for $\theta = 1 - 2r\varpi \ge -\eta_a$.

Substep (iii). Next, we turn to the second claim of (B.182). By singling out the two cases $|x| \ge |y|$ and $|x| < |y|$, we deduce from (B.153) that in both cases $r \le 1$ and $r > 1$ we have

$$x, y \in [-u_n/2, u_n/2] \implies |k_n(x,y)| \le K \left|\frac{y}{u_n}\right|^r \left(\frac{|x|}{u_n} \wedge 1\right)^{(p-r)\wedge 1}.$$

Therefore

$$\begin{aligned}
&\sum_{s \in ((i-1)\Delta_n, S(n,i)]} |k_n(Y_{s-}^{n,i}, \Delta Y_s^n)| \\
&\le \frac{K}{u_n^r} \int_{I(n,i) \times \{z:J(z) \le u_n^r/2\}} \left(\frac{|Y_{s-}^{n,i}|}{u_n} \wedge 1\right)^{(p-r)\wedge 1} J(z)\, \underline{p}(ds, dz).
\end{aligned}$$

The expectation of the above equals the expectation of the same integral, but with respect to the compensator q. Combining this with the fact that $B^n_t = \int_0^t b^n_s \, ds$ with a process b^n satisfying $|b^n_t| \le K/u_n^{(r-1)^+}$ by (B.176), whereas $|g'_n(x)| \le \frac{K}{u_n}\big(\frac{|x|}{u_n} \wedge 1\big)^{p-1}$, we readily obtain

$$\mathbb{E}(|\xi^n_i|) \le K \int_{I(n,i)} \mathbb{E}\Big(\frac{1}{u^r_n}\Big(\frac{|Y^{n,i}_s|}{u_n} \wedge 1\Big)^{(p-r)\wedge 1}$$
$$+\frac{1}{u^{r\vee 1}_n}\Big(\frac{|Y^{n,i}_s|}{u_n} \wedge 1\Big)^{p-1} ds\Big) ds.$$

Then (B.179) and Hölder's inequality yield

$$\mathbb{E}(|\xi^n_i|) \le \begin{cases} K\Delta_n^{1-\varpi+(1-r\varpi)\frac{(p-1)\wedge r}{r}} & \text{if } r \le 1 \\ K\Delta_n^{(1-r\varpi)(1+\frac{(p-r)\wedge 1}{r})} & \text{if } r > 1. \end{cases}$$

Hence the second part of (B.182) holds for $\theta = -\eta_a$.

Sub-step (iv). Since $\chi^n_i = 0$ when $r \le 1$ it remains to prove the third part of (B.182) when $r > 1$. By (A.70) and (B.176) we have

$$\mathbb{E}(|\chi^n_i|^2) \le Ku_n^{2-r} \mathbb{E}\Big(\int_{I(n,i)} g'_n(Y^{n,i}_s)^2 \, ds\Big)$$
$$\le Ku_n^{-r} \mathbb{E}\Big(\int_{I(n,i)} \Big(\frac{|Y^{n,i}_s|}{u_n} \wedge 1\Big)^{2p-2} ds\Big).$$

We apply (B.179) again to obtain $\mathbb{E}(|\chi^n_i|^2) \le K\Delta_n^{(1-r\varpi)\left(1+\frac{(2p-2)\wedge r}{r}\right)}$, hence the third part of (B.182) for $\theta = \frac{1}{2}\big((1-r\varpi)\frac{(2p-2)\wedge r}{r} - r\varpi\big)$, which is not smaller than $-\eta_a$ (recall $p > r \vee 1$).

Putting all these partial results together, we deduce that (B.180) holds for $j = 2$, with $\theta_2 \ge -\eta_a$.

Step 8. Now we prove (B.180) for $j = 1$. In case (b) we have $r \le 1$ and $Z_t = \int_0^t z_s \, ds$ for some bounded process z_s. Since

$$|g_n(x+y) - g_n(x)| \le K\Big(\big(\frac{|y|}{u_n} \wedge 1\big)^p + \frac{|y|}{u_n}\big(\frac{|x|}{u_n} \wedge 1\big)^{p-1}\Big). \tag{B.183}$$

it follows from (B.178) and (B.179) plus Hölder's inequality when $p-1 < r$ that (B.180) for $j = 1$ holds with $\theta_1 = (p-1-p\varpi) \wedge \big((1-r\varpi)\frac{(p-1)\wedge r}{r} - \varpi\big)$, which is not smaller than $-\eta_b$.

Finally consider case (c) with $\varpi < \frac{1}{2}$. We have $Z_t = X^c_t + \int_0^t z_s \, ds$ for some bounded process z_s. Then exactly as previously, and upon using Hölder's inequality and the property $\mathbb{E}(|\Delta^n_i Z|^q) \le K_q \Delta_n^{q/2}$ for any $q > 0$, we obtain

$$\mathbb{E}(|\zeta^n_i(1)|) \le K_\varepsilon\big(\Delta_n^{p(1-2\varpi)/2} + \Delta_n^{(1-2\varpi)/2+(1-r\varpi)\frac{(p-1)\wedge r}{r}}\big)$$

Therefore (B.182) holds for $j = 1$ when $\theta_1 = \left(\frac{p}{2} - 1 - p\varpi\right) \wedge \left((1 - r\varpi)\frac{(p-1)\wedge r}{r} - \varpi - \frac{1}{2}\right)$, which is not smaller than $-\eta_c$. This completes the proof. $\qquad\square$

Next, we derive a useful corollary:

Corollary B.19. *Let g satisfy (B.153) for some $p > 2$ and $u_n \asymp \Delta_n^\varpi$ for some $\varpi \in \left(0, \frac{p-2}{2p}\right)$ (hence $\varpi < \frac{1}{2}$).*
(a) There exists a number $\chi \in \left(\frac{1}{2}, 1\right)$ depending on ϖ and p, such that we have, as soon as (H-r) holds for some $r \in [0, 2]$:

$$
\begin{aligned}
u_n^{r\chi}\left(J(g_\pm; \Delta_n, u_n) - J(g_\pm; u_n)\right) &\overset{u.c.p.}{\Longrightarrow} 0 \\
u_n^{r\chi}\left(J(g_\pm; \Delta_n, u_n) - \tilde{J}(g_\pm; u_n)\right) &\overset{u.c.p.}{\Longrightarrow} 0.
\end{aligned}
\tag{B.184}
$$

(b) There exists a number $\chi' > 0$ depending on ϖ and p, such that if (H-r) holds for all $r \in (0, 2]$, we have

$$
\frac{1}{\Delta_n^{\chi'}}\left(J(g_\pm; \Delta_n, u_n) - J(g_\pm; u_n)\right) \overset{u.c.p.}{\Longrightarrow} 0.
\tag{B.185}
$$

Proof. For the first part of (B.184), and in view of (B.171), it is enough to show the existence of $\chi \in \left(\frac{1}{2}, 1\right)$ such that $r\chi\varpi > \eta_c(p, r, \varpi)$ for all $r \in [0, 2]$ (with p, ϖ being fixed). Since $p > 2$ and $\varpi < \frac{p-2}{2p}$, any χ in $\left(\frac{1}{2}, 1\right)$ and bigger than $\frac{6\varpi-1}{4\varpi}$, which is smaller than 1, solves our problem.

The second part of (B.184) readily follows from the first part, plus (B.156), which one can apply with $\beta_\pm = r$, plus the fact that $\chi > \frac{1}{2}$, implying $r\chi > \frac{\beta_\pm}{2}$.

For (b), we apply (B.171), and notice that under our conditions on p and ϖ we have $\eta_c(p, r, \varpi) < 0$ when r is close enough to 0. $\qquad\square$

We are now ready for the Law of Large Numbers and the Central Limit Theorem for $J(g; \Delta_n, u_n)$. Recall that Assumptions (L$_+$) and (L$_-$) are defined in Subsection 11.2.4.

Theorem B.20. *Let $u_n \asymp \Delta_n^\varpi$ for some $\varpi > 0$.*
(a) Assume (L$_+$) and let g be a function satisfying (11.13), with the exponent p. Then we have the following convergence in probability, locally uniform in time:

$$
u_n^{\beta_+} J(g_+; \Delta_n, u_n) \overset{u.c.p.}{\Longrightarrow} v_g(\beta_+) A^{(+)},
\tag{B.186}
$$

provided one of the following two conditions holds (with the convention

$\frac{1}{0} = \infty$):

    (i) $p > 2$ and $\varpi < \frac{1}{2(1+\beta-\beta_+)} \wedge \frac{p-2}{2(p-\beta_+)}$

    (ii) $\sigma \equiv 0$ and

$$
\begin{cases}
\beta < 1 \Rightarrow \begin{cases} p > 1 \\ \varpi < \frac{1}{1+\beta-\beta_+} \wedge \frac{p-1}{p-\beta_+} \end{cases} \\[2ex]
\beta \geq 1 \Rightarrow \begin{cases} p > \beta \\ \varpi < \frac{1}{\beta(\beta+1-\beta_+)} \wedge \frac{p-\beta}{\beta(p-\beta_+)} \\ \quad \wedge \frac{1}{2(\beta-\beta_+)} \wedge \frac{2p-2}{\beta(\beta+2p-2-2\beta_+)^+}. \end{cases}
\end{cases}
\tag{B.187}
$$

The same holds under (L_-), provided we replace $g_+, \beta_+, A^{(+)}$ by $g_-, \beta_-, A^{(-)}$.

    (b) Assume (L_+) with $\beta'_+ < \beta_+/2$ and let $g^1, \ldots, g^q$ be functions satisfying (B.153) with the same p. The q-dimensional processes with components $u_n^{-\beta_+/2}\left(u_n^{\beta_+} J(g_+^j; \Delta_n, u_n) - v_{g^j}(\beta_+)A^{(+)}\right)$ converge stably in law to the same limiting process $\mathcal{Z}^+$ as in Theorem B.17, under each one of the following two conditions:

    (i) $p > 2$ and $\varpi < \frac{1}{2+2\beta-\beta_+} \wedge \frac{p-2}{2p-\beta_+}$

    (ii) $\sigma \equiv 0$ and

$$
\begin{cases}
\beta < 1 \Rightarrow \begin{cases} p > 1 \\ \varpi < \frac{2}{2+2\beta-\beta_+} \wedge \frac{2p-2}{2p-\beta_+} \end{cases} \\[2ex]
\beta \geq 1 \Rightarrow \begin{cases} p > \beta \\ \varpi < \frac{1}{\beta(\beta+1-\beta_+/2)} \wedge \frac{p-\beta}{\beta(p-\beta_+/2)} \\ \quad \wedge \frac{1}{2\beta-\beta_+} \wedge \frac{2p-2}{\beta(\beta+2p-2-\beta_+)}. \end{cases}
\end{cases}
\tag{B.188}
$$

The same holds under (L_-), provided we replace $g_+^j, \beta_+, A^{(+)}$ by $g_-^j, \beta_-, A^{(-)}$.

    (c) If (L_+) and (L_-) hold (so we can take $\beta = \beta_+ \vee \beta_-$ in both assumptions), with $\beta'_+ < \beta_+/2$ and $\beta'_- < \beta_-/2$, and if (B.188) holds with β_+ and also with β_- instead of β_+, we have the stable convergence in law of the $2q$-dimensional processes with components $u_n^{-\beta_+/2}\left(u_n^{\beta_+} J(g_+^j; \Delta_n, u_n) - v_{g^j}(\beta_+)A^{(+)}\right)$ and $u_n^{-\beta_-/2}\left(u_n^{\beta_-} J(g_-^j; \Delta_n, u_n) - v_{g^j}(\beta_-)A^{(-)}\right)$ to $(\mathcal{Z}^+, \mathcal{Z}^-)$, as defined in Theorem B.17 again.

    Notice that the conditions (B.187) and (B.188) involve β, as well as β_+ when we only have (L_+); since $\beta \geq \beta_+$, these conditions are more stringent than if they featured β_+ everywhere instead of β. The reason is that, even though in (a) above, for example, we are not interested in negative jumps, those enter the increments $\Delta_i^n X$, hence also their positive parts $(\Delta_i^n X)^+$. Therefore we need a kind of control on negative jumps, which necessitates (B.187) with β and not simply β_+.

Proof. (a) In view of Theorem B.16, it is enough to show that (B.171) holds with $\eta = \beta_+ \varpi$. By Lemma 11.8 we know that (H-r) holds for any $r > \beta$. Then Proposition B.18 yields the result, provided we have $\varpi < \frac{1}{2}$ when σ is not identically 0, and

$$\beta_+ \varpi > \begin{cases} \eta_b(p, \beta, \varpi) & \text{if } \sigma \equiv 0, \ \beta < 1 \\ \eta_a(p, \beta, \varpi) & \text{if } \sigma \equiv 0, \ \beta \geq 1 \\ \eta_c(p, \beta, \varpi) & \text{otherwise.} \end{cases} \tag{B.189}$$

Note that here we have written $\eta_a(p, \beta, \varpi)$ for example, instead of $\eta_a(p, r, \varpi)$ for some $r > \beta$, but the two formulations are equivalent because $r \mapsto \eta_a(p, r, \varpi)$ is continuous and non-decreasing. It is easily checked that, in view of the definitions of η_a, η_b, η_c, and since we also must have $p > \beta \vee 1$, (B.187) and (B.189) are equivalent.

(b) We apply Theorem B.17, so now we have to check that (B.171) holds with $\eta = \beta_+ \varpi / 2$. Therefore it is enough to show that (B.188) is equivalent to the properties in (B.189), except that the left side is now $\beta_+ \varpi / 2$: this is again an easy check.

(c) When both (L$_+$) and (L$_-$) hold, we apply the second part of Theorem B.17 for the joint convergence, in exactly the same way as above. $\square$

B.6 Proofs for Chapter 11

B.6.1 Proof of Theorems 11.11, 11.12, 11.18, 11.19, and Remark 11.14

Step 1. We use common notation for all four theorems. The function g satisfying (B.153) with some p, and the number $\gamma > 1$, are fixed, and we associate the following function, which again satisfies (B.153) with the same p:

$$h(x) = g(x/\gamma), \quad \text{so } v_h(\beta) = v_g(\beta)/\gamma^\beta.$$

We assume at least (L$_+$), with $0 \leq \beta'_+ < \beta_+ \leq \beta < 2$; in this case the process $A^{(+)}$ is well defined, and we set

$$Z^{n,1} = u_n^{\beta_+} J(g_+; \Delta_n, u_n) - v_g(\beta_+) A^{(+)},$$
$$Z^{n,2} = u_n^{\beta_+} J(h_+; \Delta_n, u_n) - v_h(\beta_+) A^{(+)}.$$

When (L$_-$) also holds, with $0 \leq \beta'_- < \beta_- \leq \beta < 2$, we recall that we can take the common value $\beta = \beta_+ \vee \beta_-$ for the constant β in both assumptions. Then $A^{(-)}$ is well defined and we set

$$Z^{n,3} = u_n^{\beta_-} J(g_-; \Delta_n, u_n) - v_g(\beta_+) A^{(-)},$$
$$Z^{n,4} = u_n^{\beta_-} J(h_-; \Delta_n, u_n) - v_h(\beta_+) A^{(-)}.$$

Recall also that (L) implies (L_+) and (L_-), with $\beta_+ = \beta_- = \beta$ and $\beta'_+ = \beta'_- = \beta'$. We thus have, according to the case, a process $Z^n = (Z^{n,j})$ which is of dimension 2 or 4.

We use the simplifying notation $\widehat{\beta}_{n+} = \widehat{\beta}_+(\gamma, g; u_n)$ and $\widehat{A}_n^{(+)} = \widehat{A}^{(+)}(\gamma, g; u_n)$ for the estimators defined in (11.33), and accordingly the estimators for negative jumps under (L_-) are denoted $\widehat{\beta}_{n-}$ and $\widehat{A}_n^{(-)}$. These estimators are properly defined on the sets

$$\Omega_{T,n}^+ = \{J(g_+; \Delta_n, u_n)_T > 0, \ J(h_+; \Delta_n, u_n)_T > 0\}$$
$$\Omega_{T,n}^- = \{J(g_-; \Delta_n, u_n)_T > 0, \ J(h_-; \Delta_n, u_n)_T > 0\}$$

and we have on the set $\Omega_{T,n}^+$:

$$\widehat{\beta}_{n+} - \beta_+ = \frac{1}{\log \gamma} \log \frac{1 + Z_T^{n,1}/v_g(\beta_+) A_T^{(+)}}{1 + \gamma^{\beta_+} Z_T^{n,2}/v_g(\beta_+) A_T^{(+)}}$$
$$\widehat{A}_n^{(+)} - A_T^{(+)} = \left(u_n^{\widehat{\beta}_{n+} - \beta_+} \frac{v_g(\beta_+)}{v_g(\widehat{\beta}_{n+})} - 1\right) A_T^{(+)} + \frac{u_n^{\widehat{\beta}_{n+} - \beta_+}}{v_g(\widehat{\beta}_{n+})} Z_T^{n,1}. \tag{B.190}$$

Analogously, under (L_-) we have on the set $\Omega_{T,n}^-$:

$$\widehat{\beta}_{n-} - \beta_- = \frac{1}{\log \gamma} \log \frac{1 + Z_T^{n,3}/v_g(\beta_-) A_T^{(-)}}{1 + \gamma^{\beta_-} Z_T^{n,4}/v_g(\beta_-) A_T^{(-)}}$$
$$\widehat{A}_n^{(-)} - A_T^{(-)} = \left(u_n^{\widehat{\beta}_{n-} - \beta_-} \frac{v_g(\beta_-)}{v_g(\widehat{\beta}_{n-})} - 1\right) A_T^{(-)} + \frac{u_n^{\widehat{\beta}_{n-} - \beta_-}}{v_g(\widehat{\beta}_{n-})} Z_T^{n,3}. \tag{B.191}$$

Finally, when (L) holds, the estimators defined in (11.16) and (11.17) are abbreviated as $\widehat{\beta}_{n,L}$ and $\widehat{A}_{n,L}^{(\pm)}$ and are given on the set $\Omega_{T,n}^+ \cap \Omega_{T,n}^-$ by

$$\widehat{\beta}_{n,L} - \beta = \frac{1}{\log \gamma} \log \frac{1 + (Z_T^{n,1} + Z_T^{n,3})/v_g(\beta) A_T}{1 + \gamma^\beta (Z_T^{n,2} + Z_T^{n,4})/v_g(\beta) A_T}$$
$$\widehat{A}_{n,L}^{(+)} - A_T^{(+)} = \left(u_n^{\widehat{\beta}_{n,L} - \beta} \frac{v_g(\beta)}{v_g(\widehat{\beta}_{n,L})} - 1\right) A_T^{(+)} + \frac{u_n^{\widehat{\beta}_{n,L} - \beta}}{v_g(\widehat{\beta}_{n,L})} Z_T^{n,1} \tag{B.192}$$
$$\widehat{A}_{n,L}^{(-)} - A_T^{(-)} = \left(u_n^{\widehat{\beta}_{n,L} - \beta} \frac{v_g(\beta)}{v_g(\widehat{\beta}_{n,L})} - 1\right) A_T^{(-)} + \frac{u_n^{\widehat{\beta}_{n,L} - \beta}}{v_g(\widehat{\beta}_{n,L})} Z_T^{n,3}$$

Step 2. Next we prove the consistency results, that is Theorems 11.11 and 11.18. The conditions on (ϖ, p) in these theorems exactly amount to (i) of (B.187). In particular, (B.186) yields

$$
\begin{aligned}
(L_+) &\Rightarrow \mathbb{P}(\Omega_T^{(\beta_+, +)} \cap (\Omega_{T,n}^+)^c) \to 0 \\
(L) &\Rightarrow \mathbb{P}(\Omega_T^{(\beta)} \cap (\Omega_{T,n}^+ \cap \Omega_{T,n}^-)^c) \to 0.
\end{aligned}
\tag{B.193}
$$

It also follows from Theorem B.20 that, for some $\varepsilon > 0$, we have

$$Z_T^{n,j} = \mathrm{o_P}(u_n^\varepsilon) \tag{B.194}$$

for $j = 1, 3$ under (L_+), and for $j = 1, 2, 3, 4$ if further (L_-) holds, and in particular under (L).

A first consequence of these two properties, jointly with (B.190) and (B.192), is that

$$
\begin{array}{llll}
(L_+) & \Rightarrow & \widehat{\beta}_{n+} - \beta_+ = \mathrm{o_P}(u_n^\varepsilon), & \text{in restriction to } \Omega_T^{(\beta_+,+)} \\
(L) & \Rightarrow & \widehat{\beta}_{n,L} - \beta = \mathrm{o_P}(u_n^\varepsilon), & \text{in restriction to } \Omega_T^{(\beta)},
\end{array}
$$

yielding in particular the consistency of $\widehat{\beta}_{n+}$ on the set $\Omega_T^{(\beta_+,+)}$ and of $\widehat{\beta}_{n,L}$ on the set $\Omega_T^{(\beta)}$, according to the case. The above also implies $u_n^{\widehat{\beta}_{n+}-\beta_+} \xrightarrow{\mathrm{P}} 1$ on $\Omega_T^{(\beta_+,+)}$, and also $v_g(\beta)/v_g(\widehat{\beta}_{n+}) \xrightarrow{\mathrm{P}} 1$ because the function v_g is differentiable. Then another application of (B.190) and (B.194) yields the consistency of $\widehat{A}_n^{(+)}$ for estimating $A_T^{(+)}$, on the set $\Omega_T^{(\beta_+,+)}$ again. The consistency of $\widehat{A}_{n,L}^{(\pm)}$ under (L) is proved in the same way. This completes the proof of Theorems 11.11 and 11.18.

Step 3. For the Central Limit Theorems 11.12 and 11.19, we observe that the conditions on (ϖ, p) in these theorems are the same as (ii) of (B.187). We only consider the case where both (L_+) and (L_-) hold, with $0 \leq \beta'_\pm < \beta_\pm$. This includes the case where (L) holds, and the case where only (L_+) holds is similar (and in fact simpler).

We reformulate (c) of Theorem B.20. As said in the previous step already, (i) of (B.188) holds. Therefore, we have the following stable convergence in law:

$$
\begin{aligned}
\left(u_n^{-\beta_+/2} Z_T^{n,1}, u_n^{-\beta_+/2} Z_T^{n,2}, u_n^{-\beta_-/2} Z_T^{n,3}, u_n^{-\beta_-/2} Z_T^{n,4} \right) \\
\xrightarrow{\mathcal{L}-\mathrm{s}} \left(\mathcal{Z}_T^1, \mathcal{Z}_T^2, \mathcal{Z}_T^3, \mathcal{Z}_T^4 \right),
\end{aligned}
\tag{B.195}
$$

where the four-dimensional random vector $\mathcal{Z}_T$ is $\mathcal{F}$-conditionally centered Gaussian, with (conditional) covariance $\Gamma^{ij} = \widetilde{E}(\mathcal{Z}_T^i \mathcal{Z}_T^j \mid \mathcal{F})$ given by

$$
\Gamma^{ij} = \begin{cases}
v_{g^2}(\beta_+) A_T^{(+)} & \text{if } i = j = 1 \\
v_{h^2}(\beta_+) A_T^{(+)} & \text{if } i = j = 2 \\
v_{gh}(\beta_+) A_T^{(+)} & \text{if } i = 1, \ j = 2 \\
v_{g^2}(\beta_-) A_T^{(-)} & \text{if } i = j = 3 \\
v_{h^2}(\beta_-) A_T^{(-)} & \text{if } i = j = 4 \\
v_{gh}(\beta_-) A_T^{(-)} & \text{if } i = 3, \ j = 4 \\
0 & \text{if } i \leq 2, \ j \geq 3.
\end{cases}
\tag{B.196}
$$

Step 4. This step is devoted to proving Theorem 11.12, so we have (L) and $\beta_+ = \beta_- = \beta$. In view of (B.192) and (B.193) and (B.195), the delta method gives us the following stable convergence in law:

$$\frac{\widehat{\beta}_{n,L} - \beta}{u_n^{\beta/2}} \xrightarrow{\mathcal{L}-\mathrm{s}} \Psi := \frac{\mathcal{Z}_T^1 + \mathcal{Z}_T^3 - \gamma^\beta(\mathcal{Z}_T^2 + \mathcal{Z}_T^4)}{v_g(\beta)(\log\gamma)\,A_T} \quad \text{on the set } \Omega_T^{(\beta)} \qquad \text{(B.197)}$$

(recall that in this case $A = A^{(+)} + A^{(-)}$). In turn, and because v_g is a C^1 function on $(0,2)$ with derivative denoted as v_g', this yields

$$\begin{aligned}
\frac{1}{u_n^{\beta/2}\log(1/u_n)}\left(u_n^{\widehat{\beta}_n - \beta} - 1\right) &\xrightarrow{\mathcal{L}-\mathrm{s}} -\Psi, \\
\frac{1}{u_n^{\beta/2}}\left(\frac{1}{v_g(\widehat{\beta}_n)} - \frac{1}{v_g(\beta)}\right) &\xrightarrow{\mathcal{L}-\mathrm{s}} -\frac{v_g'(\beta)}{v_g(\beta)^2}\,\Psi
\end{aligned} \qquad \text{(B.198)}$$

on $\Omega_T^{(\beta)}$ again, and jointly with the convergence (B.197). Now, if we use (B.192) and the boundedness in probability of $n^{-\beta/2}\,Z_T^n$, we deduce the joint stable convergence in law of the left side of (11.21) toward $\left(\Psi, -A_T^{(+)}\,\Psi, -A_T^{(-)}\,\Psi\right)$.

The variable Ψ is, conditionally on $\mathcal{F}$ and in restriction to $\Omega_T^{(\beta)}$, centered Gaussian and, by (B.196), its (conditional) variance V is

$$\frac{v_{g^2}(\beta) + \gamma^{2\beta}\,v_{h^2}(\beta) - 2\gamma^\beta\,v_{gh}(\beta)}{v_g(\beta)^2\,(\log\gamma)^2\,A_T},$$

which equals $\overline{v}_g(\beta,\gamma)/A_T$ by a simple calculation. This completes the proof of Theorem 11.12.

Step 5. Next we prove (b) of Theorem 11.19, in the same way as in the previous step. By (B.190), (B.191), (B.193) and (B.195) we have the following joint stable convergence in law, on the set $\Omega_T^{(\beta+,+)} \cap \Omega_T^{(\beta-,-)}$:

$$\begin{aligned}
&\left(\frac{\widehat{\beta}_{n+} - \beta_+}{u_n^{\beta_+/2}}, \frac{\widehat{\beta}_{n-} - \beta}{u_n^{\beta_-/2}}\right) \\
&\xrightarrow{\mathcal{L}-\mathrm{s}} (\Psi_+, \Psi_-) := \left(\frac{\mathcal{Z}_T^1 - \gamma^{\beta_+}\mathcal{Z}_T^2}{v_g(\beta)(\log\gamma)\,A_T^{(+)}}, \frac{\mathcal{Z}_T^3 - \gamma^{\beta_-}\mathcal{Z}_T^4}{v_g(\beta)(\log\gamma)\,A_T^{(-)}}\right)
\end{aligned}$$

Then, as in (B.198), we have

$$\begin{aligned}
\frac{1}{u_n^{\beta_\pm/2}\log(1/u_n)}\left(u_n^{\widehat{\beta}_{n\pm} - \beta_\pm} - 1\right) &\xrightarrow{\mathcal{L}-\mathrm{s}} -\Psi_\pm, \\
\frac{1}{u_n^{\beta_\pm/2}}\left(\frac{1}{v_g(\widehat{\beta}_{n\pm})} - \frac{1}{v_g(\beta)}\right) &\xrightarrow{\mathcal{L}-\mathrm{s}} -\frac{v_g'(\beta)}{v_g(\beta)^2}\,\Psi_\pm,
\end{aligned}$$

on $\Omega_T^{(\beta+,+)} \cap \Omega_T^{(\beta-,-)}$ again, and jointly with the previous convergence. Then, exactly as in the previous step, we deduce the stable convergence in law of the left side of (11.35) toward the limit

$(\Psi_+, \Psi_-, -A_T^{(+)} \Psi_+, -A_T^{(-)} \Psi_-)$. It remains to observe that, by (B.196), the two variables Ψ_+ and Ψ_- are, conditionally on $\mathcal{F}$, two independent centered Gaussian variables with variances $\overline{v}_g(\beta, \gamma)/A_T^{(+)}$ and $\overline{v}_g(\beta, \gamma)/A_T^{(-)}$, and the proof is complete.

Step 6. It remains to show the statement of Remark 11.14. The estimators for $A_T^{(+)}$ now satisfy, instead of (B.192),

$$\widehat{A}_{n,L}^{(+)} - A_T^{(+)} = \frac{1}{v_g(\beta)} Z_T^{n,1}, \quad \widehat{A}_{n,L}^{(-)} - A_T^{(-)} = \frac{1}{v_g(\beta)} Z_T^{n,3}. \quad (B.199)$$

The result readily follows from the convergence (B.195).

B.6.2   Proof of Theorem 11.21

Step 1. We assume (L-j-ε) for some $j \geq 2$ and $\varepsilon > 0$, and we use all notation preceding Theorem 11.21. By localization, we may assume that the processes L_t and $a_t^{i\pm}$ are all bounded. Since (L) holds with $\beta = \beta_1$ and (i) of (B.187) holds, as in Theorem B.20 we have the fundamental convergence result:

$$u_n^{\beta_1/2} \left(J(g_\pm; \Delta_n, u_n) - J(g_\pm : u_n) \right) \overset{\text{u.c.p.}}{\Longrightarrow} 0. \quad (B.200)$$

Another useful property follows from (11.39) and $\beta_i - \beta_{i+1} > \varepsilon$ for $i = 1, \dots, j-1$ and $\beta_1 - \beta_j < 1$, which imply $\beta_i - \beta_{i+1} > \varepsilon > \left(\frac{\varepsilon}{2}\right)^{k-i} (\beta_i - \beta_{k+1})$ when $i < k \leq j$:

$$\begin{aligned} 1 &\leq i < k < j \\ &\Rightarrow u_{n,i}^{\beta_i - \beta_{i+1}} \log \frac{1}{u_{n,i}} = o\big(u_{n,k}^{\beta_i - \beta_{k+1}}\big) = o\big(u_{n,k}^{\beta_k - \beta_{k+1}}\big). \end{aligned} \quad (B.201)$$

Observe also that if (11.38) holds for β_{j+1}, it also holds for any β'_{j+1} bigger than β_{j+1} and smaller than β_j. Therefore, since $\beta_j > \beta_1/2$, it is no restriction to assume that $\beta_{j+1} \geq \beta_1/2$.

Step 2. We can apply (B.161) to the functions g_+ and g_-, to deduce from (11.38) and the boundedness of the processes a_t^{i+} and a_t^{i-} and L_t that, instead of (B.162), and for all $u \in (0, 1]$, we have

$$\left| u^{\beta_1} \widetilde{J}(g_\pm, u)_t - \sum_{i=1}^{j} u^{\beta_1 - \beta_i} v_g(\beta_i) A_t^{i\pm} \right| \leq K t u^{\beta_1 - \beta_{j+1}}.$$

Moreover, (B.159) holds, and it implies $u_n^\chi M(u_n) \overset{\text{u.c.p.}}{\Longrightarrow} 0$ for all $\chi > \beta_1/2$, and the same if we replace g_+ by g_-. Thus, recalling $\beta_{j+1} \geq \beta_1/2$, we deduce that, as long as $w_n \downarrow 0$,

$$J(g_\pm; \Delta_n, w_n)_T - \sum_{i=1}^{j} \frac{1}{w_n^{\beta_i}} v_g(\beta_i) A_T^{i\pm} = O_P(w_n^{-\beta_{j+1}}). \quad (B.202)$$

Step 3. In this step, we prove (11.42) when $i = 1$. A simple calculation, using the property $A_T^i > 0$ for $i = 1, 2$ and (B.202) with $w_n = u_n$ and with $w_n = \gamma u_n$, yields

$$
\begin{aligned}
\widetilde{\beta}_n^1 &= \beta_1 + u_n^{\beta_1 - \beta_2} \frac{v_g(\beta_2)\, \overline{A}_T^2}{(\log \gamma)\, v_g(\beta_1)\, \overline{A}_T^1} \left(1 - \gamma^{\beta_1 - \beta_2}\right) + \mathrm{o_P}(u_n^{\beta_1 - \beta_2}) \\
&= \beta_1 - u_n^{\beta_1 - \beta_2}\, H_1 + \mathrm{o_P}(u_n^{\beta_1 - \beta_2}).
\end{aligned}
$$

This gives the first part of (11.42). It also implies that

$$
\begin{aligned}
u_n^{\widetilde{\beta}_n^1} &= u_n^{\beta_1} e^{-(\widetilde{\beta}_n^1 - \beta_1)\log(1/u_n)} \\
&= u_n^{\beta_1}\left(1 + H_1 u_n^{\beta_1 - \beta_2} \log(1/u_n) + \mathrm{o_P}(u_n^{\beta_1 - \beta_2}\log(1/u_n))\right).
\end{aligned}
$$

Since v_g is differentiable on $(0, 2)$, we also have $v_g(\widetilde{\beta}_n^1) - v_g(\beta_1) = \mathrm{O_P}(u_n^{\beta_1 - \beta_2})$. Therefore in view of (B.202) we obtain the second part of (11.42).

Step 4. Now we suppose that (11.42) holds for all $i \leq k - 1$, for some $k \in \{2, \ldots, j-1\}$, and in this step we show that it also holds for $i = k$. We have the following identity, for all $y = (y_1, \ldots, y_{k+1})$ and $r = 1, \ldots, k+1$ (and $I(k, l)$ is defined before (11.39)):

$$
\sum_{l=0}^{k-1} (-1)^l \gamma^{-l y_r} \sum_{J \in I(k-1, l)} \gamma^{\sum_{j \in J} y_j} = \prod_{l=1}^{k-1}\left(1 - \gamma^{y_i - y_r}\right),
$$

hence

$$
\sum_{l=0}^{k-1} (-1)^l \gamma^{-l y_r} \sum_{J \in I(k-1, l)} \gamma^{\sum_{j \in J} y_j} = \begin{cases} 0 & \text{if } r \leq k - 1 \\ G(k, y, \gamma) & \text{if } r = k \\ G'(k, y, \gamma) & \text{if } r = k + 1 \end{cases}
$$

where $G(k, y, \gamma) = \prod_{i=1}^{k-1}\left(1 - \gamma^{y_i - y_k}\right)$ and $G'(k, y, \gamma) = \prod_{i=1}^{k-1}(1 - \gamma^{y_i - y_{k+1}})$. Therefore, (B.202) applied to $w_n = x\gamma^l u_{n,k}$ and the definition (11.40) of $U^n(k, x)$ yield (upon a tedious but straightforward calculation) that, for all $x \geq 1$ fixed, and with $\underline{\beta} = (\beta_1, \ldots, \beta_{k+1})$,

$$
\begin{aligned}
U^n(k, x) &= \sum_{r=1}^{k-1} \frac{v_g(\beta_r)\, A_T^r}{(x\, u_{n,k})^{\beta_r}} \sum_{l=0}^{k-1}(-1)^l \left(\gamma^{-l\beta_r} - \gamma^{-l\widetilde{\beta}_n^r}\right) \sum_{J \in I(k-1, l)} \gamma^{\sum_{j \in J} \widetilde{\beta}_n^j} \\
&+ \sum_{r=k}^{k+1} \frac{v_g(\beta_r)\, A_T^r}{(x\, u_{n,k})^{\alpha_r}} \sum_{l=0}^{k-1}(-1)^l \gamma^{-l\beta_r} \sum_{J \in I(k-1, l)} \left(\gamma^{\sum_{j \in J} \widetilde{\beta}_n^j} - \gamma^{\sum_{j \in J} \beta_j}\right) \\
&+ \frac{v_g(\beta_k)\, A_T^k}{(x\, u_{n,k})^{\beta_k}} G(k, \underline{\beta}, \gamma) + \frac{v_g(\beta_{k+1})\, A_T^{k+1}}{(x\, u_{n,k})^{\beta_{k+1}}} G'(k, \underline{\beta}, \gamma) + \mathrm{o_P}(u_{n,k}^{-\beta_{k+1}})
\end{aligned}
$$

(we used the property $\beta_{k+2} < \beta_{k+1}$, because $k \le j-1$). The functions $z \mapsto \gamma^{-lz}$ are C^∞. The induction hypothesis gives $\widetilde{\beta}_n^i - \beta_i = O_P(u_{n,i}^{\beta_i-\beta_{i+1}})$ for $i=1,\dots,k-1$, hence by (B.201) we get

$$1 \le r \le k-1 \;\Rightarrow\; \gamma^{-l\beta_r} - \gamma^{-l\widetilde{\beta}_n^r} = o_P(u_{n,r}^{\beta_r-\beta_{r+1}}) = o_P(u_{n,k}^{\beta_r-\beta_{k+1}})$$

$$0 \le l \le k-1,\; J \in I(k-1,l) \;\Rightarrow\; \gamma^{\sum_{j\in J}\widetilde{\beta}_n^j} - \gamma^{\sum_{j\in J}\beta_j} = o_P(u_{n,k}^{\beta_{k-1}-\beta_{k+1}}).$$

Therefore we finally obtain

$$
\begin{aligned}
U^n(k,x) &= \frac{v_g(\beta_k)\,A_T^k\,G(k,\underline{\beta},\gamma)}{(x\,u_{n,k})^{\beta_k}} + \frac{v_g(\beta_{k+1})\,A_T^{k+1}\,G'(k,\underline{\beta},\gamma)}{(x\,u_{n,k})^{\beta_{k+1}}} \\
&\quad + o_P(u_{n,k}^{-\beta_{k+1}}) \\
&= \frac{v_g(\beta_k)\,A_T^k\,G(k,\underline{\beta},\gamma)}{(x\,u_{n,k})^{\beta_k}}\left(1 + \frac{H_k\,\log\gamma}{\gamma^{\beta_k-\beta_{k+1}}-1}(xu_{n,k})^{\beta_k-\beta_{k+1}} \right. \\
&\quad \left. + o_P(u_{n,k}^{\beta_k-\beta_{k+1}})\right),
\end{aligned}
\tag{B.203}
$$

where the last equality comes from the definition of H_k in (11.41). Then exactly as in Step 3, a simple calculation shows the first half of (11.42) for $i=k$.

For the second part of (11.42), as in Step 3 again, and using also the differentiability of the function $1/v_g$ on $(0,2)$, we first deduce from the above that

$$
\frac{u_{n,k}^{\widetilde{\beta}_n^k}}{v_g(\widetilde{\beta}_n^k)} = \frac{u_{n,k}^{\beta_k}}{v_g(\beta_k)}\left(1 + H_k\,u_{n,k}^{\beta_k-\beta_{k+1}}\log(1/u_{n,k}) \right.
\left. + o_P(u_{n,k}^{\beta_k-\beta_{k+1}}\log(1/u_{n,k}))\right).
$$

Therefore it is enough to show that

$$
\frac{u_{n,k}^{\beta_k}}{v_g(\beta_k)}\left(J(g_\pm;\Delta_n,u_{n,k})_T - \sum_{i=1}^{k-1} v_g(\widetilde{\beta}_n^i)\,\widetilde{A}_n^{i\pm}\,u_{n,k}^{-\widetilde{\beta}_n^i}\right) = A_T^{k\pm} + o_P(u_{n,k}^{\beta_k-\beta_{k+1}}\log(1/u_{n,k})).
$$

Taking (B.202) with $w_n = u_{n,k}$ into consideration, this amounts to proving that, for $i=1,\dots,k-1$,

$$
v_g(\widetilde{\beta}_n^i)\,\widetilde{A}_n^{i\pm}\,u_{n,k}^{\beta_k-\widetilde{\beta}_n^i} - v_g(\beta_i)\,A_T^{i\pm}\,u_{n,k}^{\beta_k-\beta_i} = o_P(u_{n,k}^{\beta_k-\beta_{k+1}}\log(1/u_{n,k})).
\tag{B.204}
$$

The induction hypothesis and the differentiability of v_g yield

$$v_g(\widetilde{\beta}_n^i)\,u_{n,k}^{\beta_k-\widetilde{\beta}_n^i} = v_g(\beta_i)\,u_{n,k}^{\beta_k-\beta_i}\left(1 + O_P(u_{n,i}^{\beta_i-\beta_{i+1}}\log(1/u_{n,i}))\right),$$

$$\widetilde{A}_n^i = A_T^i + O_P(u_{n,i}^{\beta_i-\beta_{i+1}}\log(1/u_{n,i})).$$

Thus, the left side of (B.204) is $O_P(u_{n,i}^{\beta_i - \beta_{i+1}} \log(1/u_{n,i}))$, which by (B.201) is $o_P(u_{n,k}^{\beta_k - \beta_{k+1}})$ when $j \leq k - 1$, and (B.204) is proved.

Step 5. It remains to prove that the variables in (11.43) are bounded in probability. The difference with the previous case is that (B.203) no longer hold when $k = j$, but it can be replaced by

$$U^n(j, x) = \frac{v_g(\beta_j) A_T^j G(j, \underline{\beta}, \gamma)}{x^{\beta_j} u_{n,j}^{\beta_j}} \left(1 + O_P(u_{n,j}^{\beta_j - \beta_{j+1}})\right).$$

The rest of the proof of Step 4 is unchanged.

B.6.3   Proof of Theorem 11.23

We use a simplifying notation: a point in D is $\theta = (x_i, y_i^+, y_i^-)_{1 \leq i \leq j}$, and we define the functions

$$F_{n,l}(\theta)^{\pm} = \sum_{i=1}^{j} y_i^{\pm} v_g(x_i)/(\delta_l u_n)^{x_i} \tag{B.205}$$

on D. The "true value" of the parameter is $\theta_0 = (\beta_i, A_T^{i+}, A_T^{i-})_{1 \leq i \leq j}$, the preliminary estimators are $\widetilde{\theta}_n = (\widetilde{\beta}_n^i, \widetilde{A}_n^{i+}, \widetilde{A}_n^{i-})_{1 \leq i \leq j}$, and the final estimators are $\widehat{\theta}_n = (\widehat{\beta}_n^i, \widehat{A}_n^{i+}, \widehat{A}_n^{i+})_{1 \leq i \leq j}$.

As in the previous proof we may and will assume $\beta_{j+1} \geq \beta_1/2$. We prove only the claims about $\widehat{\beta}_n^i$ and $\widehat{A}_n^{i+}$, the one about $\widehat{A}_n^{i-}$ being proved in the same way.

Step 1. For $m \geq 2$ we set $G_m = (1, \infty)^{m-1}$, a point in G_m being denoted as $\overline{\delta} = (\delta_2, \ldots, \delta_m)$. For $1 \leq k \leq j$ and $\overline{\delta} \in G_{2k}$, and with the convention $\delta_1 = 1$, we let $\Sigma(\overline{\delta})$ be the $2k \times 2k$ matrix with entries

$$\Sigma(\overline{\delta})_{l,i} = \begin{cases} \delta_l^{-\beta_i} & \text{if } 1 \leq i \leq k \\ \delta_l^{-\beta_{i-k}} \log \delta_l & \text{if } k+1 \leq i \leq 2k. \end{cases} \tag{B.206}$$

The aim of this step is to show that the set Z_k of all $\overline{\delta} \in G_{2k}$ for which the matrix $\Sigma(\overline{\delta})$ is invertible satisfies $\lambda_{2k}((Z_k)^c) = 0$, where λ_r is the Lebesgue measure on G_r.

When $1 \leq m \leq 2k$ and $\overline{\delta} \in G_{2k}$, we denote by $\mathcal{M}_m(\overline{\delta})$ the family of all $m \times m$ sub-matrices of the $m \times 2k$ matrix $(\Sigma(\overline{\delta})_{l,r} : 1 \leq l \leq m, 1 \leq r \leq 2k)$. A key fact is that $\mathcal{M}_m(\overline{\delta}) = \mathcal{M}_m(\overline{\delta}_m)$ only depends on the restriction $\overline{\delta}_m = (\delta_2, \ldots, \delta_m)$ of $\overline{\delta}$ to its first $m - 1$ coordinates. Moreover, $\Sigma(\overline{\delta})_{1i}$ equals 1 if $i \leq k$ and 0 otherwise: so the entries of the first column of any $M \in \mathcal{M}_m(\overline{\delta})$ are 0 or 1, and $\mathcal{M}'_m(\overline{\delta})$ denotes the subset of all $M \in \mathcal{M}_m(\bar{\delta})$ for which $M_{1,i} = 1$ for at least one value of i. Finally, R_m stands for the set of all $\bar{\delta}_m \in G_m$ such that all $M \in \mathcal{M}'_m(\bar{\delta}_m)$ are invertible. Since $\mathcal{M}'_{2k}(\bar{\delta})$ is the singleton $\{\Sigma(\bar{\delta})\}$, we have $Z_k = R_{2k}$.

If $m \geq 2$ and $\bar{\delta}_m = (\delta_2, \ldots, \delta_m) \in G_m$ and $M \in \mathcal{M}'_m(\bar{\delta}_m)$, by expanding along the last column we see that

$$\det(M) = \sum_{i=1}^{k} \delta_m^{\beta_i} \left(a_i + a_{k+i} \log \delta_m\right), \qquad (B.207)$$

where each a_r is of the following form: either (i) a_r is plus or minus $\det(M_r)$ for some $M_r \in \mathcal{M}_{m-1}(\bar{\delta}_m)$ (for m values of r), or (ii) $a_r = 0$ (for the other $2k - m$ values of r). Note that we can also have $a_r = 0$ in case (i), and since $M \in \mathcal{M}'_m(\bar{\delta}_m)$ there is at least one a_r of type (i) with $M_r \in \mathcal{M}'_{m-1}(\bar{\delta}_m)$.

When at least one a_r in (B.207) is not 0, the right side of this expression, as a function of δ_m, has finitely many roots only, because all β_i's are distinct. Since $\mathcal{M}'_1(\bar{\delta})$ is the 1×1 matrix equal to 1, it follows that, with $(\bar{\delta}_{m-1}, \delta_m) = (\delta_2, \ldots, \delta_{m-1}, \delta_m)$ when $\bar{\delta}_{m-1} = (\delta_2, \ldots, \delta_{m-1})$, and recalling that λ_2 is the Lebesgue measure on $(1, \infty)$:

- $m = 2 \Rightarrow \lambda_2((R_2)^c) = 0$
- $m \geq 3,\ \bar{\delta}_{m-1} \in R_{m-1}$ \hfill (B.208)
  $\Rightarrow \lambda_2\big(\delta_m : (\bar{\delta}_{m-1}, \delta_m) \notin R_m\}\big) = 0.$

Since

$$\lambda_m((R_m)^c) = \int_{G_{m-1}} \lambda_2\big(\delta_m : (\bar{\delta}_{m-1}, \delta_m) \notin R_m\}\big) \lambda_{m-1}(d\bar{\delta}_{m-1}),$$

which equals $\int_{R_{m-1}} \lambda_1\big(\delta_m : (\bar{\delta}_{m-1}, \delta_m) \notin R_m\}\big) \lambda_{m-1}(d\bar{\delta}_{m-1})$ if $\lambda_{m-1}((R_{m-1})^c) = 0$, when $m \geq 3$, we deduce from (B.208), by induction on m, that indeed $\lambda_m((R_m)^c) = 0$ for all $m = 2, \ldots, 2k$. Recalling $Z_k = R_{2k}$, the result follows.

Since the claim of the theorem holds for all $(\delta_2, \ldots, \delta_L)$ outside a λ_L-null set only, and $L \geq 2k$, we thus can and will assume below that the numbers δ_l are such that $\bar{\delta}_{2k} = (\delta_2, \ldots, \delta_{2k}) \in Z_k$, hence $\Sigma(\bar{\delta}_{2k})$ is invertible, for all $k = 1, \ldots, j$.

Step 2. Our assumptions on the preliminary estimators yield that the set Ω_n on which $\|\tilde{\theta}_i^n - \theta_0\| \leq u_n^\eta$ satisfies $\mathbb{P}(\Omega_n) \to 1$. So below we argue on the set Ω_n, or equivalently (and more conveniently) we suppose $\Omega_n = \Omega$. By localization, we may also assume that $\frac{1}{C} \leq A_T^i \leq C$ for all i and some constant $C > 1$ (recall $A_T^i > 0$ by our hypothesis). Then $\hat{\theta}_n$ converges pointwise to θ_0, which belongs to all the sets D_n.

We set $h_n = \log(1/u_n)$ and

$$y_i^n = A_T^{i+}(\widehat{\beta}_n^i - \beta_i), \quad z_i^n = \widehat{A}_n^{i+} - A_T^{i+} - y_i^n h_n, \quad a_i^n = |y_i^n| h_n + |z_i^n|.$$

We have $a_i^n \leq K u_n^n h_n$ because $\Omega_n = \Omega$. Since v_g is a C^∞ positive function on $(0, 2]$, with first derivative denoted as v_g', an expansion of $(x, w) \mapsto w v_g(x)/(\delta_l u_n)^x$ around (β_i, A_T^{i+}) yields for all l

$$\frac{\widehat{A}_n^{i+} v_g(\widehat{\beta}_i)}{(\delta_l u_n)^{\widehat{\beta}_n^i}} - \frac{A_T^{i+} v_g(\beta_i)}{(\delta_l u_n)^{\beta_i}}$$
$$= \frac{1}{(\delta_l u_n)^{\beta_i}} \left(v_g(\beta_i) z_i^n + v_g(\beta_i) y_i^n \log \delta_l + v_g'(\beta_i) y_i^n + x_{i,l}^n \right) \qquad (B.209)$$

for suitable variables $x_{i,l}^n$ satisfying

$$|x_{i,l}^n| \leq K|y_i^n| h_n (|z_i^n| + |y_i^n|) \leq K|y_i^n| h_n a_i^n \leq K(a_i^n)^2.$$

Combining (B.202) and (B.205), we see that

$$J(g_+; \Delta_n, \delta_l u_n)_T - F_{n,l}^+(\theta_0) = O_P(u_n^{-\beta_{j+1}}),$$

and of course the same estimate holds for $J(g_-; \Delta_n, \delta_l u_n)_T - F_{n,l}^-(\theta_0)$. Since

$$\Phi_n(\theta) = \sum_{l=1}^L w_l \left(\left(J(g_+; \Delta_n, \delta_l u_n)_T - F_{n,l}^+(\theta) \right)^2 \right.$$
$$\left. + \left(J(g_-; \Delta_n, \delta_l u_n)_T - F_{n,l}^-(\theta) \right)^2 \right),$$

we deduce $\Phi_n(\theta_0) = O_P(u_n^{-2\beta_{j+1}})$. Since $\theta_0 \in D_n$ and $\widehat{\theta}_n$ minimizes Φ_n over D_n, we also have $\Phi_n(\widehat{\theta}_n) = O_P(u_n^{-2\beta_{j+1}})$, hence $F_{n,l}^\pm(\theta_0) - F_{n,l}^\pm(\widehat{\theta}_n) = O_P(u_n^{-\beta_{j+1}})$ for all l (recall that $w_l > 0$). In view of (B.205) and (B.209), this implies in particular

$$\sum_{i=1}^j \frac{1}{(\delta_l u_n)^{\beta_i}} \left(v_g(\beta_i) z_i^n + (v_g'(\beta_i) + v_g(\beta_i) \log \delta_l) y_i^n + x_{i,l}^n \right)$$
$$= O_P(u_n^{-\beta_{j+1}}). \qquad (B.210)$$

Step 3. Taking k between 1 and j, we consider the $2k$-dimensional vectors $\zeta(k, n)$ and $\xi(k, n)$ with components (for $l = 1, \ldots, 2k$):

$$\zeta(k, n)_l = \sum_{i=1}^k \frac{1}{(\delta_l u_n)^{\beta_i}} \left(v_g(\beta_i) z_i^n + (v_g'(\beta_i) + v_g(\beta_i) \log \delta_l) y_i^n \right)$$

$$\xi(k, n)_l = \begin{cases} (v_g(\beta_l) z_l^n + v_g'(\beta_l) y_l^n) u_n^{-\beta_l} & \text{if } 1 \leq l \leq k \\ v_g(\beta_{l-k}) y_{l-k}^n u_n^{-\beta_{l-k}} & \text{if } k+1 \leq l \leq 2k. \end{cases}$$

With matrix notation and (B.206) and recalling $\overline{\delta}_{2k} = (\delta_2, \ldots, \delta_{2k})$, we have $\zeta(k, n) = \Sigma(\overline{\delta}_{2k}) \xi(k, n)$, and since the matrix $\Sigma(\overline{\delta}_{2k})$ is invertible we can write

$$\xi(k, n) = \Sigma(\overline{\delta}_{2k})^{-1} \zeta(k, n). \qquad (B.211)$$

Next, we have

$$\frac{1}{(\delta_l u_n)^{\beta_i}} \left| v_g(\beta_i) z_i^n + (v_g'(\beta_i) + v_g(\beta_i) \log \delta_l) y_i^n + x_{i,l}^n \right| \leq \frac{K a_i^n}{u_n^{\beta_i}},$$
$$\frac{|x_{i,l}^n|}{(\delta_l u_n)^{\beta_i}} \leq \frac{K(a_i^n)^2}{u_n^{\beta_i}},$$

hence (B.210) and $a_i^n \leq K u_n^n h_n \leq K/h_n^2 \leq K$ yield

$$|\zeta(k,n)_l| \leq K \left(\sum_{i=1}^{k-1} (a_i^n)^2 u_n^{-\beta_i} + \frac{a_k^n}{h_n^2} u_n^{-\beta_k} + \sum_{i=k+1}^{j} a_i^n u_n^{-\beta_i} \right)$$
$$+ O_P(u_n^{-\beta_{j+1}}).$$

By (B.211) the variables $\xi(k,n)_l$ satisfy the same estimate. Since $a_k^n \leq (|\xi(k,n)_k| + |\xi(k,n)_{2k}| h_n) u_n^{\beta_k}$,

$$a_k^n \leq C h_n \left(\sum_{i=1}^{k-1} (a_i^n)^2 u_n^{\beta_k - \beta_i} + \frac{a_k^n}{h_n^2} + \sum_{i=k+1}^{j} a_i^n u_n^{\beta_k - \beta_i} \right)$$
$$+ O_P(h_n u_n^{\beta_k - \beta_{j+1}})$$

for some constant C. When n is large enough, $C/h_n \leq \frac{1}{2}$, and we deduce

$$a_k^n \leq 2C h_n \left(\sum_{i=1}^{k-1} (a_i^n)^2 u_n^{\beta_k - \beta_i} + \sum_{i=k+1}^{j} a_i^n u_n^{\beta_k - \beta_i} \right) \tag{B.212}$$
$$+ O_P(h_n u_n^{\beta_k - \beta_{j+1}}).$$

Step 4. In view of the definition of y_i^n and z_i^n, to get boundedness in probability for the first two sequences in (11.44), and recalling that in this proof we assume $\beta_{j+1} \geq \beta_1/2$, it is clearly enough to prove the existence of a number $\nu > 0$ such that, for all $i = 1, \ldots, j$, we have

$$a_i^n = O_P(h_n^\nu u_n^{\beta_i - \beta_{j+1}}). \tag{B.213}$$

To this aim, we introduce the following property, denoted $(P_{m,q,r})$, where r runs through $\{1, \ldots, j\}$ and $m, q \geq 1$, and where we use the notation $\zeta_r = \beta_r - \beta_{r+1}$:

$$i = 1, \ldots, r \implies a_i^n = O_P\big(h_n^m \left(u_n^{\beta_i - \beta_r + q\zeta_r} + u_n^{\beta_i - \beta_{r+1}} \right)\big). \tag{B.214}$$

Since $a_i^n \leq K$, applying (B.212) with $k = 1$ yields $a_1^n = O_P(h_n u_n^{\beta_1 - \beta_2})$, which is $(P_{1,1,1})$.

Next, we suppose that $(P_{m,q,r})$ holds for some $r < j$, and for some $m, q \geq 1$. Letting first $k = r + 1$, we deduce from (B.212) that, since again $a_i^n \leq K$,

$$a_k^n = O_P \Big(h_n^{1+2m} \sum_{i=1}^{k-1} \left(u_n^{\beta_k - \beta_i + 2(\beta_i - \beta_r + q\zeta_r)} + u_n^{\beta_i - \beta_{r+1}} \right)$$
$$+ h_n \sum_{i=k+1}^{j} u_n^{\beta_k - \beta_i} + h_n u_n^{\beta_k - \beta_{j+1}} \Big) \tag{B.215}$$
$$= O_P \Big(h_n^{1+2m} \left(u_n^{\beta_k - \beta_r + 2q\zeta_r} + u_n^{\zeta_r} + u_n^{\beta_k - \beta_r + 2} \right) \Big),$$

where the last line holds because $k = r+1$ and $h_n > 1$ for n large enough and the sequence β_i is decreasing. This in turn implies, for $k = r+1$ again,

$$a_k^n = O_P\left(h_n^{r+2-k+2m}\left(u_n^{\beta_k - \beta_r + 2q\zeta_r} + u_n^{\beta_k - \beta_{r+1}}\right)\right). \tag{B.216}$$

Then, exactly as above, we apply (B.212) with $k = r$, and (B.214) and also (B.216) with $k = r + 1$, to get that (B.216) holds for $k = r$ as well. Repeating the argument, a downward induction yields that indeed (B.216) holds for all k between 1 and $r + 1$. Thus (B.214) holds with q and m substituted with $2q$ and $r + 1 + 2m$. Hence $(P_{m,q,r})$ implies $(P_{r+1+2m,2q,r})$. Since obviously $(P_{m,q,r}) \Rightarrow (P_{m,q',r})$ for any $q' \in [1, q]$, by a repeated use of the previous argument we deduce that if $(P_{m,1,r})$ holds for some $m \geq 1$, then for any $q' \geq 1$ we can find $m(q') \geq 1$ such that $(P_{m(q'),q',r})$ holds as well.

Now, assuming $(P_{m,q,r})$ for some m, q, r, we take $q' = \frac{\zeta_{r+1}}{2\zeta_r} \vee 1$ and $m' = m(q')$. What precedes yields $(P_{m',q',r})$, hence (B.215) holds for all $k \leq r + 1$, with q' and m'. In view of our choice of q', this implies that $(P_{r+1+m',1,r+1})$ holds. Since $(P_{1,1,1})$ holds, we see by induction that for any $r \leq j$ there exists $m_r \geq 1$ such that $(P_{m_r,1,r})$ holds.

It remains to apply (B.214) with $r = j$ and $m = m_r$ and $q = 1$, and we get (B.213) with $\nu = m_j$. This completes the proof.

B.7   Proofs for Chapter 12

Proof of Lemma 12.2. It is convenient below to replace the process $A(p)_t = \sum_{s \leq t} |\Delta X_s|^p$ by $A'(p)$ which, together with $\widetilde{A}'(p)$, is defined as

$$A'(p)_t = \sum_{s \leq t} |\Delta X_s|^p \wedge 1, \qquad \widetilde{A}'(p)_t = \int_0^t ds \int (|x|^p \wedge 1)\, F_s(dx).$$

Those two processes $A'(p)$ and $\widetilde{A}'(p)$ are increasing, and finite-valued when $p \geq 2$. When $p < 2$ we have to be more careful. Let $R = \inf(t : A'(p)_t = \infty)$ and $R' = \inf(t : \widetilde{A}'(p)_t = \infty)$. Then $A'(p)$ is finite càdlàg on $[0, R)$ and, if $R < \infty$, infinite on (R, ∞) and $A'(p)_{R-} \leq A'(p)_R \leq A'(p)_{R+} = \infty$, both inequalities being possibly strict. As for $\widetilde{A}'(p)$, it is finite continuous on $[0, R')$, infinite on (R', ∞), left-continuous at R' when $R' < \infty$, but again $\widetilde{A}'(p)_R < \infty$ is possible.

However, we have the following property:

$$\{A'(p)_S < \infty\} = \{\widetilde{A}'(p)_S < \infty\} \text{ a.s.,}$$
for any finite random time S. \hfill (B.217)

To see this, we set $R_n = \inf(t : A'(p)_t \geq n)$ and $R'_n = \inf(t : \widetilde{A}'(p)_t \geq n)$, and observe that $A'(p)_{R_n} \leq n+1$ and $\widetilde{A}'(p)_{R'_n} \leq n$. This entails $\{A'(p)_S < \infty\} = \cup_{n\geq 1}\{S \leq R_n\}$ and $\{\widetilde{A}'(p)_S < \infty\} = \cup_{n\geq 1}\{S \leq R'_n\}$. Since $\widetilde{A}'(p)$ is the predictable compensator of $A'(p)$, we have $\mathbb{E}(\widetilde{A}'(p)_\tau) = \mathbb{E}(A'(p)_\tau)$ for any stopping time τ, hence $A'(p)_{R'_n} < \infty$ and $\widetilde{A}'(p)_{R_n} < \infty$ a.s., and (B.217) follows.

We now prove (a). In view of (B.217), it suffices to show that, almost surely, we have $\widetilde{A}'(0)_T = \infty$ on the set $\Omega_T^{(iia)}$. By the very definition of γ_T this is true when $\gamma_T > 0$, hence on the set $\Omega_T^{(i,\gamma>0)}$. If $\liminf_{x\to 0} (\overline{F}_t(x^{1+\rho}) - \overline{F}_t(x)) = \infty$ we have $F_t(\mathbb{R}) = \infty$. Therefore $\widetilde{A}'(0)_T = \infty$ on the set $\Omega_T^{(i,\gamma=0)}$, and (a) holds.

From now on, we assume (L). By Fubini's theorem,

$$\int_0^\infty (|x|^p \wedge 1) F_t(dx) = p \int_0^1 y^{p-1} \overline{F}_t(y) \, dy$$

for all $p > 0$. If $a_t^{(+)} + a_t^{(-)} > 0$ we have $\liminf_{y\downarrow 0} y^\beta \overline{F}_t(y) > 0$, hence the above yields that $\int_0^1 y^{p-1} \overline{F}_t(y) = \infty$ for all $p \leq \beta$. Thus on the set $\Omega_T^{(\beta)} = \{A_T > 0\}$ we have $\widetilde{A}'(p)_T = \infty$ for all $p \leq \beta$, hence $A'(p)_T = \infty$ almost surely by (B.217), and (c) of the lemma follows.

We can now prove (b). When $A_t > 0$ almost surely for all $t > 0$, we obviously have $\gamma_t = \beta$ a.s. for all $t > 0$, whereas $x^\beta \overline{F}_t(x) \leq L_t + a_t^{(+)} + a_t^{(-)}$ if $x \in (0,1]$ by (11.2), hence (J) clearly holds. When $\beta' = 0$ we have $\gamma_t = 0$ when $A_t = 0$ and $\gamma_t = \beta$ if $A_t > 0$: then $\sup_{s\leq t} x^{\gamma_t+\varepsilon} \overline{F}_t(x) \leq L_t + \sup_{s\leq t}(a_s^{(+)} + a_s^{(-)})$ for any $\varepsilon > 0$ and $x \in (0,1]$, and (J) holds again. This completes the proof of (b).

Finally, we prove (d) and assume $\beta' = 0$ again. We have that $\alpha_t = F_t(\mathbb{R}) 1_{\{a_t^{(+)}=a_t^{(-)}=0\}}$ is smaller than L_t. Therefore $\widetilde{A}'(0)_T \leq TL_T < \infty$ on the set $\{A_T = 0\}$ and, by (B.217) again, $A'(0)_T$, which is the number of jumps on $[0,T]$, is a.s. finite on this set. Since $\Omega_T^{(\beta)} = \{A_T > 0\}$ and $\Omega_T^{(ia)} = \{\widetilde{A}'(0)_T = \infty\}$, we deduce $\Omega_T^{(ia)} \subset \Omega_T^{(\beta)}$ almost surely. By virtue of (a) and (b) it thus remains to show that $\Omega_T^{(\beta)} \subset \Omega_T^{(i,\gamma>0)}$ almost surely. On the set $\Omega_T^{(\beta)}$ we have $\gamma_T = \beta > 0$ and the set $\Gamma_T = \{t \in [0,T] := a_t^{(+)} + a_t^{(-)} > 0\}$ has positive Lebesgue measure. Now, if $t \in \Gamma_T$, and by (11.2) with $\beta' = 0$, we have $\overline{F}_t(x) - \overline{F}_t(u) \geq \eta/x^\beta$ for all $x \in (0, u/2]$ for all $u > 0$ small enough and some $\eta > 0$ depending on (ω, t); this readily implies that for $t \in \Gamma_t$ we have $G(q, u)_t \to \infty$ as $u \downarrow 0$ for all $q < \beta$. We deduce $\Omega_T^{(\beta)} \subset \Omega_T^{(i,\gamma>0)}$, and the proof is complete. $\qquad\square$

The proof of Theorem 12.5 requires two preliminary lemmas. In this theorem, (K-2) is assumed, but for further reference these lemmas are stated under weaker assumptions. We write

$$\widetilde{X}_t = X_0 + \int_0^t (b_s - \bar{b}_{s \wedge S}) \, ds + \int_0^t \sigma_s \, dW_s,$$

where

$$S = \inf \left(t : \int_0^t ds \int_{\{|\delta(s,z)| \le 1\}} |\delta(s,z)| \lambda(dz) = \infty \right),$$
$$t \le S \;\Rightarrow\; \bar{b}_t = \int_{\{|\delta(t,z)| \le 1\}} \delta(t,z) \lambda(dz)$$

(S as in (A.4)). The process $\widetilde{X}$ satisfies (HC) and (H′), as soon as X satisfies (H-2) and (H′); however, if (H′) fails and (H-2) holds for X, then (H-2) may fail for $\widetilde{X}$. We associate with $\widetilde{X}$ the processes defined by (10.37), which we denote below as $\widetilde{B}([p,k],\Delta_n)$ and $\widetilde{B}(p,k\Delta_n)$.

Lemma B.21. *Assume (H-2) and (H′), and let $u_n \asymp \Delta_n^{\varpi}$ for some $\varpi \in (0, \frac{1}{2})$. Then for any $p > 0$ and any $k \ge 1$ we have in restriction to the set $\Omega_T^{(fa)}$ (recall $g_p(x) = |x|^p \wedge (2-x)^+$)*

$$\begin{aligned}
u_n^p J([g_p, k], \Delta_n, u_n)_T - \widetilde{B}([p,k], \Delta_n)_T &= o_{\mathrm{P}}(\Delta_n^{\frac{p-1}{2}}) \\
u_n^p J(g_p, k\Delta_n, u_n)_T - \widetilde{B}(p, k\Delta_n)_T &= o_{\mathrm{P}}(\Delta_n^{\frac{p-1}{2}}).
\end{aligned}$$
(B.218)

Proof. By localization we may assume (SH-2) for $\widetilde{X}$. Define $S_0 = 0$ and $S_q = \inf(t > S_{q-1} : \Delta X_t \ne 0)$ for $q \ge 1$. We may have $S_q = 0$ for all q; however, on the set $\Omega_T^{(fa)}$ there are Q jumps on $[0,T]$ (with Q a random integer), and we do have $S_Q \le T \le S_{Q+1}$ (we may also have $S_q = T$ for all $q > Q$), and we do have $S_Q \le T \le S_{Q+1}$, and also $0 < S_1 < \cdots < S_{Q-1} < S_Q$ if $Q \ge 1$. Hence, on the set $\Omega_T^{(fa)}$, we have for all $t \le T$

$$X_t = \widetilde{X}_t + \sum_{q=1}^Q \Delta X_{S_q} 1_{\{S_q \le t\}}.$$

In view of (A.67), $\mathbb{E}(|\Delta_i^n \widetilde{X}|^r) \le K\Delta_n^{r/2}$ for all $r > 0$. Thus, if we take some $\varpi' \in \left(\varpi \vee \frac{p-1}{2p}, \frac{1}{2} \right)$ we see that $\mathbb{P}(|\Delta_i^n \widetilde{X}| > \Delta_n^{\varpi'}) \le K\Delta_n^2$ by Markov's inequality applied with $r = \frac{4}{1-2\varpi'}$. Moreover, $S_q - S_{q-1} > 0$ and $|\Delta X_{S_q}| > 0$ for all $q = 1, \ldots, Q$, on the set $\Omega_T^{(fa)}$. Hence, upon taking n large enough to have $ku_n \ge \Delta_n^{\varpi'}$, and using the Borel-Cantelli lemma, we obtain

$$\mathbb{P}(\Omega_T^{(fa)} \cap (\Omega_n)^c) \to 0, \quad \text{with } \Omega_n \text{ the set on which:}$$
$$\begin{cases} q \le Q \;\Rightarrow\; S_q - S_{q-1} > k\Delta_n, \; |\Delta X_{S_q}| > 3u_n \\ i = 1, \cdots, [T/\Delta_n] \;\Rightarrow\; |\Delta_i^n \widetilde{X}| \le \Delta_n^{\varpi'} \le \frac{u_n}{k}. \end{cases}$$

Now, on Ω_n and for any $i \leq [T/\Delta_n] - k + 1$, we have $|\widetilde{X}_{(i+k-1)\Delta_n} - \widetilde{X}_{(i-1)\Delta_n}| \leq k\Delta_n^{\varpi'}$, and also $|X_{(i+k-1)\Delta_n} - X_{(i-1)\Delta_n}| = |\widetilde{X}_{(i+k-1)\Delta_n} - \widetilde{X}_{(i-1)\Delta_n}| \leq u_n$ for all i except at most Qk values, for which $|X_{(i+k-1)\Delta_n} - X_{(i-1)\Delta_n}| = |\widetilde{X}_{(i+k-1)\Delta_n} - \widetilde{X}_{(i-1)\Delta_n} + \Delta X_{S_q}|$ for some $q \leq Q$, implying $|X_{(i+k-1)\Delta_n} - X_{(i-1)\Delta_n}| > 2u_n$. Since $g_p(x) = 0$ when $|x| \geq 2$ and $g_p(x) = |x|^p$ when $|x| \leq 1$, it follows that both left sides in (B.218) are smaller in absolute value than $Qk^{p+1}\Delta_n^{p\varpi'}$. This, together with $\mathbb{P}(\Omega_T^{(fa)} \cap (\Omega_n)^c) \to 0$, implies the result.   □

Lemma B.22. *Assume (J), and let g satisfy (B.153) for some $p > 2$ and $u_n \asymp \Delta_n^{\varpi}$ for some $\varpi \in (0, \frac{p-2}{2p})$. Then there exists $\varepsilon > 0$ such that for any $T > 0$ (recall (B.155) for the definition of $\widetilde{J}(g; u)$)*

- $u_n^{(1-\varepsilon)\gamma_T} \, \sup_{t \leq T} |J(g; \Delta_n, u_n)_t - J(g; u_n)_t| \xrightarrow{\mathbb{P}} 0$
  on $\{\gamma_T > 0\}$
- $u_n^{(1-\varepsilon)\gamma_T} \, \sup_{t \leq T} |J(g; \Delta_n, u_n)_t - \widetilde{J}(g; u_n)_t| \xrightarrow{\mathbb{P}} 0$ (B.219)
  on $\{\gamma_T > 0\}$

and

$$\frac{1}{\Delta_n^\varepsilon} \sup_{t \leq T} |J(g; \Delta_n, u_n)_t - J(g, u_n)_t| \xrightarrow{\mathbb{P}} 0 \quad \text{on } \{\gamma_T = 0\}. \quad (B.220)$$

Proof. We begin with (B.219). We consider the number $\chi = \chi(\varpi, p)$ constructed in Corollary B.19, and the result will hold with any choice of ε in $(0, 1 - \chi)$. We pick α in the (non-empty) interval $(\frac{\chi}{1-\varepsilon}, 1)$, and also an integer $m > (2/\alpha) \vee (1/\varepsilon)$, and we set $z_1 = 2 - 1/m$ and $z_j = \alpha z_{j-1}$ for $j \geq 2$. The intervals $(z_{j+1}, z_j]$ for $j \geq 1$ form a partition of $(0, 2 - 1/m]$, and since $\gamma_T < 2$ and m is arbitrarily large, for getting (B.219) on $\{\gamma_T > 0\}$ it is enough to prove it separately on each set $\Omega_T^j = \{z_{j+1} < \gamma_T \leq z_j\}$.

Below, $j \geq 1$ is fixed. The process γ_t is optional and increasing (not necessarily càdlàg, though), so the left limit γ_{t-} is predictable and we can set

$$\overline{X}_t = X_0 + \int_0^t b_s ds + \int_0^t \sigma_s dW_s$$
$$+ \int_0^t 1_{\{\gamma_{s-} \leq z_j\}} \int x 1_{\{|x| \leq 1\}} (\mu - \nu)(ds, dx)$$
$$+ \int_0^t 1_{\{\gamma_{s-} \leq z_j\}} \int x 1_{\{|x| > 1\}} \mu(ds, dx).$$

This process obviously satisfies (J), with a global BG index $z_j \wedge \gamma_t$ instead of γ_t. Moreover, on the set Ω_T^j we have $\overline{X}_t = X_t$ for all $t \leq T$. Hence it is enough to prove the result for $\overline{X}$ instead of X. Or, in other words, we can assume that X itself satisfies (J) with $\gamma_t \leq z_j$ for all t, and thus also (L′) for any $\beta > z_j$, hence (H-r) for any $r > z_j$ as well by Lemma 11.8. In particular, $r = \frac{z_{j+1}(1-\varepsilon)}{\chi}$ satisfies $r > z_j$, hence we have (B.184) for this specific value of r.

It remains to observe that, on Ω_T^j, we have $\gamma_T(1-\varepsilon) > z_{j+1}(1-\varepsilon) = r\chi$; we then readily deduce (B.219) on Ω_T^j from (B.184).

The proof of (B.220) is analogous: we define $\overline{X}$ as above, except that we take $z_j = 0$, hence $\overline{X}_t = X_t$ for all $t \leq T$ if $\gamma_T = 0$. Thus it is enough to prove the result for $\overline{X}$, or equivalently for X when $\gamma_t = 0$ identically, and consequently we have (H-r) for all $r > 0$ by the same argument as above. Hence (B.220) follows from (B.185).   □

Proof of Theorem 12.5. The proof goes through several steps.

Step 1. We begin with (a). Since X satisfies (K-2), the process $\widetilde{X}$ defined before Lemma B.21 satisfies (KC), hence the variables $\widetilde{B}([p,k], \Delta_n, u_n)_T$ and $\widetilde{B}(p, k\Delta_n, u_n)_T$ satisfy (10.39) and (10.46) (on the set Ω). Now, another way of writing (B.218) is

$$\frac{1}{\sqrt{\Delta_n}} \left(\Delta_n^{1-p/2} u_n^p J([g_p, k], \Delta_n, u_n)_T - \Delta_n^{1-p/2} \widetilde{B}([p,k], \Delta_n)_T \right) \xrightarrow{\mathbb{P}} 0$$

on the set $\Omega_T^{(fa)}$ and the same for $J(g_p, k\Delta_n, u_n)_T$. Therefore $u_n^p J([g_p, k], \Delta_n, u_n)_T$ and $u_n^p J(g_p, k\Delta_n, u_n)_T$ satisfy (10.39) and (10.46) in restriction to the set $\Omega_T^{(fa,W)}$, and (a) of Theorem 12.5 is exactly the same as the convergences (10.41) (the cases of $\Omega_T^{(cW)}$) and (10.48).

Step 2. The proof of (b) is more complicated. For any $j = 1, \dots, k$ we set

$$J_n^j = \sum_{i=1}^{[(1-j+T/\Delta_n)/k]} g_p\big((X_{(j-1+ki)\Delta_n} - X_{(j-1+k(i-1))\Delta_n})/u_n\big). \quad \text{(B.221)}$$

For homogeneity of notation below, we write $J_n^0 = J(g_p; \Delta_n, u_n)_T$ and $J_n^{k+1} = \frac{1}{k}\left(J_n^1 + \dots + J_n^k \right)$ (no longer given by (B.221), of course), hence $J_n^1 = J(g_p; k\Delta_n, u_n)_T$ and $J_n^{k+1} = J([g_p, k]; \Delta_n, u_n)$.

Under (J) we take $\varepsilon > 0$ as in Lemma B.22, and under (L) we choose χ as in (B.184) and $r \in (\beta, \beta/\chi)$ (so in particular (H-r) holds by Lemma 11.8); with these numbers, Lemma B.22 and (B.184) yield the following for $j = 0$:

$$U_n^j := v_n \left(J_n^j - Z_n \right) \xrightarrow{\mathbb{P}} 0 \quad \text{(B.222)}$$

on the set Ω_0, where

$$
\begin{cases}
\text{under (L):} & \Omega_0 = \Omega_T^{(\beta)}, & v_n = u_n^{r\chi}, & Z_n = \widetilde{J}(g_p, u_n)_T \\
\text{under (J):} & \Omega_0 = \Omega_T^{(i,\gamma>0)}, & v_n = u_n^{\gamma T(1-\varepsilon)}, & Z_n = \widetilde{J}(g_p, u_n)_T \\
\text{under (J):} & \Omega_0 = \Omega_T^{(i,\gamma=0)}, & v_n = \Delta_n^{-\varepsilon}, & Z_n = J(g_p, u_n)_T.
\end{cases}
$$

Upon replacing Δ_n by $k\Delta_n$ we get the same when $j = 1$. When $2 \le j \le k$ and in the last case we obtain instead that $v_n \left(J_n^j - (J(g_p, u_n)_{T+(j-1)\Delta_n} - J(g_p, u_n)_{(j-1)\Delta_n} \right) \xrightarrow{\ \mathbb{P}\ } 0$. However, the expectations of the nonnegative variables $J(g_p, u_n)_{(j-1)\Delta_n}$ and $J(g_p, u_n)_{T+(j-1)\Delta_n} - J(g_p, u_n)_T$ are smaller than $K\Delta_n$, whereas $\Delta_n/v_n \to 0$, hence (B.222) also holds for $j = 2, \ldots, k$. A similar argument shows (B.222) in the first and second cases as well, for $j = 2, \ldots, k$. Finally, by summation over j, we deduce (B.222) for $j = k+1$ also.

Step 3. With the previous notation, we observe that our statistics become

$$
S^{(\text{FA-PV1})}(p, k, \Delta_n, u_n) = \frac{J_n^{k+1}}{J_n^0}, \qquad S^{(\text{FA-PV2})}(p, k, \Delta_n, u_n) = \frac{J_n^1}{J_n^0}.
$$

At this point, suppose that we have proven the following property, with v_n and Ω_0 as in (B.222):

$$
v_n Z_n \xrightarrow{\ \mathbb{P}\ } +\infty \quad \text{on the set } \Omega_0. \tag{B.223}
$$

Combining this with (B.222), we deduce that $\Omega_0^n = \Omega_0 \cap \{Z_n > 0\}$ satisfies $\mathbb{P}(\Omega_0^n) \to \mathbb{P}(\Omega_0)$, and on Ω_0^n we have $J_n^j = Z_n(1 + V_n^j)$, where V_n^j equal $U_n^j/v_n Z_n$ on Ω_0^n and 0 otherwise. We have $V_n^j \xrightarrow{\ \mathbb{P}\ } 0$, and the previous test statistics are equal to $(1 + V_n^{k+1})/(1 + V_n^0)$ and $(1 + V_n^1)/(1 + V_n^0)$ on Ω_0^n, respectively, hence their convergence in probability to 1 in restriction to Ω_0 becomes obvious.

Step 4. It thus remains to prove (B.223), and in the case under (L) with $\Omega_0 = \Omega_T^{(\beta)}$ it is a simple consequence of $r\chi < \beta$ and of (B.162).

Next, we consider the case $\Omega_0 = \Omega_T^{(i,\gamma>0)}$, under (J). In view of the definition (12.5) of g_p we have for $0 < q < p$ and $u > 0$

$$
\int g_p(x/u) \, F_t(dx) \;\ge\; \frac{1}{u^p} \int_{\{|x| \le u/2\}} |x|^p \, F_t(x)
$$

$$
= \frac{p}{u^p} \int_0^{u/2} y^{p-1} \big(\overline{F}_t(y) - \overline{F}_t(u) \big) \, dy
$$

$$
\ge \frac{p}{p-q} \frac{G(q,u)_t}{2^{p-q} u^q},
$$

the equality following from Fubini's theorem, and the last inequality from the definition (12.3). We deduce from (B.155) and (12.4) and Fatou's lemma that $u_n^q Z_n \to \infty$ on the set $\Omega_T^{(i,\gamma>0)} \cap \{\gamma_T > q\}$, for any $q \in (0,p)$. This implies $v_n Z_n \to \infty$ on the set $\Omega_T^{(i,\gamma>0)} \cap \{\gamma_T(1-\varepsilon) < q < \gamma_T\}$, for any $q \in (0,p)$ and with $v_n = u_n^{\gamma_T(1-\varepsilon)}$. Since $p > 2 > \gamma_T$, (B.223) follows in the case $\Omega_0 = \Omega_T^{(i,\gamma>0)}$.

Step 5. Finally, consider $\Omega_0 = \Omega_T^{(i,\gamma=0)}$, under (J). We choose $\rho \in (0, \varepsilon/2p\varpi)$, and we set $G(x)_t = \overline{F}_t(x^{1+\rho}) - \overline{F}_t(x)$ and denote as Γ the set of all $t \in [0,T]$ such that $G(x)_t \to \infty$ as $x \to 0$. We also introduce a counting process H^n and its compensator $\widetilde{H}^n$ by

$$ H_t^n = \sum_{s \le t} 1_{\{u_n^{1+\rho} < |\Delta X_s| \le u_n\}}, \qquad \widetilde{H}_t^n = \int_0^t G(u_n)_s \, ds. $$

On the set $\Omega_T^{(i,\gamma=0)}$ the Lebesgue measure of Γ is positive, hence Fatou's lemma gives us

$$ \widetilde{H}_T^n \to \infty \quad \text{on the set} \quad \Omega_T^{(i,\gamma=0)}. \tag{B.224} $$

Set $S_n = \inf(t : H_t^n > 0)$. We have $H_{S_n}^n \le 1$, so $\mathbb{E}(\widetilde{H}_{S_n}^n) = \mathbb{E}(H_{S_n}^n) \le 1$ and thus

$$ \mathbb{P}(\{S_n \ge T\} \cap \Omega_T^{(i,\gamma=0)}) \le \mathbb{P}(\widetilde{H}_{S_n}^n > A) + \mathbb{P}(\Omega_T^{(i,\gamma=0)} \cap \{\widetilde{H}_T^n \le A\}) $$
$$ \le \frac{1}{A} + \mathbb{P}(\Omega_T^{(i,\gamma=0)} \cap \{\widetilde{H}_T^n \le A\}). $$

So, $\mathbb{P}(\{S_n \ge T\} \cap \Omega_T^{(i,\gamma=0)}) \to 0$ follows from (B.224) by choosing first A large and then n large. Since $\{H_T^n = 0\} = \{S_n > T\}$, we deduce

$$ \mathbb{P}(\Omega_{T,q}^{(i,\gamma=0)} \cap \{H_T^n = 0\}) \to 0. \tag{B.225} $$

Now, if $H_T^n \ge 1$ and since $g_p(x) = |x|^p$ if $|x| \le 1$, we have $Z_n = J(g_p, u_n)_T \ge u_n^{p\rho}$, which is bigger than $\Delta_n^{\varepsilon/2}$ for all n large enough by virtue of $u_n \asymp \Delta_n^\varpi$ and of the choice of ρ. Therefore $v_n Z_n \ge 1/\Delta_n^\varepsilon$ on the set $\{H_T^n \ge 1\}$, and we conclude (B.223) from (B.225). $\square$

Proof of Theorem 12.8. We again have several steps.
Step 1. We first consider the behavior on the alternative set $\Omega_T^{(fa,W)}$. Exactly as in the proof of Theorem 12.5, on this set one may replace $u_n^q J(g_q; \Delta_n, u_n)$ and $(\gamma u_n)^q J(g_q; \Delta_n, \gamma u_n)$ by $\widetilde{B}(q, \Delta_n)$ (for any $q > 0$, see Lemma B.21 and before) and then use the property $\Delta_n^{1-q/2} \widetilde{B}(q, \Delta_n)_T \xrightarrow{\mathbb{P}} C(q)_T$, see for example (10.39), applied for the continuous process

$\widetilde{X}$. Applying this with q equal to p and p' readily gives the second convergence in (12.14).

Denote by V_n^{ij} the $(i,j)^{\text{th}}$ term in the sum (12.15), and consider for example the term $(i=1, j=4)$. The same argument as above yields

$$V_n^{1,4} \sim -\frac{\widetilde{B}(p+p', \Delta_n)_T}{\widetilde{B}(p, \Delta_n)_T \, \widetilde{B}(p', \Delta_n)_T},$$

hence $V_n^{1,4}/\Delta_n \xrightarrow{\mathbb{P}} -C(p+p')_T/C(p)_T \, C(p')_T$ on the set $\Omega_T^{(W)}$. A similar convergence holds, with the same normalization, for all other terms, and the second convergence in (12.16) follows because $\Delta_n/u_n^\beta \to 0$.

Step 2. For the results in restriction to the null hypothesis set $\Omega_T^{(\beta)}$, the proofs are mostly similar to those in Subsection B.6.1. To simplify notation we write $S_n = S^{(\text{IA-PV})}(p, p', \gamma, \Delta_n, u_n)$. We use the functions h_j, l_j and g defined in (12.12) and (12.13). We also need the four-dimensional process Z^n with components

$$Z^{n,j} = u_n^\beta J(l_j; \Delta_n, u_n) - A.$$

By definition of the l_j's, we have $J(g_p; \Delta_n, \gamma u_n) = \gamma^{-\beta} v_{g_p}(\beta) \, J(l_1; \Delta_n, u_n)$ and $J(g_p; \Delta_n, u_n) = v_{g_p}(\beta) \, J(l_2; \Delta_n, u_n)$, and similar relationships for the power p'. Therefore

$$S_n = \frac{(A_T + Z_T^{n,1})(A_T + Z_T^{n,3})}{(A_T + Z_T^{n,2})(A_T + Z_T^{n,4})}. \tag{B.226}$$

Recall that $\varpi \le \frac{1}{4}$, whereas $p > p' \ge 4$. First, we can apply (11.18) to obtain $Z_T^{n,j} \xrightarrow{\mathbb{P}} 0$ for $j = 1,2,3,4$, implying the first convergence in (12.14). A second consequence of (11.18) is that, considering again separately all terms V_n^{ij} in the sum (12.15), we have $u_n^{-\beta} V_n^{ij} \xrightarrow{\mathbb{P}} v_{h_i h_j}(\beta)/v_{h_i}(\beta) \, v_{h_j}(\beta) \, A_T$ on the set $\Omega_T^{(\beta)}$. Using the definition (12.13) of g, it is easy to check that $\sum_{i,j=1}^4 v_{h_i h_j}(\beta)/v_{h_i}(\beta) \, v_{h_j}(\beta)$ is indeed equal to $v_g(\beta)$, hence we have the first convergence in (12.16).

Step 3. When $\beta' < \frac{\beta}{2}$ in (L), and since (B.188) with $\beta_+ = \beta_- = \beta$ holds here for p and p' by hypothesis, we can apply Theorem B.20 to get the stable convergence in law of the processes $u_n^{-\beta/2} Z^n$ to a limiting process $\mathcal{Z}$ defined on an extension $(\widetilde{\Omega}, \widetilde{\mathcal{F}}, (\widetilde{\mathcal{F}}_t)_{t\ge0}, \widetilde{\mathbb{P}})$ of $(\Omega, \mathcal{F}, (\mathcal{F}_t)_{t\ge0}, \mathbb{P})$ and which, conditionally on $\mathcal{F}$, is a continuous centered Gaussian martingale with variance-covariance given by

$$\widetilde{\mathbb{E}}(\mathcal{Z}_t^i \, \mathcal{Z}_t^j \mid \mathcal{F}) = v_{l_i l_j} \, A_t.$$

Coming back to (B.226), an application of the delta method allows us to deduce that $u_n^{-\beta/2}(S_n - 1)$ converges stably in law, in restriction to the set $\Omega_T^{(\beta)}$, to the variable

$$\mathcal{S} = \frac{1}{A_T}\left(\mathcal{Z}_T^1 - \mathcal{Z}_T^2 + \mathcal{Z}_T^3 - \mathcal{Z}_T^4\right).$$

This variable is, conditionally on $\mathcal{F}$ and in restriction to $\Omega_T^{(\beta)}$, centered normal with (conditional) variance V given by (12.13). This completes the proof of Theorem 12.8. □

B.8   Proofs for Chapter 13

Without surprise, the proofs for Section 13.1 are simple modifications of those for Chapter 12.

Proof of Theorem 13.1. We start with (a) and (b), which we prove together. We set $f(x) = |x|^p$ and $F(x_1,\dots,x_k) = |x_1 + \cdots + x_k|^p$ on $\mathbb{R}^k$. Recalling (13.3), we see that $f(x)\mathbf{1}_{\{|x|\leq 1\}} \leq g_p(x) \leq f(x)\mathbf{1}_{\{|x|\leq 2\}}$. Hence, by a simple calculation, and with the notation (A.11) and (A.12),

$$\begin{aligned}
\Delta_n^{p/2-1}B'(f,\Delta_n,u_n) &\leq u_n^p J(g_p;\Delta_n,u_n)\\
&\leq \Delta_n^{p/2-1}B'(f,\Delta_n,2u_n),\\
\Delta_n^{p/2-1}B'([F,k],\Delta_n,u_n) &\leq u_n^p J([g_p,k];\Delta_n,u_n)\\
&\leq \Delta_n^{p/2-1}B'([F,k],\Delta_n,2u_n).
\end{aligned} \tag{B.227}$$

Since $\rho_{c_s}(F) = k^{p/2}c_s^{p/2}$ and $p < 2$, we deduce from Theorem A.3 that

$$\begin{aligned}
u_n^p\Delta_n^{1-p/2}J(g_p;k\Delta_n,u_n) &\overset{\text{u.c.p.}}{\Longrightarrow} k^{p/2-1}C(p),\\
u_n^p\Delta_n^{1-p/2}J([g_p,k];\Delta_n,u_n) &\overset{\text{u.c.p.}}{\Longrightarrow} k^{p/2}C(p),
\end{aligned}$$

which immediately yields (13.4) in restriction to the set $\Omega_T^{(W)} = \{C(p)_T > 0\}$.

Next, we apply Theorem A.14, upon observing that the conditions on r and ϖ are satisfied (here $\underline{w} = p$). We first deduce from (A.49) and (A.50) and (B.227) that the joint CLT for the processes $u_n^p\Delta_n^{1-p/2}J([g_p,k];k\Delta_n,u_n)$ and $u_n^p\Delta_n^{1-p/2}J(g_p;\Delta_n,u_n)$ and $u_n^p\Delta_n^{1-p/2}J(g_p;k\Delta_n,u_n)$ is the same as the joint CLT for the processes $B'([f,k],\Delta_n,u_n)$ and $B'(f,\Delta_n,u_n)$ and $B'(f,k\Delta_n,u_n)$. Second, we deduce from the same theorem that the CLT for the latter is the same as if X were continuous. Therefore Step 1 of the proof of Theorem 12.5 gives (b).

We now turn to (c), and assume (L) with some β. By our usual argument, proving (13.5) on $\Omega_T^{(\beta)} \cap \Omega_T^{(noW)}$ amounts to proving (13.5) on $\Omega_T^{(\beta)}$, when we additionally suppose that the volatility σ_t vanishes identically. So below we assume $\sigma_t \equiv 0$.

Recall that (K-r), hence (H-r), holds for some $r < 1$, so in view of Lemma 11.8 we necessarily have $\beta < 1$ in (L). When $\varpi \leq \frac{p-1}{p}$ (hence $\varpi < \frac{1}{2}$), we thus have (ii) of (11.19), hence by (11.18) we have $u_n^\beta J(g_p; \Delta_n, u_n)_T \xrightarrow{\mathbb{P}} v_{g_p}(\beta) A_T$. The same convergence holds for $J(g_p; k\Delta_n, u_n)_T$, whatever $k \geq 2$. Moreover $J([g_p, k]; \Delta_n, u_n)_T$ is the sum of the k variables J_i^n defined in (B.221), which is $J(g_p; k\Delta_n, u_n)_T$ when $i = 0$ and otherwise have a similar structure, we deduce that $J([g_p, k]; \Delta_n, u_n)_T \xrightarrow{\mathbb{P}} k v_g(\beta) A_T$. At this point, (13.5) is obvious. □

Proof of Theorem 13.2. The claims about the asymptotic sizes of the two critical regions follows in the usual way from (b) of Theorem 13.1, plus the fact that if $V_n = B(2p, \Delta_n, u_n)_T / (B(p, \Delta_n, u_n)_T)^2$, then variables $\alpha(p, k)_i (m_m)^2 V_n / m_{2p}$ for $i = 1, 2$ converge in probability to the conditional variances of $\mathcal{S}_{(c)}^{(J-PV1)}(p, k)$ and $\mathcal{S}_{(c)}^{(J-PV1)}(p, k)$, respectively, in restriction to the set $\Omega_T^{(W)}$ (this is a consequence of (6.27)).

For the alternative consistency, we have to establish the asymptotic behavior of V_n, on the set $\Omega_T^{(\beta)}$, when (L) holds with some $\beta < 1$ (because (K-r) holds for some $r < 1$), and when $\sigma_t \equiv 0$: the argument for this is as in Step 2 of the previous proof. We use (B.227) plus the fact that $\Delta_n^{p/2-1} B'(f, \Delta_n, u_n) = B(p, \Delta_n, u_n)$ to obtain

$$V_n \leq \frac{2^p J(g_{2p}; \Delta_n, u_n)_T}{(J(g_p; \Delta_n, u_n/2)_T)^2}.$$

We also have $(lu_n/2)^\beta J(g_{lp}; \Delta_n, lu_n/2)_T \xrightarrow{\mathbb{P}} v_{g_{lp}}(\beta) A_T$ for $l = 1, 2$, again as in the previous proof. We deduce that $V_n \xrightarrow{\mathbb{P}} 0$ on the set $\Omega_T^{(\beta)}$. Since the statistics $S^{(FA-PV1)}(p, k, \Delta_n, u_n)$ and $S^{(FA-PV2)}(p, k, \Delta_n, u_n)$ converge to 1 in probability on $\Omega_T^{(\beta)}$ and $1 > k^{p/2-1}$ here, the property $\mathbb{P}(\mathcal{C}_n \cap \Omega_T^{(\beta)}) \to \mathbb{P}(\Omega_T^{(\beta)})$ follows, and the proof is complete. □

Proof of Theorem 13.4. For (b) and for (13.8) and (13.10) in restriction to $\Omega_T^{(noW)} \cap \Omega_T^{(\beta)}$, and by the usual argument, we can assume that the volatility is identically 0. Then, for these cases, the present theorem is proved exactly as Theorem 12.8. Note, however, that here we need to fulfill the condition (ii) of (B.188) with $\beta_- = \beta_+ = \beta$, for the power $p > 2$ occurring in the definition of the statistic $S^{(IA-PV)}(p, 2, \gamma, \Delta_n, u_n)$, and also for the power 2 which appears as well in this definition, and this for all $\beta \in (0, \beta_0)$. This results in the condition $\varpi \leq \frac{2}{4-\beta_0}\left(1 \wedge \frac{2-\beta_0}{\beta_0}\right)$.

For (13.8) in restriction to $\Omega_T^{(W)} \cap \Omega_T^{(\beta)}$ we apply (a) of Theorem B.20 and so we need condition (i) of (B.187) for all $\beta_- = \beta_+ = \beta \in (0, \beta_0)$. This amounts to having $\varpi \leq \frac{p-2}{2p}$, and it gives us

$$\frac{J(g_p; \Delta_n, \gamma u_n)_T}{J(g_p; \Delta_n, u_n)_T} \xrightarrow{\mathbb{P}} \gamma^{-\beta} \qquad \text{on } \Omega_T^{(W)} \cap \Omega_T^{(\beta)}.$$

For the ratio of the two terms involving g_2 we need another argument. We observe that $g_2(x) = x^2 \wedge (2-x)^+$ yields

$$\widehat{C}(\Delta_n, u_n) \leq u_n^2 J(g_2; \Delta_n, u_n) \leq \widehat{C}(\Delta_n, 2u_n), \qquad (B.228)$$

whereas $\widehat{C}(\Delta_n, u_n) \xrightarrow{\mathbb{P}} C_T$ by (6.23), hence

$$\frac{J(g_2; \Delta_n, u_n)_T}{J(g_2; \Delta_n, \gamma u_n)_T} \xrightarrow{\mathbb{P}} 1 \qquad \text{on } \Omega_T^{(W)}.$$

Therefore, the second part of (13.8) holds, under the above-specified condition on ϖ. The proof of the second part of (13.10) is similar: under $\varpi \leq \frac{p-2}{2p} \wedge \frac{1}{4}$, and since $h_i h_j$ satisfies (11.13) with an exponent equal at least to 4, we have $u_n^\beta J(h_i h_j; \Delta_n, u_n)_T \xrightarrow{\mathbb{P}} U^{i,j}$ and analogously $u_n^\beta J(h_i; \Delta_n, u_n)_T \xrightarrow{\mathbb{P}} U^i$ when $i = 1, 2$, in restriction to $\Omega_T^{(W)} \cap \Omega_T^{(\beta)}$, for some positive variables $U^{i,j}, U^i$. On the other hand, (B.228) implies $u_n^2 J(h_i; \Delta_n, u_n)_T \xrightarrow{\mathbb{P}} U^i C_T$ when $i = 3, 4$. Combining all these convergences, one readily deduces the second part of (13.10) with V equal to $\sum_{i,j=3}^{4} U^{i,j}/U^i U^j$ on the set $\Omega_T^{(W)} \cap \Omega_T^{(\beta)}$, and to 1 outside.

It remains to check that the condition on ϖ given in the theorem implies all the conditions on ϖ stated above, and the proof is complete. □

B.9 Proofs for Chapter 14

B.9.1 Proofs for Section 14.1

Proof of (14.7). As usual, we need a joint CLT for the numerator and the denominator of $S^{(\mathrm{CoJ})}(k, \Delta_n)$, which is the ratio $B(h, [k], \Delta_n)_T / k B(h, \Delta_n)_T$ and with $h(x) = (x^1 x^2)^2$ as given by (14.4). This CLT is provided by Theorem A.9, for the two-dimensional test function f with components $f^1(x_1, \ldots, x_k) = k h(x_1)$ and $f^2(x_1, \ldots, x_k) =$

$h(x_1 + \cdots + x_k)$. Recalling (A.37) and (A.38), and with the notation (A.31), an elementary calculation shows the stable convergence in law of

$$\left(\frac{1}{\sqrt{\Delta_n}} (kB(h, \Delta_n)_T - kh * \mu_T), \right.$$
$$\left. \frac{1}{\sqrt{\Delta_n}} (B(h, [k], \Delta_n)_T - kh * \mu_T) \right) \xrightarrow{\mathcal{L}-s} (\mathcal{U}_T^1, \mathcal{U}_T^2), \tag{B.229}$$

where (below $\sigma_{T_q} \Psi_{q,+}$ for example is the vector with components $(\sigma_{T_q} \Psi_{q,+})^i = \sum_{j=1}^{d'} \sigma_{T_q}^{ij} \Psi_{q,+}^j)$

$$\mathcal{U}_T^1 = 2k \sum_{q \geq 1: T_q \leq T} \Delta X_{T_q}^1 \Delta X_{T_q}^2$$
$$\times \left(\sqrt{\kappa_q} \left(\Delta X_{T_q}^2 (\sigma_{T_q-} \Psi_{q,-})^1 + \Delta X_{T_q}^1 (\sigma_{T_q-} \Psi_{q,-})^2 \right) \right.$$
$$\left. + \sqrt{1 - \kappa_q} \left(\Delta X_{T_q}^2 (\sigma_{T_q} \Psi_{q,+})^1 + \Delta X_{T_q}^1 (\sigma_{T_q} \Psi_{q,+})^2 \right) \right)$$
$$\mathcal{U}_T^2 = \mathcal{U}_T^1 + 2 \sum_{q \geq 1: T_q \leq T} \Delta X_{T_q}^1 \Delta X_{T_q}^2$$
$$\times \left(\sum_{1 \leq l < j \leq k} \left(\Delta X_{T_q}^2 (\sigma_{T_q-} \Psi_{q,l-j})^1 + \Delta X_{T_q}^1 (\sigma_{T_q-} \Psi_{q,l-j})^2 \right) \right.$$
$$\left. + \sum_{1 \leq j < l \leq k} \left(\Delta X_{T_q}^2 (\sigma_{T_q} \Psi_{q,l-j})^1 + \Delta X_{T_q}^1 (\sigma_{T_q} \Psi_{q,l-j})^2 \right) \right)$$

(recall that (T_q) is a sequence of stopping times which weakly exhausts the jumps of X, and $\kappa_q, \Psi_{q,j}, \Psi_{j\pm}$, with $q \geq 1$ and $-k+1 \leq j \leq k-1$ are defined on an extension of the space, are independent of $\mathcal{F}$ and mutually independent, with κ_q uniform on $(0,1)$, and all other variables $\mathcal{N}(0, I_{d'})$-distributed, d' being the dimension of the Brownian motion driving the process X).

Thus $\mathcal{U}_T^2 - \mathcal{U}_T^1$, being a linear combination of the variables $\Psi_{q,j}$ with no variables κ_q involved, is conditionally on $\mathcal{F}$ a centered Gaussian variable, and its conditional variance is, upon a straightforward calculation,

$$F = \frac{4k^3 - 6k^2 + 2k)(2k-1)}{3} \sum_{s \geq T} (\Delta X_s^1 \Delta X_s^2)^2 \left((\Delta X_s^1)^2 (c_{s-}^{22} + c_s^{22}) \right.$$
$$\left. + (\Delta X_s^2)^2 (c_{s-}^{11} + c_s^1) + 2\Delta X_s^1 \Delta X_s^2 (c_{s-}^{12} + c_s^{12}) \right).$$

Now, (B.229), the property $B(h, \Delta_n)_T \xrightarrow{\mathbb{P}} h * \mu_T$ and the delta method give us (14.7) with

$$\mathcal{S}^{(\text{CoJ})} = \frac{\mathcal{U}_T^2 - \mathcal{U}_T^1}{k\, h * \mu_T}$$

in restriction to the set $\Omega_T^{(Coj)} = \{h * \mu_T > 0\}$. From what precedes, we see that this variable is $\mathcal{F}$-conditionally centered Gaussian, with conditional variance given by (14.8), which is $V = F/k^2 (h * \mu_T)^2$. □

Proof of (14.6). We suppose first that, in addition to (H-2) and (P), the two components X^1 and X^2 never jump together; in other words, (A.39) holds. We are thus in a position to apply Theorem A.10, with the same two-dimensional test function f as in Step 1 above. Below we use the notation of this theorem, and in particular the processes H_t and H'_t. We deduce

$$\left(\tfrac{1}{\Delta_n} kB(h, \Delta_n)_T, \tfrac{1}{\Delta_n} B(h, [k], \Delta_n)_T \right)$$
$$\xrightarrow{\mathcal{L}-s} (k\widetilde{\mathcal{U}}^1_T + kH_T, \widetilde{\mathcal{U}}^2_T + k^2 H_T) \tag{B.230}$$

for some variables $(\widetilde{\mathcal{U}}^1_T, \widetilde{\mathcal{U}}^2_T)$. Since h and the test function f satisfy (A.37) and (A.38), and with the notation (A.29), these variables take the form

$$\widetilde{\mathcal{U}}^1_T = \sum_{q\geq 1:\, T_q\leq T} \left((\Delta X^1_{T_q} R^2_{q,0})^2 + (\Delta X^2_{T_q} R^1_{q,0})^2 \right)$$

$$\widetilde{\mathcal{U}}^2_T = k\widetilde{\mathcal{U}}^1_T + \sum_{q\geq 1:\, T_q\leq T} \left((\Delta X^1_{T_q})^2 \Big(\sum_{j,l=1}^{k} R^2_{q,j-l} 1_{\{l\neq j\}} \Big)^2 \right. \tag{B.231}$$
$$\left. + (\Delta X^2_{T_q})^2 \Big(\sum_{j,l=1}^{k} R^1_{q,j-l} 1_{\{l\neq j\}} \Big)^2 \right).$$

Note that obviously the two variables $\widetilde{\mathcal{U}}^1_T$ and $\widetilde{\mathcal{U}}'_T = \widetilde{\mathcal{U}}^2_T - k\widetilde{\mathcal{U}}^1_T$ are non-negative. They are also $\mathcal{F}$-conditionally independent, because the variables $R_{q,j}$ are $\mathcal{F}$-conditionally independent by construction when q and j vary. Furthermore, we easily deduce from (A.29) and (P) that for each q and j and for any numbers a, b, the variable $(aR^2_{q,j})^2 + (bR^1_{q,j})^2$ has $\mathcal{F}$-conditionally a density, unless $a = b = 0$, in which case it is identically 0. Recalling the process H' of (A.40), we can summarize these findings as follows:

- the variables $\widetilde{\mathcal{U}}^1_T$ and $\widetilde{\mathcal{U}}'_T$
  are $\mathcal{F}$-conditionally independent
- both have $\mathcal{F}$-conditionally a density on $\{H'_T > 0\}$ (B.232)
  and vanish on $\{H'_T = 0\}$.

Since $H_T > 0$, whereas $\widetilde{\mathcal{U}}^1_T \geq 0$ and $\widetilde{\mathcal{U}}'_T \geq 0$, we deduce from (B.230) that

$$S^{(\mathrm{CoJ})}(k, \Delta_n) \xrightarrow{\mathcal{L}-s} \widetilde{\mathcal{S}}^{(\mathrm{CoJ})} = \frac{k\widetilde{\mathcal{U}}^1_T + \widetilde{\mathcal{U}}'_T + k^2 H_T}{k\widetilde{\mathcal{U}}^1_T + k H_T}. \tag{B.233}$$

What precedes shows the first part of (14.6), and we still need to show $\mathbb{P}(\widetilde{\mathcal{S}}^{(\mathrm{CoJ})} = 1) = 0$. For this we observe that $\widetilde{\mathcal{S}}^{(\mathrm{CoJ})}$ equals k on the set $\{H'_T = 0\}$, whereas in restriction on the set $\{H'_T > 0\}$, it has $\mathcal{F}$-conditionally a density, by virtue of its form (B.233) and of the properties

(B.232) (recall that H_T is $\mathcal{F}$-measurable). Then it almost surely does not take the value 1, and this completes the proof of $\mathbb{P}(\widetilde{\mathcal{S}}^{(\mathrm{CoJ})} = 1) = 0$.

It remains to remove the additional assumption (A.39), and this is where we need Assumption (CoJ). We do as for the proof of (10.10), on page 339: since $\Omega_T^{(noCoj)} \subset \{\tau > T\}$, where $\tau = \inf(t : \Delta X_t^1 \Delta X_t^2 \neq 0)$ is the the first time of occurrence of a common jump, according to the same argument it is enough to show the existence of another semimartingale X' satisfying (H-2) and also

$$ t < \tau \;\Rightarrow\; X_t = X_t', \qquad t > 0 \;\Rightarrow\; \Delta X_t'^1 \Delta X_t'^2 = 0. \qquad (B.234) $$

We set

$$ Y_t \;=\; \Delta X_\tau \, 1_{\{\tau \le t\}}, \qquad X_t' \;=\; X_{t\wedge\tau} - Y_t + \int_{t\wedge\tau}^t \sigma_s \, dW_s. $$

By the definition of τ, (B.234) holds. So it remains to prove that X' satisfies (H-2) and (P). Since (P) is obvious, this amounts to proving that Y satisfies (H-2). Observe that if $\Gamma = \{(\omega, t, z) : \delta^1(\omega, t, z)\delta^2(\omega, t, z) \neq 0, \; t \le \tau(\omega)\}$ (a predictable set), we can rewrite Y as

$$ Y_t = (\delta \, 1_\Gamma) * \underline{p}_t = \int_0^t b_s' \, ds + (\delta \, 1_\Gamma \, 1_{\{\|\delta\|\le 1\}}) * (\underline{p} - \underline{q})_t + (\delta \, 1_\Gamma \, 1_{\{\|\delta\|>1\}}) * \underline{p}_t, $$

where $b_t' = \int_{\{\|\delta(t,z)\|\le 1\}} \delta(t, z) \, 1_\Gamma(t, z) \, \lambda(dz)$. This is always true, in the sense that the process b_t' above is always well defined and locally integrable. But under (CJ), this process b_t' is obviously locally bounded: it is then clear that Y satisfies (H-2), and the proof is complete. $\qquad\square$

Proof of Theorem 14.1. Let $\mathcal{C}_n$ and $\mathcal{C}_n'$ be the critical regions defined by (14.10). We know that $V_n \xrightarrow{\;\mathbb{P}\;} V$, hence $V_n' \xrightarrow{\;\mathbb{P}\;} V$ as well (because $w_n \to \infty$), in restriction to the set $\Omega_T^{(Coj)}$. Then, it readily follows from (14.7) that, as in all previous tests in this book, the asymptotic levels of both $\mathcal{C}_n$ and $\mathcal{C}_n'$ are equal to α for testing the null hypothesis $\Omega_T^{(Coj)}$.

Since $w_n \Delta_n \to 0$, the consistency of the critical regions $\mathcal{C}_n'$ for the alternative hypothesis is a trivial consequence of (14.6). $\qquad\square$

Proof of (14.12) and of Theorem 14.5. Equation (14.12) is nothing else than the convergence (B.230) restricted to the first component, divided by k; so it holds under the additional assumption (A.39), and without it as well (on $\Omega_T^{(noCoj)}$ of course) by the argument of the end of the proof of (14.6) above.

Since $\widehat{H}_n + \widehat{H}_n' \xrightarrow{\;\mathbb{P}\;} H_T + H_T'$ and $H_T' \ge 0$ and $H_T > 0$ (because of (P)), we have the stable convergence in law, restricted to $\Omega_T^{(noCoj)}$

of the standardized statistics $S^{(\text{NoCoJ})}/(\widehat{H}_n + \widehat{H}'_n)$ to a variable whose $\mathcal{F}$-conditional mean equals 1; the first claim of Theorem 14.5 is then obvious. Finally, in restriction to the alternative set $\Omega_T^{(Coj)}$ we still have $\widehat{H}_n + \widehat{H}'_n \overset{\mathbb{P}}{\longrightarrow} H_T + H'_T$, with a finite limit, together with the second part of (14.11). These facts clearly imply the consistency of the tests for the alternative.   □

Proof of Theorem 14.6. We use Theorem B.11 with the variables

$$Y = S_{(d-j)}^{(DiJ)} = H_T + \sum_{m \geq 1: T_m \leq T} \left((\Delta X_{T_m}^2 R_{m,0}^1)^2 + (\Delta X_{T_m}^1 R_{m,0}^1)^2 \right)$$

$$Y_n = \widehat{H}_n + \sum_{i=k_n+1}^{[T/\Delta_n]-k_n} \left((\Delta_i^n X^2 \widetilde{R}_{i,0}^{n,1})^2 + (\Delta_i^n X^1 \widetilde{R}_{i,0}^{n,1})^2 \right) 1_{\{\|\Delta_i^n X\| > u_n\}},$$

where the two-dimensional variables $\widetilde{R}_{m,0}^n$ are $\widetilde{R}_{m,0}^n = \sqrt{\kappa_m}\, \widetilde{\sigma}_{m-k_n}^n \Psi_{m-} + \sqrt{1 - \kappa_m}\, \widetilde{\sigma}_{m+1}^n \Psi_{m+}$. These are like (B.116) and (B.120), with $\gamma = \gamma_n = 1$ and $\gamma' = \gamma'_n = 0$ and $\gamma'' = H_T$ and $\gamma''_n = \widehat{H}_n$ and $k = 1$ (so $\mathcal{L} = \{(0,0)\}$) and finally the functions $g_{0,0}(x,y) = (x^2 y^1)^2 + (x^1 y^2)^2$ for $x,y \in \mathbb{R}^2$ and $g'_{0,0} \equiv 1$. The conditions of Theorem B.11 are thus satisfied with $r = 2$ and $p = 1$, and we deduce that the $\mathcal{F}$-conditional distributions Γ_n and Γ of Y_n and Y, respectively, satisfy (B.121).

As in (B.233), the law $\Gamma(\omega,.)$ admits a positive density on $(0,\infty)$ as soon as the path $t \mapsto X_t(\omega)$ has at least a jump on $[0,T]$, hence for all $\omega \in \Omega_T^{(noCoj)} \cup \Omega_T^{(Coj)}$. In the same way, $\Gamma^n(\omega,.)$ has a density as soon as at least one increment $\Delta_i^n X$ does not vanish, that is, for almost all ω. Therefore, substituting $\mathbb{R}$ with $\mathbb{R}_+$, we have (B.127) almost surely on $\Omega_T^{(noCoj)}$. It follows, again as on page 561, that the functions $x \mapsto G^x$, G_n^x which are the inverses of $x \mapsto \Gamma([0,x])$, $\Gamma_n([0,x])$ satisfy

$$\forall \varepsilon > 0, \quad \sup_{x \in [0, 1-\varepsilon]} |G_n^x - G^x| \overset{\mathbb{P}}{\longrightarrow} 0 \quad \text{on } \Omega_T^{(d-j)} \cup \Omega_T^{(Coj)}. \tag{B.235}$$

(The difference from (B.128) is due to the fact that Γ and Γ_n are supported by $\mathbb{R}_+$ here.) At this stage, one can reproduce the proof of Steps 3–5 of the proof of Theorem 10.12, page 563, upon replacing everywhere the absolute quantiles by the ordinary quantiles, upon taking $T_n = S^{(\text{NoCoJ})}(\Delta_n)/\Delta_n$ and upon arguing in restriction to the set $\Omega_T^{(noCoj)} \cup \Omega_T^{(Coj)}$ always. This leads to the first claim of Theorem 14.6.

For the second claim, about alternative consistency, we deduce from (B.235) and (B.130) that

$$\widetilde{\mathbb{P}}(Z_n^\alpha > G^{2\alpha} \mid \mathcal{F}) \overset{\mathbb{P}}{\longrightarrow} 0 \quad \text{on } \Omega_T^{(noCoj)} \cup \Omega_T^{(Coj)}.$$

Since $G^\alpha < \infty$ almost surely, we deduce that the sequence of random variables Z_n^α restricted to $\Omega_n^{(c-j)}$ is bounded in probability. Since on this set $S^{(\mathrm{NoCoJ})}(\Delta_n)$ converges in probability to a positive random variable, we readily deduce $\widetilde{\mathbb{P}}(\mathcal{C}_n \cap \Omega_T^{(Coj)}) \to \mathbb{P}(\Omega_T^{(Coj)})$, which the desired result.

$\square$

B.9.2   Proofs for Section 14.2

By the usual localization argument, we may and will assume throughout (SK-r), instead of (K-r). We write the triple (X, σ, c) as in (B.67), and $d = 1$ here. Of course, in order to accommodate σ and c together with X, we cannot assume in general that W is one-dimensional (as is stated in Section 14.2), but we may take it to be two-dimensional, and such that the two-dimensional process σ has its second component σ^2 vanishing identically, so $c_t = (\sigma_t^1)^2$. In (B.70), and we have (B.71) for some bounded and λ-integrable function J on E.

We need a sequence of stopping times weakly exhausting the jumps of X, and we make a specific choice: for each integer $m \geq 1$ we denote by $(S(m, p) : p \geq 1)$ the successive jump times of the counting (Poisson) process $\underline{p}([0, t] \times \{z : m^{-1/r} < J(z) \leq (m-1)^{1/r}\})$. Then we relabel the double sequence $(S(m, p) : m, p \geq 1)$ as a single sequence $(S_q : q \geq 1)$, which clearly exhausts the jumps of X and satisfies $0 < S_q < \infty$.

The key point is a mild extension of Theorem 8.8 (in case $\tau < \frac{1}{2}$ and $d = 1$ only), to the effect that the convergence holds *jointly* for the sequence k_n and the sequence wk_n, for any integer $w \geq 2$. This extension is explicitly proved in Jacod and Todorov (2010) and its proof, being also a straightforward extension of the proof of Theorem 13.3.3 of [JP], is thus omitted.

More specifically, let $k_n \asymp \Delta_n^{-\tau}$ and $u \asymp \Delta_n^{\varpi}$ with (in connection with a in (14.19)):

- if $a > 0$ or if $r = 0$:
$$\left\{ \begin{array}{l} 0 < \varpi < \frac{1}{2} \\ 0 < \tau < (\varpi(4 - 2r)) \wedge \frac{2-r}{r} \wedge \frac{1}{2} \\ \frac{1}{4-r} < \varpi < \frac{1}{2} \wedge \frac{1}{2r} \\ 0 < \tau < (\varpi(4 - r) - 1) \wedge \frac{1}{2}. \end{array} \right. \qquad \text{(B.236)}$$
- otherwise:

Then under (SK-r) (hence also under (K-r)) for some $r \in [0, 2)$ and for any integer $w \geq 2$ we have the following stable convergence in law:

$$\sqrt{k_n} \left(\left(\widehat{c}(S_q-; k_n, u_n) - c_{S_q-} \right), \left(\widehat{c}(S_q; k_n, u_n) - c_{S_q} \right), \right.$$
$$\left. \left(\widehat{c}(S_q-; wk_n, u_n) - c_{S_q-} \right), \left(\widehat{c}(S_q; wk_n, u_n) - c_{S_q} \right) \right)_{q \geq 1}$$
$$\overset{\mathcal{L}-s}{\longrightarrow} \sqrt{2} \left(c_{S_q-} \Psi_{q-}, c_{S_q} \Psi_{q+}, \frac{1}{w} c_{S_q-} (\Psi_{q-} + \sqrt{w-1}\, \Psi'_{q-}), \right.$$
$$\left. \frac{1}{w} c_{S_q} (\Psi_{q+} + \sqrt{w-1}\, \Psi'_{q+}) \right)_{q \geq 1}.$$
(B.237)

Next, we introduce a good deal of notation to be used for the proofs of Theorems 14.9 and 14.11. Recalling the stopping times $S(m, q)$ used to specify the sequence (S_p), for any $m \geq 1$ we denote by $\mathcal{T}_m$ the set of all p's such that $S_p = S(m', q)$ for some $q \geq 1$ and some $m' \in \{1, \ldots, m\}$. Recalling the integer $w \geq 2$, we set

$$I(n, i) = ((i-1)\Delta_n, i\Delta_n],$$
$$i(n, q) = \text{the unique integer such that } S_q \in I(n, i(n, q))$$
$$L(n, m) = \{i(n, q) : q \in \mathcal{T}_m\},$$
$$L'(n, m) = \mathbb{N}^* \backslash I(n, m)$$

and

$$\Omega_{n,t,m} = \bigcap_{p \neq q,\, p,q \in \mathcal{T}_m} \{S_p > t, \text{ or } S_p > 3wk_n \Delta_n \text{ and } |S_p - S_q| > 6wk_n \Delta_n\}.$$

We write X as $X = X' + X''$, where

$$X'_t = X_0 + \int_0^t b''_s ds + \int_0^t \sigma_s\, dW_s,$$

$$b''_t = \begin{cases} b_t + \int_{\{|\delta(t,z)|>1\}} \delta(t, z)\, \lambda(dz) & \text{if } r > 1 \\ b_t - \int_{\{|\delta(t,z)|\leq 1\}} \delta(t, z)\, \lambda(dz) & \text{if } r \leq 1, \end{cases}$$

and

$$X'' = \begin{cases} \delta * (\underline{p} - \underline{q}) & \text{if } r > 1 \\ \delta * \underline{p} & \text{if } r \leq 1. \end{cases}$$

Then, for any integer $m \geq 0$ we set

$$\Gamma_m = \{z : J(z) \leq m^{-1/r}\}, \qquad \gamma_m = \int_{\Gamma_m} J(z)\, \lambda(dz)$$
$$X'(m)_t = X_0 + \int_0^t b''(m)_s\, ds + \int_0^t \sigma_s\, dW_s,$$
$$b''(m)_t = \begin{cases} b''_t - \int_{(\Gamma_m)^c} \delta(t, z)\lambda(dz) & \text{if } r > 1 \\ b''_t & \text{if } r \leq 1 \end{cases}$$
$$X''(m) = \begin{cases} (\delta 1_{\Gamma_m}) * (\underline{p} - \underline{q}) & \text{if } r > 1 \\ (\delta 1_{\Gamma_m}) * \underline{p} & \text{if } r \leq 1 \end{cases}$$
$$Y(m)_t = (\delta 1_{(\Gamma_m)^c}) * \underline{p}_t,$$
$$\overline{Y}(m) = X'(m) + X''(m) = X - Y(m),$$
(B.238)

and

$$\Omega'_{n,t,m} = \{|\Delta_i^n \overline{Y}(m)| \leq \frac{2}{m}, \ |\Delta_i^n X'(m)| \leq u_n/2 \text{ for all } i = 1, \ldots, [t/\Delta_n]\}.$$

Note that $\Gamma_0 = E$, $b''(0) = b''$, $Y(0) = 0$, $X'(0) = X'$ and $X''(0) = X''$. When $r \leq 1$, we can also define those quantities when $m = \infty$, in which case $\Gamma_\infty = \{z : J(z) = 0\}$, $b''(\infty) = b''$, $Y(\infty) = X''$, $X'(\infty) = X'$ and $X''(\infty) = 0$. We have $k_n \Delta_n \to 0$, and $\overline{Y}(m)$ is càdlàg with jump sizes smaller than $1/m$, and $\mathbb{E}(|\Delta_i^n X'(m)|^{8(1-\varpi)}) \leq K\Delta_n^2$ (recall that $\varpi < \frac{1}{2}$ and that $b''(m)$ is bounded), implying by Markov's inequality that $\mathbb{P}(|\Delta_i^n X'(m)| > u_n/2) \leq K\Delta_n^2$. Thus, for all $t > 0$, $m \geq 1$ we have

$$\lim_{n\to\infty} \mathbb{P}(\Omega_{n,t,m}) = 1, \qquad \lim_{n\to\infty} \mathbb{P}(\Omega'_{n,t,m}) = 1. \qquad (B.239)$$

Next, we recall that the time horizon T is fixed. For $m \geq 1$ we set

$$
\begin{aligned}
M(n,m) &= L'(n,m) \cap \{k_n + 1, k_n + 2, \ldots, [T/\Delta_n] - k_n\} \\
D^n(m) &= \sum_{q \in \mathcal{T}_m, S_q \leq T} f(\Delta_{i(n,q)}^n X) \\
&\quad \times g(\widehat{c}(S_q-; k_n, u_n), \widehat{c}(S_q; k_n, u_n) \mathbf{1}_{\{|\Delta_{i(n,q)}^n X| > u_n\}} \\
\overline{D}^n(m) &= \sum_{i \in M(n,m)} f(\Delta_i^n \overline{Y}(m)) \\
&\quad \times g(\widehat{c}(k_n, u_n)_{i-k_n}, \widehat{c}(k_n, u_n)_{i+1}) \mathbf{1}_{\{|\Delta_i^n \overline{Y}(m)| > u_n\}} \\
A(m) &= \sum_{q \in \mathcal{T}_m, S_q \leq T} f(\Delta X_{S_q}) \, g(c_{S_q-}, c_{S_q}), \\
\overline{A}(m) &= A(f, g)_T - A(m) \\
G^n(m) &= D^n(m) - A(m), \\
\overline{G}^n(m) &= \overline{D}^n(m) - \overline{A}(m).
\end{aligned}
\qquad (B.240)
$$

We define $M'^n(n,m)$, $D'^n(m)$, $\overline{D}'^n(m)$, $G'^n(m)$ and $\overline{G}'^n(m)$ analogously, with wk_n instead of k_n, and finally we set

$$
\begin{aligned}
\eta_{q-}^n &= \sqrt{k_n} \left(\widehat{c}(S_q-; k_n, u_n)^n - c_{S_q-} \right), \\
\eta_{q-}^n &= \sqrt{k_n} \left(\widehat{c}(S_q; k_n, u_n) - c_{S_q} \right), \\
\eta_{q-}'^n &= \sqrt{k_n} \left(\widehat{c}(S_q-; wk_n, u_n) - c_{S_q-} \right), \\
\eta_{q-}'^n &= \sqrt{k_n} \left(\widehat{c}(S_q; wk_n, u_n) c_{S_q} \right).
\end{aligned}
$$

With all this notation, we are ready to start the proofs.

Proof of Theorem 14.9. We need several steps. Below, we assume (B.236).

Step 1. We write $\widetilde{\mathcal{U}}(m)$ and $\widetilde{\mathcal{U}}'(m)$ for the processes (14.21), when the sum is extended over all $q \in \mathcal{T}_m$ only. In this step we prove the following stable convergence in law, for each fixed m:

$$\left(\sqrt{k_n}\, G^n(m), \sqrt{k_n}\, G'^n(m)\right)$$
$$\xrightarrow{\mathcal{L}-\mathfrak{s}} \left(\widetilde{\mathcal{U}}(m)_T, \frac{1}{w}\left(\widetilde{\mathcal{U}}(m)_T + \sqrt{w-1}\,\widetilde{\mathcal{U}}'(m)_T\right)\right). \tag{B.241}$$

To this end we first observe that

$$G^n(m) = \textstyle\sum_{q\in\mathcal{T}_m,\, S_q\le T}\zeta_q^n,$$
$$G'^n(m) = \textstyle\sum_{q\in\mathcal{T}_m,\, S_q\le T}\zeta_q'^n,$$

where

$$\zeta_q^n = f(\Delta_{i(n,q)}^n X)\, g(\widehat{c}(S_q-;k_n,u_n),\widehat{c}(S_q;k_n,u_n))$$
$$\times 1_{\{|\Delta_{i(n,q)}^n X|>u_n\}} - f(\Delta X_{S_q})\, g(c_{S_q-},c_{S_q})$$
$$\zeta_q'^n = f(\Delta_{i(n,q)}^n X)\, g(\widehat{c}(S_q-;wk_n,u_n),\widehat{c}(S_q;wk_n,u_n))$$
$$\times 1_{\{|\Delta_{i(n,q)}^n X|>u_n\}} - f(\Delta X_{S_q})\, g(c_{S_q-},c_{S_q}).$$

We also set

$$\overline{\zeta}_q^n = f(\Delta X_{S_q})\big(\partial_1 g(c_{S_q-},c_{S_q})\eta_{q-}^n + \partial_2 g(c_{S_q-},c_{S_q})\eta_{q+}^n\big)$$
$$\overline{\zeta}_q'^n = f(\Delta X_{S_q})\big(\partial_1 g(c_{S_q-},c_{S_q})\eta_{q-}'^n + \partial_2 g(c_{S_q-},c_{S_q})\eta_{q+}'^n\big). \tag{B.242}$$

Recall that a sequence of càdlàg functions of the form $y_n(t) = \sum_{q\ge 1} a(q)_n 1_{\{t\ge s(q)_n\}}$ converges for the Skorokhod topology to the limit $y(t) = \sum_{q\ge 1} a(q) 1_{\{t\ge s(q)\}}$, where the sequences $s(q)_n$ and $s(q)$ indexed by q are positive strictly increasing and converging to infinity, as soon as for each q we have $s(q)_n \to s(q)$ and $a(q)_n \to a(q)$. Then, we can apply (B.237) and the definitions of $\widetilde{\mathcal{U}}(m)$ and $\widetilde{\mathcal{U}}'(m)$, plus $\mathbb{P}(S_q = T) = 0$ for all q, to deduce that

$$\sum_{q\in\mathcal{T}_m,\, S_q\le T} (\overline{\zeta}_q^n, \overline{\zeta}_q'^n) \xrightarrow{\mathcal{L}-\mathfrak{s}} \left(\widetilde{\mathcal{U}}(m)_T, \frac{1}{w}\left(\widetilde{\mathcal{U}}(m)_T + \sqrt{w-1}\,\widetilde{\mathcal{U}}'(m)_T\right)\right).$$

This and the fact that the number of $q \in \mathcal{T}_m$ such that $S_q \le T$ is finite and independent of n imply that proving (B.241) amounts to show that for each $q \in \mathcal{T}_m$ we have

$$\sqrt{k_n}\,\zeta_q^n - \overline{\zeta}_q^n \xrightarrow{\mathbb{P}} 0, \qquad \sqrt{k_n}\,\zeta_q'^n - \overline{\zeta}_q'^n \xrightarrow{\mathbb{P}} 0. \tag{B.243}$$

These two properties are proved similarly, so we only show the first one. First, $\widehat{c}(S_q\pm;k_n,u_n) = c_{S_q\pm} + \eta_{q\pm}^n/\sqrt{k_n}$, and the sequences $\eta_{q\pm}^n$ are bounded in probability for each q by (B.237). Thus a Taylor expansion of the function g yields

$$\sqrt{k_n}\, f(\Delta X_{S_q})\,\big(g(\widehat{c}(S_q-;k_n,u_n),\widehat{c}(S_q;k_n,u_n)) - g(c_{S_q-},c_{S_q})\big) - \overline{\zeta}_q^n \xrightarrow{\mathbb{P}} 0.$$

This also implies that the sequence $g(\widehat{c}(S_q-; k_n, u_n), \widehat{c}(S_q; k_n, u_n))$ is bounded in probability. Hence, by virtue of the definition of ζ_q^n, in order to obtain (B.243) it suffices to show that

$$\sqrt{k_n}\left(f(\Delta_{i(n,q)}^n X) 1_{\{\Delta_{i(n,q)}^n X| > u_n\}} - f(\Delta X_{S_q})\right) \xrightarrow{\mathbb{P}} 0,$$

which is obviously implied by the following two properties (recall $f(0) = 0$ and $f \geq 0$):

$$\begin{aligned}
\sqrt{k_n}\left(f(\Delta_{i(n,q)}^n X) - f(\Delta X_{S_q})\right) &\xrightarrow{\mathbb{P}} 0 \\
\sqrt{k_n}\, f(\Delta_{i(n,q)}^n X) 1_{\{\Delta_{i(n,q)}^n X| \leq u_n\}} &\xrightarrow{\mathbb{P}} 0.
\end{aligned} \qquad \text{(B.244)}$$

To prove this, we use (SK-r) and apply (A.67) to the process $\overline{Y}(m)$, with its improvement (A.77) relative to the filtration $(\mathcal{G}_t^{(m)} = \mathcal{G}_t^{\Gamma_m^c})$ defined by (A.76), plus the fact that the random integer $i(n,q)$ is $\mathcal{G}_0^{(m)}$-measurable, to get $\mathbb{E}(|\Delta_{i(n,q)}^n \overline{Y}(m)|^2) \leq K\Delta_n$, which yields

the sequence $\dfrac{1}{\sqrt{\Delta_n}}\Delta_{i(n,q)}^n \overline{Y}(m)$ is bounded in probability. (B.245)

We also observe that $\Delta_{i(n,q)}^n X = \Delta X_{S_q} + \Delta_{i(n,q)}^n \overline{Y}(m)$. Since (14.16) holds when $a > 0$, the function f is almost surely differentiable at the point ΔX_{S_q} by (14.19). Then the first part of (B.244) holds because of (B.245) and the property $k_n \Delta_n \to 0$, and the second part also holds on the set $\{\Delta X_{S_s} \neq 0\}$ because $\mathbb{P}(\Delta X_{S_q} \neq 0, |\Delta_{i(n,q)}^n X| \leq u_n) \to 0$. Finally, $f(x) \leq Kx^2$ when $|x| \leq 1$ by (14.19) again, so when $\Delta X_{S_q} = 0$ we have $f(\Delta_{i(n,q)}^n X) \leq K|\Delta_{i(n,q)}^n \overline{Y}(m)|^2$ for n large enough, and we conclude the second part of (B.244) on $\{\Delta X_{S_s} = 0\}$ from (B.245) again.

Step 2. In this short step we prove the theorem when $a > 0$, and also when $a = 0$ and (K-0) holds (the finite activity case for the jumps of X). For this, we observe that

$$\begin{aligned}
D(f, g; k_n, u_n, \Delta_n)_T &= D^n(m) + \overline{D}^n(m) \\
D(f, g; wk_n, u_n, \Delta_n)_T &= D'^n(m) + \overline{D}'^n(m)
\end{aligned} \qquad \text{(B.246)}$$

on the set $\Omega_{n,T,m}$.

Suppose first that $a > 0$, so $f(x) = 0$ when $|x| \leq a$. If we take $m > 2/A$ we see that on the set $\Omega'_{n,T,m}$ we have $\overline{D}^n(m) = \overline{D}'^n(m) = 0$. We also have $\widetilde{\mathcal{U}}_T = \widetilde{\mathcal{U}}(m)_T$ and $\widetilde{\mathcal{U}}'_T = \widetilde{\mathcal{U}}'(m)_T$ everywhere, as well as $\overline{A}(m) = 0$. Then the result follows from (B.239), (B.241), and (B.246).

Second, suppose that (K-0) holds. In this case, the set $\{z : J(z) > 0\}$ is λ-integrable and we can use $m = \infty$ above. Then of course $\widetilde{\mathcal{U}}_T =$

$\tilde{\mathcal{U}}(\infty)_T$ and $\tilde{\mathcal{U}}'_T = \tilde{\mathcal{U}}'(\infty)_T$ and $A(\infty) = A(f,g)_T$, whereas the first part of (B.239) still holds with $m = \infty$. Furthermore, since $\varpi < \frac{1}{2}$, we know that for all n large enough (depending on ω) we have $|\Delta_i^n \overline{X}(\infty)| = |\Delta_i^n X'| < u_n$ for all $i = 1, \dots, [T/\Delta_n]$, so that $\overline{D}^n(\infty) = \overline{D}'^n(\infty) = 0$. Then again the result follows from (B.241), and (B.246).

Step 3. Now we assume $r > 0$ and $a = 0$. Exactly as for (14.22), and by the boundedness of c_t, the properties of f in (14.19), and the property $|\Delta X_{S_q}| \leq \frac{1}{m}$ if $q \in \mathcal{T}_m$, we have for all $m \geq 1$

$$
\begin{aligned}
\widetilde{\mathbb{E}}\big(|\tilde{\mathcal{U}}_T - \tilde{\mathcal{U}}(m)_T|^2 \mid \mathcal{F}\big) &\leq \sum_{s \leq T} f(\Delta X_s) G(c_{s-}, c_s) \mathbf{1}_{\{|\Delta X_s| \leq 1/m\}} \\
&\leq K \sum_{s \leq T} |\Delta X_s|^2 \mathbf{1}_{\{|\Delta X_s| \leq 1/m\}}.
\end{aligned}
$$

This goes to 0 as $m \to \infty$ because $\sum_{s \leq T} |\Delta X_s|^2 < \infty$, and it follows that $\tilde{\mathcal{U}}(m)_T \xrightarrow{\mathbb{P}} \tilde{\mathcal{U}}_T$, and in the same way, $\tilde{\mathcal{U}}'(m)_T \xrightarrow{\mathbb{P}} \tilde{\mathcal{U}}'(1)_T$, as $m \to \infty$. Therefore, in view of (B.239), (B.241) and (B.246) it remains to prove that for all $\eta > 0$,

$$
\lim_{m \to \infty} \limsup_{n \to \infty} \mathbb{P}\big(\sqrt{k_n}\,|\overline{G}^n(m)| > \eta\big) = 0, \qquad (B.247)
$$

and the same for $\overline{G}'^n(m)$. These two properties being similar, we prove (B.247) only below.

Letting $H(n,m) = (0,T] \backslash \big(\cap_{i \in M(n,m)} I(n,i) \big)$ and $c_i^n = c_{i\Delta_n}$ and $c_i'^n = c_{(i-1)\Delta_n}$, we see that $\sqrt{k_n}\,\overline{G}^n(m) = \sum_{j=1}^{4} V(m,j)^n$, where

$$
V(m,j)^n = \begin{cases}
\sum\limits_{i=1}^{[T/\Delta_n]} \zeta(m,j)_i^n & \text{if } j = 1,2,3 \\[2mm]
-\sqrt{k_n} \sum\limits_{s \in H(n,m)} f(\Delta\overline{Y}(m)_s)\, g(c_{s-}, c_s) & \text{if } j = 4
\end{cases}
$$

with

$$
\begin{aligned}
\zeta(m,1)_i^n &= \sqrt{k_n}\, f(\Delta_i^n \overline{Y}(m)) \mathbf{1}_{\{|\Delta_i^n \overline{Y}(m)| > u_n\}} \\
&\quad \times \big(g(\widehat{c}(k_n, u_n)_{i-k_n}, \widehat{c}(k_n, u_n)_{i+1}) - g(c_i'^n, c_i^n)\big) \mathbf{1}_{\{i \in M(n,m)\}} \\
\zeta(m,2)_i^n &= \sqrt{k_n}\, \big(f(\Delta_i^n \overline{Y}(m)) \mathbf{1}_{\{|\Delta_i^n \overline{Y}(m)| > u_n\}} \\
&\quad - \sum_{s \in I(n,i)} f(\Delta\overline{Y}(m)_s)\big) g(c_i'^n, c_i^n) \mathbf{1}_{\{i \in M(n,m)\}} \\
\zeta(m,3)_i^n &= \sqrt{k_n}\, \big(\sum_{s \in I(n,i)} f(\Delta\overline{Y}(m)_s) \\
&\quad \times \big(g(c_i'^n, c_i^n) - g(c_{s-}, c_s)\big)\big) \mathbf{1}_{\{i \in M(n,m)\}}.
\end{aligned}
$$

Recalling $f(x) \leq Kx^2$ for $|x| \leq 1$, whereas $|\Delta\overline{Y}(m)_s| \leq \frac{1}{m}$ and $g(c_{s-}, c_s)$ is bounded, we see that $0 \leq -V(m,4)^n \leq K\sqrt{k_n} \sum_{s \in H(n,m)} |\Delta\overline{Y}(m)_s|^2$. Now, the compensator of the jump measure of $\overline{Y}(m)$ is the same, relative to $(\mathcal{F}_t)$, and relative to the filtration $(\mathcal{G}_t^{(m)})$ defined in Step 1. Since the random set $H(n,m)$ is $\mathcal{G}_0^{(m)}$-measurable, with length smaller than $\Delta_n(2k_n + Q(m))$, where $Q(m)$ is the $(\mathcal{G}_0^{(m)}$-measurable and finite) number of q in $\mathcal{T}_m$ such that $S_q \leq T$, we deduce

$$
\begin{aligned}
\mathbb{E}(|V(m,4)^n| \mid \mathcal{G}_0^m) &\leq K\sqrt{k_n}\, \mathbb{E}\Big(\int_{H(n,m)} ds \int_{\Gamma_m} |\delta(s,z)|^2\, \lambda(dz) \mid \mathcal{G}_0^m\Big) \\
&\leq K\sqrt{k_n}\, \Delta_n(2k_n + Q(m)).
\end{aligned}
$$

Since $k_n^{3/2}\Delta_n \to 0$, this and Markov's inequality yield $V(m,4)^n \xrightarrow{\mathbb{P}} 0$ as $n \to \infty$, for all m. Therefore (B.247) will follow, if we can prove the existence of sets $\Omega(n,m,j)$ satisfying for $j = 1,2,3$

$$
\begin{aligned}
&m \text{ large enough} \quad \Rightarrow \quad \lim_{n\to\infty} \mathbb{P}(\Omega(n,m,j)) = 1 \\
&\lim_{m\to\infty} \limsup_{n\to\infty} \mathbb{E}\Big(1_{\Omega(n,m,j)} \sum_{i=1}^{[T/\Delta_n]} |\zeta(m,j)_i^n|\Big) = 0.
\end{aligned} \tag{B.248}
$$

Step 4. In this step we prove (B.248) for $j = 1$. On the set $\Omega'_{n,T,m}$, for all $i \leq [T/\Delta_n]$ such that $|\Delta_i^n \overline{Y}(m)| > u_n$ we have $|\Delta_i^n \overline{Y}(m)| \leq |\Delta_i^n X''(m)| \leq \frac{2}{m} + \frac{u_n}{2} \leq 1$ as soon as $u_n \leq 1$ and $m \geq 4$; since $f(x) \leq Kx^2$ if $|x| \leq 1$ and g has bounded derivatives, we deduce $|\zeta(m,1)_i^n| \leq K\zeta(m,4)_i^n$, where

$$
\begin{aligned}
\zeta(m,4)_i^n &= \sqrt{k_n}\,|\Delta_i^n X''(m)|^2 \big(|\widehat{c}(k_n, u_n)_{i-k_n} - c_i'^n| \\
&\quad + |\widehat{c}(k_n, u_n)_{i+1} - c_i^n|\big) 1_{\{i \in M(n,m)\}}.
\end{aligned}
$$

Then in view of (B.239), we see that (B.248) for $j = 1$ and $\Omega(n,m,1) = \Omega_{n,T,m} \cap \Omega'_{n,T,m}$ will hold if the second part of (B.248) for $j = 4$ holds with $\Omega(n,m,4) = \Omega_{n,T,m}$.

In restriction to the $\mathcal{G}_0^{(m)}$-measurable set $\{i \in M(n,m)\}$, the variables $\widehat{c}(k_n, u_n)_{i-k_n}$, $\widehat{c}(k_n, u_n)_{i+1}$, $c_i'^n$ and c_i^n are the same as if they were computed with $\overline{Y}(m)$ instead of X. Then, using the improvement (A.77), we see that (B.89) and (B.90) hold relative to the filtration $(\mathcal{G}_t^{(m)})$, in restriction to the $\mathcal{G}_0^{(m)}$-measurable set $\{i \in M(n,m)\}\cap\Omega(n,m,4)$. So, these estimates and the property $\mathbb{E}(|c_{(i-1)\Delta_n} - c_{(i-k_n)\Delta_n}|^2 \mid \mathcal{G}_0^{(m)}) \leq Kk_n\Delta_n$, which again holds in restriction to $\{i \in M(n,m)\}$, imply that on $\{i \in M(n,m)\} \cap \Omega(n,m,4)$ we have

$$
\begin{aligned}
&\mathbb{E}(|\widehat{c}(k_n, u_n)_{i-k_n} - c_i'^n|^2 \mid \mathcal{G}_0^m) + \mathbb{E}(|\widehat{c}(k_n, u_n)_{i+1} - c_i^n|^2 \mid \mathcal{G}_{i\Delta_n}^m) \\
&\quad \leq K\big(\tfrac{1}{k_n} + k_n\Delta_n + \Delta_n^{(4-r)\varpi-1}\big) \leq \frac{K}{k_n},
\end{aligned} \tag{B.249}
$$

where the last inequality is implied by (B.236). On the other hand, (A.67) improved as above yields $\mathbb{E}(|\Delta_i^n X''(m)|^2 \mid \mathcal{G}_{(i-1)\Delta_n}^m) \leq K\Delta_n\gamma_m$

on the set $\{i \in M(n,m)\}$. Then, since $\widehat{c}(k_n, u_n)_{i-k_n} - c_i'^n$ and $\Delta_i^n X''(m)$ are measurable with respect to $\mathcal{G}_{(i-1)\Delta_n}^m$ and $\mathcal{G}_{i\Delta_n}^m$, respectively, we obtain by successive conditioning and Cauchy-Schwarz inequality that $\mathbb{E}(\zeta(m,4)_i^n 1_{\Omega(n,m,4)}) \leq K\Delta_n \gamma_m$. Since $\gamma_m \to 0$ as $m \to \infty$, we deduce (B.248) for $j = 4$.

Step 5. Now we prove (B.248) for $j = 3$, with $\Omega(n,m,3) = \Omega$, so the first part is obvious. Since $|\Delta \overline{Y}(m)_s| \leq \frac{1}{m}$, as in the previous step we have $|\zeta(m,3)_i^n| \leq K(\zeta(m,5)_i^n + \zeta(m,6)_i^n)$, where

$$\begin{aligned}
\zeta(m,5)_i^n &= \sqrt{k_n} \sum_{s \in I(n,i)} |\Delta \overline{Y}(m)_s|^2 |c_{s-} - c_i'^n| \\
\zeta(m,6)_i^n &= \sqrt{k_n} \sum_{s \in I(n,i)} |\Delta \overline{Y}(m)_s|^2 |c_i^n - c_s|.
\end{aligned}$$

So it is enough to prove (B.248) for $j = 5,6$, and with $M(n,m)$ substituted with $\{1, \ldots, [T/\Delta_n]\}$. The process $|c_{s-} - c_i'^n| 1_{s > (i-1)\Delta_n}$ is predictable, hence

$$\begin{aligned}
\mathbb{E}(\zeta(m,5)_i^n) &= \sqrt{k_n}\, \mathbb{E}\Big(\int_{(i-1)\Delta_n}^{i\Delta_n} \int_{\Gamma_m} |c_{s-} - c_i'^n| \delta(s,z)^2 \underline{p}(ds, dz) \Big) \\
&= \sqrt{k_n}\, \mathbb{E}\Big(\int_{(i-1)\Delta_n}^{i\Delta_n} |c_{s-} - c_i'^n| ds \int_{\Gamma_m} \delta(s,z)^2 \lambda(dz) \Big) \\
&\leq K k_n^{1/2} \Delta_n^{3/2},
\end{aligned}$$

where the last inequality comes from (A.68). For $j = 6$ we use again (A.68) to get

$$\begin{aligned}
\mathbb{E}(\zeta(m,6)_i^n) &= \sqrt{k_n} \sum_{q \geq 1} \mathbb{E}\big(|\Delta \overline{Y}(m)_{S_q}|^2 |c_i^n - c_{S_q}| 1_{S_q \in I(n,i)} \big) \\
&\leq K k_n^{1/2} \Delta_n^{1/2} \sum_{p \geq 1} \mathbb{E}\big(|\Delta \overline{Y}(m)_{S_q}|^2 1_{S_q \in I(n,i)} \big) \\
&\leq K k_n^{1/2} \Delta_n^{3/2}.
\end{aligned}$$

Then (B.248) for $j = 5,6$ and $\Omega(n,m,j) = \Omega$, hence for $j = 3$ as well, follows because $k_n \Delta_n \to 0$.

Step 6. Now we start proving (B.248) for $j = 2$. Set

$$\begin{aligned}
\zeta(m,7)_i^n &= \sqrt{k_n}\, g(c_i'^n, c_i^n) \Big(f(\Delta_i^n \overline{Y}(m)) 1_{\{\Delta_i^n \overline{Y}(m)| > u_n\}} \\
&\quad - \sum_{s \in I(n,i)} f(\Delta \overline{Y}(m)_s) 1_{\{\Delta \overline{Y}(m)_s| > u_n\}} \Big).
\end{aligned}$$

We have

$$\begin{aligned}
|\zeta(m,2)_i^n - \zeta(m,7)_i^n| &\leq K \sqrt{k_n} \sum_{s \in I(n,i)} |\Delta \overline{Y}(m)_s|^2 1_{\{|\Delta \overline{Y}(m)_s| \leq u_n\}} \\
&\leq K k_n^{1/2} u_n^{2-r} \sum_{s \in I(n,i)} |\Delta X_s|^r,
\end{aligned}$$

and $\mathbb{E}\big(\sum_{s\in I(n,i)} |\Delta X_s|^r\big) \leq K\Delta_n$ by (SH-r). Since $\tau < \varpi(4 - 2r)$ we deduce that

$$\lim_{n\to\infty} \mathbb{E}\Big(\sum_{i=1}^{[T/\Delta_n]} |\zeta(m,2)_i^n - \zeta(m,7)_i^n| \Big) = 0$$

and it remains to prove (B.248) for $j = 7$.

Step 7. This step is devoted to an auxiliary result, for which m and some number $l \in (1, 1/2r\varpi)$ are *fixed* (this is possible by (B.236)). We also suppose that m is large enough, so that $\gamma_m \leq 1$. We will be mainly concerned with the process $\overline{Y}(m)$, so we freely use the filtration $(\mathcal{G}_t^m)$ instead of $(\mathcal{F}_t)$ below, which does not change the characteristics of the semimartingale $\overline{Y}(m)$. We write $v_n = [(u_n)^{-l}]$. Since $u_n \to 0$ and $u_n v_n \to \infty$ and $\Delta_n v_n^r \to 0$, we can and will also suppose below that n is big enough for having $1/v_n < u_n < 1/m$ and $\Delta_n v_n^r \leq 1$. We complement the notation (B.238) with

$$\begin{aligned}
&\Gamma_n' = \Gamma_m \cap (\Gamma_{v_n})^c = \{v_n^{-1/r} < J \leq m^{-1/r}\}, \\
&Y^n = (\delta\,1_{\Gamma_n'}) * \underline{p}, \qquad Z^n = (J^{1/r}\,1_{\Gamma_n'}) * \underline{p}, \\
&b_t^n = \begin{cases} -\int_{\Gamma_n'} \delta(t,z)\,\lambda(dz) & \text{if } r > 1 \\ 0 & \text{if } r \leq 1, \end{cases} \\
&B_t^n = \int_0^t b_s^n\,ds, \qquad N_t^n = \underline{p}([0,t] \times \Gamma_n'), \\
&\overline{Y}^n = \overline{Y}(m) - Y^n = X'(m) + X''(v_n) + B^n \\
&G(n,i) = \big\{|\Delta_i^n \overline{Y}^n| \leq \tfrac{u_n}{2}\big\} \cap \big\{\Delta_i^n N^n \leq 1\big\}.
\end{aligned} \qquad (B.250)$$

First, N^n is a Poisson process with parameter $\lambda(\Gamma_n') \leq K\gamma_m v_n^r$, hence

$$\mathbb{P}(\Delta_i^n N^n \geq 2 \mid \mathcal{G}_{(i-1)\Delta_n}^{(m)}) \leq (\Delta_n \lambda(\Gamma_n'))^2 \leq K\Delta_n^{2-2rl\varpi}. \qquad (B.251)$$

Second, we have $\Delta_n v_n^r \leq \Delta_n^{1-rl\varpi} \leq 1$ and $|b_t^n| \leq v_n^{r-1}\gamma_m$ when $r > 1$ and $b_t^n = 0$ if $r \leq 1$ and $|b''(m)_t| \leq Km$. Then by (A.74), strengthened according to (A.77), we have after a simple calculation, and as soon as $\Delta_n \leq 1/m^2$, so $m\Delta_n^p \leq \Delta_n^{p/2}$ for all $p \geq r$,

$$\mathbb{E}(|\Delta_i^n \overline{Y}^n|^p \mid \mathcal{G}_{(i-1)\Delta_n}^{(v_n)}) \leq K_p(\Delta_n^{p/2} + \Delta_n^{1+(p-r)l\varpi}). \qquad (B.252)$$

This applied with p large enough and Markov's inequality yield

$$\mathbb{P}(|\Delta_i^n \overline{Y}^n| > u_n/2) \leq K\Delta_n^2. \qquad (B.253)$$

Next, on the set $G(n,i)$, we have $|\Delta_i^n \overline{Y}^n| \leq u_n/2$ and $|\Delta_i^n Y^n| \leq 1/m$, and also $|\Delta \overline{Y}(m)_s| \leq u_n$ for all $s \in I(n,i)$, except possibly when

$\Delta_i^n N^n = 1$, in which case this may fail for a single value of s for which $\Delta \overline{Y}(m)_s = \Delta_i^n Y^n$ (whose absolute value may be smaller or greater than u_n). In other words, on $G(n,i)$ we have

$$\zeta(m,7)_i^n = \sqrt{k_n}\, g(c_i'^n, c_i^n)\Big(f(\Delta_i^n Y^n + \Delta_i^n \overline{Y}^n) 1_{\{|\Delta_i^n Y^n + \Delta_i^n \overline{Y}^n| > u_n\}}$$
$$-f(\Delta_i^n Y^n) 1_{\{|\Delta_i^n Y^n| > u_n\}}\Big) 1_{\{|\Delta_i^n Y^n| \leq 1/m, |\Delta_i^n \overline{Y}^n| \leq u_n/2\}}.$$

The following estimate, when $u \in (0, 1/m)$, is easy to prove, upon using (14.19):

$$|x| \leq \tfrac{1}{m},\ |x'| \leq \tfrac{u}{2}$$
$$\Rightarrow \big|f(x+x')1_{\{|x+x'|>u\}} - f(x)1_{\{|x|>u\}}\big| \leq K\big(|x|\,|x'| + (|x| \wedge u)^2\big).$$

Therefore, since c and thus $g(c_i'^n, c_i^n)$ are bounded,

$$|\zeta(m,7)_i^n| \leq K\sqrt{k_n}\,\big(|\Delta_i^n Y^n|\,|\Delta_i^n \overline{Y}^n| + (|\Delta_i^n Y^n| \wedge u_n)^2\big) \qquad (B.254)$$

on $G(n,i)$.

Apply (A.75) with $p = 2$ and $\chi = \varpi$ to obtain

$$\mathbb{E}\big((|\Delta_i^n Y^n| \wedge u_n)^2 \mid \mathcal{G}_{(i-1)\Delta_n}^{(m)}\big) \leq K\Delta_n^{1+(2-r)\varpi}.$$

On the other hand, $\mathbb{E}(|\Delta_i^n \overline{Y}^n| \mid \mathcal{G}_{(i-1)\Delta_n}^{(v_n)}) \leq K\sqrt{\Delta_n}$ follows from (B.252) with $p = 2$ and the Cauchy-Schwarz inequality. We also have $|\Delta_i^n Y^n| \leq \Delta_i^n Z^n$ and $\Delta_i^n Z^n$ is $\mathcal{G}_0^{(v_n)}$-measurable; moreover Z^n has the same form as the process Z of (A.74), with the same J as here, and with $r = 1$ and $w = \sup J$ and $\alpha \leq K v_n^{(r-1)^+}$, hence $\mathbb{E}(|\Delta_i^n Z^n|) \leq K\Delta_n^{1-(r-1)^+ l\varpi}$. Thus

$$\mathbb{E}(|\Delta_i^n Y^n|\,|\Delta_i^n \overline{Y}^n|) \leq \mathbb{E}\Big(\Delta_i^n Z^n\, \mathbb{E}(|\Delta_i^n \overline{Y}^n| \mid \mathcal{G}_{(i-1)\Delta_n}^{(v_n)})\Big)$$
$$\leq K\Delta_n^{3/2-(r-1)^+ l\varpi}.$$

Putting all these estimates together, we deduce from (B.254) that

$$\mathbb{E}\big(|\zeta(m,7)_i^n| 1_{G(n,i)}\big) \leq K\sqrt{k_n}\,\big(\Delta_n^{1+(2-r)\varpi} + \Delta_n^{3/2-(r-1)^+ l\varpi}\big). \quad (B.255)$$

Step 8. Now we are ready to prove (B.248) for $j = 7$. We take $\Omega(n,m,7) = \cap_{1\leq i\leq [T/\Delta_n]} G(n,i)$. Putting together (B.251), (B.253) and (B.255), and recalling $2rl\varpi < 1$, we get

$$\mathbb{P}(\Omega(n,m,7)^c) \leq \sum_{i=1}^{[T/\Delta_n]} \mathbb{P}(G(n,i)^c) \leq KT(\Delta_n + \Delta_n^{1-2rl\varpi})$$
$$\mathbb{E}\Big(1_{\Omega(n,m,7)} \sum_{i=1}^{[T/\Delta_n]} |\zeta(m,7)_i^n|\Big) \leq \sum_{i=1}^{[T/\Delta_n]} \mathbb{E}(|\zeta(m,7)_i^n| 1_{G(n,i)})$$
$$\leq K\sqrt{k_n}\,T(\Delta_n^{(2-r)\varpi} + \Delta_n^{1/2-(r-1)^+ l\varpi})$$

The first expression goes to 0 because $l < 1/2r\varpi$; the second goes to 0 for an appropriate choice of l, because when l decreases to 1, then $1 - 2(r - 1)^+l\varpi \to 1 - 2(r - 1)^+\varpi$, which is bigger than τ by (B.236). Thus (B.248) holds for $j = 7$, and the proof is complete.   □

Proof of Theorem 14.11. The proof is basically the same as the previous one. We assume (B.236) and (SK-r), as before.

Step 1. For any $w \geq 1$ we write $\widetilde{\mathcal{U}}(w, m)$ for the processes (14.24), when the sum is extended over all $q \in \mathcal{T}_m$ only. The aim of this step is to prove that, for each fixed m, and with the notation (B.240):

$$(k_n D^n(m), k_n D'^n(m)) \xrightarrow{\mathcal{L}-\mathrm{s}} (\widetilde{\mathcal{U}}(1, m)_T, (\widetilde{\mathcal{U}}(w, m)_T) \qquad (B.256)$$

on the set $\Omega_T^{(A,dj)}$. For this, we follow the argument of Step 1 of the previous proof, with a few changes. Since $g(y, y) = 0$ and $f(x) = 0$ when $x \notin A$, we now have $G^n(m) = D^n(m)$ and $G'^n(m) = D'^n(m)$ on $\Omega_T^{(A,dj)}$. We define ζ_q^n and $\zeta_q'^n$ as before, and replace (B.242) by

$$\overline{\zeta}_q^n = \tfrac{1}{2} f(\Delta X_{S_q}) \left(\partial_{11}^2 g(c_{S_q-}, c_{S_q})(\eta_{q-}^n)^2 + \partial_{22}^2 g(c_{S_q-}, c_{S_q})(\eta_{q+}^n)^2 \right.$$
$$\left. + 2\partial_{12}^2 g(c_{S_q-}, c_{S_q})\eta_{q-}^n \eta_{q+}^n \right)$$
$$\overline{\zeta}_q'^n = \tfrac{1}{2} f(\Delta X_{S_q}) \left(\partial_{11}^2 g(c_{S_q-}, c_{S_q})(\eta_{q-}'^n)^2 + \partial_{22}^2 g(c_{S_q-}, c_{S_q})(\eta_{q+}'^n)^2 \right.$$
$$\left. + 2\partial_{12}^2 g(c_{S_q-}, c_{S_q})\eta_{q-}'^n \eta_{q+}'^n \right).$$

Then, we have

$$\sum_{q \in \mathcal{T}_m, S_q \leq T} (\overline{\zeta}_q^n, \overline{\zeta}_q'^n) \xrightarrow{\mathcal{L}-\mathrm{s}} (\widetilde{\mathcal{U}}(1, m)_T, \widetilde{\mathcal{U}}(w, m)_T),$$

and it is thus enough to prove the following, instead of (B.243):

$$k_n \zeta_q^n - \overline{\zeta}_q^n \xrightarrow{\mathbb{P}} 0, \qquad k_n \zeta_q'^n - \overline{\zeta}_q'^n \xrightarrow{\mathbb{P}} 0,$$

on the set $\Omega_T^{(A,dj)} \cap \{S_q \leq T\}$.

Once more, only the first part of (B.243) will be proved. Recall that $g(y, y) = \partial_j g(y, y) = 0$, whereas $c_{S_q-} = c_{S_q}$ when $f(\Delta X_{S_q}) > 0$, on the set $\Omega_T^{(A,dj)} \cap \{S_q \leq T\}$. So, now, we use a second order Taylor expansion to get

$$k_n f(X_{S_q}) g(\widehat{c}(S_q-; k_n, u_n), \widehat{c}(S_q; k_n, u_n)) - \overline{\zeta}_q^n \xrightarrow{\mathbb{P}} 0$$

on the set $\Omega_T^{(A,dj)} \cap \{S_q \leq T\}$, and it remains to prove that, instead of (B.244),

$$k_n \left(f(\Delta_{i(n,q)}^n X) - f(\Delta X_{S_q}) \right) \xrightarrow{\mathbb{P}} 0,$$
$$k_n f(\Delta_{i(n,q)}^n X) 1_{\{\Delta_{i(n,q)}^n X| \leq u_n\}} \xrightarrow{\mathbb{P}} 0.$$

This is proved exactly as (B.244), upon using $k_n\sqrt{\Delta_n} \to 0$ instead of $k_n\Delta_n \to 0$.

At this stage, we deduce that our theorem holds when $a > 0$, or when $r = 0$, in exactly the same way as in Step 2 of the previous proof.

Step 2. From now on, we assume $r > 0$ and $a = 0$. We prove $\widetilde{\mathcal{U}}(w, m)_T \xrightarrow{\;\mathbb{P}\;}$ $\widetilde{\mathcal{U}}(w)_T$ for any integer w as in Step 3 of the previous proof, and, instead of (B.247), it thus remains to show that for all $\eta > 0$,

$$\lim_{m\to\infty} \limsup_{n\to\infty} \mathbb{P}\big(\{k_n\,|\overline{G}^{\,n}(m)| > \eta\} \cap \Omega_T^{(A,dj)}\big) = 0, \qquad (\text{B.257})$$

and the same for $\overline{G}^{\,\prime n}(m)$, and again we prove (B.247) only.

We have $\overline{G}^{\,n}(m) = \overline{D}^{\,n}(m)$ on $\Omega_T^{(A,dj)}$. Therefore, with the notation

$$\rho(m,1)_i^n = k_n\,f(\Delta_i^n\overline{Y}(m))\,1_{\{\Delta_i^n\overline{Y}(m)|>u_n\}}$$
$$\times g(\widehat{c}(k_n,u_n)_{i-k_n},\widehat{c}(k_n,u_n)_{i+1})\,1_{\{i\in M(n,m)\}},$$

it remains to prove the existence of sets $\Omega(n,m,1)$ such that the following holds for $j = 1$:

$$\Omega(n,m,1) \subset \Omega_T^{(A,dj)}$$
$$m \text{ large enough} \quad\Rightarrow\quad \lim_{n\to\infty}\mathbb{P}(\Omega(n,m,j)) = \mathbb{P}(\Omega_T^{(A,dj)}) \qquad (\text{B.258})$$
$$\lim_{m\to\infty}\limsup_{n\to\infty}\mathbb{E}\Big(1_{\Omega(n,m,j)}\sum_{i=1}^{[T/\Delta_n]}|\rho(m,j)_i^n|\Big) = 0.$$

On $\Omega'_{n,T,m}$, arguing as for $\zeta(m,1)_i^n$ in Step 4 of the previous proof, plus a Taylor expansion of g around the points of the diagonal, together with $g(y,y) = \partial_i g(y,y) = 0$, we see that for all $i \le [T/\Delta_n]$ we have $|\rho(m,1)_i^n| \le K(\rho(m,2)_i^n + \rho(m,3)_i^n)$, where

$$\rho(m,2)_i^n = k_n\,|\Delta_i^n X''(m)|^2\big(|\widehat{c}(k_n,u_n)_{i-k_n} - c_i'^n|^2$$
$$+ |\widehat{c}(k_n,u_n)_{i+1} - c_i^n|^2\big)1_{\{i\in M(n,m)\}}$$
$$\rho(m,3)_i^n = k_n\,|\Delta_i^n X''(m)|^2\,|\Delta_i^n c|^2.$$

Hence, in view of (B.239), and upon taking $\Omega(n,m,1) = \Omega(n,m,2) \cap \Omega(n,m,3) \cap \Omega'_{n,T,m}$ we are left to prove that (B.258) holds for $j = 2,3$, for suitable sets $\Omega(n,m,j)$.

For $j = 2$, this is proved as in Step 4 of the previous proof, with $\Omega(n,m,2) = \Omega_{n,T,m} \cap \Omega_T^{(A,dj)}$: indeed, we have (B.249), and successive conditioning yields $\mathbb{E}(\rho(m,2)_i^n\,1_{\Omega(n,m,2)}) \le K\Delta_n\gamma_m$. Using $\gamma_m \to 0$ as $m \to \infty$ and (B.239), we deduce (B.258) for $j = 2$.

Step 3. At this stage it remains to show (B.258) for $j = 3$, and we will prove the stronger claim

$$\mathbb{E}\Big(1_{\Omega_T^{(A,dj)}} \sum_{i=1}^{[T/\Delta_n]}|\rho(m,3)_i^n|\Big) \to 0 \qquad (\text{B.259})$$

as $n \to \infty$, for each m. So below we *fix* m. We take $l = 1/r\varpi$, and use the notation $v_n = [(u_n)^{-l}]$ and (B.250), and for simplicity later we also write

$$Z(4)^n = B^n, \quad Z(5)^n = X''(v_n), \quad Z(6)^n = Y^n,$$

so $X''(m) = \sum_{j=4}^{6} Z(j)^n$, and we associate the variables

$$\rho(m,j)_i^n = k_n \, |\Delta_i^n Z(j)|^2 \, |\Delta_i^n c|^2.$$

It is thus enough to prove (B.259) when $j = 4, 5, 6$. First, we have $|\Delta_i^n Z(4)^n| \le K\Delta_n^{1-l\varpi(r-1)^+}$ and thus by (A.68) we get $\mathbb{E}(\rho(m,4)_i^n) \le K\Delta_n^{2-l(r-1)^+\varpi}$, and (B.259) for $j = 4$ holds.

Next, we can apply (B.252) with $X''(v_n)$ instead of $\overline{Y}^n$, with the effect of dropping the first summand on the right side. Thus $\mathbb{E}(|\Delta_i^n Z(5)|^p) \le K_p\Delta_n^{1+(p-r)l\varpi} = K_p\Delta_n^{p/r}$ for all $p \ge r$. This and (A.68) and Hölder's inequality yield that, for any $\theta > 0$, we have $\mathbb{E}(\rho(m,5)_i^n) \le K_\theta k_n \Delta_n^{1+2/r-\theta}$. Since $\tau < 1 < 2/r$, we deduce (B.259) for $j = 5$.

Finally, we set $Y(n,i)_t = \sum_{(i-1)\Delta_n < s \le t} |\Delta Y_s^n|$ for $t \in I(n,i)$. Observe that

$$|\Delta_i^n Z(6)^n|^2 \le Y(n,i)_{\Delta_n}^2 = \sum_{s \in I(n,i)} \left(|\Delta Y_s^n|^2 + 2Y(n,i)_{s-}|\Delta Y_s^n| \right).$$

Thus, since $\Delta c_s = 0$ when $\Delta Y_s^n \ne 0$ for all $s \le T$ on the set $\Omega_T^{(A,dj)}$, we see that

$$\rho(m,6)_i^n \le K(\rho(m,7)_i^n + \rho(m,8)_i^n + \rho(m,9)_i^n)$$

for all $i \le [T/\Delta_n]$ on this set, where

$$\rho(m,7)_i^n = k_n \sum_{s \in I(n,i)} |\Delta Y_s^n|^2 \, |c_{s-} - c_i'^n|^2 + \sum_{s \in I(n,i)} |\Delta Y_s^n|^2 \, |c_i^n - c_s|^2$$

$$\rho(m,8)_i^n = k_n \sum_{s \in I(n,i)} Y(n,i)_{s-} |\Delta Y_s^n| \, |c_{s-} - c_i'^n|^2$$

$$\rho(m,9)_i^n = k_n \sum_{s \in I(n,i)} Y(n,i)_{s-} |\Delta Y_s^n| \, |c_i^n - c_s|^2,$$

and it remains to show (B.259) for $j = 7, 8, 9$.

Since $|\Delta Y_s^n| \le |\Delta \overline{Y}(m)_s|$, we have $\rho(m,7)_i^n \le \sqrt{k_n} \, (\zeta(m,5)_i^n + \zeta(m,6)_i^n)$, with the notation of the previous proof, hence by virtue of Step 5 of that proof we obtain the estimate $\mathbb{E}(\rho(m,7)_i^n) \le K k_n \Delta_n^{3/2}$, so (B.259) holds for $j = 7$ because $k_n \sqrt{\Delta_n} \to 0$. For the cases $j = 8, 9$ we use the same argument as in this Step 5 again, thus getting

$$\mathbb{E}(\rho(m,8)_i^n) \le K k_n \int_{I(n,i)} \mathbb{E}\big(Y(n,i)_{s-} |c_{s-} - c_i'^n|^2\big) \, ds \int_{\Gamma_n'} J(z) \, \lambda(dz)$$

$$\le K k_n v_n^{(r-1)^+} \int_{I(n,i)} \mathbb{E}\big(Y(n,i)_{s-} |c_{s-} - c_i'^n|^2\big) \, ds$$

and

$$\begin{aligned}
\mathbb{E}(\rho(m,9)_i^n) &\leq K k_n \Delta_n \, \mathbb{E}\left(\sum_{s \in I(n,i)} Y(n,i)_{s-}^{r-1} \, |\Delta Y_s^n| \right) \\
&\leq K k_n \Delta_n \, \mathbb{E}\left(\sup_{s \leq i\Delta_n} (Y(n,i)_s)^2 \right).
\end{aligned}$$

Observe that $Y(n,i)$ has the same form as the process Z of (A.74), with $w = 1$ and (J', r') given by $J' = J 1_{\{J > 1/v_n\}}$ and $r' = 1$, hence the number α there satisfies $\alpha \leq K v_n^{(r-1)^+}$. Since $v_n \asymp \Delta_n^{-1/r}$, we obtain

$$\mathbb{E}\left(\sup_{s \leq i\Delta_n} (Y(n,i)_s)^2 \right) \leq K \Delta_n^{1-2(r-1)^+/r}.$$

Using $\mathbb{E}(|c_{s-} - c_i'^n|^4) \leq K \Delta_n$ and Cauchy-Schwarz inequality, one deduces

$$\mathbb{E}(\rho(m,8)_i^n) + \mathbb{E}(\rho(m,9)_i^n) \leq K k_n \Delta_n^{2-2(r-1)^+/r}.$$

Then (B.259) readily follows for $j = 15, 16$ by virtue of (B.236). This completes the proof of the theorem. $\qquad\square$

Bibliography

AïT-SAHALIA, Y. (2002). Telling from discrete data whether the underlying continuous-time model is a diffusion. *The Journal of Finance*, **57** 2075–2112.

AïT-SAHALIA, Y. (2004). Disentangling diffusion from jumps. *Journal of Financial Economics*, **74** 487–528.

AïT-SAHALIA, Y., FAN, J. and LI, Y. (2013). The leverage effect puzzle: Disentangling sources of bias at high frequency. *Journal of Financial Economics*, **109** 224–249.

AïT-SAHALIA, Y. and JACOD, J. (2008). Fisher's information for discretely sampled Lévy processes. *Econometrica*, **76** 727–761.

AïT-SAHALIA, Y. and JACOD, J. (2009a). Estimating the degree of activity of jumps in high frequency financial data. *Annals of Statistics*, **37** 2202–2244.

AïT-SAHALIA, Y. and JACOD, J. (2009b). Testing for jumps in a discretely observed process. *Annals of Statistics*, **37** 184–222.

AïT-SAHALIA, Y. and JACOD, J. (2010). Is Brownian motion necessary to model high frequency data? *Annals of Statistics*, **38** 3093–3128.

AïT-SAHALIA, Y. and JACOD, J. (2011). Testing whether jumps have finite or infinite activity. *Annals of Statistics*, **39** 1689–1719.

AïT-SAHALIA, Y. and JACOD, J. (2012a). Analyzing the spectrum of asset returns: Jump and volatility components in high frequency data. *Journal of Economic Literature*, **50** 1005–1048.

AïT-SAHALIA, Y. and JACOD, J. (2012b). Identifying the successive Blumenthal-Getoor indices of a discretely observed process. *Annals of Statistics*, **40** 1430–1464.

AÏT-SAHALIA, Y., JACOD, J. and LI, J. (2012). Testing for jumps in noisy high frequency data. *Journal of Econometrics*, **168** 207–222.

AÏT-SAHALIA, Y. and MANCINI, L. (2008). Out of sample forecasts of quadratic variation. *Journal of Econometrics*, **147** 17–33.

AÏT-SAHALIA, Y. and MYKLAND, P. A. (2003). The effects of random and discrete sampling when estimating continuous-time diffusions. *Econometrica*, **71** 483–549.

AÏT-SAHALIA, Y. and MYKLAND, P. A. (2004). Estimators of diffusions with randomly spaced discrete observations: A general theory. *Annals of Statistics*, **32** 2186–2222.

AÏT-SAHALIA, Y., MYKLAND, P. A. and ZHANG, L. (2005). How often to sample a continuous-time process in the presence of market microstructure noise. *Review of Financial Studies*, **18** 351–416.

AÏT-SAHALIA, Y., MYKLAND, P. A. and ZHANG, L. (2011). Ultra high frequency volatility estimation with dependent microstructure noise. *Journal of Econometrics*, **160** 160–175.

AKGIRAY, V. and LAMOUREUX, C. G. (1989). Estimation of stable-law parameters: A comparative study. *Journal of Business and Economic Statistics*, **7** 85–93.

ALDOUS, D. (1978). Stopping times and tightness. *Annals of Probability*, **6** 335–340.

ALDOUS, D. J. and EAGLESON, G. K. (1978). On mixing and stability of limit theorems. *Annals of Probability*, **6** 325–331.

ALVAREZ, A., PANLOUP, F., PONTIER, M. and SAVY, N. (2012). Estimation of the instantaneous volatility. *Statistical Inference for Stochastic Processes*, **15** 27–50.

ANDERSEN, T. G. and BENZONI, L. (2009). Realized volatility. In *Handbook of Financial Time Series* (T. G. Andersen, R. A. Davis, J.-P. Kreiss and T. Mikosch, eds.). Springer-Verlag, 555–575.

ANDERSEN, T. G. and BOLLERSLEV, T. (1998). Answering the skeptics: Yes, standard volatility models do provide accurate forecasts. *International Economic Review*, **39** 885–905.

ANDERSEN, T. G., BOLLERSLEV, T., DIEBOLD, F. X. and LABYS, P. (2001). The distribution of exchange rate realized volatility. *Journal of the American Statistical Association*, **96** 42–55.

ANDERSEN, T. G., BOLLERSLEV, T., DIEBOLD, F. X. and LABYS, P. (2003). Modeling and forecasting realized volatility. *Econometrica*, **71** 579–625.

ANDERSEN, T. G., BOLLERSLEV, T. and DOBREV, D. (2007). No-arbitrage semimartingale restrictions for continuous-time volatility models subject to leverage effects, jumps and i.i.d. noise: Theory and testable distributional implications. *Journal of Econometrics*, **138** 125–180.

ANDERSEN, T. G., BOLLERSLEV, T. and MEDDAHI, N. (2004). Analytic evaluation of volatility forecasts. *International Economic Review*, **45** 1079–1110.

ANDERSEN, T. G., BOLLERSLEV, T. and MEDDAHI, N. (2005). Correcting the errors: Volatility forecast evaluation using high frequency data and realized volatilities. *Econometrica*, **73** 279–296.

ANDERSEN, T. G., BOLLERSLEV, T. and MEDDAHI, N. (2011). Market microstructure noise and realized volatility forecasting. *Journal of Econometrics*, **160** 220–234.

ANDERSEN, T. G., DOBREV, D. and SCHAUMBURG, E. (2012). Jump-robust volatility estimation using nearest neighbor truncation. *Journal of Econometrics*, **169** 75–93.

ANDREOU, E. and GHYSELS, E. (2002). Rolling-sample volatility estimators: Some new theoretical, simulation, and empirical results. *Journal of Business and Economic Statistics*, **20** 363–376.

BALL, C. A. and TOROUS, W. N. (1983). A simplified jump process for common stock returns. *Journal of Financial and Quantitative Analysis*, **18** 53–65.

BALL, C. A. and TOROUS, W. N. (1984). The maximum likelihood estimation of security price volatility: Theory, evidence, and applications to option pricing. *Journal of Business*, **57** 97–112.

BANDI, F. M. and RENÒ, R. (2011). Nonparametric stochastic volatility. Tech. rep., Johns Hopkins University.

BANDI, F. M. and RENÒ, R. (2012). Time-varying leverage effects. *Journal of Econometrics*, **169** 94–113.

BANDI, F. M. and RENÒ, R. (2013). Price and volatility co-jumps. Tech. rep., Johns Hopkins University.

BANDI, F. M. and RUSSELL, J. R. (2008). Microstructure noise, realized volatility and optimal sampling. *Review of Economic Studies*, **75** 339–369.

BANDI, F. M. and RUSSELL, J. R. (2011). Market microstructure noise, integrated variance estimators, and the accuracy of asymptotic approximations. *Journal of Econometrics*, **160** 145–159.

BANDI, F. M., RUSSELL, J. R. and YANG, C. (2008). Realized volatility forecasting and option pricing. *Journal of Econometrics*, **147** 34–46.

BARNDORFF-NIELSEN, O. E. (1977). Exponentially decreasing distributions for the logarithm of particle size. *Proceedings of the Royal Society of London, A*, **353** 401–419.

BARNDORFF-NIELSEN, O. E. (1998). Processes of normal inverse Gaussian type. *Finance and Stochastics*, **2** 41–68.

BARNDORFF-NIELSEN, O. E., GRAVERSEN, S. E., JACOD, J., PODOLSKIJ, M. and SHEPHARD, N. (2006). A central limit theorem for realised bipower variations of continuous semimartingales. In *From Stochastic Calculus to Mathematical Finance, The Shiryaev Festschrift* (Y. Kabanov, R. Liptser and J. Stoyanov, eds.). Springer-Verlag, 33–69.

BARNDORFF-NIELSEN, O. E., HANSEN, P. R., LUNDE, A. and SHEPHARD, N. (2008). Designing realized kernels to measure ex-post variation of equity prices in the presence of noise. *Econometrica*, **76** 1481–1536.

BARNDORFF-NIELSEN, O. E., HANSEN, P. R., LUNDE, A. and SHEPHARD, N. (2011). Multivariate realised kernels: Consistent positive semi-definite estimators of the covariation of equity prices with noise and non-synchronous trading. *Journal of Econometrics*, **162** 149–169.

BARNDORFF-NIELSEN, O. E. and SHEPHARD, N. (2002). Econometric analysis of realized volatility and its use in estimating stochastic volatility models. *Journal of the Royal Statistical Society, B*, **64** 253–280.

BARNDORFF-NIELSEN, O. E. and SHEPHARD, N. (2004). Power and bipower variation with stochastic volatility and jumps. *Journal of Financial Econometrics*, **2** 1–37.

BARNDORFF-NIELSEN, O. E. and SHEPHARD, N. (2005). Power variation and time change. *Theory of Probability and Its Applications*, **50** 1–15.

BARNDORFF-NIELSEN, O. E. and SHEPHARD, N. (2006). Econometrics of testing for jumps in financial economics using bipower variation. *Journal of Financial Econometrics*, **4** 1–30.

BASAWA, I. V. and BROCKWELL, P. J. (1982). Nonparametric estimation for nondecreasing Lévy processes. *Journal of the Royal Statistical Society, B*, **44** 262–269.

BATES, D. S. (1991). The crash of '87: Was it expected? The evidence from options markets. *The Journal of Finance*, **46** 1009–1044.

BAUWENS, L. and GIOT, P. (2001). *Econometric Modeling of Stock Market Intraday Activity*. Kluwer.

BAUWENS, L. and HAUTSCH, N. (2009). Modelling financial high frequency data using point processes. In *Handbook of Financial Time Series* (T. G. Andersen, R. A. Davis, J.-P. Kreiss and T. Mikosch, eds.). Springer-Verlag, 953–982.

BELOMESTNY, D. (2010). Spectral estimation of the fractional order of a Lévy process. *Annals of Statistics*, **38** 317–351.

BIAIS, B., GLOSTEN, L. and SPATT, C. (2005). Market microstructure: A survey of microfoundations, empirical results, and policy implications. *Journal of Financial Markets*, **8** 217–264.

BIBINGER, M. (2012). An estimator for the quadratic covariation of asynchronously observed Itô processes with noise: Asymptotic distribution theory. *Stochastic Processes and Their Applications*, **6** 2411–2453.

BIBINGER, M., HAUTSCH, N., MALEC, P. and REISS, M. (2013). Estimating the quadratic covariation matrix from noisy observations: Local method of moments and efficiency. Tech. rep., Humboldt-Universität Berlin.

BIBINGER, M. and REISS, M. (2014). Spectral estimation of covolatility from noisy observations using local weights. *Scandinavian Journal of Statistics*, **41** 23–50.

BIBINGER, M. and WINKELMANN, L. (2013). Econometrics of cojumps in highfrequency data with noise. Tech. rep., Humboldt-Universität Berlin.

BILLINGSLEY, P. (1999). *Convergence of Probability Measures*. 2nd ed. Wiley.

BLACK, F. (1976). Studies of stock price volatility changes. In *Proceedings of the 1976 Meetings of the American Statistical Association*. 171–181.

BLACK, F. (1986). Noise. *The Journal of Finance*, **41** 529–543.

BLUMENTHAL, R. M. and GETOOR, R. K. (1961). Sample functions of stochastic processes with stationary independent increments. *Journal of Mathematics and Mechanics*, **10** 493–516.

BOS, C. S., JANUS, P. and KOOPMAN, S. J. (2012). Spot variance path estimation and its application to high-frequency jump testing. *Journal of Financial Econometrics*, **10** 345–389.

BROCKWELL, P. J. and BROWN, B. (1980). High-efficiency estimation for the positive stable laws. *Journal of the American Statistical Association*, **76** 626–631.

BROWNLEES, C. T. and GALLO, G. M. (2010). Comparison of volatility measures: A risk management perspective. *Journal of Financial Econometrics*, **8** 29–56.

CAI, T. T., MUNK, A. and SCHMIDT-HIEBER, J. (2010). Sharp minimax estimation of the variance of Brownian motion corrupted with Gaussian noise. *Statistica Sinica*, **20** 1011–1024.

CAMPBELL, J. Y. and HENTSCHEL, L. (1992). No news is good news: An asymmetric model of changing volatility in stock returns. *Journal of Financial Economics*, **31** 281–318.

CARR, P., GEMAN, H., MADAN, D. B. and YOR, M. (2002). The fine structure of asset returns: An empirical investigation. *Journal of Business*, **75** 305–332.

CARR, P. and WU, L. (2003a). The finite moment log stable process and option pricing. *The Journal of Finance*, **58** 753–777.

CARR, P. and WU, L. (2003b). What type of process underlies options? A simple robust test. *The Journal of Finance*, **58** 2581–2610.

ÇINLAR, E. and JACOD, J. (1981). Representation of semimartingale Markov processes in terms of Wiener processes and Poisson random measures. In *Seminar on Stochastic Processes*. Birkhauser, Boston, 159–242.

CHRISTENSEN, K., KINNEBROCK, S. and PODOLSKIJ, M. (2010). Pre-averaging estimators of the ex-post covariance matrix in noisy diffusion models with non-synchronous data. *Journal of Econometrics*, **159** 116–133.

CHRISTENSEN, K., OOMEN, R. C. and PODOLSKIJ, M. (2011). Fact or friction: Jumps at ultra high frequency. Tech. rep., University of Heidelberg.

CHRISTENSEN, K. and PODOLSKIJ, M. (2007). Realized range-based estimation of integrated variance. *Journal of Econometrics*, **141** 323–349.

CHRISTIE, A. A. (1982). The stochastic behavior of common stock variances: Value, leverage and interest rate effects. *Journal of Financial Economics*, **10** 407–432.

CLÉMENT, E., DELATTRE, S. and GLOTER, A. (2013). An infinite dimensional convolution theorem with applications to the efficient estimation of the integrated volatility. *Stochastic Processes and Their Applications*, **123** 2500–2521.

CLÉMENT, E., DELATTRE, S. and GLOTER, A. (2014). Asymptotic lower bounds in estimating jumps. *Bernoulli, forthcoming.*

CLÉMENT, E. and GLOTER, A. (2011). Limit theorems in the Fourier transform method for the estimation of multivariate volatility. *Stochastic Processes and Applications*, **121** 1097–1124.

COMTE, F. and GENON-CATALOT, V. (2009). Nonparametric estimation for pure jump Lévy processes based on high frequency data. *Stochastic Processes and Their Applications*, **119** 4088–4123.

COMTE, F. and GENON-CATALOT, V. (2011). Estimation for Lévy processes from high frequency data within a long time interval. *Annals of Statistics*, **39** 803–837.

CONT, R. and MANCINI, C. (2011). Nonparametric tests for pathwise properties of semimartingales. *Bernoulli*, **17** 781–813.

CORRADI, V., DISTASO, W. and SWANSON, N. R. (2009). Predictive density estimators for daily volatility based on the use of realized measures. *Journal of Econometrics*, **150** 119–138.

CORRADI, V., DISTASO, W. and SWANSON, N. R. (2011). Predictive inference for integrated volatility. *Journal of the Americal Statistical Association*, **106** 1496–1512.

CORSI, F. (2009). A simple approximate long-memory model of realized volatility. *Journal of Financial Econometrics*, **7** 174–196.

CORSI, F. and AUDRINO, F. (2012). Realized covariance tick-by-tick in presence of rounded time stamps and general microstructure effects. *Journal of Financial Econometrics*, **10** 591–616.

CORSI, F., PIRINO, D. and RENÒ, R. (2010). Threshold bipower variation and the impact of jumps on volatility forecasting. *Journal of Econometrics*, **159** 276–288.

CORSI, F., ZUMBACH, G., MÜLLER, U. A. and DACOROGNA, M. M. (2001). Consistent high-precision volatility from high-frequency data. *Economic Notes*, **30** 183–204.

CUCHIERO, C. and TEICHMANN, J. (2013). Fourier transform methods for pathwise covariance estimation in the presence of jumps. Tech. rep., ETH Zurich.

DACUNHA-CASTELLE, D. and FLORENS-ZMIROU, D. (1986). Estimation of the coefficients of a diffusion from discrete observations. *Stochastics*, **19** 263–284.

DAHLHAUS, R. and NEDDERMEYER, J. C. (2013). Online spot volatility-estimation and decomposition with nonlinear market microstructure noise models. *Journal of Financial Econometrics forthcoming*.

DELATTRE, S. and JACOD, J. (1997). A central limit theorem for normalized functions of the increments of a diffusion process, in the presence of round-off errors. *Bernoulli*, **3** 1–28.

DELLACHERIE, C. and MEYER, P.-A. (1982). *Probabilities and Potential B: Theory of Martingales*. North-Holland.

DOHNAL, G. (1987). On estimating the diffusion coefficient. *Journal of Applied Probability*, **24** 105–114.

DOLÉANS, C. (1969). Variation quadratique des martingales continues à droite. *Annals of Mathematical Statistics*, **40** 284–289.

DOVONON, P., GONÇALVES, S. and MEDDAHI, N. (2013). Bootstrapping realized multivariate volatility measures. *Journal of Econometrics*, **172** 49–65.

DUFFIE, D. and GLYNN, P. (2004). Estimation of continuous-time Markov processes sampled at random time intervals. *Econometrica*, **72** 1773–1808.

DUFOUR, J.-M., GARCIA, R. and TAAMOUTI, A. (2012). Measuring high-frequency causality between returns, realized volatility, and implied volatility. *Journal of Financial Econometrics*, **10** 124–163.

DUMITRU, A.-M. and URGA, G. (2012). Identifying jumps in financial assets: A comparison between nonparametric jump tests. *Journal of Business and Economic Statistics*, **30** 242–255.

DUMOUCHEL, W. H. (1971). *Stable Distributions in Statistical Inference*. Ph.D. thesis, Department of Statistics, Yale University.

DUMOUCHEL, W. H. (1973a). On the asymptotic normality of the maximum-likelihood estimator when sampling from a stable distribution. *Annals of Statistics*, **1** 948–957.

DUMOUCHEL, W. H. (1973b). Stable distributions in statistical inference: 1. Symmetric stable distributions compared to other symmetric long-tailed distributions. *Journal of the American Statistical Association*, **68** 469–477.

DUMOUCHEL, W. H. (1975). Stable distributions in statistical inference: 2. Information from stably distributed samples. *Journal of the American Statistical Association*, **70** 386–393.

DURBIN, J. (1959). Efficient estimation of parameters in moving-average models. *Biometrika*, **46** 306–316.

EASLEY, D. and O'HARA, M. (1992). Time and the process of security price adjustment. *The Journal of Finance*, **47** 577–605.

EBERLEIN, E. and KELLER, U. (1995). Hyperbolic distributions in finance. *Bernoulli*, **1** 281–299.

EMBRECHTS, P., KLÜPPELBERG, C. and MIKOSH, T. (1997). *Modelling Extremal Events*. Springer-Verlag.

ENGLE, R. F. and NG, V. K. (1993). Measuring and testing the impact of news on volatility. *The Journal of Finance*, **48** 1749–1778.

ENGLE, R. F. and RUSSELL, J. R. (1998). Autoregressive conditional duration: A new model for irregularly spaced transaction data. *Econometrica*, **66** 1127–1162.

ETHIER, S. N. and KURTZ, T. G. (1986). *Markov Processes: Characterization and Convergence*. John Wiley and Sons.

FAMA, E. F. (1965). The behavior of stock market prices. *Journal of Business*, **38** 34–105.

FAN, J. and WANG, Y. (2008). Spot volatility estimation for high-frequency data. *Statistics and Its Interface*, **1** 279–288.

FAN, Y. and FAN, J. (2011). Testing and detecting jumps based on a discretely observed process. *Journal of Econometrics*, **164** 331–344.

FELLER, W. (1951). The asymptotic distribution of the range of sums of independent random variables. *The Annals of Mathematical Statistics*, **22** 427–432.

FENECH, A. P. (1976). Asymptotically efficient estimation of location for a symmetric stable law. *Annals of Statistics*, **4** 1088–1100.

FEUERVERGER, A. and McDUNNOUGH, P. (1981a). On efficient inference in symmetric stable laws and processes. In *Statistics and Related Topics* (M. Csörgö, D. A. Dawson, J. Rao and A. Saleh, eds.). North Holland, 109–122.

FEUERVERGER, A. and McDUNNOUGH, P. (1981b). On the efficiency of empirical characteristic function procedures. *Journal of the Royal Statistical Society, B*, **43** 20–27.

FIGLEWSKI, S. and WANG, X. (2000). Is the "leverage effect" a leverage effect? Tech. rep., New York University.

FIGUEROA-LÓPEZ, J. (2009). Nonparametric estimation for Lévy models based on discrete-sampling. In *Optimality: The Third Erich L. Lehmann Symposium* (J. Rojo, ed.), vol. 57. IMS Lecture Notes – Monograph Series, 117–146.

FIGUEROA-LÓPEZ, J. and HOUDRÉ, C. (2006). Risk bounds for the non-parametric estimation of Lévy processes. In *High Dimensional Probability* (E. Giné, V. Koltchinskii, W. Li and J. Zinn, eds.), vol. 51. IMS Lecture Notes – Monograph Series, 96–116.

FIGUEROA-LÓPEZ, J. E. and NISEN, J. (2013). Optimally thresholded realized power variations for Lévy jump diffusion models. *Stochastic Processes and Their Applications*, **123** 2648–2677.

FLORENS-ZMIROU, D. (1993). On estimating the diffusion coefficient from discrete observations. *Journal of Applied Probability*, **30** 790–804.

FOSTER, D. and NELSON, D. B. (1996). Continuous record asymptotics for rolling sample variance estimators. *Econometrica*, **64** 139–174.

FRENCH, K. R. and ROLL, R. (1986). Stock return variances: The arrival of information and the reaction of traders. *Journal of Financial Economics*, **17** 5–26.

FRENCH, K. R., SCHWERT, G. W. and STAMBAUGH, R. F. (1987). Expected stock returns and volatility. *Journal of Financial Economics*, **19** 3–29.

FUKASAWA, M. (2010a). Central limit theorem for the realized volatility based on tick time sampling. *Finance and Stochastics*, **34** 209–233.

FUKASAWA, M. (2010b). Realized volatility with stochastic sampling. *Stochastic Processes and Applications*, **120** 829–852.

FUKASAWA, M. and ROSENBAUM, M. (2011). Central limit theorems for realized volatility under hitting times of an irregular grid. *Stochastic Processes and Applications*, **122** 3901–3920.

GALLANT, A. R., HSU, C.-T. and TAUCHEN, G. T. (1999). Using daily range data to calibrate volatility diffusions and extract the forward integrated variance. *The Review of Economics and Statistics*, **81** 617–631.

GARMAN, M. B. and KLASS, M. G. (1980). On the estimation of price volatility from historical data. *Journal of Business*, **53** 67–78.

GATHERAL, J. and OOMEN, R. C. (2010). Zero-intelligence realized variance estimation. *Finance and Stochastics*, **14** 249–283.

GENÇAY, R., BALLOCCHI, G., DACOROGNA, M., OLSEN, R. and PICTET, O. (2002). Real-time trading models and the statistical properties of foreign exchange rates. *International Economic Review*, **43** 463–491.

GENON-CATALOT, V. and JACOD, J. (1994). Estimation of the diffusion coefficient of diffusion processes: Random sampling. *Scandinavian Journal of Statistics*, **21** 193–221.

GENON-CATALOT, V., LARÉDO, C. and PICARD, D. (1992). Nonparametric estimation of the diffusion coefficient by wavelets methods. *Scandinavian Journal of Statistics*, **19** 317–335.

GHYSELS, E. and SINKO, A. (2011). Volatility forecasting and microstructure noise. *Journal of Econometrics*, **160** 257–271.

GLOSTEN, L. R. (1987). Components of the bid-ask spread and the statistical properties of transaction prices. *The Journal of Finance*, **42** 1293–1307.

GLOSTEN, L. R. and HARRIS, L. E. (1988). Estimating the components of the bid/ask spread. *Journal of Financial Economics*, **21** 123–142.

GLOTER, A. (2000). Estimation du coefficient de diffusion de la volatilité d'un modèle à volatilité stochastique. *C.R. Acad. Sciences Paris*, **330** 243–248.

GLOTER, A. and JACOD, J. (2001a). Diffusions with measurement errors: I - Local asymptotic normality. *ESAIM P&S*, **5** 225–242.

GLOTER, A. and JACOD, J. (2001b). Diffusions with measurement errors: II - Optimal estimators. *ESAIM P&S*, **5** 243–260.

GOBBI, F. and MANCINI, C. (2012). Identifying the Brownian covariation from the co-jumps given discrete observations. *Econometric Theory*, **28** 249–273.

GONÇALVES, S. and MEDDAHI, N. (2009). Bootstrapping realized volatility. *Econometrica*, **77** 283–306.

GOTTLIEB, G. and KALAY, A. (1985). Implications of the discreteness of observed stock prices. *The Journal of Finance*, **40** 135–153.

GRIFFIN, J. E. and OOMEN, R. C. (2008). Sampling returns for realized variance calculations: Tick time or transaction time? *Econometric Reviews*, **27** 230–253.

GRIFFIN, J. E. and OOMEN, R. C. (2011). Covariance measurement in the presence of non-synchronous trading and market microstructure noise. *Journal of Econometrics*, **160** 58–68.

GRIGELIONIS, B. (1971). On the representation of integer-valued random measures by means of stochastic integrals with respect to the Poisson measure. *Lithuanian Mathematics Journal*, **11** 93–108.

HALL, P. (1992). *The Bootstrap and Edgeworth Expansion.* Springer.

HALL, P. and HEYDE, C. C. (1980). *Martingale Limit Theory and Its Application.* Academic Press.

HANSEN, L. P. (1982). Large sample properties of generalized method of moments estimators. *Econometrica*, **50** 1029–1054.

HANSEN, P. R. and LUNDE, A. (2006). Realized variance and market microstructure noise. *Journal of Business and Economic Statistics*, **24** 127–161.

HARRIS, L. (2003). *Trading and Exchanges: Market Microstructure for Practitioners.* Oxford University Press.

HARRIS, L. E. (1990a). Estimation of stock price variances and serial covariances from discrete observations. *Journal of Financial and Quantitative Analysis*, **25** 291–306.

HARRIS, L. E. (1990b). Statistical properties of the Roll serial covariance bid/ask spread estimator. *The Journal of Finance*, **45** 579–590.

HARRIS, L. E. (1991). Stock price clustering and discreteness. *Review of Financial Studies*, **4** 389–415.

HASBROUCK, J. (1991). Measuring the information content of stock trades. *The Journal of Finance*, **46** 179–207.

HASBROUCK, J. (1993). Assessing the quality of a security market: A new approach to transaction-cost measurement. *Review of Financial Studies*, **6** 191–212.

HASBROUCK, J. (2007). *Empirical Market Microstructure.* Oxford University Press, New York, NY.

HAUTSCH, N. (2004). *Modelling Irregularly Spaced Financial Data: Theory and Practice of Dynamic Duration Models.* Lecture Notes in Economics and Mathematical Systems 539, Springer.

HAUTSCH, N. (2012). *Econometrics of Financial High-Frequency Data.* Springer.

HAUTSCH, N. and PODOLSKIJ, M. (2010). Pre-averaging based estimation of quadratic variation in the presence of noise and jumps: Theory, implementation, and empirical evidence. *Journal of Business & Economic Statistics,* **31** 165–183.

HAYASHI, T., JACOD, J. and YOSHIDA, N. (2011). Irregular sampling and central limit theorems for power variations: The continuous case. *Annales de l'Institut Henri Poincaré – Probabilités et Statistiques,* **47** 1197–1218.

HAYASHI, T. and KUSUOKA, S. (2008). Consistent estimation of covariation under nonsynchronicity. *Statistical Inference for Stochastic Processes,* **11** 93–106.

HAYASHI, T. and YOSHIDA, N. (2005). On covariance estimation of nonsynchronously observed diffusion processes. *Bernoulli,* **11** 359–379.

HAYASHI, T. and YOSHIDA, N. (2008). Asymptotic normality of a covariance estimator for nonsynchronously observed diffusion processes. *Annals of the Institute of Statistical Mathematics,* **60** 367–406.

HAYASHI, T. and YOSHIDA, N. (2011). Nonsynchronous covariation process and limit theorems. *Stochastic Processes and Applications,* **121** 2416–2454.

HESTON, S. (1993). A closed-form solution for options with stochastic volatility with applications to bonds and currency options. *Review of Financial Studies,* **6** 327–343.

HILL, B. M. (1975). A simple general approach to inference about the tail of a distribution. *Annals of Statistics,* **3** 1163–1174.

HOFFMANN, M. (1999a). Adaptive estimation in diffusion processes. *Stochastic Processes and Their Applications,* **79** 135–163.

HOFFMANN, M. (1999b). Lp estimation of the diffusion coefficient. *Bernoulli*, **5** 447–481.

HOFFMANN, M. (2002). Rate of convergence for parametric estimation in a stochastic volatility model. *Stochastic Processes and Their Applications*, **97** 147–170.

HOFFMANN, M., MUNK, A. and SCHMIDT-HIEBER, J. (2012). Adaptive wavelet estimation of the diffusion coefficient under additive error measurements. *Annales de l'Institut Henri Poincaré – (B)*, **48** 1186–1216.

HOFFMANN-JØRGENSEN, J. (1993). Stable densities. *Theory of Probability and Its Applications*, **38** 350–355.

HUANG, X. and TAUCHEN, G. T. (2005). The relative contribution of jumps to total price variance. *Journal of Financial Econometrics*, **4** 456–499.

IKEDA, S. S. (2014). Two-scale realized kernels: A univariate case. *Journal of Financial Econometrics, forthcoming*.

JACOD, J. (1979). *Calcul stochastique et problèmes de martingales*. Lecture Notes in Mathematics 714, Springer-Verlag.

JACOD, J. (1996). La variation quadratique du Brownien en présence d'erreurs d'arrondi. *Astérisque*, **236** 155–162.

JACOD, J. (2000). Non-parametric kernel estimation of the coefficient of a diffusion. *Scandinavian Journal of Statistics*, **27** 83–96.

JACOD, J. (2008). Asymptotic properties of realized power variations and related functionals of semimartingales. *Stochastic Processes and Their Applications*, **118** 517–559.

JACOD, J. (2012). Statistics and high frequency data. In *Statistical Methods for Stochastic Differential Equations* (A. L. Matthieu Kessler and M. Sorensen, eds.). Taylor and Francis, 191–310.

JACOD, J., KLÜPPELBERG, C. and MÜLLER, G. (2013a). Functional relationship between price and volatility jumps and their consequences for discretely observed data. *Journal of Applied Probability*, **49** 901–914.

JACOD, J., KLÜPPELBERG, C. and MÜLLER, G. (2013b). Testing for non-correlation between price and volatility jumps. Tech. rep., TUM Munich.

JACOD, J., LEJAY, A. and TALAY, D. (2008). Estimation of the Brownian dimension of a continuous Itô process. *Bernoulli*, **14** 469–498.

JACOD, J., LI, Y., MYKLAND, P. A., PODOLSKIJ, M. and VETTER, M. (2009). Microstructure noise in the continuous case: The pre-averaging approach. *Stochastic Processes and Their Applications*, **119** 2249–2276.

JACOD, J. and MYKLAND, P. A. (2012). Adaptive pre-averaging. Tech. rep., University of Chicago.

JACOD, J. and PODOLSKIJ, M. (2013). A test for the rank of the volatility process: The random perturbation approach. *Annals of Statistics*, **41** 2391–2427.

JACOD, J. and PROTTER, P. (1998). Asymptotic error distributions for the Euler method for stochastic differential equations. *Annals of Probability*, **26** 267–307.

JACOD, J. and PROTTER, P. (2011). *Discretization of Processes*. Springer-Verlag.

JACOD, J. and REISS, M. (2013). A remark on the rates of convergence for integrated volatility estimation in the presence of jumps. *Annals of Statistics, forthcoming*.

JACOD, J. and ROSENBAUM, M. (2013). Quarticity and other functionals of volatility: Efficient estimation. *Annals of Statistics*, **41** 1462–1484.

JACOD, J. and SHIRYAEV, A. N. (2003). *Limit Theorems for Stochastic Processes*. 2nd ed. Springer-Verlag.

JACOD, J. and TODOROV, V. (2009). Testing for common arrivals of jumps for discretely observed multidimensional processes. *Annals of Statistics*, **37** 1792–1838.

JACOD, J. and TODOROV, V. (2010). Do price and volatility jump together? *Annals of Applied Probability*, **20** 1425–1469.

JEGANATHAN, P. (1982). On the asymptotic theory of estimation when the limit of the loglikelihood is mixed normal. *Sankya, Ser. A*, **44** 173–212.

JIANG, G. J. and KNIGHT, J. (1997). A nonparametric approach to the estimation of diffusion processes – with an application to a short-term interest rate model. *Econometric Theory*, **13** 615–645.

JIANG, G. J. and OOMEN, R. C. (2008). Testing for jumps when asset prices are observed with noise – A "swap variance" approach. *Journal of Econometrics*, **144** 352–370.

JING, B.-Y., KONG, X.-B. and LIU, Z. (2012). Modeling high-frequency financial data by pure jump processes. *Annals of Statistics*, **40** 759–784.

JING, B.-Y., KONG, X.-B., LIU, Z. and MYKLAND, P. A. (2011). On the jump activity index for semimartingales. *Journal of Econometrics*, **166** 213–223.

KALNINA, I. (2011). Subsampling high frequency data. *Journal of Econometrics*, **161** 262–283.

KALNINA, I. and LINTON, O. (2008). Estimating quadratic variation consistently in the presence of endogenous and diurnal measurement error. *Journal of Econometrics*, **147** 47–59.

KARATZAS, I. and SHREVE, S. E. (1991). *Brownian Motion and Stochastic Calculus*. Springer-Verlag.

KINNEBROCK, S. and PODOLSKIJ, M. (2008). An econometric analysis of modulated realised covariance, regression and correlation in noisy diffusion models. Tech. rep., CREATES, Aarhus.

KOIKE, Y. (2013). Limit theorems for the pre-averaged Hayashi-Yoshida estimator with random sampling. Tech. rep., University of Tokyo.

KOOPMAN, S. J. and SCHARTH, M. (2013). The analysis of stochastic volatility in the presence of daily realized measures. *Journal of Financial Econometrics*, **11** 76–115.

KOUTROUVELIS, I. A. (1980). Regression-type estimation of the parameters of stable laws. *Journal of the American Statistical Association*, **75** 918–928.

KRISTENSEN, D. (2010). Pseudo-maximum likelihood estimation in two classes of semiparametric diffusion models. *Journal of Econometrics*, **156** 239–259.

LARGE, J. (2011). Estimating quadratic variation when quoted prices change by a constant increment. *Journal of Econometrics*, **160** 2–11.

LE CAM, L. and YANG, G. L. (1990). *Asymptotics in Statistics.* Springer-Verlag.

LEE, S. S. and HANNIG, J. (2010). Detecting jumps from Lévy jump diffusion processes. *Journal of Financial Economics*, **96** 271–290.

LEE, S. S. and MYKLAND, P. A. (2008). Jumps in financial markets: A new nonparametric test and jump dynamics. *Review of Financial Studies*, **21** 2535–2563.

LÉPINGLE, D. (1976). La variation d'ordre p des semi-martingales. *Zeitschrift für Wahrscheinlichkeitstheorie und Verwandte Gebiete*, **36** 295–316.

LI, J. (2013). Robust estimation and inference for jumps in noisy high frequency data: A local-to-continuity theory for the pre-averaging method. *Econometrica*, **81** 1673–1693.

LI, Y. and MYKLAND, P. A. (2007). Are volatility estimators robust with respect to modeling assumptions? *Bernoulli*, **13** 601–622.

LI, Y., MYKLAND, P. A., RENAULT, E., ZHANG, L. and ZHENG, X. (2009). Realized volatility when sampling times are possibly endogenous. Tech. rep., University of Chicago.

LIEBERMAN, O. and PHILLIPS, P. C. (2008). Refined inference on long memory in realized volatility. *Econometric Reviews*, **27** 254–267.

LO, A. W. and MACKINLAY, A. C. (1990). An econometric analysis of nonsynchronous trading. *Journal of Econometrics*, **45** 181–211.

MADAN, D. B., CARR, P. P. and CHANG, E. E. (1998). The Variance Gamma process and option pricing. *European Finance Review*, **2** 79–105.

MADAN, D. B. and SENETA, E. (1990). The Variance Gamma (V.G.) model for share market returns. *Journal of Business*, **63** 511–524.

MADHAVAN, A., RICHARDSON, M. and ROOMANS, M. (1997). Why do security prices change? *Review of Financial Studies*, **10** 1035–1064.

MAHEU, J. M. and MCCURDY, T. H. (2011). Do high-frequency measures of volatility improve forecasts of return distributions? *Journal of Econometrics*, **160** 69–76.

MALLIAVIN, P. and MANCINO, M.-E. (2002). Fourier series methods for measurement of multivariate volatilities. *Finance and Stochastics*, **6** 49–61.

MALLIAVIN, P. and MANCINO, M.-E. (2009). A Fourier transform method for nonparametric estimation of multivariate volatility. *Annals of Statistics*, **37** 1983–2010.

MANCINI, C. (2001). Disentangling the jumps of the diffusion in a geometric jumping Brownian motion. *Giornale dell'Istituto Italiano degli Attuari*, **64** 19–47.

MANCINI, C. (2004). Estimating the integrated volatility in stochastic volatility models with Lévy type jumps. Tech. rep., Università di Firenze.

MANCINI, C. (2009). Nonparametric threshold estimation for models with stochastic diffusion coefficient and jumps. *Scandinavian Journal of Statistics*, **36** 270–296.

MANCINI, C., MATTIUSSI, V. and RENÒ, R. (2012). Spot volatility estimation using delta sequences. Tech. rep., Università di Firenze.

MANCINO, M.-E. and SANFELICI, S. (2008). Robustness of Fourier estimator of integrated volatility in the presence of microstructure noise. *Computational Statistics and Data Analysis*, **52** 2966–2989.

MANCINO, M.-E. and SANFELICI, S. (2011). Estimating covariance via Fourier method in the presence of asynchronous trading and microstructure noise. *Journal of Financial Econometrics*, **9** 367–408.

MANCINO, M.-E. and SANFELICI, S. (2012). Multivariate volatility estimation with high frequency data using Fourier method. In *Handbook of Modeling High-Frequency Data in Finance* (F. G. Viens, M. C. Mariani and I. Florescu, eds.). Wiley, 243–294.

MANDELBROT, B. (1963). The variation of certain speculative prices. *Journal of Business*, **36** 394–419.

MEDDAHI, N. (2002). A theoretical comparison between integrated and realized volatility. *Journal of Applied Econometrics*, **17** 479–508.

MERTON, R. C. (1976). Option pricing when underlying stock returns are discontinuous. *Journal of Financial Economics*, **3** 125–144.

MEYER, P.-A. (1976). Un cours sur les intégrales stochastiques. In *Séminaire de Probabilités X*, Lecture Notes in Mathematics 511. Springer, 245–400.

MÜLLER, H.-G., SEN, R. and STADTMÜLLER, U. (2011). Functional data analysis for volatility. *Journal of Econometrics*, **165** 233–245.

MUNK, A. and SCHMIDT-HIEBER, J. (2010). Nonparametric estimation of the volatility function in a high-frequency model corrupted by noise. *Electronic Journal of Statistics*, **4** 781–821.

MYKLAND, P. A. and ZHANG, L. (2006). ANOVA for diffusions and Itô processes. *Annals of Statistics*, **34** 1931–1963.

MYKLAND, P. A. and ZHANG, L. (2008). Inference for volatility-type objects and implications for hedging. *Statistics and Its Interface*, **1** 255–278.

MYKLAND, P. A. and ZHANG, L. (2009). Inference for continuous semi-martingales observed at high frequency. *Econometrica*, **77** 1403–1445.

NELSON, D. B. (1991). Conditional heteroskedasticity in asset returns: A new approach. *Econometrica*, **59** 347–370.

NEUMANN, M. H. and REISS, M. (2009). Nonparametric estimation for Lévy processes from low-frequency observations. *Bernoulli*, **15** 223–248.

NISHIYAMA, Y. (2008). Nonparametric estimation and testing time-homogeneity for processes with independent increments. *Stochastic Processes and Their Applications*, **118** 1043–1055.

NOLAN, J. P. (1997). Numerical computation of stable densities and distribution functions. *Communications in Statistics – Stochastic Models*, **13** 759–774.

NOLAN, J. P. (2001). Maximum likelihood estimation and diagnostics for stable distributions. In *Lévy Processes: Theory and Applications* (O. E. Barndorff-Nielsen, T. Mikosch and S. I. Resnick, eds.). Birkhäuser, 379–400.

NOVIKOV, E. (1994). Infinite divisible distributions in turbulence. *Physical Review E*, **59** R3303–R3305.

OGAWA, S. and HOANG-LONG, N. (2010). Real-time estimation scheme for the spot cross volatility of jump diffusion processes. *Mathematics and Computers in Simulation*, **80** 1962–1976.

OGAWA, S. and SANFELICI, S. (2011). An improved two-step regularization scheme for spot volatility estimation. *Economic Notes*, **40** 107–134.

O'HARA, M. (1995). *Market Microstructure Theory*. Blackwell Publishers.

OOMEN, R. C. (2005). Properties of bias corrected realized variance in calendar time and business time. *Journal of Financial Econometrics*, **3** 555–577.

OOMEN, R. C. (2006). Properties of realized variance under alternative sampling schemes. *Journal of Business and Economic Statistics*, **24** 219–237.

PARKINSON, M. (1980). The extreme value method for estimating the variance of the rate of returns. *Journal of Business*, **53** 61–68.

PARTHASARATHY, K. (1967). *Probability Measures on Metric Spaces*. Academic Press.

PATTON, A. J. (2011). Volatility forecast comparison using imperfect volatility proxies. *Journal of Econometrics*, **160** 246–256.

PHILLIPS, P. C. B. and YU, J. (2007). Information loss in volatility measurement with flat price trading. Tech. rep., SMU.

PODOLSKIJ, M. and VETTER, M. (2009). Estimation of volatility functionals in the simultaneous presence of microstructure noise and jumps. *Bernoulli*, **15** 634–658.

PODOLSKIJ, M. and ZIGGEL, D. (2011). New tests for jumps in semimartingale models. *Statistical Inference for Stochastic Processes*, **13** 15–41.

PRESS, S. J. (1967). A compound events model for security prices. *Journal of Business*, **40** 317–335.

PRESS, S. J. (1972). Estimation in univariate and multivariate stable distributions. *Journal of the American Statistical Association*, **67** 842–846.

PROTTER, P. (2004). *Stochastic Integration and Differential Equations: A New Approach.* 2nd ed. Springer-Verlag.

RACHEV, S. and MITTNIK, S. (2000). *Stable Paretian Models in Finance.* Wiley.

REBOLLEDO, R. (1979). La méthode des martingales appliquée à la convergence en loi des processus. *Mémoires de la Société Mathématique de France*, **62**.

REISS, M. (2011). Asymptotic equivalence for inference on the volatility from noisy observations. *Annals of Statistics*, **39** 772–802.

REISS, M. (2013). Testing the characteristics of a Lévy process. *Stochastic Processes and Their Applications*, **123** 2808–2828.

RENÒ, R. (2008). Nonparametric estimation of the diffusion coefficient of stochastic volatility models. *Econometric Theory*, **24** 1174–1206.

RÉNYI, A. (1963). On stable sequences of events. *Sankyā Series A*, **25** 293–302.

REVUZ, D. and YOR, M. (1994). *Continuous Martingales and Brownian Motion.* 2nd ed. Springer-Verlag.

ROBERT, C.-Y. and ROSENBAUM, M. (2011). A new approach for the dynamics of ultra-high-frequency data: The model with uncertainty zones. *Journal of Financial Econometrics*, **9** 344–366.

ROBERT, C.-Y. and ROSENBAUM, M. (2012). Volatility and covariation estimation when microstructure noise and trading times are endogenous. *Mathematical Finance*, **22** 133–164.

ROGERS, L. and SATCHELL, S. (1991). Estimating variance from high, low and closing prices. *Annals of Applied Probability*, **1** 504–512.

ROLL, R. (1984). A simple model of the implicit bid-ask spread in an efficient market. *The Journal of Finance*, **39** 1127–1139.

ROSIŃSKI, J. (2007). Tempering stable processes. *Stochastic Processes and Their Applications*, **117** 677–707.

SHIMIZU, Y. (2010). Threshold selection in jump-discriminant filter for discretely observed jump processes. *Statistical Methods and Applications*, **19** 355–378.

SIAS, R. W. and STARKS, L. T. (1997). Return autocorrelation and institutional investors. *Journal of Financial Economics*, **46** 103–131.

SINGLETON, K. (2001). Estimation of affine asset pricing models using the empirical characteristic function. *Journal of Econometrics*, **102** 111–141.

SIZOVA, N. (2011). Integrated variance forecasting: Model based vs. reduced form. *Journal of Econometrics*, **162** 294–311.

SKOROKHOD, A. V. (1956). Limit theorems for stochastic processes. *Theory of Probability and Its Applications*, **1** 261–290.

SUN, Y. (2006). Best quadratic unbiased estimators of integrated variance in the presence of market microstructure noise. Tech. rep., UCSD.

TANIAI, H., USAMI, T., SUTO, N. and TANIGUCHI, M. (2012). Asymptotics of realized volatility with non-Gaussian ARCH(∞) microstructure noise. *Journal of Financial Econometrics*, **10** 617–636.

THEODOSIOU, M. and ZIKES, F. (2011). A comprehensive comparison of alternative tests for jumps in asset prices. Tech. rep., Central Bank of Cyprus.

TODOROV, V. and TAUCHEN, G. T. (2010). Activity signature functions for high-frequency data analysis. *Journal of Econometrics*, **154** 125–138.

UBUKATA, M. and OYA, K. (2009). Estimation and testing for dependence in market microstructure noise. *Journal of Financial Econometrics*, **7** 106–151.

VETTER, M. (2010). Limit theorems for bipower variation of semimartingales. *Stochastic Processes and Their Applications*, **120** 22–38.

VETTER, M. (2011). Estimation of integrated volatility of volatility with applications to goodness-of-fit testing. Tech. rep., Ruhr-Universität Bochum.

VETTER, M. (2012). Estimation of correlation for continuous semimartingales. *Scandinavian Journal of Statistics*, **39** 757–771.

WANG, D. C. and MYKLAND, P. A. (2012). The estimation of the leverage effect with high frequency data. *Journal of the Americal Statistical Association, forthcoming.*

WOERNER, J. H. (2011). Analyzing the fine structure of continuous-time stochastic processes. In *Seminar on Stochastic Analysis, Random Fields and Applications VI.* Progress in Probability 63, Springer, 473–492.

XIU, D. (2010). Quasi-maximum likelihood estimation of volatility with high frequency data. *Journal of Econometrics,* **159** 235–250.

YU, J. (2005). On leverage in a stochastic volatility model. *Journal of Econometrics,* **127** 165–178.

ZHANG, L. (2006). Efficient estimation of stochastic volatility using noisy observations: A multi-scale approach. *Bernoulli,* **12** 1019–1043.

ZHANG, L., MYKLAND, P. A. and AÏT-SAHALIA, Y. (2005). A tale of two time scales: Determining integrated volatility with noisy high-frequency data. *Journal of the American Statistical Association,* **100** 1394–1411.

ZHANG, L., MYKLAND, P. A. and AÏT-SAHALIA, Y. (2011). Edgeworth expansions for realized volatility and related estimators. *Journal of Econometrics,* **160** 190–203.

ZHOU, B. (1996). High-frequency data and volatility in foreign-exchange rates. *Journal of Business & Economic Statistics,* **14** 45–52.

ZOLOTAREV, V. M. (1986). *One-dimensional Stable Distributions.* Translations of Mathematical Monographs 65, American Mathematical Society.

ZOLOTAREV, V. M. (1995). On representation of densities of stable laws by special functions. *Theory of Probability and Its Applications,* **39** 354–362.

ZU, Y. and BOSWIJK, P. (2014). Estimating realized spot volatility with noisy high-frequency data. *Journal of Econometrics, forthcoming.*

ZUMBACH, G. O., CORSI, F. and TRAPLETTI, A. (2002). Efficient estimation of volatility using high frequency data. Tech. rep., Olsen & Associates.

Index

adapted (to a filtration), 6
adaptive pre-averaging, 247
Assumption (A), 302
Assumption (CoJ), 454
Assumption (D-q), 303
Assumption (DD-2), 316
Assumption (GN), 221, 497
Assumption (H$'$), 479
Assumption (H$'$), 330
Assumption (H-r), 170, 330, 478
Assumption (H-Lr), 454
Assumption (HC), 170, 479
Assumption (J), 431, 480
Assumption (K-r), 193, 268, 330, 479
Assumption (KC), 230, 268, 479
Assumption (KCC), 275, 480
Assumption (L), 396, 480
Assumption (L$'$), 399
Assumption (L$_+$), 415
Assumption (L$_+''$), 579
Assumption (L$_-$), 416
Assumption (L$_-''$), 580
Assumption (L-j), 420
Assumption (P), 193, 330, 454, 480
Assumption (SGN), 503
Assumption (SH-r), 502
Assumption (SK-r), 503, 532
Assumption (SKC), 503, 532
Assumption (SKCC), 503, 532
Assumption (SP), 503
Assumption (WN), 221

asymptotic size (of a test), 153
asymptotically efficient, 136
asymptotically variance-efficient, 135

Blumenthal-Getoor index, 31, 141
Brownian motion, 5, 7
Brownian semimartingale, 10
Burkholder-Gundy inequalities, 40

càdlàg (right-continuous with left-hand limits), 16
Cauchy process, 22
characteristic exponent (of a Lévy process), 18
characteristic triple (of a Lévy process), 18
characteristics (of a semimartingale), 43
compensated Poisson process, 21
compound Poisson process, 21
consistent tests, 152
continuous martingale part of a semimartingale, 10, 38

diffusion coefficient, 14
diffusion process, 12
drift coefficient, 14

Edgeworth expansion, 203
Epps effect, 314
exhausting and weakly exhausting sequences of stopping times, 488

657

filtered extension of a probability space, 46
filtered probability space, 6
filtered product extension of a probability space, 46
filtration, 3, 6
filtration generated by a process, 6
finite activity (for the jumps of a process), 31
finite-dimensional stable convergence in law, 269
first modified characteristic, 150
fixed times of discontinuity, 53
flat top kernels, 250

$\mathcal{G}$-stable convergence in law, 95
gamma process, 24
globally even (function), 492
Grigelionis form of an Itô semimartingale, 47

identifiable, 133
identifiable (parameter), 147
index (of a stable process), 22
infinite activity (for jumps), 31, 429
infinitely divisible, 17
Itô semimartingale, 10, 45
Itô's formula, 11, 40

jump activity index, 31
jump measure (of the process X), 26

LAN property, 135
law of iterated logarithm, 8
leverage effect, 279
Lévy Characterization Theorem, 7
Lévy measure, 18
Lévy modulus of continuity, 7
Lévy process, 5, 16

Lévy process relative to a filtration, 16
Lévy-Itô decomposition of a Lévy process, 33
Lévy-Khintchine formula, 18
local martingale, 9
local spot volatility estimator, 266
local time, 290
local uniform convergence in probability (u.c.p.), 9
localization, 502
localizing sequence of stopping times, 9
locally bounded process, 10, 37, 503

martingale, 6
maximum likelihood estimator (MLE), 86, 136
Merton's model, 116
mixed renewal schemes, 304
modulated Poisson scheme, 304
moments of a Lévy process, 19
multi-scales realized volatility (MSRV), 237, 253
multipower, 192

pairwise identifiable, 133
parameter, 146
Parzen kernel, 252
Poisson measure relative to a filtration, 26
Poisson process, 20
Poisson random measure, 24, 30
polarization identity, 40
power variations, 109
pre-averaging, 238
predictable, 27
process with conditionally independent increments, 54

process with independent incre-
    ments, 53
progressively measurable, 6

quadratic covariation, 39
quadratic variation, 10, 39
quarticity, 85, 173

realized quadratic variation, 11
realized volatility, 84, 171

scaling property, 22
semimartingale, 35
Skorokhod space, 96, 147
Skorokhod topology, 96
spot Blumenthal-Getoor index, 151
spot characteristics (of an Itô semi-
    martingale), 45
stable convergence in law, 93
stable convergence in law in restric-
    tion to a set, 95
stable process, 23
stochastic differential equation, 14
stochastic integral, 28
stopping time, 6

strong asymptotic size, 153
strongly predictable time, 302
subordinator, 23
successive Blumenthal-Getoor in-
    dices, 142
successive Blumenthal-Getoor in-
    tensities, 142
symmetrical stable process, 22

tempered stable process, 24
time-changed regular scheme, 310
triangular kernel, 240
truncated power variations, 110
truncated realized volatility, 180
two scales realized volatility
    (TSRV), 233

uniform rate, 158

very good filtered extension, 47

weak asymptotic size, 153
weight function, 239, 497
white noise, 268
Wiener process, 5